February 23–27, 2013
San Antonio, Texas, USA

Association for
Computing Machinery

Advancing Computing as a Science & Profession

CSCW 2013

Proceedings of the 2013 ACM Conference on

Computer Supported Cooperative Work

Sponsored by:

ACM SIGCHI

Vol. 2 of 2

Association for
Computing Machinery

Advancing Computing as a Science & Profession

The Association for Computing Machinery
2 Penn Plaza, Suite 701
New York, New York 10121-0701

Volume 2
ISBN: 978-1-4503-1331-5 (Digital)
ISBN: 978-1-4503-2099-3 (Print)

Additional copies may be ordered prepaid from:

ACM Order Department
PO Box 30777
New York, NY 10087-0777, USA

Phone: 1-800-342-6626 (USA and Canada)
+1-212-626-0500 (Global)
Fax: +1-212-944-1318
E-mail: acmhelp@acm.org
Hours of Operation: 8:30 am – 4:30 pm ET

Printed in the USA

CSCW 2013 Chairs' Welcome

It is our great pleasure to welcome you to the *2013 ACM Computer Supported Cooperative Work – CSCW'13*. This year's conference continues its tradition of being the premier forum for research on online collaboration, social computing, and social media studies. CSCW meets a wide range of research interests, from technical communication systems building to ethnographic studies of computer-mediated collaboration in the wild. The mission of the conference is to share novel research in these domains of interest in order to advance the state of the art in CSCW.

CSCW is committed to innovation in all aspects of research. This year's conference marks the second year in which the conference used a revision cycle in the paper reviewing process. The goal of this process is to increase quality of accepted papers and grow the program to better reflect the richness of our field. 390 paper submissions were received, 139 of which were accepted for publication after going through two rigorous review cycles. This year also marks the first year in which page length limits and the Papers/Notes distinction were eliminated, resulting in an overall modest increase in the length of papers. In all, the changes to the authoring and reviewing process have generated more papers of higher quality. *CSCW '13* also has tracks for posters, demos, videos, workshops, panels, and a doctoral consortium, all of which are seeing tremendous participation. The workshops alone, for instance, have attracted almost 150 participants. For the first time, CSCW this year will have an open format "unconference" track where attendees can explore ideas in greater depth. We will also have a fitness track to start each day with some collaborative healthy activity.

In addition to the stellar technical program, *CSCW'13* hosts two exciting keynote speakers, Ron Burt and Jascha Franklin-Hodge. Ron will open the conference with a discussion of his research on volatility and advantage in networks, while Jascha will close the conference with an in-the-trenches look at modern digital democracy. Other highlights outside the papers program include a posters and videos reception and the main conference reception, both of which should provide time to connect with your fellow CSCW researchers.

Putting together *CSCW'13* was a team effort. We first thank the authors for providing the content of the program. We are grateful to the program committee, who worked hard in reviewing papers and providing feedback for authors. We heard from many authors and reviewers that the reviewing process truly helped improve the final papers. We thank the conference committee, from the papers chairs to the treasurer to the webmaster, an incredible group of people who donated countless hours of their time. We also thank Lisa Tolles at Sheridan Communications, Yvonne Lopez at RegOnline, and Ashley Cozzi and Stephanie Sabal from ACM for all of their assistance with arrangements, registration, and printing. Special thanks go out to John and Joanne Lateulere for their invaluable help with conference planning and management. Finally, we thank our sponsors ACM and SIGCHI, and generous corporate supporters, Facebook, Microsoft Research, NSF, Grand NCE, IBM Research, Yahoo! Labs, and Google.

We hope that you find this program interesting and thought provoking and that the conference provides you with a valuable opportunity to share ideas with other researchers and practitioners from institutions around the world.

Amy Bruckman
CSCW'13 General Chair
Georgia Institute of Technology, USA

Scott Counts
CSCW'13 General Chair
Microsoft Research, USA

Table of Contents

Mining Social Media Data

Monday February 25 *(14:30-16:00)*

Teams

Monday February 25 *(14:30-16:00)*

Games

Monday February 25 *(16:30-18:00)*

Collaboration and Sharing in Scientific Work

Monday February 25 *(16:30-18:00)*

Crowdsourcing

Tuesday February 26 *(9:00-10:30)*

Local Is Where It's At

Tuesday February 26 *(9:00-10:30)*

Working Together

Tuesday February 26 *(9:00-10:30)*

Computer-Mediated Communication

Tuesday February 26 *(9:00-10:30)*

VOLUME 2

Understanding People's Practices in Social Networks

Tuesday February 26 *(9:00-10:30)*

Wikipedia Supported Cooperative Work

Tuesday February 26 *(11:00-12:30)*

Ideology, Politics, and Social Curation: Recent Work on Twitter

Tuesday February 26 *(11:00-12:30)*

Not Lost in Translation?

Tuesday February 26 *(11:00-12:30)*

Big Issues for CSCW to Consider

Tuesday February 26 *(14:30-16:00)*

Technology to Support Family Connections

Tuesday February 26 *(14:30-16:00)*

Searching: Better Together?

Tuesday February 26 *(14:30-16:00)*

Q&A

Wednesday February 26 *(14:30-16:00)*

Crowding Out the Competition

Wednesday February 27 *(9:00-10:30)*

Computer Supported Young People

Wednesday February 27 *(9:00-10:30)*

Roles

Wednesday February 27 *(11:00-12:10)*

Alternative Contexts for Collaboration

Wednesday February 27 *(11:00-12:10)*

CSCW 2013 Conference Organization

General Chairs:	Amy Bruckman *(Georgia Institute of Technology, USA)* Scott Counts *(Microsoft Research, USA)*
Program Chairs:	Cliff Lampe *(University of Michigan, USA)* Loren Terveen *(University of Minnesota, USA)*
Panels Chairs:	Darren Gergle (*Northwestern University, USA*) Sian Lindley (*Microsoft Research, USA*)
Workshops Chairs:	Jeremy Birnholtz *(Northwestern University, USA)* Andy Crabtree *(University of Nottingham, UK)*
Videos Chairs:	Sasa Junuzovic *(Microsoft Research, USA)* Carman Neustaedter *(Simon Fraser University, Canada)*
Interactive Posters Chairs:	Gary Hsieh *(Michigan State University, USA)* Chen Zhao *(Microsoft Research, USA)*
Demonstrations Chairs:	Dan Cosley *(Cornell University, USA)* Travis Kriplean *(University of Washington, USA)*
Doctoral Colloquium Chairs:	Geraldine Fitzpatrick *(Vienna University of Technology, Austria)* David McDonald *(University of Washington, USA)*
Open Space Chairs:	Eric Gilbert *(Georgia Institute of Technology, USA)* Jenn Thom-Santelli *(IBM Research, USA)*
Publications & Proceedings Chairs:	Aleksandra Sarcevic *(Drexel University, USA)* Bryan Semaan *(University of Hawaii, USA)*
Social Interaction & Publicity Chairs:	Andrea Forte *(Drexel University, USA)* Reid Priedhorsky *(Los Alamos National Lab, USA)*
Treasurer:	Nic Ducheneaut *(Ubisoft, USA)*
Student Volunteer Chairs:	Brian Keegan *(Northwestern University, USA)* Jenn Marlow *(Carnegie Mellon University, USA)*
Fitness Chairs:	Andrew Miller *(Georgia Institute of Technology, USA)* Sarita Yardi *(University of Michigan, USA)*

Program Committee (continued):

Gary Olson *(University of California, Irvine, USA)*
Sameer Patil *(Helsinki Institute for Information Technology/ Indiana University, Finland/USA)*
Erika Poole *(Pennsylvania State University, USA)*
Reid Priedhorsky *(Los Alamos National Laboratory/University of Minnesota, USA)*
Emilee Rader *(Michigan State University, USA)*
David Randall *(University of Siegen/Manchester Metropolitan University, Germany/UK)*
Madhu Reddy *(Pennsylvania State University, USA)*
Jennifer Rode *(Drexel University, USA)*
Mary Beth Rosson *(Pennsylvania State University, USA)*
Aleksandra Sarcevic *(Drexel University, USA)*
Frank Shipman *(Texas A&M University, USA)*
Chengzheng Sun *(Nanyang Technological University, Singapore)*
John Tang *(Microsoft Research, USA)*
Jennifer Thom *(IBM Research, USA)*
Zachary Toups *(Texas A&M University, USA)*
Hao-Chuan Wang *(Cornell University, USA)*
Rick Wash *(Michigan State University, USA)*
Naomi Yamashita *(NTT Communication Science Laboratories, Japan)*
Jun Zhang *(Pitney Bowes/University of Michigan, USA)*

CSCW 2013 Additional Reviewers

Agustina Agustina
Ban Al-Ani
Morgan Ames
Ken Anderson
Adrienne Andrew
Judd Antin
Gabriela Avram
Phoebe Ayers
Naveen Bagalkot
Brian Bailey
Kalika Bali
Nelson Baloian
Jakob Bardram
Barbara Rita Barricelli
Archer Batcheller
Scott Bateman
Eric Baumer
Natalie Bazarova
Andrew Begel
Bo Begole
Rachel Bellamy
Nicholas Berente
Michael Bernstein
Matthew Bietz
Jeffrey Bigham
Christian Bird
Torger Bjornrud
Joshua Blumenstock
Mark Blythe
Alexander Boden
Johan Bollen
Elizabeth Bonsignore
Marcela Borge
Marcos Borges
Alan Borning
Nathan Bos
Claus Bossen
Guillaume Bouchard
Mohamed Bourimi
Joel Brandt
Andy Brooks
Barry Brown
Jed Brubaker
Peter Brusilovsky
Jenna Burrell
Ayse Buyuktur
Daragh Byrne
Federico Cabitza
Kelly Caine
Stefan Carmien
Marcelo Cataldo
Melissa Cefkin
Zebin Chen
Yunan Chen
Jilin Chen
Marisa Cohn
Sunny Consolvo
Stephane Conversy
Eric Cook
Henriette Cramer
Lorrie Cranor
Jonathon Cummings
Mary Czerwinski
Laura Dabbish
Elizabeth Daly
Laurie Damianos
Catalina Danis
Munmun De Choudhury
Cleidson de Souza
David Dearman
Dominique Decouchant
Nicholas Diakopoulos
E.Ilana Diamant
Joan DiMicco
Xianghua Ding
Gavin Doherty
Jonathan Donner
Andre Doucette
Steven Dow
Jill Drury
Gaurav Dubey
Nicolas Ducheneaut
Therese Dugan
Casey Dugan
Henry Been-Lirn Duh
Shree Durga
Erik Duval
Achim Ebert
Andy Echenique
Kate Ehrlich
Nicole Ellison
Ingrid Erickson
Thomas Erickson
Jerry Fails
Robert Farrell
Rosta Farzan
Mirko Fetter
Joel Fischer
Danyel Fisher
Rowanne Fleck
Benjamim Fonseca
Jodi Forlizzi
Jacob Foster
Marcus Foth
Mike Fraser
Susan Fussell
Krista Galyen
R. Kelly Garrett
Deborah Gears
R. Stuart Geiger
Aaron Genest
Elizabeth Gerber
Werner Geyer
Fabien Girardin
Christophe Giraud-Carrier
Jennifer Golbeck
Gloria Gomez
Tijana Gonja
Victor Gonzalez
Walkyria Goode
Nicholas Graham
Raphael Grasset
Judith Gregory
Catherine Grevet
Erik Gronvall
William Griswold
Jonathan Grudin
Ning Gu
Rosanna Guadagno
David Gurzick
Francisco Gutierrez
Eben Haber

Aaron Halfaker
William Hamilton
Jeff Hancock
Benjamin Hanrahan
Thomas Hansen
David Harley
richard harper
Christopher Harris
Steve Harrison
Drew Harry
Bjorrn Hartmann
Andrea Hartzler
Kirstie Hawkey
Gillian Hayes
Brent Hecht
Libby Hemphill
Felienne Hermans
Valeria Herskovic
Morten Hertzum
Jonna Hakkila
Brian Hilligoss
Serena Hillman
Starr Roxanne Hiltz
Jon Hindmarsh
Pamela Hinds
Erik Hofer
Eve Hoggan
Nic Hollinworth
HrÌ¦nn Holmer
Henry Holtzman
James Howison
Lee Humphreys
CJ Hutto
Kori Inkpen
Keisuke Inoue
Joshua Introne
Lilly Irani
Petra Isenberg
Isa Jahnke
Lian Jian
Hao Jiang
Jinlei Jiang
Marina Jirotka
Aditya Johri
Julie Jones
Elisabeth Joyce
Tejinder Judge
Nicolas Jullien
Sanjay Kairam
Santosh Kalwar
Matthew Kam
Sep Kamvar
Bridget Kane
Victor Kaptelinin
Karrie Karahalios
Azmina Karimi
Natascha Karlova
Brian Keegan
Kerstin Keil
Patrick Kelley
Aisling Kelliher
Juho Kim
Jeffrey Kim
Taemie Kim
Jennifer King
Matthew King
Peter Kinnaird
David Kirk
Lorraine Kisselburgh
Aniket Kittur
Funda Kivran-Swaine
Styliani Kleanthous
Mark Klein
Scott Klemmer
Cory Knobel
Shin'ichi Konomi
Joseph Konstan
Vassilis Kostakos
Yong Ming Kow
Adam Kramer
Robert Kraut
Erin Krupka
Pavel Kucherbaev
Anand Kulkarni
Diana Kusunoki
Carl Lagoze
Shyong Lam
Cliff Lampe
Airi Lampinen
Walter Lasecki
Lydia Lau
Tessa Lau
Eric Laurier
Edith Law
Shaun Lawson
Christopher Le Dantec
Lucian Leahu
David Lee
Matthew Lee
Alison Lee
Charlotte Lee
Thomas Lento
Gilly Leshed
Qinying Liao
Brian Lim
Jih-Hsuan Tammy Lin
Sian Lindley
Janne Lindqvist
Greg Little
Tracy Liu
Ying Liu
Sophia Liu
Huanglingzi Liu
Kai-Uwe Loser
Tun Lu
Andres Lucero
Paul Luff
Stephan Lukosch
Alina Lungeanu
Kurt Luther
Kalle Lyytinen
Allan MacLean
Rachel Magee
Brian Magerko
Paul Maglio
Jalal Mahmud
Nasim Mahmud
Scott Mainwaring
Peter Mambrey
Lena Mamykina
Jennifer Mankoff
Osama Mansour
Gabriela Marcu
Gary Marsden
Paul Marshall
Catherine Marshall
Andrea Marshall
Christopher Mascaro
Winter Mason
Michael Massimi
Ashwin Mathew

Matthew Mayernik
Michelle Mazurek
Nora McDonald
Gregor McEwan
Claudia MÌ_ller
Andrew Miller
Zara Mirmalek
Tanushree Mitra
Pascal Molli
Wendy Moncur
Andrew Monk
Andres Monroy-Hernandez
Jonathan Morgan
Florian Mueller
Gabriel Mugar
Sean Munson
Bilge Mutlu
Brad Myers
Lennart Nacke
Dawn Nafus
Yiftach Nagar
Hideyuki Nakanishi
Kevin Nam
Tooba Nasir
Mark Newman
Duyen Nguyen
Jeffrey Nichols
Jeffrey Nickerson
Sylvie Noel
David Novick
Petteri Nurmi
Erick Oduor
Judith Olson
Elisa Oreglia
Felipe Ortega
Jahna Otterbacher
Tyler Pace
Xinru Page
Joyojeet Pal
Aditya Pal
Leysia Palen
Katherine Panciera
Carolyn Pang
Katrina Panovich
Hugo Paredes
Andrea Parker
Fabio Paterno
Sharoda Paul
Helen Petrie
Emmanuel Pietriga
Niels Pinkwart
Jose Pino
Volkmar Pipek
Anne Marie Piper
Enrico Piras
Bernd Ploderer
John Pollak
Wanda Pratt
Nathan Prestopnik
Michael Prilla
Daniele Quercia
Alexander Quinn
Andrew Raij
Rebecca Randell
Yolanda Rankin
Stuart Reeves
Tim Regan
Markus Rester
David Ribes
Romain Robbes
Lionel Robert
Michelle Rogers
John Rooksby
Carolyn Rose
Chiara Rossitto
Dana Rotman
Mark Rouncefield
Karen Ruhleder
Paul Russo
Kathy Ryall
Daisuke Sakamoto
Antti Salovaara
Nithya Sambasivan
Christian Sandvig
Cheryl Savery
Steve Sawyer
Florian Schaub
Lauren Scissors
James Scott
Stacey Scott
Melinda Sebastian
Magy Seif El-Nasr
Abigail Sellen
Bryan Semaan
Shilad Sen
Chirag Shah
N. Sadat Shami
Kalpana Shankar
Nikhil Sharma
Aaron Shaw
Cuihua Shen
Haifeng Shen
Patrick Shih
Irina Shklovski
Gavin Sim
Bart Simon
Leif Singer
Roger Slack
Madeline Smith
Jacob Solomon
Clay Spinuzzi
Tad Stach
Kate Starbird
Charles Steinfield
Gunnar Stevens
Cristiano Storni
Fred Stutzman
Ozge Subasi
Bongwon Suh
Elisabeth Sylvan
Anna-Liisa Syrjanen
Federico Tajariol
Charlotte Tang
Karen Tang
Anthony Tang
Andrea Tartaro
Yla Tausczik
Ahmed Tawfik
Nick Taylor
Jaime Teevan
Paul Tennent
Monica Tentori
Loren Terveen
William Thies
Elizabeth Thiry
Peter Tolmie
Bill Tomlinson
Mercan Topkara
Khai Truong
Manfred Tscheligi
Simon Tucker

Kathleen Tuite
Kristene Unsworth
Jan Van den Bergh
Max Van Kleek
Ravi Vatrapu
Alcides Velasquez
Theresa Velden
Kaisa Vaananen-Vainio-Mattila
Sarah Vieweg
Jesse Vig
Jessica Vitak
Juergen Vogel
Amy Voida
Mihaela Vorvoreanu
Maja Vukovic
Patrick Wagstrom
Jing Wang
Yi-Chia Wang
Hao Wang
Nadir Weibel
Suzanne Weisband
Andrew West
Ryen White
Mark Whiting
Jason Wiese
Andrea Wiggins
Heather Willever-Farr
Max Wilson
Susan Winter
Volker Wulf
Susan Wyche
Lu Xiao
Bin Xu
Yun Yang
Sarita Yardi Schoenebeck
Svetlana Yarosh
Chen Ye
Jude Yew
Zhen Yue
Mi Zhang
Qiping Zhang
Shengdong Zhao
Xiaomu Zhou
Dingyun Zhu
John Zimmerman

CSCW 2013 Sponsor & Supporters

Sponsor: SIGCHI

Supporters (Hero): NSF

Supporters (Benefactors): facebook; Microsoft Research

Supporters (Contributors): grand (Graphisme, animation et nouveaux médias / Graphics, Animation and New Media); IBM Research; Yahoo! Labs

Supporters (Friends): Google

The Post that Wasn't: Exploring Self-Censorship on Facebook

Manya Sleeper, Rebecca Balebako, Sauvik Das, Amber Lynn McConahy, Jason Wiese, Lorrie Faith Cranor

Carnegie Mellon University
Pittsburgh, PA
{msleeper, balebako, sauvik, amberlynn, wiese, lorrie}@cmu.edu

ABSTRACT

Social networking site users must decide what content to share and with whom. Many social networks, including Facebook, provide tools that allow users to selectively share content or block people from viewing content. However, sometimes instead of targeting a particular audience, users will self-censor, or choose not to share. We report the results from an 18-participant user study designed to explore self-censorship behavior as well as the subset of unshared content participants would have potentially shared if they could have specifically targeted desired audiences. We asked participants to report all content they thought about sharing but decided not to share on Facebook and interviewed participants about why they made sharing decisions and with whom they would have liked to have shared or not shared. Participants reported that they would have shared approximately half the unshared content if they had been able to exactly target their desired audiences.

Author Keywords

Social networking sites; usability; privacy; self-censorship

ACM Classification Keywords

H.1.2 User/Machine Systems: Human factors

INTRODUCTION

Social Networking Site (SNS) users make decisions about what content to share and with whom. Sharing inappropriately can result in consequences ranging from regret to job loss [20]. SNSs provide tools that allow users to share content with some people and block other people from viewing content. However, sometimes instead of targeting a particular audience, users will self-censor or choose not to share.

Lampinen et al. describe self-censorship as one of the techniques SNS users rely on to manage the co-existence of different social groups on SNSs [13]. Self censorship is an important ability; SNS users choose not to post content for a variety of reasons, including to protect their own and others' privacy and to prevent regret [12, 13, 20, 22]. In this paper we explore users' self-censorship decisions on Facebook, as well as the types of content they choose to self-censor.

While self-censorship can be a desirable behavior both on- and offline, users sometimes choose to self-censor on SNSs because available access-control tools don't meet their needs. For a subset of self-censored content, users choose not to share because they would like only specific audiences to see the content, and those audiences are difficult, or impossible, to target given current interface design. We focus on understanding this subset of self-censored content and the potential impact of optimizing selective sharing tools to allow users to share this content with their preferred audiences.

Selective sharing [9] occurs when users can share with only their desired audiences, by selecting people to share with or block. We look specifically at sharing that could potentially have occurred if participants had been able to target exactly their desired audiences (optimal selective sharing). Our intention is to explore the potential ability of tools to allow users to share a subset of currently unshared content.

This paper has two primary contributions. Self-censorship has been established as a means for preserving SNS privacy but has not been thoroughly examined. We seek to expand understanding of types of, and reasons for, self-censorship on SNSs by examining self-censorship on Facebook. Second, we provide insight into the subset of self-censored content users could potentially share given improved SNS selective sharing mechanisms, as well as the types of tools that would be necessary to allow users to share this content. Previous work tended to focus on shared content; by focusing on unshared content, we provide additional insight for creating selective-sharing tools.

To address these issues we examined the types of Facebook content that users were not sharing, and why. Specifically, we looked at the following research questions:

- **Q1:** What types of content are users currently not sharing?
- **Q2:** Why do users choose not to share different types of content?
- **Q3:** What subset of content that users currently don't share (unshared content) could potentially be shared if they could

exactly target their intended audiences (i.e., given optimal selective sharing mechanisms)?

- **Q4:** What attributes typify the groups with whom users would like to selectively share currently unshared content?

We ran a weeklong, 18-participant, diary study during which we asked participants to send us Facebook posts they thought about posting but decided not to share. We used an in-lab interview to gather additional information about the content. We found that participants chose not to share a variety of types of content, especially entertainment and personal content. Participants would have shared approximately half of the unshared content if they were able to share with or block some combination of specific individuals, groups of individuals, and more ambiguous, attribute-defined groups.

RELATED WORK

Prior work on SNS user behavior, online identity management, and grouping for online privacy informed our study. We expand on prior work by examining unshared content and by looking at a subset of self-censored content to understand the interplay between sharing decisions and grouping for audience management.

User behavior on social networks

Users behave in risky ways when using SNSs, often due to audience mismanagement. Reynolds et al. found that Facebook users' behaviors did not coincide with their privacy concerns [17]. Stutzman and Kramer-Duffield compared intended audiences to actual audiences on friend networks, in a privacy context. They found that friends-only privacy settings could include "weak tie" relationships that presented privacy challenges [19].

Users can also regret SNS posts. Wang et al. found that one of the reasons Facebook users regretted posts was visibility to unintended audiences. Self-censorship was among the responses that they saw [20]. We complement this work on sharing regrettable content by exploring the subset of content users self-censor.

Identity management

Farnham and Churchill showed that users often manage multiple identities when sharing online. Users behave differently based on the social groups with which they interact, many of which are affiliated with different social roles [5]. These findings suggest that SNSs would benefit from tools that enable users to create appropriate boundaries for sharing.

When users make sharing decisions on SNSs, they are often trying to control how they present themselves. On Twitter, Marwick and boyd observed the tendency of users to collapse multiple audiences into a single context. The imagined audience with which the users interacted affected their sharing behaviors, including levels of self-censorship [14]. Strater and Lipford found that this perceived audience tended to narrow over time, often falling out of line with users' actual privacy settings [18]. Lampinen et al. found that Facebook users identified with multiple groups that co-existed on Facebook and used proactive strategies, including self-censorship, to manage this "group co-presence" [13].

SNS users also try to manage interpersonal boundaries on SNSs. On Facebook, they use mechanisms not formally built into the interface. These strategies include using self-censorship to avoid disclosing inappropriate information about others [12]. Wisniewski et al. also found that users employed "coping mechanisms," such as posting less content, to manage social boundaries on SNSs [22].

Grouping

One way to manage audiences is to create groups of individuals to share with or block from viewing content. Karr-Wisniewski et al. included group creation as a boundary regulation mechanism that allows users to define "relationship boundaries" on several SNSs [10].

Olson et al. found that access preferences for different types of content depended on the types of information they contained and the people who would potentially view them, thus making sharing conducive to grouping [16]. Kelley et al. asked users to create groups of their Facebook friends and found that common groups included "general friends," "college," "other education," "family," and "work." Static groups created ahead of time tended not to perform well when faced with real-time sharing decisions, suggesting a need for dynamic grouping [11]. Wiese et al. also found that "self-reported closeness," co-location, "frequency of communication," and common contacts were predictive features of sharing behavior [21]. Looking at Google+ circle names, Kairam et al. found that the majority of groups could be sorted into some combination of "life facet" (e.g., "work" and "school") and "tie strength" ("strong tie" and "weak tie") groups [9].

Mechanisms have been proposed to automatically support users' abilities to create groups on SNSs. Jones and O'Neil compared an automated SCAN clustering algorithm to groups created using card sorting and found that human-created groups outperformed algorithm-created groups in best and worst cases [8]. Fang and LeFevre explored the possibility of an interactive tool for specifying privacy preferences by asking users to make sharing decisions about a subset of their friends [4]. ReGroup is a more interactive machine-learning tool that looks for patterns in who users choose to share with through continually updated groups; users preferred it to an equivalent Facebook-style interface [1].

The underlying goal of these systems and studies was to understand sharing decisions and the groups with whom users wanted to share. In this work, we also examine unshared content. We explicitly explore reasons users do not share and the groups of people with whom a subset of this unshared content could potentially be shared.

METHODOLOGY

We wanted to determine what users were not sharing, and why (Q1,2), as well as the subset of unshared content that could potentially be shared using optimal selective sharing (Q3). We also wanted to explore attributes of the groups with whom our participants would have wanted to selectively share or block from viewing this subset of unshared content (Q4).

The study had two phases and took place in April and May of 2012. First, participants took part in a weeklong diary study during which they used SMS messaging to report all instances of unshared content on Facebook (i.e., content intentionally self-censored). Participants also filled out nightly surveys to further describe unshared content and any shared content that they decided to post on Facebook. Next, qualified participants took part in in-lab interviews. The interview provided more details about reported, unshared content and a better understanding of participants' decisions on when to share. We asked about participants' reasons for deciding against sharing, as well as the people, if any, participants hoped would see or wanted to block from viewing their content.

We iteratively coded each piece of unshared and shared content that we were able to ask participants about in the final interviews (122 piece of unshared and 83 pieces of shared content) for types of content, the types of groups the participant wanted to share with or block from viewing the content, and the participant's reasons for not sharing.

Recruitment and Demographics

We recruited 18 participants from a campus participant pool website, Craigslist, flyers, and a targeted Facebook ad. They were screened online for high English proficiency, a minimum age of 18, at least 6 months of Facebook use, frequent Facebook use (more than once per week), texting regularly (at least once per week), and having frequently held back content on Facebook (at least 3 pieces of unshared content over the past week). Thirty potential, qualified participants were sent online instructions for participating in the diary study, including 8 students. Nineteen of the 30 recruited participants completed at least one nightly survey, and 16 out of 30 completed the full study including the final interview. Two additional qualified student participants received the link to the instructions from friends and participated in the full study, resulting in 18 participants.

Participants ranged in age from 20 to 51. Ten were female, and seven were students. Table 1 summarizes participant demographics. Participants were compensated $20 for the final interview and $2 per nightly survey completed, up to a total of $34. We also reimbursed $6 for parking.

Diary Study

The diary study lasted seven days. Participants had continuous access to a set of online instructions. Participants sent SMS text messages whenever they thought "of things that they would like to post on Facebook but decide[d] not to post." They were asked to describe the potential post and include the type of post it would have been (e.g., wall post, photo, link, etc). This SMS-based approach was based on the technique used by Brandt et al. [2].

Every night, each participant was also sent a link to an online survey, which contained questions for each piece of unshared content. Participants could provide more detailed descriptions of unshared content and reasons for not posting. Participants were also prompted with questions about the people with whom they would have liked to share or would have liked to block from viewing each item. These questions were open ended, allowing participants to either name specific individuals or define their own notions of the people that would have constituted a "group" for sharing. The interface allowed participants to add additional unshared content, so they were not bound by the SMS messaging system. The survey also asked participants to describe content they had shared that day (shared content). If a participant had not shared any content, they were asked to fill out an auxiliary question about why they had not shared. We hoped to ensure a baseline level of effort and minimize incentives not to report.

Code	*Age*	*Gender*	*Occupation*	*Unshared items*	*Shared items*
P01	20	F	engineering student	7	4
P02	26	M	engineering student	8	4
P03	20	M	bus admin student	1	3
P04	33	F	social science student	24	0
P05	30	M	dental student	4	3
P06	26	M	unemployed	2	2
P07	23	F	non-profit	13	5
P08	29	F	art/writing/journalism	3	11
P09	25	F	non-profit	1	8
P10	28	M	human resources	10	4
P11	26	M	unemployed	6	7
P12	25	F	art/writing/journalism	4	5
P13	51	F	bus/mgt/fin	9	7
P14	24	F	lab mgr	8	1
P15	24	M	art/writing/journalism	2	7
P16	32	F	unemployed	12	8
P17	22	M	architecture student	4	2
P18	21	F	engineering student	4	2

Table 1. Participant demographics

We used this diary study and survey system because users can think of unshared content throughout the day, and we wanted to capture this as it occurred. This technique also allowed a participant to provide a quick "digest" of unshared content through the SMS system, and, if they were busy, return to the survey at a more convenient time to provide details.

Semi-Structured Interview

Participants who completed at least four surveys qualified for a final, in-lab interview (18 participants). We chose a semi-structured approach, which allowed us to capture similar types of data across all the interviews while maintaining the flexibility to explore the varied content reported. The interviews each lasted approximately one hour and occurred in a lab. One researcher served as the primary interviewer and interacted with the participant. A second researcher served primarily as a note taker. All interviews were audio recorded.

We used participants' shared and unshared content to explore our four research questions. We went through each piece of unshared content, and the participant's nightly survey responses, and probed for details on the content, reasons for wanting to share and not sharing, and, when relevant, details about the groups the participant would potentially have wanted to share with or block. For example, we asked the participant to describe the unshared content in more detail, to further explain why they decided not to post it, and to expand on their relationships with or common characteristics of the people they would have wanted to share content with or block. We also asked participants about their willingness to share each item, given selective sharing mechanisms, as well as for additional details on shared content and a series of questions on SNS usage and privacy habits.

Prior to study launch, we refined our methodology by piloting with 10 additional participants who are not included in analyses.

Data coding and analysis

To analyze the data, we looked at each piece of nightly survey content that we were able to discuss with participants during the final interviews. We removed any content that we were unable to discuss in the interviews, either because the participant did not complete enough nightly surveys to qualify for the interview or because the participant submitted too many items to allow for discussion of all content (only P04, who submitted 52 pieces of unshared and 32 pieces of shared content). Table 1 lists the number of shared and unshared items included in the analyses for each participant. We coded each item for the type of content, the participant's reason for not sharing, and the types of people with whom the participant would have wanted to share and/or block (where relevant). Our coding process was based on that used by Kairam et al. to code content shared on Google+ [9] as well as the technique used by Naaman et al. to code Twitter data [15].

To create codes, two researchers each independently coded a random selection of 50 items, using data from the nightly surveys and notes from the interviews. Based on those codes, the researchers collaboratively created a set of high level codes and independently coded the majority of the remaining data. The two researchers then iteratively coded all the data with updated codes two additional times. Between each iteration, the researchers updated the coding scheme based on shortcomings from the previous round. Using the final codes, the researchers went through their independent codings and discussed and agreed on any codes that differed. This process produced the set of codes used in the analyses.

Analyses presented in this paper are intended to be entirely qualitative. Numbers are intended to illustrate results from the sample but are not meant to indicate statistical significance or quantitative generalizeability. Examples are only intended to illustrate trends seen during the study.

RESULTS

Participants self-censored a variety of types of content, especially those related to external material (content unrelated to the participant), like entertainment. They most commonly chose not to share because they were trying to control how they presented themselves, and they would have shared about half of unshared content, given optimal selective sharing. The groups participants wanted to use for this optimal selective sharing included specific individuals, specific groups of individuals, as well as more dynamic groups that depended on context.

In this section we outline the types of unshared content, the reasons participants chose not to share, how much of that content would have been amenable to selective sharing, and the characteristics of the groups that would have been necessary

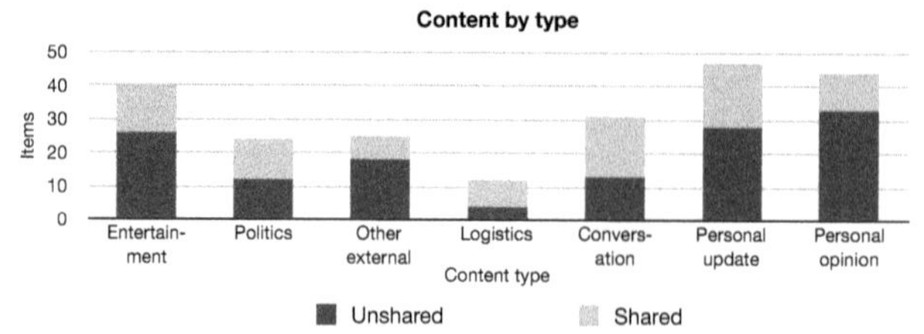

Figure 1. Shared and unshared content by type

to allow participants to have selectively shared that subset of unshared content.

Q1: Types of unshared content

We coded shared and unshared items into one or more of seven categories. We split items based on whether they were external content (e.g., entertainment, politics, or other external content), personal information, or related to planning or conversation. This led to three external categories: **entertainment**, **politics**, and **other**; two personal content categories: **personal update** and **personal opinion**; and categories for **conversational** content and **logistics**. Figure 1 shows the number of unshared and shared items in each category. These categories were roughly based on those Kairam et al. used for reasons to share Google+ content [9]. Items could be coded in multiple categories.

External content

External content included references unrelated to the participant. It could be intended to entertain, inform others, or allow the individual to express an opinion about the outside world. There were three subcategories: **entertainment**, **politics**, and **other**. We also noted when it included an opinion.

Entertainment: Examples included references to or articles about movies, television, sports, or music. This category contained 21% of unshared and 17% of shared content (26 and 14 items respectively). Unshared entertainment content tended to contain more material that could potentially offend. Several items contained explicit language or drug references. P17, for example, considered sharing a "weird" video that included drug-related content, but decided not to because her "family in Austin is really religious... they would've called [her] about it."

Half of unshared entertainment items included opinions, as opposed to three shared items. In contrast, shared entertainment content tended to advertise without a stated opinion. For example, several participants posted to advertise concerts.

Politics: Content that referenced politics, current events, or activism was coded as politics, which included 10% of unshared and 15% of shared content (12 items each). The majority of the unshared political content was considered potentially controversial. P04, for example, decided not to post a "Link to article about young black republicans" to try to avoid controversy. On the other hand, shared content trended more toward current events. P12, for example, "posted a link to an article about the slow recovery from the BP Oil Spill in Louisiana." She explained "it was one of the few instances when there was something kind of political and I put it up anyway," because it "was the true story and what's seen."

Other external content: This category included items that referenced content not related to the participant, entertainment, or politics. It included facts, quotes, pictures, and jokes, and included 15% of unshared and 9% of shared content (18 and 7 items respectively). Many sharing decisions depended on context. For example, P18 considered sharing "a recipe for a cake I saw posted by a friend from high school" but decided not to share because "I haven't spoken to her in a while and it would be awkward."

Personal content

Personal content related to a participant's life or general opinions and included **personal updates** and **personal opinions**.

Personal updates: These were items that described something that happened in a participant's life. Examples included content about the participant's day or about events the participant took part in, including photos. Personal updates made up 23% of the unshared and shared content (28 and 19 items respectively). Participants often decided not to post personal updates because they were too "frivolous" or not "creative" enough. For example, P10 thought about posting "Kicking ass and taking names!!! Happy Monday!!!" but decided not to because it was "very vague very generic, didn't think it was very creative." Participants also didn't post because they felt their personal updates were too negative or sounded like they were "whining." P16, for example, thought about posting about a fight between her and her boyfriend but decided not to because it was "grumpy." Shared personal updates tended to be relatively positive or straightforward.

Personal opinions: Opinions unrelated to external content were coded as personal opinions. These included how the participant generally felt about life, such as "having a stressful day," or more general opinions such as "We are way too old to be celebrating 420 day." Personal opinions included 27% of unshared and 13% of shared items (33 and 11, respectively). As with updates, many unshared personal opinions tended to be negative. Participants also worried that some might offend or start an argument. For example, P05 considered posting about how she disapproved of the Pokemon tattoo her brother-in-law was considering but decided against the post "because he wouldn't have liked it and it really wouldn't have made a difference anyway."

Conversation and planning

Conversational: This category included conversational niceties without additional content, such as birthday wishes or replies to posts that did not include additional content. This category included 11% of unshared and 22% of shared content (13 and 18 items respectively). Participants tended to not post conversational content based on potential social awkwardness. For example, P07 thought about wishing a friend happy birthday but decided not to because she hadn't "talked to him in a long time."

Logistics: Logistics included posts related to making plans. More were shared (8 items, 10%) rather than unshared (4 items, 3%). When participants didn't share, it tended to be due to offline, social reasons. For example, P05 decided not to discuss lunch plans because he didn't know one of the people involved in the conversation well enough.

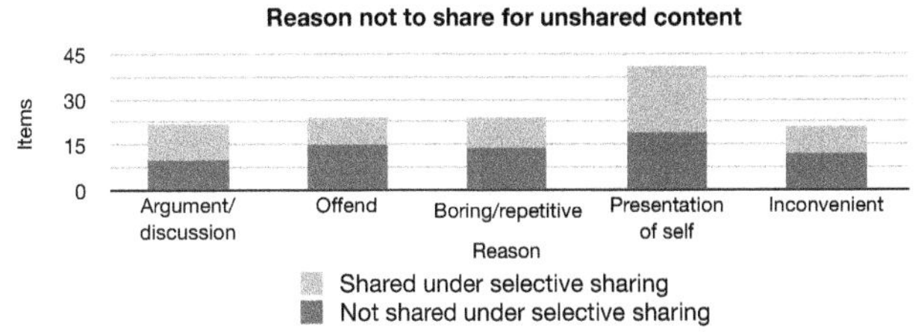

Figure 2. Reasons not to share unshared content

Q2: Reasons for not sharing

We were also interested in reasons for self-censorship. We asked in the surveys and the final interview, for each unshared item, why participants decided not to share. Responses tended to fall into one or more of five categories:

- **Argument/discussion**: Didn't want to start or participate in an argument or discussion.
- **Offend**: Didn't want to offend or hurt someone.
- **Boring/repetitive**: Felt the content was redundant, boring, or not interesting enough.
- **Presentation of self**: Felt the content went against the way the participant wanted to present him/herself (e.g., "seemed silly" or "don't like to post that kind of thing").
- **Inconvenient**: Prevented from posting due to time or technology (e.g., location made it difficult to post).

Figure 2 summarizes the number of items in each category. Presentation-of-self issues were most common (34%, 41 items) by a small margin; however, the remaining reasons each applied to approximately 20% of items. Percentages add up to over 100% because some items were not shared for multiple reasons.

Several reasons emerged more frequently for different types of content. Approximately half of entertainment and personal updates weren't shared because of presentation-of-self concerns, and slightly over half of political items weren't shared because participants didn't want to start or participate in arguments or discussions. Almost half of personal updates also weren't shared because participants were worried that the items would be boring or repetitive.

Q3: Potential for selective sharing

Participants would potentially have shared a subset of the unshared content if they could have exactly targeted particular audiences under optimal selective sharing. To isolate this subset, we used two Likert scale questions to judge participants' willingness to share given an optimal ability to selectively share with desired audiences. For each item of unshared content for which a participant provided a potential group that they would have liked to have shared with or blocked, we asked the participant to imagine that they either "could have shared this content only with" the people they wanted to share it with or could have "prevent[ed]" the people they didn't want to see it from viewing the content. To increase generalizability, we did not specify the interface that would be used to share the content, only that it would exactly target desired audiences. Responses were on a five-point Likert scale where a one was "very unlikely" and a five was "very likely." We consider a participant who indicated above a three for either question to have been potentially willing to share given optimal selective-sharing mechanisms. If a participant answered above a three for sharing and/or blocking selected people, we analyzed the people with whom the participant indicated they wanted to share and/or block. Overall, 60 out of 122 unshared items (49%) would have potentially been shared given optimal selective sharing. Of those, 57 would have been shared if the participants could have shared with only a desired set of people, and 25 would have been shared if the participants could have blocked people from viewing content. Figure 3 shows each participant's potential willingness to share given optimal selective-sharing tools.

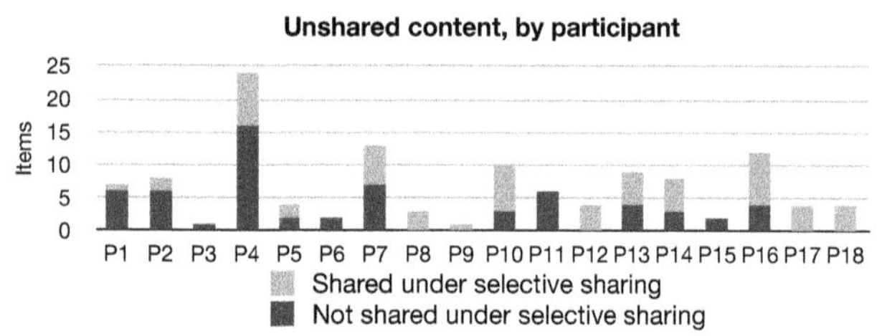

Figure 3. Unshared content participants were willing or unwilling to share, given optimal selective sharing

Although our small sample limits the generalizeability of these results, this indicates that participants could have potentially shared a relatively large subset of their self-censored content if they could have exactly targeted desired audiences.

Types of content for selective sharing

Participants would potentially have selectively shared approximately half of each type of content. External content tended to be amenable to selective sharing because participants wanted to share items with people who would have been interested and block people who might have been offended. For example, P08 considered posting "a lot of angry status updates" during a hockey game she was watching but decided not to because others were already doing so. She would have posted if only her hockey friends had been able to see the posts because they would have been interested. This was common for unshared entertainment content, which participants often felt only a subset of people would be interested in and/or other people might be offended by. A similar dynamic occurred with political content, with more of an emphasis on avoiding debate. This might have been expected because participants often decided not to share such political content to avoid argument or discussion.

Approximately half (15 out of 28 items) of personal updates would have potentially been shared with optimal selective sharing. Participants often wanted to share with people who were "close friends" or who they saw regularly who would understand or appreciate the posts. For example, P16, who considered posting about a fight with her boyfriend, only wanted to share with a small group of friends because "they can relate, because they know more about me and we talk about more personal things with each other." Participants would have potentially shared 42% of personal opinions (14 items) given optimal selective sharing. In several cases, participants wanted to share opinions with people who would understand the context. P07, for example, wanted to post "don't have pets if you're not prepared to take care of them!!!" after a bad experience cat sitting but only wanted mutual friends of the person who the post was directed at to see it.

Items for which participants wanted to control presentation of self or didn't want to start an argument or discussion were most amenable to selective sharing (slightly over half). Participants tended to want to share items with presentation-of-self issues with close friends or people who would be interested in or understand the content. For example, P07 thought about posting about her frustrations at her babysitting job to get advice, but chose to self-censor because she didn't think babysitting was "cool." She would have preferred to share only with particular people who also babysat. Participants who chose not to share because they didn't want to get involved in an argument or discussion tended to want to share with people who agreed or thought the same way about potentially controversial content. P04, for example, considered posting a link to an article about "cohabitation and divorce." She decided against posting because she had a lot of Facebook friends who were religious Christians who disapproved of cohabitation, and she wanted to avoid a long discussion.

Q4: Types of groups

For participants to selectively share the desired subsets of content, they would need to be able to specify, using the interface, the individuals or groups with whom they wanted to share. We asked participants to specify who they did and did not want to view each unshared item, so we could understand the kinds of groups participants would need to create to express their optimal selective-sharing preferences. We looked at the number of people in, and characteristics of, the groups.

Number of people in group

We coded the people with whom participants did or did not want to share each item into one or more of the following: a **specific person** (e.g., "my sister," "Tim"); **specific people** defined as a countable set of people (e.g., a group of ten close friends); or an **ambiguous group** defined by one or more attributes or relationships (e.g., "hockey friends"). Percentages add up to over 100% because participants sometimes specified multiple sets of people they wanted to share with or block (e.g., a specific person and an ambiguous group).

Participants specified individuals or groups with whom they wanted to share for 92 out of the 122 unshared items (75%). For the remaining items they were willing to share with everyone or weren't willing to share with anyone. Of the groups associated with the 92 pieces of content, we looked at those with which participants would have shared given optimal selective sharing (53/92 items). Of the groups that would have been useful for selective sharing, 47% (25) were ambiguously defined, 30% (16) were groups of specific people, and 33%

(17) were specific individuals. Participants specified individuals or groups to block from viewing content for 57 items (47%). Of these, participants said that blocking 23 of the groups would allow them to share the content items under optimal selective sharing. Of these groups that would have been useful for selective sharing, 74% (17) were ambiguously defined, 13% (3) were specific groups of people, and 26% (6) were specific individuals.

These results partially imply that our participants were not using Facebook's current custom privacy settings. Participants indicated that they wanted to share with single individuals or specific people, which could be done on Facebook. Participants' reasons for not doing so are further addressed in the Discussion. More ambiguous groups also accounted for a relatively large percent of potentially useful groups. They tended to be attribute-based and consisted of both concrete groups (e.g., classmates) and more context-specific groups (e.g., people who would disagree with a post). Such groups would require more extensive user effort or new tools. For example, a user could set up a school-based group ahead of time but might have more difficulty creating a group defined by people's feelings toward a topic.

Group characteristics

We also looked at characteristics associated with the individuals and groups with whom the participants would have liked to have selectively shared. We coded each individual or group into one or more of the following categories:

- **Work/school**: Work or school at any stage of the participant's life (e.g., coworkers, classmates, high school).
- **Demographics**: Age, gender, geography, race (e.g., younger relatives, male/female).
- **Family**: Relatives (e.g., mother, extended family).
- **Close friends**: Close relationships (e.g., close friends, people seen on a regular basis, boyfriend/girlfriend).
- **Not close friends**: Lacking close relationships (e.g., "not close to," someone never met, "frenemies").
- **Relationship to post**: Interested in the post, felt a certain way about the post, personally relevant to the post (e.g., "feel the same way as me," person the post was directed at, interested in the content).

A summary of the characteristics of the groups associated with the items participants would have been willing to share if they could have targeted or blocked specified people is in Tables 2 and 3. These categories are similar to those that emerged in other work on grouping [9, 11, 13, 21].

Based on the 53 items that participants said that they would have been willing to share if they could have shared with selected individuals, the most frequent attribute was the person or group's relationship to the post (62%, 33 items). It was slightly more likely to occur for a specific person or ambiguous groups. Participants tended to want to share only with people at whom the content was directed or people who would be interested in an item. For example, P08 "had tickets

SHARED	Total	Specific person	Specific group	Ambiguous group
Work/school	17	0	6	11
Demographics	10	2	4	6
Family	6	3	2	3
Close	9	3	6	0
Not close	2	1	1	1
Relationship to post	33	11	11	16
Total items	**53**	**17**	**16**	**25**

Table 2. Characteristics of groups participants wanted to share with for optimal selective sharing, by type of group

BLOCKED	Total	Specific person	Specific group	Ambiguous group
Work/school	8	1	2	6
Demographics	4	0	0	4
Family	2	0	2	1
Close	1	1	0	0
Not close	7	2	0	6
Relationship to post	13	5	1	10
Total items	**23**	**6**	**3**	**17**

Table 3. Characteristics of groups participants wanted to block for optimal selective sharing, by type of group

to an advanced screening of The Avengers and almost posted about how excited [she] was to see it using a bunch of profanity." She wanted to share it with her friends who liked comic books and video games and was "sure I would have posted it if it was just like the people I know like it would've seen it." But, as she pointed out, "I don't have a group for comic book friends, mostly because I don't know who would like it, there are people who like things I don't know about." Determining these more complex, ambiguous relationships to posts that rely on time-of-post decisions would be relatively difficult.

The second most common attribute was work/school (32%, 17 items), which only occurred for groups of specific people and ambiguous groups. For specific groups of people, this attribute tended to be associated with a close group of friends that included people from school. Such specific groups would be relatively easy to define using a selective-sharing mechanism, because they are at least partially defined by a concrete common attribute. When participants defined more ambiguous groups using work/school, they tended to be people who would be interested in the content and who either currently went to school or worked with the participant or went to school with the participant in the past. P08, for example, wanted to share content about a hockey game with "hockey friends," who also tended to be college friends. Defining these more ambiguous groups would be more difficult with current tools and might not be encompassed by the work/school attribute.

Relationship to post also occurred most frequently for the 23 items that participants would have been willing to share if they could have blocked a specific group of individuals (56%, 13 items). Again, it was more likely for specific people and ambiguous groups. For specific people, participants tended to want to block the person who originally posted the content they were planning to comment on or people who might be offended. For example, P12 considered posting "some links to articles I read on NPR and WeArePowerShift.org - very political stuff." She didn't mind the general public seeing the content, but wanted to block her boyfriend's dad and other conservative friends from viewing it.

Work/school was also the second most common attribute for people participants wanted to block. However, for blocking selected people, but not for sharing with selected people, "not close friends" emerged as the third most common attribute. This attribute characterized specific individuals and ambiguous groups. Participants tended not to want to share more personal content with people who didn't know them as well. For example, P14 considered posting about a stressful day but didn't want to share it with people she wasn't as close to. As she put it "if they're better friends with you then they don't necessarily care if you're venting or complaining." Such groups would be relatively difficult to capture using current tools because they tended to be context-specific. They ranged from friends-of-friends to the "frenemies" P13 considered too "weird" to know about her evening plans.

LIMITATIONS

This study had several primary limitations. First, it was qualitative, limited to a small sample, and did not consider unshared content in a cross-cultural context. Conclusions, therefore, lack broad generalizability. Our sample also skewed young. This age skew partly reflects SNSs; in 2010, approximately three-quarters of SNS users were 35 or younger [7]. However, future work examining differences in self-censorship across age levels would also be interesting.

Using a diary study also introduced bias. Participants were aware of the purpose of the study; as part of a "study on Facebook usage" they were asked to report "everything you think about sharing on Facebook but decide not to post." Texting in content and filling out surveys likely primed them to think about Facebook, unshared content, and audiences. When asked, participants did not feel they had changed their behavior due to the study. However, about a third mentioned being more aware of what they posted and unshared content. This may have pushed them to think more about self-censorship.

The study structure also relied on self-reported data based on hypothetical scenarios. Actual behavior does not always match what participants say they will, or mean, to do. These issues could be partially addressed in future studies by designing studies to focus on actual behavior. One possibility would be to examine the differences in types and levels of sharing that occur under different interface designs or when a user is instructed to share in different manners (e.g., posting only for oneself, for close friends, etc). Focusing on behavior might reduce the limitations of self-reported hypothetical data and could allow for less priming.

Finally, this study was only able to capture a subset of self-censored content. There is a spectrum of how likely a user would be to post an unshared item, which ranges from content they are almost prepared to post (e.g., at the keyboard and have fully composed) to vague ideas that they decide they probably shouldn't post. Responses to this study mostly included more fully-thought-out ideas, although there were some vague thoughts. It likely missed more of what people self-censor before ideas are fully developed.

Participants may also have been less likely to report sensitive or embarrassing content. To reduce participants' sensitivity, we avoided face-to-face interaction until after the diary study. We believe this was at least partially successful; participants reported some potentially sensitive items that included profanity, political opinions, and drug references. There is also likely content that is so sensitive that it is self-censored in an ingrained way and was not captured. Future work might accompany an approach like this by using a survey to try to probe more ingrained self-censorship by asking participants if they would consider posting content on a variety of more extreme topics (e.g., sexual content, violence, etc.).

DISCUSSION AND CONCLUSIONS

Participants self-censored content, often because they wanted to manage how they presented themselves to various audiences or to avoid argument or discussion. They indicated that they would have potentially shared about half of this self-censored content, across content types, given the ability to optimally target audiences. The people participants wanted to share with, or block, ranged from those captured by current Facebook privacy controls to ambiguous, context-specific groups that would require more sophisticated mechanisms. We discuss why participants seemed not to use Facebook's custom privacy settings, participants' uses of alternatives to self-censorship, and some high-level design suggestions for capturing selective sharing preferences.

Reasons for not using Facebook custom privacy settings

In general, participants didn't use Facebook's custom privacy settings to control who could see content. At the time of the study (April-May 2012), Facebook offered the ability to set the visibility of a post to the general public, friends-only, lists of friends defined either automatically by Facebook or manually by the user, or a post-specific list of people. Users could set a default to public, friends, or a custom list. Most participants used a friends-only default setting. Some, like P03, felt that friends should be able to "see everything," while others, like P15, assumed that anything posted on Facebook was available for a general audience. A few participants had set up friend lists at some point but tended to have used them once or set them up and then stopped maintaining them. P18, for example, had used the friend lists feature when it first appeared but hadn't continued to actively use them. This behavior is consistent with the literature. Kelley et al. found that users tended not to want to use previously created groups for sharing [11], Strater and Lipford found that users both had trouble understanding Facebook privacy settings and tended not to revisit them once set up [18], and Karr-Wisniewski et al. found that users did not use provided grouping tools [10].

Several participants found Facebook's grouping and privacy features too confusing or difficult to use. P01, for example, hadn't recently adjusted her settings, even though she realized Facebook had changed their privacy settings, and said that "it kind of worries me that I haven't messed with it." She both found the settings confusing, admitting that "I'm not really sure how lists work" and felt that Facebook was something she quickly logged on and checked, not something she sat down and used long enough to bother with the settings. P08 pointed out that she frequently posted status updates from the Facebook mobile app on her phone, where "it's easier to just not post than to go in and mess with the settings."

Other participants didn't trust Facebook. Some didn't trust Facebook to maintain their privacy settings. P16 put it "Like maybe one day they'll just take off all the permissions, like just for fun... so I never know if that's going to happen, since Facebook seems to have a negative track record in most people's minds, I just try to censor myself." Other participants didn't trust themselves to configure the privacy settings and understand how they would propagate.

This suggests that for preferences that could have been captured by Facebook's current tools, users might require better, built-in, education about Facebook's privacy controls, a better interface, or an overall increased level of trust in Facebook's data privacy. One potential direction might be to increase the visibility of available tools and their impact on sharing. Many participants seemed confused about available custom privacy settings and friend lists and how they could be used; increasing transparency could increase their abilities to use such tools and might potentially increase trust in Facebook.

Alternatives to self-censorship

Lampinen et al. describe strategies SNS users rely on to mitigate the co-presence of multiple social groups on SNSs. One of these strategies is self-censorship. However, users also rely on other strategies, including choosing "channels of communication" and dividing up who can see what content [13] both of which our participants described.

Consistent with "dividing the platform," Facebook includes "group pages" that allow users to post content to particular groups. Unlike the other privacy features, participants used the group pages to post content for particular, self-selected groups. Several participants used groups affiliated with interests, school, or work to post and read content, participate in discussions, and advertise events to interested people.

Stutzman and Hartzog also describe how SNS users can choose to use different social network services to maintain "privacy, identity, utility, and propriety" [6]. Participants mentioned using different channels of communication as ad hoc privacy controls to varying degrees. Some used chat for more private communications. Others used locked and unlocked Twitter accounts to post personal content they felt was unfit for Facebook. Several felt they could better limit who was following their content on Twitter. P08 for example, was friends with her young sisters on Facebook, and said "I have been kind of watching things I post [on Facebook] because they're on it a lot, so I'm trying not to swear as much or post a whole lot of crazy things." Instead, she would "post it somewhere else like on my Twitter or on my blog or something" where she felt her sisters couldn't find the content as easily. Such behavior was in line with Stutzman and Hartzog's observation that SNS users relied on a strategy of "practical obscurity" to make it difficult to find certain accounts and maintain privacy [6]. Other participants felt they could better track who viewed Twitter content, even with public accounts. This might indicate a desire for a simpler sharing interface. Participants tended to be wary of how their content would be shared through friends of their friends on Facebook.

Potential improvements to selective sharing

Participant interest in selectively sharing currently self-censored content (approximately half of currently unshared items) suggests a desire for selective sharing tools that would allow them to share with the groups encompassed by their desired audiences. To allow users to share such content would require interface tools that captured the more ambiguous groups participants wanted to target for selective sharing. They would require context-specific information or information often unknown to the user. As outlined in Related Work, machine learning solutions are being developed to help users dynamically create groups. Facebook provides a rich dataset for machine learning, including posts, group pages, likes and a user's own and friends' profile data.

Participants often wanted to share with or block audiences that were relevant to posts. This might require tools that could target groups related to topics people are interested in or might disagree with. Defining these traits could require discovering traits, like "geeky comic book friends" or friends with liberal political views that users might not know themselves but might find useful for sharing. One potential method would be to rely on self-identification. For example, a user could indicate that she wanted to share with "comic book lovers" and wait for people to indicate an interest. Alternatively, a user or algorithm could try to identify characteristics that typified a trait. Such a system might be similar to the Hummingbird system for Twitter. Hummingbird uses Twitter hashtags to allow users to indicate the topics of their tweets and then request and approve others' requests for access by topic [3]. Participants also sometimes wanted to just target individuals involved in a conversation around a post; future tools could make it easier for users to limit a post's audience to people who had previously been involved in a conversational thread. Some combination of these tools could help facilitate users' abilities to target content to people relevant to posts.

Conclusions

Participants chose to self-censor a variety of different types of content. We found that participants most commonly self-censored external content, especially items related to entertainment, closely followed by personal content, including personal opinions and updates. Participants most often tended to self-censor to better control presentation of self. Of the content participants chose to self-censor, they indicated that they would have shared slightly over half if they had been able to exactly target their desired audiences. However, to allow participants to exactly target these audiences would require tools that could specify such desired audiences. We found that participants wanted to target specific individuals and groups of specific people that could potentially be captured using current interface tools but also wanted to share with or block more ambiguously-defined, often context-dependent groups that would be more difficult to target. Across categories these groups were most frequently characterized by their relationship to the content, including relevance to the post or participation in a conversation around the item.

Based on the content participants indicated that they would share if given the opportunity for optimal selective sharing, there may be opportunities to create improved selective sharing tools both by improving the usability of tools to target individuals and specific groups and by creating selective sharing tools for dynamic group creation.

ACKNOWLEDGEMENTS

This material is based upon work supported by the National Science Foundation under Grants No. 0946825 and DGE-0903659, as well as the ARCS Foundation. We thank Patrick Gage Kelley, Michelle Mazurek, and Blase Ur for their assistance.

REFERENCES

1. S. Amershi, J. Fogarty, and D. Weld. Regroup: interactive machine learning for on-demand group creation in social networks. CHI '12, pages 21–30, New York, NY, USA, 2012. ACM.
2. J. Brandt, N. Weiss, and S. R. Klemmer. txt 4 l8r: lowering the burden for diary studies under mobile conditions. CHI EA '07, pages 2303–2308, New York, NY, USA, 2007. ACM.
3. E. D. Cristofaro, C. Soriente, G. Tsudik, and A. Williams. Hummingbird: privacy at the time of Twitter. Oakland '12. IEEE, 2012.
4. L. Fang and K. LeFevre. Privacy wizards for social networking sites. WWW '10, pages 351–360, New York, NY, USA, 2010. ACM.
5. S. D. Farnham and E. F. Churchill. Faceted identity, faceted lives: social and technical issues with being yourself online. CSCW '11, pages 359–368, New York, NY, USA, 2011. ACM.
6. S. Frederic and H. Woodrow. Boundary regulation in social media. CSCW '12, pages 769–778, New York, NY, USA, 2012. ACM.
7. K. N. Hampton, L. S. Goulet, L. Rainie, and K. Purcell. Social networking sites and our lives. *Pew Internet*, June 2011.
8. S. Jones and E. O'Neill. Feasibility of structural network clustering for group-based privacy control in social networks. SOUPS '10, pages 9:1–9:13, New York, NY, USA, 2010. ACM.
9. S. Kairam, M. Brzozowski, D. Huffaker, and E. Chi. Talking in circles: selective sharing in Google+. CHI '12, pages 1065–1074, New York, NY, USA, 2012. ACM.
10. P. Karr-Wisniewski, D. Wilson, and H. Richter-Lipford. A new social order: mechanisms for social network site boundary regulation. AMCIS 2011, 2011.
11. P. Kelley, R. Brewer, Y. Mayer, L. Cranor, and N. Sadeh. An investigation into Facebook friend grouping. Interact 2011, pages 216–233. Springer Berlin / Heidelberg, 2011.
12. A. Lampinen, V. Lehtinen, A. Lehmuskallio, and S. Tamminen. We're in it together: interpersonal management of disclosure in social network services. CHI '11, pages 3217–3226, New York, NY, USA, 2011. ACM.
13. A. Lampinen, S. Tamminen, and A. Oulasvirta. "All my people right here, right now": management of group co-presence on a social networking site. GROUP '09, pages 281–290, New York, NY, USA, 2009. ACM.
14. A. E. Marwick and D. Boyd. I tweet honestly, I tweet passionately: Twitter users, context collapse, and the imagined audience. *New Media & Society*, 13(1):114–133, 2010.
15. M. Naaman, J. Boase, and C.-H. Lai. Is it really about me?: message content in social awareness streams. CSCW '10, pages 189–192, New York, NY, USA, 2010. ACM.
16. J. S. Olson, J. Grudin, and E. Horvitz. A study of preferences for sharing and privacy. CHI EA '05, pages 1985–1988, New York, NY, USA, 2005. ACM.
17. B. Reynolds, J. Venkatanathan, J. Gonçalves, and V. Kostakos. Sharing ephemeral information in online social networks: privacy perceptions and behaviours. Interact 2011, pages 204–215. Springer, 2011.
18. K. Strater and H. R. Lipford. Strategies and struggles with privacy in an online social networking community. BCS-HCI '08, pages 111–119, Swinton, UK, UK, 2008. British Computer Society.
19. F. Stutzman and J. Kramer-Duffield. Friends only: examining a privacy-enhancing behavior in Facebook. CHI '10, pages 1553–1562, New York, NY, USA, 2010. ACM.
20. Y. Wang, G. Norcie, S. Komanduri, A. Acquisti, P. G. Leon, and L. F. Cranor. "I regretted the minute I pressed share": a qualitative study of regrets on Facebook. SOUPS '11, pages 10:1–10:16, New York, NY, USA, 2011. ACM.
21. J. Wiese, P. G. Kelley, L. F. Cranor, L. Dabbish, J. I. Hong, and J. Zimmerman. Are you close with me? are you nearby?: investigating social groups, closeness, and willingness to share. UbiComp '11, pages 197–206, New York, NY, USA, 2011. ACM.
22. P. Wisniewski, H. Lipford, and D. Wilson. Fighting for my space: coping mechanisms for SNS boundary regulation. CHI '12, pages 609–618, New York, NY, USA, 2012. ACM.

Widespread Underprovision on Reddit

Eric Gilbert
School of Interactive Computing & GVU Center
Georgia Institute of Technology
gilbert@cc.gatech.edu

ABSTRACT
Many online communities ask their members to do work for the good of everyone on the site. On social voting sites like Reddit, this means that users judge a stream of incoming links by voting them up or down. The links with the most up-votes bubble up to the main page, pointing everyone toward the best content. A threat to all sites designed this way, however, is underprovision: when too many people rely on others to contribute without doing so themselves. In this paper, we present findings suggesting that widespread underprovision of votes is happening on Reddit, arguably the internet's largest social voting community. Notably, Reddit overlooked 52% of the most popular links the first time they were submitted. This suggests that many potentially popular links get ignored, jeopardizing the site's core purpose. We conclude by discussing possible reasons behind it, and suggest future research on social voting sites.

Author Keywords
social navigation; reddit; voting; free riding; underprovision

ACM Classification Keywords
H5.3. Group and Organization Interfaces; Asynchronous interaction; Web-based interaction.

INTRODUCTION
Reddit, one of the most visited sites on the web[1], is a social voting site that calls itself the "voice of the internet." In the site's own words,

> Reddit is a source for what's new and popular on the web. Users like you provide all of the content and decide, through voting, what's good and what's junk. Links that receive community approval bubble up towards #1, so the front page is constantly in motion and (hopefully) filled with fresh, interesting links. [23]

In short, since you can't follow everything published on the web, you call upon the aggregate wisdom of Reddit's votes to find places on the web worth visiting.

[1] `http://www.alexa.com/siteinfo/reddit.com`
At the time of this writing, Alexa ranks Reddit as the 121st most visited site worldwide and the 54th most visited in the United States.

CSCW'13, February 23–27, 2013, San Antonio, Texas, USA.

Many other online communities also employ this design pattern, known in the academic literature as "social navigation" [7, 8]. Sites like Digg [17] and Hacker News [11] have affordances nearly identical to Reddit's. On Slashdot, members vote to moderate comments [16]. For every product review it receives, Amazon asks its customers, "Was this review helpful to you?" The reviews with the most helpful votes jump to the top so that other customers see them first [10]. On eBay, buyers rate sellers (and vice versa) in the hope of separating the reputable ones from people you shouldn't trust [13]. These votes are public goods, provided for the benefit of everyone in the community [19].

However, what if too few people vote? On Reddit, for example, people might choose to simply visit the popular content without voting on the stream of new links pouring into the site. It takes time and energy to wade through all those new links. After all, if most of them were good, we wouldn't need Reddit. If too many people free ride off of everybody else, the quality of the site will eventually degrade, perhaps to the point where Reddit can no longer surface the best content submitted to the site.

All social production communities experience this situation to an extent [4], a concept known as underprovision. Despite the threat of underprovision quickly turning into a "tragedy of the commons" [12], many online and offline communities overcome widespread underprovision via a combination of social norms, repeated interaction and reputation mechanisms [5, 20, 26]. Studies of Wikipedia [21], Slashdot [16] and eBay [25], for example, all depict flourishing communities that experience some underprovision, yet don't allow it overwhelm the community.

However, discussions among redditors (the name Reddit community members give to themselves) alerted us to possible, significant underprovision on their site. Reddit is primarily a link-sharing site, but also has sections devoted purely to discussion, such as the popular *AskReddit* subreddit (i.e., a sub-community). Redditors expressed concern that their links go completely unnoticed by the community. Meanwhile, someone else submitting the same link later would go to the front page. As Reddit runs on a reputation currency called "karma," redditors complained that this was unfair. For example, one redditor writes:

> yes. this is what's frustrating. an innocuous, earnest submission with absolutely no activity whatsoever is just . . . vexing. it feels like . . . if you delete it and do it again later, it might work . . . I guess I'm just grateful when it works. it's such an incredible resource when the comments are flowing, but if your post gets buried for whatever reason, it's painfully anti-climactic.

Comments like this one inspired the statistical work we present here. In this paper, we present a study of underprovision on Reddit. Examining both page view data and duplicate submissions, we arrive at the conclusion that widespread underprovision of votes is likely happening on the site. Notably, Reddit overlooked 52% of the most popular links the first time they were submitted. This suggests that many potentially popular links (i.e., ones the Reddit community would value) are ignored, jeopardizing Reddit's core purpose.

We conclude by discussing possible reasons behind the underprovision of votes we observe on Reddit. In particular, we discuss candidate answers to the following question: Which design elements, if any, invite the underprovision we see? While we can offer no conclusive answers with this short paper, we hope to invite lines of work that can investigate this deeper research question.

METHOD

In this paper, we present two types of statistical evidence addressing underprovision on Reddit: page view data and an analysis of duplicate submissions.

Page Views

To gain precision around issues of underprovision, we first performed an analysis of page view data we collected from Reddit. We wanted to understand how many people actually look at the new links flowing into the site. As noted earlier, Reddit organizes its design around the most popular content; you have to seek out the queue of brand new submissions. The ratio of new submission page views to popular content page views would give us a first-order view of where attention flows on Reddit.

While sites like Alexa [2] can provide aggregate traffic for a site, fine-grained page-view data among subsections of a site is hard to come by unless you have access to site logs. However, we employed a workaround in focusing on a particular subcommunity within Reddit: the *pics* subreddit. Reddit's second-largest subcommunity by membership [24], *pics* lets users share pictures from around the internet. *pics* has more than 2.1M subscribers, accounting for roughly 3.6% of Reddit's total subscriptions, and its contributions very often make their way to site's most popular page. While the image content varies widely, redditors share the majority of their images using the image-sharing site `imgur.com` (a statistic we derived from our data). While Reddit does not provide page view data, `imgur.com` shows page views to users.

In this paper, we compare the page views that new *pics* images receive with how many the most popular *pics* images receive. While imperfect—it only measures a segment of Reddit—this result will give us insight into the site's distribution of attention. Between April 25, 2011 and May 11, 2011, we crawled the most popular *pics* images and the *pics* new queue every 10 seconds, recording every `imgur.com` link. Our dataset consists of page view statistics for the 14,864 images submitted to *pics* and the 648 most popular images during these 17 days. These particular 17 days were not a significant aspect of the study; rather, they allowed us to study Reddit over time while collecting enough data to draw conclusions.

Other referring sites. One potential confound with the approach just described is that people can visit an imgur picture by referral from any site on the web, or simply by typing its URL directly into their browser. Without access to imgur's server logs (and their associated HTTP referrer data), it is impossible to say how much of an image's traffic originates from Reddit. However, it is important to consider that a Redditor created imgur expressly for the Reddit community to share images, calling it "My Gift to Reddit" [18]. While imgur has branched out to other online communities since then, in a recent interview given to *The Wall Street Journal*, imgur's founder stated that Reddit referrals still dominate imgur's traffic [9]. Therefore, while we cannot achieve the kind of precision we would normally like, we see it as reasonable to examine page views of imgur images linked from Reddit for a first-order estimate of where attention flows on the site. We argue that despite noise at the individual image level (i.e., it would be hard to answer "Did this image get popular because of Reddit?"), this noise washes out between groups at the scale of tens of thousands of data points.

Duplicate Submissions

If enough people monitor the Reddit new queue, then truly good content should rarely go overlooked. (This is a variant of *Linus's Law*: "Given enough eyeballs, all bugs are shallow" [22].) In the second phase of our work, we crawled Reddit every ten seconds between April 25 and May 11, acquiring over a gigabyte of text. This time, however, we crawled the Reddit main page and its overall new queue. Our dataset consists of the 172,030 links submitted to Reddit and the 9,370 links that appeared on the most popular page during these 17 days. We will search this dataset for links which ultimately became popular, but were submitted earlier by someone else. These earlier links—good by definition because they ultimately became very popular—went overlooked by the community.

Ground truth data. This method allows us to construct ground truth data: links that ultimately became popular (even if they were overlooked the first few times) are precisely what Reddit values. However, our approach disregards links that could have been popular if only they had attracted Reddit's attention. Future work might consider overcoming this limitation by sending new Reddit links en masse to Mechanical Turk, for example. For the time being, we argue that the approach presented here will provide the research community with a conservative estimate of the proportion of valuable, yet overlooked content.

RESULTS

The median page views for an image put on the *pics* new queue (but one which did not end up becoming popular) is 557. The median page views for a popular image, on the other hand, is 148,911. Put another way, an image which ends up on the most popular page receives greater than two orders of magnitude more views than one that does not, Wilcoxon $W = 9{,}008{,}436$, $p < 10^{-15}$. As is typical for quantitative social data, these p-values hold less meaning than the magnitude of the differences between groups. Figure 1 illustrates this finding graphically, showing the log-scale distributions of both groups induced via Gaussian kernel density estimates.

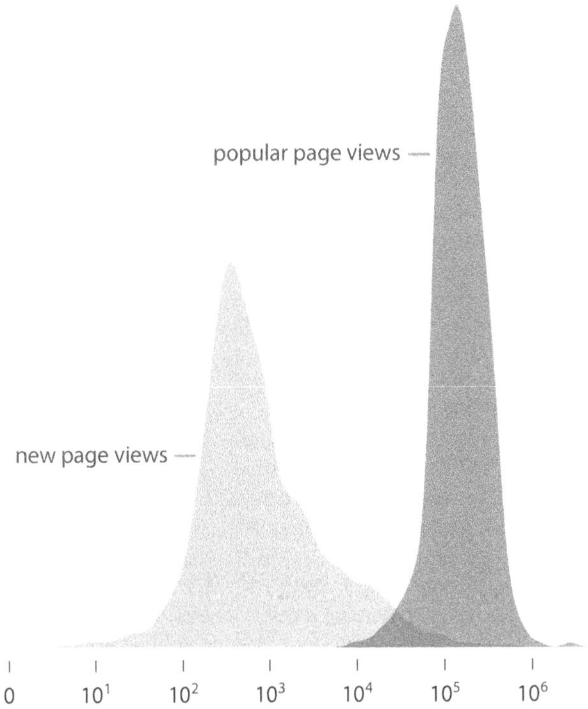

Figure 1. Page view distributions for new *pics* images versus most popular images. On average, the most popular images receive two orders of magnitude more page views than images on the new queue. (The distributions were induced via Gaussian kernel density estimates.)

Gaussian kernel density estimates smooth datasets in an attempt to expose a more continuous, more realistic picture of the underlying distribution [6].

Duplicate Submissions

Of the 9,370 most popular links we collected, we were able to identify when 5,186 first appeared in the new queue. (Since it takes time for a link to become popular, our process of crawling the new queue requires time to find ultimately popular links.) Of these 5,186 most popular links, someone else had submitted the same link earlier in 2,672 cases. In other words, 51.52% of the links destined for the most popular page had been submitted by someone else earlier (within our 17-day window). Those previous links went overlooked by nearly the entire Reddit community.

Figure 2 presents the distribution of times a most popular link had been submitted earlier by someone else. For instance, in 1,717 cases (33.1%) exactly one person submitted the same link earlier. A single link in our dataset had 54 prior submissions before finally finding popularity, probably the result of a bot slipping through Reddit's automated defenses. Figure 2, while only showing cases zero through five, seems to exhibit the long-tail form (e.g, log-normal, power-law, stretched exponential, etc.) characteristic of social data. This formulation of the data is too sparse, however, to confirm which exact shape it takes.

DISCUSSION

By combining these statistical approaches, we see a picture of underprovision emerge. Our *Duplicate Submissions* data present perhaps the most direct evidence. If you submit a

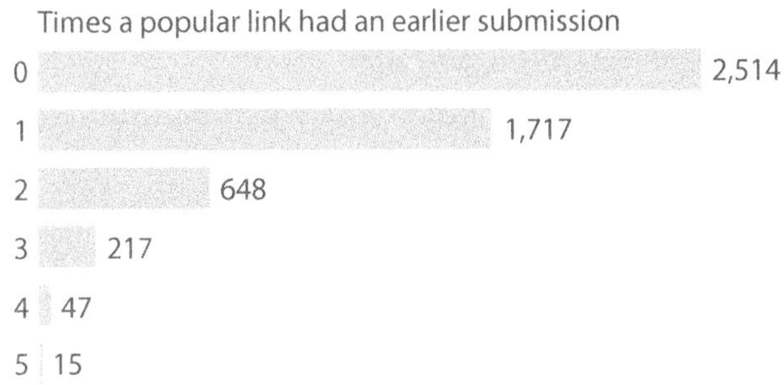

Figure 2. The distribution of how many times 5,186 most popular links had been submitted earlier by someone else. For example, in 648 cases two other people had submitted the same link earlier. Less than half of Reddit's most popular links (2,514/5,186 = 48.48%) get noticed on their first submission to the site.

great link to Reddit, more than half the time someone else will get the karma associated with the upvotes.

We find it surprising that such a stark difference exists between attention paid to the new queue and attention paid to the most popular content. This remains true when you sum over both groups: the total page views given to the most popular images is more than four times that given to new images, despite the fact that this dataset contains 22.9 times more new images than most popular images.

Redditors often lament the presence of bots in the community, something we shouldn't ignore. Bots upvote links they favor and downvote ones they do not, en masse. Of course, any large online community will have to contend with them. Yet, one interpretation of the bot problem comes from the work presented here: Reddit may be susceptible because too few people look at new content, like a market with too few competitors. We know from previous work, for example, that a small number of colluding cliques can drive what emerges on Digg's front page, another social voting site [17].

We examined links which ultimately ended up popular to construct ground truth. We needed to conclusively call the link "good." However, our findings imply that many links that could reach popularity never get noticed, beyond the duplicate submissions examined here. Perhaps community members want multiple submissions to infer the worth of a link. In other words, redditors may monitor every link, yet purposely withhold their vote until they see a link for the second or third time. While we see this as a less viable explanation, we should investigate the impact this practice could have on those that get ignored in the early stages of a link's submission.

Design Implications

These early data suggest that widespread underprovision of votes is happening on Reddit. We next turn to possible explanations. What features of Reddit's design could generate widespread underprovision of votes? Is it specific to Reddit or something found more generally among social navigation systems? Each possibility below suggests a different design intervention, yet we caution that this space needs deeper empirical work before targeting specific design strategies. We instead use our data, along with theory and design criticism, to introduce starting points for new design-oriented research questions about social voting sites.

Could Reddit's design disincent searching the new queue? It seems axiomatic for a social voting site: most of the content submitted to it isn't any good. Redditors have a strong incentive to drop in on the site for its most popular content and ignore the firehose of new submissions. Most of the time, they will find something funny, interesting or inspiring. They would find exactly the opposite on the new queue: mostly bad jokes, uninteresting blog posts and uninspiring stories. Imagine the wasted effort a redditor would have to expend wading through all the noise flowing into Reddit.

In our dataset, 9,370 of the 172,030 links submitted to Reddit became popular (5.4%). Even if the true rate of good content is twice what we see currently on the site (i.e., roughly 11%), the enterprising redditor would face a deluge of bad content. Perhaps Reddit's fundamental design idea—showing by default the good content that others promote from the firehose of the internet—leads to underprovision. Perhaps the firehose is simply too much for too many people.

Perhaps because the voting mechanism isn't social? In previous work, researchers have found many large, successful online communities that overcome underprovision problems. However, earlier research has focused on designs that include conversations among community members: discussions on Slashdot or reviews on eBay, for instance. The Reddit voting mechanism isn't conversational. You vote with a click and go away. Perhaps this difference explains the discord with existing online communities research.

Could the subcommunity architecture reward poachers? Subreddits let users find smaller communities more in tune with their interests. The subreddits vary in size and topic, ranging from hundreds of thousands of subscribers to just a handful [24]. While this design follows best practices [14], as it shields redditors from the parts of the internet they don't care about, it also makes poaching possible. For example, imagine that a redditor posts a great link to a subreddit with 15 subscribers. Someone else in bigger subreddit can then cross-post it. The link submitted to the bigger subreddit probably has a greater chance of success.

Does someone else sell it better? When you post a link to Reddit, you also give it title. The site suggests that the title reflect where the link points, but it also gives the redditor room to comment. Titles are often witty, timely and sometimes reflect Reddit's idiosyncratic values. Perhaps the second or third submitter of the same link comes up with a better title, piquing everyone's interest in a way the original submitter did not.

Do redditors vote on the underlying link or on how well someone sells the title? In our data, while most resubmitted links have different titles, we find that most contain a majority of words from the original submission. If re-titling significantly explains our findings, then the mechanism is probably subtle. This question deserves investigation, as its answer could underpin how much voting mechanisms hinge on subtle, small design choices like letting user provide titles. Other sites, such as Hacker News, often moderate submissions whose titles do not mirror the target's title tag.

Or, do some redditors post at the wrong time? It seems likely that during certain times of day or under certain conditions (e.g., during periods of peak usage), the likelihood of having your link noticed could go down. In our data, we find effects for time-of-day, with popular links posted in the morning hours much more likely to get ignored than those in the afternoon and evening. At the same time, many fewer links are posted during morning hours, so it remains unclear how much simple external forces like time-of-day account for popular submissions going unnoticed on Reddit.

Theoretical Implications

Above, we explore design-oriented research questions that may help shed light on our findings. We believe the present research also suggests new directions for CMC theory. Researchers have consistently found vastly skewed participation curves in social systems (e.g., power-law, stretched exponential, log-normal, etc.), both offline and online [1, 15]. Sometimes this is framed as a result of a process of preferential attachment happening on underlying social networks [3]. Consider that voting participation patterns skew this way, too. Do different skews (i.e. exponents, in the power-law framing) lead to different proportions of overlooked, yet valuable content on social voting sites?

On Reddit, we see roughly half of all valuable content overlooked on its first submission. Researchers might leverage this work to contrast this finding with other social voting sites, like Digg and Hacker News. How does this "overlooked proportion" vary with broader participation skews, presuming different ones on different sites? Moreover, researchers can take our results as a point of departure for community-wide studies. Does such a high-rate of overlooked, valuable content result in high turnover among newcomers? How do people gauge when and what they should submit in the face of such high rates of failure?

CONCLUSION

Large online communities often overcome the threat of underprovision via a combination of social norms, repeated interaction and reputation mechanisms. However, in this paper we document a case of widespread underprovision within a major online community.

We hope that researchers will see directions for new research in this work, perhaps developing interventions to solve underlying design problems. For example, if the social voting design truly disincents searching the new queue, a strategy of investable reputation (i.e., something akin to buying stock in a great, but unknown company) might resolve the problem. We look forward to future work addressing these issues.

ACKNOWLEDGEMENTS

We would like to thank the Social Spaces group at Illinois, as well as the comp.social lab at Georgia Tech. Tony Bergstrom and Tanushree Mitra contributed valuable feedback on early drafts. Google helped support this work.

REFERENCES

1. L. Adamic and B. Huberman. Zipf's law and the Internet. *Glottometrics*, 3(143–150), 2002.
2. Alexa. http://alexa.com. Retrieved June 1, 2012.
3. A. Barabási and R. Albert. Emergence of Scaling in Random Networks. *Science*, 286(5439):509–512, 1999.
4. Y. Benkler. *The Wealth of Networks: How Social Production Transforms Markets and Freedom*. Yale University Press, 2006.
5. F. Berkes, D. Feeny, B. McCay, and J. Acheson. The Benefits of the Commons. *Nature*, 340(6229):91–93, 1989.
6. R. Cao, A. Cuevas, and W. Gonzalez Manteiga. A Comparative Study of Several Smoothing Methods in Density Estimation. *Computational Statistics & Data Analysis*, 17(2):153–176, 1994.
7. A. Dieberger, P. Dourish, K. Höök, P. Resnick, and A. Wexelblat. Social navigation: techniques for building more usable systems. *Interactions*, 7(6):36–45, 2000.
8. P. Dourish and M. Chalmers. Running Out of Space: Models of Information Navigation. In *Proc. CHI*, 1994.
9. L. Gannes. Interview: Imgur's Path to a Billion Image Views Per Day. http://dthin.gs/JgKPqL. Retrieved August 27, 2012.
10. E. Gilbert and K. Karahalios. Understanding Deja Reviewers. In *Proc. CSCW*, pages 225–228, 2010.
11. Hacker News. http://news.ycombinator.com. Retrieved June 1, 2012.
12. G. Hardin. The Tragedy of the Commons. *Science*, 162(3859):1243–1248, 1969.
13. T. Khopkar, X. Li, and P. Resnick. Self-selection, Slipping, Salvaging, Slacking, and Stoning: The Impacts of Negative Feedback at eBay. In *Proc EC*, pages 223–231, 2005.
14. A. Kim. *Community building on the web*. Peachpit Press, 2000.
15. J. Laherrere and D. Sornette. Stretched exponential distributions in nature and economy: "fat tails" with characteristic scales. *The European Physical Journal B-Condensed Matter and Complex Systems*, 2(4):525–539, 1998.
16. C. Lampe and P. Resnick. Slash(dot) and Burn: Distributed Moderation in a Large Online Conversation Space. In *Proc. CHI*, pages 543–550, 2004.
17. K. Lerman and A. Galstyan. Analysis of Social Voting Patterns on Digg. In *Proc. WOSN*, pages 7–12, 2008.
18. My Gift to Reddit. http://redd.it/7zlyd. August 27, 2012.
19. M. Olson. *The Logic of Collective Action: Public Goods and the Theory of Groups*. Harvard University Press, 1974.
20. E. Ostrom. *Governing the Commons: The Evolution of Institutions for Collective Action*. Cambridge University Press, 1999.
21. R. Priedhorsky, J. Chen, S. Lam, K. Panciera, L. Terveen, and J. Riedl. Creating, destroying, and restoring value in Wikipedia. In *Proc. GROUP*, pages 259–268, 2007.
22. E. Raymond. *The Cathedral and the Bazaar: Musings on Linux and Open Source by an Accidental Revolutionary*. O'Reilly & Associates, Inc., 2001.
23. Reddit. http://www.reddit.com/help/faq#Whatisreddit. Retrieved June 1, 2012.
24. Redditlist. http://redditlist.com. Retrieved June 1, 2012.
25. P. Resnick and R. Zeckhauser. Trust Among Strangers in Internet Transactions: Empirical Analysis of eBay's Reputation System. *Advances in Applied Microeconomics*, 11:127–157, 2002.
26. M. Smith and P. Kollock. *Communities in Cyberspace*. Psychology Press, 1999.

Users and Nonusers: Interactions between Levels of Facebook Adoption and Social Capital

Cliff Lampe
School of Information
University of Michigan
105 S. State St.
Ann Arbor, MI 48109
cacl@umich.edu

Jessica Vitak
College of Information Studies
University of Maryland
4105 Hornbake Bldg, South Wing
College Park, MD 20742
jvitak@umd.edu

Nicole Ellison
School of Information
University of Michigan
105 S. State St
Ann Arbor, MI 48109
enicole@umich.edu

ABSTRACT
Although Facebook is the largest social network site in the U.S. and attracts an increasingly diverse userbase, some individuals have chosen not to join the site. Using survey data collected from a sample of non-academic staff at a large Midwestern university (N=614), we explore the demographic and cognitive factors that predict whether a person chooses to join Facebook. We find that older adults and those with higher perceived levels of bonding social capital are less likely to use the site. Analyzing open-ended responses from non-users, we find that they express concerns about privacy, context collapse, limited time, and channel effects in deciding to not adopt Facebook. Finally, we compare non-adopters against users who differ on three dimensions of use. We find that light users often have social capital outcomes similar to, or worse than, non-users, and that heavy users report higher perceived bridging and bonding social capital than either group.

Author Keywords
Facebook; social network sites; social capital; technology adoption

ACM Classification Keywords
H.5.3. Group and Organization Interfaces – Web-based Interaction

INTRODUCTION
Social network site (SNS) use has grown significantly in the United States in recent years. In 2005, only 8% of U.S. Internet-using adults were members of an SNS, but by 2011 that percentage had grown to 65% [30], largely dominated by membership on Facebook. However, that leaves 35% of that population who have chosen not to join a SNS. While some of this lack of adoption may result from lack of access to Internet tools or a lack of skills associated with using these services, differences between adopters and non-adopters of SNSs may also be explained by differences in individual characteristics and motivations. Given the growing body of literature that suggests SNS use is associated with benefits such as social capital gains [6, 15, 44] and increases in well-being [45], we feel it is important to better understand patterns around non-adoption and social capital and self-esteem patterns associated with no use, low use, and high use of the site.

While there have been multiple studies of SNS users in college populations [21, 24], in general adult populations [6, 17], and in organizations [38, 42], these studies have focused on current users, rather than on differences between users and non-users of these sites. In one notable exception, Hargittai [21] examined differences between undergraduate users and non-users of SNSs. She identified demographic predictors of site use and looked not only at adoption vs. non-adoption but also differences among specific sites (e.g., Facebook vs. MySpace). Likewise, recent longitudinal research by Brandtzaeg [5] looking at Norwegian's Internet use over a three-year period found that, compared with non-users, SNS users have more face-to-face interactions, more acquaintances, and higher bridging social capital, although they also report higher loneliness.

There have been multiple models of technology adoption proposed in the literature [1, 10, 11, 18, 46], many of which have been applied to social software use in an organizational setting. However, compared to organizational groupware adoption patterns, we expect social media sites like Facebook will be associated with different usage and adoption patterns given the greater selection of tools available and differences in user characteristics and site features. A common theme in models of technology adoption points to the complex interplay between features of the system, social structures like norms and influence, and individual demographic and cognitive factors like motivation, literacy, and efficacy [11]. It is also unclear from this literature what adoption means. For example, simply creating a Facebook account is unlikely to have the same effects as using it regularly.

In what ways are Facebook users and non-users different, and how are heavy users distinct from light users? To answer those questions, we conducted a survey of non-academic staff at a large university. Given that Facebook use can be quite heterogeneous, we look at both heavy and light users of Facebook, comparing their characteristics to each other as well as to non-users and identifying social capital and well-being outcomes associated with these different levels of use.

LITERATURE REVIEW

SNS use is growing across a diverse set of people. In the United States, 65% of Internet-using adults have a profile on a SNS [30]. When looking at specific age demographics, those in the 30-49 age range increased from 25% adoption in 2008 to 70% in 2011, and those in the 50-64 bracket went from 11% in 2008 to 51% in 2011. While this is a notable increase in use over a short amount of time, 35% of Internet-using adults still have not joined a SNS. As another example of the changes in this area, Twitter was used daily by only 2% of Internet-using Americans in November 2010, yet by May 2012 was used by 8% daily and 15% overall, with even more stark increases in use by young adults, residents of urban areas, and African Americans [40].

How and why people use Facebook is important because research has shown a wide range of potentially positive outcomes from that use [50]. Facebook use has been associated with increases in social capital [15], political mobilization [43] and participation [22, 48]; information seeking both within organizations [31, 42] and in more everyday settings [25, 32]; and in educational settings [4, 27, 37].

SNSs can fill a variety of user needs, and multiple studies have applied the Uses and Gratifications perspective to account for the heterogeneous ways in which people use Facebook. For example, Joinson [23] applied this approach to understand how Facebook members used the site, finding some users were mainly interested in interpersonal communication, while others were more invested in picture sharing or playing games. Also applying a Uses and Gratifications lens, Papacharissi and Mendelson [33] showed how different motivations were associated with levels of social capital reported by Facebook users. Smock et al. [41] studied how college students' uses of and gratifications derived from Facebook were associated with use of and efficacy toward different Facebook features.

How individuals use the site to connect with others, and who these connections are, also varies across users. Hampton et al. [20] conducted phone surveys with Facebook users, and matched those survey responses with Facebook server data. They found that "most people get more than they give" in relation to attention from others because a small group of power users are actively engaged in behaviors like commenting, liking, and tagging the content of others. Backstrom et al. [2] used Facebook server data to show how users divided attention (as measured by Wall posts, messages, and profile views) across their Facebook network and found heterogeneous strategies that were stable by individual. Some people would spend their attention on a small group of people in their network, while others would spread their attention more equally across connections. Similarly, Ellison et al. [15] found that Facebook users employed three different "connection strategies" regarding who they connected with on the site, and these practices had implications for users' perceived social capital levels. Burke et al. [6] found that people who did not actively engage with their networks had higher levels of reported loneliness and lower social capital outcomes. Brandtzaeg [5] divided SNS users into five use clusters based on how they described their site behaviors (e.g. Lurkers, Socializers, Debaters, Sporadics and Advanced) and found difference in loneliness and bridging social capital between those groups. The heterogeneity of motivation to use and type of use likely means that people have different outcomes resulting from their participation.

Given the increasing percentage of the population across demographics that have started to use Facebook, non-adoption is an issue that becomes increasingly important, as these non-adopters may be opting out of significant opportunities for communication. The studies described above have identified a range of potential positive outcomes and new ways of interacting with social systems, enabled by these tools. Understanding why users choose not to participate in these opportunities may help to identify the impact of non-adoption. Additionally, it is clear that Facebook use is far from monolithic, and comparing non-users of the site to users as a single block may miss some subtleties in that variety of use. We have identified three types of use to compare users across—non-users, light users, and heavy users—which we see as a first step in adding nuance to the perception of Facebook participation.

Technology Adoption

Why might some people adopt a site like Facebook while others do not? What differences exist between those who log in multiple times a day versus those who go days without checking in? Researchers have identified several models of why people adopt technology in general, and social software more specifically. Grudin [18, 19] looked at adoption of groupware in organizational settings and found that issues like network effects and difficulty in evaluating outcomes of use had an effect on overall adoption of groupware. In particular, he highlights the importance of not designing socio-technical systems where there is a "disparity between who does the work and who gets the benefit" and describes the cost-benefit analysis that groupware users make when they decide whether to use a technology. DeSanctis and Poole [11] describe Adaptive Structuration Theory, pointing to a complex interplay between individual, group and technological features that predict when a technology will be developed. Diffusion of Innovations Theory [35] adopts a social learning perspective, proposing that people adopt a technology after observing others (especially influential others) using that technology and receiving benefit from it.

Often used to explore organizational-level adoption, a common model of information technology adoption is the Technology Acceptance Model (TAM) [10, 46], which argues that people assess two major dimensions of a technology as they decide whether to adopt it: perceived ease-of-use and perceived usefulness. In this model, potential users evaluate the tension between how hard or easy a system is to use versus the benefits they can receive from the system. In relation to the decision about whether or not to use Facebook, TAM would predict that people are assessing two aspects of the site when making adoption decisions: how difficult Facebook is to use and the possible benefits (or usefulness) of site use. The original work on TAM focused on how information technology could facilitate work processes, but more recent studies have also looked at social benefits of adoption [9]. Although TAM has often been accused of over-simplifying the adoption process [3] and being overly-embedded in rational choice paradigms [28], it does provide a baseline model for describing some of the factors that may influence adoption.

Adoption of Facebook

Few studies have looked at how people decide whether or not to adopt social media in general, or Facebook in particular. Hargittai [21] did early work looking at how factors like race, gender, and socio-economic status affected adoption of multiple SNS platforms. She found, for example, that Facebook users were more likely to be White and from more affluent socio-economic backgrounds. However, these data were collected in 2006 when Facebook was still limited to university networks and, as shown above, there has been a large-scale changes in the SNS userbase since they were collected. Brandtzaeg [5] has done a more recent study looking SNS users and non-users, as well as comparing different categories of Facebook users. He found that bridging social capital is different between users and non-users, but used a measure of social capital that assess network diversity, rather than outcomes from connections. In addition, while he did not directly measure bonding social capital, he found that Facebook users had more acquaintances and more face-to-face interactions with their close friends than non-users.

One reason there has been little work exploring non-adopters of Facebook is because research in this area has been dominated either by studies of undergraduate students, a population that does not typically include enough non-users to support comparative analyses, or by studies that are based on Facebook server-level data, which are limited to Facebook users. While the Pew Internet & American Life Project has provided multiple descriptive studies of SNS use [20, 39, 40], few of them involve multivariate analysis of relationships between variables.

METHODS

In order to compare characteristics of Facebook users and non-users, we invited, via email, a random sample of 2149 non-academic staff at a large, Midwestern university to participate in an online survey regarding their use of online communication tools in February 2011; all participants were also invited to provide an email address to be entered into a raffle for one of ten $15 Amazon gift cards. We received usable responses from 614 people; after removing undelivered invitations, the response rate was calculated to be 28.9%. Of that sample, 22% (134) were not Facebook members. Our sample – non-academic staff members of a university – presumably have Internet access on campus (at campus computer labs if not in their local workplace) and thus constitute an appropriate sample for exploring motivations for non-use that does not stem from lack of access. In addition to their presumed access at the workplace – a college campus – the vast majority of our sample (93.8%) reported having an Internet-connected computer at home. Thus access is unlikely to be the primary reason why they do not use the site.

Unless otherwise noted, all scale variables detailed below were measured using Likert-type response options ranging from 1 (Strongly Disagree) to 5 (Strongly Agree).

Variables Measured for Members and Non-members

Our survey instrument included demographic, psychological, and perception-based measures in order to test differences between Facebook members and non-members. Across the entire sample, participants were more likely to be female (66%), White (83%) and 45 years old on average (SD = 11). They reported spending a median of 3.49 hours per day on the Internet, and 72.1% had a college degree or higher. Ninety-five percent reported having access to high-speed Internet, and 90% had a computer in the home.

Internal use characteristics

Internet Self-Efficacy [29] captures individuals' perceptions of their ability to understand a variety of Internet-based concepts and perform various Internet-based tasks. The 7-item scale (M = 3.68, SD = .80) was highly reliable (α = .93).

Self-esteem has consistently shown to be related to Facebook users' engagement with the site (e.g., [13, 15]). In this study, we included Rosenberg's [36] 7-item Self-Esteem Scale (α = .86, M = 4.33, SD = .56) to capture individuals' self-esteem.

Perception of Facebook's Usefulness

Perceptions of Facebook's Usefulness is an original scale (two items; α = .91, M = 3.60, SD = .88) intended to capture both Facebook users' and non-users' perceptions of Facebook's general utility ("Facebook is a useful site" and "I see benefits in joining Facebook").

Social capital
Participants were asked a series of questions to capture their perceived access to social capital resources through interactions with members of their social network. Social capital is often delineated into two types: bridging social capital, which is characterized by access to new people and ideas, inclusivity, and expanded world views; and bonding social capital, which typically includes more dense networks of support that are inward-looking in nature and more likely to be associated with emotional support and more significant forms of mobilization (such as a large financial loan) Putnam [34]. Bridging social capital is important for mobilizing generalized reciprocity—the belief that people do good things for a person or society without specific expectation of repayment (e.g., donating blood)—while bonding social capital is key to specific reciprocity and mobilizing solidarity within a group.

The scales used in this survey were adapted from Williams' [49] Internet Social Capital Scales (ISCS), with participants instructed to "think about your entire social network, including relatives, close and distant friends, coworkers and acquaintances" when reporting their level of agreement with statements such as "Interacting with people in my social network makes me want to try new things" and "There are several people in my social network I trust to help solve my problems." Note that in contrast to other versions of these scales, we did not specify a particular context (such as the original scales' "offline" and "online" contexts) in order to use the same items for both Facebook users and non-users. The bridging social capital measure (10 items, $\alpha = .88$; $M = 3.74$, $SD = .58$) captures aspects including contact with diverse others and feeling part of a broader group, while the bonding social capital scale (10 items, $\alpha = .84$, $M = 3.49$, $SD = .63$) is focused on social and emotional support as well as "big favors."

Variables Measured for Facebook Members Only
Previous research suggests that use of Facebook is strongly heterogeneous for members [20]. In order to compare different levels of use with non-use, we asked Facebook users questions related to three different dimensions of Facebook use. We created categorical variables for light and heavy types of each type of use by grouping the lowest and highest quartile of each of the variables.

Time spent on Facebook
The amount of time someone spends using Facebook is a standard measure of overall use that has been used in other Facebook research [7, 8, 16]. In this study, Facebook members were asked to respond to a question which asked, "In the past week, on average, how many minutes PER DAY have you spent actively using Facebook?" We were careful to indicate that we were interested in active use, as opposed to just having the site open on one's screen. On average, users reported spending 34 minutes on the site per day (median = 15, $SD = 47.90$). The lowest quartile of reported use was 5 minutes per day or less, while the highest quartile of reported use was 45 minutes or more per day.

"Actual" and Total Friends on Facebook
Other work [15] has found that in determining the effects of network size on social capital, the number of "actual friends" respondents report having in their Facebook network was a stronger predictor of outcome measures such as social capital than the total number of Facebook connections one has made. The authors speculated that actual friends are likely to be "individuals with whom the user has a stronger offline connection" and that users may configure their settings to hide content from "non-actual" friends (and, conversely, may also have their content hidden from these individuals), potentially minimizing the social capital benefits associated with "non-actual" friends. Another factor contributing to this lack of visibility is technical: Facebook's algorithm hides content from some Friends, and non-actual Friends (weaker ties) are probably more likely to be categorized as irrelevant to a particular user (and thus hidden). In this survey, Facebook users were asked, "Approximately how many TOTAL Facebook friends do you have?" and "Approximately how many of your TOTAL Facebook friends do you consider actual friends?" On average, respondents reported having 76 actual friends (median = 40, $SD = 101$) and 207 total Friends (median = 120, $SD = 288$); therefore, examining median responses, Facebook users reported that approximately one-third of their total Facebook network was comprised of actual friends. Similar to [15], we did not define what "actual friends" meant in order to tap into individual understandings of friendship.

Signals of Relational Investment (SRI)
SRI is a scale comprised of five items related to the respondents' reported likelihood of engaging in behaviors that signal attention to specific Friends in their Facebook network. This scale ($\alpha = .901$, $M = 3.55$, $SD = .83$) has been used in previous work [14, 26] and has been validated through confirmatory factor analysis ($X^2 = 7.91$, $p > .05$; RMSEA = .05; CFI = 1.00; GFI = .99). SRI probes the extent to which subjects report that they "try to respond" to Friends when they post requests for information and advice or make less explicit articulations of social support needs, such as posting about having a bad day. A fifth item in the scale asks about posting "happy birthday" on a Friend's Wall. We argue [14, 26] that responding to these requests constitute relationship maintenance activities, in that users are explicitly signaling that they are attending to specific individuals in their network and engaging in a mediated form of "social grooming" [12] with these specific ties. Previous research [26] found SRI to be highly correlated with perceptions of bridging social capital, and similar attention-signaling behaviors such as commenting on Friends' updates have been shown to be related to social capital [6]. Breaking reported SRI into quartiles, the lowest

quartile had a value of 3.20 or less on the scale, while the highest quartile had a value of 4.00 or higher.

RESULTS

In order to explore how Facebook non-users are different from users, we present three analyses. First, we conduct a binary logistic regression comparing non-users against all users in our sample, to identify high-level differences between these two groups. Next, we present data from open-ended responses from non-users responding to a question about why they don't use Facebook. Finally, we present three ANOVAs highlighting differences between non-users of Facebook and either light or heavy users.

Predicting Members and Non-members

In order to determine which individual characteristics were associated with whether a participant reported being a Facebook member or not, we employed binary logistic regression (see Table 2), which shows how each independent variable affects the likelihood that someone responded either yes or no to being a Facebook member. Of the demographic variables described above, only age was a statistically significant predictor of membership. Being older had a slightly negative association with being a member of Facebook, which is consistent with descriptive studies of overall SNS use [30]. A correlation matrix of non-demographic variables included in this model are presented in Table 1.

Internet efficacy, self-esteem, and bridging social capital were not significantly related to the likelihood of being a Facebook member in this model; however, two variables were significant in this model. First, the more strongly one agreed with statements about how useful Facebook was, the more likely s/he was to use the site. Second, in an unexpected finding given previous literature on this topic, bonding social capital was a strong **negative** predictor of being a Facebook member.

Qualitative Data from Non-Users

The 134 participants who reported not having a Facebook account were asked to explain why they had chosen to refrain from participating in Facebook. The majority (91%) provided a response, which we then analyzed through an iterative process to establish a taxonomy of reasons for non-use. First, a research assistant on the project read through each of the responses and identified six main categories of responses. The second author then reviewed the categorization scheme and collapsed two of the categories due to redundancy: a category called "Not interested" was collapsed into the "Lack of interest" category, in light of the conceptual overlap between these categories and the fact that many responses spanned these codes. Finally, all responses were reviewed for correct categorization. The five final categories were: time constraints, the impersonality of communication online, privacy concerns, context collapse, and a general lack of interest. When responses reflected multiple themes, this was reflected in the coding process (i.e., they received multiple codes).

As a whole, a dominant theme of these responses evoked the sense that using the site was not worth it – either due to the costs (in time or effort) of site use, the lack of value associated with site use, or the sense that even if using Facebook did involve some positive outcomes, they did not outweigh the negative outcomes of use. For instance, one participant wrote, "I tried it a couple of times, and while there are very clear benefits to Facebook, I found that it wasn't for me in terms of time spent using it." Similarly, another noted, "[The site] creates more social problems than it's worth." While some remarked on its value for sharing information or for communicating with younger family members who use the site as their "major method of communication," they ultimately identified as non-users. Below we describe each of these themes in more detail.

	Self Esteem	FB Usefulness	Bridging	Bonding
Internet Efficacy	0.10**	0.11**	0.07*	0.04
Self Esteem		0.01	0.17**	0.19**
FB Usefulness			0.28**	0.14**
Bridging				0.38**
Bonding				

Table 1: Kendall's Tau correlations of variables for both users and non-users. * <.05 **<.01

Variable name	Beta	S.E.	Sig	Exp (B)
Sex (Male)	-0.179	0.293	0.542	0.836
Age	**-0.043**	**0.014**	**0.004**	**0.961**
Ethnicity (NonWhite)	-0.515	0.360	0.152	0.598
Education	-0.065	0.123	0.598	0.937
Weekly Internet Use	-0.025	0.050	0.616	0.976
Internet Efficacy	0.336	0.185	0.069	1.400
Self Esteem	-0.294	0.237	0.216	0.746
Facebook Usefulness	**1.344**	**0.163**	**0.001**	**3.833**
Bridging SC	0.323	0.286	0.259	1.381
Bonding SC	**-0.463**	**0.223**	**0.038**	**0.630**
Constant	-1.67	1.571	0.915	0.846

Table 2: Binary logistic regression predicting likelihood of being a Facebook member. Nagelkerke R^2 = 0.36. Bolded lines are significant predictors at a .05 alpha or lower.

Time Constraints. Many participants referenced their busy schedules and suggested that using Facebook would require more time and energy than they had available. Some noted the "time suck" aspect of use, with one saying, "I believe it is a huge waste of time and it takes away from productivity in the workplace." Several specifically referenced spending extensive time on their computers for work and wanting to avoid doing the same while at home. For example, one participant said, "I feel that I do not have time to be online, work, and spend time with my family."

Channel Effects. Participants noted what they perceived to be the impersonal nature of interactions facilitated by the site, and some compared Facebook interactions to having face-to-face interactions with a friend, which they saw as more authentic, private, and personal. For example, one participant wrote, "I feel these types of interactions to be extremely impersonal. I would much rather speak to another person; much more can be accomplished through a simple conversation." Another noted, "I prefer talking face to face or on the phone. My personal friends deserve a private conversation." Some highlighted what they saw as differences between "real" friendships and those found online, as this participant explained: "I find Facebook 'relationships' and social interactions to be superficial and a gossip mine. I would prefer to have real relationships with a smaller group of people. I feel secure with who I am and don't need 8,000 'friends.'"

Privacy. Privacy concerns played a role in many non-users' comments. Perhaps fueled by media stories describing the privacy concerns associated with Facebook and other social media, participants voiced concerns about sharing private data in they perceived to be a public space. For some, even knowledge of the privacy settings was not enough: "Personally, I think it's creepy. Even with the privacy guards in place, people can stalk you from your friends' sites." Others referenced privacy concerns explicitly, with comments like "They [Facebook] are in the business of making money, not securing my privacy... I am not a product to be sold" or which referenced "Facebook's disregard for users privacy and concerns."

Context Collapse. Context collapse concerns have been identified in previous studies of Facebook users [47]. Context collapse encapsulates users' desire to maintain boundaries between various dimensions of their identity, which some users see as increasingly difficult as the number of people using the site grows. This concern was directly mentioned by only two participants, although others indirectly referenced related concerns. Participants' comments specifically referenced the desire to separate professional and personal aspects of their identity: "too much overlap between work and personal life on Facebook" and "Professional reasons—to keep boundaries around my personal and professional lives." A third participant indirectly referenced a related issue: one of time management. The participant wrote, "time on the PC after work, be it Facebook or something else, takes away from time with my spouse and children. I try to be available while at home and 'on-task' at work." In a related comment, one participant didn't want to signal to his/her children that Facebook was a desirable activity by having an account: "I discourage my 13-year-old and 11-year old from joining such sites (because I distrust that their peers and maybe they, themselves, behave as well on-line as they do in face-to-face interactions), so I don't want to make it seem desirable to them." While these comments fall outside more narrow conceptualizations of context collapse, they do echo concerns about aspects of one's identity or online behaviors spilling into other dimensions of one's life.

Lack of Interest. For some participants, there was simply no compelling reason for them to join the site. They failed to "see any value in sharing the minutiae of my daily life with a bunch of strangers and seeing their asinine comments or whether they 'like' my statements" and did not want to "display [their] personal lives for everyone to see." One participant commented, "I don't want 'one more place' to have to check mail at," while another said, "[I] don't see how it could add value to my life." Several people simply said, "Not interested." Lack of interest may be a cover for more complex concerns about use, like those described above. In cases where people had concerns like privacy or context collapse, and potentially a mix of concerns, they might find it simpler to frame their concerns as a lack of interest.

Comparing Non-Members with Light and Heavy Users

In comparing non-users of Facebook to users, we are intentionally simplifying the concept of "use," looking only at adoption vs. non-adoption. Other studies, however, have shown that Facebook use is quite heterogeneous [23, 33]. Thus in this section we break out use into two levels and compare them to each other and to non-users in order to gain a more nuanced understanding of different kinds of users. In this section we describe analyses examining responses from three types of participants: non-users, light users, and heavy users of the site.

Variables		SRI		FB Time		Actual Friends	
		Mean	F	Mean	F	Mean	F
Age	Non	49.74[a]	15.21***	49.74[a]	37.78***	49.74[a]	53.85***
	Light	46.12[b]		47.85[a]		49.32[a]	
	Heavy	43.19[c]		39.46[b]		39.07[b]	
Education	Non	5.01[a]	2.09	5.01[a]	1.26	5.01[a]	0.25
	Light	5.14[a]		5.05[a]		5.08[a]	
	Heavy	4.92[a]		4.87[a]		5.08[a]	
Weekly Internet Use	Non	2.96[a]	0.44	2.96[a]	7.88***	2.96[a]	8.66***
	Light	3.08[a]		2.44[a]		2.60[a]	
	Heavy	3.24[a]		3.73[b]		3.95[b]	
Internet Efficacy	Non	3.43[a]	7.49***	3.43[a]	11.07***	3.43[a]	11.32***
	Light	3.72[b]		3.67[b]		3.58[a]	
	Heavy	3.78[b]		3.91[c]		3.89[b]	
Self Esteem	Non	4.34[a]	0.18	4.34[a]	0.82	4.34[ab]	4.76**
	Light	4.30[a]		4.27[a]		4.20[a]	
	Heavy	4.34[a]		4.36[a]		4.41[b]	
FB Usefulness	Non	3.12[a]	127.09***	3.12[a]	86.63***	3.12[a]	82.96***
	Light	3.44[b]		3.53[b]		3.48[b]	
	Heavy	4.11[c]		4.11[c]		4.06[c]	
Bridging Social Capital	Non	3.57[a]	28.10***	3.57[a]	17.50***	3.57[a]	27.31***
	Light	3.57[a]		3.57[a]		3.53[a]	
	Heavy	3.98[b]		3.95[b]		4.00[b]	
Bonding Social Capital	Non	3.64[a]	10.82***	3.64[a]	6.01**	3.64[a]	25.53***
	Light	3.42[b]		3.39[b]		3.22[b]	
	Heavy	3.80[a]		3.71[a]		3.85[c]	

Table 3: ANOVA comparisons of non-users, light users, and heavy users of Facebook. Superscript letters show groupings based on Tukey's B post hoc tests. * p<.05, ** p<.01, *** p<.001

Table 3 presents the results of three one-way ANOVAs comparing mean responses to our independent variables across our categories of use. These variables, described above in more detail, are Signals of Relational Investment (SRI), number of minutes spent per day on Facebook, and the number of "actual" friends within their Friend network. The ANOVA shows whether the means of the distinct groups are different overall; post-hoc analyses (Tukey's B) identify the specific means that are significantly different.

The three types of users are different across our three dimensions of use on many of the independent variables we included. Older people were more likely to be a non-user or a light user across all three dimensions of use, even though due to the nature of our population, the means differ by only a span of ten years. Weekly Internet Use was different in both the "Time on FB" and "Actual Friends" conditions. Light users in these two categories reported less weekly Internet use than either non- or heavy users. No differences were found across education level for different types of users.

Differences in Internet efficacy were consistent in that across all types of users, a participant with more reported efficacy was more likely to be a Facebook user, and more likely to be more engaged in different types of site use. Regarding self-esteem, the only significant difference between the types of users was for actual friends, with people who reported lower numbers of actual friends reporting lower self-esteem than either those who reported more actual friends or those who were non-users.

Reported beliefs about Facebook's usefulness were different across all groups in all dimensions of use, with heavy users reporting the highest values for this scale, and non-users reporting the lowest. For bridging social capital, both the non-users and light users in each dimension of use reported statistically similar levels of bridging social capital, whereas heavy users consistently reported more bridging social capital than the other two groups. As a reminder, both social capital scales presented here are for the social networks of the respondents overall, not just their Facebook networks.

We see a different pattern in relation to bonding social capital. For bonding social capital, across all types of users, light users reported less bonding social capital than either heavy users or non-users. In other words, those who become members of Facebook but don't use it in an active or intense fashion (as measured by time on site, engagement in SRI, and number of "actual friends" on the site) report less value from their overall social network in regards to the emotional support and other aspects of bonding social capital (which are typically associated with close ties). Even though the differences between means are not very large (for example 3.53 vs. 3.34 on a 5-point scale), the fact that these results are based on use of a scale that aggregates multiple questions regarding bonding social capital means that these are relatively robust results.

DISCUSSION

In this paper, we sought to understand the ways in which people who decided not to become members of Facebook (or who were members but stopped using the site) differ from those who were members, as well as differences between non-users, light users, and heavy users of the site.

Using binary logistic regression to calculate which individual characteristics are associated with whether a person is a Facebook member or not, we find that age, perceptions of Facebook's usefulness, and general bonding social capital are strong predictors. Internet efficacy was not significantly associated with the likelihood of being a Facebook member, indicating that participants' confidence about their ability to use Internet technology was unlikely to be an explanation for non-adoption.

When asked about why they had chosen to not use Facebook, non-adopters responses fell into five categories, with an overall theme being that these participants did not see benefits of joining or felt that the benefits of participating were not worth the costs (either in terms of time, context collapse concerns, privacy concerns, or other potential negative outcomes). These sentiments are consistent with the Technology Acceptance Model, which describes how people need to be able to identify the usefulness of the tool to be motivated to adopt it. This model also explains that identification of benefits can also include weighing risks of use as well. While previous literature has framed that as switching or learning costs, in a system like Facebook they may include concerns about privacy or context collapse. Although most of the comments evidenced concerns about other people (what they might find out), some participants who had used Facebook in the past wrote about how the affordances of the site affected them in ways they were not comfortable with (e.g., "I found I was using it to be nosy"; "I was on Facebook for about three days and did not like being that 'connected' 24/7"). Because we only asked whether participants were currently using the site, we were unable to distinguish in our analysis between those who used the site and then stopped from those who never tried the site. Future research on non-users may wish to explore differences between these two groups in terms of the kinds of benefits and risks of site use that they articulate.

One stated reason for not using the site was that participants did not see its "value." This is of particular interest given previous empirical research articulating a link between perceived social capital and site use. Given the strong link between bridging social capital, which is associated with weak ties, we speculate that as the population of Facebook users becomes more heterogeneous, these bridging social capital benefits (such as exposure to different perspectives) could become more robust as more diversity is introduced into the content shared on the site. Similarly, as use of the site becomes more normative, users may increasingly use it as a platform for sharing information and organizing events and may overlook those few acquaintances who are not on the site. Similar to concerns about the digital (access) divide, which argued that as more people come online, those who didn't would be increasingly left out, Facebook non-users may find themselves at a disadvantage. Future research should explore how experiences of non-users change over time.

Another consistent finding in Facebook studies is that motivations for use, and norms for appropriate use, are heterogeneous amongst users [23, 27]. Papacharissi and Mendelson [33] previously showed that different motivations to use Facebook had different relationships to bridging and bonding social capital. As we explore different motivations and types of uses, we're likely to find more differences like these, as the complex interplay between social systems, individual beliefs and capacities, and technical affordances continue to interact with one another.

Given extant literature on this topic, the difference in bonding social capital between non-users and light users of Facebook was surprising. Facebook non-users and heavy users reported higher bonding social capital than light users in terms of Signals of Relationship Investment and time spent on the site, and all three types of users were different in their number of "actual friends," though again people who reported fewer actual friends had less bonding social capital than not only those who reported more, but than those who weren't Facebook users at all. These data are correlational, so we cannot make causal claims about this relationship. As suggested above, it may be that there is a baseline level of use necessary for accessing the kinds of social resources associated with bonding social capital, such as meaningful emotional support. For instance, someone who discloses a support need on the site (such as a health condition), but then does not log back in for a few days may be less likely to see supportive messages when they would be most meaningful. They may also be less likely to see instances of resource exchanges between other members of their network, when seeing those exchanges could shape perceptions of their ability to access their network in the future. Other explanations may lie in third variable explanations – the existence of other important characteristics (like loneliness) which we didn't measure but which may affect the overall calculus of bonding social capital processes. Future research should focus on light users of the site to see how their perceptions and practices differ from "power" users.

It may be that participating at a very low level means increased time and effort costs on the part of the users without increases in social capital or other benefits of site use. Future work should explore this notion of a threshold effect – the level of activity at which social capital benefits are realized. The notion of a threshold effect is evidenced in some of our qualitative data. For instance, one participant (who identified as a non-user) explained, "I have started to join facebook (sic) but am not willing to put personal info out there about myself so my kids said 'why bother, mom?'"

Bonding social capital is typically associated with close friends, and thus network composition may be especially powerful when considering benefits and costs. It may be that these non-users do not have close friends on the site and thus do not see potential gains in regards to emotional support or other "big favors" associated with bonding social capital. Future research could go beyond measures of total and actual friends to include consideration of very close friends on the site. Alternatively, it could be that non-users have many strong ties, but in the absence of Facebook have used other tools to maintain relationships, in which case moving to Facebook would risk these established patterns.

For bridging social capital, analysis reveals slightly different patterns, in that light and non-use of the site was associated with lower levels of reported social capital than was heavy use. This was consistent across all three of our dimensions of use. Given previous work on this topic, we would expect to see differences between light and non-use of the site. Similarly to the bonding social capital differences, it could be that there is a threshold of use that is necessary to see benefit, or that some type of social learning occurs for heavier users that is missed by light users. It is worth noting that these light users represent the lowest quartile of use in each category, so we do not know at what level of use the bridging social capital benefits are realized.

However, why is there a difference in the patterns between bridging and bonding social capital? In both cases, heavy users reported the most social capital, but non- and light users were similar in their perception of bridging social capital, but not in terms of their bonding social capital. One explanation might be a "channel replacement" phenomenon, where for heavy users Facebook replaces other channels and allows them to access and groom a wider set of ties associated with social capital of both types. People who don't have access to Facebook may not have this "channel replacement" effect that facilitates bridging social capital, but do have access to other tools that help foster bonding social capital. All communication tool choices are made in the context of other available tools to meet a goal, and it could be that more tools facilitate bonding social capital than bridging.

Limitations

Surveys as a method of collecting data are dependent on self-reported data and respondent recall of past behaviors. However, Hampton et al. [20] found when matching survey responses to Facebook server data on the same behaviors that recall was actually very good regarding Facebook activities. Many of our variables, like Facebook usefulness and the social capital questions, are not dependent on recall. Although Hargittai's [21] work points out that looking only at aggregated SNS use statistics does not enable us to explore differences concerning specific site usage preferences, given the growing userbase and large body of scholarship that focus on Facebook, we focus only on this site in this study. Additionally, we only look at social capital as an outcome for Facebook use, when other outcomes might show different effects.

While the open-ended question in the survey provided some data expressed in the respondents' interpretation of their behavior, the use of dialogic interviews might have helped us to unpack their sense of "usefulness" to a greater extent. Future studies might include more in-depth interviews with non-users in order to more fully explore how and why they see the site as useful or not.

CONCLUSION

While use of social network sites, and Facebook in particular, has grown rapidly over the past several years, there are many people who have decided not to join these sites. Even for those who do join, they may experience benefits in different ways based on how they use it. By examining people who have decided not to adopt Facebook, and comparing their social capital scores with light and heavy users across three dimensions, we show that sometimes light use leads to the same or worse outcomes as non-use. The concept of "use" of a social computing system remains a complex interplay between individual and social factors, but our results indicate that membership alone is not sufficient to receive all benefits of use.

ACKNOWLEDGMENTS

This work was supported in part by the National Science Foundation (HCC 0916019). We would like to thank

Rebecca Gray for her help in data collection and analysis. We also thank Brandon Brooks and Yumi Jung for help in data collection.

REFERENCES

1. Ackerman, M. The Intellectual Challenge of CSCW: The Gap between Social Requirements and Technical Feasibility. in Carroll, J. ed. *Human Computer Interaction in the New Millennium*, ACM Press, New York, NY, 2001.
2. Backstrom, L., Bakshy, E., Kleinberg, J., Lento, T.M. and Rosenn, I., Center of Attention: How Facebook Users Allocate Attention Across Friends. in *Fifth International AAAI Conference on Weblogs and Social Media (ICWSM)*, (Barcelona, 2011).
3. Bagozzi, R.P. The Legacy of the Technology Acceptance Model and a Proposal for a Paradigm Shift. *Journal of the Association for Information Systems*, *8* (4). 244-254.
4. Barkhuus, L. and Tashiro, J. Student socialization in the age of facebook *Proceedings of the 28th international conference on Human factors in computing systems*, ACM, Atlanta, Georgia, USA, 2010.
5. Brandtzaeg, P.B. Social networking sites: Their users and social implications—a longitudinal study. *Journal of Computer-Mediated Communication*, *17*. 467-488.
6. Burke, M., Kraut, R. and Marlow, C. Social capital on facebook: differentiating uses and users *Proceedings of the 2011 annual conference on Human factors in computing systems*, ACM, Vancouver, BC, Canada, 2011, 571-580.
7. Burke, M., Marlow, C. and Lento, T., Feed me: Motivating newcomer contribution in social network sites. in *ACM Conference on Human Factors in Technical Systems*, (Boston, MA, 2009), ACM Press.
8. Burke, M., Marlow, C. and Lento, T. Social network activity and social well-being *Proceedings of the 28th international conference on Human factors in computing systems*, ACM, Atlanta, Georgia, USA, 2010.
9. Cheunga, C.M.K., Chiua, P.-Y. and Leeb, M.K.O. Online social networks: Why do students use facebook? *Computers in Human Behavior*, *27* (4). 1337-1343.
10. Davis, F.D. Perceived usefulness, perceived ease of use, and user acceptance of information technology. *MIS Quarterly*, *13* (3). 319-340.
11. DeSanctis, G. and Poole, M.S. Capturing the Complexity in Advanced Technology Use: Adaptive Structuration Theory. *Organization Science*, *5* (2).
12. Donath, J.S. Signals in social supernets. *Journal of Computer Mediated Communication*, *13* (1). 12.
13. Ellison, N., Steinfield, C. and Lampe, C. The benefits of Facebook "friends:" Social capital and college students' use of online social network sites. *Journal of Computer Mediated Communication*, *12* (4). article 1.
14. Ellison, N., Vitak, J., Gray, R., Lampe, C. and Brooks, B. Cultivating Social Resources on Facebook: Signals of Relational Investment and their Role in Social Capital Processes *iCS-OII 2011 "A Decade in Internet Time" Symposium.* , Oxford, UK, 2011.
15. Ellison, N.B., Steinfield, C. and Lampe, C. Connection Strategies: Social Capital Implications of Facebook-enabled Communication Practices. *New Media & Society*, *13*. 873-892.
16. Gilbert, E. and Karahalios, K. Predicting tie strength with social media *Proceedings of the 27th international conference on Human factors in computing systems*, ACM, Boston, MA, USA, 2009.
17. Golder, S., Wilkinson, D. and Huberman, B.A., Rhythms of Social Interaction: Messaging within a Massive Online Network. in *3rd International Conference on Communities and Technologies (CT2007)*. (East Lansing, MI, 2007), Springer.
18. Grudin, J. Groupware and social dynamics: Eight challenges for developers. *Communications of the ACM*, *37* (1). 93-104.
19. Grudin, J., Why CSCW applications fail: problems in the design and evaluationof organizational interfaces. in *ACM conference on Computer-supported cooperative work*, (Portland, OR, 1988), ACM Press, 85-93.
20. Hampton, K., Sessions-Goulet, L., Marlow, C. and Rainie, L. Why most Facebook users get more than they give, Pew Research Center's Internet & American Life Project, Washington DC, 2012.
21. Hargittai, E. Whose Space? Differences Among Users and Non-Users of Social Network Sites *Journal of Computer Mediated Communication*, *13* (1).
22. Johnson, T. and Perlmutter, D. The Facebook Election: New Media and the 2008 Election Campaign. *Mass Communication and Society*, *12* (3).
23. Joinson, A.N., Looking at, looking up or keeping up with people?: motives and use of facebook. in *Conference on Human Factors in Computing Systems (CHI)*, (Florence, Italy, 2008), ACM Press, 1027-1036.
24. Lampe, C., Ellison, N. and Steinfield, C., Changes in Use and Perception of Facebook. in *ACM Conference on Computer-Supported Cooperative Work (CSCW)*, (San Diego, CA, 2008), ACM Press.
25. Lampe, C., Vitak, J., Gray, R. and Ellison, N., Perceptions of Facebook's Value as an Information Source in *30th International Conference on Human*

Factors in Computing Systems (CHI), (Austin, TX, 2012), ACM Press.

26. Lampe, C., Vitak, J., Gray, R. and Ellison, N., Perceptions of Facebook's Value as an Information Source. in *CHI - Conference on Human Factors in Computing*, (Austin, TX, 2012), ACM Press.

27. Lampe, C., Wohn, D.Y., Vitak, J., Ellison, N.B. and Wash, R. Student use of Facebook for organizing collaborative classroom activities. *International Journal of Computer-Supported Cooperative Learning*, *6* (3). 329-347.

28. LaRose, R. The Problem of Media Habits. *Communication Theory*, *20* (2). 194-222.

29. Larose, R., Mastro, D. and Eastin, M.S. Understanding Internet Usage. *Social Science Computer Review*, *19* (4). 395-413.

30. Madden, M. and Zickuhr, K. 65% of Online Adults Use Social Networking Sites, Pew Internet & American Life Project, Washington, DC, 2011.

31. Morris, M.R., Teevan, J. and Panovich, K. What do people ask their social networks, and why?: a survey study of status message q&a behavior *Proceedings of the 28th international conference on Human factors in computing systems*, ACM, Atlanta, Georgia, USA, 2010.

32. Panovich, K., Miller, R. and Karger, D. Tie strength in question & answer on social network sites *Proceedings of the ACM 2012 conference on Computer Supported Cooperative Work*, ACM, Seattle, Washington, USA, 2012, 1057-1066.

33. Papacharissi, Z. and Mendelson, A. Toward a new(er) sociability: Uses, gratifications and social capital on Facebook. in Papathanassopoulos, S. ed. *Media perspectives for the 21st century*, Routledge, New Tork, 2011, 212-230.

34. Putnam, R.D. *Bowling Alone*. Simon & Schuster, New York, 2000.

35. Rogers, E.M. *Diffusion of Innovations*. The Free Press, New York, 1995.

36. Rosenberg, M. *Society and the Adolescent Self-image*. Wesleyan University Press, Middletown, CT, 1989.

37. Selwyn, N. Faceworking: exploring students' education-related use of Facebook *Learning, Media and Technology*, *34* (2). 157-174.

38. Skeels, M.M. and Grudin, J. When social networks cross boundaries: a case study of workplace use of facebook and linkedin *Proceedings of the ACM 2009 international conference on Supporting group work*, ACM, Sanibel Island, Florida, USA, 2009.

39. Smith, A. Why Americans use social media, Pew Research Center's Internet & American Life Project, Washington, DC, 2011.

40. Smith, A. and Brenner, J. Twitter Use 2012, Pew Research Internet & American Life Project, Washington, D.C., 2012.

41. Smock, A.D., Ellison, N.B., Lampe, C. and Wohn, D.Y. Facebook as a toolkit: A uses and gratification approach to unbundling feature use. *Computers in Human Behavior*, *27* (6). 2322-2329.

42. Teevan, J., Morris, M.R. and Panovich, K., Factors Affecting Response Quantity, Quality, and Speed for Questions Asked via Social Network Status Messages. in *ICWSM - International Conference on Weblogs and Social Media*, (Barcelona, Spain, 2011).

43. Tufekci, Z. and Wilson, C. Social Media and the Decision to Participate in Political Protest: Observations From Tahrir Square. *Journal of Communication*, *62* (2). 363-379.

44. Valenzuela, S., Park, N. and Kee, K.F. Is there social capital in a social network site?: Facebook use and college students' life satisfaction, trust and participation. *Journal of Computer-Mediated Communication*, *14*. 875-901.

45. Valkenburg, P.M., Peter, J. and Schouten, A.P. Friend networking sites and their relationship to adolescents' well being and social self-esteem. *CyberPsychology and Behavior*, *9*. 584-590.

46. Venkatash, V., Morris, M.G., Davis, G.B. and Davis, F.D. User Acceptance of Information Technology: Toward a Unified View. *MIS Quarterly*, *27* (3). 425-478.

47. Vitak, J. and Ellison, N. There's a network out there you might as well tap': Exploring the benefits of and barriers to exchanging informational and support-based resources on Facebook. . *New Media & Society*.

48. Vitak, J., Zube, P., Smock, A., Carr, C.T., Ellison, N. and Lampe, C. It's Complicated: Facebook Users' Political Participation in the 2008 Election. *Cyberpsychology, Behavior, and Social Networking*, *14* (3). 107-114.

49. Williams, D. On and Off the 'Net: Scales for Social Capital in an Online Era *Journal of Computer Mediated Communication*, *11* (2).

50. Wilson, R.E., Gosling, S.D. and Graham, L.T. A Review of Facebook Research in the Social Sciences *Perspectives on Psychological Science, in Press*.

Uses & Gratifications of a Facebook Media Sharing Group

Mayur Karnik, Ian Oakley, Jayant Venkatanathan, Tasos Spiliotopoulos and Valentina Nisi
Madeira Interactive Technologies Institute, University of Madeira
Campus da Penteada, Funchal, Portugal
{mayurkarnik, ian.r.oakley, vjayant, tspiliot, valentina.nisi}@gmail.com

ABSTRACT
This paper explores uses and gratifications of a content community on a social network service – a music video sharing group on Facebook. In a two-stage study, 20 users first generated words or phrases to describe how they used the group, and what they enjoyed about their use. These phrases were coded into 34 questionnaire items that were then completed by 57 new participants. Factor analysis on this data revealed four gratifications: contribution; discovery; social interaction and entertainment. These factors are interpreted and discussed, leading to design implications and guidelines aimed at informing the design of future online services that combine media sharing with social interaction to create online systems based on a rich and meaningful object-centered sociality.

Author Keywords
Social Media; Music; Groups; Uses & Gratifications.

ACM Classification Keywords
H.5.3 [Information Interfaces and Presentation]: Group and Organization Interfaces: Web-based interaction.

General Terms
Design.

INTRODUCTION
Social media is core part of the modern Internet experience. According to Forrester research, 75% of Internet users accessed social media in summer 2008, up from 56% in 2007 [12]. More recent figures indicate that between 79% (Europe) and 86% (US) of online adults engage with social media [8] and Facebook, currently the most popular site, reports more than 900 million monthly active users [9]. To achieve this widespread appeal, Social Network Sites (SNS) focus on enabling their users to communicate and interact with one another in diverse ways and for diverse ends. Indeed, Facebook excels at this, offering a wide range of features including: browsing user profiles; direct messaging services; casual gaming; posting media content and; participating in online groups and forums. Beyond being highly successful, researchers have argued that SNS exert a positive effect on the society by, for example, allowing individuals to manage a wide network of weak ties and thus boost their bridging social capital [2]. Others have gone further and suggested that SNS have the potential to fundamentally change the nature of our social lives, on both interpersonal and community levels [4].

However, the rapid advent of SNS has raised questions as to the fundamental motivations driving their use – what makes them so popular and what needs are they meeting? One approach to answering such questions has been to adopt methods typically used to explore the motivations underlying the consumption of more traditional media. In particular, Uses and Gratifications theory (U&G) [21], which relates to the how and why of media use, has been extensively deployed. For instance, Lampe et al. [14] used a U&G approach to show that different motivations for use were associated with different patterns of contribution in online content generation communities. Similarly, Joinson [11] studied Facebook and identified a core set of fundamental uses and gratifications for the site while Park et al. [16] focused on Facebook Groups and uncovered a distinct set of uses and gratifications specific to this feature.

This last study highlights a key issue, eloquently expressed by Smock et al. [20] in their argument that uses and gratifications in SNS are relevant not to entire sites, but to specific *unbundled* subsets of site features, such as status updates, messaging services or media sharing. This assertion helps ground the observation that SNS are a rapidly moving target on which novel uses dynamically evolve as new features are introduced. However, the rollout of such functionality is typically tied not to observed user needs, but to technical factors such as increases in computational power, network bandwidth and the sophistication of web technologies. Thus, it is often unclear what value SNS users gain from novel features and services. This paper argues that in order to understand the true worth of such extensions, explaining their use and guiding their evolution, focused investigations that consider them at a granular, unbundled, level are currently required.

Reflecting this point, this paper investigates a widespread interaction pattern in SNS - sharing social media objects such as videos and engaging in conversations around them - that has been enabled due to recent technological advancements. This behavior represents a form of object-centered sociality - a term proposed by Knorr-Cetina [13]. This paper argues that forums organized around such artifacts as a *focus* will engender novel behaviors, not only in the media sharing practices overtly supported but also in

CSCW '13, February 23–27, 2013, San Antonio, Texas, USA.

the type and nature of the interpersonal connections fostered among members [6].

We seek to investigate the veracity of this assertion through a study that makes three contributions. These are, firstly, to explore and extend the claim that examining unbundled SNS features exposes novel aspects of use. Secondly, to offer a nuanced account of the role that social media objects play in creating communities on SNS. Specifically, this paper adopts the position that such objects, in contrast to profile and user information, can become an axis around which novel forms of online social interaction occur [15] and seeks to provide a first characterization of this behavior. Finally, this paper synthesizes this material to identify design guidelines to inform the creation of future SNS media sharing communities or social apps. To achieve these objectives, this paper reviews related work and then describes a multi-method analysis of 'Saturday Morning Classics' (SMC) a small Facebook group (comprised of friends and friends-of-friends) dedicated to sharing music videos. It closes with a discussion and a set of design implications derived from this work.

RELATED WORK

Although SNS are widespread, understanding why and how people use them remains a substantial challenge. Researchers have suggested that uses and gratifications theory is a useful technique to address this problem. For instance, Joinson [11] identified seven unique gratifications for Facebook use: social connection; shared identities; photographs; content; social investigation; social network surfing and; status updating. While such sweeping conclusions have value, recent work has argued that a finer grained approach may be more informative – essentially the notion is that, in complex services, different features or feature sets may meet very different needs [20]. Park et al.'s [16] study of Facebook groups supports this point. Their U&G study identified four unique factors (socializing, entertainment, self-status seeking and information) that differ substantially from those described in Joinson's work. The current paper seeks to explore this issue further by investigating (as Park et al. suggest) whether groups with different types of focus will support different motives for (and elicit different patterns of) use.

Kaplan and Haenlein categorize SNS (e.g. Facebook, Twitter) and content communities (e.g. Youtube, Wikipedia) as distinct forms of social media [12]. Although extensive research has been carried out in these two areas [e.g. 4, 18], services at their intersection have attracted relatively little attention. Today, enabled by inter-operable media sharing tools, such hybrids are becoming increasingly common. For example, services such as Pinterest (pinterest.com/) allow users to curate and share media from various Internet sources around self-selected topics (e.g. art, recipes, grooming, etc). Similarly Foursquare (foursquare.com/) allows strangers to engage in conversations about and around specific places. Both services include their own SNS features but also integrate with Facebook to ensure wide dispersal and dissemination of user activities. Motivated by such innovative examples, this paper suggests that content communities on SNS represent a novel type of group that is not only likely to elicit interesting usage patterns but that is also worthy of independent study in and of itself.

This paper focuses on music videos, social media objects that are commonly shared and discussed on SNS. This prevalence reflects the fact that music is a ubiquitous part of our everyday lives [3], serving as a powerful tool for expressing, understanding and sharing identity [1]. Indeed, although the consumption of music is typically seen as a leisure activity, music and related discussions have also been portrayed as important elements in creating and maintaining friendship networks [19]. Online communities are also reported to boost desirable exposure to novel music [7]. With these facts in mind, this paper focuses on music sharing as an example activity through which to explore the broader space of content communities on SNS.

'SATURDAY MORNING CLASSICS' FACEBOOK GROUP

SMC is an online experiment to construct and study a small music sharing community. It is an open Facebook group created specifically for this research in February 2011. It takes the form of a forum for posting and discussing "classic" music videos hosted on media archiving websites such as Youtube and Vimeo. As a specific type of content was targeted, the group was seeded with initial media by the researchers in order to develop critical mass in the community [10]. The group was initially populated through direct invitations but later expanded through referrals by existing members and via approving direct requests to join the group. The group's privacy settings were 'Open' so that new members could easily join and current members could broadcast their activities publically on their newsfeeds.

To support study of this group, a Facebook application was developed. This scanned through the group and extracted attributes such as number of posts, relationship graphs within the group and the degree of social interaction (indicated by likes and comments). The open privacy settings facilitated direct access to this data - it was entirely public. As of May 2012, the group had 167 members, who had posted 833 items relating to classic music from various genres, regions and cultures. These posts elicited 836 "likes" from other members and 355 comments. After establishing these characteristics, study of the group took place via surveys to understand the uses and gratifications in a typical 2-stage process [11]. In Study 1, users were asked to generate lists of words or phrases that represented their uses and gratifications. In Study 2, a questionnaire based on these items was generated, numerical responses captured and factor analysis used to reveal clustered profiles of distinct uses and gratifications.

STUDY 1: EXPLORATORY STAGE

Participants

Participants were selected from a list of group members sorted according to the frequency with which they posted videos. Requests to complete an online survey were sent out to every alternate individual in this sequence in an attempt to ensure that responses were elicited from users with different levels of engagement with the group. Users who had never posted videos were excluded from this preliminary study to ensure that feedback was captured from those who had directly engaged with the group. Ultimately, 35 invitations were distributed and 20 complete responses returned.

Materials

The online survey included demographics (age, gender, occupation, nationality) and usage measures for Facebook and the SMC group (time spent, visit frequency, number of friends, length of usage). We adapted Stafford's free text entry questions [21] (also deployed by Joinson [11]), and asked participants to respond to the following questions:

- What is the first thing that comes to your mind when you think about what you enjoy most when using the SMC Facebook group?
- What other words describe what you enjoy about using the SMC Facebook group?
- Using single, easy-to-understand terms, what do you use the SMC Facebook group for?
- What uses of the SMC Facebook group are most important to you?

Results

Respondents answered the questions in words and phrases. As in prior work [11], two raters collaboratively sorted the responses based on affinity and identified themes from the emergent clusters. The broad themes identified were: *discovery* (e.g. exposure to music from different cultures, finding rare songs); *social interaction* (likes, browsing user profiles); *content* (e.g. listening to music, watching videos) and *nostalgia* (e.g. remembering past events and people).

STUDY 2: IDENTIFYING USES & GRATIFICATIONS

Item Generation

In total 34 items[1] were generated with six to eight items drawn from each of the four themes identified in Study 1. Duplicate items were discarded and wording was kept as close to the source content as possible. A 7-point Likert scale, labeled from 'Strongly Disagree' to 'Strongly Agree' was used to elicit all responses.

Participants

Survey requests were sent out to 85 group members who had not participated in Study 1. 57 participants responded to these requests and completed the survey - 37 males and 20 females. 25 members were in the age group of 21-30, 29 were aged between 31-40 and three were more than 40 years old. More than 80% of the respondents had been using Facebook for more than 2 years; 65% had been SMC members for between 6-9 months and 27% for between 3-6 months. We interpreted this to indicate familiarity with the SNS features and the SMC group in particular.

Results

Exploratory factor analysis on this data was conducted. The initial analysis (varimax rotation) yielded 7 components with Eigenvalues over 1, explaining 79% of the variance. However, an examination of the Scree plot's "elbow" and the distribution of unique loadings led to further reduction and four factors (explaining 61% of the variance) were eventually retained. These were termed: *contribution*, *discovery*, *social interaction* and *entertainment*. Based on the convention of using only loadings greater than 0.5, six markers were identified for Factors 1 and 2, five for Factor 3 and three for Factor 4. A total of 14 items were discarded. The factors are described in Tables 1-4 and as follows:

Factor 1 contained items that relate to participating in the group by *contributing* to and *commenting* on the content. Members reported valuing sharing their knowledge of music by posting videos and participating in conversations around music. These conversations were in the form of comments, often as suggestions about similar or related content or expressions of appreciation about particular media items. This factor relates to users who viewed themselves as collaboratively contributing to an archive of music.

Factor 2 contained items that refer to *discovery* of new music. Items relating to discovering rare songs and music from foreign cultures loaded most strongly. In addition, users valued re-discovering music they had not listened to in a long time. Interestingly, items related to immediate emotional responses also loaded in this factor, suggesting that discoveries often triggered a pleasant emotional response.

Factor 3 contained items related to *social* aspects of using the group. Receiving appreciation (via 'likes') scored the highest loading while showing such appreciation also featured, although not as strongly. Other items loading strongly related to accessing the public profiles of others and to check for mutual friends of SMC posters whom they did not know.

Factor 4 contained items related to *entertainment*. Members appreciated the music genre ("classic") that the group represents. This finding complements Park et al.'s [16] notion that entertainment is a valued gratification reported by users of Facebook groups. Interestingly, listening to music posted by friends also loaded in this factor.

DISCUSSION

The study described in this paper set out to reveal uses and gratifications pertaining to media sharing groups on a social network. The results revealed four main uses and gratifications that people derived from the SMC Facebook group: contribution, discovery, social interaction and

[1] Complete survey available on request to corresponding author

entertainment. The latter two match two of the factors uncovered in Park et al.'s [16] study of Facebook groups. However, the current work's focus on groups as content communities resulted in the emergence of two novel factors: contribution and discovery. This suggests that media sharing groups represent a unique context, in terms of the motivations that drive use, in social networks. It is worth unpacking and discussing the factors in detail. In order to do so most effectively, we merge qualitative observations of behaviors on the group with data from the U&G study.

The fact that contribution served as a key gratification among group members indicated a pleasurable commitment to the social archival, curation and discussion of media content. Conversations on the group often took playful non-verbal forms like 'replying' to content by posting semantically similar content – users responded to media by posting complimentary (or occasionally contradictory) content. This dynamic attracted considerable attention on the site – post threads tended to develop in rapid spurts of activity. It also served a key role in developing and fleshing out particular topics, memes and (ultimately) the group identity. These behaviors suggest, in line with Knorr-Cetina's [13] assertions about object-oriented sociality, that social interaction around media objects has the potential to instantiate in novel forms. An SNS content community allows people to directly and engagingly express their (good) taste and demonstrate their knowledge of a topic. It is worth noting that this finding is likely to have been influenced by the relatively tightly knit nature of SMC – it was largely composed of friends and friends-of-friends.

The discovery of new content was a second novel driver for participation in the group. This is obviously tightly tied to the group's topic – musical discovery is a popular leisure activity both on and offline [1]. It also relates to Garg et al.'s notion [7] that, in the presence of peers, people engage in discovery through observational learning. The social mechanisms of posting, commenting, viewing and following in the group facilitated this activity and stand in stark contrast to the algorithm-based recommendation features common to online music services such as Grooveshark (grooveshark.com) and Last.fm (last.fm). In other words, musical discovery in the group was socially mediated and this proved to be compelling enough to serve as a strong gratification and driver for use. The cultural diversity of the group members (14 nationalities were represented) also contributed to this factor by spurring members' interest in the broad origins of the posted content.

The third factor identified, 'social interaction', mirrored in Park et al's [16] work, also links to what Strafford identified as a gratification that differentiates the Internet from more traditional media – its capacity to serve as a social environment [21]. Direct observations of behaviors on the group and examinations of the final network graphs of members supported this assertion. For example, two

Factor 1: Contribution ($\alpha = 0.90$)	**Mean (SD)**	**Loading**
I often comment on music posted by others on SMC.	2.44 (1.48)	0.775
I like to share my knowledge of music on SMC.	3.16 (1.72)	0.765
I like adding to collection of songs on SMC by posting a song when others post music on a specific theme.	3.75 (1.66)	0.692
I like to share music on SMC.	3.89 (1.87)	0.682
I like the discussion that take place on SMC	4.11 (1.58)	0.645
I like to share videos on SMC.	3.46 (1.80)	0.662

Table 1. Factor 1 – Contribution

Factor 2: Discovery ($\alpha = 0.91$)	**Mean (SD)**	**Loading**
I like discovering music from foreign cultures through SMC.	4.91 (1.84)	0.858
I find music through SMC that I haven't heard in a long time.	5.67 (1.41)	0.513
I like listening to the music people post on SMC.	4.72 (1.64)	0.577
Often the music posted on the group surprises me.	4.72 (1.50)	0.553
Often a song posted on SMC changes my mood in the day.	3.84 (1.74)	0.543
I discover rare songs through SMC.	5.12 (1.68)	0.709

Table 2. Factor 2 – Discovery

Factor 3: Social Interaction ($\alpha = 0.89$)	**Mean (SD)**	**Loading**
I am often keen to see if what I posted on SMC has been liked by others.	3.74 (2.10)	0.801
I often browse the public profiles of people I don't know when they post music on SMC.	2.89 (1.95)	0.782
I like to find out who are my mutual friends when someone unknown to me posts music on SMC.	3.86 (1.95)	0.706
I often try to understand what and why members post certain kind of music on SMC.	3.70 (2.02)	0.594
I often 'like' music posted by others on SMC.	3.56 (1.90)	0.585

Table 3. Factor 3 - Social Interaction

Factor 4: Entertainment ($\alpha = 0.85$)	**Mean (SD)**	**Loading**
I like the music genre that the group represents.	5.07 (1.44)	0.786
The music posted on the group makes me joyful.	4.46 (1.40)	0.629
I like listening to music my friends post on the group.	4.40 (1.66)	0.537

Table 4. Factor 4 - Entertainment

cases were noted in which group members became Facebook friends during the course of the study and after discussing or otherwise engaging around a particular artist or musical genre. While our data is a snapshot of the network and does not allow us to trace the complete evolution of friendship ties between members of the group over time, these anecdotal observations suggest that social media objects can act as foci [6] to facilitate the formation of ties.

Before moving on, it is worth contrasting the presence of social interaction as a factor driving use in SMC against Smock et al.'s [20] assertion that participation in Facebook groups is primarily motivated by expressive information and that social engagement plays a limited role. To explain this discrepancy, we note that Smock's study is agnostic as to the nature of the groups considered. Accordingly, we suggest that the results of the current study provide evidence that SNS content communities form a distinct type of group in which social interaction is a valued driver.

The final factor unearthed in this study was entertainment. This is clearly coupled to the nature of the content – users visited the group to watch music videos. Although this is unsurprising, the other factors highlight distinctions between the qualities of the entertainment sought compared to that available via more traditional channels. Essentially, the group provided socially vetted, tightly themed and personally curated content – the group members valued these qualities.

In summary, the results of this study strongly support the assertion that the nature and type of a group fundamentally shape the motivations that drive its use. This reinforces Smock et al.'s argument for the need to study unbundled SNS features [20] and, indeed, suggests that this point be extended to not only consider specific technical features (e.g. groups) but also distinctions between the different topics and foci for which such functionalities can be used (e.g. media sharing via civic or political engagement). Specifically, the work presented in this paper suggests that groups with different kinds of foci will exhibit different patterns of use in order for their users to achieve different types of gratification. This paper also catalogued and discussed the particular motivations for participating in an SNS content community and now moves on to instantiate those findings as design themes to inform the future construction of such services.

IMPLICATIONS FOR DESIGN

Designing for Contribution

Contribution of content and commentary was a key motivation for using SMC. Media sharing services should be designed to best encourage and reward contribution or participation. The literature suggests a variety of techniques for achieving this. Rotman et al. [17], in their study of content curation communities highlight the need to find an active subset within the community and also the need to attribute content to the users who post it. Lampe et al. [14] reinforce this point by arguing that registered users (as opposed to anonymous users) are motivated by a sense of affiliation and identity and are likely to be more committed. These observations speak to the power of combining content communities with meaningful on-site user identities, such as those inherently present in SNS. Such hybrid sites are likely to engender high levels of participation. Moving beyond such foundational points, another trend from the study reported here was the prominence of response chains where a first post elicited a rapid sequence of related material. It was clear that users enjoyed exploring and extending connections and relations among media, and future site designs in this space should explicitly support such activities. For example, one way this could be achieved would to support the collective construction and compilation of playlists, an idea analogous to the content collections of Pinterest (pinterest.com/) but currently unsupported in music-themed online services.

Designing for Discovery

Social media systems need focus on enabling users to discover new content and then to collectively archive this material. This observation ties into Garg et al.'s [7] work showing the positive influence online peers exert on the diffusion of music. However, this idea stands in stark contrast to current implementations offered in online music services that emphasize algorithm-based music discovery (e.g. genre matching) rather than social approaches. Elaborating on this point, the work in this paper indicates that acts of contributing and discovering were tightly intertwined, in that users posted videos and discovered closely related content when other members responded and replied with their own posts and media. This natural dynamic represents a valuable type of highly focused social filtering that could be exploited in future system designs.

Designing for Social Interaction

The combination of content communities and SNS offers novel possibilities for social interaction. Comments, approvals ("likes") and the posting of media responses were all commonplace and valued – indeed, users reported directly seeking the community's endorsement of taste that such activities and responses imply. Designs in this space should emphasize such object-centered sociality by facilitating, for example, the posting of media replies and the navigation around chains of such content. Farzan et al. [5] show how designs that encourage relationships among members or emphasize the community as an entity both increase commitment and retention of group members. Linking this idea to Rotman et al.'s [17] recommendation to target active subgroups within communities, designers could create team-based roles to encourage playful forms of participation. A second novel social interaction highlighted in SMC is investigations of individuals with similar (or simply interesting) taste – indentifying such people, and allowing users to explore their posts and contributions, may help create more compelling social experiences.

CONCLUSIONS

This paper argues that media sharing groups on Facebook represent a unique intersection between social networking sites and content communities. The study presented in this paper revealed contribution, discovery, social interaction and entertainment to be the key gratifications met by such systems – the key drivers of use. The novel nature of these factors suggests there is value in Smock et al.'s [20] notion that SNS features should be analyzed in discrete, unbundled, chunks rather than via examinations of entire services. The factors also represent a valuable exploration of design space intersecting SNS and content communities. This work also led to guidelines and recommendations that future designers of media sharing tools may find valuable.

Limitations of this work include its modest (but typical) sample size; most Facebook groups are small. Accordingly, future work will extend investigations to a larger set of groups, validate the findings presented here and explore issues such as the impact of privacy settings or groups with more diverse demographics. Ultimately, this research will empower users to connect more easily, seamlessly and closely with the media content that they want, seek and like.

ACKNOWLEDGEMENTS

This work was supported by Madeira Life, a project co-funded by the regional government of Madeira (MADFDR-01-0190-FEDER_001) and ZON Multimedia. Additional support was provided by the Portuguese Foundation for Science and Technology (FCT) through grant CMU-PT/SE/0028/2008 (Web Security and Privacy) and PhD scholarship SFRH/BD/65908/2009. We would like to thank Nuno David Santos for his technical contributions and the members of the 'Saturday Morning Classics' Facebook group for their continued participation and support.

REFERENCES

1. Brown, B., Sellen, A. J., and Geelhoed, E. Music sharing as a computer supported collaborative application. In *Proc. ECSCW 2001.*
2. Burke, M., Kraut, R., and Marlow, C. Social capital on Facebook: Differentiating uses and users. In *Proc. CHI 2011*, 571–580.
3. Denora, T. Music in Everyday Life. Cambridge; New York: Cambridge University Press, 2000. 181 pp.
4. Ellison, N. B., Lampe, C., and Steinfield, C. FEATURE: Social network sites and society: current trends and future possibilities. Interactions 16, 1 (Jan 2009), 6-9.
5. Farzan, R., Dabbish, L.A., Kraut, R.E., and Postmes, T. 2011. Increasing commitment to online communities by designing for social presence. In *Proc. CSCW '11*
6. Feld, S.L., The focused organization of social ties. The American Journal of Sociology, 1015–1035, 1981 3, 12
7. Garg, R., Smith, M. D., Telang, R., "Discovery of Music through Peers in an Online Community," In *Proc. HICSS*, 2001.
8. http://blogs.forrester.com/gina_sverdlov/12-01-04-global_social_technographics_update_2011_us_and_eu_mature_emerging_markets_show_lots_of_activity (Retrieved on 27/08/2012).
9. http://newsroom.fb.com/content/default.aspx?NewsAreaId=22 (Retrieved on 27/08/2012).
10. Jacob, S., and Wash, R. 2012. Bootstrapping wikis: developing critical mass in a fledgling community by seeding content. In *Proc. CSCW '12.*
11. Joinson, A. Looking at, looking up or keeping up with people?: motives and use of facebook. In *Proc. CHI 2008,* ACM Press (2008), 1027-1036.
12. Kaplan, A. M. and Haenlein, M. (2010). Users of the world, unite! The challenges and opportunities of Social Media. Business Horizons, 53 (1), 59-68.
13. Knorr-Cetina, K. Sociality with objects: Social relations in post-social knowledge societies, Theory, Culture and Society 14, 4 (1997), 1-30.
14. Lampe, C., Wash, R., Velasquez, A., and Ozkaya, E. Motivations to participate in online communities. In *Proc. CHI, 2010.*
15. McCarthy, J. Bridging the gaps between HCI and social media. interactions 18, 2 (March 2011), 15-18.
16. Park, N., Kee, K. F., and Valenzuela, S. (2009). Being immersed in social networking environment: Facebook groups, uses and gratifications, and social outcomes. Cyberpsychology and Behavior 12, 729-733.
17. Rotman, D., Procita, K., Hansen, D., Parr, C.S., Preece, J. Supporting Content Curation Communities: The Case of the Encyclopedia of Life. In JASIS&T, 63, 6 (2012), 1092–1107.
18. Rotman, D., and Preece, J. The 'WeTube' in YouTube – creating an online community through video sharing. Int. J. Web Based Communities 6, 3 2010, 317-333.
19. Singh, S., Jackson, M., Waycott J., and Beekhuyzen, J. Downloading vs Purchase: Music Industry vs Consumers, Springer Link (2006).
20. Smock, A.D., Ellison, N.B., Lampe, C., and Wohn, D.Y. Facebook as a toolkit: A uses and gratification approach to unbundling feature use. Computers in Human Behavior 27, 6 (2011), 2322–2329.
21. Stafford, T.F., Stafford, M.R., & Schkade, L.L. Determining uses and gratifications for the internet. Decision Sciences, 35, (2004), 259–288.

"Welcome!": Social and Psychological Predictors of Volunteer Socializers in Online Communities

Gary Hsieh*, Youyang Hou†, Ian Chen*
*Communication Arts and Sciences, †Department of Psychology
Michigan State University
{garyh, houyouya, chenyira}@msu.edu

Khai N. Truong
Department of Computer Science
University of Toronto
khai@cs.toronto.edu

ABSTRACT
Volunteer socializers are members of a community who voluntarily help newcomers become familiar with the popular practices and attitudes of the community. In this paper, we explore the social and psychological predictors of volunteer socializers on reddit, an online social news-sharing community. Through a survey of over 1000 reddit users, we found that social identity, prosocial-orientation and generalized reciprocity are all predictors of socializers in the community. Interestingly, a user's tenure with the online community has a quadratic effect on volunteer socialization behaviors—new and long-time members are both more likely to help newcomers than those in between. We conclude with design implications for motivating users to help newcomers.

Author Keywords
Volunteer Socialization; Online Communities; reddit

ACM Classification Keywords
H.5.3. Collaborative computing

INTRODUCTION
As a newcomer to an online community, we are often clueless about how we should behave and how to use the available features. Sometimes, we get lucky—someone voluntarily welcomes us and helps us understand the community, teaches us the expected social norms, and even introduces us to new friends. Because he or she helped socialize us to the community, we are able to quickly become active and contributing members. However, sometimes, we are not so lucky. It may take a lot of embarrassments before we finally become comfortable in the community, assuming that we have not given up already.

Despite the important role that socialization plays in helping newcomers in online communities, relatively little is known about those who volunteer their time to socialize newcomers. Much research on socialization has focused on two things: (1) the tactics used for socialization—how an organization or community can best socialize newcomers [e.g., 1] and (2) the content gained from socialization—what is learned during socialization [e.g., 18]. However, a key research gap that has not been addressed is who are these volunteer socializers? Do most members eventually volunteer as socializers over time, or are certain people more likely to assume the role of socializers? What are some of the factors that may influence users to help newcomers?

Understanding volunteer socializers is a timely problem as we grow increasingly reliant on online communities for information and social support [41]. Unlike traditional organizations, online communities often do not have institutionalized and formal newcomer-socialization processes in place [18,23]. Even for online communities where there are established mentorship programs, because newcomers can join the community at anytime, the newcomers' first (and often only) impression depends heavily on members who provide help voluntarily. If we can better understand why people undertake the task of socializing newcomers, we may more effectively users to help socialize the newcomers.

To study volunteer socializers, we conducted two surveys on a social news sharing community, reddit (www.reddit.com). In the first survey, with 129 responses, we developed a scale to identify socializers. Then through a more elaborate survey with 1174 responses, we found that personal identification with the community, prosocial-orientations and generalized reciprocity are all predictors of volunteer socialization. How much time per day a user spends on the community, however, is not a significant predictor. Interestingly, membership tenure has a curvilinear effect—new and long-time members are both more likely to help newcomers than those in between.

This work offers several contributions. On the theoretical side, this work provides a first step in understanding the antecedents for individuals to voluntarily help out newcomers in a community. On the applied side, the various predictors found can help designers and community builders to encourage more newcomer socialization. In addition, we also introduce a 7-item newcomer socialization behavior scale that can help future work in identifying volunteer socializers.

VOLUNTEER SOCIALIZERS

Socialization is the process through which newcomers acquire the behaviors and attitudes essential to playing their roles in a group or an organization [47]. It is through socialization that newcomers are welcome to the community and learn the skills and knowledge that are necessary for them to become full-fledged members.

The importance of socialization has been recognized in organizational setting. The socialization process contributes greatly to the newcomers' successful adaptation to an organization in the initial period of their entering the organization. For example, it has been shown that socialization reduces newcomers' anxiety and uncertainty [43,78] and thus decreases role ambiguity and role conflict [7,39]. Socialization also benefits several other "proximal outcomes" of adjustment such as role clarity, perceived job and perceived organization fit [15,39,62]. From the long-term perspective, successful socialization also greatly benefits some "distal outcomes" of the newcomers. Studies have shown that socialization positively relates to job attitudes such as job satisfaction, organizational commitment, and intention to remain [3,7,10,64]. Additionally, newcomers show better work performance [10,36,64] and are less likely to turnover from the organization [2,62].

Recent research has turned to the study of socialization in online communities. These studies have found that the benefits of socialization also extend to the online context—socialization can increase newcomers' likelihood to participate in the future [5,20,27,42]. However, unlike traditional organizations, there is often no institutionalized socialization processes in online communities. For example, studies on WikiProjects, the task-oriented groups in Wikipedia, showed that newcomers are rarely assigned mentors nor are they given clear guidance on how to behave in the project [20]. Even in production-oriented environments, such as Python's open-source software development community, socialization is informal, and newcomers learn by simple trial and error [23]. Due to the lack of centralized administration or any "managers" who are responsible for socializing newcomers, socialization has becomes heavily reliant on volunteer socializers – users who help socializer newcomers even though they are not paid or asked to do so.

Due to this reliance of online communities on volunteer socializers, it is important to understand what leads people to volunteer to help newcomers. The closest to studying volunteer socializers are prior research on the naturally emerged mentorship between a newcomer and a senior member in the work setting (informal mentorships) [14,19,54,55]. However, only limited studies have explored why people volunteer and assume the role of mentors. For example, some have found that informal mentorships develop due to perceived competence and interpersonal comfort [4,38,40,54]. What has been missing is an understanding of social and psychological factors that predict people's likelihood to volunteer. If we can understand what influences people to help newcomers, we may (1) more effectively motivate people to help newcomers and (2) identify these volunteers and offer them tools to more effectively mentor newcomers.

In this paper, we hypothesize that people's likelihood to be volunteer socializers in online communities is influenced by their identity with the community, their personal prosocial values, generalized reciprocity, their tenure and opportunities for socializing newcomers.

Social Identity

According to the social identity theory, people seek to classify themselves and others into social categories by membership, affiliation, age, gender culture and others [6,76]. Through this process of self-categorization, individuals are able to locate or define themselves in the social environment.

One of the consequences of social identity is that it can enhance support or commitment to groups in which the individuals "belong". Social identity implies a sense of emotional involvement with the group. It suggests attachment and emotional commitment [e.g.,11,26], and can foster loyalty and citizenship behaviors [e.g.,11,46]. Applying social identity theory, Mael and Ashforth found that alumni's identification with their alma mater predicted the alumni's recruitment of students, donation to that institution and attendance at functions [44].

Extending to online communities, social identity has been found to increase general contribution and commitment in the group [49]. Through this heightened attachment and commitment to the community, social identity may motivate members to socialize newcomers to grow and increase the prominence of the community while ensuring that the newcomers learn and internalize the values and beliefs of the community. Thus:

H1. Members' positive social identity will predict their likelihood to socialize newcomers.

Personal Prosocial Values

Volunteer socialization can be thought of as a prosocial act [24], where the volunteer is trying to help or benefit the newcomer. From that perspective, much research has shown that individual's prosocial orientations may help predict their volunteering behaviors [e.g.,17,45]. Prosocial orientation can predict volunteerism as prosocial individuals experience strong empathy towards others, have a strong sense of personal and social responsibility, and believes in their capability to help (self-efficacy) [56].

In this work, we use prosocial values from Schwartz's Value Theory. Values are "desirable, trans-situational goals, varying in importance that serve as guiding principles in people's lives" [50]. Schwartz et al. derived 10 basic human values from their study of people's value priorities from 67 countries [67]. Out of which, self-transcendent values of universalism and benevolence are designed to measure prosocial orientations [71] and have been found to predict prosocial behaviors in various contexts [12,65,69]. As explained by Schwartz, self-transcendence values lead individuals to care about societal poverty and others' welfare [70]. "Benevolence values may increase perception of need, empathic concern, and perspective taking in relation to members of one's in-group; universalism may do the same in relation to out-group members and strangers." [p.13,70] In addition, self-transcendence values may also positively influence self-efficacy beliefs to prosocial behavior—the more people value others' welfare, the more likely they will strive to develop the abilities to help others [16].

Therefore, we posit that these prosocial orientations can also influence members' likelihood of helping newcomers:

H2a. Members' prosocial values will positively predict their likelihood to socialize newcomers.

Prior research suggests that social identity moderates the psychological process and motivations underlying helping and volunteering behaviors [22,57,67,75]. In particular, shared group membership facilitated the translation of dispositional factors into actual helping behaviors [75]. This could mean that prosocial values would more strongly influence newcomer socialization for members who more strongly identify with their community.

H2b. Social identity will moderate the effect of prosocial value orientation on being a newcomer socializer.

Generalized Reciprocity

Generalized reciprocity is the exchange of goods and services where the giver does not know who will make a return (or how or when) [25,63]. It is more commonly referred to as "pay it forward." Real world examples of generalized reciprocity include blood banks and food banks, where people contribute expecting that they would receive aid when they themselves are in need [see 48 for review].

In the context of communities, generalized reciprocity contributes to social capital and has been used to explain why people contribute to communities even though they could just choose to free ride on others' efforts and contributions. According to theories of collective action, individuals forgo their tendency to free ride due to the influence of social capital [e.g.,58]. Instead of maximizing individual-based capital, individuals try to enhance the resources embedded in a social structure—social capital. One of the key sources of social capital is the norm of generalized reciprocity, where individuals are willing to help others with the expectation that down the road, someone will return the favor. Previous research has used the concept of generalized reciprocity to explain why people contribute e.g., knowledge [79] and files [35] online.

Along the same vein, generalized reciprocity may also play a role in influencing volunteer socialization in an online community. A basic norm of reciprocity is a sense of mutual indebtedness—individuals usually reciprocate the benefit they received from others to ensure ongoing exchanges [72]. Therefore, if members of a community are themselves socialized by others, they may be more likely to pay it forward and help other newcomers.

H3. Members who were socialized by others will be more likely to help socialize newcomers.

Opportunities and Tenure

Another set of predictive factors may relate to how frequent and how long someone has participated in the online community.

Perceived need is an antecedent of empathy. If people were to volunteer to help socialize newcomers, they must first notice newcomers. In addition, increase in perceived need has been shown to increase volunteerism [e.g., 29]. The more time a member spends in the community, the more likely they will be exposed to newcomers' requests for help, which could increase their likelihood to socialize newcomers.

H4. Members who spend more time per day in the community are more likely to socialize newcomers.

Research on the effects of membership duration (tenure) on participation is not definitive. Some findings suggest that tenure in an online community actually predicts lower participation as users become "bored, disappointed or otherwise less enthusiastic" [13,52]. Whereas findings from other studies suggest that interacting with others in the community overtime may increase their connection to others and increase in participation [34]. Other evidence also showed that tenure modulated the many motivation factors regarding their effect on community participation [53]. If we view volunteer socialization as a type of online community participation, then it is unclear if and how tenure predicts members' willingness to help socialize newcomers. Therefore, we proceed with a general research question exploring the relationship between tenure and socializing.

RQ. Can and how does a member's tenure predict the degree to which they socialize newcomers?

REDDIT.COM

In this work, we focus on reddit.com, one of the most visited, if not the most visited social news site. Social news sites are a form of online communities where members submit stories and the stories are ranked based on popularity. At the time of our study, reddit ranked 8th in the personalized news category ranking by Alexa, and 115th overall in the world. More than 34.8 million people visit reddit.com per month.

Additionally, reddit.com is a broad and diverse "community of communities." The site has over 100,000 subforums, which support users from different cities or universities, or those who are interested in specific TV shows, video games, sports, and even world problems. Over 8,400 of these subreddits have over 100 subscribers[1].

Reddit's interface has remained relatively unchanged since its initial launch. Users can submit links or stories, and other users can comment on the submitted content. Users can also vote on the submitted content, and their up or down votes can increase or decrease the content's visibility. Users can accumulate "karma" points by submitting links that other people like and vote for; this number offers the user no value, but is intended to "be a reminder of [her] legacy."

There are two key reasons why reddit is chosen as the focus of this work. First, while it is one of the fastest growing social media sites, it has not yet gained much research attention. The functions of reddit are simple but representative of a wide range of different online communities. Like most other sites, it enables users to submit content, comments, maintain a profile, and curate content. Thus, the findings from the study of reddit may be generalizable to other online communities. Second, unlike other online communities that focus on specific interests or topics, reddit welcomes users with a wide-range of interests through their subreddit design. For example, r/askreddit works like a Q&A site where people post questions and others answer the question by commenting, while r/worldnews is essential a world news aggregator where users post link from major news site from all over the world. This enables us to examine socialization using a potentially more diverse user base.

SOCIALIZER SCALE DEVELOPMENT

In the first phase of the project, we developed a scale to identify volunteer socializers. To develop our scale, we examined existing literature on socialization and mentorship to consolidate the set of behaviors that would constitute as socializing.

Scale Items

Research suggests that there are two major functions of mentoring and socialization: psychological functions and career functions [40,49]. Psychological functions address the interpersonal aspects of a mentoring relationship. It involves providing an acceptance role, friendship role, counseling role, or a role modeling function. On the other hand, career functions help enhance protégé's career advancement, and it includes sponsoring, coaching, protecting, providing challenge assignments, and increasing protégé's visibility.

Our approach to identifying socializers is to measure the degree to which an individual has served these functions to newcomers. Prior work has developed scales to measure mentorship functions [51,60]. However, these scales were developed to measure mentor roles from the perspective of the protégés. In addition, it was heavily situated in the traditional organizational context, assuming that the goal of mentorship is career advancement. Therefore, while we draw upon these scales, we also made significant modifications in our socializer scale.

Most notably, we removed *sponsoring* and *providing challenging assignment* sub-functions from our survey. This is because most online communities are not career-oriented. There tend to be little hierarchical structure and established roles in online communities. It is unclear what advancement would mean to online community members.

Then, we focused on seven of the sub-areas identified, found examples of such behaviors on reddit, and developed a 5-point Likert question item for each sub-area (ranging from 1-strongly disagree to 5 strongly agree). The four are are "psychological" functions and the last three are "career" functions.

- *Acceptance-and-confirmation*. To provide positive feedback and compliments. An example is when a reddit user (redditor) responded to another with "welcome newfound redditor" [2]. Our survey item is: *I have welcomed newcomers on reddit*.
- *Counseling*. To discuss personal matters of concern. An example is when a redditor provided emotional support to a newcomer who has a bad habit of overdosing[3]. Our survey item is: *I have provided emotional support to newcomers*.
- *Friendship*. To help establish a social relationship with the newcomer. An example is when a redditor invited a newcomer to join their gaming team[4]. Our survey item is: *I have tried to build friendships with newcomers*.
- *Role modeling*. To serve as an example to newcomers regarding attitude, values and behavior. Unlike other roles, this is less tied to any specific instances, and more about gaining respect and recognition over time. Our

[1] http://blog.reddit.com/2012/01/2-billion-beyond.html

[2] http://www.reddit.com/r/AskReddit/comments/mqg9v/why_do_i_need_karma_newbie_to_reddit/c3327av

[3] http://www.reddit.com/r/depression/comments/k5d36/hey_newbie_with_a_bad_habit_of_oding/

[4] http://www.reddit.com/r/bf3pc/comments/tloze/newbie_looking_for_some_friends_to_play_bf3/

	Accept.	Counsel.	Friend.	Role M.	Exposure	Coaching	Protect.	Mean	Std	Factor Loading
Accept.	1							2.96	1.22	0.54
Counsel.	0.48	1						2.48	1.15	0.59
Friend.	0.62	0.61	1					2.50	1.11	0.77
Role M.	0.47	0.48	0.65	1				2.44	1.07	0.57
Exposure	0.34	0.45	0.66	0.53	1			2.14	1.09	0.54
Coaching	0.57	0.53	0.51	0.49	0.50	1		2.87	1.30	0.56
Protect.	0.54	0.65	0.70	0.53	0.56	0.54	1	2.60	1.20	0.69

Table 1. Correlations, mean, standard deviation and factor loading of 7-items socializer scale from the initial survey.

survey item is: *I can feel the respect and admiration from newcomers.*

- *Exposure and visibility.* To enhance the visibility of the newcomer to other members of the community. An example of this includes the creation of a specific thread for newcomers to post their questions[5]. Our survey item is: *I have made newcomers more visible to other reddit users.*
- *Coaching.* To offer strategies for becoming an effective member of the community. An example is when a redditor wrote a newbie guide[6]. Our survey item is: *I have explained to newcomers how to use and/or how to behave on reddit.*
- *Protection.* To help shield newcomers from negative comments. An example is when a redditor wrote "I know the other guy was being rude about it, but there are a lot of good resources in the sidebar. It's a good place to start!"[7]. Our survey item is: *I have defended and/or protected newcomers from other reddit users.*

Initial Survey

We conducted an initial survey of the reddit community to test our scale. We deployed our survey to two subreddits that are related to the universities where the authors work; these have about 2800 subscribers. We only targeted these subreddits for the testing and validation of our scale. Doing so also helped establish credibility within the reddit community for the larger deployment where we tested our hypotheses (the second phase of the project). Reddit users were told that participants would be entered into a drawing for one of multiple $100 Amazon Gift Cards (4 participants received gift cards). They were also told that instead of collecting the gift card, they will have the option to donate the $100 to a charity of their choice.

After cleaning up the results where we removed incomplete responders and those who failed our consistency checks (low variance across all items and high discrepancies between duplicate items), we had 132 responses (out of 236 who started to take our survey and 164 who completed the survey). As expected, most of our survey participants are affiliated with the Universities. 97% are between the ages of 18 and 29. 74% of participants are male.

Socializer Scale Results

The 7-item scale achieved very high reliability (α=0.89). Principle component factor analysis with varimax rotation was used to examine the empirical structure of these items. The items all loaded on a single factor (see Table 1). This suggests that the two major functions of mentoring—psychological functions and career functions—may not be distinct in a social online communities setting as it may be in the traditional work setting.

Besides the high reliability, we also sought to validate our scale through three different methods. First, we tested our scale against the survey respondents' perception of socialization. At the start of our survey, we asked the respondents a likert question of: "Do you help newcomers adopt the behaviors and/or attitudes essential to being a member of reddit?" The correlation between our response and our 7-question item was significant ($r(130)=0.62$, $p<0.001$).

Second, we asked respondents to list the number of newcomers they have helped socialize on reddit. The average ratings from our socializer scale for those who have helped new redditor users are significantly higher ($t(130)=3.10$, $p=0.002$).

Third, we scraped the reddit site and collected our survey responders' 1000 most recent comments (1000 limitation imposed by the site design). We then checked how frequently those comments were in response to a post or a comment whose poster has joined within 30 days of posting (a newcomer). Due to the non-normal distribution of posting frequencies, we analyzed the correlation using Spearman's correlation. There is a weak correlation between those who are more likely to respond to these newcomers, provided a higher socializer rating ($r_s(130)=0.15$, $p=0.10$). These convergent tests of self-

---

[5] http://www.reddit.com/r/Eve/comments/ck8kq/collective_newbie_question_thread/

[6] http://www.reddit.com/r/self/comments/d0bia/newbies_newbie_guie_to_reddit/

[7] http://www.reddit.com/r/LucidDreaming/comments/ssjem/help_points_for_a_newbie/c4gnla5

reported and behavior data and the high reliability provided sufficient support for our next phase of study.

STUDY OF PREDICTORS OF SOCIALIZERS

To test our hypotheses on the predictors of socializers, we deployed a survey on reddit. The survey was posted a general subreddit, r/self. We also cross-posted our survey on other subreddits in order to attract more redditors (total of ~84,000 subscribers). Again, respondents were entered into the drawing for one of multiple $100 Amazon Gift Cards or donation gifts.

Measures

The survey contained various psychological and social scales, questions about reddit usage, and basic demographic questions to measure our dependent and independent variables.

Socializer Scale

We used the 7-item socializer scale as discussed in the previous section. The average of the items were used as the dependent variable in our analysis (α=0.89). Survey respondents were directed to these questions only if they have seen a newcomer on reddit (either a user claims to be new, or that her profile indicates that she just joined). Once again, the items loaded on a single dimension.

Social Identity Scale

We used a 6-item scale adopted from [21] to measure social identity. This 6-items scale focused on 3 dimensions: cognitive, affective, and evaluative. The average of all of the items were used as the independent variable of social identity (α=0.76).

Portrait Value Questionnaire (prosocial values)

We used the 21-item short version of the Portrait Value Questionnaire developed by Schwartz and colleagues [68]. The questionnaire measures 4 high-level value dimensions: self-transcendence, self-enhancement, openness-to-change, and conservation. Self-transcendence emphasizes concern for the welfare and interest of others, and it is used as our prosocial values measure (α=0.66). Schwartz explains that the "low" reliability is because the questionnaire items are designed to measure different underlying goals of the values [68]. As per their instructions, we used the normalized version of the rating for our analysis as these value ratings highlight the relative, and not absolute strengths of the values to each individual.

Generalized Reciprocity

Survey respondents were asked to what degree they themselves were socialized by others when they first joined the reddit community, from 0-never to 4-a great deal.

General Usage

Survey respondents were also asked to report their general usage of reddit. Of which, we used the items "how much time on average do you spend on reddit daily" and "when did you first sign up on reddit" (month/year) as independent variables in our analysis. Due to the skewed nature of reddit-tenure, a log-transformation was applied on the number of months a survey taker has been a redditor. We chose to use the self-reported tenure, as we did not want to limit our findings to only those who have are willing to share their reddit IDs. In addition, some redditors may have over time changed their accounts or chosen to use a "throw-away" account for the survey (an account that is created with no past comments linking them to who they are), in which cases the account's membership date would not be a valid indicator of actual membership tenure.

Demographic Questions

Basic demographic questions, such as age, gender, education, income, and location of residence area, were also included in the survey.

Results and Analysis

After removing incomplete responses and those that were completed too quickly (<5 minutes) or failed our consistency checks (low variance across all items and high discrepancies between duplicate items), we ended up with 1305 survey responses. We limit our analyses to only those responders who have seen a post by a newcomer while using reddit—who has had at least one opportunity to help socialize the newcomers (1174).

The majority of our respondents identified themselves as male (64%), between the ages of 21 and 29 (54%), and had at least some college education (>80%). On average, these users had been members of reddit for 20 months and were fairly heavy users, spending between 1 to 4 hours on the site per day (68%). Our respondents provided a nice range of user-tenure, offering a mix of new users (9% just joined reddit in the past month), and senior members (5% have been with reddit for more than 50 months).

Our dependent measure of socializing behaviors had a bi-modal distribution, where the second mode (centered around 1, out of the 5 point scale) is much smaller than the first mode (centered around 3). Therefore, to test our hypotheses, we analyze our data three ways. First, we used an OLS regression model with the data as is. Second, we excluded the samples with the average of 1 socializer score in the regression to remove the second mode. Third, we employed a multinomial logistic regression (mlogit in stata) to compare across 3 tiers, low, medium and high socializers (1 to <2, 2 to 4, 4+). Social identity, prosocial values, generalized reciprocity, daily time spent on reddit, tenure and the quadratic effect of tenure as the independent variables. The interaction effect of prosocial values and social identity was also included. We also tested various control variables: whether or not the redditor is an administrator in a subreddit, their age and gender. None of the control variables were found to be significant and are not discussed henceforth.

Newcomer Socialization			R^2=0.19			
	Mean	S.D.	Est.	Std. Err	Std. Beta	Prob
Social Identity	2.75	0.65	0.25	0.04	0.20	<0.001
Prosocial (Self-transcendence)	0.86	0.64	0.17	0.04	0.14	<0.001
Social Identity*Prosocial			0.03	0.05	0.01	
Reciprocity	1.90	0.88	0.30	0.03	0.33	<0.001
Time spend daily	4.50	0.98	-0.01	0.02	-0.01	
Tenure (log)	1.19	0.35	0.08	0.07	0.04	
Tenure (log)*Tenure (log)			0.27	0.14	0.06	<0.05

Table 2. Regression model predicting newcomer socialization behaviors.

The predictor variables were similar across the three analyses methods. Here, we report on the first method—an OLS regression model using all the data. The results are summarized in Table 2. The model is statistically significant F(7,1065)=36.6, p<0.001) and collinearity test shows that the main effects were not highly correlated.

A number of our hypotheses were supported. We hypothesized that social identity (H1), prosocial values (H2a), and general reciprocity (H3) are positive predictors of socializers and our results supported these hypotheses. Respondents who identify with the reddit community, hold prosocial values, and were themselves socialized by other redditors, are more likely to help socialize newcomers on reddit. The interaction effect of social identity and prosocial values, however, was not significant. This suggests that social identity does not moderate the effects of prosocial values on volunteer socialization (H2b not supported).

We also hypothesized that time spent on reddit is a positive predictor of socializing; our results did not support this hypothesis (H4). Finally, our research question tries to examine whether tenure also predict socializing (RQ). We found that while tenure is not a significant predictor of socializing, the quadratic effect of tenure does show that there is a curvilinear effect of membership-length on volunteer socialization. Results suggest that new and long-time members of reddit are more likely to perform socialization behaviors than medium-tenured users. Possible reasons are examined in the discussion section.

DISCUSSION

Attracting and socializing newcomers has been identified as an important problem for online communities [20,23,27]. However, due to the lack of organizational structures in the online communities, much of the newcomer socialization has relied on volunteer socializers—members who voluntarily help out newcomers in these communities. Given the growing importance of volunteer socialization, it has become necessary to understand the underlying factors that influence people to volunteer.

Our results suggest that contextual factors do influence the likelihood of volunteer socialization. Specifically, when members identify with the particular community, and if they were themselves socialized by others within the community, they become more likely to help newcomers.

At the same time, our results also indicate dispositional factors that predict socialization behaviors. Our results showed that individuals who hold prosocial values are more likely to help socialize newcomers. Further, we did not find that social identity moderates the effect of prosocial values on socialization behaviors. This means that individuals holding prosocial values are more likely to socialize newcomers in a community, regardless of how strongly they identify with the particular community. Their willingness to help newcomers also does not amplify when they identify with the community.

Unlike what we have hypothesized, we did not find an effect of socialization opportunities on socialization behaviors. One possible reason is that being exposed to socializing opportunities alone is not sufficient to motivate members to help newcomers. However, given prior research showing that perceived need increase helping behaviors [e.g., 29], a more plausible explanation may be that time spent on site may not be an accurate measure of socialization opportunities. A more direct measure of how frequently members actually notice a newcomer asking for help may turn out to be a significant predictor of socialization behaviors.

Our exploration on the effect of membership tenure on socialization led to the finding that tenure has a quadratic prediction effect on socializers. Prior findings from online community participation suggest that participation may be highest at the start of members' tenure or when they have become senior, full-fledged members. Our results suggest that both may be true when it comes to members' participation in socialization newcomers. Newer members who have recently gone through the learning stage can perhaps more closely identify with the newcomers, which make them more motivated to help those users. In addition, they may also feel more motivated to demonstrate their membership status and helping newcomers to signal that they are no longer newcomers themselves. On the other hand, senior members perhaps also feel more obligated to welcome and socialize newcomers as they hold a lot of institutional knowledge that others do not have. There may also be self-selection factors at play. Long-time members who are still using the site are perhaps more vested in the community—others might have gotten bored have already dropped out over time. Additional, longitudinal research is needed to better understand the underlying causes of the curvilinear relationship.

Since the examined predictors were measured differently (e.g., different Likert options for the scale), we are cautious in making any strong claims about the relative strengths of the different factors examined. However, using the standardize beta coefficients, it appears that one unit change in reciprocity has the strongest effect on socialization of newcomers, then social identity, prosocial values, and then the quadratic effect of tenure. Future research can confirm this experimentally by manipulating some of these factors to better assess the effectiveness of these factors in encouraging newcomer socialization.

While the focus of this work is in the online community setting, our results also provide a starting point for understanding general factors in predicting volunteer socialization in offline and organizational settings. Prior research has identified reasons why informal mentors select certain individuals as protégés (e.g., interpersonal comfort), but our findings also offer a set of general factors. Extending our work to the organizational context could be particularly useful as informal mentorship in organizational settings are actually more effective and lead to longer-term relationships than assigned mentorship [59]. We should point out, however, that key differences do existing between online communities and corporate organizations and it would be important to explore how these differences (e.g., anonymity/pseudonymity, social versus career-oriented) lead to differences in socializer predictors. As our exploratory factor analyses of the socialization scale indicated, the distinction between psychological and career functions of socialization identified in traditional work settings may not be as strong in the online social community setting.

Practical Contributions

This research offers two key practical contributions. First, results from this research enable us to identify volunteer socializers. We have developed a 7-item scale to identify these members of the community. While more validation is needed, this scale can be useful to researcher or designers as a general measure for assessment of the "health" of an online community. Specifically, this measure indicates of how active the community is at supporting newcomers and can suggest the potential rate of acceptance and integration of new members to the community.

In the near future, knowing what psychosocial factors predict volunteer socializing behaviors may allow us to build computational models to automatically identify these volunteers. We can then offer tools or training to facilitate these volunteers to more effectively socialize the newcomers.

In addition to identifying socializers, understanding the predictors of socializers can also lead to strategies to foster more volunteer socialization in online communities. First, given that generalized reciprocity is found to be a predictor of newcomer socialization (potentially the strongest of the factors we examined), one potential design to encourage more volunteer socialization is to remind members of how others have helped them when they first joined the community. Such a reminder may encourage members to help newcomers as they were once helped.

Alternatively, online communities may also leverage shared social identity to encourage volunteer socialization. Recent research has explored the use of common identity to facilitate the building of online communities [61]. For example, providing members with more community level information or using interface that highlights homogeneity between members may help increase identity-based attachment. This design has been shown to motivate member participation (e.g., visits and attachment to the community), but findings from our study also suggest that through strengthening identity-based attachment, members may also be more likely to voluntarily help newcomers.

LIMITATIONS AND GENERALIZABILITY

Our respondents self-selected into taking our surveys, which may have introduced sampling bias in our data. Certain types of users (e.g., with different value-orientations) may be more likely to respond to online survey requests than others. In addition, with our cross-sectional data, we cannot draw conclusive causal inferences. Additional research with longitudinal data should help validate our findings.

Studies involving a single site also have its limitations. However, since reddit is a broad community with a fairly diverse set of subcommunities (subreddits), we believe the predictive factors we found may generalize to other online and offline communities. However, community-specific features are likely to alter the effect size of the factors. For example, communities that attract a higher number of prosocial-oriented users (such as volunteer communities) are more likely to report higher correlations between social identity and prosocial values, hence affecting the predictive power of each of those factors.

CONCLUSION

In this paper we explored the predictors of volunteer socializers and found both contextual and dispositional factors. Users who identify more strongly with the community and who have been socialized by other users are more likely to help newcomers. In addition, users who hold prosocial values are dispositionally more likely to be volunteer socializers. Future work should apply these findings to identify and support volunteer socializers.

ACKNOWLEDGMENTS

We thank all the reviewers for their helpful comments, BITLab members at Michigan State University for their feedback throughout the process, and Tim Levine for his suggestions with data analyses.

REFERENCES

1. Ahuja, M. K., & Galvin, J. E. (2003). Socialization in virtual groups. *Journal of Management*, 29(2), 161.
2. Allen, D. G. (2006). Do organizational socialization tactics influence newcomer embeddedness and turnover? *Journal of Management*, 32(2), 237.
3. Allen, N. J., & Meyer, J. P. (1990). Organizational socialization tactics: A longitudinal analysis of links to newcomers' commitment and role orientation. *Academy of Management Journal*, 847- 858.
4. Allen, T. D., Poteet, M. L., & Burroughs, S. M. (1997). The Mentor's Perspective: A Qualitative Inquiry and Future Research Agenda. *Journal of Vocational Behavior*, 51(1), 70–89
5. Arguello, J., Butler, B. S., Joyce, E., Kraut, R., Ling, K. S., & Wang, X. (2006). Talk to me: Foundations for successful individual-group interactions in online communities. *Proceedings of the SIGCHI conference on Human Factors in computing systems,* 959-968
6. Ashforth, B. E. & Mael, F. (1989). Social identity theory and the organization. *Academy of management review*, 20-39
7. Ashforth, B.E. & Saks, A. M. (1996). Socialization tactics: Longitudinal effects on newcomer adjustment. *Academy of Management Journal*, pp. 149-178.
8. Baard, P. P., Deci, E. L., & Ryan, R. M. (2004). Intrinsic need satisfaction: A motivational basis of performance and well-being in two work settings. *Journal of Applied Social Psychology*, 34, 2045- 2068.
9. Barrick, Murray R. & Michael Mount. (1991). The Big Five Personality Dimensions and Job Performance: A Meta-Analysis. *Personnel Psychology*, 44, 1–26.
10. Bauer, T. N., Bodner, T., Erdogan, B., Truxillo, D. M., & Tucker, J. S. (2007). Newcomer adjustment during organizational socialization: A meta-analytic review of antecedents, outcomes, and methods. *Journal of Applied Psychology*, 92(3), 707.
11. Bergami, M., & Bagozzi, R. P. (2000). Self-categorization, affective commitment, and group self-esteem as distinct aspects of social identity in an organization. *British Journal of Social Psychology*, 39(4), 555–577.
12. Bond, M. H., & Chi, V. M. Y. (1997). Values and moral behavior in Mainland China. *Psychologia*, 40, 251-264
13. Brandtzæg, P. B., & Heim, J. (2008). User loyalty and online communities: why members of online communities are not faithful. In *Proceedings of the 2nd international conference on INtelligent TEchnologies for interactive enterTAINment,* article 11.
14. Burke, R. J. (1984). Mentors in Organizations, *Group and Organization Studies*, 9, 353-372.
15. Cable, D. M., & Parsons, C. K. (2001). Socialization tactics and person-organization fit. *Personnel Psychology*, 54(1), 1-24.
16. Caprara, G. V., & Steca, P. (2007). Prosocial agency: The contribution of values and self–efficacy beliefs to prosocial behavior across ages. *Journal of Social and Clinical Psychology*, 26, 218–239.
17. Carlo, Gustavo, Morris A. Okun, George P. Knight, and Maria Rosario T. de Guzman. 2005. The Interplay of Traits and Motives on Volunteering: Agreeableness, Extraversion and Prosocial Value Motivation. *Personality and Individual Differences 38*: 1293-1305.
18. Chao, G. T., O'Leary-Kelly, A. M., Wolf, S., Klein, H. J., & Gardner, P. D. (1994). Organizational socialization: Its content and consequences. *Journal of Applied Psychology*, 79(5), 730-743.
19. Chao, G. T., Walz, P., & Gardner, P. (1992). Formal and informal mentorships: a comparison on mentoring functions and contrast with nonmentored counterparts. *Personnel Psychology*, 45(3), 619–636
20. Choi, B., Alexander, K., Kraut, R. E., & Levine, J. M. (2010). Socialization tactics in wikipedia and their effects. *Proceedings of the 2010 ACM conference on Computer supported cooperative work*, 107-116
21. Dholakia, U. M., Bagozzi, R. P., & Pearo, L. K. (2004). A social influence model of consumer participation in network-and small-group-based virtual communities. *International Journal of Research in Marketing*, 21(3) 241-263.
22. Dovidio, J. F., Gaertner, S. L., Validzic, A., Matoka, K., Johnson, B. & Frazier, S. (1997). Extending the Benefits of Recategorization: Evaluations, Self-Disclosure, and Helping. *Journal of Experimental Social Psychology*, 33(4), 401-420.
23. Ducheneaut, N. (2005). Socialization in an open source software community: A socio-technical analysis. *Computer Supported Cooperative Work*, 14(4) 323-368.
24. Eisenberg, N., Fabes, R. A. and Spinrad, T. L. (2007). Prosocial Development. *Handbook of Child Psychology*. 646-718.
25. Ekeh, P.P., (1974). *Social Exchange Theory: The Two Traditions*. Harvard University Press, Cambridge, MA.

26. Ellemers, N., Kortekaas, P., & Ouwerkerk, J. W. (1999). Selfcategorization, commitment to the group, and group self-esteem as related but distinct aspects of social identity. *European Journal of Social Psychology*, *29*, 371– 389.

27. Farzan, R., Pal, A., Kraut, R. & Konstan, J. (2012). Socializing volunteers in an online community: A field experiment. In *Proceedings of the ACM conference on Computer-Supported Cooperative Work.*

28. Finkelstein, M. A., Penner, L. A., & Brannick, M. T. (2005). Motive, role identity, and prosocial personality as predictors of volunteer activity. *Social Behavior and Personality: an international journal*, 33, 403-418

29. Fisher, R. J., & Ackerman, D. (1998). The Effects of Recognition and Group Need on Volunteerism: A Social Norm Perspective. *Journal of Consumer Research*, 25(3) 262-275

30. Galegher, J. Sproull, L., & Kiesler, S. (1998). Legitimacy, authority, and community in electronic support groups. *Written communication*, 15, 493-530

31. Hertel, G., Niedner, S., & Herrmann, S. (2003). Motivation of software developers in Open Source projects: an Internet-based survey of contributors to the Linux kernel. *Research policy*, 32, 1159-1177

32. Hogg, M. A. & Abrams, D. (1988). *Social identifications: A social psychology of intergroup relations and group processes*. Psychology Press

33. Halbesleben, J. R. B., Bowler, W. M., Bolino, M. C., & Turnley, W. H. (2010). Organizational Concern, Prosocial Values, or Impression Management? How Supervisors Attribute Motives to Organizational Citizenship Behavior. *Journal of Applied Social Psychology*, 40(6), 1450-1489.

34. Huberman, B. A., Romero, D. M., & Wu, F. (2009). Crowdsourcing, attention and productivity. *Journal of Information Science*, 35(6), 758-765.

35. Jian, L., & Mackie-Mason, J. K. (2008). Why share in peer-to-peer networks? *Proceedings of the 10th international conference on Electronic commerce*, No. 4

36. Jones, G. R. (1986). Socialization tactics, self-efficacy, and newcomers' adjustments to organizations. *Academy of Management Journal*, 262-279.

37. Joyce, E., & Kraut, R. E. (2006). Predicting continued participation in newsgroups. *Journal of Computer-Mediated Communication*, 11(3), article 3

38. Kalbfleisch, P. J., & Davies, A. B. (1993). An interpersonal model for participation in mentoring relationships, *Western Journal of Communication,* 57(4)

39. Kim, T. Y. Cable, D.M. & Kim, S.P. (2005). Socialization tactics, employee proactivity, and person-organization fit. *Journal of Applied Psychology*, vol. 90, 232.

40. Kram, K. E., & Isabella, L. A. (1985). Mentoring Alternatives: The Role of Peer Relationships in Career Development. *The Academy of Management Journal*, 28(1) 110-132

41. Kraut, R. E., & Resnick, P. (2011). *Evidence-based social design: Mining the social sciences to build online communities*. MIT Press.

42. Lampe, C. A. C., Johnston, E., & Resnick, P. (2007). Follow the reader: filtering comments on slashdot. *Proceedings of the SIGCHI conference on Human factors in computing systems,* 1253-1262

43. Lester, R.E. (1987). Organizational culture, uncertainty reduction, and the socialization of new organizational members. *Culture and communication: Methodology, behavior, artifacts, and institutions*, vol. 105, p. 113.

44. Mael, F. & Ashforth, B. E. (1992). Alumni and Their Alma Mater: A Partial Test of the Reformulated Model of Organizational Identification, *Journal of Organizational Behavior 13*, 103–23.

45. Matsuba, M. K., Hart, D., & Atkins, R. (2007). Psychological and social-structural influences on commitment to volunteering. *Journal of Research in Personality*. 41, 889-907

46. Meyer, J. P., Stanley, D. J., Herscovitch, L., & Topolnytsky, L. (2002). Affective, continuance, and normative commitment to the organization: A meta-analysis of antecedents, correlates, and consequences. *Journal of Vocational Behavior*, *61*, 20– 52.

47. Mizruchi, M. S. (1993). Cohesion, equivalence, and similarity of behavior: a theoretical and empirical assessment. *Social Networks*, 15(3) 275-307

48. Moody, M. (2008). Serial Reciprocity: A Preliminary Statement. *Sociological Theory*, 26(2) 130–151

49. Musicant, D. R., Ren, Y., Johnson, J. A., & Riedl, J. (2011). Mentoring in Wikipedia: a clash of cultures. In *Proceedings of the 7th International Symposium on Wikis and Open Collaboration*, 173-182.

50. Nguyen, D., & Rose, C. P. (2011). Language use as a reflection of socialization in online communities. *Proceedings of the Workshop on Language in Social Media.*

51. Noe, R. A. (1988). An investigation of the determinants of successful assigned mentoring relationships. *Personnel Psychology*, 41, 457-479.

52. Nov, O., Naaman, M., & Ye, C. (2009). Motivational, structural and tenure factors that impact online community photo sharing. *Proceedings of AAAI International Conference on Weblogs and Social Media.* San Jose, CA.

53. Nov, O., Naaman, M., & Ye, C. (2010). Analysis of participation in an online photo-sharing community: A multidimensional perspective. *Journal of the American*

Society for Information Science and Technology, 61(3), 555-566.

54. Olian, J.D., Carroll, S.J., Giannantonio, C.M., & Feren, D.B. (1988). What do proteges look for in a mentor? Results of three experimental studies. *Journal of Vocational Behavior*, 33(1), 15–37

55. Ostroff, C. & Kozlowski, S.W. (1993). The role of mentoring in the information gathering processes of newcomers during early organizational socialization. *Journal of Vocational Behavior*, 42(2), 170-183.

56. Penner, L.A., Fritzsche, B.A., Craiger, J.P., Freifeld, T.R. (1995). Measuring the prosocial personality. In *Advances in Personality Assessment*. Volume 10, ed. J Butcher, CD Spielberger. 147–63. Hillsdale, NJ: LEA.

57. Penner, L. A., & Finkelstein, M. A. (1998). Dispositional and structural determinants of volunteerism. *Journal of Personality and Social Psychology*, 74(2), 525.

58. Putnam, Robert D. (1995), "Bowling Alone: America's Declining Social Capital," *Journal of Democracy*, *6* (January), 65–78.

59. Ragins, B. R., & Cotton, J. L. (1999). Mentor functions and outcomes: A comparison of men and women in formal and informal mentoring relationships. *Journal of Applied Psychology*, 84, 529-550.

60. Ragins, B. R., & McFarlin, D. (1990). Perception of mentor roles in cross-gender mentoring relationships. *Journal of Vocational Behavior*, 37, 321-339.

61. Ren, Y., F. M. Harper, S. Drenner, L. Terveen, S. Kiesler, J. Riedl, R. E. Kraut. (2012). Building member attachment in online communities: Applying theories of group identity and interpersonal bonds. Forthcoming. *MIS Quarterly*.

62. Riordan, C. M., Weatherly, E. W., Vandenberg, R. J., & Self, R. M. (2001). The effects of preentry experiences and socialization tactics on newcomer attitudes and turnover. *Journal of Managerial Issues*, 13(2), 159-176.

63. Sahlins, Marshall (1972), *Stone Age Economics*. Chicago: Aldine Atherton.

64. Saks, A. M., Uggerslev, K. L., & Fassina, N. E. (2007). Socialization tactics and newcomer adjustment: A meta-analytic review and test of a model. *Journal of Vocational Behavior*, 70(3), 413-446.

65. Schwartz, S. H. (1990). Individualism-collectivism: Critique and proposed refinements. *Journal of Cross-Cultural Psychology*, 21, 139- 157.

66. Schwartz, S. H. (1992). Universals in the content and structure of values: Theoretical advances and empirical tests in 20 countries. *Advances in experimental social psychology*, 25(1): 1-65.

67. Schwartz, S. H. (1994). Are there universal aspects in the structure and contents of human values? *Journal of social issues* 50(4): 19-45.

68. Schwartz, S. H. (2002). A Proposal for Measuring Value Orientations across Nations. Chapter 7 in the *Questionnaire Development Package of the European Social Survey*.

69. Schwartz, S. H. (2007). Universalism Values and the Inclusiveness of Our Moral Universe. *Journal of Cross-Cultural Psychology*, 2007, 38: 711

70. Schwartz, S. H. (2010). Basic Values: How they motivate and inhibit prosocial behavior. In Mario Mikulincer & P. R. Shaver (Eds.), *Prosocial motives, emotions, and behavior: The better angels of our nature*: 221-241. Washington, DC: American Psychological Association.

71. Schwartz, S. H., & Bilsky, W. (1990). Toward a theory of the universal content and structure of values: Extensions and cross-cultural replications. *Journal of Personality and Social Psychology*, 58, 878-891

72. Shumaker, S. A., & Brownell, A. (1984). Toward a theory of social support: Closing conceptual gaps. *Journal of Social Issues*, *40*(4), 11-36.

73. Simon, B., Stürmer, S., & Steffens, K. (2000). Helping individuals or group members? The role of individual and collective identification in AIDS volunteerism. *Personality and Social Psychology Bulletin*, 26(4), 497-506.

74. Snyder, M., Omoto, A. M., & Lindsay, J. J. (2004). Sacrificing time and effort for the good of others. In A. G. Miller (Ed.), *The social psychology of good and evil* (pp. 444–468). New York: The Guilford Press.

75. Stürmer, S., Snyder, M., & Omoto, A. M. (2005). Prosocial emotions and helping: the moderating role of group membership. *Journal of Personality and Social Psychology*, 88(3), 532.

76. Tajfel, H. T. Turner, J. C. (1986). The social identity theory of intergroup behavior. *Psychology of Intergroup Relations*, 7-24.

77. Tidwell, M. V. (2005). A social identity model of prosocial behaviors within nonprofit organizations. *Nonprofit Management and Leadership*, 15, 449-467

78. Turner, T. C., Smith M., Fisher, D., & Welser H. T. (2005). "Picturing Usenet: Mapping Computer-Mediated Collective Action." *Journal of Computer Mediated Communication* 10 (4).

79. Wasko, M. M., & Faraj, S. (2005). Why Should I Share? Examining Social Capital and Knowledge Contribution in Electronic Networks of Practice. *MIS Quarterly*, 29(1) 35-57.

Tea & Sympathy: Crafting Positive New User Experiences on Wikipedia

Jonathan T. Morgan, Siko Bouterse, Sarah Stierch, Heather Walls
Wikimedia Foundation
{jmorgan, sbouterse, sstierch, hwalls}
@wikimedia.org

ABSTRACT
We present the Teahouse, a pilot project for supporting and socializing new Wikipedia editors. Open collaboration systems like Wikipedia must continually recruit and retain new members in order to sustain themselves. Wikipedia's editor decline presents unique exigency for evaluating novel strategies to support newcomers and increase new user retention in such systems, particularly among demographics that are currently underrepresented in the user community. In this paper, we describe the design and deployment of Teahouse, and present preliminary findings. Our findings highlight the importance of intervening early in the editor lifecycle, providing user-friendly tools, creating safe spaces for newcomers, and facilitating positive interactions between newcomers and established community members.

Author Keywords
User experience; new users; Wikipedia; gender; socialization; collaboration

ACM Classification Keywords
H.5.3. Information Interfaces and Presentation (e.g., HCI): Group and organization interfaces.

General Terms
Human Factors; Design; Measurement.

INTRODUCTION
SubSubPop23 has just joined Wikipedia and is excited about editing. The first article she creates is about her favorite San Francisco street artist, a local legend who recently died. But when she logs in a few days after starting her article to continue working, she sees that it has been tagged for immediate removal from Wikipedia because of "a lack of notability" and "few reliable sources". She feels confused, unfairly singled out, and frustrated. But above all, she is concerned that she is about to lose all of her work. She clicks through the links on the deletion message, and tries to make sense of the process for contesting this decision. She finds the process to be overly complicated, and the whole experience feels impersonal. What does she need to do to save her article? What counts as notable on Wikipedia? How does she add a reliable source? Who does she need to convince to keep her article online while she works on it? Will anyone even respond to her inquiries before they delete her article?

The scenario above illustrates some of the challenges of being a new user in an established online community. All open collaboration systems require a pool of volunteer contributors to function. Since all participants in such systems will eventually stop contributing, a steady stream of newcomers must join the community in order to maintain productivity. In systems like Wikipedia where 0.01% of editors contribute 44% of the encyclopedia's value [25], it is critical that some of these participants move from the periphery of the community to the center and become 'Wikipedians'—power editors who not only write and edit articles but also perform critical quality assurance and community organizing roles such as coordinating group work, fighting vandalism and recruiting and socializing the next generation of editors [1].

Historically, the English language Wikipedia has been effective at recruiting and retaining new editors. The community grew from hundreds of active editors in 2001 to a peak of 51,418 active editors in March of 2007 [29]. The contributions of many volunteers have propelled the encyclopedia to a high level of quality and comprehensiveness [10].

Editor decline: newcomer rejection and the gender gap
However, after 2007, Wikipedia's exponential growth stalled and the population of active editors (those who make more than 5 edits per month) began to decline. Research has shown that this decline is likely due in part to a growing resistance within the community towards new contributions and new contributors [26]. Moreover, the overall proportion of edits that are subsequently reverted by other editors has increased year by year, and this increase in reversions disproportionately affects occasional contributors, creating a growing disparity between the proportion of reverted edits by editors who make fewer than 10 edits per month and higher-volume contributors [26].

CSCW '13, February 23–27, 2013, San Antonio, Texas, USA.

The Increasing rejection of new editors

The likelihood of rejection for new editors has also increased as the encyclopedia has aged [12], a phenomenon that can have a powerful demotivating effect on newcomers: it leads them to edit less and stop contributing sooner [13].

The increased scrutiny to which new editors are subjected is understandable given that Wikipedia's increasing popularly has made the encyclopedia more vulnerable to vandalism and self-interested editing. However, recent work [12] has demonstrated that the proportion of newcomers who edit in 'good faith' has in fact held relatively constant since 2006, even as the rate at which these newcomers are rejected has risen in step with overall rejection rates.

Taken together, these findings suggest that while new editors in 2012 are no less capable of high quality contributions than previous generations of newcomers, the community appears to increasingly dismiss the efforts of good faith newcomers who would benefit the encyclopedia by continuing to contribute.

A persistent gender gap

Another probable factor contributing to editor decline is the encyclopedia's inability to recruit and retain editors from outside the traditional demographics. According to a 2011 survey [30] of 5,287 current and former contributors, the average Wikipedian is around 30 years old, male, computer-savvy, and lives in the U.S. or Europe. Nowhere is the homogeneity of the community more evident than in its gender distribution: although the community has aged and grown somewhat more geographically diverse since its inception, the proportion of female editors has remained very low. The 2011 editor survey reported that only 8.5% of active editors are women [30].

Another recent study [19] of new editors found the proportion of female newcomers to be 16%, nearly double the site-wide average. This suggests that the attrition rate for female editors is even higher than for newcomers in general. The same study also found that female newcomers tended to participate at a lower rate than their male counterparts overall, see their edits reverted at a higher rate, and leave sooner. Post-hoc analysis of data gathered from a previous survey [11] of over 50,000 Wikipedia readers and editors contextualizes these findings: female editors rated their satisfaction with editing lower than men on average, citing negative social factors (such as the degree of conflict and hostility they experienced) at a higher rate than male editors [4].

The gender gap has had a quantifiable impact on the quality and coverage of the encyclopedia: articles on topics of interest to female editors received less coverage than those of interest to male editors, and articles within those topic areas were shorter on average [19]. The persistent gender gap represents a significant missed opportunity for increasing the pool of dedicated Wikipedians.

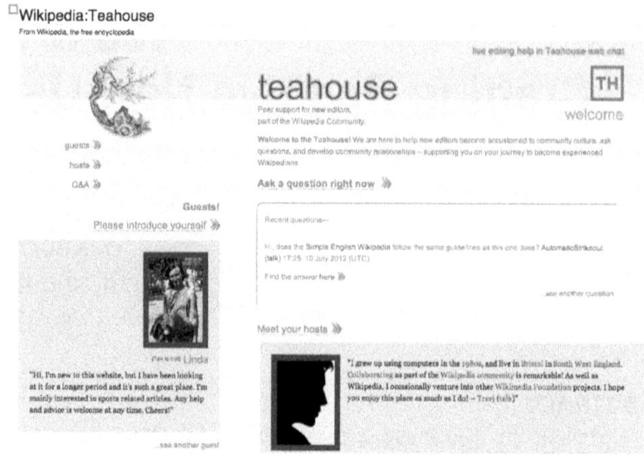

Figure 1: The Wikipedia Teahouse main page

The decline in the average tenure of new editors and the community's inability to retain female editors point to potential systemic flaws in the new user experience of Wikipedia, particularly the way the community socializes new contributors. Increasing the overall proportion of new editors who become Wikipedians, and boosting female participation in particular, requires new solutions to old challenges.

TEAHOUSE: A PLACE FOR NEW EDITORS

In this paper, we will first identify several common challenges that new editors face—isolation, intimidation and limited opportunities for socialization—and highlight their potential impact on female editors in particular. We then propose a comprehensive strategy for addressing these challenges through early outreach and social support, which we have implemented in a new support space on Wikipedia called the Teahouse[1].

The Teahouse (**Figure 1**) is designed to boost overall editor retention and narrow the gender gap in a scalable, sustainable way: it provides early, positive socialization opportunities for more new editors and creates a 'safe zone' for interactive community support. New editors who might otherwise stop editing are provided with proactive help to learn the ropes of Wikipedia.

At the Teahouse, new editors (called *guests*) have the opportunity to introduce themselves and have their questions answered by patient, friendly Wikipedians, called *hosts*. A welcoming atmosphere and simple, user-friendly tools reduce intimidation and isolation, and an active volunteer base encourages sustained community involvement.

We will present data from the Teahouse pilot period, from February 27th through October 11th 2012. We report overall participation data and results from four editor surveys deployed during the pilot. We compare the reported satisfaction scores of male and female participants. We also compare the experience of participating in the Teahouse *Q&A board* with another help space, the Wikipedia *Help Desk*.

[1] http://en.wikipedia.org/wiki/WP:Teahouse

We then analyze the impact of Teahouse participation on new editors' subsequent editing activities. We conclude with a discussion of the broader significance of the Teahouse and the limitations of our pilot study, and outline possible next steps for research and design.

Challenge #1: missed opportunities for socialization

Moving from a newcomer in an online community to a power user involves a series of difficult transformations. Ducheneut [6] found that successfully becoming a full-fledged member of an OSS project involved a complex process wherein the new member acquired relevant expertise, constructed an in-project identity based around valued work, and learned how to participate successfully in the political life of the community. Bryant describes a similar transformative process involving the acquisition of local expertise and identity formation among new editors who go on to become highly active Wikipedians [1].

Unfortunately, the vast majority of Wikipedia newcomers do not make this transformation. 60% of new account creators never make a single edit after their first day, and even among the newcomers who are most active during their first 24 hour period, only 8% go on to become Wikipedians: editors who have made at least 250 edits [23]. Common struggles that new editors face include finding tasks to do [17], locating help resources, learning the 'wikitext' markup language [20] and navigating Wikipedia's complex system of policies and guidelines [2].

In many organizations, formal mechanisms such as new member orientations and mentorship programs exist to help shepherd newcomers through this identity transformation and promote the adoption of pro-social norms [22]. While community-created mentorship programs exist on Wikipedia, these programs operate on a relatively small-scale. A study of one of the most successful programs, Adopt-a-User, found that it had served approximately 1,000 new editors between 2006 and early 2011 [21]. However, during that same period more than 7,000 new users created an account and made 10 or more edits *each month* [29]. While one-on-one mentorship affords a high degree of personal interaction and a high quality of support, the coordination cost of implementing it at the scale necessary to reach a substantial percentage of good-faith newcomers may be prohibitive.

Other support mechanisms on Wikipedia may also promote pro-social behavior and improve editor retention. Unfortunately, these mechanisms are not always easy for new editors to find. Joining WikiProjects (topic-focused, small group collaborations among editors) can provide a sense of belonging and motivate contribution [7], and tools like SuggestBot can help users find useful tasks that match their interests [5], but new editors may not be aware that these opportunities exist. They are not suggested to new editors by default, and links to these and other potentially helpful community-created resources are not prominently surfaced within the interface.

Figure 2: Teahouse invite template messages for declined AfC submitters (top) and for brand new editors (bottom)

Strategy: Offer support to more newcomers, earlier

The high and rapid newcomer attrition rate described by Research by Panciera [23] suggests that there is a very narrow window of opportunity for new editor outreach and socialization: most new editors stop editing within their first day, before they know their way around well enough to find the help they need or learn how to productively contribute. Contacting these editors before they give up or lose interest, ideally within the first 24 hours, and alerting them to opportunities for editing support and human interaction could increase the number of newcomers who go on to become Wikipedians.

In order to help Teahouse hosts reach out to more new editors during the critical first 24 hours, we wrote a script that published an automated daily report of 'promising' newcomers to a wiki page,. Following previous research [12, 23] on early editing patterns associated with an increased probability of retention, the report contained a sample of new editors who had joined within the past 24 hours and had made at least 10 edits. We excluded editors whose accounts were currently blocked from editing for vandalism or disruptive behavior. Hosts viewed the contribution histories of these editors and selected those they wanted to invite to the Teahouse. This report facilitated invitation of 40-60 new editors per day.

Teahouse hosts were also encouraged to monitor the new editor contributions filter[2] and the Feedback Dashboard[3] for potential invitees, and to invite newcomers who had recently had draft articles declined by the Articles for Creation committee.

Previous research has also shown that using personalized welcome messages and including contextually-relevant information in invitations can encourage participation in online communities [3, 15]. We designed several personalize-able Teahouse invite templates for hosts to place on new editors' talk pages. For example, newcomers who were invited after having a proposed article declined by the Arti-

[2] https://en.wikipedia.org/w/index.php?title=Special:Contributions&contribs=newbie
[3] http://en.wikipedia.org/wiki/Special:FeedbackDashboard

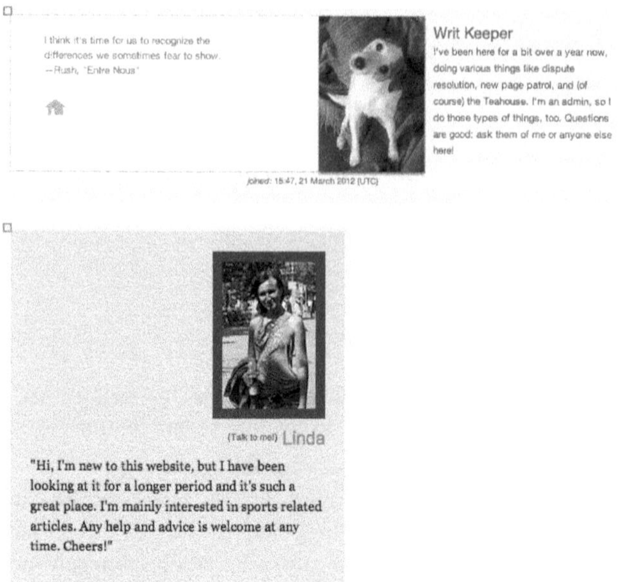

Figure 3a: Host (top) and Guest (bottom) profiles.

cles for Creation committee received a different invitation than newcomers who were identified as candidates for invitation on the daily invitee report (**Figure 2**).

Challenge #2: new editor isolation and intimidation

Being a newcomer in an online community can be intimidating. A survey of peripheral participants in MSN bulletin board communities found that among the primary reasons that "lurkers" did not participate publicly were: confusion about how to use the software, concern about being the target of aggression or hostility, and uncertainty about whether the community was a good 'fit' for them [24].

New editors often don't initially perceive Wikipedia as a community at all [1] and even when they do, their initial interactions with community members are likely to be negative. Like SubSubPop23, the only form of socialization that many new editors experience before leaving Wikipedia comes in the form of generic warning messages informing them that they've done something wrong, or terse notices that their edits have been reverted. These messages are often delivered by automated 'bots' rather than by real people. Such anonymous, negative socialization tactics are of limited utility for promoting constructive editing behaviors or boosting editor retention [12].

As SubSubPop23's story illustrates, the new editor experience of Wikipedia can be an unsettling combination of anonymous and hostile. This, too, has increased over time. The proportion of new editors whose first interaction with Wikipedia is via a generic message left by an automated script or tool has increased to over 80%, from less than 40% in 2006. The proportion of first contact messages that are warnings rather than welcomes was 65% in 2010 and has increased year by year [13].

Figure 3b: The Teahouse Q&A board.

Many Wikipedians also experience Wikipedia as a hostile environment. A survey of 1200 former editors conducted in 2010 [31] found that 27% of former contributors cited the rudeness or stubbornness of other editors as their primary reason for leaving, and among highly active editors (those who made more than 10 edits a month) the proportion was 53%.

Female editors may experience Wikipedia's combative culture even more acutely. In previous studies, female editors have reported feeling uncomfortable with antagonistic exchanges among Wikipedians, and they cite conflict as a reason for ceasing to contribute more often than their male counterparts [4]. Female editors also report a desire for a more collaborative, less conflict-driven editing experience, and for more social interaction in general [5].

Strategy: Opportunities for positive socialization

Collier [4] advocates design improvements to promote more female contribution to Wikipedia: forums to facilitate social or educational discussion separate from the hypercritical, debate-style discourse of article talk pages [28], as well as features for surfacing potential common interests and fostering more direct collaboration. We believe that these same features would benefit new editors in general by introducing them to the people behind the encyclopedia in a more friendly way, and providing a supportive, engaging environment for learning.

The Teahouse is an attempt to improve the new editor experience of Wikipedia by meeting the immediate needs of new users, as well as a gradualist strategy for changing the culture and demographics of the editing community and reversing the editor decline.

Features: Profiles and Social Q&A

The Teahouse space is built around two primary activities. On the *Guests* page, new editors can introduce themselves by creating a simple profile, and also browse profiles created by other new editors and by Teahouse hosts (**Figure 3a**).

On the *Q&A board,* guest can ask, read, and answer questions (**Figure 3b**).

Self-introduction is a common newcomer behavior in online communities, and has been shown to elicit positive responses from other community members [2], but social interaction for its own sake is sometimes discouraged on Wikipedia[4]. The Teahouse Guests page provides a safe space for newcomers for introduce themselves and 'meet' other new editors.

Asking questions can be intimidating for newcomers [24], but intimidation can be reduced if newcomers are provided with clear cues for how to participate, and know what kinds of reaction to expect when they do. While many Q&A sites follow a transaction model, with information seekers (often lurkers or newcomers) eliciting factual information from 'Answer people' [27], other 'social Q&A' forums host more personal, collegial, and interactive discussions [14] and even micro-collaborations [8] among multiple seekers and providers. The Teahouse Q&A board is designed to make new editors feel comfortable asking any question they might have, and to provide opportunities for constructive social interaction. Hosts were asked to follow a set of five simple guidelines (**Figure 4**) in order to make the Q&A experience less intimidating and more engaging for guests.

The technical mechanisms for creating a profile or asking a question in the Teahouse are designed to reduce barriers to entry, encouraging new editors to jump in and participate. However, since the Teahouse is intended to provide opportunities for learning, most interactions do require users to edit a page. We attempt to simplify more complex tasks through clear, contextual prompts and structured workflows.

Pilot study

We will evaluate the success of our attempt to improve the new editor experience and boost participation by newcomers and female editors in the sections below. The goal of our analysis is two-pronged: first, we analyze survey data on the *experience* of participating in Teahouse for new editors, female editors and veteran Wikipedians. Then we analyze the impact of the Teahouse in two ways: we compare the dynamics of the Teahouse Q&A board with a more tranditional help forum, the Wikipedia Help Desk, and we compare the subsequent editing activities of Teahouse visitors with invited newcomers who did not participate.

DEPLOYMENT AND DATA ANALYSIS

The Teahouse was developed with support from the Wikimedia Foundation by a four-member team consisting of a project manager, a UX researcher, a visual designer and a community organizer who was a veteran Wikipedian with experience in outreach initiatives for female editors. To ensure a baseline of community involvement in the project, we approached 20 Wikipedians with a history of new user outreach at the beginning of the pilot and invited them to sign up as hosts. Of those invited at the outset, 15 subsequently participated. Although we undertook no further recruitment initiatives, many more hosts signed up and participated during the pilot period, and other experienced Wikipedians participated by inviting new users to the Teahouse and answering questions on the Q&A board without formally joining the project.

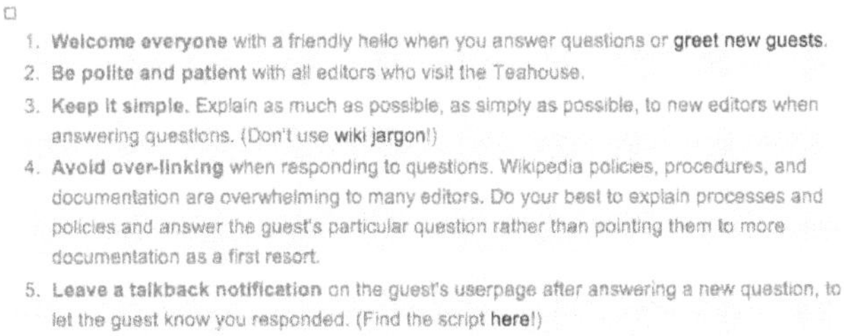
1. **Welcome everyone** with a friendly hello when you answer questions or **greet new guests**.
2. **Be polite and patient** with all editors who visit the Teahouse.
3. **Keep it simple.** Explain as much as possible, as simply as possible, to new editors when answering questions. (Don't use **wiki jargon**!)
4. **Avoid over-linking** when responding to questions. Wikipedia policies, procedures, and documentation are overwhelming to many editors. Do your best to explain processes and policies and answer the guest's particular question rather than pointing them to more documentation as a first resort.
5. **Leave a talkback notification** on the guest's userpage after answering a new question, to let the guest know you responded. (Find the script **here**!)

Figure 4: Host guidelines for the Teahouse *Q&A Board*

Data collection

We tracked editor activity on the Teahouse using a live mirror database of Wikipedia. We considered an editor to be a 'new editor' if they had fewer than 100 edits at the time of their first edit to either the Q&A board or the Guests page. 100 edits is a standard benchmark used by the Wikimedia Foundation for inexperienced editors [32].

We tracked which new editors received Teahouse invitations, what kind of invitation they received, and whether or not they subsequently visited the Teahouse. We logged a total of 7339 invitations sent by Teahouse hosts between February 27th and May 27th, 2012. The overall response rate for tracked invitations was 4.5%. This low response rate illustrates one of the challenges of trying to reach out to newcomers very early, before the natural 'winnowing' process described by Panciera [23] takes effect: many new editors listed on the daily invitee reports may have stopped editing for good before they noticed that they had received an invitation.

Survey data

We surveyed distinct samples of Teahouse guests during the 5th, 11th, and 26th week of the pilot period. We also surveyed experienced Wikipedian participants (including hosts) during week 11. We report responses from 196 Teahouse guests and 71 experienced Wikipedians.

The guest survey included questions related to satisfaction with the Teahouse, as well as general questions related to challenges of being a new editor. Respondents were asked to rate their satisfaction with the answers they received on the Q&A board, with the experience of creating a guest profile, and with the Teahouse as a whole on a 5-point Likert scale ("Very dissatisfied" to "Very satisfied"). We also elicited specific feedback on Teahouse features from guests. Guests were asked (but not required to disclose) their gender, and 92% of respondents did so. The experienced editor survey focused on satisfaction, general impressions and specific feedback. In this paper, we report survey results

[4] http://en.wikipedia.org/wiki/WP:NOTSOCIALNETWORK

related to guest and experienced editor satisfaction, and compare satisfaction between male and female guests.

Dynamics of Teahouse Q&A board vs. Wikipedia Help Desk
In order to assess whether the Q&A board provided a more interactive experience than other Wikipedia Q&A forums, we compared it with the Wikipedia Help Desk, an active community-run forum that also fields many questions from new editors. To assess whether the Teahouse provided a qualitatively different Q&A experience than the Help Desk, we compared a sample of 500 questions asked on the Q&A board between February 27th and August 18th, 2012 with 500 Help Desk questions from the same time period.

For this analysis, we compare the time between the question and its first response, the number of answers per question, and the number of times the original poster replied within their own question thread. We excluded questions asked by editors who were not logged in at the time they posted their question. We also excluded any edits made by Bots, as well as minor edits. When analyzing number of responses by the questioner within their own question thread, we excluded subsequent edits made by the questioner less than 5 minutes after their original post.

Retention of Teahouse visitors vs. non-visitors
To assess the impact of Teahouse participation on subsequent editing activities and editor retention, we compared the subsequent editing activities of a sample of 252 Teahouse visitors with 260 new editors who did not visit.

Teahouse hosts chose which new editors to invite on a case-by-case basis, introducing an invitation bias into our sample: hosts likely avoided inviting new editors whose early edits showed blatant tendencies towards vandalism, for instance. This makes meaningful comparison between the editing patterns of Teahouse visitors and a random sample of all new editors a challenge. Instead, we compared a sample of Teahouse visitors with a random sample of editors who were invited to the Teahouse by a host, but did not visit.

All editors in our *visitors* sample had been invited to visit the Teahouse between February 27th and May 27th, 2012 and had subsequently visited the Teahouse prior to June 10th. Editors in our *invitees* sample were invited during the same time period, but did not subsequently edit either the Q&A Board or Guests page. To control for the possibility that some of these invitees had stopped editing before they saw the invitation, we removed any invitees who had not made at least 1 edit to Wikipedia after their date of invitation from our sample. We analyzed edits made by these editors between the day after invitation and November 23rd, 2012, excluding any edits they made to the Teahouse itself from our analysis.

FINDINGS

Between February 27th and October 11th, 2012 1,098 new editors participated in the Teahouse, at an average rate of 34 per week. We counted a new editor as a participant if they made at least one edit to the Q&A board or the Guests page. Guests asked 1,381 questions and created 420 profiles. 77 Wikipedians participated as hosts during the pilot, and an average of 21 hosts participated each week. Hosts participated in a variety of ways: answering questions, sending out invitations to new editors, creating Teahouse barnstars [18] to award to new editors and to one another, and writing custom scripts and templates to make their work easier.

Editor satisfaction

New editors enjoyed their Teahouse experience. 71% of new editors surveyed said that they were "Satisfied" or "Very satisfied" with their Teahouse experience, versus only 5% who said they were "Dissatisfied" or "Very dissatisfied". When asked to describe what in particular they liked about their experience, new editors cited a range of factors, from the promptness and quality of the answers they received to the friendly atmosphere and the ease of use. A sample of guest responses is listed below.

> *Help from people who do not criticize.*
>
> *Cool message when I first became a Wikipedia editor on my talk page and a really nice lady. Easy to post an answer and the community responded quickly.*
>
> *Courteous, detailed and prompt responses.*

Survey responses by experienced editors mirror those of new editors. 70% of experienced editors surveyed (hosts and non-hosts) said that they were "Satisfied" or "Very satisfied" with their Teahouse experience, versus 5% for "Very dissatisfied" or "Dissatisfied".

When asked to describe what in particular they liked about their experience on the Teahouse, experienced editors also cited the promptness and quality of the answers they read or received and the friendly atmosphere. Many respondents indicated that they believed that the Teahouse was having a positive impact on newcomers, primarily by functioning as a friendly 'safe zone', and that the Teahouse was beneficial to the community as a whole. As one editor eloquently put it:

> *There is nothing extraordinary about [the Teahouse]. It just needs to exist and is fundamental to the Wikipedia experience.*

Other responses from Wikipedians included:

> *I liked that the Teahouse is a ground for new users so they have lots of support, and that hosts and new users interact a lot with each other.*
>
> *Learning from others, in addition to sharing my own knowledge. Non-confrontational.*

Participation by female editors

Survey responses indicate that female newcomers participated in the Teahouse at a high rate. While Lam [19] found that 16% of new editors were women in 2009, 32% (57/178) of new editor survey respondents who disclosed their gender identified as female. This may indicate that we were successful in our goal of engaging new female editors. However, it is difficult to get accurate gender data on Wikipedia editors, and without comparative data on the overall gender breakdown of new editors during our study period, we cannot say definitively whether women participated in the Teahouse at a higher-than-expected rate.

To determine whether women found the Teahouse more or less engaging than men, we conducted independent-sample t-tests comparing their responses related to satisfaction with Q&A board answers, Guests page profiles and the overall Teahouse experience. The results of these analyses are presented in **Table 1.** We found no statistically significant differences between men and women's satisfaction with the Teahouse, although women did rate their satisfaction with the answers they received on the Q&A board lower than men to a marginally significant degree (M_{women} = 4.04, SD = 1.13 versus M_{men} = 4.33, SD = 0.78), t(124) = 1.71, p = 0.089.

Qualitative survey responses and our own observations suggest room for improvement in Teahouse's Q&A and peer support model if the project is to effectively address the needs of female editors. The three female editors who rated the quality of their answers lowest stated:

> *Talk talk talk which wasn't much use except for ONE person.*
>
> *It didn't help me with what I wanted to do.*
>
> *My question was ignored.*

These responses reflect our own observation that the quality of an answer in the Teahouse may vary depending on the host. Furthermore, as most Teahouse hosts who were active in the Q&A forum are male, we believe that there may be further gender dynamics to be explored in terms of the host/guest interaction.

Impact of social Q&A

The Teahouse Q&A board was designed to make the process of asking a question into an opportunity for positive socialization, not just an information transaction. Teahouse guests asked 1.6 questions on average, and 23% of guests asked multiple questions. Survey responses indicate that both new and experienced editors found Teahouse Q&A to be engaging, and recognized it as an effective mechanism for positive new editor socialization.

We performed independent sample t-tests to compare the average time between when a question was asked and the first response, the number of responses per question, and the number of posts by the original questioner within the question thread. Results are listed in **Table 2.**

Gender	n	Q&A	Profiles	Overall
Female	57	4.04	3.74	3.93
Male	121	4.33	3.78	3.86

Table 1: Average guest satisfaction by gender. Differences are not significant.

Forum	Response Time (minutes)	# answers*	# questioner responses*
Teahouse	56.66	3.12	1.04
Help Desk	23.44	2.55	0.6

Table 2: Interactivity of Teahouse Q&A board vs. Help Desk. Significant differences are marked with an asterisk.

We found no significant difference in response times between the two forums ($M_{teahouse}$ = 56.66, SD = 460.46 versus $M_{helpdesk}$ = 23.44, SD = 229.05), t(998) = 1.44, p = 0.15.

However, Teahouse questions did receive significantly more answers than Help Desk questions ($M_{teahouse}$ = 3.12, SD = 2.54 versus $M_{helpdesk}$ = 2.55, SD = 2.01), t(998) = 3.91, $p < 0.01$. Teahouse questioners also posted significantly more responses in their own question thread than Help Desk questioners ($M_{teahouse}$ = 1.04, SD = 1.79 versus $M_{helpdesk}$ = 0.6, SD = 0.99), t(998) = 4.89, $p < 0.01$.

Q&A guests seldom offered peer support

We hoped that because the Teahouse Q&A board deemphasized the boundary between information seekers (guests) and 'experts' (hosts) in favor of a more collaborative model, new users would feel comfortable jumping in and answering questions, in addition to asking them. While the Teahouse was more successful at eliciting newcomers to answer questions than the Help Desk, the number of newcomers who participated in a discussion around a question asked by another editor was low. Overall, only 11% of new editors who participated in the Q&A board posted in a question thread started by someone else.

Survey responses from new editors shed some light on this low level of peer support activity. Of those respondents who indicated why they had not answered a question on the Teahouse, 25% stated that they did not know they were allowed to, and 47% stated that they either did not see any questions to which they knew the answer, or felt they were too inexperienced to answer a question. No respondents stated that they could not figure out how to answer a question. However, during the pilot period we observed several guests asking questions about how to answer a question, suggesting that confusion or intimidation with the editing interface may have contributed to the low level of peer support.

Group	Total edits*	Weeks active*	Article edits*	Articles edited*	Discussion space edits*
Visitors	260.81	7.62	260.81	84.76	62.7
Nonvisitors	57.12	5.37	57.12	14.31	8.12

Table 3: Editing activity by Teahouse visitors and invited non-visitors, March – November 2012. Significant differences are marked with an asterisk.

Creating new opportunities for more direct interaction among Teahouse guests could help create more solid social bonds and support editor retention by fostering a greater sense of community among cohorts of editors. We intend to explore different interface design strategies and feature enhancements in the future to encourage more peer support.

Impact of participation

The ultimate goal of the Teahouse is not to bring new editors to the Teahouse, but to increase the number of editors who become frequent, high-volume contributors to Wikipedia. We performed independent sample t-tests to determine whether Teahouse visitors made more edits overall, whether they made more edits to articles, whether they edited more individual articles, and whether they participated more in 'talk' namespaces.

Teahouse visitors make more edits overall, and edit longer

Teahouse visitors made significantly more subsequent edits to Wikipedia than non-visitors ($M_{visitors}$ = 388.71, SD 1683.21 versus $M_{invitees}$ = 75.97, SD = 281.52), t(510) = 2.95, $p < 0.01$. Visitors also made at least 1 edit during more weeks, post-invite, than invitees ($M_{visitors}$ = 7.62, SD 8.74 versus $M_{invitees}$ = 5.37, SD = 6.64), t(510) = 3.29, $p < 0.01$.

Teahouse visitors make more edits, to more articles

Visitors also made significantly more edits to the article namespace of Wikipedia ($M_{visitors}$ = 260.81, SD 1331.49 versus $M_{invitees}$ = 57.12, SD = 223.56), t(510) = 2.43, $p < 0.05$. And they edited significantly more articles than invitees ($M_{visitors}$ = 84.76, SD 412.9 versus $M_{invitees}$ = 14.31, SD = 47.13), t(510) = 2.73, $p < 0.01$.

Teahouse visitors participate more in discussion spaces

Teahouse visitors made significantly more edits to pages within the primary 'discussion' namespaces of Wikipedia (User Talk, Article_Talk and Wikipedia_Talk) than invitees ($M_{visitors}$ = 62.7, SD 282.9 versus $M_{invitees}$ = 8.12, SD = 33.58), t(510) = 3.09, $p < 0.01$. Edits made to a user's own User_talk page were excluded from this analysis.

Kittur [16] found a similar increase in talk page participation for editors who joined WikiProjects, which they attributed to an increase in coordination work resulting from the editors becoming more engaged in group activities in these small topic-focused collaboration efforts. Since Teahouse is intended to socialize newcomers in such pro-social norms of interaction, we are encouraged to see that more Teahouse guests go on to 'talk before they type'. However, since participating in the Teahouse was voluntary, we cannot say whether these editors are engaging in a higher level of talk page activity than they would have otherwise. It may be that editors who chose to participate in a social space like the Teahouse were already more inclined towards socializing and collaboration than those who declined to participate. Even if this is the case, our findings suggest that participating in the Teahouse gave these editors more opportunities to learn how to collaborate productively, and provided them with additional incentives to continue participating.

The elevated activity level of Teahouse visitors is a promising sign of sustained engagement with Wikipedia. We intend to continue tracking the participation of Teahouse visitors and non-visitors over time in order to determine whether Teahouse participation has a measurable long-term impact on editor retention, editing activities and quality of contribution.

DISCUSSION

Wikipedia needs more Wikipedians. Increasing a newcomer's awareness of the community behind the encyclopedia and creating more opportunities for positive experiences that both meet her immediate needs and teach her community norms in an engaging and supportive setting will help her tackle the confusion, frustration and conflicts to come.

Wikipedia also needs more *different* Wikipedians. Increasing the diversity of the community will not only increase the quality and completeness of the encyclopedia, it will increase the likelihood that any new member of the community will find like-minded collaborators and feel like they fit in.

Teahouse, a new editor support space, consists of a relatively simple set of tools, norms and procedures that frame the new editor experience in a new way. We have shown that both new editors and Wikipedians find the space itself and the activities it supports to be engaging and worthwhile, and provided evidence that Teahouse offers opportunities for positive socialization, social interaction, and interactive editor support that other support spaces and tried-and-true socialization strategies do not. And we have shown that Teahouse guests edit more and edit longer than non-visitors with similar early activity patterns.

CONCLUSION

Our analysis, though limited and preliminary, suggests that early outreach and social support are promising tools for community diversification and new editor retention. While the needs of Wikipedia newcomers are not necessarily equivalent to those of new users in other peer-production communities, they are reflective of them. The level of involvement in the Teahouse by new and experienced community members gives us confidence in the impact, scalability, and sustainability of gradualist, community-powered solutions for addressing complex sociotechnical problems like the Wikipedia editor decline.

Participation patterns in online collaborative communities may be cyclical or follow a more regular growth-peak-decline trajectory. Communities also evolve over time. On Wikipedia, socialization tactics that worked during the growth period do not appear to be as effective in the context of the current decline. In some cases, substantial top-down technological intervention may be the best way to attract new users or shift community dynamics. However in volunteer communities, where users are apt to rebel en mass if they feel manipulated or taken for granted by the technology owners [9], supporting bottom-up, community-driven solutions may prove more effective and sustainable. Community solutions like the Teahouse can also be effective test beds, allowing designers, community managers and community members to try out new ideas in a lightweight way, while building community consensus around social or technological changes that might otherwise be seen as disruptive.

Future work

The Teahouse is not going away any time soon. Community members and Foundation staff are already at work planning Teahouses on other Wikimedia wikis, starting with the Arabic Wikipedia. Ideas from the Teahouse are also being adopted in other parts of the community: the Help Desk has implemented a 'talkback' message system to alert questioners of a response, and other editors have begun to discuss the creation of local, offline Teahouse meetups.

For the English Wikipedia Teahouse, our future work will focus primarily on boosting female participation, facilitating more peer support, and developing mechanisms for connecting new editors with both relevant and engaging tasks and potential collaborators.

ACKNOWLEDGMENTS

The authors thank the CSCW reviewers for the exemplary peer support and mentorship they provided us. We also thank the Hosts of the Teahouse for their hard work and dedication to improving the new user experience of Wikipedia.

REFERENCES

1. Bryant, S.L., Forte, A., and Bruckman, A. Becoming Wikipedian: transformation of participation in a collaborative online encyclopedia. *In Proc. GROUP 2005, ACM Press (2005), 1–10.*
2. Butler, B., Joyce, E., and Pike, J. Don't look now, but we've created a bureaucracy: The nature and roles of policies and rules in Wikipedia. In *Proc. CHI 2008*, ACM Press (2008), 1101.
3. Choi, B., Alexander, K., Kraut, R.E., and Levine, J.M. Socialization tactics in Wikipedia and their effects. In *Proc. CSCW 2010,* ACM Press (2010), 107.
4. Collier, B. and Bear, J. Conflict, criticism, or confidence: an empirical examination of the gender gap in Wikipedia contributions. In *Proc. CSCW 2012,* ACM Press (2012), 383–392.
5. Cosley, D., Frankowski, D., Terveen, L., and Riedl, J. SuggestBot: using intelligent task routing to help people find work in Wikipedia. In *Proc. IUI 2007*, ACM Press (2007), 32–41.
6. Ducheneaut, N. Socialization in an Open Source Software Community: A Socio-Technical Analysis. *Comput. Supported Coop. Work 14*, 4 (2005), 323–368.
7. Forte, A., Kittur, N., Larco, V., Zhu, H., Bruckman, A., and Kraut, R.E. Coordination and beyond: social functions of groups in open content production. In *Proc. CSCW 2012*, ACM Press (2012), 417–426.
8. Gazan, R. Microcollaborations in a social Q&A community. *Information Processing & Management 46*, 6 (2009), 693–702.
9. Gazan, R. Redesign as an act of violence: disrupted interaction patterns and the fragmenting of a social Q&A community. In *Proc. CHI 2011*, ACM Press (2011), 2847–2856.
10. Giles, J. Special Report–Internet encyclopaedias go head to head. *Nature 438*, 15 (2005), 900–901.
11. Glott, R., Schmidt, P., and Ghosh, R. Wikipedia survey--overview of results. *United Nations University: Collaborative Creativity Group*, 2010. http://www.wikipediasurvey.org/docs/Wikipedia_Overview_15March2010-FINAL.pdf.
12. Halfaker, A., Geiger, R.S., Morgan, J., and Riedl, J. The Rise and Decline of an Open Collaboration System: How Wikipedia's reaction to sudden popularity is causing its decline. *American Behavioral Scientist (in press)*, .
13. Halfaker, A., Kittur, A., and Riedl, J. Don't bite the newbies: how reverts affect the quantity and quality of Wikipedia work. In *Proc. WikiSym 2011*, ACM Press (2011), 163–172.
14. Hansen, D.L. Overhearing the crowd: an empirical examination of conversation reuse in a technical support community. In *Proc. C&T 2009*, ACM Press (2009), 155–164.
15. Harper, F.M., Frankowski, D., Drenner, S., et al. Talk amongst yourselves: inviting users to participate in online conversations. In *Proc. IUI 2007*, ACM Press, (2007), 62–71.

16. Kittur, A., Pendleton, B., and Kraut, R.E. Herding the cats: the influence of groups in coordinating peer production. In *Proc. WikiSym 2009*, ACM Press (2009), 7:1–7:9.
17. Krieger, M., Stark, E.M., and Klemmer, S.R. Coordinating tasks on the commons: designing for personal goals, expertise and serendipity. In *Proc. CHI 2009*, ACM Press (2009), 1485–1494.
18. Kriplean, T., Beschastnikh, I., and McDonald, D.W. Articulations of wikiwork: uncovering valued work in Wikipedia through barnstars. In *Proc. CSCW 2008*, ACM Press (2008), 47–56.
19. Lam, S. (Tony) K., Uduwage, A., Dong, Z., et al. WP:Clubhouse?: an exploration of Wikipedia's gender imbalance. In *Proc. WikiSym 2011*, ACM Press (2011), 1–10.
20. Morgan, J.T., Geiger, R.S., Pinchuck, M., and Shawn Walker. New user help requests. http://meta.wikimedia.org/wiki/Research:NewUserHelp-FullResearchReport.
21. Musicant, D.R., Ren, Y., Johnson, J.A., and Riedl, J. Mentoring in Wikipedia: a clash of cultures. In *Proc. WikiSym 2011*, ACM Press (2011), 173.
22. Ostrom, E. Collective action and the evolution of social norms. *The Journal of Economic Perspectives*, (2000), 137–158.
23. Panciera, K., Halfaker, A., and Terveen, L. Wikipedians are born, not made: a study of power editors on Wikipedia. In *Proc. GROUP 2009*, ACM Press (2009), 51–60.
24. Preece, J., Nonnecke, B., and Andrews, D. The Top 5 Reasons For Lurking: Improving Community Experiences For Everyone. *Computers in Human Behavior 20*, 2 (2004), 201–223.
25. Priedhorsky, R., Chen, J., Lam, S. (Tony) K., Panciera, K., Terveen, L., and Riedl, J. Creating, destroying, and restoring value in Wikipedia. In *Proc. GROUP 2007*, ACM (2007), 259–268.
26. Suh, B., Convertino, G., Chi, E.H., and Pirolli, P. The singularity is not near: slowing growth of Wikipedia. In *Proc. WikiSym 2009*, ACM Press (2009), 10.
27. Turner, T.C., Smith, M.A., Fisher, D., and Welser, H.T. Picturing Usenet: Mapping Computer-Mediated Collective Action. *Journal of Computer-Mediated Communication 10*, 4 (2005).
28. Viegas, F.B., Wattenberg, M., Kriss, J., and Van Ham, F. Talk Before You Type: Coordination in Wikipedia. In *Proc. HICSS 2007*, IEEE Computer Society (2007), 78.
29. Wikipedia Statistics English. http://stats.wikimedia.org/EN/TablesWikipediaEN.htm.
30. Editor Survey 2011. *Wikimedia Foundation*. http://meta.wikimedia.org/wiki/Editor_Survey_2011/.
31. Former Contributors Survey. *Wikipedia Strategic Planning Initiative*. http://strategy.wikimedia.org/wiki/Former_Contributors_Survey_Results.
32. Wikimedia Foundation: Definition of Research Terms. http://upload.wikimedia.org/wikipedia/commons/0/09/Definitions_of_Research_Terms.pdf.

Making Peripheral Participation Legitimate: Reader Engagement Experiments in Wikipedia

Aaron Halfaker
GroupLens Research
University of Minnesota
200 Union St. S.E.
Minneapolis, MN 55455
halfaker@cs.umn.edu

Oliver Keyes
Wikimedia Foundation
149 New Montgomery St.
3rd Floor
San Francisco, CA 94105
okeyes@wikimedia.org

Dario Taraborelli
Wikimedia Foundation
149 New Montgomery St.
3rd Floor
San Francisco, CA 94105
dario@wikimedia.org

ABSTRACT

Open collaboration communities thrive when participation is plentiful. Recent research has shown that the English Wikipedia community has constructed a vast and accurate information resource primarily through the monumental effort of a relatively small number of active, volunteer editors. Beyond Wikipedia's active editor community is a substantially larger pool of *potential* participants: readers. In this paper we describe a set of field experiments using the *Article Feedback Tool*, a system designed to elicit lightweight contributions from Wikipedia's readers. Through the lens of social learning theory and comparisons to related work in open bug tracking software, we evaluate the costs and benefits of the expanded participation model and show both qualitatively and quantitatively that peripheral contributors add value to an open collaboration community as long as the cost of identifying low quality contributions remains low.

Author Keywords

Wikipedia; Social learning; Legitimate peripheral participation; quatitative; experiment; participation; open production

ACM Classification Keywords

H.5.3. Information Interfaces and Presentation (e.g. HCI): Group and Organization Interfaces

INTRODUCTION

Open collaboration systems like Wikipedia require a stable pool of volunteer contributors to remain productive. Without volunteers to occupy necessary roles, these systems would cease to function. The success of an open collaboration project appears to be highly correlated with the number of participants it maintains[7]. In order to maintain the pool of contributors, newcomers must be continually socialized into the organization[22, 18].

Participation in peer production

Participation in online communities tends to manifest as a long-tail distribution[27]; a tiny, active minority produces most of the content while the majority of community members produces very little individually. Beyond the contributing population is an often overlooked population of users who do not contribute, commonly referred to as "lurkers". Despite the fact that lurkers do not contribute, their numbers tend to dwarf the rest of the community by orders of magnitude. The primary reason for lurking in online communities has been identified as the lack of a perceived "information benefit" in increasing their effort to contribute[17, 5, 12], yet in some communities, a substantial proportion of lurkers are simply not aware that they can participate[1, 16].

Recent work has shown that the English Wikipedia, an online encyclopedia often held as a prototypical example of open collaboration, has a particularly steep long-tail of participation[27]. Through an analysis of Wikipedia's historical edit logs, Priedhorsky et al. estimated that the most active 0.1% of contributors produce nearly half of the encyclopedia's value[19]. According to the Wikimedia Foundation's official statistics[1] report for March of 2012, the encyclopedia was edited by 113,304 editors and a comScore[2] report for the same month shows 1.47 billion unique visitors. These numbers suggest that the English Wikipedia's consumers outnumber producers by 10,000 to 1. Given what the current contributors have been able to achieve – a vast and highly accurate encyclopedia – the consumers of Wikipedia would represent a massive potential workforce if even a small percentage of them could be coerced to contribute productively.

Research in collaborative computing has explored effective mechanisms for boosting participation in online communities. For example, Beenen et al. used insights from the collective effort model (CEM) to increase participation in a movie recommender via email requests[2]. Rashid et al. extended their study by replacing the email requests with visual queues within the user interface[20]. Within Wikipedia, Cosley et al. showed the effectiveness of a task routing system designed to decrease the cost of finding *where* to contribute in order to boost contributions of current Wikipedians[6]. Wash and Lampe showed that directly asking users for comments on

[1] `http://stats.wikimedia.org/EN/TablesWikipediaEN.htm`
[2] `http://comscore.com`

news articles could temporarily increase participation without reducing the quality of comments[25]. However, none of these studies examined the process of transitioning from non-participant to participant.

Supporting peripheral participation

Social learning theory gives us a framework for understanding how newcomers to a community transition from non-participation to participation – i.e. from consumer to producer. In their highly cited work on how newcomers approach "communities of practice", Lave & Wenger describe the process by which initiates begin participation on the periphery of a community by performing simple and low risk, yet productive tasks that they refer to as legitimate peripheral participation (LPP)[15]. As newcomers gain experience, they become more familiar with the tasks, vocabulary and norms of the community, and by doing so, they are able to confidently expand their level of participation. Recent work by Preece & Shneiderman applies this framework to online communities by defining a set of roles that users adopt as they transition from the periphery of the community (reader) to its center (leader). Specifically, they recommend that online communities should be designed to "support legitimate peripheral participation so that readers can gradually edge into contributing"[18].

The open source software community has engineered a model for supporting a type peripheral participation in the form of open issue tracking software. Through such systems, users who do not have the knowledge, time or interest in directly contributing code to a project may submit bug reports and feature requests to the developers. Through the use of such systems, participation is expanded from the a relatively small number of producers (developers) to a much more numerous group of consumers. This contribution medium allows these consumers to learn about the norms and practices of a community by interacting at the periphery. In an analysis of the growth of the developer community around the Freenet project, an open source file sharing platform, Von Krogh et al. describes a "joining script" where some newcomers post bug reports and feature requests before attempting substantial participation. Newcomers who follow this sequence of activities are more likely to be granted privileged access to the source code repository[24].

Such expanded participation models allow prospective contributors to make simple and low risk, yet productive contributions, and by doing so, the workload for maintaining the community product is distributed more evenly among its stakeholders. When such participation is high in quality, it can reduce the workload of the small percentage of prolific contributors by spreading a time-consuming production activity (e.g. bug detection and reporting) over more individuals. This reduction in workload for the primary contributors is particularly valuable for volunteer communities where effort is the primary currency of progress.

When viewed this way, Wikipedia is not keeping pace with developments in collaborative computing that leverage peripheral participation. Although Bryant et al. uncovered, through a series of interviews with highly active Wikipedia editors, that social learning theory matches the way that editors view their integration into the Wikipedia community[4], the most peripheral type of activity they describe is making edits to fix mistakes. Antin and Cheshire argue that reading the encyclopedia should be viewed as a form a legitimate participation by showing evidence that experienced readers of Wikipedia know more details about the editing community[1], but they do not explain how reading is "productive", a condition of legitimate peripheral participation as described by Lave & Wenger[15]. MediaWiki, the software that runs Wikipedia, affords no half-step from reader to editor and recent work suggests newcomers are finding it increasingly difficult to transition into productive editors. In an analysis of the predictors of newcomer retention, Halfaker et al. showed that desirable new editors are likely to have their first few contributions rejected and that this rejection is a strong predictor that newcomers will give up on editing entirely[11, 9]. Given that lurkers in other communities have reported fear of strong, negative reactions[12] as their reason for not contributing, it seems likely that many Wikipedia readers don't contribute due to a reasonable fear of rejection.

However, opening up peripheral participation to a larger pool of users doesn't always come for free. The net value of expanding participation often depends on the associated cost of filtering and moderating a larger volume of contributions. A recent analyses of bug reports by casual users in large-scale open source software projects suggest that the mismatch between what users report and what developers find useful can undermine the value of broader participation [3]. A related study reports that core developers in software projects find higher value in smaller groups of highly committed bug reporters than in a larger group of unengaged contributors [13]. Given these concerns, it is essential to consider both a potential increase in participation and the moderation concerns when vetting extensions to participation.

Article feedback

Motivated by decreasing levels of newcomer retention in the English Wikipedia's contributor community[26, 21], the we worked with the Wikimedia Foundation to develop a half-step between reading and editing in the form of an extension to the Wikipedia's software called the *Article Feedback Tool* (AFT). This tool allows readers to submit feedback about encyclopedia articles to editors via the standard web interface. Like bug tracking software, AFT allows the community's consumers to communicate their concerns to the community's producers in a simple, low risk way. Submitting feedback to an article's editors can also be productive; like bug reports, feedback can be used by the producers as a mechanism for identifying problems and missed opportunities in articles. In this way, we view AFT as an extension of the contribution model of Wikipedia that supports a new mode of legitimate peripheral participation.

In this paper we extend the online participation literature and examine an aspect of LPP in Wikipedia through a set of field experiments (performed live on the English Wikipedia) designed to test AFT's effectiveness in eliciting participation from readers and encouraging the conversion from reader to

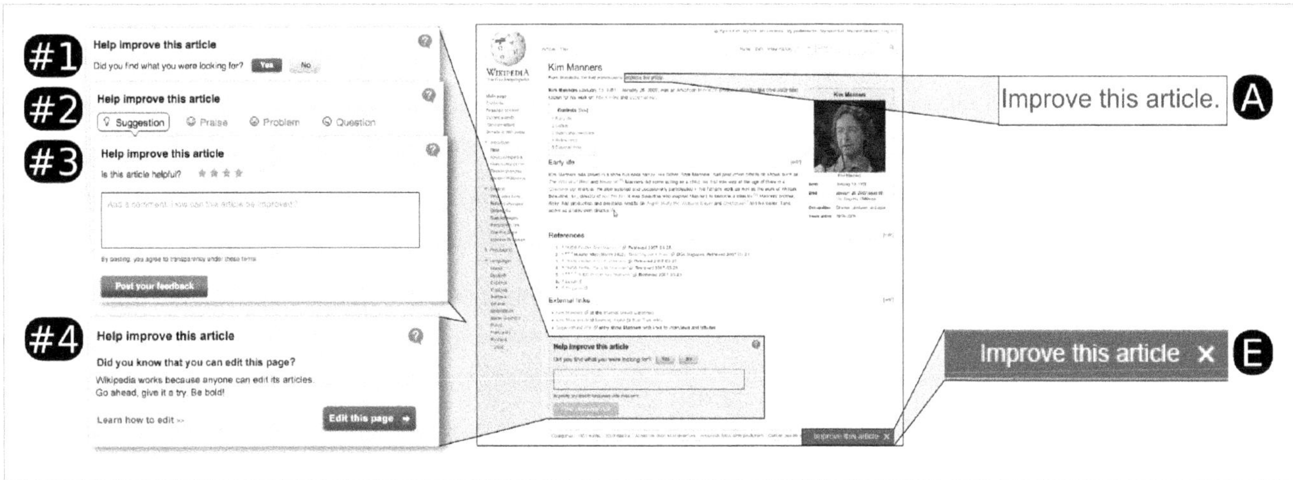

Figure 1: **The Article Feedback Tool's interface components.** The components of the AFT interface are called out from Wikipedia's article viewing interface. An article on Kim Manners, one of the randomly sampled articles, is loaded. **#1-3** represent different versions of the article feedback forms. **#4** represents the edit invitation form, a request for the reader to try editing the page. **A** and **E** represent links inserted into the page to direct readers to the feedback form.

editor. We also analyze the utility and productivity of the increased participation in the context of Wikipedia's quality control mechanisms.

THE ARTICLE FEEDBACK TOOL

The *Article Feedback Tool*[3] is an extension of Wikipedia's user interface that affords readers of an article the ability to submit feedback about that article to the editors. When a reader views an article, a small form appears after the content asking the reader to "Help improve this article". Figure 1 displays the different versions of this form that were tested as part of the present study. Each form consists of two components: a question prompt, which we refer to as an "elicitation", followed by a free-form text box. The feedback forms differ only by their elicitations:

- Form 1 asks the reader if she found what she was looking for: yes or no.
- Form 2 allows the reader to pick from 4 types of feedback she might give in the text box: suggestion, praise, problem or question.
- Form 3 asks the reader to rate the article on a 1-5 scale.

To evaluate the feedback form's effect on the conversion from reader to editor, we introduced a fourth type of form for comparison. Form 4 doesn't accept feedback; instead, the form invites the reader to make a contribution by editing the article using a UI of exactly the same size and location as the feedback forms.

Since many Wikipedia articles are very long, the feedback forms are often hidden beneath pages of scrolling. To allow for more straightforward access to the form and encourage more readers to leave feedback, we designed two prominent links (labelled A and E in figure 1) that act as shortcuts to the form. When a reader clicks on a prominent link, the form is loaded as an overlay on the page – allowing a reader to access the form without having to scroll. Although Link A appears at the top of the article, it is relatively hidden by the boilerplate statement "From Wikipedia, the free encyclopedia". Link E is intended to be much more likely to catch a reader's attention by (1) taking up more space, (2) making clear that it is a button and (3) remaining visible to the reader by staying fixed to the bottom of the window as she scrolls through the article.

When performing our experiments (described in Experiments and Results), we mixed and matched these interface components to form experimental conditions that test the effects that each component has on the quality and quantity of participation.

RESEARCH QUESTIONS

In this section we motivate three research questions that drive our analysis to understand the effectiveness of AFT as a mechanism for eliciting useful feedback and converting readers to Wikipedia editors.

RQ1: How do different elicitations affect the volume and utility of feedback?

A larger pool of contributors isn't necessarily better. Although Wash and Lampe found that increasing participation by asking readers for comments on news articles did not decrease comment quality[25], these comments were not judged for their *usefulness* to the journalists. When Bettenburg et al. measured the usefulness of bug reports to developers, they found that reports by casual users were less useful due to mismatches between user and developer concerns[3]. We hypothesize that focusing readers toward the concerns of Wikipedia editors when eliciting feedback will encourage submissions that are more useful to editors. Conversely, we expect designing the feedback form around the concerns of Wikipedia readers may encourage more readers to submit feedback at the cost of decreased utility to editors.

[3] `http://www.mediawiki.org/wiki/Article_feedback`

We expect to find a tradeoff between the quantity and quality of participation whereby elicitations that receive more feedback submissions will do so by encouraging submissions that are less useful to editors, or more precisely:

- Asking readers whether they found what they were looking for (form 1) should increase participation since the question directly addresses readers' concerns but decrease utility since many of those concerns will not be shared by editors.
- Asking readers to categorize their feedback (form 2) should elicit more useful feedback by giving cues to readers about what types of feedback are expected but decrease participation due to the increased transaction cost of requiring the reader to provide meta-information.
- Asking readers to rate the article (form 3) should increase the quality of comments by encouraging readers to consider the the article's quality within the context of the encyclopedia (editors' concern) but decrease participation by forcing readers into the role of experts.

H1.1: Form elicitations that increase participation will do so at the cost of the decreased utility of submissions.

RQ2: How does the prominence of the elicitation affect the volume and utility of feedback?

The design decision to place the feedback forms after an article was strategic. Given that most articles in Wikipedia contain enough content to require scrolling the browser window, feedback forms positioned at the bottom of the article are hidden such that only readers who have scrolled through the article will ever see them appear on the screen. Presumably, these readers are particularly suited to leaving feedback because they should be more likely to have examined some content from the article before seeing the form. However, there may be readers who would have submitted valuable feedback, but never realized they could because they didn't scroll through the entire article.

By presenting a prominent link to the feedback form, we provide an alternate route to leaving feedback that does not require the reader to scroll through the article and we expect that the prominent placement will capture the attention of more readers. We expect that by making feedback forms more prominent, we will increase the number of submissions at the cost of decreasing the overall usefulness of submissions.

H2.1: The volume of feedback submissions will increase with prominence.

H2.2: The utility of feedback submissions will decrease with prominence.

RQ3: How does the presence of the feedback interface affect new editor conversion?

A prominent invitation to leave feedback as opposed to making a productive edit to an article may undermine the "sofixit"[4] and "be bold"[5] culture of Wikipedia that encourages individuals who feel that an article should be changed to boldy edit the article themselves. Further, even for a reader whose interest in making an edit herself was held constant despite submitting feedback, the act of submitting feedback should "cannibalize" some of her finite time and effort that could have been put towards more direct participation in the form of an edit. If this is true, the presence of AFT may actually be counterproductive.

H3.1: The presence of AFT will decrease the rate of new editor conversions.

As a stopgap measure, presenting the reader with an invitation to edit (form 4 in figure 1) after submitting feedback should encourage potential new editors to continue through the normal process of "boldly" making an edit themselves. However, such an invitation to edit might also short circuit the normal process of peripheral participation by encouraging a reader to make the transition to editing before they've lurked for long enough to understand the norms and goals of the community.

H3.2: New editors who are invited to start editing articles will be less productive than editors who start by their own volition.

METHODS

The article sample

To explore our three research questions, we performed three distinct experiments on the English Wikipedia. For each experiment, the AFT interface components were loaded on a 0.6% random sample of encyclopedia articles. All readers who viewed these articles were randomly assigned to experimental conditions (described in Experiments and Results). We used browser cookies to extend the continuity of experimental groups between sessions and internet connections (IP addresses) so that readers would remain within the same experimental condition through the duration of an experiment.

To minimize the potentially disruptive impact of testing AFT on a live website, the same random sample of articles was used for all three experiments. However all users were rebucketed between experiments to control for a potential ordering bias.

Feedback utility

In order to address the research questions postulated in Research Questions, we required a way to determine which of the feedback submissions were useful to editors. The judgement of experienced Wikipedia editors to perform this evaluation was invaluable in determining the usefulness of feedback since, by design, they will be responsible for making use of feedback after it has been submitted, so they will know best which feedback submissions are useful. In other words, we consider their judgement to be a direct measure of utility. We

[4] `http://en.wikipedia.org/wiki/Template:sofixit`
[5] `http://en.wikipedia.org/wiki/WP:BOLD`

organized a group of Wikipedian volunteers interested in determining the overall utility of AFT via requests posted on the documentation page[6] and several IRC sessions.

To support these Wikipedian evaluators, we built a user interface to present a feedback submission in the context in which it was submitted while hiding details about the experimental condition from which feedback was submitted. For each feedback submission loaded into this user interface, the version of the article at the time feedback was submitted is loaded into an article preview pane, and the feedback text that was submitted is loaded into the feedback text pane. The rater was instructed to use an evaluation form to answer two questions:

Is this useful? Raters were instructed to mark a feedback submission as "useful" if they could imagine making use of this feedback to edit the article[7].

What's the intent? Raters were instructed to categorize the intent of the feedback. They could select zero to many options from: *suggestion*, *praise*, *question*, *issue*, *irrelevant* and *abuse*. These categories were decided upon through a pilot run in cooperation between the researchers and a subset of the raters.

20 Wikipedians participated in this hand-coding process. We randomly assigned work such that each feedback submission was rated by exactly two different Wikipedians. Each Wikipedian rated between 50 and 350 feedback submissions.

New editor productivity

To measure the productivity of newly converted editors, we examine their contributions to encyclopedia articles during their first week of tenure. We assume that an edit is "productive" if it is not reverted by another editor within 48 hours.

We identify reverted edits by looking for subsequent revisions that completely discard the changes of a new editors' revisions using the approach for determining "identity reverts" described by Halfaker et al. Their work suggests that the proportion of reverted edits is a useful proxy for the quality of an editor's work in most cases [10]. Given Wikipedia's efficient vandal-fighting system (see [8] for an overview), most unproductive edits should be reverted within moments, so 48 hours should be ample time to capture a reverting edit. We consider an editor to be "productive newcomer" if she makes at least one productive edit to an encyclopedia article within a week of her conversion.

To understand the cost of the increasing non-productive edits, we examined *how* these newcomer edits were reverted. The Wikipedia community's approaches to reverting damaging contributions can be organized into three categories:

- *manual* - Human editors revert edits directly via the web interface. Reverts performed manually require the most human effort.
- *semi-automated* - Wikipedians have developed a suite of tools to make the process of identifying and reverting damage require less human effort. Contributions revert by wikipedians using semi-automated tools require less effort than manual reverts.
- *automated* - Autonomous computer programs commonly referred to as "bots" monitor recent changes and perform reverts without human input. Contributions reverted by bots require essentially no human effort.

Advantageously, the automated and semi-automated tools identify themselves by leaving structured comments along with the revisions they make. Through the use of a set of regular expressions on these edit comments, we are able to categorize reverts into the above three categories. Reverts performed by user accounts with a bot "flag" were classified as *automated.* Reverts performed using Huggle[8], Twinkle[9], Popups[10], Rollback[11] or STiki[12] were classified as *semi-automated.* All other reverts were classified as *manual.* We examined the proportion and raw number of reverts that are caught by each tool to understand the cost of non-productive newcomer contributions.

EXPERIMENTS AND RESULTS

RQ1: How do different elicitations affect the volume and utility of feedback?

To explore this research question, we randomly divided readers into three exprimental conditions – one for each of the three feedback forms (1-3 from figure 1). For each condition, the appropriate feedback form appeared at the end of the encyclopedia article. Note that neither of the prominent links were used for this experiment.

Results

We considered different designs of the AFT as treatments applied to the same population of articles and measured the amount of daily feedback submissions generated in response of each treatment for the duration of the experiment (Dec. 27th - Jan 24th, 2012). Figure 2 plots the median submissions per day over the last two weeks of the experimental period. The first two weeks were discarded to limit the effect of novelty for the new feedback interface. Forms 1, 2 and 3 generated a total of 1666, 1539 and 1148 feedback submissions respectively. We used a one-way analysis of variance to test the null hypothesis that the means of these treatments are equal. The test allows us to reject the null hypothesis at $\alpha = 0.01$ ($F(2, 42) = 6.57, p = 0.003$). Post-hoc comparisons using the Tukey range test indicates that the means for form 1 ($M = 111, SD = 32.3$) and form 2 ($M = 102.6, SD = 27.4$) were significantly higher than form 3 ($M = 76.5, SD = 20.5$) at $\alpha = 0.05$. However, the

[6] `http://en.wikipedia.org/wiki/Wikipedia:Article_Feedback_Tool`

[7] Raters were allowed to select a checkbox named "unsure" if they didn't feel confident about their rating.

[8] `http://enwp.org/WP:HG`

[9] `http://enwp.org/WP:TW`

[10] `http://enwp.org/WP:Popups`

[11] `http://enwp.org/WP:Rollback`

[12] `http://enwp.org/WP:STiki`

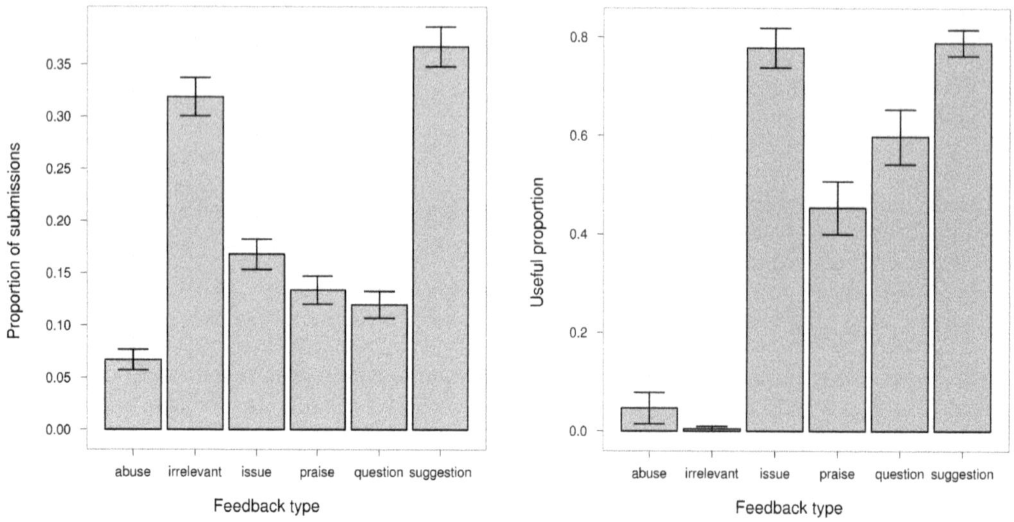

(a) **Proportion of feedback types**. (b) **Utility of feedback types**.

Figure 3: (left) The proportion of feedback submitted is plotted by intention as determined by at least one Wikipedian. (right) The proportion of useful feedback is plotted for each type. These plots draw aggregate proportions from feedback submitted through all three experimental conditions.

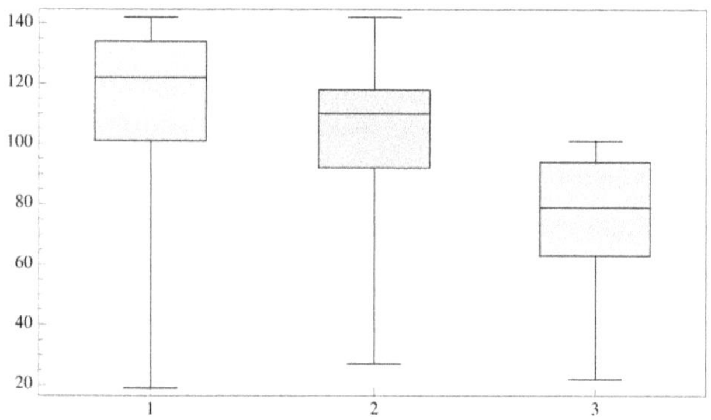

Figure 2: **Quantity of feedback by experiment.** The median daily feedback submissions per day is plotted for the last two weeks of the experiment with box limits at the 25% - 75% quantiles and bar limits at the most extreme observed values.

rate of feedback submissions for form 1 did not significantly differ from form 2.

Next, we looked at the utility of feedback submissions via the three forms as determined by our Wikipedian evaluaters. A random sample of up to 250 feedback submissions was gathered for each condition such that no two submissions came from the same article over the entire experimental period[13]. This sampling approach was used to produce statistics that reflect the expected utility of feedback submissions per article by controlling for the overrepresentation of popular articles. To measure the quality of feedback submitted, we examined the proportion of useful feedback submissions as determined via hand coding by multiple Wikipedians, as described in Methods.

To combine the two ratings per feedback submission into a single assessment, we employed three aggregation strategies:

- **someone**: useful to at least one Wikipedian
- **both**: useful to both Wikipedians
- **strict**: useful to both Wikipedians and neither was unsure

We found the three rating aggregation strategies to compare similarly between experimental conditions, so we opt to only report the proportion of feedback determined useful by both Wikipedians ("both" strategy).

The differences between the proportion of useful feedback submitted between the three interfaces varied insignificantly around 0.45. Of the three conditions, the most substantial difference was observed between form 2 (0.436) and 3 (0.469), however a χ^2 test found that difference to be insignificant ($p = 0.604$).

We also found a relatively strong consistency between the apparent intentions of feedback submitted via the three interfaces with a couple of exceptions: a χ^2 test showed that form 2 elicited a significantly more useful issues than form 1 ($\Delta = 0.225, p = 0.035$) and form 1 elicited a significantly higher proportion of questions than form 3 ($\Delta = 0.100, p = 0.005$). Although these differences are statistically significant, the difference in useful issues could be considered insubstantial and may have come about by chance given the number of statistical tests performed to identify differences (6 types of feedback * 2 tests * 2 conditions = 24 tests).

[13]Form 3 didnt elicit feedback submissions across enough distrinct articles during this period, so we were only able to sample 143 submissions.

To explore a potential mismatch between the types of feedback readers were likely to submit and the types of feedback Wikipedians found useful, we merged the feedback submitted via the three interfaces to compare the aggregate rate of feedback types and utility. Figures 3a and 3b show some substantial differences between the feedback submitted by readers and the feedback that Wikipedians found useful. As an example, the proportion of feedback determined irrelevant by Wikipedians was the second most frequent type (31.9%) while the proportion of irrelevant feedback that was marked useful was vanishingly small (0.5%) and could be attributed to rater error given that it represents a single submission labelled both useful and irrelevant.

Figures 3a and 3b also shows some similarities. For example, suggestions appear to be both the most prevalent (36.7%) and useful (78.9%) submission type.

The relatively small proportion of abuse is also worth noting. Only 6.6% of feedback was determined to be submitted in bad-faith. To put this into context, 10.0% of anonymous edits to encyclopedia articles are explicitly labelled as vandalism when they are reverted[11].

Discussion

Although the elicitation directed towards readers' concerns (form 1) did elicit more participation than the form directed toward editors' concerns (form 3), there was not a signficiant difference in the proportion of useful feedback. This result refutes hypothesis 1.1 and suggests that the strategy of directing readers towards editor interests – at least in this case – did not affect the usefulness of their participation.

However, we did see a slight effect on the intentions of submitted feedback. We observed a significantly lower proportion of questions submitted via form 3 which asks readers to rate an article. We suspect that, to evaluate the quality of an article, readers must put themselves in the role of an expert – someone qualified to perform an evaluation. Assuming readers who have legitimate questions would be less likely to adopt this role, it makes sense to see both a lower proportion of questions submitted and fewer overall submissions for form 3. Given the relatively high overall utility of questions (59.7% useful), this suggests that a substantial number of useful questions may not have been submitted by readers in this condition.

RQ2: How does the prominence of the elicitation affect the volume and utility of feedback?

Given that the results reported in the last section suggest that the different forms had no substantial effect on the utility of submissions and our Wikipedian hand-coders preferred form 1, we continue our experimentation using only that form. To look for changes in the utility of feedback submitted based on the amount of reader participation, we performed another experimental run using links "A" and "E" described in figure 1 in an attempt to increase the prominence of the feedback form. We re-shuffled readers into three new experimental conditions:

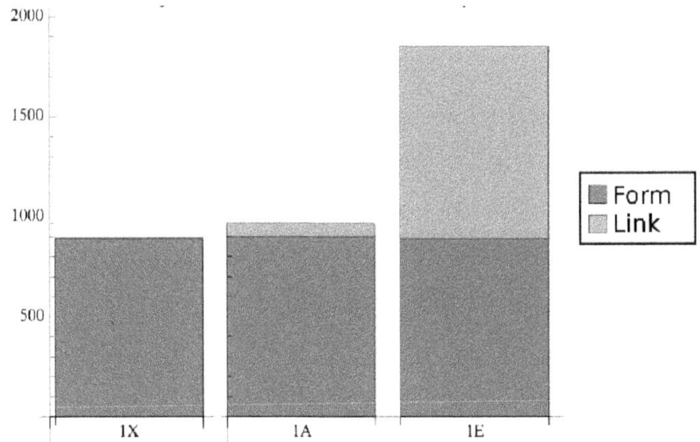

Figure 4: **Volume of feedback by experiment.** The raw amount of feedback submitted via the three experimental conditions is plotted by whether the feedback was submitted via the prominent link or via the form at end of articles.

- **1X**: Form 1 loads only on the bottom of the article.
- **1A**: Same as 1X but includes link A
- **1E**: Same as 1X but includes link E

Results

To ensure that the prominent links A and E were serving their intended function, we measured the total amount of feedback submitted over the period between April 5 and April 19 (15 days).

As figure 4 shows, the prominent link appears to have been effective in eliciting more feedback. While all cases elicited approximately the same amount of feedback directly via the form at the bottom of the article as the non-prominent condition (1X), the feedback submitted via the prominent link itself appears to purely supplement the total amount of feedback submitted (1X: 892, 1A: 967 and 1E: 1851). In the case of 1E, the prominent link apparently increased the rate at which feedback was submitted by about 91%.

To look for differences in the utility of feedback submitted via each of the experimental conditions, we randomly sampled 300 feedback submissions per condition and asked our Wikipedian coders to rate their usefulness. The differences between the proportion of useful feedback submitted between the three interfaces varied insignificantly around 0.42. A χ^2 of the largest observed difference between the conditions 1X (no link) and 1A (less prominent link) was insignificant ($\Delta = 0.065, p = 0.124$). If the prominence of the interface caused a decline in the utility of feedback, we would expect to see a more substantial dip in the proportion of useful feedback in the 1E condition given the amount of additional feedback submitted.

However, we did observe a significant difference in utility based on the whether the feedback originated via the form at the bottom of the article or the prominent link E. Figure 5 plots the proportion of useful feedback submitted for each experimental interface by whether it originated via the form

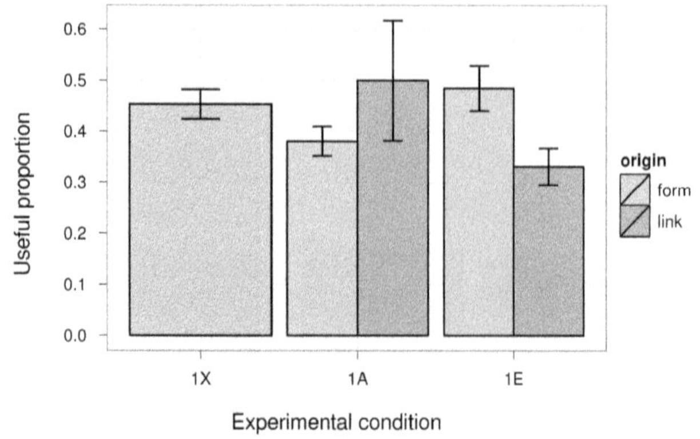

Figure 5: **Utility of feedback by origin.** The proportion of useful feedback is plotted for each condition by the origin from which it was submitted with standard error bars. Note that the large error bars around the proportion of useful feedback submitted via the link in the 1A condition is due to the small amount of feedback sampled in that condition (n=18).

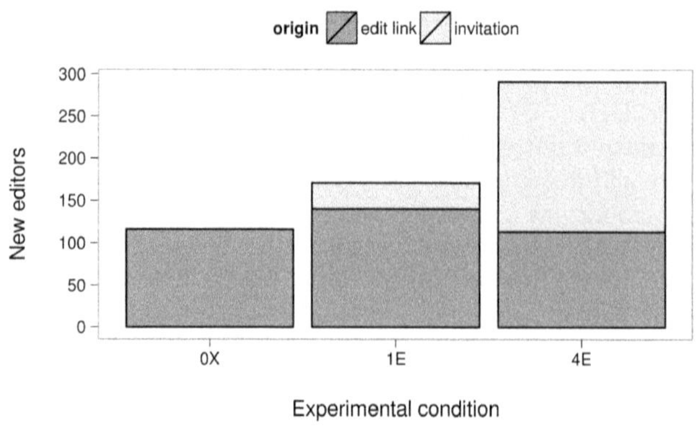

Figure 6: **New users by origin.** The number of new editors is plotted and stacked by the origin of their first edit. "edit link" refers to the standard vector for accessing the edit pane. "invitation" refers to form 4 which invites the user to make an edit.

at the bottom of the article or the prominent link. The proportion of useful feedback submitted via the most prominent link (1E) was significantly lower than the feedback submitted via the corresponding form ($\Delta = 0.153, p = 0.010$). This appears to be partially due to complaints about the prominent link submitted via the prominent link. After the experiment, we received messages from some concerned users that felt the prominent link was distracting. Out of the 8 feedback comments submitted via 1E's link by registered editors, only 1 feedback submission was determined to be useful while the rest were useless protests of the presence of the feedback interface.

Discussion

Increasing the prominence of the feedback form increased the volume of contributions in the expected way, affirming hypothesis 2.1. The results above suggest that the rate at which feedback is submitted can be nearly doubled by introducing prominent link E into the interface.

Surprisingly, we also found that expanding participation by making the interface more prominent did not affect the overall proportion of useful submissions, thus refuting hypothesis 2.2. We had hypothesized that increasing participation arbitrarily via a more obvious interface would elicit participation from readers who were increasingly less interested in contributing constructively, and therefore, utility would fall. However, we found no significant change in the proportion of useful feedback submitted despite more than doubling the amount of submissions. This result suggests that there are many potentially productive contributors available who may simply not be aware of their ability to contribute and that hiding the means to contribute is not an effective mechanism for improving the utility of contribution.

However, we did observe that feedback submitted via the most prominent link was of lower utility than that submitted directly via the form. Although it is tempting to conclude that the prominent link itself elicits lower utility submissions, it is important to note that the overall utility of submissions through the most prominent condition (1E) was not significantly lower than the 1X condition despite the fact that the prominent link nearly doubled the rate at which feedback was submitted. Given the slightly larger proportion of useful feedback submitted directly via the 1E form than the 1X form, we suspect that the underlying cause of this disparity is a re-routing of less useful feedback (that would have been submitted anyway) through the prominent link.

RQ3: How does the presence of the feedback interface affect new editor conversion?

To look for a potential cannibalization effect of AFT on new editor conversions, we re-shuffled readers into three new experimental conditions:

- **0X**: Control condition (no feedback form or link)
- **1E**: Feedback form 1 displayed at the bottom of the article, with prominent link E. Users were presented with edit invitation form 4 after successfully submitting feedback (indirect invitation)
- **4E**: Edit invitation form 4 displayed at the bottom of the article, with prominent link E (direct invitation)

Results

To measure new editor conversions, we observed user activity for the period between April 27th and May 7th 2012. During this observation period, both the direct invitation (4E) and indirect invitation (1E) conditions saw more new editors conversions than the control case. Figure 6 shows that a similar number of new editors originated via the standard vector (edit link) in the treatment conditions (1E: $n = 140$, 4E: $n = 113$) as in the control condition (0X: $n = 116$). The new editors whose first edit originated via the invitations to edit (1E: $n = 31$, 4E: $n = 178$) only appear to supplement these numbers.

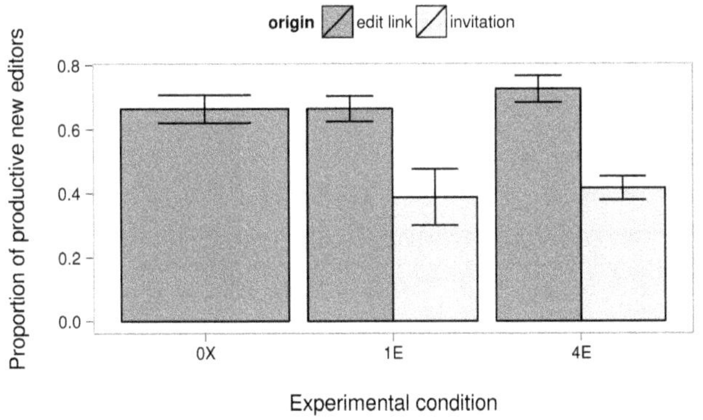

Figure 7: **Proportion of productive new users by origin.** The proportion of new editors who made at least one productive contribution in their first week is plotted by the origin of their first edit for the three experimental conditions.

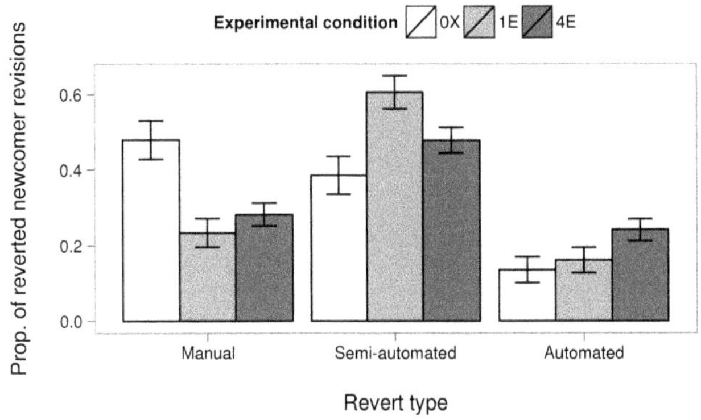

Figure 8: **The cost of non-productivity**. The proportion of newcomer revisons reverted for each experimental condition by how the revision was reverted.

To test if this increase in conversion was significant, we approximated the view-to-editor conversion rate by drawing 95% confidence intervals around the approximate views that each experimental condition received based on the total number of views that the sample received during the observation period (9,424,041). The random function which assigned readers to experimental conditions can be represented as a binomial proportion where the underlying probability of assignment to any one condition is $\frac{1}{3}$. Therefore, we can divide the total views and draw confidence intervals using the binomial approximation to a normal distribution($\frac{9424041}{3} = 3141347 \pm 945.47$). We used this confidence interval to perform a conservative χ^2 test that appropriately reduces the likelihood of a type I statistical error. Let u_1 and u_2 be set of new users such that $|u_1| > |u_2|$ we performed the following test:

$$\chi^2(\frac{|u_1|}{3141347+945.47}, \frac{|u_2|}{3141347-945.47})$$

The conservative χ^2 test found the difference in the rate of new editor conversions to be significant for all three cases (0X < 1E: $p = 0.002$, 1E < 4E: $p < 0.001$). This suggests that the indirect invitation condition (1E) converted significantly more views to new editors than control condition and the direct invitation condition (4E) converted significantly more views to new editors than both 1E and the control.

To explore the productivity of new editors conversions via the experimental conditions, we performed an analysis of the first week of contributions made by each new editor to look for productive contributions as described in Methods. We define a "productive editor" as a new editor who made at least one edit to an article that was not reverted within 48 hours by another editor.

As figure 7 shows, editors who originated via the invitation to edit through both the direct and indirect call to action were significantly less likely to make productive contributions in their first week than those who originated through the edit links within the same condition (1E: $\Delta = 0.277, p = 0.008$; 4E: $\Delta = 0.310, p < 0.001$). When comparing only those new editors who originated via the edit link between experimental conditions, the proportion of productive new editors varied insignificantly around 0.68. These results suggest that new editors who originated via an invitation to edit are about half as likely to contribute productively in their first week as those editors who originated via the standard vectors.

To examine the cost of introducing more unproductive newcomer contributions to Wikipedia, we classified the reverted newcomer editors in each condition into *manual*, *semi-automated* and *automated* as described in Methods. As figure 8 suggests, a χ^2 test found that a significantly smaller proportion of unproductive newcomer edits were reverted manually in both the 1E($\Delta = -0.25, p < 0.001$), and 4E($\Delta = -0.19, p = 0.001$) conditions. We also see that a significantly larger proportion of 1E revisions were reverted with semi-automated tools($\Delta = 0.219, p = 0.002$) and that a significantly larger proportion of 4E revisions were reverted with fully automated tools($\Delta = 0.134, p = 0.019$) when compared to the control. These differences suggest that Wikipedia's damage filtering systems (automated and semi-automated tools) are making up for some of the increased cost of damage due to the invitation to edit.

Discussion

The results described in this section are a solid refutation of hypothesis 3.1. Even without including those editors who saw the edit invitation, (insignificantly) more new editors made their first contribution in the 1E condition through the standard vectors to the edit pane (edit link) than in the control case. The indirect call to action appeared to only supplement new editor conversions. Further, this class of new editors appears to be just as likely to be productive in their first week of tenure as those who started editing via the control case.

However, there appears to be a cost to boosting conversions via invitations to edit – at least initially. A substantially smaller proportion of editors originating via the invitation made a productive contribution in their first week of edit activity.

RQ1: How do different elicitations affect the volume and utility of feedback?		
H1.1	unsupported	Although form 1 and form 2 elicited more feedback submissions than form 3, the quality of submissions was insignificantly different.
RQ2: How does the prominence of the elicitation affect the volume and utility of feedback?		
H2.1	supported	The prominent link conditions elicited significantly more feedback than the control.
H2.2	unsupported	Although feedback submitted via the prominent links was less useful, the overall differences were insignificant.
RQ3: How does the presence of the feedback interface affect new editor conversion?		
H3.1	unsupported	The presence or absence of the feedback interface had no observed effect on the rate of new editor conversions through the standard vectors.
H3.2	supported	New editors whose first edits originated via an invitation were substantially less likely to contribute productively in their first week.

Table 1: A summary of our hypotheses and findings.

As we suspected, the edit invitation strategy is a double-edged sword. Although the invitation appears to have effectively convinced substantially more readers to try their hand at editing, these invited editors were less likely to make productive contributions in their early wiki-career than those who started editing on their own. This result supports hypothesis 3.2.

Social learning theory suggests that newcomers to a community tend to go through a natural process by which they learn about a community and build confidence before expanding their contribution pattern[18]. It seems likely that explicitly inviting new editors to contribute would artificially inflate their confidence and speed up the process of introduction to the community which would naturally lead to more mistakes – at least initially.

Our analysis suggests that, at least in part, Wikipedia's efficient damage filtering mechanisms reduce the cost of the increase in unproductive newcomer contributions. Although we can assume that the cost in human effort of a few more automated reverts is essentially zero, the cost of operating the semi-automated reverting tools is unclear. Without such understanding, it's difficult to reason about just how much Wikipedia's damage filtering mechanisms make up for the increase in unproductive newcomer contributions.

CONCLUSIONS

In this paper, we examined a strategy for increasing participation from Wikipedia's consumers (readers) through a set of experiments performed using the Article Feedback Tool, an extension of the software that allows encyclopedia readers to make simple and low risk, yet productive, contributions – thereby supporting legitimate peripheral participation. Table 1 summarizes the results of our three experiments in the context of the research questions and hypotheses stated in Research Questions.

Although we hypothesized a trade-off between the quality and quanity of participation, our observations of such an effect were inconsistent. While we were able to boost the rate of feedback submissions both by aligning AFT's feedback forms to readers concerns and by making the interface more prominent to readers, we did not observe a decrease in the quality ("useful"ness as determined by Wikipedian raters) of feedback submitted. This result reflects the findings of Wash and Lampe[25] and suggests that there are many potentially productive non-contributors available who may simply be unaware of their ability to contribute and that obfuscating the mechanism for contribution is not an effective mechanism for improving the quality of contribution. In other words, increasing transactional costs either through requiring the reader to occupy a certain role or through obfuscating the ability to contribute do not appear to be effective strategies for increasing contribution quality for this low investment type of contribution. On the contrary, both our results and those of Wash and Lampe[25] suggest that participation can be increased by making the means of contribution more prominent without sacrificing quality with simple and straightforward contribution types like comments and feedback.

However, when we invited editors to edit articles via an explicit invitation, those supplemental new editors were less likely to be productive in their first week of tenure in Wikipedia. Editing an encyclopedia is a more demanding type of contribution than leaving a comment or submitting feedback, because editors must both contribute novel encyclopedic information and work within Wikipedia's complicated set of policies and guidelines – a requirement that new editors tend to struggle to meet[9]. Under the framing of legitimate peripheral participation, we might expect potential new editors to naturally go through a lurking process by which they build a situated understanding of the Wikipedia community and their place within it before making their first contribution – an assertion supported by [1]. When viewed this way, the invitation to contribute could be short circuiting the natural "joining script"[24] of new Wikipedia editors. If this is true, other systems with non-trivial contribution difficulty should see a similar effect.

It is useful to understand the value of AFT's invitation to new editors to the Wikipedia community's goals from a system-level perspective. In order to draw a data-based recommendation on whether AFT's invitation to edit should be released at a larger scale or not, both the value of new productive contributions and the cost of unproductive contributions must be accounted for. Systems with a high value on new contributions/contributors and/or efficient filters for dealing with unwanted contributions will be more likely to benefit from invitations despite the increase in unproductive edits.

Related work by Geiger et al. suggests that the English Wikipedia's automated and semi-automated anti-vandal tools are a efficient and scalable solution to the problem of moderation[8]. Our analysis suggests that these tools are effectively reducing the increased cost of unproductive contributions via the invitation to edit. In this context, it seems likely that the invitation to edit represent a net benefit to Wikipedia despite the larger proportion of unproductive edits. Related works examining Slashdot's distributed moderation system [14] and YouTube's copyright infringement detection algorithms[23] suggest a trend toward efficient, distributed and automated curation mechanisms in Web 2.0 systems that may also reduce the cost of such unwanted contributions in other systems.

ACKNOWLEDGEMENTS

We gratefully acknowledge the support of the National Science Foundation under grants IIS 09-68483 and IIS 11-11201. We would also like to thank the Wikimedia Foundation and the following Wikipedians for their work evaluating feedback submissions: Salim Fadhley, Fluffernutter, GorillaWarfare, Adam Hyland, Jamietw, John Minthorne, Tom Morris, Osarius, Rohit Patnaik, Utar and Whiteguru.

REFERENCES

1. Antin, J., and Cheshire, C. Readers are not free-riders: reading as a form of participation on wikipedia. In *CSCW '10*, ACM (New York, NY, USA, 2010), 127–130.
2. Beenen, G., Ling, K., Wang, X., Chang, K., Frankowski, D., Resnick, P., and Kraut, R. E. Using social psychology to motivate contributions to online communities. In *CSCW '04*, ACM (New York, NY, USA, 2004), 212–221.
3. Bettenburg, N., Just, S., Schröter, A., Weiss, C., Premraj, R., and Zimmermann, T. What makes a good bug report? In *SIGSOFT '08*, ACM (New York, NY, USA, 2008), 308–318.
4. Bryant, S. L., Forte, A., and Bruckman, A. Becoming wikipedian: Transformation of participation in a collaborative online encyclopedia. In *GROUP '05*, ACM (New York, NY, USA, 2005), 1–10.
5. Butler, B., Sproull, L., Kiesler, S., and Kraut, R. E. Community effort in online groups: Who does the work and why? *Human-Computer Interaction Institute* (2007), 90.
6. Cosley, D., Frankowski, D., Terveen, L., and Riedl, J. Suggestbot: using intelligent task routing to help people find work in wikipedia. In *Proceedings of the 12th international conference on Intelligent user interfaces*, IUI '07, ACM (New York, NY, USA, 2007), 32–41.
7. Ducheneaut, N. Socialization in an open source software community: A socio-technical analysis. In *CSCW '05*, ACM (New York, NY, USA, 2005), 323–368.
8. Geiger, R. S., and Ribes, D. The work of sustaining order in Wikipedia: The banning of a vandal. In *CSCW '10*, ACM (New York, NY, USA, 2010), 117–126.
9. Halfaker, A., Geiger, S., Jonathan, M., and Riedl, J. The rise and decline of an open collaboration system: How Wikipedia's reaction to sudden popularity is causing its decline. *American Behavioral Scientist* (in-press).
10. Halfaker, A., Kittur, A., Kraut, R., and Riedl, J. A jury of your peers: Quality, Experience and Ownership in Wikipedia. In *WikiSym '09*, ACM (New York, NY, USA, 2009), 1–10.
11. Halfaker, A., Kittur, A., and Riedl, J. Don't bite the newbies: How reverts affect the quantity and quality of Wikipedia work. In *WikiSym '11*, ACM (2011), 163–172.
12. Katz. Luring the lurkers. http://news.slashdot.org/story/98/12/28/1745252/luring-the-lurkers, Dec 1998.
13. Ko, A. J., and Chilana, P. K. How power users help and hinder open bug reporting. In *CHI '10*, ACM (New York, NY, USA, 2010), 1665–1674.
14. Lampe, C., and Resnick, P. Slash(dot) and burn: distributed moderation in a large online conversation space. In *CHI '04*, ACM (New York, NY, USA, 2004), 543–550.
15. Lave, J., and Wenger, E. *Situated learning: Legitimate peripheral participation*. Cambridge University Press, 1991.
16. Nonnecke, B., and Preece, J. Why lurkers lurk. In *Americas Conference on Information Systems* (2001).
17. Nonnecke, B., and Preece, J. Silent participants: Getting to know lurkers better. *From usenet to CoWebs* (2003), 110–132.
18. Preece, J., and Shneiderman, B. The reader-to-leader framework: Motivating technology-mediated social participation. *AIS Trans HCI 1 1*, 1 (2009), 13–32.
19. Priedhorsky, R., Chen, J., Lam, S., Panciera, K., Terveen, L., and Riedl, J. Creating, destroying, and restoring value in Wikipedia. In *GROUP'07* (Sanibel Island, FLorida, USA, 2007).
20. Rashid, A. M., Ling, K., Tassone, R. D., Resnick, P., Kraut, R., and Riedl, J. Motivating participation by displaying the value of contribution. In *CHI'06*, ACM (New York, NY, USA, 2006), 955–958.
21. Suh, B., Convertino, G., Chi, E. H., and Pirolli, P. The singularity is not near: Slowing growth of Wikipedia. In *WikiSym '09*, ACM (New York, NY, USA, 2009), 1–10.
22. Taraborelli, D., and Roth, C. Viable Web communities: Two case studies. In *Viability and Resilience of Complex Systems*, G. Deffuant and N. Gilbert, Eds. Springer, 2011, 75–105.

23. Tartelton, G. The politics of platforms. *New Media & Society 12*, 3 (2010), 347–364.

24. Von Krogh, G., Spaeth, S., and Lakhani, K. Community, joining, and specialization in open source software innovation: a case study. *Research Policy 32*, 7 (2003), 1217–1241.

25. Wash, R., and Lampe, C. The power of the ask in social media. In *CSCW '12*, ACM (New York, NY, USA, 2012), 1187–1190.

26. Wikimedia. Editor trends study. `http://strategy.wikimedia.org/wiki/Editor_Trends_Study`, March 2011.

27. Wilkinson, D. Strong regularities in online peer production. In *Ecommerce '08*, ACM (2008), 302–309.

Using Edit Sessions to Measure Participation in Wikipedia

R. Stuart Geiger
School of Information
University of California, Berkeley
102 South Hall, Berkeley CA 94703
stuart@stuartgeiger.com

Aaron Halfaker
Grouplens Research
University of Minnesota
200 Union St. S.E., Minneapolis, MN 55455
halfak@cs.umn.edu

ABSTRACT
Many quantitative, log-based studies of participation and contribution in CSCW and CMC systems measure the activity of users in terms of output, based on metrics like posts to forums, edits to Wikipedia articles, or commits to code repositories. In this paper, we instead seek to estimate the amount of time users have spent contributing. Through an analysis of Wikipedia log data, we identify a pattern of punctuated bursts in editors' activity that we refer to as *edit sessions*. Based on these edit sessions, we build a metric that approximates the labor hours of editors in the encyclopedia. Using this metric, we first compare labor-based analyses with output-based analyses, finding that the activity of many editors can appear quite differently based on the kind of metric used. Second, we use edit session data to examine phenomena that cannot be adequately studied with purely output-based metrics, such as the total number of labor hours for the entire project.

ACM Classification Keywords
H.5.3 [**Information Systems**]: Group and Organization Interfaces—*computer-supported collaborative work*

Keywords
Labor; activity; work; work practices; Wikipedia; peer production; labor-hours; sessions; quantitative methods

INTRODUCTION

Measuring Wikipedia
In less than a decade, Wikipedia has grown from a frequently ridiculed experiment to one of the world's most popular websites. The online encyclopedia has reached near-ubiquity among Internet users and is often invoked as a synecdoche for user-generated content communities, crowdsourcing, peer production, and Web 2.0. As such, it is hardly surprising that a number of high-impact statistics demonstrating the project's unexpected success are frequently mentioned in the public sphere. As of April 2012, there have been 528 million edits made to the English-language version and a total of 1.29 billion edits across all language versions [23]. Other commentators describe the project in terms of its article content, not the amount of work put into those articles, and such figures are equally daunting: 19 million encyclopedia articles contain 8 billion words in 270 languages, and the English-language Wikipedia alone has 3.9 million articles containing 2.5 billion words. [30]

While most of these and other statistics are backed up by a substantial amount of empirical research, estimations of the total number of labor-hours contributed to Wikipedia are one notable exception. However, this has not stopped champions of the project from stating with more and less certainty that Wikipedia is one of the largest projects in human history. Yet in his 2010 book *Cognitive Surplus,* [24] Clay Shirky makes the opposite argument: he first estimates that 100 million labor-hours have contributed to Wikipedia, but then compares this amount of time with the absolutely staggering statistic that Americans spend 200 billion hours watching television each year. Shirky's argument is that we spend a substantial amount of time on activities like television, which effectively waste our collective brainpower on acts of consumption as opposed to projects like Wikipedia, which foster creativity and collaboration.

While the total number of labor hours that have been contributed to Wikipedia is an interesting bit of trivia, measuring contributions in terms of labor hours is a novel approach to not only studying Wikipedia, but other CSCW and CMC platforms and communities. Casting contributions to a peer production platform like Wikipedia in terms of labor hours, as opposed to a metric based on the number of contributions or posts, radically reframes how we conceptualize users. If we are interested in measuring users in terms of how prolific or active they are, then previous quantitative methods are rather well-developed and deployed. This is especially the case considering the vast and often public records that log and document activity in wikis, open source software projects, message boards, forums, citizen science projects. However, if we are interested in understanding the volunteers of peer production projects in terms of their level of investment or engagement, we have been traditionally limited to surveys, interviews, time diaries, and other approaches which do not scale very well.

In this paper, we introduce a novel method for estimating the amount of time that users contribute to projects like Wikipedia, using the concept of edit sessions – which are punctuated bursts of editing activity captured by log data – as a way of identifying continuous periods of work on the wiki. This approach is not merely useful for arriving at a far more accurate estimation of the total number of labor-hours contributed to Wikipedia, but more importantly, it can be used to measure the activity of editors at a variety of scales. This approach provides an alternative to how most large-scale quantitative studies of not only Wikipedia but other CSCW platforms have operationalized activity using output-based metrics. Most notably, our analysis of labor-hours contributed by different cohorts of editors sheds new light on the project's oft-discussed growth and decline. [8,15,27] Specifically, we find that editors who joined the project in 2006 have not only contributed more labor-hours to the project than any other annual cohort, but continue to out-perform all other cohorts in 2012.

Measuring labor and work in CSCW

The most common way in which work in Wikipedia is measured is through edit counts, where one edit to a wiki document is considered one fungible unit of work. In most of the accounts of Wikipedia's power law inequalities – that is, how 1% of the editors contribute 55% of the content – edit counts are used. [27] Total bytes or words contributed in edits have also been used in order to arrive at a more nuanced figure. In addition, output-based metrics that examine how long edits persist are becoming quite popular when studying Wikipedia editors. [1,9,21,22]

However, many Wikipedia researchers have been moving away from raw edit count metrics in recent years. The main reason behind this stems from the realization that all edits are not equal. For example, the kinds of tasks and activities that predict whether editors become administrators has been modeled, with the results indicating that in many cases, the kind of contributions made matters more than the raw number. [4] One trend is towards using structured traces and articulations of work, such as barnstars and warning templates, to qualitatively and quantitatively measure the kinds of work that editors are rewarded and punished for performing. [6,7,12,19] Another trend is to measure editors by the number or edits or words that persist in articles, so that a spammer who makes thousands of edits which are always instantly removed ranks lower than an less active editor whose few contributions form the basis of the project's most edited and viewed articles. [9,10,21,22]

This tendency to use output-based metrics is not unique to studies of Wikipedia, as many large-scale quantitative studies of discussion forums [13], learning environments [16], recommender systems [17], open source software development, and other platforms often reduce interaction to one or occasionally two fungible units of activity. These are usually based on whatever kind of contribution is natively supported in the software platform. Wilkinson's study of peer production communities [29] is an excellent example of this, as he compares the power law distributions of activity in Wikipedia, Digg, Bugzilla, and Essembly. In Wikipedia, he examines articles created and edits to articles; in Bugzilla, bugs submitted and comments made; in Digg, stories submitted and 'diggs' to stories; and in Essembly, resolves proposed and votes cast.

These output-based metrics are quite useful in measuring work practices and the distribution of labor across content creation communities, which, as Wilkinson argues, often follows a power law distribution. However, we take from Barabasi's insight that that human activity is often not randomly or normally distributed, but instead occurs in bursts. [2] Reconceptualizing work and contributions in terms of time as opposed to content may seem counter-intuitive given that communities like Wikipedia are organized around producing content. Yet as we show in the later sections, labor-based metrics give us quite a different view of who Wikipedia's top contributors are, for example.

METHODOLOGY

Beyond 'editcountitis': the story of a mixed-methodological collaboration

Before detailing our quantitative methodology, we wish to note that this study was the result of a methodological collaboration between the authors: one of us is a qualitative ethnographer and the other is quantitative computer scientist. Furthermore, both of us have been long-term editors of Wikipedia and members of the Wikipedian community, in addition to having studied Wikipedia for some time. Our decision to measure the activity of Wikipedians in terms of labor-hours was inspired by a number of qualitative and ethnographic observations we made about the ways in which Wikipedians quantify and aggregate their own labor practices. We believe that our quantitative methodology independently verifies the veracity of the edit session metric, but we wish to detail our motivation to provide context as well as to inspire future lines of mixed-method research.

Wikipedians have developed a number of ways to measure the relative contributions made by each editor. The simplest and easiest of these is the edit count, which as previously mentioned, is also a metric widely used by Wikipedia researchers. However, we have found that many Wikipedians, particularly veteran editors and administrators, know quite well that a Wikipedian's edit counts do not necessarily reflect the amount of time, energy, and effort they have contributed to the project. A widely-circulated essay on "Editcountitis" succinctly summarizes this view:

> Editcountitis is used humorously to suggest a belief that a Wikipedian's overall contribution level can be measured solely by their edit count. This is a phenomenon which some think may be harmful to processes such as requests for adminship, as well as to the Wikipedia community in itself. The problems with using edit counts to measure relative level of experience

> are that it does not take into account that users could have an extensive edit history prior to registering an account (posting anonymously), and that major and minor edits are counted equally, regardless of whether the edit is a typo fix, or the creation of a full article. Furthermore, edit counts do not judge the quality of the edits, as insightful comments on talk pages and acts of vandalism are counted equally. Hence, it is not always a reliable way of telling how experienced or worthy a user truly is. [28]

Our edit session metric is a direct response to the claims of editcountitis by Wikipedians; we see our metric as one of many tools that researchers and editors can use to measure the labor of Wikipedians. A qualitative, ethnographic study of the ways in which Wikipedians measure and value their own activities would be quite revealing and could further ground this line of research. However, such a study is outside of the scope of this paper, which is to establish a new metric for quantifying the labor practices in peer production communities. We should note that we have begun conducting preliminary qualitative interviews with Wikipedians about these issues in order to inform this quantitative research, and in future research, we aim to introduce the edit sessions metric and study how it affects the relationships between Wikipedians and their work practices.

From edit sessions to labor hours

In this section, we describe and justify the metric we use to estimate the labor hours spent by editors working on Wikipedia: the *edit session*. Our intent is to estimate, in a consistent manner, the total amount of time a user has spent contributing to a site like Wikipedia. We use the concept of an activity session, a technique that is commonly used to track and categorize website visitor activity. [20] While sessions are usually tracked via page view data, we track editor activity based on revision histories and logging data. This metric only includes work that is done by editors on http://en.wikipedia.org, and we can only identify editor activity based on their editing history. Well-founded privacy concerns in the Wikipedian community prohibit us from using page view data to track individual users as they perform actions which do not result in an edit – such as reading a long discussion without making a comment – and we note this as a limitation later in the paper. However, for researchers who have access to these data, our methodology can certainly take advantage of access logs to provide an even more sophisticated analysis.

Defining edit sessions

Within the log data of Wikipedia, a user's edits appear as a stream of events with associated timestamps. In order to divide the stream edit activity into contiguous sessions of edits, the time between edit events (inter-edit time) can be examined and a method for identifying boundaries in the stream must be employed. We define an edit session as *a sequence of edits made by an editor where the difference between the time at which any two sequential edits are saved is less than one hour*. In other words, a set of edits S is an edit session if:

$$\forall e_1, e_2 \in S: I(e_1) = I(e_2) - 1 \rightarrow T(e_2) - T(e_1) \leq \alpha$$

where:

$I(e)$ = the index of edit e in a sequence of edits

$T(e)$ = the time at which edit e occurred in seconds

α = the maximum time between edits (one hour)

To gather edit sessions for the English Wikipedia, we used a backup copy of the project's MySQL database to process all page revisions sorted by the time in which they occurred and processed them sequentially. While stepping forward through revisions, we identified the start and end of edit sessions by tracking the "user_text" (username for registered editors, IP address for anonymous editors) and last edit timestamps. When the last edit timestamp for a individual became stale (> 1 hour old), we conclude that an session ended at the time of their last edit. This processing approach allows us to compute the edit sessions for a user in the same amount of time and complexity as the commonly used edit counters ($O(n)$).

Figure 1 illustrates an example edit session produced by applying this method. Toby Bartels' first edit in this session occurred at 00:11, with edits at 00:20, 00:29, and 00:47. While this editor made edits before and after this session, but they took place more than 60 minutes before the first

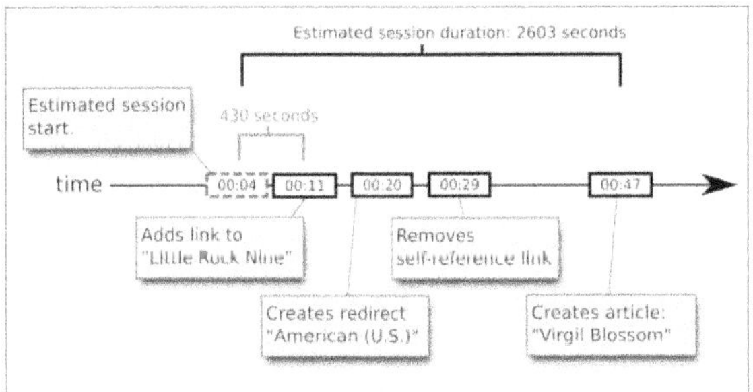

Figure 1. Estimated session length for Toby Bartels. Edits made by "Toby Bartels" are plotted and annotated over time for a session he completed on September 4th, 2010. The estimated session start time is plotted at 430 seconds before the user's first edit.

edit at 00:11 and more than 60 minutes after the last edit at 00:47. As this example illustrates, there are a variety of tasks which the user performs during this time on a number of different pages.

Vetting the one hour cutoff

Preliminary work that looked at edit sessions in a more limited context simple placed a cutoff on inter-edit time at 1 hour under the assumption that the largest edits will take about an hour to complete, so any more time between edits meant that the editor left of site. We tested the validity of this cutoff time by analyzing the time between edits for a random sample of 1 million revisions, which were then filtered to exclude edits from unregistered and bot users as well as the first edit by a registered user. With the remaining 821,749 revisions, we retrieved the time between the sampled revision and the previous revision from that user. This produced a long tail distribution that we suspected to be log-normal, so we bucketed inter-edit time logarithmically to produce the empirical histogram in Figure 2.

We suspected that the histogram was a result of summing at least two log-normal distributions representing within session time and between session time, so we fit the summed distributions using an expectation maximization (EM) algorithm. It turns out that we achieved a much better fit with three distributions than with two. We suspect that the smallest inter-edit times, overlaid in red, correspond to within-session edits and is on the order of minutes, making up a bulk of the revisions sampled. The second, overlaid in blue, corresponds to time between edit sessions and is on the order of days, while the third, overlayed in green, corresponds to extended breaks from the project (or "wikibreaks") and is on the order of months. As the dashed line in Figure 2 shows, the hour cutoff is just under the intersection of the inter-session and between-session distributions. To ensure that the 1 hour cutoff behaves reasonably over time, we graphed the fitted means and standard deviations for the history of Wikipedia (Figure 3).

The consistency of these fits indicate that the distribution of within-session and between-session inter-edit time stays largely consistent since the project gained critical mass and began its exponential growth phase. [27] These analyses suggest that the 1 hour cutoff appropriately divides within-session edits from between session edits and is useful throughout the history of the Wikipedia project. This consistency is especially striking considering that the pattern of inter-edit times has been generally unaffected by the many changes which have occurred in the community, such as the growing and shrinking size of the editor base, the development of policies and bureaucracies, the evolution of tasks in and around article writing, and various technical developments and new features. In addition, the distribution of the time between edits suggests that editors in Wikipedia follow a "Barabasi queueing" [2] model in which edits are largely concentrated in contiguous sessions as opposed to being normally or randomly distributed, which we suspect will also hold in other peer production projects.

Estimating edit session duration

From an edit session, we derive the session duration as a proxy to the amount of time an editor actually spent working on Wikipedia. We assume that, in between the edits they make, editors are performing legitimate wiki-work, and therefore, we can estimate their labor hours by measuring the time taken to complete their session. A naive way to derive session duration from an edit session is to simply find the difference in time between the first and last edits in the session. However, this approach does not account for the amount of time that the first edit in a

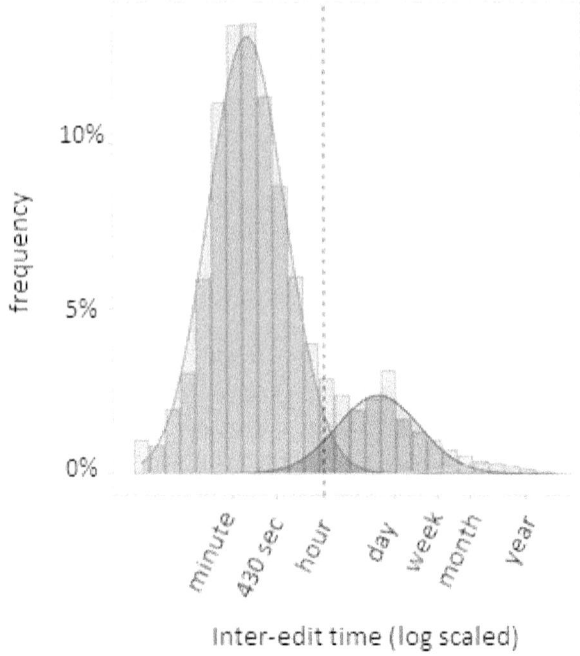

Figure 2. Histogram of time between users edits with an EM fit of three log-normal distributions corresponding to within-session, between-session, and extended session breaks.

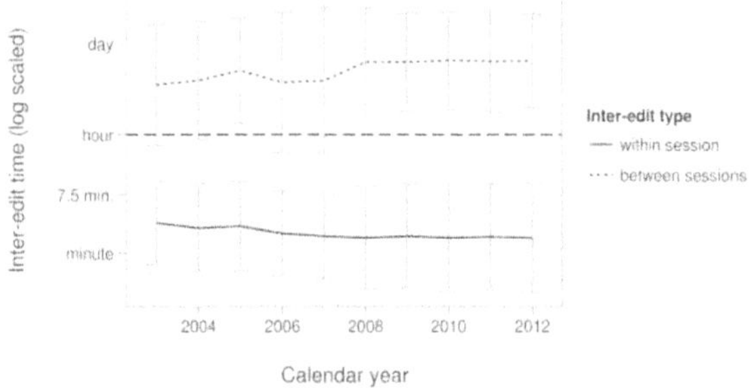

Figure 3. EM fitted means and standard deviations of within and between session inter-edit times over time (wikibreaks excluded).

session required to make, and therefore, sessions that contain only one edit would appear to have required zero labor-hours. To account for the time that the temporal bounds of edit sessions do not capture, we calculated the average time between edits across all sessions that contained more than one edit, which was 430 seconds. We combine the difference in time between the first and last session edits with 430 seconds (see "Estimated session start" in Figure 1) to produce an estimated session duration.

RESULTS

Analyses derived from edit session data

Out of the 528 million edits in the English-language version of Wikipedia from January 2001 to April 2012, we identified 423 million edits that were not made by automated bots. Iterating through these edits, we identified 114 million distinct edit sessions by 33.6 million distinct registered and anonymous editors. Of these, 60.6 million edits (14.3% of all edits) were made outside of a continuous edit session and were assigned the duration of 430 seconds, the average time between edits in a multi-edit session, as explained in the methodology section. The median session length was 10 minutes, and as Figure 2 illustrates, the distribution of sessions is highly skewed towards short sessions, although some notable outliers exist. For example, our dataset includes a 1251 minute session by a Wikipedian who spent nearly 21 continuous hours contributing to articles, participating in discussions and sending messages to other users during a marathon of editing in December of 2006.

Most sessions are much shorter, as 83.4% of all edit sessions were less than 30 minutes in length. As Figure 4 illustrates, there is a slight increase in the mean session duration from 27.3 to 33.6 minutes between sessions performed in editor's first month and sessions performed in their 2nd year. The mean session time for edits performed in a editor's second year stays relatively consistent from that point forward. This indicates that as Wikipedians editors mature, they edit in slightly longer sessions, but do not substantially change their session habits. Due a long tail of session length, the median session length is substantially lower than the mean across editors of all tenure.

Edit session data can be used to reveal interesting aspects of the work practices of contributors to peer production projects. Figure 5 plots the average session length per day of the week, finding that there is a small but noticeable pattern. Edit sessions on weekends tend to be longer than those during the middle of the week, suggesting that for at least some Wikipedians, weekends are spent on longer and more complex tasks. Figure 6 plots the average session length per month, showing that the longest edit sessions are in the summer and winter months. Taking into account Western work and education cycles, these analyses lend support to a hypothesis that Wikipedians edit for longer periods of time during periods of leisure and vacation.

Edit counts versus labor hours

The rate at which an editor saves revisions to pages can vary substantially based on their wiki-work habits and the kind of activity they are engaged in. Even when working on a single article, some editors save changes every minute while others will not save their changes until they have finished the task at hand. Furthermore, 3rd party tools like AutoWikiBrowser and Huggle pre-script similar tasks and allow editors to make several revisions per minute, or even every few seconds in some cases. It is assumed that more edits typically corresponds to more labor, but only if editors are doing the same type of work with the same editing habits. To demonstrate this, we compared edit counts versus edit session metrics, first determining the top 20 editors in March 2012 by edit count (Figure 7). These editors performed a total of 259,516 edits, or 7.87% of all the edits from registered editors that month. Applying our metric to the top 20 editors by edit count, we found that they account for 4,276.5 labor hours in March 2012, or

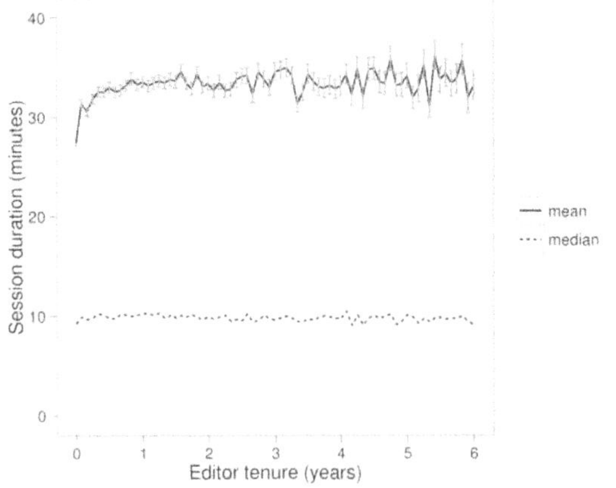

Figure 4. Mean and median session duration by number of years the editor has been registered.

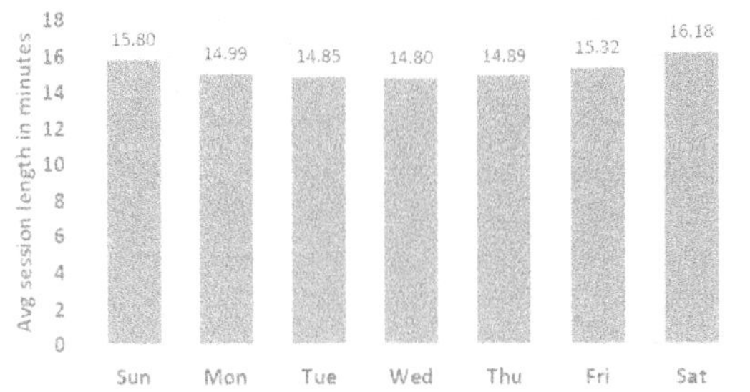

Figure 5. Average edit session length by day of week, 2001-12

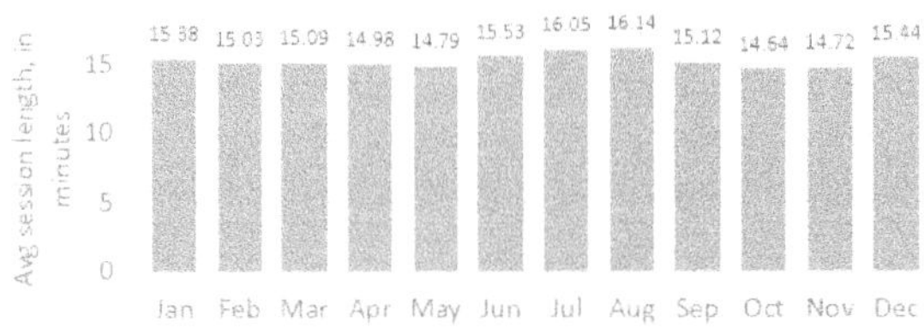

Figure 6. Average edit session length by month, 2001-12

	Top editors by edits		Top editors by edit sessions		
	Username	edits	Username	edits	hours
1	Koavf	43997	**Materialscientist**	**7472**	**453.2**
2	Waacstats	33402	Jtmorgan	1231	402.9
3	Hmains	17176	**Kwamikagami**	**9088**	**356.3**
4	Rich Farmbrough	17169	TonyTheTiger	6152	344.0
5	Bgwhite	14531	ACP2011	2218	337.2
6	Courcelles	13832	Pinethicket	3894	317.7
7	Fortdj33	12919	Armbrust	6288	311.0
8	VasuVR	12095	P.T. Aufrette	6257	306.4
9	BD2412	9801	**Koavf**	**43997**	**302.2**
10	Cloudz679	9779	Derek R Bullamore	4228	290.0
11	Kwamikagami	9088	MathewTownsend	1807	280.8
12	Muboshgu	8098	Crisco 1492	2747	278.5
13	Tassedethe	7976	Alarbus	1669	277.5
14	Materialscientist	7472	**Rich Farmbrough**	**17169**	**274.8**
15	John of Reading	7415	Alan Liefting	5970	274.3
16	DBigXray	7405	**BD2412**	**9801**	**273.2**
17	Ssriram mt	7100	Sitush	4421	270.7
18	Woohookitty	7099	**DBigXray**	**7405**	**270.2**
19	Allens	6757	**Allens**	**6757**	**270.1**
20	Fram	6405	**Cloudz679**	**9779**	**249.9**

Figure 7. Top 20 editors in March 2012 by edits and sessions

1.5% of the total labor hours from registered editors that month.

As an alternative ranking, we retrieved all the editors who, according to our edit session metric, contributed a total of at least 8 hours of labor a day per day in March 2012. In all, 20 registered editors met this 248 hour threshold, and the lists (Figure 7) are quite different. There is a small amount of overlap (Jaccard index = 0.29) that suggests these metrics are making a similar but certainly not identical measurement. For sample, the highest editors in both rankings appear in both lists. However, the same is not true for either of the second-highest ranked editors. These differences suggest that edit count and edit sessions are measuring editor labor differently, but why choose one over the other? We contend that measuring labor with edit sessions benefits over edit count in two important ways: (1) labor hours should be comparable between editors performing a wide range of different tasks in Wikipedia and (2) measuring work in hours is more intuitive. To demonstrate this intuitive nature, we pose a question. Which tells us more about an editor such as MatthewTownsend and his investment and motivations: that he made 1,807 edits in March 2012, or that in that time period, he edited Wikipedia for an average of 9 hours per day, *every day*?

For researchers and community members who are interested in identifying the most dedicated and invested contributors, both the raw number of labor hours and the number of sessions which last longer than a standard work day provide an alternative metric. This is one of the many kinds of analyses that edit session data can be used to generate. For example, Figure 9 plots the raw number and proportion of edit sessions over 8 hours in length since 2004. This shows a different view of the project's much-discussed decline (Figure 8, see [15,27]), indicating that there is only a slight decline in the number of times Wikipedians engage in quite lengthy, dedicated editing sessions. This is useful because it indicates that core editors are continuing to invest substantial amounts of time in the project, suggesting that the decline may result from a loss of the more peripheral and casual contributors. In fact, the steady rise in the proportion of edit sessions lasting longer than 8 hours is in line with recent work demonstrating that the project's decline stems from a failure to recruit and retain newcomers as opposed to a mass exodus from the project's most longstanding and dedicated contributors. [8]

Comparing labor across user cohorts

An interesting use of our labor-hour metric is to compare the total labor hours between groups of Wikipedians depending on how long they have been editing Wikipedia. We bucket registered users into annual cohorts based on when each user made their first edit and tracked their aggregate labor hours over time. Figure 10 plots the stacked total labor hours for each cohort up to April, 2012. Editors who started in 2006 spend the most time editing Wikipedia. Even in 2012, editors who joined the project in 2006

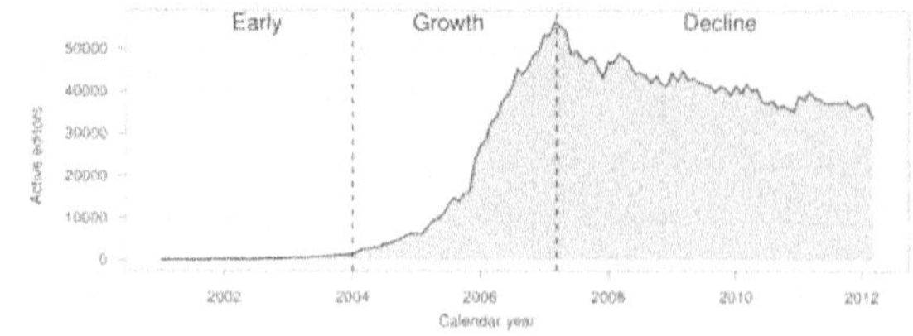

Figure 8. Wikipedia's growth and decline. The number of active editors, defined as over 5 edits per month, data from [8].

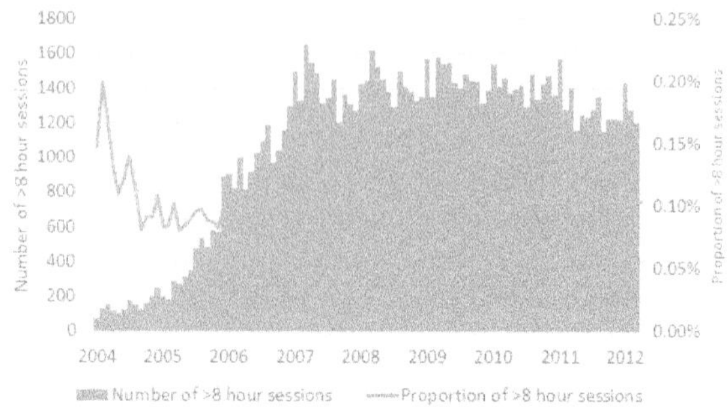

Figure 9. Number and proportion of extended edit sessions (>8 hours) over the history of Wikipedia since 2004.

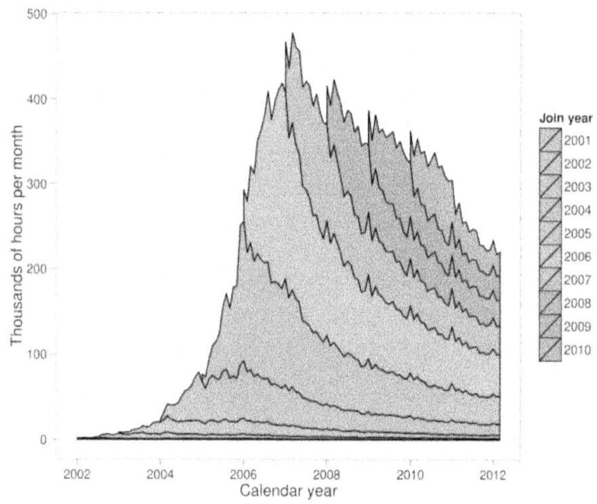

Figure 10. Labor-hours contributed to English Wikipedia per month, by registered user cohorts from 2001-2010.

collectively spend more time editing Wikipedia than any other cohort. The total labor hours contributed by the cohort of 2006 in March 2012 is 41,583 while the next highest (the 2007 cohort) is 30,598. In contrast, the 2011 cohort is quite low, at 16,122 hours.

Computing total labor hours contributed

Our approach also enables us to replicate Shirky and Wattenberg's back of the envelope estimations about the total number of labor hours contributed to Wikipedia. Labor-hour (or man-hour) calculations for large-scale projects are typically found in back-of-the-envelope calculations, not rigorous analysis of actual work performed – such analysis is usually impossible. Labor-hour calculations are typically derived by multiplying the number of employees who work on a project in a given week by the average length of their work week, and then multiplying that figure by the number of weeks spent on the project. While this can be slightly complicated when some workers are employed for different amounts of time (part vs. full time) or when the number of workers changes in a new phase of the project, most modern megaprojects are administered in such a way that these labor patterns are well-documented.

For example, a well-documented and often-repeated labor-hour estimation is that of the Empire State Building, which took 3,000 laborers a total of 7 million labor-hours to construct. [14] Figures for the construction of the Channel Tunnel report a total 170 million labor-hours, [5] while estimations of the Great Pyramid at Giza range from 880 million [25] to 3.5 billion labor-hours. [26] The first edition of the *Encyclopedia Britannica* was written and published by 3 employees authoring 24 pages a week for 100 weeks, [11] which is around 12,000 labor-hours assuming 40 hour work week. Alternatively, labor hours have been used as the basis of studies of software development and project management, such as in Brooks' influential *The Mythical Man-Month* [3], where he argues that adding more labor to a project does not necessarily speed up the project – in fact, it can often slow a project down.

Summing the duration of all continuous editing sessions and single edit sessions, we identified 41,018,804 total labor-hours expended in the English-language version of Wikipedia. As Figure 11 shows, the number of labor-hours per month experiences a comparable exponential growth and decline as in editing that has been discussed extensively [8,15,27]. At the peak of the project's growth, approximately 675,000 labor-hours were contributed each month, but this has fallen to approximately 425,000 labor-hours in 2012. This graph also illustrates a similar distribution between the number of labor-hours contributed by registered and anonymous editors: 27.43% of all labor-hours were from anonymous editors, compared to 25.83% of all edits. Extrapolating to all language version of Wikipedia based on the total number of edits made to each project, we estimate that 61,706,883 total labor-hours have been contributed in edit sessions for non-English language Wikipedias, for a total of 102,673,683 total labor-hours to all Wikipedia versions.

OBJECTIONS AND LIMITATIONS

Although this approach simplifies all facets of the wiki-work into interactions that change the content of the wiki's pages, we argue that this approach to measuring work hours is robust to the most common types of wiki-work. Yet the most immediate objection to such a metric is that there is little ancillary data to support the assumption that a user is active during the time between edits. This is mitigated by the fact that in Wikipedia, nearly all actions within the MediaWiki software platform are represented by an edit to a page. [6,7] This is because the platform is notoriously lacking in built-in features. While the MediaWiki platform

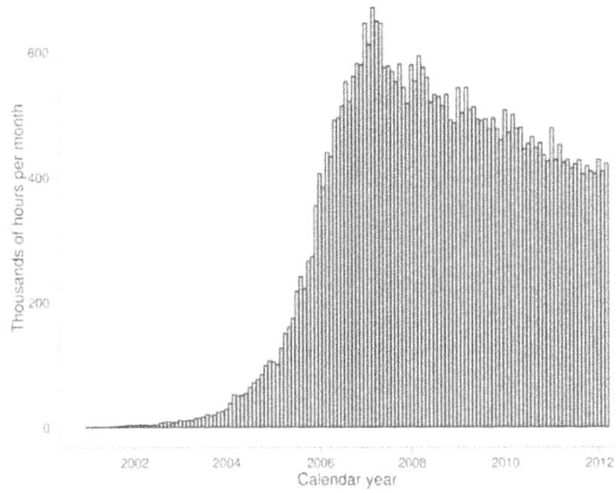

Figure 11. Total monthly labor hours over the history of Wikipedia for all registered, human editors.

supports discussion spaces, meta-discussion spaces, user-to-user messaging, user profiles, quality control procedures, task discovery and assignment mechanisms, administrative queues, newsletters, and many other tasks beyond simple encyclopedia editing, all of these features are represented as pages that can be edited.

For example, when an administrator blocks a user, it is customary to edit the user's talk page (where anyone can leave them a message) and leave a templated message indicating that the user has been blocked. [6] When a user requests that an administrator temporarily protect an article from editing, they do so by editing a specialized page, and it is customary for the responding administrator to edit this page as well, marking the request as approved or rejected and removing it from the queue. Almost all of these activities are represented as edits to pages and are, therefore, included in our analysis of edit sessions. As such, an edit session should capture article editing activity as well as communication and coordination activities across the system. However, this prolific logging of social and organizational activity is quite specific to Wikipedia and grounded through ethnographic fieldwork. Because of this, researchers seeking to use our edit session metric should first understand what kind of activity is logged.

Labor which occurs but is not measured

We must stress that Wikipedians perform a number of activities which are critically important to the encyclopedia project but are completely invisible in this calculation. The most revealing aspect of this can be seen in our algorithm's estimation for the number of hours spent in edit sessions by Wikipedia's co-founder Jimmy Wales: 869 hours – or just under 22 full-time work weeks – since January 2001. First, this estimation completely neglects the amount of work Jimmy Wales has put into Wikipedia behind the scenes. However, it is lower than expected given that he spends much of his time resolving disputes and building consensus, tasks which involve reading a substantial amount of existing dialogue before stating one's own opinion. A better figure to showcase Wales' dedication would be that out of the ~4,100 days since Wikipedia was founded, he has made an edit almost every other day – 1,993 distinct days in total.

There are many different ways in which Wikipedians contribute labor to the encyclopedia project that never result in even a single edit. These kinds of activities are entirely unaccounted for in our analysis, and include: carefully reviewing articles for errors and finding none; looking up a source to see if it is accurate, and finding it is; reading various policies, guidelines, and the manual of style; and keeping up with various project-wide debates and controversies without weighing in. Furthermore, many editors do not edit in continuous sessions, spending dozens or even hundreds of hours in activities that result in just one edit. These include activities like: writing a full-length article in a text editor and submitting it in one edit; searching for historical documents in archives; reading an entire book to verify a source; reviewing hundreds of comments in a controversy before weighing in; traveling to a remote location to take a photograph. Another potential issue is that anonymous editors are treated as distinct editors, such that one hundred editors can all simultaneously be in a continuous edit session at the same library or institution, but they are treated as one editor. There are also a variety of activities that take place outside of http://wikipedia.org, such as the project's hundreds of mailing lists and IRC channels, editor-to-editor communication over personal channels like e-mail or IM, in person meetups, and the annual Wikimania conference. However, we must note that most of these activities are also not directly captured by current methodologies that rely on output-based metrics.

Possible over-estimations of labor

First, our inter-edit cutoff for sessions is one hour, and while we argue the validity of this value in section 2.2, it could be argued that this is too long of a time period. Hypothetically, an editor could make an edit, head to lunch, and then 59 minutes later, return home and respond to a message sent to them. If this occurs in less than 60 minutes, we assume they have been working the whole time. However, this raises a more fundamental question as to what labor is in a post-industrial society: is time spent 'on break' time spent working? Traditionally, labor-hours are the time that all laborers spend directly working on or supporting a project, which rarely includes the time each worker spends while on a scheduled break, paid vacation, commuting, etc.

Multitasking and rapid task switching are now ubiquitous [18], and many people edit Wikipedia while performing other tasks, such as watching television or even talking with friends and family on the telephone. This complicates our understanding of the edit session as a metric of discrete, continuous labor contributed to the encyclopedia project. For example, an editor who spends an hour editing Wikipedia and watching television may actually just be editing during the commercial breaks, spending the other 45 minutes focused on the TV. Or in an extreme case, an editor could be gainfully employed at some unrelated workplace, and spend thirty seconds every half hour editing an article. If they did this all work day, it would appear in our metric as eight continuous hours of labor contributed to Wikipedia when only four minutes were expended. However, we can complicate this example even more: what if this user is patrolling a high-profile article for vandalism and has put themselves 'on call' for eight hours, using a notification tool to help them review every edit made to this article within one minute?

FUTURE WORK

This study has exclusively studied the English-language Wikipedia, and future research is necessary to further validate the use of edit sessions as a way of analyzing activity in both Wikipedia and other collaboration platforms. Diary studies or surveillance-based techniques, in which users are recorded or record their own behavior, could provide another form of validation to the edit session metric. Furthermore, it would be interesting to see what kinds of activity are not included in edit sessions but are recorded by Wikipedians, as discussed in section 4.2.

Future research can use the session approach to explore the differences and similarities between different classes and types of users, as well as the different kinds of activity which are performed. We noted that one of the longest edit sessions in our dataset was from a Wikipedian who was engaged more in communication and dispute resolution than article editing itself. Qualitative coding of a sample of edit sessions and both extremes could reveal substantial differences between how editors engage with a peer production project. Future research could also use statistical modeling to classify sets of similar users based on their edit session behaviors, asking, for example, if editors who are engaged in dispute resolution, counter-vandalism, or article construction tend to have many short sessions or a few long sessions.

The concept of the activity session is not unique to Wikipedia, and a study of contributions to fast-paced crowdsourcing platforms like Galaxy Zoo and NASA click-workers would likely result in a drastically reduced value for the average time between sessions, as well as the three different distributions of breaks between edits. Yet we expect that this threefold distribution of breaks within sessions, breaks between sessions, and extended breaks would appear in any peer production community. Based on this framework, it would be quite revealing to compare the kind, number, and duration of between session and extended session breaks.

CONCLUSION

This paper has introduced and explained the concept of the edit session as a way of estimating the number of labor-hours that Wikipedians spend continuously contributing to the encyclopedia project. Our metric is a more robust and revealing way of operationalizing editors' contributions, activities, and levels of investment than pure edit counts and other output-based metrics. Edit sessions are also more intuitive than edit counts, and labor-based metrics provide for a more robust comparison between editors, independent of the kinds of activities that editors perform. Session data also provides for interesting studies of interaction and activity in CSCW sessions, such as daily and seasonal periodicity as well as queuing behaviors. Examining other peer production communities using a labor-hours approach may also prove fruitful, and comparing other communities to Wikipedia might reveal interesting similarities and differences. Further research is also necessary to validate this method to real-world activity, possibly using diary studies or other modes of observational research.

ACKNOWLEDGMENTS

This work would not have been possible without the support of our research groups, the Wikimedia Foundation, NSF grants IIS 09-68483 and IIS 11-11201, as well as the constructive comments from the CSCW reviewers.

REFERENCES

1. Adler, B.T., Alfaro, L. de, Pye, I., and Raman, V. Measuring Author Contributions to the Wikipedia. *Proc WikiSym 2008*, ACM Press (2008).
2. Barabási, A.-L. The origin of bursts and heavy tails in human dynamics. *Nature 435*, 7039 (2005), 207–211.
3. Brooks, F.P. *The Mythical Man-Month*. Addison-Wesley, 1995.
4. Burke, M. and Kraut, R. Taking up the mop: identifying future wikipedia administrators. *Proc CHI 2008*, ACM (2008), 3441–3446.
5. Cutler, D. Facts on the Channel Tunnel. *Reuters*, 2010. http://www.reuters.com/article/2010/10/07/siemens-eurostar-tunnel-idUSLDE69623720101007.
6. Geiger, R. and Ribes, D. The work of sustaining order in wikipedia: the banning of a vandal. *Proc CSCW 2010*, ACM (2010).
7. Geiger, R.S. and Ribes, D. Trace Ethnography: Following Coordination Through Documentary Practices. *Proc HICSS 2011.*, IEEE (2011).
8. Halfaker, A., Geiger, R.S., Morgan, J.T., and Riedl, J. The Rise and Decline of an Open Collaboration System. *American Behavioral Scientist.* (In press). Accessed online 27 Aug 2012 at http://halfaker.info/archive/halfaker12rise.pdf
9. Halfaker, A., Kittur, A., Kraut, R., and Riedl, J. A Jury of Your Peers: Quality, Experience and Ownership in Wikipedia. *Proc WikiSym 2009*, ACM Press (2009).
10. Halfaker, A., Kittur, A., and Riedl, J. Don't bite the newbies: how reverts affect the quantity and quality of Wikipedia work. *Proc WikiSym 2011*, ACM (2011).
11. Kogan, H. *The Great EB: The Story of the Encyclopædia Britannica.* University of Chicago Press, Chicago, 1958.
12. Kriplean, T., Beschastnikh, I., and McDonald, D. Articulations of wikiwork: uncovering valued work in wikipedia through barnstars. *Proc CSCW 2008*, ACM (2008), 47–56.
13. Lampe, C. and Resnick, P. Slash(dot) and burn: distributed moderation in a large online conversation space. *Proc CHI 2004*, ACM (2004), 543–550.
14. Langmead, D. and Garnaut, C. *Encyclopedia of Architectural and Engineering Feats*. ABC-CLIO, 2001.
15. van Liere, D. and Fung, H. *Editor Trends Study*. 2011. Accessed 13 April 2012 from http://strategy.wikimedia.org/wiki/Editor_Trends_Study
16. Lipponen, L., Rahikainen, M., Lallimo, J., and Hakkarainen, K. Patterns of participation and discourse in elementary students' computer-supported collaborative learning. *Learning and Instruction 13*, 5 (2003), 487–509.
17. Ludford, P.J., Cosley, D., Frankowski, D., and Terveen, L. Think different: increasing online community participation using uniqueness and group dissimilarity. *Proc CHI 2004*, ACM Press (2004), 631–638.
18. Mark, G., Gonzalez, V.M., and Harris, J. No task left behind?: examining the nature of fragmented work. *Proc CSCW 2005*, ACM Press (2005).
19. McDonald, D.W., Javanmardi, S., and Zachry, M. Finding patterns in behavioral observations by automatically labeling forms of wikiwork in Barnstars. *Proc WikiSym 2011*, ACM Press (2011).
20. Mongomery, Alan, L., Li, S., Srinivasan, K., and Leichty, J.C. Modeling Online Browsing and Path Analysis Using Clickstream Data. *Marketing Science 23*, 4 (2004), 579–595.
21. Panciera, K., Halfaker, A., and Terveen, L. Wikipedians are born, not made: a study of power editors on Wikipedia. *Proc GROUP 2009*, ACM (2009), 51–60.
22. Priedhorsky, R., Chen, J., Lam, S.T.K., Panciera, K., Terveen, L., and Riedl, J. Creating, destroying, and restoring value in wikipedia. *Proc GROUP 2007*, ACM Press (2007), 259–268.
23. S23. WikiStats: List of Wikipedias. 2012. http://s23.org/wikistats/wikipedias_html.php.
24. Shirky, C. *Cognitive Surplus: Creativity and Generosity in a Connected Age*. Penguin, New York, 2010.
25. Smith, C.B. Program Management B.C. *Civil Engineering 69*, 6 (1999).
26. Smith, N. Classic Projects: Great Pyramid at Giza. *Engineering and Technology Magazine 6*, 1 (2011).
27. Suh, B., Convertino, G., Chi, E., and Pirolli, P. The Singularity is Not Near: Slowing Growth of Wikipedia. *Proc WikiSym 2009*, ACM (2009).
28. Wikipedia contributors. "Wikipedia:Editcountitis." *Wikipedia.* http://enwp.org/W:ITIS, accessed 7 Dec 2012.
29. Wilkinson, D.M. Strong regularities in online peer production. *Proc EC 2008*, ACM Press (2008), 302.
30. Zachte, E. *Wikipedia Statistics*. 2012. Accessed 13 Apr 2012, http://stats.wikimedia.org/EN/TablesWikipediaZZ.htm

Structures of Broken Ties: Exploring Unfollow Behavior on Twitter

Bo Xu, Yun Huang
Northwestern University
2145 Sheridan RD, TECH C210
Evanston, IL, 60208, U.S.A.
{bo.xu, yun}@northwestern.edu

Haewoon Kwak
Telefonica Research
Diag. 00 Plaza de Ernest Lluch i Martín, Barcelona, Spain
kwak@tid.es

Noshir S. Contractor
Northwestern University
2145 Sheridan RD, TECH D241
Evanston, IL, 60208, U.S.A.
nosh@northwestern.edu

ABSTRACT
This study investigates unfollow behavior in Twitter, i.e. people removing others from their Twitter following lists. Considering the interdependency and dynamics of unfollow decisions, we use actor-oriented modeling (SIENA) to examine the impacts of reciprocity, status, embeddedness, homophily, and informativeness on tie dissolution. Focusing on ordinary users in tightly-knitted user groups, the results show that relational properties play key roles in the emergence of unfollow behavior: mutual following relations and common followees reduce the likelihood of unfollowing. And unfollow tends to be reciprocal: when a user is unfollowed by someone, he or she will unfollow back. However, there is no evidence of the impacts of homophily based on common interests and informativeness of interactions. The findings suggest that Twitter has many heterogeneous user groups and relational and informational factors may not be applicable universally.

Author Keywords
Unfollow relations; tie dissolution; Twitter; actor-oriented modeling (SIENA); snowball sampling.

ACM Classification Keywords
H.5.m. Information interfaces and presentation (e.g., HCI): Miscellaneous.

INTRODUCTION
As a social networking service Twitter helps people to stay connected and share their status through short text messages [6]. With the rapid development all over the world, it has soon become new media for broadcasting and commercial applications. Although many ordinary users socialize with their friends, family, and co-workers in Twitter, famous figures and companies have adopted the media platform to maintain, improve, and promote their public relations. Thus, relation building and information retrieval becomes the two major motivations that drive people to use Twitter [8].

CSCW '13, February 23–27, 2013, San Antonio, Texas, USA.
Copyright 2013 ACM 978-1-4503-1331-5/13/02...$15.00.

Previous studies show that both relational and informational factors are important for all users in maintaining following relations in Twitter [10]. However, no research has distinguished the two: whether they have the impact at the same time or they exist in different user groups? To be more specific, do all users use Twitter for both relational and informational purposes or do various types of Twitter users have different motivations? This paper explores the different impacts of relational and informational factors on user relations in Twitter.

In Twitter, users can take two steps to establish and maintain their relations with others. When joining Twitter, users may subscribe to others' tweets, known as *follow*, and become followers of other users. Later on, users are free to unsubscribe and remove others from their following lists, known as *unfollow*. Follow and unfollow decisions are distinct and based on different information and reasons.

While a substantial body of studies has investigated the creation and maintenance of network ties, very little research focuses on the dissolution of network ties [13]. Unfollow on Twitter is therefore an excellent opportunity to help us understand the concerted effort to dissolve relations. Further, we focus on unfollow behavior because we believe unfollow decisions are more rational than follow decisions. Twitter's internal suggestions and the prevalence of social toolbars make follow actions as simple as one-click even without visiting Twitter's website. It is possible to follow many users quickly and therefore the follow decisions could be influenced by many external factors. In contrast, the decision of removing specific following relations is more consistent since it is likely based on previous interactions with the targets. Moreover, users' unfollow behavior indicates that they actually read tweets and manage their relations accordingly. The noises in the data due to inactive users can be reduced by studying unfollow.

Tie formation and dissolution are the two equally important factors that drive the structural evolution of a network but the process of tie dissolution is not well covered in the literature perhaps due to the lack of longitudinal data. Most ties in real life decay gradually so that it is very difficult to define the point of a "formal breakup" [11]. However, online social networking services such as Twitter provide temporal information of online relations. Through multiple snapshots of following relations in Twitter, we can detect the breakup of following ties and therefore study the unfollow behavior.

Kwak et al. [9] study unfollow behavior in a Korean Twitter community and find that reciprocity, informativeness, and the overlap of relationships are crucial in the decision to unfollow. This indicates that Twitter, as a whole, is both relational and informational. Kivran-Swaine et al. [7] analyze the structural properties that correlate with unfollow behavior using logistic regression. They conclude that reciprocity and transitivity is most influential to unfollow behavior. However their model does not incorporate the attributes of Twitter users.

Previous research performs logistic regression analysis on the entire user population and assumes that they all have the same behavioral pattern no matter which type of groups they belong to. This paper aims to provide more insightful ideas about user behavior within different user groups. Individuals' motivations of using Twitter may vary from group to group. Unfollow behavior in tightly knitted communities is not the same as that in superstar fan groups. Unfollowing a friend and unfollowing a celebrity should have different reasons. Thus, it is problematic to use the entire population to analyze heterogeneous users since some of them may be influential outliers and distort the results.

Using logistic regression, previous studies assume that unfollow activities are independent of each other. However, users' decisions are related to others' behavior in Twitter. Some users are likely to be unfollowed by many others for the same reasons such as spam. These unfollow decisions against the same user are correlated because of the influence of the common factor. Another example is reciprocal unfollow: when users are unfollowed by others they are likely to unfollow back in response.

This paper investigates different impacts of relational and informational factors on unfollow behavior in Twitter. We focus on ordinary users in tightly knitted user groups and analyze the dynamics of their unfollow relations using a longitudinal dataset with multiple snapshots of Twitter following relations.

We use SIENA, an actor-oriented model, to address the interdependency among unfollow relations and utilize the longitudinal samples [20]. Compared to logistic regression, SIENA assumes that users represented by nodes in a network play a crucial role in changing their ties to others according to their own attributes, others' attributes, and the relations among them. This method of social network analysis incorporates the interdependency of individual decisions through specific network structures. Moreover, SIENA is a dynamic model which uses multiple snapshots of a network at different time points and therefore captures temporal patterns among users, i.e. the tendency for users' unfollow and then re-follow actions in a period of time.

THEORIES AND HYPOTHESES

Different user groups are established based on different types of social bonds. Wittel [23] argues that "community entails stability, coherence, embeddedness and belonging. It involves strong and long-lasting ties, proximity and a common history or narrative of the collective." Communities consist of narrational relations, i.e. relation-oriented and more durable social bonds. However, if the relations in a network are primarily informational and based on ephemeral exchange of data, this network is considered as expressing network sociality rather than a community. Most computer-based virtual communities, working groups, and new media are typical examples of network sociality in which social bonds are created on an informational basis [23].

Previous studies on Twitter show that *reciprocity* [16], *social status* [2], *embeddedness* [21], *homophily* [12] and *informativeness* [8] play key roles in the process of tie formation. This reveals the social network and news media perspectives of Twitter [8]. However, it is not clear whether social networks and media are two *sides* of Twitter or two *parts* of Twitter. In other words, do users use Twitter for both relational and informational purposes at the same time or do various groups of Twitter users have different motivations?

The following paragraphs review five theories of relation building: reciprocity, social status, and embeddedness as relational motivations, and topic-homophily and informativeness as informational motivations. We adopt this set of theoretical frameworks of tie formation to characterize tie dissolution on Twitter. These five factors of relation building may not be applicable for all user groups in Twitter. In tightly knitted user groups studied in this paper, following relations reflect users' social ties and relational factors should play a dominant role in maintaining following ties.

Reciprocity

Reciprocity means behaving towards someone in the manner in which they behave toward you. Paying back a favor and returning a smile with a smile are examples of reciprocal behavior [16]. Previous studies show that reciprocity, as a source of social cohesion, creates stronger mutual ties and increases the stability and equilibrium of the society [3, 18]. In Twitter, mutually following relations enable two users to follow each other's updates, which increase their communication frequency and lead to more stable relations. From this perspective, we have:

Hypothesis 1: Users are less likely to unfollow those who follow them.

On the other hand, reciprocal exchange can also happen in negative interactions. In reciprocal relations, the breaking of one tie indicates decreasing social cohesion between the two. Therefore, it is very likely that the other party will unfollow back in return:

Hypothesis 2: Users are more likely to unfollow those who unfollow them.

Social Status

Status shows the influence and popularity of an individual in a community. According to preferential attachment theory [1], people tend to be better integrated with a social network by connecting to popular nodes in it.

In Twitter, users with many followers are often considered more "powerful." For example, some celebrities have millions of followers and their tweets diffuse much faster and wider in the network. Users with a higher status tend to spend more time on Twitter in order to retain their followers. Therefore other users are more likely to maintain the relations with them.

Hypothesis 3.1: Users with more followers are less likely to be unfollowed.

At the same time, high-status users usually are more serious in managing their relations and followees. They may have a higher tendency to terminate unnecessary relations.

Hypothesis 3.2: Users with more followers are more likely to unfollow.

Embeddedness

Embeddedness is the degree to which individuals are enmeshed in a social network. According to Granovetter [4], the structural embeddedness of a tie between two individuals can be measured by the overlap of social ties between them. In the context of collaboration networks, Newman et al. [14] show that more common neighbors lead to a higher probability of collaboration. Onnela et al. [15] also find a positive correlation between tie strength and the number of common friends.

Since more than 90% of following relations in our sample are mutual, the number of common followees can be used as an approximation of common friends. Therefore the users with more common followees are more embedded in the network.

Hypothesis 4: Users are less likely to unfollow those with whom they share more common followees.

Topic-Homophily

Homophily is the tendency of people to associate with similar people rather than dissimilar ones [11, 12]. By doing so, they avoid potential areas of conflict in the relationship [17].

Weng et al. [22] discover that Twitter users are more likely to follow those who are similar in the topics of their tweets. Kwak et al. [8] report that many respondents in their survey state that they unfollow people because they are not interested in the topics of their tweets, irrespective of the quality.

Many Twitter users include hashtags, that is, the keywords or topics prefixed by the # symbol, in their tweets to label and categorize tweets. In this paper, we use the number of common hashtags as a measure of topic-homophily between users. The more hashtags the two users share in common, the more similarity between them. If the motivation of Twitter following is informational, people are more likely to maintain the relations with similar others for data exchange.

Hypothesis 5: Users are less likely to unfollow those who are interested in similar topics.

Informativeness

Kwak et al. [8] explain the nature of interactions between Twitter users from an informativeness perspective. Informativeness can be measured by the frequency of interactions and data exchange between users in Twitter. Users express their interest in others through interactions such as reply, retweet, mention, and favorite. If people use Twitter relations for information exchange, they are more likely to keep following those who they interacted with.

Hypothesis 6: Users are less likely to unfollow those whom they have retweeted, mentioned, replied, or favorited.

DATA DESCRIPTION

Since cultural beliefs about relationships may vary, we focus on a set of users in the same cultural context. Based on a sample population of *697,628* Korean Twitter users, we took four snapshots of their following relations on June 25th 2010, September 3rd 2010, April 26th 2011, and September 19th 2011. We consider the dissolution of a tie between snapshots as an unfollow relation: a directed link from user A to user B if A followed B but stopped following at the next time point. In this way, the dissolution of following relations is modeled by the emergence of unfollow relations in an unfollow network. For example, there were almost seven hundred thousand users and 34 million following relations on June 25th, 2010, 73.6% of which are mutual. On April 26th, 2011, 858,702 following relations disappeared are used to construct an unfollow network. By comparing the four snapshots, we construct three unfollow networks at different time points: time 1 on September 3rd, 2010, time 2 on April 26th, 2011, and time 3 on September 19th, 2011.

The degree distribution of the first snapshot of following relations is illustrated in Figure 1. The picture shows that the nodes with degree 2,000 or less follow the power law distribution similar to the findings in Java et al. [6]. Users with more than 2,000 followers are mostly superstars and commercial users. Since the aim of this paper is to study user behavior in ordinary user groups, we exclude these users from our analysis.

Due to the heterogeneous structures in Twitter networks, we use one-wave snowball sampling to extract closely connected user groups [5]. The sampling method includes two steps: selecting a sample population based on a seed user and identifying unfollow relations for the sample. First we randomly select a user with 1,000 to 2,000 followers as the seed and find all his or her followers in the first snapshot. Based on their following relations, some outliers with extreme degrees are removed (about 2.5%). And then the unfollow relations among these users are extracted from the three unfollow networks. This approach decomposes the huge Twitter network into many small communities and focuses on the unfollow activities at a normalized level.

We generate 104 random snowball samples. Each sample is estimated independently using SIENA models and all results are combined in a macro-level between-community analysis by using meta-analysis [19].

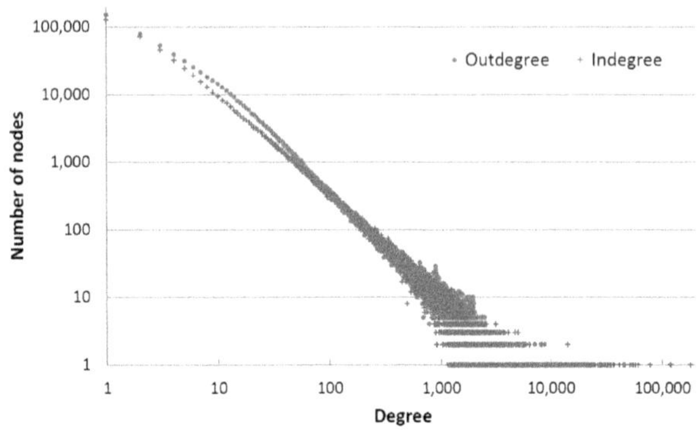

Figure 1. Indegree and outdegree distributions of follow networks on June 25th 2010.

In SIENA models, each user (i.e. sender) makes a decision to form or remove an unfollow relation to another user (i.e. receiver) at each time point based on sender's attributes, receiver's attributes, and the relations between them. Four network statistics are included as control variables to handle the interdependency among the unfollow relations.

MODEL AND RESULTS

As in logistic regressions, SIENA models characterize the impact of explanatory variables on the log odds of links. A positive coefficient in estimation indicates that a larger-valued corresponding explanatory variable leads to a higher tie probability, conditional on all other effects in the model. Table 1 summarizes our model results of the meta-analysis.

The results show that the reciprocity plays a critical role both based on following relations and unfollow relations. Mutual following ties have a negative and significant impact on unfollow relations. When two users follow each other mutually, the odds ratio of one unfollowing another is only 0.63, i.e. exp(-0.46), of those without mutual following relations. Mutual ties indeed make relations stronger and more cohesive. However, if one user in mutual following relations unfollows the other, the unfollowed user is very likely to unfollow back in return. The odds ratio of reciprocal unfollowing is 10.49 times, i.e. exp(2.81-0.46), of that of one-way unfollowing. Both Hypotheses 1 and 2 are supported.

As with following, unfollowing is directed with a sender who initiates the action and a receiver who is unfollowed. Receiver's number of followers has a negative impact on unfollow relations and sender's number of followers has a positive impact. High status users, who have more followers, are less likely to be unfollowed but more likely to unfollow others. Both Hypotheses 3.1 and 3.2 are supported.

Parameters	Estimate (S.E.)	
Relational factors:		
Mutual following ties	-0.46*(.038)	H1: Supported
Reciprocal unfollow	2.81*(.12)	H2: Supported
# Followers (receiver)	-0.05*(.004)	H3.1:Supported
# Followers (sender)	0.09*(.013)	H3.2:Supported
# Common followees	-0.13*(.049)	H4:Supported
Informational factors:		
# Common Hashtag	-0.01 (.008)	H5:Not supported
# Replies	0.004 (.002)	H6:Not supported
# Retweets	-0.009 (.005)	H6:Not supported
# Mentions	0.02 (.009)	H6:Not supported
# Favorites	0.01 (.006)	H6:Not supported
Unfollow network structures as control variables:		
Rate (time 1 to time 2)	32.55*(3.855)	
Rate (time 2 to time 3)	12.93*(1.290)	
Density	-1.97*(.234)	
In-star effect	0.31*(.023)	

Note: * indicates p<0.05, # followers and # common followees are in thousands.

Table 1. Summary of model results.

As predicted in Hypothesis 4, the number of *common followees* has a negative impact on unfollow relations. People following many common users are less likely to unfollow each other.

Contrary to Kwak et al. [8], the number of *common hashtags* has no significant impact. There is no evidence that the common interests reduce the likelihood of unfollowing. The topic-homophily effect proposed in Hypothesis 5 is not supported. Similarly, we do not find any significant impacts of *replies*, *retweets*, *mentions,* and *favorites* on unfollow behavior. Hypotheses 5 and 6 are not supported.

Other than the ten explanatory variables drawn from the hypotheses discussed above, *Rate 1*, *Rate 2*, *Density,* and *In-stars effect* are also included to control for the network structures during the Monte Carlo Markov Chain Simulation in SIENA [20]. Compared to logistic regression models, SIENA models consider important network structures when examining the impacts of explanatory variables. *Rate 1* (*Rate 2)* captures the base-line change rates of unfollow relations between time 1 and time 2 (time 2 and time 3). The positive Rate 1 indicates that more unfollow relations are observed at time 2 compared to time 1. *Density*, like the constant (or intercept) in logistic regressions, controls for the number of edges in the networks. The negative coefficient of *density* suggests that the unfollow networks are sparse and people are less likely to unfollow others randomly. In fact only 2.5% of following relations have dissolved in ten months. *In-star effect* controls for the in-degree distribution. The positive coefficient of *in-stars effect* indicates that users are more likely to be unfollowed by many others at the same time. This result demonstrates the interdependency among the unfollow relations.

DISCUSSION

Consistent with previous empirical research, our analysis indicates that relational factors have strong influences on unfollow decisions in Twitter. As predicted by Hypotheses 1-4, reciprocity, status, and embeddedness are key properties that affect user behavior of maintaining following relations. Twitter users seek cohesion and equilibrium when managing their relations and tend to keep reciprocal relations. Only 0.26% of mutual following ties disappeared within 10 months in our samples. This suggests that mutually following friends are unlikely to unfollow each other. High status users with more followers are more serious and active in posting tweets and organizing their following relations. Thus, they are less likely to be unfollowed and more likely to unfollow others. Users connected by many common friends (e.g. followees) are embedded in a strong network structure. These entangled social bonds contribute to the persistence of their relations.

However, the impact of information exchange is inconclusive. Hypotheses 5 and 6 are not supported and topic-homophily and informativeness has no significant impact on unfollow in our sample groups. Although the results contradict previous studies [10], this study demonstrates that by focusing on some parts of the Twitter network, the influences of relational and informational factors can be disentangles.

We believe that Twitter has many heterogeneous user groups and it is not appropriate to model different types of behavior using the entire population as a whole. Using the samples of tightly connected user groups, we show that the relations in these groups are more likely to reflect users' pre-existing social bonds in reality, which represent long lasting, narrative relations. Therefore, informational factors such as the content and frequency of their interactions may not affect the persistence of their following ties.

The measurement issue could be another potential reason for the lack of informational motivations in these groups. Since we did not perform semantic analysis on tweets, the measures used may not fully capture the informational factors of user behavior. For example, common hash tags indicate the overlapping of keywords users tweeted and retweeted but may not truly reveal their shared interests. Similarly, the numbers of replies, retweets, mentions, and favorites measure the frequency of interactions but not the information exchanged.

Our findings also suggest that users make decisions according to other's behavior in Twitter. Previous studies consider each unfollow action as independent and use logistic regressions to model the decisions. Using SIENA models, we show that unfollow decisions are correlated and the network structures have critical impacts: unfollow decisions are highly reciprocal and clustered. For example, the breakup of one tie in a pair of mutual following relations will lead to the breakup of the other. 8% of unfollow relations are in pairs (i.e. reciprocal to each other), which is significantly higher than random chances. Ignoring the interdependency of relations in the Twitter network may lead to wrong conclusions.

CONCLUSION

This paper studies the dissolution of following relations in Twitter. Based on the findings in tightly connected user groups, we show that only relational motivations have significant impacts on maintaining following relations but the impact of topic-homophily and informativeness is not significant. This suggests that relational and informational factors may not influence all users at the same time. It is likely that Twitter has many types of sub-groups with different motivations.

We use small and tightly connected user groups to explore the differences of relational and informational factors in tie dissolution and find relation-oriented groups in Twitter. For other types of users, such as followers of celebrities and interest groups, information oriented motivations such as common interests may have a dominant impact on unfollow behavior. Limited by the sampling methods and focal population, this study cannot reveal the reason why individual interactions such as replies, retweets, mentions, and favorites have no impact on maintaining following ties. Future research will evaluate and compare unfollow patterns in Twitter user groups of different types and sizes. The snowball sampling and meta-analysis used in this paper may provide an adequate approach to study the heterogeneous groups in a large network.

ACKNOWLEDGMENTS

This study was supported by the National Natural Science Foundation (Grant No. CNS-1010904, OCI-0904356, & IIS-0841583) and Army Research Lab (W911NF-09-02-0053), the National Natural Science Foundation of China (No. 90924020), MOE project of Humanities and Social Sciences (No. 11YJA630044), and the Innovation Foundation of BUAA for PhD Graduates. We thank Wonjae Lee and Sue Moon for preparing data sets and CSCW reviewers for providing helpful comments on previous versions.

REFERENCES

1. Barabasi, A. L., Albert, R., Emergence of Scaling in Random Networks, *Science* 286 (5439) (1999) 509-512.
2. Emerson, R. M., Power-Dependence Relations, *American Sociological Review 27* (1) (1962) 31-41.

3. Gouldner, A. W., The Norm of Reciprocity: A Preliminary Statement, *American Sociological Review* 25 (2) (1960) 161-178.
4. Granovetter, M., Economic Action and Social Structure: The Problem of Embeddedness, *Readings in Economic Sociology,* Blackwell Publishers Ltd, 2008, pp. 63-68.
5. Gruzd, A., Wellman, B., Takhteyev, Y., Imagining Twitter as an Imagined Community, *American Behavioral Scientist* 55 (10) (2011) 1294-1318.
6. Java, A., Song, X., Finin, T., Tseng, B., Why we twitter: understanding microblogging usage and communities, *Proceedings of the 9th WebKDD and 1st SNA-KDD 2007 workshop on Web mining and social network analysis*, 2007.
7. Kivran-Swaine, F., Govindan, P., Naaman, M., The impact of network structure on breaking ties in online social networks: unfollowing on twitter, in *Proc. CHI 2011*, ACM Press (2011), 1101-1104.
8. Kwak, H., Chun, H., Park, H., Moon, S., What is twitter, a social network or a news media, *in Proc. www 2010*, ACM Press(2010), 591-600.
9. Kwak, H., Chun, H., Moon, S., Fragile Online Relationship: A First Look at Unfollow Dynamics in Twitter, in *Proc. CHI 2011*, ACM Press (2011), 1091-1100.
10. Kwak, H., Moon, S., Lee, W., More of a receiver than a giver: Why do people unfollow in Twitter, in *Proc. ICWSM 2012*, AAAI Publications (2012).
11. Martin, J. L., Yeung, K.-T., Persistence of close personal ties over a 12-year period, *Social Networks* 28 (2006) 331-362.
12. McPherson, M., Smith-Lovin, L., Cook, J. M., Birds of a Feather: Homophily in Social Networks, *Annual Review of Sociology* 27 (2001) 415-444.
13. Monge, P., Contractor, N., *Theories of Communication Networks*, Oxford University Press, Oxford, UK, 2003.
14. Newman, M. E. J., Clustering and preferential attachment in growing networks, *Physical Review E* 64 (2001) 025102.
15. Onnela, J. P., Saramaki, J., Hyvonen, J., Szabo, G., Lazer, D., Kaski, K., Kertesz, J., Barabasi, A. L., Structure and tie strengths in mobile communication networks, in *PNAS* (2007), 7332-7336.
16. S.A., Golder., Yardi, S., Structural Predictors of Tie Formation in Twitter: Transitivity and Mutuality, in *IEEE Social Computing* (2010), 88-95.
17. Sherif, M., Superordinate Goals in the Reduction of Intergroup Conflict, *American Journal of Sociology* 63 (4) (1958) 349-356.
18. Simmel, Georg, *On individuality and social forms: Selected writings*, University of Chicago Press, 1971.
19. Snijders, T. A. B., Baerveldt, C., A multilevel network study of the effects of delinquent behavior on friendship evolution, *The Journal of Mathematical Sociology* 27 (2-3) (2003) 123-151.
20. Snijders, T. A. B., van de Bunt, G. G., Steglich, C. E. G., Introduction to stochastic actor-based models for network dynamics, *Social Networks* 32 (1) (2010) 44-60.
21. Wasserman, S. a. F., K., *Social network analysis: Methods and applicaitons*, Cambridge University Press, 1994.
22. Weng, J., Lim, E.-P., Jiang, J., He, Q., TwitterRank: finding topic-sensitive influential twitterers, in *Proc. WSDM 2010*, ACM Press (2010), 261-270.
23. Wittel, A., Toward a Network Sociality, *Theory, Culture & Society* 18 (6) (2001) 51-76.

What's Congress Doing on Twitter?

Libby Hemphill, Jahna Otterbacher, and Matthew A. Shapiro
Illinois Institute of Technology
3301 S Dearborn St, Chicago IL, 60616
{libby.hemphill, jahna.otterbacher, mshapir2}@iit.edu

ABSTRACT
As Twitter becomes a more common means for officials to communicate with their constituents, it becomes more important that we understand how officials use these communication tools. Using data from 380 members of Congress' Twitter activity during the winter of 2012, we find that officials frequently use Twitter to advertise their political positions and to provide information but rarely to request political action from their constituents or to recognize the good work of others. We highlight a number of differences in communication frequency between men and women, Senators and Representatives, Republicans and Democrats. We provide groundwork for future research examining the behavior of public officials online and testing the predictive power of officials' social media behavior.

CATEGORIES AND SUBJECT DESCRIPTORS
K.4.1 [**Computers and Society**]: Public Policy Issues

KEYWORDS
Congress; Twitter; social media; political communication; automated classification

INTRODUCTION
As of March 2012, members of the U.S. House of Representatives had 407 active, verifiable Twitter accounts, while members of the U.S. Senate had 97. Those 504 accounts, and the thousands more who respond to them, generate thousands of tweets per day. Given this level of activity, it's natural to ask, what are they doing on Twitter? And how does their tweeting matter?

Twitter has garnered public attention for its use in a number of socio-political events such as social demonstrations [16], presidential debates [14, 48], and campaigning [37]. Earlier studies of political communication in social media explored the content of tweets from Congress [20], connections among political blogs [1], and political position among candidates for public office [37]. Because Twitter is relatively new, the landscape of Congressional communication (compared to print media and the Congressional Record, for instance) has only recently become mature enough to study. Few systematic studies of how public officials use this new method of communicating with the public exist, and we contribute to that body of literature by providing detailed understanding of how public officials use social media. We also contribute to literature on social media- research methods by demonstrating successful approaches to automatic classification of social media content.

Our findings suggest that officials frequently use Twitter to advertise their political positions and to provide information but rarely to request political action from their constituents or to recognize the good work of others. Rules governing public officials' social media and web presences are evolving[1], and our analysis reveals the conventions developing through officials' regular use of Twitter.

RELATED LITERATURE
Most of the existing research on Congress's use of internet and social media communication focuses on elections and campaigning [15, 21, 24, 47, 50, 54]. Candidates' websites, for instance, have received a great deal of attention, as they provide information about the candidate and his or her positions and often encourage individuals to either volunteer or donate to the campaign [50]. While managing their own websites provides a great deal of freedom for candidates, the candidates limit the number of issues they present there, and they engage their opponents on only a few issues most salient to the public [15]. Incumbents provide more information about their policy positions than their opponents, and all candidates tend to engage in "position taking" more often than "issue dialogue" [54].

Together, these findings suggest that candidates use their websites to promote themselves rather than to engage their opponents or their constituents. Their disagreements with opponents are implicit in these "position taking" statements where they outline their own views without referencing their opponents. These patterns of engagement with opponents and interactions with constituents represent departures from offline political communication [54].

---

[1] For instance, see the Committee on House Administration's Regulations governing official Social Media and Secondary web site content: http://democrats.cha.house.gov/official-social-media-and-secondary-web-sites

Research on online political communication dramatically increased following the 2004 elections in the U.S., when candidates' websites received a great deal of attention. Since then, social media outlets such as Twitter and Facebook have received more attention from politicians, voters, and researchers in both the U.S. and abroad. Recent examinations of Twitter's role in recent elections in Brazil [18] and Iran [16], for instance, found that the impact in Iran's elections remains unclear [16], while a strong social media presence provided an edge for candidates in Brazil's lower house of Congress [18].

Beyond election campaigns, researchers are beginning to examine the role of social media in every day communication [32] and in policy debates [28, 33]. Recent results indicate that Korean officials use Twitter to communicate with one another rather than with their constituents [29], and we found similar patterns of communication among U.S. officials.

Much of the popular press coverage of social media use for political communication centers around transparency and increasing officials' accountability [45, 49] or the fleeting nature of social media content [17]. Officials' strategies for employing social media are evolving, but it's becoming clear that allowing MOCs to communicate directly with their constituents impacts political parties' efforts to present a consistent brand [23].

Though candidates' websites are now well understood, existing literature does not adequately explain how the U.S. Congress is using Twitter, whether that use differs from their approaches to more permanent communication platforms like print media, or whether Congress' Twitter use marks an increase in responsiveness or transparency. Golbeck and colleagues [20] provided the first overview of MOCs' Twitter use, finding that Congress used Twitter mostly to distribute information, especially to link to other sources such as their blogs. The behaviors Golbeck and colleagues identified, though, did not suggest that Congress was providing increased government transparency or responsiveness through their use.

Austin [2] proposed that communication between humans is often much more than a means to transfer information from a speaker to a hearer. We are often trying to achieve a particular goal when we speak, and these underlying actions are referred to as being speech acts [3]. Similarly, a question of particular interest in our work is what an official achieves (or tries to achieve) when he or she posts a given tweet. In other words, we can approach the analysis of officials' tweets using the concept of the speech act.

We provide an expanded and detailed account of the speech acts members of Congress (MOCs) make via Twitter and discuss the implications of their social media behavior for online political engagement more broadly.

METHODS

Data Collection

We first identified verifiable Twitter accounts for members of Congress, then collected their tweets for a period of time and qualitatively coded a subset of tweets for actions that officials performed through posting the tweet. Using the Twitter Database Server [22] and Twitter-collectors [25], we gathered three sets of tweets between August 2011 and February 2012. First, we gathered a subset of 791 total tweets from the top 10 and bottom 10 users in each of three categories: tweets, followers, and friends. We used that subset of extreme users' tweets to gather a diverse set of tweets accomplishing a number of different actions in order to develop our coding scheme for "Action" (described in detail in the next section). We expected behaviors among the most and least active users to differ enough to provide a more diverse sample than a simple random sampling method could guarantee.

Then, we gathered another subset of 526 tweets from all active public officials with which to check our coding scheme and to train the automated classifier. Once we developed a robust classifier, we gathered 30,373 original tweets posted by 380 elected Congressmen between December 22, 2011 and February 29, 2012. This analysis is part of an ongoing project to examine the relationships among Twitter conversations and offline political behavior, and only those officials who mentioned or were mentioned by another official during the data collection period are included in this last dataset. The 30,373 tweets include all tweets, except explicit retweets, posted by those 380 officials who mentioned or were mentioned by others during that time period.

Coding for Action

When manually coding the subset of 791 tweets described above, we excluded retweets and duplicate tweets. We used three rounds of inductive coding to develop a robust coding scheme for the action taken in tweets. The resulting scheme used six codes – narrating, positioning, directing to information, requesting action, giving thanks, and other – to categorize the kind of action taken in a tweet. Codes were not mutually exclusive, meaning a tweet could be coded as exhibiting more than one action. For example, "With massive debt, why are taxpayers funding wine tasting? Washington's spending addiction continues http://t.co/2QaYJmo," a tweet from Jim DeMint, was coded as both positioning and directing to information. It's clear that DeMint disagrees with this use of public funds (i.e., positioning), and he also suggests that his followers examine the article at the link provided for more information. Cohen's kappa [13] scores for each code show reliable (>= 0.70) inter-coder agreement [34]. The code definitions, examples, and kappas are reported in Table 1. Positioning and directing to information were by far the most common actions exhibited on Twitter.

Code	Definition	Example	Cohen's kappa	N (%)
Narrating	Telling a story about their day, describing activities	"headed up to the Fox News camera for an interview" (Rep. Ron Paul, R-TX)	0.83	2,069 (7%)
Positioning	Situating one's self in relation to another politician or political issue, may be implied rather than explicit	"A9: Theoretically, not realistically. HC spending is growing 4x inflation and driving our debt. Let's tackle the real threat. #ryanttv" (Rep. Paul Ryan, R-WI)	0.87	6,728 (22%)
Directing to information	Pointing to a resource URL, telling you where you can get more info	"Harkin Announces More Than $300,000 for Housing in Tama County http://1.usa.gov/lf6Aem" (Sen. Tom Harkin, D-IA)	0.70	12,468 (41%)
Requesting action	Explicitly telling followers to go do something online or in person (not just visiting a link but asking them to do something like sign a petition, apply, vote) - look for action verbs	"RSVP to my Immigration Forum with Rep. Luis Gutierrez this Saturday in Brooklyn http://t.co/qTcWugs" (Rep. Yvette Clark, D-NY)	0.70	299 (1%)
Thanking	Says nice things about or thanks someone else, e.g. congratulations, compliments	"@rmartindc Thanks. MoC's handwriting is probably on par with M.D.'s. Glad I could make your job easier." (Rep. John Shimkus, R-IL)	0.90	667 (2%)
Other	Doesn't fit in any other Action category, or one can't tell what they're doing	"@jfor441 Will do!" (Rep. Jason Chaffetz, R-UT)	N/A	N/A

Note. Cohen's kappa values refer to the reliability of hand-coded tweets used to train the classifier. N (%) reports the output of the automatic classifier.

Table 1. Definitions, Examples, Reliability, and Distribution of Qualitative Action Codes

Earlier work about how Congress users Twitter [20] uses a similar coding scheme – the Golbeck scheme – but provides only percent agreement measures of reliability. Percent agreement is an overly liberal measure of inter-coder reliability because it does not account for chance agreement [38]. We originally tried to apply their coding scheme to our larger dataset but were unable to reach acceptable agreement using Cohen's kappa scores. The main problem in applying the Golbeck scheme is the difficulty in determining which tweets do *not* fall in their information category. We updated Golbeck's [20] scheme in a number of important ways:

- We allowed tweets to fall into multiple categories rather than in mutually exclusive categories. We noticed that many tweets were explicitly accomplishing more than one communication activity (e.g., pointing to a resource and staking a political position). Such multi-purpose tweeting is not uncommon [35]. Though posts are limited to 140 characters, Twitter users are remarkably effective at accomplishing multiple communication activities within a single tweet.
- We distinguished "positioning" from "information" in order to compare communication on Twitter with communication elsewhere, such as websites [54] because we recognize the differences between providing opinions and publicizing resources.
- We refined the "requesting action" category to refer to tweets that demanded effortful activities such as participating in community events rather than low-effort activities such as reading a statement. In other words, we exclude slacktivism activities from "requested actions" when coding tweets. Slacktivism, a shortening of "slacker activism", is used to describe activities that require little effort but still provide activists with a sense of accomplishment or engagement [16]. In our schema, only "active" actions are included in requesting action, allowing us to examine how often public officials encourage their followers to actively engage in the political process or get involved in a social issue.

- We ignored questions of audience (Golbeck's "communication" codes) because we could not reach agreement on the audiences implied in such short posts.

Automated Classification

We used the second manually labeled dataset of 526 tweets mentioned in Section 3.1 to reevaluate our coding scheme and to train binary classifiers for each of the following five action codes: narrative, positioning, provide information, request action, and thanks. We did not train classifiers for the code "other," since tweets that are not assigned to one of the other five codes are automatically labeled as "other."

To train and evaluate our classifiers, we used MALLET (Machine Learning for LanguagE Toolkit) [39] and experimented with three supervised learning trainers in order to develop three classifiers: naïve Bayes, decision tree, and maximum entropy. In each case, the words appearing in a tweet are its features, and the classifier is a function that maps the features onto the output classes (i.e., action codes). In other words, we infer the intended action or speech act of the tweeter using only the word frequencies in the respective tweet. For each classifier, we experimented with two representations of the text of the tweets: the raw text and the text with stop words removed. For each classifier, we used MALLET's default English stop words.

The maximum entropy classifier performed best. Maximum entropy models begin with the assumption that uniform distributions are preferred (i.e., assume a 50/50 chance that a tweet is "narrative" or not). They use training data to learn constraints to be applied to this distribution. Nigam and colleagues report that in many cases, maximum entropy outperforms naïve Bayes, however, it does have a tendency toward overfitting in cases where data is sparse (i.e., when there are only few positive examples of a tweet of a given class). The accuracy statistics for our classifier's performance with the training data of 526 tweets are reported in Table 3.

We used supervised trainers, which means that we used a set of tweets labeled for the action code we wanted to predict. The algorithm was then applied to a test set of tweets, and the predicted classification labels were compared to the (manually created) truth data. We conducted a 10-fold cross-validation procedure for each of the six classifiers. For each of 10 iterations, 0.90 of the tweets are randomly assigned to the training set, and 0.10

Classifier	Narr	Posit	Info	ReqAc	Thank
MaxEnt	0.83 -0.05	0.71 -0.06	0.91 -0.03	0.91 -0.03	0.95 -0.03
No stop words	0.80 -0.07	0.71 -0.07	0.91 -0.04	0.91 -0.03	0.93 -0.04

Table 3. Mean (s.d.) Classification Accuracy on Test Data Using 10-fold Cross-validation Procedure

	N	Median	S.D.	Range
Overall	35,361	1,090	2,134	18-8,893
By Females	5,535	760	873	60-3,677
By Males	29,826	1,155	2,262	18-8,893
By Republicans	21,253	1,228	2,544	51-8,893
By Democrats	13,648	825	799	18-3,005
By Independents	460	3,372	0	3,372
By Representatives	28,834	1,055	2,266	18-8,893
By Senators	6,527	1,219	1.396	165-5,927

Table 2. Frequencies of tweets by gender, party, and chamber

of the tweets to the test set. We observed that stop word removal did not help improve performance of the classifiers. This seems to suggest that with texts this short, how tweeters use non-content, functional words may contain useful information.

RESULTS

General Twitter behavior

Frequency of tweeting is not normally distributed among members of Congress or within gender, chamber, or party groups (see Table 2). We included all group dummy variables (male, Republican, and Senate) and a "days in office" variable in regression analyses to compare frequency of tweets among groups (see Table 4). Our results show significant main effects for all four variables. Male, Republican, Representative and longer tenure predict more tweeting. Clearly there are other factors that influence frequency of tweets; even when including all four variables, the model explains only 10% of the variance.

Speech acts on Twitter

Our analysis of the content of tweets, (see Table 1), shows that *providing information* is the most common action accomplished in officials' tweets (41%), followed by *positioning* (22%), *narrative* (7%), *thanking* (2%), and *requesting action* (1%).

Many tweets fell into more than one category. For instance, "Unemployment rate is 9.1%. Democrats promised 'stimulus' spending binge would keep it below 8% http://j.mp/pnalhs #wherearethejobs" both positioned the author against the stimulus spending by pointing out a perceived failure and provided additional information by pointing to a URL with more information. Similarly, "I am on live with Drew Skaggs on WLGC talking about the #debtlimit and our plan to cut spending. Listen in: http://goo.gl/b62Wi" narrated the author's activities (as a guest on a radio show), his position on economic policy (cutting spending) and provided additional information by including a URL.

	Model 1	Model 2	Model 3	Model 4
Male	943.309***	597.863***	593.203***	585.361***
	(30.83)	(30.67)	(30.68)	(30.46)
Republican		1110.179***	1105.994***	1201.930***
		(22.76)	(22.78)	(22.99)
Senate			-113.932***	-134.147***
			(28.00)	(27.81)
Days in Office				0.077***
				(0.00)
Constant	1080.438***	704.562***	732.038***	427.333***
	(28.31)	(28.47)	(29.25)	(31.92)
r2	0.026	0.087	0.088	0.101
*** p<0.001				

Table 4. Comparing tweeting frequency across groups

We make three additional observations about the overlaps of Twitter action. First, tweets that provide information often link to news articles, mainly statistics or a world event:

- This @WashingtonPost story is very interesting if true. Iranian lawmaker says Obama proposed talks... http://t.co/8n6YbZmI (Rep. Paul Gosar, R-AZ)
- The Bureau of Labor Statistics reports today that the US economy added 200,000 jobs in Dec. Unemployment falls to 8.5%. http://t.co/WHZO7RaR (Rep. Andre Carson, D-IN)

Second, officials often used narrative tweets to mention a TV or Radio appearance:

- I'm talking to CNN's @randikayecnn at 1:15pm ET and MSNBC's @mitchellreports at 1:45pm ET"please tune in! #nhprimary #FITN (Rep. Debbie Wasserman Schultz, D-FL)

Third, many of the position tweets had a very partisan tone, placing blame or accusing the other party or president:

- President Obama is again bypassing Congress-this time to give amnesty to an untold number of illegal immigrants- http://t.co/KhqoQBCQ (Rep. Walter Jones, R-NC)
- House Republicans refused to let me speak on House floor today. GOP needs to return to work on #payrolltaxcut. Video: http://t.co/YwZFxwWb (Rep. Jim Moran, D-VA)

Because we are specifically examining politicians, we distinguish between tweets about political positions and tweets about general information. Making this distinction between informative tweets and positioning tweets likely accounts for the marked decline in the proportion of information tweets we observed compared to Golbeck's earlier reports [20].

DISCUSSION

Comparing behavior among groups

Gender, Party, Chamber, and Tenure

Our results indicate that a member's gender, party affiliation, chamber, and tenure in Congress all have strong effects on his/her frequency of tweeting. We see large variance in tweeting frequency in all groups, though (see Table 2). Women in Congress are often cast as quite distinct from men in Congress [e.g., 3,40], but research on members' web sites revealed that these stereotypes did not hold. Rather, our findings confirm existing research that women can be just as explicit about their engagement in power struggles and in the diversity of issues about which they care [44]. Our current analysis does not allow us to explore whether women engage in different communication actions than men, but we did identify a significant difference in the volume of their communication – in Congress, women are decidedly less active on Twitter than are men. Instead,

As social media becomes an increasingly significant source of political news, the dominance of male voices becomes more problematic. Our results suggest that Republicans, Representatives, and men dominate most of the conversation, and future work will examine the implications of these imbalances.

Illustrative example tweeters

We noticed differences between the distributions of actions in our training sample and the larger sample, most notably decreases in narrating and positioning. We expect that the users whose tweets we used to develop our coding scheme, those most and least active on Twitter, differ in their actions from other users. It's possible that users around the median for participation are using Twitter more conversationally. However, when we compare prolific and minimally active tweeters[2], we see similar patterns of action. Table 5 and Figure 1[3] show that among minimally active tweeters (Reps. Alexander and Biggert), providing information remains the most common action, followed by positioning. Prolific tweeters (Reps. Issa and Ross) exhibit similar patterns, yet moderately active tweeters' (Reps. Cravaack and Ros-Lehtinen) patterns are different. Rep. Cravaack accomplished positioning more often than providing informatiWhile Rep. Ros-Lehtinen shows an even greater contrast between the rates of positioning and providing information: Rep. Cravaack tweeted positions only slightly more often than information. We do not claim to generalize statistically from this sample of six, rather we leverage these users to illustrate some of the differences suggested by our large-scale analysis.

Tweet Content

Our content analysis results (summarized in the last column of Table 1) differ somewhat from earlier results on the content of Congress's tweets [20, 53]: we found a lower proportion of information tweets and identified a specific type of politically charged tweet action. Some of the differences between earlier results and ours can be explained by differences in coding schemes. Though the absolute proportions of Congress's activities on Twitter have changed over time, the relative proportions have not. For instance, though earlier work predicted that as adoption increased, behaviors would change [19], we confirmed that providing information is the most common action, followed by policy or position tweets.

Public officials use Twitter in campaigning [21, 53, 54] and rely on web-based media for a variety of communication activities including "issue dialogue" and "position taking" [54]. Distinguishing between positioning and providing information allows us to compare the tweets to other forms of communication such as candidate websites. We found that, even though they were not engaged in explicit public campaigning activities during our study period, members of Congress often used Twitter to publicly position themselves. According to Xenos and Foot [54], this kind of public position, a hallmark of traditional offline campaigning, is common in campaign websites. Our results indicate that position taking is common on Twitter as well, suggesting that candidates are using Twitter to implicitly campaign throughout their tenure. While perhaps not surprising, this finding is interesting because it indicates that public officials do not alter their communication strategies between media but rather use a common strategy across media (e.g., websites, speeches, Twitter). Given the remarkable differences between the audience, length of content, frequency of updates, and reach among various media, a single strategy for all is surprising.

Official	Tweets	Followers	Friends
Rep. Rodney Alexander (R-LA)	18	1319	171
Rep. Judy Biggert (R-IL)	26	5514	224
Rep. Chip Cravaack (R-MN)	253	2377	1246
Rep. Ileana Ros-Lehtinen (R-FL)	312	9235	10
Rep. Dennis Ross (R-FL)	976	3648	1114
Rep. Darrell Issa (R-CA)	1208	36,819	22,524

Table 5 Numbers of Tweets, Followers, and Friends for Examples of Minimally Active, Moderately Active and Prolific Tweeters

What effects do current events have on Congress's Twitter behavior?

A number of events that occurred during our sample's timeframe may have impacted our results. During part of

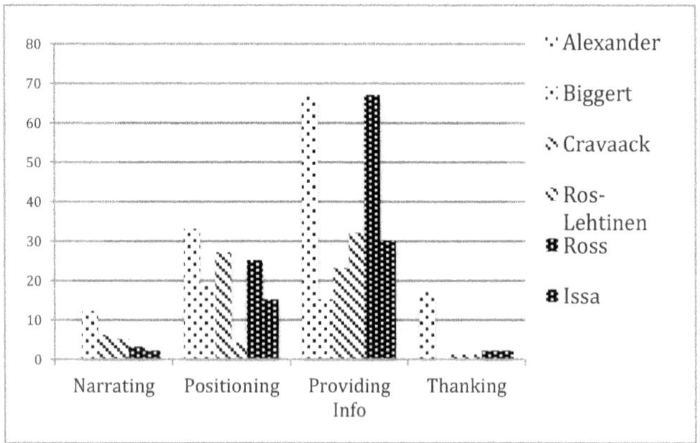

Figure 1. Comparing actions between prolific and minimally active tweeters. Tweeters are arranged left to right from least active to most active. The Y-axis indicates the percentage of a users' tweets that were assigned a given action by the automatic classifier. Users are grouped into three pairs – minimally active, moderately active, and prolific – indicated by the fill patterns within the bars.

[2] In an effort to minimize variability among our example tweeters, we use only Republican members of the House in this section.

[3] We excluded requesting action in Figure 1 because none of these six example users tweeted requesting action.

this period, Congress was in winter recess, and some research suggests they behave quite differently when not in session [19]. Other events that happened between December 2011 and February 2012 and may have influenced what Congress tweeted about include budget debates, SOPA and PIPA, the first caucuses and primaries, and Gabrielle Giffords stepping down.

Some officials even took to Twitter to talk about Twitter itself during the SOPA and PIPA debates. These conversations provided a number of interesting examples of positioning tweets, and the wide public debate about these bills may have produced more positioning tweets than we would have seen in another sample. For instance, Rep. Joe Walsh (R – IL) voiced his opposition: "Thank God twitter isn't blocked today so I can tell you that I refuse to vote for #SOPA. #uncensored #StopSOPA". Rep. Lynn Westmoreland (R – GA) and Rep. Louise Slaughter (D – NY), respectively, voiced theirs as well and acknowledged hearing from their constituents: "Getting lots of calls on #SOPA and #PIPA. I oppose both bills because of their unintended consequences. http://t.co/ngjLiMQp" and "To clarify, I oppose both #SOPA and #PIPA. The many tweets you've sent me today are the best proof that these bills should be stopped". While on the side that supported the legislation, Rep. Darrell Issa (R – CA) posted "Got some great news for you...we've just released #PIPA in the Madison platform at http://t.co/lkiF4nOB: http://t.co/Rteeze7L #SOPA #OPEN."

What isn't Congress doing on Twitter?

What Congress is *not* doing via social media is also interesting. For example, very few tweets requested action. Our results indicate that public officials rarely (only 352 of 30,373 tweets) request that their followers actively engage. Earlier research suggests great promise for social media in increasing civic engagement [55], but our results suggest it is as best underutilized and at worst not used at all.

It seems Congress uses social media as a broadcast forum rather than as an engagement tool. Much of the conversation about the role of social media in political communication revolves around transparency [6–8, 30] and civic engagement [11, 55], but we saw no evidence of Congress using Twitter to increase either transparency or engagement. Of course, the scale of Twitter activity among officials implicitly creates transparency, especially when officials reveal their daily activities through narrating (e.g., "The H.R. 3630 Conference Committee just concluded our first meeting. Read my opening remarks here: http://t.co/ByceoXM1" [Rep. Tom Price, R – GA]) or providing information about floor ("On my way to the House Floor to discuss the rise in poverty in America. We need #jobs. Pass HR 3638 - Restore American Dream for 99% Act" [Rep. Barbara Lee, D – CA]) and media appearances ("I'll be discussing the dangers of Rx drug abuse on CNN w/ @Soledad_OBrien tomorrow at 8 a.m. EST. I hope you'll tune in." [Rep. Mary Bono Mack, R - CA). Officials often point their followers to results of votes and committee meetings ("Here's the roll call for the Call of the House, also known as the quorum call. Quorum calls officially are used... http://t.co/XsEpESjN" - [Rep. Justin Amash, R – MI]), but the potential to increase transparency via social media remains.

We also see relatively few narrative tweets. Of course, the rules governing how Congress may use social media[4] and websites limit the kinds of communication they attempt, and so the prevalence of providing information is not surprising. Similarly, the lack of narrative among public officials' may be because rules prohibit communications that are not germane to the official and representational duties. However, just as most Twitter users do, even members of Congress use Twitter to share mundane details of their activities: "I just got up to 663 in #DoodleJump!!! Beat that!" (Sen. John McCain, R - AZ).

FUTURE WORK

Our results suggest a number of interesting avenues for future work. For instance, we are not able to discuss what positions public officials take or whether they discuss only a few key issues online. Additionally, the limited time of our data collection prevented us from making comparisons longitudinally or between campaign season and regular, off-season governance.

Our data will allow us to explore relationships among the various kinds of measurable activities. For instance, we will be able to determine whether the level of twitter activity influences the kinds of actions officials accomplish – e.g., are frequent tweeters more likely to use positioning statements while infrequent tweets mainly provide information? As our examples show, different distributions of action appear across different levels of activity, and this point must be addressed in future analyses.

Our results raise questions about the relationship between pro-social actions such as thanking and potentially alienating actions such as positioning. Some previous research has examined the concepts of "civility" and "politeness" in online political discussions [40, 43, 46], and future work should examine officials' language more closely in order to better understand the relationship between *language* and *behavior*. Specifically, we predict that pro-social language is a good predictor of political centrism, and we intend to include this measure in later regressions to test the predictive power of a civility scale. Those regressions will be the main focus of our next stage of research during which we will test the predictive power of social media behavior, namely that an official's social media behavior can be used to predict his offline behavior such as voting and communication strategy. In this way, we can examine theories of political communication related to agenda setting [41], market segmentation of political

[4] http://democrats.cha.house.gov/official-social-media-and-secondary-web-sites

messages [42], and shifting communication vehicles over time [9, 10, 31]. Looking even farther ahead, this can be the basis for later tests of motivated reasoning by examining citizens who follow high-tweeting members of Congress.

We excluded retweets from our automated results because they present unique coding challenges. Retweets are repeated, unoriginal content, and the lack of variance makes it difficult to compare them to original content. For instance, we cannot assume that a retweet constitutes an endorsement of the original tweet. In fact, some officials make it clear that not all retweets are endorsements by including a disclaimer in their Twitter profiles. Officials' retweeting and modified tweeting behaviors remain to be examined in order to determine officials' intentions when reusing others' content.

The social activity trail officials leave by using Twitter is also ripe for study. For instance, officials' conversation networks may reveal their connections with other officials, appointees, the public, lobbyists, etc. Using social network analysis to examine Twitter relationships and behaviors is increasingly common [4, 12, 51, 52], and our future work will explore public officials' social media networks.

CONCLUSION

As Twitter becomes a more common means for officials to communicate with their constituents, it becomes more important that we understand just how that communication relates to other political activities and what kinds of communication are accomplished via social media. Our findings indicate that officials frequently use Twitter to advertise their political positions and to provide information but rarely to request political action from their constituents or to recognize the good work of others. Congress appears to use Twitter as yet another broadcast mechanism rather than as a way to engage in dialogue with the public or as a "call to action" to organize constituents. Though Twitter and its use are often cast as "social computing," among Congress, the "social" is less pronounced than we expected.

Future work will examine the relationships between the networks created through Twitter activity and political coalitions, and among the language used and the governing behaviors. 2012 offers a unique opportunity to examine campaigning behavior in order to compare campaign communication and social interaction with everyday governance. Ours is not the first study to examine Twitter use by the U.S. Congress, but we do offer an essential update based on a larger, more inclusive dataset, robust coding scheme, and comparisons among groups of MOCs. We have provided additional groundwork for future research examining the behavior of public officials online and its impacts on the relationship between public officials and their constituencies.

ACKNOWLEDGEMENTS

This material is based on work supported by the Illinois Institute of Technology (IIT) Social Networks Research Group and the IIT Graduate College.

REFERENCES

1. Adamic, L.A. and Glance, N. 2005. The political blogosphere and the 2004 U.S. election: Divided they blog. *Proc. LinkKDD '05*, 36–43.
2. Austin, J.L. 1962. *How to do things with words.* Oxford University Press.
3. Bach, K. 1998. Speech acts. *Routledge Encyclopedia of Philosophy*. E. Craig, ed. Routledge.
4. Bakshy, E. et al. 2011. Everyone's an influencer: Quantifying influence on Twitter. *Proc. WSDM '11,* 65–74.
5. Berkman, M.B. and O'Connor, R.E. 1993. Do Women Legislators Matter?: Female Legislators and State Abortion Policy. *American Politics Research*. 21, 1, 102–124.
6. Bertot, J. 2010. Using ICTs to create a culture of transparency: E-government and social media as openness and anti-corruption tools for societies. *Government Information Quarterly*. 27, 3, 264–271.
7. Bertot, J. and Jaeger, P. 2010. Social media technology and government transparency. *Computer*. 43, 11, 53–59.
8. Bertot, J.C. et al. 2010. Crowd-sourcing transparency: ICTs, social media, and government transparency initiatives. *Proceedings of the 11th Annual International Digital Government Research Conference on Public Administration Online: Challenges and Opportunities*.
9. Bimber, B. 2003. *Information and American democracy: Technology in the evolution of political power*. Cambridge University Press.
10. Blumler, J.G. and Kavanagh, D. 1999. The Third Age of political communication: influences and features. *Political Communication*. 16, 3, 209–230.
11. Campbell, S.W. and Kwak, N. 2011. Political involvement in "mobilized" society: The interactive relationships among mobile communication, network characteristics, and political participation. *Journal of Communication*. 61, 6, 1005–1024.
12. Cha, M. et al. 2010. Measuring user influence in twitter: The million follower fallacy. *Proc. ICWSM '10,* 10–17.
13. Cohen, J. 1960. A coefficient of agreement for nominal scales. *Educational and Psychological Measurement*. 20, 1, 37–46.
14. Diakopoulos, N. and Shamma, D. 2010. Characterizing debate performance via aggregated Twitter sentiment. *Proc. CHI '10*, 1195-1198.
15. Druckman, J.N. et al. 2010. Issue engagement on congressional candidate web sites, 2002—2006. *Social Science Computer Review*. 28, 1, 3–23.
16. Gaffney, D. 2010. #iranElection: Quantifying online activism. *Proc. WebSci10*.

17. Garber, M. 2012. A year after the Egyptian revolution, 10% of its social media documentation is already gone. *The Atlantic*.
18. Gilmore, J. 2012. Ditching the pack: Digital media in the 2010 Brazilian congressional campaigns. *New Media & Society*. 14, 4, 617–633.
19. Glassman, M.E. et al. 2009. Social networking and constituent communication: Member use of Twitter during a two-week period in the 111th Congress (Report No. R40823).
20. Golbeck, J. et al. 2010. Twitter use by the U.S. Congress. *Journal of the American Society for Information Science and Technology*. 61, 8, 1612–1621.
21. Graf, J. 2008. New media-The cutting edge of campaign communications. *Campaigns on the Cutting Edge*. R. Semiatin, ed. CQ Press. 48–68.
22. Green, A. 2011. Twitter database server (Beta 0.10), http://140dev.com/free-twitter-api-source-code-library/twitter-database-server/.
23. Groeling, T. 2010. *When Politicians Attack: Party Cohesion in the Media*. Cambridge University Press.
24. Gulati, G.J. and Williams, C.B. 2007. Closing the gap, raising the bar: Candidate web site communication in the 2006 campaigns for congress. *Social Science Computer Review*. 25, 4, 443–465.
25. Hemphill, L. 2011. Twitter-collectors (144e2f0f6), https://github.com/casmlab/Twitter-collectors.
26. Hemphill, L. and Otterbacher, J. 2012. Learning the lingo? Gender, prestige and linguistic adaptation in review communities. *Proc. CSCW '12,* 305-314.
27. Herring, S.C. 2003. Gender and power in online communication. *The Handbook of Language and Gender*. J. Holmes and M. Meyerhoff, eds. Blackwell Publishers. 202–228.
28. Howard, P.N. 2005. *New media campaigns and the managed citizen*. Cambridge University Press.
29. Hsu, C. and Park, H.W. 2012. Mapping online social networks of Korean politicians. *Government Information Quarterly*. 29, 2, 169–181.
30. Jaeger, P.T. and Bertot, J.C. 2010. Transparency and technological change: Ensuring equal and sustained public access to government information. *Government Information Quarterly*. 27, 4, 371–376.
31. Jenkins, H. 2006. *Convergence culture*. New York University Press.
32. Kim, M. and Park, H.W. 2012. Measuring Twitter-based political participation and deliberation in the South Korean context by using social network and Triple Helix indicators. *Scientometrics*. 90, 1, 121–140.
33. Klotz, R. 2007. Internet campaigning for grassroots and astroturf support. *Social Science Computer Review*. 25, 1, 3–12.
34. Krippendorff, K. 2004. Reliability in Content Analysis. *Human Communication Research*. 30, 3, 411–433.
35. Kwak, H. et al. 2010. What is Twitter, a social network or a news media? Categories and subject descriptors. *Proc. WWW '10,* 591-600.
36. Lam, S.K. et al. 2011. WP: Clubhouse? An exploration of Wikipedia's gender imbalance. *Proc. WikiSym '11,* 1–10.
37. Livne, A. et al. 2011. The party is over here: Structure and content in the 2010 election. *Proc. ICWSM '11.*
38. Lombard, M. et al. 2002. Content Analysis in Mass Communication: Assessment and Reporting of Intercoder Reliability. *Human Communication Research*. 28, 4, 587–604.
39. McCallum, A.K. 2002. MALLET: A maching learning for language toolkit, http://mallet.cs.umass.edu/.
40. McClain, C. 2009. Debating restrictions on embryonic stem cell research. Politics and the Life Sciences: The Journal of the Association for Politics and the Life Sciences. 28, 2 , 48–68.
41. McCombs, M. 2004. Setting the agenda: The mass media and public opinion. Polity Press.
42. Mullainathan, S. and Shleifer, A. 2005. The market for news. *American Economic Review*. 95, 4, 1031–1053.
43. Ng, E.W.J. and Detenber, B.H. 2006. The impact of synchronicity and civility in online political discussions on perceptions and intentions to participate. *Journal of Computer-Mediated Communication*. 10, 3.
44. Niven, D. and Zilber, J. 2001. Do Women and Men in Congress Cultivate Different Images? Evidence from Congressional Web Sites. *Political Communication*. 18, 4, 395–405.
45. Noveck, B.S. 2011. What's in a name? Open gov and good gov. *Huffington Post*.
46. Papacharissi, Z. 2004. Democracy online: Civility, politeness, and the democratic potential of online political discussion groups. *New Media & Society*. 6, 2, 259–283.
47. Schneider, S.M. and Foot, K.A. 2006. Web campaigning by U.S. presidential primary candidates in 2000 and 2004. *The Internet Election: Perspectives on the Web's Role in Campaign 2004*. A. Williams and J. Tedesco, eds. Rowman & Littlefield. 21–36.
48. Shamma, D. et al. 2009. Tweet the debates: Understanding community annotation of uncollected sources. *Proc. ICWSM '09.*
49. Southall, A. 2012. White House ethics hub goes live online. *New York Times*.
50. Trammell, K.D. et al. 2006. Evolution of Online Campaigning: Increasing Interactivity in Candidate Web Sites and Blogs Through Text and Technical Features. *Mass Communication and Society*. 9, 1, 21–44.
51. Tumasjan, A. et al. 2011. Election forecasts with Twitter: How 140 characters reflect the political landscape. *Social Science Computer Review*. 29, 4, 402–418.

52. Weng, J. et al. 2010. TwitterRank: Finding topic-sensitive influential Twitterers. *Proc. WSDM '10*, 261 - 270.
53. Williams, C.B. and Gulati, G.J. 2011. Communicating with constituents in 140 characters or less: Twitter and the diffusion of technology innovation in the United States Congress. *SSRN*, http://ssrn.com/paper=1817053.
54. Xenos, M.A. and Foot, K.A. 2005. Politics as usual, or politics unusual? Position taking and dialogue on campaign websites in the 2002 U.S. Elections. *Journal of Communication*. 55, 1, 169–185.
55. Xenos, M.A. and Moy, P. 2007. Direct and differential effects of the internet on political and civic engagement. *Journal of Communication*. 57, 4, 704–718.

Is News Sharing on Twitter Ideologically Biased?

Jonathan Scott Morgan
School of Journalism
Michigan State University
404 Wilson Road
East Lansing, MI 48824
morga125@msu.edu

M. Zubair Shafiq
CSE Department
College of Engineering
Michigan State University
East Lansing, MI 48824
shafiqmu@msu.edu

Cliff Lampe
School of Information
University of Michigan
105 S. State St
Ann Arbor, MI 48109
cacl@umich.edu

ABSTRACT
In this paper we explore effects of perceived ideology of news outlets on consumption and sharing of news in Twitter. Selective exposure theory suggests that when given access to a broad range of information, people will tend to consume and share news that confirms their existing beliefs and biases. We find that users share news in similar ways regardless of outlet or perceived ideology of outlet, and that as a user shares more news content, they tend to quickly include outlets with opposing viewpoints. This suggests that while perceived ideology does not inspire most Twitter users to treat liberal or conservative news outlets differently, it is a factor in their news consumption and sharing. Specifically, users in our sample who sent multiple tweets tended to increase the ideological diversity in news they shared within two or three tweets, and users' information diversity increased as their number of tweets sent increased.

Author Keywords
Twitter; online discussion; information flow; political discourse; journalism; Social Computing and Social Navigation; Computer-Mediated Communication; Social Networking Site Design and Use.

ACM Classification Keywords
H.5.3 [Group and Organization Interfaces]: Web-based interaction.

INTRODUCTION
As social media sites become increasingly popular, more and more everyday communication is migrating from established mediums like email and the telephone to the social web. This personal information joins increasing amounts of other types of information that government and other organizations are making available online, creating an immense storehouse of information that people are interacting with, linking to and referencing across many information channels, both mediated and unmediated.

This wealth of information is theoretically invaluable for citizens in a democracy. Those with an Internet connection have access to an unprecedented diversity of thought, fact, and opinion. Access and use are not the same, however. Bounded rationality is defined by Simon as "rational choice that takes into account the cognitive limitations of the decision-maker - limitations of both knowledge and computational capacity." [38] In the context of a democratic public sifting through this wealth of information to inform civic and electoral decisions, bounded rationality suggests that the public has limited time and cognitive resources to devote to its civic duties, and so will use simplifying strategies when informing civic decisions.

One such simplifying strategy that is theorized to affect news consumption is selective exposure [35,41]. Selective exposure suggests that the Internet's overwhelming news options and ability to choose content without editorial intervention make online news consumers more likely to consume and share news that confirms their preformed biases and avoid news that does not, in order to ease the cognitive burden of analyzing and internalizing discordant information. Some scholars argue that the ease of personalizing content choices on the Internet may increase the likelihood of selective exposure [40]. In addition, examination of links between conservative and liberal blogs showed relatively few references between blogs of different ideologies, potentially indicating that some type of selective exposure was occurring [1].

Online social network sites may help increase exposure of users to news of different types. Most people interact in these online communities with friends or colleagues who have different political ideologies [7,22,32]. The lower switching costs of changing from one online news source to another might also make people more likely to seek out diverse viewpoints online than they would be in other contexts where switching is more costly.

In this study, we capture Tweets that reference 12 popular news outlets across a spectrum of perceived ideology, from liberal to conservative. We examine traits of tweeters, message cascades, and tweets to look for differences in news sharing based on outlets or perceived ideology. We then examine diversity of perceived source ideology in news tweets shared by Twitter users to see if news sharing choices provide evidence of underlying selective exposure.

LITERATURE REVIEW

There have been a number of studies recently that deal with how people interact and share information using the Internet and social media sites [1,4,18,19,31]. Within Twitter, for example, people have recently studied how hashtags evolve [13], the spread of information in general [25,27,44] and political information in particular [33,37], and the collaborative potential of conversation [21]. In this study, we examine the interactions between multiple channels (journalism and Twitter), the cognitive burden that results as more diverse information is placed online and integrated across channels, and ways that participants in these channels deal with this cognitive burden.

Multiple Interconnected Channels

In the broader sense of mediated communication using the Internet, each of these social network sites and collaborative technologies is one of many interconnected channels for information consumption and sharing on the Internet. Studies of these sites, however, with some notable exceptions [23,24,26,42], tend to limit themselves to a single channel's content and interactions, even though it is clear that these sites are more and more being used to share information across multiple channels, both mediated and unmediated.

A substantial portion of the "user-generated content" on social media sites is content shared from another channel – images aggregated in Pinterest, for example, likes and recommendations of articles in Facebook, or URLs, videos, and images shared in Twitter. The increasing number of mechanisms that make it easier to share content between these sites is creating richer online interactions that span multiple channels. As information channels become more interconnected, there is a need to better understand motivations for and patterns of multi-channel sharing, to learn ways we can design around both adaptive and maladaptive sharing.

Twitter and News

Twitter is a micro-blogging service that allows users to broadcast 140-character messages, called tweets. The Twitter application has a number of affordances that facilitate its use in news gathering and discussion. Users can follow each other to subscribe to each other's tweets. Any message can be easily re-tweeted, causing it to be resent by a user to all of their followers [44]. Hashtags, categories assigned to tweets, preceded by a pound sign ("#"), can be placed anywhere in a tweet, providing a flexible way to target tweets for a variety of purposes [13,23,33]. URLs in tweets are automatically shortened, allowing for links to news to be easily shared within the tweet character limit [5]. And at-mentions, explicit references to a user's Twitter username preceded by an at sign ("@"), allow tweets to target and reference users [21].

Twitter makes sharing information easy, and this helps make a genuine bi-directional exchange in discussion of news between news outlets and Twitter users. News outlets quote tweets and reporters use twitter in their news-gathering, while many twitter users share and discuss news articles [3,6,39]. This interaction has become an important part of coverage of and reaction to news events, including politics, and elections [9,37] and natural disasters [39,43].

Information Overload and Bounded Rationality

There is also a need to examine how users of increasingly interconnected systems make sense of the rich network of information these linked channels create. Simon's bounded rationality adapts the economic theory of subjective expected utility (SEU) to more realistically account for the cognitive limits of the human brain. SEU conceptualizes people as understanding all possible outcomes and their probabilities, then deciding among them based on maximizing a utility function. Simon believes this entails too heavy a computational burden on decision-makers, and looks for "procedures for choosing that are computationally simpler, and that can account for observed inconsistencies in human choice patterns." [38] These procedures include: making do with information found most easily (satisficing); relying on sources used in the past; and, when seeking diverse information, using relatively simple heuristics to choose information sources that simplify decision-making, but could also substantially limit actual source diversity.

Perceived Ideology of News

When examining the ideological diversity of outlets included in news sharing, one must first decide how to categorize news outlets' ideological position. In American journalism, there is often a substantial difference between the perception of slant or bias in a given news outlet [15,29] and the concrete instances of bias in the news they produce [2,14,16,36]. One bad article about a popular topic or person could pre-dispose whole classes of people to assuming an outlet is biased, even when that outlet is otherwise mostly neutral. This perception effect is also exacerbated by the trend of political parties and political partisans methodically asserting that the press is politicized and partisan, regardless of the truth of stories, when journalists make news that the parties do not like [12]. We understand the difference between perception of ideological slant and concrete analysis of content. In this study, we categorize news outlets based on the public's perception of their bias, since perceptions of the similarity or differences with news outlets play a central role in use of selective exposure to choose news content.

Selective Exposure and Ideological Homogeneity

Selective exposure is one of many heuristics that people may use to deal with cognitive overload. Selective exposure is the tendency to limit information exposure to messages that are compatible with already held attitudes or interests, and to avoid information that might cause cognitive dissonance [8,35].

Some researchers are concerned that as more and more of the sources of information for political discourse (and the venues in which political discourse occur) are accessed via the Internet, the public will respond to increasing amounts of information by seeking out and perpetuating ideological homogeneity - selectively exposing themselves only to like-minded individuals and information sources, leading to an increasingly ill-informed and polarized body politic [40]. Adamic and Glance found the political blogosphere to be polarized in this way in 2004, with homogeneous groups of liberal and conservative bloggers linking to and reading each other, but rarely linking to posts or blogs of the opposite ideology [1].

This fear is not universally accepted, however [10,17,35], and research indicates that most people interact with others in their networks who are of different political ideologies [7,22,32]. In fact, people who may not expose themselves to seemingly contrary news in the mass media channels (e.g. a liberal might avoid watching Fox News on cable) may be exposed to that content by maintaining a diverse social network in online systems.

As people share information in Twitter, they are often choosing to share links to news stories. These news stories may come with a perceived or actual bias that confirms the beliefs of the person sharing that link. Consequently, if selective exposure is at play as a heuristic by which people decide to share information, we would expect them to only share news from sources that confirm those biases.

RESEARCH QUESTIONS

RQ1: How do people share news on Twitter?

RQ2: Is news from news outlets that are perceived to be ideologically similar shared similarly?

RQ3: Are Twitter users more likely to share multiple news items from news outlets that have similar perceived ideology or from outlets with diverse ideologies?

METHODS

To examine the ways that tweets from news outlets across the spectrum of political ideologies in America are included in Twitter conversations, we first selected 12 news outlets broken into three ideological categories: liberal, conservative, and a third category of outlets that are either neutral or are not American, and so are a foreign control. For each outlet, we gathered a week's worth of tweets that contained either a link to news content published on their web site or a formal at-mention of the outlet's Twitter username. We carried out a series of outlet-to-outlet comparisons to create a baseline of variance across outlets, and to make sure that there were differences between the tweets of the different outlets. We also grouped the outlets by ideology (our three categories from above) and a simple measure that compared number of uses to number of tweets in the sample (to assess diversity of those tweeting), then implemented the same comparisons among these groupings, to see how much of the variance between the individual outlets could be explained by ideology or homogeneity of those who tweeted about each outlet. Finally, we shifted focus to the users in our data set, examing the range of outlets each user shared content from to see if sharing behaviors provided evidence of users' ideological or political biases manifesting in selective exposure.

News Outlet Selection and Categorization

For this study, we used Twitter's spritzer feed (a 1% random sample of tweets matching any filter criteria passed to the API) to collect data. Given this limited sample of tweets, we chose national news outlets that would have a larger volume of tweets.

We used the 2010 biennial news consumption survey conducted by The Pew Research Center for the People & the Press [46] as a first source for popular news sources for our three ideological categories: liberal, conservative, and neutral/control. One method the Pew survey uses to examine ideology in news is to ask those it surveys their ideological perspective: liberal, moderate, or conservative. It then asks these same people about their news consumption habits, including use of major popular news outlets, and breaks out consumption based on the proportions of overall readership for each outlet that self-reports liberal, conservative, or moderate/other.

To categorize outlets based on their perceived ideology, we took all outlets with a roughly 2-to-1 liberal-to-conservative audience ratio and added them to our "liberal" category (MSNBC, The New York Times, NPR, and CNN), and added those with the same ratio of conservative to liberal to our "conservative" category (Fox News, Wall Street Journal). We ignored the percentage of consumers that self-reported moderate, since that classification is ambiguous. We also selected one outlet with roughly equal liberal and conservative consumption (USA Today) to be the first member of our "moderate/neutral/control" group.

We then chose a few non-traditional outlets that are relatively new to fill out the ideological categories, adding the Drudge Report to our conservative group and the Huffington Post to the liberal group, and added a few other large outlets to the control/neutral group: BBC News, CBS News, and the Washington Post.

Data Collection

To examine the differences in sharing between tweets from our twelve news outlets, we gathered 1,378,336 tweets from the Twitter spritzer feed (a 1% random sample of tweets matching any filter criteria passed to the API) from February 28, 2012 to March 8, 2012. For each outlet, we ran a separate tweet collector implemented with the tweetstream python module [20] against Twitter's streaming API. We conceptualize exposure to a news outlet broadly as including both exposure to news by an outlet and exposure to and awareness of information about an outlet itself, so each collector filtered the overall tweet stream based on the presence of either a URL referencing content on that outlet's web site (indicated by URLs that contained either the organization's web address or their URL shortening domain) or the Twitter username of the outlet's highest level news Twitter account. Only 805 tweets in the

News Outlet	Domain Name	URL Shortener	Twitter User	Tweet Count
BBC	bbc.co.uk/news/	bbc.in	@bbcnews	21,658
CBS News	cbsnews.com	t.co	@cbsnews	35,856
CNN	cnn.com	on.cnn.com	@cnn	470,988
Drudge Report	drudgereport.com	drudge.tw	@drudge_report	9,895
Fox News	foxnews.com	fxn.ws	@foxnews	69,879
Huffington Post	huffingtonpost.com	huff.to	@huffingtonpost	186,325
MSNBC	msnbc.msn.com	on.msnbc.com	@msnbc	152,196
New York Times	nytimes.com	nytm.es	@nytimes	131,329
NPR	npr.org	n.pr	@nprnews	16,843
USA Today	usatoday.com	usat.ly	@usatoday	34,118
Wall Street Journal	online.wsj.com	on.wsj.com	@wsj	189,126
Washington Post	washingtonpost.com	wpo.st	@washingtonpost	60,123

Table 1: News outlet selection details

sample were from outlet usernames, which is a relatively small number given the size of the sample. The list of outlets and the filter strings we used for each is in Table 1. Because we chose outlets based on their perceived ideological bias and did not take size or popularity into account, some of the outlets in our study are very different in terms of newsgathering resources and popularity. This caused the number of tweets in a week for each outlet to vary, and to vary widely in some cases.

Analysis

Operationalizing Selective Exposure

In this study, we define exposure broadly as any exposure to either a news outlet or the news created by that outlet, independent of attitude or valence toward the outlet or type of information shared. To investigate selective exposure, we look at news sharing behaviors to see if they provide evidence of underlying attitudes affecting news exposure. Our data doesn't provide explicit information on attitudes, beliefs, or biases of the twitter users we are studying, but information that is shared must have been consumed at some level, and so homogeneity or diversity of ideology in news tweets shared does at least provide information on a subset of each user's news consumption choices, and so has the potential to contain evidence of selective exposure.

Traits of Tweets

We computed 7 different traits per tweet for use in our analysis: retweet count, follower count and count of those the user follows, and user mention count, hashtag count, url count, and tweet text length. We chose these traits to capture at a high level and include in our analysis three concepts: an idea of how far the tweet spread (retweet count); structural traits of the social context and network of the tweeter (follower count – those whom the tweeter influences - and count of those the user follows – those who influence the tweeter); and manifest traits of the content of the tweet itself (user mention count, hashtag count, url count, and tweet text length). See Table 2 for descriptive statistics of these computed traits.

We examined differences in the distributions of these traits across news outlets and categories of news outlets. We also used these traits in logistic regressions to predict the outlet or category to which a given tweet belonged, and to investigate if spread of a tweet, network of the tweeter, or traits of tweet text could help to predict which tweets belonged to which outlet or category.

Categorizing Tweets By Heterogeneity

In addition to our categorization based on perceived ideology of news outlets, we also generated a basic statistic to assess the overall heterogeneity of the people who shared information. The heterogeneity score for each outlet was the ratio of the number of unique users who tweeted that outlet's content to the total number of tweets related to that outlet. This score ranges from 0 to 1, and outlets were clustered into three non-overlapping categories: low (between 0.46 and 0.52: CNN, Fox News, MSNBC, Wall Street Journal), medium (between 0.58 and 0.60: BBC, Drudge, Huffington Post), and high (between 0.66 and 0.70: CBS, NYTimes, USA Today, Washington Post; and NPR with 0.78). A score approaching 1 indicates that more users are responsible for sharing of the outlet's news, and so each user shares fewer items, where a score of 1 would indicate that each tweet for the outlet is sent by a unique user. A score approaching zero indicates that fewer people are responsible for the distribution that outlet receives in Twitter. We call this a heterogeneity score - a reflection of whether those who tweet an outlet's content are a small group sharing many items each (similar to what Adamic and Glance [1] found liberal and conservative bloggers to be, sharing with each other) or a larger group of people sharing fewer items each.

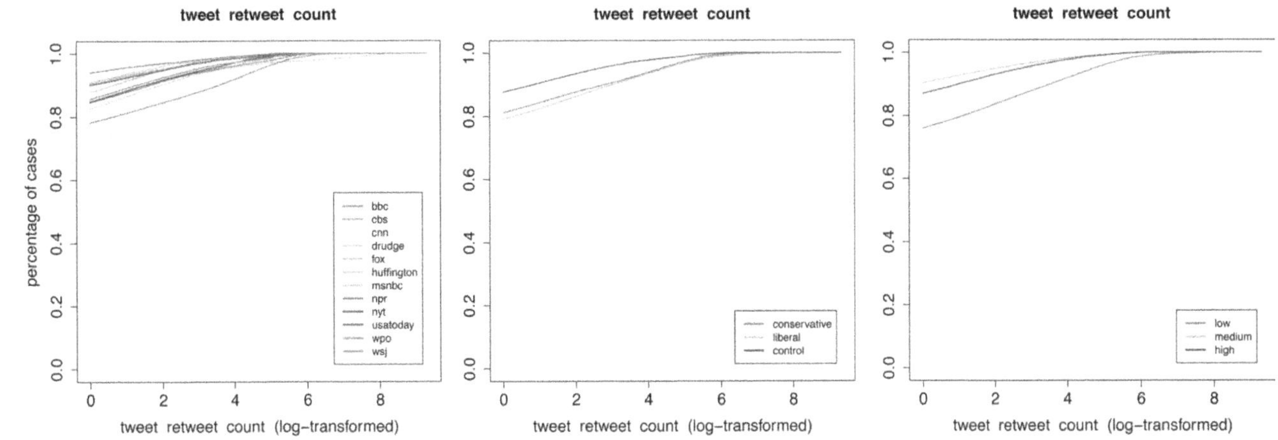

Figure 1: Normalized Cumulative Distribution Function (CDF) plots of retweet count broken out by organization, ideology, and heterogeneity (in that order, from left to right).

CDF Plots and the Two-Sample K-S Test

To assess differences between distributions for news outlets and categories of news outlets, we compared the distributions of the aforementioned tweet traits using normalized Cumulative Distribution Function (CDF) plots and the two-sample Kolmogorov-Smirnov test (K-S test) of similarity of distributions. These methods and statistics are not particularly well-known in this field, and so we'll describe them briefly now before we outline our analysis.

A CDF plot is an alternate way of visually presenting a distribution of data. It takes the counts in a histogram and cumulatively sums them as the function moves from left to right over the X-axis, then plots the cumulative sum as the Y-value for each X. CDF plots make visual comparison of distributions easier, but when differences are subtle (as in our data – see Figure 1), a more precise measure of difference between distributions is needed.

The K-S test is a non-parametric test for the equality of distributions that uses the points from a CDF plot to approximate and compare underlying distributions. It is sensitive to differences in locations and shapes of distributions. The K-S statistic that results runs from 0 to 1, where 0 indicates that points from two CDFs reflect an identical underlying distribution and 1 indicates no overlap between the underlying distributions represented by the two samples, indicating that they are entirely distinct [45].

Comparing Outlets and Outlet Categories

To assess presence of variance in tweets across outlets, we generated CDFs of the aforementioned traits of tweets across individual outlets, outlet categories based on their perceived ideology, and outlet categories based on the heterogeneity or diversity of people referencing their name and content. Figure 1 shows CDF plots for retweet count broken out by news outlet, ideology, and heterogeneity. We then used these CDF plots to compute K-S statistics for all possible pairs of the news outlets and pairs of categories.

Predicting Outlet and Category Membership

To look at the variance between news outlets and between categories that each of our traits explained, we also implemented logistic regression to see how well our 7 trait variables could predict a given tweet being from a given news outlet or category. We implemented this using SPSS Multinomial Logistic Regression (MLR), which performs a series of binomial logistic regressions across all combinations of a categorical variable using a single sample from the overall data set, allowing per-unit assessment, but also accruing information to create overall estimates of the model, including an estimated R-squared value.

Examining Sharing Behaviors of Users

Since selective exposure is typically identified in individuals, we concluded our analysis by aggregating traits of tweets from each user in our sample to look for patterns of sharing behaviors. Our goal was to find evidence of selective exposure in users' sharing behaviors, i.e. whether users select news outlets they include in tweets based on the perceived ideology of the outlet.

RESULTS

Traits of Tweets

In addition to our conceptual groupings, the traits we computed for tweets fall into two categories: those that are inherently range-limited by a given tweet being at most 140 characters (tweet text length, URL count, hashtag mention count, and user mention count), and those that are not (retweet count, user's follower count and count of people the user follows).

None of the traits were normally distributed, and most appeared to have a power law distribution, so they were log-normalized when used in regression.

	Retweet Count	Follower Count	Following Count	User Mentions	Hashtag Count	URL Count	Text Length
Minimum	0	0	0	0	0	0	3
Maximum	11,032	9,744,612	554,667	17	28	6	353
Mean	18.63	5,166.54	278.54	1.00	.62	.83	107.02
- SE of Mean	*.109*	*91.754*	*4.290*	*.001*	*.001*	*.000*	*.026*
Median	.00	225.00	5.00	1.00	.00	1.00	113.00
Mode	0	0	0	1	0	1	140
Std. Dev.	127.944	107,721.506	5,036.580	1.093	1.480	.537	30.480
Variance	16,369.645	11,603,922,894.819	25,367,141.753	1.194	2.191	.288	929.000
Skewness	17.416	46.915	84.436	2.761	4.120	.157	-.713
- SE of Skewness	*.002*	*.002*	*.002*	*.002*	*.002*	*.002*	*.002*
Kurtosis	472.850	2,551.441	8,673.320	14.588	22.606	2.058	-.380
- SE of Kurtosis	*.004*	*.004*	*.004*	*.004*	*.004*	*.004*	*.004*

Table 2: Descriptive statistics for data calculated per tweet. Standard Error (SE) of Mean, Skewness, and Kurtosis are in italics in a separate row beneath each statistic.

Measures of centrality of all of the traits indicated variance both in the data set as a whole (see Table 2) and across categories. In addition, the ranges of a given trait sometimes differed substantially within categories, e.g. the mean of the retweet count ranges from 1.61 to 44.84 for different outlets and the maximum ranges from 161 to 11,032. Therefore, it was difficult to compare the variance across groupings using measures of centrality alone. To better assess the differences between the distributions of traits for different outlets and groupings of outlets, we sought more sophisticated ways of visualizing and analyzing differences in distributions.

Differences Between Outlets and Outlet Categories

Distribution Differences: CDF plots and K-S Statistics

The visual inspection of normalized CDF plots across outlets showed that while the shapes of the plot lines were similar, suggesting a similar underlying distribution, the slopes and magnitudes varied across news outlets, suggesting minor differences in distributions. The distributions were too close to visually assess the precise magnitude of these differences.

Tweet Trait	Max K-S	Mean K-S	Median K-S
Retweet Count	0.254	0.080	0.066
Follower Count	0.158	0.067	0.064
Following Count	0.209	0.072	0.062
User Mentions	0.419	0.162	0.134
Hashtag Count	0.292	0.111	0.100
URL Count	0.398	0.172	0.180
Text Length	0.190	0.095	0.089

Table 3: K-S statistic summary by tweet trait.

A comparison of K-S statistic values indicated that while some individual news outlets have substantially different distributions for certain traits, the average K-S statistic value for a given trait is never above 0.2, and only 2 of 7 make it above 0.1 (see Table 3 for more details). Some traits have maximum K-S values of around 0.3 or higher (user mention count, K-S = 0.419; URL count, K-S = 0.398; hashtag count, K-S = 0.292), indicating substantially different distributions among the outlets for these tweet traits. The modest mean and median K-S statistics across all traits suggest that these substantial differences are exceptions and that overall these distributions are similar.

K-S statistic values across outlets also indicate that while there are substantial differences in certain traits between outlets, the distributions of the outlets' tweet traits are mostly similar. All outlets have a maximum K-S statistic value, including all traits, of between 0.279 and 0.419 – some larger than others, but all in the range of K-S statistic values that indicate only moderate difference. However, their mean and median K-S statistic values are around 0.1 (see Table 4 for more details). While there are some substantial differences in distributions of traits between outlets, they are spread evenly among the outlets, and no outlet has a mean K-S statistic value is above 0.139.

Categorization of outlets based on ideology and heterogeneity of tweeters show even more modest amounts of differences between the underlying distributions of the traits. Across outlet categories based on ideology, all K-S statistic values are below 0.1, so clustering based on

News Outlet	Max K-S	Mean K-S	Median K-S
BBC	0.398	0.139	0.112
CBS News	0.338	0.098	0.085
CNN	0.311	0.111	0.095
Drudge Report	0.355	0.119	0.098
Fox News	0.279	0.100	0.088
Huffington Post	0.373	0.106	0.084
MSNBC	0.336	0.091	0.084
New York Times	0.419	0.127	0.100
NPR	0.384	0.089	0.072
USA Today	0.398	0.111	0.088
Wall Street Journal	0.351	0.085	0.066
Washington Post	0.419	0.125	0.108

Table 4: K-S statistic summary by outlet.

ideology actually seems to mask the differences in traits between outlets. Therefore, it is not useful in explaining the between-outlet distribution differences. Across outlet categories based on heterogeneity, we observe more variance in distributions of traits, with some K-S statistic values around 0.12, and a few values above 0.2. Overall, the K-S statistic values of around 0.2 are still modest.

Logistic Regression

To further explore the variance between news outlets and the amount of that variance our categorizations of news outlets explained, we also implemented Multinomial Logistic Regression to investigate how well these 7 traits could predict a given tweet being from a given news outlet or outlet category.

All three logistic regression models had chi-squared values that indicated statistically significantly fit, $p < .001$, likely because of the size of our data set. Low Pearson correlations among predictors (highest Pearson's $r = 0.281$, then -0.236, then 0.199, and the rest were less than absolute value of 0.072), relatively high tolerance values (all above 0.867), and Variance Inflation Factor values (VIF ranges from 0 to positive infinity, where large values indicate inflation of standard error due to collinearity) between 1 and 1.154 all indicate no violation of MLR's collinearity assumption.

Given the size of our data set, we also assessed model fit using a test that is more robust to large sample sizes than chi-squared. Chance criteria for assessing model fit, adapted from discriminant analysis [34], compares a model's accuracy to that expected by chance to determine the quality of the model. It is not affected by sample size. In discriminant analysis, the specific test used depends on how equally divided the cases are among the different groupings [28]. In multivariate logistic regression, it is accepted to use the Proportionate Chance criteria regardless of comparative cell sizes. Using this criteria, a model is a good fit when its *Actual Accuracy* is greater than its *Chance Accuracy + 25%*. The individual news outlet model passed the proportionate test, with an actual accuracy of 0.635, a full ten percent greater than the goal of 0.535. The other models were close, but did not meet this criteria (Table 5).

Grouping	Actual Accuracy	Chance Accuracy + 25%
Outlet	***0.635***	0.535
Ideology	0.826	***0.876***
Heterogeneity	0.756	***0.759***

Table 5: Proportionate Chance criteria – MLR model Actual Accuracy compared to Chance Accuracy + 25%.

Grouping	Cox and Snell	Nagelkerke
Outlet	0.228	0.243
Ideology	0.08	0.117
Heterogeneity	0.114	0.152

Table 6: Cox and Snell and Nagelkerke Pseudo R-Squared values for logistic regression models by outlet, ideology,

Though the ideology and heterogeneity models are poor fits, the Cox and Snell [11] and Nagelkerke [30] pseudo R-squared values (see Table 6) are in line with the trends observed in K-S statistics. Grouping tweets by outlet explains a similar amount of variance as an R-Squared of between 0.23 and 0.24 would represent in a linear regression model, a respectable amount given the sparse sample and the basic nature of traits being analyzed. Grouping by ideology and heterogeneity explained proportionately much less, and as with distribution comparisons, while heterogeneity is the better explainer of variance in tweet traits of the two, it is not better by much.

For the outlet model, SPSS "Likelihood Ratio Tests" indicated that all predictors were significant parts of the model, $p < .001$. None of the predictors had standard errors over 2, which suggests that there were no numerical anomalies with the model.

News Selection at the User Level

In our sample, 81% of users shared tweets from only one outlet. Of the 19% who shared more than one tweet, 44% shared 2, and so 56% of users who shared news from more than one source shared from 3 or more.

Liberal news is more prevalent in this sample than news from conservative or control outlets in terms of numbers of both tweets and users. 77% of users included outlets we categorized as liberal in the tweets they forwarded, either alone or in combination with other ideologies. This fits with the numerical prevalence of tweets from liberal outlets, in particular CNN (69% of tweets were from liberal outlets, 34% overall were from CNN).

It is interesting to note that as people share more tweets, however (see Table 7), their sharing quickly becomes more diverse, and the proportions of people who only share from one ideology drop quickly: to 63% of people who share 2 or more, to 40% when 5 or more tweets are sent, and approaching 30% as number of tweets increases further. Even given the prevalence of liberal tweets, this highlights that as people share more tweets, they are more likely to include news outlets with diverse ideologies, and it isn't just the heaviest tweeters who share from liberal, conservative, and our control – 23% of users who share 5 or more tweets share from all three of our groups.

This trend becomes evident starting when users share 2-3 tweets, and could indicate that while the limited data we've created might not predict our ideological categories well, the categorizations have some merit. Our control group seems not to be very salient – most of the diversity comes from sharing both liberal and conservative tweets, not from including the outlets in our control group – and people tend to include news from both liberal and conservative outlets pretty quickly as they share more.

DISCUSSION

First, this study has limitations. Our data set included a limited number of news outlets and was only a 1% sample of tweets. Though it spanned multiple days, it did not include data from multiple points in time to support longitudinal analysis. Our method of sampling by perceived ideology of outlet resulted in inclusion of outlets with substantially different magnitudes of Twitter sharing traffic, which complicated analysis. We did not differentiate between links to a news outlet's articles and mentions of an outlet's name, and these two types of references to an outlet's content could be part of very different types of conversation, though we assert that they are both evidence of at least some exposure to the news outlet. We only captured the most basic of information on the tweets we gathered. We didn't analyze the Twitter users to assess different user types or goals. Perceived ideology of a news outlet is complicated, also, and our method of assigning ideology did not have much explanatory power in our data.

Even with these limits, we did learn something about how Twitter users share news. Both our distribution analysis and the logistic regression results suggest that there are a few reasonably substantial differences in tweets across outlets. Overall, however, we observed that people seem to share news in similar ways, regardless of outlet, and the traits we examined did not indicate a substantial difference between outlets. Though our ideology-based categorization might not have been perfect, our sample did include news from a range of ideological perspectives, and the similarity of sharing across these outlets suggests that selective exposure is not a strong actor at the outlet level.

The lack of difference across our categorizations also supports the idea that selective exposure lacks power in influencing news outlet choice when sharing tweets. Grouping tweets by perceived ideology of outlets and our basic measure of heterogeneity both resulted in K-S statistic values smaller than those when outlets were compared, and MLR models for the categories were poor fits and were rejected outright. Therefore, these categorizations were not much help in explaining differences in our tweet data.

Information on users' sharing behaviors also provided indirect refutation of selective exposure, and suggested that even though our ideological categorization did not explain differences in sharing, it does have at least some validity. People who share more than one tweet seem pretty quickly to include news from different ideologies in the news they share, the opposite of what selective exposure would predict. A substantial percentage shared tweets from 3 or more outlets, especially given the limited snapshot present in a 1% sample. Moreover, as number of tweets increased, the percentage of users who included multiple ideologies quickly increased (half of all users who shared 3 tweets included outlets with different ideologies). This could indicate that switching costs are low enough in consuming and sharing online news that people are more likely to explore and share different points of view online, even if they are prone to selective exposure in other venues. It

Min Tweets	Users	Only Control	Only Lib.	Only Cons.	Only 1	Lib. + Cons.	Cons. + Control	Lib. + Control	Only 2	1 or 2	All 3
1	597,536	0.094	0.663	0.132	0.889	0.049	0.006	0.036	0.091	0.98	0.02
2	178,810	0.036	0.513	0.08	0.628	0.162	0.021	0.12	0.304	0.933	0.067
3	91,232	0.022	0.42	0.061	0.503	0.203	0.018	0.144	0.365	0.868	0.132
4	58,445	0.018	0.365	0.053	0.436	0.215	0.014	0.148	0.376	0.813	0.187
5	41,960	0.016	0.329	0.05	0.395	0.216	0.012	0.146	0.374	0.769	0.231
6	32,240	0.016	0.303	0.049	0.367	0.213	0.01	0.143	0.366	0.734	0.266
7	25,982	0.015	0.286	0.049	0.35	0.208	0.009	0.137	0.354	0.704	0.296
8	21,599	0.015	0.272	0.049	0.336	0.203	0.008	0.133	0.344	0.68	0.32
9	18,314	0.015	0.263	0.05	0.328	0.197	0.008	0.127	0.331	0.659	0.341
15	8,694	0.016	0.23	0.061	0.307	0.169	0.006	0.105	0.279	0.586	0.414

Table 7: Distribution of tweets across ideological spectrum as number of tweets shared increases.

could also indicate that people are less affected by selective exposure in general than was previously thought, and more representative data in services like Twitter, even though it is not perfectly representative of the population as a whole, is detailed enough that it is helping us get a more accurate representation of the public.

CONCLUSION

Many researchers have studied Twitter's role in politics and political discussion. In this study, we focus on the role news articles and organizations play in online discussion, how users share news articles, and what those sharing behaviors suggest about the character of the conversation on Twitter, the role news plays in online discussion, and how users filter information. In this study we have shown that Twitter users tend to share news without bias toward or against the perceived ideology of news outlets. While selective exposure might be a strong influence at some level, in the sample of tweets we examined, it does not seem to strongly influence choice of news outlet. Twitter users even seem to actively include news from outlets of different perceived ideology as they share more news, counter to what selective exposure would predict.

There are a number of ways to move this research forward: methods that better take social context and network patterns of sharing into account, for example; better assessing and including traits of users; or including more nuanced analysis of content of tweets and content of things linked by tweets, to better detect the tone of tweets, tweets that are about the same topic, similar topics, etc., and so differentiate between types of information.

Even so, this study indicates that a simplistic model of Twitter news consumers being inchoate and guided by selective exposure is incorrect, and the more nuanced and open-minded information consumer our work implies bears substantial further study.

ACKNOWLEDGEMENTS

The authors would like to thank Iman Barjasteh, Alex X. Liu and Hayder Radha for their help and advice on the analysis in this paper. This work has been supported by the National Science Foundation under Grant IIS-0968495.

REFERENCES

1. Adamic, L.A. and Glance, N. The Political Blogosphere and the 2004 U.S. Election: Divided They Blog. *ACM LinkKDD-2005*, ACM Press (2005).
2. Alterman, E. *What Liberal Media?: The Truth about Bias and the News*. Basic Books, 2004.
3. An, J., Cha, M., Gummadi, K.P., Crowcroft, J., and Quercia, D. Visualizing Media Bias through Twitter. *Sixth International AAAI Conference on Weblogs and Social Media*, (2012).
4. Antin, J. and Cheshire, C. Readers are not free-riders: reading as a form of participation on wikipedia. *Proceedings of the 2010 ACM conference on Computer supported cooperative work*, ACM (2010), 127–130.
5. Antoniades, D., Polakis, I., Kontaxis, G., et al. we.b: the web of short urls. *Proceedings of the 20th international conference on World wide web*, ACM (2011), 715–724.
6. Armstrong, C.L. and Gao, F. Now Tweet This How News Organizations Use Twitter. *Electronic News 4*, 4 (2010), 218–235.
7. Bakshy, E., Rosenn, I., Marlow, C., and Adamic, L. The Role of Social Networks in Information Diffusion. *arXiv:1201.4145*, (2012).
8. Baran, S.J. and Davis, D.K. *Mass Communication Theory: Foundations, Ferment, and Future*. Wadsworth Publishing, 2008.
9. Bruns, A. and Burgess, J. #Ausvotes: How twitter covered the 2010 Australian federal election. *Communication, Politics & Culture 44*, 2 (2011), 37.
10. Chaffee, S.H., Saphir, M.N., Graf, J., Sandvig, C., and Hahn, K.S. Attention to Counter-Attitudinal Messages in a State Election Campaign. *Political Communication 18*, 3 (2001), 247–272.
11. Cox, D.R. and Snell, E.J. *Analysis of Binary Data, Second Edition*. CRC Press, 1989.
12. Crawford, C. *Attack the Messenger: How Politicians Turn You Against the Media*. Rowman & Littlefield, 2007.
13. Cunha, E., Magno, G., Comarela, G., Almeida, V., Gonçalves, M.A., and Benevenuto, F. Analyzing the dynamic evolution of hashtags on Twitter: a language-based approach. *Proceedings of the Workshop on Languages in Social Media (LSM 2011)*, Association for Computational Linguistics (2011), 58–65.
14. D'Alessio, D. and Allen, M. Media bias in presidential elections: a meta-analysis. *Journal of Communication 50*, 4 (2000), 133–156.
15. Eveland, W.P. and Shah, D.V. The Impact of Individual and Interpersonal Factors on Perceived News Media Bias. *Political Psychology 24*, 1 (2003), 101–117.
16. Fico, F., Richardson, J.D., and Edwards, S.M. Influence of Story and Structure on Perceived Story Bias and News Organization Credibility. *Mass Communication & Society 7*, 3 (2004), 301–318.
17. Garrett, R.K. Echo chambers online?: Politically motivated selective exposure among Internet news users. *Journal of Computer-Mediated Communication 14*, 2 (2009), 265–285.
18. Gruhl, D., Guha, R., Liben-Nowell, D., and Tomkins, A. Information diffusion through blogspace. *Proceedings of the 13th international conference on World Wide Web*, ACM (2004), 491–501.
19. Halvey, M.J. and Keane, M.T. Exploring social dynamics in online media sharing. *Proceedings of the 16th international conference on World Wide Web*, ACM (2007), 1273–1274.

20. Halvorsen, R. tweetstream - simple twitter streaming API. https://bitbucket.org/runeh/tweetstream/src.

21. Honey, C. and Herring, S.C. Beyond Microblogging: Conversation and Collaboration via Twitter. *42nd Hawaii International Conference on System Sciences, 2009. HICSS '09*, IEEE (2009), 1–10.

22. Horrigan, J.B., Garrett, K., and Resnick, P. *The Internet and Democratic Debate*. Pew Internet & American Life Project, 2004.

23. Huang, J., Thornton, K.M., and Efthimiadis, E.N. Conversational tagging in twitter. *Proceedings of the 21st ACM conference on Hypertext and hypermedia*, ACM (2010), 173–178.

24. Kittur, A. and Kraut, R.E. Beyond Wikipedia: coordination and conflict in online production groups. *Proceedings of the 2010 ACM conference on Computer supported cooperative work*, ACM (2010), 215–224.

25. Kwak, H., Lee, C., Park, H., and Moon, S. What is Twitter, a social network or a news media? *Proceedings of the 19th international conference on World wide web*, ACM (2010), 591–600.

26. Lerman, K. and Ghosh, R. Information Contagion: An Empirical Study of the Spread of News on Digg and Twitter Social Networks. *Proceedings of the Fourth International AAAI Conference on Weblogs and Social Media*, AAAI Press (2010), 90–97.

27. Van Liere, D. How far does a tweet travel?: Information brokers in the twitterverse. *Proceedings of the International Workshop on Modeling Social Media*, ACM (2010), 6:1–6:4.

28. Marcoulides, G.A. and Hershberger, S.L. *Multivariate Statistical Methods: A First Course*. Psychology Press, 1997.

29. Morris, J.S. Slanted Objectivity? Perceived Media Bias, Cable News Exposure, and Political Attitudes. *Social Science Quarterly 88*, 3 (2007), 707–728.

30. Nagelkerke, N.J.D. A Note on a General Definition of the Coefficient of Determination. *Biometrika 78*, 3 (1991), 691–692.

31. Preece, J. and Shneiderman, B. The Reader-to-Leader Framework: Motivating Technology-Mediated Social Participation. *AIS Transactions on Human-Computer Interaction 1*, 1 (2009), 13–32.

32. Rainie, L. and Smith, A. *Pew Internet Social networking sites and politics*. Pew Research Center's Internet & American Life Project, 2012.

33. Romero, D.M., Meeder, B., and Kleinberg, J. Differences in the mechanics of information diffusion across topics: idioms, political hashtags, and complex contagion on twitter. *Proceedings of the 20th international conference on World wide web*, ACM (2011), 695–704.

34. Schwab, A.J. Multinomial Logistic Regression: A Problem in Personnel Classification. http://www.utexas.edu/courses/schwab/sw388r7/Tutorials/RulonMulitNomialLogisticRegressionProblem_doc_html/026_The_Classification_Matrices_as_a_Measure_of_Model_Accuracy.html.

35. Sears, D.O. and Preedman, J.L. Selective Exposure to Information: A Critical Review. *Public Opinion Quarterly 31*, 2 (1967), 194–213.

36. Shah, D.V., Watts, M.D., Domke, D., Fan, D.P., and Fibison, M. News Coverage, Economic Cues, and the Public's Presidential Preferences, 1984-1996. *Journal of Politics 61*, 4 (1999), 914.

37. Shamma, D.A., Kennedy, L., and Churchill, E.F. Tweet the debates: understanding community annotation of uncollected sources. *Proceedings of the first SIGMM workshop on Social media*, ACM (2009), 3–10.

38. Simon, H.A. Bounded Rationality. In J. Eatwell, M. Milgate and P. Newman, eds., *Utility and Probability*. W. W. Norton & Company, 1990, 15–18.

39. Starbird, K., Palen, L., Hughes, A.L., and Vieweg, S. Chatter on the red: what hazards threat reveals about the social life of microblogged information. *Proceedings of the 2010 ACM conference on Computer supported cooperative work*, ACM (2010), 241–250.

40. Sunstein, C.R. *Republic.com 2.0*. Princeton University Press, 2009.

41. Sweeny, K., Melnyk, D., Miller, W., and Shepperd, J.A. Information avoidance: Who, what, when, and why. *Review of General Psychology 14*, 4 (2010), 340–353.

42. Tsagkias, M., De Rijke, M., and Weerkamp, W. Linking online news and social media. *Proceedings of the fourth ACM international conference on Web search and data mining*, ACM (2011), 565–574.

43. Vieweg, S., Hughes, A.L., Starbird, K., and Palen, L. Microblogging during two natural hazards events: what twitter may contribute to situational awareness. *Proceedings of the 28th international conference on Human factors in computing systems*, ACM (2010), 1079–1088.

44. Yang, Z., Guo, J., Cai, K., et al. Understanding retweeting behaviors in social networks. *Proceedings of the 19th ACM international conference on Information and knowledge management*, ACM (2010), 1633–1636.

45. Young, I.T. Proof without prejudice: use of the Kolmogorov-Smirnov test for the analysis of histograms from flow systems and other sources. *Journal of Histochemistry & Cytochemistry 25*, 7 (1977), 935–941.

46. *Ideological News Sources: Who Watches and Why - Americans Spending More Time Following the News*. The Pew Research Center for the People & the Press, 2010.

Tweets Are Forever: A Large-Scale Quantitative Analysis of Deleted Tweets

Hazim Almuhimedi[a], Shomir Wilson[a], Bin Liu[a], Norman Sadeh[a], Alessandro Acquisti[b]
[a]School of Computer Science, [b]Heinz College
Carnegie Mellon University
{hazim,shomir,bliu1,sadeh}@cs.cmu.edu, acquisti@andrew.cmu.edu

ABSTRACT
This paper describes an empirical study of 1.6M deleted tweets collected over a continuous one-week period from a set of 292K Twitter users. We examine several aggregate properties of deleted tweets, including their connections to other tweets (e.g., whether they are replies or retweets), the clients used to produce them, temporal aspects of deletion, and the presence of geotagging information. Some significant differences were discovered between the two collections, namely in the clients used to post them, their conversational aspects, the sentiment vocabulary present in them, and the days of the week they were posted. However, in other dimensions for which analysis was possible, no substantial differences were found. Finally, we discuss some ramifications of this work for understanding Twitter usage and management of one's privacy.

Author Keywords
Privacy; Social Networks; Deletion

ACM Classification Keywords
H.3.1. Information Systems: Information Storage and Retrieval: Content Analysis and Indexing

INTRODUCTION
Online social networks such as Twitter, Facebook, Google+, and LinkedIn have established themselves as channels for a variety of communications between individuals. Archival formats in social networks, known by terms such as *news feeds* or *timelines*, often allow the users to view the histories of their peers' posts. Since one's communication history is on display for others to browse or scrutinize, it is natural that online social networks often (or almost always) include some mechanism for users to delete posts that they previously made. Reasons to do this are numerous: posts may include typos, factual errors, stale information, reconsidered ideas, or regretted statements. Sometimes deletions are superficial in nature, but in other cases they may have serious ramifications, as recognized by the European Commission's draft of a "right to be forgotten" [1].

When a post is deleted from an online social network, users generally assume that the post will no longer be available for anyone to see. However, this is not necessarily true, as evidence may persist of the post and its content in less visible ways. Twitter, through its API service, provides a particularly rich and accessible stream of data on deleted posts. By following the posts (*tweets*) of a user and other messages from the API, one can reconstruct which tweets the user decides to delete without losing any data associated with them. By tracking a large number of users whose posts are public, it is thus possible to observe large-scale patterns in deletion behavior. These patterns can inform the design of online social networks to help users better manage their content.

The fact that Twitter users sometimes delete tweets seems intuitive—if not obvious—but the ramifications of deletion have received little attention. Specifically, we wish to address the following questions:

- *What differences exist between deleted and undeleted tweets?* For instance, are certain properties of tweets (e.g., location tags, reply frequencies) correlated with likelihood of deletion? Might there be patterns in sentiments or topics among deleted tweets?

- *How often are tweets deleted for superficial reasons?* These include typos, simple rephrasings, spam generators, and mass deletions. Some superficial deletions may represent a waste of effort that could be prevented with enhancements to Twitter clients, while others may involve little or no action on the part of a human user.

- *What are some of the additional reasons that people delete tweets?* Answering the above two questions may provide some insight (albeit indirect) into user intentions. A comprehensive account of reasons for deletion might be impossible, given the challenges of reconstructing users' motivations and specific circumstances. However, some hypotheses can be formulated by examining the properties of deleted tweets *en masse*.

This paper describes the first large-scale empirical study of deleted tweets gathered from the Twitter online social network. A corpus of approximately 1.6M deleted tweets was gathered over a continuous one-week period from a set of approximately 292K users who made their posts available to the general public. The same users' persistent undeleted tweets also were gathered, providing a comparative set. Several features of the two sets of tweets were contrasted, including the source clients, tweet content, quantity of replies, and the presence of geotagging information. The researchers found that many of the properties of deleted tweets in aggregate differed from undeleted tweets, while others were indistinguishable. Finally, some implications of these findings are discussed, along with some directions for future work.

TWITTER

The reader is likely to be familiar with Twitter already, but for completeness, below is an overview of the service and its terminology.

Twitter is an online social network that allows users to post 140-character long messages, known as *tweets*. A user can *follow* other users (sometimes informally referred to as their *friends*, as in many similar networks) to easily receive their tweets in an aggregated news feed. By default, all tweets are public and accessible by anyone who browses Twitter's website. However, a user can *protect* their account and only allow a selected group of approved followers to view their tweets. For this study, the researchers only gathered data from public Twitter accounts.

A Twitter user can engage in a conversation by replying to a tweet posted by another user or by *mentioning* a user; both methods use the convention of including "@username" in the reply tweet or mentioning tweet. Additionally, a Twitter user can *retweet* another user's tweet if it is public, thus passing it along to her followers. To assign a topic to a tweet, Twitter users follow the convention of using *hashtags* (e.g., "#topic"). Tweets frequently contain URLs to websites or images, and they are sometimes tagged with location metadata.

Tweet Deletion

Twitter users are able to delete tweets that they have posted. Upon deletion, the tweet disappears from the user's timeline and from their follower's timelines as well. A deleted tweet effectively disappears from the results of searching Twitter, although a short delay sometimes occurs between deletion and disappearance. A *status deletion notice*[1] is distributed via the Twitter streaming API to relevant users' clients so that they, in turn, remove deleted tweets from their records. A user also may delete a retweet through an undo mechanism, although this does not delete the original retweeted post, since it belongs to a different user. On the other hand, if the author of a tweet that has been retweeted deletes it, then all retweets are deleted as well.

Twitter does not provide a bulk-deletion of user's tweets. It provides, however, a one-click bulk-deletion of all location data that were attached to user's tweets, without deleting the tweets. By clicking on the "Delete all location information" button on user's account settings page, all locations attached to all previous tweets are deleted. A "location deletion notice", which includes a "user ID" and an "up-to-status ID", will be sent to third party clients so they, in turn, can delete the location information of tweets from their back-end data stores.

[1]https://dev.twitter.com/docs/streaming-apis/messages

RELATED WORK

A large volume of research has been conducted on Twitter, including social network topology and properties [13, 11] as well as user classifications, behaviors, and topics of tweets [27, 26, 11, 10, 12]. The contents of tweets have been a particular focus of recent research. Such efforts have involved manual coding of small samples [17], utilizing the crowd [2] and automatic topic modeling for large samples [19].

Tweet deletion has received little direct attention in previous studies, although we note one prior effort focused on this topic. Hovey [9] created a tool to recover and display deleted tweets, with statistics on their lifespans and most frequently occurring keywords. Although he explored applying natural language processing methods to deleted tweets, no results were reported. Our work differs from Hovey's in many dimensions, including the volume of the collected data, the reported comparisons between deleted and undeleted tweets, temporal and spatial analysis of deleted tweets, and the keyword-based analysis of tweet content.

Prior studies have demonstrated that users of online social networks delete their posts to manage social consequences and maintain their privacy. Wang et al. showed that Facebook users most commonly handle regrettable posts by deleting them [25]. Boyd showed that deleting posts is a "structural" strategy that teens use to minimize the social consequences of their posts, rather than taking advantage of an online social network's privacy controls [5]. Other methods of image management by teenagers include deletion of other users' posts that might cause embarrassment (e.g., making fun of one's interests) [5] and deleting posts that present a negative image of oneself to other readers [14]. Tufekci determined that 81.3% of Facebook users delete information from their profiles due to privacy or visibility concerns, and women are more likely than men to do so [24]. Some Facebook users who are concerned about privacy delete all their posts periodically [20].

Although most social networks offer deletion functionality, data is not necessarily removed immediately or erased completely. Bonneau and Cheng [4, 7, 8] separately demonstrated that deleted photos on Facebook were still accessible after the user requested their removal, almost a month and a year later, respectively. More recently, Facebook solved this problem, and deleted photos are erased within a month. Twitter deletes photos and posts instantaneously [7], but it also allows third party applications to access and archive users' tweets. No guarantee can be made that third parties will comply with users' deletions, and a few services have attempted to archive deleted tweets for public viewing. Among them were *Undetweetable* and *Tweleted*, although neither of these remains operational due to actions taken by Twitter. *Politwoops* is a recent service dedicated to storing and recovering tweets deleted by politicians. It started in the Netherlands and now

Total number of users	292,293
Total number of all posted tweets	67,295,171
Total number of undeleted tweets	65,677,499
Total number of deleted tweets	1,617,672
Number of users who tweeted at least 1 tweet	222,185
Number of users who deleted at least 1 tweet	144,816

Table 1: Totalized statistics on the tweets in our dataset.

Statistic	Mean	Median	Std. Dev.
Followers	1,281	305	30,114
Following	541	289	2,235
Account Age (mo.)	21	20	11

Table 2: Statistics on the users in our dataset.

has 13 different international versions including one in the U.S.

In summary, although prior research linked deletion of posts in social networks with privacy and social concerns, the phenomenon has not been examined using a volume of data comparable to the present study, nor with attention to the metadata associated with deleted tweets. We believe that this large-scale, multifaceted examination is a necessary step in exploring the ramifications of deleted user content.

DATA COLLECTION

Using Twitter's streaming API, we first collected a random set of users who matched the following criteria: (1) their account was at least a month old; (2) the user had posted at least 10 tweets; (3) the user had at least 10 followers and 10 following; and (4) the first tweet we received through the API was in English (as determined by the Google Translate and Microsoft Translator APIs) and not a retweet. This resulted in a set of approximately 292K users, whom we followed via the streaming API for one continuous week (2012-03-14 through 2012-03-20). This allowed us to receive all public tweets posted by those users as well as retweets posted by them, replies to their tweets by their followers, and retweets of their tweets. In addition, we collected metadata for each tweet such as hashtags, URLs, user mentions, and location information. When a user deleted a tweet, a deletion notice was sent via the API containing identifiers for the user and the specific tweet. Similar deletion notices were sent for each tweet when a user removed the location information from all of their tweets. These deletion notices allowed us to divide the tweets in our dataset into those that were deleted and those that were not.

All Users

Statistic	Mean	Median	Std. Dev.
Deleted Tweets	7.2	1	43
Undeleted Tweets	296	168	374

Deletion-Active Users

Statistic	Mean	Median	Std. Dev.
Deleted Tweets	11	3	53
Undeleted Tweets	387	259	403

Table 3: Statistics on the numbers of deleted and undeleted tweets per user in our dataset. "Deletion-active" users are those who deleted at least one tweet during the data collection period.

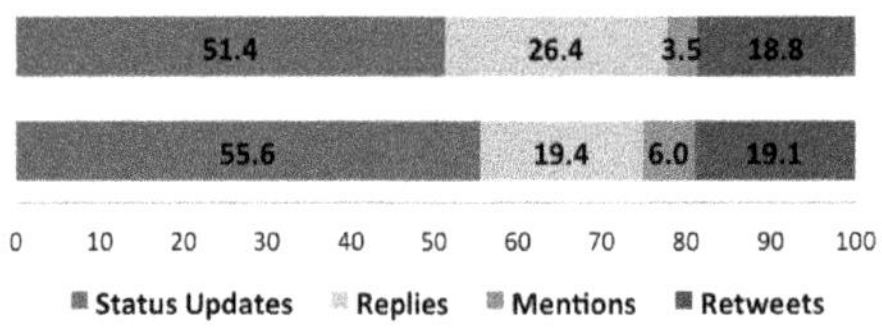

Figure 1: Breakdown of deleted (bottom) vs. undeleted tweets (top).

Table 1 lists some total figures for our dataset, and Table 2 shows some descriptive statistics on the included users. The mean numbers of followers and followees were skewed by very small numbers of public figures and automated accounts, respectively. In comparison to other studies of the Twitter population, our sample appears to be slightly biased toward users who have more followers and fewer followees [22, 6], perhaps because such accounts are more active and thus had posted the requisite number of tweets for our collection criterion.

GENERAL ANALYSIS

Breakdown of Deleted vs. Undeleted Tweets

The 67.2M collected tweets consist of approximately 65.6M (97.6%) undeleted tweets and 1.6M (2.4%) deleted tweets. Tweets were sorted into one of four mutually exclusive categories: retweets, replies, tweets that mention other users, and *status updates* (i.e., tweets that fit none of the preceding categories). Replies that mentioned other users were labeled solely as replies.

Figure 1 shows the breakdown of deleted and undeleted tweets among these categories. Compared to undeleted tweets, deleted tweets contain more status updates (55.6% vs. 51.4%), mentions (6% vs. 3.5%), and retweets (19.1% vs. 18.8%), but deleted tweets contain fewer replies (19.4% vs. 26.4%). The distributions of deleted and undeleted tweets differ significantly among the four categories of tweets ($\chi^2 = 64789.2$, $df = 3$, p-value <0.05). Pairwise per-category differences between deleted and undeleted tweets were all significant as well.[2] From a conditional probability perspective, given that a tweet is a mention or a status update, its likelihood of being deleted is slightly higher than if it is a reply or retweet.

Deleted vs. Undeleted Tweets Per User

Not all users had tweeted or deleted a tweet during the one week period. Table 3 presents some statistics on the quantities of deleted and undeleted tweets per user. Of those 292,293 Twitter users we tracked, 76% had posted at least one tweet during the monitoring period, and 49.5% deleted at least one tweet during the same period. Out of all users who posted at least once, only 65% of them deleted at least one tweet during the same period. Figures 2 and 3 show the distributions

[2]We applied Bonferroni correction for all per-category (i.e. multiple comparison) statistical tests throughout this paper.

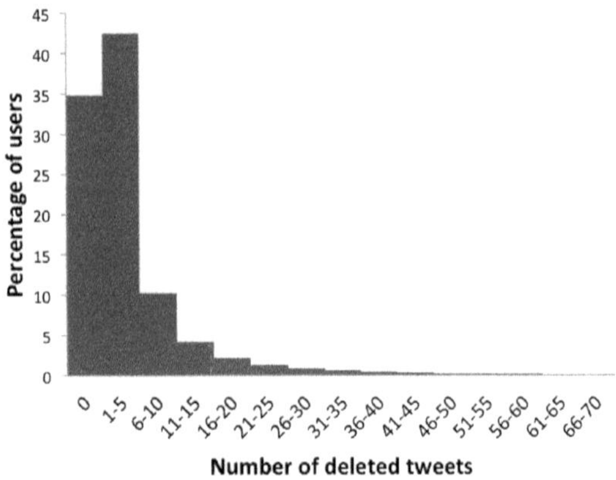

Figure 2: The percentage of users per number of deleted tweets.

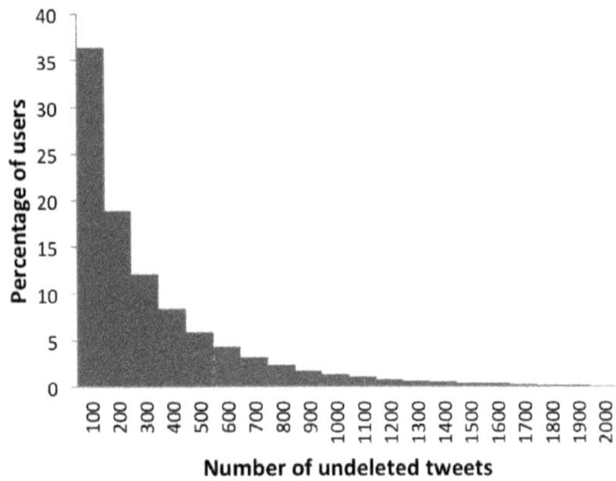

Figure 3: The percentage of users per number of undeleted tweets.

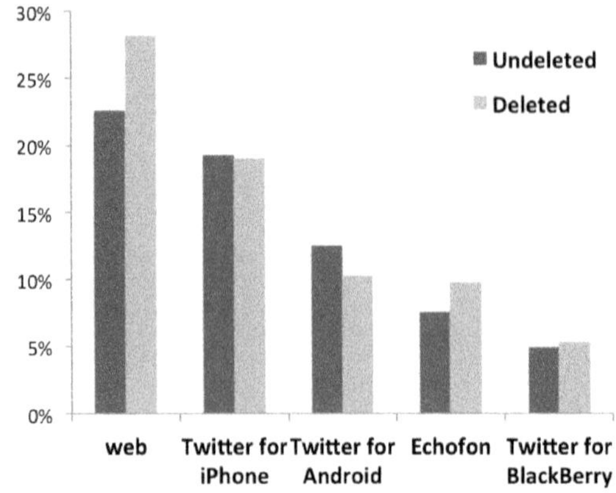

Figure 4: Top 5 clients for deleted vs. undeleted.

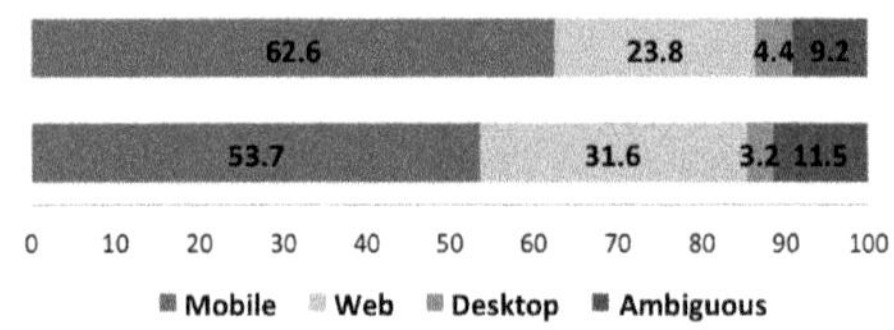

Figure 5: Source of deleted (bottom) vs. undeleted (top) tweets.

of users across quantities of deleted and undeleted tweets, respectively.

Included in our dataset were a few unusually active users. The two top users deleted 4,848 and 3,326 tweets, respectively. The first account was a bot account, and its tweets were posted and deleted automatically.[3] All its deleted tweets had the same pattern: mentioning a number of random users with no textual content. The second account was a regular account but for a very active user. However, by excluding the deleted retweets, the number of deleted tweets for this user dropped by 71% from 3,326 to only 971.

Sources of Deleted vs. Undeleted Tweets

Tweets are posted from a variety of official and third-party clients. In total, deleted tweets were posted from 1,252 unique clients, while undeleted tweets were posted from 3,395 unique clients. However, 99% of deleted and undeleted tweets were posted from 110 and 132 unique clients, respectively. The top five clients for both deleted and undeleted tweets were identical; the percentages, however, were different. Figure 4 shows the percentages of deleted and undeleted tweets from each of the top five clients. The Twitter website and the official Twitter apps dominate the sources of both deleted and undeleted tweets. The website was the source of the single largest percentage of deleted and undeleted tweets, with 28% and 23%, respectively. Only one non-official Twitter client, Echofon, was among the top five sources of deleted and undeleted tweets. Echofon has Mac, Windows, iPhone, and iPad clients as well as a Firefox extension.

We sorted the sources of 99% of deleted and undeleted tweets into web, mobile, and desktop client categories, in order to determine whether a greater proportion of deleted tweets originated from one of them. Web-originating tweets were posted from the official Twitter website, Twitter buttons on other sites, or other web clients and applications such as TwitLonger or Like My Tweet. The mobile category refers to tweets that were posted from mobile devices (including posts via mobile websites), and the desktop category refers to non-web based desktop clients. If the source of a tweet is not clear,[4] the source is labeled as ambiguous. The majority of deleted and undeleted tweets were posted from mobile or web clients. 31.6% of deleted tweets were posted from web sources, whereas 23.8% undeleted tweets were posted from web sources. 53.7% of deleted tweets were posted from mobile clients, whereas 62.6% of undeleted tweets were posted from mobile clients. Figure 5 shows the percentages of deleted and undeleted tweets for all four categories.

[3]It was not possible to methodically remove bot accounts from the dataset, due to their highly varied behaviors. However, even this extremely active account produced only 0.3% of all tweets in the dataset.

[4]One example is Echofon, which refers to multiple clients. All of them use an identical source tag ("Echofon") for tweets, thus making it hard to identify the tweet source.

The distributions of deleted and undeleted tweets differ significantly among the four types of Twitter clients ($\chi^2 = 74789.7, df = 3$, p-value <0.05). Comparing deleted to undeleted tweets in every type of Twitter client, deleted tweets were posted significantly more often from web clients ($\chi^2 = 52532.6, df = 1$, p-value <0.05) and significantly less often from web ($\chi^2 = 52532.6, df = 1$, p-value <0.05) and desktop ($\chi^2 = 5475.8, df = 1$, p-value <0.05) clients.

Replies to Deleted and Undeleted Tweets

It is natural to expect that deleted tweets are less likely to receive replies, and this was found to be true. However, not all deleted tweets went unnoticed by the Twitter community. 11% of deleted tweets initiated conversations (i.e., received one or more replies) prior to their deletion. These conversations varied in message volume. The mode of the number of replies was one (covering 89% of deleted tweets that received any replies), the mean was 1.2, the median was 1, and the maximum was 524. For comparison, 27% of undeleted tweets started conversations, with a mode of one (covering 93% of undeleted tweets that received any replies), a mean of 1.1, a median of 1, and a maximum of 838. Deleted and Undeleted tweets differ significantly in the number of replies they receive (χ^2, p-value <0.05).

Those conversations initiated by deleted tweets were rarely voluminous. The three deleted tweets that generated the most replies received 524, 263, and 176 of them, respectively. All three consisted of offers to follow users, and two of them proposed to do so in return for liking the author's tweets via third party services. Large numbers of people replied to these tweets to ask to participate. The tweet that generated the fourth most replies was a user's announcement that a university had rejected her admission application; her followers replied with sympathy and requests for more information. A full examination of the topics and contents of conversation-provoking deleted tweets was beyond the scope of this study, although it might be fruitful for future research.

To examine the connection between conversations and deletion rate, we compared the percentage of tweets with zero replies that were deleted to the percentage of tweets with one or more replies that were deleted. 2.9% of tweets with zero replies were deleted, and 1.0% of tweets with one or more replies were deleted. This difference was statistically significant ($\chi^2 = 157413.9, df = 1$, p-value <0.0001). This may suggest Twitter users are reluctant to delete their posts once they have received replies, or tweets that provoke replies tend to contain content that the user is less likely to delete.

SUPERFICIAL DELETIONS

Using cues in tweet content and metadata, we identified tweets that were deleted for two particularly superficial reasons: *typos or rephrasing* and *spam*. Typos and rephrasing comprise about 17% of deleted tweets, while spam comprises 1%. Below, we describe the heuristics used to assign these labels.

Topic	Keyword count	Keyword source
Alcohol and drug use	847	WordNet (alcohol.n.01, drink.n.02, drug_of_abuse.n.01)
Sexual activity	157	WordNet (sexual_activity.n.01)
Religion and politics	273	WordNet (god.n.01, politics.n.02, religion.n.01, religion.n.02)
Offensive comments	349	noswearing.com keyword list

Table 4: Selected topics and sources for keyword coverage investigation. For topics with WordNet as a source, all hyponyms were gathered for the indicated lemmas. Keyword counts include both single words and collocations (e.g., both *alcohol* and *alcoholic beverage*).

Topic	Tweet Coverage (%)	
	Deleted	Undeleted
Alcohol and illegal drug use	1.69	1.94
Sexual activity	7.96	7.38
Religion and politics	0.0964	0.178
Offensive comments	9.97	10.4

Table 5: Coverage by the keyword lists for selected topics over deleted and undeleted tweets.

Deleting for Typos and Rephrasing

Twitter users sometimes delete tweets and replace them with similar ones to correct misspellings, missing mentions, missing hashtags, or other small issues, as previously noticed by Hovey [9]. Users also may replace tweets to make changes that are semantically substantial but limited in scope (e.g., replacing a one word obscenity with a milder term). We assigned the *typos or rephrasing* label to all tweets apparently deleted for these reasons, and detected them as follows.

If a deleted tweets is *similar* to any K subsequent tweets from the same user, it is labeled a typo or replacement. We define similarity using a combination of edit distance (i.e., Levenshtein distance [15]) and cosine similarity. Edit distance is applied to detect deletions due to changes such as misspellings and missing hashtags, since it measures character-level similarity between tweets. To identify changes in word order, cosine similarity was utilized to take into consideration word-level similarity. To tweak parameters used in this procedure, we manually gathered 200 deleted tweets that contained typos or rephrasing and 200 tweets that did not. We then experimented with different distance and similarity thresholds, and determined that an edit distance of 5, a cosine similarity of 0.6, and a scanning memory of K = 3 were optimal.

Spam

Twitter identifies twenty different classes of spamming behaviors, including aggressive following and unfollowing, using or publicizing services that sell followers, and unsolicited

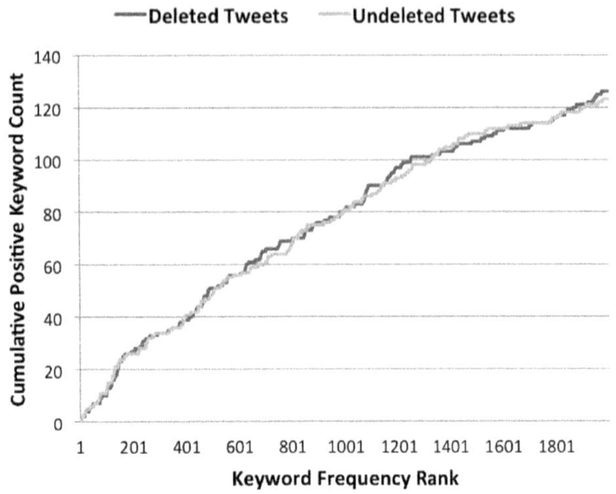

Figure 6: Cumulative distributions of positive-sentiment keywords over frequency-ranked keywords in tweets.

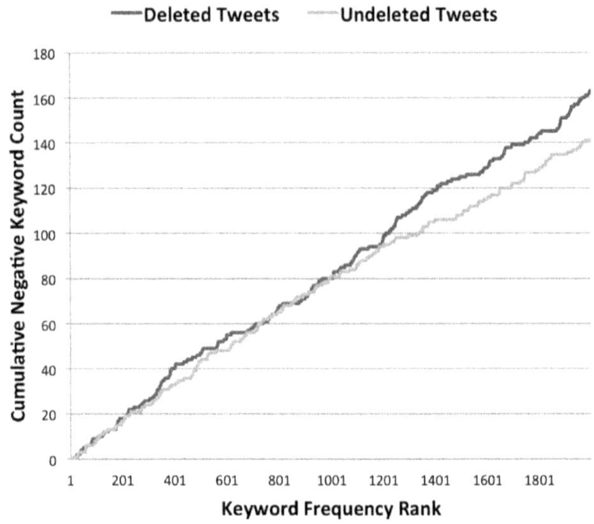

Figure 7: Cumulative distributions of negative-sentiment keywords over frequency-ranked keywords in tweets.

replies or mentions.[5] By focusing on those behaviors that related to the sources and contents of tweets, we were able to identify a lower bound for the percentage of spam among deleted tweets. We manually classified Twitter clients into those that produced only spam and those that did not. A client was considered a spam producer if it promoted or provided a service that claimed to give users more followers, or the client produced a large number of unsolicited replies or mentions.

Just above 1% of deleted tweets came from 14 sources that matched at least one of the above conditions. Most of these identified sources tweeted links that Twitter flagged as spam. Nearly all of the tweets from these sources (over 99%) promoted services that claimed to give users more followers, although a few were mentions and replies. Examples of spam tweets include *"GET MORE FOLLOWERS I WILL FOLLOW YOU BACK IF YOU FOLLOW ME - http://shortlink [Like it? http://shortlink]"*, *"I just gained 100+ followers from @user GO Follow her if you need more followers"*, and *"@user #hitfollowteam @user #rt @user"*. It is important to note that our approach to identifying spam among deleted tweets is a conservative one and should only be regarded as a lower bound.

Lexical Analysis

One of our motivations for examining deleted tweets was the study of regret in online social networks, since a link between regretted content and some fraction of deleted content seems plausible. Although regrettable content is subjective (perhaps highly so) and tweets may be deleted for a variety of other reasons, it was hypothesized that some stereotypically regrettable topics might appear with greater frequency in deleted tweets than in undeleted tweets. In this section we present a preliminary evaluation of that hypothesis, as well as some related results on sentiment analysis.

[5]The Twitter Rules; `https://support.twitter.com/articles/18311`

We decided to take a lexical approach to measuring topic frequency, as more advanced methods (such as latent Dirichlet allocation [3] for topic modeling) did not produce sensible results on the available data. Four stereotypically regrettable topics were selected, as a subset of those identified from interviews with Facebook users by Wang, et al.: alcohol and illegal drug use, sexual activity, religion and politics, and offensive comments [25]. Lists of keywords and collocations were constructed for each of those topics. Table 4 shows further information on each topical keyword list. The coverage of these keyword lists (i.e., the percentage of tweets that contained at least one word from a given list) was then calculated for approximately 10,000 randomly chosen deleted and undeleted tweets, respectively. Words in tweets were stemmed prior to the coverage calculations.

Table 5 shows the coverage of each keyword list on the sets of deleted and undeleted tweets. By this measure, it appears that the two sets are roughly equal in occurrences of the selected topics. Since word sense disambiguation was not performed, it initially seemed possible that certain polysemous words (e.g., "love" in the keyword list for sexual activities) had dominated coverage and obscured actual differences between the two populations. However, manually examining the top occurring keywords for each topic did not reveal such a pattern. It is either the case that more advanced methods are necessary to determine differences between deleted and undeleted tweets for these topics, or such differences are too subtle to detect.

Finally, a different keyword-based approach was used to assess differences in sentiment between deleted and undeleted tweets. The top 2,000 most frequently occurring words in deleted and undeleted tweets (respectively) were scanned for occurrences of words in AFINN-111, an annotated list of words that frequently express positive or negative sentiment in online social network posts [18]. Figure 6 and Figure 7 show cumulative distributions of positive and negative words in the frequency-ranked lists of words in deleted and undeleted tweets. Differences were expected to be subtle, since tweets widely vary in vocabulary and topics.

It appears that positive words occur with roughly the same distribution across the frequency rankings for both sets of tweets, though a slight difference appears between ranks 401 and 601. For negative words, a greater difference emerges past rank 1,200 and persists through the end of the examined frequencies. It appears that deleted tweets share much of the same sentiment vocabulary with undeleted tweets, although there is a possibility of more negative words in the *long tail* of the frequency distribution.

TEMPORAL ANALYSIS

Tweet deletion notices do not contain timestamps that indicate when users took actions to delete tweets. We observed that deletion notices sometimes appear in the Streaming API slightly prior to the tweets they refer to, and this raised concerns about the time difference between receiving a deletion notice and the actual deletion. To determine the accuracy of the deletion timestamp as an estimate of the actual time of deletion, we conducted an experiment in which we posted 100 tweets and deleted them immediately. We recorded times for posting, deletion, and receiving deletion notices. Then, we calculated the differences between actual deletions and receptions of the deletion notices. Mindful of possible differences in responsiveness due to changing server loads and network congestion, we conducted this experiment at several different times throughout the day. We concluded that the average time difference between deleting a tweet and receiving its deletion notice is negligible.

The results of this experiment suggest that the time of receiving a deletion notice is an accurate estimate of the time of actual deletion. For clarity, the remainder of this section implicitly assumes that theory

How Fast Is a Tweet Deleted?

Figure 8 shows a breakdown of tweet deletion over days with a maximum of one week, as this was the duration of our data collection.[6] However, a large fraction of tweets were deleted within a much shorter period of time. About 17% of tweets were deleted within 30 seconds, 22% within a minute, 58.6% within 30 minutes, and 65.2% within an hour. On average, tweets were deleted 8.45 hours after they were posted with a standard deviation of 20.85 hours.

Although most tweets were deleted shortly after they were posted, the duration between posting and deleting a tweet differs significantly for tweets that received the two superficial deletion labels. Tweets labeled as typos and rephrasing are the fastest to be deleted, with a mean of two hours and a standard deviation of ten hours. Spam tweets are deleted, on average, five hours after being posted with a standard deviation of 11 hours. Tweets that are not spam or typos and reposts,

[6] Some tweets may have been deleted more than seven days after they were posted, but those deletions exceeded the tracking period of the study.

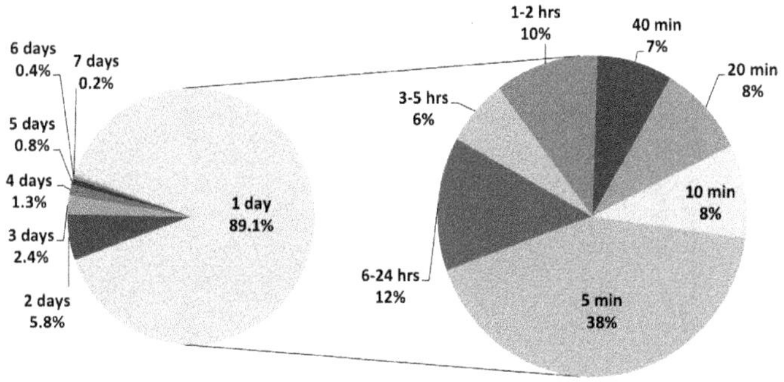

Figure 8: How fast is a tweet deleted?

on the other hand, are the slowest, with a mean time to deletion of 10 hours and a standard deviation of 10 hours. The differences between the lifespans of deleted tweets in these three populations are statistically significant (Kruskal-Wallis test, p-value$<$0.05).

The relationship between the posting frequency of a user and how rapidly they delete tweets is illustrated in Figure 9. Greater variation in lifespan toward the right side of the graph was the result of increasing sparsity in the data (i.e., fewer users who posted at greater frequencies). There appeared to be an inverse relationship between posting frequency and time to deletion, especially for frequencies less than 200. We observed that the same relationship appears between *deletion frequency* and time to deletion. Intuitively, this suggests that Twitter users who post (and delete) more often also respond more quickly when they sense a reason to delete a tweet.

Analysis Over Days of the Week

We hypothesized that the rate of tweet deletion might increase on the weekends, due to social factors generally absent in the workplace. Although it was not possible to verify the motivations behind deletions, the rate was indeed greater than average on Saturdays and Sundays. On a per-day basis, Sunday had the largest percentage of deleted tweets (15.7%) and Tuesday had the smallest percentage of them (12.9%). 70% of deleted tweets were posted during weekdays, and 30% were posted during the weekend. Figure 10 shows this breakdown. Averaging over days as appropriate, the difference in the fraction of deleted tweets posted on a weekday and a weekend day was statistically significant ($\chi^2 = 924.3, df = 1$, p-value $<$0.05). Thursday was the peak day for spam, with 15.3% of the weekly total for its label, while the peak for typos and rephrasings was on Sunday at 15.3%.

The Sunday peak reinforces but does not prove our hypothesis for the weekly distribution of deleted tweets, which will require further study. However, the relative dearth of deleted tweets on Tuesday was unexpected and not readily explainable.

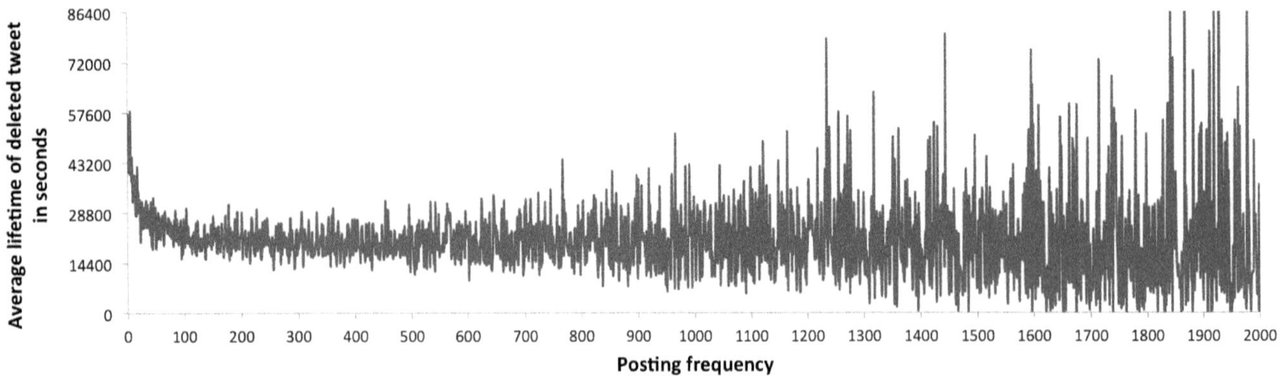

Figure 9: The relationsip between users' posting frequencies and the average lifespans of their deleted tweets.

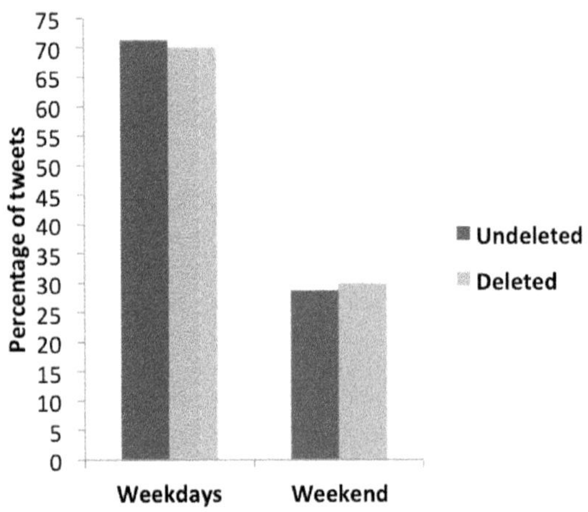

Figure 10: Distribution of deleted vs. undeleted tweets on weekdays and weekend days.

Bulk Deletion

Twitter does not provide a bulk-deletion operation for one's tweets, and some third party applications have been developed for this purpose. Tweeteraser, TwitWipe, Delete Multiple Tweets, Delete My Tweets, and the iPhone applications Delete Your Tweets and Tweeticide are some examples. We attempted to identify bulk deletions in the dataset for two reasons: to determine how widely bulk deletion is used to manage one's Twitter history and to determine the impact of this deletion tactic on our dataset, since it minimizes the element of human intervention in each deletion.

To determine the impact of bulk deletion on the composition of our dataset, we conducted an experiment to determine what fraction of tweets were deleted by bulk deletion services. To do this, we created a chronological record of each user's deletions and experimented with thresholds for time differences between deletions to identify segments of bulk deletion. We assume that the number of tweets in a bulk deletion (K) is relatively high, since otherwise the user would delete tweets manually. At the same time, the time elapsed (T) from the first event to the last in a bulk deletion set must be very small, since the process is automatic. We experimented with different values of K and T, and some of the results are shown in Table 6.

This experiment shows that when $K>5$, the number of bulk-deleted tweets decreases sharply, regardless of the value of T. Overall, it appears that a very small percentage of deleted tweets were the result of bulk deletion services. This suggests that bulk deletion has a negligible impact on the results in this paper. Due to the short period of this study, we are not able to make any conclusion regrading whether or not bulk deletion is a common tactic to manage one's Twitter history.

SPATIAL ANALYSIS OF DELETED TWEETS

Prior research has shown that users care about their location privacy and the granularity at which they disclose their locations in different contexts [21, 16]. In this section we first examine the relationship between location tags and tweet deletion, and then categorize the locations of deleted and undeleted tweets using a service provided by Foursquare.

Location Sharing on Twitter

Tweeting with location is disabled by default, and users can enable and disable the feature on a per-tweet basis. Twitter's default setting for location granularity is city- or neighborhood-level; however, more fine-grained information sometimes appears in tweets from third party clients. For instance, some third party clients allow a user to share their exact longitude and latitude in a tweet.

There are two ways to delete location information: a user may delete the tweet tagged with the information, or they may delete *all* location information attached to all of their previous tweets, leaving those tweets otherwise unaltered. Twitter does not provide the ability to merely remove the location from a single tweet, which forces users to delete and repost their tweets to accomplish that.

Deleted vs. Undeleted Tweets with Location

A total number of 494,018 undeleted tweets with locations attached were posted by 12,474 distinct users. For users who posted at least one location, the mean number of tweets posted with location was 40, the median was one, and the standard deviation was 115. However, approximately 50%

K	T	Instance of Bulk Deletion	% of Deleted Tweets
5	1s	327	0.020
10	1s	118	0.007
20	1s	37	0.002
5	5s	1265	0.078
10	5s	377	0.023
20	5s	120	0.007
5	10s	2046	0.126
10	10s	57	0.035
20	10s	163	0.010
5	15s	2670	0.165
10	15s	743	0.046
20	15s	197	0.012

Table 6: Bulk deletion experiments.

of those users posted eight or less tweets with locations (median = 8). The maximum number of tweets with location per user is 4,454, while the minimum was one tweet per user. The mean number of deleted tweets with location per user was 3.5 tweets, and the maximum was 307. The average ratio of deleted tweets to undeleted tweets with location per user is 3:10. 77.5% of deleted tweets with location were posted from Twitter's official mobile clients (iPhone, Android, Blackberry, Windows, iPad, and mobile web), 6.6% from FourSquare, and 6.4% from TweetCaster. The other 9.5% were posted from a variety of clients including UberSocial (Android and Blackberry) and Instagram.

Although it happened rarely, we observed Twitter users deleting location information without deleting the accompanied tweets.[7] 286 instances of bulk deletion of location information were invoked by 268 users. Although most users (252, or 94%) invoked this action only once, a small number of users (16, or 6%) invoked it more than once: 15 users invoked it twice, and one user did three times.

Tweets that explicitly share exact coordinates of a residence appear in both the deleted and undeleted sets. Such tweets contain text such as "I'm home", "I'm at grandma's house", or "At my friend Alice's house", and they are tagged with exact coordinates as well as other metadata such as the city and state. A manual examination of a random sampling of these coordinates confirmed that they point to residential locations.

Location Analysis via Foursquare

We hypothesized that deletion rates would vary depending on the locations at which tweets are posted, since some locations are more private or sensitive than others. We were able to test this hypothesis using the Foursquare API, which provides a reverse geocoding service to translate location information (i.e., longitude and latitude) into venues. Foursquare places each venue into one of nine categories: "Arts & Entertainment", "College & University", "Food", "Nightlife Spots", "Great Outdoors", "Professional & Other Places", "Residences", "Shops & Services", and "Travel & Transport".

[7]This data is from a different week (2012-05-16 through 2012-05-22).

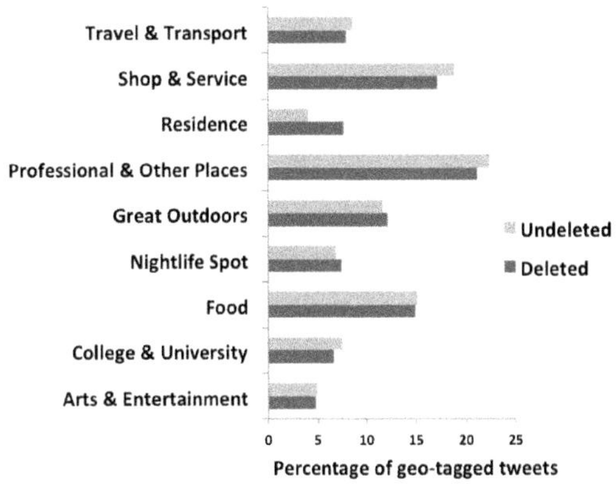

Figure 11: Distribution of venues' categories of location information attached to deleted and undeleted tweets

Using the reverse geocoding service, it was possible to assign these venue categories to locations associated with 7,604 deleted tweets (89% of all deleted tweets with locations) and 423,673 undeleted tweets (86% of all undeleted tweets with locations).

Figure 11 shows the distribution of venue categories for geo-tagged deleted and undeleted tweets. Overall, the difference between these distributions is statistically significant ($\chi^2 = 683.5, df = 8$, p-value <0.05). More specifically, the percentages of deleted and undeleted tweets in the "Residence" category (respectively 7.7% and 4%) differ significantly ($\chi^2 = 258.5, df = 1$, p-value <0.05). The difference between the percentages at "Shop & Service" (17% deleted, 19% undeleted) is also significant ($\chi^2 = 8741.4, df = 1$, p-value <0.0001). The other by-category differences were not found to be statistically significant. Notably, these findings agree with those from a prior study of location sharing. Toch et al. [23] determined that residences are particularly private places, where users of location sharing services are more reticent to announce their presence.

DISCUSSION

Our analysis shows that tweet deletion is a frequent event for a large number of users, and it spans a variety of types of information posted on Twitter. Overall, about 2.4% of all tweets are deleted and about 50% of all users deleted at least one tweet during the weeklong monitoring period. Users deleted tweets that chiefly contained text, tweets with images or locations attached, and location information attached to prior tweets.

The results from the previous sections suggest these answers to the research questions posed in the introduction:

- *The differences between deleted and undeleted tweets are distinct in some dimensions and subtle or nonexistent in others.* Substantial differences appeared in the distributions of clients used to post tweets, the locations of posts (determined via FourSquare), and the quantities of replies that they generated. Slight, inconclusive differences were observed in sentiment vocabulary and how tweets connected to the rest of the Twitter community via mentions and retweets. Substantial differences were expected in the distributions of stereotypically regrettable topics, but these were not observed, perhaps due to the sheer volume and variety of reasons tweets are deleted.

- *A substantial fraction of deleted tweets are deleted for superficial reasons.* Together, typos, rephrasing, and spam account for 18% of deleted tweets. Bulk deletions, however, comprise only a tiny fraction of the sample population. This answer comes with the caveat that small changes in a tweet's textual content (counted as "rephrasings") sometimes may have a dramatic impact on its meaning.
- *It is possible to speculate some common reasons why users delete tweets, but further investigation–including the collection of first-hand explanations of deletions–will be necessary to validate any hypotheses.* Tweets from residences seemed more likely to be deleted than those from many other kinds of locations, possibly reflecting a concern for location privacy. Tweets from web clients were more likely to be deleted than those from other sources, suggesting they are often the source of unwanted tweets that did not meet our criteria for spam.

Similarities Between Deleted and Undeleted Tweets

Our analysis shows that deleted and undeleted tweets are largely similar in terms of content, weekday and weekend volume, and volume of tweets with location information attached.

Our lexical analysis of the two sets of tweets revealed that they were fairly similar. For topics that stereotypically might provoke greater deletion, no substantial differences were observed. Although it is likely that some tweets were deleted as a result of containing those topics, more sophisticated methods or further contextual information (beyond what is available on Twitter) will be necessary to discern them. Keyword-based sentiment analysis revealed no differences in positive-sentiment vocabulary, although a slight difference may exist in negative-sentiment vocabulary. Further study will be necessary to determine whether this difference is meaningful. A longer period of data collection combined with more sophisticated topic and sentiment analysis also may produce more substantial results.

Prior to this study, we had informally hypothesized that the percentage of tweets deleted would be significantly higher from mobile devices, due to the challenges of posting (e.g., difficulties with entry methods, cognitive burden from one's surroundings). However, this was not the case, as deletion instead consumed a greater fraction of tweets posted from non-mobile sources. This could be due to the more spontaneous nature of interaction with mobile devices, in contrast with more deliberate interactions with fixed-web devices, on which users may curate their posts with greater ease.

Reasons for Deletion

The relative lifespans of spam tweets and typo or rephrasing tweets followed prior intuitions. Posts that needed to be corrected were deleted and replaced relatively quickly, while spam lasted longer, and deleted tweets that satisfied neither of those labels lasted even longer. It is possible that some spam deletions occur because spammers repost their messages (to elevate their positions in followers' timelines), although this was not verified. More advanced methods, and possibly large-scale hand labeling, will be necessary to discern structure in the remaining 82% of tweets that received neither of those two labels.

Although attempts to identify distinct topics among deleted tweets were unsuccessful, our analysis did show slightly more high-frequency negative keywords in deleted tweets than in undeleted tweets. We hypothesize a link between this difference and *regret* as a reason for deletion. Other researchers [25, 5] have studied the causal link between regret and deletion on Facebook, and their results are likely to apply to Twitter as well.

Deleting a Tweet Does Not Mean It Is Completely Gone

Deleting a tweet fails to guarantee that it will not be stored elsewhere in repositories outside of the Twitter service. Countless third party applications, such as search engines and clients, access and store users' tweets via Twitter's streaming API. Enforcing deletion across all applications is a challenge, and currently there is no mechanism to assure adherence, even if Twitter demands such compliance. The availability of deleted tweets raises security and privacy implications, both from tweets' textual contents and their location tags. It is incumbent upon Twitter to ensure that users are aware of the limitations of deletion.

Services and entities that archive deleted tweets would find themselves at odds with a proposed reform to the European Commission's data protection rules, which (as of early 2012) includes a *right to be forgotten*: "If an individual no longer wants his personal data to be processed or stored by a data controller, and if there is no legitimate reason for keeping it, the data should be removed from their system" [1]. Although the reform is presently only a draft, it demonstrates the consideration that deletion has received, and that some view the option it represents as a fundamental right.

CONCLUSION AND FUTURE WORK

To our knowledge, this was the first large-scale study of deleted data from a social network. Our comparisons have illustrated several differences between deleted and undeleted tweets in aggregate, as well as a few unexpected similarities. This study was initially motivated by one of our continuing research goals, to design intervention techniques that "nudge" users to avoid posting tweets that they might regret in the future. The results of this study show that metadata such as location and source client can be pieces of the puzzle to generate effective interventions, while interventions based upon content analysis alone are unlikely to work.

In addition to our intended goal, a few other applications of these findings are possible. Twitter-tailored spelling detection and correction could prevent the necessity of many deletions and reposts, saving users time and improving their experience. Appropriate training data for this task is readily available in large quantities via the streaming API. Spam filtering by tweet source also appears to be a feasible, albeit with low recall and high precision.

ACKNOWLEDGMENTS

This research was supported in part by the National Science Foundation under grants CNS-101276 and CNS-0905562, in part by CyLab at Carnegie Mellon under grants DAAD19-02-1-0389 and W911NF-09-1-0273 from the Army Research Office, in part by Google and in part by King Abdulaziz City for Science and Technology.

REFERENCES

1. European Commission - Press Release: Commission proposes a comprehensive reform of data protection rules to increase users' control of their data and to cut costs for businesses, 2012-01-24.
2. André, P., Bernstein, M., and Luther, K. Who gives a tweet?: Evaluating microblog content value. In *Proc. CSCW* (2012).
3. Blei, D. M., Ng, A. Y., and Jordan, M. I. Latent dirichlet allocation. *The Journal of Machine Learning Research* (2003), 993–1022.
4. Bonneau, J. Attack of the zombie photos. *Light Blue Touchpaper http://www.lightbluetouchpaper.org/2009/05/20/attack-of-the-zombie-photos/* (2009).
5. Boyd, D., and Marwick, A. E. Social privacy in networked publics: Teens' attitudes, practices, and strategies. *A Decade in Internet Time: Symposium on the Dynamics of the Internet and Society* (2011).
6. Cheng, A., and Evans, M. Inside Twitter: An in-depth look inside the Twitter world. *Sysomos http://www.sysomos.com/insidetwitter* (2009).
7. Cheng, J. Are "deleted" photos really gone from Facebook? Not always. *Ars Technica http://arstechnica.com/business/2009/07/are-those-photos-really-deleted-from-facebook-think-twice* (2009).
8. Cheng, J. Three years later, deleting your photos on Facebook now actually works. *Ars Technica http://arstechnica.com/business/2012/08/facebook-finally-changes-photo-deletion-policy-after-3-years-of-reporting/* (2012).
9. Hovey, P. Real-time recovery and visualization of deleted tweets. Master's thesis, University of California, 2010.
10. Huberman, B., Romero, D., and Wu, F. Social networks that matter: Twitter under the microscope. *First Monday* (2008).
11. Java, A., Song, X., Finin, T., and Tseng, B. Why we twitter: Understanding microblogging usage and communities. In *Proc. of WebKDD and SNA-KDD* (2007).
12. Krishnamurthy, B., Gill, P., and Arlitt, M. A few chirps about Twitter. In *Proc. WOSN*, ACM (2008).
13. Kwak, H., Lee, C., Park, H., and Moon, S. What is Twitter, a social network or a news media? In *Proc. WWW* (2010).
14. Lampe, C., Ellison, N. B., and Steinfield, C. Changes in use and perception of Facebook. In *Proc. CSCW* (2008).
15. Levenshtein, V. Binary codes capable of correcting deletions, insertions, and reversals. In *Soviet Physics Doklady* (1966).
16. Lin, J., Benisch, M., Sadeh, N., Niu, J., Hong, J., Lu, B., and Guo, S. A comparative study of location-sharing privacy preferences in the U.S. and China. Tech. rep., Carnegie Mellon University - CyLab, 2012.
17. Naaman, M., Boase, J., and Lai, C. Is it really about me?: Message content in social awareness streams. In *Proc. CSCW* (2010).
18. Nielsen, F. Å. A new ANEW: Evaluation of a word list for sentiment analysis in microblogs. *ArXiv e-prints - arXiv:1103.2903* (2011).
19. Ramage, D., Dumais, S., and Liebling, D. Characterizing microblogs with topic models. In *Proc. ICWSM* (2010).
20. Raynes-Goldie, K. Aliases, creeping, and wall cleaning: Understanding privacy in the age of Facebook. *First Monday* (2010).
21. Sadeh, N., Hong, J., Cranor, L., Fette, I., Kelley, P., Prabaker, M., and Rao, J. Understanding and capturing people's privacy policies in a mobile social networking application. *Personal Ubiquitous Computing* (2009).
22. Sysomos. Twitter Statistics for 2010: An in-depth report at Twitter's growth 2010, compared with 2009. *http://www.sysomos.com/insidetwitter/twitter-stats-2010/* (2010).
23. Toch, E., Cranshaw, J., Drielsma, P. H., Tsai, J. Y., Kelley, P. G., Springfield, J., Cranor, L., Hong, J., and Sadeh, N. Empirical models of privacy in location sharing. In *Proc. Ubicomp* (2010).
24. Tufekci, Z. Facebook, youth and privacy in networked publics. In *Proc. ICWSM* (2008).
25. Wang, Y., Norcie, G., Komanduri, S., Acquisti, A., Leon, P. G., and Cranor, L. F. "I regretted the minute I pressed share": A qualitative study of regrets on Facebook. In *Proc. SOUPS* (2011).
26. Wu, S., Hofman, J., Mason, W., and Watts, D. Who says what to whom on Twitter. In *Proc. WWW* (2011).
27. Zhao, D., and Rosson, M. How and why people Twitter: The role that micro-blogging plays in informal communication at work. In *Proc. Group* (2009).

Understanding Informal Communication in Multilingual Contexts

Chien Wen Yuan[1], Leslie D. Setlock[1], Dan Cosley[2], Susan R. Fussell[1,2]
Departments of Communication[1] and Information Science[2]
Cornell University
{cy294, lds87, drc44, srf72}@cornell.edu

ABSTRACT

Informal communication in organizations has many benefits, but people who are not native speakers of the organization's common language may find it hard to interact informally. In an interview study of nine native English-speaking and 33 non-native English-speaking students at a large U.S. university, we explore how native language shapes patterns of informal interaction. We found that non-native speakers generally preferred interacting informally with fellow speakers of their own native language as opposed to native English speakers, which hinders communication and collaboration between groups. Three factors led to this "clustering" effect: issues of common ground, feelings of social obligation to other speakers of one's native language, and desires to build social networks within a language group. Four factors led to greater motivation for cross-language interaction: a desire to build bridging capital, physical proximity, one-on-one or small-group interaction, and an established work relationship. The findings suggest ways that communication tools might reduce barriers to informal interaction between speakers of different native languages.

Author Keywords

Informal communication, cultural differences; multilingual communication

ACM Classification Keywords

H.5.m. Information interfaces and presentation (e.g., HCI): Miscellaneous.

INTRODUCTION

Informal communication in organizations has many benefits, including the development of new interpersonal relationships, awareness of others' activities, and information exchange [22, 31]. For example, researchers might find new collaborators, or students may discover job possibilities. However, people may be fluent enough to work in a multicultural organization yet be limited in their comfort with colloquial, spontaneous conversation. In this case, they may choose instead to interact with fellow speakers of their own native language during breaks, meals, and social events. This splintering or clustering effect could create barriers to relationship development, awareness and information exchange between speakers of different native languages. The goals of this paper are to understand how native language shapes patterns of informal interaction in an English-speaking organization for both native and non-native speakers and to identify opportunities for designing new tools to facilitate multilingual interaction in organizations.

As global organizations increasingly bring together people from around the world to work on common problems [15, 32, 45], they face challenges due to linguistic diversity. Similarly, in educational contexts, students from around the world work together in labs, in departments, and on campus. In such contexts, problems have been shown to arise from differences in communication styles [e.g., 3, 45], relationship norms [e.g., 23, 37], negotiation strategies [e.g.,1], methods of dealing with conflict [e.g., 37], preferred media [36], and technological proficiency [e.g., 18], which can result in misattribution of others' intentions [14] and difficulty establishing trust [28].

Multilingual organizations can use a variety of strategies to support communication among members, including human and machine translation, selection of a common language (*lingua franca*) such as English, and intensive language training for all employees [21]. Choosing English as a common language is frequently the strategy of choice for many reasons, including the role of English in higher education, colonization, political considerations, and cultural influence [e.g., 50]. Using a common language reduces the need for expensive human or machine translation, while effective language training means that, in principle, no members of the organization should be marginalized because of their native language.

However, there is evidence that speaking a common language can have negative consequences for non-native speakers. Non-native speakers may fear appearing incompetent if they seem to misunderstand conversational partners, and therefore may not request needed clarification [25, 39]. People may form within-language cliques [9, 35, 49] for the ease of conversational grounding, as in Figure 1. Non-native speakers may also lack culturally specific knowledge needed to engage in informal communication that is fundamental to maintaining awareness, developing relationships, and coordinating activities on the fly [35, 49]. At the same time, native speakers may be hesitant to engage in informal communication with non-native speakers because of concerns about the addressee's fluency, creating further clustering [e.g., 5, 25, 56].

In this paper, we explore the effects of using English as a *lingua franca* in a multilingual U.S. academic environment on both native and non-native English speakers. We first review what the literature on informal communication in organizations says about the effects of being a non-native speaker on such communication. Then, we describe and report on themes from an in-depth interview study with interviewees from a variety of linguistic backgrounds. Non-native speakers formed the within-language cliques reported by other studies, and for some of the same reasons of language fluency and lack of cultural common ground.

However, non-native interviewees also provided a number of novel insights about forces that both pushed them away from interaction with native English speakers, such as the large size and rapid conversational pace of many informal group settings, and pulled them toward interaction with members of their own language community, such as feelings of social obligation. For native English speakers, not knowing other cultures' norms for appropriate interaction pushed them away from cross-cultural communication. Interviewees also identified conditions that promoted greater informal interaction between native and non-native speakers, including personal career motivations and proximate, structured opportunities for interaction.

These forces affected participants' choices around informal multi-lingual interaction at multiple levels: individual-level forces that affected the development of relationships with specific people, group-level forces that shaped decisions about which group of people to interact with, and interaction-level forces that hindered informal communication in the moment. Thus, we close by exploring ways to use and adapt existing technologies to reduce barriers at each of these levels, with the goal of giving both native and non-native speakers more flexibility in meeting their needs around cross-lingual and cross-cultural communication in organizations.

BACKGROUND

Informal Communication

In collocated organizations, informal interactions in such places as cafeterias and hallways are essential for promoting awareness of others' activities [e.g., 22, 31] and building valuable interpersonal ties [13]. The ability to converse socially is important for developing trust [28] and establishing shared identity and context [27].

However, studies suggest that informal interaction may be challenging for less fluent individuals, whose language training may have focused on task-related terminology. These individuals may communicate well in formal situations such as meetings but have difficulty with the casual chitchat that is essential for informal information exchange and relationship development [25, 34, 49, 51].

Figure 1. Clustering by language (left, English; right, Chinese) in a campus social space.

Costs of Speaking a Non-Native Language

Formal knowledge of a non-native language does not always lead to successful communication in that language. Processing messages in a foreign language imposes direct costs, decreasing the cognitive resources available for a task [47, 48]. Perceived communication competence can also affect people's willingness to communicate. Those who perceive themselves deficient in speaking a non-native language might experience anxiety in social settings, which might lead to less willingness to communicate and a lower frequency of communication [35, 53].

Not communicating, however, also has costs. English fluency is a major source of power in multilingual teams, affecting negotiations, debate, and other job functions [e.g., 36]. Misunderstandings related to non-native language use also lead to reduced trust [26] and poorer interpersonal relationships within the workplace [10, 16, 43].

Non-Native Speakers May Avoid Informal Communication

Research suggests that less fluent individuals may hold back from participating in conversations in an effort to manage their self-presentation [5, 39]. For example, Tange and Lauring's study of a multilingual Danish firm in which English was the corporate language found that non-native English speakers reported shunning "non-essential" interactions in English [49].

Research also suggests that people who are less fluent in a non-native language prefer communicating more formally via email rather than spontaneously via IM so that they can carefully construct their thoughts [44, 45]. This behavior, while adaptive, reduces their ability to coordinate on the fly with fellow members of the organization. It is also not a feasible strategy in many face-to-face informal settings.

Further, native language based subgroups or cliques may develop [34, 49]. In organizations that use English as a common language, non-native employees often use their native language for informal talk at meals and other social occasions, excluding those who speak the common language [9, 49] while failing to build their own English skills. This avoidance of informal conversation in the *lingua franca* is problematic because the network ties and information exchange that informal communication facilitates stay bounded within language communities or are channeled through a fluent bilingual speaker [2].

THE CURRENT STUDY

The goal of the current study is to explore in depth the factors that affect how people interact informally within and across language groups. By understanding these factors, we hoped to develop new design ideas for tools to support informal communication in multilingual organizations. We focused on students studying at a large U.S. university because in 2009 there were more than 250,000 foreign students studying in the U.S. in the areas of science and engineering alone [5]. As a result, classes, academic research labs, and other campus activities are likely to include students, faculty, and post-doctoral fellows from a variety of linguistic backgrounds.

METHOD

Participants

We recruited 42 interviewees through student mailing lists and international student associations at a large, culturally diverse university in the northeastern U.S. (23 male, 19 female). We had a total of nine English speakers and 33 non-native English speakers from China (11), Taiwan (9), South Korea (9), Japan (1), Thailand (1), Indonesia (1), and Nepal (1) who had been in the U.S. for less than five years. We focused on a sample of East Asians, which provides a valuable complement to prior research conducted in Finnish and Danish companies [e.g., 4, 20] and it is representative of many current real-world multilingual groups. Students from China, Taiwan, and South Korea comprise the three largest international student groups at the school, and interviewees from these countries had a sizeable population of fellow students who spoke the same native language. The students from Japan, Thailand, Indonesia, and Nepal were part of relatively small populations of native speakers. (There are also a significant number of Indian students, but they were not included in the study due to the extensive study of the English language in Indian educational systems.)

Interviewees were studying in a wide variety of fields, including Engineering, Economics, Architecture, Business, Anthropology, Statistics, Biology, Philosophy, and Design. Eight were undergraduates, 19 were Master's students, 13 were Doctoral students, and 2 were staff members who used to be students at the university.

Materials

The interviews explored interviewees' experiences of interacting with peers who do or do not speak the same native language. For the international interviewees, the focus was on when and how they used English in informal contexts such as class breaks, meals, or social events outside of school. We asked about their interactions with those who spoke the same native language, with speakers of other non-English native languages, and with native-English speaking American students. We also asked about the topics they talked about, how conversations were initiated, and who they turned to for task-related and other kinds of information. The question sets for American interviewees were similar but inquired about only two groups: those who speak English as a native language and those who speak it as a non-native language.

Procedure

Participants were interviewed one-on-one, in English, by the first author (a native speaker of Mandarin Chinese and fluent in English). Before the interview, participants were briefed about the purpose of the study and instructed to answer the questions according to their own personal experiences. They were then interviewed following our interview protocol. When necessary the interviewer asked follow-up questions to understand specific responses. Interviews lasted 45-60 minutes; participants were then thanked and compensated $15 for their time.

Interviews were audio-recorded using a Olympus WS-331M digital recorder and transcribed using a modified version of Jefferson's [29] system, in which false starts, pauses, and other disfluencies were noted but the exact length of pauses and detailed prosodic information was not. For ease of reading, we have removed disfluencies from the excerpts presented below.

We used an iterative, grounded theory approach [24] to identify and organize recurring themes that emerged after multiple iterations of coding and analysis. During the analysis process, we first sorted the data into meaningful categories of phenomena, such as interviewees' general social activities, activities in short breaks, interaction with different groups of people, and language use in social situations. From the categories, important themes were derived and are presented in the following section.

RESULTS

Four central themes emerged that shape interaction across language boundaries among international respondents: problems in common ground and language comprehension; feelings of social obligation toward members of one's own language and culture; a desire to build rich friendships for social capital; and the positive benefits of prior structured experiences with native English speaking Americans. These themes are not mutually exclusive, or exhaustive of the themes in the transcripts, but they provide a useful framing of interviewees' experiences. Another theme, cultural awareness, emerged on the American respondents' side but was not identified by international interviewees.

Common Ground and Community Co-Membership

The first theme that ran through the interviews of non-native English speakers revolved around what Clark and colleagues [11, 12] have called *common ground*, or shared knowledge and beliefs that help ensure that messages are understood as intended. Non-native English speakers reported three types of problems with respect to common ground that influence the interaction level of informal communication: idiomatic English usage, American cultural referents, and English conversational routines.

Informal and Idiomatic English

One important source of common ground is shared knowledge of a language, which for informal interaction includes idioms, jargon, and slang. Interviewees pointed out that informal English was quite different than what they had learned in formal English classes, and their lack of familiarity with idiomatic phrases was a handicap to informal (but not work) communication.

> [N]ative speakers sometimes use a lot of idioms sometimes I cannot totally understand what they are saying. (I16, Taiwan)

> I don't know about the slangs or English they talk between friends ... (I22, Korea)

In addition, the fast pace of informal exchanges, especially in large group settings, proved challenging to non-native English speakers.

> I think I made several friends, native friends, here. And I like to talk to them but if like attending some party or some something like this … I know it's a good chance for me to know people, talk with people. I just a little afraid … I just see all the people around me. They're just chatting, chatting and talking, talking. Well, I just can't understand. (I1, China)

Although interactions among international students who spoke different native languages posed similar challenges for conversational grounding, interviewees reported less trouble in these interactions. Non-native English speakers found it easier to communicate in English in a group that includes other non-native English speakers, or people who are also new to the American culture. In part, this is because the playing field was leveled because all parties to the conversation were speaking in a non-native language.

> [I]nternational students basically can understand—English is their non-native language so they try to use formal vocabularies and good expressions. (I16, Taiwan)

> [For international students] English is merely a non-native language. So there aren't really terms that are so culture-infused that we couldn't really understand between each other. So we were using really text-book English … So they don't have much cultural references and like slangs. I think that's an important distinction between communication amongst international students and communication between American students and international students. (I26, Korea)

Shared Cultural Referents

The quote above also highlights a second important source of common ground: co-membership in a community or culture that shares certain knowledge, beliefs, and opinions [12]. For example, American college students are likely to know (and discuss) TV shows like *Saturday Night Live*, while students from other countries may not have heard of the show or know what it is about. Lack of cultural referents combined with language anxiety left non-native interviewees feeling "lost" in English-based social activities.

> If I hang out with American students, I will feel a little bit less confident. I would think that I'm not that good in English, I'm not that good in expressing myself and I don't know much about you and I don't know what I would like to talk with you. (I20, Korea)

> [J]oining conversation at a party, sometimes you need to encourage yourself to join in because they are speaking very quickly, and so they are laughing … I want to join that kind of conversation, but my English sometimes very slow, and then … I cannot understand their punch line, so I cannot share laughing. (I23, Japan)

Some interviewees also expressed frustration that their American peers had unrealistic expectations about the degree to which cultural referents would be shared across nations and cultures.

> I have this one class … one of the [American] students … had an example and the rest of class were like *what are you talking about?* And then the [American] professor was like *you have to know that* and we just feel like *come on we're from another country how can we know that?* … So sometimes it's just hard to communicate… sometimes you just don't know what they're talking about. (I9, China)

Even when American cultural referents were mutually understood, non-native speakers sometimes found the topics less interesting than things they might discuss with members of their own linguistic and cultural communities.

> So my background is all in Chinese. It's a cultural background I don't think that can change a lot when you are grownup so it's still important to have people from your own cultural background to talk and discuss things you can share interest with … if I come in here with American students, they will talk about movies, sports that type I'm not interested in and that's probably just because a different background. And also we might have different political views and so it's more comfortable to discuss deeper topics with people from your own country. (I6, China)

In contrast to their experiences with American students, interviewees felt that shared elements of culture between Asian countries and the experience of being an international student in America provided ready topics for conversation among international students with different native languages.

> I think I am much more familiar to talk with some international student from Japan or Korea. We are all in Asia so we have similar culture … (I24, Taiwan)

> [M]ost of my close friends are Asian, even [though] we cannot speak the same native language … even when we communicate in English, we can understand each other easier than when we try to understand Americans. (I25, Thailand)

Within language groups, topics of conversation ranged widely from personal to purely business and had more depth in conversation content than conversations with native English speakers.

> Well, seriously I haven't talked with American friends … We just say *hi* and … share the greetings and how things going on and that's it. We never talk about our deeper conversation. (I16, Korea)

Knowledge of Conversational Routines

Finally, common ground includes understanding certain conversational conventions such as turn-taking rules [42] and norms for appropriate conversational content in various informal settings. Interviewees had often not learned such aspects of English in their formal language training and found it challenging to identify expectations. One source of difficulty was how to respond to formulaic questions that Americans usually answer in a routinized way (e.g., responding to *how are you?* with *fine*) rather than as a true question-answer pair.

> Sometimes in daily conversation there is *what's up*? or *how are you doing?* … at first I do not know how to respond … like *what's up?* sometimes I have to think about it. (I5, China)

> It's my impression, but I feel like Americans are not comfortable with silence, so they try to do small talk, and I don't really like that, because, Korean culture, we don't do small talk, like *How are you?* and we don't ask those things. (I33, Korea)

Social Obligation

Whereas gaps in common ground between speakers of different native languages create a kind of push away from informal interaction among Americans and international students, feelings of social obligation provide a pull toward greater interaction within a language/cultural group. Our Asian respondents, especially those who were members of relatively large language communities such as the Chinese and Korean students, reported having a strong sense that they *should* choose to interact with those from their own linguistic background when given the choice.

> Actually, I do want to explore the opportunity to interact with foreign friends but … there's so many Chinese students and … they are going to say *hey come sit here. Come talk with me* or something like that and it's just very uncomfortable to say *ok no. I do not want to talk to you today. I want to talk with some foreign friends*. (I3, China)

> I have to hang out with Chinese. I'm in the Association and I don't feel you are comfortable if you abandon your own people. (I4, China)

> It's just much easier to get a Korean friend, and also Koreans think it's really important for Koreans together. There's the Korean community. (I30, Korea)

Although the majority of interviewees from China, Korea and Taiwan expressed this group-level motivation of social obligation, there was a small minority who were motivated to interact with Americans due to their personal ambitions and career goals of staying in the U.S.—goals that were sometimes in conflict with the pull forces of their community. For example, one participant stressed the need to acquire strong English skills for a future career.

> I was trying to practice my English. That's why I mostly hung out with people [who] speak English, like people from Europe mostly. (I11, China)

Others sought experience with U.S. culture, again with future job opportunities in mind.

> I want to interact with American although it's not that easy … about career and if you want to work in here or you want to live in here you definitely want to … you could really have some friends in here. (I24, Taiwan)

> I think it's important to get exposed to diverse environment, and I'm thinking of getting a job here first so it can help me definitely. So it's more like dutiful. I feel more obliged to hang out with them and get used to their culture, but like personally and emotionally not really. (I29, Korea)

These attempts to reach out across cultures and languages were not always viewed positively by other members of the same language community.

> There are definitely some people [who interact with Americans]. I will not be like that … Well, like my friend in the class, that particular girl who likes to hang out with Americans. I believe she has a task. That's her responsibility to bridge those gaps. It's not mine <laughter>. (I4, China)

Interviewees who were members of small campus language communities, such as the Japanese, Nepalese, or Indonesian interviewees, reported being more open to mingling with people from other linguistic and cultural backgrounds, most likely because they did not have a large in-group toward which they felt strong social obligations.

> Thai students … have pot luck party about twice per semester. So I not meet them that often. I think part of the reason is because I am the only one Thai [college name] student and 80% of Thai students are undergrad students. So they hang out a lot together … And other 20% … they don't hang out at all. (I25, Thailand)

Social Network and Relationship Development

In addition to reporting feelings of social obligation toward those with whom they already had established ties, our non-native English speaking interviewees were concerned with building new social networks and developing social capital. Many came to the U.S. knowing few other people, and strove for both bonding social capital that provided emotional support and bridging social capital that could enhance their future career prospects [40].

Building Bonding Social Capital

Because of concerns about being able to converse fluently with Americans, non-native speakers rarely initiated social talk with their American classmates or friends. In some cases, they avoided going to English-language social events altogether. Consequently, they saw little commonality that could be used to build relationships with American peers. Instead, they put effort into making new friends within their own language group, through a variety of informal social activities and campus organizations.

> When I first came to [school], I didn't know a lot of Koreans around campus, but I started to go to church group, and I also worked for Korean Grad Student Association, so I got to know more Koreans, and I feel more comfortable being with them, because we speak same language, and we share the similar culture (I33, Korea)

Our interviewees pointed out that they found it difficult to share similar experiences with their American peers, because Americans and Western European students preferred different types of social activities.

> A lot of Americans, they just want to go for a drink, but I don't like to drink alcohol so if they wanted to go clubbing or go to bars, I just don't want to go because I don't like to drink. (I18, Taiwan)

Furthermore, since free time was short, interviewees felt that they had to focus their relationship-building efforts where they were most likely to succeed:

> So it needs time to build the relationship. And it's not easy to build relationship with everyone. So … you have limited people that you can approach, and you not see them all the time. (I25, Thailand)

Building Bridging Social Capital

Bridging social capital consists of ties between people in heterogeneous groups that are more useful for information exchange than emotional bonding [40]. The types of bridging ties our interviewees sought were linked to their individual career aspirations. For those hoping to stay in the U.S. after graduating, ties with Americans were highly valued:

> I think you have to seek the chance to interact with people from other origins just to broaden your view or just to build up your experience. And maybe the next time you get the chance to talk about … in business … I think those are valuable experiences. (I3, China)

These interviewees, who were usually from professional schools such as Law, International Relationships, Business, or Human Resources, were more likely to attend English language social events because they actively sought job opportunities in the U.S. or they needed to learn how to deal with people of different cultures to meet the requirements of their desired job.

> [I]f I want to work in Human Resources, especially in a globalized companies it's very important to know people from different countries not just in U.S. or other European countries so I think it's really essential … (I17, Taiwan)

For others, who hoped to return to their home country after a perhaps lengthy absence, bridging ties with members of their own linguistic community offered not only bonding connections in the present but also paved a way leading to the future after they return.

> [C]ommunicating with these people from China definitely help me to have better knowledge of the current situation in China right now. Because I'm thinking about going back to China eventually some time and I will definitely spend time trying to adapt to the environment there then and since I've been outside of China for so long and that's going to take some time and these are definitely going to help me. (I11, China)

Students from larger same-language groups thus had choices about who to interact with and why, and tensions between group cohesion and expanding networks, bridging and bonding, shaped people's choices. Students from smaller same-language groups had less choice: their willingness—and need—to interact with people from other linguistic backgrounds also pushed them to expand their social networks, and to reach out more than other students.

> I try to make opportunities, "Oh, this is good weather," very simple topic. <laughs> I mean, otherwise, yeah, everybody is just focusing on research or classes. I'm sharing with three people, yeah, American people and Canadian people. But they're just focusing on studies or … few don't say anything, just no conversation, and then that's it, so I try to make opportunity to, "Hey, how it's going?" (I23, Japan)

Prior Experience in Structured Contexts

While uniformly agreeing that it was difficult to build new friendships with native English-speaking Americans, our interviewees did provide some insights into when these friendships were most likely to flourish. Three interaction-level factors in particular were mentioned throughout the interviews as supportive of relationship-building across language boundaries: physical proximity, one-on-one or small-group interaction, and an established work relationship.

Physical Proximity

International interviewees said that being in the same environment supported building social relationships, just as it does within English speaking communities [22, 51].

> I think it usually starts with a class, when I take classes with [native English speakers]. And all of my close international friends were in choir, which had a really social and close atmosphere, so we had more opportunities to talk to each other rather than academic classes. And because it's a music class it we have a common topic to start a conversation, so that was a beginning part. And I think conversations just lead us through a closer relationship. (I29, Korea)

Unfortunately, however, these relationships often did not outlast the time the individuals were collocated:

> I used to share my office with other Americans in this department, but my office changed last semester, but, when I was spending most of time there, I was around Americans all the time and we had a lot of conversations about professors, yeah … it helps a lot. It gives me more a chance to speak with [American students], and that's makes me more comfortable speaking with them, and I eventually hang out with them later after work, and I used to go ski, snowboarding with my office American mates. But, after moving my office, I feel really distant from them, cause of less interaction. (I33, Korea)

One-on-One Interactions

Our non-native English speaking respondents felt it was easier to get to know native English speakers when conversation was one-on-one or in small groups. In a social setting with many native speakers and simultaneous conversations, the non-native speakers found it hard to participate. They also felt their English-speaking partners were more attentive to their needs in one-on-one settings.

> So if I hang out with my American classmates, if we go out in a group then I would be more unlikely to speak because they'll do most of the talking themselves but if I hang out just one or two of them and then I have more room to express myself and then they'll just listen and it's easier for me to communicate with just one or two of them … (I19, Taiwan)

Established Work Relationships

Respondents also suggested that relationships were more likely to develop when people worked together on a project, because the mutual knowledge provided through work could form the basis for conversation.

> I need to order something. Or our equipment is broken. So I have to go to a technician talk about how this could happen or could you draw something for me … And well he's the one that wants to talk but he won't come to you and say *hey I want to talk to you*. It's like you come to him and say something and you just start talking. So it's like during the repairing stuff for whatever he will be like *oh what do you think of this blah blah blah* or *that blah blah blah*. Or sometimes we will talk about vacations stuff like that. (I9, China)

Native English Speakers' Viewpoints

We now turn to the interviews with native English-speaking Americans. In our analysis, we sought to identify the extent to which the themes developed based on interviews with non-native speakers could also be found in the interviews with native speakers. Our data suggest that many, but not all, of the push and pull forces that influence interaction across language barriers are shared by all members of multilingual organizations. Given that the emergent themes for native and non-native speakers only partially overlapped, we chose to juxtapose rather than merge their viewpoints. This allows us to explore each group's perspective independently, without being constrained to only the overlapping themes. The data also show some awareness among the English speaking majority of the challenges faced by non-native speakers.

Common Ground and Community Co-membership

Native speakers did not consider the language proficiency of non-native speakers as a serious issue in informal communication. But they echoed the non-native speakers' points about a lack of shared common ground derived from cultural membership. The native speakers saw this lack of common ground as a barrier to initiating conversation with non-native speakers.

> It might be easier to make friends with Americans more quickly than it might be for international students, because I think we'll have more superficial things in common … for example, if I'm from the Midwest in the United States, Ohio, and my friend's from Michigan, you know, that's a kind of superficial thing, like there's a rivalry between my school and his school, and so like we beat you in football, blah, blah, blah. And like those superficialities make it easier to like instigate conversation. Whereas if I meet someone from like Nepal, I don't know anything about Nepal. I can't say my school beat your school in football. (I36, US)

The native speakers also expressed awareness that American cultural norms and referents might be problematic for non-native speakers, making it harder for them to understand informal English conversations.

> So there's language proficiency, but there are a lot of cultural nuances as well when you talk [to] people from another culture (I42, US).

Some native English speakers expressed awareness that communicative norms differed and some understanding of factors (age, status, etc.) that guide those norms.

> In terms of age and hierarchy a lot of international people that I know are much more sensitive to the subtleties and hierarchy. And in terms of respect and authority, they have a greater sensitivity in their

> behavior, and language, and body language to all of those issues. (I36, US)

> When [international students] talk to American students they don't expect them to know anything about Chinese culture or Chinese language. So the fact that this is something that I've been studying for a while and just something that I've accumulated through self-interest like my ability to sort of like throw out facts really I guess engenders me to them. They're like, "Oh hey, this is a guy that I can say stuff and he'll understand it. I don't have to like try to pretend to be an American student to him. He's pretending to be a Chinese student to me it's a lot easier for me." (I40, US)

Social Obligation

American interviewees did not report feeling that they had obligations to any specific group members, in the way that non-native speakers reported feeling obligated toward fellow speakers of their native language. Most likely, this is because the native English speakers were in the majority in almost all contexts within the organization, and thus speaking to another native English speaker would not seem like an active choice but rather the norm. In addition, none of our native English speaking interviewees seemed to have considered that social obligation might be important to their non-native colleagues.

Social Network and Relationship Development

Native English speakers also did not raise issues of social network development as either an impetus or a barrier to interaction across language barriers. It is possible that most of the individuals who the native English interviewees would think of in this regard are also native English speakers (professors, senior students, alumni) so there was no conflict with their default patterns. They likewise did not seem to consider that this would be an important factor for non-native speakers.

Prior Experience in Structured Contexts

Our non-native speaking interviewees suggested that physical proximity, one-on-one interactions, and structured relationships were factors that increased the probability of interaction across language barriers. Some of these factors were also noted by the English speaking interviewees, especially as regards to the effects of physical collocation.

> Generally, because we're in a university environment, we can talk about [non-native English speaking acquaintances'] classes and what they're interested in doing, and that gets you a lot of mileage right there, because there's a lot of things to talk about. Or people's experiences with a certain class, how they did, how they felt about that, did they understand that concept, da da da. So I'd say that's the most common thing. (I37, US)

> I think a lot comes out in conversation at dining halls. Like you don't have anything really to talk about … Eventually you'll talk about where are you from, and like what did you do before [this university]. And so I think like, especially in my dorm on my floor, like we would all go to dining halls together as a group. So I think like you find out a lot about the group like just in informal conversation, like just people talking back and forth to each other, like trying to get to know each other and stuff. (I41, US)

The English speaking interviewees also showed some realization that the ideal structures for interaction might vary between native and non-native speakers.

> Some of [my Chinese friends] told me that they really valued one-on-one time. If you go somewhere with a friend, and you pay attention to them, then that's something that's very valued. But if you say, "Hey, come to this party. There'll be 30 people there." Then I think especially because this friend was not very good with English, he didn't really wanna come to a large group hangout, because he thought he would just kind of get lost in the background (I42, US).

DISCUSSION

In this paper, we used a grounded theory approach to explore experiences of native and non-native speakers in English-speaking informal settings. We found that non-native speakers showed a strong preference for interacting informally within their own language community rather than across language boundaries. This is consistent with the language clustering Tange and Lauring observed in a Danish multinational firm [49], suggesting that this kind of clustering is not unique to the academic environment, or to specific language communities.

We identified several factors that influenced how non-native English speakers interact within or across language groups. Interaction-level problems like how to establish common ground, especially with respect to English slang and American cultural referents, made it hard for non-native speakers to engage in informal communication with native English speakers. While all non-native interviewees passed the minimum standard of language proficiency test set by the school, colloquial English doesn't always resemble the usage or vocabulary the students' learned in preparation for studying abroad. In other words, fluency or a high spoken test score does not indicate comfort and smoothness in informal communication. Non-native speakers expressed a lack of confidence in colloquial English, leading them to prefer spending meals, breaks, and other unstructured time with other members of their own language community.

Moreover, group-level factors could contribute to this clustering effect. The number of other students on campus speaking one's native language, accompanied with a sense of social obligation to this language community, influenced how much emphasis non-native speakers placed on building relationships within their own language community versus across language communities. Non-native speakers also expressed a tradeoff between building relationships within and beyond their own language community, consistent with Ying's [56] findings that Taiwanese students considered social capital to be a finite resource. This preference for interaction within one's own language community, however, was not universal. Seeking to expand one's social network as an individual-level factor drives those with a greater motivation to stay in the U.S. after graduation, or who were members of small language communities, to try to develop friendships with Americans.

Although issues of common ground and the desire for social relationships within one's own language community worked against informal interaction across language boundaries, there were four factors of different levels that increased the likelihood of informal interaction between our non-native English speaking interviewees and native English speaking Americans. Other than an individual's pursuit of a career in the U.S,, on the interaction level, non-native speakers found it easier to establish relationships with Americans if they were physically close (e.g. adjacent offices), or if there was a formal work relationship (e.g., lab mates). On the group level, non-native speakers tend to socialize more across groups if group size was very small.

For the native English speakers, one factor that influenced their interaction with non-native speakers was a lack of "cultural common ground," or a shared understanding of appropriate conversational topics and interactional processes in other cultures. To some extent, however, they felt that these problems could be reduced through better cultural awareness. Such awareness does not mean a full grasp of cultural norms from other countries; instead, it is a recognition and understanding that there may be different norms, and where these differences are most likely to arise. Adaptations followed by cultural awareness, such as acting according to non-native speakers' familiar way, can help interaction with non-native speakers.

Despite an awareness of possible cultural barriers, native English speakers might not be aware of the profoundness of the language issues faced by non-native speakers and how these issues might impede potential interaction. Like the non-native speakers, native English interviewees also thought that having structured interactions, such as working on the same group project or being members of the same lab, made it easier to interact across language communities.. Possible adaptations like prompt detection of miscommunication by offering explanations of culture-ridden referents, slowing down while talking in groups, or using fewer idioms, can alleviate non-native speakers' language issues.

Although we did not directly measure the outcomes of linguistic clustering on non-native English interviewees' participation in the English language academic community, we can surmise from previous research [e.g., 30] that this lack of informal interaction across language groups will influence important organizational processes, including the development of new collaborations, informal awareness of colleagues' activities, and information exchange.

One implication of our results is that organizations need to think carefully about their informal relationship-building activities. For example, in one department studied in this paper with a very large number of graduate students from Asia, the faculty organized a large weekly get together at a local bar. According to our interviewees, this is precisely the type of event at which clustering, rather than informal interaction across language barriers, is likely to occur.

Tool Support for Informal Interaction

In addition to more carefully chosen opportunities for face-to-face interaction within an organization, CMC tools play an important role in both work and educational multilingual contexts. In work contexts, CMC tools are used to facilitate geographically distributed teams [15, 32, 45]. In educational contexts, CMC tools for online learning such as Blackboard, Moodle, and Piazza are increasingly used to complement classroom instruction [46]. Further, evidence suggests that non-native speakers often prefer CMC to face-to-face interaction [e.g., 44, 46].

Thus, CMC tool design may allow global organizations to help non-native speakers be more comfortable and more effective members. This does not mean that systems should *enforce* cross-lingual interaction: although effective communication and diverse participation can be important for both the organization and the long-term success of individual members, participants often had values that led them to interact with same-culture and same-language partners. Instead, our goal is to support these values and encourage people to reflect on them, while mitigating barriers to cross-lingual interaction such as the lack of shared cultural referents or awareness of language difficulties that participants highlighted.

We structure our discussion around barriers at the level of choosing cultural groups, of fostering individual relationships, and of supporting particular interactions.

Groups: Facilitating Awareness of Culture

At the level of social groups, our non-native English speaking interviewees said it was easier to communicate with fewer participants, more room to talk, and more attention devoted to the conversation. CMC tools could partially recreate these conditions by manipulating either the composition or the perception of group sizes. Familiar examples include supporting parallel conversations in discussion and chat spaces through providing separate topics, as in Babble [20]. The Mad Hatter system [4] helped participants experience large physical gatherings as a set of smaller, more manageable conversations, while Talking in Circles does a similar job in a virtual space [41]. A number of techniques, including subgrouping, recommendations, filtering, and awareness interfaces, can help CMC tools create more intimate and attentive environments to support cross-lingual communication.

But participants didn't just want subgroups: they wanted subgroups that met relational goals and fulfilled social obligations. Sometimes this meant reaching across languages or cultures, but other times it required supporting the same-culture community. Thus, recommendation tools seem less appropriate than tools that support awareness of others' linguistic and cultural backgrounds. Especially in dynamic environments, social proxies [20] augmented with such information might help people in a multilingual organization quickly see groups, topics, and places where people of different backgrounds are most active, allowing them to make choices that suit their current goals.

CMC tools might also encourage people to reflect on these goals and obligations by providing aggregate views of their interaction history with people of different linguistic and cultural backgrounds. Since such activity data is more useful with information to help interpret it [32], the tool might also explicitly present information about the value of bilingual networks for building bridging social capital in organizations [2] and provide indicators of this capital. Following the lead of the Search Dashboard, which used comparisons to expert behavior to guide searchers [5], systems might also present the interaction history and social network of successful peers or leaders in the organization as points of comparison to support reflection and suggest behavior.

Individuals: Supporting Relationship Development

At the level of individual relationships, interviewees said that a structured work context helped them develop knowledge about each other, facilitating more natural and spontaneous informal conversation. CMC tools might help create shared contexts, referents, and structures for conversation in a number of ways. Recommender systems might play a useful role here, as part of a virtual buddy system that augments existing language partner matching programs on campuses by recommending other-language partners with shared interests. This would likely increase their chance of having common ground for mutually interesting and understandable conversation. Such a system might be especially useful for members of minority cultural groups such as our Thai and Indonesian participants, who had to reach out beyond their own community because of a lack of numbers.

The communication channel itself might help structure activities and provide referents. Shared activities at a distance, such as physical exercise [38], might work as icebreakers that help people cross language and cultural barriers by both structuring and constraining interactions. The channel might also organize conversation around artifacts that serve as shared referents, as in the SocialTV system's use of television shows as a platform for social activity [19]. Online educational tools also often structure group activities around specific topics, and the combination of collaborative learning and social presence leads to satisfying outcomes for students [46]. Further, in both educational and icebreaker contexts, interaction partners are often chosen by an external authority such as the teacher or host. CMC-enabled icebreakers and training tools can also delegate partner choice to the system, perhaps reducing feelings of social obligation while allowing organizations to encourage cross-lingual interactions.

CMC tools might also manipulate features of the channel to create feelings of social presence and proximity that might elicit greater informal interaction across language groups, based on our participants' own experiences of the value of proximity. For instance, abstract representations of presence [e.g., 20, 41] or actual video-conferencing [e.g., 30] may both increase this sense of presence.

Interactions: Enhancing Grounding and Empathy

At the level of individual conversations, non-native speakers needed help with cultural references and colloquial language. Systems might provide information relevant to current context such as status updates, IM conversations, or emails in order to build this common ground. For instance, IdeaExpander extracted keywords from an IM conversation to retrieve pictures that supported multi-cultural brainstorming [52]. Displaying a collage of pictures and text relevant to ongoing conversation might contextualize cultural referents and provide information to help resolve ambiguity, translation errors, and other fluency issues. Another way to address fluency issues would be to exploit real-time machine translation tools that allow people to converse in their native languages [54, 55]. And, though we have focused on CMC, physical spaces might also be augmented with a combination of speech recognition and ambient displays to present icebreakers and conversational referents.

Native speakers were aware of these cultural differences, but were relatively insensitive to language difficulties even though these were a major problem for non-native speakers. Techniques that analyze the conversation and present information about potential difficulties might help people realize and react when fluency issues are affecting an interaction. This idea is based on earlier systems that displayed relative levels of activity in a group conversation, leading participants to change their speaking behavior [16] and reflect on the conversation [5]. To address potential barriers to fluent conversation, systems might measure the rate of speech, rate of topic changes, presence of idiom and slang, measures of formality or reading level, and other indicators of linguistic complexity. Presenting these metrics along with target or typical values of these indicators for native and non-native speakers could help raise awareness of both specific problematic moments and the general need to be sensitive to linguistic ability. The design would need to present this data in a way that doesn't reflect badly on non-native speakers, but done well it might lead to more sensitive and effective cross-lingual interaction.

LIMITATIONS AND FUTURE DIRECTIONS

One of the limitations of the study is that the interviewees were recruited from a university, which while culturally diverse is relatively homogenous in terms of age and occupation and does not draw from all cultures equally. In particular, we focused on the experiences of members of the most common language communities, so we can provide no insights into the experiences of speakers of other languages such as Arabic, which are sizeable communities in many global organizations. In addition, as the study was conducted at a university, the results cannot be automatically generalized to other organizational settings. To address this limitation, we plan to follow up this work with a more extensive interview and survey study in a corporate environment that includes a greater diversity of language communities.

In addition, we used English for all of our interviews because we wanted to ensure consistency in the semi-structured interview process. We don't think that the language used in the interviews strongly affected the results because all interviewees self-identified as fluent in English, and they were all used to using English in similar contexts as students in the U.S. We also conducted a pilot study in Mandarin with native Mandarin speakers while we were developing the interview protocol. Interviewees using Mandarin reported themes and experiences almost identical to those reported by our study interviewees using English.

Furthermore, because we only interviewed people in an American English-speaking organization, we cannot speak to the experiences of non-native speakers in organizations that use other languages as their lingua franca, or which are situated in other countries. We are currently conducting a parallel study of native and non native Mandarin speakers studying in Taiwan in order to tease apart these issues.

Finally, for most of our interviewees, language and culture were inextricably intertwined and it can be difficult to identify which problems arise from cultural differences and which arise from language barriers and how language proficiency might help with cultural familiarity. To the extent that members of a variety of cultures and language groups expressed similar sentiments regarding inter-lingual interaction, however, we hope that we have captured general experiences of being a non-native speaker rather than specific characteristics of an interviewee's cultural background. To try to disentangle culture from language, future interview studies might include participants who were more or less fluent in English while holding cultural background and experience in the U.S. constant.

CONCLUSION

This study examined the factors that affect informal communication between speakers of different native languages who are members of a single large English speaking organization. Our findings indicate several forces that push people away from interaction across language boundaries, such as problems in conversational grounding, social obligations towards members of one's own language community, and the desire to develop relationships with people who speak the same native language. The findings also suggest that certain factors promote greater interaction across language boundaries, including physical proximity and structured interactions with native English speakers. Tools that provide structure and presence with support for awareness of others' linguistic and cultural background may be a promising approach for supporting informal interaction in multi-lingual organizations.

ACKNOWLEDGMENTS

This research was funded in part by National Science Foundation grant # 1025425. The material is also based in part on work supported by the National Science Foundation, while Susan Fussell was working at the Foundation. Any opinion, findings, and conclusions or recommendations expressed in this material are those of the authors and do not necessarily reflect the views of the National Science Foundation. We thank Lydia Wright and Sarah Sanders for their assistance transcribing the interviews.

REFERENCES

1. Adair, W. L., Okumura, T., & Brett, J. M. (2001). Negotiation behavior when cultures collide: The United States and Japan. *Journal of Applied Psychology, 86*, 371–385.
2. Andersen, H., & Rasmussen, E. (2004). The role of language skills in corporate communication. *Corporate Communication: An International Journal, 9*, 231–242.
3. Anwati, D., & Craig, A. (2006). Behavioral adaptation within cross-cultural virtual teams. *IEEE Transactions On Professional Communication, 49*, 44–56.
4. Aoki, P. M., Romaine, M., Szymanski, M. H., Thornton, J. D., Wilson, D., & Woodruff, A. (2003). The mad hatter's cocktail party: a social mobile audio space supporting multiple simultaneous conversations. In *Proceedings of CHI 2003*, 425–432.
5. Barner-Rasmussen, W., & Bjorkman, I. (2007). Language fluency, socialization and inter-unit relationships in Chinese and Finnish subsidiaries. *Management and Organizational Review, 3*, 105–128.
6. Bateman, S., Teevan, J., and White, R. W. (2012). The search dashboard: how reflection and comparison impact search behavior. In *Proceedings of CHI 2012*, 1785 - 1794.
7. Bergstrom, T., and Karahalios. K. (2007). Conversation Clock: Visualizing audio patterns in co-located groups. In *Proceedings of HICSS 2007*, 78.
8. Bernstein, M. S., Marcus, A., Karger, D. R., & Miller, R. C. (2010). Enhancing directed content sharing on the web. In *Proceedings of CHI 2010*, 971–980.
9. Charles, M., & Marschan-Piekkari, R. (2002). Language training for enhanced horizontal communication: A challenge for MNCs. *Business Communication Quarterly, 65*, 9–29.

10. Chevrier, S. (2003). Cross-cultural management in multinational project groups. *Journal of World Business, 38*, 141–149.
11. Clark, H. H., & Brennan, S. E. (1991). Grounding in Communication. In L. B. Resnick, R. M. Levine & S. D. Teasley (Eds.), *Perspectives on Socially Shared Cognition* (pp. 127–149). Washington, DC: APA.
12. Clark, H. H., & Wilkes-Gibbs, D. (1986). Referring as a collaborative process. *Cognition, 22*, 1–39.
13. Constant, D., Sproull, L., & Kiesler, S. (1996). The kindness of strangers: The usefulness of electronic weak ties for technical advice. *Organization Science, 7*, 119–135.
14. Cramton, C. D. (2001). The mutual knowledge problem and its consequences in geographically dispersed teams. *Organization Science, 12*, 346–371.
15. DeSanctis, G., & Monge, P. (1998). Communication processes for virtual organizations. *Journal of Computer Mediated Communication, 3*(4).
16. DiMicco, J. M., Pandolfo, A., and Bender, W. (2004). Influencing group participation with a shared display. In *Proceedings of CSCW 2004*, 614-623.
17. DiStefano, J. J., & Maznevski, M. L. (2000). Creating value with diverse teams in global management. *Organizational Dynamics, 29*, 45–61.
18. Dubé, L., & Paré, G. (2001). Global Virtual Teams. *Communications of the ACM, 44(12)*, 71–73.
19. Ducheneaut, N., Moore, R. J., Oehlberg, L., Thornton, J. D., & Nickell, E. (2008). SocialTV: Designing for distributed, social television viewing. *International Journal of Human-Computer Interaction, 24*, 136–154.
20. Erickson, T., Smith, D., Kellogg, W., Laff, M., Richards, J. & Bradner, E. (1998). Socially translucent systems: Social proxies, persistent conversation and the design of "Babble." In *Proceedings of CHI 1998*, 72–79.
21. Feely, A.-J., & Harzing, A. W. K. (2003) Language management in multinational companies. *Cross-Cultural Management: An International Journal, 10*, 37–52.
22. Festinger, L., Shachter, S., & Back, K. (1950). *Social Pressures in Informal Groups*. NY: Harper.
23. Gibbs, J. L. (2009). Culture as kaleidoscope: navigating cultural tensions in global collaboration. In *Proceedings of ICIC 2009*, 89–98.
24. Glaser, B. G., & Strauss, A. L. (1967). *The Discovery of Grounded Theory: Strategies for Qualitative Research*. New York: Aldine de Gruyter.
25. Harzing, A-W., & Feely, A. J. (2008). The language barrier and its implications for HQ-subsidiary relationships. *Cross-cultural Management: An International Journal, 15*, 49–61.
26. Henderson, J. K. (2005). Language diversity in international management teams. *International Studies of Management and Organization, 35*, 66–82.
27. Hinds, P. J., & Mortensen, M. (2005). Understanding conflict in geographically distributed teams: The moderating effects of shared identity, shared context, and spontaneous communication. *Organization Science, 16*, 290–307.
28. Jarvenpaa, S. L., & Leidner, D. E. (1999). Communication and trust in global virtual teams. *Organization Science, 10*, 791–815.
29. Jefferson, G (1984). Transcript notation. In J. M. Atkinson and J. Heritage (Eds.) *Structures of Social Action: Studies in Conversation Analysis*. Cambridge: Cambridge University Press.
30. Kirk, D. S., Sellen, A. & Cao, X. (2010). Home video communication: Mediating 'closeness'. In *Proceedings of CSCW 2010*, 135–144.
31. Kraut, R., Egido, C., & Galegher, J. (1990). Patterns of Contact and Communication in Scientific Research Collaborations. In J. Galegher, Kraut, R., & Egido, C. (Ed.), *Intellectual Teamwork*. Hillsdale, NJ: LEA.
32. Leshed, G., Cosley, D., Hancock, J. T., and Gay, G. (2010). Visualizing language use in team conversations: designing through theory, experiments, and iterations. In *Proceedings of CHI 2010*, 4567-4582.
33. Lipnack, J., & Stamp, J. (1997). *Virtual Teams: Reaching Across Space, Time and Organizations with Technology*. NY: John Wiley & Sons.
34. Luo, Y., & Shenkar, O. (2006). The multinational corporation as a multilingual community: Language and organization in a global context. *Journal of International Business Studies, 37*, 321–339.
35. MacIntyre, P. D., Noels, K. A., & Clement, R. (1997). Biases in self-ratings of non-native language proficiency: The role of language anxiety. *Language Learning, 47*, 265–287.
36. Massey, A., Montoya-Weiss, M., Hung, C., & Ramesh, V. (2001). When culture and style aren't about clothes: Perceptions of task-technology "fit" in global virtual teams. In *Proceedings of Group 2001*, 207–213.
37. Morris, M. W., Podolny, J., & Sullivan, B. N. (2008). Culture and coworker relations: Interpersonal patterns in American, Chinese, German, and Spanish divisions of a global retail bank. *Organization Science, 19*, 517–532.
38. Mueller, F., Agamanolis, S., & Picard, R. (2003). Exertion interfaces: sports over a distance for social bonding and fun. In *Proceedings of CHI 2003*, 561–568.
39. Olson, G. M., & Olson, J. S. (2000). Distance matters. *Human Computer Interaction, 15*, 139–178.

40. Putnam, R. (2000). *Bowling alone: The collapse and revival of American community*. NY: Simon and Schuster.

41. Rodenstein, R., & Donath, J. S. (2000). Talking in circles: Designing a spatially-grounded audio-conferencing environment. In *Proceedings of CHI 2000*, 81–88.

42. Sacks, H., Schegloff, E., & Jefferson, G. (1978). A simplest systematics for the organization of turn-taking for conversation. *Language, 50*, 696–735.

43. Sarbaugh-Thompson, M., & Feldman, M. S. (1998). Electronic mail and organizational communication: Does saying "hi" really matter? *Organization Science, 9*, 685–698.

44. Setlock, L. S., & Fussell, S. R. (2010). What's it worth to you? The costs and affordances of CMC tools to Asian and American users. In *Proceedings of CSCW 2010*, 341–350.

45. Shachaf, P. (2008). Cultural diversity and information and communication technology impacts on global virtual teams: An exploratory study. *Information Management, 45*, 131–142.

46. So, H.-J., & Brush, T. A.. (2008). Student perceptions of collaborative learning, social presence and satisfaction in a blended learning environment: Relationships and critical factors. *Computers & Education, 51*, 318–336.

47. Takano, Y., & Noda, A. (1993). A temporary decline of thinking ability during foreign language processing. *Journal of Cross-Cultural Psychology, 24*, 445–462.

48. Takano, Y., & Noda, A. (1995). Interlanguage dissimilarity enhances the decline of thinking ability during foreign language processing. *Language Learning, 45*, 657–681.

49. Tange, H., & Lauring, J. (2009). Language management and social interaction within the multilingual workplace. *Journal of Communication Management, 13*, 218–232.

50. Tietze, S. (2004). Spreading the management gospel–in English. *Language & Intercultural Communication, 4*, 175–189.

51. Veinott, E., Olson, J., Olson, G., & Fu, X. (1999). Video helps remote work: Speakers who need to negotiate common ground benefit from seeing each other. In *Proceedings of CHI 1999*, 302–309.

52. Wang, H-C., Fussell, S. R., & Cosley, D. (2011). From diversity to creativity: Stimulating group brainstorming with cultural differences and conversationally-retrieved pictures. In *Proceedings of CSCW 2011*, 265–274.

53. Yashima, T. (2002). Willingness to communicate in a non-native language: The Japanese EFL context. *The Modern Language Journal, 86*, 54–66.

54. Yamashita, N., & Ishida, T. (2006). Effects of machine translation on collaborative work. In *Proceedings of CSCW 2006,* 515-523.

55. Yamashita, N., Inaba, R., Kuzuoka, H., & Ishida, T. (2009). Difficulties in establishing common ground in multiparty groups using machine translation. In *Proceedings of CHI 2009*, 679-688.

56. Ying, Y-W. (2002). Formation of cross-cultural relationships of Taiwanese international students in the United States. *Journal of Community Psychology, 30*, 45–55.

Lost in Transmittance: How Transmission Lag Enhances and Deteriorates Multilingual Collaboration

Naomi Yamashita[1], Andy Echenique[2], Toru Ishida[3], Ari Hautasaari[3]

[1] NTT Communication Science Labs.
Kyoto, Japan.
naomiy@acm.org

[2] University of California, Irvine
apexinandy@gmail.com

[3] Kyoto University
ishida@i.kyoto-u.ac.jp
arihau@ai.soc.i.kyoto-u.ac.jp

ABSTRACT
Previous research has shown that audio communication is particularly difficult for non-native speakers (NNS) during multilingual collaborations. Especially when audio signals become distorted, NNS are overburdened by not only having to communicate with imperfect language skills, but also compensating for the deteriorations. Under these faulty audio conditions, NNS need to pay extra time and effort to understand the conversation. In order to give NNS more time to process conversations, we tested the insertion of silent gaps (from 0.2 to 0.4 seconds) between conversational turns. First, gaps were inserted into a previously taped conversation, resulting in a significant improvement of NNS's understanding of the conversation. Second, gaps were inserted during a real-time audio conference by adding artificial delay between native speakers. The results show that the added delays have a combination of beneficial and detrimental effects for both native and non-native speakers. The findings have implications towards how audio conferencing can be improved for NNS.

Author Keywords
Audio conferencing, non-native speakers, mental resource, silent gaps, delay.

ACM Classification Keywords
H.5.3 [**Group and Organization Interfaces**]: Computer-supported cooperative work, Synchronous interaction.

INTRODUCTION
Audio conferencing is one of the most highly used communication tools in global enterprises and social organizations. It is very cost-effective, convenient, and allows rapid decision making among people in different locations.

Even though the use of audio conferencing continues to grow very rapidly, conference calls impose an excessive burden on non-native speakers (NNSs) [13, 15, 16]. In an audio conference, it is generally difficult to follow everyone's speech; audio quality is typically low, some terms or even some voices cannot be heard, and there tends to be extraneous noise. It is also sometimes difficult to identify who is speaking. Research has demonstrated that non-native speakers have particular difficulty perceiving speech in such imperfect conditions because they cannot instantly come up with a range of alternative possibilities once they miss a term [13, 16]. According to Rogers, "even true bilinguals cannot reach the ability of monolinguals in the presence of noise [17]." It is thus important for system designers to consider the plight of non-native speakers in imperfect audio conditions.

To date, however, virtually no research has focused on supporting non-native speakers in audio conferences. Although researchers have proposed novel solutions to improve the current audio conference (e.g., improving sound quality and adding visual cues [3, 4]), those approaches are not specifically designed for non-native speakers.

Our interest is in supporting non-native speakers in audio conferences. As a preliminary investigation to capture the difficulty they face when joining an audio conference, we conducted a small survey and a follow-up interview in the Japanese computer science research community. Seven researchers who play an active role in their respective communities (such as HCI, HRI, AI) participated in the investigation. All have served as international committee members more than ten times and have attended at least three audio conferences. The average length of their overseas experience was two years.

From the questionnaire results, we found that their perceived comprehension and production levels of speech during conference calls were much lower than in face-to-face meetings (Tables 1 and 2). Although the sample size is too small to derive any conclusions, astonishingly, 70% of the professionals who are considered to be Japanese representatives of various technical fields feel that they cannot contribute even half of what they want to say. The interesting point is that they seem to face particular difficulty in audio conferences, while they feel comfortable using a second language in face-to-face meetings.

Table 1. NNS's perceived ability to follow conversation.

Comprehension level (%)	0-20	20-40	40-60	60-80	80-100
Face-to-face	0	0	1	2	4
Audio conf.	0	0	4	2	1

Table 2. NNS's perceived ability to make an utterance.

Utterance level (%)	0-20	20-40	40-60	60-80	80-100
Face-to-face	0	0	3	2	2
Audio conf.	3	2	0	1	1

Inspired by these questionnaire results, this study explores ways to support the verbal activities of such high-skilled, non-native speakers in audio conferences. Since most of these people could comprehend and contribute in face-to-face meetings, we believe their language skills are sufficiently high; if the same meeting were held face-to-face, their performance would have been better. Rather than a problem of their language skills, the problem is the lack of resources for concurrently processing multiple demanding tasks [1, 20]; when they are using their resources to compensate for the missed cues/information in an audio conference, their ability to think about the conversational content and to analyze the forthcoming input (such as phonetic analysis and parsing an ongoing conversation) is likely to decline [20]. Under such condition, non-native speakers will usually be left behind in a conversation.

Based on the previous works, we hypothesized that giving non-native speakers more time to understand the conversation would reduce their mental load. We developed the idea of inserting frequent silent periods for non-native speakers to compensate for the high demand on their mental resources. Ideally, those silent periods should allow non-native speakers to deal both with incomplete information and language processing in a timely manner (without being left behind in the conversation).

In this paper, we examine whether adding short silent gaps between native speakers' conversational turns improves non-native speaker's verbal activities. We explored this issue in two stages. First, we examined whether inserting small gaps in a pre-recorded meeting actually improved non-native listener's comprehension; second, we examined whether inserting small gaps in a real-time audio conference by adding artificial delays only among native speakers improved the non-native speakers' comprehension and production of speech. Note that the artificial delay allowed non-native speakers to listen to native speaker's speech earlier than other native speakers, which gave the non-native speakers a small break between utterances during which they could process the speech.

This study is important in two ways. First, we demonstrate that gaps as short as 0.2-0.4 seconds added between native speakers' conversational turns did indeed improve non-native listener's comprehension. Second, we report on how the small gaps were produced by controlling the amount of transmission delays between native and non-native speakers and how it affected native and non-native speakers' conversation. Although transmission delay is a common issue that has been studied for years [19], to our knowledge, no research has investigated its effects on conversation between native and non-native speakers.

In the remainder of this paper, we first draw on prior research that guided our work. Next, we describe our iterative studies and present the results for each study. Finally, we conclude with a discussion on the implications of our findings and some issues raised by them.

RELATED WORK

Audio conferencing is difficult not only for non-native speakers but also for native speakers. Indeed, previous research has pointed out various problems in audio conferencing. Many are related to the audio itself, such as poor audio quality, noise, and the inability to identify speakers. Others are related to the attendee's behavioral issues (e.g., speakers tend not to check others for their understanding) or technical issues (e.g., attendees are unable to check who is attending the meeting) [27].

Researchers have suggested many techniques for dealing with those problems. Many researchers have tried to improve the audio quality in audio conferences, starting with the reduction of reverberation. For example, previous works [9, 25] suggested that spatialized audio enhanced attendees' comprehension of speech by enabling them to distinguish between background noise and the focal speaker's voice. Researchers have also attempted to augment audio conferences with such visual cues as video images of attendees and/or expression buttons. Video images (spatialized video) have proven particularly useful in multiparty conversations: smoother turn-takings [24], and increased attendee involvement and ability to keep track of the conversation [7]. Besides adding a video channel, Yankelovich added a private chat channel so that attendees can consult with others without disturbing the main conversation [26]. In addition, for those who missed small parts of the conversation, Junuzovic et al. proposed an "accelerated instant replay" function [8], which allows the attendees to catch up on missed content.

Some of these techniques could be useful for non-native speakers as well. For example, spatialized audio also appears beneficial to non-native attendees by extracting speech information from background noise [5]. For augmenting audio conferencing with visual cues, Veinott studied non-native English speaking pairs and found that video images facilitated mutual understanding by helping them assess each other's state of understanding [23]. While other techniques such as additional chat channels and accelerated instant replay might also be useful to non-native speakers (for asking others for clarification and catching up with the discussion), we must keep in mind that non-native speakers are already overwhelmed with multiple parallel processes such as linguistic processing (i.e. speech recognition, production of a foreign language, and recovering from the missed conversational context when necessary) and intensive thinking, which is typically accompanied by internal speech in their native language [20, 14], which could also be the target of linguistic processing. Thus, techniques that require further intensive work for non-native speakers are likely to be ineffective - it might even decrease performance. Instead, a technique that reduces the burden on non-native speakers would be desirable.

CURRENT STUDY

In this paper, we explore the ways for reducing the burden of non-native speaking attendees in an audio conference. Since the main problem of our target users (i.e., non-native attendees whose language skill is sufficiently high to participate in a face-to-face meeting in their second language) lies on the high demand on their resources to run multiple processing, we consider how to provide them with additional resources (e.g., processing power, time). As our first step, we attempt to supplement non-native attendees with additional processing time. We considered two ways for their support: either to slow down the conversation or to insert frequent silent gaps between speeches. Because the latter approach seemed more natural (i.e. people are usually exposed to silent gaps caused by transmission delay), we employed the latter approach for this study.

We carried out two studies to examine whether the short silent gaps improved the non-native speaker's verbal activities. The first study investigated the effects of short gaps on non-native speaker's perceived comprehension effort and actual comprehension level when they were manually inserted in a pre-recorded meeting. The second study explored their effects on non-native speakers' comprehension and production of speech when inserted in a real-time audio conference. The difference between the two studies is whether the short gaps were studied in an interactive situation.

STUDY 1: DO SHORT GAPS IMPROVE NON-NATIVE LISTENER'S COMPREHENSION?

The first experiment measured the effects of three different silent gaps (0, 0.2, or 0.4 seconds) on comprehension and perception of comprehension effort. To see whether the short gaps had similar effects on native speakers, the scores were compared between native and non-native speakers.

Method

Participants

Ten native English speakers and ten non-native English speakers were recruited for this study. The native speakers were born and raised in an English speaking country. The non-native speakers were all Japanese. Their English proficiency levels varied, but all had studied English for more than six years. Most were confident in their English skills; eight described themselves as proficient. Their average overseas experience in English speaking countries was 0.8 years.

Experimental Design

Each participant engaged in three listening tasks. The three tasks differed in their listening materials and in the length of silent gaps (0, 0.2, or 0.4 seconds). The order of the listening materials and the length of gaps were counterbalanced across participants.

Task Materials

As a pre-recorded meeting, we used the meeting corpus released by the Linguistic Data Consortium (LDC)[1]. The meeting consisted of four native English speakers discussing how "9-11" affected their lives and how innovative technologies might help prevent terrorism. The audio data was collected using two personal microphones attached to each meeting member (i.e. a close-talking noise-canceling boom microphone and an omni-directional lapel microphone) and several table microphones covering 360 degrees. Since each channel was recorded in a separate file (Figure 1, second and third top), we could independently handle each member's speech. This allowed us to change the timing of each member's speech by manually shifting each member's utterances and eventually mixing them all together (see bottom of Figure 1 and 2).

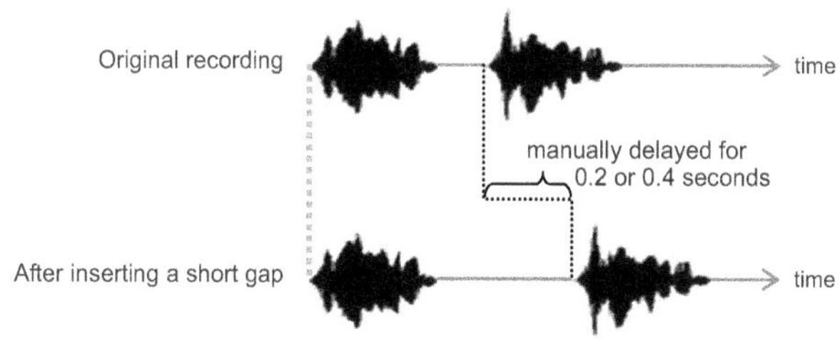

Figure 1. Insertion of short gaps

For the listening task material, we first randomly clipped three fragments from the meeting data. Each fragment lasted about 45 seconds with 10 to 11 speaker switches, 4 or 5 of them being overlapped with one another. We then prepared three versions for each fragment: no changes, a 0.2 second gap, or a 0.4 second gap inserted in between every speech. Note that the length of the latter two fragments

---

[1] http://www.ldc.upenn.edu/

became approximately 2 (or 4) seconds longer than the original version due to the insertion of gaps.

Note also that when there was an overlap between two speakers' utterances, the speech overlaps were resolved but the actual gap produced in the modified recording was less than 0.2 seconds (or 0.4 seconds) (Figure 2).

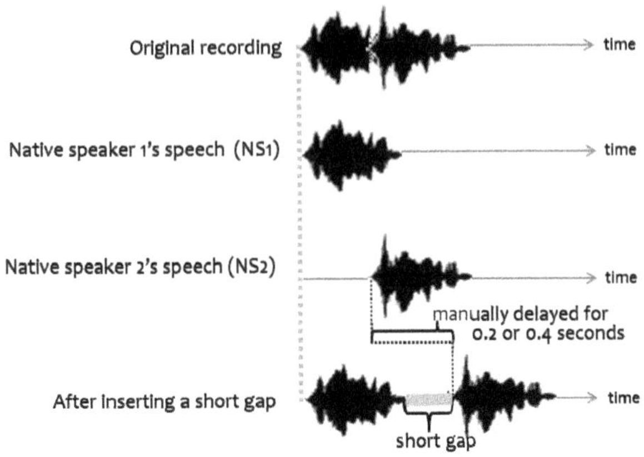

Figure 2. Resolving speech overlaps.

Tasks

The task was a simple listening task in which participants listened to each fragment (with different gaps) and rated their comprehension - after listening to each fragment, the participants were given a transcript, and were asked to mark all sentences or words they were able to follow. The native English speakers were provided with an English transcript while the Japanese participants were provided with transcripts translated into Japanese.

Procedure

Participants were first provided with a brief introduction to the study, including the topic of the recorded meeting and the experiment procedures. Note, however, that the differences between the three tasks were not explained to the participants to avoid any influence it may have on the outcomes.

After the introduction, the participants worked on a sample listening task to familiarize themselves with the actual experiment task. The fragment of the sample task was also extracted from the same meeting data. No changes were made (no silent gaps were added) to the sample task.

Next, the participants carried out a series of three trials. During the trials, they were allowed to take notes although they were only allowed to play each fragment once. Upon completion of each task, the participants filled out post-task questionnaires about their perception of their comprehension effort. After all three tasks, they were interviewed about the differences they have noticed among the trials.

Results

Below, we examine the effects of short gaps on non-native speaker's comprehension using two measures - in the first analysis, objective measures were used to compare actual comprehension level between the conditions; then, subjective measures were used to compare participant's comprehension effort. Throughout the paper, performance results (using objective measures) were analyzed in a repeated measures ANOVA, and survey results (using subjective measures) were analyzed in a non-parametric Friedman test, unless specified.

Each participant's comprehension level for each task was measured by calculating the rate of words he/she was able to follow by counting the number he/she marked in the trial and dividing it with the total number of words in the fragment.

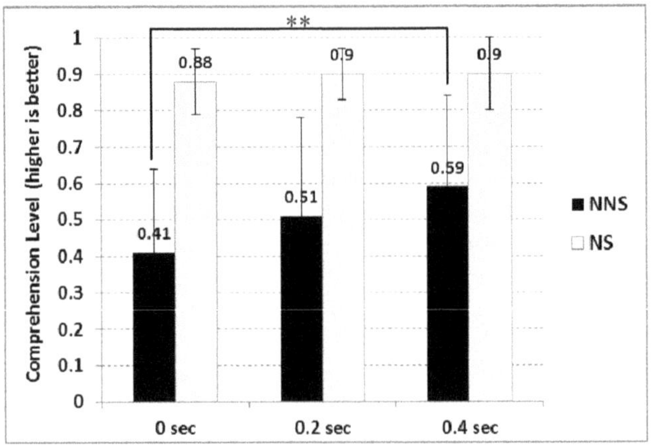

Figure 3. Mean comprehension scores by gap.

Overall, the comprehension level of the native English speakers ("NS") remained high throughout the conditions, while comprehension of the Japanese participants ("NNS") increased as silent gaps were added (Figure 3). A repeated measures ANOVA using gap lengths as repeated factors indicated a significant main effect of the gaps ($F[2, 18]= 5.91$, $p<.05$). A Bonferonni post hoc test indicated that the difference was significant between gaps of 0 and 0.4 seconds ($p<.01$). No significant difference was found for the native English speakers.

Next, we measured the participants' perception of comprehension effort using the questionnaire results on a five-point Likert scale. The results showed that the Japanese participants felt the tasks became easier as the length of the gap increased (Figure 4). A Friedman test indicated that this effect was significant ($\chi^2[2]=10.47$, $p<.01$). Post hoc tests (Wilcoxon Signed-Rank Test with Bonferroni correction) indicated that the difference was significant between gaps of 0 and 0.4 seconds ($p<.01$) and slightly different between gaps of 0.2 and 0.4 seconds ($p=.06$). Similar to the comprehension scores, no significant difference was found on comprehension effort for the native English speakers.

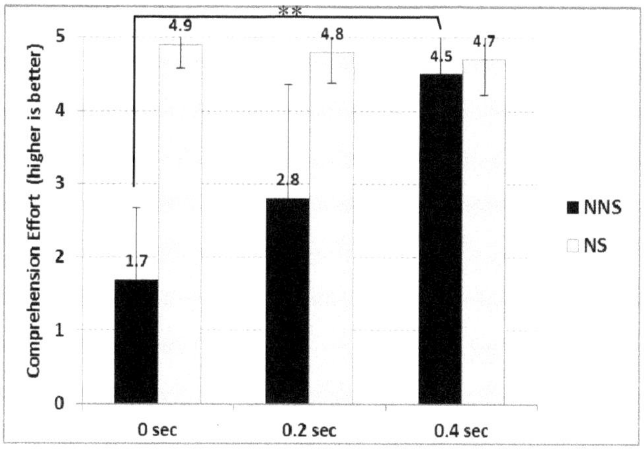

Figure 4. Mean ratings of perception for comprehension effort.

In the post-experimental interview, participants made some interesting comments about the differences between the trials. Many native English speakers commented that they felt the conversation (particularly with 0.4 gaps) somewhat awkward and unnatural, although it did not seem to affect their comprehension/effort. Meanwhile, many Japanese mentioned that conversation slowed down for some sessions and were easier to follow. They seemed surprised when notified that it was not the conversation speed but the silent periods inserted between conversational turns.

Additionally, some of the Japanese participants mentioned that they felt the conversation particularly fast and difficult to follow when there was a conversation overlap. Since the manually inserted gaps often eliminated the overlaps as in Figure 2, the elimination of overlaps might also have helped the Japanese participants follow the conversation with less effort.

In summary, inserting short gaps and resolving the overlaps between speeches helped the non-native speakers follow the conversation with less effort.

STUDY 2: HOW DO SHORT GAPS AFFECT REALTIME CONVERSATION?

Although silent gaps during conversation appear effective for non-native speakers, inserting frequent gaps is usually difficult during ordinary verbal activities - asking native speakers to temporarily halt before making an utterance is unrealistic. In our second study, we inserted the gaps by controlling the transmission delays between native and non-native speakers.

Figures 5 and 6 illustrate how the gaps were produced by adding artificial delays among native speakers. The direct sound waves of a speaker's voice are shown in black, and the sound waves that have passed through the network (i.e., sound waves heard at the listener's site) are shown in gray. Note that these examples show the case of zero network delay. Figure 5 shows that non-native speakers listen to native speaker NS1's voice ahead of other native speakers because the artificial delay is added among native speakers. This allows the non-native speaker to process NS1's speech ahead of the other native speakers, which eventually provides them with additional processing time. The gap is not only expected to increase non-native speakers' comprehension but also to allow them to prepare their own utterance.

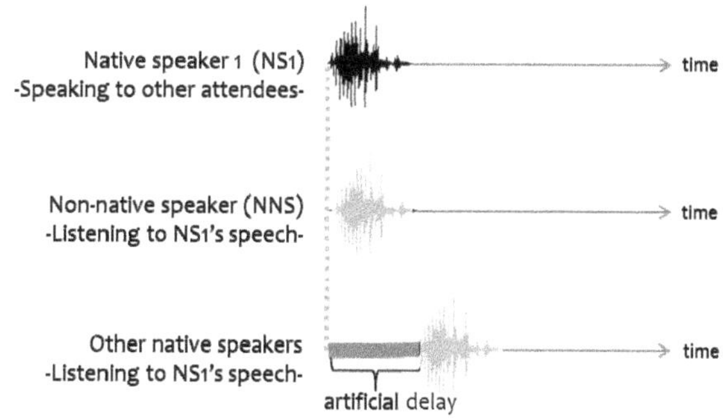

Figure 5. Providing NNS with additional processing time by inserting artificial delay among NSs.

The artificial delay inserted among native speakers is not only expected to supplement non-native speakers with additional processing time, but also to allow them to hear each utterance more thoroughly by reducing/resolving conversational overlaps (Figure 6).

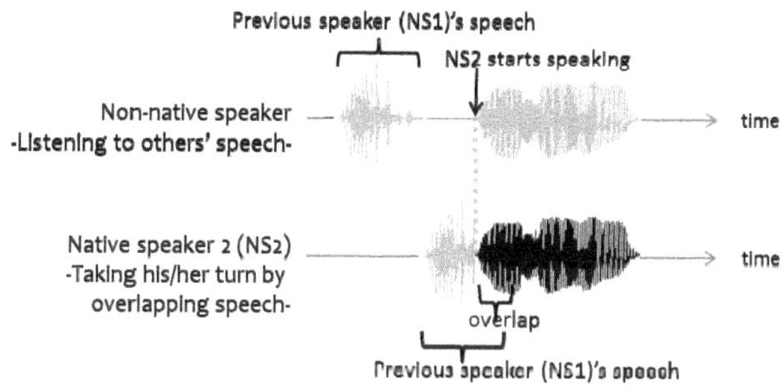

Figure 6. Resolving conversation overlaps between NSs.

While the short gaps are expected to be useful for non-native speakers, we must also pay attention to their effects on native speakers. In fact, previous research has significantly demonstrated the negative impacts of network delay on communication [6, 10, 22]. For example, Krauss et al. demonstrated that an audio delay of 0.3 seconds can have a detrimental effect on the communication process, and delays as large as 0.9 seconds can drastically impact a pair's ability to communicate [10]. Similarly, Tang et al. found that a delay of 0.57 seconds make turn-taking difficult to negotiate [22]. In summary, previous work on audio delay indicates that people hardly notice the delay if it is shorter than 0.2 seconds; delays between 0.2 and 0.4 seconds pose little if any problems; but delays longer than 0.45 seconds can severely impact communication and coordination processes.

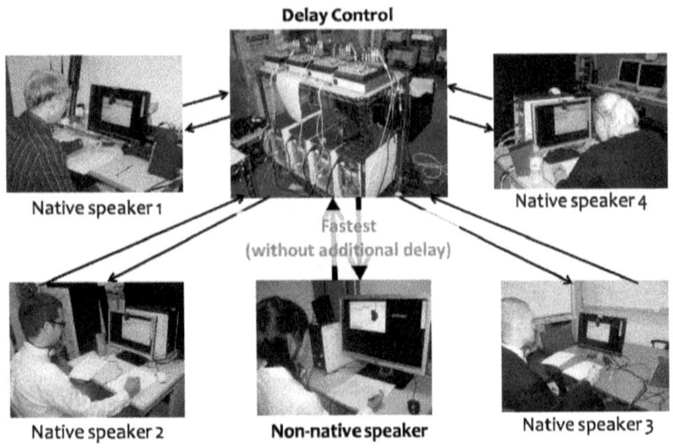

Figure 7. Five participants (4 NSs and 1 NNS) working on a decision making task over Skype with delay control.

In our second study, we examine the effects of adding artificial delays of 0.2 or 0.4 seconds among native speakers voice relay (Figure 7 and 8), which presumably have a small impact on native speakers' conversations. We were interested to know whether the small gaps would actually improve the non-native speakers' verbal activities without hindering the native speakers. Specifically, we sought to answer the following questions:

- Does our delay mechanism work as expected? – Does it actually produce small gaps and reduce conversation overlaps in a real-time audio conference.
- How does the mechanism affect communication among native speakers? – Does turn-taking get difficult, and do the native speakers feel more frustrated as the delay increase?
- Does the scheme improve non-native speakers' verbal activities? – Can we see an increase in their perceived comprehension and in their production of speech?
- How does our delay mechanism affect consensus building among native and non-native speakers?

Method

Participants

Fourteen groups of five adults (70 participants) were newly recruited for this study. Fifty-six were native English speakers, and fourteen were non-native speakers. The non-native speakers were Japanese participants whose English skills were sufficient to have daily conversations in English. Their TOEIC scores exceeded 860, and the average length of their overseas experience was 1.6 years.

Experimental Design

Five-person groups (four native speakers and one non-native speaker) participated in three decision making tasks with different silent periods: 0, 0.2, and 0.4 seconds. Groups of five were selected due to their ability to be small enough for participants to collaborate while still not being so small that participants will be chosen to take the floor by default. The order of the discussion topics and gap lengths were counterbalanced across participants.

Tasks

As a discussion topic, we chose a series of survival tasks (on a desert, at the arctic, and on the moon) [11] that are widely used for training group development. In these tasks, participants imagine that they have been stranded at one of these locations. Several items are presented, and each participant ranks the items for importance to survival. After ranking them individually, their discussion generates a group solution through an audio conference. Each task contained fifteen items, but for simplification, we excluded the items that are not used in daily conversations (such as a "large piece of insulating fabric") and randomly chose six items from the remaining pool.

Apparatus

Skype was used as the audio conferencing software. The Skype interface was displayed on each participant's screen. There was approximately 0.2 seconds of network plus Skype latency between the clients. Artificial delays were added using an audio delay device (Figure 7 and 8). In other words, a native speaker's speech arrived at other native speakers' site with 0.2, 0.4, or 0.6 seconds delay while it arrived at the non-native speakers' site with 0.2 seconds delay regardless of the conditions.

Figure 8 shows the wire diagram of the system used in the study. It illustrated how delays were inserted only among native speakers.

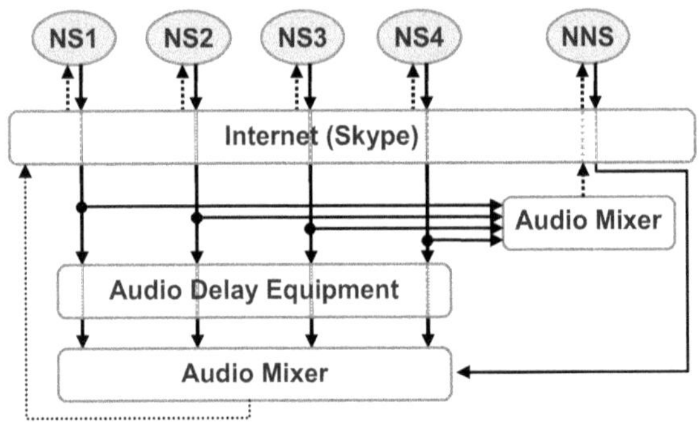

Figure 8. Wire diagram of the system.

During the experiment, conversations were recorded using Tapur, which is an exclusive Skype recorder. Tapur was installed on each client because it allowed us to store the exact voice data exchanged at each site.

Procedure

Procedure (1): On arrival, participants completed experimental consent forms and then moved to five separate rooms. After a short phonetic test, they were introduced to each other over Skype.

Procedure (2): The following procedure was repeated three times with different amounts of delay introduced among native speakers: Participants were given five minutes to rank the six task items by themselves and to write down their solutions. Next, participants were given 15 minutes to generate a group solution. In the discussion, they were told to have a free-style conversation (i.e. with no chairman) because we were interested in investigating the effects of our delay mechanism on non-native speakers' unprompted turn-taking behaviors (e.g., whether it would allow them to produce more utterances without being prompted). After a group solution was determined, participants were separated and asked to rank their second individual rankings to determine the possible influence of the group discussion. Participants also completed post-task questionnaires about the conversations they had just experienced. Similarly to the first study, the participants were not notified about the differences between the trials.

Procedure (3): Following the completion of the three tasks, participants completed a final questionnaire and were interviewed about the differences between the three trials.

Results

Production of Small Gaps

First, we examined if our delay mechanism actually produced small silent gaps and reduced conversation overlaps at the non-native speaker's site[2]. To this end, speaker switches between native speakers were classified into two groups: the ones with no overlaps and the ones with overlaps. Speaker switches in the former group were used to examine if the mean length of gaps increased, and those in the latter group were used to see if the mean length of overlaps reduced.

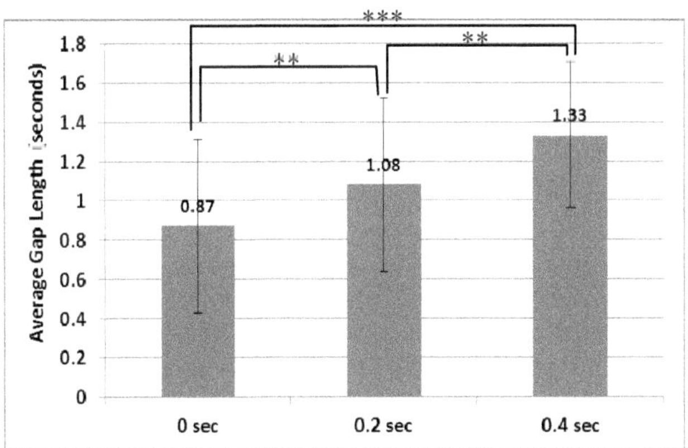

Figure 9. Mean length of gaps between native speakers' speech by delay scheme.

Figure 9 shows the average gap lengths of speaker transitions between native speakers. As expected, the results showed a steady increase in the average length of gaps between native speakers' speech as the delay increased. A repeated measures ANOVA indicated that the differences between the trials were significant ($F[2, 26]=24.09$, $p<.001$). A Bonferonni post hoc test indicated that the difference was significant between gaps of 0-0.2 seconds ($p<.01$), 0.2-0.4 seconds ($p<.01$), and 0-0.4 seconds ($p<.001$).

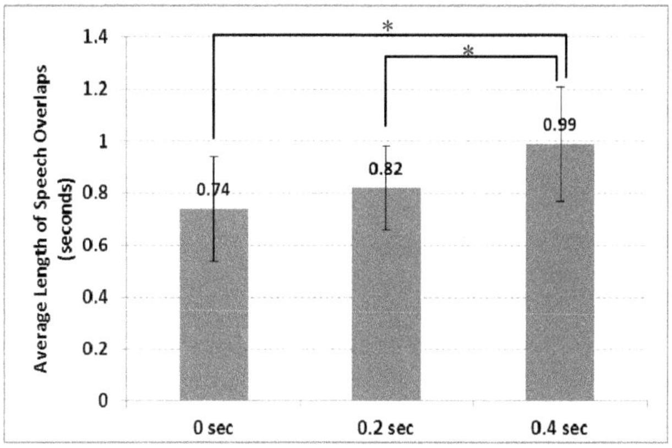

Figure 10. Mean length of overlaps between native speakers' speech by delay.

Similarly, we also measured the overlap lengths among native speakers' speech. Although we expected a constant decrease, the average length of speech overlaps increased as the delays increased (Figure 10). A repeated measures ANOVA indicated that the differences between the trials were significant ($F[2, 26]=9.70$, $p=.001$). A Bonferonni post hoc test indicated that the difference was significant between gaps of 0-0.4 seconds ($p<.05$) and 0.2-0.4 seconds ($p<.05$).

This was mainly caused by the increase in speech overlaps where multiple native speakers started talking simultaneously to take their next turn without noticing that another participant was taking their turn due to the longer delay (see Table 3 top row; further explanation provided below).

Effects on Native Speakers

Overall, we found a trend showing that native speakers had trouble taking their turns as delays increased. Table 3 shows evidences that support this tendency.

Table 3. Native speakers having difficulties in taking their turns as delays increase.

	0 sec	0.2 sec	0.4 sec
Percentage of conversations initiated simultaneously	22%	33%	41%
Frequency of speaker switches (# of speaker switches per min.)	7.8	7.3	6.6
Speaking effort (5pt Likert scale: higher is better)	4.2	4.2	4.0
Comprehension effort (5pt Likert scale: higher is better)	4.4	4.5	4.3
Frustration (5pt Likert scale: lower is better)	1.7	1.8	2.1

[2] All the analysis presented in this paper was conducted using the data stored at the NNS's client, unless specified.

(1) *Increase in simultaneous speech when multiple NSs start talking*: Native speakers in the delayed trials sometimes started talking without noticing that others had already started their speech because of the delayed arrival of other native speakers' speech. This caused an overlap in the beginning of their speech. The frequency of such overlapped speech was measured by first counting the number of incidences where multiple native speakers started talking to take their next turn in each trial, and then dividing it with the total number of speaker switches during each trial. Table 3 shows a steady increase in the average frequency of such incidences as the delays increase. A repeated measures ANOVA indicated a significant main effect for delay ($F[2,26]=11.58$, $p<.001$). A Bonferonni post hoc test indicated that the difference was significant between gaps of 0-0.2 seconds ($p<.05$) and 0-0.4 seconds ($p<.01$).

(2) *Decrease in the frequency of speaker switches among NSs*: Speaker switches were measured in order to identify the difficulty of turn taking. If speaker switching is low, it indicates a lower level of interactivity between speakers. Coding for this measure only counted instances when new speakers took the floor, excluding utterances that were not completed. The frequency of speaker switches between native speakers decreased as delay increased (Table 3). A repeated measures ANOVA indicated a significant main effect of delay ($F[2,26]=3.79$, $p<.05$). The difficulties in their turn-taking may be due to the increase in overlap and long pauses caused by delay. We found many instances in which native speakers continued talking because others could not take the turn at the right timing. The following excerpt[3] captures this tendency:

Excerpt 1 (0.4 second trial):

NS1: When you say fishing kit what do you mean↑ exactly↓ (0.8) uh:: well what do you have in mind when you say FISHING KIT↑(1.4)

NS2: Pro [bably ro::d and]

NS1: [Mosquito netting is] pretty thin it could rip (.) I mean you know (0.9) well it it it's pretty (0.2) I don't think it's uh good for uh::: for for catching fish.

(3) *Increase in NS's frustration*: From the post-experimental interview, it revealed that overlaps occurring in the early stage of speech occasionally sounded rude because they felt like someone broke into their speech without listening to the entire argument. This seemed to increase their frustration during the discussion. Table 3 shows the average scores of native speaker's perceived comprehension effort, speaking effort, and frustration. Results show that the scores of the 0.4 sec delay is consistent in being the worst of all trials. A Friedman test indicated a significant main effect of delay for frustration ($\chi2[2]=7.23$, $p<.05$). Post hoc tests (Wilcoxon Signed-Rank Test with Bonferroni correction) indicated that the difference was significant between gaps of 0-0.4 seconds ($p<.05$).

[3] [ ] indicates where overlaps take place; ↑ and ↓ indicates rising and falling intonation; : indicates an extension of sound; ( ) indicates a silent gap timed in tenths of a second.

Effects on Non-native Speakers

Overall, we found a trend that non-native speakers performed the best and preferred the 0.2 second trial. The 0.4 second trial was consistently the worst of all trials in terms of non-native speaker's performance and preference. Similarly to the previous section, we will show evidence that supports this tendency (Table 4).

Table 4. Non-native speakers performing best with 0.2 second delay trial.

	0 sec	0.2 sec	0.4 sec
Average rate of spontaneous speech	0.76	0.81	0.69
Speaking effort (5pt Likert scale: higher is better)	3.1	3.4	2.3
Comprehension effort (5pt Likert scale: higher is better)	4.1	4.1	3.5
Frustration (5pt Likert scale: lower is better)	2.9	2.7	3.1

(1) *Increase in NNS comprehension effort*: Based on our first study, we had initially expected that non-native speakers' comprehension effort would decrease as delay increase, because the artificial delays create gaps. However, it turned out that non-native speakers made slightly more effort to comprehend the discussion as delay increased (Table 4). A Friedman test indicated that this effect was borderline significant ($\chi2[2]=5.52$, $p<.06$).

(2) *Rise and drop in the rate of NNS's spontaneous speech*: The degree to which non-native speakers were eager to speak during the trials was measured by the rate of their spontaneous speech, which was calculated by first counting the number of non-native speakers' spontaneous speech (opposed to speech prompted by native speakers) and then dividing it with their total number of utterances. Table 4 shows that non-native speakers spontaneously spoke the most in the 0.2 sec trial and the least in the 0.4 sec trial. A repeated measures ANOVA indicated a borderline significant effect of delay ($F[2, 26]=3.23$, $p=.056$).

(3) *Drop and rise in perceived effort of producing an utterance*: Although the actual difference in the proportion of non-native speaker's spontaneous speech was subtle, it appeared that non-native speakers felt strongly that it was easier to produce an utterance in the 0.2 second trial and difficult in the 0.4 second trial (Table 4). A Friedman test indicated that this effect was

significant ($\chi^2[2]=6.59$, $p<.05$). Post hoc tests (Wilcoxon Signed-Rank Test with Bonferroni correction) indicated that the difference was significant between gaps of 0.2 and 0.4 seconds ($p<.05$). In the post-experimental interview, one non-native speaker explained her reluctance to speak "*(In the 0.4 second trial,) they started to jump onto others' conversation. At times, it sounded like they didn't want to listen to others' opinions. [...] So, I felt reluctant to cut into the conversation. I just tried to concentrate on following their conversations.*"

In sum, even though our delay mechanism successfully created silent gaps between native speakers' speech, increased speech overlaps (caused by multiple native speakers trying to take their next turns) appeared to have a negative effect on non-native speakers. The negative effects grew apparent in the 0.4 second trials.

Effects on Consensus Building

Finally, we investigated whether our delay mechanism affected consensus building - how much the participants actually agreed with the group ranking, whether the agreement levels differed between native and non-native speakers, and whether the agreement levels varied across different delay conditions.

Table 5. NS and NNS's agreement levels of group ranking.

	0 sec	0.2 sec	0.4 sec
Average correlation between NS and Group rankings	0.90	0.89	0.91
Average correlation between NNS and Group rankings	0.68	0.88	0.77

We first calculated the correlation (Spearman's coefficient) between each participant's second individual ranking and the group ranking. Each correlation score indicates the participant's agreement level (i.e. degree of ranking similarity), ranging from -1 (complete opposite) to 1 (identical). We then compared the average correlation scores between native and non-native speakers using the Wilcoxon test (Table 5). Results indicated that non-native speakers were significantly less convinced by the group ranking than the native speakers when delay was not added ($p<.05$). The gaps between native and non-native speakers became less prominent in conditions with 0.2 or 0.4 sec delay (both n.s.). The gap found in 0 sec condition may becaused by the difference in their comprehension and speaking skills where non-native speakers have difficulties arguing back and defending their opinions at the right timing.

We further ran a Friedman test to see if the correlation scores varied across delay conditions. Results indicated that the effect of delay was not significant. Although not significant, non-native speakers seemed to be most convinced by the group ranking in 0.2 sec delay (Table 5). The result is consistent with the pattern found in the previous section where 0.2 sec delay was preferred and performed the best by the non-native speakers.

DISCUSSION

There are five main findings from our two studies:

- Reducing overlaps and inserting small gaps in a previously recorded meeting significantly improved the comprehension (Figure 3) and perceived effort (Figure 4) for non-native speakers when following the conversation. Similar effects were not found for native speakers.
- Our delay mechanism (i.e. adding artificial delays among native speakers) successfully inserted small gaps among native speakers' speech in a real-time audio conference (Figure 9). However, the speech overlaps did not decrease as expected, but increased along with delay (Figure 10).
- Native speakers had trouble taking their turns as delays increased (Table 3): Due to the delay, speakers were unaware when they would talk simultaneously or over the speech of others. This created higher instances of simultaneous speech as delay increased which usually ended with speakers ending their utterances abruptly. This resulted in lower frequency of turn-taking between native speakers. Native speakers' perceived efforts (both for comprehension and speaking) also grew substantially with 0.4 second delay.
- Non-native speakers spontaneously spoke the most in the 0.2 second delay condition (Table 4). Their perceived speaking effort was also the lowest with 0.2 second delay. Their perceived frustration also followed a similar pattern – 0.2 sec delay being the best and 0.4 sec delay being the worst. Regarding the non-native speakers' comprehension effort, although we expected it to decrease, it remained similar between the 0 and 0.2 second delays, and increased in the 0.4 second delay.
- Non-native speakers were significantly less convinced by the group solution than the native speakers when delay was not added. The agreement level of non-native speakers improved when delays were added - gaps between native and non-native speakers became less prominent in conditions with 0.2 or 0.4 sec delay.

Below, we explain our findings and discuss some design opportunities and directions for future work.

Explanations of the Findings

How did the gaps in a pre-recorded meeting affect NS and NNS's comprehension?

There are two possible reasons why the gaps worked well on non-native speakers when they were inserted in a pre-recorded meeting. First, the gaps allowed for more time to process incoming information, placing less demands on the listener's mental resources. Second, inserting gaps in between utterances resulted in less overlaps in conversation. This improved the overall conversation clarity and reduced the effort needed to compensate for the missed parts of the conversation caused by speech overlaps. In short, the gaps between utterances allowed the non-native speakers to have a longer window to make out the meaning of each utterance before focusing on the following content.

Though the insertion of gaps improved comprehension for non-native speakers, the same benefits were not seen for native speakers. For native speakers, their comprehension scores were always high, perhaps indicating that they did not require much mental resource to understand the conversation. Thus, an improvement in comprehension (both in terms of score and effort) would not have been seen even when their mental resources were conserved.

How did the added delays affect NS and NNS's communication in a real-time meeting?

As previous literature indicated, our second study demonstrated that the added delays negatively affected the native speakers. The number of overlaps in the beginning of their speeches increased and there were also awkwardly long pauses as illustrated in Excerpt 1. We suspect that such difficulties in turn-taking led them to fewer speaker switches and increased frustration.

For the non-native speakers, it appeared that there were both beneficial and detrimental effects because of the added delays on non-native speakers. The beneficial aspects were that the delays were successful in creating gaps (Figure 9) where non-native speakers could utilize to process the language and think of what to speak. It also gave them an opportunity to participate in the conversation before other native speakers, resulting in a higher rate of spontaneous speech (Table 4). The detrimental effects were found for longer delays. This includes longer, more disruptive speech overlaps that occurred more frequently.

Why didn't the gaps improve NNS comprehension in a real-time meeting?

Non-native speakers were able to follow the conversations with less effort when the gaps were inserted in a pre-recorded meeting. However, those gaps appeared insufficient for improving their comprehension effort in a real-time audio meeting. We infer that the changes caused by the delay in the native speakers' conversation impacted the non-native speakers, requiring more attention and effort to follow the conversation.

Another consideration is the difference in the characteristics of overlapping speech, which might have affected the non-native speakers' comprehension effort - in the 0.2 second trial, the average number of words in an overlapping speech was approximately 1 or 2 words while that of the 0.4 second trial was around 2 to 3 words. Although this difference might look subtle, the participants' reaction to the overlaps was quite different. In the 0.2 second trial, when participants started talking together, they soon noticed the overlaps, halted, and then often repeated their utterance. In contrast, participants in the 0.4 second trial were more likely to be interrupted in the middle of their sentences. In such cases, they typically continued their speech or just halted without repeating their utterance. The excerpts below capture the tendency:

Excerpt 2 (0.2 second trial):

NS1: Ok=

NS2: =Yeah (.)

NS1: So [anyway]

NS3: [I:::] I need I need the brandy

Excerpt 3 (0.4 second trial):

NS1: my argument towards [the knife is tha:::t]

NS2: [the thing that kill you] the fastest is dehydration (0.8) so:::

NS1: yeah (.)

NS3: water or dead

The missed part (i.e. overlapped speech) in 0.4 second trial looks much more difficult to compensate than the 0.2 second trial, which had possibly led them to much higher comprehension effort and frustration.

Design Implications

Our findings and the above discussions suggest recommendations for the design of future audio conferencing systems to support non-native speakers. Since gaps were beneficial but overlaps overshadowed those effects for non-native speakers, a function that inserts gaps without increasing overlaps might better support their verbal communication in an audio conference.

For example, one solution for inserting gaps without increasing overlaps during audio conferencing would be to combine push-to-talk (PTT) functionality with our delay mechanism. The PTT function is commonly used to block out any possible background noise when there are a large number of participants, but moreover, works as a behavioral trigger to avoid overlaps in discussions [18]. An artificial delay interval combined with PTT functionality might reduce the negative effects of native speaker overlaps in longer delay settings. This would thus increase the positive effects of longer delays for non-native speakers in NS-NNS audio conferencing while still keeping overlaps to a minimum.

CONCLUSIONS AND FUTURE DIRECTIONS

Previous literature has shown the negative impacts of transmission delays on communication between collaborators with the same native language. Yet little is known about how these delays would affect multilingual collaborations. Our studies provide insight into the effects of delays on communication among native and non-native speakers. By looking at how the delays have affected non-native speakers in isolation as well as native and non-native speakers in a group, we have been able to identify how comprehension and participation are affected. When listening to discussions with embedded delays (i.e. gaps), non-native speakers were capable of understanding the discussion content with greater accuracy. In a group, a short delay (0.2 second) also assisted non-native speakers by creating more opportunities to participate in the conversations. However, as the delay increased to 0.4 second the positive effects of the speech delay that assisted non-native speakers were overshadowed by the negative effects experienced by the native speakers, such as increased speech overlaps.

For future studies, we are interested in expanding our study to other language speaking participants. For example, the Japanese participants may be having difficulties collaborating in English due to the differences in grammatical structures [21]. Adjusting both the native language background of the participants and/or the language used to communicate may yield different results.

These studies illustrate how in a group interaction, higher delays deteriorate communication between native and non-native speakers. Especially when connections span oceans and continents, the combination of even seemingly minute delays along with imperfect language skills create a very taxing situation for non-native speakers. Yet even these imperfect short delay conditions, which have always been considered entirely detrimental, have given some insight into ways to enhance communication between native speakers and non-native speakers. We do not support extending delays, but neither can their benefits be overlooked. We hope that this work illustrates the impact these delays/gaps have on collaboration in the hopes that future work in this field will consider its effects.

ACKNOWLEDGMENTS

We are grateful to Hideaki Kuzuoka for his comments on an earlier draft of the paper. We would also like to thank Linsi Xia and Masanobu Ishimatsu for their assistance in running the experiment. Finally, we thank the anonymous reviewers for their constructive comments and suggestions.

REFERENCES

1. Broadbent, D. *Perception and communication.* Oxford: Pergamon, 1958.
2. Clark, H. H. & Schaefer, E. F. Collaborating on contributions to conversations. *Language and Cognitive Processes, 2*, 1987, 19-41.
3. Ding, X., Erickson, T., Kellogg, W. A., Levy, S., Christensen J., Sussman, J., Wolf, T. V., Bennett, W. E. An Empirical Study of the Use of Visually Enhanced VoIP Audio Conferencing: The Case of IEAC. *Proceedings of CHI*, 2007, 1019-1028.
4. DiMicco, J. M, Hollenbach, K., and Bender, W. Using visualizations to review a group's interaction dynamics, *Proceedings of CHI*, 2006, 706-711.
5. Ezzatian, P., Avivi, M., Schneider, B. Do non-native listeners benefit as much as native listeners from spatial cues that release speech from masking? *Speech Communication, 52*, 2010, 919-929.
6. Gutwin, C. The effects of network delay on group work in shared workspaces, *Proceedings of ECSCW*, 2001, 299-318.
7. Inkepen, K., Hegde, R., Czerwinski, M. and Zhang, Z. Exploring spatialized audio & video for distributed conversations, *Proceedings of CSCW*, 2010, 95-98.
8. Junuzovic, S., Inkepen, K., Hegde, R., Zhang, Z., Tang, J. and Brooks, C. What did I miss? In-Meeting Review using Multimodal Accelerated Instant Replay (AIR) Conferencing. *Proceedings of CHI*, 2011, 513-522.
9. Kilgore, R., Chignell, M. and Smith, P. Spatialized Audioconferencing: What are the Benefits? *Proceedings of CASCON*, 2003, 135-144.
10. Krauss, R. M. and P. Bricker. Effects of transmission delay and access delay on the efficiency of verbal communication. Journal of the Acoustical Society of America, 41 (2), 1967, 286-292.
11. Lafferty, J. C., Eady, P. M., & Elmers, J. The Desert Survival Problem. Plymouth, Michigan. Experimental Learning Methods, 1974.
12. Li, H. Z., Yum, Y., Yates, R., Aguilera, L., Mao, Y. and Zheng, Y. Interruption and Involvement in Discourse: Can Intercultural Interlocutors be Trained? *Journal of Intercultural Communication Research*, Vol. 34, No. 4, 233-254.
13. Luisa, M., Lecumberri, G., Cooke, M., Culter, A. Non-native speech perception in adverse conditions: A Review. *Speech Communication*, 52, 2010, 864-886.
14. Macnamara, J. and Kushnir, S. L. Linguistic independence of bilinguals: The input switch. *Journal of Verbal Learning and Verbal Behavior, 10*, 1971, 480-487.
15. Mayo, L., Florentine, M., Buus, S. Age of Second-language acquisition and perception of speech in noise. *Journal of Speech, Language, and Hearing Research*, Vol. 40, No. 3, 1997, 686-693.
16. Nabelek, A.K., Donahue, A.M., Perception of consonants in reverberation by native and non-native listeners. *Journal of Acoustical Society of America, 75*, 1984, 632-634.
17. Rogers, C., Lister, J., Febo, D., Besing, J., Abrams, H. Effects of bilingualism, noise and reverberation on speech perception by listeners with normal hearing. *Applied Psycholinguistics*, 27, 2006, 465-485.

18. Sawhney, N. and Schmandt, C. Nomadic radio: speech and audio interaction for contextual messaging in nomadic environments. *TOCHI*, 2000, 353-383.

19. Short, J., Williams, E. & Christie, B. The Social Psychology of Telecommunications. London: John Wiley, 1976.

20. Takano, Y. and Noda, A. A temporary decline of thinking ability during foreign language processing. *Journal of Cross-Cultural Psychology*, 24, 1993, 445-462.

21. Tanaka, H. Turn Projection in Japanese Talk-in-Interaction. *Research on Language and Social Interaction, 33,* (1), 2009, 1-38.

22. Tang, J.C., and Isaacs, E.A. Why do users like video? Studies on multimedia-supported collaboration. Sun Microsystems Laboratories, Inc., Mountain View, CA, 1992.

23. Veinott, E., Olson, J., Olson, G., and Fu, X. Video Helps Remote Work: Speakers Who Need to Negotiate Common Ground Benefit from Seeing Each Other. *Proceedings of CHI*, 1999, 302-309.

24. Vertgaal, R., Van der Veer, G. C. and Vons, H. Effects of Gaze on Multiparty Mediated Communication. *Proceedings of Graphic Interface 2000*, Morgan Kaufmann Publishers, (2000), 95-102.

25. Yankelovich, N., Kaplan, J., Provino, J., Wessler, M., DiMicco, J. M. Improving Audio Conferencing: Are Two Ears Better than One? *Proceedings of CSCW*, 2006, 333-342.

26. Yankelovich, N., McGinn J., Wessler, M., Kaplan, J. and Provino, J. and Fox, H. Private Communications in Public Meetings. *Proceedings of CHI*, 2005, 1873-1876.

27. Yankelovich, N., Walker, W. Roberts, P., Wessler, M., Kaplan, J. and Provino, J. Meeting Central: Making Distributed Meetings More Effective. *Proceedings of CSCW*, 2004.

Machine Translation vs. Common Language: Effects on Idea Exchange in Cross-Lingual Groups

Hao-Chuan Wang
Department of Computer Science &
Institute of Information Systems and Applications
National Tsing Hua University
Hsinchu, Taiwan 30013
haochuan@cs.nthu.edu.tw

Susan R. Fussell[1,2], Dan Cosley[2]
[1]Department of Communication,
[2]Department of Information Science
Cornell University
Ithaca, NY 14850, USA
{sfussell, drc44}@cornell.edu

ABSTRACT
Diversity among members of international teams can be a valuable source of novel ideas. However, to reap these benefits, groups need to overcome communication barriers that stem from differences in members' native languages. We compare two strategies for overcoming these barriers: the use of English as a common language, and the use of machine translation (MT) tools that allow each person to communicate in his or her own native language. Dyads consisting of one English-speaking American and one native Mandarin-speaking Chinese participant exchanged ideas to perform brainstorming tasks, either through English or using MT. We found that MT helped the non-native English speakers produce ideas but that both native and non-native English speakers viewed MT-mediated messages as less comprehensible than English messages. The findings suggest it can be effective to support cross-lingual communication with asymmetric design, using MT technology to help people produce messages in their native languages, while leaving incoming messages untranslated and leveraging people's second language proficiency for comprehension.

Author Keywords
Machine translation; idea exchange; cross-lingual communication; computer-mediated communication

ACM Classification Keywords
H5.3 **[Group and Organization Interface]:** Computer-supported cooperative work

General Terms
Experimentation, Human Factors

INTRODUCTION
International groups perform various tasks that require idea generation, such as problem solving and design. Such teamwork can be found in numerous domains, such as the human genome project [4] and joint space exploration [5]. One important motivation for internationalizing work of this sort is the need to combine knowledge and expertise across cultures in order to diversify the knowledge accessible to groups and to better identify alternative ideas and solutions.

National and cultural diversity in global teams both provides benefits and creates obstacles. Diversity in concepts and ways of thinking can expand the knowledge base of a group and stimulate the generation of new ideas [28]. However, diversity in social norms, communicative styles, and languages spoken can be detrimental to communication. For tasks like problem solving and design, barriers in communication may interfere with the production and exchange of ideas, thereby eliminating the potential benefits of conceptual diversity for tasks.

Of the various constraints that can hamper idea exchange across nations and cultures, the language barrier is one that may be especially worth trying to overcome. Many global organizations have members who speak a wide variety of native languages [9][19]. People in these organizations have generally had training in the common language of the organization (often English), but they may have less than

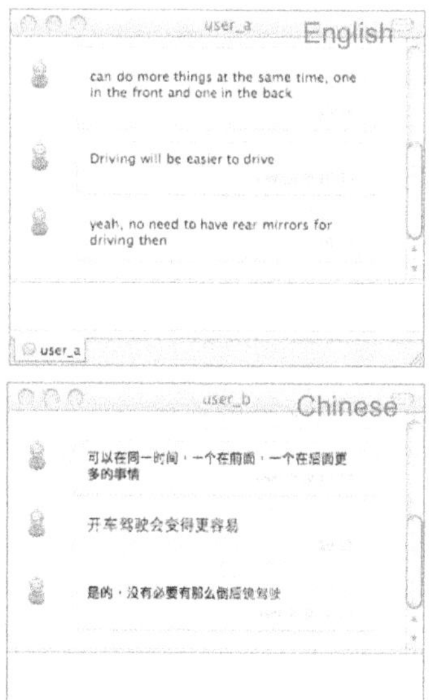

Figure 1. Using machine translation to enable idea exchange between people using different native languages.

perfect proficiency that can negatively affect interpersonal and work processes [12][26]. Even when they are proficient, there is evidence that people find it cognitively taxing to communicate in a second language [24][25].

Technical work in natural language processing (NLP) suggests an alternative approach for bridging language gaps in international groups. Rather than making everyone use a common language, machine translation (MT) can be used to allow everyone to speak in his or her own native language. The integration of MT services and computer-mediated communication tools like instant messaging (IM) allows people to communicate, at least in principle, with others who speak different languages while producing and receiving messages in their native language (Figure 1).

However, as with second language use, MT imposes costs. Current MT services still sometimes produce erroneous translations or words unsuited to the communication context (e.g., by translating *computer bug* into the equivalent of *computer insect*), or by forming poor sentence compositions (e.g. by translating the Chinese sentence "*还需要跟上海那边确认来不来得及*," equivalent to "*Still need to confirm with the Shanghai side to see if there is enough time to make it*," into the English translation "*Need to keep Shanghai there confirm that I time*"). MT can make it difficult for group members to establish mutual knowledge or common ground [3], particularly when teams must refer to objects and entities in a workspace. As a result, studies have shown that when communication requires coming to agreement on objects of reference, using MT is less efficient than using a shared second language [29][30].

Previous comparisons of MT and second language use have focused primarily on overall outcomes of communication and collaborative work (e.g., agreeing on labels for objects). Less is known about which aspects of the communication process MT supports well or badly. For instance, MT might be differentially useful for message production versus comprehension. It may be easier for a native Mandarin speaker to produce "*还需要跟上海那边确认来不来得及*" than the English equivalent, but its translation could be very difficult to a native English speaking partner to understand.

A second unanswered question concerns the possible benefits of using one's native language in MT-mediated communication. Studies suggest native language use is more socially and cognitively advantageous than second language use [24][26]. However, it is unknown if *MT-enabled native language use* will also work well, because the advantages of using one's own native language use might be outweighed by the costs imposed by MT errors.

In this paper, we report results of a lab study comparing MT-enabled versus English language communication in conversations between native-English speaking Americans and native Mandarin speaking Chinese nationals. We ask people to perform a brainstorming task with a partner who speaks a different native language. This domain allows us to examine (a) whether using MT to enable native language use benefits idea production and comprehension for non-native English speakers, and (b) whether MT affects communication behaviors when the language used is unchanged but incoming messages are mediated by MT.

As we will show, MT influenced idea exchange for both Chinese and American participants. Allowing Chinese speakers to produce messages in their native language was indeed beneficial; they produced more new ideas when communicating in Chinese over MT than when using English. In addition, although American participants used English and produced similar numbers of ideas in both the MT and English-only conditions, MT changed the way they communicated. Americans were less talkative, producing fewer conversational turns and words, when using MT than when using English as a common language. Finally, Americans and Chinese participants saw MT as less comprehensible than English-mediated conversation.

These asymmetries between production and consumption, and between native and non-native speakers, advance current understandings of how MT affects teamwork and contribute to the design of cross-lingual communication that includes MT. Rather than seeing MT as categorically inferior to second language use, our results suggest that there are tradeoffs between MT-enabled and second language communication for certain processes and tasks. Understanding these tradeoffs can improve the design of CMC tools that leverage these asymmetries, interleaving MT and second language use to get the best of both worlds.

BACKGROUND

We begin by identifying two lines of research that are especially relevant to cross-lingual communication: one showing the costs of using a non-native common language to communicate, and the other revealing the detrimental effects of MT on the development of shared knowledge in groups. Neither of these lines of work has directly addressed using MT to enable idea exchange in multilingual groups. We review this literature to develop specific hypotheses for MT-mediated versus second language use in idea exchange and test them in the current study.

Costs of Using Non-Native Common Languages

People from different cultural backgrounds often speak different native languages. Global organizations often solve this problem by requiring people to speak a common language (e.g., English), but this may disadvantage group members who speak a different native language as well as negatively impact group work.

This is because second language use imposes communicative inefficiencies and cognitive costs. Because second language speakers tend to have more limited linguistic resources (e.g., constrained vocabulary size), they often have to use more complex communication strategies such as rephrasing or repeating previous utterances to bridge the gap between their second language proficiency and their communicative intentions [7]. The extra effort required to manage these more complex strategies appears to decrease the cognitive resources people have available. Studies show that expressing messages in a second language leads to worse performance in a parallel problem-solving task [24][25]. Misunderstandings in communication caused by second language use can also lead to long-term consequences for group work, including reduced trust [13] and poorer interpersonal relationships at work [2][6].

Taking the communicative and cognitive constraints that second language use imposes, using a non-native common language such as English thus may not be ideal for international cross-lingual communication.

Effects of Machine Translation on Communication

The increasing availability of MT tools such as Google Translate (http://translate.google.com) makes it important to evaluate and assess the benefits and constraints of MT-mediated communication. In general, studies to date have shown that translation errors can hinder communication, especially when establishing joint understanding is key to the success of the task [14][29][30].

Yamashita and colleagues looked at Chinese-Japanese dyads using MT to collaborate on figure-matching tasks. Each of the participants has the same set of tangram figures, but in different orders, and they have to use language to communicate and match their orders of the figures (e.g., "your figure number 5 is my number 3"). Compared to using English as a common language, participants using MT couldn't efficiently use language to refer to the tangram objects or to understand others' referring expressions. MT mediation required participants to use longer sentences to accomplish their communication needs, even after multiple trials with the same objects, suggesting that people had difficulty establishing shared understanding over MT [29]. This is even more difficult in multiparty communication (e.g., three-person groups consisting of Chinese, Japanese, and Korean participants) [30] because translation errors and inconsistencies across multiple language pairs make it challenging for people to trace the status of understanding of other people, exacerbating communication problems.

Production and Comprehension in Cross-Lingual Communication

Using a common language or using MT are two readily available options for cross-lingual communication if we do not consider options that involve a third person (e.g., manual translation) for reasons of cost and privacy.

The two options pose different tradeoffs. Using a non-native common language may make it harder to produce and share ideas to others and more cognitively taxing to think. Using MT, on the other hand, may hinder comprehension. Translation problems can make it hard for people to accurately understand what their partners mean and to repair misunderstandings. However, using MT requires no second language proficiency, and may possibly avoid at least some of the costs of non-native language use.

Thus, MT—at least at its current level of sophistication—is most useful when reducing the cognitive costs of producing ideas is more valuable than the cost of misunderstandings. Determining this requires not just attention to overall outcomes, but to considering production and consumption separately. Previous studies used tasks that rely on referring expressions to align the perspectives of participants and achieve a well-defined solution (e.g., [29][30]). In such tasks, meaningful units of analysis are sequences of conversational turns (e.g., questioning-answering pairs) rather than individual utterances, and thus it is less feasible to use these tasks for the purpose of looking at aspects of production and comprehension separately.

THE CURRENT STUDY

To allow studying both the production and comprehension of messages, we chose to study the effects of MT on cross-lingual brainstorming groups. Group brainstorming tasks require groups to generate as many new ideas as possible [21][23]. Because the goal is ideational productivity, brainstorming tasks provide a natural driving force for group members to produce messages that externalize their ideas. The ideas shared by other group members may have a beneficial stimulation effect, helping people retrieve rare concepts from memory and think of ideas that they may not have generated alone [23][28]. Overall, idea exchange activities between group members, including both processes of production and comprehension, are central to group brainstorming. This makes group brainstorming an ideal task for our research purpose, because production and comprehension can be measured separately at the individual level through a combination of observed idea generation and questionnaires about comprehensibility.

Design of the Study

We asked American-Chinese dyads to brainstorm either in their native languages over MT (MT-mediated groups) or in English as a common language (English-mediated groups). The study recruited Chinese participants with Mandarin as their native language but who were also fluent or nearly fluent in English as a second language, possessing the proficiency for using English to communicate. From a participant-centric point of view, there is an asymmetry in language processing over these two types of mediation. Table 1 shows the modes of language processing (language for producing and consuming ideas) for American and Chinese participants under different mediation conditions.

American participants read and type in their native language in both English- and MT-mediated groups. However, Chinese participants read and type in a second language (English) over English mediation and in their native language (Chinese) when using MT. Using different types of mediation thus implies a greater change in language processing modes for Chinese participants.

Table 1. Modes of language processing for American and Chinese over English- and MT-mediated communication.

	English-mediation	MT-mediation
American	Type: Native (English) Read: Native (English)	Type: Native (English) Read: Native (Translated)
Chinese	Type: Non-Native (English) Read: Non-Native (English)	Type: Native (Chinese) Read: Native (Translated)

In this asymmetric configuration, comparing Chinese participants' behaviors and perceptions in MT-mediated versus English-mediated groups can reveal the effects of MT-enabled native language use on idea production and comprehension. Similarly, because American participants use their native language in both conditions, the difference between conditions is that MT mediation can affect the quality of incoming messages. Thus, we can examine how MT influences idea production and comprehension independently from native versus second language use.

Hypotheses

Based on the literature and the issues we discussed earlier, we pose a number of hypotheses. First, for the Chinese participants, who will produce and receive messages in Mandarin in the MT condition vs. English as the common language, we predict:

H1: Chinese participants will generate more ideas during brainstorming when using MT than when using English as a common language. Although poorly translated messages may be a burden, the benefit of being able to express ideas in one's native language may compensate for the cost. In other words, MT-enabled native language use will lead to higher idea productivity than second language use.

H2: Chinese participants will consider messages exchanged in MT-mediated groups to be less comprehensible than those exchanged in English-mediated groups due to translation problems introduced by MT. That is, MT-enabled native language use will lead to poorer comprehension because the cost of translation errors will outweigh the benefit of receiving messages in one's native language.

For American participants, who will produce and receive messages in English in both conditions, we predict:

H3: American participants will generate fewer ideas in MT-mediated groups than in English-mediated groups. This is because American participants won't receive the benefit of native language use in MT-mediated groups. However, receiving translated messages may require more effort to process and lead to lower idea productivity.

H4: American participants will consider messages exchanged less comprehensible in MT-mediated than in English-mediated groups because of translation errors.

METHOD

Two-person groups consisting of one American participant with English as a native language and one Chinese participant with Mandarin as a native language performed group brainstorming using a text-based instant messaging (IM) chat client. Each dyad was assigned to one of two conditions: using MT to communicate (*MT-mediation*) or using English to communicate (*English-mediation*). The dyads performed two structurally similar brainstorming tasks, to allow for better generalization to different brainstorming topics. The task order was counterbalanced.

For MT-mediation groups, participants typed messages in their own native languages (English or Chinese), with the IM server translating the messages using Google Translate and displaying the messages in their partners' chat windows in the partner's native language. Google Translate was accessed through the API during the period of time of the study (February to April 2011). For English-mediation groups, participants typed and saw all messages in English.

Procedure

Participants were brought to two separate rooms and instructed about the brainstorming topics and provided with four conventional brainstorming rules: (a) the more ideas the better; (b) the wilder the ideas the better; (c) combination and improvement of ideas is better; and (d) avoid evaluating others' ideas [21]. They were instructed to brainstorm with their partners over a text chat. They were not informed about their partner's identity or background. Groups brainstormed for 15 minutes for each task.

Participants

Participants consisted of 64 students (70% female) from a large U.S. university and the surrounding community. Half were self-identified Americans who had lived in the U.S. or Canada for more than 10 years and spoke English as their native language. The other half were self-identified Chinese who spoke Mandarin as their native language but who were fluent or near-fluent in English. Although the Chinese participants were all currently studying or working in the U.S., the majority had grown up in China (97%) and been in the U.S. for less than 2 years (77%). Note that although some degree of bilingual ability is common in the multilingual organizations we aim to support, the time spent in the U.S. means that this population might have better English skills than other native Chinese speakers. This works against our hypotheses that MT will affect message production and comprehension, thus creating a conservative test of the hypotheses.

Participants were randomly assigned to brainstorming groups and experimental conditions. All groups were dyads, consisting of one American participant and one Chinese participant. In total, there were 32 two-person groups (17 MT-mediated groups and 15 English-mediated groups).

Tasks

Teams performed two brainstorming tasks of equivalent difficulty. The "extra thumb" and the "extra eye" questions, which have been used in many studies [27][28], ask participants to brainstorm about the benefits and difficulties for people having a hypothetical extra thumb or an extra eye at the back of their heads in the future.

Measures

Our key dependent measures were the productivity of ideation (H1 and H3) and the comprehension of messages (H2 and H4). To enable an exploratory analysis looking at how type of mediation influences message production overall, we also measured talkativeness during the tasks.

Because the study involved Chinese participants typing in Chinese in the MT-mediated groups, not all conversational data was in English. To enable analyses and comparisons of outcomes across conditions, a Chinese-English bilingual translator manually translated the Chinese utterances into English. A second bilingual speaker read the original Chinese inputs and corresponding translations and decided that the overall translation quality was satisfactory. This allowed further English-based data coding and analyses.

Productivity

To measure productivity, we adopted a two-level coding strategy proposed in a previous study [28]. At the first level, coders classified whether each conversational turn contained an idea or not. Turns coded as containing an idea were then coded as either duplicates (minor variations of an idea already contributed) or having originality (ideas not yet proposed in the session).

To assess intercoder reliability, two coders independently coded sample conversations from six randomly selected groups, accounting for 19% of the data. Inter-coder agreement was very good at the level of whether or not there was an idea present (Cohen's Kappa=.82) and satisfactory at the second level of whether the idea was novel (Cohen's Kappa=.63) One useful criterion for interpreting Kappa considers Kappa values between .61 and .80 substantial, and above .81 almost perfect [8][16]. Thus we used the number of turns coded as containing original ideas as a measure of productivity.

Comprehensibility

To assess the general comprehensibility of messages in each condition, we asked participants to answer three questions after each brainstorming trial: "I could understand other members' ideas", "I am confident that other group members understood my ideas", and "I didn't understand what other group members said". Ratings of the three items using 7-point Likert scales were averaged as a single measure (Cronbach's alpha=.89).

Talkativeness

There are two straightforward measures for talkativeness during brainstorming: the number of words typed and the number of chat turns generated. Because our analytical strategy of manually translating Chinese utterances into English for the purpose of data coding might distort counts of the number of "words", we looked at both the number of turns and the number of words in our analysis for ensuring the reliability of behavioral patterns observed.

RESULTS

The units of analysis were individuals, because the hypotheses concerned how MT influences individuals' production and comprehension. However, because they worked in dyads, we used mixed model ANOVAs to account for possible interdependencies caused by repeated measures or social influences between group members [15]. This type of mixed model adjusts the estimation of variance and typically provides more conservative results. Note that in mixed models, it is standard to estimate degrees of freedom by using Satterthwaite's approximation. Non-integer degree of freedom results may occur (see [18]).

Our basic analytical model, which we used across multiple dependent measures, treated brainstorming task, individual, and group as random variables. Brainstorming task was nested within participant, and participant was nested within group. Linguistic background (American or Chinese), type of mediation (MT or English), and brainstorming trial (first or second) were independent fixed variables.

Productivity

To test H1 and H3, we conducted a mixed model ANOVA using the number of original ideas as the dependent variable. Figure 2 shows idea productivity by American and Chinese participants in MT- and English-mediated groups.

Overall, there was a main effect of linguistic background: American participants produced more original ideas than Chinese participants ($F[1,30]=8.7$, $p<.01$). This difference may involve different communication styles, such as Chinese participants adopting a relatively "high-context" style and thus verbalizing fewer ideas [10]. However, this line of inquiry is not directly relevant to our hypotheses.

There was a marginal effect of brainstorming trial, where people tended to produce more ideas during the second trial than the first ($F[1,60]=3.3$, $p<.1$). There was also an interaction effect between trial and type of mediation ($F[1,60]=4$, $p<.05$). Participants in MT-mediated groups

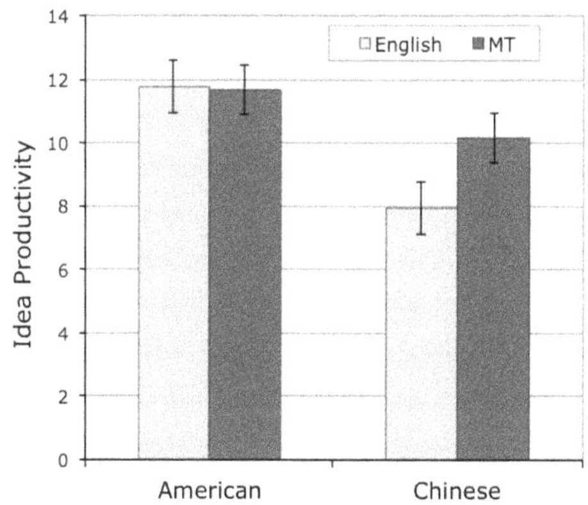

Figure 2. Idea productivity by Americans and Chinese in MT- and English-mediated groups.

produced more ideas in the second trial ($F[1,60]=7.8$, $p<.01$), while participants in English-mediated groups did not differ in idea productivity across trials ($F[1,60]=.01$, *n.s.*). There were no other main or interaction effects.

We then took a deeper look to test H1, which asked whether MT-enabled native language use was beneficial to idea production. A contrast analysis focusing on Chinese participants' productivity showed that there was a trend for Chinese participants in MT-mediated groups to produce more original ideas than those working in English-mediated groups (see Figure 2; $F[1,59.3]=2.6$, $p=.1$). This effect of native language was significant in the second brainstorming trial. A further contrast analysis showed that Chinese participants in MT-mediated groups produced significantly more original ideas than those in English-mediated groups in the second trial (first trial: $F[1,96.4]=.3$, *n.s.*; second trial: $F[1,96.4]=5$, $p<.05$). Thus there is some evidence in support of H1: there was benefit to expressing ideas in one's native language compared to a non-native language.

We also looked at whether MT, without the benefit of native language use (i.e., for English speakers), was detrimental to idea production. A contrast analysis focusing on American participants' productivity showed no difference between American participants generating ideas using MT or using English ($F[1,59.3]=.004$, *n.s.*). The effect of MT on American participants' productivity was uniform across brainstorming trials (first trial: $F[1,96.4]=.5$, *n.s.*; second trial: $F[1,96.4]=.2$, *n.s.*). H3 was thus not supported. Receiving machine-translated messages did not reduce productivity for native language speakers.

Comprehensibility

To test hypotheses H2 and H4, we conducted a mixed model ANOVA using ratings of comprehensibility as the dependent variable. Figure 3 shows perceived comprehensibility by American and Chinese participants in MT- and English-mediated groups.

Again, there was a main effect of linguistic background: Chinese participants in general rated comprehensibility higher than American participants ($F[1,60]=37.1$, $p<.0001$).

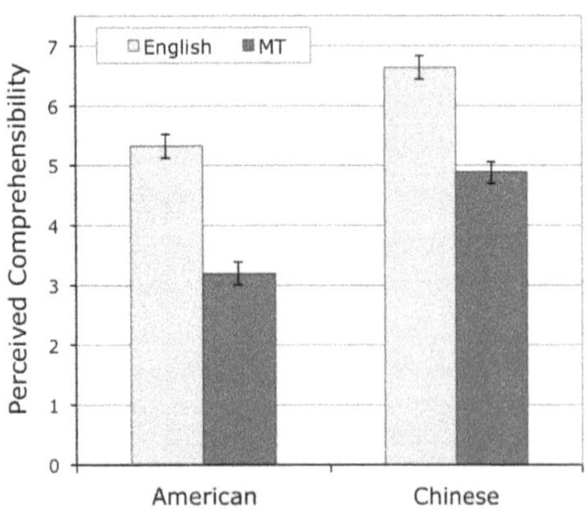

Figure 3. Perceived message comprehensibility by Americans and Chinese in MT- and English-mediated groups.

As messages received by American participants were either English messages produced by second language speakers (Chinese) or translated by MT, one possibility is that there is a large gap between the quality of these messages and Americans' proficiency, leading to lower comprehensibility ratings from Americans. However, this difference may also involve cultural styles of responding to surveys [11] and is not our main focus in this analysis.

What is relevant is the main effect of MT mediation. Participants rated English-mediated messages easier to understand than MT-mediated messages, regardless of their linguistic backgrounds ($F[1,60]=61.9$, $p<.0001$). There was no interaction effect between mediation and linguistic background ($F[1,60]=.5$, *n.s.*), and no main or interaction effects associated with brainstorming trial (all Fs < 1).

To test H2, a contrast analysis focusing on Chinese participants' ratings showed that Chinese participants in MT-mediated groups rated messages as less comprehensible than Chinese participants in English-mediated groups ($F[1,60]=25.4$, $p<.0001$). The effect of MT was uniform across brainstorming trials. It was more difficult to understand machine-translated messages than English-mediated messages even though translations were in one's native language. MT-enabled native language use reduced perceived comprehensibility, supporting H2.

A contrast analysis focusing on American participants showed that MT also negatively influenced American participants' ratings of message comprehensibility ($F[1,60]=37$, $p<.0001$). The pattern was consistent across brainstorming trials. H4 was thus supported.

Exploratory Analyses of Production Behaviors

In our analyses of productivity, we found that MT-enabled communication was beneficial for participants for whom English was not a native language; at the same time, MT had no negative consequences on the productivity of native English speakers. Thus it appears that there is value to use MT to mediate intercultural idea exchange.

However, the analyses of comprehensibility reveal that messages mediated by MT were less comprehensible than those mediated by English, for both American and Chinese participants (H2 and H4 supported). Whether or not the incoming messages are in one's native language does not appear to be a problem for comprehension, whereas less than perfect translations can have a significant negative impact on people's understanding of messages.

When combining these two sets of findings, it remains unclear whether and how disrupted translation influences the process of message production. Poor translation did not affect task performance (idea productivity), but how do people handle incoming messages when they are difficult to understand? What is the impact of people's perceptions of incomprehensibility on their production behaviors?

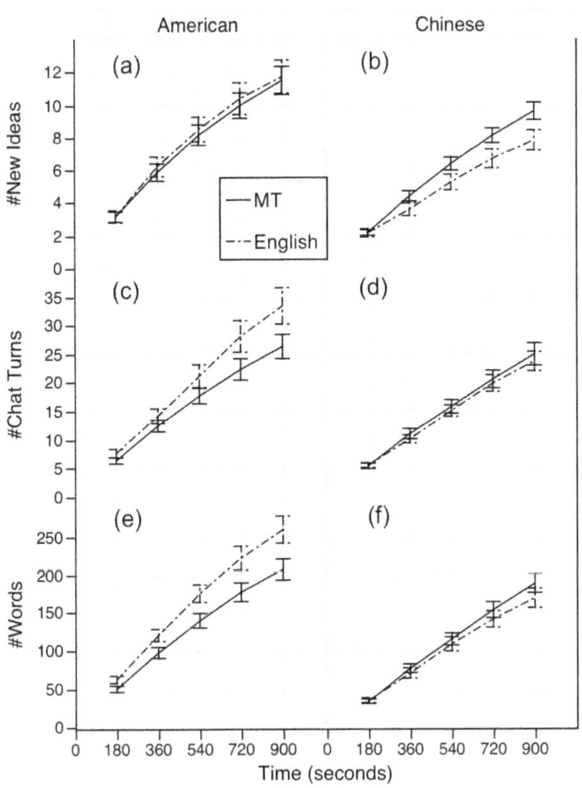

Figure 4. Production behaviors (idea productivity and talkativeness) over time.

To explore this issue, we looked at participants' patterns of production over time during the brainstorming session. Figure 4 shows several production measures over time, including the accumulated numbers of original ideas (Figure 4a and 4b), chat turns (Figure 4c and 4d), and words (Figure 4e and 4f). The time-based graphs allow us to see the consistency of production behaviors and whether people adapt their behaviors at different phases of interaction. Overall, people's production behaviors appear to be consistent over time in all conditions, thus it is safe to focus on behaviors assessed at the end of sessions.

Figure 4a and 4b visually confirm what we learned from the earlier analyses of productivity. MT enhanced idea productivity when it enabled native language use and did not harm productivity for native English speakers.

However, it did affect their talkativeness. In Figure 4c and 4e, American participants in MT-mediated groups appeared to be less talkative, producing fewer chat turns and words, than Americans in English-mediated groups. Mixed model ANOVAs using numbers of words and turns measured at the end of sessions (900 seconds) as dependent variables confirmed this observation. There was a trend that American participants tended to produce fewer turns over MT mediation than with English ($F[1,50.4]=2.6$, $p=.1$). American participants also produced fewer total words total over MT mediation than with English ($F[1,58.9]=3.92$, $p<.05$). Brainstorming trial did not change this pattern.

In contrast to Americans' decreased talkativeness over MT, Chinese participants in MT-mediated and English-mediated groups did not differ in their numbers of chat turns ($F[1,50.4]=.08$, *n.s.*) or words ($F[1,58,9]=.5$, *n.s.*). This can be seen in Figure 4d and Figure 4f.

These patterns provide further information about how disrupted translation subsequently influences one's own production behaviors. When the language used is kept constant, it appears that the influence of MT is more on communication style (talkativeness) rather than on performance (idea productivity). In other words, in MT-mediated communication American participants may have developed ways of communicating differently from what they do in regular English-based conversation. We will discuss this finding and its implications next.

DISCUSSSION

We examined the influence of MT-mediated versus English communication in brainstorming conversations between native English speaking Americans and native Mandarin speaking Chinese. Measures of production behaviors and perceptions of comprehensibility give a clearer picture of the benefits and drawbacks of using MT for idea exchange.

One important message is that MT tends to support cross-lingual groups by enabling people to produce ideas in their native language. Previous studies evaluating MT-mediated communication primarily focused on how translation problems affect certain holistic measures of communication (e.g., the process of grounding) [29]. The current study identifies that the effects of MT on production and comprehension are *asymmetrical*. Although both this study and previous work show that MT lowers comprehensibility of messages, it can boost idea productivity through native language use, as supported by the trend of Chinese participants' increasing ideation performance in this study.

The study also shows that the benefit of MT-enabled native language on productivity is particularly prominent in the second brainstorming trial, which may suggest that prior experience of collaborating over MT (e.g., the first trial) can help people better benefit from MT-enabled native language use for idea production. Learning and the development of coping strategies may be involved in this process. Future work looking into this issue may help further reveal the value and cost of MT-enabled native language use and suggest ways to improve MT technology.

The results demonstrate the practical value of using MT to mediate cross-lingual idea exchange, in that machine-translated messages at least did not negatively influence American participants' ideation performance. Although previous work found that MT can hamper group work that requires the establishment of common ground [29], one practical implication derived from the current study is that current MT may be more useful for tasks that focus more on productive expression of ideas than on the alignment of perspectives among group members.

Re-Coupling Production and Comprehension

Although brainstorming tasks permit us to analytically decouple production and comprehension of ideas for the purposes of testing our hypotheses, group brainstorming is still a group activity that requires members to communicate their ideas to one another. Theoretical models and studies show that interaction in groups can influence one's own thinking and behaviors [17][23]. Therefore, it is reasonable to think that errors in machine-translated messages may still impact aspects of production behaviors, even if idea productivity stays at the same level.

The exploratory analysis shown in Figure 4 suggests that translation quality influences communication style rather than performance. Americans' decreased talkativeness over MT may be a result of a different conversational process or strategy for handling translation errors. The following excerpt shows a scenario in which machine-translated messages triggered the American to seek clarification.

Chinese: But I do not think a better force.
(original: *但是我觉得不会更好用力.*
manual translation: *But I think it won't be easier to exert force.)*

American: huh?

Chinese: But I think even more advantages.
(original: *但是我觉得好处更多.*
manual translation: *But I think there are a lot of advantages too.)*

American: than disadvantages?

The need to ask questions to repair understanding may change the priority of various types of conversational moves that people may take in brainstorming such as elaboration of ideas and socialization (see [27] for a coding scheme). This in turn may influence other social outcomes in groups, such as attribution and trust. Future research is needed to look at how the use of MT affects communication styles and shapes social outcomes in group work.

It will also be interesting to take a deeper look at the difference between comprehending messages in a second language versus translated by MT. Either second language mediation or MT mediation can hinder comprehension and production, but possibly through very different mechanisms. Studies with more careful controls of message content and level of comprehension of the content can help us understand the difference. Deliberately degrading the comprehensibility of messages to varying degrees can be another possible approach to explicitly study how comprehension affects production.

Transforming MT-Mediated Idea Exchange

Although receiving machine-translated messages did not reduce overall task performance, it appears that people might not be able to engage in efficient idea exchange over MT and perform brainstorming in a synergistic sense. As the conversational episode just shows, translation problems can distract people from effective idea exchange.

One possible way to increase the value of MT for idea exchange is the theoretical perspective of "word-based priming". From this perspective, poorly translated messages may still be cognitively stimulating and helpful because they contain keywords useful for triggering concepts and facilitating memory retrieval [1][20]. This "word-as-prime" or "word-as-retrieval-cue" theoretical approach also underlies certain theories of conversation [22] and group brainstorming [23], positing that unconscious cognitive processing is important for language use and idea generation.

To increase the benefits of MT, it might also be possible to change the presentation of translated messages, such as highlighting key words while de-emphasizing function words and syntactical errors, in order to promote the unconscious aspects of cognitive processing.

Asymmetry for Cross-Lingual Communication Design

The study also has implications for the design of cross-lingual communication tools that go beyond idea exchange. The fact that MT-enabled native language use releases one language constraint (production) but not another (comprehension) suggests a divide-and-conquer strategy, dealing with needs of production and comprehension separately by leveraging different technical or social mechanisms.

For example, we might redesign our setting, preserving the MT-enabled native language use component while reducing the translation part. For Chinese participants capable of using English as a second language, requiring them to both type and read ideas in Chinese over MT is not the only option. People might express ideas in their native language, with the system only translating bilingual Chinese speakers' ideas to English, leaving native English speakers' ideas untranslated. This design may better match the language skills of different cultures, allowing people to receive the benefit of producing ideas in their own native languages while avoiding comprehension problems introduced by MT.

Limitations of the Current Study

One consideration for future study is that Chinese participants' English proficiency may interact with type of mediation—MT may be more helpful to both non-native speakers and their partners when English fluency is low. In this study, Chinese participants identified themselves as fluent or nearly fluent English speakers, and were randomly assigned to groups. Thus, individual difference in English proficiency is unlikely to influence our results. However, to further understand the role of second language skills in cross-lingual communication, explicit measurement and control of linguistic proficiency is needed.

The current study also only looks at Chinese-American dyads where English is the designated common language. To generalize the results, it will be beneficial to look at

Chinese-American dyads where Chinese becomes the common language, and other types of cross-lingual dyads that involve other languages.

For simplicity and generalizability, the current work does not control for individual differences. Future studies may benefit from controlling certain variables, such as language proficiency and familiarity with MT, to obtain clearer patterns of the effects of MT.

CONCLUSION

This paper presents a laboratory study looking at tradeoffs around MT-enabled native language use for cross-lingual idea exchange. The design of the study allows us to explore the benefits and constraints imposed by MT in group communication. Results show that MT tends to be beneficial rather than detrimental for idea production when it enables people to speak their own native language. However, machine-generated translations hinder comprehension. The work provides a fresh understanding of the roles of MT on cross-lingual idea exchange, with two main contributions. First is the finding that MT-enabled native language use tends to increase productivity in divergence-oriented domains. Second is the observation that MT has effects on production and comprehension asymmetrically. Our findings suggest that the classic view that MT obstructs teamwork is too coarse and that more study of the processes by which MT affects teamwork are needed. We also believe that applying these insights may lead to the design of CSCW tools that leverage these asymmetries to support idea exchange in particular and cross-lingual communication in general.

ACKNOWLEDGEMENT

This research was funded in part by National Science Foundation grants #0845351 and #1025425. The material is also based in part on work supported by the National Science Foundation, while Susan Fussell was working at the Foundation. Any opinion, findings, and conclusions or recommendations expressed in this material are those of the authors and do not necessarily reflect the views of the National Science Foundation. We thank Meaghan Frank, Johna Seo and Monica Chen for their assistance. We thank anonymous reviewers for their valuable comments that contribute to the improvement of this work.

REFERENCES

1. Bargh, J. A. & Chartrand, T. L. (1999). The unbearable automaticity of being. *Amer. Psychologist*, *54*, 462–479.
2. Chevrier, S. (2003). Cross-cultural management in multinational project groups. *J. World Business*, *38*.
3. Clark, H. H. (1996). *Using Language*. Cambridge Press.
4. Collins, F. S., Morgan, M., & Patrinos, A. (2003). The human genome project: Lessons from large-scale biology. *Science*, *300*, 286–290.
5. Culhane, J. L., & Worms, J. C. (2001). Improving the effectiveness of international collaboration in space science. *Space Policy*, *17*, 179–186.
6. DiStefano, J. J. & Maznevski, M. L. (2000). Creating value with diverse teams in global management. *Organizational Dynamics*, *29*, 45–61.
7. Dornyei, Z., & Scott, M. L. (1997). Communication strategies in a second language: Definitions and taxonomies. *Language Learning*, *47*, 173–210.
8. Everitt, B. (1996). *Making sense of statistics in psychology: A second-level course.* Oxford Univ. Press.
9. Frederiksson, R., Barnr-Rasmussen, W., & Piekkari, R. (2006). The multinational corporation as a multilingual organization: The notion of a common corporate language. *Corporate Communications, 11*, 406–423.
10. Hall, E. (1976). *Beyond Culture*. New York, NY: Doubleday/Anchor Books.
11. Hamamura, T., Heine, S. J., & Paulhus, D. L. (2008). Cultural differences in response styles: The role of dialectical thinking. *Personality and Individual Differences*, *44*, 932–942.
12. Harzing, A-W., & Feely, A. J. (2008). The language barrier and its implications for HQ-subsidiary relationships. *Cross Cultural Management, 15,* 49–61.
13. Henderson, J. K. (2005). Language diversity in international management teams. *International Studies of Management and Organization*, *35*, 66–82.
14. Jiang, H. & Singley, K. (2009). Exploring bilingual, task-oriented, document-centric text. *Proceedings of Group 2009* (pp. 229–232). NY: ACM Press.
15. Kenny, D. A., Mannetti, L., Pierro, A., & Livi, S. (2002). The statistical analysis of data from small groups. *J. Personality and Social Psych.*, *83*, 126–137.
16. Landis, J. R. & Koch, G. G. (1977). The measurement of observer agreement for categorical data. *Biometrics*, *33*, 159–174.
17. Levine, J. M., & Moreland, R. L. (1990). Progress in small group research. *Annual Rev. Psych.*, *41*, 585–634.
18. Littell, R., Milliken, G. A., Stroup, W. W., & Wolfinger, R. D. (1996). *SAS system for mixed models*. SAS Inst.
19. Luo, Y. & Shenkar, O. (2006). The multinational corporation as a multilingual community: Language and organization in a global context. *Journal of International Business Studies, 37*, 321–339.
20. McNamara, T. P. (2005). *Semantic Priming: Perspectives from Memory and Word Recognition*. New York, NY: Psychology Press.
21. Osborn, A. (1957). *Applied Imagination*. NY: Scribner.
22. Pickering, M. J., & Garrod, S. (2004). Toward a mechanistic psychology of dialogue. *Behavioral and Brain Sciences*, *27*.
23. Stroebe, W., Nijstad, B. A., & Rietzschel, E. F. (2010). Beyond productivity loss in brainstorming groups: The

evolution of a question. *Advances in Experimental Social Psychology*, *43*, 157–203.

24. Takano, Y. & Noda, A. (1993). A temporary decline of thinking ability during foreign language processing. *Journal of Cross-Cultural Psychology*, *24*, 445–462.

25. Takano, Y. & Noda, A. (1995). Interlanguage dissimilarity enhances the decline of thinking ability during foreign language processing. *Lang. Learn.*, *45*, 657–681.

26. Tange, H. & Lauring, J. (2009). Language management and social interaction within the multilingual workplace. *Journal of Communication Management*, *13*, 218–232.

27. Wang, H-C., Fussell, S. R., & Setlock, L. D. (2009). Cultural difference and adaptation of communication styles in computer-mediated group brainstorming. *Proc. CHI 2009* (pp. 669–678). NY: ACM Press.

28. Wang, H-C., Fussell, S. R., & Cosley, D. (2011). From diversity to creativity: Stimulating group brainstorming with cultural differences and conversationally-retrieved pictures. *Proc. CSCW 2011* (pp. 265–274).

29. Yamashita, N. & Ishida, T. (2006). Effects of machine translation on collaborative work. *Proc. CSCW 2006* (pp. 515–523). NY: ACM Press.

30. Yamashita, N., Inaba, R., Kuzuoka, H., & Ishida, T. (2009). Difficulties in establishing common ground in multiparty groups using machine translation. In *Proc. CHI 2009* (pp. 679–688). NY: ACM.

"Could Someone Please Translate This?" – Activity Analysis of Wikipedia Article Translation by Non-Experts

Ari Hautasaari
Department of Social Informatics
Kyoto University
Yoshida-Honmachi, Sakyo-Ku,
Kyoto, 606-8501, Japan
arihau@ai.soc.i.kyoto-u.ac.jp

ABSTRACT
Wikipedia translation activities aim to improve the quality of the multilingual Wikipedia through article translation. We performed an activity analysis of the translation work done by individual English to Chinese non-expert translators, who translated linguistically complex Wikipedia articles in a laboratory setting. From the analysis, which was based on Activity Theory, and which examined both information search and translation activities, we derived three translation strategies that were used to inform the design of a support system for human translation activities in Wikipedia.

Author Keywords
Wikipedia; translation; activity analysis; non-experts.

ACM Classification Keywords
H.5.2 [Information Interfaces and Presentation]: User Interfaces – Evaluation/methodology; J.5 [Computer Applications]: Arts and Humanities – Language translation.

General Terms
Human Factors; Design.

INTRODUCTION
Wikipedia is the largest collaboratively edited online encyclopedia available, and the sixth most visited website in the world[1]. Unsurprisingly, almost 60% of the traffic is directed to the English language Wikipedia. The English Wikipedia is the largest in terms of number of articles (close to four million), and active contributors. Together with the German, French and Dutch Wikipedias, the four language versions are the only ones with over one million articles. Combined, there are currently close to 22 million articles in 285 languages, and 34 million registered users in the multilingual Wikipedia[2].

Currently, 6,912 living languages, including sign languages, exist in the world, and in some countries, such as Indonesia, hundreds of languages are spoken by the people [12]. In this light, aiming to provide information equally in all languages seems like a daunting task to undertake. The only way to realistically achieve such a goal would be to rely on volunteer contributors, such as in Wikipedia, to translate existing content. However, even when focusing on the currently existing language versions of Wikipedia, the number of active contributors, especially in the smaller Wikipedias with fewer than 1,000 articles, is very low. The question is; how can we support the Wikipedia contributors translating articles in the multilingual Wikipedia?

Wikipedia Translation
First, we need to define what we mean by Wikipedia translation. In this study, "Wikipedia translation" refers to the activities related to translating Wikipedia article pages. Wikipedia translation can also include the translation of non-encyclopedic pages, such as WikiProject pages, and even discussion pages attached to each Wikipedia article [15].

Wikipedia articles can be overtly complex in linguistic terms, as is evident from the existence of the Simple English Wikipedia[3], which includes English Wikipedia articles written in simplified language. In previous research [31], the main differences identified between the Simple English Wikipedia articles and the corresponding English Wikipedia articles were the less frequent use of complex words, and decreased variety of syntactic structures in the Simple English versions. Furthermore, the language used in conceptual articles was found to be more complex compared to biographical and object-based articles [31].

The language complexity in Wikipedia articles becomes increasingly apparent in translation tasks. As Wikipedia is a collaboratively edited encyclopedia, translation of articles is also a collaborative effort. In previous research, this aspect of Wikipedia translation was studied through the analysis of discussion contributions in translated Wikipedia articles

[1] http://www.alexa.com/siteinfo/wikipedia.org

[2] http://meta.wikimedia.org/wiki/List_of_Wikipedias

[3] http://simple.wikipedia.org/wiki/Main_Page

[14]. The main problem during a translation task that required the translators to consult the Wikipedia community for help was identified as the translation of names, proper nouns and transliteration, as opposed to resolving the syntactic and semantic structure of the translated text.

Various supporting systems have been developed for the Wikipedia translation community, ranging from machine translation supported article editors, such as Microsoft's WikiBhasha[4], to translation workflow management [9, 23]. Machine translation has also been proposed as a viable solution to overcome some challenges when translating complex Wikipedia articles to multiple languages with the help of monolingual domain experts [15]. Machine translation techniques also enable cross-language information retrieval from websites [2], and multilingual collaboration in online environments [30]. "The aim of using computers for translation is not to emulate or rival human translation but to produce rough translations which can serve as drafts for published translations, as gists for information gathering, and as cross-language communication aids" [17]. For high quality translation a human translator is still required to be kept as part of the translation process.

While Wikipedia article translation is a collaborative effort, there has been little previous work done regarding the activities of individual volunteer translators. This study focuses on the individual actions of Wikipedia translators as components of collaborative translation work in Wikipedia, and gives a first glimpse on how the needs of individual non-expert translators can be accommodated in a Wikipedia translation support tool [13].

RESEARCH QUESTIONS

The research questions in this study were derived from the existing work regarding Wikipedia translation [14]. In the previous work, the discussion contributions of Wikipedia contributors were analyzed to identify what type of problems in article translation process require community interaction in the Wikipedia discussion pages. After further investigating the existing literature, we found that there is very little research focusing on the translation process of individual Wikipedia translators.

Although translation studies are by no means a new field, studies conducted with non-professional translators tend to include students of translation as subjects. This led us to conclude that we do not know *how* volunteer Wikipedia contributors translate articles. Hence, our initial research question was:

> RQ1. How do non-expert Wikipedia translators conduct translation work?

The second and third research questions were clarified during a preliminary data analysis, where we noted the extensive need to access online resources during the translation process.

> RQ2. What are the information needs of non-expert translators?

> RQ3. How are the information needs resolved in an online environment?

This study is exploratory in the sense that we do not take a strict standpoint of translation studies, but focus on the human-computer interaction in Wikipedia article translation. Through an Activity Theoretical approach, we aim to explain the translation process of individual non-expert translators, and the process of resolving information needs during a task of Wikipedia article translation. Based on the analysis results, we draw design implications for a Wikipedia translation support tool.

RELATED WORK

Previous studies have concluded that professionals and non-professionals show different types of behavior during a translation task [8, 18, 21]. In [26], Lörscher gives a brief comparison of the differences in professional and non-professional translation processes. The main differences found were that non-professionals tend to be more form-oriented, focus on translation as a problem solving task, and tend to include formulating problems in the translated text [27]. In [32], the cost of crowdsourcing translations is shown to be lower than when using professional translators, while still keeping the quality up to par.

Different language versions of a Wikipedia article can include a great deal of unique information. Omnipedia[5] is one project that aims to bring the information in the multilingual Wikipedia articles available to users in their native language. Previous studies have revealed that monolingual users are not aware of the multitude of information not available in their own language, while also highlighting the importance of culturally-aware hyperlingual applications [3, 6, 16]. In [6], the authors recommend a user-driven approach to Wikipedia translation, where cultural differences in different language Wikipedias are respected, and mechanical translation is supported by machine translation.

METHODOLOGY

Theoretical Background – Activity Theory

According to Activity Theory (AT), human activity is always directed towards an object, which exists outside the human. Activity Theory defines a three-level hierarchy for human activities: Activity-Action-Operation. Activities are always directed towards a motive. Activities are divided in

[4] http://www.wikibhasha.org

[5] http://omnipedia.northwestern.edu

to Actions, which are directed towards specific goals. Actions are again divided to Operations, which are lower-level units executed and adjusted to specific conditions of the context, and often internalized to a point where people may not be aware how they are performed.

Human activity is mediated through artifacts, with which humans interact with objects. Artifacts can range from physical objects, such as carpenter tools, to psychological artifacts, such as language and signs. Human activity is also collaborative. Humans do not act in a vacuum, but engage in collaborative processes with other people. In collaborative activities, different people conduct different actions belonging to an activity, aligning the goals of each action towards the objective of the activity through communicative artifacts. Activity Theory recognizes the evolving nature of human activities: Activities, actions and operations, the relationships between the activities, mediating artifacts, and socio-cultural context are constantly changing. This means that an activity can become an action, and an action can become an operation when the goals change [25].

For an in-depth introduction and discussion on Activity Theory and it's application to HCI design see: [11, 22, 24].

Activity Analysis

Activity Analysis aims to provide a detailed description of human activity conducted within the constraints and resources of the real-world setting. As detailed in [4], Activity Analysis consists of a qualitative study, an observation phase, and a detailed analysis of activity patterns based on Activity Theory.

In this study, the qualitative phase included a video recording of the activity. The focus of this study is on the activity system of Wikipedia article translation, and we began the analysis by collecting data on the following:

Activity – The Wikipedia article translation activity, actions, operations, actors, and artifacts used in the translation activity.

Person – Activities and actions of individual non-expert translators conducting the translation activities.

Artifacts – The use of specific tools for mediating activities and actions in Wikipedia article translation.

In the observation phase, we created a coding schema for the analysis of the collected data based on Activity Theory. The schema was focused on the following characteristics of the Wikipedia translation task:

Activity – Identifying all the activities included in the translation task based on the motive and object of work.

Action – All actions performed as a part of an activity.

Operations – Manual operations performed as a part of an action.

Context – Context of each action including the time of action occurrence during an activity, and the artifacts used to mediate the action.

Actors – Non-expert translators conducting the activities. In this study, each translator was working individually.

The created coding schema allowed the identification of activities, actions, the starting time and end time of each subsequent action, details on the operations, tools used to perform and actors performing each action.

The specific activities were distinguished from actions, and other activities, by observing the *object* of the task in the given context. In Article Translation Activity, the object is the translated article. As discussed in detail later, the object of the task could change to a single word, phrase or information item, and the activity was then defined as a Information Search Activity.

EXPERIMENTAL DESIGN

The task for the experiment participants was to translate an English Wikipedia article to Chinese. The criteria for choosing the articles for this experiment were:

1. There was no existing translation in the Chinese language Wikipedia [6] or in the Chinese collaboratively edited online encyclopedia, Baidu Baike[7].
2. Length of each article/passage is no more than 500 English words.
3. Each article represents a different domain (i.e., no two articles are about computer science).
4. The article content is representative of the general Wikipedia article language complexity, and does not have a version in the Simple English Wikipedia[8].

The length of each translation task was limited to no more than one hour thirty minutes. To fit this timeframe, the length of each English passage was set to a maximum of 500 words. "Akan Volcanic Complex" and "Ying Huang" were complete Wikipedia articles, whereas "Crowdsourcing" included two sections of the full article not available in the Chinese language Wikipedia or Baidu Baike to match the set article translation length (Table 1). The source articles were uploaded to a Wiki-server dedicated for this experiment.

Participants

The experiment participants were university graduate students of various fields hired specifically for this task. The group consisted of 15 Chinese native speakers, with at

[6] http://zh.wikipedia.org

[7] http://baike.baidu.com

[8] http://simple.wikipedia.org/wiki/Main_Page

least a score of 61 in TOEFL iBT[9] or 500 in TOEFL PBT[10] academic English aptitude test.

Article	Number of words	Average translation time
Akan Volcanic Complex http://en.wikipedia.org/wiki/Akan_Volcanic_Complex	490**	93 minutes
Ying Huang http://en.wikipedia.org/wiki/Ying_Huang	466**	82 minutes
Crowdsourcing* http://en.wikipedia.org/wiki/Crowdsourcing	412**	93 minutes

* *"Web-based Crowdsourcing" and "Collaboration".*
** *On December 12th 2011.*

Table 1: Articles for translation.

In this paper, the term "non-expert translator" refers to the experiment participants who were A) not professional translators, or have not received training in translation, and B) not domain experts with extensive knowledge on the topics of the articles being translated. With this choice of terminology, we aim to differentiate the subjects in this study from non-professional translators, who have often been subjects in previous translation studies (e.g., [1, 20]). The participants in this study represent bilingual "Site Visitors", or casual users, who are potential contributors and one target user group for Wikipedia translation support tools [9].

Experiment Task

We asked each translator to create a translated Chinese language Wikipedia article from the source article. The participants were only given basic instructions on how to create a new Wikipedia article page and a brief tutorial to the interface options in the MediaWiki software.

Each participant was randomly assigned to one of the three articles as a translator. Hence, each article was translated by five individual non-expert translators during the experiment. The participants were given identical laptop computers, which were cleaned of any page history, cache and auto-filling options.

Data Collection

We recorded the computer screen of each participant for the full duration of the experiment task. In addition, we collected the browsing history and the final translated Chinese article from each participant. In previous studies, the think-aloud method has been used to collect data from translators during a translation task, but we opted to rely on the video recording due to previous inconclusive evidence on the effect of think-aloud method on the translation product [19]. Overall, we collected approximately 18 hours of video material, 15 fully translated articles, and the browsing history of each of the 15 participants.

Data Annotation

After the experiment, each video recording was annotated for activities, actions and operations during the article translation process. Each operation was identified by a mouse-click (such as changing a browser window) or keystroke (such as typing a letter), which were highlighted in the video log, but not on the participants' screen. Each action was given a timestamp based on the video recording (excluding administrative tasks). In total, we identified 16 actions during a translation activity, and 23 operations belonging to one or more actions.

ACTIVITY ANALYSIS OF WIKIPEDIA ARTICLE TRANSLATION BY NON-EXPERTS

Translation Strategies

We annotated the individual actions of each experiment participant during the Article Translation Activity, where the object is defined as the translated article. The annotation schema is illustrated in Table 2. Based on the Activity Analysis, we derived three distinct strategies used by non-expert Wikipedia translators.

	Action ID	Action Description
(C)	14	Refine machine translation input
	13	Machine translate words/phrases
	12	Refine word/phrase in dictionary search
	11	Search word/phrase in dictionary
	10	Refer to knowledge resources (Wikipedia, online articles, publications...)
	9	Scan search engine results
	8	Refine search engine search terms
	7	Search engine query
(B)	6	Post-edit machine translated sentence in target article
	5	Compare machine translation result to original text
	4	Machine translate full sentences
	3	Read own translation (proofread)
	2	Translate sentence
	1	Read source article
(A)	-1	Open resources (text editor, web pages...)
	-2	Create target language page

Table 2: Activity Analysis coding schema for Actions in Wikipedia article translation. (A) Tool management. (B) Sentence translation. (C) Information search.

[9] Test of English as a Foreign Language: Internet-based test

[10] Test of English as a Foreign Language: Paper-based test

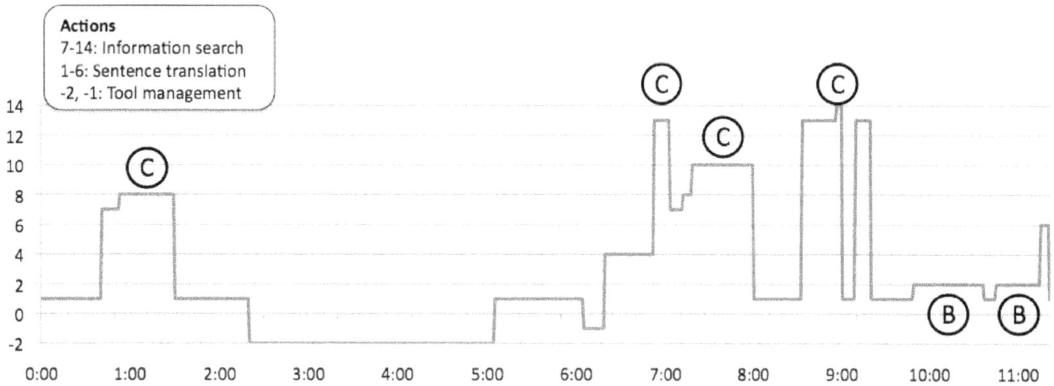

Figure 1: Temporal action sequence of *Search First Then Translate* strategy. (C) Search for word translations, or information about source language words or phrases (B) Translate sentences based on previous search results in target page.

Each participant was exclusively identified to adopt one of the three strategies in different stages of the article translation process. The identified translation strategies have some similarities with the translator types described in [7]. However, in [7], dictionaries and online resources were not allowed for the translators, and the strategies described in this paper are representative of individual non-expert Wikipedia translators.

In the following sections, the Wikipedia translation strategies are illustrated with an action sequence of three different translators translating the title and the first paragraph in the "Akan Volcanic Complex" article:

Akan Volcanic Complex
Akan Volcanic Complex is a volcanic group of volcanoes that grew out of the Akan caldera. It is located within Akan National Park, about 50km Northwest of Kushiro in eastern Hokkaidō, Japan.

Search First Then Translate Strategy
Figure 1 represents the action sequence for a translator type who searches unknown words in the source article first, then translates whole sentences or paragraphs. (C) indicates the information search actions during a translation task. In this example, the translator uses a search engine to find a definition for a word, machine translates words and phrases using Google Translate, and finally when the translator has resolved the meaning and Chinese translation for all the unknown words in the paragraph, conducts the sentence translation action (B).

Translate-Search-Translate Strategy
Figure 2 represents the action sequence for a translator type who translates sentences in increments, while looking for word translations or related information in between sentence translation actions. (C) indicates the actions during which the translator conducts a dictionary search, translates words in a machine translator or searches the meaning of an English word in a search engine. As illustrated in Figure 2, the information search actions are done in parallel with the translation of sentences (B). In other words, the translator would conduct an information search action whenever he/she encountered an unknown word in the source text while translating the same sentence.

Paraphrase Machine Translation Strategy
Figure 3 represents the action sequence for a translator type who paraphrases machine translation results as the main translation action. (B1) indicates the sequences where the translator uses a machine translation tool to translate complete sentences. (B2) indicates an action where the translator paraphrases the machine translation result to increase the quality of the translated sentence. The translator evaluates the machine translation quality during both actions, and conducts information searches for word translation or for additional information about the words or phrases when the machine translation result alone does not suffice for an accurate translation.

Learning Effects on Choosing a Translation Strategy
The translators spent the longest amount of time on actions related to sentence translation. These included reading the source article, paraphrasing machine translation results as well as translating the sentences by hand. Similarly to previous work conducted on professional translators [10], the non-expert Wikipedia translators required a wide range of tools to perform the task. In this experiment, translators spent on average 24.22% of total article translation time conducting information search actions with no significant difference between strategies (Table 3).

Activity	*Actions*	*% of article translation*
Sentence translation	(1-6)	66.46%
Information search	(7-14)	24.22%
Tool management	-1, -2	9.32%

Table 3: Time spent on different activities during Wikipedia article translation.

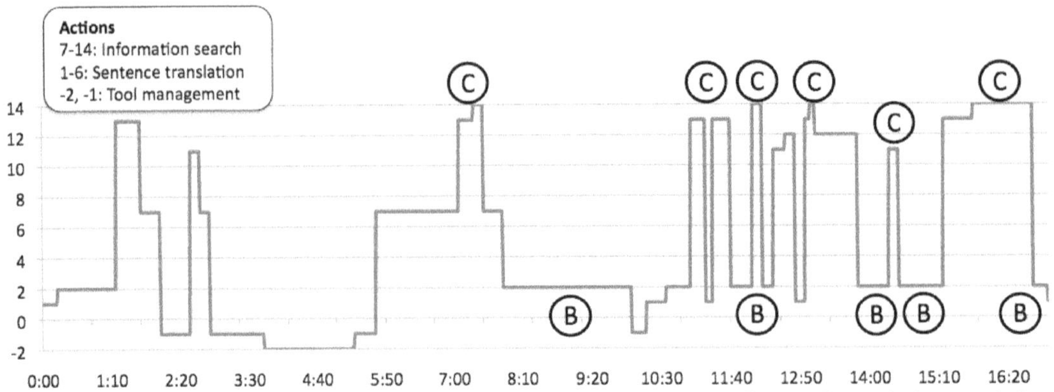

Figure 2: Temporal action sequence of *Translate-Search-Translate* strategy. (C) Search for word translations, or information about source language words or phrases (B) Translate sentences based on previous search results in target page.

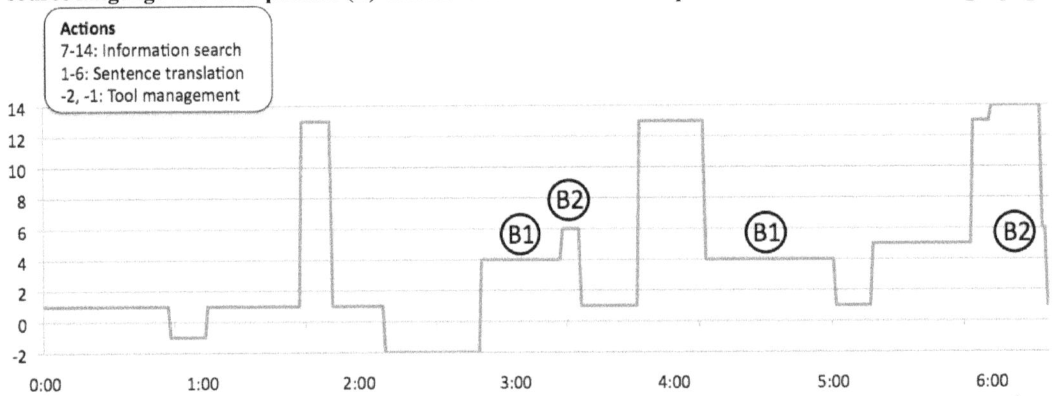

Figure 3: Temporal action sequence of *Paraphrase Machine Translation* strategy. (B1) Translate full sentences in a machine translator. (B2) Paraphrase machine translation result in target page.

There was no distinguishable trend in the choice of the initial translation strategy, and five of the participants did not modify their strategy during the translation task. However, three translators of the "Crowdsourcing" article began with *Translate-Search-Translate* strategy and later modified their strategy to *Paraphrase Machine Translation.* Two of the translators began with *Paraphrase Machine Translation* and did not modify their initial strategy (Table 4).

Based on the Activity Analysis, and the source article content, it became apparent that the "Crowdsourcing" article included longer paragraphs and more complete sentences than the other two articles. Furthermore, it was faster for translators to paraphrase the full machine translated sentences, which did not include a large amount of specialized words, or names and proper nouns. "Akan Volcanic Complex" and "Ying Huang" included over 40 words that could be considered specialized (incl. names and proper nouns), whereas the "Crowdsourcing" article included only 17 specialized words. Based on these observations, we concluded that *Paraphrase machine translation* can be a more desirable strategy for translating conceptual articles than biographical articles in Wikipedia, even though the English language might be more complex [31]. The effectiveness of each translation strategy could be determined from the translation time and quality of the translated article, but it is out of the scope of this paper.

Translator ID	Translation Task	Initial Strategy	Modified Strategy
1	Akan Volcanic Complex	Paraphrase MT	Search First
2	Akan Volcanic Complex	Search First	Search First
3	Akan Volcanic Complex	Search First	Paraphrase MT
4	Akan Volcanic Complex	Search First	Translate-Search
5	Akan Volcanic Complex	Translate-Search	Translate-Search
6	Ying Huang	Paraphrase MT	Paraphrase MT
7	Ying Huang	Paraphrase MT	Paraphrase MT
8	Ying Huang	Translate-Search	Translate-Search
9	Ying Huang	Paraphrase MT	Translate-Search
10	Ying Huang	Translate-Search	Translate-Search
11	Crowdsourcing	Translate-Search	Paraphrase MT
12	Crowdsourcing	Paraphrase MT	Paraphrase MT
13	Crowdsourcing	Translate-Search	Paraphrase MT
14	Crowdsourcing	Paraphrase MT	Paraphrase MT
15	Crowdsourcing	Translate-Search	Paraphrase MT

Table 4: Learning effects in translation strategy choice.

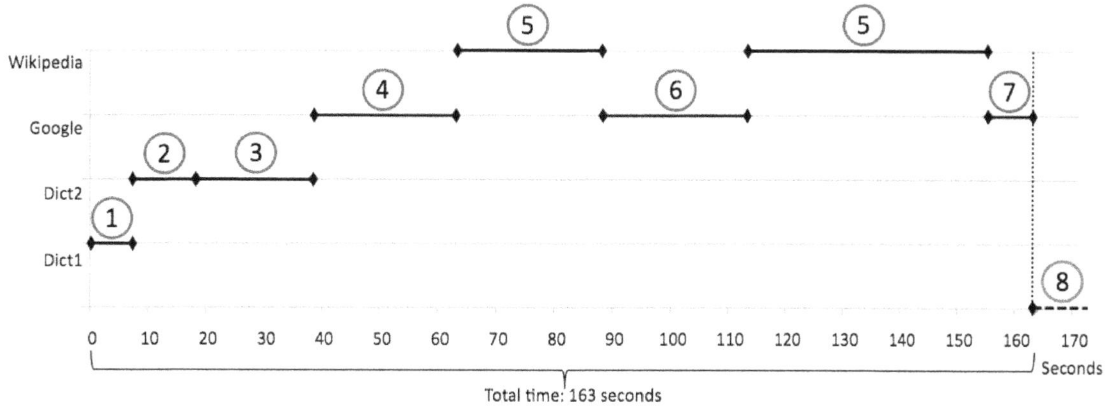

Figure 4: Temporal pattern of information search for Chinese translation of "*crowdfunding*". (1) Search "*crowdfunding*" in Dictionary 1. (2) Search "*crowdfunding*" in Dictionary 2. (3) Paraphrase search term to "*crowdfund*". (4) Search "*crowdfunding*" in Google. (5) Read English Wikipedia article on "Crowd Funding". (6) Scan Google search results for "*crowdfunding*". (7) Search "*collective cooperation*" copied from "Crowd Funding" article in Google. (8) Read article without resolving the Chinese translation.

INFORMATION SEARCH DURING A WIKIPEDIA TRANSLATION TASK

As described in [25], activities can become actions, or actions can become activities when the goals change. In the Activity Analysis of the Wikipedia translation task, information search was denoted as a series of actions belonging to the translation activity (Table 2, (C)). In this section, we analyze information search as a separate activity, where the *object* of the activity is one information item (e.g., word or phrase).

For information search activity the following are defined:

Activity – Information search: Search a Chinese translation of a word, phrase, name or a proper noun from online resources. Search additional information about a word or a phrase being translated.

Object – Information object: Chinese translation of a word or a phrase; definition of a word or a phrase; transliteration of an English name or a proper noun in Chinese.

Artifacts – Online language and search tools: Search engines in Chinese and English, online multilingual dictionaries, machine translators (for word or phrase translation), Wikipedia, Baidu Baike, online publications.

The precondition to engage in an information search activity was that the first tool used would not produce a result valued high enough by the translator (no result, clearly wrong result, too many results). The translator would then choose another tool, modify the search terms, or finally try to find an explanation in the source or target language on the meaning of the original word (i.e., try to find enough additional information to successfully translate the given word when no direct translation could be found).

The example in Figure 4 is extracted from the "Crowdsourcing" article translation, and it represents a typical case of information search activity during a Wikipedia article translation task. The translator begins the information search activity by consulting a dictionary for direct word translation for "*crowdfunding*". When no result is found, the translator searches the same word from another dictionary without a result. The translator then paraphrases the search term by shortening it to "*crowdfund*". When this does not yield a result, the translator searches for additional information on the topic in English through Google and Wikipedia. At the end of the activity, the translator is unable to find a proper translation for the word, or a satisfactory definition on the meaning in the English term.

A simple case of information search *action* found through the Activity Analysis was the search of a single word in a dictionary, or through a machine translator. On average, the translators were engaged 23.32% of the time in single search actions, and 76.67% of the time in information search activities for one information item, such as one word.

Similarly to [14], the transliteration of English names to Chinese proved to be time consuming for the translators of "Akan Volcanic Complex" and "Ying Huang". These two articles included place names, proper nouns and names of people, which could not be directly translated with available online dictionaries or machine translators. When transliterating English names and proper nouns to Chinese, translators need to choose characters with similar phonemic representation [28, 29]. The non-expert translators, however, were unwilling to transliterate the names and proper nouns unless they found a reference through an information search activity. In cases where direct equivalent was not found, the translators gave up on the information search and used the non-translated English word directly in the translated Chinese language article.

The Activity Analysis revealed that non-expert translators conduct short sporadic word searches in dictionaries or machine translators, as is apparent especially in the *Translation-Search-Translate* strategy (Figure 2). The key finding here is that non-expert translators tend to engage in the time-consuming information search activities only when the first initially highly valued tool returns an unsatisfactory result.

DESIGNING A TRANSLATION SUPPORT SYSTEM FOR WIKIPEDIA

In this section, we focus on the derived design implications specifically for a *Wikipedia translation support system*, and illustrate how Activity Analysis was applied for designing a collaboratively edited multilingual dictionary tool for supporting complex translation tasks in Wikipedia.

Design for Multiple Activities

Wikipedia is essentially a collective intelligence platform, where users engage in multiple types of activities [9]. In previous approaches to support Wikipedia translation, the focus has been on mechanical translation, often with the help of machine translation (e.g., [23]). However, as we reflected on the actions taken by the participants during a Wikipedia article translation activity (Table 2) and the translation strategies of individual translators (Figures 1, 2 and 3), it became obvious that article translation includes multiple activities in sequences, not just mechanical translation.

Based on this observation, we defined the first requirement for our prototype as "support multiple activities, rather than just mechanical translation". Furthermore, rather than adapting to separate activities, we defined a system that has the same functionality whether the user is reading the source article, translating an article or proofreading the translated text.

Design for Continuous Action

As can be seen in Figures 1, 2 and 3, all translation strategies require the translators to hop between multiple *types* of tools when searching for information (dictionaries, machine translators, search engines and information resources). The second requirement for our prototype was that it is "usable in any Wikipedia page, and only in any Wikipedia page". Furthermore, we observed that users tend to spend a lot of time changing between actions, such as reading an article to viewing a dictionary. Hence, we defined a requirement stating "in order to view a dictionary entry, the current action/activity should not be interrupted".

A solution derived from the Activity Analysis is a pop-up page element reacting to mouse-over operations, displaying existing multilingual dictionary entries for the words in a Wikipedia article body text. The designed page element was defined to include an added feature to support information search by displaying search engine results using the highlighted word and it's existing translations as search terms. The first two design implications are aimed to lower the number of interactions needed to access the multilingual information online during different translation activities in Wikipedia, such as in information search activities (Figure 4).

Design for Context Awareness

The Activity Analysis revealed, that even when using the *Paraphrase Machine Translation* strategy (Figure 3), translators had to search word translations from other information resources (Figure 4). This is partly due to the fact that, currently, machine translators do not handle the context of the translated sentence very well, and often give inappropriate word translations as a result (word polysemy). For example, the word "*crowdfunding*" in Figure 4 can be translated in at least three different ways: 众筹 (zhong chou), 集体融资 (ji ti rong zi), and 大众集资 (da zhong ji zi). In this case, the first option is the correct one given the domain of the article, while the last two are technically not incorrect, but less appropriate.

Based on this observation and the frequency of information search activities, we defined a requirement for our prototype to "include only one translation for each word given the context of the article". We define the context of a dictionary entry by using category-tags associated with an article being translated and the tags added to each domain specific dictionary. Furthermore, the inter-wiki links associated with category pages are used to preserve the context in the multilingual articles. Each entry is displayed with additional information on the source dictionary (name) and domain (categories) in order for users to determine whether an entry is appropriate given the context of the article. We defined that conflicts in the context specific dictionary entries are to be resolved by the community to keep the human in the loop, as mentioned in [17].

Design for Knowledge Sharing

It should be taken in to consideration how human actions create value in multilingual collective intelligence platforms, such as Wikipedia. Even though direct collaboration is possible through the Wikipedia discussion pages [14], indirect collaboration is much more common [5]. The changes in the source and target articles, as well as any resources should be reflected to all collaborators in the multilingual and monolingual dimensions.

"Akan Volcanic Complex" and "Ying Huang" articles both included over 40 specialized words, whereas the "Crowdsourcing" article included 17 specialized words. Non-expert translators, as opposed to bilingual domain experts, need to put considerable effort on resolving all the correct word translations (e.g., Figure 4). Based on this observation, we defined a requirement for our prototype to "support reusability of the resolved word translations". In other words, support knowledge sharing by enabling article translators as well as domain experts to contribute translations of words to domain specific dictionaries.

Our prototype was designed so that any new unique multilingual dictionaries would be visible in any Wikipedia article in any language, thus making them available to translators as well as "Site Visitors" [9]. Furthermore, we included full history and versioning function to each dictionary to foster collaboration in the dictionary creation process. In the nature of Wikipedia, we included a discussion function to each dictionary page, with a possibility to translate messages to other languages with machine translation.

By combining the previous design implications, we created a prototype of a user edited multilingual domain specific dictionary to support multiple translation activities in Wikipedia directly in the standard MediaWiki interface, which we shall report in a future paper.

CONCLUSION

Wikipedia translation activities aim to increase the quality of the multilingual Wikipedia via article translation, especially in languages where the active contributors do not include domain experts in certain topics. However, previous studies have not answered one of the central questions in system design for Wikipedia translation support: *How* do individual Wikipedia contributors translate articles?

In this study, we identified three translation strategies of bilingual non-expert English to Chinese translators. We also found indications that paraphrasing machine translation results can be a more desirable strategy for translating conceptual articles than biographical articles for non-experts. This suggests that the current support systems may be effective only for certain type of articles or translators.

Translators engage in time-consuming information search activities when a translation of a word, especially proper nouns and names, cannot be resolved through the initial dictionary or machine translation service. The information needs of translators are met through multiple separate online resources, and translators need to put considerable effort into finding the relevant information online.

The results of the Activity Analysis were used to define design implications for a Wikipedia translation support system. The implications discussed in this paper included; i) design for multiple activities, not just mechanical translation, ii) design for continuous action in Wikipedia, rather than external tools iii) design for context awareness in the monolingual and multilingual dimensions of the Wikipedia article space, and iv) design for knowledge sharing to include domain experts in the collaborative translation. These guidelines were applied to a design of a support system for human translation activities in Wikipedia.

In order to support the needs of non-expert Wikipedia translators, we enable domain experts to work as resource providers to support non-expert translators through knowledge sharing via multilingual domain specific dictionaries directly in Wikipedia. We also included assisted information search about multilingual dictionary entries as one element of the supporting tool to reduce the time spent on information search activities, and to reduce interruptions during translation tasks.

Limitations and Future Work

As this was an exploratory study on the actions taken by individual non-expert translators in Wikipedia, a number of limitations were identified. Although we collected a large amount of data, the number of participants could have been higher to better address individual differences. We found that the three articles chosen for this experiment were a good fit for a laboratory experiment, considering time and resource limitations, but were not representative of very long and elaborative Wikipedia articles. Furthermore, in this study we focused only on English to Chinese translation by bilingual participants. With different language pairs, and with translators from different cultural and linguistic backgrounds, the results might be different. Most notably, in certain language pairs, problems with transliteration of proper nouns and names are unlikely to occur.

This study is one part of a multidisciplinary approach to better understand the framework of Wikipedia translation in the multilingual and multicultural dimensions. In the future work, the developed support system will be introduced and evaluated in more detail. We will also observe how the activities identified in this study reflect to Wikipedia translation "in the wild", and how our approach affects the work practices of real-life Wikipedia translators.

ACKNOWLEDGMENTS

This research was partially supported by a Grant-in-Aid for Scientific Research (S) (24220002, 2012-2016) from Japan Society for the Promotion of Science (JSPS), and Kyoto University Global COE Program: Informatics Education and Research Center for Knowledge-Circulating Society, and Strategic Information, and Communications R&D. A special thanks to Linsi Xia, NTT Communications, for the help with Chinese translations.

REFERENCES

1. Al-Dabbagh, U. The 'Explicitation Hypothesis' and nonprofessional translators: A case study. *IJAES, 9* (2008), 85-106.
2. Ballesteros, L. and Croft, W.B. Phrasal translation and query expansion techniques for cross-language information retrieval. In *Proc. SIGIR 1997*, ACM Press (1997), 84-91.
3. Bao, P., Hecht, B., Carton, S., Quaderi, M., Horn, M. and Gergle, D. Omnipedia: Bridging the Wikipedia language gap. In *Proc. CHI 2012,* ACM (2012), 1075-1084.
4. Bardram, J. and Doryab, A. Activity Analysis - Applying activity theory to analyze complex work in hospitals. In *Proc. CSCW 2011*, ACM (2011), 455-464.
5. Bryant, S.L., Forte, A. and Bruckman, A. Becoming Wikipedian: Transformation of participation in a collaborative online encyclopedia. In *Proc. GROUP 2005*, ACM (2005), 1-10.

6. Callahan, E.S. and Herring, S.C. Cultural bias in Wikipedia content on famous persons. *J. Am. Soc. Inf. Sci. Technol.*, 62, 10 (2011), 1899-1915.

7. Carl, M., Dragsted. B. and Jakobsen, A.L. A taxonomy of human translation styles. *Translation Theory 16, 2* (2011). http://www.translationjournal.net/journal/56taxonomy.htm.

8. Carl, M. and Buch-Kromann, M. Correlating translation product and translation process data of professional and student translators. In *Proc. EAMT 2010,* European Association for Machine Translation (2010). http://mt-archive.info/EAMT-2010-Carl.pdf.

9. Désilets, A., Gonzalez, L., Paquet, S. and Stojanovic, M. Translation the Wiki way. In *Proc. The 2006 International Symposium on Wikis 21, 23* (2006), 19-32.

10. Domas White, M., Matteson, M. and Abels, E.G. Beyond dictionaries: Understanding information behavior of professional translators. *Journal of Documentation 64, 4* (2008), 576 – 601.

11. Engeström, Y. Activity theory and individual and social transformation. In *(eds.) Engeström, Y., Miettinen, R. and Punamäki, R. L. Perspectives on Activity Theory,* Cambridge University Press (1999), 19-38.

12. Gordon, R.G. Jr. Ethnologue: Languages of the World, 15th ed., SIL International (2005).

13. Grudin, J. Why CSCW applications fail: Problems in the design and evaluation of organizational interfaces. In *Proc. CSCW 1988*, ACM (1988), 85-93.

14. Hautasaari, A. and Ishida, T. Analysis of discussion contributions in translated Wikipedia articles. In *Proc. ICIC 2012*, ACM (2012), 57-66.

15. Hautasaari, A., Takasaki, T., Nakaguchi, T., Koyama, J., Murakami, Y. and Ishida, T. Multi-language discussion platform for Wikipedia translation. In *(ed.) Ishida, T. The Language Grid - Service-Oriented Collective Intelligence for Language Resource Interoperability*, Springer (2011), 231-244.

16. Hecht, B. and Gergle, D. The tower of Babel meets web 2.0: User-generated content and its applications in a multilingual context. In *Proc. CHI 2010,* ACM (2010), 291-300.

17. Hutchins, J. Computer-based translation in Europe and North America, and its future prospects. *JAPIO 20th anniversary,* Japan Patent Information Organization (2005), 156-60.

18. Jakobsen, A. L. and Schou, L. Logging target text production with Translog. *Copenhagen Studies in Language, 24* (1999), 9-20.

19. Jääskeläinen, R. Focus on methodology in think-aloud studies on translating. In *(eds.) Tirkkonen-Condit, S. and Jääskeläinen, R. Tapping and Mapping the Processes of Translation and Interpreting: Outlooks on empirical research*, John Benjamins Publishing Company (2000), 71-82.

20. Jääskeläinen, R.H. Translation assignment in professional versus non-professional translation: Think-aloud protocol study. In *(Ed.)* Se'*quinot, C. The Translation Process*, H.G. Publications (1989), 87-98.

21. Jääskeläinen, R. Automatised processes in professional vs. non-professional translation: A think-aloud protocol study. In *(ed.) Künzli, A. Empirical Research into Translation and Interpreting: Processes and Products,* Neuchâtel: Université de Neuchâtel (1988), 89-109.

22. Kaptelinin, V. and Nardi, B.A. Acting with technology: Activity theory and interaction design. The MIT Press (2006).

23. Kumaran, A., Datha, N., Ashok, B., Saravanan, K., Ande, A., Sharma, A., Vedantham, S., Natampally, V., Dendi, V. and Maurice, S. WikiBABEL: A system for multilingual Wikipedia content. *AMTA Workshop* (2010). http://amta2010.amtaweb.org/AMTA/papers/7-01-04-KumaranEtal.pdf.

24. Kuutti, K. Activity theory as a potential framework for human-computer interaction research. In *(ed.) Nardi, B.A. Context and Consciousness: Activity Theory and Human-Computer Interaction*, MIT Press (1996), 17-44.

25. Leont'ev, A. The problem of activity in psychology. *Soviet Psychology 13, 2* (1974), 4-33.

26. Lörscher, W. The translation process: Methods and problems of its investigation. *Meta: Translators' Journal 50, 2* (2005), 597-608.

27. Lörscher, W. A. Psycholinguistic analysis of translation processes. *Meta: Translators' Journal 41, 1* (1996), 26-32.

28. Virga, P. and Khudanpur, S. Transliteration of proper names in cross-lingual information retrieval. In *Proc. MultiNER 2003,* ACL (2003), 57-64.

29. Wan, S. and Verspoor, C.M. Automatic English-Chinese name transliteration for development of multilingual resources. In *Proc. COLING 1998,* ACL (1998), 1352-1356.

30. Yamashita, N. and Ishida, T. Effects of machine translation on collaborative work. In *Proc. CSCW 2006,* ACM (2006), 515-524.

31. Yasseri, T., Kornai, A. and Kertesz, J. A practical approach to language complexity: A Wikipedia case study. *arXiv:1204.2765v1 [cs.CL]* (2012), 1-14. http://arxiv.org/pdf/1204.2765v2.pdf.

32. Zaidan, O.F. and Callison-Burc, C. Crowdsourcing translation: Professional quality from non-professionals. In *Proc. ACL HLT 2011*, ACL (2011), 1220–1229.

Social Navigation for Loosely-Coupled Information Seeking in Tightly-Knit Groups using WebWear

Scott Bateman[†‡], Carl Gutwin[†], Gordon McCalla[†]

[†]Department of Computer Science
University of Saskatchewan
Saskatoon, Saskatchewan

[‡]Department of Computer Science & IT
University of Prince Edward Island
Charlottetown, Prince Edward Island

sbateman@upei.ca, gutwin@cs.usask.ca, mccalla@cs.usask.ca

ABSTRACT
Many web-based information-seeking tasks are set in a social context where other people's knowledge and advice improves success in finding information. However, when tightly-knit contacts (friends, family, colleagues) are not available, information seeking becomes more difficult. Inspired by previous work in social navigation, we developed WebWear, a system that collects and displays traces of activity for tightly-knit groups. WebWear allows people to use contextual knowledge of contacts' interests and activities to interpret the meaning of the traces, improving their usefulness. In a comparative study, we found that WebWear helped people complete information-seeking tasks more accurately, without requiring additional effort. A one-week field trial found that WebWear was both usable and useful, and that privacy concerns were reduced in the small-group context. WebWear shows that small-scale social navigation systems are feasible, and that they can improve the effectiveness of information seeking on the World-Wide Web.

Keywords
Social navigation; collaborative information seeking

ACM Classification Keywords
H.5.3 [**Group and Organization Interfaces**]: *CSCW*

INTRODUCTION
Many information-seeking tasks on the World-Wide Web are set in a social context of the knowledge and activities of people around us, and we often make use of this context to simplify and improve our information-seeking behavior. For example, we may visit websites that others have mentioned during a conversation, or try a particular social media service because a colleague uses it, or choose subtasks in collaborative work based on what we know of others' current activities.

In these situations, we communicate with tightly-knit groups of contacts (friends, family, or colleagues) to seek advice and obtain the knowledge we need in order to most effectively complete our tasks. This knowledge is not always essential (that is, the work is loosely-coupled and can often continue even without the other person's input [12]), but, when available, it can provide substantial benefits in efficiency and effectiveness. Tightly-knit groups, then, are groups of contacts who know one another and share common information seeking interests. The contacts in these groups are willing to share information to help one another accomplish their tasks with more success.

CSCW '13, February 23–27, 2013, San Antonio, Texas, USA.

However, since people have few tight-knit contacts, they are not always available to provide information when needed – people may be physically away, or too busy to interrupt. In these situations, we lose the benefit of others' experience and guidance. The unavailability of contacts leads to collaborative work being less efficient or effective. In some cases this causes annoyance and inconvenience (e.g., "I can't find the article John was telling me about, I will have to ask him about it tomorrow"); in other cases it can lead to more severe problems and task failures (e.g., "I can't find the online form Sally told me to complete before tonight's deadline, and her flight just left").

Although CSCW researchers have studied several aspects of web-based collaboration, existing solutions are still insufficient to solve the problems described here. First, collaborative information seeking systems (e.g., [10,18,24]) are traditionally oriented towards more tightly-coupled and focused collaboration, and the explicit-collaboration approach often does not match the loose coupling of web tasks [1]. Second, social navigation systems (e.g., [6,25,26]) traditionally take a view that is much broader than that of a tightly-knit group, leading to information that is difficult to interpret because it cannot be contextualized through personal knowledge of the provider.

We have developed a third approach – called WebWear – that fits between these existing paths: WebWear focuses on support for loosely-coupled information-seeking tasks in which a tightly-knit group of contacts can provide valuable knowledge and advice. WebWear uses a basic idea of social navigation – collecting traces of activity from other users – but only gathers information from people within the tightly-knit group, allowing the viewer to better interpret the traces based on knowledge of the people in the group, their preferences and habits, and their current activities.

We have developed a working WebWear system that gathers, stores, and visualizes traces of shared web activity (Figure 1). WebWear works in a standard browser and uses passive methods for gathering and displaying information – which can better support loosely-coupled information-seeking tasks. To test the effectiveness of this approach, we conducted a user study and an initial field trial. In the user study, participants carried out realistic information-seeking tasks in a hypothetical small-workgroup setting. We compared WebWear, a broad social-navigation display, and a standard browser. We found that WebWear led to significant improvements in task success, user confidence, and preference, without requiring additional effort. These results show the potential benefit that can be gained when social-navigation systems are built on a smaller scale: when information comes from known contacts, navigation traces become more interpretable and more useful.

We also deployed WebWear in a small field trial with sixteen users, to test real-world usefulness and to explore issues of overlap and privacy. The study showed that there were numerous times that people encountered others' traces, and that there were several situations where this information was valuable to the user. Although participants had privacy concerns, these did not prevent them from actively using WebWear, and users reported diminished concerns due to the workgroup context.

Our work provides three main contributions. First, we present a new kind of social navigation system that is designed specifically for tightly-knit groups. Second, we show that the contextualization possible in this approach improves web-based information-seeking tasks. Third, we demonstrate a working and freely-available WebWear system, and provide initial evidence that the approach can be deployed successfully in the real world.

RELATED WORK

Information Seeking Tasks

Information seeking is "a process in which humans purposefully engage, in order to change their state of knowledge ([16], p.5)". Pirolli and Card identified two loops that take place during information seeking [23]: a *foraging* loop where useful information is identified; and, a *sensemaking* loop where the identified information is consolidated with current knowledge. The concept of *information scent* describes the "(imperfect) perception of the value, cost, or access path of information sources obtained from proximal cues, such as WWW links [3]." Thus, the information scent for alternative paths on the Web can be improved by providing informative proximal cues, which in turn improves information access [26].

Loosely-Coupled Collaboration

Kraut and colleagues observed that most workplace interactions (81%) occur in an informal, unplanned, and opportunistic fashion [15]. Similar patterns have been observed in collocated information-seeking; e.g., in one study, 62% of collaborations occurred without pre-planning [1]. These kinds of collaborations often involve *loosely-coupled work* [15]. Coupling describes the amount of work that people can do individually before they require communication or actions from another person [12]. In loosely-coupled work, communication with collaborators must be low-cost, because the collaboration is often secondary to the underlying task; if the cost of communication is too high, people will simply not engage in collaboration [1,2,15,22].

It has been observed in loosely-coupled situations that traces of work left in the physical environment are a preferred channel of communication [2,22]. Traces in shared documents or work artifacts allow collaborators to communicate indirectly about the work they have undertaken [22], cost little to gather (since they are stored as a result of performing other primary tasks), and are easy for others to discover and retrieve [22]. Researchers have suggested that digital environments should, therefore, represent traces of work, since these are an important part of collaboration in physical environments [2].

Based on this previous work, we describe *loosely-coupled information seeking tasks* as tasks in which other people can provide advice or guidance, but where direct communication between an information seeker and a guide may not be practical or possible.

Social Search and Collaborative Information Seeking

Social search encompasses any scenario where people work together to seek information on the Web [4,8,10,18]. Social interaction in web search is a common occurrence [4,8,18]; for example, a recent survey found that 59% of search respondents shared the results of their most recent search [8]. Even when search is solitary, the underlying task can involve communication and collaboration with others [4, 8]: before searching – to help describe and focus what is sought; during search – to receive guidance and advice on avenues to pursue; and after search – to share what has been found. However, most existing search systems do not support any form of collaboration [10,16]. This leads people to adopt workarounds [10]; e.g., exchanging URLs by email [1].

Research in *collaborative information seeking* addresses situations where users have "explicitly-shared information needs" ([10], p.47), and actively work together to fulfill these needs. Work in this area has produced systems that support different forms of collaboration (see [18] for a review), including: collocated, synchronous distributed, and asynchronous distributed collaborations. This research has produced several successful systems (e.g, [19,20,24]); however, the focus on "explicitly-shared information needs", means that they are oriented towards pre-planned work and more tightly-coupled interaction. As described above, however, most collaboration occurs in an unplanned way, and may be better supported by lower-cost solutions that fit into existing individual tools and practices.

Computational Wear

Hill and colleagues [13] described the idea of *computational wear* – capturing "on computational objects the events that comprise their use" ([13], p.3). They developed tools that visualize traces of reading and editing history for people working on a shared document. Their goal was to allow people to easily answer questions about who wrote and edited different parts of the document [13].

Computational wear shows that interaction traces provide implicit communication that can reduce the need for direct communication. Further, it provides a potential solution for loosely-coupled collaborations, because traces can be created at low cost and can be used in an informal fashion. However, there has been little work on how systems could be designed to enable appropriate sharing of traces in real-world web-based information seeking.

Social Navigation

Social navigation describes how people can be guided through an information space based on the direct advice or interpreted actions of others [7]. The idea of indirect social navigation from interpreted behavior (e.g., computational wear) led to Web systems such as Footprints [25], CoWeb [6], or Scented Widgets [26] (which show traces in a user interface). These systems provide visualizations of others' use of paths and links – they augment the information scent in the environment, providing information about social activity that allows users to make inferences about the choices made by others. Studies showed that these systems can reduce the navigation steps needed [25] and can increase the number of alternatives explored [26].

However, these social navigation systems typically aggregate the behavior of all users [9], limiting what can be inferred from the traces and what questions can be answered. For example, a system showing the navigation behavior of a large group can indicate general visitation patterns and popularity [25], but is less useful for specific questions that are set into a local social context.

Some social navigation systems that offer narrower support are in active use on several social networking websites (e.g., Facebook, Twitter, or Academia.edu), and on search engines (e.g., Bing or Google). These systems provide indirect social navigation from the traces of a seeker's social networking contacts. For example, Facebook displays contacts' reading behavior on particular news sites, and Google displays social annotations from Google+ next to search results. These systems narrow social navigation support, by providing details of *who* and *when*. These systems are limited in scope, however, because they work only for certain types of behavior and on certain websites. For example, Facebook only displays friends' history for certain sites (e.g., Yahoo! News). This means the scope of the activity does not extend to most information-seeking tasks, which can occur over many different websites. Whether current narrow systems that have a limited scope can provide support in typical information-seeking tasks is unclear.

DESIGNING WEBWEAR

The goal of WebWear is to support loosely-coupled Web information seeking that occurs within a social context, by providing narrow social navigation support throughout information seeking tasks. Here we describe four aspects of the design: tasks, information, gathering, and display.

What tasks should be supported?

Previous research has identified several kinds of collaborative information seeking that are relevant to loosely-couple scenarios:

- *Following*: purposefully repeating someone else's actions [6] to find an object of shared interest.
- *Division of labor*: dividing up work so that there is reduced duplication of effort [18].
- *Seeding*: traces left purposefully for discovery by a collaborator (e.g., [22]).
- *Serendipity:* unexpected encounters with a trace that provides useful information [25].

Direct communication tasks are also a common part of loosely-coupled work; however, in WebWear we focus on implicit information rather than explicit communication.

What information do people need in these tasks?

Much of what people need for loosely-coupled information tasks has been examined in research on group awareness (e.g., [12]). Providing the appropriate level of awareness in collaborative information seeking has been shown to facilitate collaboration [24]; as described above, current social navigation systems may provide information at too high a level for tasks that exist in a social context.

Therefore, supporting information-seeking in tightly-knit groups involves showing traces from the group, at all stages of a person's information seeking activities, including starting points such as search engines. Further, support can be narrowed by providing awareness information that relates to activity from the past [11], including *what* activities were carried out, *who* performed them, *where* on the web they went, and *when* the activity happened.

What can be gathered from web interactions?

Browsers can be instrumented to capture a wide variety of user behavior, from details of scrolling behavior to the pages users bookmark (see [14] for a review). However, the use of most web browser functionality – including how bookmarking functionality is used, how many tabs are used, or if a page has been printed – is highly idiosyncratic.

We therefore focused our attention on the basic unit of interaction on the Web – the webpage visit. Regardless of how a user makes use of their browser, everyone must visit pages in order to find and gather information. Therefore, we limited our data to what can be collected from time-stamped URLs with a user identifier. This simple data can provide rich awareness of the information seeking process, including: what pages were visited, who visited the pages, when a visit occurred, how long a visit lasted, and the content of search queries (from the query string of a URL). User-specific URLs are, of course, a potential privacy concern; we discuss this issue further later in the paper.

How can the information be displayed?

Design Constraints

Support for loosely-coupled collaboration must be low cost (both to gather and interpret), and should fit within existing work practices, due to the discretionary nature of loosely-coupled collaboration. Thus, WebWear must work within established interaction patterns based on webpages, web browsers, and common tools such as search engines.

Design Factors

Location: External versus Internal to the page. Previous work on collaborative information seeking has provided support widgets that display or summarize participants' activities (e.g., [19,20,24]), which allows a large amount of detailed information to be displayed (e.g., using a sidebar). In contrast, work on information scent often augments webpages to provide proximal cues (e.g., [6,21]), allowing users to see additional information scent within the page. However, the internal approach means that only limited information can be displayed without obscuring webpage content. We chose an internal approach using graphical representations to allow better integration with existing tools such as search engines; in addition, when no trace information is available, users can fall back to using webpages as they normally would.

Style of Augmentation: Artifact Encoding vs. Glyph. Graphical objects (glyphs) can be placed near the artifacts of interest (i.e., pages and links) [6], or information can be encoded into the representation of the artifacts themselves (e.g., changing the font size of links [4]). We decided to use glyphs to encode the information: although glyphs can occlude information on the page, they can be consistently displayed without altering a page's style and functionality.

Information to Display. Information seeking on the Web often involves a combination of page visits, search engine queries, and decisions about which search results to visit. We wanted to display only information relevant to making choices in this process [26]; therefore, we include information about the page currently visited, the links that can be chosen on the page, and, when search is available, information that supports query formulation. We show two basic elements that are initially visible in the glyphs: whether or not a contact has visited a particular page, and an indicator of interest in that page (a review indicators of interest from interaction data can be found in [14]).

WebWear

The WebWear system is an add-on for the Chrome browser that collects and adds trace visualizations to web pages (see Figure 1, source code: https://github.com/scottbateman/WebWear). WebWear provides glyphs that encode the number of contacts who visited a page or a link, and the recency of the visit. If no glyph is present, it means that none of the users' contacts have visited the page.

Page-Level Glyphs. The basic glyph used in WebWear is a small colored bar. Bars representing visits to the current page are colored purple. The fill of the bar represents the number of unique contacts who visited a page (see Figure 2). The bars fade away over time to indicate the recency of the last visit. The bar is darkest if the visit occurred in the last few days, and fades to its lightest if the visit was over a month old. Glyphs are 8x10-pixel marks for page-level visitation and are placed at the right of each link (Figure 1 and Figure 2). A larger version of the glyph (300x15 pixels) is shown at the top of the page to indicate visitation to the page currently being viewed (Figure 1).

Figure 1. WebWear displayed on a search results page. 1) Glyphs representing visitation to the current page (purple) and website (green). 2) Activity glyphs on a link. 3) Detail popup after hovering on a glyph. 4) Scrollbar overview showing glyph locations on the page.

Figure 2. Left: glyphs indicating the number of unique visitors to a link in WebWear. Right: glyphs as displayed in the BroadNav condition of the study.

Website-Level Glyphs. To increase the likelihood of encountering useful information, WebWear provides a second indicator that aggregates the activity on all pages visited on a given website. Website-level aggregation was chosen because visits to a particular website are likely to have some tasks or information needs in common. We used the same visual encoding as the page-level glyphs, but colored these bars green (Figure 1).

Details-on-Demand. All glyphs are interactive, and can provide details about the represented activity. Mousing over a glyph produces a popup that shows a recency-ordered list of visitors, and an overview of their visitation for the page or website. The popup displays the total number visits on the website, the number of pages visited, the total amount of time spent, and when the last visit occurred. A list of the occurrence and duration of each individual visit can also be displayed. Popups relating to website visits show a recency-based list of pages visited on that site. Further, a sparkline visualization in the popup allows users to get a sense of the activity of all contacts' visits to a page or website in the last month (see Figure 3).

Overview. Because some pages are long, and users may not be able to see all glyphs at once, we added an overview display showing the vertical position of all glyphs on the page. A grey overlay next to the scrollbar displays purple and green marks indicating the vertical position of page-level and website-level glyphs. Clicking any of the marks scrolls to that glyph.

Contact Filtering. Users can filter the traces by selecting and de-selecting contacts in the WebWear control menu located on the browser toolbar.

Figure 3. Details popup for activity on wikipedia.org, showing details of all contacts' visits to the website.

Group-based Query Completion. For any page that uses a standards-based query field (i.e., with an HTML name attribute value of "q"), WebWear also provides a recency-based query completion list based on the query history of contacts (Figure 4). The group-query completion overrides existing query completion. Clicking on the search field displays the most recent queries executed by all contacts, providing a simple way to see the activity of all users. Letters typed in the field updates the filter. The query completion works effectively on Google, Bing, and Yahoo, and also in site-specific search fields for sites such as stackoverflow.com. Group search activity is shared across all search fields, regardless of the site where it came from.

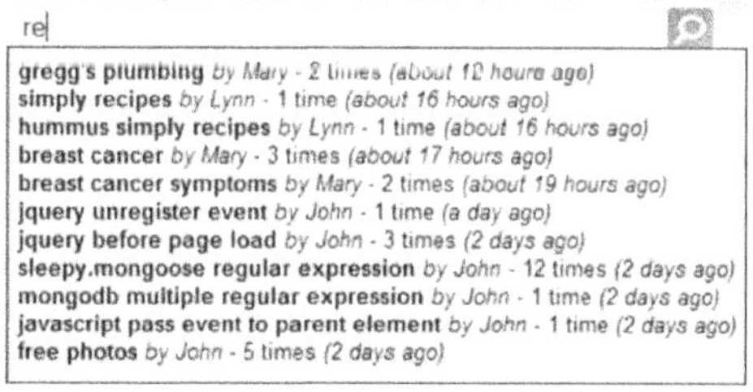

Figure 4. Group-based query completion displayed on Bing; a recency-based based on the queries of contacts.

Controlling WebWear. Because users may want to turn off the sharing of traces in particular situations, WebWear can be turned off through checkboxes located in the WebWear menu. Users can selectively turn off sharing traces and seeing others' traces. The system is turned off completely when the browser is placed in privacy mode. If sharing is enabled, WebWear collects webpage visits for the current user, and stores them on a remote server.

EMPIRICAL USER STUDY OF WEBWEAR

To evaluate our primary hypothesis – that smaller-scale social navigation information can improve information seeking in tightly-knit groups – we carried out a user study that asked participants to perform web-based information tasks in a variety of different conditions. The study was designed to answer two main questions:

- Whether the small-group interaction histories in WebWear improve task performance compared to either no history, or broad social-navigation information; and,
- Whether the WebWear visualizations (as described above) are easy to access and interpret for users, when used in a real web browser and a realistic task context.

Study Methods

Interface Conditions

We tested three different interfaces in the study: a normal browser, a broad social-navigation display, and WebWear.

- *Normal browser* was an unchanged version of the Chrome web browser (version 19.0.1084.52).
- *Broad social navigation (BroadNav)* is a visualization of link popularity that was similar to the simple bar visualizations used in WebWear, and appeared on all pages (Figure 2). Popularity information was simulated with Google PageRank data (obtained by querying the Google Toolbar webservice for each link). PageRank approximates the likelihood of randomly visiting a page. While it is only weakly correlated with real world page visitation [17], as an approximation it provides a reasonable stand-in for true link visitation counts.
- *WebWear* was implemented as described above (see Figure 1). Information traces were pre-determined for the tasks used in the study; traces were pre-recorded and made visible for three members of the participant's task workgroup (described below).

Tasks and Scenarios

For the experiment, participants were asked to imagine working with a hypothetical group, which included: Mary, a close friend to the participant; John, a friendly colleague and a computer programmer; and, Lynn, the group's manager and mentor. Participants carried out two kinds of tasks: *follow* and *divide* tasks. These two task types (as introduced above) were selected for our evaluation because both have been a focus of previous work, are extremely common in real-world workgroup collaborations, and can occur in planned or unplanned scenarios. First, *follow* tasks involved following up on a lead or comment provided by a member of the person's scenario workgroup, and finding a specific article or site that had been mentioned or discussed by the other person. In follow tasks, we were interested in whether participants could successfully find specific items that had been partially identified by another person. For example, one of the follow task descriptions was:

John tells you that he saw a great book of bird photographs on Amazon that the office should buy for Mary's birthday. Mary has a lot of bird books, but John says he knows she doesn't have any 'coffee table' books like this, and it only costs about $38. You are in charge of buying the present, so you decide to try and find the book John had seen.

Second, *division* tasks involved completion of a group task, where the workgroup investigates a particular topic or area; in these tasks there were no specific answers (as in follow tasks), but rather the group's job was to cover the area efficiently. In division tasks, we were interested in whether people would be able to organize and coordinate the task, and whether people would be able to avoid duplication of work. For example, one division task description was:

Your colleague Mary has a history of breast cancer in her family. Over lunch last week, together you decided to research breast cancer symptoms together. You are trying to get a wide coverage from different sources, so you are trying to each collect URLs for three introductory articles that mention common breast cancer symptoms. You plan to look at these together tomorrow. Of course, it would be useful to find different articles than Mary does.

The tasks were presented in the context of a hypothetical scenario in which the participant was a member of a workgroup, and that they had a set of tasks on a to-do list that they wanted to finish at the end of the day. The scenario indicated that the other members of the workgroup were not available for direct communication, meaning that the participant had to complete the tasks using only the information available from the scenario and the interface.

Two minor constraints were imposed on participants: first, they were asked to use only a single tab to reduce the variability in behavior between participants; second, they were asked to start each task from the Google search page.

Participants and Apparatus

Twenty-four participants (14 women, 10 men, mean age=26.1 years) were recruited from a local university. Eighteen were students from a range of disciplines, others were researchers (5) or software engineers (1); none were familiar with the research project. Participants all reported searching the Web at least once a day and spending at least 2 hours/day using a computer, during a normal workday.

The study used a standard version of the Chrome browser, running on a recent Windows 7 PC, and a 1920x1080 LCD monitor. The WebWear condition used the actual system as described above, but with small modifications. For example, simulated traces were added for the workgroup, which included activities that contained overlapping and non-overlapping traces to the experimental tasks; and, gathering was turned off.

Design and Procedure

The study used a 3x2 within-participants design with two factors: *Interface* (*normal* browser, *BroadNav* for broad social navigation, or *WebWear*) and *Task* Type (*follow* or *divide*). Participants carried out six tasks in total: both task types in each of the three interfaces.

Participants first completed a demographics survey, and were given a handout that introduced them to the hypothetical scenario and collaborators. They were then given a practice task using the normal browser. They next completed one of the three interface condition blocks (balanced with a Latin square), which included both a *follow* and a *divide* task (alternating order between participants). Before each of the BroadNav and WebWear interface blocks, participants were given a short tutorial (approximately 5 minutes), where they were introduced to the new interface and asked to perform a random query to show how they system displayed information. They were then given an additional practice task. The experimenter interacted with the participant during the practice tasks and pointed out the displayed information in the context of the task. Participants then completed the two experimental tasks. After each task they completed a short questionnaire concerning their experiences, and after the WebWear and BroadNav interfaces they completed a second questionnaire that asked their opinions of the interface. At the end of the session, participants were asked about their preferences.

The study system gathered two types of data for each task. *Performance data* included completion time for the task and an accuracy score for their final task result (participants were given 1 point if they correctly identified the webpage in follow tasks, and 1 point if they did not duplicate any answers in divide tasks). *Subjective data* came from the three questionnaires, which were composed of 7-point Likert-scale statements and free-text questions.

Data Analysis

Performance data was analyzed using RM-ANOVA, and post-hoc tests used Bonneferoni corrections for multiple comparisons. Because the accuracy score was a binary value, we initially transformed accuracy scores using the Aligned Rank Transform [27]. Subjective responses were analyzed using Friedman's test, and post hoc comparisons were done using the Wilcoxon signed-rank test. However, because Friedman's is a one-way test only, we split our task-related questionnaire data by task type, and looked for differences between interfaces under the different task conditions. We did not look at the differences in task type data, as we were mainly interested in participants' subjective responses to interface, not task type.

Results

We present our results organized by our main hypotheses about success and effort in completing the tasks. We first present performance data and subjective responses, and then report on experiences and preferences.

Were participants more successful with WebWear?

Participants completed their work more successfully when using WebWear (see Figure 5). There was a main effect of Interface on accuracy score ($F_{2,46}$=13.76, p<.001) and task type ($F_{1,23}$=6.29, p<.05), but there was no interaction effect between interface and task type ($F_{2,46}$=2.11, p>.05). Pairwise comparisons show that participants were significantly more accurate in completing the task with WebWear than with either BroadNav (p<.005) or the normal browser (p<.001). There was no difference in accuracy between BroadNav and normal (p>.05). Participants were significantly more accurate in completing the divide tasks than the follow tasks (p<.05).

Participants also felt more certain about having successfully completed the task when using WebWear. In follow tasks, participants felt more certain about having found the correct webpage (Figure 5). In divide tasks, participants felt more certain about having not duplicated any answers (Figure 5). There was a significant effect of Interface on certainty about divide tasks ($\chi^2(2)$=39.78, p<.001). Pairwise comparisons show that participants were more certain with WebWear than with BroadNav (z=-2.94, p<.005) and normal (z=-3.63, p<.001). Participants were also significantly more certain with BroadNav than normal (z=-2.27, p<.05). There was a significant effect of Interface on certainty for follow tasks ($\chi^2(2)$=18.25, p<.001); pairwise comparisons show that participants were significantly more certain with WebWear than BroadNav (z=-4.07, p<.001) or normal (z=-3.32, p<.001), and more confident with BroadNav than normal (z=-2.78, p≤.005).

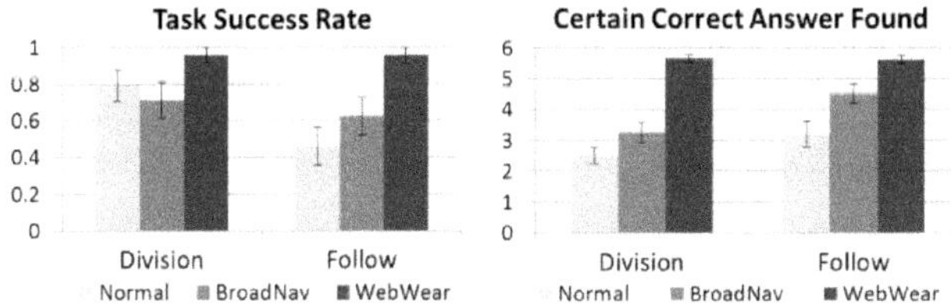

Figure 5. (Left) Task success rate. (Right) Subjective certainty about task success.

Did participants require less effort when using WebWear?

To consider efficiency, we looked at the time taken to complete the task, subjective perceptions of efficiency, and subjective need for communication with a collaborator.

Completion times are shown in Figure 6. There was a main effect of Interface on completion time ($F_{2,46}$=20.89, p<.001). Pairwise comparisons show that BroadNav was slower than both WebWear (p<.001) and normal (p<.001), but that there was no difference observed between WebWear and normal (p>.05). There was no effect of task type on completion time ($F_{1,23}$=.32, p>.05), with divide tasks (*mean*=2.9 min., *SEM*=.19) taking roughly the same amount of time as follow tasks (*mean*=2.7 min., *SEM*=.35). There was no interaction effect observed ($F_{2,46}$=.56, p>.05).

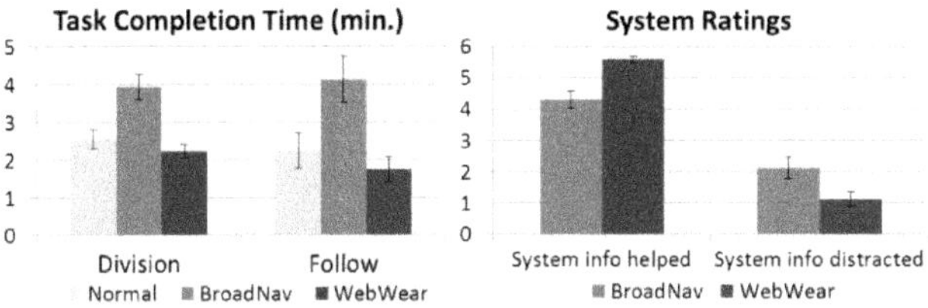

Figure 6. (Left) Average task completion time. (Right) Participant ratings of the system being helpful and distracting.

Participants felt they were most efficient when using WebWear (see Figure 7). There was a significant effect of Interface for both divide tasks ($\chi^2(2)$= 10.84, p<.005) and for follow tasks ($\chi^2(2)$= 13.92, p<.001). For divide tasks, participants felt they were more efficient with WebWear than both BroadNav (z=-2.65, p<.01) and normal (z=-2.81, p≤.005). There were no differences between Normal and BroadNav (z=-.84, p>.05). For follow tasks, participants again felt they were more efficient with WebWear than both BroadNav (z=-3.39, p≤.001) and normal (z=-3.21, p≤.001), but there was no observed difference between Normal and BroadNav (z=-.24, p>.05).

Participants felt less need for communication when using WebWear (see Figure 7). There was an effect of Interface for both divide tasks ($\chi^2(2)$= 25.42, p<.001), and for follow tasks ($\chi^2(2)$=11.17, p<.005). For division tasks, the perceived need to communicate was lower for WebWear than both BroadNav (z=-3.31, p≤.001) and normal (z=-4.01, p<.001). Participants also felt they needed to communicate less with BroadNav than normal (z=-2.07, p<.05). For follow tasks, again the perceived need to communicate was lower for WebWear than both BroadNav (z=-2.86, p<.005) and normal (z=-3.84, p<.001), but there was no difference between BroadNav and normal (z=-.68, p>.05).

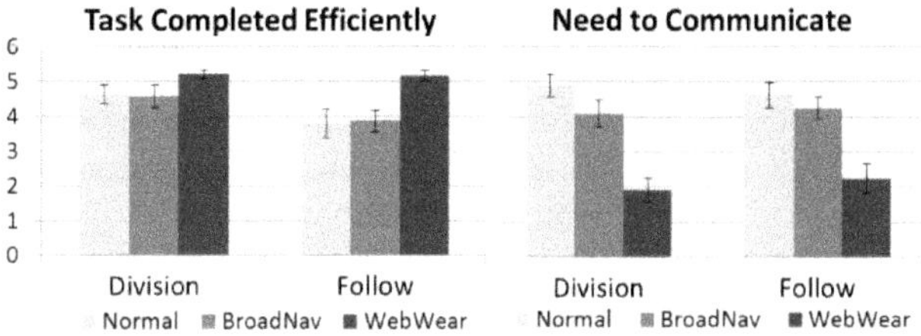

Figure 7. (Left) Participant agreement with having completed the task efficiently. (Right) Ratings of needing to communicate to be successful in the task.

Perceived Usefulness of WebWear and BroadNav

Participants felt that the information available in both WebWear and BroadNav was useful in completing the tasks (Figure 6), but they rated the information in WebWear as being significantly more helpful (z=-3.447, p<.001). Participants also felt that the information displays in both BroadNav and WebWear did not get in the way or distract participants from their work (see Figure 6); however, they felt that WebWear was significantly less distracting than BroadNav (z= -2,55, p<.05). Finally, 22 of the 24 participants felt that WebWear was the best tool for the type of tasks seen in the study, and 22 agreed that they would use WebWear for information seeking activities (*mean agreement*=5.13, *SEM*=0.26, *max*=6, *min*=0).

FIELD TRIAL

To better understand issues of WebWear's use in the real world, we also held an initial one-week field trial within our research lab. We were interested in three main issues:

- would people's information-seeking activity overlap, providing opportunities for WebWear to be used;
- would WebWear lead to useful experiences;
- what are peoples' impressions of, and concerns with, sharing activities during their real-world searches.

Sixteen members of our lab (1 professor, 1 visiting researcher, 10 graduate students, 4 undergraduates; none of them authors) installed the WebWear extension and used it on their lab computers for one week. Typical work activities for this group cover a wide range of HCI and computer science topics. Trial participants were given a 10-minute tutorial about how WebWear worked; none had previously used or seen it. Participants completed an optional survey four times during the week, which asked about their experiences. At the end of the week, we held an hour-long group interview. The deployed WebWear system was the same as described above, but additionally provided a facility for participants to view and permanently delete any of their own traces from the system.

Participants were relatively active during the week of the trial, sharing 6140 page visits and 1022 searches. Participants reported that encountering others' traces was frequent, and 88% of the surveys report exploring other users' activities. Three participants even reported changing their search behavior so that they could encounter traces more often – rather than searching by typing a query in to the address bar in Chrome as they normally do, they would first visit the Google homepage, so that they could see WebWear's group-query completion (Figure 4).

Trial participants found WebWear useful in several ways. First, many participants reported that WebWear was useful for maintaining an awareness of the activities of others. For example, "While looking for tutorials on … XNA I did notice, thanks to WebWear, that [P12] had also been searching for this topic. I didn't even realize that [P12] was using XNA in his project. Now I guess if I run into anything major, I at least know someone who may have also been dealing with the same topic."

Further, even in this brief trial, we counted three instances of unplanned follow or divide collaborations. An example of a follow task: "[P15] had visited Dexsoft, a 3D model website, and had discussed with me the category of models that she would like me to look at. When I visited the Dexsoft website I hardly had to look around the website to find the models she was talking about because I just followed her WebWear 'footprints'."

An example of a division task arose when P8 asked P10 if he knew how to solve an issue with a Bluetooth dongle. P10 did not have an answer and returned to his desk, deciding only later to search for an answer to try to help P8. As P10 started his search he saw P8's queries, and selected different search terms to explore a different path, now knowing that she had already searched without success. These examples illustrate real-world cases of the tasks used in our user study, and also provide evidence that loosely-coupled tasks can be supported through shared traces.

Finally, all field-trial participants agreed that there was potential value in being able to share traces both to maintain awareness and to help coordinate tasks. In the group discussion, many people still reported being wary of privacy despite having mainly positive experiences during the trial. The privacy concerns related mostly to the fear of unwanted activity accidentally being entered into the browser, or other participants misinterpreting the context of search activity. Not all participants experienced these concerns, though, and some reported forgetting about the data collection because they were not overly worried.

All participants agreed that the work context was suitable for sharing traces, and while some concerns with sharing existed, no one reported having a bad experience in using WebWear, and were open to using it in the future.

DISCUSSION

The empirical user study provides three main results:

1. People were significantly more accurate in finding answers with WebWear than with either a normal browser or with a broad social-navigation system, and were significantly more confident in their answers.
2. The increased accuracy did not come at the cost of additional effort: tasks were faster in WebWear than in BroadNav and no slower than the normal browser. Participants also reported a reduced need to communicate than with the other systems.
3. People subjectively felt that they were more efficient with WebWear, that the information it presented was helpful and did not distract from their tasks, and that they would like to use it in appropriate contexts.

The initial field trial of WebWear in real use provided three further findings:

4. There was enough overlap in people's real-world browsing that participants were able to make use of WebWear on numerous occasions over one week;
5. Participants reported several cases where they found WebWear information useful, both for specific loosely-coupled information-seeking tasks, and for maintaining awareness of others in the workgroup;
6. All sixteen participants indicated that while privacy from passive tracking remained a concern, using WebWear did not unduly intrude on their privacy, and there were benefits to sharing in a work context.

In the following sections, we provide explanations for these main results, and then discuss issues surrounding the real-world deployment of WebWear.

Explanations for Main Results

The results observed in our user study support our main hypothesis – that trace information is more useful in loosely-coupled collaborative tasks when contextualized to a tightly-knit group. WebWear combines lessons from social navigation and collaborative information seeking, and our studies show that this combination provides good support for loosely-coupled information-seeking tasks.

Why did WebWear work in the user study?

WebWear provided three main tools that led to the successful results in our user study. First, group-query completion allowed users to see if their search terms aligned with those of their contacts. This was useful in both follow and divide tasks. In follow tasks, users could repeat queries to match the results of a previous collaborator; in divide tasks, they could formulate unique queries to get results that had not been seen by their collaborators. Second, the activity glyphs next to links allowed users to quickly identify pages that they should visit or avoid.

Third, the popup details on the glyphs provided appropriate information that allowed users to confirm if an activity was of interest or not. Most often, simply seeing *who* had left the trace was all that was needed (and the user portraits available in the system gave this information at a glance). Further, the details for websites (Figure 3) provided a useful way to quickly find a known target. For example, to complete the "bird book" task (described above) a user could simply visit amazon.com, look at the website popup, and see the list of pages John had visited on Amazon. This form of contextual history provides a natural way for people to quickly find history of interest.

Were the user study tasks biased towards WebWear?

The specific task types examined in this work (loosely-coupled information seeking tasks) have not been previously examined, and show the limitations of many previous social navigation systems. We selected experimental tasks that could be successfully completed by our participants without information from tightly-knit contacts. These tasks did prove more difficult without WebWear; however, this only means that WebWear successfully supports this type of loosely-coupled task. Our literature review suggests that loosely-coupled information seeking may be a more common use case than explicit forms of collaboration, but exactly how often systems like WebWear may be able to lend support during typical information seeking is an important open question.

Why did broad social navigation not work?

Broad social navigation (BroadNav) was no better than a normal browser for most tasks, and was significantly slower than the other interfaces. Reasons for these results may arise from the issue of introduced cost. While we intended our design of WebWear and BroadNav to have a low cost (small glyphs that were easily ignored), it is likely that participants needed more time to consider them. BroadNav offered information that was too general for our tasks (e.g., participants wanted to find John's bird book, not the book that was most popular); therefore, time spent considering BroadNav information was not beneficial. This effect could diminish with more training – that is, users could learn to only attend to the glyphs for certain tasks. Attending to the information of WebWear also introduced a cost, but this was offset by the benefit provided.

While we could have designed other tasks that would suit BroadNav (e.g., "Find the most globally popular webpage describing attractions in Vancouver"), the value of general social navigation systems has already been established – and our interests were in showing the value of the approach behind WebWear.

WebWear in the Field Trial

In the field trial, it was clear that the most-frequently used feature was group query completion. Participants would visit the Google main page and click on the query box to see what other participants had recently been searching for. Several participants reported that this feature gave them an increased sense of awareness about others' activities. Participants also reported frequently checking the activity traces of other participants when they were encountered. The indicators did not always provide task assistance (there were relatively few shared projects going on at the time), but were still followed out of curiosity. For example, several participants reported looking at one another's traces on YouTube. These participants reported not having seen anything of major interest, suggesting that shared traces on sites like YouTube, which cover many topics, may be too broad for most encounters.

Did WebWear lead to new information seeking behavior?

In both studies, we found that people adopted behavior that was different from their normal search behavior. First, as reported above, people worked in ways that would allow them to encounter traces as part of the normal search practices. Second, we observed several cases where people would formulate queries in the search box without executing them, to see if they could find someone else's past query. Finally, we also saw a few people become momentarily confused when activity traces didn't appear where they were expected on search result pages. In these cases participants seemed to have incorporated expectations of WebWear-style information into their model of information scent on web pages. This problem arose due to inexperience with the system, but highlights the importance of making the source and display of trace information simple and easy to understand.

Generalizing the Results and Deployment Issues

There are four main issues in generalizing our results: overlap, usefulness, tightly-knit groups, and privacy.

Overlap of Traces

The sparseness of traces is an important potential issue for small workgroups – given the size of the Web it could be that traces are encountered too infrequently to be useful. However, two principles provide some indication that there will be reasonable overlap. First, there are a set of common starting points (e.g., search engines) that increase overlap and provide opportunities for shared encounters. WebWear's group-query completion was designed with this in mind, and the field trial showed that this feature was frequently used, and in the ways that we intended.

Second, a defining characteristic of tightly-knit groups such as workgroups is that they have shared goals, interests, and tasks (even when working in loosely-coupled fashion). These overlaps should translate into people visiting some of the same regions of the web. In our field trial, we saw clear examples: 9 of 16 people had visited stackoverflow.com (a programming help website) within the 1-week trial. This and other examples suggest that there is adequate overlap within many small groups. However, in future work we will test this hypothesis through longer term studies with several different workgroups.

Providing Useful Information

Our work shows that traces can be successfully displayed and used, but there are situations where traces may not provide valuable information. For example, one of the known challenges of social navigation systems is *herding* (i.e., blindly following others' trails) [9]. Herding is a problem if a trace leads to a poor decision being made.

Further, as previously discussed, there is a cost to interpreting information, so the benefits of making traces easy to encounter and explore must also be considered in terms of the quality of the information. For example, we did not expect a great deal of overlap in our field trial, due to the wide range of activities that people were working on. However, the (green) website glyphs that can appear next to each of the links on a page actually appeared quite often on certain search result pages, which participants did not find overly useful. Systems like WebWear must balance between broadening the possibility of encountering traces and ensuring that the information is still valuable.

There are, however, several design possibilities that can be explored to address this specific issue. For example, a simple approach would be to narrow our website-level traces. Currently, we present website activity for all traces on a top level domain (e.g., google.com); this could be narrowed by including the full domain (e.g., the website would be separated for traces on sites like news.google.com and maps.google.com). However, we have some evidence from our field trial that curiosity leads people to investigate more indicators than necessary (which could partially be an effect of novelty). With more familiarity, and because loosely-coupled collaboration is discretionary, people can decide on a case-by-case basis whether the information provided by WebWear is useful. Further, the interpretation context will help people to determine whether information is valuable or spurious (e.g., "I know Mary is not an expert in biochemistry, so I won't follow her trail in this area").

Privacy

Concerns about privacy have often been the main barrier to the deployment of some awareness systems. Because WebWear passively collects people's interaction history, it could in some cases feel like surveillance. In addition, WebWear attaches people's names to particular actions, meaning that there is no anonymity like there is with broad social navigation. Therefore, systems like WebWear should be used carefully. There are several examples that suggest the technique can work in some cases, however.

First, people have different degrees of willingness to share information about themselves with different kinds of contacts [5]. For example, people are more willing to share with their spouse, friends, and family; therefore, there may be settings and groups of contacts where people are willing to share, even if they would not share with all contacts.

Second, people treat work situations and work browsing very differently from more private settings such as the home. At work (e.g., in an open-plan office) it is easy for people to see what sites are in people's web browsers; therefore, there is a general change in the kinds of browsing that people do at work. This can lead to a greater willingness to have interaction history shared.

Third, people may actually want to share some of their interaction histories. For example, people may wish to highlight a website or demonstrate an expert route through a set of material; examples such as Twitter indicate that some people are quite willing to selectively share their activities with others.

Fourth, it is always possible to switch off the information-gathering aspects of WebWear; this can help to mitigate privacy concerns since people know they will not always be tracked. Further privacy-protection mechanisms could be explored (as discussed below). Last, the ability to edit the recorded information and delete items can help people recover from inadvertent sharing of private activity.

The initial field study provides at least limited evidence that these factors do provide a workable solution to privacy problems. Of the people who initially volunteered, all sixteen completed the one-week trial, indicating that there are people out there who are amenable to this degree of sharing (within a small workgroup). Privacy was a main interest in the group discussion, and some participants did report concerns for their privacy during the field trial. Concerns were not important enough, however, to prevent active sharing by all participants. Further, several participants stated that they do not see their work setting as providing a great deal of privacy anyway, and so they already carry out work on the Web with the expectation that others will be able to see their activities.

Participants were interested in discussing activity sharing during the group interview and felt that logical extensions to WebWear might include whitelists and blacklists to define how personal data should be shared (e.g., I may be willing to share activity on Wikipedia, but keep all my YouTube activity private). However, a few participants were skeptical that such mechanisms could be added without requiring undue effort on the part of a user, and felt that the current on/off mechanism would actually be best. Future work should focus on low-effort and simple sharing mechanisms, because concerns about privacy and decisions about sharing may change on a task-by-task basis, and would likely evolve over time.

Identifying, Maintaining, and Targeting Tightly-Knit Groups

Perhaps the greatest protection for privacy is the targeting of WebWear to tightly-knit groups, groups with mutual trust among members. In our studies we used WebWear with a particular tightly-knit group: a small workgroup. Field trial participants agreed that the use of WebWear in the workplace would be useful and appropriate.

Even though we saw real examples of support provided by WebWear, there were likely situations where participants could have used some guidance, but none was available. With a larger number of contacts available, a user would have a higher likelihood of receiving support when it was needed, by being able to access the experiences of more people. At the same time, in the real world people may be part of several distinct tightly-knit groups, and it seems likely that WebWear users would want to share different activities with different groups. This raises several questions: How might someone create and maintain separate tightly-knit groups? How could different types of information-seeking activities be targeted to different groups? Should a user see a group's traces if the user is not themselves sharing with the group? What should happen to shared history after a member leaves the group?

In this work, the context of a single tightly-knit group allowed us to first focus on assessing the WebWear approach in general. Future work should aim to better understand the nature of information seeking and information sharing in tightly-knit groups – groups of people that have shared interests, have some level of trust, and are willing to share activities to benefit one another. The findings could lead to answers to the questions raised above, and increase the number of situations where people could benefit from each other's previous work.

CONCLUSION

In this paper we presented WebWear, a system that collects and displays traces of shared activity to support information seeking in tightly-knit groups. We showed that WebWear allows people to use contextual knowledge of contacts' interests and activities to interpret the meaning of shared traces. Through two studies we showed that WebWear can improve accuracy and confidence in completing previously untested loosely-coupled collaborative information-seeking tasks, and provided initial evidence that the approach can be successfully deployed in real-world scenarios. WebWear shows that small-scale social navigation systems are feasible, and that they can improve the effectiveness of information seeking on the World-Wide Web.

ACKNOWLEDGEMENTS

This work was supported by NSERC, the GRAND NCE, and the Walter C. Sumner Memorial Foundation.

REFERENCES

1. Amershi, S. & Morris, M.R. Co-located Collaborative Web Search: Understanding Status Quo Practices. Proc. *CHI*, 2009, 3937-3640.
2. Bellotti, V., & Bly, S. Walking Away from the Desktop Computer: Distributed Collaboration and Mobility in a Product Design Team, Proc. *CSCW*, 1996, 209-18.
3. Card, S., Pirolli, P., Van der Wege, M., Morrison, J. B., Reeder, R.W., Schraedley, P.K., & Boshart, J. Information scent as a driver of web behavior graphs. Proc. *CHI*, 2001, 498–505.
4. Chi, E. Information Seeking Can Be Social. *IEEE Computer*, 42(3), March, 2009, 42-46.
5. Davis, S. & Gutwin, C. Using relationship to control disclosure in awareness servers. Proc. *GI*, 2005, 145-52.
6. Dieberger, A. & Lonnqvist, P. Visualizing Interaction History on a Collaborative Web Server. Proc. *Hypertext* 2000, 221-22.
7. Dourish, P. & Chalmers, M. Running out of space: Models of information navigation. Proc. *HCI*, 1994.
8. Evans, B.M., & Chi, E. An elaborated model of social search. *IPM*, 46 (6), 2010, 656-78.
9. Goecks, J. *Understanding the Social Navigation User Experience*. PhD Dissertation. Georgia Tech. 2009.
10. Golovchinsky, G., Qvarfordt, P., & Pickens, J. Collaborative information seeking. *IEEE Computer*, 42(3), 2009, 47-51.
11. Gutwin, C. & Greenberg, S. A Descriptive Framework of Workspace Awareness for Real-Time Groupware. *CSCW*, (11)3, 2002, 411-446.
12. Gutwin, C., Greenberg, S., Blum, R., Dyck, J., Tee, K., & McEwan, G. Supporting Informal Collaboration in Shared-Workspace Groupware. *JUCS*, 14(9), 2008, 1411-34.
13. Hill, W.C., Hollan, J.D., Wroblewski, D., McCandless, T. Edit wear and read wear. Proc. *CHI*, 1992, 3-9.
14. Kelley, D., & Teevan, J. Implicit feedback for inferring user preference: a bibliography. *SIGIR Forum*, 37(2), 2003, 18-28.
15. Kraut, R., Fish, R., Root, R., & Chalfonte, B., Informal Communication in Organizations: Form, Function, and Technology, in R. Baecker, *Readings in Groupware and Computer Supported Cooperative Work*, 1993.
16. Marchionini, G. *Information Seeking in Electronic Environments*. Cambridge University Press. 1995.
17. Meiss, M.R., Menczer, F., Fortunato, S., Flammini, A., & Vespignani, A. Ranking web sites with real user traffic. Proc. *WSDM*, 2008, 1067-75.
18. Morris, M.R., & Teevan, J. Collaborative Web Search: Who, What, Where, When, and Why. Morgan and Claypool Publishers, San Rafael, CA, USA, 2010.
19. Morris, MR. & Horvitz, E. SearchTogether: an interface for collaborative web search. Proc. *UIST*, 2007, 3-12.
20. Morris, M.R. and Horvitz, E. S3: Storable, Shareable Search. Proc. *Interact*, 2007, 120-123.
21. Olston, C. & Chi, E. ScentTrails: Integrating browsing and searching on the Web. *TOCHI*. 10(3), 2003,177-97.
22. Pinelle, D., & Gutwin, C. Designing for loose coupling in mobile groups. Proc. *GROUP*, 2003, 75-84.
23. Pirolli, P., & Card, S. The sensemaking process and leverage points for analyst technology as identified through cognitive task analysis. Proc. *Intelligence Analysis*, 2005.
24. Shah, C. & Marchionini, G. Awareness in collaborative information seeking. *JASIS*, 61, 2010, 1970–86.
25. Wexelblat, A. & Maes, P. Footprints: history-rich tools for information foraging. Proc. *CHI*, 1999, 270-77.
26. Willett, W., Heer, J., & Agrawala, M. Scented Widgets: Improving Navigation Cues with Embedded Visualizations. *IEEE Vis*, 13(6), 2007, 1129-1136.
27. Wobbrock, J., Findlater, L., Gergle, D. & Higgins, J. The Aligned Rank Transform for Nonparametric Factorial Analyses Using Only ANOVA Procedures. Proc. *CHI*, 2011, 143-146.

Analyzing the Quality of Information Solicited from Targeted Strangers on Social Media

Jeffrey Nichols*, Michelle X. Zhou*, Huahai Yang*, Jeon Hyung Kang†, Xiaohua Sun‡

*IBM Research – Almaden
650 Harry Road
San Jose, CA 95120
{jwnichols,mzhou,hyang}@us.ibm.com

†USC ISI
4676 Admiralty Way
Marina del Rey, CA 90292
jeonhyuk@usc.edu

‡Tongji University
Shanghai, China
xsun@tongji.edu.cn

ABSTRACT
The emergence of social media creates a unique opportunity for developing a new class of crowd-powered information collection systems. Such systems actively identify potential users based on their public social media posts and solicit them directly for information. While studies have shown that users will respond to solicitations in a few domains, there is little analysis of the quality of information received. Here we explore the quality of information solicited from Twitter users in the domain of product reviews, specifically reviews for a popular tablet computer and L.A.-based food trucks. Our results show that the majority of responses to our questions (>70%) contained relevant information and often provided additional details (>37%) beyond the topic of the question. We compare the solicited Twitter reviews to other user-generated reviews from Amazon and Yelp, and found that the Twitter answers provided similar information when controlling for the questions asked. Our results also reveal limitations of this new information collection method, including its suitability in certain domains and potential technical barriers to its implementation. Our work provides strong evidence for the potential of this new class of information collection systems and design implications for their future use.

Author Keywords
Social Q&A; crowdsourcing; Twitter; product reviews

ACM Classification Keywords
H.5.2

General Terms
Algorithms; Experimentation; Human Factors

INTRODUCTION
Hundreds of millions of people express themselves every day on public social media, such as Twitter. This creates a unique opportunity for building a brand new class of crowd-powered information collection systems, which *actively* solicit information from the right people at the right time based on their public social media posts. For example, if a person just tweeted about getting a sandwich from a food truck, such a system can ask her to provide additional details about her experience. This approach offers several advantages over other crowd-powered information collection systems, such as social Q&A [3]. First, it can collect information about an event, such as a robbery, soon after that event occurred. Second, it can collect information from people who are most likely to share their "visceral reaction" to an event [4]. Third, it can also collect information from a range of people across a particular dimension of a population (e.g., liberal vs. conservative).

Although this approach and its feasibility have been demonstrated in a few domains [1, 12], there are still many unknowns about the approach that need to be explored. One unknown is the level of information *quality* obtainable through this collection method. While there is abundant research effort on studying the quality of crowd-sourced information, especially in the form of social Q&A systems [5, 8, 9, 10, 16, 17], there are differences in this new approach that may influence the outcomes:

- Answers are *actively* solicited from strangers, who have not opted-in *a priori* and most likely have no social or organizational ties to the question asker. This may causes strangers to be less likely to respond, but it may also cause the responses that are received to be more objective and balanced, because the information providers are not self-selected and may have fewer intrinsic motivations for providing information [4].
- Information exchange occurs mainly between the asker and answerer, without any moderation by a larger group. This removes the potential reputation and filtering benefits of typical Social Q&A sites, like Quora, to govern the quality of crowd-sourced information.
- Potential information providers are chosen based on their social media content, which may be misleading about their true ability to provide quality information.

To rigorously assess the quality of information collected using this approach, we have designed and conducted a set of experiments that focus on two aspects. First, we focus on analyzing the quality of crowd-sourced information collected from targeted strangers on Twitter. Second, we focus on collecting reviews about "experienced goods"— products or services of which characteristics are difficult to observe in advance but can be learned after consumption [11]. By focusing in these directions, we contain the scope of our study and focus on collecting data that can rigorously and externally validated. A consequence of this choice is our experimental scenario does not explore the true potential of such information collection systems, which is to solicit time-sensitive information from a diverse population. Such information is unfortunately more subjective and difficult to validate externally.

We collect reviews about two "goods": a popular tablet computer and Los Angeles-area food trucks. We chose to focus on the product reviews domain for two reasons. First, products and services are a frequent topic of conversations among Twitter users, thus making it easier for us to find product owners or users of a service from whom we can solicit information. Second, other sources of product and service reviews are available, such as Amazon and Yelp, which can provide external validation for the reviews collected from Twitter. We chose these two particular goods because both inspired a reasonable volume of messages on Twitter but are fairly different from each other.

This paper presents our study design and results to answer three sets of questions:

1. Will strangers respond to our questions with relevant responses? What types of responses will we receive and what information will they contain? If we do not receive a relevant response, what might be the cause?
2. How does the quantity of information collected on Twitter compare with reviews on Amazon or Yelp when controlling for the specific questions asked?
3. How do people perceive the quality of information collected on Twitter versus that of Amazon or Yelp? Which reviews do people find more useful, objective, balanced, and trustworthy?

To address the first set of questions, we designed and conducted a live Q&A experiment on Twitter by manually identifying Twitter users who appeared to own the popular tablet computer or had recently visited one of the food trucks. Each of these users was asked to answer at least one question about the product or service they had used. The results demonstrate the feasibility of our approach: overall we received 369 responses (37.7% overall response rate) from strangers on Twitter, and 76.5% of the responses contained relevant answers.

To answer the second and third sets of questions, we designed and conducted a mixed-method study that assessed both quantity and quality of our Twitter answers against reviews collected from Amazon and Yelp, both objectively and subjectively. The comparisons show that the Twitter answers provided similar information when controlling for the questions asked. More importantly, the results reveal the advantages and disadvantages of our approach against existing crowd-powered systems, like Amazon and Yelp. Based on this finding, we discuss important design implications for building a new class of smart, crowd-powered information systems that leverage public social media.

RELATED WORK

Our work is related to two main research efforts: Social Q&A and studies on the answer quality of Social Q&A.

Social Q&A Systems

There are several different categories of Social Q&A systems. One type is web-based community Q&A (CQA) sites, such as Yahoo! Answers[1], Answers.com[2], StackOverflow[3], and Quora[4]. At these sites, askers post their questions and self-selected volunteers provide answers to the questions. Another type is instant messaging-based Q&A services, including Aardvark [7] and IM-an-Expert [17]. Such services route questions in real-time to users with matching, but often self-described, expertise. Compared to these efforts, our approach focuses on *actively* identifying and engaging suitable answerers based on estimates of their expertise gleaned from their public social media posts.

A third type of Q&A takes place on social networks, such as Twitter and Facebook, where users broadcast questions to their own social networks through their status update messages. These questions are likely to be seen only by users' Facebook friends or Twitter followers, many of whom may not know the answer, but this method may be preferable to some because users tend to trust the opinions of people they know more than those of strangers [10, 14]. To leverage a larger crowd, a few Q&A services on social networks also involve strangers in the answering process, such as TweetQA[5] and AskOnTwitter[6]. While these services allow users to find questions that have been answered in others' social networks, they do *not* allow the users to ask questions of strangers directly.

Closer to our work, there are systems that are targeting strangers to answer questions based on their social media content. For example, Moboq[7] utilizes Sina Weibo (a China-based service similar to Twitter) to identify and send location-based questions to strangers. Bulut et al. [1] crowd-sourced answers to location-based inquiries from users identified to be in a particular location either by their Twitter profiles or by their posts made automatically to Twitter from Foursquare. Nichols et al. explored asking questions of strangers on Twitter in two domains [12]: airport security wait time tracking and digital camera product

[1] http://answers.yahoo.com/
[2] http://answers.com/
[3] http://www.stackoverflow.com/
[4] http://www.quora.com/
[5] http://www.tweetqa.com/
[6] http://www.askontwitter.com/
[7] http://www.moboq.com/

reviews. Compared to these efforts, where the analysis of answer quality is limited, our focus in this paper is to rigorously examine answer quality under different conditions.

Answer Quality in Social Q&A

Harper et al. studied the quality of various Q&A services, and found that services that collected answers from *a group* outperformed services that routed questions to "expert" individuals [5]. Jeon et al. reanalyzed Harper et al.'s data specifically for services, such as Google Answers, where the asker could offer a reward for answering their question and found that while response time was affected by the reward, there was no effect on quality [9]. Hsieh et al. confirmed this result using a different data set from a different paid Q&A site, Mahalo Answers [8]. Our work builds on the notion that quality answers can be sourced for non-expert unpaid groups, and examines these findings in the context of answerers recruited from public social media.

Zhu et al. propose a set of 13 questions that can be used to evaluate the quality of an answer [18], and Shah et al. conducted an experiment using workers on Mechanical Turk to annotate a Q&A corpus from Yahoo! Answers with these 13 questions [16]. Shah et al. found that these answers strongly correlated with asker's ratings of the answer in the corpus. We also used a survey approach with Mechanical Turk workers to measure the quality of our Twitter responses. While our questions differ from those of Zhu et al., most of the same concepts, such as truthfulness, are present in our questions.

Shah et al. also experimented with automatically predicting quality ratings of answers using features such as answer length, number of answers, and properties of answerers' profiles [16]. Unfortunately, many of these features are sparse or unavailable when analyzing strangers on public social media, and thus we could not make use of these models in our work.

There are also two studies that have looked at answer quality of Q&A on social networks. Paul et al. conducted an in-depth study of questions asked on Twitter, examining the response rate and relevance of the responses [13]. Panovich et al. studied tie strength and the quality of responses received from friends to questions posted as Facebook status updates [14]. The results show that answers from people with stronger ties provide slightly more informational answers than those from people with weaker ties. Unlike our approach that utilizes strangers to answer questions, both of these studies focus on Q&A scenarios that revolve around users' social networks. Their results may serve as interesting point of comparison however.

DATA COLLECTION

For the purpose of our experiments, we collected data for two products: one for a popular tablet computer at the time we asked questions (Samsung Galaxy 10.1) and another for food trucks based in the Los Angeles area. For each product, we needed to determine both the set of questions to ask and our method for finding the potential answerers using the public Twitter stream.

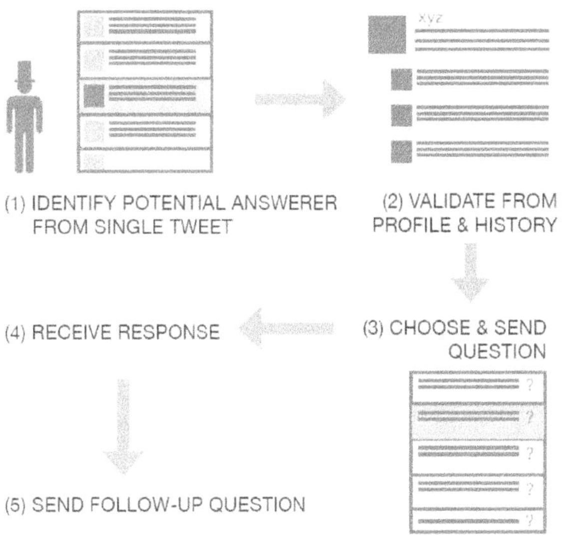

Figure 1. Question asking process flow used in our studies.

Twitter Data Collection

To collect responses from strangers on Twitter, we developed an experimental system where a human operator monitors the Twitter stream, identifies suitable strangers on Twitter, and then sends questions to them. The same human operator asked all of the questions for the studies described in this paper.

Experimental System Overview

Figure 1 shows the main question-asking flow used for collecting reviews for both products. The first step for the human operator was to identify potential answerers by watching a filtered feed of publicly posted Twitter status updates that was updated in real time. Filtering was primarily done by keywords related to the scenario, though spam filters and other scenario-specific heuristics were applied to eliminate as many irrelevant tweets as possible. The tweets of users who had previously been asked a question were also filtered to prevent the operator from accidentally engaging with the same user more than once. When the human operator identified a potential answerer, he would examine the user's profile and recent tweets, verify that user was a good candidate, and then send the user a question. Questions were sent as @replies to one of the answerers' recent relevant tweets, thus giving the answerers some context for why that question was directed to them.

The operator would also monitor Twitter for responses to questions. Up to two questions were asked of each answerer, and if the answerer responded to the first question then a second question would be sent. The operator could send custom responses to users who asked follow-up questions back to the question-asking account. Note that not

Table 1. Questions asked for the Tablet. The 1st question was prefaced with "Trying to learn about tablets...sounds like you have Galaxy Tab 10.1." The 2nd question was prefaced with "Thanks!". The "Rnd" column indicates in which round that question was used.

Q#	Rnd	Question Text
1a	1	How fast is it? Does it ever noticeably lag?
1b	2	How fast is it?
2a	1	How does it feel? Does it seem solid?
2b	2	How does it feel?
3a	1	How is the display? Readable in sun or from angle?
3b	2	How is the display?
4a	1	How is the camera quality? (both front and back)
4b	2	How is the camera quality?
5a	1	How are the speakers? Is the sound quality acceptable?
5b	2	How are the speakers?
6a	1	How is the battery life? How long does it take to charge?
6b	2	How is the battery life?
7a	1	Where do you use yours most? (home, work...)
7b	2	Where do you use yours most?
8a	1	Who would you recommend it for? (techie, novice...)
8b	2	Who would you recommend it for?
9	2	How easy is it to carry around?
10	2	Are you finding all of the apps that you want?
11	2	Is it easy to personalize the device for your use?
12	2	What do you use it for the most?
13	2	How easy is it to connect to other devices?

every user was sent a follow-up question, particularly in cases where they responded that they did not own the tablet or had not visited the food truck, or if their response came in long after the initial question was asked.

For both products, a set of questions was chosen in advance. In general, the next question to ask was chosen randomly by the operator with a weight towards questions that had so far received the fewest responses. A *question-tracking* view in the dashboard let the operator track how many times each question had been answered. Our goal was to collect roughly the same number of responses to each question. All tweets received and sent by our system were collected in a database for later analysis.

Collecting Tablet Reviews

We chose a consumer electronics product for our study because there is a great deal of discussion around such products on Twitter. Tablets seemed like a particular good choice because they were popular products at the time, and the particular device that we chose (Samsung Galaxy Tab 10.1) was among the most popular in the tablet category at the time. One negative to choosing this particular device, which we did not anticipate until after we began, is that Samsung has a line of Galaxy-branded products that also include phones. This made the task of identifying potential answerers more challenging, and may be in part responsible for the resulting lower response rates compared to previous work [12] and the food truck scenario (see Table 3).

We could have chosen the Apple iPad instead of the Galaxy Tab, but at the time spam about the iPad was quite common, which might have had two negative effects. First, it would have made it more difficult to find appropriate answerers due to the high volume of spam tweets about iPads. Second, users might have been more likely to disregard our question as a spam because they might have already received many spam messages about iPads.

We conducted two separate rounds of questioning for the Galaxy Tab, and the questions we chose are shown in Table 3. For the first round, we chose questions based on reading expert tablet reviews from Cnet.com and Engadget.com, and our own intuitive notions of what might be important to a purchaser of a tablet. The questions we wrote were all composed as a general question followed by some form of clarification, because we felt such questions would be easier for users to answer. After sending these questions to a number of users, we decided to add a second round of questions for two reasons. First, we wanted to ensure that our questions covered all of the major types of information commonly discussed in Amazon reviews to facilitate the content comparison between the Twitter and Amazon reviews. For this purpose, we analyzed the top-50 Amazon reviews for the Galaxy Tab 10.1 to identify the top-10 major aspects of information revealed about the tablet. Based on our findings, we added questions #9-13. Second, we removed the clarification phrases from our 1st round of questions to explore whether and how answer behavior would change if more open-ended versions were used.

For the first round of questioning, the initial question sent to a user was chosen from questions #1-6, and the follow-up question was either #7 or #8. We chose this approach because we felt the latter questions were more open-ended and might be too difficult to ask initially. For the second round of questioning, we removed this restriction and the operator randomly selected questions as described earlier.

All questions for this scenario were sent from the Twitter account **@tabletsqa**. The first round of questions took place on September 11-14, 2011, and the second round took place between October 5, 2011 and January 5, 2012.

Collecting Food Truck Reviews

We chose food truck reviews for our second scenario because of the increasing popularity of gourmet food trucks and the use of Twitter by many food truck owners to broadcast their trucks' locations and converse with their customers. Many users when talking about a food truck on Twitter will use its Twitter handle instead of its proper name (e.g., "grlldcheesetruk" instead of "Grilled Cheese Truck"), which makes filtering for conversations about specific trucks much easier. Los Angeles has a large vibrant food truck community, and we thus focused on trucks specifically in this area. We collected a list of 90 active L.A.-based trucks' Twitter handles by browsing web pages and Twitter lists dedicated to the topic.

In order to maximize the number of answers that could be collected, we did not filter the list of 90 trucks. Due to the

Table 2. Questions asked for the Food Trucks. The 1st question was prefaced with "Interested in <food truck handle>...sounds like you've eaten there." The 2nd one had no preface.

Q#	Question Text
1	What do you prefer to order?
2	Are there vegetarian options?
3	Is the menu large or small (for a food truck)?
4	How is the service?
5	Does the price match the amount of food you get?
6	Is it clean?
7	Does it move a lot, or is it often in the same places?
8	How far would you travel to get food from this truck?

popularity of the trucks however, most of our answers are for three: grlldcheesetruk, GrillEmAllTruck, and kogibbq.

The questions asked in this scenario are shown in Table 2. These questions were chosen based on our experience and intuition of what might be interesting to a prospective customer of a food truck. Unlike for the tablet questions, we conducted only one round of question asking and we also chose not to include a second clarification question for any of our questions. Initially our phrasing included the food truck Twitter handle using the @ symbol, which notifies the food truck owner that we mentioned their account. Due to the number of questions being sent, we later removed the @ symbol to avoid creating too many mentions that might spam the truck owners. Use of the @ symbol in our tweets did lead to responses from several food truck owners in addition to the potential answerers we were targeting. Questions were sent using the weighted random method from the Twitter account **@foodtruckqa**. Questions were asked during the period of September 16-28, 2011.

Data Collection from Amazon and Yelp

To compare the quality of the product reviews collected from targeted strangers on Twitter to a baseline, we collected a set of user-generated reviews on Amazon and Yelp.

From Amazon, we first collected the top-50 rated most useful reviews of the Samsung Galaxy Tab 10.1. By carefully examining these reviews, we found that the top 10 reviews covered 8.7 key features of the tablet (e.g., display, performance, and software) on average, while the next 10 reviews covered only 3.9 features already in the top 10 reviews. The reviews rated below the top 20 contained even less information. We thus decided to use the top 10 reviews as our comparison data set for the tablet scenario.

From Yelp, we collected the first page of reviews in Yelp-sort order (a ranking that combines usefulness, recency, and other factors), for the three most popular food trucks mentioned previously: *Kogi BBQ*, *The Grilled Cheese Truck*, and *Grill Em All*. This collection contained 40 reviews for each truck, which we examined using the same approach as for the Amazon reviews. Based on our analysis, we selected the top 10 reviews of each truck for comparison.

CONTENT ANALYSIS METHODOLOGY

We examined the content of collected reviews and analyzed their quality in two methods: hand coding the reviews for an objective content analysis, and a survey conducted on Mechanical Turk for a subjective analysis.

Review Coding

To help understand the user responses and to compare the content of the reviews collected on Twitter with those from Amazon and Yelp, we hand-coded all reviews from all sources to answer two main questions:

1. How did the Twitter users respond to our questions? This question gets at more generic aspects of the responses, such as whether users provided a relevant answer, or whether they asked us a question back, etc.
2. What types of information do the reviews contain, and how do the Twitter responses compare to those collected from Amazon and Yelp in terms of their content? This question requires more scenario-specific coding to match the different information types conveyed in the different types of reviews.

We coded the reviews using an open coding approach, guided by our research questions (see the Introduction). For the tablet reviews, four coders coded each collected tweet and each Amazon review independently and then discussed their coding and reconciled the differences. Similarly, for the food truck reviews, two coders first coded each collected tweet and each Yelp review independently, and then reconciled their differences through discussion.

Through this process, our coding scheme evolved to contain two types of codes to address our first two sets of research questions. Twitter-specific codes about users' response behavior are shared across the Twitter reviews for both products, aiming at answering the first set of questions. For example, one Twitter-specific code indicates whether a response is relevant to the question. To answer the second set of questions, domain-specific codes were created to describe particular types of information contained within a review. For example, one tablet-specific code indicates that a user mentioned that the display was bright, and one food truck-specific code indicates the cleanliness of the truck. As a result, our scheme included 10 Twitter-specific codes, 86 informational codes about tablets, and 29 about food trucks. The informational codes were grouped into a hierarchy with 9 top-level topics for each product type, which were used to construct the survey described below.

Mechanical Turk Studies

To assess users' perceived quality of the reviews collected from different sources to answer our third set of research questions, we designed and conducted a survey study using Amazon Mechanical Turk. Four different surveys were constructed for each combination of review types (Twitter and Amazon/Yelp reviews) and products (tablet and food truck). The first page of each collected basic demographic information, such as age, and information about the turker's experience with the product under survey.

The turker was then asked to read the complete set of reviews corresponding to the particular survey. For example, all Twitter reviews about the 3 LA-area food trucks, or the top 10 Amazon reviews about the Samsung Galaxy Tab 10.1. The reviews were displayed in a separate browser window so the turker could refer to them throughout the survey. Each survey consisted of multiple pages, each corresponding to the top-level topic identified in our collected Twitter reviews for that product. For each topic, the turker was asked to use the reviews that they just read to come up with at least 5 keywords to describe the topic. This exercise not only was intended to test the turkers' comprehension of the reviews, but it also forced the turkers to carefully read all the reviews before answering any survey questions.

After completing each topic page, the turker were asked 5 5-point Likert scale questions about the reviews:

- *Usefulness*: how well have the reviews provided overall and relevant ideas about the product that may affect your buying decision?
- *Objectiveness*: how well do the reviews provide unbiased information about the product?
- *Trustworthiness*: how much do you trust the reviews?
- *Balance*: how well do the reviews cover multiple aspects, including pros and cons?
- *Readability*: how easy is it to understand the reviews?

After completing the survey, the turker was given a code to enter into the Mechanical Turk web site to receive payment.

To ensure the quality of the survey, we allowed only turkers located in United States and with greater than 96% approval ratings to participate. A browser cookie was checked to ensure that a turker filled out only one of the four surveys. Each turker response was individually screened to ensure the quality of answers. The four surveys were posted until we received 36 valid responses to each. A total of 19 work assignments were rejected, primarily due to the submission of incorrect completion codes. Some surveys were rejected for copying/pasting or entering random text in the responses. Each approved response was paid $2.00. Among the respondents, 57% were male; 49% were between age 20 and 30, 22% between age 30 and 40, and 21% above 40.

TWITTER RESPONSE RESULTS

To address our first set of research questions, we examined the response rate and time of the Twitter users in our experiment and compare them with previous work. We then analyzed the response quality based on our coding.

Response Rate and Time

In previous work [12], it was found that response rates and times differ for the first question asked and any follow-up questions, so here we break out results by the order in which a user saw a question. Table 3 shows the response

Table 3. Summary of response statistics for both products.

	Questions	Responses	Response Rate (%)	Median Response Time (min)	% Responses in 30 Min	95% Responses Received In (hrs)
Tablet						
Q1	633	183	29%	180.5	36%	128
Q2	117	75	64%	23.3	52%	39
Food Truck						
Q1	171	70	41%	34.7	46%	128
Q2	57	41	72%	32.1	49%	21

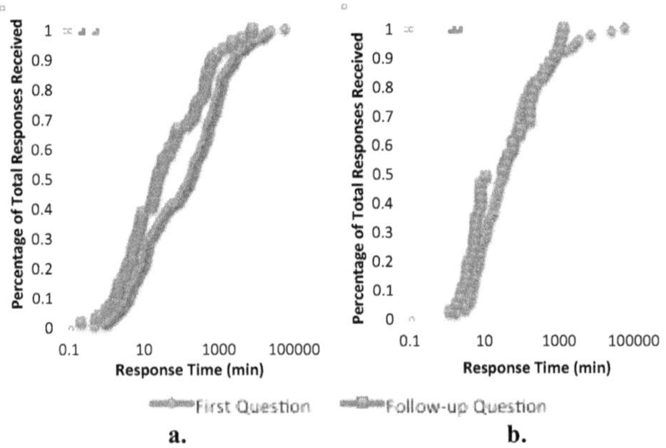

Figure 2. Response times for the (a) Tablet scenario, and (b) Food Truck scenario.

rates and times, broken down by product and question order. Figure 2 shows the response time behavior for both tablet and food truck.

The response rates and times for food truck are comparable to previous results that obtained an average response rate of 42% and received 44% of responses in 30 minutes [12]. The first question in the tablet scenario has both a noticeably lower response rate and slower response times. The lower response rates may be due to the greater difficulty in identifying users who owned a Galaxy Tab 10.1 as compared to other products in the Galaxy line, as questions sent to owners of the wrong product were less likely to receive a response. It is not clear what would lead to the longer response times. We examined the difference between the two rounds of Q&A for the tablet to see if a change between the two might account for these differences. However, response rates were nearly identical for both rounds (34.9% for both) despite more than twice as many questions being asked in the second round (209 questions were sent in the first round vs. 541 in the second round).

Table 4. Summary of answer coding statistics.

	Response Count	Relevant Answer	Wrong Answer But Useful Info	Multi- Message Response	Average Info per Response	Off-topic Info per Response
Tablet	258	71%	19%	3%	1.82	0.48
Food Truck	111	82%	6%	6%	1.69	0.46

Table 5. Summary of reasons for low quality answers.

	# Irrelevant Responses	No Experi-ence	Didn't know or understand	Thinks we're a bot
Tablet	75	63%	11%	7%
Food Truck	20	25%	30%	0%

Response Quality

Table 4 presents our analysis of the relevance of the Twitter responses that we received, as determined from hand coding. The majority of responses for both products provided answers to the questions asked. Even when the specific question was not answered, the answerer often provided useful additional information.

Table 5 shows a breakdown of the responses that failed to answer the question. In the tablet scenario, the majority of irrelevant responses (63%) came from users who had no experience with the device we asked about. This verifies that identifying users of the Galaxy Tab 10.1 was difficult for our human operator, which likely led to a decrease in response quality. Two other causes can be attributed to the irrelevant responses: 1) some users did not understand our questions (11%), and 2) some believed that a bot sent the questions (7%). However, these two cases combined occurred in only 5% of the overall responses (19 out of 369).

Table 6 shows some actual responses that we received to our questions. We examined the number of information pieces contained in each response, and found for both products that users on average provided more than one piece of information per response. While the majority of this extra information seems relevant to the response, such as providing evidence for a claim (Table 6a), users would occasionally provide other information that was not directly asked for, such as about a different feature that was not mentioned (Table 6). In about 40% of responses for the tablet and 87% for the food truck, the users gave a summary statement about the product (e.g., "great device!").

COMPARING QUANTITIES OF INFORMATION

To objectively compare the *quantities of information* contained in the two sets of reviews for each product, we applied Shannon's information theory [15] to our human coding of the amount and type of information contained in each set of reviews (Twitter, Amazon, and Yelp).

Specifically, we computed Shannon entropy *H(X)* to measure the average amount of information in *bits* contained in each set of reviews (e.g., Twitter tablet reviews) [15]. Here *X* is an *information point*, a random variable with values ranging over all the features of a data set (e.g., the display of the tablet or the location of the food truck). *H(X)* was calculated using a shrinkage entropy estimator [6]. We computed the entropy for the four review data sets (Table 7). To make a fair comparison, here we limit the entropy analysis to only information points that exist in both sets.

For both products, the Twitter reviews contained slightly less information than their web-based counterparts. To better understand the differences in their information quantity, we also calculated the relative entropy (KL divergence) between each two sets [2], which suggests the corresponding review sets contain similar amounts of information for their common information points.

Table 6. Questions and answers sent as part of our experiments with Twitter user names anonymized.

a.	**foodtruckqa:** "Is it clean?"
	user1: "yes. They have a health grade of A."
b.	**tabletsqa:** "How fast is it?"
	user2: "Its fast. More flexibility than ipad. Allows SIM card."
c.	**foodtruckqa:** "Does the price match the food you get?"
	user3: "yupp the best tots and hot dogs on the planet"
d.	**foodtruckqa:** "What do you prefer to order?"
	user4: "Chow fun, chimales are my faves, but it's all good. In alley off 6th at Main tonight."

Table 7. Information entropy computed based on the hand-coded content including only information points occurred in both of a scenario's review sets.

	Tablet		Food Truck	
	Amazon	Twitter	Yelp	Twitter
Information (bits)	4.09	3.73	3.27	3.02

MECHANICAL TURK COMPARISON RESULTS

In Mechanical Turk studies, we examined how people perceive the quality of data collected from different sources.

Tablet Results

On average, turkers finished reading and answering questions for the Amazon reviews in 26.5 minutes, Twitter reviews in 25.8 minutes. A *t* test showed no significant difference between the two.

Turker Background

Among our subjects, 68% did not own any tablet; 58% did not know anything about the tablet under review, and only 5% had a lot of experience with the tablet. However, 68% of the readers did have plans to buy a tablet at some point in

Table 8. Turker's subjective rating of review quality for Tablet reviews

	Amazon	Twitter	Mann-Whitney	p
Usefulness	3.19	2.64	868.5	0.006
Objectiveness	2.94	2.53	814.5	0.042
Trustworthiness	2.94	2.39	861.0	0.008
Balance	3.00	2.11	936.0	0.001
Readability	2.92	2.61	741.5	0.270

the future. On a 5-point Likert scale, the turkers were asked how often they search and consult online reviews before a purchase (0 being "never" and 4 being "always"). The median answer was 3 "often", with mean=3.32, sd=0.78.

Subjective Ratings of Review Quality

Table 8 summarizes the results of the five final questions in our survey, where turkers were asked to rate the reviews in five aspects on a 5-point likert scale (1 being most negative and 5 being most positive). Mean ratings and Mann-Whitney U statistics of comparison are shown. Since the turkers rated Amazon reviews consistently higher than Twitter reviews in all five aspects, we re-examined both sets of reviews. We found that Amazon reviews provided more details (e.g., one's experience with the tablet) and context (e.g., comparing the Galaxy tablet to iPad) about the tablet. The comments from the turkers confirmed these findings. Amazon reviews are also better written compared to the informal text in Twitter responses, which may be another factor affecting the ratings (e.g., trustworthiness).

As mentioned by Gilbert and Karahalios [4], there are professionals who write elaborate reviews to gain social capital on sites like Amazon. We examined the profiles of the 10 reviewers of the top-10 reviews used in our study. Seven out of ten reviewers had written at least ten reviews (23 reviews per person on average) on Amazon on various topics (e.g., electronics and computers). Five of them were also highly ranked among the millions of reviewers on Amazon. In contrast, we selected Twitter answerers merely based on their mention of "Galaxy tablet" in their tweets. Our ongoing work is performing an in-depth analysis of Twitter users based on their social media posts and social behavior to infer their intrinsic traits, including personality and motivations, which will form the basis for us to select those who are *willing*, *able*, and *ready* to answer our questions. However, this topic is beyond the scope of this paper. This also suggests that building a better profile of social media users (e.g., knowing a person who has extensive experience with multiple devices) and more careful selection of answerers might help improve the quality of responses.

Comparison of Perceived Content

To understand turkers' comprehension of targeted reviews, we asked them to use a list of keywords to describe each of the nine topics covered by the reviews. For each topic, we then compared the two sets of turker-entered keywords based on their reading of the Twitter and Amazon reviews.

Depending on the topic, the overlap between the two sets of keywords differed, which may imply the amount of content perceived by the turkers differed. For example, the *build* topic of the tablet is rather broad, covering multiple facets, such as look, feel, and weight of the device. In this case, the turkers used more keywords to describe the build of the tablet after reading the Amazon reviews. In contrast, our Twitter questions solicited information about the build from only three facets (Table 1, questions 2a, 2b, and 9). Compared to the build topic, the two sets of keywords generated for the display topic overlapped greatly. This suggests that our 2 questions about displays were sufficient to cover what was said in the Amazon reviews.

While the overlap between the two turker-generated keyword sets varied by topics, we see a clear trend: the more specific the topic is, the greater the overlap is between the two keyword sets. As discussed more later, this implies that our Twitter-based information solicitation is more suitable for clearly defined topics compared to broad topics.

Food Truck Results

On average, turkers finished reading and answering questions about the Yelp reviews in 19.9 minutes and the Twitter reviews in 16.8 minutes. A t test finds no significant difference, with $t = 1.73$, $p = 0.08$.

Table 9. Turker's subjective rating of review quality for Food Truck reviews

	Yelp	Twitter	Mann-Whitney	p
Usefulness	2.86	2.56	734.0	0.309
Objectiveness	2.17	2.08	672.0	0.783
Trustworthiness	2.58	2.14	800.5	0.071
Balance	2.47	1.72	921.0	0.002
Readability	2.89	2.11	896.0	0.004

Subjective Rating of Review Quality

Table 9 summarizes the five aspects of review quality as judged by the turkers. As can be seen, the Twitter responses are not significantly different from the Yelp reviews in term of perceived usefulness and objectiveness. The Yelp reviews were perceived slightly more trustworthy compared to the Twitter responses, but it is not statistically significant. The Yelp reviews are perceived to be significantly more balanced and readable than Twitter responses.

Note that the perceived difference between the two sets of reviews for the tablet is larger than that of the food trucks. Again, this may imply the suitability of domains for this method of information collection. In the tablet case, we asked more generic questions (e.g., how is the display) versus more personalized experience in the food truck case (e.g., what they prefer to order).

Comparison of Perceived Content

We compared the two turker-generated keyword sets for each of the nine topics about the food trucks based on Twitter and Yelp. The results were similar to that of the tablet.

DISCUSSION

The results of our experiments show both the advantages and limitations of this new information collection approach.

Advantages

We have seen that greater than 70% of the responses to our questions contained relevant information, and many answers contained additional information beyond what was asked. We also saw that many of the cases in which we received irrelevant answers were due to targeting strangers who did not have the background or experience to answer the question. This is encouraging because it suggests we may be able to further improve quality by better choosing strangers to target or focusing on scenarios where the challenge of targeting is less difficult.

Our entropy-based analysis of information quantity suggests that the Twitter method produces similar information to other methods for the questions asked. This suggests that our approach could be more valuable if we also involve a crowd in question selection. For example, our system can collect reader-driven product reviews by allowing review readers to select the questions. This would differ greatly from the current state of the art where reviews are primarily writer-driven. Our food truck reviews provide some evidence that this could work already, as certain features of food trucks, like *cleanliness*, were not frequently discussed in the Yelp reviews that we looked at.

Limitations

A key negative result is that the Mechanical Turk users who took our surveys found the Twitter-based reviews universally lacking in balance, a feature we hypothesized would be a strength of our approach. Comments from turkers who took our survey suggest that concrete examples of positive or negative experiences would be desirable to include in the reviews, as well as more background about the users who are providing the reviews. This might be addressable by structuring our question asking to draw out scenarios and background information, which we did not attempt here.

Design Implications

Our findings suggest several important design considerations for building such a system.

Domain Suitability

A unique advantage of our approach is its *agility*: we solicit information from the right people at the right time on social media. This implies that our method could be better used to collect information that existing systems cannot offer. Given the dynamic nature of social media, our approach is particularly suitable for collecting *time-sensitive*, *context-specific* information (e.g., the current wait time at a popular restaurant). Due to the constraints of social media interaction (e.g., length of a tweet), our experimental results also indicate that our work is more effective for collecting information along a narrow dimension (e.g., the display vs. the build of a tablet) associated with an *easy-to-identify* entity (a specific food truck vs. a tablet in varied sizes). The latter criterion also helps reduce the difficulty in identifying the right users. In short, our approach could be applied to answer questions that are not easily possible to answer with existing systems (e.g., the crowd mood at an event) or to supplement existing systems, like Amazon and Yelp, to collect missing (e.g., cleanliness) information.

Selection of Target Answerers

Looking forward, if our method is to become useful, then it will likely be necessary to automate or greatly streamline the answerer selection process. Improved methods of user profiling are needed to identify users that are *willing*, *able*, and *ready* to provide the requested information. Such methods should also identify a diverse crowd from which balanced information can be collected (e.g., positive and negative reviews of a product). Not only will these considerations help address the current deficiencies in our approach (e.g., the perceived a lack of balance in our Twitter reviews), but they can also help improve the quality of solicited answers. For example, we could ask a person who has gone to several food trucks to provide a comparison or ask people with different backgrounds about their opinion of a product.

Questioning Method

The question method directly affects the quality of responses received. In our tablet scenario, for example, we asked "*Where do you use yours most?*" One person responded, "*elaborate 'where'. As in apps or where I usually use my tab.*" A more targeted question such as, "*What apps do you use the most?*" may solicit more useful responses regarding the usage of the tablet. We could also consider structuring questions to elicit more balanced and useful responses. For example, in the food truck scenario, when asking "*what do you prefer to order*," adding "*tell us also what you dislike*" may help solicit a more balanced answer. In this same domain, we would obtain more useful rating about the price-to-value ratio of a food truck, if we ask users how often they frequent the food truck or whether they have visited other trucks.

Since our approach engages with strangers on social media, a challenging research question is how to maximize the information gain while minimizing the cost. For example, a multi-step conversation may allow the system to acquire more information and accommodate platform restrictions (e.g., number of characters allowed per message), but users may dislike engaging in a long conversation with a stranger.

Another key ingredient toward automation is to decide how many times a question should be sent. The amount of information obtained may not grow linearly as the number of responses grows. Monitoring the information entropy of the responses (i.e., the amount of information gained) as they are collected may help with making this decision, and carefully crafting or dynamically adjusting questions may even allow the system to optimize the rate of information gain.

CONCLUSION

In this paper, we explored the quality of crowd-sourced information that is actively solicited from strangers based on their public social media status updates. We found that users answered questions at rates similar to those found previously, the answers contained information relevant to the question over 70% of the time, and over 37% of answers provided additional details beyond the specific question asked. The information collected was also similar to that of other sources when controlling for the set of questions that were asked. While our work demonstrates the potential of this new type of information collection systems, our finding that users preferred traditional reviews suggests that challenges still remain in selecting questions and answerers, or displaying the content in a more acceptable fashion, in order to produce a better review experience.

ACKNOWLEDGEMENTS

Research was sponsored by the U.S. Defense Advanced Research Projects Agency (DARPA) under the Social Media in Strategic Communication (SMISC) program, Agreement Number W911NF-12-C-0028. The views and conclusions contained in this document are those of the author(s) and should not be interpreted as representing the official policies, either expressed or implied, of the U.S. Defense Advanced Research Projects Agency or the U.S. Government. The U.S. Government is authorized to reproduce and distribute reprints for Government purposes notwithstanding any copyright notation hereon.

REFERENCES

1. Bulut, M.F., Yilmaz , Y.S., and Demirbas, M. "Crowdsourcing Location-based Queries," in *PerCol 2011*.
2. Cover. T., and Thomas, J., (2006) *Elements of Information Theory*. Wiley.
3. Gazan, R. Social Q&A. *J. of the Amer. Soc. for Info Science & Technology,* 62(12): 2301-2312.
4. Gilbert, E. and Karahalios, K. "Understanding déjà reviewers", in *CSCW 2010*: 225-228.
5. Harper, F.M., Raban, D., Rafaeli, S., and Konstan, J.A. "Predictors of answer quality in online Q&A sites," *CHI'08*: 865-874.
6. Hausser, J. and Strimmer, K. (2009) "Entropy inference and the James-Stein estimator, with application to nonlinear gene association networks," In *J. Mach. Lear. Res.* 10: 1469-1484.
7. Horowitz, D. and Kamvar, S.D. "The anatomy of a large-scale social search engine," *WWW'10*: 431–440.
8. Hsieh, G., Kraut, R.E., and Hudson, S.E. "Why pay?: exploring how financial incentives are used for question & answer," *CHI'10*: 305-314.
9. Jeon, G.Y., Kim, Y-M., and Chen, Y. "Re-examining price as a predictor of answer quality in an online q&a site," *CHI'10*: 325-328.
10. Morris, M.R., Teevan, J., and Panovich, K. "What do people ask their social networks, and why?: A survey of status message q&a behavior," *CHI '10*:1739-1748.
11. Nelson, P. Information and Consumer Behavior, 78(2) *Journal of Political Economy* 311-329 (1970).
12. Nichols, J. and Kang, J.H. "Asking Questions of Targeted Strangers on Social Media," *CSCW'12*: 999-1002.
13. Paul, S.A., Hong, L., and Chi, E.H. "Is Twitter a Good Place for Asking Questions? A Characterization Study," *ICWSM'11 Posters*.
14. Panovich, K., Miller, R.C., and Karger, D. "Tie Strength in Question and Answer on Social Network Sites," *CSCW'12*: 1057-1066.
15. Shannon, C. E. "A Mathematical Theory of Communication". *Bell Sys.Tech. J.* 27 (3): 379–423, 1948.
16. Shah, C. and Pomerantz, J. "Eval. and predicting answer quality in community Q&A," *SIGIR'10*: 411-418.
17. Richardson, M. and White, R.W. "Supporting Synchronous Social Q&A Throughout the Question Lifecycle," *WWW'11*: 755-764.
18. Zhu, Z., Bernhard, and D., Gurevych, I. (2009) "A Multi-dimensional Model for Assessing the Quality of Answers in Social Q&A Sites," Tech. Rep. TUD-CS-2009-0158, Technische Universität Darmstadt.
19. Zhuang, L., Jing, F., and Zhu, X. "Movie review mining and summarization," *CIKM'06*: 43-50.

Personality-Targeted Design: Theory, Experimental Procedure, and Preliminary Results

Oded Nov
Polytechnic Institute of New York University
Brooklyn, New York
onov@poly.edu

Ofer Arazy
University of Alberta
Edmonton, Alberta, Canada
ofer.arazy@business.ualberta.ca

ABSTRACT
We introduce a framework for personality-targeted design. Much like a medical treatment applied to a person based on his specific genetic profile, we make the case for theory-driven personalized UI design, and argue that it can be more effective than design applied equally to the entire population. In particular, we show that users' conscientiousness levels determine their reactions to UI indicators of critical mass. We created a simulated social recommender system in which participants answer a short personality questionnaire and are subsequently presented with a picture of a pet that purports to be the "best match" for their personality. We then manipulated the UI by providing indicators of the existence and the lack of critical mass. We tested whether the interaction between personality and UI design affects users' participation. The findings validate our hypothesis, showing that manipulation of the critical mass indicators affect high-conscientiousness and low-conscientiousness participants in opposite directions.

Author Keywords
Social psychology; theory-driven design; personality; conscientiousness; critical mass; diffusion of responsibility.

ACM Classification Keywords
H.5.m. Information interfaces and presentation (e.g., HCI): Miscellaneous.

General Terms
Human Factors; Design

INTRODUCTION
Recent years have seen a substantial growth in the scale and scope of social technologies, which are based on technology-mediated social participation [45]. Consequently, researchers have been stressing the need to develop theories that will guide practice, which is to date, guided to a large extent by intuition, trial and error [29, 45]. Current studies on the factors that drive social participation tend to take one of the following approaches:

- **Experimental, design-based research** in which controlled experiments are used to test the effect of design features (primarily focusing on UI design) on user performance. Typically, such studies build on social psychology theories to inform design choices [6, 12, 13, 17, 30, 47]. This approach enables researchers to draw conclusions about design effectiveness. However, to date, studies based on this approach did not take into account differences in users' idiosyncratic attributes, such as their personalities or motivations; in other words, to follow a medical metaphor, this is equivalent to testing the effectiveness of a medical treatment by providing it to all patients, regardless of their specific genetic make-up.
- **Individual differences research** in which contributors' personal attributes, such as motivations or personality traits are identified, often using self-report surveys, and correlated with data on participation levels quality and quantity [25, 36-38, 49, 50]. This approach enables researchers to identify a relatively large number of relevant personal attributes directly, using validated instruments, and then develop and test theories about the relationships between personal attributes, attitudes and participation. A disadvantage of this approach, however, is that the research design is often cross-sectional, and causality is difficult to establish. Furthermore, such studies usually do not involve direct testing of system design effectiveness.

The objective of the present study is to develop, implement and test a novel approach, which builds on the strengths of these two approaches. We combine controlled experiments, design manipulations, surveys, and system data, to test the effectiveness of design features that target participants' idiosyncratic personal attributes. While the proposed approach is applicable in a variety of settings, in the present study we focus on social recommender systems and participants' rating and feedback activities.

We address the following general research question: are there differences in the effects of design interventions targeting users' idiosyncratic personal attributes traits on users' participation? Using the medical metaphor mentioned above, the proposed approach is analogous to a medical treatment that is applied to an individual based on his specific genetic profile. The extant research on personalization [7, 18, 19, 21, 31], often focuses on users' past experiences and interaction. Our approach here focuses on more fundamental user attributes such as personality traits.

To address the research questions, we developed for the present study a simulated online recommender system called PetMatch.[1] PetMatch is presented to its users as a research project in need of feedback from users: its landing page invites participants to answer a very short personality questionnaire, and a simulated recommender system returns a picture of a pet that purports to present the "best match" for the participant's personality (see Figure 1). The PetMatch environment facilitates a 2X2 factorial experimental design consisting of: (1) measurement of personal attributes (through a short questionnaire), (2) design intervention, and (3) opportunities for users to rate the accuracy of the recommendation and provide verbal feedback (see Table 1). As such, PetMatch serves as a platform on which to address research questions concerning the interactions between personal attributes, design choices, and user participation.

In the present study, we present findings from an experiment focusing on the interaction between the personality trait of conscientiousness (a known predictor of helping behavior in various social settings), design choices involving indicators of high and low levels of critical mass, and their joint effects on user participation.

	Experimental Interventions	
Personal Attributes	*Design intervention: low level*	*Design intervention: high level*
Low level of personal attribute	Outcomes for: low attribute X low intervention	Outcomes for: low attribute X high intervention
High level of personal attribute	Outcomes for: high attribute X low intervention	Outcomes for: high attribute X high intervention
	Experimental Outcomes	

Table 1. Experimental conditions: personal attributes and interventions.

BACKGROUND

The CSCW field has a long tradition of social psychology-driven design research, often using controlled experiments [6, 13, 17, 30, 47]. In such studies, the effectiveness of design features is tested in online environments. For example, drawing on social comparison theory, [6] showed in an online experiment that when users of MovieLens, a movie recommender system, receive information about others' contribution, users below the median increase their participation, whereas those above the median do not decrease their ratings. Similarly, [30] and [33] found that users contributed more when they were reminded of their contribution's uniqueness. A different approach to studying user participation involves personal attributes such as motivations or personality traits. In such studies, attributes are identified, often using self-report surveys, and correlated with users' participation data [25, 49, 50]. For example, the "Big Five" personality factors were found to be useful predictors of internet use [35], and participation in social media sites [4, 8].

Participation in online environments was studied extensively, leading to the identification of various factors that encourage participation. Perceived critical mass – a user's subjective belief that there is a large number of other users who participate in a community or adopt a new technology – was shown has a positive effect on the user's own participation behavior [34, 46, 52]. However, in contrast, extant social psychology research shows that the higher the number of people present in a situation or taking part in a collective effort, there is a higher likelihood of social loafing [28] and diffusion of responsibility [14, 20], such that each one of the people present feels less personal responsibility, and less compelled to help. This phenomenon applies to online settings as well [1, 5, 11].

While prior research focused on factors such as group homogeneity [40] and group interaction [16], we attempt to reconcile the contrasting evidence by focusing on the role of personality. Specifically, we study the role of conscientiousness (being responsible, dependable, planful, organized, and persistent, [2, 23]), one of the Big Five personality factors [9, 22]. Prior studies of personality and social behavior showed the important role the conscientiousness trait plays in explaining helping behavior that is relevant to the present study. Specifically, it was found that conscientiousness was the best personality trait predictor of organizational citizenship behavior [26, 43] (discretionary behavior which promotes the effective functioning of the organization but is not part of the formal reward system [42, 44]), and that it was negatively related to social loafing [26]. These two outcome variables are closely related to the dependent variable in our study, and thus we expect the relationship between consciousness and participation to generalize to the setting of our study.

Building on these prior findings and using our experimental platform, we test the hypothesis that perceived low level of critical mass will discourage diffusion of responsibility among participants characterized by high conscientiousness resulting in increased participation, while a perception of

[1] The system is referred to here as PetMatch in line with the CSCW blind review guidelines. The real name is searchable online and will inform the reviewers of the researchers' identities.

the existence of critical mass will decrease participation in this population. This is because people characterized by high conscientiousness tend to be responsible and self-disciplined [10, 48], and therefore, we hypothesize, they will act more responsibly in the face of a request for help - such as the researchers' request to rate users' pet match as part of a research project - when they see that there are fewer others who may be available to do so (i.e. low critical mass experimental condition). When facing a situation in which there is an indication that others have already provided help (i.e. high critical mass condition), the need for help would seem less important, and highly conscientious people are expected to feel less obliged to help (resulting in increased diffusion of responsibility and decreased participation). Participants characterized by low conscientiousness, on the other hand, are more likely to exert effort when there is social pressure on them from others to do so [3, 24]. Therefore, we hypothesize, they will be more likely to participate when faced with an indication of a large number of other participants who already rated (i.e. high critical mass indicator), but less likely to participate in the absence of such indication (i.e. low critical mass indicator).

METHOD

In what follows we outline the details of the experimental procedure used in the present study.

Personal attributes condition: conscientiousness

Participants were recruited in the authors' universities among undergraduate and graduate students. In addition, students were asked to share the invitation to participate in the study with their friends and family, and many of them shared the PetMatch link with their contacts via social media. The participants were led to believe that PetMatch is part of an academic research project involving the development of a technique to match respondents' personality traits and the pet that would suit them most. This was communicated to participants in a recruitment email, and on the PetMatch site itself. Participants were not compensated for their participation.

The PetMatch landing page invites participants to answer a very short personality questionnaire. Self-report surveys are commonly used in social science research to identify personal attributes, and have been used extensively in HCI and CSCW studies [27, 35, 38, 39, 41, 51]. The two conscientiousness questionnaire items used a 7-point Likert scale and were adapted from the Ten Item Personality Instrument [23], a short version of the Big Five instrument which has been validated and tested numerous times in prior studies [15].

After filling out the short questionnaire and answering two demographic questions (age, gender), respondents were presented with their purported "best match" (see Figure 1): an image of an animal based on the responses to the survey questions, such that each combination of responses was consistently associated with a specific pet image. Unbeknownst to the respondents, PetMatch in fact presented pet images arbitrarily, with no real attempt to match images to personalities.

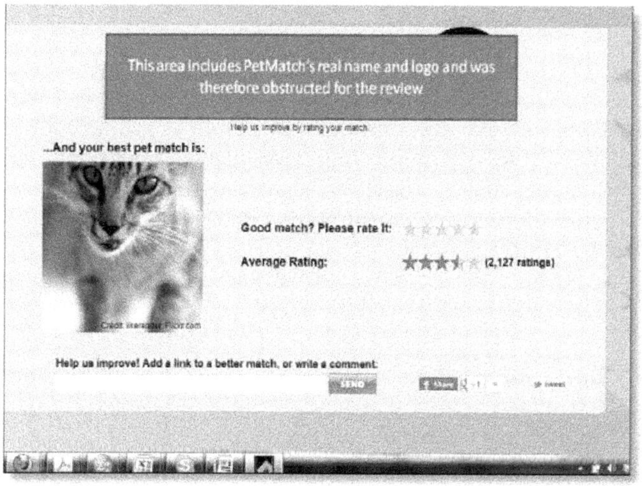

Figure 1. PetMatch screenshot (the logo is obstructed for review purposes).

A post-hoc median split was performed such that respondents whose conscientiousness score was above the sample median were classified as high-conscientious and those below the median as low-conscientious respondents.

Design intervention: perceived critical mass

In addition to the image, respondents were also presented with information about the average rating for the particular pet image presented to them, as well as the number of ratings received so far (along the lines of UI design common on popular recommender systems such as Amazon or Netflix). Unbeknownst to the respondents, the average rating was fixed at 3.5 (out of 5), and the count and average rating indicators were in effect an experimental manipulation. The number of ratings received served as an indicator of critical mass. Perceived critical mass is a subjective and context-specific concept [32, 52], and we therefore set two levels of critical mass in the experiment, assigned randomly to participants: a high value of prior ratings (2,127) represented a high level of critical mass, and a low value (26 ratings) represented a low level of critical mass. These low and high values were established based on a pre-study in which we described the experimental design to three of our colleagues, and asked for their opinions on critical mass values which would be believable in the context of this study. The values of 26 and 2,127 represented the averages for the responses we received.

To further validate the low and high values in the experiment, we administered an additional experiment, this time using Amazon Mechanical Turk. In this experiment, participants were directed to a webpage describing a simple scenario fairly similar to PetMatch: in this scenario, the participant heard about a web site where users rate movies, and visits it to check out a movie they are curious about. The participant then finds that the movie received the rating of 3.5 stars out of 5, based on X reviews (where X is manipulated by the researchers and is randomly assigned the values of either 2,127 or 26 ratings – the low and high critical mass PetMatch values). Having seen these ratings, the subject is asked to what extent they agree with a statement that the movie reviews website has reached a critical mass of users. Responses range from 1 (strongly disagree) to 4 (Neutral) to 7 (strongly agree) on a Likert scale. 78 people took part in this validation experiment. The low critical mass anchor (26 ratings) received the average score of 2.44 out of 7, and the high critical mass anchor (2,127 ratings) received the average score of 5.11. A t-test was used to compare the means, and difference between them was found to be significant ($p<0.001$). Furthermore, both scores were significantly ($p<0.001$) lower and higher (respectively) than the "Neutral" perceived critical mass value. The results therefore support the assumption that the two anchors represent high and low levels of perceived critical mass anchors.

In summary, at this stage respondents were assigned to one of the four experimental conditions described in Table 1.

Respondents' participation (outcome variables):

In addition to the image indicators described, respondents were presented with two participation opportunities that would help the project: (1) a request to rate the quality of the match on a five-star scale, and (2) a request to provide verbal feedback: a comment or a link to a better match (see Figure 1). Respondents' decision on whether to perform these actions or not served as a measure of the participation outcome variables.

To test the hypothesis, we performed a comparison between the average participation rates in all four conditions. In addition, to validate the hypothesis that the interaction between the dimensions (interventions x personal attributes) explains participation rather than just its separate dimensions, we performed two distinct bivariate correlations, one between participation and the critical mass manipulation, and the other between participation and conscientiousness. We also performed logistic regressions for both outcome variables, without the independent variables' interaction.

RESULTS

Overall, 459 people used PetMatch, of which 53.2% were women. The average age was 31.2 (stdev=10.7). Cronbach's alpha was 0.72, representing satisfactory reliability. Participation data of respondents in the experimental conditions were compared in order to identify the differences between the proportions of respondents who participated (by rating or by providing verbal feedback) vs. those who did not. Overall, 46.8% of the participants provided rating and 21.7% provided verbal feedback. However, patterns of participation differed across experimental conditions. These are discussed below.

Logistic regression analyses were performed to test a full model with two independent variables, the interaction between them, as well as demographics (age and gender). The dependent variables were (i) whether respondents rated or not (Rated=1, Not Rated=0), and (ii) whether respondents provided verbal feedback (Feedback=1, No Feedback=0). The independent variables were conscientiousness level (high and low - above and below the median, respectively) and perceived critical mass (high and low). The results of running the full regression are presented in Table 2. Logistic regression: rating The overall model for Rated was significant ($\chi2(5)=13.0$, $p<.05$). The main effects of conscientiousness and perceived critical mass on rating were both positive but only conscientiousness was significant. The interaction between the independent variables was negative and significant.

IV	B	S.E.	Wald $\chi2$	p
Age	.012	.011	1.165	.281
Gender	-.280	.246	1.292	.256
Conscientiousness	1.023	.383	7.131	.008
Critical mass	.518	.395	1.716	.190
Conscientiousness X Critical mass	-1.115	.506	4.860	.027

Table 2. Logistic regression: rating.

As expected, the interaction (see Figure 2) was such that participants characterized by high conscientiousness were more likely to rate when there was perceived low critical mass (i.e. when participants perceived that few others were available to rate). Low conscientiousness participants, on the other hand, were more likely to rate when faced with an indication of a large number of other participants (i.e. perceived high critical mass).

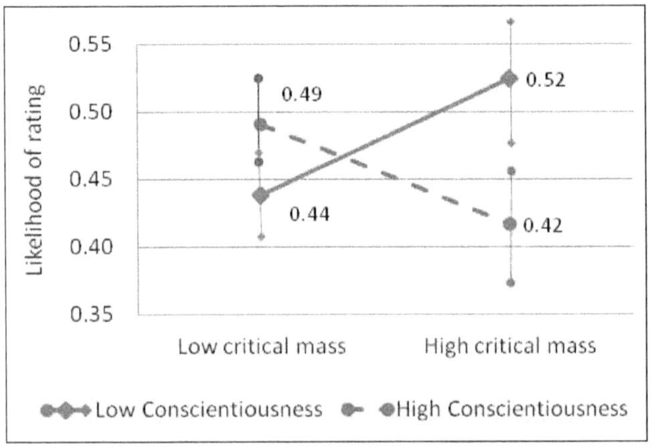

Figure 2. Likelihood of rating in each of the experimental conditions (horizontal lines represent error bars).

An alternative logistic regression model using verbal feedback as a dependent variable yielded similar results (see Table 3): the overall model was significant ($\chi 2(5)=16.9$, $p<.01$). The main effects of conscientiousness and perceived critical mass were positive, but conscientiousness was weakly significant and perceived critical mass was not significant. The interaction between the independent variables was significant and negative.

IV	B	S.E.	Wald $\chi 2$	p
Age	.041	.012	10.837	.001
Gender	-.098	.291	.114	.736
Conscientiousness	.805	.451	3.191	.074
Critical mass	.430	.469	.840	.359
Conscientiousness X Critical mass	-1.200	.603	3.965	.046

Table 3. Logistic regression: verbal comment.

Here too, the interaction was such that participants characterized by high conscientiousness were more likely to provide verbal feedback when there was perceived low critical mass, and low conscientiousness participants were more likely to contribute when faced with an indication of a large number of other participants (see Figure 3).

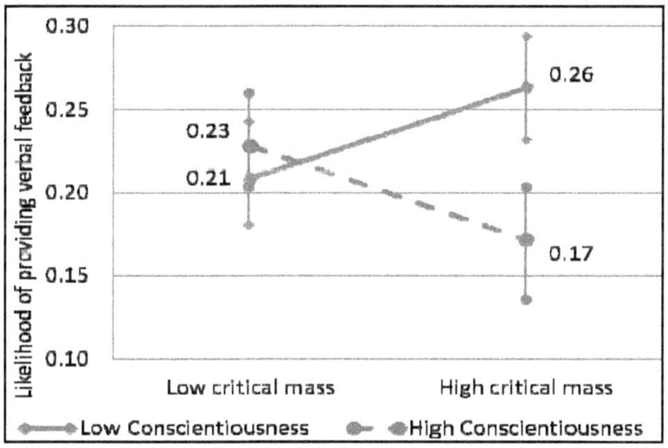

Figure 3. Likelihood of providing verbal feedback in each of the experimental conditions.

Overall, for both outcome variables the interactions were significant in the expected direction, thus supporting our hypotheses.

The bivariate correlations, performed between participation and the critical mass manipulation, and between participation and conscientiousness showed no significant correlations. Furthermore, logistic regressions performed for both outcome variables without the interactions, revealed insignificant main effects for both independent variables. Both analyses confirmed the hypothesis that it is the interaction rather than the main effects that explains participation.

DISCUSSION AND CONCLUSIONS

The design intervention we tested was shown to have a different effect on people with different levels of the conscientiousness personality traits, illustrating the potential value of personality-targeted design. Future research in this direction may help transforming the way we understand technology-mediated social participation and help improve the ways social systems attract, retain and encourage members' participation.

The findings of the present study have implications for developing and managing social systems, and in particular, recommender systems. A direct implication from our findings is that in recommender systems, when considering the user population at large, we cannot necessarily expect indicators of community's activity (e.g. critical mass) to affect participation for the entire population. This insight puts into question the common practice by web site designers to provide indicators of others' behavior. Only when we consider users' personal attributes do we see the effects of critical mass indicators. Interestingly, the effects for highly-conscientiousness and less-consciousness users were in opposite directions, stressing further the need to get an indication of users' personality before presenting community activity indicators. More broadly, our proposed approach to personalized design highlights the need to tailor design features to personality, such that the front end and back-end design features fit users' particular personal attributes. Such tailoring may simply involve making visible, or not, information such as the number of other users who already participated. Personalized content delivery is now common practice, yet few – if any – online communities provide personalized UI based on user's personal attributes. A practical implication of our approach is the need to get an indication of users' personality. While the survey approach used in this study is possible, there may be less intrusive methods for automatically detect aspect of users' personal attributes. Such methods can try to measure invariable traits and dispositions (i.e. creating a user profile), or even capture users' transient preferences and attitudes such that the UI is not only personalized across users but also tailored to a users' particular attitude at particular point in time.

ACKNOWLEDGMENTS

This work was partially supported by NSF award IIS 1149745. We would like to thank Erez Heiman for his contribution to the site design, and Durga Bhavani and Manasa Ranjitha Alla for research assistance.

REFERENCES

[1] Alnuaimi, O. A., *et al.*,2010 "Team Size, Dispersion, and Social Loafing in Technology-Supported Teams: A Perspective on the Theory of Moral Disengagement," *Journal of Management Information Systems,* vol. 27, pp. 203-230.

[2] Barrick, M. R., *et al.*,1993 "Conscientiousness and performance of sales representatives: Test of the mediating effects of goal setting," *Journal of Applied Psychology,* vol. 78, p. 715.

[3] Bolino, M. C., *et al.*,2010 "Citizenship under pressure: What's a "good soldier" to do?," *Journal of Organizational Behavior,* vol. 31, pp. 835-855.

[4] Buffardi, L. E. and Campbell, W. K.,2008 "Narcissism and social networking web sites," *Personality and Social Psychology Bulletin,* vol. 34, pp. 1303-1314.

[5] Butler, B.,2001 "Membership Size, Communication Activity, and Sustainability: A Resource-Based Model of Online Social Structures," *Information Systems Research,* vol. 12, pp. 346-362.

[6] Chen, Y., *et al.*,2009 "Social Comparisons and Contributions to Online Communities: A Field Experiment on MovieLens," *American Economic Review,* vol. 100, pp. 1358-1398.

[7] Chu, W. and Park, S.-T., "Personalized recommendation on dynamic content using predictive bilinear models," presented at the Proceedings of the 18th international conference on World wide web, Madrid, Spain, 2009.

[8] Correa, T., *et al.*,2010 "Who interacts on the Web?: The intersection of users' personality and social media use," *Computers in Human Behavior,* vol. 26, pp. 247-253.

[9] Costa, P. and McCrae, R.,1992 "NEO Personality Inventory–Revised (NEO-PI-R) and NEO Five-Factor Inventory (NEO-FFI) Professional Manual," *Odessa, FL: Psychological Assessment Resources,*

[10] Costa, P. T., *et al.*, *Revised neo personality inventory (neo pi-r) and neo five-factor inventory (neo-ffi)*: Psychological Assessment Resources Odessa, FL, 1992.

[11] Counts, S.,2007 "Group-based mobile messaging in support of the social side of leisure," *Computer Supported Cooperative Work (CSCW),* vol. 16, pp. 75-97.

[12] Dabbish, L., *et al.*, "Fresh faces in the crowd: turnover, identity, and commitment in online groups," presented at the Proceedings of the ACM 2012 conference on Computer Supported Cooperative Work, Seattle, Washington, USA, 2012.

[13] Dabbish, L. and Kraut, R.,2008 "Awareness displays and social motivation for coordinating communication," *Information Systems Research,* vol. 19, pp. 221-238.

[14] Darley, J. M. and Latane, B.,1968 "Bystander intervention in emergencies: diffusion of responsibility," *Journal of Personality and Social psychology,* vol. 8, p. 377.

[15] Ehrhart, M. G., *et al.*,2009 "Testing the latent factor structure and construct validity of the Ten-Item Personality Inventory," *Personality and Individual Differences,* vol. 47, pp. 900-905.

[16] Esteban, J. and Ray, D.,2001 "Collective action and the group size paradox," *American political science review,* vol. 95, pp. 663-672.

[17] Farzan, R., *et al.*, "Increasing commitment to online communities by designing for social presence," in *ACM 2011 Conference on Computer Supported Cooperative Work (CSCW)*, Hangzhou, China, 2011, pp. 321-330.

[18] Felfernig, A., *et al.*, "Personalized user interfaces for product configuration," in *Proceedings of the 15th international conference on Intelligent user interfaces*, Hong Kong, China, 2010, pp. 317-320.

[19] Galitz, W. O., *The essential guide to user interface design: an introduction to GUI design principles and techniques*: Wiley, 2007.

[20] Garcia, S. M., *et al.*,2002 "Crowded minds: The implicit bystander effect," *Journal of Personality and Social psychology,* vol. 83, p. 843.

[21] Gauch, S., *et al.*,2007 "User profiles for personalized information access," *The adaptive web,* pp. 54-89.

[22] Goldberg, L. R.,1993 "The structure of phenotypic personality traits," *American psychologist,* vol. 48, p. 26.

[23] Gosling, S. D., *et al.*,2003 "A very brief measure of the Big-Five personality domains* 1," *Journal of Research in personality,* vol. 37, pp. 504-528.

[24] Grant, A. M.,2008 "The significance of task significance: Job performance effects, relational mechanisms, and boundary conditions," *Journal of Applied Psychology,* vol. 93, p. 108.

[25] Hertel, G., *et al.*,2003 "Motivation of software developers in Open Source projects: an Internet-based survey of contributors to the Linux kernel," *Research Policy,* vol. 32, pp. 1159-1177.

[26] Hoon, H. and Tan, T. M. L.,2008 "Organizational citizenship behavior and social loafing: The role of personality, motives, and contextual factors," *The Journal of psychology,* vol. 142, pp. 89-108.

[27] Johnsen, K., *et al.*, "The validity of a virtual human experience for interpersonal skills education," in *SIGCHI conference on Human factors in computing systems*, 2007, pp. 1049-1058.

[28] Karau, S. J. and Williams, K. D.,1993 "Social Loafing: A Meta-Analytic Review and Theoretical Integration," *Journal of Personality & Social Psychology,* vol. 65, pp. 681-706.

[29] Kraut, R., *et al.*,2010 "Scientific Foundations: A Case for Technology- Mediated Social- Participation Theory," *IEEE Computer,* vol. 43, pp. 22-28.

[30] Ling, K., *et al.*,2005 "Using Social Psychology to Motivate Contributions to Online Communities," *Journal of Computer-Mediated Communication,* vol. 10,

[31] Liu, J., *et al.*, "Personalized news recommendation based on click behavior," presented at the Proceedings of the 15th international conference on Intelligent user interfaces, Hong Kong, China, 2010.

[32] Lou, H., *et al.*,2000 "Perceived critical mass effect on groupware acceptance," *European Journal of Information Systems,* vol. 9, pp. 91-103.

[33] Ludford, P. J., *et al.*, "Think Different: Increasing Online Community Participation Using Uniqueness and Group Dissimilarity," in *ACM SIGCHI Conference on*

Human Factors in Computing Systems, Vienna, Austria, 2004, pp. 631-368.
[34] Markus, M. L.,1987 "Toward a “Critical Mass” Theory of Interactive Media Universal Access, Interdependence and Diffusion," *Communication Research,* vol. 14, pp. 491-511.
[35] McElroy, J. C., *et al.*,2007 "Dispositional factors in internet use: Personality versus cognitive style," *MIS Quarterly,* vol. 31, pp. 809-820.
[36] Nov, O., *et al.*, "Volunteer computing: a model of the factors determining contribution to community-based scientific research," in *Proceedings of the 19th International World Wide Web Conference - WWW 2010.*, 2010, pp. 741-750.
[37] Nov, O., *et al.*, "What drives content tagging: the case of photos on Flickr," in *CHI '08: 26th annual SIGCHI conference on Human factors in computing systems* 2008, pp. 1097-1100.
[38] Nov, O. and Ye, C., "Community photo sharing: Motivational and structural antecedents," in *29th International Conference on Information Systems (ICIS)*, 2008, p. 2009.
[39] Nov, O. and Ye, C., "Personality and technology acceptance: Personal innovativeness in IT, openness and resistance to change," in *41st Annual Hawaii International Conference on System Sciences*, Waikoloa, HI, 2008, pp. 448-448.
[40] Oliver, P. E. and Marwell, G.,1988 "The Paradox of Group Size in Collective Action: A Theory of the Critical Mass. II," *American Sociological Review,* pp. 1-8.
[41] Oreg, S. and Nov, O.,2008 "Exploring motivations for contributing to open source initiatives: The roles of contribution context and personal values," *Computers in Human Behavior,* vol. 24, pp. 2055-2073.
[42] Organ, D. W., *Organizational citizenship behavior: The good soldier syndrome.* Lexington, MA: Lexington Books, 1988.
[43] Organ, D. W.,1994 "Personality and organizational citizenship behavior," *Journal of Management,* vol. 20, pp. 465-478.
[44] Podsakoff, P. M., *et al.*,2000 "Organizational citizenship behaviors: A critical review of the theoretical and empirical literature and suggestions for future research," *Journal of Management,* vol. 26, pp. 513-563.
[45] Preece, J. and Shneiderman, B.,2009 "The Reader-to-Leader Framework: Motivating technology-mediated social participation," *AIS Transactions on Human-Computer Interaction,* vol. 1, pp. 13-32.
[46] Raban, D. R., *et al.*, "An empirical study of critical mass and online community survival," in *ACM 2011 Conference on Computer Supported Cooperative Work (CSCW)*, Savannah, GA, 2010, pp. 71-80.
[47] Ren, Y., *et al.*,2007 "Applying common identity and bond theory to design of online communities," *Organization Studies,* vol. 28, pp. 377-408.
[48] Renn, R. W., *et al.*,2011 "Empirical examination of the individual-level personality-based theory of self-management failure," *Journal of Organizational Behavior,* vol. 32, pp. 25-43.
[49] Roberts, J., *et al.*,2006 "Understanding the Motivations, Participation, and Performance of Open Source Software Developers: A Longitudinal Study of the Apache Projects," *Managenent Science,* vol. 52, pp. 984-999.
[50] Schroer, J. and Hertel, G.,2009 "Voluntary engagement in an open web-based encyclopedia: Wikipedians and why they do it," *Media Psychology,* vol. 12, pp. 96-120.
[51] Seay, A. and Kraut, R., "Project massive: self-regulation and problematic use of online gaming," in *CHI 2007: ACM conference on human factors in computing systems*, 2007, pp. 829-838.
[52] Van Slyke, C., *et al.*,2007 "Perceived critical mass and the adoption of a communication technology," *European Journal of Information Systems,* vol. 16, pp. 270-283.

Photographer Paths: Sequence Alignment of Geotagged Photos for Exploration-based Route Planning

Abdallah El Ali
ISLA, University of Amsterdam
Amsterdam, The Netherlands
a.elali@uva.nl

Sicco N. A. van Sas
University of Amsterdam
Amsterdam, The Netherlands
sicco@ddo.nl

Frank Nack
ISLA, University of Amsterdam
Amsterdam, The Netherlands
nack@uva.nl

ABSTRACT
Urban mobility analysis of geotagged photos can unlock mobility patterns of users who took these photos, which can be used for exploration-based city route planners. Applying sequence alignment techniques on 5 years of geotagged Flickr photos in Amsterdam (The Netherlands) allowed creating walkable city routes based on paths traversed by multiple photographers (or photographer paths). To evaluate our approach, we conducted a user study with Amsterdam residents to compare our routes with the most efficient and popular route variations. Drawing on experience questionnaire data, web survey responses, and user interviews, our results show that our photographer paths were perceived as most stimulating and suitable for city exploration. Moreover, while digital aids based on photographer paths can potentially aid city exploration, their acceptance in mainstream route planners likely depends on their visualization. From our proof-of-concept approach and user study findings, we discuss the potential of data-driven exploration-based city route planners.

Author Keywords
Exploration-based route planning; sequence alignment; geotagged photos; UGC; urban computing

ACM Classification Keywords
H.5.2 Information interfaces and presentation: Theory and methods; H.4 Information Systems Applications

INTRODUCTION
We are not always in a hurry to get from point A to point B. Sometimes we take a longer route because it is more scenic, more interesting, or simply to avoid the mundane [12]. While expert tour guides (e.g., Lonely Planet[1]) tell us what to see and do, they are geared towards recommending destinations and tour guide offers, not generating route plans or journeys. In fact, research has focused extensively on tourism, and replete with how to develop mobile technology (or electronic mobile guides) to support travelers and tourists in 'what to do' [13, 3]. For current route planning services (e.g., Google Maps[2]), the generated routes are tailored towards providing shortest paths between any two locations. However, city pedestrians, whether tourists or locals, may not always want the fastest route – this is strengthened when for example considering the buzz surrounding Foursquare's[3] launch of the Explore functionality that recommends places based on friends' check-ins. In other words, given the right context and time, people do wish to wander into hitherto unfamiliar or unconventional paths. However, there is surprisingly little work in CSCW and geographic HCI [11] that addresses this gap: how can we build city route planners that automatically compute route plans based not on efficiency, but on people's trailing city experiences? Importantly, how do these experiences influence our route preferences and perception of urban spaces?

With the unbridled adoption of location-aware mobile devices that permit geotagging multimedia content, places and routes can now be ubiquitously micro-profiled with geotagged user-generated content. This geotagged data comes from mobile social media services (e.g., Flickr[4], Twitter[5]), and relates to the actions and experiences of thousands of people at different locations. In line with a recent SIG meeting discussing the research opportunities of geographic HCI and the rise and use of User-Generated Content (UGC) [11], we believe this geotagged data can be used not only for revealing the social dynamics and urban flow of cities [15], but also unlock fragments of user intentions and experiences at places and transitions between them. This data can provide a latent source for generating exploration-based routes traversed in a city that are not based on travel efficiency.

In this paper, we focus on sequences of geotagged photos, which we show can allow computing city paths that represent the history of where the photographers of these photos have been. By using this latent information on photographer paths, we believe this unlocks novel application and research avenues for data-driven exploration-based route planners.

RESEARCH QUESTIONS
Our main research question is: how can we *automatically* generate walkable route plans in a city for residents that would like to *explore a city*? Specifically, what existing data sources and which methods can be used to generate such

[1]http://www.lonelyplanet.com/ ; last retrieved: 08-11-2012

[2]http://www.maps.google.com/ ; last retrieved: 08-11-2012
[3]https://foursquare.com/ ; last retrieved: 08-11-2012
[4]http://www.flickr.com/ ; last retrieved: 08-11-2012
[5]http://www.twitter.com/ ; last retrieved: 08-11-2012

routes, and how are these routes perceived in comparison with both the popular and fast routes in a city? While our target user group is city residents (defined as having lived in the city for at least one year), our contributions as will be shown later also apply to tourists who wish to discover off-beat paths when visiting a city.

To define what constitutes an interesting walkable route, we reasoned that the mobility behavior of city photographers tells us something about worthy alternative routes in a city. The underlying assumption here is that locations of photographs are potentially interesting as the photographer(s) found it worthwhile to take a picture there. For this purpose, the image photo-sharing site Flickr provides a suitable data source given that many images are geotagged.[6] Here, we focus on users that do not have any specific interest or do not want to supply this interest and they just want to be given an interesting route from A to B, which we suspect city photographers (be they locals or tourists) can help unravel.

To avoid making the user supply preferences, we wanted to automatically generate routes based on where people traveled within a city. But not every route may be interesting, so we focused on routes made up of locations were people took pictures, given our assumption that taking a picture somewhere depicts an interesting location. One such route made out of photographs from a single photographer is insufficient, so ideally we want multiple photographers that took pictures at the same locations in the same sequence, i.e. took the same route and found similar things photo-worthy along the same locations. Thus, we needed a method that handles not only where photographers have been, but importantly, in what order they have been there and to what extent their movements resemble the movements of other city photographers. To achieve this, we use sequence alignment (SA) methods. These methods are borrowed from bioinformatics and later adapted to time geography to systematically analyze and explore the sequential dimension of human spatial and temporal activity [20]. We hypothesize that the aligned routes traversed by multiple city photographers (or 'photographer paths') provide desirable paths for pedestrians wishing to explore a (familiar) city. Furthermore, while we are concerned with route planning using both mobile devices and desktops, here we focus on pre-trip route plans, which usually involves viewing routes on a desktop.

Our work yields two main research contributions: a) a novel data-driven methodology for generating walkable route plans based on photographers' paths in a city and b) an empirical understanding (based on quantitative and qualitative assessments) of how users perceive these photographer paths in comparison with today's efficiency driven route planners and popular routes. Additionally, we provide a preliminary investigation on the role that digital information aids on a map (e.g., Points-of-Interest (POIs), photos, comments, etc.) play in influencing people's decisions about which route to take for exploring a city.

[6]Around 520,00 geotagged photos tagged with 'Interesting' in Amsterdam alone (retrieved on 30-05-2012).

The rest of the paper is structured as follows: we give a review of related work, followed by our Photographer Paths approach and alignment experiments. We then present a user study (consisting of a lab and web-based study) to evaluate the different route plans and importance of digital information aids in influencing users' perception of city routes. We then present and discuss our results, future work and conclude.

RELATED WORK

Given our interest in both generating and consuming UGC-generated routes, this paper draws from various related work, including time geography, urban modeling techniques, and importantly route planners.

Time Geography

Time geography dates back to Hägerstrand [9], who stressed the importance of taking into account temporal factors in spatial human activities. This gave rise to a space-time path visualization which shows the movement of an individual graphically in the spatial-temporal environment when one collapses the 3D space and uses perpendicular direction on a 2D map to represent time.

Essentially, time geography seeks to analyze patterns of human activity using space-time paths in an objective, structural manner (e.g., aligning sequences of activities by visitors to the Old City of Akko [20]). The idea behind this is to visualize human movement and interactions between individuals on a 2-D plane where the x- and y- axis represent geographic coordinates (longitude and latitude, respectively) and the z-axis represents time. This so-called space-time "aquarium" is used for analysis and evaluation of social dynamics and activity distribution across space and time. This is useful for analysis of aligned sequences of human activity, where the activity of concern here is the photo-taking behavior by photographers of the geotagged images retrieved from the Flickr photo-sharing site. In short, we use these representational methods to analyze sequences of photo-taking activities, where we later use alignments for generating walkable city routes based on these photographer paths.

Photo-based City Modeling

Given the iconic correspondence between photographs and reality, we believe photo sharing services like Flickr provide a window into the unique perspectives of city photographers. If we consider Flickr photo features, thousands of photos shared by photographers come contextualized with textual user-defined tags and descriptions, geotags (latitudes and longitude coordinates), and time-stamps (date and time of day).

[21] used the varied photos taken by multiple photographers of the same scene along a path as controls for image-based rendering, allowing automatic computation of orbits, panoramas, canonical views, and optimal paths between 3D scene views. Relatedly, [23] used a game-based crowdsourcing approach to constructing 3D building models, based on contributions from a community of photographers around the world. In this work however, we are not concerned with 3D

scene views (e.g., Google Street View[7]), only with the generation and perception of route plans plotted on a 2D map.

Using Flickr data alone, computational approaches have been developed to understand tourist site attractiveness based on geotagged photos [8], constructing travel itineraries [7] and landmark-based travel route recommendations [16], and generating personalized Point-of-Interest (POI) recommendations based on the user's travel history in other cities [6]. All these approaches however focus primarily on describing locations and/or landmarks at these locations, and not on within-city routes that connect them irrespective of popular landmarks. Closer to the present approach, [18] mine sequences of locations from Flickr geotags – however, their focus is on recommending the most popular tourist places in a city.

Non-efficiency Driven Route Planners

Relevant here is whether there is work on route planners that go beyond finding routes that optimize commute efficiency. [17] developed a system to automatically generate travel plans based on millions of geotagged photos and travelogues, which was tailored towards providing city tourists with popular attractions/landmarks and popular routes between them. Relatedly, [4] mined people's attributes from photos to provide personalized travel route recommendations; however, their method was aimed at finding personalized hotspots, not for exploring off-beat paths in a city.

[1] categorized travel trips from people based on geotagged images taken and the accompanying tags and photo titles, allowing development of an application for searching frequent trip patterns. While the goal here was catering for users that wish to learn more about the most frequently visited places in a city, we are interested in automatically computing route plans for exploring a city based on sequences of photographers' movements. Relatedly, [12] present a method comprising a user survey and subsequent clustering analysis to classify route selection criteria for bicyclists. Here, they found that bicyclists most favored fast and safe routes, followed by simple and attractive ones in an urban environment. Finally, using a crowdsourcing approach, [26] developed the Mobi system which allows people to collaboratively create and edit itinerary plans in cities, thus showing the merits of human computation tasks to provide rich plans. In our work however, we try to automate the process of providing exploration-based route plans in a city.

PHOTOGRAPHER PATHS

Approach: MSA of Arbitrarily Long Sequences

To align the geotagged photos, we used the ClustalTXY [25] alignment software. ClustalTXY is suitable for social science research, as it makes full use of multiple pairwise alignments, where alignments are computed for similarity in parallel – in other words, it makes use of a progressive heuristic to apply multiple sequence alignment (MSA) [25]. Furthermore, ClustalTXY allows representing up to 12-character words, which allows us to uniquely represent small map regions containing the geotagged photos.

[7]www.google.com/streetview/ ; last retrieved: 08-11-2012

MSA is done in 3 stages: first, pairwise alignments are computed for all sequences. Then these aligned sequences are grouped together in a dendogram based on similarity. Finally, the dendogram is used as a guide for multiple alignment. To deal with differences in sequence length, ClustalTXY adds gap openings and extensions to sequences. Opening is the process of adding a gap between two previously gapless words and extension is the process of adding another gap in between two words which already had a gap.

Throughout the paper, 'words' are synonymous with 'locations' and 'nodes', where a given term is used depending on the context of discussion. The more aligned sequences that contain the same words, the more popular is a particular word. Thus, the most interesting sequences are distilled by finding matching sequences of popular words in the alignment results. In our approach, we map each location in a sequence to a cell in a partitioned grid map where each cell corresponds to an indexed location unit (e.g., 125 x 125 m cell). For example, a route containing 5 locations would thus be `BcEtSgQlQn`, where `Bc` constitutes the first word (i.e., a location). Furthermore, all repeated words were trimmed down to one (e.g., `FyEjEjEjYfWyFs` would become `FyEjYfWyFs`). We use a simple grid-based approach instead of a mean-shift clustering approach (cf., [5]) in order to allow for locations photographers visited that may not otherwise contain many data points. We then apply MSA to the photographer routes (consisting of sequences of their photos' locations) to find the aligned location sequences. These are used for selecting matching segments of sequences across photographers – we call these exact matches *photographer route segments* (PRSs).

Dataset

We used the Flickr API to retrieve geotagged photos within Amsterdam, The Netherlands (17.3 km N-S and 24.7 km E-W)[8] over a 5-year period (Jan. 2006 - Dec. 2010), with the following attributes: owner ID, photo ID, date and timestamp, tags, latitude, longitude and the accuracy of the coordinate. This resulted in a database of 426,372 photos.

Preprocessing

We included in our database only photos with geo-coordinates with near-street accuracy or better (accuracy 14-16 in Flickr attributes). We inferred the sequences taken by photographers from the time and geotags of their photos. Each photo in the sequence had to be taken within 4 hours from the previous photo. Sequences were constrained to having at least two or more different locations (or nodes), where each location corresponds to a cell on the grid. Given early experiments, we used a grid cell size of 125 x 125 m. We also now focused our grid on the city center of Amsterdam as most routes were in this area and this would speed up alignment computation. The city center could be described using a grid of 26 by 26 cells, so 2-letter words were sufficient. These steps resulted in a dataset of 1691 routes, which had an average length of 9.92 words (min = 2, max = 124). There were

[8]The area is based on the Amsterdam region as currently defined in the Flickr API (bounding box: 4.7572, 52.3178, 5.0320, 52.4281; centroid: 4.8932, 52.3731).

1130 unique photographers, where on average each photographer contributed 1.50 routes to the dataset.

Sequence Alignment

Main parameters in MSA are gap opening and extension values. In bioinformatics these values correspond to a penalty for splitting a DNA or protein sequence, which needs to be restricted in order to retain informative groups of sequences of nucleotides or amino acids. In our case this analogy does not hold and we want to match as many words as possible, therefore we set both values to 0. Alignment for this 125m dataset took approximately 7 hours on a single core server.

To find photographers paths from PRSs, we set constraints for selecting PRSs having *at least 4* photographers having *at least* 2 aligned nodes (or locations/words). This choice was motivated by the resulting PRSs from our 5-year dataset (see Fig. 1), where having more photographers per route segment took precedence over number of locations (or nodes). These 2 or more aligned nodes form the PRSs. Photographers could have made different photos in between nodes, but they must have visited the locations in the same order and within 4 hours between each visited location. After applying these constraints, we had 231 PRSs (visualized in Fig. 2) with an average length of 2.61 nodes and a maximum PRS length of 4 nodes.

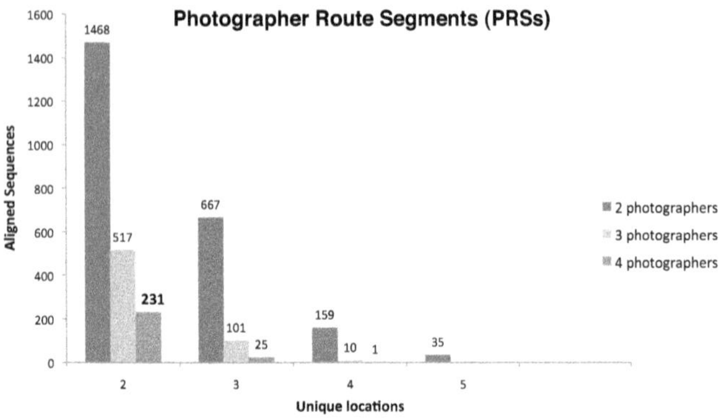

Figure 1. Aligned sequences (PRSs) in Amsterdam over a 5-year period for different numbers of unique photographers and locations. Our PRS set choice value ('231 sequences') is shown in bold.

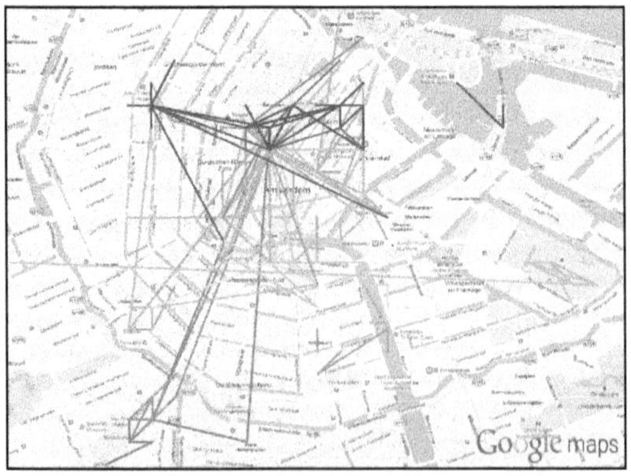

Figure 2. 231 PRSs of alignments of 4 photographers and 2 unique locations in Amsterdam city center. ***Best seen in color.***

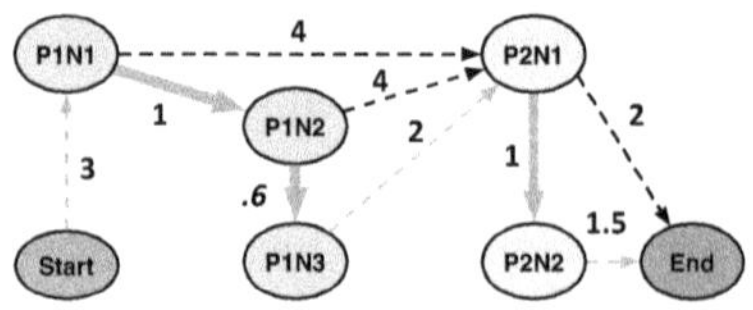

Figure 3. Example of PRS aggregation. 'P1N2' stands for node 2 of PRS 1. Numbers indicate inter-node distance. ***Best seen in color.***

PRS Aggregation

Next step was to develop a method which uses these PRSs to generate routes from a given start location to a user specified destination. We used an implementation of Dijkstra's shortest path algorithm[9] to find the shortest route along the PRSs. Recall that a PRS is a transition between two or more locations/nodes based on sequences of at least 4 photographers, where a PRS is calculated from the aligned sequences of the ClustalTXY alignment.

Dijkstra's algorithm requires a network of edges between nodes, with a specified cost for traversing each edge. We thus had to specify how our PRSs would both connect within themselves and to each other. Every edge cost is set to the distance between the nodes. However, if all nodes were to be connected with each other, then Dijkstra's algorithm would simply output the direct connection between the start node and the end node as a route, so we set a maximum distance for edges between and within PRSs. Dijkstra's algorithm finds the shortest path between nodes, but we wanted to steer the algorithm to make use of as many transitions between nodes within each PRS as possible, even if this meant a detour, because these transitions are more representative of the actual paths of photographers. To solve this, we required that at least two nodes were used in each PRS, thus at least one edge within a PRS is always used. After this hard constraint, Dijkstra's algorithm connects a PRS to another PRS, because using a third node within the original PRS will usually result in a longer route. The final route would thus be made out of PRSs where only two nodes within each PRS are used. To maximize the number of nodes within each PRS, we gave discounts [range 0-1] to the distances of every edge (beyond the first edge) used within a PRS, forcing Dijkstra's algorithm to incorporate extra edges within the PRS.

A simplified PRS aggregation task using these methods is shown in Fig. 3. The thick solid lines show the edges between the nodes within PRSs, while the thin dashed lines show the connections between the PRSs and the user specified start and end nodes. Dijkstras algorithm would normally find the following shortest path Start-P1N1-P2N1-End with a cost of 9, but due to the constraint of at least two nodes per PRS and the discounted edge cost (0.6 (cost) * 1 (original weight) = 0.6; shown in italics) between P1N2-P1N3, a different route is selected. The recommended route (green edges or Start-P1N1-P1N2-P1N3-P2N1-P2N2-End) will now make use of all the PRS edges.

We applied this algorithm on our chosen PRS set (4 photographers, 2 locations), to create two different photographer

[9]http://code.activestate.com/recipes/119466-dijkstras-algorithm-for-shortest-paths/ ; last retrieved: 08-11-2012

routes in the city center of Amsterdam: one made up of 9 PRSs with 11 total connections (where black route segments are gaps filled for completing the route), that runs from Central Station to Museumplein (CM). The other was made up of 4 PRSs with 6 total connections (again black route segments are route gaps filled), and runs from Waterlooplein to Westerkerk (WW). These routes are visualized in Fig. 4.

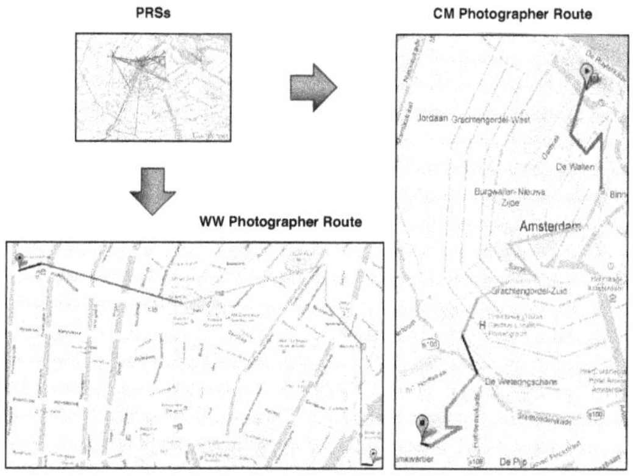

Figure 4. Our chosen PRS set after applying the modified Dijkstra's algorithm resulted in two 'crude' photographer routes (where individual PRSs are color coded): a) Central Station to Museumplein (CM) route b) Waterlooplein to Westerkerk (WW) route. ***Best seen in color.***

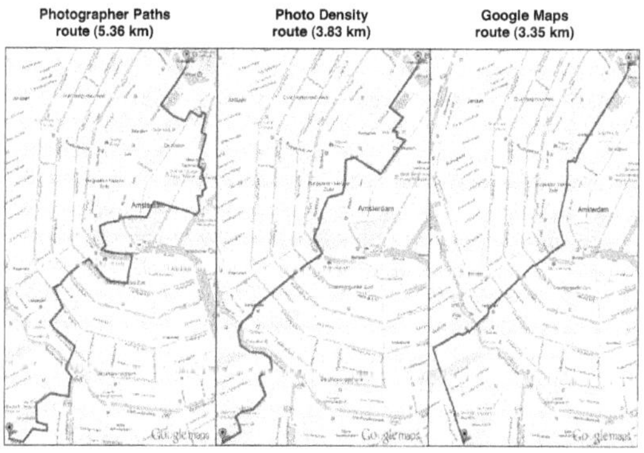

Figure 5. Visual comparison of the generated routes from Central Station to Museumplein. ***Best seen in color.***

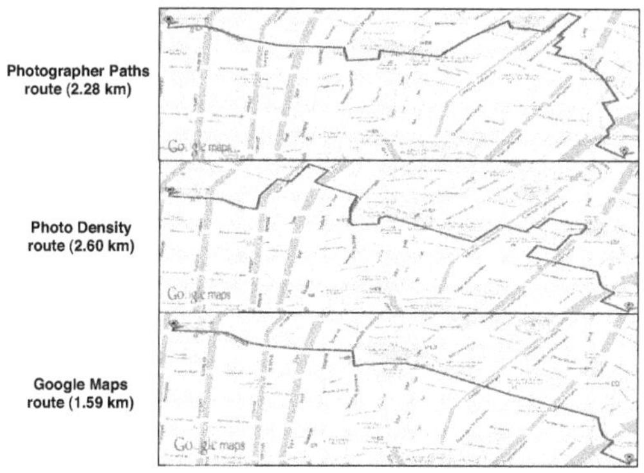

Figure 6. Visual comparison of the generated routes from Waterlooplein to Westerkerk. ***Best seen in color.***

Results

To turn the 'crude' photographer routes given by our adapted Dijkstra's algorithm into walkable routes, these routes were mapped to a Google Maps map where we took the shortest walking distance between each route node (or location). This resulted in walkable photographer paths. The Photographer Paths (PP), Photograph Density (PD), and Google Maps (GM) route variations for our chosen two routes, Central Station to Museumplein (CM) and Waterlooplein to Westerkerk (WW) route are shown in Fig. 5 and Fig. 6, respectively. Explanation and motivation for the PD and GM route variations is given below.

USER EVALUATION

Laboratory-based study

Study Design

We wanted to evaluate whether our Photographer Paths (PP) route variations are indeed preferred by users for exploration-based route planning. While previous work (e.g., [14]) addressed how to evaluate the usability of electronic mobile guides (which may include route planners), there are no established standards on how to best evaluate a service that provides alternative walkable city routes from a human-centered perspective, especially since POI selection accuracy and routing efficiency are not suitable measures for the desirability of the service. However there is work that addresses similar problems. [19] evaluated location-based stories generated automatically from Wikipedia[10] by making use of a Likert-type questionnaire. [22] evaluated their mobile guide in a cultural heritage setting by means of participant observation, questionnaires, and semi-structured interviews. [16] used a quantitative approach where they compared their photographer behavior model against three probabilistic models to account for the accuracy of their personalized route recommendations.

To evaluate whether our route variations are perceived by users as desirable alternatives to current efficiency-based route planners, we chose a user-centered mixed-methods approach that includes both quantitative and qualitative measures. While our target user group included both city residents and tourists, here we focus on expert evaluations from city residents. To test whether our approach provides not just a novel method for generating routes, but routes that city residents would rate as preferable for an exploration scenario, we chose to compare our generated route variation with two other route variations that have a similar start and end destination. Our baseline comparison was a route based on the density of photographs taken per grid cell, where we assumed that this would provide a route plan through the most touristic hotspots within Amsterdam. This was chosen instead of a route that connects a density of all POIs as a POI-density based route would require further differentiating between the kinds of POIs, which is not the aim of a route planner that generates routes automatically without requesting user preferences. For each scenario, participants (who were city residents) had to evaluate the routes in Amsterdam.

Two routes were tested, each with 3 variations: Photographer Paths (PP) route, a Photo Density (PD) variation as baseline,

[10]http://www.wikipedia.org/ ; last retrieved: 08-11-2012

and a Google Maps (GM) efficiency-based route variation. For each route, participants were given scenarios. For the first scenario, participants had to imagine being in the company of local friends on a sunny Saturday between 14-15:00 o'clock, where they wished to walk from Central Station to Museumplein (CM route). For the second scenario, participants had to imagine being in the company of a friend (a local) on a cloudy, Sunday evening between 19-20:00, where this friend just returned from a vacation and they now wished to catch up at a café near Westerkerk (WW route). While both scenarios emphasized there was time to spare, we expected participants to favor efficiency in the WW route.

PD route was created by drawing a path between grid cells containing the highest density of geotagged photos taken in Amsterdam in 5 years, for the hour corresponding to each scenario given to participants (14-15:00 and 19-20:00, respectively). The restriction by hour was set so paths between cells remains meaningful, as plotting a 5-year dataset of geopoints makes it difficult to differentiate between choosing one cell over another. This route served as a popular and touristic route baseline by which to measure our PP route against.

We set up a within-subjects experimental design, where route variation is the independent variable, and measured dependent variables are: a) perceived quality of the presented route variations for each route (CM and WW) b) participants' route preferences and c) subjective reports on what they thought about the generated routes. To measure perceived quality of the route variations, we adapted the AttrakDiff2™ [10] questionnaire[11] so that participants can reflect on the presented routes and give us a quantitative measure of the hedonic and pragmatic aspects of each route variation. AttrakDiff2 measures pragmatic and hedonic qualities by allowing participants to provide ratings on a 7-point semantic differential scale for 28 attributes[12], resulting in 4 quality dimensions: 1) Pragmatic Quality (PQ), which measures usability of a product (or in our case routes). Here, PQ gives insight into how well users can achieve their goal given each route 2) Hedonic Quality - Identification (HQ-I), which gives insight into the extent that users can identify with a given route 3) Hedonic Quality - Stimulation (HQ-S), which gives insight into the extent that a route stimulates users with novelty and enables personal growth 4) Attractiveness (ATT), which provides a global value and quality perception of a route, or in other words, perceived attractiveness.

To get further insight into participants' perception of the route variations, we had a two part semi-structured interview at the end of each testing session, where users could give their feedback directly on their route preferences and inform us what information types they find valuable in deciding whether or not a route affords exploration. For the first part, participants were asked to give their opinion on which route variation they preferred for each route, and what they thought about routes based on photographer paths. In the second part of the interview, they were provided with examples of different digital information aids and asked which (or a combination of) they found useful for exploring a city. These were: a plain Google Maps route, Foursquare POIs (that include short textual comments left by others) along a route, a route with Flickr photos, our PP route segments (made up of PRSs) that shows via color coding the different route segments that make up the photographer paths (see Fig. 4), and a route showing multiple photo geopoints (i.e., PD route). Finally, they were asked about the applied potential of this kind of route planning service.

The need to investigate information types (even if not the primary aim of our study) relates to the need for transparency and intelligibility in ubiquitous computing systems [24]. On one hand, to make a fair user perception comparison between routes generated by route planners means that further information cannot be provided on a route variation. This is because we risk comparing the effects of information type on route preference, and not the quality of the route itself. On the other hand, in an actual route planner system, users should be given the option to understand 'why' a given route is generated, which is why we had to simultaneously investigate digital information aids in different kinds of media.

Participants

15 participants (10 male, 5 female) aged between 21-35 (M_{age} = 29.2; SD_{age}= 3.3) were recruited. Only participants who had lived in Amsterdam for at least one year were recruited, to ensure that they were able to adequately judge the presented route variations. Our participant sample spanned 9 different nationalities. Most participants claimed to know Amsterdam fairly well (10/15), where the rest knew it either very well (2/15) or just average (3/15). Many (10/15) had a technical background (e.g., Computer Science), and all were familiar with route planning services, where most (10/15) reported using route planners at least once a week.

Prototype, Setup & Procedure

To test the route variations, an interactive web-based prototype route planner interface was shown to each participant. The interface was adaptable to mobile devices, but testing route preferences on a mobile device was not important as participants were selecting a route based on pre-trip preferences, which usually involves viewing routes on a desktop. The study was conducted at the User Experience lab at XYZ university. Each session took approximately 45 min. to complete. To facilitate discussion and eventual consensus regarding our interview questions amongst participants, participants were interviewed in groups of three. For the first part of the study, each participant was seated in front of a laptop, where they each interacted (zooming, panning) with the route planner interface. For the interview, participants were allowed and encouraged to discuss and answer the questions in a collaborative manner.

Before the study session, each participant filled a background information form, signed an informed consent form, and read through detailed instructions for performing the task. In each task, a participant had to inspect 3 route variations (PP, PD,

[11] AttrakDiff2™ is a questionnaire originally developed to measure the perceived attractiveness of interactive products based on hedonic and pragmatic qualities. However, the measured bipolar qualities that apply to interactive products can also apply to city routes, making for a suitable domain generalization.

[12] Only one attribute-pair was changed to fit our study: Technical-Human was replaced with Slower-Faster for the PQ dimension.

GM) for each route (CM, WW). The order of presentation of both routes and route variations were counterbalanced and then randomized (after first presented variation) across participants. After inspecting each route variation, a participant had to fill in the 'same' adapted AttrakDiff2™ questionnaire, marking their responses with the corresponding route variation number so their responses where relative to one another. Participants were asked to give their first, spontaneous response. After all three participants finished inspecting all route variations, they were given the semi-structured interview. After the interview, each participant was offered a small monetary reward and thanked for their time.

Web Survey

To test if there is an immediate difference between the generated route variations (PP, PD, and GM), we constructed a short web-based survey to compare each of the route variations for the CM and WW routes. This survey was meant to be short and easy to fill, and to provide a rough idea of whether people consider route plans based on alternative city routes useful, and to collect data on what they find useful digital information aids for exploration. Basic demographic information (age, gender, years in Amsterdam, familiarity with route planners) was asked, and thereafter participants had to choose which route variations they would follow given our two respective scenarios (as in the lab-based study). Here however, there were two main differences to the lab study: a) maps showing each route were static images, and so participants could not zoom in on a location and b) all routes and route variations were shown on a single screen, so order effects were not accounted for.

For the survey, 82 participants (55 male, 27 female) aged between 17-62 (M_{age}= 27.6; SD_{age}= 6.1) responded. Most (44/82) lived in Amsterdam for more than 3 years, some (15/82) between 1-3 years, and the rest either less than a year (11/82) or only visited Amsterdam before (12/82). All were familiar with route planners and GPS-based systems. All participants were considered here, as we were interested in immediate reactions to the presented variations and questions about digital information aids.

Results

Perceived Route Quality

Responses on the modified AttrakDiff2 in the lab study were analyzed within groups, per generated route. For each category, one-way repeated measures ANOVA tests were conducted comparing results from all route variations. Means, standard deviations, confidence intervals, significance, and (partial) eta-squared values for each tested route variation for each route (CM and WW) are shown in Table 1. For the CM route, a repeated measures ANOVA showed significant differences in the responses across quality dimensions for only PQ, HQ-S, and ATT. For the WW route, a repeated measures ANOVA showed significant differences in the responses across quality dimensions for only PQ and HQ-S. Post-hoc pairwise comparisons (with Bonferroni correction[13]) between each variation (PP, PD, GM) were conducted in every case.

[13]Backward-corrected SPSS© Bonferroni adjusted p-values are reported.

	Dimension	Route Variation	M	SD	CI	P-value	η^2_p
CM Route	**PQ**	**PP**	-1.5	.1	[-2,-1]	**p<.001**	
		PD	.4	1.0	[-.1,.9]	$F(2,28) = 38.9$	.7
		GM	1.7	1.1	[1.2,2.2]		
	HQ-I	PP	.5	.8	[.1,.9]	p = .262	
		PD	.4	.7	[.04,.7]	$F(2,28) = 1.4$	.1
		GM	-.01	.9	[-.5,.4]		
	HQ-S	**PP**	1.2	.8	[.8,1.6]	**p<.001**	
		PD	.2	.9	[.1,.3]	$F(1.3,19.4) = 21.3$	.6
		GM	-1.1	1.1	[-1.7,-.6]	(corr. G-G ϵ= .69)	
	ATT	***PP***	.9	1.2	[.4,1.6]	**p<.05**	
		PD	.8	1.0	[.3,1.3]	$F(2,28) = 4.8$	.2
		GM	-.4	1.4	[-1,.3]		
WW Route	**PQ**	***PP***	-.9	1.4	[-1.6,-.2]	**p<0.01**	
		PD	-1	1.2	[-1.6,-.4]	$F(2,28)$	.7
		GM	2.3	.9	[1.9,2.8]	= 38.18	
	HQ-I	PP	.1	.6	[-.2,.4]	p = .591	
		PD	.3	.5	[.05,.5]	$F(2,28) = .5$	.04
		GM	.3	.7	[-.01,.7]		
	HQ-S	***PP***	.5	1.0	[-.01,1]	**p<.001**	
		PD	.7	.9	[.2,1.3]	$F(2,28) = 17.3$	.5
		GM	-1.4	1.1	[-2,-.9]		
	ATT	PP	.3	1.1	[-.3,.8]	p = .877	
		PD	.3	1.0	[-.2,.9]	$F(2,28) = 1.3$	.01
		GM	.5	1.0	[-.04,1]		

Table 1. Descriptive statistics (N=15) for each route variation (PP, PD, GM) under each tested route (CM and WW) for each AttrakDiff2 dimension: PQ = Pragmatic Quality, HQ-I: Hedonic Quality-Identity, HQ-S: Hedonic Quality-Stimulation, ATT: Attractiveness.

Where significant, dimensions are represented in bold, and where a particular pairwise comparison is not significant, the dimensions are in (additional) italics.

For the CM route, participants perceived clear differences across all route variations for the PQ. It is not surprising that the GM variation scored the highest here, given that the route is based on efficiency. Nor is it surprising that our PP variation scored the lowest, given the length of the route. However, it is surprising to see that the PD variation significantly differed from both the PP and GM variation, as it is close in length to the GM variation, yet still considered not pragmatic. This can be partially explained by the fact that the PD route variation runs through all the heavily touristic areas, which may not be very practical to take. For the PP and PD variations, responses for HQ-I were around zero, however there were no significant differences between any of the variations. This suggests that all participants identified with the route variations similarly, but perhaps overall it may be that those variations were not ones that our sample of participants identified with.

For the HQ-S, there were significant differences between all tested route variations, where our PP variation scored the highest. This finding is in line with our hypothesis that photographer paths can provide a stimulating and novel route variation in a city. The mean responses for the PD variation are around zero, which shows that for our participants who are living in Amsterdam, the popular aspect of the PD variation was not stimulating (but nor was it found to be as completely dull and boring as the GM route). Finally, there were significant differences in ATT between PP and GM and between PD and GM route variations, however not between PP and PD. The fastest GM variation was rated the lowest. Here, we would have expected our PP variation to be rated higher than the PD variation, however it could be that participants found the PD variation attractive depending on the company they are with (given the scenario); as they later mention in the interviews, they could be with touristic friends in which case they would find the popular route variations more attractive for the sake of tourism.

For the WW route, participants perceived clear differences for the PQ dimension between the GM route variation and both our PP variation and the PD variation. The GM route variation was not surprisingly rated as the most pragmatic, however here the PD variation was on par with our PP variation. For the HQ-I, there were again no significant differences between any of the route variations, were all responses had a mean around zero. This again suggests that identifying with the generated routes was not important for our participants. For the HQ-S, the GM variation was again rated the lowest, however this time there were no significant differences between our PP variation and the PD variation. This was likely due to the overall short distance between Waterlooplein and Westerkerk, where little room was left for identifying stimulating qualities of the routes. Importantly, in line with the scenario, participants here did not value stimulating qualities of the route variations, as one going to a café with a friend back from vacation on a cloudy day is not a situation that affords a stimulating route variation. This is further confirmed by considering the ATT dimension, where the GM route variation was now rated higher than it was for the CM variation, which indicates that participants valued the short distance for the GM variation. However, given that there were again no significant differences, it seems to still be that all route variations are attractive enough to take, even under efficiency-driven scenarios.

Route Preference

All but one participant in the lab study found the scenarios quite realistic. The one participant objected that it would have been clearer if the gender of friends in the scenarios was given. In the lab-based study, after inspecting all route variations for each route, participants were asked which variation they would follow (if any) and why (convenient, interesting, scenic, or other response). For the CM route, most participants (9/15) chose to follow our PP route variation, where the rest picked the PD (4/15) and GM (2/15) variations. For all cases where participants picked the PP variation, they stated it was more scenic. This is in line with our hypothesis that the PP variation provides a favorable route to take in a city one has time to explore. During the interviews, participants mentioned that they found the PP variation attractive and suitable for the scenario (P3: *"I liked the second route variation [PP] given it was nice weather so perfect for exploration."*; P12: *"One of the routes [PP] was long and took many detours, and I thought that was a very attractive route!"*).

Also some reported that the PD route variation (as well as the GM variant) to be very touristic, which they did not like (P5: *"I would obviously not go through the Kalverstraat as it is very touristic.. the first [GM] and last [PD] route took me through there, and I think that is not really Amsterdam."*). Still, others found the PP route too long (P10: *"I thought the [PP] route was too long, my feet would fall off!"*) and preferred something in the middle between the PP and GM variations (P14: *"If I want to see the city, I would go for the [PD] one."*). In the web survey, most participants said they would follow the GM route (40/82), followed by the PD route (23/82) and the PP route (10/82), where the rest chose neither (9/82). The difference in findings here can be explained either because participants did not inspect the routes carefully or take the scenarios seriously, or perhaps more likely those that lived in Amsterdam already knew their own specific routes, which they take by commuting by bicycle and largely avoiding touristic areas (where both PP and PD route variations pass through). Unlike the lab study, the experimenter could not steer participants to stick with the scenario – this was evident by most comments left in the free-form box form (e.g., *"I would not easily walk these routes... who in amsterdam walks? ;)"*; *"I would use cycling routes."*). Nevertheless, they highlight that alternative route plans may take time to be accepted as city exploration aids (alongside routes suggested by expert travel guides) in both familiar and unfamiliar cities.

For the WW route, most participants (10/15) in the lab study favored the GM route variation, followed by the PD variation (4/15) and in one case neither one. For all participants that picked GM, they stated it was more convenient. This was not surprising under the WW scenario, where it was a cloudy evening and meeting a friend returning from a vacation. Indeed, later in the interviews this was mentioned explicitly (P3: *"You are going for coffee so you just want to get there, unlike in the first [CM] scenario where it is a nice day and you have time."*). Here, it was also mentioned that our PP route variation and PD both went off to the Red Light District, which may not be desirable for them (P11: *"Second [GM] route was very simple and straightforward... Red light part is more interesting for tourists."*). In the web survey, most participants said they would follow the GM route (67/82), followed by the PD route (6/82) and the PP route (3/82), where the rest chose neither (6/82). Favoring the GM variation for the WW scenario is in line with the findings of the lab-based study.

Digital Information Aids for City Exploration

During the post-test interview, participants were asked about digital information aids they would find useful when deciding to take a route in a city for exploration purposes. They were asked explicitly about what they thought about information that tells you how many persons (particularly city photographers) took a given route segment over a certain time period (e.g., 1 year). Around half (8/15) found such information useful for exploring a city one already knows, some where not quite sure (4/15), some thought it depended on who those photographers were (2/15), and one thought this is not something for him. In the second part of the interview (after participants saw examples of different digital information aids), many (10/15) found our PP information type attractive (e.g., P4: *"Nice to find corners that I don't really know."*). This was visualized by coloring the different segments of a route on a map and stating how many photographers took a segment over time (for us, 4 photographers through 2 locations over a 5 year period). However, many of those participants

(6/10) also stated that they would combine this information with photos (3/6) and POIs (3/6). While some mentioned that the PP information is useful for exploring a familiar city (P8: *"[PP] information is useful if you are familiar with the city."*), still others thought it redundant (P3: *"Hard to see why I'd use a map in a city I already know."*).

In the web survey, we gained further insight into what digital aids people find useful in helping them explore a city. These are (ordered by count of mentions): POIs along a route (51x), route distance (51x), comments along a route (ranked by highest ratings or recency) (24x), expert travel guides (22x), photos of route segments (17x), no digital aids (13x), number of photographers that took a given path over a time period (9x), number of photos along a route over a time period (9x). While we expected that established aids such as POIs and distance are useful indicators for planning personal routes, it was surprising that there were only few reports of the usefulness of photographer paths to guide exploring a city. This was also evident with photo counts along a route, which is also a novel information aid. This may be because participants are not familiar with such novel aids, especially since in the web survey (to avoid biasing route preference and save time), they were not provided with visualizations of how this information may be visualized. Considering the findings of the lab-study and web survey, it seems that photographer paths as city exploration aids have potential, but stating it without visualizing how it could intelligibly augment an alternative route plan (as was done in the lab-based study) may have influenced its immediate adoption by participants in the web study.

Use of Non-Efficiency Driven Route Planners

Finally, participants were asked what they thought about future route planning applications that generate alternative walkable routes in a city, both locally and abroad, and whether they would use them. Most participants (13/15) were positive about such applications (P7: *"Yes. Helps you to explore more and discover different things, gives you another option."*; P4: *"Yes, especially for a specific corner of a city."*), where the remaining two brought to question why they would use such apps in a city they already knew (P12: *"I would like it more for a city that I don't already know."*; P14: *"Google Maps is enough."*). Responses on what these route planners should be based included: personalized route plans (e.g., in accordance with route travel history) and preset route plans (e.g., museum route, market route, etc.). Together, the responses from participants highlight that a new generation of route planners aimed for exploring cities is desirable.

DISCUSSION

Study Limitations

In this paper, we have presented a novel approach based on sequence alignment methods to generate exploration-based route plans in a small-sized city like Amsterdam. Our lab-based user test provided strong evidence that our generated route plans are of potential interest to city dwellers especially by way of hedonic stimulation, under an exploration-based scenario. However, while most participants mentioned they would follow our PP route variation in the CM scenario, this was not the case for the web survey. This brought to question not only whether such a quick survey was able to sufficiently provoke reflection on the given scenarios and routes, but also that alternative city route plans may not be immediately accepted by both locals and visitors to a city. Furthermore, without providing intelligible explanations (cf., [24]) as was done in the lab-study (visualizing the digital aids on the generated route plans) for why a route was given may have made it difficult for potential users to make an informed judgment.

Another limitation is the real-world evaluation of the generated routes. While we have tried to tease out the differences between each route on participants' route preferences in a lab-based and web-based study, we may not immediately generalize to how participants would react to such routes if used in real-time in an actual situation with a working prototype. A related issue is that the number of route variations presented is limited to two, where participants' reactions may differ in such cases. Nevertheless, the findings from the lab-study provide strong evidence that photographer paths have potential for generating desirable route plans in the city, and importantly highlight the merits of an automatic data-driven approach based on geotagged photographs in a city.

Towards Automatic Exploration-based Route Planners

We started from the question of how human sequential movement patterns can be leveraged as an indicator of interest, and attempted to answer this by relying on a data-driven approach that borrows SA methods from bioinformatics and time geography. Our approach goes against the established human-centered literature on catering for user needs, where typical mobile recommender studies (e.g., [2]) begin with distilling requirements from observing and interacting with users. Here, it can be argued that such a quantitative approach may drastically oversimplify our human needs for exploring a city. However, we wanted to compute routes based on paths taken by photographers in a city *automatically*, without burdening the user to tell us her desires.

Under the foregoing motivation, we have created an opportunity to consider a currently unused information type obtained from geotagged images to guide exploration-based route planning in a city: the number of city photographers that took a given route segment over a certain time period. With this proof-of-concept approach, we have shown it is possible to leverage social geotagged data to cater for the hard problem of automatically generating exploration-based route plans.

FUTURE WORK & CONCLUSIONS

Future work should take the work presented here into the real-world, where a functional prototype that generates photographer paths can be deployed in situ on a large-scale. This would allow (crowdsourced) data collection on more route variations than the ones considered here, and allow for grid cell sizes that are determined by the size of the considered street network (and not fixed to a size like 125 x 125m as considered here). The resulting bigger sample size would better support the alignment-based method presented, and the merits of data-driven exploration-based route planners in general.

In this paper, we have presented a proof-of-concept approach that uses sequence alignment methods and the digital footprints of city photographers (obtained through Flickr) to compute exploration-based route plans within a small-sized city like Amsterdam. From our user study with Amsterdam residents, we found that our photographer paths are promising for city exploration. We hope to have set the stage for further experimentation with data-driven approaches to tackle the hard problem of automatically generating 'interesting' route plans for exploring both familiar and unfamiliar cities.

ACKNOWLEDGEMENTS

Authors thank Eurostar (E5262) SmartInside Project for its support.

REFERENCES

1. Arase, Y., Xie, X., Hara, T., and Nishio, S. Mining people's trips from large scale geo-tagged photos. In *Proc. MM '10*, ACM (2010), 133–142.
2. Bellotti, V., Begole, B., Chi, E. H., Ducheneaut, N., Fang, J., Isaacs, E., King, T., Newman, M. W., Partridge, K., Price, B., Rasmussen, P., Roberts, M., Schiano, D. J., and Walendowski, A. Activity-based serendipitous recommendations with the magitti mobile leisure guide. In *Proc. CHI '08*, ACM (2008), 1157–1166.
3. Brown, B., and Chalmers, M. Tourism and mobile technology. In *Proc. ECSCW '03*, Kluwer Acad. (2003), 335–355.
4. Cheng, A.-J., Chen, Y.-Y., Huang, Y.-T., Hsu, W. H., and Liao, H.-Y. M. Personalized travel recommendation by mining people attributes from community-contributed photos. In *Proc. MM '11*, ACM (2011), 83–92.
5. Clements, M., Serdyukov, P., de Vries, A., and Reinders, M. Finding wormholes with flickr geotags. In *Advances in Information Retrieval*, C. Gurrin, Y. He, G. Kazai, U. Kruschwitz, S. Little, T. Roelleke, S. Rüger, and K. van Rijsbergen, Eds., vol. 5993 of *LNCS*. Springer, 2010, 658–661.
6. Clements, M., Serdyukov, P., de Vries, A. P., and Reinders, M. J. Using flickr geotags to predict user travel behaviour. In *Proc. SIGIR '10*, ACM (2010), 851–852.
7. De Choudhury, M., Feldman, M., Amer-Yahia, S., Golbandi, N., Lempel, R., and Yu, C. Automatic construction of travel itineraries using social breadcrumbs. In *Proc. HT '10*, ACM (2010), 35–44.
8. Girardin, F., Calabrese, F., Fiore, F. D., Ratti, C., and Blat, J. Digital footprinting: Uncovering tourists with user-generated content. *IEEE Pervasive Computing 7* (2008), 36–43.
9. Hägerstrand, T. What about people in Regional Science? *Papers in Regional Science 24*, 1 (1970), 6–21.
10. Hassenzahl, M., Burmester, M., and Koller, F. AttrakDiff: Ein Fragebogen zur Messung wahrgenommener hedonischer und pragmatischer Qualität. *Mensch & Computer 2003. Interaktion in Bewegung* (2003), 187–196.
11. Hecht, B., Schöning, J., Erickson, T., and Priedhorsky, R. Geographic human-computer interaction. In *Proc. CHI '11 EA*, ACM (2011), 447–450.
12. Hochmair, H. Towards a classification of route selection criteria for route planning tools. *Developments in Spatial Data Handling* (2004), 481–492.
13. Kenteris, M., Gavalas, D., and Economou, D. Electronic mobile guides: a survey. *Personal and Ubiquitous Computing 15* (2011), 97–111.
14. Kjeldskov, J., Graham, C., Pedell, S., Vetere, F., Howard, S., Balbo, S., and Davies, J. Evaluating the usability of a mobile guide: the influence of location, participants and resources. *Behaviour and Information Technology 24*, 1 (2005), 51–65.
15. Kostakos, V., Nicolai, T., Yoneki, E., O'Neill, E., Kenn, H., and Crowcroft, J. Understanding and measuring the urban pervasive infrastructure. *Personal Ubiquitous Comput. 13*, 5 (2009), 355–364.
16. Kurashima, T., Iwata, T., Irie, G., and Fujimura, K. Travel route recommendation using geotags in photo sharing sites. In *Proc. CIKM '10*, ACM (2010), 579–588.
17. Lu, X., Wang, C., Yang, J.-M., Pang, Y., and Zhang, L. Photo2trip: generating travel routes from geo-tagged photos for trip planning. In *MM '10*, ACM (2010), 143–152.
18. Okuyama, K., and Yanai, K. A travel planning system based on travel trajectories extracted from a large number of geotagged photos on the web. In *PCM* (2011).
19. Schöning, J., Hecht, B., and Starosielski, N. Evaluating automatically generated location-based stories for tourists. In *CHI EA '08*, ACM (2008), 2937–2942.
20. Shoval, N., and Isaacson, M. Sequence alignment as a method for human activity analysis in space and time. *Annals of the Association of American Geographers 97*, 2 (2007), 282–297.
21. Snavely, N., Garg, R., Seitz, S. M., and Szeliski, R. Finding paths through the world's photos. In *SIGGRAPH '08*, ACM (2008), 15:1–15:11.
22. Suh, Y., Shin, C., Woo, W., Dow, S., and Macintyre, B. Enhancing and evaluating users' social experience with a mobile phone guide applied to cultural heritage. *Personal Ubiquitous Comput. 15* (August 2011), 649–665.
23. Tuite, K., Snavely, N., Hsiao, D.-y., Tabing, N., and Popovic, Z. Photocity: training experts at large-scale image acquisition through a competitive game. In *CHI '11*, CHI '11, ACM (2011), 1383–1392.
24. Vermeulen, J. Improving intelligibility and control in ubicomp. In *Proc. Ubicomp'10*, ACM (2010), 485–488.
25. Wilson, C. Activity patterns in space and time: calculating representative hagerstrand trajectories. *Transportation 35* (2008), 485–499.
26. Zhang, H., Law, E., Miller, R. C., Gajos, K. Z., Parkes, D. C., and Horvitz, E. Human computation tasks with global constraints. In *CHI'12*, ACM (2012), 217–226.

Supporting Creative Collaboration in Globally Distributed Companies

Raja Gumienny, Lutz Gericke, Matthias Wenzel, Christoph Meinel
Hasso Plattner Institute
Prof.-Dr.-Helmert-Str. 2-3, Potsdam, Germany
{raja.gumienny, lutz.gericke, matthias.wenzel, meinel}@hpi.uni-potsdam.de

ABSTRACT
Creative ways of working with whiteboards and sticky notes are growing in popularity even in global companies. However, digital tools for enabling these ways of working, especially for geographically distributed teams, have still not been adopted in these companies. We present Tele-Board, a web-based digital whiteboard and sticky note system and describe how it was used in a large company at three locations. From system log data and interviews recorded after three months of use, we found that idea generation and feedback collection can be facilitated if a system offers real-time synchronous editing as well as asynchronous input. Interestingly, the users who were *not* located at the company's headquarters regarded the tool as very beneficial and used it more than their colleagues at the headquarters. We provide a detailed analysis of the study and important points for fostering the adoption of creative tools in large companies.

Author Keywords
distributed teams; remote collaboration; global work; professional communication; idea generation

ACM Classification Keywords
H.5.3. Group and Organization Interfaces: Synchronous interaction, Asynchronous interaction, Computer-supported cooperative work

INTRODUCTION
Collaborative work over geographic distances is common practice for most employees of large global enterprises [20]. Many meetings include participants from multiple locations worldwide [6, 14]. Although a variety of tools for supporting different working modes exist, the most commonly used tools are still audio conferences (for synchronous communication) and e-mail (for asynchronous communication) because they are readily available and easy to use [22, 32].

Still, some ways of working, such as collaborative brainstorming or sketching ideas on a whiteboard, cannot be completely supported in remote situations using standard tools. But this way of working is becoming more and more prevalent. It is even seen in larger companies who seek to introduce methods such as design thinking [2] in order to increase their innovative potential [21]. Though whiteboard and brainstorming applications have been developed and researched for decades (e.g. [17, 19, 25, 33]), they have not been widely adopted in larger companies [15]. It was our goal to investigate whether and how this situation could be changed.

We developed Tele-Board, a digital whiteboard and sticky note software system. It supports design thinking over geographic distances and aims to improve the communication and collaboration for globally distributed teams [9]. In order to determine how well it suits the needs of a corporate environment, we deployed our system at three locations of a large IT company. The study lasted three months.

In this paper, we present our findings on how team members at the different locations used Tele-Board and the benefits they saw in using it for their daily work. Though we thought the team would mainly use the system for synchronous remote meetings, they often used it asynchronously as well. By working asynchronously, they could prepare meetings in advance, enter feedback whenever they liked, and bridge time zones. Contrary to our expectations, we found that users at the company's subsidiaries used the system more frequently than those users at the headquarters. Furthermore, they found that the tool could save them time. The team in this study did not use any digital whiteboard hardware. This was due to organizational and economic reasons. Still, they appreciated our whiteboard and sticky note system for idea generation and feedback sessions, even on their standard computers.

RELATED WORK
In order to support working modes such as design thinking [2], we had been looking for tools that offered the possibility of writing or scribbling on a whiteboard. This included sticky notes or similar objects. An additional requirement was that it be possible to work at different locations simultaneously with the interactions synchronized at some point. During this collaborative work an awareness of the remote partner, as described by Gutwin & Greenberg [10], must be preserved.

There is a large body of research on digital whiteboard applications, but these applications often focus only on co-located use, e.g. [13, 24, 25, 26] or do not offer sticky notes or similar tools that provide the possibility to add ideas and information [12, 17, 30, 31, 33]. A good example of a system that combines these two attributes – remote collaboration and

CSCW '13, February 23–27, 2013, San Antonio, Texas, USA.
Copyright 2013 ACM 978-1-4503-1331-5/13/02...$15.00.

sticky notes – is the *Designer's Outpost* from Klemmer et al. [19]. In this system, users can work with physical sticky notes that are captured by a special camera setup and digitized. In the *Distributed Designer's Outpost* from Everitt et al. [7] the system was augmented with shadows that made it possible to see remote people standing at a digital whiteboard. However, we consider the digitization of paper sticky notes as too slow and cumbersome. Additionally, inconsistency problems arise when the digital version of a sticky note is moved and the paper version stays in its place.

We see *Clearboard* [17] as a good model for our system regarding two crucial points: conveying workspace awareness [10] and connecting a remote video image with the content on a whiteboard. Clearboard provides a "reference space" [4] for pointing and gesturing in order to improve communication and uses real video and not only shadows as *VideoWhiteboard* [33] or *Distributed Designer's Outpost* [7]. The main drawback of *Clearboard* is the missing functionality of manipulating the other person's drawings and any other artifacts they created. We believe this functionality is very important for distributed collaboration.

Neither these systems nor any comparable ones are in use in companies today. In the early nineties, the *DOLPHIN* groupware application was introduced for meetings in corporate environments [29]. It was designed for co-located use but could also connect with remote users or meeting rooms and offered several whiteboard functions and the possibility to create notes. The system had all functions that are important for creative meetings over distances, but its use has been discontinued.

Global companies that apply Design Thinking today, such as Procter & Gamble, use a TelePresence video conference system [1]. This system conveys the feeling of sitting around a table together. However, this solution is not available to the majority of the teams because dedicated TelePresence rooms entail a great deal of expensive equipment. Additionally, there is still no common creative workspace between the subsidiaries of a company for sharing artifacts similar to traditional whiteboards and sticky notes.

In order to share artifacts, people in corporate environments mainly use file sharing and desktop sharing systems for their meeting related content [27, 34]. But these systems allow editing to only one user at a time. Others can contribute only via audio or must wait their editing turn. With this "one at a time" mode, distributed and reciprocal synchronous collaboration is not possible. Even though research has proven that real-time and synchronous connectivity is important for successful collaboration [26, 28], standard meetings in large companies still rely on the tools described above. In their research, Yankelovich et al. proposed the *Meeting Central* prototype for improving the effectiveness of distributed meetings [34]. However, the available applications remain similar to the existing tools. For example, the desktop sharing application still only gives one user the possibility to "take control".

Other research on collaboration in corporate environments has mainly focused on social software such as blogs and social networking sites (e.g. Muller et al. [23] give an overview of different tools) or social file sharing in an enterprise [27].

A particularly big problem for the adoption of digital whiteboard systems is the special setup required. Such a setup is not easy to implement in large companies where meeting rooms are always changing [15]. Additionally, in a lot of meetings, people have a variety of different professional backgrounds and do not have time to learn how to use new tools [6]. The lack of time on the part of participants means that even if new tools may benefit users, they do not easily find their way into most companies [22].

Although we designed Tele-Board to be used with digital whiteboard hardware, and ideally with an integrated videoconferencing for deictic references [9], it was very important to us that it could be used with normal computers as well. In the following section, we introduce Tele-Board and the Tele-Board features that were most relevant for the team of our study.

TELE-BOARD

Tele-Board is a tool that supports creative teamwork, such as design thinking, even if team members are located at different locations. As it is our main objective to support distributed teams, all actions that take place at one whiteboard instance are automatically transferred to all other connected whiteboards that show the same content. Sticky notes can be created directly at a digital whiteboard or with a variety of other devices, as for example, a smartphone, a digital pen, or a laptop. All users can create sticky notes at the same time in order to enable parallel work and prevent "production blocking" [16, 26, 28].

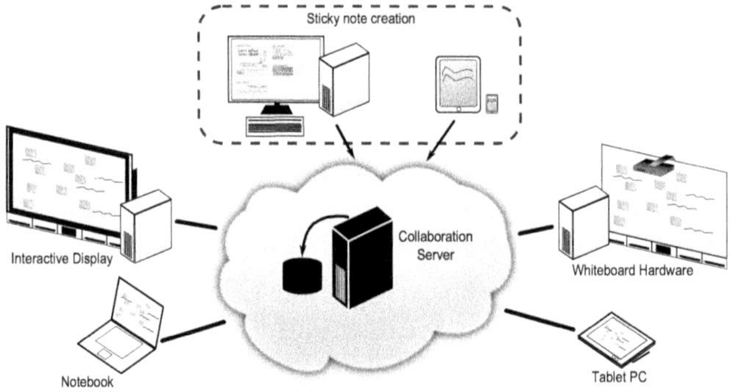

Figure 1. The Tele-Board software system architecture. All connected devices are synchronized via the central collaboration server. The whiteboard client software can run on a variety of hardware devices. These are displayed next to the server component. Sticky notes can be created with the help of mobile devices acting as digital sticky note pads (e.g. tablets or smartphones) or in the Web portal.

The components of the Tele-Board software system are the *Web portal*, *whiteboard client*, *digital sticky note pads*, and *server component*, which run on a variety of hardware devices (for an example see Figure 1). Originally, we thought that teams would want to use Tele-Board at large displays with touch and pen input options, in order to recreate the experience of working at a traditional whiteboard. But we learned that employees at large companies could not imagine having a dedicated meeting room with interactive whiteboard hardware. For them, it was essential to use a whiteboard application on their standard computers as well. Therefore, we made sure that our system ran on every computer and did not require any special installation or setup.

Web Portal

In the Tele-Board Web portal, users can manage *projects* and *panels* in order to organize their work and control access rights. Only users who are assigned to a project by a project administrator can see it in their list. Working inside a project, users can create various panels that represent virtual whiteboard spaces.

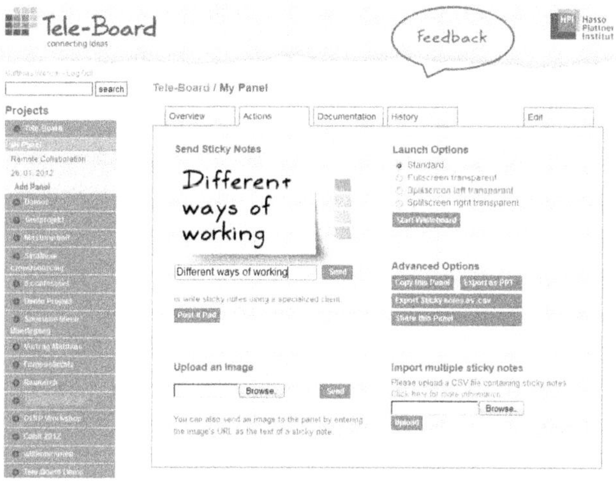

Figure 2. The Tele-Board Web portal (demo system). The left menu shows all projects and panels the user is assigned to. Every panel has different tab views: on the Overview Tab a feed of recent activities is shown, on the Actions Tab the user can write sticky notes, upload picture and access export functions.

Each project and each panel has its own *activity feed* on the *overview tab*. Here, one can see who worked on a project or panel at what time and read or write comments. On the overview tab, one can also see the latest state of the panel and open the whiteboard client with one click.

Several panel-specific functions are available on the *actions tab* of a panel (see Figure 2). The most important one is writing sticky notes and sending them to the panel. Another important function is adding pictures. Users can either upload an image from their computer or paste an image URL in the sticky note text input field. In the second case, the image from the web will appear in the whiteboard client. It is also possible to copy a panel and then continue in a separate "branch" with the same content. Additionally, users can export a graphical representation of the whole whiteboard surface or the texts of all sticky notes as a CSV file and share the panel with non Tele-Board users by sending a link to the panel.

The fourth tab view is the *history tab*, which is especially important for asynchronous work. Starting from the most current state of a panel, users can go back to any state of the whiteboard content (see also the Server Component section below) and continue working there or download or share this state.

Whiteboard Client

The Tele-Board whiteboard client is the digital equivalent of a traditional whiteboard. It is a Java application and can therefore be opened on most computers. Users just need to go to a panel page in the web portal and start the whiteboard client. The respective panel content will be loaded automatically.

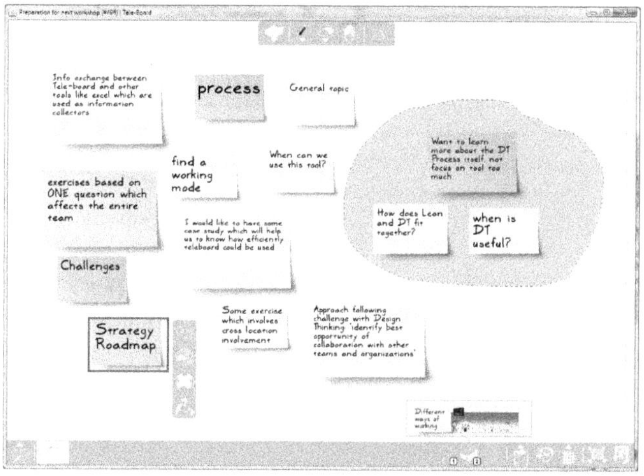

Figure 3. The Tele-Board whiteboard client. It offers standard whiteboard application functionality such as writing with a pen, erasing and panning the surface. It is possible for users to create sticky notes and perform several operations with selected sticky notes, for example copy, cluster, delete, recolor. Sticky notes and images from the Web portal or mobile clients arrive at the bottom of the whiteboard client and can be dragged to the working area.

The top menu offers basic functions such as creating new sticky notes, the pen mode for writing, the erase mode for deleting pen strokes and the move mode for panning the whiteboard surface. Sticky notes can be selected directly. A context menu offers more advanced functions such as, copy, cluster, delete, and recolor (see Figure 3). A cluster of whiteboard elements can also be created by encircling them. This means, it is possible to move around several sticky notes and pen strokes.

Sticky notes and images sent from the web portal, or a mobile device, arrive in a dedicated area at the bottom of the whiteboard client. From there, the user can drag them onto the whiteboard surface.

Digital Sticky Note Pad

As a digital equivalent for paper sticky notes, we offer different applications for writing sticky notes on mobile devices. Though we regard this way of creating sticky notes as an important part of the Tele-Board system, it could not be used by the team because the required devices were not available to them.

Server Component

The Server Component connects all parts of the Tele-Board system (see Figure 1). All events are transferred as Extensible Messaging and Presence Protocol (XMPP) messages and this keeps whiteboard clients synchronized. That is to say, all users who open the whiteboard client of the same panel, always see the same content and can work on the same items.

In order to keep the server's database consistent, we implemented a "last writer wins" strategy [18]. However, there is also the option of stopping the synchronization of whiteboard panning and zooming. Users can work at different areas of the virtual whiteboard without disturbing each other. All pen strokes and sticky notes are still synchronized.

Besides synchronizing all clients, the server component also stores all events in a database, which is the basis for the history tab in the Web portal. For more information, see [8]. When users send new sticky notes with mobile devices or via the Web portal, they are stored in a queue until they are dragged onto the whiteboard. That is to say, users can create sticky notes without opening the whiteboard client and add them later or even let other users add the notes to the board.

ORGANIZATIONAL AND DEPLOYMENT CONTEXT

As described above, Tele-Board was mainly developed for creative ways of working, such as design thinking. In 2011, an initiative for introducing design thinking was started in a large global IT company. In general, the goal was to use a *"human-centered approach to problem solving that helps people and organizations become more innovative and more creative,"* [2] as it was introduced by the design firm IDEO and applied at companies like Procter & Gamble [21]. After seeing a demonstration of Tele-Board, a team manager at this company decided to use it for his newly created team working between Germany, Italy, and India.

For his team, the manager had two incentives to apply design thinking and to use Tele-Board. Following the corporate strategy, he wanted his team to work in a more user- and customer-centered manner and be more creative in general. Additionally, he was looking for a way that his distributed team could work together more closely and make use of their diverse cultural backgrounds in addressing different markets. The first difficulty was that team members were in three different locations and two time zones. Additionally, the team was set up recently and consisted of people who did not know each other earlier. The members also brought different levels of expertise with them regarding their new tasks.

As part of an IT company, the team's job was to create preconfigured parts of a larger software that are ready to use at once by the customer. Though some software adjustments had to take place, most members of the team never did any coding. While some were involved in coding, others worked exclusively on general configuration, documentation, or translation. In their meetings, it was very important to make arrangements with each other and coordinate tasks. All team members worked on several pre-configured software parts at any given time. This work also involved people from outside of the team, some of whom were located in other countries, e.g. China, or the United States. There was a biweekly global team meeting where organizational topics and new ideas were discussed with the manager. Before our study, the team used video conferencing as the means of communication and oftentimes also a desktop sharing application.

Although the manager saw a demonstration of Tele-Board with digital whiteboard hardware and acknowledged the advantages of it, he told us that he could not provide this hardware at each location and that it was also not realistic to reserve the same meeting room (with this hardware) all of the time. Therefore, he wanted his team to start using Tele-Board with their standard laptops.

For the study, we worked with a team of 25 people (13 female), with 15 of them located at the company's headquarters in Germany (DE), 2 in Italy (IT) and 8 in India (IN). While no team member was a native English speaker, it was the language used in meetings. The team members came from different academic backgrounds. This resulted in teamwork that was quite interdisciplinary. During the course of our study, 5 people from another department joined the team. On average, the length of service with the company was higher for the German team members (on average 13.5 years) than those from India (avg. 6.3 years) and Italy (avg. 8.5 years). Differences in expertise and addition of new members to the team necessitated knowledge transfer across locations.

Two months before the beginning of the study, we conducted interviews with 6 people out of the team (2 female, 4 male; 4 Germans, 2 Indians) for about 30 minutes each. We wanted to find out more about their current challenges with regard to global teamwork and what they expected from a more creative way of working and a new tool.

Challenges for the Team

Working in a newly created team, with three different work locations and various levels of expertise, was viewed as a challenge by the members. Thus, with new working methods and a new tool they expected to improve international collaboration and teamwork in general. They wished to work in a more user-centered way, and with the introduction of design thinking they hoped to get in touch with more stakeholders who were involved in creating pre-configured software packages. As these packages are sold worldwide, they saw their diverse set of knowledge and contacts in different countries as an opportunity for building better solutions. However, from collaboration on past and present projects they knew that distributed collaboration was not always easy. Although two interviewees said that they could clarify some issues over the phone or via instant messaging, others saw calling their remote colleagues as a hurdle:

"Perhaps it's the distance and the time difference, but you don't just pick up the phone and say: I have to tell you an idea I just had. That just doesn't work. I mean, you don't want to steal someone's time with any vague idea." (DE7)

With co-located colleagues one could just walk by the office and see if the colleague had time. But this was not always possible, for example if the colleague kept different working hours. As also reported by other researchers [6, 32], time zone differences were a *"major pain point" (DE3)* in collaborative work. However, the team we studied saw it as an advantage that they needed to deal with only two time zones with a time difference of less than five hours. In fact, they hoped to leverage the longer time span of working hours.

Another difficulty for the communication with other locations was language barriers. As already stated above, no one spoke

English as the first language and therefore spoke with an accent. This could be hard for others to understand and consequently lead to misunderstandings. The same was true for formulating ideas and thoughts in English:

"When you have an idea or want to say something spontaneously in another language, you first have to think: now, how do I phrase this? And this is not only our problem that we have to speak English, it's the same for people in India and Italy. Nobody can speak their first language and I think this is indeed a little handicap." (DE7)

Especially the topic of idea generation and collecting the points of view from people with diverse backgrounds and countries is seen as a great advantage of global teamwork. However, the interviewees said that this is difficult over distances with their current tools. Of course, standard office applications can be used, but the coordination is difficult and they cannot share ideas outside of these applications:

"We had a meeting two weeks ago with a colleague at another location in Germany. While one was drawing something on a whiteboard, the person who was not in the room was lost, because he could not follow the sense of the discussion." (DE3)

As underscored in this example, informal collaboration is generally poorly supported in current systems [11]. However, it was quite important for the team, because they needed to *"get the new colleague on board" (DE4)* and this often happened via informal exchanges within or between offices next to each other:

"The state of knowledge is still very different. I'm quite new in the team and the colleagues in India and Italy as well. But I am lucky that I'm here in Germany and there are many people who have been here for a longer time and really know a lot. No matter if it's about organizational stuff or domain knowledge, I have it directly at my office and that's really convenient." (DE7)

How much and in which way Tele-Board could fulfill the stated expectations of the team and their manager and support distributed collaboration in their office setting was examined via server logs and interviews after three months of use.

EVALUATION

Tele-Board was introduced to the team in a workshop at the beginning of February 2012 where all of the functions were shown in detail and the participants could practice using them. Afterwards, the team started to use Tele-Board during their daily work.

In this section, we will first report on some usage statistics from the system's log files. Afterwards, we outline the findings from interviews with most of Tele-Board's users.

Usage Statistics

To create the following diagrams we analyzed the log file data from February 13 until May 11, i.e. twelve weeks. Twenty-five members of the team (15 from Germany, 8 from India, 2 from Italy; 13 female, 12 male) had user accounts, though 5 of them (DE9, DE10, DE11, DE15, IN8) joined the team only after about 6 weeks.

In the first three weeks, only three to four people used the systems, but in the following weeks more and more users were involved and whiteboard events increased. During Easter vacation time in Europe the number of users dropped, but afterwards we saw a continuous increase of users and whiteboard events again.

Working across time zones

Time zone differences can be a challenge for teams at different locations. But as Tele-Board also supports asynchronous ways of working, we were interested in the distribution of working hours. Figure 4 shows the aggregated number of users for every hour of the day for the entire 12-week period. For example, we can see that all users in India had worked with the system between 12:30 pm and 4:30 pm local time at some point during the study period. Between 8:30 am and 9:30 am at least half of the users connected to the system one or more times.

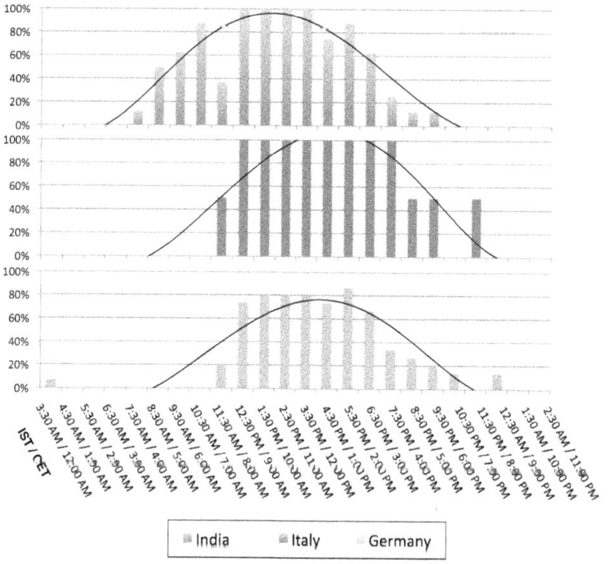

Figure 4. Distribution of user involvement throughout the hours of the day and over the whole study period. Locations are distinguished by colors; the two involved time zones are Central European Time (CET) and Indian Standard Time (IST).

The team mostly followed the pattern of typical working hours from about 9am to 5pm local time. Apparently, the overlapping synchronous work time was used more intensively than the time spent working alone. This often meant that the Indian team members were working until 6:30 pm or longer. In further research, we want to investigate if this intense synchronous use can also be observed in teams that have fewer overlapping working hours. We expect to see more asynchronous work because it is likely that people prefer working during the standard office hours at their time zone, as we can partly see with the Indian team members.

Different usage patterns

Figure 5 shows a selection of panels and how they were used from week 4 until the end of the study period. The size of the circles indicates how many users were involved each day and the colors show the location of the respective users.

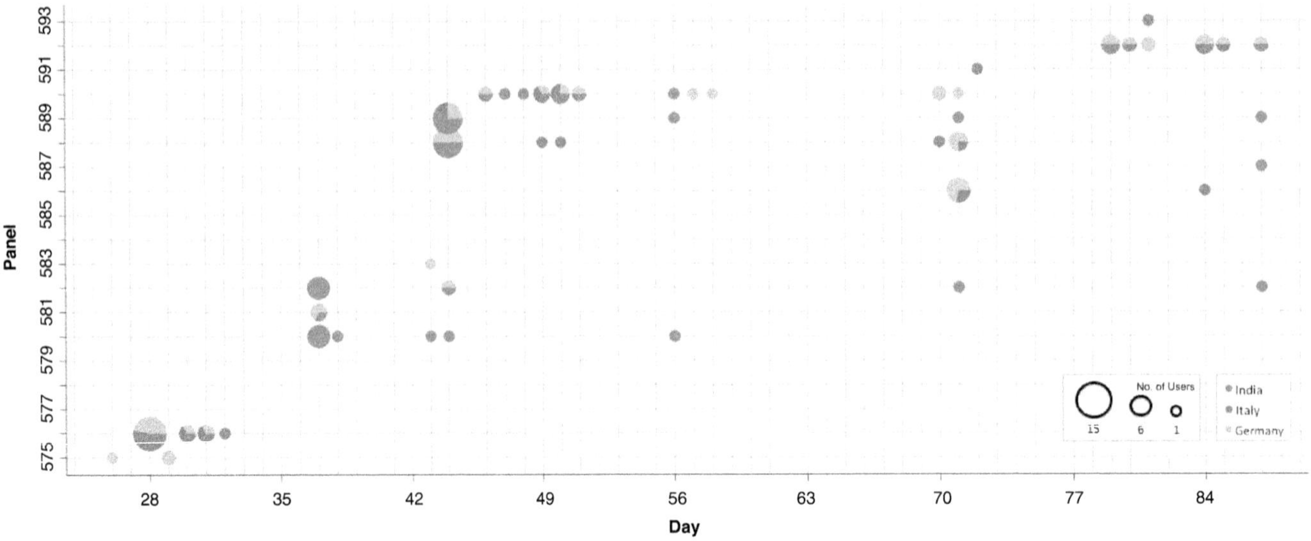

Figure 5. A selection of panels and their user involvement structure over time. The size of each circle displays the number of users active on a certain day on a certain panel. The colors indicate how many people from different locations collaborated with each other. Some panels were only used in a few synchronous global team meetings while other panels were used by only a few participants asynchronously.

The interactions on the panels reveal different usage patterns. It seems, for example, that panel 590 was used for a long-term feedback collection activity. In contrast, Panel 589 appears to be used primarily as an idea sketchpad during a meeting on that one day. After this point, however, it only served to document meeting recap (see "Results from Interviews section for more details). Looking at the different panels, we can see that there is no single way of working with Tele-Board; rather people shifted between working alone, in small groups, and in larger groups. They used the panels during different time periods and manipulated the content asynchronously as well as synchronously.

Giving users the possibility for easy transition between working together and alone in order to facilitate "loose and tight coupling" is important for distributed groupware [10]. Our users also appreciated that Tele-Board not only provided one way of working but several (see subsection "Support for Different Ways of Working").

As an indicator of collaboration among Tele-Board users, we examined how many people worked with the same content, i.e., the same sticky notes. It turned out that almost half of all sticky notes created during the study period were moved/modified by at least 2 people over the course of the study, with the highest number of users editing as many as 8 sticky notes (average: 2.08, SD: 1.44).

Activity per location

The most interesting fact we could derive from the log data was that the activity of all Tele-Board users was not evenly distributed across the different locations (see Figure 6). For all interactions with the system – number of sticky notes created, number of whiteboard events, number of whiteboard client sessions, and session duration – were higher for users at the company's subsidiaries in India and Italy. Although there were some very active users at the headquarters in Germany, others contributed little or nothing. However, four of the five new users who joined the team after half of the study period are located in Germany. This difference in contribution is also reflected in the median and standard deviation values of the different activities (see Table 1).

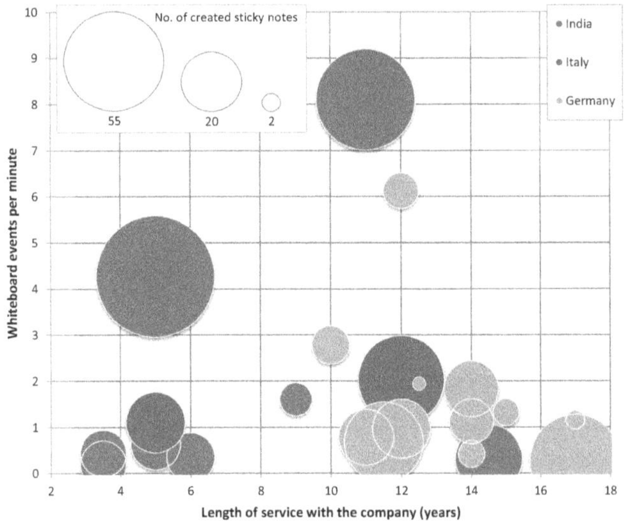

Figure 7. The level of activity of all Tele-Board users in relation to their length of service with the company. Each user is represented as one circle. The number of sticky notes created is expressed by the size of the circles. Based on their location on the y-axis, the circles also show whiteboard activity in terms of whiteboard events / session duration.

Because the length of service with the company in Germany is higher on average, we examined whether there is a relationship between the length of service and Tele-Board activity (see Figure 7). In this figure, the size of the circles shows the number of sticky notes a user created (each circle represents a user). The y-axis indicates the ratio between whiteboard

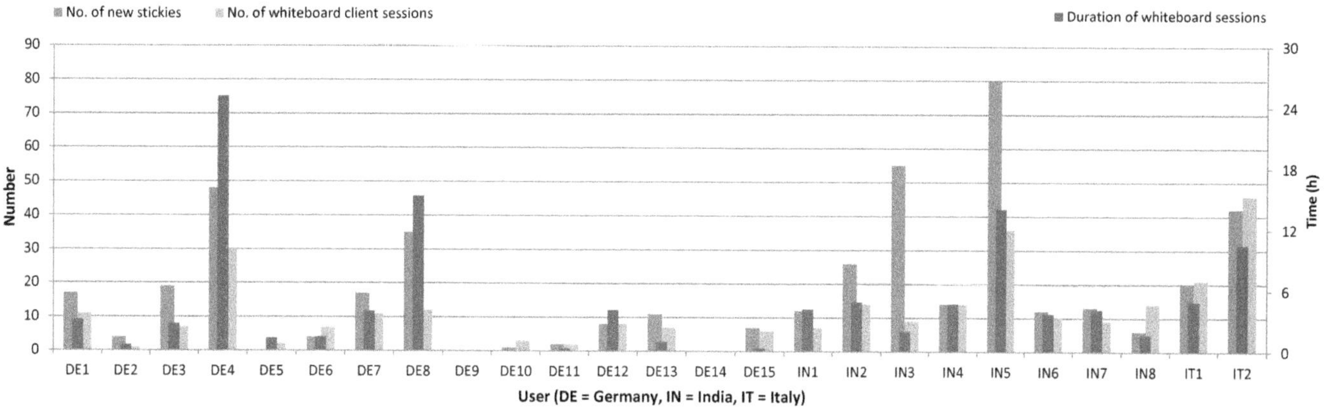

Figure 6. Activity of all Tele-Board users. The left y-axis indicates the number of whiteboard client sessions (orange) and the number of created sticky notes (blue) per user. The right y-axis and the red bars show how many hours each participant used Tele-Board within the three months of our study.

events (i.e., every interaction with the whiteboard client) and session duration (i.e., whiteboard events per minute). This shows how active users were after starting the whiteboard client. Please note that three German users do not appear in this figure because they did not write any sticky notes. Though the statistical values in the table show that the German users generated fewer whiteboard events, started the whiteboard client less often, and wrote fewer sticky notes, a lot of them used the whiteboard actively once they initiated a session. This is indicated by the ratio of whiteboard events per minute. However, we could not observe a relationship between activity and length of service with the company.

Location		No. of sticky notes	No. of whiteboard events	No. of whiteboard sessions	Session duration (hours)
DE	AVG	11.5	181.7	7.1	3.9
	MED	7.0	108.0	7.0	1.2
	SD	14.0	230.9	7.5	0.3
IN	AVG	27.3	651.4	14.1	4.9
	MED	13.5	129.0	12.0	4.1
	SD	26.3	1225.4	9.3	1.2
IT	AVG	31.0	803.5	33.5	7.7
	MED	31.0	803.5	33.5	7.7
	SD	15.6	675.3	17.7	0.2

Table 1. Average, median, and standard deviation values for all activities with the Tele-Board system per location for the study period of twelve weeks.

We believe that the main reason for the variation in Tele-Board use across locations is based on the difference in potential benefits, as described by Gutwin et al.'s study on informal collaboration [11]. As mentioned by user DE7 in the *Challenges for the Team* section, there are many domain experts at the headquarters and the German users can meet them informally on the floor or go to their office with a question. Therefore, the benefit of using Tele-Board is not as high at the headquarters as it is at the subsidiaries and maybe not *"worth the effort of initiating and joining into a collaborative session"*[11]. Especially with regard to knowledge exchange, users at the subsidiaries see Tele-Board as a place where they can ask questions and discuss them. Instead of spending time writing e-mails, users saved time by utilizing Tele-Board instead. As the analysis of the interviews in the next section shows, the difference in activity across locations corresponds to the differences in opinions on the usefulness and effectiveness of Tele-Board.

Results from Interviews

We conducted semi-structured interviews with 20 members of the team (10 male and 10 female). 11 interviewees came from Germany, 7 from India, and 2 from Italy. As 4 interviewees (DE9, DE10, DE11, IN8) were new to the team, they did not use Tele-Board yet, but talked about their first impressions and experiences from former collaborative remote work. Each interview lasted approximately 30 minutes. Interview questions focused on the usage of Tele-Board and general communication within the team and with stakeholders outside of the team. The interviews with the German interviewees were conducted face-to-face, while the interviews with team members from India and Italy were conducted over the phone. All interviews were recorded and transcribed. We used open-coding techniques to discover patterns and recurring topics [5]. The main topics we identified in the analysis are described below.

Support for Different Ways of Working

In response to our query regarding use of Tele-Board, the interviewees said that they used it primarily during team meetings in the phases of generating ideas / brainstorming and collecting feedback. All users created sticky notes in the same way: in the web portal by typing the note's content with their keyboard (see Figure 2). All users liked Tele-Board for idea collection in particular, because it worked *"just like a whiteboard, a virtual one, as it is intended." (DE6)* For synchronous work, the team members typically did a silent brainstorming and afterwards discussed and grouped their ideas:

"Normally we have a topic for the meeting, and we agree with the participants to allow some time to post the ideas on the board and then we go back into an all-together mode. Normally these are remote, of course, so we are not sitting in the same room anyway. Then we rearrange the ideas on the board and we start sharing and commenting and working on the ideas that are already posted on the board." (IT2)

Ten out of the sixteen active users told us that they also used Tele-Board for asynchronous work. DE4, for example, first posted his ideas on a whiteboard panel and later presented them in a project team meeting to other stakeholders. In most other cases, a meeting organizer created a panel and sent the link to it with the meeting request and asked all participants to post agenda topics or questions on sticky notes. In the meeting, everyone opened the panel and went through all topics on the notes. Feedback collection could occur the other way around, i.e., someone created a panel during a meeting and all participants were asked to post their feedback after the meeting (see Figure 5). This transition between different ways of working was not available in the other tools that the team was using and was greatly appreciated.

Influence on Efficiency

In the former section, we saw that the team used Tele-Board for idea generation and communicating synchronously and asynchronously. But, as in the case with all new tools a company implements, the real question is how efficiently the tool supported employees in their daily work. Though we uncovered different points of view, half of the interviewees stated that Tele-Board saved them time because more people could work together simultaneously. Because of this, meeting minutes and documentation could be omitted and e-mail correspondence could be decreased.

"Earlier we used to just have an open discussion where anyone who has an idea on a particular topic, presents his or her ideas, and the minutes are taken by one person and finally at the end of the meeting all ideas discussed are sent out as minutes by this person; which is time consuming. It's additional effort for a person to capture the ideas, put them in minutes and send it out. And not all of them speak up during a meeting if they have some ideas. Some of them tell their ideas, some of them don't.

Now that we are extensively using Tele-Board for idea collection, I find that the time for those exercises has drastically been reduced. Because everyone just puts in their ideas and it just takes 2 min. and then it's already in there. Now the person who is hosting the meeting only needs to collect the ideas and put it in a proper grouping. The tool has improved the idea collection phase." (IN2)

Interestingly, we heard such statements from only two people located at the company's headquarters. Additionally, eight out of the nine interviewees who worked at the subsidiaries said that Tele-Board saved time. This shows that the benefit of Tele-Board was considered higher by the Italian and Indian users and corresponds with the usage statistics of more activity at these locations (see Figures 6 and 7).

Most interviewees agreed that there were situations when it was neither efficient nor helpful to use Tele-Board. Such situations included one-on-one phone calls, short meetings where to-dos were discussed (IN1, IN7), as well as document review and project status meetings (IT2, DE2). As the tasks of all team members within their project work were diverse (DE6), some interviewees told us that they rarely had meetings where they could "think out of the box" (DE2, DE5, DE6) and use of Tele-Board could be beneficial.

Conversely, other users saw no advantage to using Tele-Board when compared with existing tools (DE2, DE5):

"I don't see the added value. Basically it's another tool for making notes. I prefer having a list and all of these sticky notes are just too much information for me if no one groups or categorizes them but just sticks them there. You always need someone who sorts them. I prefer having it structured. I prefer a list that I can work from. Otherwise I have to read everything first, then structure it and that's cumbersome." (DE5)

In general, there were different points of view as to how much Tele-Board could and should help structure a meeting. Some thought it helped structure brainstorming and idea grouping (IN3, IN7, IN8, DE7, IT2), while one user criticized what he saw as the unstructured format of the meeting (DE3) and yet another thought it was good to have more flexibility (DE1).

Some users saw advantages in the asynchronous work as time zone differences could be bridged and it was easier to go on working at a whiteboard panel at any point in time (IT2, DE1, IN1), see Figure 4.

"Sometimes it helps when you are working with colleagues from other locations and you have been doing some tasks and they have to follow up, because of the time difference it's always better you use the tool and you post what you have completed, so you don't wait. Because we have to wait until the German colleagues come in the afternoon. Instead we can just start in the morning, based on what the German colleagues or others have posted. That might help in going faster." (IN1)

Another point where users told us that Tele-Board saved time and effort was with respect to the "clean desktop" policy of the company: all employees are always supposed to wipe off whiteboard content or take away flip-chart sheets and this was not necessary with a virtual whiteboard (DE1, DE11).

Influence on Communication and Collaboration

Though some interviewees perceived that the communication within the team was already very good (DE6, IN2), others saw further improvements due to the use of the new tool. For example, one user found that the tool was advantageous for quieter people. The possibility to communicate was easier when it involved posting a sticky note and explaining it afterwards (DE7). In general, several people agreed that Tele-Board encouraged communication (IN1, IN2, IN7) because people were more comfortable speaking freely (IN5): They lost their inhibitions to say something if they could post it first (DE4, IT1). Especially for asynchronous feedback rounds, participants liked the "anonymous" appearance of sticky notes though it was possible to track the author of the sticky note. Interestingly, the feeling of anonymity praised by some was viewed by one participant as potentially inhibiting users from posting (DE2).

Having everybody's input in *written* format was important to many users (DE11, DE3, DE5, IN6, IN7, IT2) in order not to forget something and to improve understanding of what people wanted to say. As stated at the beginning, problems with audio connections and accents of non-native speakers sometimes hampered communication (IT2, DE5, IN7). This is consistent with the findings of Yankelovich et al. [34]. In such cases, written sticky notes can assist in communication:

"When we talk over the phone, it might be that their voice is not clear and we could not understand them properly. In that case Tele-Board was very helpful because we have written format and we get to see what they really want to tell us." (IN7)

Overall, the manager of the team also saw an improvement in mutual understanding:

"The understanding is definitely better than before. I mean, I see their results. And when I talk to them separately at regularly scheduled meetings I can tell that they are talking less about different things. The big picture is more consistent. It's better, but not perfect." (DE8)

Interplay with other tools

Tele-Board offered a new way of working and the whiteboard and sticky note metaphor was different from other digital tools used in the company. It was our goal to introduce a virtual whiteboard for remote collaboration which was, as one user described it, *"a perfect addition to the other tools"* (DE6).

As the team formerly used MS Excel for collecting ideas and feedback, some interviewees compared Tele-Board to this tool. One user expressed the feeling that she used it like she used Excel, just with easier clustering (DE7). The team saw the main difference and advantage as the ability to enter data simultaneously or in *"real-time"* (IN1, IN2, IT2). Others thought it was easier to use than other tools because everyone knew the analog equivalent and it was more fun to use because of its colors and playful character (DE4, DE1).

"[..] it's very receptive, because it's colorful, it's sorted, you can concentrate on the visuals and that's easier to remember than words on an Excel sheet. We did it with Excel before and the rows and columns don't stick in your head. But if you remember the colorful stickies you can say: yes, the pink topic was below the orange one, it stays into your head as a picture." (DE1)

Regardless of whether people liked working with whiteboards and sticky notes, we often heard that they always had to transfer the content into a MS Office document. As the manager put it: *"It's good for collecting ideas as a first step towards a solution. But it has to go on..."* (DE8). Tele-Board could be *"a mind map where it is easy to add links and documents"* (DE8) or as some participants stated: *"a Powerpoint slide-deck"* (IN2, DE5, DE6).

An additional question to participants was how much they used video conferencing for their remote work. Most of them said that they usually did not use it for their project work, because it was difficult to get a video conferencing room at each location. For this reason, especially in the case of small meetings, video conferencing was seen as not worth the effort. But they also said, it was not very important to see the faces if they saw the same content on the screen (IN2, IN6, IN8, DE4, DE5, DE6, IT1, IT2). One user thought it could even have a negative effect during brainstorming because one is distracted by the faces (DE3), which is consistent with other research [3].

Tool Introduction

Introducing new tools in a corporate environment is challenging because employees do not have much time and are compelled to learn several new tools, especially at the beginning (DE2, DE9).

In our case, the manager of the team promoted the use of Tele-Board from the beginning (DE8). Some team members accepted it passively (IN8, DE3, DE6) while others viewed it negatively *"I think a lot of people use Tele-Board because our manager wants it"* (DE2) or positively *"It is good that our manager forces us to use it, someone has to convince the others"* (DE9).

Several users saw it as an advantage that the use of Tele-Board was not difficult to learn (DE6, IT1, IN8) and that new users could start working right away after the main features were explained to them. These features were: creating sticky notes and adding them to a board, changing the color of sticky notes, creating clusters, creating a panel, and starting a project. We heard from the new team members that it was not too difficult to learn how to use Tele-Board (DE11, IN8).

Members of the team thought that they could get feedback from other stakeholders (e.g. product owners or consultants) more easily and on a regular basis if these stakeholders also had a Tele-Board account (IN1). As the tool was only introduced to team members, no automatic routine for creating other users was set up. However, Tele-Board could certainly help in collaborating with people outside of the company as well. As the manager put it:

"In a world with less budget and possibilities to travel to a customer, a platform for quick exchange is very valuable. It may help to faster get an understanding for the customer's needs." (DE8)

DISCUSSION

From usage statistics as well as interviews, we can tell that Tele-Board became part of the team's repertoire of work tools during our study. Though the time they used it (in terms of session duration) may not seem to be high compared to the total working time, we detected whiteboard activity on 46 of the 60 working days (12 weeks of 5 days). Considering that main working time is dedicated to composing and building suitable software packages, we were happy to see that team members included Tele-Board quite frequently in the range of tools for their internal communication and collaboration.

Interviewees stated that they did *not* use Tele-Board for meeting types such as status updates or document review meetings or one-on-one phone calls. For these kinds of meetings, existing tools in a corporate environment do the job and Tele-

Board does not aim to be their substitute. With Tele-Board we provided the team with a tool that complements existing tools with new functions (DE6). Now, they had the possibility to generate ideas and input at the same time, and they could also continue working on the same content at a later point in time, whenever convenient.

Several users thought that Tele-Board saved time because it allowed them to work together in real-time without anyone having to wait for others to finish. Work was shared, which also meant that no one was burdened by having to write documentation or minutes of the meeting.

We could also see that Tele-Board improved team collaboration. The manager confirmed that mutual understanding (e.g., of the project contents) increased when using Tele-Board. A second improvement was the feeling of shared experience and sense of co-presence that working on the same whiteboard gave team members [3]. The *written* format of sticky notes, in contrast to audio-only meetings, was another advantage for communication among team members because it mixed verbal and visual communication. Moreover, working with the same artifacts simplified the verbal communication and made interaction more efficient [10]. Our interviewees confirmed this and stated that it was easier to understand others and express one's own opinion. Additionally, quieter participants were more likely to be heard.

Of course, other tools also provide the possibility to share in written format, but they either do not support real-time participation (e.g. MS Office products) or show input in a linear format (e.g. instant messengers). With the help of sticky notes, Tele-Board allows the possibility of rearranging and sorting one's own input as well as the input of others. The team used this option for creating schedules and plans for meetings or for collecting questions they had for other stakeholders. Oftentimes, similar ideas appeared, but then they could be grouped together and a shared interest in this topic became visible. Additionally, sticky notes encourage going from structured meetings and data sharing to the *"far messier tasks of generating ideas and building consensus around them"*[2], which is desirable when a company wants to apply design thinking or similar methods.

Tele-Board combines advantages of synchronous collaboration with the possibility of asynchronous input. Users could easily start working before a meeting or go on working after a joint session with their colleagues. From usage statistics and interview statements we saw that the team actually followed such work practices (see Figure 5): some panels were mainly used for one joint meeting; others were used repeatedly over time. Additionally, entering ideas whenever they occurred made the team less dependent on different time zones and office hours (see Figure 4).

By complementing existing tools, Tele-Board offered a new communication channel that was used by team members, especially at the subsidiaries. Feedback from interviews and usage numbers from log files showed that users from Italy and India interacted more with Tele-Board than users from the headquarters in Germany (see Figure 1). As domain and task experts were located mostly at the headquarters, German users did not have the same motivation to use a digital tool for knowledge exchange as the Italian and Indian users did. German users could simply take a question directly to a colleague. By contrast, an Indian user told us that he and his colleague used Tele-Board to collect questions on a panel and then discussed them with more experienced colleagues in Germany.

From this study, we learned that a prerequisite for using a tool like Tele-Board is easy availability to all team members. The manager told us that a whiteboard software tool that is available only on dedicated whiteboard hardware and in special meeting rooms will not be used very often. If, in the future, the hardware becomes available on a general basis, the Tele-Board software could support work practices that are more similar to working at traditional whiteboards. Nevertheless, it is essential that Tele-Board remains available to users on standard computers as well. Moreover, we should make Tele-Board accessible to those outside the team and also to consultants or customers outside the company, in order to improve collaboration and foster user-centered work practices.

Limitations

Our study was conducted with a single team in one company and was influenced by the structure and composition of this team. From the 25 users there were only 20 active users because 5 people joined the team only after half of the study period. Future work in other organizations and teams is needed to verify if the results are similar or if advantages and disadvantages of Tele-Board differ across teams and contexts. More users from various locations and in different areas of work are necessary in order to draw generalizable conclusions.

CONCLUSION

In this paper, we presented the Tele-Board system, which offers the possibility of fostering creativity in globally distributed teams in corporate environments. We conducted a three month usage study with a team in a large IT company based in three locations on two continents that used Tele-Board for its work. We collected quantitative data from usage logs as well as qualitative data from interviews with the users.

We learned that the "optimal" system setup we created in our lab could not simply be deployed in a company as is. It needed to be adjusted to a user's daily environment and equipment, which meant standard computers instead of digital whiteboards and sticky note hardware.

However, users could still benefit from the system because it enabled them to engage in real-time idea generation and feedback sessions over distances. It also provided them with a platform for knowledge exchange anytime they wanted to use it. Tele-Board supports a smooth transition between synchronous and asynchronous work: a user can either work along at a panel asynchronously or several users can connect to the same panel to work synchronously. Everyone could choose his or her preferred way of working, depending on the respective (team) situation. System log data and interview results showed that both ways of working were used by the team. It was therefore important that they were able to shift easily between working alone and working together [10].

Moreover, in the interviews we found that a shared workspace and its artifacts simplified verbal communication and understanding due to the written format of sticky notes. The graphical note appearance of sticky notes made them ideal for arranging and sorting.

Interviews as well as log data showed that Tele-Board users at company subsidiaries used this extra communication tool considerably more than those at the company's headquarters. Tele-Board provided a potentially promising channel of communication to improve joint work across company branches. This is an area we will examine further in our ongoing research.

ACKNOWLEDGMENTS

We thank all interviewees for their time and Sharon Nemeth, Kim Philip, Sean Gustafson and Holger Rhinow for their help with this paper. We also thank the HPI-Stanford Design Thinking Research Program for funding and supporting this project.

REFERENCES

1. Cisco TelePresence, Procter & Gamble case study. `http://www.cisco.com/en/US/services/ps6887/ps10672/External_CaseStudy_Procter_Nov2009.pdf`.
2. Brown, T. *Change by Design: How Design Thinking Transforms Organizations and Inspires Innovation.* HarperBusiness, 2009.
3. Brubaker, J. R., Venolia, G., and Tang, J. C. Focusing on Shared Experiences: Moving beyond the camera in video communication. In *Proc. DIS '12*, ACM Press (2012), 96–105.
4. Buxton, W. Mediaspace - Meaningspace - Meetingspace. In *Media Space 20 + Years of Mediated Life*, S. Harrison, Ed., Computer Supported Cooperative Work. Springer, London, 2009, ch. 13, 217–231.
5. Corbin, J. M., and Strauss, A. Grounded theory research: Procedures, canons, and evaluative criteria. *Qualitative Sociology 13*, 1 (1990), 3–21.
6. Espinosa, J., and Pickering, C. The Effect of Time Separation on Coordination Processes and Outcomes: A Case Study. In *Proc. Hawaii International Conference on System Sciences (HICSS'06), Volume 1*, IEEE (2006), 25.2.
7. Everitt, K., Klemmer, S. R., Lee, R., and Landay, J. Two worlds apart: bridging the gap between physical and virtual media for distributed design collaboration. In *Proc. CHI '03*, no. 5, ACM Press (2003), 553–560.
8. Gericke, L., Gumienny, R., and Meinel, C. Message capturing as a paradigm for asynchronous digital whiteboard interaction. In *Proc. CollaborateCom '10*, IEEE Computer Society (2010), 1–10.
9. Gumienny, R., Gericke, L., Quasthoff, M., Willems, C., and Meinel, C. Tele-Board : Enabling Efficient Collaboration In Digital Design Spaces. In *Proc. CSCWD '11*, IEEE Computer Society (2011), 47–54.
10. Gutwin, C., and Greenberg, S. A Descriptive Framework of Workspace Awareness for Real-Time Groupware. *Computer Supported Cooperative Work (CSCW) 11*, 3 (2002), 411 – 446.
11. Gutwin, C., Greenberg, S., Blum, R., Dyck, J., Tee, K., and McEwan, G. Supporting Informal Collaboration in Shared-Workspace Groupware. *Journal of Universal Computer Science - J.UCS 14*, 9 (2008), 1411–1434.
12. Hailpern, J., Hinterbichler, E., Leppert, C., Cook, D., and Bailey, B. P. TEAM STORM: demonstrating an interaction model for working with multiple ideas during creative group work. *Creativity and Cognition* (2007), 193–202.
13. Hilliges, O., Terrenghi, L., Boring, S., Kim, D., Richter, H., and Butz, A. Designing for collaborative creative problem solving. *Creativity and Cognition '07* (2007), 137–146.
14. Hinds, P., and McGrath, C. Structures that work: social structure, work structure and coordination ease in geographically distributed teams. In *Proc. CSCW '06*, ACM Press (2006), 343–352.
15. Huang, E. M., Mynatt, E. D., Russell, D. M., and Sue, A. E. Secrets to Success and Fatal Flaws: The Design of Large-Display Groupware. *IEEE Computer Graphics and Applications 26*, 1 (2006), 10–17.
16. Hymes, C. M., and Olson, G. M. Unblocking brainstorming through the use of a simple group editor. In *Proc. CSCW '92*, ACM Press (1992), 99–106.
17. Ishii, H., and Kobayashi, M. ClearBoard: a seamless medium for shared drawing and conversation with eye contact. In *Proc. CHI '92:*, ACM Press (1992), 525–532.
18. Johnson, P. R., and Thomas, R. H. RFC0677: The Maintenance of Duplicate Databases. *Internet RFCs* (1975), 1–11.
19. Klemmer, S. R., Newman, M. W., Farrell, R., Bilezikjian, M., and Landay, J. A. The designers' outpost: a tangible interface for collaborative web site. In *Proc. UIST '01*, ACM Press (2001), 1–10.
20. Koehne, B., Shih, P. C., and Olson, J. S. Remote and alone: coping with being the remote member on the team. In *Proc. CSCW '12*, ACM Press (2012), 1257–1266.
21. Martin, R. L. *The design of business: why design thinking is the next competitive advantage*. Harvard Business Press, 2009.
22. Matthews, T., Whittaker, S., Moran, T., and Yuen, S. Collaboration personas: a new approach to designing workplace collaboration tools. In *Proc. CHI '11*, ACM Press (2011), 2247–2256.

23. Muller, M., Ehrlich, K., Matthews, T., Perer, A., Ronen, I., and Guy, I. Diversity among enterprise online communities: collaborating, teaming, and innovating through social media. In *Proc. CHI '12*, ACM Press (2012), 2815–2824.

24. Mynatt, E. D., Igarashi, T., Edwards, W. K., and LaMarca, A. Flatland: new dimensions in office whiteboards. In *CHI '99: extended abstracts on Human factors in computing systems* (1999), 346–353.

25. Pedersen, E. R. n., McCall, K., Moran, T. P., and Halasz, F. G. Tivoli: an electronic whiteboard for informal workgroup meetings. In *Proc INTERACT '93 and CHI '93, ACM Press* (1993), 391–398.

26. Prante, T., Magerkurth, C., and Streitz, N. Developing CSCW tools for idea finding - empirical results and implications for design. In *Proc. CSCW '02*, ACM Press (2002), 106–115.

27. Shami, N. S., Muller, M., and Millen, D. Browse and discover: social file sharing in the enterprise. In *Proc. CSCW '11*, ACM Press (2011), 295–304.

28. Shih, P. C., Nguyen, D. H., Hirano, S. H., Redmiles, D. F., and Hayes, G. R. GroupMind: supporting idea generation through a collaborative mind-mapping tool. In *Conference on Supporting Group Work* (2009), 139–148.

29. Streitz, N. A., Geiß ler, J., Haake, J. M., and Hol, J. DOLPHIN: Integrated Meeting Support across Local and Remote Desktop Environments and LiveBoards. In *Proc. CSCW '94*, ACM Press (1994), 345–358.

30. Tang, A., Boyle, M., and Greenberg, S. Display and presence disparity in Mixed Presence Groupware. In *Proc. AUIC '04*, vol. 28, ACM Press (2004), 73–82.

31. Tang, A., Neustaedter, C., and Greenberg, S. VideoArms: Embodiments for Mixed Presence Groupware. In *Proc. HCI '06*, Springer London (2006), 85 – 102.

32. Tang, J., Zhao, C., and Cao, X. Your time zone or mine?: a study of globally time zone-shifted collaboration. In *Proc. CSCW '11*, ACM Press (2011), 235–244.

33. Tang, J. C., and Minneman, S. VideoWhiteboard: video shadows to support remote collaboration. In *Proc. CHI '91*, ACM Press (1991), 315–322.

34. Yankelovich, N., Walker, W., Roberts, P., Wessler, M., Kaplan, J., and Provino, J. Meeting central: making distributed meetings more effective. In *Proc. CSCW '04*, ACM Press (2004), 419–428.

Redistributing Leadership in Online Creative Collaboration

Kurt Luther,[1] Casey Fiesler,[2] Amy Bruckman[2]

[1] HCI Institute
Carnegie Mellon University
5000 Forbes Ave., Pittsburgh, PA 15213 USA
kluther@cs.cmu.edu

[2] GVU Center
Georgia Institute of Technology
85 5th St. NW, Atlanta, GA 30332 USA
casey.fiesler@gatech.edu, asb@cc.gatech.edu

ABSTRACT

In this paper, we integrate theories of *distributed leadership* and *distributed cognition* to account for the roles of people and technology in online leadership. When leadership is distributed effectively, the result can be success stories like Wikipedia and Linux. However, finding a successful distribution is challenging. In the online community Newgrounds, hundreds of collaborative animation projects called "collabs" are started each year, but less than 20% are completed. We suggest that many collabs fail because leaders are overburdened and lack adequate technological support. We introduce Pipeline, a collaboration tool designed to support and transform leadership, with the goal of easing the burden on leaders of online creative projects. Through a case study of a six-week, 30-artist collaboration called Holiday Flood, we show how Pipeline supported redistributed leadership. We conclude with implications for theory and the design of social computing systems.

Author Keywords

Social computing; online creative collaboration; creativity support tools; distributed leadership; distributed cognition.

ACM Classification Keywords

H.5.3 **[Information Interfaces and Presentation]**: Group and Organization Interfaces --- *collaborative computing; computer-supported cooperative work; theory and models; web-based interaction.*

INTRODUCTION

Effective leadership is a key ingredient in many forms of successful online creative collaboration. Many open-source software (OSS) projects are headed by "benevolent dictators" such as the Linux kernel's Linus Torvalds [33]. Polymath, the online collaboration that solved a significant open problem in mathematics, was led by two prominent mathematicians [7]. Collaborative art projects such as the *Virtual Choirs* [1], *Star Wars Uncut* [31], or *The Johnny Cash Project* [11] are as often credited to their auteurs as the crowds who authored the content.

These projects are well known because they were successful. Their creators were effective at recruiting and motivating volunteers, providing a creative vision, dividing up work, and other essential leadership behaviors. But what happens when leaders aren't as effective? In the Newgrounds community of Flash animation enthusiasts, hundreds of collaborative projects called "collabs" are started each year, but leaders of these projects frequently become overburdened, and less than 20% result in a finished animation [21,22].

We might look to leadership theory to explain why such failures occur, but theories of leadership in online creative collaboration are not yet well developed, particularly with respect to designing technological support. One promising option is *distributed leadership* (DL), a theory originating in education research that construes leadership as a set of behaviors that can be distributed across all members of a group, not just formal leaders [13,32]. While DL is well suited for analyzing leadership structures in traditional organizations, its ability to account for the role of technology or provide design implications is limited. To address this limitation, we integrate DL with *distributed cognition* (DCog), a theory embraced by the CSCW community for analyzing how cognitive processes can be distributed across people, artifacts, and time [17,19].

Using this theoretical framework, we argue that many Newgrounds collabs failed because leaders were overburdened and unable to effectively redistribute their responsibilities among other members or technologies. We propose that technology designed for *redistributing leadership* could ease the burden on leaders and allow for more complex creative projects. To explore this idea, we created Pipeline, a web-based tool for supporting and transforming leadership in online creative projects. We present a detailed case study of one Pipeline project, a collaborative artwork called Holiday Flood, to show how Pipeline supported and transformed leadership. We conclude with implications for theory and design of social computing systems.

This paper makes three main contributions to CSCW. First, it synthesizes the relative strengths of DL and DCog to provide a more complete theoretical perspective on online leadership that accounts for both the role of technology and the experiences of people. Second, it presents a new system and design implications for redistributing leadership in online creative collaboration when existing leadership configurations are ineffective. Third, it provides a detailed case study of how such a system is used in a real-world context to illustrate its strengths and areas for improvement.

BACKGROUND

Distributed Leadership

A growing body of research has challenged the premise of a "heroic" individual leader and instead argued that leadership is often distributed across members of a group. Distributed leadership (DL) decouples leadership roles from leadership behaviors, proposing that group members without formal or "legitimate" leadership status can and do act as leaders [32]. The focus then shifts to understanding how, why, when, etc. certain members perform certain leadership behaviors. Most research under the DL banner has been conducted by United Kingdom-based scholars and focuses on traditional organizations in education and healthcare [5]. Computer-mediated contexts such as online creative collaboration have not yet received much attention from DL scholars. A notable exception is Zhu et al.'s investigation of shared leadership in Wikipedia [35,36]. They found that while "legitimate" (formally appointed) leaders like administrators are more influential overall, regular members also substantially influence others via leadership behaviors.

While not discussed in terms of DL, other research has shown evidence of distributed or decentralized leadership in online creative collaboration. Wikipedia has a "benevolent dictator," co-founder Jimmy Wales, but governance on the site has become decentralized over time, with sub-communities adopting their own, sometimes conflicting, policies [10]. Like Wikipedia, many popular open-source software projects, such as the Linux kernel, embrace more decentralized governance over time [33]. Projects like the Apache web server embrace council-style leadership structures, where authority rotates among a small group [24], and research suggests that OSS projects with more utility-oriented goals lend themselves to decentralized leadership [26]. Finally, a study of the online mathematics collaboration Polymath found that though the project's two formal leaders were essential to its success, regular members also made significant contributions [7]. Our work extends this prior research by exploring how it could inform the design of technological support for online leaders.

Distributed Cognition

Distributed cognition (DCog) is a theory about cognition "in the wild"; i.e., how information is gathered and processed in the real world [19]. It asserts that cognition is a social, embodied process, and cannot be divorced from the culture in which it is situated. The theory considers systems of functional relationships between components, which can include individuals, groups, tools, computers, and other elements, and is chiefly concerned with how information moves between them, and over time.

Distributed cognition's origins lie in cognitive science, as a response to a prevailing school of thought holding that cognition takes place only inside the human brain. Hollan et al. [17] argued that distributed cognition could also serve as a new foundation for HCI research and design. Halverson [16] analyzed the utility of distributed cognition in the context of CSCW, comparing it to activity theory, and identified some key advantages of distributed cognition. Distributed cognition is flexible, allowing the unit of analysis to be determined by the phenomenon, and including both people and artifacts in analyses without privileging either. Distributed cognition is also highly data-driven and presents data in a way that is convenient for informing system design.

These attributes make distributed cognition a valuable theory for understanding collaborative processes when a large proportion of communication is mediated, such as in online communities. Recently, scholars have begun to think about online creative collaboration, such as Wikipedia, in terms of distributed cognition. For example, Geiger and Ribes [12] analyzed vandalism detection on Wikipedia—a system of vandals, vandal fighters, and software tools—and argued that non-human agents such as vandalism-detection bots occupy significant social roles.

Integrating DL and DCog

DL and DCog originated in different disciplines and have generally been considered separately. In this paper, we argue that combining elements from both theories can offer new insights into the design and study of social computing systems.

DL and DCog share some core concepts but there are notable differences as well. One similarity is that both theories assume a unit of analysis that is dependent on context, dynamically reconfigurable, and informed by empirical data. For DCog, the unit of analysis is a cognitive process and it is "delimited by the functional relationships among the elements that participate in it" [17]. For DL, the unit of analysis is the activity of leadership, which is composed of leadership behaviors that can be performed by any member of a group. DCog and DL are also similar in that both seek to broaden the unit of analysis beyond the individual. DL "does not privilege the work of particular individuals or categories of persons, nor is there a presumption about which individual's behavior carries more weight with colleagues" [13]. It also "allows for the possibility that all organization members may be leaders at some stage" [13]. Similarly, DCog "does not privilege the individual" [16] and holds that cognitive processes can be "distributed across members of a social group" [17].

DCog differs from DL in that it allows for cognitive processes to be distributed across artifacts and time as well as people. Consequently, it has proven especially applicable for analyzing systems that include a substantial technological component [16,17]. DL remains focused on people, and though it acknowledges that leadership can change over time [13], it does not account for the role of non-human systems in leadership. Researchers have also established DCog as a valuable source of design considerations for new systems (e.g. [4]). While DL may also make valuable contributions to system design, we were unable to find any examples of such attempts.

On the other hand, because DL is more human-centered than DCog, it is better suited for providing insight into *why* the human elements of the system behave the ways they do. DL studies typically involve in-depth, phenomenological interviews with leaders that explore both the rationale behind decisions as well as their practical effects. This includes, for example, the role of power and influence, though this is still a nascent area of research [14]. DL studies have also sought to identify different patterns of leadership and understand the sociocultural forces that created them (e.g. [5,8,13]). Because DCog is concerned mainly with functional relationships among elements, it is only able to account for the externally observable consequences of emotions, motivations, etc. experienced by individuals within the system [16].

In summary, both DL and DCog assume a unit of analysis that is dependent on context, informed by empirical data, changing over time, and broader than the individual. They differ in that DL is more human-centered, providing greater insight into the "whys" of human behavior in a system, while DCog, which includes non-human artifacts in its analysis, is better equipped to provide design implications. We propose that an integrated theory combining the strengths of DCog and DL can bring a valuable new perspective to social computing research and design.

Leadership Behaviors

As mentioned above, DL fundamentally argues that leadership roles can be separated from leadership behaviors. Therefore, in order to analyze DL in a particular context, it is necessary to first identify which leadership behaviors are the focus of the analysis. Throughout this paper, we discuss leadership using the five behaviors for managing work identified by Yukl, in his review of leadership research in organizational behavior [34]. These task-oriented behaviors—planning, problem solving, clarifying, informing, and monitoring—reflect the broader theoretical view of leadership as a process of initiating structure for followers. In the rest of the section, we briefly define each of the behaviors according to Yukl.

Planning

According to Yukl, planning is "deciding what to do, how to do it, who will do it, and when it will be done" [34]. The activity of planning is generally a cognitive one, though the leader may involve others in the planning process. Thus, it is easiest to identify planning when the leader is actually implementing the plans. Planning takes many forms, including strategic and operational planning. Two sub-types with particular relevance to this paper are action planning, defined as "determining how to implement a strategy or carry out a project in an effective manner," and contingency planning, which is "the development of procedures for reacting…to unavoidable problems and crises." In contrast to problem solving (discussed below), planning is not reactive and has a long-term orientation [34].

Problem Solving

The leadership behavior of problem solving "involves identifying work-related problems, analyzing them in a systematic but timely manner, and acting decisively to implement solutions and deal with crises" [34]. Unlike planning, which has a long-term orientation, problem solving is about dealing with emergencies and other situations that occur unexpectedly and require immediate attention. Leaders who are effective problem solvers are especially apt at being decisive and taking responsibility for a problem rather than avoiding it or excessively "buck-passing" (making somebody else responsible) [34].

Clarifying Roles and Objectives

Clarifying, according to Yukl, "is the communication of plans, policies, and role expectations" [34]. He identifies four sub-types of clarifying behaviors: (1) defining job responsibilities, (2) setting performance goals, (3) assigning tasks, and (4) providing instructions for doing a task. This latter sub-type can involve behaviors such as providing feedback on members' work and offering demonstrations of best practices [34].

Informing

The leadership behavior of informing "involves the communication of task-relevant information needed by subordinates, peers, superiors, or outsiders" [34]. A leader who is an effective informer is able to expose project members to the information they need and avoid wasting their time with information that isn't relevant to them. The leader is essentially a curator, processing all the information that passes through the project, pulling out the bits that are meaningful to certain members, and sharing it with them in a timely fashion [34].

Monitoring

Monitoring "involves gathering information about the operations of the manager's organizational unit," including elements such as progress, individual performance, and the success of various endeavors [34]. Monitoring provides the information to be used for the planning and problem solving behaviors described above.

In the following section, we describe the context of our study, Newgrounds collabs, and explain how leaders of these projects struggle to perform these behaviors.

STUDY CONTEXT: COLLABS

The context of our research into distributed leadership is the "collab," a collaborative project organized over the Internet with an artistic, expressive, or entertainment-oriented goal, such as a movie, game, or artwork. Previous work focused on the challenges for collab leaders on Newgrounds,[1] a popular online community of Flash animation enthusiasts [21,23]. A follow-up study examined success factors in collabs and found that more than 80% of collabs fail to produce a completed work [22]. This percentage suggests significant opportunities for improvement, as most collab members define success as completing the project.

Why do so few collabs succeed? First, collabs bring with them a number of challenges common to artistic and expressive collaboration in general. These include *completion* (work can only be made public if it is finished and polished); *originality* (members strive for originality, which is necessarily riskier because it eschews familiar conventions [2]); *subjectivity* (fundamentally subjective media like visual art and storytelling rarely have one clear best approach); and *ownership* (members must reconcile their own creative visions with the group's best interest) [21].

These general challenges of creative collaboration are complicated by the challenges of online, distributed collaboration and other characteristics of the Newgrounds community. Distance matters, and collab work, like other types of collaborative design, is often tightly coupled [27]. Collabs also require diverse groups to find common ground and work together: amateurs and professionals, novices and experts, artists and programmers. Furthermore, collab members are volunteers, so they frequently drop out when work or "real life" take priority.

Finally, the technology used by Newgrounds members to organize collabs is poorly suited to the task. Most collabs are organized in the Newgrounds forums—one thread per collab—which were originally designed for conversation but have since been appropriated for collaboration. Threads quickly balloon to dozens or hundreds of replies, becoming almost impenetrable to newcomers. The chronological ordering of replies causes individual posts to be quickly buried beneath a flurry of unrelated replies, and the forums support minimal file sharing (one image upload per post).

In this environment, leaders struggle to perform leadership behaviors. *Monitoring* members' progress is already difficult because geographic distribution makes direct observation impossible. Furthermore, as Yukl notes, monitoring is "most difficult when work involves unstructured, unique tasks for which results can be determined only after a long time interval" [34], a description that applies to the animation and visual art requirements of many collabs. Since monitoring supplies the information for *planning* and *problem solving*, a lack of information makes these leadership behaviors difficult to perform. Leaders consume large amounts of time *informing* and *clarifying* because members miss answers to their own questions or other relevant posts, and the forum software prevents leaders from editing their own posts to add clarification. Consequently, leaders must frequently repost the same information or deal with the resulting confusion.

In addition to these leadership behaviors, collab leaders also assume additional responsibilities not normally associated with leadership (e.g. managing project files). Thus, many leaders propose relatively simple projects and adopt centralized, top-down leadership styles, simply to minimize coordination and communication. For example, one of the most popular collab structures requires members to submit short animations based around a theme, which the leader edits into a single movie. This simple structure allows members to work almost entirely independently and in parallel.

These challenges weigh on all collab members, but most intensely on the leader, who, in a vicious cycle, typically invests the most time and effort in the collab and therefore has the most to lose. It follows that the leader is also the most likely member of the collab to become overburdened. When leaders become overwhelmed, they often quit, and their collabs fail shortly afterward. We suggest that one of the most promising avenues for improving collab success is to focus on the leader, who is both the most influential member of the collab and the most likely to benefit from a design intervention. *Our hypothesis is that new technology can be designed to ease the burden on collab leaders by supporting and transforming the work they do as leaders.* Specifically, the technology could *support* leadership by helping leaders perform their roles more easily, and *transform* leadership by redistributing some leader responsibilities more broadly across the group.

Better technological support could ease the burden on leaders, increase communication between members, open up new leadership styles, and result in more successful, complex, creative projects. To explore these ideas, we built and launched Pipeline, a web-based collaboration tool for supporting and transforming leadership. In the next section, we describe the Pipeline system and explain how its major features are designed with redistributed leadership in mind.

PIPELINE

Designing for Decentralization and Automation

Our goal with Pipeline was to provide a tool that helps online leaders redistribute some of their responsibilities in order to avoid becoming overwhelmed. The literature on DCog and DL provides some theoretical insights into how to accomplish this. From DL and DCog, we borrow the idea that leadership and cognitive processes can be distributed across members of a social group. This suggests *decentralization* as a design principle: Pipeline should allow leaders to easily share their responsibilities with other members of the project. From DCog, we borrow the idea that cognitive processes can also involve coordination with

[1] http://www.newgrounds.com/

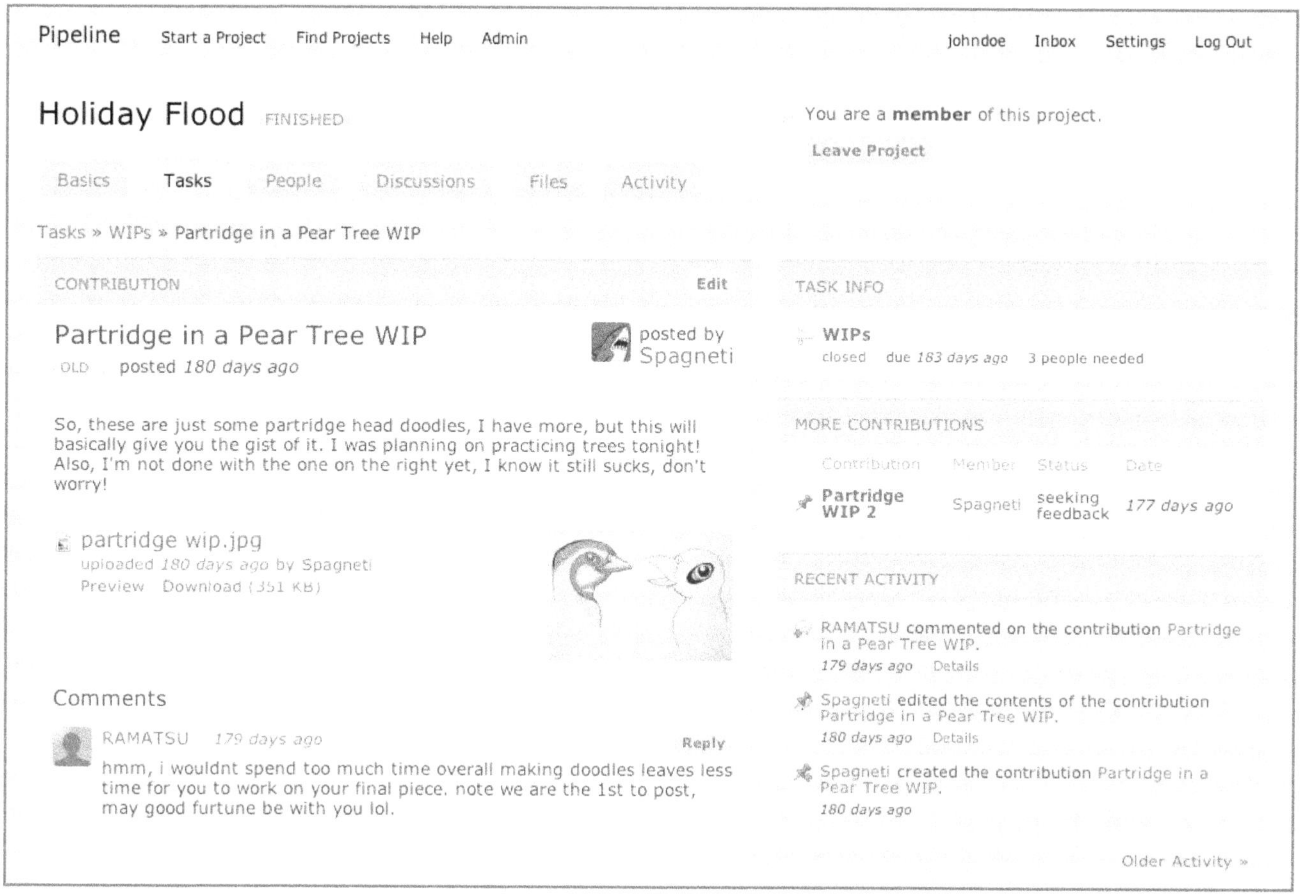

Figure 1. The Pipeline tasks system. This screenshot depicts a task contribution. The left column displays (from top to bottom) the metadata, contents, and comments for this version of the contribution. The right column lists (from top to bottom) the contribution's parent task, other versions of this contribution, and recent activity for the contribution.

artifacts, and extend this notion beyond cognitive processes to include leadership. This suggests the design principle of *automation*, meaning that Pipeline itself should be able to assist with leadership as a non-human agent, much as, for example, bots and scripts perform social roles in combating Wikipedia vandalism [12]. Finally, since DL and DCog emphasize that distributions can happen over time, Pipeline should allow leaders to reconfigure decentralization and automation in real time, in response to changing circumstances.

System Overview

Pipeline[2] is a web-based collaboration tool built with PHP, MySQL, and jQuery. It was not designed to be a new online creative community nor a new host for finished projects; these needs are already well served by existing sites like YouTube, DeviantArt, and Newgrounds. Instead, Pipeline is meant to provide collaboration support that integrates with existing online communities. It is free, open source software released under the GPL and available on GitHub. A moderately technical person can install a new Pipeline instance for any online community in a few minutes, similar to the process used by the popular blogging software Wordpress. Alternatively, our research group's web server hosts Pipelines for several popular creative communities, including Newgrounds.

Pipeline's basic structure borrows many familiar concepts from other social software, such as user profiles, private messages, and a dashboard. Projects are the cornerstone of Pipeline. Any registered user can start a new project or find one to join by browsing a list of public projects. Users can also create private projects that are visible only to invited members. The key features of Pipeline projects that enable decentralization and automation are the trusted members system, the tasks system, and the activity feeds, which we describe below.

Trusted Member System

Pipeline uses the concept of "trust" to distribute leadership within a project. Content creation, e.g. joining open tasks, sharing work in progress, leaving feedback on others' work, and participating in discussions, is open to all project members. However, *articulation work* [20,29], e.g. creating

[2] http://pipeline.cc.gatech.edu/

tasks or editing high-level project settings like deadlines, specs, and rules, is limited to trusted members.

When a user creates a new Pipeline project, she can choose which members to trust, if any. On one extreme, the creator could trust only herself, potentially replicating the top-down, centralized approach to leadership seen in most collabs. On the other extreme, the creator could trust all project members, granting full technical permissions to everyone. In this case, the project could resemble a wiki, relying on social rather than technical controls to influence member behavior. Beyond these extreme options, project creators could also trust any subset of members, from a small group of close friends to all but a handful of novices, for example. Trusted status can be granted or revoked at any time, allowing for dynamic adjustments of leadership distribution throughout the project's lifespan.

Tasks System
Pipeline provides a lightweight tasks system to help project members organize their work (Figure 1). Only trusted members can create tasks, and each task has a "task leader" responsible for ensuring the task gets done. This feature is meant to encourage decentralization, but not at the expense of members' free choice. Most Pipeline users are volunteers, and being able to self-select for tasks is both an important motivator and a highly efficient mechanism for dividing up work in online collaboration [3]. Hence, the design of Pipeline encourages members to claim work for themselves rather than assigning work to others. For example, there is no explicit software support for assigning work to project members; instead, members find work by browsing a list of open tasks and joining those that appeal to them. When a trusted member creates a new task, the default option is to lead the task herself.

Any project member can join a task and make contributions to it. Each contribution can include attached files in many popular media formats, including Flash animation, video, audio, images, and text documents, some of which Pipeline compresses or streams for quick previewing in the web browser. Members can iterate on their contributions by posting new versions, which Pipeline links together visually. Members can also leave feedback on any version of a contribution in the form of threaded comments.

Activity Feeds
Pipeline keeps comprehensive, fine-grained histories of user behavior. More than 40 types of events are stored, including users creating or editing projects, tasks, contributions, file uploads, discussions, and comments; users joining or quitting projects and tasks; and users inviting, banning, or trusting other members. Pipeline's database also stores sufficient metadata for each event to allow a project's complete history to be reconstructed.

One benefit of these histories is to aid our research efforts, but more importantly, Pipeline shares this information with users in order to increase the visibility, awareness, and accountability of their actions—i.e., to facilitate *social translucence* among users [9]. Group awareness is critical to successful collaboration, but it can be difficult and time-consuming to maintain, particularly when members are geographically distributed, as in online collaboration [15]. Pipeline seeks to automate some of the more tedious aspects of group awareness previously handled by leaders by making member behavior more socially translucent, i.e., displaying it as "recent activity" feeds. These feeds appear as a sidebar on most pages and are context-sensitive, showing only events related to the current page. Each project also includes a dedicated activity page where members can filter and explore the project's complete history. For most event types, users can zoom in on an event's details, e.g. the complete text of a comment or the "diff" of an edit to a task's description. Users can also set up customized email notifications for when certain event types occur, such as new comments on their contributions, or changes to a task they joined.

It is worth noting that while most user actions are logged, some events are hidden from activity feeds to protect users' privacy (e.g. events related to private messages). The goal with social translucence is not transparency but rather effective use of constraints, such as the balance between privacy and visibility, and helping users understand these constraints [9]. To this end, Pipeline uses a simple privacy model: all project members (creator, trusted, regular) see exactly the same set of events.

Comparisons to Similar Systems
Pipeline differs from other web-based collaboration tools, such as Asana, Basecamp, Podio, and Teambox, in that Pipeline's features encourage users to work with people they may not already know. It supports public projects and its trusted member system (described below) offers flexible permissions to help such projects succeed. Additionally, while most collaboration tools are proprietary and charge monthly fees, Pipeline is free, open-source, and designed to integrate with existing online communities.

Pipeline also bears similarities to peer production tools. Its purpose is similar to software development host Github, but Pipeline aims for breadth rather than depth, supporting a variety of creative domains. Pipeline also draws inspiration from the wiki platform MediaWiki, but even in its most wiki-like configurations, Pipeline provides more structure than MediaWiki's defaults. Finally, Pipeline's task system resembles those of crowdsourcing marketplaces like Amazon Mechanical Turk, but unlike these systems, Pipeline assumes users will directly interact with each other and are driven by intrinsic motivations rather than payment.

Development Process and Launch
The design of Pipeline began in earnest in the fall of 2009. We created low-fidelity HTML mockups and solicited feedback via email from a subset of interviewees from our

initial studies of collabs. After receiving this feedback and modifying our designs, we spent most of 2010 developing a working prototype. In early 2011 we released our prototype, Pipeline 1.0, to a small group of beta testers. We spent the summer developing a major revision based on feedback from the beta period. We launched Pipeline 2.0 in October 2011, advertising in creative communities such as Newgrounds, Kongregate, DeviantArt, and Vimeo. In November 2011, we released the Pipeline source code on GitHub. Since then, the Pipelines on our web server have attracted more than 350 registered users and 90 projects, including Flash movies and games, films and videos, transmedia story development, and even Minecraft texture packs. In the rest of the paper, we focus on a case study of one Pipeline project, Holiday Flood, a six-week visual art collaboration between 30 artists from around the world.

METHODS

Because DCog is a theory for understanding cognition in the wild, much DCog-based research takes the form of detailed case studies of real-world phenomena (e.g. [12,16,17,18]). We take a similar approach, using primarily qualitative methods to provide a rich description of the process by which leadership was distributed in Holiday Flood. For this case study, we collected and analyzed three sources of data: activity logs from the Pipeline project where Holiday Flood was organized, discussion about Holiday Flood in the Newgrounds Art Forum, and in-depth interviews with active members of Holiday Flood.

Pipeline Server Logs

The main source of data for this case study was the set of activity logs for Holiday Flood's Pipeline project. Pipeline logged a total of 1,155 events for Holiday Flood between November 9, 2011 (project start) and December 25, 2011 (project end). This count omits non-project-specific events, such as users registering for Pipeline, sending private messages, or updating their profiles. It also omits 15 events generated by the researchers (mostly related to Pipeline bug reports and feature requests).

Newgrounds Art Forum

The Newgrounds forums provided a secondary source of data for this research. The creator of Holiday Flood announced the Pipeline project, recruited members, and posted occasional updates in a thread in the Newgrounds Art Forum. From November 9 to December 27, 2011, this thread accumulated 144 replies and, as of May 2012, more than 5,100 views.

In-depth Interviews

A final source of data for this study was a series of in-depth, semi-structured interviews [30] with the five most active Holiday Flood members. We interviewed the project creator (Renae) twice, first when the project was halfway done, and again when the project was finished. We also interviewed four other members after the project was finished. Participants were interviewed either via Skype or instant message, whichever they preferred, and were not compensated for their time. Skype interviews were audio-recorded with participants' permission and fully transcribed. Interviews lasted an average of 105 minutes each (min: 35, max: 167), for a total of 627 minutes (10.5 hours). Our questions focused on participants' experiences with the Holiday Flood project, including the role of leadership, division of labor, feedback and communication patterns, attitudes towards the finished product, and benefits and drawbacks of using Pipeline.

Using Real Names

Since many of our participants view themselves as artists, it is potentially unethical to deny them credit for their work by anonymizing them [6]. Throughout this paper, we refer to participants by their Pipeline usernames, with two exceptions. We use interviewees' real names instead of their usernames if they requested it. We also do not name participants who dropped out of Holiday Flood, to avoid embarrassing them.

CASE STUDY: HOLIDAY FLOOD

The story of Holiday Flood's success is worth telling per se, but it also sheds light on how Pipeline supported and transformed leadership in a real-world example of online creative collaboration. In the following sections, we first describe the result of Holiday Flood, and then present a rich description of the process by which it was created.

The Holiday Flood

On the morning of December 12, 2011, a 19-year-old artist with the username Ashman submitted an illustration of a drummer to the Newgrounds Art Portal. Later that day, another drummer illustration appeared, authored by a different young artist, ZaneZanesorrow. At the time, few visitors to the Portal made note of these artworks among the dozens of others submitted that day.

By Christmas Eve, 28 artists from around the world had submitted 24 artworks (two per day) illustrating the lyrics of "The Twelve Days of Christmas," a traditional carol. Each artwork incorporated a special thumbnail image and was tagged with the same obscure keyword: "ohfl1". Viewers who noticed and clicked on this tag discovered that the thumbnails were actually puzzle pieces. This action aligned all the puzzle pieces in the proper sequence, revealing a hidden message: a large, festively illustrated "Season's Greetings" poster, complete with the signatures of all 28 artists (Figure 2). Thus, the Holiday Flood artworks comprised not only a visual interpretation of the "Twelve Days of Christmas" song, but also a kind of digital Advent calendar. Traditionally, these calendars anticipate the arrival of Christmas with a collection of doors on a card, one opened each day, revealing parts of an image or story.

Finally, on Christmas Day, "Operation Holiday Flood," an interactive art gallery, appeared in the Newgrounds Flash Portal.[3] It was a compilation of all 24 artworks, complete with a custom arrangement of the classic song.

In many ways, Holiday Flood was a success. Artists completed and submitted their works within their 12-hour windows, the thumbnails lined up correctly, and the interactive gallery was finished by Christmas Day, all according to plan. The Newgrounds community responded well to their efforts: most artworks received high ratings and positive reviews, and the gallery won an award for being one of the top-rated submissions on December 25.

Previous Floods

Since October 2010, two moderators of the Newgrounds Art forum, Renae (username: ReNaeNae) and Robert Westgate (username: TurkeyOnAStick), had organized a series of events called "Flood the Portal Fridays." In a typical flood, Renae or Robert would announce a theme (e.g. frogs, facial hair), a specially created thumbnail image, and a time frame, usually the first Friday of each month at 6 o'clock EST. Artists were invited to create an artwork based on the theme, submit it within the specified time frame, and include the provided thumbnail image. The result was a "flood" of new artwork to the Art Portal, unified by the theme, thumbnail, and a custom tag (e.g. "ftpf12" for "Flood the Portal Fridays 12," the twelfth such flood). The floods were a lightweight form of collaboration intended to build a sense of community among Newgrounds artists and encourage submissions to the Art Portal. As Renae observed:

> *With regular floods, it's just for fun...nothing more comes of it than covering the page with the same thumbnail, so...it's not that big of a deal if you skip out.*

As the end of 2011 approached, Renae wanted to organize a new, more ambitious type of flood. Meanwhile, we had just released Pipeline to the public, and Renae had been an early beta tester. She decided (without prompting from us) to use Pipeline to organize the new flood, which would be called "Holiday Flood" and based on a Christmas theme.

Designing the Holiday Flood

Renae's plan for Holiday Flood was more complex than previous floods in several ways. Previous floods were openly publicized on the Art Forum, but Holiday Flood would be, as much as possible, organized in secret. Holiday Flood would occur in a particular sequence, not just at a particular date and time. Rather than being identical, the artworks' thumbnails would be unique puzzle pieces that, when fitted together, revealed a hidden holiday greeting poster. Finally, Holiday Flood would not only be released as individual submissions to the Art Portal, but also collected together in a submission to the Flash Portal.

Figure 2. The result of Holiday Flood. Each of the 24 artworks contained a thumbnail with the artist's signature. Searching for the tag "ohf11" displayed all the thumbnails in order of submission, revealing the hidden "Season's Greetings" poster.

One of the first issues Renae encountered was how to recruit members for a secret project. She wanted to recruit from the Newgrounds Art Forum without spoiling the surprise for those who opted out. The simplest option might have been to privately invite a group of familiar artists, but Renae wanted Holiday Flood to be open to the entire community, at least initially. Her solution was to frame Holiday Flood as a kind of secret mission. On November 9, she created a thread in the Art Forum titled, "Operation Holiday Flood 2011," describing a *"top secret"* project for which she needed to recruit a large number of *"agents."* Anyone who betrayed the mission's secrets would be punished severely, she warned, adding, "*This is Christmas dammit! We're not messing around!*"

[3] http://www.newgrounds.com/portal/view/586537

Simultaneously, Renae created a private project on Pipeline as a counterpart to the public thread on Newgrounds. Private projects on Pipeline are visible only to members, providing a space for Holiday Flood artists to work in secret. Renae instructed interested users to create Pipeline accounts and post their usernames in the public thread. She then sent invitations to the Pipeline accounts listed in the thread, on a first-come, first-served basis. Within a few days, Renae had recruited almost 30 artists, and she had to turn away several others. According to the information self-reported in their profiles, the recruits were mostly male and mostly in their 20s. They represented at least 12 countries on 5 continents, with the majority concentrated in North America and Europe.

Renae gave "trusted" status to two members of Holiday Flood beyond herself. The first was Robert, her fellow Art Forum moderator and frequent flood organizer. Renae also trusted BlueJay, a 25-year-old artist from the Netherlands.

Managing the Artists

For Holiday Flood to succeed, four major tasks needed to be completed. The 24 artworks, two for each of the 12 Days of Christmas, had to be claimed by artists and created. The hidden holiday greeting poster had to be created, divided into 24 "puzzle piece" thumbnails, and reintegrated into the finished artworks. The finished artworks needed to be submitted in a particular sequence at particular dates and times. Finally, all of the artworks, as well as original music, needed to be collected and integrated for a Flash gallery.

Creating the Artworks

Renae created a task on Pipeline titled "CLAIM YOUR PART!." For the task's instructions, Renae had divided up the 12 Days of Christmas into 24 slots, two for each day. She asked the artists to each claim one of the slots, on a first-come, first-served basis, and create an artwork based on that slot's theme.

Renae took a straightforward divide-and-conquer approach to this task, intending each slot to be claimed by one artist. Yet three slots were each claimed by pairs of artists working in a partnership. In "Buurds" and "Three Calling Birds," one artist drew the line art, and the other colored it in. For "Buurds" (Figure 3, top) one of the Four Calling Birds artworks, Fifty-50 provided the Angry Birds-inspired line art and Larkatosa colored it. "Three French Hens" by CosmicDeath and Kashi, which shows a hen bearing the three colors of the French flag and the word "trois," was also a line art-coloring partnership.

The third partnership, "Captain Sauron" (Figure 3, bottom) by MajesticBob and Kinsei, was more complex than the others. A collage of tangible and digital artwork, the final product combined a digital illustration and a custom-built picture frame. The illustration depicted characters from *Lord of the Rings* wearing rings from the *Captain Planet* television show, while the picture frame included

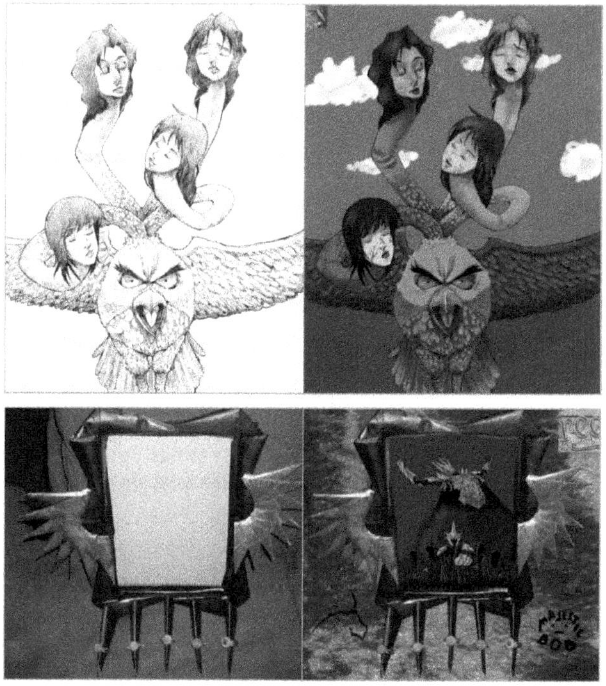

Figure 3. Two examples of partnerships. The top pair depicts Four Calling Birds by Fifty-50 (left, line art) and Larkatosa (right, coloring). The bottom pair depicts Five Golden Rings by MajesticBob (left, physical art) and Kinsei (right, digital art).

handcrafted copies of the rings shown in the illustration. While MajesticBob was responsible for the tangible portion of the artwork, both partners contributed to the digital portion. He explained:

> *I hand made the rings and the frame. Kinsei did the Picture. I cropped and fitted the pic into the frame and I did the color streams and [Photo]shopped the wind ring... Kinsei cleaned up the background and [Photo]shopped the rest of the rings.*

After all the artwork slots were claimed, Renae created another task called "WIPs", a.k.a. works-in-progress, with a deadline of December 12 (12 days before Christmas Eve). In this task, she encouraged artists to share drafts of their artworks and critique other members' work. This task served multiple purposes. It gave artists an opportunity to improve their work prior to submission, but it also provided progress updates, signaling which artists were more or less likely to make the deadline. About half of the artists shared a WIP before posting their completed artworks.

Creating the Poster and Thumbnails

In addition to creating the 24 artworks mentioned above, Holiday Flood also required a Season's Greetings poster (Figure 4), which would be divided up into puzzle pieces, one for each artwork. Renae created a task for the poster at the start of Holiday Flood, around the same time as the task for creating the artworks.

Figure 4. Evolution of the "Season's Greetings" poster. From left to right, Gabriel created the first two versions. Robert continued the development with the next two versions. Renae elaborated on Robert's concept to create the final version on the far right.

Initially, the poster task was ill-defined. No one had decided what the poster was supposed to look like, aside from Renae's vague instructions: *"a greeting card type thing... with all of our signatures on it."* Also, no one had volunteered to work on it. After some discussion within the task, Gabriel (username: ZombieMonkey), a 19-year-old Canadian artist, made the first rough drafts. He posted several versions on Pipeline, receiving detailed feedback from Renae and Robert after each.

After about a week, Robert felt that Gabriel's work had progressed as far as it could, and asked him to share his source files on Pipeline. Robert then used those source files to create a series of revisions that were generally agreed to be improvements. Gabriel himself admitted that *"[Robert] took my image and just made it so much better looking. I mean, it just looks so good now. Mine was a little bit cartoony and he just made it look so beautiful."* Robert spent nearly three weeks working on the poster, but as the Holiday Flood deadline approached, he found himself lacking the time to complete it. He recalled:

> *I polished it further and further until I couldn't really work on the image any more because I had my own stuff to do. All of those files were on Pipeline and then [Renae], because she wanted to polish up the image further, she took those files from Pipeline and edited that image further to be the finalized design.*

The last step was to collect the artists' custom signatures so they could be superimposed onto the poster. Robert created a new task requesting every member to submit an image containing his or her signature. Once all signatures were submitted, Renae used Photoshop to divide up the poster into 24 equal-sized puzzle pieces, or "thumbnails," and overlay a signature onto each. She then attached all the thumbnail files to a new task, so that artists could incorporate them into their finished artworks. As artists confirmed downloading their thumbnails, Renae manually checked them off the list by editing the task description.

Deploying the Artworks

With the artworks and their corresponding thumbnails completed, the next task was to release them on a particular schedule. Each of the 24 artworks needed to be submitted, or "deployed," within a 12-hour window. There were several possible failure modes. If an artist submitted late, the artwork wouldn't appear on the correct Day of Christmas. If an artist mixed up the order or didn't submit at all, the thumbnails wouldn't line up properly. The geographic distribution of artists, living in numerous time zones across a dozen countries, added to the challenge.

To assist with deployment, Renae created a task called "Deployment Schedule." For each of the 12 days, it listed who was responsible for submitting. As artists submitted, Renae or Robert updated the task, writing "CHECK" next to the artists' names and linking to their submissions on Newgrounds. This process gave artists a clear, updated reference as to who was done and who was up next.

Completing the Flash Gallery

With all of the artworks complete and deployment underway, the interactive art gallery could now be created. Renae took the lead developing the gallery, and in the last few days before Christmas, she posted frequent updates in a task called "Flash Submission," and artists responded with rapid feedback and bug reports. Renae had invited bakeroflongo, a 30-year-old musician from Boston, to provide a custom arrangement of the "12 Days of Christmas" song. After adding his music to the Flash gallery, Renae submitted the finished product to Newgrounds on Christmas Day.

DISCUSSION

Holiday Flood was a successful project, but how much of its success can be attributed to Pipeline? In the following section, we discuss ways that Pipeline supported and transformed (redistributed) leadership in Holiday Flood, focusing on Yukl's leadership behaviors reviewed above:

planning, problem solving, clarifying, informing, and monitoring.

Planning

Holiday Flood's leaders had extensive experience planning previous floods and collabs, and they brought this experience to bear on Holiday Flood. For example, Robert noted that contingency planning (in his words, *"risk management,"*) was an important practice he had developed over the years:

> *To be honest, whenever I handle projects, I tend to think of these problems early on, anyway, and try and come up with, well, risk management really. Try and work out how to control and mitigate those problems rather than encounter them and cry because we didnt think it would happen.*

Some leadership behaviors like this one are likely more attributable to Robert and Renae's experiences than any affordances of Pipeline. Yet, there is evidence that Pipeline had a major impact on the planning process. Both leaders emphasized that Pipeline's technological support emboldened them to plan a much more complex, elaborate flood. Robert explained:

> *Renae wanted to do something for Christmas, and...because this type of project needs a bit more management on the site, because you've also got to look after the order of the thumbnails coming into the Art Portal, as well as trying to make sure people actually come up with work, rather than doing absolutely nothing. So basically that project needs a lot more management, and that's why we brought Pipeline into it.*

Renae agreed, *"Holiday Flood was all planned and plotted...it's the reason we needed Pipeline. [I] doubt it would have worked out any other way."*

These quotes suggest that Holiday Flood's leaders felt that Pipeline made it possible to organize a new type of flood, one that was too difficult or ambitious to attempt previously. Much of the collaboration in Holiday Flood was highly interdependent, with the added complication that everything had to be completed in secret by a certain deadline. The entire process was filled with potential bottlenecks due to dependencies. If any of these steps had been omitted or seriously delayed, Gabriel explained, *"the whole thing would've been ruined,"* a sentiment shared by all of our interviewees.

Several features of Pipeline may have supported these more elaborate plans. The "Start a Project" interface was designed to use scaffolding to help leaders include key structural/planning elements in their new projects. This tool, coupled with each project's Basics tab, communicated the most important information about the project to members. Robert recalled, *"At the start of the project, [Renae] outlined how she was going to run the project, which was a simple idea which needed to be fleshed out."*

Following this, the leaders used Pipeline's task system to implement these "actions plans," in Yukl's words, and share them with members. The general consensus was that implementing similar plans on the Newgrounds forums would have been very difficult or impossible. In Luwano's words:

> *To be honest [Holiday Flood] would simply not have been possible without [Pipeline]. Getting 24 people to draw their pics would have been possible on NG, but arranging all the thumbnails and setting up the schedule would not have been possible there.*

Some of Pipeline's benefits are real, but others could have been imagined. The perceived advantages of Pipeline may have catalyzed a high level of enthusiasm among members and a desire to attempt something elaborate. More projects must be studied to tease apart the perceived and actual benefits provided by the software.

Problem Solving

Overall, Holiday Flood's leaders encountered few emergencies and minimized the need to engage in problem solving. Potentially, this was the result of the leaders drawing on their past experience and engaging in effective contingency planning. However, some problems did arise and the leaders dealt with them successfully. The most frequent and recurring emergencies were drop-outs. When artists claimed a slot for one of the Twelve Days of Christmas and then failed to deliver, Renae and Robert worked to quickly find replacements. Early in the project, they responded to drop-outs by inviting new members recruited on the Newgrounds forums. However, when the artist responsible for Twelve Drummers Drumming dropped out four days before deployment was scheduled to begin, the impending deadline created additional pressure. Renae took responsibility by posting a breathless plea for help on Newgrounds: *"The project has taken a critical hit... the entire operation is now in danger."* But Holiday Flood had been shrouded in secrecy for weeks, so finding an external replacement on such short notice proved to be challenging. Rather than a new recruit, it was an existing member, ZaneZanesorrow, who quickly drew up an "Emergency Drummers" artwork. *"It saved the whole project, basically,"* recalled Gabriel. Thus, both a leader and a regular member ultimately shared responsibility for solving the problem.

In the above examples, Renae responded by working to find others to claim open slots. Other times, Holiday Flood's leaders solved the problem by doing the work themselves. One of the best examples of leaders solving problems directly involves the Season's Greetings poster. As described above, when Gabriel became too busy to complete the poster, Robert and Renae stepped in and made the necessary improvements themselves, in a process of collaborative iteration. Pipeline's support for file sharing, commenting, and multiple versions facilitated this form of direct problem solving, as the leaders could download and modify Gabriel's work-in-progress without even contacting him. If Gabriel was too busy to finish the artwork, he was likely also too busy to share his work materials. Without Pipeline, it may have been more expedient for the leaders, unable to gauge his progress, to start over with someone else.

Clarifying Roles and Objectives

Defining Job Responsibilities

Pipeline helped leaders define job responsibilities most significantly through the trusted member system. The software gave trusted members access to tools for supporting articulation work, while regular members were limited by the system to content creation. The evidence suggests that overall, this division of labor worked well for Holiday Flood. Regular members enjoyed the creative freedom they sought while trusted members retained the authority to keep the project focused and organized. In BlueJay's opinion, *"[S]tuff might have gotten cluttered if everyone could start tasks etc."*

Leadership theory emphasizes the importance of clarifying roles, but Holiday Flood provides an example of a context where it was sometimes useful to allow for multiple interpretations. The notion of "trust" provided a valuable degree of ambiguity about the role of trusted members that might be harder to achieve with more traditionally power-laden concepts like "moderator" or "leader." Particularly online, where participation is often voluntary, leaders have a strong incentive to avoid flaunting their authority. For example, Reagle's [28] theory of "authorial leadership" describes the somewhat paradoxical relationship between "benevolent dictators," such as Wikipedia's Jimmy Wales and Linux's Linus Torvalds, and the egalitarian-minded communities they lead. Similarly, Holiday Flood's trusted members did not view themselves as authoritarians despite their extra permissions, authority, and influence. Robert reflected:

> *Even though I had a bit more of a major role, as a guy looking after the thumbnails or the other guy [BlueJay] who was meant to look after the Flash project, I didn't really see that role as a really significant one in the overall project. I still thought of that as on the same level as a contributor making a picture and sticking a thumbnail over top of it.*

The non-leaders we interviewed concurred with this view. They found the subjective experience of participating in the project to be egalitarian and empowering and saw the leaders primarily as organizers whose goal was to facilitate progress. While they agreed that Renae and Robert had authority, they found it directed mainly at preserving the project's basic structure rather than influencing artists' creative decisions. BlueJay felt that the leaders were *"mostly making sure everyone stuck to the schedule...kept the Pipeline a bit organized, making threads/tasks for stuff etc. [whereas] generating ideas and deciding on them was mostly done in consultation with everyone."*

Setting Performance Goals

Pipeline helped leaders set performance goals primarily through the Basics tab and task management system. Early in the project, Renae described the project's overall goals in the Pitch section of the Basics tab. As the project progressed, she created tasks for all major components of the project. For eight of the nine tasks, she also supplied a deadline, which further clarified the expectations for those tasks.

Assigning Tasks

As mentioned above, Pipeline encourages self-selection for tasks by preventing leaders from directly assigning work to members. This design decision appeared to be a good match for the Newgrounds community and Holiday Flood in particular. For example, one of the first tasks Renae created was titled, "CLAIM YOUR PART!," in which she encouraged members to sign up for artwork slots on a first come, first served basis. Members were pleased with their selections, as evidenced by excited comments on the task and the fact that all artworks were completed. Meanwhile, leaders were free to focus on responsibilities other than matching artists with tasks and dealing with those who were unsatisfied with their assignments.

Providing Instructions for Tasks

The leaders of Holiday Flood provided instructions to members throughout the project. Pipeline supported this practice in several ways. Tasks were designed with several fields for including instructions, such as the number of people needed for a task, and a plain-text "Instructions" area for more detailed information.

Yukl notes that providing feedback is another important component of the leadership behavior of providing instruction [34]. Traditionally, formal leaders provided most or all of the feedback to collab members because the limitations of the Newgrounds forum made it difficult for members to share their work or exchange feedback among themselves. Most had to wait for audience reviews of the finished product, or they could email their files to the project's leader and request comments.

In contrast, Pipeline provided each contribution with a dedicated area for file sharing, iteration, and discussion. Many members were able to share rough drafts and receive comments prior to the deadline, from both leaders and regular members. As a result, feedback was more evenly distributed among the group. BlueJay explained:

> *In previous floods people usually provided feedback after everything had been submitted to the portal. With other art collabs the amount of feedback is usually pretty much limited to the collab organizer. For the Holiday Flood people uploaded and got more feedback on WIPs.*

BlueJay's impression is supported by the data. We analyzed the Pipeline logs and found that members of Holiday Flood had posted 114 comments on contributions that were not their own. Of these, less than half (50 comments, or 44%) were posted by Renae and Robert. In other words, the majority of feedback on works-in-progress was provided by regular members, not formal leaders.

Informing

Pipeline was designed with the goal of helping to organize the information flow and supporting leaders as informers. Each project has a Discussion tab, which allows members to participate in forum-style discussions that are organized by topic, rather than as one chronological list. Renae used this feature several times to make general announcements to the Holiday Flood membership.

Other Pipeline features sought to help automate certain aspects of informing. Yukl notes that leaders can increase effective informing by "improv[ing] direct access by others to relevant information" [34]. Pipeline is intended to support this direct access by connecting members to the content that matters to them. For example, the Tasks tab displays the user's tasks first, and Recent Activity feeds are contextual, showing only the events that are relevant to the surrounding content. Our intention was that Pipeline would automate some of this tedious informing work, easing the burden on leaders and freeing them to focus on other tasks. Our inspiration for this idea was Hutchins' analysis of DCog in airplane cockpits, where he describes how small instrument markers called "speed bugs" do not actually help pilots remember significant airspeeds, but instead store the information so that pilots need not remember it at all, and can focus on other matters [18]. He writes, "The beauty of devices like speed bugs is that they permit these reconfigurations of functional systems in way that reduce the requirements for scarce cognitive resources." Similarly, we hoped that Pipeline could provide tools that, like an aircraft's speed bugs, reduced the requirements for scarce cognitive resources. Holiday Flood raised two issues with this line of thinking that prompted me to unpack the goal of "easing the burden on leaders," which may have been overly simplistic.

First, many of our design choices for automating leadership behaviors in Pipeline had the unexpected consequence of actually distributing small but significant bits of work to non-leaders. For example, instead of leaders collecting members' files and providing feedback, members uploaded their files directly to Pipeline so that anyone in the project could comment. Instead of leaders answering questions about the project's structure, members could explore the open tasks to answer their own questions. Instead of leaders manually updating member lists, members clicked "Join" or "Leave" buttons and Pipeline updated the member list accordingly. In general, Pipeline encouraged Holiday Flood's members to interact regularly with the site so that it could capture this activity and share it with other members in the form of recent activity feeds. Instead of automating leadership behaviors (e.g. informing and monitoring), it may be more accurate to say that Pipeline was improving the social translucence of these leadership behaviors.

Second, there were unexpected benefits to having human leaders act as informers. For example, some leaders manually updated tasks when members made a contribution, even as Pipeline updated the task automatically. While the leaders' manual efforts and the task system both communicated the same progress information, they were not redundant because the manual updates contained additional information: the leaders were paying attention to the artists' progress. The automatic updates were quicker and more reliable, but the manual ones provided valuable motivation. Robert explained:

> *[It was] very helpful for everybody really, just to make sure that people are contributing and that there is some active progression on the site. Not only because it's a clear sign that the leader is very much motivated with the project, but that other people also have that motivation as well.*

Hence, it is important to consider the tradeoffs of automating leadership behaviors, as sometimes even tedious work is more effectively done by human leaders. This finding bears similarities to attitudes towards authorship in online remix communities, where manual crediting is viewed as essential even when the system automatically attributes remixed content [25].

Monitoring

Pipeline supports monitoring most significantly through its Recent Activity feeds, email notifications, and the underlying infrastructure that logs user behavior. As mentioned above, this infrastructure caused many member activities that previously happened off-site or went uncaptured to become socially translucent, and therefore available for other users to interpret. Additionally, the fact that Recent Activity feeds were visible to all project members, not just leaders, meant that monitoring was transformed into a more distributed leadership behavior. Leaders could more easily monitor the progress of members, but now members could also monitor the leaders and one another.

While the Recent Activity feeds helped redistribute some aspects of monitoring, other Pipeline features also supported more traditional, leader-driven monitoring. One example is the Discussion tab, which Renae used to organize two "roll calls" on November 18 and December 5 in order to smoke out drop-outs. In these discussions, Renae required every member of Holiday Flood to check in and post a brief update before a certain deadline—otherwise, they would be banned from the project. As described above, Renae followed through on this promise and banned a handful of unresponsive members, taking advantage of both

Pipeline's tools for communication and for cutting off communication.

CONCLUSION AND IMPLICATIONS

Leadership plays a significant role in the success or failure of online creative collaboration. When leaders have proper technological support and assume a manageable workload, they can lead complex creative collaborations with significant impact. These success stories include the world's largest encyclopedia, some of its most popular and useful software, and compelling, award-winning art and entertainment. However, many other promising efforts fail because leaders are overburdened. In the Newgrounds community, the challenges of online creative collaboration and poor technological support contributed to a culture of simple projects and top-down, centralized leadership styles. Leaders who attempted more ambitious projects ended up dealing with many of the complications that arose themselves, with little help from technology or other members. In this paper, we developed a theoretical framework to understand how leadership could be redistributed; described the design of Pipeline, a web-based tool informed by this framework; and presented a case study showing how the tool was used in a real-world context, a successful online artistic collaboration.

The case study revealed that Holiday Flood's leaders organized a highly ambitious project and were rewarded by success. To understand Pipeline's role in this success, we analyzed leadership in the project through the theoretical lens of Yukl's five leadership behaviors. While the leaders, Renae and Robert, brought extensive leadership experience to the project and drew upon that experience, their efforts were also streamlined and emboldened by Pipeline.

For the most part, Pipeline served to support Renae and Robert's top-down, centralized leadership style. Its "Start a Project" tool and Basics tab assisted with early planning and structure for Holiday Flood, while the software's overall capabilities encouraged the leaders to strive for something more complex and interdependent. Pipeline helped leaders solve problems by providing quick access to members' works in progress. While Pipeline's trusted member system helped clarify roles by limiting permissions of regular members, it also provided a valuable degree of ambiguity that deemphasized power relationships. The software supported leaders' informing behaviors by helping them communicate important information to members via discussions, and leaders also used discussions to initiate "roll calls" that helped them monitor progress.

There is also evidence that Pipeline transformed some aspects of leadership by redistributing certain leadership behaviors across a broader set of Holiday Flood members. Assigning tasks is an important leadership behavior identified by Yukl [34], yet unlike most project management tools, Pipeline does not allow leaders to assign tasks. Rather, Pipeline's design draws inspiration from peer production theory and encourages users to self-select for tasks. Holiday Flood's leaders created tasks and asked members to claim ones that appealed to them, reducing the leaders' coordination efforts and leveraging the motivations and self-knowledge of members. Another leadership behavior identified by Yukl, providing feedback, was redistributed via Pipeline's support for comments, file sharing, and iteration such that more than half of all Holiday Flood feedback was provided by non-leaders. Finally, the Recent Activity feeds in Pipeline helped redistribute the leadership behaviors of informing and monitoring by encouraging members to make their actions more socially translucent, and displaying this behavior in meaningful, context-sensitive ways.

Overall, the Holiday Flood case study suggested that Pipeline can be a powerful tool for both supporting and transforming leadership in online creative collaboration. However, more studies of additional projects are needed to understand its strengths and limitations, and tease apart the interrelationships between leader expertise, domain requirements, and technological support.

The major theoretical implication of this work is that online leadership can be redistributed to make it more effective. Previous work established that leadership can be distributed in online creative collaboration [35,36]. We extend this work by integrating theories of distributed leadership (DL) and distributed cognition (DCog) to show how technology can help redistribute leadership. This integration furthered the development of DL by introducing technology as a means of distributing leadership, and pushed DCog forward by showing how its constructs can be used for analyzing and designing for leadership, not just cognition.

According to Halverson [16], theories that are useful for CSCW have four important attributes: inferential power, application power, descriptive power, and rhetorical power. Our proposed framework helped us *infer* that leaders could be more effective, and projects more complex, if leadership was redistributed in Newgrounds collabs. It helped us *apply* the theory of DL to online creative collaboration by informing our design considerations for Pipeline (e.g. decentralization and automation). It helped us *describe* the Holiday Flood creation process using a case study that focused on the interplay between people (formal leaders, other members) and technologies (Pipeline, Newgrounds). And finally, it provided *rhetorical* power by helping us map observed phenomena in Holiday Flood to theoretical constructs (e.g. leadership behaviors, leader legitimacy, and social translucence).

This work also suggests a major design implication. Systems supporting online creative collaboration should assume formal leaders exist, but also help them redistribute leadership across the entire group as needed. In the case of Holiday Flood, Pipeline helped Renae and Robert organize a complex artistic collaboration by helping them decentralize some tasks traditionally handled by leaders, such as giving feedback and sharing progress reports, across nearly 30 other members. Other projects may have the opposite problem, where leadership is too distributed to be effective and needs to be concentrated among a smaller number of formal leaders. By providing tools like Pipeline's "trust" system that allow members to customize leadership models for each project, or even make real-time adjustments within one project, system designers will encourage a richer variety of creative processes and outcomes from users.

ACKNOWLEDGMENTS

We wish to thank the participants in this study, Pipeline users and beta testers, and the Newgrounds staff and community. Boris de Souza, Chris Howse, and Kevin Ziegler made substantial contributions to the design and development of Pipeline. Scott Counts, Jill Dimond, Betsy DiSalvo, Ellen Do, Eric Gilbert, Wendy Kellogg, Sarita Yardi, and our anonymous reviewers provided valuable feedback on this paper. This research is supported by NSF award CreativeIT-0855952.

REFERENCES

1. Adair, M. Eric Whitacre's Virtual Choir will be unveiled Thursday. *The Los Angeles Times*, 2011. http://latimesblogs.latimes.com/culturemonster/2011/04/eric-whitacre-virtual-choir-revealed.html.
2. Becker, H.S. *Art Worlds*. University of California Press, 1984.
3. Benkler, Y. Coase's Penguin, or Linux and the Nature of the Firm. *Yale Law Journal 112*, 3 (2002), 369–446.
4. Boland, R.J., Tenkasi, R.V., and Te'eni, D. Designing Information Technology to Support Distributed Cognition. *Organization Science 5*, 3 (1994), 456–475.
5. Bolden, R. Distributed Leadership in Organizations: A Review of Theory and Research. *International Journal of Management Reviews 13*, 3 (2011), 251–269.
6. Bruckman, A. Studying the amateur artist: A perspective on disguising data collected inhuman subjects research on the Internet. *Ethics and Inf. Technol. 4*, 3 (2002), 217–231.
7. Cranshaw, J. and Kittur, A. The polymath project: lessons from a successful online collaboration in mathematics. *Proceedings of the 2011 annual conference on Human factors in computing systems*, ACM (2011), 1865–1874.
8. Edwards, G. Concepts of Community: A Framework for Contextualizing Distributed Leadership. *International Journal of Management Reviews 13*, 3 (2011), 301–312.
9. Erickson, T. and Kellogg, W.A. Social translucence: an approach to designing systems that support social processes. *ACM Trans. Comput.-Hum. Interact. 7*, 1 (2000), 59–83.
10. Forte, A., Larco, V., and Bruckman, A. Decentralization in Wikipedia Governance. *Journal of Management Information Systems 26*, 1 (2009), 49–72.
11. Galant, R. Software brings Johnny Cash back to life. *CNN*, 2011. http://articles.cnn.com/2011-04-21/opinion/koblin.data.art_1_images-compelling-data-users?_s=PM:OPINION.
12. Geiger, R.S. and Ribes, D. The work of sustaining order in wikipedia: the banning of a vandal. *Proceedings of the 2010 ACM conference on Computer supported cooperative work*, ACM (2010), 117–126.
13. Gronn, P. Distributed leadership as a unit of analysis. *The Leadership Quarterly 13*, 4 (2002), 423–451.
14. Gronn, P. The future of distributed leadership. *Journal of Educational Administration 46*, 2 (2008), 141–158.
15. Gutwin, C., Penner, R., and Schneider, K. Group awareness in distributed software development. *Proceedings of the 2004 ACM conference on Computer supported cooperative work*, ACM (2004), 72–81.
16. Halverson, C.A. Activity Theory and Distributed Cognition: Or What Does CSCW Need to DO with Theories? *Comput. Supported Coop. Work 11*, 1-2 (2002), 243–267.
17. Hollan, J., Hutchins, E., and Kirsh, D. Distributed cognition: toward a new foundation for human-computer interaction research. *ACM Trans. Comput.-Hum. Interact. 7*, 2 (2000), 174–196.
18. Hutchins, E. How a cockpit remembers its speeds. *Cognitive Science 19*, 3 (1995), 265–288.
19. Hutchins, E. *Cognition in the Wild*. A Bradford Book, 1996.
20. Kriplean, T., Beschastnikh, I., and McDonald, D.W. Articulations of wikiwork: uncovering valued work in wikipedia through barnstars. *Proceedings of the ACM 2008 conference on Computer supported cooperative work*, ACM (2008), 47–56.
21. Luther, K. and Bruckman, A. Leadership in online creative collaboration. *Proceedings of the ACM 2008 conference on Computer supported cooperative work*, ACM (2008), 343–352.
22. Luther, K., Caine, K., Ziegler, K., and Bruckman, A. Why it works (when it works): success factors in online creative collaboration. *Proceedings of the 16th ACM international conference on Supporting group work*, ACM (2010), 1–10.
23. Luther, K., Diakopoulos, N., and Bruckman, A. Edits & credits: exploring integration and attribution in

online creative collaboration. *Proceedings of the 28th of the international conference extended abstracts on Human factors in computing systems*, ACM (2010), 2823–2832.

24. Mockus, A., Fielding, R.T., and Herbsleb, J.D. Two case studies of open source software development: Apache and Mozilla. *ACM Trans. Softw. Eng. Methodol. 11*, 3 (2002), 309–346.

25. Monroy-Hernández, A., Hill, B.M., Gonzalez-Rivero, J., and boyd, danah. Computers can't give credit: how automatic attribution falls short in an online remixing community. *Proceedings of the 2011 annual conference on Human factors in computing systems*, ACM (2011), 3421–3430.

26. Nakakoji, K., Yamamoto, Y., Nishinaka, Y., Kishida, K., and Ye, Y. Evolution patterns of open-source software systems and communities. *Proceedings of the International Workshop on Principles of Software Evolution*, ACM (2002), 76–85.

27. Olson, G.M. and Olson, J.S. Distance matters. *Hum.-Comput. Interact. 15*, 2 (2000), 139–178.

28. Reagle, J.M. Do as I do: authorial leadership in wikipedia. *Proceedings of the 2007 international symposium on Wikis*, ACM (2007), 143–156.

29. Schmidt, K. and Bannon, L. Taking CSCW seriously: Supporting articulation work. *Computer Supported Cooperative Work 1*, 1 (1992), 7–40.

30. Seidman, I. *Interviewing As Qualitative Research: A Guide for Researchers in Education And the Social Sciences*. Teachers College Press, 2006.

31. Stelter, B. An Emmy for Rebuilding a Galaxy. *The New York Times*, 2010. http://www.nytimes.com/2010/08/28/arts/television/28uncut.html.

32. Thorpe, R., Gold, J., and Lawler, J. Locating Distributed Leadership. *International Journal of Management Reviews 13*, 3 (2011), 239–250.

33. Weber, S. *The Success of Open Source*. Harvard University Press, 2004.

34. Yukl, G.A. *Leadership in Organizations*. Prentice Hall College Div, 1997.

35. Zhu, H., Kraut, R., and Kittur, A. Effectiveness of shared leadership in online communities. *Proceedings of the ACM 2012 conference on Computer Supported Cooperative Work*, ACM (2012), 407–416.

36. Zhu, H., Kraut, R.E., Wang, Y.-C., and Kittur, A. Identifying shared leadership in Wikipedia. *Proceedings of the 2011 annual conference on Human factors in computing systems*, ACM (2011), 3431–3434.

From Organizational to Community Creativity: Paragon Leadership & Creativity Stories at Etsy

Tyler Pace, Katie O'Donnell, Natalie DeWitt, Shaowen Bardzell, Jeffrey Bardzell
Indiana University
919 E 10th St, Bloomington, IN 47408 USA
{tympace, kaodonne, nkdewitt, selu, jbardzel} @ indiana.edu

ABSTRACT
With the rise of massive scale, globally distributed creative communities, such as Deviant Art, Etsy, and Minecraft, the role of creative leadership in sociotechnical systems is worth investigating. This paper presents a case study of one strategy Etsy, one such online creative community, uses to articulate the creative dispositions of the community's exemplar members: Featured Seller interviews. For this study, we report on a combined content analysis and close reading of Featured Seller interviews on Etsy.com, followed up with member check interviews. Our analysis highlights the demographics of featured sellers, the ways in they express their identities and creative processes, and how they position themselves within the broader Etsy community. Our findings demonstrate that Etsy's administrators provide both a platform and scaffolding for community leaders to co-articulate with them the creative ideals they believe will strengthen the bonds of the Etsy community.

Author Keywords
Craft; art; creativity; community; paragon; leadership; Etsy; content analysis

ACM Classification Keywords
H5.m. Information interfaces and presentation (e.g., HCI): Miscellaneous.

INTRODUCTION
Creativity is a prized human trait, and not surprisingly it has been broadly theorized and studied in nearly every modern academic discipline. Creativity research is a p articularly mature area in psychology, where empirical studies since the Second World War have incrementally contributed to an increasingly powerful theoretical account of human creativity in diverse situations and contexts, including developmental creativity in children, creativity in the fine arts, creativity in everyday life, and professional creativity in the sciences, law, and other professions.

CSCW '13, February 23–27, 2013, San Antonio, Texas, USA.
Copyright 2013 ACM 978-1-4503-1331-5/13/02...$15.00.

Given the emergence of socio-technical systems as an important research area in HCI and CSCW [3], it is not surprising that organizational theories of creativity would be explored as an important topic of interest within that area [11, 12, 13]. Derived primarily from empirical studies of organizations—corporate, government, non-profits, etc.—such theories are optimized to contribute to interaction design for those types of organizations. A key component of these organizational theories is the role of leaders in shaping, promoting, and embodying creativity for the organization at large. In psychology, *creativity* is understood as "the ability to produce work that is both novel (i.e., original, unexpected) and appropriate (i.e., adaptive concerning task constraints)" [30], and extends beyond artistic creativity also to include diverse forms of innovation and problem-solving throughout everyday life.

With the rise of massive scale, globally distributed and decentralized creative communities, such as Deviant Art, Etsy, Pinterest, and Minecraft, which are managed by organizations and have features and structures that are analogues of traditional organizational structures, the role of the creative leader is worth revisiting. Yet it is difficult to evaluate the efficacy of creative leaders in massive decentralized communities, in part because not enough empirical research is available about such communities.

In this paper, we describe our research on Etsy, an online community devoted to buying and selling crafts. With over 15 million members and $63 million in sales each month, the Etsy community is massive and successful in terms of craft items listed, viewed, and sold [8, 9]. While there are many factors that contribute to Etsy's economic success, this paper focuses on the growing number of publicly acknowledged and promoted sellers that help influence and shape the creative skills and dispositions of Etsy crafters throughout the community. A key strategy employed by Etsy administrators is to identify and promote its exemplar members is their use of the ongoing "Featured Seller" interviews. In brief, each Featured Seller interview highlights a successful member of Etsy community using a structured interview format. These interviews are then made available to the broader Etsy community via a high profile position on the official Etsy.com website. For clarity throughout this paper, we will use *Etsy community* (or *Etsy-comm*) to refer to the collectivity of all the site's buyers, sellers, users, lurkers, etc. We use *Etsy corporate* (or *Etsy-corp*) to refer to the business that owns the brand and platform; and we use *Etsy.com* to refer to the technology platform itself.

This paper reports on a content analysis [14] of the corpus of these interviews. This analysis sheds light on Etsy-corp's emergent efforts to highlight exemplar members as a type of paragon leadership [27] in the community as one means of supporting creativity in a massive community. We focus our analysis on three dimensions of creative leadership found in the interviews: establishing identities as creators, articulating sources of inspiration, and reinforcing the broader community. These interviews, we argue, help Etsy-corp develop a coherent community vision and ethos, strategically (yet with restraint) strengthening the bonds of the loosely coupled millions that make up its community. Our research contributes to the study of massive scale creative communities by offering preliminary evidence as to how exemplar community members, in collaboration with site owners, may co-articulate desirable skills and dispositions that work to influence the broader membership of an online community of creators.

From Organizational Creativity to Online Communities of Creators

Organizational theories of creativity seek to identify and explain optimal team composition, leadership strategies, work environments, failure tolerance, organizational culture, etc. [23, 24, 25, 33]. Work in HCI and CSCW has carried these themes forward into interaction design. Fischer and colleagues [11, 12, 13] have investigated the relationships between social structures (e.g., communities of practice and communities of interest) and technological resources (e.g., boundary objects and collaboratories) as supports for organizational creativity. Farooq et al. [10] continue this work on organizational creativity noting the desirability of studying and designing for everyday long-term creative efforts and collaborations as opposed to anticipating the mythical "lightning bolt" moments of inspiration. Further, Davenport and Mazalek [6] explore the artful role of the designer (and researcher) in shaping new creative domains and communities through the development of innovative technologies.

One aspect of organizational creativity that is frequently emphasized in the literature is creative leadership. A recent article on organizational creativity [21] describes work on creative leadership as "a burgeoning body of research," and the authors' synthesis indicates that leaders that promote organizational creativity have the following attributes: "tolerance for ambiguity, ability to assess and be comfortable with risk; ability to quickly and effectively assess an individual; ability to balance passion and objectivity; and ability to change" [21]. Another key aspect of leadership in creative organizations is to define roles for the organization as a whole as well as teams and individuals within it [23]; roles help define relationships among members and facilitate decentralized collaborations. Leadership also creates (dis-)incentive structures that can affect organizational creativity [31], e.g., by stifling creativity through transactional reward structures that reward well defined goal achievement, rather than innovation and change. Finally, leaders in their roles as domain experts also take on the role of the creativity gatekeeper insofar as they often decide what gets to count as "creative" and what is preserved as an exemplar creative achievement for the future [4, 5].

In addition to the aforementioned organizational capacities of leaders (i.e., role definition [23], incentive structures [31], & gatekeeping [4, 5]), creative leaders may also serve as "role models" who lead-by-example through their day-to-day actions and dispositions [27]. Role models come in the form of impersonal "paragons" who are admired and emulated from a distance as well as personal "mentors" who influence emerging creativity in a more direct fashion [27]. One of the central means by which paragons influence the creativity of their followers is through the embodiment and reproduction of *creativity stories* that work to convey a message about the skills and dispositions that are best suited for encouraging creativity and success within their respective organizations [26, 27]. For these stories to be successful, they must (1) address individual and group identity, (2) appeal to the experiences of the audience, (3) operate in an organizational structure, and (4) be embodied by the actions of the leader [26, 27].

However, the empirical work on which these theories of creative leadership are based was grounded predominantly in twentieth-century professional organizations. These organizations tended to situate their members within strong organizational relationships that might not exist in massive creative communities. Many members of the organizations favored in traditional creativity research share a similar past, in the sense that they have similar backgrounds (e.g., collegiate degrees and professional knowledge). They share a similar present, in their physical, technical, and social environments. And they share a disposition toward the future, e.g., through organizational visions, mission statements, career trajectories, etc.

In the past decade, the rise of network-based creative communities, from e-science platforms to YouTube, provide an increasingly viable alternative to the traditional hierarchical organization. One emerging theoretical formulation of this type of community is Sylvan's [31] online community of creators (OCOC). According to her definition, an OCOC is a social network site that involves (1) individuals sharing their own creations, (2) discussion of one another's work, and (3) an association of creators with their creations. In [32], Sylvan identifies Flickr, Vimeo, and deviantART as paradigmatic examples. Membership in these communities is looser, in the sense that shared backgrounds, environments, and visions are more diluted. The Etsy community, too, fulfills the formulation of an online community of creators with its emphasis on creators and their creations, support of a loosely networked membership, and minimal organizational oversight. This paper works to provide early evidence of how strategies for creative leadership that were applied in traditional organizations, in particular the role of paragon leaders and creativity stories, may be renewed, rejected, or otherwise reinterpreted in OCOCs.

Etsy as a Site for Massively Networked Creativity

Etsy is an online marketplace where people buy and sell vintage and handmade goods, as well as art and craft supplies. Etsy-corp's mission statement characterizes Etsy as a "community that actively supports one another in the shared goal of offering alternatives to mass-produced objects," with a focus on connecting buyers and sellers in a meaningful way [8]. In addition to Etsy-corp's goal of supporting a consumer-conscious community, it also facilitates the sharing of craft related skills among members, assists sellers in improving business practices, and fosters the growth of an online community for "all things handmade."

Most importantly, as alluded to in our naming conventions, Etsy can be distinguished from the types of organizations typically researched under the auspices of organizational creativity due to a hybrid organizational structure that separates, in part, Etsy's corporate entity and Etsy's broader community of crafter-sellers, what we refer to as Etsy-corp and Etsy-comm, respectively. Etsy-corp is managed by a CEO and a team of administrators, but these corporate leaders do not work in the same industry or domain as Etsy's crafter-sellers. Running a massive-scale e-commerce and community platform requires a different set of skills and dispositions than running a small handwork business. For Etsy's crafter-sellers, creative leadership is unlikely to be found in Etsy-corp's CEO, community managers, or engineers, (creative as they may be), which make up the bulk of the company, but is instead located within the community of crafter-sellers itself.

As a result, Etsy.com offers important empirical opportunities for studying massive-scale organizational creativity because of its hybrid organizational structure and its successes as an online community of creators. Further, Etsy.com has made available a d ataset that, among other things, sheds light on Etsy-corp's emerging efforts to support its community by enabling that community to disseminate its own creativity stories that are embodied in and reproduced through the crafter-seller community's exemplar members. That dataset is the corpus of its Featured Seller interviews.

According to a research collaborator at Etsy-corp, up to three sellers a week are selected as "featured sellers" (note that as of summer 2012, Etsy-corp renamed them "featured stores") through a curated committee process among Etsy-corp staff, during which storefronts, merchandise, and photography are evaluated according to ideals that Etsy-corp wishes to promote. These include community participation, policy and guideline compliance, individual creative voice, and commercial success. Once selected, the featured sellers are invited to answer a variety of text-based, committee-selected questions about their hobbies, goals, Etsy-comm experiences, and creative work.

As noted, the 600 expert interviews constitute a promising corpus for understanding the sort of leadership Etsy-corp and the featured sellers co-articulated for this massive-scale creativity community. However, there is a complication. Over the course of six years of interviews, Etsy-corp changed the questions. For the most part, the changes in the questions were slow and incremental. It is also clear from the changes that Etsy-corp refined the question sets in an ongoing effort to refine and clarify the ideals that they wish Etsy-comm to embody. In our analysis, we characterize both the question changes and more importantly their implications for how we understand these leaders.

RESEARCH DESIGN

The central empirical contribution of this work derives from a content analysis [14] of the Featured Seller interviews posted to Etsy.com from 2005 to 2010. There are 612 total interviews in the archive with a random sample of 237 interviews analyzed to establish a confidence interval of 95%

Code Theme	Code Category	Brief Description	# Codes	% Correct	Kripp. Alpha*
Demographics	Gender	Male, Female, or Transgender.	303	98.54	.79
	Craft Partnership	Store operated by more than one seller.	50	96.52	.71
	Training	Type of training received in craft or other skills.	586	92.51	.70
	Family	Live-in family members or pets.	436	98.52	.60
	Job Status	Current profession and employment status.	392	92.45	.63
Identity	--	Self-identified status as a creator.	307	74.66	.62
Process	Tools	Non-consumable items used in the creative process.	173	94.81	.57
	Product	Products produced and sold by the featured seller.	413	92.35	.55
	Materials	Consumable items used in the creative process.	393	96.74	.65
	Inspiration	Sources of inspiration in the creative process.	223	89.34	.61
Community	Advice	Advice given to other creators.	689	89.95	.67
	Technology	Discussion of technologies that support membership in an online creative community.	799	91.37	.61

Table 1: Breakdown of relevant coding categories. Only codes/categories discussed in this paper are listed. *Calculated via the Coding Analysis Toolkit [CAT]. α > .55 used for this study.

+/- 5%. The number of interviews included in the final sample reflects the distribution of the total number of interviews per year. Table 2 offers a breakdown of the total number, sample number, and percent distribution of interviews by year.

Year	Total # Interviews	Sample # Interviews	% of Total Distribution
2005*	8	3	1.31
2006	41	16	6.70
2007	95	37	15.52
2008	155	60	25.33
2009	156	60	25.49
2010	157	61	25.65
Total	*612*	*237*	*100.0*

Table 2: Breakdown of featured seller interviews by year. *Partial year. Interviews began on Oct. 6, 2005.

The coding system employed in this study was developed through three iterative test codings of small random samples of interviews. For the initial coding system, the coding team (composed of three of the authors) independently evaluated a random sample of 20 interviews from years 2005-2010 and developed separate coding systems. These initial coding systems were collaboratively merged to produce a single shared coding system and were further developed through two additional iterations in which the coding team applied the shared coding system to a new random sample of 10 interviews each. In sum, the final coding system was developed through three iterations and across 40 random interviews. Interviews used during the development stage were removed from the interview data set before selection of the final sample. Additionally, a coding manual was developed in tandem with each iteration of the coding system to serve as a unifying reference for the coding team.

The final coding system includes 42 unique codes organized into 13 categories and 5 themes. Table 2 offers a breakdown of code themes, categories, and code descriptions. For this study, codes, categories, and themes relate to each other as follows:

- A *code* represents the smallest unit of analysis and is employed directly by the coder when coding the interview text.
- A *category* is a group of tightly related codes. For example, Gender is a category containing the codes of Male, Female, and Transgender.
- A *theme* is a critical grouping of code categories developed by the research team for the purposes of data analysis. Themes will be discussed in more detail in the findings and discussion sections.

The final coding process was conducted independently by each member of the coding team for all interviews in the final sample. In order to facilitate valid and reliable codes at the completion of the project, interviews were coded randomly, not chronologically, to prevent the privileging of a particular date range in the dataset. Also, to combat coder fatigue, each coder started in a different, evenly separated position in the dataset and a coding schedule was utilized. In total, the coding team applied 7,522 codes to 2,537 quotations across the 237 interviews in the final sample. Atlas.Ti, a Computer Assisted Qualitative Data Analysis Software package, was used by the coding team to code the interviews and manage the code data.

Codes were validated using the Coding Analysis Toolkit (CAT) [2]. Codes were uploaded to the CAT system online and validated by an adjudication team comprised of the original coding team. To control for validation by a coding team, the code details and history were not made available to the coding team during the validation process. The adjudicators could not see which coder(s) applied the codes under validation. Further, the final codes were validated in a random order. Table 3 presents a summary of coder and code correctness post-validation.

	Avg. % Correct	(%) SD
Coders	91.1	1.57
Codes	90.45	9.8

Table 3: Coder and code correctness post-validation.

Additionally, Table 1 offers a breakdown of the number of codes, percent valid, and a Krippendorff's Alpha measurement of intercoder agreement. Agreement levels of $\alpha > .55$ were considered satisfactory for further analysis given the following study conditions.

- The interview data is volatile. The nature of the questions and responses changes over time.
- Interviews were coded as they appear on the Etsy.com website and interview text was not pre-selected for coders. The coding team was responsible for both identifying key text and then applying codes to the text.

After validation, the invalid codes were removed and the valid code data was exported for analysis in SPSS.

Interview Question Phases

To aid in analysis of the interview corpus, the research team analyzed all interviews' questions posed in the dataset to document the amount of variance in the questions over time. Our analysis of the questions and their changes was conducted through the method known as *explication de texte* or, more commonly, a close reading. An analytic method originating in the humanities [20], close reading refers to the careful and critical examination of rhetorical devices, style, and other thematic and formal elements of a text. We critically analyzed Featured Seller interview questions to identify significant rhetorical changes across the history of the interviews to help situate the interview data. These rhetorical changes are considered evidence of emergent strategy by Etsy-corp to refine its creativity stories to better highlight desirable skills and dispositions within the crafter-seller community.

Phase	Start Date	End Date	# Interviews
Phase 1	Oct. 6, 2005	June 24, 2007	91
Phase 2	June 25, 2007	Jan. 10, 2008	56
Phase 3	Jan. 11, 2008	Dec. 31, 2010	465

Table 4: Significant question changes cluster into three phases in Etsy Featured Seller interviews from 2005-2010.

In total, the team identified 23 questions changes wherein two sets of interview questions occurring at different times were considered to contain substantial rhetorical differences (e.g., changes in question content or structure). To account for the question changes in our analysis, we divided the interviews into a timeline segmented into three major question phases, shown in Table 4. In the findings section, we will discuss how specific question changes work together over time to shape the nature of the interview responses and the efforts of Etsy-comm's creative leaders.

Member Check Interviews

Following the content analysis, we conducted member check interviews [17] with featured sellers selected at random from our final sample of Featured Seller interviews. In total, we invited 73 featured sellers to participate in member check interviews and received 8 initial responses resulting in 5 completed interviews. The member check interviews were conducted remotely through email and chat clients. Interview questions were based on the claims and findings derived from our content analysis project. These interviews are not meant to compose a significant sample with respect to the total number of featured sellers, but rather the goal of the member check interviews was to validate our understanding of the Featured Seller interviews with community members that were most central to the process, i.e., featured sellers themselves.

FINDINGS

In the following, we present and interpret Featured Seller interview coding data by code theme (refer back to Table 2 for a breakdown of code themes): *Featured Sellers*, which collectively identifies key demographic attributes and characteristics of the sellers that Etsy-corp chose to feature; *Identity*, which explores the two most common forms of identity (i.e., artist and crafter) expressed by the featured sellers; *Process*, which explores trends into how the featured sellers articulate their work practices, and finally *Community*, which explores advice giving and support in a community that blurs the professional-amateur distinction. We also present the results of our member check interviews, which validate and also add nuance to the findings of our content analysis. The implications of these findings and their relation to creative leadership will be presented in the Discussion section.

Featured Sellers

Understanding the types of people selected as featured sellers provides insight into the demographics most salient in the community members who are identified and promoted by Etsy-corp as exemplar members. Table 5 presents key demographic data on the featured sellers.

Demographic Category	Code	% of Interviews
Gender*	Female	90.7
	Male	23.6
Craft Partnership	--	18.1
Training	General Aptitude	79.3
	Art/Craft Degree	57.0
	Family Legacy	38.0
	Other Degree	22.4
	Self-Taught	15.6
Job Status	Full Time Crafter/Artist	36.3
	Stay at Home Parent	13.5

Table 5: Demographics of Etsy's featured sellers
***Gender is not exclusive due to Craft Partnerships.**

The demographic data offers a number of insights into the backgrounds and experiences of the featured sellers. First, featured sellers are overwhelmingly female (90.7%) suggesting that Etsy-corp carries forward the traditional gendered association (at least in the contemporary West) of craft work with females. Further, member check interview participants offered similar claims regarding the female-centric perspective of Etsy and the broader North American craft community.

"the crafting world in general is quite female dominated" [Female 1; Member Check]

"a pretty feminine community overall" [Female 2; Member Check]

"Although it's always interesting to see what the men are up to on Etsy, I'm most excited about supporting the female makers..." [Female 3; Member Check]

Second, in *contrast* to the mainstream Western notion of craft as amateur work [1], the featured sellers are predominantly professional, with the simple majority (57%) holding a formal degree in craft or art disciplines and a significant minority (22.4%) claiming professional training in other fields. Member check interviews revealed that training provides desirable social capital that featured sellers can leverage for economic and social gains.

"Etsy is all about selling & one upping each other... and having a trained background is just one more competitive edge" [Female 2; Member Check]

Finally, the demographics note that only 36.3% of featured sellers are employed full-time through their craft or art work despite both the overall economic success of Etsy.com and their special status within the community as featured members. Combining professional degrees with nights/weekends work, the featured sellers are a p ro-amateur group. However, member check interview participants noted that full-time employment as an artist or crafter is more fluid than the Featured Seller interviews suggest.

"For a while I was making my boxes full time, and was being rather successful at it with projected gross annual sales in excess of $75,000, but then the economy took a turn" [Male 1; Member Check]

In addition to establishing certain demographic characteristics, featured sellers construct the content of their interviews around a number of key discursive categories. These categories are present across the majority of interviews regardless of the changing nature of the questions. Table 6 lists eight discursive categories identified in this study. Almost uniformly, featured sellers establish their expertise and, in part, validate their status as a featured seller through their unprompted discussion of training (94.9%). Participants in our member check interviews suggested a number of motivations for discussing their training in the Featured Seller interviews.

"Featured sellers talk about their training because it helps to define who they are at that moment..." [Male 1; Member Check]

"When you've paid thousands upon thousands of dollars for a very specific education, you're usually quite proud of it..." [Female 2; Member Check]

"If you're a working artist, trying to explain your job to other people makes you sound a little bit like a flake ... a lot of people need to make it clear that they are doing more than 'stringing beads'" [Female 1; Member Check]

Collectively, the member check interviews reveal a desire to professionalize art and craft through associations with formal education, career trajectories, and work—and they do so with full awareness of common prejudices against craft creativity, as the "stringing beads" example shows. Further, this professionalism and the seller's "successful" status are leveraged to provide advice (96.6%) to readers wishing to one day become featured sellers.

Beyond expertise, featured sellers frequently touch on their personal lives and aspirations via a discussion of their family (87.3%) and goals (87.3%). Furthermore, demographic statements concerning *Family* and *Training Legacy* (i.e., training received from a family member in an art or craft) increase by 11% and 10.4% across the question phases.

Code Category	% of Interviews
Advice	96.6
Training	94.9
Family	87.3
Goals	87.3
Materials	83.5
Job Status	83.1
Inspiration	78.5
Creative Identity	77.6

Table 6: Dominant discursive categories in the interviews.

In addition to personal life, professional life and experience are brought to the interviews through regular discussions of job status (83.1%), craft materials (83.5%), and design inspiration (78.5%). Finally, featured sellers frequently position their work and identity with respect to art (77.6%). However, and in contrast to the prior discursive categories, Etsy-corp prompted the frequent reflection on art through specific alterations of the interview questions. These changes are discussed in the next section.

For Etsy-corp and its featured sellers, the foregrounding of commercial success and professional pedigrees may work to professionalize craft, deemphasizing craft as a hobby and situating it instead within commerce and idealizations of consumerism. This may help explain a number of empirical results, e.g., that while craft is culturally constructed in the West as a hobby, a "culture of prosperous excess," predominantly female, and an amateur activity [1], 68.4% of featured sellers talk about their college education, and only 15.6% of them claim to be self-taught; that whereas only 4% of Etsy users are male [7], 23.6% of Etsy featured sellers are male; and that 77.6% of them use the language of "art," rather than or in addition to "craft" [9]. Together, these findings point to negotiations about forms of membership and identity in the Etsy community, with a particular emphasis on the relations and tensions between art and craft, and artist and crafter, as key roles available to members of Etsy's creative community.

Identity

As noted in the previous section and in Table 6, featured sellers frequently discuss themselves as creators in terms of both their creations and their own identities as crafters and/or artists (77.6%). This regular reflection on the values of craft, art, and one's identity as (or not as) an *artist* represents a central yet divergent property of the identity of the featured sellers. Over time, the Featured Seller interview questions have focused on this question and foregrounded a discussion among the featured sellers concerning the merits of *artist* and *crafter* as types of identities assumed by members of the Etsy community.

Phases 1 and 2 of the Featured Seller interviews asked: "What is the first thing you remember making by hand? How and why did you make it?" In phase 3, sellers were asked: "What first made you want to become an artist?" Phase 3's version is leading in two ways: it asserts that featured sellers have already become artists, and it asserts that this is a good outcome (i.e., that they *wanted* to be artists).

The overall estimated increase in the *Identity* theme is approximately 14.7% with the most active period of reflection occurring in Phase 3, the final question phase (85.4%). For reference, Table 7 offers a breakdown of coding themes and categories with the percent of interviews in each question phase containing the associated codes. Additionally, Table 7 includes the Gamma measure of association as well as a total estimated percent change in the codes from the first to last question phase.

At the code level, there are several significant relations between question phases and *Identity* codes. The *Identity* theme includes the following significant code and question phase relations:

- *Art Embrace*: Featured sellers who identify as artists increased by 11.2% across the phases.
- *Art Growth*: Featured sellers who "grew," "developed," as/into or otherwise "became" an artist increased by 7.3% across the phases.
- *Art Refusal*: Featured sellers who refuse the title of artist increased by 6.8% across the phases.

The Art Refusal code is of special significance as it only appears in phase 3, when Etsy-corp implemented the leading question to ask about becoming an artist. Prior to this question, featured sellers were able to volunteer their statuses as artists, and many did, but in phase 3, they were all practically required to position themselves and their work with respect to art. As a result, a new discursive strategy emerged wherein some featured sellers denounced any formal ties to art. The following interview quote is representative regarding the way featured sellers reject the label of artist as a means to embrace the skill of craft:

"I feel a bit silly and embarrassed calling myself an artist. I would be proud, though, to be considered a craftsperson... It seems the word craft has taken a be ating somewhere along the line, but to me, it conjures up the honorable and noble idea of taking the time and care to craft a beautiful decorative or useful item." [Female; Feb. 5, 2010]

At other times, the art-refusing featured sellers appear to be humbly reacting to the (lingering) cultural status of art:

"It's strange to think of myself as an 'artist'" [Female; Jan. 22, 2010]

"I've never been too comfortable with the title of artist as I've always thought of myself as a de signer." [Female; March 13, 2009]

"I still don't feel like an artist, but I was always creating things, sewing and painting." [Female, April 28, 2010]

"I've always been uncomfortable calling myself an artist but that has more to do with insecurities than anything." [Male & Female; June 4, 2010]

"I truly don't consider myself an artist, but I am creative." [Female; Aug. 25, 2010]

"I'd feel misleading to call myself an artist. I prefer to consider myself a crafty lady with fun ideas that I bring to life." [Female; Oct. 20, 2010]

As demonstrated by these quotes and the interview codes, the relationship between art and craft remains one rife with tensions and implications for understanding the identity struggle exemplified by the featured sellers. The identity struggle espoused in the interviews embodies, in part, a recent and growing shift in the relation between art and craft, wherein art seems to continue to enjoy more esteem than craft, but craft is beginning to make a comeback [19, 26]. The connotations of art-as-intellect and craft as-embodiment in many ways remain, but the cultural and economic capital associated with those connotations is shifting, as embodied knowledge practices are increasingly appreciated [15, 26].

Member check interview participants validated our findings that art versus craft identities and connotations are actively negotiated within the broader Etsy community.

"There's a gray line between being an artist and be ing simply a crafter" [Male 1; Member Check]

"I like the ... challenge of making something & sending it on to a new home almost immediately. Selling prints & fine art is a tough life ... In the end, I do need to make a living from it." [Female 2; Member Check]

"I really love craft and folk art, and am inspired by people who make something because they need to make that thing even though they haven't been trained to do so" [Female 1; Member Check]

"I don't really care for the term 'crafters' because it denotes an amateur status to the work and insults what you're trying to do..." [Female 4; Member Check]

In their position as exemplars within Etsy's creative community, the featured sellers embody different positions within a broader debate about the acceptable types of creative identity in the Etsy community. Together, culturally unresolved tensions between art(ist) and craft(er) may help to inspire, attract, and define the paths to membership in the Etsy community.

Process

Discussion of the process of creative work—and in particular the inspirations and materials involved in such work (as noted in Table 6)—is a major topic within the interviews. The dominance of such concerns notwithstanding, the *Process* theme actually declined by 7.3% across the phases. This decrease is more than compensated for by a corresponding increase in the *Community* theme. Table 8 offers a breakdown of the *Process* and *Community* themes.

Code Theme	Code Categories	% Phase 1	% Phase 2	% Phase 3	% Est. Change	Gamma	*df*, X^2 *[N = 237]*
Identity	Artist: Accept	43.9	44.4	68	12.1	.431	2, 10.757
	Artist: Refusal	0.0	0.0	13.5	6.8	1.00	2, 8.85
Process	Materials	100.0	100.0	78.1	-11.0	-.398	6, 16.08
	Inspiration	100.0	100.0	71.3	-14.4	-.731	12, 69.83
Community	Technology	65.9	83.3	100.0	17.1	.874	4, 108.37
	Advice	97.6	61.1	100.0	1.2	.726	4, 110.70

Table 7: Breakdown of significant associations (p < .01) between code categories and % of interviews with the codes per phase.

Questions regarding the featured seller's process begin with the first interview where Etsy posed the related questions of "What inspires you? Where do your ideas come from?" and "What are your favorite materials?" However, beginning with the phase 3, the specific questions about inspiration and materials are replaced with, "Please describe your creative process." Whereas the questions in phases 1 and 2 decomposed the creative process into widely recognized constituents—inspiration and materials—in phase 2 Etsy reformulated a more abstract and less operational prompt. Featured sellers correspondingly spoke with less reference to these specific dimensions of their creative process, materials, and inspirations.

The following *Process* related codes exhibit significant changes across the question phases.

- *Tools*: Descriptions of non-consumable items used in the craft process increased by 11.3% across the phases.
- *Product*: Mentions of the craft or art products sold by the seller increased by 10.3% across the phases.
- *Inspiration Etsy*: Mentions of Etsy.com or other Etsy sellers as sources of inspiration decreased by 2.6% across the phases.
- *Inspiration Nature*: Mentions of nature and the environment as sources of inspiration decreased by of 11.4% across the phases.
- *Inspiration People*: Mentions of non-family and non-Etsy sellers as sources of inspiration decreased by 19.4% across the phases.
- *Inspiration Other*: Miscellaneous citations of inspiration that did not fit into other Inspiration categories decreased by 21.6% across the phases.
- *Material Other*: Citations of miscellaneous consumable items that did not fit into other Material categories decreased by 12.9% across the phases.

As stated earlier, our analysis of the *Process* theme reveals an overall decline in the extent to which featured sellers discuss their creative process. However, even though the frequency of *Process* related codes may be in an overall decline, many featured sellers note the transformative and supportive role of the Etsy community itself in facilitating their growth and performance as a crafter, as seen in the following interview excerpts:

"The way people on Etsy work together on projects inspires me." [Female; April 25, 2007]

"Etsy ... has made me feel part of a bigger world as well as providing a source of inspiration, suggestions, and hints for every aspect of ... creating my art." [Female; July 16, 2007]

"I am ... constantly amazed and inspired by the creativity of other ... Etsy sellers." [Female; Sept. 30, 2009]

"I get really excited when I ... see new stores open ... and I treasure the folks who gave me support and direction along the way." [Male; Sept. 13, 2007]

"Featured seller interviews...we read these religiously and find them very inspirational." [Female & Female; January 9, 2009]

Member check participants also highlighted the role of the Etsy community in influencing their professional development. In particular, the member check interviews revealed the underlying social and economic pressures that are delivered through the Etsy community and how these pressures push sellers to improve and expand their skills and operations.

"I actively push myself to improve my techniques because of etsy. There are a lot of sellers on etsy, and eventually original work gets copied, or emulated, and I really want to stay ahead of that curve." [Female 1; Member Check]

"I believe my art and craft skills have improved greatly alongside my business skills, as Etsy has allowed me to create and sell my work on a regular basis. Painting full time is continuing to improve my craft, and feedback from the Etsy community helps me hone my skills. [Female 5; Member Check]

As shown in the interviews, there is a trend away from the featured sellers discussing the personal, intimate, and intangible dimensions of craft-centric creative process (e.g., inspirations, insights from nature or from an embodied engagement with craft materials) and an increasing emphasis on the role of Etsy.com as a socio-technical platform for defining and supporting a community and the creative work of its members. This focus on Etsy as a *Community* is addressed in the following section.

Community

Pursuant to Etsy-corp's mission of elevating the social and economic status of creative handwork, the Featured Seller interviews contain discussions of how to improve the seller's competence in operating an Etsy.com store specifically and a handwork business more broadly, but also increasingly provide insight into how to operate as a successful member of an online creative community. As a theme, mentions of *Community* increase by 17.1% across the 3 interview question phases. As noted earlier, while the frequency of statements about *Process* declines over time, discussions of *Community* increase. The overall growth of the *Community* theme across the question phases is influenced in part by a

Code Theme	Phase 1	Phase 2	Phase 3	Gamma	(%) Est. Change	*df*, X^2 *[N = 237]*
Identity	56.1	50.0	85.4	.608	14.7	2, 25.043
Process	6.1	6.4	4.6	-.505	-7.3	14, 41.66
Community	6.0	5.0	9.5	.868	17.1	8, 135.29

Table 8: Breakdown of significant associations ($p < .05$) between code themes and question phases.

number of interview question changes. Changes to the interview questions will be discussed below in relation to the code categories most impacted by the questions changes.

Advice: Phase 1 interviews included this question to prompt featured sellers to offer business advice: "Any tips for selling handmade stuff?" Phase 2 i nterviews added a second question, "What have been the most valuable lessons learned from other artists on Etsy?" By phase 3, the advice-oriented questions underwent a substantive revision, replacing earlier questions with: "How do you p romote your work?" and "What advice would you give to artists who are new to Etsy?" Phase 3 introduced two places for featured sellers to offer advice, even while they were simultaneously framing their interviews around questions of "artists" and "work," instead of the more folksy "handmade stuff" of the earlier question phases.

Technology: Phase 1 interviews included the question "Any Etsy feature requests?" and in phase 3 that question was replaced with "What are your favorite features on Etsy? What new features would like to see?" Again, the combination of a leading question and an operationalization of an abstract idea has obvious pragmatic benefits for Etsy-corp as an organization seeking to support and improve the output of its members.

At the code level, a number of relations developed between *Community* related codes and the question phases. The following codes demonstrate significant relations.

- *Technology General*: Citations of technology not specific to Etsy.com increased by 28.3% across the phases.
- *Technology Etsy*: Citations of technology specific to Etsy.com increased by 20.2% across the phases.
- *Advice Practical*: Specific and actionable advice given to the reader and other sellers increased by 14.7% across the phases.
- *Advice Orientation*: Attitudinal or dispositional advice given to readers increased by 5.3% across the phases.

Furthermore, *Technology* and *Advice* increase across the interview question phases; both categories peak in Phase 3, with 100% of interviews containing technology and advice related statements. However, the estimated change across the question phases is different for the categories with *Technology* increasing by 17.1% and *Advice* by 1.2%.

It is important to note that the featured sellers frequently framed their discussions of technology, especially of Etsy.com, as fundamental to their success. Typical passages from interviews discussing Etsy as a technical resource highlight how various technical features of Etsy.com (and other sites like Twitter and Facebook) can be leveraged to both increase professional skill as a business owner and creative skill as a craftsperson. Below are examples:

"The critique forums have given me some crucial information about my listings and my shop --- you just give some reviews, and then you get some reviews in return." [Male; February 20, 2009]

"Read as much as possible about being successful at Etsy by ... reading blogs by other successful shop owners, and observing how other successful shops handle their business." [Female & Male; April 26, 2010]

"Spend a whole lot of time on the site and use everything you can to your advantage. 'Favorite' other artists, read everything you can, use the tools--like showcase--to your advantage. It really comes down to really using the site, literally, not just seeing it as an e-commerce tool." [Female; January 12, 2009]

Common to these quotes, and the interviews as a whole, is a view of Etsy.com and its users as a thriving, supportive online creative community and not "just ... an e-commerce tool." Accordingly, as exemplar members of this community, many featured sellers provide encouraging and supportive advice about investing in Etsy as a community of like-minded creators. As exemplified in the following quotes, the featured sellers embody participation that helps to maintain and develop Etsy's community of creators [27, 28].

"Become involved in the Etsy community straight away. Don't be afraid to share info, make friends, reach out for help." [Female; January 4, 2010]

"Etsy is its own supportive community with thousands of creative people networking with each other, sharing the same passion, TO CREATE!" [Female; January 18, 2008]

"I love that Etsy is a real community. We as users care so much about our Etsy 'clubhouse' and prove it by speaking up loudly to voice our concerns and successes. I meet Etsians in real-life and feel a real connection. This ain't no eBay." [Female; May 30, 2008]

Member check interview participants further highlighted the importance of Etsy's community to the growth and success of their stores. In particular, the member check participants validated the sense of safety and confidence that the Etsy community offers to new crafter-sellers.

"just building up a marketplace ... has helped immensely ... also getting together with other artists has been essential... it's strange to have a huge connection of virtual friends, but many are very important to me" [Female 1; Member Check]

"the most touching aspect ... were the hundreds of convos [messages] *I received from people ... to receive the endorsement of so many people really validated what I was doing and gave me the confidence to continue to grow the business."* [Female 3; Member Check]

The increasing focus on Etsy.com as a tool for inspiration and a platform for organizing a community is a distinct trend in our data. This multi-faceted perspective on Etsy (both the site and its community) is shared across Etsy's featured sellers. Further, developing and sharing this worldview of Etsy is framed as a key requirement and benefit of membership in Etsy's community of crafter-sellers.

DISCUSSION

Summarizing our findings from an analysis of the Etsy Featured Seller interviews at a high level, we have seen the following:

- They are semi- or fully professional crafter-artists, with degrees and professional skills, in contrast to traditional stereotypes of craft as amateurish and hobbyist.
- They are engaged in an activity of identity and role definition which navigates and defines the relations and tensions between art(ist) and craft(er) as key roles in the Etsy community.
- They embody a view of Etsy as e-commerce tool, virtual community, and inspirational resource.

Together, these findings constitute, in part, a creativity story [28, 29] told through the words of the Etsy community's exemplar members. Further, in as much as the featured sellers are used to promote this creativity story, they may also be leveraged as paragon leaders [27] who provide valuable identity and behavior modeling from a distance.

As a generative template for creativity stories, the Featured Seller interview seemingly meet the aforementioned requirements of (1) addressing individual and group identity, (2) appealing to the experiences of the audience, (3) operating in an organizational structure, and (4) being embodied by the actions of the leader [28, 29]. Discussions of individual and group identity, especially with respect to the roles of crafter and artist, are a central theme in the interviews. Further, these discussions of identity are rooted in the experiences of crafter-sellers as they work to integrate and extend their handwork, small-business skills, and community network to improve the social and economic visibility of Etsy and their stores. To meet the organizational structure and embodied leadership requirements for a successful creativity story, Etsy-corp has modified the traditional creativity story format (one leader to many followers) [28, 29] by leveraging a strategy for paragon leadership in a decentralized organization.

Instead of members of Etsy corporate attempting to embody the desirable skills and dispositions to operate a handwork e-store, they instead identify and promote exemplar members as paragon leaders. These paragons need not be leaders in the sense that they themselves implement appropriate organizational policies and incentive structures, but rather in that they offer leadership-by-example through the creativity stories they tell about themselves, their handwork, and the crafter-seller community. Further, by providing many paragons, Etsy-corp is able to present a generalizable model of the skills and dispositions that are constitutive of success (as defined by Etsy corporate) to the crafter-seller community, while leaving room for individual crafter-sellers to interpret and act on the creativity stories in ways that best suit their individual contexts (a strategy echoed by Simonton [27] for the optimal use of paragons).

At the heart of Etsy-corp's recognition and promotion of its exemplar members via the Featured Seller interviews sits an organizational strategy for defining and communicating desirable skills and dispositions in hopes of positively influencing the community at large. Such strategies are not uncommon in HCI, with Ling et al. [16] and Preece and Shneiderman [22] recently demonstrating the utility of using social and organizational psychology-informed design strategies, including behavior modeling, as effective means for motivating and increasing involvement within online communities. Further, Luther and Bruckman [18] highlight the importance of supporting alternative styles of leadership in online communities, especially in "open-ended" domains like Etsy's crafter-seller community.

Managing and supporting creativity in massive online communities of creators will likely require new and modified strategies informed by existing literatures on social and organizational creativity and their design oriented counterparts in HCI and CSCW. Etsy-corp provides an example of one such strategy in its Featured Seller interviews. The creative leadership strategy of modeling desirable skills and dispositions through creativity stories as told by the Etsy community's paragon members may help to develop an increasingly coherent community vision and ethos, while strategically (but with restraint) strengthening the bonds of the loosely coupled millions that make up the crafter-seller community, contributing usefully to a organizational structure and culture of creativity.

CONCLUSION

The goal of this paper is to contribute to organizational creativity in massive-scale socio-technical systems research in HCI by offering an empirical look at an apparently successful example of decentralizing leadership in an online creative community. We report on a combined content analysis and close reading of Featured Seller interviews on Etsy.com. Our analysis sheds light on the demographic characteristics of Etsy's creative leaders while also revealing the ways in which these leaders discuss their creative identities, creative processes, and their relation to the broader creative community. Further, we demonstrate how Etsy-corp uses these interviews to provide a stage to paragon leaders, and to shape their performances while on it, so that these leaders can embody and co-articulate Etsy-corp's emerging vision of an ideal online craft commerce community. Specifically, we found that this interview-mediated and emergent co-articulation of creative ideals was used to strengthen the bonds of a decentralized community of creators and, eventually, support both craft and commercial creativity within that community.

ACKNOWLEDGEMENTS

This research was funded in part by the NSF IIS Creative IT grant (#1002772) and the Intel Science and Technology Center for Social Computing grant. We would also like to thank the AC and the reviewers for their thoughtful reviews.

REFERENCES

1. Adamson, G. (2007) *Thinking through Craft*. Berg, UK.

2. Coding Analysis Toolkit (CAT). http://cat.ucsur.pitt.edu.
3. Consortium for the Science of Sociotechnical Systems. http://sociotech.net/
4. Csikszentmihalyi, M. (1996) *Creativity: Flow and the Psychology of Discovery and Invention*. Harper Perennial. New York, USA.
5. Csikszentmihalyi, M. (1999) Implications of a Systems Perspective for the Study of Creativity. In Sternberg, R. (Ed.), *Handbook of Creativity*. Cambridge University Press, UK.
6. Davenport, G. and Mazalek, A. (2004) Dynamics of Creativity and Technological Innovation. *Digital Creativity*, 15 (1), 21-31.
7. Etsy Blog: Results of the Blog Reader Survey. http://www.etsy.com/storque/etsy-news/survey-says-the-results-of-the-blog-reader-survey-are-here-7223/.
8. Etsy Press Kit. http://www.etsy.com/press/kit/.
9. Etsy Statistics: Weather Reports. http://www.etsy.com/storque/search/tags/weather-report/.
10. Farooq, U., Carroll, J., and Ganoe, C. (2007) Supporting Creativity with Awareness in Distributed Collaboration. *Proc. of ACM GROUP'07,* ACM Press, 31-40.
11. Fischer, G. (2005). Distances and diversity: Sources for social creativity. *Proc. of ACM Creativity & Cognition*. ACM Press, 128-136.
12. Fischer, G., Giaccardi, E., Eden, H., Sugimoto, M., and Ye, Y. (2005) Beyond binary choices: integrating individual and social creativity. *International Journal of Human-Computer Studies*, 64 (4/5), 482-512.
13. Fischer, G. and Shipman, F. (2011) Collaborative Design Rational and Social Creativity in Cultures of Participation. *Human Technology*, 7 (2), 164 187.
14. Krippendorff, K. (2003) *Content Analysis: An Introduction to Its Methodology*. Sage Publications.
15. Levine, F. and Heimerl, C. (2008) *Handmade Nation: The Rise of DIY, Art, Craft, and Design*. Princeton Architectural Press. New York, USA.
16. Ling, K., Beenen, G., Ludford, P., Wang, X., Change, K., Li, X., Cosley, D., Frankowski, D., Terveen, L., Rashid, A.M., Resnik, P., and Kraut, R. (2005) Using Social Psychology to Motivate Contributions to Online Communities. *Journal of Computer-Mediated Communication*, 10 (4), article 10.
17. Lincoln, Y., Guba, E. (1985) *Naturalistic Inquiry*. Sage Publications, Newbury Park, CA.
18. Luther, K. and Bruckman, A. (2008) Leadership in online creative collaboration. *Proc. of CSCW '08.* ACM Press, 343-352
19. McCullough, M. (1996) *Abstracting Craft: The Practiced Digital Hand.* The MIT Press.
20. Ogden, C. and Richards, I.A. (1923) *The Meaning of Meaning*. Mariner Books, New York.
21. Puccio, G. and Cabra, J. (2010) Organizational Creativity: A Systems Approach. In Kaufman, J. and Sternberg, R. (Eds.), *The Cambridge Handbook of Creativity*. Cambridge University Press, UK.
22. Preece, J. and Shneiderman, B. (2009) The Reader-to-Leader Framework: Motivating Technology-Mediated Social Participation. *AIS Transactions on Human-Computer Interactions*, (1) 1, 482-512.
23. Runco, M. (2006) *Creativity: Theories and Themes: Research, Development, and Practice*. Elsevier Academic Press. London, UK.
24. Sawyer, R.K. (2010) Individual and Group Creativity. In Kaufman, J. and Sternberg, R. (Eds.), *The Cambridge Handbook of Creativity*. Cambridge UP, UK.
25. Sawyer, R.K. (2006) *Explaining Creativity: The Science of Human Innovation*. Oxford University Press, UK.
26. Sennett, R. (2008) *The Craftsman*. Yale University Press. New Haven, USA.
27. Simonton, D.K. (1988) Creativity, Leadership, and Chance. In Sternberg, R. (Eds.), *The Nature of Creativity*. Cambridge University Press, New York, NY, USA.
28. Sternberg, R. (2007) A Systems Model of Leadership. *American Psychologist* 62 (1), 34-42.
29. Sternberg, R. (2005) The WICS Model of Organizational Leadership. *Center for Public Leadership Paper Series*. http://dspace.mit.edu/handle/1721.1/55937
30. Sternberg, R., & Lubart, T.I. (1999) The Concept of Creativity: Prospects and Paradigms. In Sternberg, R. (Ed.) *Handbook of Creativity*. Cambridge University Press.
31. Sylvan, E. (2010) Predicting influence in an online community of creators. *Proc. of CHI'10*, ACM Press, 1913-1916.
32. Sylvan, E. (2008) *The Sharing of Wonderful Ideas: Influence and Interaction in Online Communities of Creators*. Doctoral Dissertation. Massachusetts Institute of Technology, Boston, USA.
33. Williams, W. and Yang, L. (1999) Organizational Creativity. In Sternberg, R. (Ed.), *Handbook of Creativity*. Cambridge University Press, UK.

The Cost of Collaboration for Code and Art: Evidence from a Remixing Community

Benjamin Mako Hill
Massachusetts Institute of Technology
77 Massachusetts Ave, Cambridge, MA
mako@mit.edu

Andrés Monroy-Hernández
Microsoft Research
One Microsoft Way, Redmond, MA
amh@microsoft.com

ABSTRACT
In this paper, we use evidence from a remixing community to evaluate two pieces of common wisdom about collaboration. First, we test the theory that jointly produced works tend to be of higher quality than individually authored products. Second, we test the theory that collaboration improves the quality of functional works like code, but that it works less well for artistic works like images and sounds. We use data from Scratch, a large online community where hundreds of thousands of young users share and remix millions of animations and interactive games. Using peer-ratings as a measure of quality, we estimate a series of fitted regression models and find that collaborative Scratch projects tend to receive ratings that are lower than individually authored works. We also find that code-intensive collaborations are rated higher than media-intensive efforts. We conclude by discussing the limitations and implications of these findings.

Author Keywords
remixing, online communities, computers and children, creativity support tools, social computing and social navigation, computer mediated communication

ACM Classification Keywords
H.5.3 Group and Organization Interfaces Information Interfaces and Presentation: Computer-supported cooperative work

INTRODUCTION
Over the last decade, researchers and theorists studying computer-supported cooperation have pointed to FLOSS, Wikipedia, and the products of remixing communities as examples of how wide scale collaboration facilitated by the Internet – "peer production" – has produced creative works of enormous value and high quality [4, 41]. A subset of this research has focused on remixing: the construction of creative products based on works created previously by others, often involving the recombination and reworking of code with images and sound. Benkler has argued that remixing is an important modality of peer production [4]. In his eponymous book on the subject, Lessig suggests that widespread remixing on the Internet represents an important cultural shift toward a more collaborative culture [29]. Broadly considered, the pattern of indirect reuse central to remixing is characteristic of peer production and a large body of Internet-based collaborative work.

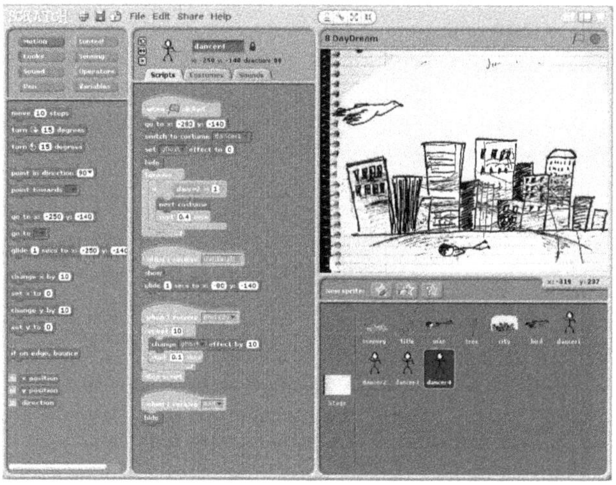

Figure 1. Screenshot of the Scratch desktop application. The leftmost column represents an inventory of "programming blocks" (shown in blue) which have been assembled into program code in the center column. The area in the top right represents the project as it will be displayed to a user interacting with the finished product. The bottom right column shows the available images that can be controlled by the code.

Others have countered that the products of peer production – and remixing communities in particular – are amateurish and of poor quality [27, 22]. Acknowledging the successful examples of GNU/Linux and Wikipedia, Benkler has advanced a nuanced argument that peer production may be particularly well suited to the creation of functional works, like operating system software, "because software is a functional good with measurable qualities" [4]. On the other hand, the last half decade has witnessed high quality peer produced artistic works such as the Grammy-nominated Johnny Cash Project music video.

Do remixes result in higher quality creative works, on average, than the products of solitary creators? Is remixing better for functional works like code than it is for creative works like art? Although these questions lie at the core of conversations about peer production, its value, and its limitations, empirical evidence has largely been missing. Internet-based remixing platforms often combine the production of both code and art, and as a result, provide a setting uniquely well suited to answering these questions.

Using peer ratings we seek the answers to these questions in Scratch – a large online remixing community where young people build, share, and collaborate on interactive animations and video games. We find that, on average, remixed projects are rated lower by members of the Scratch community than projects that are the work of a single creator. Additionally, we find that remixes involving artistic creations are less positively evaluated than programmatic works.

BACKGROUND

The possibility or promise of high quality products, like FLOSS and Wikipedia, has been central to interest in peer production [4, 29, 41]. Benkler has argued that peer production results in high quality projects because the Internet has lowered costs associated with contribution, attracting many lightly motivated contributors [4]. Discussing FLOSS, Raymond suggests that contributors will be able to find and fix shortcomings to produce software that is superior to alternatives produced by individuals or firms [35]. Moreover, there is empirical evidence that supports the argument that increased collaboration leads to higher-quality products in peer production. For example, studies of Wikipedia have suggested that vandalism is detected and removed within minutes or seconds [40] and that high quality articles in Wikipedia, by several measures, tend to be produced by more intense collaboration [43, 23, 12].

That said, we also know that collaborative work is not always better. To cite just one influential example, the rich literature on brainstorming has suggested that, in many cases, groups produce fewer, lower quality, ideas than the same number of individuals working alone [9]. In a baccalaureate speech, Yale President A. Whitney Griswold once expressed this sentiment: "Could Hamlet have been written by a committee, or the Mona Lisa painted by a club? Could the New Testament have been composed as a conference report? Creative ideas do not spring from groups. They spring from individuals. The divine spark leaps from the finger of God to the finger of Adam" [13].

In the literature on peer production and remixing, some have expressed skepticism that increased collaboration will result in better products – the strongest criticisms calling into question the fundamental promise of the phenomena. Keen has argued that the openness of peer production and remixing to participation leads to products that are amateurish and of low quality [22]. In a critique of what he calls "online collectivism," Lanier points to several shortcomings in peer production and suggests that Wikipedia is sterile and lacks a single voice: "[A] voice should be sensed as a whole. You have to have a chance to sense personality for language to have its full meaning. Personal Web pages do that, as do journals and books" [26]. Echoing Griswold, Lanier points out that even in successful collective processes, like scientific endeavors, it is, "individual scholars [that] matter, not just the process or the collective." Previous studies of remixing have shown that factors associated with increased remixing of projects are associated with "cheaper" and easier forms of work, perhaps by lowering costs and attracting dabblers whose contributions involve less complexity and effort [16].

But although remixing and peer production have been the subject of a growing body of research, few studies have attempted to compare the quality of resulting remixes and none has questioned the assumption, fundamental to much of the interest in peer production, that collaboration in the form of remixing leads to higher-quality works. This leads us to our first research question:

RQ1: Are remixes, on average, higher quality than single-authored works?

One response to the critiques of Keen, Lanier, and Griswold is to suggest the peer production *can* result in high-quality artifacts, but only for certain types of creative goods. After all, Griswold's archetypes of works that cannot be created by a committee are all from the arts.

Of course, many great works of art are produced by multiple authors. The King James translation of the Bible was, literally, written by a committee. Even singularly authored works, like the poetry and stories of T.S. Eliot and Raymond Carver, involved deep collaboration with influential editors [15]. Research from the psychology literature on creativity has shown that creativity is highly embedded in social contexts [2, 8].

And although peer production's functional products are more widely known, high quality art has also been peer produced. The Johnny Cash Project [21] aggregated thousands of peer produced drawings to create a Grammy-nominated music video. Work by Luther [30] has shown how artistic work is produced in vibrant remixing communities. Recent work looking at the design of virtual objects has shown that remix-style collaboration leads to better designs than when individuals work alone [44]. If artistic products are less visible in peer production and remixing, it might be because the tools necessary to collaborate over the Internet have, historically, been better suited for producing technical products like programming code. New collaborative media and design tools produced over the last decade have shifted that *status quo*.

But, it is undeniable that the poster children of peer production are more "functional" than Griswold's archetypes. For example, Nature's widely cited study evaluated Wikipedia's quality by counting factual errors [11]. Raymond speaks of additional contributors revealing and fixing "bugs" [35]. Works of art may be more or less positively received, but their evaluation is more subjective. Computing researchers have suggested that supporting group work in creative tasks like design or art remains a major challenge and an open area for research [39, 10, 32].

In general, crowdsourcing systems have tended to focus on "less creative" tasks that can be easily divided and objectively evaluated – qualities often missing from creative works like media and film [31]. This can make artistic creations more difficult to manage [30]. Even successful crowd-produced art like Sheep Market [24] and the Johnny Cash Project asked participants to contribute a small well-defined piece of an individual's broader vision. Lanier argues that collectives are

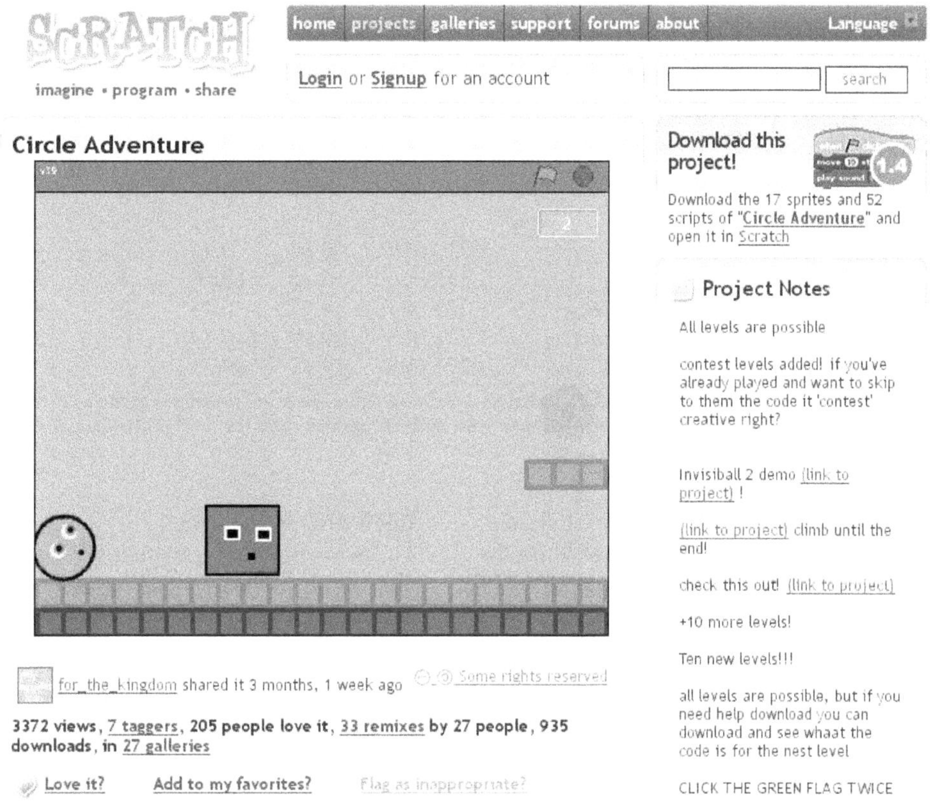

Figure 2. Example of a web page for a single Scratch project. (Accessed: May 29, 2012)

more effective than individuals at tasks like setting market prices, but less effective at others, saying, "when a collective designs a product, you get design by committee, a derogatory expression for a reason" [26]. Keen is also doubtful of collective writing and design when he asks, "can a collaboration of amateur voices create an authoritative, coherent fictional narrative?" His answer: "I doubt it" [??]

That said, previous work has struggled to compare artistic and more functional products in a single setting or community. Peer production may be able to create high-quality art, while performing less well than it would with a more functional goal. Additionally, remixers may be able to create great works of art, but show more interest in contributing to more functional tasks when it comes time to collaborate because it leads to smoother social interactions. This conflicting evidence leads us to our second research question:

> *RQ2: Are code-intensive remixes, on average, higher quality than media-intensive remixes?*

Of course, operationalizing and quantifying quality – especially concerning subjective products like art – is difficult and controversial. Some studies on peer production have suggested simple popularity metrics, like views or downloads, as proxies for quality [7]. Others have taken advantage of peer rating systems to help evaluate and rate content [25]. We will follow the latter, rating-based, approach. That said, in results that are not presented here, we experimented with similar analyses using popularity-based quality measures and found substantively similar results.

SCRATCH

To answer our research questions, we look to the Scratch online community: a public and freely accessible website where a large community of users create, share, and remix interactive media. The community was built to support users of the Scratch programming environment: a freely downloadable desktop application with functionality similar to Adobe Flash [36]. A screenshot of the Scratch programming environment is shown in Figure 1. Crucial to our analysis, Scratch is designed to allow users to build projects integrating images, music, sound and other media with programming code [36]. Scratch was designed by the Lifelong Kindergarten Group at the MIT Media Lab as a platform for creative learning, and aims to introduce young people to computer programming. Much of the practice, and promise, of peer production and remixing has been located in communities of young technology users [29, 19, 33], which makes Scratch an ideal platform to study.

From within the Scratch authoring environment, creators can publish their projects on the Scratch online community website hosted at MIT.[1] As of May 2012, more than one million users had created accounts on the website and more than one-third of these users had shared at least one of more than 2.5 million total projects. Any web visitor can create an account, which becomes active immediately. The nature of Scratch projects shared in the community varies widely and includes

[1] `http://scratch.mit.edu`

Variable	N	Mean	SD	Min	Max
Dependent Variables					
Loveits within 1 yr. ($loveits_p$)	1,271,085	0.64	6.53	0	1,320
Question Predictors					
Number of blocks ($blocks_p$)	1,271,085	110.52	573.45	0	25,2237
Sum of images and sounds ($media_p$)	1,271,085	22.88	70.03	1	11,624.00
Remix status ($isremix_p$)	1,271,085	0.17	0.37	0	1
Controls					
User is female ($female_u$)	1,270,519	0.34	0.48	0	1
User age in years (age_{up})	1,240,014	16.46	10.66	4	74.92
Account age in months ($joined_{up}$)	1,271,085	4.17	6.43	0	49.37
Users' previous loveits ($prevlovits_{up}$)	1,271,085	29.29	146.79	0	1,2287
Views within 1 yr. ($views_p$)	1,271,085	14.17	69.26	0	1,1287

Table 1. Summary statistics for variables used in our analysis. Measures with the subscript p are measured at the level of the project while measures with the subscript u are measured at the level of the user. Measures with both are measured at the level of the user at the time that the project was shared.

everything from interactive greeting cards to fractal simulations to animated stories and video games. Projects on the Scratch website vary enormously in complexity in terms of both code and media.

The community is visited by more than half a million people each month[2] who can browse material on the website and interact with projects directly from their web browsers. Visitors must create accounts to remix projects or contribute by publishing, commenting, showing support (i.e., giving "loveits"), tagging, or flagging projects as inappropriate. Most of the community's users self-report their ages ranging between 8 and 17 with 13 being the median age for new accounts. Thirty-five percent of users of the online community self-report as female.

Central to the purposes of our study, the Scratch online community is designed as a platform for collaboration through remixing. Influenced by theories of constructionist learning in communities [34] and communities of practice [28], the Scratch website seeks to help users learn through exposure to, and engagement with, others' projects. The commitment to remixing is deep and visible in Scratch. The name "Scratch" is a reference to hip-hop DJs' practice of remixing. Every project shared on Scratch is available for download and remix by any other user, through a prominent download button. Additionally, every project is licensed under a Creative Commons license, explained in "kid friendly terms," that explicitly allows reuse. Administrators and community members actively encourage remixing.[3]

Remixing in Scratch represents a wide range of collaborative modalities, from experimentation, to bug-fixing, to socialization, to coordination within semi-formal organizations, to meme-spreading. For example, organized groups with formal membership use remixing to build projects serially over extended periods of time [3]. Although we lack good knowledge of the distribution of types of remixing, we believe that Scratch remixes include a broad range of the types of cooperative information production studied by human-computer interaction researchers.

[2]`http://quantcast.com/scratch.mit.edu`
[3]`http://info.scratch.mit.edu/License_to_play`

DATA AND MEASURES

The Scratch online community is built on top of a database-driven web application that stores an extensive range of metadata on projects, users, and interactions on the website. This database also identifies, tracks, and presents data on whether projects are created through remixing. Additionally, the website stores each of the "raw" Scratch project files, which can be further analyzed to reveal details, such as projects' programming code and media elements. Our dataset is constructed by combining exported metadata about Scratch's users, projects, and interactions, with algorithmic analyses of each project to measure complexity in both code and media.

Our unit of analysis is the Scratch project and our dataset includes every project shared on the Scratch online community from the moment the first project was shared in Scratch on March 5, 2007 through April 1, 2011 – a total of 1,685,353 projects. We omit 19,796 projects for which we do not have data on the amount of code or media because of technical errors in our analytic tools or because of corruption in the project files. We also omit 395,728 projects (24% of the total) which have been removed from the public website by the author. In robustness checks not reported in this paper, we include these hidden projects in our analyses and find that our results are unchanged.

To operationalize quality we use user ratings. In particular, we use a count of *loveits* which are analogous to "liking" or "upvoting" in other social media platforms and which are a indication that a user with an account appreciates a project. Each user can only "love" a project once and can remove her "loveit" from a project later. Users cannot publicly express dislike with a similar mechanism. Loveits are public in the sense that the author of a Scratch project can see which users "loved" her own projects and in the sense that the total number of *loveits* a project has received is visible on the Scratch website next to each project (see Figure 2). This measure of quality is in line with previous work that has suggested the validity of peer rating systems [25] as well as with studies that have used crowd workers for measuring subjective qualities of creative work such as visualizations [14] and photos, [5] which have been shown to be reliable in those contexts.

We operationalize functional complexity of projects as the number of programming *blocks*. Blocks, also shown in Figure 1, are analogous to tokens or symbols in the source code of computer programs. Blocks are similar to, but more granular than, source lines of code, which have a long history of use as a measure of both complexity and effort in software engineering [42, 1]. We operationalize the artistic intensity of projects as the sum of the number of distinct images and sounds (*media*).

We operationalize collaborativeness using a dummy variable, *isremix*, that indicates whether a project is, itself, a remix of another project. Although this is a crude measure of collaborativeness, only 10.9% of projects are remixed at all and only 1.4% are remixed more than once. As a result, this dichotomous measure captures most variation in collaborativeness in Scratch. It is important to note that this variable only measures material being copied and, as a result, does not capture "conceptual" remixing such as employing a Disney or Nintendo character in a new Scratch game, borrowing material from any source outside Scratch, or inspiration from sources inside Scratch without downloading and copying a project.

We also include a range of controls. For each user, we include self-reported measures of gender, which we have coded as a dichotomous variable (*female*); date of birth, which we have coded as age in years at the moment that each project was shared (*age*), which may indicate sophistication of the user; and the age of each account (*joined*), which may indicate a user's level of experience with Scratch. We are concerned that the prominence of projects' creators may drive positive ratings. To control for prominence, we employ a count the total previous loveits that a project's author had received (*prevloveits*) at the moment that the project in question was shared. The variable is measured at the project level, but is aggregated across all projects previously shared by a user when a user shares the project in question.[4]

Finally, depending on how we conceptualize quality, the popularity of projects may represent an important confounding variable. Our measure of exposure, *views*, reflects the number of visits to a project by logged-in users on the Scratch website. Scratch projects are visible publicly to individuals without accounts but these visits are not recorded and do not count in the tabulation of views. Views, like loveits, are publicly displayed on the Scratch website under each project (see Figure 2). In addition to viewing, logged-in users can download projects to their own computers. In robustness checks not presented here, we found that *downloads* had a similar, but weaker, moderating effect as our control for *views* with an identical pattern of results. Summary statistics for each of our measures are shown in Table 1.

ANALYSIS

Our analytic strategy involves the estimation of fitted regression models on our count of *loveits* one year after creation. In both the models we present, we include interaction terms between *isremix* and our measures of project complexity *code* and *media*. Both complexity measures, as well as our measure of prominence (*prevloveits*) are highly skewed, but a started log transformation results in an approximately normal distribution in each case.

One of the challenges of using loveits as a measure of quality is that it may simply measure exposure. Of course, many social media systems use quality measures that are closely related to, or reflect, popularity. That said, more popular projects may receive more loveits only because they are more exposed. As a result, controversial projects, or those reusing elements taken from popular culture, might be viewed more frequently, and receive more loveits, despite the possibility that they are otherwise of lower quality.

We can address this concern by controlling for *views*, our measure of exposure. In Model 1, we do not include a measure of views. These results might be more easily comparable to metrics used in many social media systems. We believe that Model 2, which controls for exposure, offers more conservative estimates. Except for the fact that Model 2 adds the control for *views*, the two models are identical.

Our formal model is shown below and includes the full set of variables including *views*:

$$\begin{aligned} loveits = \beta_0 + \beta_1 \log blocks + \beta_2 \log media + \\ \beta_3 isremix + \beta_4 \log blocks \times isremix + \\ \beta_5 \log media \times isremix + \beta_6 age + \beta_7 joined + \\ \beta_8 female + \beta_9 \log prevloveits + \beta_{10} \log views \end{aligned}$$

Poisson regression is frequently used for count dependent variables like *loveits* but, as is common with counts, there is an over-dispersion of zeros in our measure. To address this over-dispersion, we use negative binomial regression to estimate both models.

Because users can upload several projects, and because many do (51% of the users in our dataset), there are concerns about correlation of standard errors between projects uploaded by the same user. We address this by fitting hierarchical mixed-effect models that estimate random intercepts for each user and cluster variance within and between users. These estimates are not reported here but are similar in the magnitude and hypothesis tests.

RESULTS

Our results are shown in Table 2. The median number of loveits a Scratch project receives after one year is 0 and more than 80% of projects do not receive a single loveit in their first year. As a result, most of the estimated effect sizes in our fitted models represent only fractions of a loveit.

In both models, the principal effects of *blocks* and *media* are positive and statistically significant. In other words, for *de novo* projects, increased complexity in either code or media is, on average, associated with more loveits. This finding is in line with previous work that has suggested that increased complexity of projects is usually associated with positive reception in remixing communities [17, 16]. For example, our

[4]Other measures of prominence include number of past views, number of past downloads, and number of past favorites. All are highly correlated with past loveits ($0.89 < \rho < 0.97$) and our results remain unchanged if we use these alternative indicators.

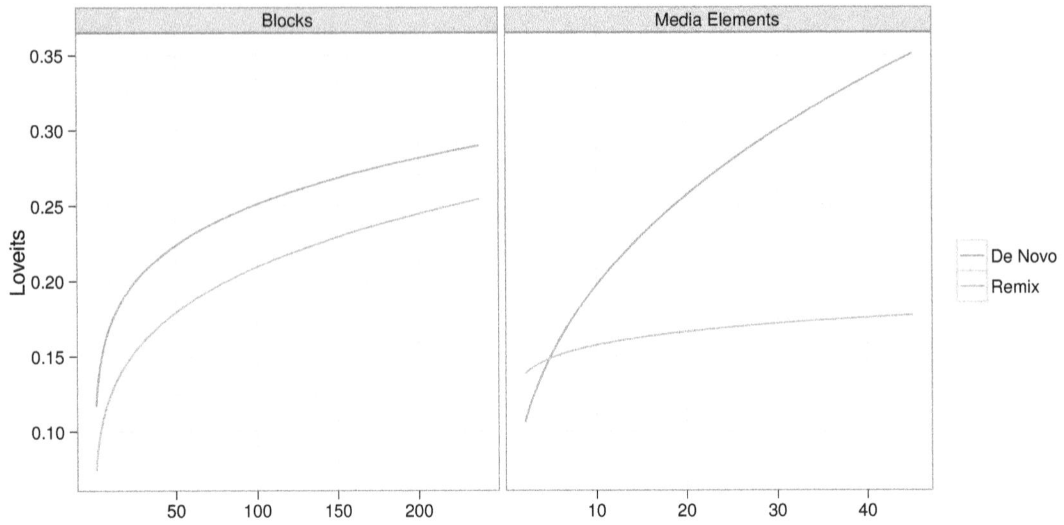

Figure 3. Two plots of estimated values for prototypical projects showing the predicted number of loveits using our estimates in Model 1. In the left panel, the x-axis varies number of blocks while holding media intensity at the sample median. The right panel varies the number of media elements while holding the number of blocks at the sample median. Ranges for each are from 0 to the 90th percentile.

Model 1 estimates that a *de novo* project with 3 blocks (10th percentile) would be expected to receive, on average, 0.15 loveits; a similar project with 237 blocks (90th percentile) would be expected to receive 0.29 loveits. The relationship between *media* and our dependent variables follows a similar pattern.

Our parameter estimate for *isremix* is positive, large, and statistically significant in Model 1, but is negative and statistically significant when we control for *views* in Model 2. That said, this coefficient should not be interpreted directly because the parameter estimates for the interaction terms between *isremix* and both measures of complexity are also statistically significant. To answer our research questions, we must consider the sum of all these effects. Because interaction effects can be difficult to interpret, plots of predicted values for prototypical individuals using the parameter estimates for Model 1, with unvarying qualities held at the sample medians, are shown in Figure 3. Prototypical plots for Model 2 are not included but show similar relationships.

Answering RQ1, our results suggest that most remixes in Scratch will be less highly rated than similar *de novo* projects. Although the principal effects of *isremixed* are positive in both models, the strong negative effect of the interaction between log *media* and *isremix* tends to overwhelm this effect. Except among the least media-intensive projects (see the far left of the right panel in Figure 3), remixes with median values of all other predictors receive less loveits, on average, than otherwise similar *de novo* projects.

Answering RQ2, we find support for claims that remixing is more effective for code-heavy projects than for media-heavy works. Across all models, the interaction between log *blocks* and *isremix* is positive, although relatively small in magnitude. The interaction between log *media* and *isremix* is negative and strongly statistically significant in both models and is much larger than the interaction term with *blocks*.

The left panel of Figure 3 visualizes predicted loveits across varying code complexity while holding media complexity at its sample median of 10. The graph visualizes Model 1's prediction that *de novo* projects will receive more loveits than remixes at all levels of code complexity. That said, as projects become more complex, the predicted gap between remixes and *de novo* projects narrows slightly.

The difference between the effects of code-intensity and media-intensity for remixes is stark: all but the least media-intensive remix projects are predicted to receive more loveits than similar *de novo* projects. An otherwise average project with a single media element is predicted to receive 0.14 loveits – slightly higher than the estimate for an identical *de novo* project (0.11). However, if the same project contained 44 pieces of media (90th percentile), it would be expected to receive 0.18 loveits – much lower than the estimate of 0.35 loveits for an otherwise similar *de novo* work.

As predicted, we find that *views* is a strong predictor of *loveits*. Parameter estimates associated with log *views* are highly statistically significant in Model 2 and larger in magnitude than any other parameter. Controlling for *views* results in a substantial increase in goodness of fit and in large decreases in the magnitude of most of the other parameter estimates; as predicted, loveits is strongly influenced by exposure. That said, the essential pattern of results – in both the signs of parameter estimates of our key question predictors and their relative magnitude – is stable across the two models. In fact, controlling for views even strengthens aspects of our findings. For example, Model 2 predicts that the effects of *loveits* will always be lower for *media* than for *blocks* in remixes, and will decrease monotonically as remixes increase in media-intensity if other variables are held constant.

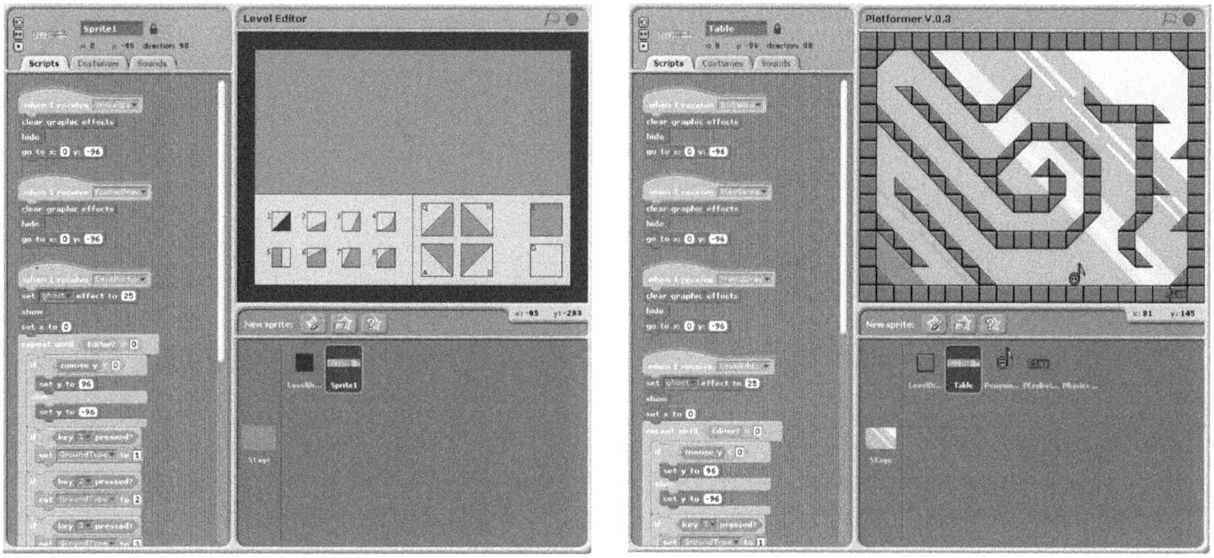

Figure 4. Example of a code-intense project (left) and a remix of that that project (right).

Our controls are also statistically significant predictors of loveits. Surprisingly, we find that find that projects by older users and users with longer tenure on the site receive fewer loveits on average – although both of these effects are extremely small in magnitude. We find that our measure of prominence ($prevloveits$) is a powerful predictor of ratings but is largely attenuated by the addition of a control for exposure; more prominent users receive more loveits because they receive more attention. Finally, controlling for exposure changes a non-significant estimate of the parameter associated with female authorship into a large, positive, and statistically significant effect. We interpret this as suggesting that girls' projects are given more positive ratings, on average, but only after we take into account the fact that they tend to be viewed less often.

These findings can be made more concrete using two examples. The first example is shown in Figure 4. In the left panel of the figure is a "simple level editing system" created, *de novo*, by a 15-year-old American boy. The project has a framework to create a game with multiple platforms. In the right panel is a remix of that project created by a 13-year-old American boy who built a full-fledged game from the original project. The remixed project had 247 blocks (near the 90th percentile of code intensity) but is near the sample median in media intensity. As our findings suggest happens on average, the code-intense remix received more loveits than its antecedent.

That example can be contrasted with a pair of media intense projects shown in Figure 5. On the left side is, once again, a *de novo* work: a project by 11-year-old boy that contained several animations of a Star Wars character that moves around the screen. A remixed version of the project, shown on the right, was created by an adult Scratch user to change the color and to replace and change a number of the the graphical elements. The remix project, very similar to its antecedent, contained 38 images (near the 90th percentile in terms of media intensity) but near the sample median in terms of code. Again, as our findings suggest happens on average in Scratch, the remix of the the media-intense project was less highly rated, receiving no loveits all, while the *de novo* project received several.

In summary: Speaking to RQ1, we find surprising evidence that remixed works are less positively rated in Scratch, on average, than similar *de novo* projects for all but the least media-intensive works. Remixes are, in general, rated less highly than the works of single authors. In answer to RQ2, we find support for the common wisdom about the relatively poor quality of remixed art. Our results suggest that remixes are more positively rated when they are code-intensive than when they are media-intensive. We find that these basic associations are attenuated by, but robust to, consideration of the effect of exposure.

LIMITATIONS

A number of important limitations and threats may affect the validity of our findings. One important concern that we have already alluded to is around our measure of quality. Most crowdsourcing and peer production research has focused on works with relatively clear and objective means of evaluation. Because we are interested in comparing works with artistic components, evaluation must be subjective. Other valid measures of quality – e.g., expert ratings – might result in different findings.

Our discussion of code and media intensity in Scratch in terms of functional versus artistic modes of production involves a series of important limitations and threats. Scratch users can use code to generate aesthetic or artistic work. Similarly, a very media intense project might serve a very functional purpose. Our independent variables measure the material of production – code and media – and do not capture conceptual models of creative production. The relationship

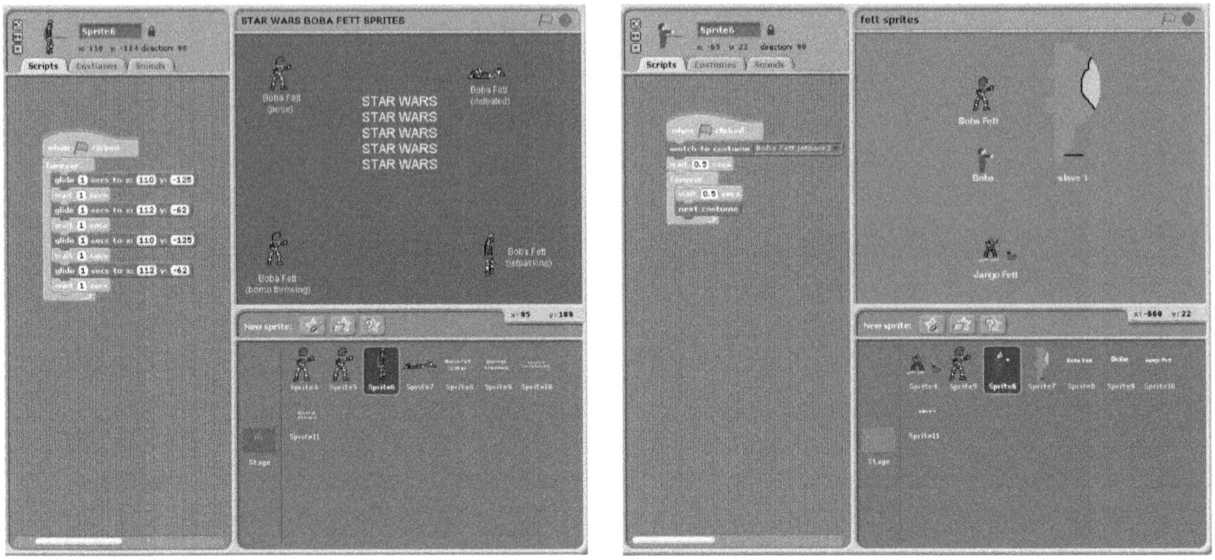

Figure 5. Example of a media-intense project (left) and a remix of that project (right).

between the tools and materials of production and the styles of products that result is a deep topic beyond the scope of this analysis. Our findings should be seen as limited in this regard.

Additionally, our empirical strategy assumes that media-intensive collaborative projects result from collaboration on the media itself. This may not always be the case. For example, a media-intensive work might be remixed entirely through addition of, or changes to, code. In that situation, the collaborative act would be collaboration on code but would be measured, in our dataset, merely as the amount of code and media in the resulting remix. Through our experience with Scratch and conversations with its administrators, we believe that remixed works will be similar to their antecedents and will involve collaboration distributed approximately proportionally across their different parts and types of content. However, we cannot reject this threat.

Previous work has shown that explicit and public expression of admiration may create self-reinforcing social dynamics [37]. A second measure, *favorites*, is a count of the number of times that a project has been listed by other users as a favorite – designed as a form of personal bookmarking. Like loveits, users can only favorite a given project once and a project being listed as a favorite is visible to both the project creator and the person "favoriting." However, unlike *loveits*, *favorites* are not displayed on project pages and are only visible by browsing to the bottom of the favoriter's profile page. As a result, this second measure is less likely to provoke concerns of self-reinforcing behaviors. Although the median number of favorites after one year is even lower than *loveits* (85% of projects are never marked as a favorite by another Scratch user), our basic pattern of results is similar when we use *favorites* as a dependent variable.

Another important threat is that our results may be driven by remixed projects competing for ratings with their antecedents. This may be the case because, although loveits are not limited, users' attention is. For example, if a game is lightly remixed and shared, there would then be two similar games in the community which would divide attention; each project would receive only a portion of the loveits that would otherwise have been given to the original. Our models controlling for exposure should help address this threat. We can gain additional confidence that this threat is not driving our results because remixed projects in our data receive many more loveits ($\mu = 4.6$) than projects which are never remixed ($\mu = 0.5$) and the difference is strongly statistically significant ($t = 46$; $p < 0.001$).

Another important limitation, common to any in-depth analysis of a single community, is generalizability beyond the empirical setting. Although our analysis only considers collaboration through remixing – one of several collaborative modalities – remixing is widely popular in contemporary youth culture. At the very least, multimedia remixing is widely practiced, in very similar forms, in other communities like Newgrounds and ccMixter [20, 18, 6, 29]. And although Scratch is a single site, it contains the works of over a million creators engaged in a wide variety of collaborative interactions. It is more difficult to speculate on how these results will generalize to adults, to other types of collaborative communities, or to different types of creative production. These remain open questions for future research.

Nevertheless, Scratch is unusual in several ways that inform questions of generalizability. For example, we can address our second research question because Scratch projects fluidly, and by design, mix artistic and functional elements in a single interface and community. This also means that Scratch projects exist in a genre that defies easy categorization. Scratch projects are rarely as purely artistic as a novel or painting and are rarely as purely functional as operating system software. Our findings should be seen as limited to this boundary area between functional and artistic works.

Although we argue that loveits are proxies for project quality, it is important to realize that loveits are constituted as social

	Model 1	Model 2
(Intercept)	-3.359^*	-4.828^*
	(0.010)	(0.008)
log *blocks*	0.166^*	0.076^*
	(0.002)	(0.002)
log *media*	0.384^*	0.086^*
	(0.004)	(0.003)
log *isremix*	0.279^*	-0.091^*
	(0.020)	(0.014)
female	0.000	0.284^*
	(0.005)	(0.004)
age	-0.006^*	-0.002^*
	(0.000)	(0.000)
joined	-0.020^*	-0.008^*
	(0.000)	(0.000)
prevloveits	0.568^*	0.076^*
	(0.002)	(0.001)
log *blocks* × *isremix*	0.059^*	0.021^*
	(0.005)	(0.004)
log *media* × *isremix*	-0.305^*	-0.103^*
	(0.009)	(0.006)
views		1.226^*
		(0.002)
θ	0.250^*	1.722^*
	(0.001)	(0.011)
N	1239470	1239470
AIC	1803040	1415524
BIC	1803570	1416101
log L	-901476	-707714

Standard errors in parentheses;
** indicates significance at $p < .01$

Table 2. Table of fitted negative binomial regression models estimating a count the number of "loveits" a Scratch project has received one year after being shared on the website.

actions within a community of creators, evaluators, and collaborators. It is important to consider that different types of remixing in Scratch may also lead to variation in the norms around appropriate expression of appreciation between subcommunities.

By bringing together a wide variety of activities, Scratch provides a unique empirical setting that makes answering our research questions possible. However, the richness, breadth, and size of Scratch comes with a cost that makes our answers necessarily contingent. We hope that future work on these issues will explore and test our findings, and these limitations, in the growing number of similar peer production communities and beyond.

DISCUSSION

Our paper contributes to the literature on peer production, remixing, and cooperative work in two key ways. First, we provide empirical evidence from a remixing community that collaborative projects are, on average, rated as being of lower quality than works of single authorship. This finding is surprising, and suggests new and important limits to very broad claims of the benefit of collaboration in remixing and peer production. Second, by using a unique dataset of content that mixes code and traditionally artistic media, we provide what we believe is the first empirical support for the common wisdom that collaboration may be more effective for functional works than for artistic media.

Our quality metric is based on community assessment but it is unclear when designers should care what a community thinks about a member's work. Remixing may be good *a priori*, if it encourages learning, promotes democratization of cultural production, or encourages problem solving. For example, the quality of remixes in Scratch might not be important if it allows people to learn and socialize. Similarly, even if remixing results in low quality products, it might, as Lessig and Benkler suggest, play a democratizing function for culture. Furthermore, the quality of remixes might be irrelevant to those innovators that are driven by a desire to solve their own problems, as theories of user innovation suggest [41]. While high quality products have been an important driver of interest in peer production, peer evaluations of quality may be less important or relevant to system designers when considered from all three of these perspectives.

Both Lanier and Keen criticize remixing and peer production not only for producing low quality work, but also for lacking originality and the ability to produce real innovation. Even Raymond raises questions about the possibility that peer production can create innovative products and suggests that, fundamentally, "insight comes from individuals" [35]. Although previous work on Scratch has shown evidence of a wide range of derivative and transformative remixes [16], the innovativeness of a given project is both difficult to ascertain and fundamentally subjective. And although we know that less original remixes result in less happy users [17], it is difficult to know to what degree user ratings reflect novelty, creativity, or the spark of innovation. Finally, although it seems reasonable to suggest that the average remix will be less innovative – by virtue of being a remix – than a similar *de novo* project, interest in remixing stems, in part, from the fundamental Schumpeterian concept of innovation through recombination [38].

Our results suggest that people rate code-based remixes more positively that media-based remixes. One possible explanation is that Scratch is more modular for code than for media. As a result, remixing of media may lead to a struggle to maintain a consistency of vision or execution in way that code-based remixing does not. This decreased consistency may be reflected in lower ratings. In broader terms, perhaps the Scratch platform is simply not well designed for artistic collaboration. As a first step, designers can address this by building systems that support more modular media to support more structured collaboration.

A second explanation is that people perceive collaboration in code in terms of objective improvements while media elements will tend to be viewed more subjectively. This subjectivity in the evaluation of projects could lead to less positive assessment on average. Although it represents a challenge, future work could address both explanations by comparing different systems and considering the structure and shape of this variation.

The creation of richer avenues for productive interaction between media and code is an important area for further work in Scratch and elsewhere. Our results suggest that collaborative creativity, already cited in the HCI literature as an important and challenging area for future research, is likely to face particularly stark challenges for more media-intensive works.

What we hope to offer in this paper is a step toward a fuller understanding of the limitations of collaboration in remixing and peer production. As others have suggested and shown, collaboration is not *always* better. In Scratch, at least, it usually results in lower peer ratings of the resulting products – particularly for media-intensive works. As supporters and advocates of remixing, we reject the blind repetition of the mantra that collaboration is better for all types of work. Instead, we believe it is crucial to learn and understand the limitations and challenges associated with these important cultural practices. With this knowledge, we hope to more effectively influence the design of social media and collaboration support systems, and to help peer production thrive.

ACKNOWLEDGMENTS

We thank the Lifelong Kindergarten Group at the MIT Media Laboratory for creating Scratch as well as the thousands of children and adult members of the Scratch online community. Scratch is a project with financial support from the National Science Foundation (Grant No. ITR-0325828), Microsoft Corp., Intel Foundation, Nokia, and the MIT Media Lab research consortia. Work in this paper was funded by the MIT Sloan School of Management, the MIT Media Lab Consortia, Microsoft Research, the Berkman Center for Internet and Society at Harvard University, NSF grants OCI-1026473 and OCI-1027848 and the Ford Foundation's Visionary Leadership gift.

REFERENCES

1. Albrecht, A. J., and Gaffney, J. E. Software function, source lines of code, and development effort prediction: A software science validation. *IEEE Transactions on Software Engineering SE-9*, 6 (Nov. 1983), 639– 648.
2. Amabile, T. M., Conti, R., Coon, H., Lazenby, J., and Herron, M. Assessing the work environment for creativity. *Academy of Management Journal 39*, 5 (Oct. 1996), 1154–1184.
3. Aragon, C. R., Poon, S. S., Monroy-Hernández, A., and Aragon, D. A tale of two online communities: Fostering collaboration and creativity in scientists and children. In *Proceedings of the seventh ACM conference on Creativity and Cognition*, C&C '09 (2009), 9–18. ACM ID: 1640239.
4. Benkler, Y. *The Wealth of Networks: How Social Production Transforms Markets and Freedom*. Yale University Press, May 2006.
5. Bernstein, M. S., Brandt, J., Miller, R. C., and Karger, D. R. Crowds in two seconds: enabling realtime crowd-powered interfaces. In *Proceedings of the 24th annual ACM symposium on User interface software and technology*, UIST '11, ACM (New York, NY, USA, 2011), 33–42.
6. Cheliotis, G., and Yew, J. An analysis of the social structure of remix culture. In *C&T 2009* (2009), 165–174.
7. Crowston, K., Howison, J., and Masango, C. Towards a portfolio of FLOSS project success measures. In *Proceedings of the Open Source Workshop of the International Conference on Software Engineering* (2004).
8. Csikszentmihalyi, M. *Creativity: Flow and the Psychology of Discovery and Invention*. Harper Perennial, May 1997.
9. Diehl, M., and Stroebe, W. Productivity loss in brainstorming groups: Toward the solution of a riddle. *Journal of Personality and Social Psychology; Journal of Personality and Social Psychology 53*, 3 (1987), 497.
10. Fischer, G. Social creativity: Turning barriers into opportunities for collaborative design. In *Proceedings of the eighth conference on Participatory design: Artful integration: interweaving media, materials and practices - Volume 1*, ACM (Toronto, Ontario, Canada, 2004), 152–161.
11. Giles, J. Internet encyclopaedias go head to head. *Nature 438*, 7070 (Dec. 2005), 900–901.
12. Greenstein, S., and Zhu, F. Is wikipedia biased? *American Economic Review 102*, 3 (May 2012), 343–348.
13. Griswold, A. W. Baccalaureate address, June 1957.
14. Heer, J., and Bostock, M. Crowdsourcing graphical perception: using mechanical turk to assess visualization design. In *Proceedings of the 28th international conference on Human factors in computing systems*, CHI '10, ACM (New York, NY, USA, 2010), 203–212.
15. Hill, B. M. *Literary collaboration and control: A socio-historic, technological and legal analysis*. Thesis, Hampshire College, Amherst, Massachusetts, May 2003.
16. Hill, B. M., and Monroy-Hernández, A. The remixing dilemma: The trade-off between generativity and originality. *American Behavioral Scientist*.
17. Hill, B. M. H., Monroy-Hernández, A., and Olson, K. Responses to remixing on a social media sharing website. In *Proc. ICWSM 2010*, AAAI (Washington, D.C., 2010), 74–81.
18. Ito, M. Technologies of the childhood imagination: Yu-gi-oh!, media mixes, and everyday cultural production. In *Structures of Participation in Digital Culture*, J. Karaganis, Ed. The Social Science Research Council, 2007.
19. Jenkins, H. *Convergence Culture: Where Old and New Media Collide*, revised ed. NYU Press, New York, Oct. 2008.
20. Jenkins, H., Clinton, K., Purushotma, R., Robinson, A., and Weigel, M. Confronting the challenges of

participatory culture: Media education for the 21st century. Tech. rep., MacArthur Foundation, Chicago, Illinois, USA, Oct. 2006.

21. Jurgensen, J. Beyond 'Thriller': reinventing the music video. *Wall Street Journal* (May 2011), J D1.
22. Keen, A. *The Cult of the Amateur: How Today's Internet is Killing Our Culture*, 3rd printing ed. Crown Business, June 2007.
23. Kittur, A., and Kraut, R. E. Harnessing the wisdom of crowds in wikipedia: quality through coordination. ACM (San Diego, CA, USA, 2008), 37–46.
24. Koblin, A. M. The sheep market. In *Proceedings of the seventh ACM conference on Creativity and cognition*, C&C '09, ACM (New York, NY, USA, 2009), 451–452.
25. Lampe, C. A. *Ratings Use in an Online Discussion System: The Slashdot Case*. PhD thesis, University of Michigan, Ann Arbor, Michigan, 2006.
26. Lanier, J. Digital maoism: The hazards of the new online collectivism. *Edge* (May 2006).
27. Lanier, J. *You Are Not a Gadget: A Manifesto*, 1 ed. Knopf, Jan. 2010.
28. Lave, J., and Wenger, E. *Situated learning: Legitimate peripheral participation*. Cambridge University Press, Sept. 1991.
29. Lessig, L. *Remix: Making Art and Commerce Thrive in the Hybrid Economy*. Penguin Press HC, Oct. 2008.
30. Luther, K., and Bruckman, A. Leadership in online creative collaboration. In *Proceedings of the 2008 ACM conference on Computer supported cooperative work*, ACM (San Diego, CA, USA, 2008), 343–352.
31. Maher, M. L., Paulini, M., and Murty, P. Scaling up: From individual design to collaborative design to collective design. In *Design Computing and Cognition '10*, J. S. Gero, Ed. Springer Netherlands, 2011, 581–599.
32. Mamykina, L., Candy, L., and Edmonds, E. Collaborative creativity. *Communications of the ACM 45*, 10 (2002), 96–99.
33. Palfrey, J., and Gasser, U. *Born Digital: Understanding the First Generation of Digital Natives*. Basic Books, Aug. 2008.
34. Papert, S. *Mindstorms: Children, computers, and powerful ideas*. Basic Books, New York, 1980.
35. Raymond, E. S. *The cathedral and the bazaar: Musings on Linux and open source by an accidental revolutionary*. O'Reilly and Associates, Sebastopol, CA, 1999.
36. Resnick, M., Maloney, J., Monroy-Hernández, A., Rusk, N., Eastmond, E., Brennan, K., Millner, A., Rosenbaum, E., Silver, J., Silverman, B., and Kafai, Y. Scratch: programming for all. *Commun. ACM 52*, 11 (2009), 60–67.
37. Salganik, M. J., Dodds, P. S., and Watts, D. J. Experimental study of inequality and unpredictability in an artificial cultural market. *Science 311*, 5762 (Feb. 2006), 854–856.
38. Schumpeter, J. A. *The theory of economic development: An inquiry into profits, capital, credit, interest, and the business cycle*. Harvard University Press, Jan. 1934.
39. Shneiderman, B. Creativity support tools. *Communications of the ACM 45*, 10 (2002), 116–120.
40. Viegas, F. B., Wattenberg, M., and Dave, K. Studying cooperation and conflict between authors with history flow visualizations. In *CHI '04: Proceedings of the SIGCHI conference on Human factors in computing systems*, ACM Press (New York, NY, USA, 2004), 575–582.
41. von Hippel, E. *Democratizing innovation*. The MIT Press, Cambridge, Massachusetts, 2005.
42. Walston, C. E., and Felix, C. P. A method of programming measurement and estimation. *IBM Systems Journal 16*, 1 (1977), 54–73.
43. Wilkinson, D. M., and Huberman, B. A. Cooperation and quality in wikipedia. In *Proceedings of the 2007 international symposium on Wikis*, ACM (Montreal, Quebec, Canada, 2007), 157–164.
44. Yu, L., and Nickerson, J. V. Cooks or cobblers?: crowd creativity through combination. In *Proceedings of the 2011 annual conference on Human factors in computing systems*, CHI '11, ACM (New York, NY, USA, 2011), 1393–1402.

The Promise and Peril of Real-Time Corrections to Political Misperceptions

R. Kelly Garrett Brian E. Weeks
School of Communication
Ohio State University
Columbus, OH 43210, USA
{garrett.258,weeks.311}@osu.edu

ABSTRACT

Computer scientists have responded to the high prevalence of inaccurate political information online by creating systems that identify and flag false claims. Warning users of inaccurate information as it is displayed has obvious appeal, but it also poses risk. Compared to post-exposure corrections, real-time corrections may cause users to be more resistant to factual information. This paper presents an experiment comparing the effects of real-time corrections to corrections that are presented after a short distractor task. Although real-time corrections are modestly more effective than delayed corrections overall, closer inspection reveals that this is only true among individuals predisposed to reject the false claim. In contrast, individuals whose attitudes are supported by the inaccurate information distrust the source more when corrections are presented in real time, yielding beliefs comparable to those never exposed to a correction. We find no evidence of real-time corrections encouraging counterargument. Strategies for reducing these biases are discussed.

Author Keywords

Credibility; Misinformation; Learning

ACM Classification Keywords

H.1.2 User/Machine Systems.

INTRODUCTION

Inaccurate information is notoriously common on the web [49, 50]. Hundreds of false or unsubstantiated claims on a host of topics, from the link between vaccines and autism to the birthplace of the President, can be found in seconds using a search engine or by perusing relevant blogs. Political misperceptions—beliefs about candidates and issues that are not supported by the best available evidence—are particularly prevalent. Survey data indicate that the more people rely on the Internet for political news, especially partisan blogs, the more false rumors they encounter [16]. This is perhaps unsurprising: the Internet is a unique communication medium, characterized by its broad reach, high speed, low cost, and by the persistence of posted information. Taken together, these attributes give voice to individuals and groups who might otherwise lack the necessary resources to share their beliefs publicly, and this exposure can grant false claims an air of legitimacy [23, 49].

There are several mechanisms that animate the flow and acceptance of misinformation [25]. Sometimes inaccurate beliefs result from a misunderstanding or a failure of memory; at other times, they are the product of politically motivated deception. Whatever their source, though, people tend to hold on to inaccurate beliefs, especially when they are consistent with their world view [25] or when they provide an explanation for an otherwise puzzling phenomenon [47]. Even individuals who strive to be impartial and who have no political axe to grind tend to be biased in their response to corrections by virtue of the mental shortcuts that they use when evaluating new information [46]. Fortunately, however, given sufficient evidence, even the most biased audiences can be moved to reject falsehoods [44].

In response to the prevalence of online misinformation, researchers have begun crafting systems designed to help people make sense of the vast array of competing claims. These systems employ a diverse array of techniques, but they share a common goal: to help users distinguish between truth and falsehoods. Of particular interest here are systems such as Dispute Finder [14], which attempt to present corrections to inaccurate information in real time. The appeal of real-time corrections is self-evident: if we can identify or correct a false statement when the user first encounters it, it is at least plausible that we could limit its influence by preventing its acceptance and further dissemination.

This paper concerns the theoretical assumptions on which systems providing real-time corrections are premised. Specifically, it describes an experimental test of the effectiveness of this approach when correcting inaccurate political information. Despite its obvious appeal, psychological theory suggests that real-time correction might not be as effective as it at first appears. There are numerous reasons to think that a system presenting corrections alongside an inaccurate statement may inadvertently provoke users into defending attitude-consistent misperceptions. In other words, there may be conditions under which this strategy could backfire, undermining corrections rather than reinforcing them. Our goal here is to test whether real-time corrections are in fact more effective than corrections that are presented after a delay.

Rather than build a working prototype to test this claim, we construct an experiment that simulates users' experience under different designs. We compare participants who are presented with an inaccurate statement and no correction to those who see a correction after a delay and to those see a message in which disputed information is highlighted and accompanied by a correction. Results indicate that although real-time corrections are sometimes better than delayed corrections, they are *less* effective when the correction poses a threat to individuals' political attitudes. We argue that this raises significant concerns about the approach employed in a number of contemporary designs; however, we also suggest that there are strategies that can help alleviate this problem. We begin by reviewing the current design space.

BACKGROUND AND RELATED DESIGN WORK

Journalists and web developers have responded vigorously to the high profile of falsehoods circulating online. Snopes, one of the earliest web sites to address this issue, provides detailed assessments of many controversial or outrageous claims found online. News organizations have followed suit, offering fact-checking sites that focus more narrowly on newsworthy political misperceptions (e.g., FactCheck.org and PolitiFact). Most recently, some organizations have experimented with crowdsourcing as a means of fact checking the news (e.g., NewsTrust's TruthSquad).

Researchers have taken up the challenge as well, looking for ways to stem the flow of misinformation online by creating technologies that can identify and, in some cases, correct inaccuracies. Not all of these systems concern political misperceptions, but the mechanisms they employ to enhance users' understanding of the information environment are relevant. Computer scientists have developed systems capable of tracking short distinctive phrases, including rumors and misinformation, as they move across the Web, documenting how they evolve and mutate [28, 48]. Other researchers focus specifically on identifying deceptive messaging. Truthy, for example, is intended to spot social-media campaigns that are orchestrated by an individual or organization, but purport to be a spontaneous expression by a large group of independent individuals [42]. Another research team has focused on detecting deceptive "opinion spam", favorable reviews written by individuals in exchange for compensation [40]. Videolyzer allows users to analyze online political videos and rate them in terms of accuracy and bias [11] and SRSR (pronounced "sourcer") aims to help journalists identify trustworthy content amidst the flood of information produced by social media [10].

Another vein of research in this area involves creating systems that can enhance individuals' understanding of a contentious issue by mapping relationships among competing claims and corresponding evidence using a mix of manual and automated processing [24, 45] (e.g., Debatepedia, DebateGraph, Cohere, considerate, and many others). Some of these systems have an explicitly evaluative component, and are intended to help users systematically review relevant data so that they might assess a claim or prediction [35] (e.g., Statement Map, Competing Hypotheses). Other systems are designed to facilitate citizens' exposure to a diverse range of information and opinions. Prototypes strive to present readers with news articles containing multiple viewpoints [41], or to tailor news aggregators in order to encourage a diverse diet of opinions [34].

Finally, there are a handful of systems that attempt to correct online misinformation at the point of contact. Perhaps the most well known of these is Dispute Finder [13, 14]. The goal of this system is to highlight inaccurate phrases on a webpage as the page is displayed. It accomplishes this with a browser plug-in that executes a simple text entailment algorithm, comparing the content of page to be displayed to a cached database of previously identified falsehoods. The corpus of claims is constructed by crawling Snopes and Politifact and through manual additions by system users. The result is a tool that allows users easy access to fact-checking information from any webpage that includes one of the disputed claims. In 2009 and 2010, a commercial service with similar objectives was also being developed. Called DotSpots, the system allowed users to annotate text on one webpage and would automatically display the annotation on other pages containing similar text. Crowdsourced fact checking was not the sole goal of the system, but the company's slogan "spot the truth, connect the dots!" suggests that this was a prominent consideration. This service, however, failed to achieve a critical mass of users, and development ended in late 2010. Nevertheless, interest in real-time corrections continues unabated, as exemplified most recently in Hypothes.is. Like its predecessors, the project aims to discourage the flow of inaccurate information, this time by creating a distributed platform for textual annotation paired with a reputation system intended to ensure the annotations are of high quality.

In sum, there is a growing collection of tools that can be used to identify, track, analyze, and potentially correct misinformation online, and several systems aim to present these corrections in real time. Which brings us to the question driving this research, namely, how effective is a real-time fact-checking approach? Research in psychology offers some insights into how we answer this question.

Political fact-checking psychology

Correcting misinformation as it is presented assumes that political learning is a simple operation, with individuals retaining information that is supported by facts and discounting or rejecting unsupported claims and falsehoods. On this view, correcting a misperception is no different than learning about a change in a weather forecast: you were expecting sun, but now the forecast calls for rain. In this scenario, updating your beliefs is straightforward and unambiguous. You were not invested in the old forecast, the meteorologist has nothing to gain from lying, and the cost of being wrong is relatively low.

Political learning, however, is rarely so simple. There are important differences between a weather forecast and a contentious political issue such as climate change. In contrast to a forecast, people are more likely to have invested effort into reaching an opinion about climate change. Furthermore, experts making the claims—those with the data and the corresponding analytic tools—have a stake in what people believe, and the costs of being wrong about the issue are high. Given this, it should be unsurprising that people cautiously approach new information on contentious topics, especially information that runs counter to their beliefs. That people argue against counterattitudinal evidence while readily accepting proattitudinal evidence is undisputed [29, 31, 51]. Several different factors may contribute to this behavior. It could be at least partially an artifact of Bayesian learning, whereby the same information has different consequences for belief depending on the individual's prior knowledge and confidence [7, 19]. But there is also compelling evidence of an affective component, whereby individuals are motivated to defend their position beyond the point of reason [43]. The result is that beliefs can diverge in response to corrections; in some extreme cases, individuals may even become more accepting of inaccurate information [39].

In short, there is significant evidence that people do not simply "learn" from fact-checking messages. Instead, individuals assess new information before storing it in memory, evaluating whether the evidence is sufficiently persuasive to merit updating their beliefs and adjusting the magnitude of the update based on both the strength of their prior convictions and of the novel evidence [54]. This is neither surprising nor fundamentally problematic—to unquestioningly accept every new claim encountered would be naïve—but the practice has important implications for how people respond to attempts to correct misperceptions. Specifically, it suggests that it may be most appropriate to view factual corrections as a form of persuasion or strategic communication [4]. After all, these messages are intended to convince the reader that they represent the truth and that claims to the contrary are false. This has important consequences for how we understand the response that corrective messages elicit.

There are some reasons to expect corrections presented at the time of exposure to perform better than those presented later, even if people vet counterattitudinal information. People are not "ambulatory encyclopedias", memorizing every fact they encounter; instead they rely on shortcuts to arrive at their decisions [30]. One important shortcut involves maintaining easily recalled summary judgments of attitudes and beliefs, while discarding much of the evidence on which the judgments are based [3, 54]. If the evidence contained in a correction is convincing enough that recipients are compelled to accept it—even if it means that they only reject parts of the misinformation—then an immediate correction should reduce the risk of individuals updating stored attitudes based on a falsehood. On this view, flagging inaccuracies before they can sway attitude is potentially useful, and real-time corrections should generally outperform delayed corrections.

What, then, is the risk? The key question is whether a correction embedded in an inaccurate message generates *more* resistance than a correction presented at a later time. There are a few reasons to think that it could. First, real-time corrections may produce heightened counterargument. Corrections presented at the time of exposure are more confrontational because they draw attention to points of controversy, directly challenging claims that some readers are inclined to believe. This can create an affective response—e.g., anger and defensiveness at being told one's views are based on lies—and can be more threatening to those inclined to believe the falsehood than are corrections not attached to specific claims. Research has shown that people generate more counterarguments to ego-threatening messages than non-threatening messages [26], and that such counterargument makes attitude-consistent evidence more accessible [6, 15, 39]. As a consequence, threat-inducing corrections are more likely to be overwhelmed by arguments in favor of a misperception than less threatening messages.

Second, correcting inaccuracies at the time of exposure could encourage users to question the credibility of the message. Real-time corrections explicitly pit two claims against one another: the misinformation and its correction. Forced to weigh these competing claims, individuals are likely to regard the attitude-consistent claims as more believable [29]. Furthermore, there is evidence that this tendency becomes stronger when the individual feels more threatened. Source derogation, for example asserting that a source is biased or that it lacks relevant expertise, is more prevalent when individuals feel their position is in jeopardy [26], and this reduces the likelihood that an individual will act in accordance with a corrective message [8].

In sum, although we do anticipate that real-time corrections should be more effective than delayed corrections overall, they may be less effective among those who are predisposed to believe the misinformation. For these individuals, corrections applied directly to an inaccurate

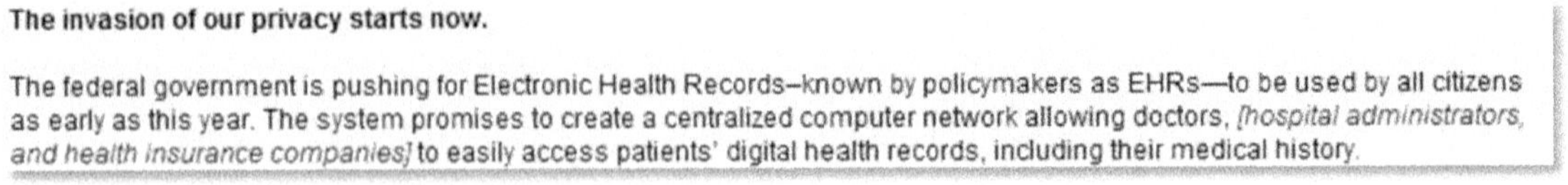
The invasion of our privacy starts now.

The federal government is pushing for Electronic Health Records–known by policymakers as EHRs—to be used by all citizens as early as this year. The system promises to create a centralized computer network allowing doctors, *[hospital administrators, and health insurance companies]* to easily access patients' digital health records, including their medical history.

Figure 1. Partial screenshot showing an embedded correction.

claim could induce greater counterargument and could lead the recipient to question the message's credibility.

EXPERIMENTAL STUDY

We conducted a between-participants experiment to examine how real-time delivery of fact checking information influences recipients' subsequent beliefs compared to other strategies. The topic of the information presented in this study was electronic health records (EHRs), an issue that had received only modest news coverage at the time of data collection (May 2011). We utilized an opt-in online panel administered by Survey Sampling International to recruit a demographically diverse sample of U.S.-based participants ($N = 574$). The sample is 49% male, has an average age of 45.8 years ($SD = 15.8$), and is racially diverse (86.9% While, 6.8% Black, 6.3% other). Participants also had a range of party affiliations (25.4% Republican, 34.7% Democrat, 28.1% Independent, 11.9% other) and of ideologies (28.4% Liberal, 35.0% Moderate, 36.6% Conservative).

Procedure

The experiment compared participants' beliefs across three conditions. In all conditions, we began by asking participants to tell us how much they knew about five contemporary policy issues, including electronic health records. Familiarity was measured on a seven-point scale, anchored by "unfamiliar with the issue" (coded as 1) and "know a great deal about the issue" ($M = 4.2$, $SD = 1.7$). We also asked participants to indicate their attitude toward the same five issues on a seven-point scale anchored by "extremely negative" (coded as 1) to "extremely positive" ($M = 4.8$, $SD = 1.6$).

Next, we asked participants to read a 443-word "news article" written by a journalist with guidance from the research team that provided a brief introduction to EHRs, describing the technology, its objectives, and current deployment levels. This information was gleaned from contemporary news stories and government sources, and was accurate to the best of our knowledge.[1] Participants were required to spend at least one minute viewing the story, though many spent substantially longer ($M = 112$s, $SD = 78$s).

The three conditions diverged at this point, varying how inaccurate information was subsequently presented and corrected. In the first condition, the *delayed correction* ($n = 191$), participants were next shown a 367-word message that contains a number of factual errors, purportedly copied from "a widely read political blog". The errors, which we inserted intentionally, include several false statements about who is allowed to access EHRs. For instance, the message claims that hospital administrators, health insurance companies, employers, and government officials have unrestricted access to personal health information. As before, participants were required to spend at least one minute viewing the story, though the average participant spent more than the minimum ($M = 93$s, $SD = 51$s).

Before presenting a correction, participants in the delayed-correction condition were asked to complete a three-minute image-comparison task. The directions stated that this would allow researchers to understand how the individual processes images, but its true function was to serve as a distractor task, clearing working memory prior to introducing the correction. Participants were presented with a pair of nearly identical images and had one minute to count observed differences before reporting their results ($M = 4.58$, $SD = 2.17$, range 0-11). Participants were then informed that there were in fact 13 differences and were encouraged to be as accurate as possible in subsequent comparisons. The comparison task was repeated twice more without feedback.

After completing the distractor task, participants were presented with a 378-word correction attributed to FactCheck.org, an award-winning non-partisan news service. The correction addressed each of the inaccuracies included in the previous message, noting for example that there are clear policies restricting access to patient health information to those involved in a patient's care. Most participants spent more than the required minute reading this article ($M = 105$s, $SD = 63$s).

In the second condition, the *immediate correction* ($n = 182$), participants were presented with an annotated version of the "blog post" described above (see Figure 1). The directions explained that, "A third-party fact-checking service has reviewed this blog post and concluded that it contains factual errors. Inaccurate statements are italicized, enclosed in [square brackets] and displayed in red. Please see the fact-checking article at the bottom of this page for more detailed information." All false information was marked in the body of the message accordingly. Below this, the fact-checking message used in the first condition was presented in its entirety. Participants were required to spend at least two minutes reading the corrected document, but most spent considerably longer ($M = 181$s, $SD = 87$s).

---

[1] Stimuli are available from the first author upon request.

The visual flagging of false claims in this condition is similar, but not identical, to Dispute Finder's interface. In Dispute Finder, the claim was highlighted in red; in this study it was printed in dark-red italicized text and enclosed in square brackets. We selected this presentation style to ensure that individuals could spot inaccuracies even if they were not easily able to see red highlighting. Also, Dispute Finder corrections appeared in a popup if the user clicked on the highlighted snippet; in contrast, corrections in this condition were always present at the bottom of the page. We know from prior online experiments that participants sometimes have difficulty managing popups, and we did not want this to be an obstacle to successful completion of the study.

In the *control condition* (n = 201), participants were only presented with the inaccurate message during the study; the correction was presented after the study was complete, during debriefing.

The study concluded with a brief questionnaire, beginning with a series of standard psychological measures. One of these was a "memory tally", which asked participants to list everything they learned about EHRs from the reading (up to ten items, M = 3.5, SD = 2.7). Next, participants were asked to indicate their feelings about each recalled item on a seven-point scale anchored by "extremely negative" (coded as 1) and "extremely positive". We then counted the number of negative items (those scored below the scale midpoint) that came to mind (M = 1.3, SD = 1.7).

Accuracy was measured by asking participants to indicate how easy or difficult it will be for each of several groups (doctors, employers, government officials, hospital administrators, insurers, pharmaceutical companies, and medical staff—listed in random order) to access EHRs using a seven-point scale anchored by "very easy" (coded as 1) and "very difficult". Responses most consistent with the fact-checking document would describe doctors and medical staff as having very easy access and everyone else as having very difficult access. Thus, the items corresponding to the first two groups were reverse coded and the seven items were summed to create an accuracy measure (α = .75, M = 28.8, SD = 8.2, range 13-49).

Finally, the questionnaire asked participants to assess the credibility of the fact-checking message by answering three questions: "How successful was the fact checking article at discrediting the claim that Electronic Health Records will allow limitless access to patient health information?", "How persuasive was the evidence given in the fact checking article that Electronic Health Records do not pose a privacy threat?", and "How credible was the fact checking article's presentation of information about Electronic Health Records?". The questions used a seven-point response scale, with higher scores corresponding to higher credibility (α = .88, M = 14.3, SD = 4.5).

Results

First we confirm that corrections can be effective, even on politically charged topics. Results indicate that individuals exposed to a fact-checking message hold more accurate beliefs than those who are not exposed. To see this, we constructed a linear regression model predicting belief accuracy by condition, treating the control as the reference category. Four cases in which the participant did not answer all the belief questions are omitted, leaving an n of 570. Interpreting model coefficients (not shown, but see Figure 2), we find that compared to the control condition participants in both the delayed-correction condition (*diff*=3.3 points, p < .001) and immediate-correction condition (*diff*=5.2 points, p < .001) score significantly higher on the accuracy measure. This establishes that these beliefs, which are colored by political interests, can change in light of new information.

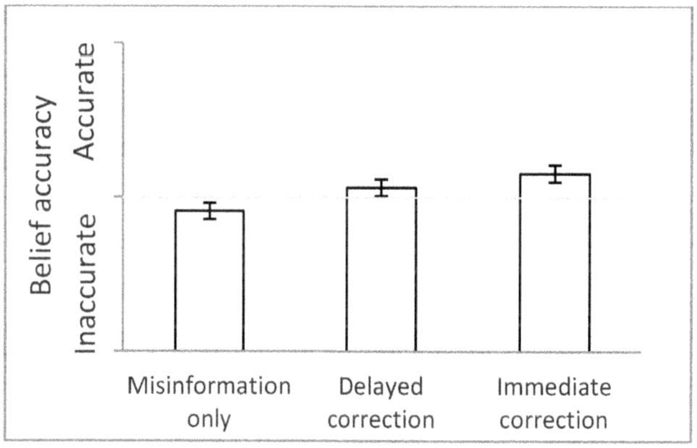

Figure 2. Predicted belief accuracy by condition based on linear regression coefficients; 95% confidence intervals shown. The grey horizontal line is the accuracy scale midpoint (28).

We also posit that immediate corrections are more effective than corrections presented after a delay, as implicitly assumed by many designers who have embraced the real-time approach. The data support this prediction as well. Visually, we see that the bar representing beliefs in the immediate-correction condition is taller than that of the delayed-correction condition. A Wald test confirms that this difference is significant. The coefficient on the immediate-correction condition is significantly larger than that of the delayed correction, $F(1, 567) = 5.31, p < .05$.

Recall, however, that we also anticipated real-time corrections having some harmful effects. More important than the modest improvements in accuracy associated with an immediate correction is the possibility that this approach might amplify the influence of attitude-based bias. The data suggest that this is the case. Adding interaction terms between condition and participants' issue favorability (mean centered) to the previously described regression allows us to test these relationships (see Table 1).

As one would expect, an individual's attitude toward Electronic Health Records prior to viewing the stimuli has a strong main effect on accuracy: the more (less) positively the individual feels about the issue, the more (less) accurate his or her beliefs. When misinformation is corrected immediately, this difference is more pronounced: correcting misinformation at the time of exposure is more effective for issue supporters, but less effective among opponents. There is, however, no evidence that issue favorability has a moderating effect in the delayed correction: the correction's influence is the same regardless of the participants' issue favorability. Figure 3 illustrates these relationships, highlighting the fact that the effectiveness of a real-time correction is due to its performance among those most inclined to reject the misinformation. Among those who oppose EHRs, the effect of the immediate correction on beliefs is statistically comparable to no correction at all.

	B	*SE*
Delayed correction [a]	3.50***	(0.78)
Immediate correction [a]	5.24***	(0.79)
Issue favorability	0.99**	(0.36)
Delayed * favorability	0.03	(0.52)
Immediate * favorability	1.07*	(0.51)
Intercept	25.92***	(0.55)

Table 1 . Linear regression predicting belief accuracy. Note $N = 570$, $R^2 = 0.14$, * $p < 0.05$, ** $p < 0.01$, *** $p < 0.001$ Favorability is mean-centered. ([a]) Misinformation-only condition is reference category.

We identified two mechanisms that might help explain the uniquely biased processing of real-time corrections. First, corrections that are presented alongside a false claim might cause issue opponents to engage in more vigorous counterargument than corrections presented later. A linear regression predicting the number of counterarguments listed during the memory-recall task, however, offers no support for this prediction (Table not shown). The coefficients on both the immediate and the delayed correction conditions are negative—$B = -.47$, $p < .01$ for the delayed correction and $B = -.72$, $p < .001$ for the immediate correction—and they are not significantly different from one another, $F(1, 571) = 2.42$, $p = .12$. In other words, individuals volunteered *fewer* negative thoughts about EHRs when exposed to a correction than not, regardless of when the correction was presented. Furthermore, issue favorability has no influence on this relationship. The interactions between issue favorability and each of the two correction conditions are non-significant. Participants in these two conditions have comparable numbers of negative thoughts in response to the correction, regardless of their prior attitude toward EHRs. Hence, there is no evidence that real-time corrections provoke heightened counterargument, even among issue opponents.

The second mechanism we identified to help explain biased responses to real-time corrections was the idea that

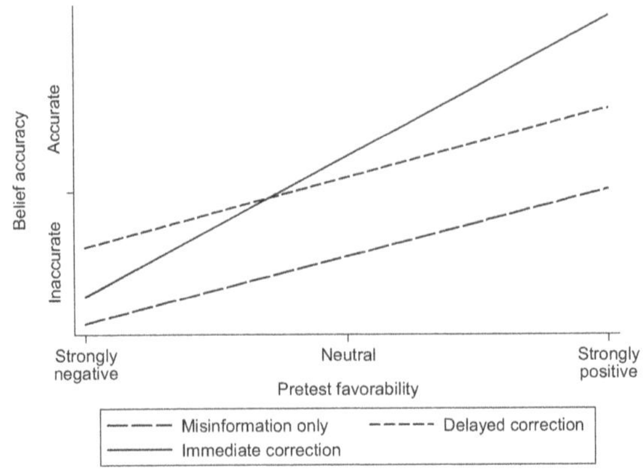

Figure 3. Predicting belief accuracy by issue favorability for each condition based on linear regression coefficients.

embedded corrections effectively pit two claims against one another, perhaps causing users to place greater focus on the credibility of the competing messages. Since credibility assessments tend to be biased by prior attitudes, focusing on them should lead EHR opponents to question the fact-checking message's credibility. The data support this explanation, as evidenced by a linear regression model predicting perceived credibility of the correction (see Table 2 and Figure 4). Consistent with prior research, we see that the more favorably an individual felt about EHRs, the more credible the correction was perceived to be. The significant interaction term indicates that this relationship is stronger in the immediate-correction condition than in the delayed-correction condition, suggesting that attitude-based biases play a bigger role when corrections are presented in real time.

	B	*SE*
Immediate correction [a]	0.79	(0.43)
Issue favorability	0.85***	(0.20)
Immediate * favorability	0.57*	(0.28)
Intercept	13.94***	(0.30)

Table 2 . Linear regression predicting message credibility. Note $N = 372$, $R^2 = 0.17$, * $p < 0.05$, *** $p < 0.001$ Favorability is mean-centered. ([a]) Delay is reference category.

Finally, we considered whether issue favorability influenced belief accuracy indirectly by shaping participants' trust of the corrective message. A mediation test using boot-strapped confidence intervals confirms this, demonstrating that the influence of issue favorability on belief accuracy is mediated by the perceived credibility of the message [21]. This holds when the correction is immediate, with a 95% confidence interval for the mediated effect between .94 and 1.97; and when it is delayed, with a

95% confidence interval between .42 and 1.35. In other words, individuals who are more favorably inclined toward EHRs view the corrections as more credible, which in turn promotes more accurate beliefs.

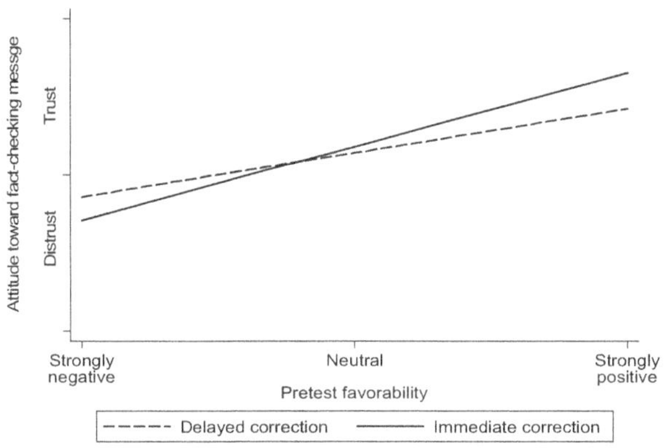

Figure 4 . Predicting credibility of correction by issue favorability for each correction condition based on linear regression coefficients.

DISCUSSION

Despite the obvious appeal of providing immediate corrections to false information online, this approach has some negative consequences that need to be addressed. Annotating a misleading message by highlighting inaccuracies and embedding fact-checking information accentuates individuals' tendency to view these corrections through an attitudinally biased lens. We should be careful not to exaggerate the significance of this behavior: real-time corrections are often as effective as traditional post-exposure correction strategies. The problem is that these techniques actually increase resistance to the correction among those whose attitudes are most strongly supported by the misperception. Thus, for example we would anticipate that systems like Dispute Finder would do little to change the beliefs of the roughly one in six Americans who, despite exhaustive news coverage and fact checking, continue to question whether President Obama was born in the U.S. [2] or whether vaccines are safe [20]. New approaches may be required when designing automated systems to promote more accurate beliefs among those whose prior attitudes leave them predisposed to hold a misperception.

Implications for Practice

We believe that the key theoretical insight for guiding future design work is our argument that people respond to fact-checking messages in ways that are comparable to their response to propaganda and persuasion. Indeed, critics at both ends of the political spectrum have labeled fact checking organizations as partisan [22, 53]. This comparison implies a more complicated view of political learning than assumed in prior design work, but it also suggests a variety of strategies from which system builders may be able to learn. Scholars who study health-behavior modification campaigns (e.g., anti-smoking campaigns) and those who work in science communication (e.g., efforts to increase public understanding of global climate change) have been grappling with similar challenges for a long time, and some of the approaches they have developed may translate. We highlight a few strategies that we believe are particularly promising.

Recommendation 1. One strategy focuses on the source of the correction. It is hardly surprising that individuals trust some sources more than others [33], and that trust in expertise varies significantly based on the attributes of both the expert and the individuals [5, 37]. For example, independent experts are generally more influential than industry representatives, but there are many individuals who tend to distrust both groups. Research suggests that likeable sources and sources that share characteristics with the message recipient are less prone to derogation [8]. Criticisms from unexpected sources are also uniquely persuasive, as when a politician criticizes one of his or her ideological allies [1].

This suggests that users may be more willing to accept corrective messages from sources that are ideologically similar, or that they choose for themselves. To accomplish the former, a system might offer corrective messages derived from and attributed to frequently used sources, or sources that the user regularly recommends to others (via Facebook Likes or Tweets, for example). Alternatively, designers might allow users to explicitly tailor which sources the correction system utilizes. An architecture that allows multiple independent groups to create their own databases of disputed claims and affords users the opportunity to opt in to one or more of these differing collections could be beneficial.

A question raised by this approach is who decides what the truth is. The political world is complex, and there are legitimate alternative interpretations of many situations. At the same time, however, there are instances when the preponderance of evidence supports one factual claim over another (e.g., President Obama was born in the U.S.; the 9/11 attacks were not a Bush-administration conspiracy). Fortunately, experts who disagree with one another ideologically often agree about the facts, though they may differ in how they present them. Thus, allowing users to select which sources they trust does not mean giving up on the question of truth. Furthermore, although there is a risk that individuals might seek out "fact-checking" sources that affirm information consistent with their ideological beliefs without regard to the evidence, while avoiding other sources, there is growing evidence that such an aversion is relatively rare [17] and a competitive media environment can help to guard against outlet bias by penalizing the reputation of sources that are consistently inaccurate [18].

Recommendation 2. Another strategy concerns how the message is framed. For example, a correction might highlight the *risks* associated with holding a misperception, the *benefits* of a more accurate belief, the *moral obligation* to weigh the evidence fairly, etc. Different frames have been shown to resonate with different audiences, and the better aligned the frame is with the recipients' ideology, the more likely the message is to be accepted [32]. For example, conservatives tend to be uniquely responsive to information framed in terms of loss, while liberals respond better to benefit frames [27]. The power of how a correction is framed should not be underestimated: some research suggests that the influence of factual content is almost entirely eclipsed by its framing. Experimental studies have shown that compared to how a message is framed, factual information has comparatively little sway on opinion formation and is more prone to being viewed as biased [12].

A fact-checking system might tailor its presentation of corrections by combining user profiles, algorithms for guessing frame preferences based on these profiles, and databases of corrections framed in a variety of ways. For example, users who consistently consume a diverse mix of ideologically oriented outlets might be uniquely responsive to a message framed in terms of the need to weigh competing evidence. Individuals who have been identified as having a high risk aversion, either through self-reports or, more likely, implicit behavior measures, would instead see corrections that emphasis the risks associated with inaccurate beliefs on the topic.

It would be crucial in such a system, however, to ensure that the factual information is consistent across the various frames least it become a propaganda tool. Furthermore, the creation of such a system poses considerable threat to user privacy. Although many search services use behavior logs to inform future results, implementing this recommendation requires careful consideration. It could, for example, be problematic to maintain a remote database of user frame-preference profiles without a mechanism for protecting the identity of those users lest the information be abused. Framing strategies are also a double-edged sword: the system imagined here could also be uniquely effective for introducing inaccuracies. Despite these risks, this approach could yield significant benefits. If we can present accurate information in ways that allow individuals to be more receptive to it while protecting user privacy and guarding against system abuse, we may be able to significantly reduce misperceptions.

Recommendation 3. The last strategy is suggested by our growing understanding of the psychological mechanisms that motivate biased processing. As noted in our initial theorizing, ego-threats have been shown to promote counterargument and source derogation. Other work has shown that self-affirmation—such as reflecting on one's positive attributes—prior to exposure to a counterattitudinal message can work in the opposite direction and reduce bias [9, 52]. Furthermore, inducing positive feelings toward the self is relatively straightforward [36]. This suggests that fact-checking systems may be more effective if corrections are timed to follow self-affirming experiences, either naturally occurring or purposefully constructed.

Fact-checking systems could monitor user-behavior, delivering corrective information after individuals have consumed content that is self-affirming, such as news stories that reinforce their political values, personal beliefs, or personal contributions to the world. Alternatively, these systems could couch the corrections in a positive message, for example acknowledging the sources that user has already consulted and complimenting the user's prior efforts to consider alternative perspectives.

It is important that the system not be perceived as manipulative or patronizing. Instead, the affirmation should be a legitimate positive experience that can help to counteract the unease that typically accompanies being corrected. It should be noted, however, that recent experimental work has raised questions about this approach. A series of studies found that although self-affirmation led participants to express more accurate beliefs, it did not augment the effects of corrective information: accuracy improvements occurred regardless of whether a correction was presented or not [38]. Nevertheless, given the somewhat inconsistent evidence on this topic, more research is merited.

Limitations

This study has several limitations. First, these results are based on a single exposure to a correction. It is possible that the effects may be more promising when users are presented with a regular stream of factual corrections, as research has shown that partisan biases do exhibit a tipping-point effect, whereby new information eventually overcomes prior predispositions [44]. Such a study could be accomplished in the lab, with an information board design providing repeated exposures over an extended period, or in the wild, through user studies (we return to this idea below).

Second, the study was conducted in the context of a single issue: electronic health records. Although the misinformation was designed to elicit negative reactions from across the political spectrum (e.g., concerns about big government for conservatives and about big business for liberals), Democrats were initially more favorable to the issue than Republicans, 5.2 versus 4.4, $t\ (434) = 5.3$, $p < .001$. Thus, it is possible that the effects seen here are limited to a particular demographic group. More research is needed, but we believe that the problems demonstrated are likely to apply across party lines, as shown in other research [39].

Third, differences between the immediate and delayed corrections could be due (at least in part) to the distractor task itself, which was only present in the latter condition. The distractor could have two possible effects. It could increase cognitive load of the task, which would artificially reduce participants' performance in the delayed condition. If this were the case, however, it would only strengthen our findings: including a distractor in both conditions would increase the relative advantage of the delayed correction over the immediate correction. The other possible effect is grounded in participants' performance on the distractor task. Participants who did well on the task, correctly identifying the number of differences between the pictures shown in the first image pair, might experience a boost in self-confidence, akin to the self-affirmation manipulations described above, and this could lead them to be more receptive to corrections. The data, however, do not support this interpretation: the correlation between the accuracy of identified differences in the distractor and the accuracy of factual beliefs was non-significant (and very small).

Fourth, it is plausible that the immediate-correction condition, in which misinformation and its rebuttal are presented simultaneously, could influence how corrections are encoded by encouraging participants to move back and forth between the two types of content. This could have one of two consequences. On one hand, the effort invested in encoding the information might lead to better memory and more robust long-terms effects of the immediate correction despite the somewhat discouraging short-term effects. On the other hand, presenting a claim and counter-claim side-by-side could prompt more effortful processing, especially among those invested in the original claim. Recent work in social psychology suggests that the more effort required to understand a statement, the less likely it is to be believed [46]. Thus, if the immediate correction produces more effortful processing than the delayed correction, it will be less persuasive. This study did not capture participants' scrolling behavior, so we cannot rule this possibility out entirely. We did, however, collect timing data. If we assume that effortful cross-content comparison is time consuming, than the preceding arguments suggest that the cumulative time participants spent on misinformation and its correction should differ by condition. Instead, we find that total viewing time in the immediate and delayed conditions is not statistically different (immediate = 182s, delayed = 191s, p = .07). Hence, there is no evidence that the effort participants' exerted to process the messages differed across conditions.

Finally, it is possible that these results are specific to the visual presentation style employed here. This seems unlikely: we can think of no theoretical reason to expect pop-ups to be more trusted or less threatening than on-screen corrections, or for red highlighting to induce less bias than red italicized text. Nevertheless, this is an empirical question that would be effectively answered with a subsequent study.

We believe that we offer reasonable evidence against each of the rival explanation identified here. Nevertheless, a real-world test of competing designs could provide useful additional evidence. Comparing the belief accuracy of individuals using a system that provides immediate corrections (perhaps built on top of the foundation offered by Dispute Finder, or promised by Hypothes.is) to one that presents a cumulative summary of corrective information after a delay would be informative. Such a test could be conducted over a period of weeks or months, shedding light on long-term dynamics. This approach would also offer greater ecological validity, helping to ensure that the effects are not a product of the experimental design.

CONCLUSION

Fostering a better informed citizenry is an admirable goal with many potential benefits, including better policy decisions, better health choices, and more. Using computer software to augment humans' ability to sift through the vast stores of online information, distinguishing fact from fiction, is a potentially crucial tool for accomplishing this. People do not have time to systematically evaluate every claim they encounter, and the value of helping them achieve an understanding that reflects the best evidence on any issue is undisputed. This paper demonstrates, however, that the complexity of building software is only part of the challenge.

Providing factual information is a necessary, but not sufficient, condition for facilitating learning, especially around contentious issues and disputed facts. As highlighted by this study, individuals are influenced by a variety of biases that can lead them to reject carefully documented evidence, and correcting misinformation at its source can actually augment the effects of these biases. Our goal is not to discourage future work in this area, but to suggest a variety of correction-presentation strategies the designers might use to help overcome these biases.

ACKNOWLEDGEMENTS

The authors also gratefully acknowledge Emily Lynch for her assistance with the design of stimuli and manipulations, and Cliff Lampe, Paul Resnick, Scott Robertson and members of the Ohio State Communication, Opinion, and Political Studies group for their thoughtful comments and suggestions. This work was funded in part by the U.S. National Science Foundation under Grant No. IIS-1149599.

REFERENCES

1. Baum, M. and Groeling, T. Shot by the Messenger: Partisan Cues and Public Opinion Regarding National Security and War. *Political Behavior*, *31*, 2 (2009), 157-186.
2. Berinsky, A.J. The Birthers Are Back. http://today.yougov.com/news/2012/02/03/birthers-are-back/.
3. Bizer, G.Y., Tormala, Z.L., Rucker, D.D. and Petty, R.E. Memory-based versus on-line processing: Implications for attitude strength. *Journal of Experimental Social Psychology*, *42*, 5 (2006), 646-653.

4. Bordia, P., DiFonzo, N., Haines, R. and Chaseling, E. Rumors Denials as Persuasive Messages: Effects of Personal Relevance, Source, and Message Characteristics. *Journal of applied social psychology, 35*, 6 (2005), 1301-1331.
5. Brossard, D. and Nisbet, M.C. Deference to Scientific Authority Among a Low Information Public: Understanding U.S. Opinion on Agricultural Biotechnology. *International Journal of Public Opinion Research, 19*, 1 (2007), 24-52.
6. Bullock, J.G. Experiments on partisanship and public opinion: Party cues, false beliefs, and Bayesian updating *Ph.D. Dissertation, Stanford University*, Stanford, CA, 2007.
7. Bullock, J.G. Partisan Bias and the Bayesian Ideal in the Study of Public Opinion. *Journal of Politics, 71*, 3 (2009), 1109-1124.
8. Byrne, S. and Hart, P.S. The ‘boomerang’ effect: A synthesis of findings and a preliminary theoretical framework. *Communication Yearbook, 33* (2009), 3-37.
9. Cohen, G.L., Aronson, J. and Steele, C.M. When Beliefs Yield to Evidence: Reducing Biased Evaluation by Affirming the Self. *Personality and Social Psychology Bulletin, 26*, 9 (2000), 1151-1164.
10. Diakopoulus, N., De Choudhury, M. and Naaman, M., Finding and Assessing Social Media Information Sources in the Context of Journalism. In *Proc. Conference on Human Factors in Computing Systems (CHI)*, ACM (2012).
11. Diakopoulus, N., Goldenberg, S. and Essa, I., Videolyzer: Quality Analysis of Online Informational Video for Bloggers and Journalists In *Proc. Conference on Human Factors in Computing Systems (CHI)*, ACM Press (2009).
12. Druckman, J.N. and Bolsen, T. Framing, Motivated Reasoning, and Opinions About Emergent Technologies. *Journal of Communication, 61*, 4 (2011), 659-688.
13. Ennals, R., Byler, D., Agosta, J.M. and Rosario, B., What is disputed on the web? In *Proceedings of the 4th workshop on Information credibility*, ACM (2010), 67-74.
14. Ennals, R., Trushkowsky, B. and Agosta, J.M., Highlighting disputed claims on the web. In *Proceedings of the 19th international conference on World wide web*, ACM (2010), 341-350.
15. Freedman, J.L. and Sears, D.O. Warning, distraction, and resistance to influence. *Journal of Personality and Social Psychology, 1*, 3 (1965), 262-266.
16. Garrett, R.K. Troubling consequences of online political rumoring. *Human Communication Research, 37*, 2 (2011), 255-274.
17. Garrett, R.K., Carnahan, D. and Lynch, E. A turn toward avoidance? Selective exposure to online political information, 2004-2008. *Political Behavior* (2011), 1-22.
18. Gentzkow, M. and Shapiro, J.M. Media bias and reputation. *Journal of Political Economy, 114* (2006), 280-316.
19. Gerber, A. and Green, D. Misperceptions about perceptual bias. *Annual Review of Political Science, 2*, 1 (1999), 189-210.
20. Harris Interactive/HealthDay. Vaccine-Autism Link: Sound Science or Fraud? . http://www.harrisinteractive.com/newsroom/pressreleases/tabid/446/mid/1506/articleid/674/ctl/readcustom%20default/default.aspx.
21. Hayes, A.F., Preacher, K.J. and Myers, T.A. Mediation and the Estimation of Indirect Effects in Political Communication Research. in Bucy, E.P. and Holbert, R.L. eds. *Sourcebook for Political Communication Research: Methods, Measures, and Analytical Techniques*, Routledge, New York, 2011, 434-465.
22. Hemingway, M. Lies, damned lies, and 'fact checking' *The Weekly Standard*, 2011.
23. Katz, J.E. Struggle in cyberspace: fact and friction in the World Wide Web. *Annals of the American Academy of Political and Social Science, 560*, 1 (1998), 194-199.
24. Kriplean, T., Morgan, J.T., Freelon, D., Borning, A. and Bennett, L., ConsiderIt: improving structured public deliberation. In *Proceedings of the 2011 annual conference extended abstracts on Human factors in computing systems*, ACM (2011), 1831-1836.
25. Kuklinski, J.H., Quirk, P.J., Jerit, J., Schwieder, D. and Rich, R.F. Misinformation and the Currency of Democratic Citizenship. *The Journal of Politics, 62*, 03 (2000), 790-816.
26. Lapinski, M.K. and Boster, F.J. Modeling the ego-defensive function of attitudes. *Communication Monographs, 68*, 3 (2001), 314-324.
27. Lavine, H., Burgess, D., Snyder, M., Transue, J., Sullivan, J.L., Haney, B. and Wagner, S.H. Threat, Authoritarianism, and Voting: An Investigation of Personality and Persuasion. *Personality and Social Psychology Bulletin, 25*, 3 (1999), 337-347.
28. Leskovec, J., Backstrom, L. and Kleinberg, J., Meme-tracking and the dynamics of the news cycle. In *Proceedings of the 15th ACM SIGKDD international conference on Knowledge discovery and data mining*, ACM Press (2009), 497-506.
29. Lord, C.G., Ross, L. and Lepper, M.R. Biased assimilation and attitude polarization: the effects of prior theories on subsequently considered evidence.

Journal of Personality and Social Psychology, *37*, 11 (1979), 2098-2109.

30. Lupia, A. and McCubbins, M.D. *The Democratic Dilemma*. Cambridge University Press, Cambridge, 1998.
31. MacCoun, R.J. and Paletz, S. Citizens' Perceptions of Ideological Bias in Research on Public Policy Controversies. *Political Psychology*, *30*, 1 (2009), 43-65.
32. Maibach, E.W., Roser-Renouf, C. and Leiserowitz, A. Communication and Marketing As Climate Change–Intervention Assets: A Public Health Perspective. *American Journal of Preventive Medicine*, *35*, 5 (2008), 488-500.
33. Moser, S.C. Communicating climate change: history, challenges, process and future directions. *Wiley Interdisciplinary Reviews: Climate Change*, *1*, 1 (2010), 31-53.
34. Munson, S.A. and Resnick, P., Presenting Diverse Political Opinions: How and How Much. In *CHI 2010* (2010).
35. Murakami, K., Nichols, E., Mizuno, J., Watanabe, Y., Masuda, S., Goto, H., Ohki, M., Sao, C., Matsuyoshi, S., Inui, K. and Matsumoto, Y., Statement map: reducing web information credibility noise through opinion classification. In *Proceedings of the fourth workshop on Analytics for noisy unstructured text data*, ACM Press (2010), 59-66.
36. Napper, L., Harris, P. and Epton, T. Developing and Testing a Self-affirmation Manipulation. *Self and Identity*, *8*, 1 (2009), 45-62.
37. Nisbet, M.C. and Scheufele, D.A. What's next for science communication? Promising directions and lingering distractions. *American Journal of Botany*, *96*, 10 (2009), 1767-1778.
38. Nyhan, B. and Reifler, J. Opening the Political Mind?: The effects of self-affirmation and graphical information on factual misperceptions, 2011.
39. Nyhan, B. and Reifler, J. When Corrections Fail: The persistence of political misperceptions. *Political Behavior*, *32*, 2 (2010), 303-330.
40. Ott, M., Choi, Y., Cardie, C. and Hancock, J.T., Finding deceptive opinion spam by any stretch of the imagination. In *Proceedings of the 49th Annual Meeting of the Association for Computational Linguistics: Human Language Technologies - Volume 1*, Association for Computational Linguistics (2011), 309-319.
41. Park, S., Kang, S., Chung, S. and Song, J., NewsCube: delivering multiple aspects of news to mitigate media bias. In *Proceedings of the 27th international conference on Human factors in computing systems*, ACM (2009), 443-452.
42. Ratkiewicz, J., Conover, M., Meiss, M., Gonçalves, B., Patil, S., Flammini, A. and Menczer, F., Detecting and Tracking the Spread of Astroturf Memes in Microblog Streams. In *Proceedings of the 20th international conference companion on World wide web* (2010), 249-252.
43. Redlawsk, D.P. Hot Cognition or Cool Consideration? Testing the Effects of Motivated Reasoning on Political Decision Making. *Journal of Politics*, *64*, 4 (2002), 1021-1044.
44. Redlawsk, D.P., Civettini, A.J.W. and Emmerson, K.M. The Affective Tipping Point: Do Motivated Reasoners Ever "Get It"? *Political Psychology*, *31*, 4 (2010), 563-593.
45. Schneider, J., Groza, T. and Passant, A. A Review of Argumentation for the Social Semantic Web. *Sematic Web journal*, *4*, 3 (to appear 2013).
46. Schwarz, N., Sanna, L.J., Skurnik, I. and Yoon, C. Metacognitive Experiences and the Intricacies of Setting People Straight: Implications for Debiasing and Public Information Campaigns. in Zanna, M.P. ed. *Advances in experimental social psychology*, Academic Press, 2007, 127-161.
47. Seifert, C.M. The continued influence of misinformation in memory: What makes a correction effective? in Brian, H.R. ed. *Psychology of Learning and Motivation*, Academic Press, 2002, 265-292.
48. Simmons, M.P., Adamic, L. and Adar, E., Memes Online: Extracted, Subtracted, Injected, and Recollected. In *Fifth International AAAI Conference on Weblogs and Social Media* (2011).
49. Stempel, C., Hargrove, T. and Stempel III, G.H. Media use, social structure, and belief in 9/11 conspiracy theories. *Journalism & Mass Communication Quarterly*, *84*, 2 (2007), 353-372.
50. Sunstein, C.R. *On rumors: how falsehood spread, why we believe them, what can be done*. Farrar, Strauss and Giroux, New York, NY, 2009.
51. Taber, C.S. and Lodge, M. Motivated Skepticism in the Evaluation of Political Beliefs. *American Journal of Political Science*, *50*, 3 (2006), 755-769.
52. van Koningsbruggen, G.M., Das, E. and Roskos-Ewoldsen, D.R. How self-affirmation reduces defensive processing of threatening health information: Evidence at the implicit level. *Health Psychology*, *28*, 5 (2009), 563-568.
53. Wemple, E. The Maddow-Politifact clash *The Washington Post*, Washington, DC, 2012.
54. Zaller, J.R. *The nature and origins of mass opinion*. Cambridge University Press, New York, 1992.

Your Process Is Showing: Controversy Management and Perceived Quality in Wikipedia

W. Ben Towne,[1] Aniket Kittur,[2] Peter Kinnaird,[2] & James Herbsleb[1]
[1]Institute for Software Research, [2]Human-Computer Interaction Institute; School of Computer Science
Center for the Future of Work; Heinz College
Carnegie Mellon University
5000 Forbes Ave, Pittsburgh, PA 15213 USA
{wbt, nkittur, kinnaird, jdh}@cs.cmu.edu

ABSTRACT

Large-scale collaboration systems often separate their content from the deliberation around how that content was produced. Surfacing this deliberation may engender trust in the content generation process if the deliberation process appears fair, well-reasoned, and thorough. Alternatively, it could encourage doubts about content quality, especially if the process appears messy or biased. In this paper we report the results of an experiment where we found that surfacing deliberation generally led to decreases in perceptions of quality for the article under consideration, especially – but not only – if the discussion revealed conflict. The effect size depends on the type of editors' interactions. Finally, this decrease in actual article quality rating was accompanied by self-reported improved perceptions of the article and Wikipedia overall.

Author Keywords

User-generated content; discussion; dispute resolution; trust; perceptions of quality

ACM Classification Keywords

H.5.3 Web-based interaction; Asynchronous interaction; Collaborative computing; Computer-supported cooperative work.

General Terms

Human Factors; Experimentation; Wikipedia; Commons-based Peer Production; Deliberation

INTRODUCTION

Technological advances in recent years, such as wikis, have enabled large-scale systems for aggregating knowledge and information from a very large number of participants, who bring a broad range of viewpoints, information, and expertise. In some systems, like Wikipedia, a significant amount of coordination communication is employed to effectively combine these contributions [11].

However, many readers of Wikipedia are unaware that this work that has gone into the creation of an article, even though these efforts represent a potential source for readers to understand and evaluate the trustworthiness of an article. For example, imagine a reader who encounters a controversial topic in Wikipedia. In one case, the reader sees only the article and must evaluate the likely bias and validity of the topic on its own. Alternatively, the reader also sees that substantial and considered discussion has taken place among the editors of the topic on how to sensitively and appropriately present it. In the latter case, the reader has additional information to judge the article quality. If the discussion seems measured and fair, the reader's evaluation of the article may improve. If, on the other hand, the reader sees unchecked biases or personal attacks among the contributors, the reader may be less likely to trust the content than if it were encountered in isolation. Readers may simply become overwhelmed by the amount of information needed to understand the article creation process. More fundamentally, increasing the visibility of the uncertain and messy process by which articles are created may undermine readers' perceptions of trust — even if that process leads to a preferred outcome [21:1–14, 111–138]. To quote John G. Saxe, "Laws, like sausages, cease to inspire respect in proportion as we know how they are made" [32]. The same may be true of user-generated content.

To examine this question, we conducted an experiment in which we surfaced various types of discussions along with content, and measured readers' perceptions of the quality of the article excerpt being discussed. We found that when discussion was provided alongside content, the quality ratings for the content were significantly lower than when no discussion was displayed, supporting the "sausage" hypothesis. When discussion involving conflict was displayed, article quality ratings were even lower. However, if the editors involved in the conflict resolved it through a positive collaboration approach, the negative effects of conflict disappeared. Participants were not generally aware of the rating-lowering effect of the discussion, and generally reported that reading the discussion raised their perceptions of both the article's quality and Wikipedia in general.

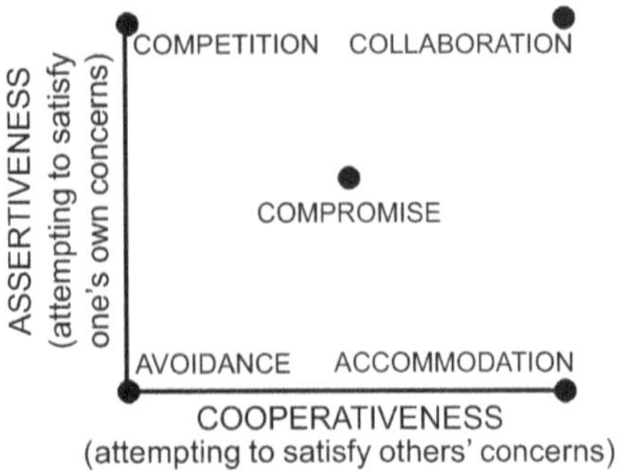

Figure 1: Two dimensional taxonomy of conflict handling modes (adapted from [24])

CONFLICT RESOLUTION STRATEGIES

Conflict has been studied from a variety of different perspectives, mostly in the context of small groups. Thomas and Kilman [24] described a framework in 1976 characterizing approaches to managing conflict, by the degree to which individuals attempt to satisfy their own concerns ("assertiveness") vs. others' concerns ("cooperativeness"). They find the five distinct conflict management strategies shown in Figure 1.

This framework has been adopted in the literature and validated several times [24:269]. It is supported by a number of other studies that independently attempt to build typologies of conflict resolution strategies and identify aspects of conflict management that are important to outcomes, such as Klein & Lu [12]'s early analysis of approaches to solving task conflicts in a cooperative interdisciplinary design team. Klein & Lu's primary conclusions are that "conflict resolution plays a central role in cooperative design...and knowledge acquisition in cooperative design presents special challenges and requires special techniques." The authors believe that new practices with parallel interaction amongst diverse concerns cannot happen without effective conflict resolution [12:169].

In this study, we examine how revealing details of the joint production process affect perceived quality of outcomes. Task conflicts have a wide range of potential effects, both positive and negative. Therefore, we explored only task conflicts, as opposed to relationship conflicts that are generally only seen to have negative effects (see e.g. [6]).

WIKIPEDIA TALK PAGES

Wikipedia is an open and free encyclopedia that anyone can edit. The encyclopedic content and editing process are well studied as an example of a large-scale open collaborative system. A "discussion" tab in the upper left corner of most article pages links to a "Talk" page where editors discuss changes to the article [30].

Viégas et al. [26] confirm Kittur et al's finding [11] that Talk and Project pages are the fastest growing parts of Wikipedia, especially with more heavily edited articles. They coded subsets of 25 article Talk pages (excluding archives) to find out what people are doing there, producing a typology that guided our choice of discussion types. They chose controversial and non-controversial topics in areas from hard science to pop culture, especially including cases with difficult coordination issues. Postings were coded for 11 binary dimensions, which were analyzed for frequency.

The most common kind of posting found in this study is "requests for coordination," with contributors asking for help and explaining why they think specific changes should be made. Over half of Talk page contributions fit this category, including 97% of the discussions coded from the Yasser Arafat page.

The next most common use was a "request for information," found in just over 10% of posts. Writers of these posts hope to tap into the knowledge of an "approachable community of experts" [26:8] on a specific topic, without necessarily having intention to edit the article. The overwhelming majority of these requests were answered, with information or links that might answer the question.

The third most common type of posting was coded as "off-topic remarks," generally users sharing trivia or personal experiences related to the article topic. The fourth most common type of posting, with 7.9% of Talk page activity, includes references to official Wikipedia guidelines, as guidance for article editing. This pattern generally followed "serious disagreements or flame wars" in response to high levels of conflict [26:8].

JUDGING THE CREDIBILITY OF INFORMATION ONLINE

A number of studies have examined factors impacting reliability perceptions of online sources, including Wikipedia. For example, Fogg et al. [4] studied over 2600 participants evaluating 100 real-world websites in 10 categories, identifying 18 top features that people consider when evaluating Web site credibility. Wikipedia fixes some of these to be the same across all articles, such as Design Look, Structure, Advertising, and Site Functionality. Other of Fogg's factors vary between articles, such as perceived information accuracy and bias, tone of writing, author motive, and readability; the discussion behind an article sometimes reveals signals about these factors. We hold most of these factors constant to focus specifically on how the presence and type of discussion influences perceptions.

Lucassen and Schraagen [16] build on this work with an experiment to discover "which elements of Wikipedia articles university students use to assess their trustworthiness." They found the major elements to be textual features such as comprehensiveness, correctness, length, and pictures. We hold these factors constant and extend the investigation to another factor, examining how the discussion behind content impacts trustworthiness evaluations when it is used.

Chesney [3] further suggests that people will rate content they are more familiar with as more credible than content on a random topic, which we observe but control for by random assignment.

Stvilia et al. studies a more objective information quality measure, noting early on that "The same information can be judged as being of different quality depending on the context of a particular use" [23:983]. This work describes a correlation between "actual" quality as measured by Featured Article status and discussion pages that are large, readable, and well-organized, but that translation of interest to this quality measure depends on the content of the discussion and whether or not a consensus has been reached [23:992]. Differences in collaboration patterns are known to lead to differences in actual quality of an article as measured by "Featured" status [9,15]. We would like to know if changing what somebody sees about the discussion correspondingly changes their perception of the article quality. Perceived quality is important for establishing legitimacy and building a more active community.

Stvilia et al. [23] call for empirical studies of information quality, suggesting the English Wikipedia as a particularly interesting case for study. We answer that call and provide empirical evidence for some of the paper's observations, noted above. That paper partially defines information quality as "noncontroversial," assuming greater capacity to objectively evaluate articles. Our extension to controversial topics serves as a building block for online deliberation systems that may eventually help people solve complex problems where objective evaluation may be impossible or less important than perceived quality.

The way that discussion around information is presented to users is an important design choice for an online community, with important consequences for how accurately the community is able to judge the credibility of information shared there. It may be, for example, that hoaxes are less likely to be discovered when discussion is separated from content, as in Wikipedia, compared to sites where discussion is front and center, such as Reddit, and that hoaxes are more likely to propagate in systems where the discussion is decentralized (as in Facebook as compared to Wikipedia or Reddit) [1,5]. It is important to understand how the visibility of discussion may change perceptions of quality in the system, and how the effects of salient discussion may depend on the content of that discussion.

A number of experiments in adding visible discussion capabilities to sites that previously did not support this kind of interaction around specific content have been tried and shown to add value. For example, Kriplean et al. [13,14] focus on grounded discussion and active listening, discussing the content even on sites that are already forums, as a means of increasing empathy and positive participation while efficiently summarizing and clarifying content.

Kittur, Suh, and Chi [10] cite significant distrust in user-generated content in current large collaborative systems, and hypothesize that readers lack sufficient information to evaluate the trustworthiness of content. They present a "Wikipedia dashboard" with visualizations of churn, reversion, and editor registration, showing who edited how much when, and found that the information raised or lowered trust ratings, depending on whether the record implied an irresponsible (e.g., many anonymous edits) or responsible process. Shneiderman [20] recommends full disclosure of sources' past performance patterns "in comprehensible and compact terms" as a means of building trust. Pirolli, Wollny, and Suh [19] extended that work with a more comprehensive view of edit histories, displaying only real data for each article in their lab experiment. They also demonstrated significant increases in article credibility ratings through exposure of editor identity and more detailed histories.

We build on this line of work by explicitly examining how readers' opinions of quality and trustworthiness may differ based only on what is exposed about the discussion that led to the content, termed content transparency [22]. In particular, we addressed the following research questions:

RQ1: What is the effect of exposing discussions about article content on perceived article quality?

Since discussion about controversial topics can reveal disagreements, inaccuracies, and possible bias, or remind readers that fallible non-expert editors created the content, revealing discussions could significantly diminish perceptions of quality (the "sausage hypothesis"). However, seeing the discussion could also show that content is being discussed and vetted at some level, which might increase perceptions of quality.

RQ2: Do different kinds of conflict resolution have different effects on perceptions of content quality?

Some aspects of the discussion, such as inequality in editors' experience levels, are known to lead to differences in rated quality, while other aspects, such as inequality of contributions, do not [2]. We investigate how differences between discussion strategies also influences rated quality.

Resolving conflict by personal attacks, threats to leave the community, or ignoring complaints seem likely to have much more of a negative effect than resolution accomplished more rationally, for example by citing policies or sources. We expected that conflicts resolved through collaboration would be seen as more likely to increase the quality of the resulting article text than other approaches to conflict resolution.

Montoya-Weiss, Massey, and Song [18] provide some hypotheses for how conflict resolution strategies in internationally distributed groups communicating asynchronously through text affect actual performance on a marketing consulting project with some time pressure. They found that avoidance and compromise behavior (as experienced by team members) significantly hurts performance, accommodation has no effect (because the text channel may not have been expressive enough to make this strategy obvious for team members to experience), and competition & collaboration correlate significantly and positively with performance. In [18], the compromise approach may have hurt performance because of its manifestation, cutting and pasting possibly contradictory content from different team members into a final team document, without integration effort.

RQ3: What do participants believe about how viewing the discussion may have changed their perceptions?

While RQ1 and RQ2 compare quality ratings from large groups of people who see different types of discussion or no discussion at all, RQ3 examines how individuals believe they are affected. In addition to their ratings of this particular article, we would like to see how the presence of discussion impacts participants' perceptions of Wikipedia overall.

We seek to discover whether the effects of different types of discussions are brought about by a deliberative process (what Kahneman calls System 2) or by a more automatic associative process (Kahneman's System 1) [7], and how these two mental systems interact to evaluate perceived quality. People are generally able to report with reasonable accuracy on System 2 activities, while associative activities generally escape awareness. A common experimental approach used to investigate especially System 1 psychology is to perform a between-subjects controlled experiment which demonstrates reliable differences caused by the manipulated variable, but where the cause of the effect never enters conscious thought (System 2), and participants may believe they were not affected or affected in the opposite direction. If we observe non-alignment between the results of RQ3 and RQ1 or RQ2, we know that at least part of the explanation must lie in what System 1 processes without the involvement of System 2.

It is possible to change the way people cognitively evaluate information, and Kahneman presents several factors known to more readily engage System 2. Simply presenting arguments has been shown to increase participants' cognitive evaluation of case descriptions in experiments evaluating the perceived legitimacy of Supreme Court decisions [17]. We extend that work by examining a source with a very different base level of credibility, examining how presentation of arguments (of different styles) may change cognitive evaluation and perceptions of quality.

EXPERIMENTS

Overview

We showed participants a segment of a collaboratively produced article and then showed them either no discussion or one of ten different discussions about the article segment. We then asked comprehension questions about the article and discussion to promote deep reading. We then asked participants to rate the article and the discussion on a number of scales, including ratings of article quality and the perceived level of conflict in the discussion. We collected data about demographics prior to the task, and collected self-report data about how the participants thought they may have been affected by seeing the discussion at the end.

Data Source

We chose Wikipedia as a ready source of data that has both a wide range of content along with publicly available discussion and resolution of disputes about the content.

We selected topics that were both controversial and had high-quality articles. We wanted controversial topics with many disputes so we could identify a number of instances of different kinds of resolution. We also wanted articles that were high quality, because low quality articles are more likely to have features visible in the writing — poor style, lack of clarity, etc. — which could dominate judgments about quality, giving our manipulations less of a chance to have observable effects.

To identify controversial topics, we looked at community-curated lists of controversial issues and pages which were explicitly tagged as controversial, displaying and linking to an appropriate notice. We only considered articles in the main project namespace. This excludes, for example, Wikipedia policies and coordination pages, and uploaded files. This process identified 3403 unique controversial articles.

We then looked for examples of articles where the collectively generated content had reached a high level of quality. As with "controversial," we looked to the Wikipedia community's identification of the highest quality articles. The community uses an assessment scale to measure article quality, on an ongoing basis through a manual process. We selected Featured Articles, which are "the best articles Wikipedia has to offer, as determined by Wikipedia's editors." [32]. This measure correlates significantly with quality assessed by external raters [9]. At the time when we copied the list, there were 3189 featured articles (<0.1%). 50 articles were listed as both "controversial" and "featured," and we selected those for further investigation.

We examined this group of 50 articles and found common topical categories: Health, Science, Religion, Politics & History, Pop Culture, and Places. We chose articles across these categories, to ensure diversity in the pool of topics. We did our best to choose topics that were not currently dominating discussions in the news, and would be unlikely to change much over the course of the study period, because news reporting during the experiment could have unpredictable effects on the results. Our selections were Autism, Pope Pius XII, Yasser Arafat, and the Cretaceous–Paleogene extinction event.

One author read through the Talk page archives of these articles to determine the specific controversies present in that article. Some issues came up many times in different Talk page discussions, and the discussions were manually open-coded for the primary topic of discussion. Then, an issue was chosen based on its presence as an important controversy in that article, but which would be unlikely to be affected by strongly charged and very diverse viewpoints of our participants. As an example, in the Yasser Arafat article, we chose the controversy about his place and date of birth (a common controversy for celebrities) rather than the ones around his sexual orientation or the use of the word "terrorist." We did this to reduce variance and maintain a relatively constant level of emotionality, since high emotionality in conflict has been shown to lead to lower quality in conflict resolution outcomes [6].

We then created ten brief vignettes illustrating Talk page discussions about the particular chosen controversy, based in part on the styles (and some original content) from the discussions we observed. We portrayed a conflict between editors and resolution through each of the five approaches described by Thomas [24]. Two pilots of this study included only conflict conditions, and found that revealing strong conflict among editors lowered perceptions of article quality. To investigate rating differences beyond those that may be caused by seeing conflict, we also composed four non-conflict discussion conditions, three of which were based on the three most common Talk page uses described by Viégas et al. [26]. The fourth shows one editor reporting on changes s/he made to the article, with no apparent controversy; a second editor leaves one word of thanks. Also based on Viégas et al. [26], we had a sixth conflict condition depicting a single editor changing an article after removing a source that was inaccurately cited, implicitly addressing Wikipedia's policies around reliable sources; the editor is a frequent Wikipedian who also uses an abbreviation "POV" derived from the abbreviation of the "Neutral Point of View" core content policy [28]. We classified this as a conflict condition based on Viégas's description that this strategy is used as a response to conflict (p. 8). A manipulation check later verified that this condition "behaved" like a conflict condition with respect to the measure of perceived conflict.

These ten vignettes were originally created for one article and then adapted for each of the other topics by substituting in the topics, sides, and sources used in discussion, aiming to maintain similarity of structure and conversational style.

Some of the discussions contained excerpts from actual interactions, though all the discussions presented were created by one of the authors to represent a certain discussion type. These discussion vignettes were written with a number of principles in mind. All were written to be short to minimize the time and attention required of participants. The vignettes were written to clearly demonstrate each of the discussion types, and were similar across article topics (within the same discussion type). Because quotes were not direct, editors' names were replaced by two-letter initials, and each topic showed discussions among nominally different editors. Links and other aspects of Wikipedia formatting were retained in the presentation of both the article and discussion segments. Links to references were retained, but the actual references were not shown, to focus participants' evaluations on the text itself. No pictures were included in the short segments of our experiment. The actual discussions used are available in the attached appendix A.

Experimental Design: Details

As suggested by Kittur et al. [8], we posted a request on Amazon's Mechanical Turk requesting participation in our study and describing the task. Turkers who accepted our task were randomly assigned to an article topic and discussion type, neither of which they had seen before. We restricted eligibility to Turkers who had at least 95% of their prior micro-tasks approved, and who were in the United States (according to their Turk profile).

In all conditions, participants were first asked some preliminary questions about their background and use of Wikipedia. They were then shown a brief segment of an article, all participants assigned to a given topic viewing the same article text. Then they were shown a discussion about the article, and the discussion type varied as an experimental manipulation. We had ten discussion types, six of which displayed conflict and four of which did not, and an 11th (control) condition where no discussion was shown. We asked comprehension questions to provide greater motivation for participants to read the passages for understanding. The passages were presented as screenshots to exactly maintain Wikipedia formatting and presentation, and prevent participants from using the browser's Find or Copy-Paste features to answer the comprehension questions.

Two pilot versions of this study (with about 500 participants each) included an extra no-discussion control condition with extra article text to equalize the amount of time a participant spends on task in the control and the discussion conditions. We found no significant differences between the controls, so we dropped the extended text condition.

Among other questions, we then asked participants to evaluate the article using seven-point Likert items, each with {{Strongly, Moderately, Slightly} {Agree, Disagree}}, Neutral, and "I don't know" options. They evaluated the article with four questions:

"Based on the excerpt shown above, I believe the article as a whole is likely to be...

well-written."

... an accurate and trustworthy source of information."

... biased." [Scale reversed for analysis.]

"Based on the excerpt shown above, I believe this article should be included in a collection of high quality articles."

The first three questions used for assessment of perceived article quality are also used in the Wikipedia Article Feedback Tool [27] version 4, which asked readers at the end of each article to "rate this page" on a scale of one to five stars on whether the article was "Trustworthy" (tooltip interpretations focused on the page having more or less reputable sources), "Objective" (tooltip interpretations ranged from "heavily biased" to "completely unbiased"), "Complete," and "Well-written." We adopt three of these same measures, omitting "complete" because we are showing participants only a small segment of the article. The wording about inclusion in a collection of quality articles is inspired by the similar dependent measure in [10].

Wikipedia's assessment tool also includes a checkbox allowing users to identify themselves as "highly knowledgeable" about an article's topic; we include this as a pre-task seven-point Likert item.

Turkers were given the option of participating again so long as we could guarantee that they would not see a discussion type or article topic more than once; in this experiment they were limited by the number of unique topics (four).

RESULTS

Participants

A total of 1348 surveys were completed by 566 unique Turk workers over the course of 26 hours. We paid $0.60 for each survey and a bonus of $0.15 to the 196 participants who participated the personal maximum of four times.

37 the 1348 surveys, completed by 15 participants, did not meet our *a priori* inclusion criteria that the worker must be in the United States (as discovered by a GeoIP lookup resolving outside the US) and those data were discarded.

Our participants were reasonably well-educated, as self-reported on a seven point scale, with 90% reporting at least some college experience, nearly a third reporting a bachelor's degree, and 16% reporting a post-graduate degree. They are also regular Wikipedia users, with over 80% reporting that they read Wikipedia "a few times per week" or more often, and over 96% reading "a few times per month" or more often. Over 85% agreed with the statement "Wikipedia articles are an accurate and trustworthy source of information." All of these factors were randomly distributed across the different experimental conditions.

A free-text box at the end, the only item explicitly labeled "optional," was filled out on 42.7% of surveys, showing that the Turkers were engaged enough to do extra work for us though it was not required for payment. 59.6% of the comments were substantive (beyond e.g. "no comments"). From this feedback, we learned in participants' words that the task was enjoyable, that it taught some of them to pay attention to their information sources, and that the pay was fair. These survey subsets were not significantly different on rated quality or on how participants thought they had been affected by reading the discussion.

To check for responses that may have been completed too hastily, we manually reviewed all responses that were completed in under three minutes, with that cutoff being slightly above one standard deviation below the mean. The comprehension question responses and overall response patterns were very similar to the remaining data, so we found no reason to exclude any other participants.

Measures

We examined the four measures of article quality (well-written, unbiased, accurate and trustworthy, and should be included in a collection of high quality articles) to see whether they did indeed all measure a similar construct (overall "quality") or whether they were independent dimensions. We found that they were significantly correlated (average $\rho = .570$; $p < .0005$), and loaded onto a single factor in a Principal Components Analysis, consistent with pilot results. Confident that there was only one underlying dimension, we then considered only the final (overall) quality question, as an interpretable measure of overall perceived quality for our primary dependent variable.

As a manipulation check, we asked participants whether a conflict was present in the discussion. Those in a conflict condition agreed fairly strongly (mean 1.78 Likert points, 95% CI [1.67, 1.88]) and those who weren't disagreed (mean −.65, 95% CI [−.83, −.46]); the difference was highly significant ($p<.0005$). The Avoidance and Competition resolutions were seen as having more conflict than the other conflict types, and referring to policies in removing a source had less, but there was a definite gap between the 95% confidence intervals for the mean measure of conflict in conflict and non-conflict conditions. These data provide evidence that the manipulation was strongly successful.

Of 1200 responses, most agreed with the pre-test statement "Anybody can edit Wikipedia," with the modal response (39%) at "strongly agree;" only 10.3% disagreed with that statement and an additional 4.5% were neutral. However, participants generally did not use Talk pages. When asked how often they read Talk pages, 23.6% said "I don't know what these are" and an additional 44.6% of the 1303 responses said "never." 20.4% read Talk pages "a few times per year" and only 11.4% read them more often.

Analysis

Where means are reported in Likert points, they are on a seven point scale coded for analysis in the range [−3,+3], and otherwise unaltered from the participants' responses. To compare subsets of the data and see if viewers rated the same article text as being of different quality based on the style of discussion they saw, we report the results of a Kruskal-Wallis one-way analysis of variance, which is a nonparametric test that permits ordinal Likert item data. Mean numeric values are reported to allow the reader to estimate effect size.

In order to ensure that our results were valid under strict statistical assumptions regarding fully independent measurements and rule out order effects, we repeated our analysis on just the first survey that each participant loaded, and identically significant effects were observed. We also replicated the analysis using ANOVA instead of Kruskal-Wallis, and again observed the same effects. Treating the data either as ordinal (Kruskal-Wallis) or interval (ANOVA), the results do not vary.

By randomly assigning participants to experimental conditions, we expected prior knowledge and perceptions about Wikipedia, the topic, and our task to be randomly distributed across conditions. We have verified that prior knowledge and trust of Wikipedia are not significantly different between the groups that we are comparing below.

RQ1: How does exposing discussions about article content affect perceived article quality?

Our first planned contrast examined whether or not exposure to the discussion (of any type) led readers to assess the article at a different quality level than readers who did not see the discussion behind it. We find that *people who saw any Talk page discussion rated quality significantly lower than those who did not see any discussion* (0.21 vs. 1.08 Likert points, $p < .0005$).

We hypothesize that if people are exposed to conflict about an issue, they would be less likely to perceive a discussion outcome as high quality. We find that *people who saw conflict conditions rated quality lower than those who saw non-conflict conditions* (−0.04 vs. 0.61 Likert points, $p<.0005$). We also compared quality ratings of those who saw non-conflict discussions with those in the control condition, and found that *even those who saw non-conflict conditions rated quality lower than those who did not see any discussion* (0.61 vs. 1.08 Likert points, $p=.011$).

RQ2: Do different kinds of conflict resolution have different effects on perceptions of content quality?

After finding the main differences between no discussion, non-conflict discussion, and conflict discussion conditions, we looked within these groups to see if particular strategies for conflict resolution led to higher or lower quality ratings than others.

We found no significant differences between quality ratings among non-conflict discussions; none were expected.

Based on the prior literature (e.g. [18]) and pilot data, we hypothesized that the "ignored complainer" in the "avoidance" strategy would lead to significantly lower quality ratings than the other discussion types, because it shows one editor complaining about low quality and nobody responding to those criticisms. Our data support this hypothesis, whether comparing to just the conflict conditions (−1.13 vs. 0.16 Likert points, $p<.0005$) or to all discussion conditions (−1.13 vs. 0.36 Likert points, $p<.0005$).

Based on prior literature that describes collaboration as the conflict resolution strategy generally leading to the best outcomes, we believed the collaboration conflict resolution strategy would be perceived as a "good" conflict resolution strategy and enhance output quality ratings, at least in comparison to other ways of resolving conflicts. We hypothesized that the collaboration condition would lead to significantly higher perceived quality than the other conflict types. Our data support this: People who saw the collaboration condition rated quality higher than those who saw other conflict conditions (0.61 vs. −0.18 Likert points, $p<.0005$). People who saw the compromise condition also rated quality higher than those who saw other conflict conditions (0.47 vs. −0.13 Likert points, $p=.004$). The compromise and collaboration conditions were not distinct from each other; they were also illustrated similarly. In fact, these two were not significantly different from the non-conflict discussion conditions in terms of quality rating, even though they were significantly different from the non-conflict discussion conditions in terms of perception of conflict (1.70 vs. −0.65 Likert points, $p<.0005$). These two resolution strategies were able to overcome the negative effects of conflict on quality ratings.

RQ3: What do participants believe about how viewing the discussion may have changed their perceptions?

Participants who saw discussion conditions were asked directly if reading the discussion affected their perceptions, and if so in what direction. The question, options, and data for each discussion condition are shown in Figure 2. Participants believed that seeing the discussion *raised* their perception of the article's quality and of Wikipedia in general, overall and for many single-discussion-condition subsets, with significant effects indicated by asterisks in the figure. The ignored complainer in the "avoidance" condition is the only one where participants were aware of the fact that reading the discussion lowered their perception of that article's quality.

Our exact significance test in these analyses examined the balance between the "raised" response options as one set and the "lowered" response options as another set, calculating how likely the actual balance between these would be if both were equally likely, akin to calculating the probability that at least a given percentage of "heads" would appear on the appropriate number of flips of a fair coin. Unless otherwise indicated, significant effects have $p<.0005$ and non-significant effects have $p>.05$.

CONCLUSIONS AND DISCUSSION

Large-scale distributed systems for collaborative content creation must have a good way of dealing with controversial topics. We have shown that the way these conflicts are dealt with, and whether that is exposed to consumers of the content, impacts how viewers perceive the quality of the content, even when its actual content is held constant.

We find evidence that surfacing discussions about content generally lowers the perceived quality of the content, and that this effect differs significantly depending on how the discussion is conducted and whether or not a conflict is revealed. However, the effect runs counter to participants'

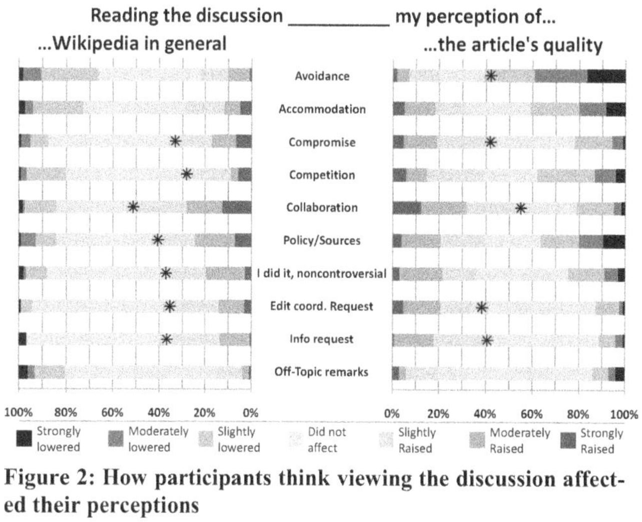

Figure 2: How participants think viewing the discussion affected their perceptions

self-reported perceptions, as participants tended to report that reading the discussion increased their perception of the article's quality and of the overall platform (here, Wikipedia) in general. The discussion which follows explores possible mechanisms that may help explain the effect.

We suspected that the quality ratings of those already familiar with Talk pages would not be affected by seeing discussion (especially non-conflict discussion) in the same way as somebody who had never seen Talk pages, because the discussion may have made the less Wikipedia-savvy people more aware of the fallibility of Wikipedia's editing process. If the presence of discussion changes how people engage with the article in a way that reduces perceived quality even among individuals already familiar with discussion pages, and the same results are observed in that subset, we would reject that explanation. To test for this, we asked at the beginning of the exercise how often participants read Wikipedia Talk pages, with results summarized above, and filtered to use only responses where people reported familiarity with Talk pages. While some statistical tests suggested the same primary results, when using non-parametric ordinal tests and strictly maintaining the limit of one observation per Turker, we did not have sufficient power to observe significant effects that would lead us to conclusively eliminate this possibility.

Our experimental design, across all conditions, aimed to engage participants in reasonably deep thinking. Our comprehension questions required all participants to read in the material in a reasonable degree of detail; our presentation of those passages as images helped force more detailed reading and engagement.

However, seeing the discussion may have engaged participants' critical thinking skills (Kahneman's System 2) more deeply than the non-discussion condition, causing them to look at the original material more skeptically, leading participants to be more critical of the article in their ratings. Interestingly, they nevertheless believed the discussion caused them to perceive the article as higher quality, perhaps because they believe they were able to make a more accurate and informed evaluation, or because System 2 included a more thoughtful understanding of "quality" than the quick intuitive judgment of System 1, which often substitutes easier questions that may have different baseline answers [7]. If this is the explanation for our results, it would suggest that designers of online collaborative content creation systems need to pay close attention to factors that influence System 2 engagement (summarized in [7]) when considering how people will perceive content quality.

As another possible explanation, we see from the design literature that people are less willing to be critical of work that they perceive to be "finished" or "complete," and more willing to offer criticism of works in progress. People are more willing to give higher-level constructive criticism about something that seems to be more "sketchy" with lower level details not yet fixed, as compared to a polished product [31]. This may be a mechanism of System 1.

All our article segments were taken from works currently listed as Featured Articles, meaning they have already reached the highest quality standard on Wikipedia, but all Wikipedia articles are in some sense incomplete [29]. Revealing the discussion might frame the article more as a "work in progress" than a completed, polished piece. This more apparent state of incompleteness could invite more criticism, as reflected in lower quality ratings, even while participants feel that reading the discussion improved their perceptions (presumably compared to other work viewed as being in a similar state of completion). We plan to check for this in a future study that manipulates the perceived completeness of collaboratively produced content, regardless of the presence or absence of discussion. If this explains our experimental results, system designers would need to attend to stylistic details that make work seem more or less polished, depending on their goals for the system.

This paper describes an experiment and a robust set of results about *how* the presence of discussion causally affects perceived quality. The results prompt questions of exactly *why* these results are observed, which must be explored in future work, before specific prescriptive advice can be given to the designers of online community platforms. The causal understanding will also have implications for designers of external tools that reveal information about the editing and production process, such as many research tools visualizing Wikipedia edit histories with the intention of impacting perceptions of trustworthiness, accuracy, quality, and community (e.g. [10, 19, 25]).

FUTURE WORK

In this work, we have found a "sausage" effect that revealing discussion generally lowers perceived article quality, with the strength of the effect depending on the presence of conflict and the way that any present conflict is resolved. This leaves open many questions about the underlying causal psychological mechanisms.

Since we studied only one context, it naturally leads one to wonder about the generality of this finding. One could readily use a similar experimental paradigm with other sources or in contexts with different signals about information quality, for example. The presence and type of discussion seems likely to interact with other factors impacting a source's credibility, such as assumed editor expertise (e.g. showing editorial discussions from a major national newspaper, or a federal agency's rule-setting work, instead of Wikipedia) or page presentation (e.g. does showing reasoned discussion behind content on a site that does not otherwise appear to be a credible source improve credibility?).

If conflict and conflict resolution strategies in discussions can be automatically detected (e.g. by a machine learning classifier), one could (a) replicate some of these findings on a larger scale, using ratings from the Wikipedia article assessment tool, and (b) proactively flag certain future discussions for moderator attention and possible intervention.

ACKNOWLEDGMENTS

The authors gratefully acknowledge support from NSF grants IIS-1111750, SMA-1064209, OCI-0943168, IIS-1149797, IIS-1217559, IIS-0968484, OCI-0943148, IIS-1111124, CNS-1040801, and from the Center for the Future of Work, Heinz College, Carnegie Mellon University. We also thank our participants and our reviewers for some very high-quality reviews.

REFERENCES

1. Y. Appelbaum. "How the Professor Who Fooled Wikipedia Got Caught by Reddit." *The Atlantic*, 2012. http://www.theatlantic.com/technology/archive/2012/05/how-the-professor-who-fooled-wikipedia-got-caught-by-reddit/257134/.
2. O. Arazy and O. Nov. "Determinants of Wikipedia Quality: The Roles of Global and Local Contribution Inequality." *Proc. CSCW*, ACM (2010), 233–236.
3. T. Chesney. "An Empirical Examination of Wikipedia's Credibility." *First Monday 11*, 11-6 (2006).
4. B.J. Fogg, C. Soohoo, D.R. Danielson, L. Marable, J. Stanford, and E.R. Tauber. "How Do Users Evaluate the Credibility of Web Sites?" *Proc. DUX*, (2003), 1.
5. M. Garber. "Abraham Lincoln Did Not Invent Facebook: How a Guy and His Blog Fooled the Whole Wide Internet." *The Atlantic*, 2012. http://www.theatlantic.com/technology/archive/2012/05/abraham-lincoln-did-not-invent-facebook-how-a-guy-and-his-blog-fooled-the-whole-wide-internet/256945/.
6. K.A Jehn. "A Qualitative Analysis of Conflict Types and Dimensions in Organizational Groups." *Administrative Science Quarterly 42*, 3 (1997), 530–557.
7. D. Kahneman. *Thinking, Fast and Slow*. Farrar, Straus and Giroux, 2011.
8. A. Kittur, E.H. Chi, and B. Suh. "Crowdsourcing User Studies with Mechanical Turk." *Proc. CHI*, ACM (2008), 453–456.
9. A. Kittur and R.E. Kraut. "Harnessing the Wisdom of Crowds in Wikipedia: Quality Through Coordination." *Proc. CSCW*, ACM (2008), 37–46.
10. A. Kittur, B. Suh, and E.H. Chi. "Can You Ever Trust a Wiki?" *Proc. CSCW*, ACM (2008), 477.
11. A. Kittur, B. Suh, B.A. Pendleton, and E.H. Chi. "He Says, She Says: Conflict and Coordination in Wikipedia." *Proc. CHI*, (2007), 453–462.
12. M. Klein and S.C.-Y Lu. "Conflict Resolution in Cooperative Design." *Artificial Intelligence in Engineering 4*, 4 (1989), 168–180.
13. T. Kriplean, M. Toomim, J. Morgan, A. Borning, and A.J. Ko. "Is This What You Meant?: Promoting Listening on the Web with Reflect." *Proc. CHI*, ACM (2012), 1559–1568.
14. T. Kriplean, M. Toomim, J.T. Morgan, A. Borning, and A.J. Ko. "REFLECT: Supporting Active Listening and Grounding on the Web through Restatement." *Proc. CSCW*, ACM (2011).
15. J. Liu and S. Ram. "Who Does What: Collaboration Patterns in the Wikipedia and Their Impact on Article Quality." *ACM Trans. Manage. Inf. Syst. 2*, 2 (2011), 11:1–11:23.
16. T. Lucassen and J.M. Schraagen. "Trust in Wikipedia: How Users Trust Information From an Unknown Source." *Proc. 4th Workshop on Information Credibility*, (2010), 19–26.
17. J.J. Mondak. "Perceived Legitimacy of Supreme Court Decisions: Three Functions of Source Credibility." *Political Behavior 12*, 4 (1990), 363–384.
18. M.M. Montoya-Weiss, A.P. Massey, and M. Song. "Getting It Together: Temporal Coordination and Conflict Management in Global Virtual Teams." *The Academy of Management Journal 44*, 6 (2001), 1251–1262.
19. P. Pirolli, E. Wollny, and B. Suh. "So You Know You're Getting the Best Possible Information: A Tool that Increases Wikipedia Credibility." *Proc. CHI*, ACM (2009), 1505.
20. B. Shneiderman. "Designing Trust into Online Experiences." *Communications of the ACM 43*, 12 (2000), 57–59.
21. H.A. Simon. *The Sciences of the Artificial*. MIT Press, 1996.
22. H.C. Stuart, L. Dabbish, S. Kiesler, P. Kinnaird, and R. Kang. "Social Transparency in Networked Information Exchange: A Theoretical Framework." *Proc. CSCW*, ACM (2012), 451–460.
23. B. Stvilia, M.B. Twidale, L.C. Smith, and L. Gasser. "Information Quality Work Organization in Wikipedia." *Journal of the American Society for Information Science and Technology 59*, 6 (2008), 983–1001.
24. Thomas, K.W. "Conflict and Conflict Management: Reflections and Update." *Journal of Organizational Behavior 13*, 3 (1992), 265–274.
25. Viégas, F.B., Wattenberg, M., and Dave, K. "Studying Cooperation and Conflict Between Authors with History Flow Visualizations." *Proc. CHI*, ACM (2004), 575–582.
26. Viégas, F.B., Wattenberg, M., Kriss, J., and van Ham, F. "Talk Before You Type: Coordination in Wikipedia." *HICSS*, (2007), 78.

27. Wikimedia Foundation. "MediaWiki Extension:ArticleFeedback." https://www.mediawiki.org/wiki/Extension:ArticleFeedback.

28. Wikipedia community consensus. "Wikipedia: Neutral Point Of View." *Wikipedia*, 2012. https://en.wikipedia.org/w/index.php?title=Wikipedia:Neutral_point_of_view&oldid=491462094.

29. Wikipedia community consensus. "Wikipedia: There Is No Deadline." *Wikipedia*, 2012. https://en.wikipedia.org/w/index.php?title=Wikipedia:There_is_no_deadline&oldid=487857034.

30. Wikipedia contributors. "Help: Using Talk Pages." *Wikipedia*, 2012. https://en.wikipedia.org/w/index.php?title=Help:Using_talk_pages&oldid=487941001.

31. Wong, Y.Y. "Rough and Ready Prototypes: Lessons from Graphic Design." *Posters and short talks of CHI*, ACM (1992), 83–84.

32. *Daily Cleveland Herald*, 1869.

Arguments about Deletion

How Experience Improves the Acceptability of Arguments in Ad-hoc Online Task Groups

Jodi Schneider
Digital Enterprise Research Institute, National University of Ireland, Galway
jodi.schneider@deri.org

Krystian Samp
Digital Enterprise Research Institute, National University of Ireland, Galway
krystian.samp@deri.org

Alexandre Passant
Digital Enterprise Research Institute, National University of Ireland, Galway
alexandre.passant@deri.org

Stefan Decker
Digital Enterprise Research Institute, National University of Ireland, Galway
stefan.decker@deri.org

ABSTRACT
Increasingly, ad-hoc online task groups must make decisions about jointly created artifacts such as open source software and Wikipedia articles. Time-consuming and laborious attention to textual discussions is needed to make such decisions, for which computer support would be beneficial. Yet there has been little study of the argumentation patterns that distributed ad-hoc online task groups use in evaluation and decision-making. In a corpus of English Wikipedia deletion discussions, we investigate the argumentation schemes used, the role of the arguer's experience, and which arguments are acceptable to the audience. We report three main results: First, the most prevalent patterns are the *Rules* and *Evidence* schemes from Walton's catalog of argumentation schemes [34], which comprise 36% of arguments. Second, we find that familiarity with community norms correlates with the novices' ability to craft persuasive arguments. Third, acceptable arguments use community-appropriate rhetoric that demonstrate knowledge of policies and community values while problematic arguments are based on personal preference and inappropriate analogy to other cases.

Author Keywords
collaboration and conflict; argumentation schemes; critical questions; online argumentation; decision-making; deliberation; peer production; Wikipedia

ACM Classification Keywords
H.5.3 Information Interfaces and Presentation: Group and Organizational Interfaces—*Collaborative computing*

INTRODUCTION
Jointly creating digital artifacts in a distributed collaboration is commonplace, for instance in distributed software development [9] and collaborative authoring [10]. Distributed online communities which produce jointly-created artifacts often need to make decisions on these artifacts, such as when an open source software product is ready for release, when a W3C recommendation is completed, or whether a Wikipedia article is acceptable for continued inclusion in the encyclopedia. Collaborators may at first rely on task independence, formal coordination, or shared mental models (sometimes acquired through informal discussion). After the creation phase, artifacts may move into revision and acceptance/rejection phases, which may draw discussion from larger groups.

CSCW '13, February 23–27, 2013, San Antonio, Texas, USA.

Decision-making often relies on generating and integrating feedback from a large group, particularly for the products of diverse, widely distributed online communities. However, these feedback discussions can be overwhelming, making it difficult to focus the discussion on the relevant aspects. Further, each community applies specific criteria to determine when artifacts are *ready to release* and *appropriate*, and what kinds of comments are relevant and helpful at a given point, meaning that only certain kinds of arguments are relevant and acceptable. Different viewpoints, from multiple people, may be submitted for consideration, and when disagreements arise, in order to make progress, resolutions must be found. The process of coming to agreement should:

- consider all relevant arguments
- be inclusive of multiple viewpoints
- minimize effort
- avoid alienating participants
- result in a high quality decision.

The English-language Wikipedia is a prime example of a collaborative authoring community, where ad-hoc voluntary groups undertake a number of tasks such as creation, editing, and deletion [4]. Deletion is a prominent activity involving significant conversations within and at the boundaries of the community [32, 20], which is made more challenging since newcomers often misunderstand the policies, such as

Wikipedia's notability[1] policy[2]. Despite numerous guidelines and a standardized workflow, disagreements are evident in deletion discussions [5]. There are an average of 500 discussions a week, and some articles are repeatedly discussed [32]. Therefore, deletion discussions are a useful first place to analyze the disagreement resolution process in order to identify common patterns.

Our work has three primary goals:

1. to identify which arguments are given in content deletion discussions
2. to investigate the differences between novices' and experts' arguments
3. to describe the structure of acceptable arguments both for keeping and for deleting content.

The outcomes of our work can be applied in several ways. Argumentation patterns, such as the argumentation schemes used in this paper [34], are needed to apply existing work on decision-making and group support systems (e.g. [11]). For socializing newcomers, externalizing acceptable argumentation patterns and making them explicit may be particularly helpful; as we show, acceptance of arguments depends in part on how well they display an understanding of community policies and values. Further, we provide evidence about the role of argumentation in online decision-making, an important topic with little previous investigation.

Following this introduction, we first present related work. Subsequently we describe the deletion process and then present our research questions and methodology. We then analyze typical arguments, explain how experience affects arguments, and describe what types of arguments are accepted. Finally, we conclude with discussion and future work.

RELATED WORK

We now review related work about team behavior, online decision-making, deletion in Wikipedia, and newcomers.

Team behavior

Team behavior has been studied in various research domains, including psychology, management science, and CSCW. Kozlowski & Ilgen review the psychology literature on groups and teams, which indicates that some types and levels of conflict are helpful in groups; that team processes and task demands should be appropriately matched; and that shared and team mental models may be important in effective task completion [22]. Further, turn-taking is important in effective group performance, at least for synchronous, in-person groups, and social sensitivity impacts the group productivity [35]. Research on virtual teams has found that "routine patterns of media use" are quickly established and thereafter are maintained, which provides a first mover advantage to establishing communication procedures [19]. Our work addresses the routine procedures used in arguing, and requires an understanding of what makes task completion successful.

[1] http://en.wikipedia.org/wiki/WP:Notability

[2] Notability issues account for over one-fifth of all deletions from the encyclopedia, as articles that do not articulate their importance are summarily deleted in great numbers without discussion or controversy [25, 15].

Online decision-making

Numerous groups – notably open source communities and some standardization bodies (e.g. the W3C[3]) – use online discussions as their primary medium for decision-making. The rhetoric of decision-making has already received some attention in these communities. For instance Chilana, Ko, and Wobbrock investigated rhetorical devices and contentiousness in bug reports, in order to raise design criteria for future bug reporting [7]. In the Python community, Barcellini, Détienne, and Burkhardt have investigated how design proposals are moved forward to successful implementation through boundary-spanning participants who are able to bridge the rhetoric of novices and experts [2]. In comparison to the typical speech-act oriented approaches, the process for argumentative analysis we describe in this paper is intensive and adds detail; in the future it could be applied to any epistemic or artifact-oriented community.

Previous Research on Deletion in Wikipedia

The arguments used in deletion discussions are of primary importance: according to community policy, decisions should be made by consensus, based on which arguments prevail. However, previous research on deletion in Wikipedia has focused primarily on the votes given and the numbers supporting each side of a discussion. Taraborelli and Ciampaglia investigated the chronological order of votes in controversial deletion discussions [32]. Schneider et al. investigated decision factors in a representative sample of deletion discussions [30]. Geiger [15] and Lam et al. [25] documented deletion statistics based on keyword logs. The bulk of decisions are made by the same regular participants: Article creators rarely (18%) participate [15]. Only 26% of all deletion debates include newcomers, and only 8% include more than one newcomer [15]. However, researchers have suggested that ensuring broad participation may be important for fighting discussion bias, one of the shortcomings of the deletion process [32]. Decisions made by large groups with diverse tenure are least likely to be overturned, while decisions made with the participation of newcomers are more likely to be reversed [24]. Our work contributes by focusing on the arguments used to make decisions and by identifying problematic aspects of newcomers' participation in deletion discussions.

Newcomers and Socialization

We now review work on newcomers in online communities, and in particular, in Wikipedia. Five problems of dealing with newcomers are addressed in [23]: recruitment, selection, retention, protection, and socialization. Newcomer socialization, and the differences between newcomer and expert performance, have been a frequent topic of research. Various socialization techniques have been tested. For instance, goal-setting, time-tables, and feedback (both personalized emails and anonymous peer feedback), along with recommended worked examples, were used to socialize newcomers to a tax Q&A community in [12].

In Wikipedia, socialization is of heightened importance because of Wikipedia's slowing growth [31, 17]. Yet socializa-

[3] See i.e. the HTML standards group Decision Policy: http://dev.w3.org/html5/decision-policy/decision-policy-v3.html

tion may also be at odds with novices' perception of the encyclopedia as an artifact, rather than a community [4]. Various of Wikipedia's socializing mechanisms have been studied, including legitimate peripheral participation [1], group membership [8, 13], and inter-editor communication [27], which can function as a deterrent to further participation as well as a socialization tactic [16]. In general, as Kraut et al. have noted, there is a tension between protecting the community (since newcomers do not know and may not be motivated to conform to community norms) and welcoming and socializing newcomers [23]. This is particularly evident when deleting content: participants are more likely to leave the encyclopedia project when content they added is deleted.[4] In quantifying differences in novices' arguments, the present study points towards interventions; we also highlight the need to maintain quality without alienating participants.

THE DELETION PROCESS

Next, we describe the deletion process, the focus of our work. Anyone can suggest that a Wikipedia article be deleted, by editing it and adding a special flag. Three main deletion procedures are used, depending on how controversial deletion is expected to be and the impact of deleting material. Under *speedy deletion*, no waiting period is required before an administrator deletes clearly inappropriate content (e.g. vandalism and spam). *Proposed deletion* is meant for uncontroversial cases; the deletion notice must remain uncontested for a seven day waiting period. *Articles for Deletion*[5] is intended for controversial articles.

Articles for Deletion Discussions

Articles for Deletion (AfD) is the most deliberative of Wikipedia's three main deletion procedures, involving community discussions to determine whether controversial articles are appropriate topics for the encyclopedia. A sample AfD discussion is shown in Figure 1. In each AfD discussion, a nominator gives a justification for deleting an article; the community discusses the merits of the article and topic, providing arguments for or against deleting the article; and a discussion closer–generally an administrator–reviews the discussion after seven days, with the intention of finding a consensus decision.

Our work focuses on AfD since these community discussions have the longest and most elaborate argumentative discussions and thus enable us to best study the deliberation process. Nominators, discussants, and closers are self-selected. While these deletion discussions are open to anyone – even IP users without a username – to read and to comment on, they are sophisticated wiki spaces with their own conventions: messages start with a bolded indication of their 'vote'[6] (*Keep*, *Delete*, *Merge*, etc.), they are signed with the poster's username or IP address, and, most importantly, messages must use appropriate rhetoric based on Wikipedia guidelines and policies.

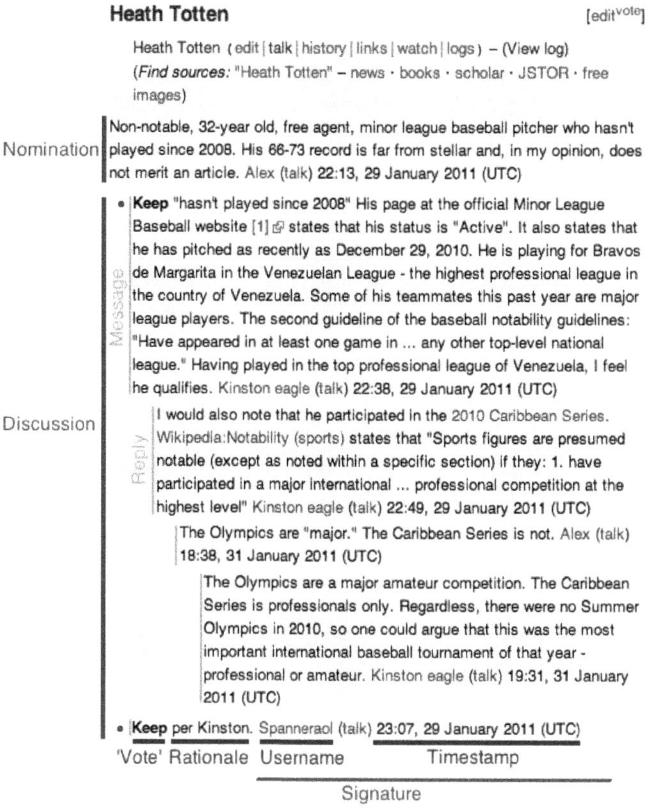

Figure 1. An extract from the deletion discussion for baseball player Heath Totten. Community discussion follows the nomination; participants can reply to the nomination or to each other. A typical message consists of a 'vote' followed by a rationale, signed with the poster's username and a timestamp.

While these 'votes' may be helpful, majority vote does not in fact determine the outcome. Rather, in the English-language Wikipedia, decisions are intended to be made by consensus, based on whether one side "substantively defeated the other's key arguments"[7]. Yet these actual arguments made in deletion discussions have not been investigated.

RESEARCH QUESTIONS

We consider three research questions about content deletion. In a corpus of user discussions called Articles for Deletion, used to decide what topics deserve articles in the English Wikipedia, we ask:

[RQ1] What arguments are given?
[RQ2] Do people with different levels of experience with Wikipedia editing or the Wikipedia deletion process provide different types of arguments?
[RQ3] Which argumentation schemes are accepted?

Next we describe the argument classification used in this study.

[4]"only 0.6 percent of those whose articles are met with deletion stayed editing, compared to 4.4 percent of the users whose articles remained" http://en.wikipedia.org/w/index.php?title=Wikipedia:Wikipedia_Signpost/2011-04-04/Editor_retention&oldid=425153383

[5]http://en.wikipedia.org/wiki/WP:Articles_for_deletion/

[6]Colloquially referred to as *!vote*, to emphasize that they are *not* votes.

[7]Policy from http://en.wikipedia.org/wiki/Wikipedia:Deletion_process#Consensus, well-summarized by an administrator's closing remarks at http://en.wikipedia.org/WP:Articles_for_deletion/List_of_common_misconceptions_(3rd_nomination)

ARGUMENTATION SCHEMES

In examining which arguments are given, we followed philosopher Douglas Walton's 2008 classification [34]. With 60 argumentation schemes collected from other scholars and from his own work, Walton's collection is the most comprehensive. Refined over more than a decade, Walton's schemes are widely used in computational argumentation since they "have provided exactly the right balance between theoretical consistency... and practical utility" [29]. Walton traces the modern use of argumentation schemes to 1953 and his own first collection of 25 argumentation schemes was published in 1995 [33], which originated in studying under what conditions traditional logical fallacies were in fact "appropriate, acceptable, and persuasive" (p11) [34].

Example Argumentation Scheme

Argumentation schemes classify the patterns used in making arguments. Walton's schemes each begin with a title and a description. For example, here is the argumentation scheme **Argument from Rules - From Established Rule** [34]:

Major Premise: If carrying out types of actions including A is the established rule for x, then (unless the case is an exception), a must carry out A.
Minor Premise: Carrying out types of actions including A is the established rule for a.
Conclusion: Therefore, a must carry out A.

To indicate possible flaws in reasoning, associated with each scheme, there are critical questions pointing to the possible counterarguments. For example, three *critical questions* accompany the Argument from Rules:

1. Does the rule require carrying out this type of action?
2. Are there other established rules that might conflict with or override this one?
3. Are there extenuating circumstances or an excuse for non-compliance?

Such critical questions can be used to guide a debate, and to ensure that all possible objections have been addressed.

Instantiating an Argumentation Scheme

Argumentation schemes are *patterns* for arguing: to use them, they must be instantiated with details. We now provide a concrete example instantiating the above example argumentation scheme Argument from Rules. We draw a (hopefully familiar) example from the rules of the road: the rule that vehicles must stop at red lights.

If stopping at a red light is the established rule for driving a vehicle, then (unless the case is an exception), drivers must stop at a red light.
Stopping at a red light is the established rule for drivers.
Therefore, drivers must stop at a red light.

Using this example, we also provide some instantiations of the critical questions above:

1. Were you driving a vehicle?
2. Did a police officer direct you to continue without stopping?
3. Were you driving an ambulance with its siren on?

Next we examine argumentation schemes in context.

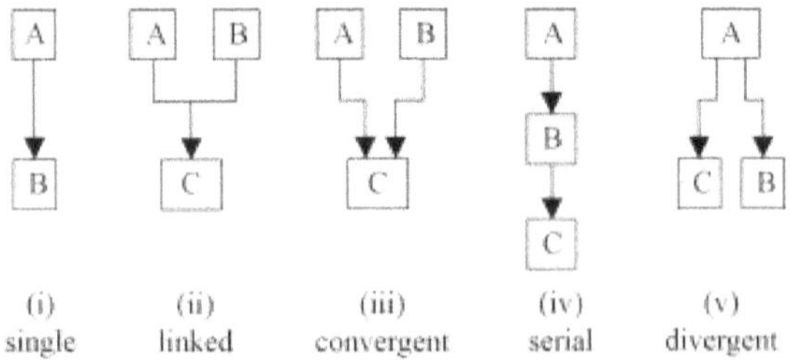

Figure 2. To reason from premises to conclusions, argumentation schemes (represented by arrows) are used. An argument may involve one or several premises, conclusions, and argumentation schemes. Diagram from Rahwan [28].

EXAMPLE ARGUMENT

Figure 1 shows the beginning of a debate about baseball player Heath Totten[8]. Six messages are shown: the nomination (1 message), a bolded 'Keep' vote (1 message), with three replies indented below it (3 messages), and a second bolded 'Keep' vote (1 message). We use this as an example for analysis below.

Analysis

This argument for keeping the article is fully articulated. It is principally an application of the Argument from Rules described above, as a policy interpretation about which guideline should be applied (baseball notability[9]). It combines this with an Argument from Evidence (see Table 1)–a sourced, factual correction (the player is currently active). Additional comments (e.g. *Some of his teammates this past year are major league players*) are given. Unusually, in this case, the connection between the rule and the evidence are made explicit: *Having played in the top professional league in Venezuela, I feel he qualifies.*

A second follow-up response, from the same person, is more typical, in that it is less explicit. It again uses the same two argumentation schemes–a Rule (baseball notability) and Evidence (played in the Caribbean series)–yet without spelling out the further claim that this evidence shows that the player meets the baseball notability guideline. As typical in conversations, this is an enthymeme: the arguer does not explicate the argument fully, and the reader must infer the implied claim that the player meets the sports guideline. Unstated and missing information adds challenges for machine processing. Yet, as evidenced by the nominator's response, for a human, there is no ambiguity here. Thus, the nominator replies, contesting that the Caribbean series qualifies under the baseball notability guideline.

In general, multiple arguments may be given in a message, and arguments can be used in various combinations, drawn from Walton's schemes (Table 1). Arguments can be related as supporting sub-arguments, or can be independent, separate arguments, as shown in Figure 2 (from [28]).

METHODOLOGY

We used Walton's 60 argumentation schemes (see the example above) as the basis for a categorization of the argu-

[8]http://en.wikipedia.org/wiki/Wikipedia:Articles_for_deletion/Heath_Totten
[9]http://en.wikipedia.org/wiki/Wikipedia:Notability_(sports)#Baseball

ments appearing in a sample corpus of deletion. To address our research questions, after determining the argumentation classifications to use, we needed a representative sample. Within this sample we needed to count the arguments presented (RQ1), determine which users were novices and what arguments they gave (RQ2), and determine which arguments were challenged (RQ3). Choosing the level at which to annotate arguments was particularly challenging, since messages can contain any number of arguments, or no argument at all. For this paper, we annotated arguments at two different levels: first, to determine which arguments were most prevalent, we used all arguments, constituted of a clause, several sentences, or the entire message. Later, to determine the main argument, we coded one main argument per message. We now detail our methodology.

Representative Sample

Our core corpus was the 72 debates begun or relisted on January 29, 2011[10]; this is a typical day, with an average number of debates[11]. Figure 1 shows a nomination and responses from a debate in our corpus. Debates include from 2 to 33 messages (stddev 6). This core corpus consists of 741 messages contributed by 244 users between the first nomination[12] on January 14 and the last close of debate on February 8. Messages in our core corpus range from about a dozen to over 4,000 characters. The scope of the sample enabled extensive manual examination, unlike previous research which merely reported deletion data based on keyword logs, using Wikipedia's classifications [15] or using rough categories, such as no content/context, notability/significance, and whether the issue was discussed or administratively deleted without discussion [25]. By contrast, we use annotation and content analysis to analyze deletion discussions and outcomes based on hand analysis of our sample, to illuminate the activity of deletion discussions, rather than to provide a fully representative record.

Iterative Annotation

We annotated arguments in four rounds, following an iterative annotation strategy [18], with the first two rounds of coarse annotation by the principal investigator, and two rounds of subsequent annotation by trained student annotators. Initially, we focused on identifying the most prevalent arguments, in the first and second rounds. To determine the most prevalent argumentation schemes, each message in the corpus was first coded by the principal investigator as a sequence of contiguous arguments selected from Walton's 60 argumentation schemes. Subsequently, the most prevalent schemes were used in the third and fourth rounds; these schemes, along with selections from the final annotation manual are shown in Table 1. To determine the main argument in each message, the same two student annotators selected one of 17 categories characterizing the message's argument strategy. This helped simplify annotation, which aided the crispness of the categorization for the third and fourth rounds, since inter-annotator agreement is particularly sensitive to boundary variation.

[10]http://en.wikipedia.org/wiki/WP:Articles_for_deletion/Log/2011_January_29

[11]based on January 2007-April 2011

[12]While debates typically last 7 days, they can be relisted for further discussion.

Our annotation guide evolved through this process. For the first round of annotation, 'A User's Compendium of Schemes' (Chapter 9 of [34]) and notes on Walton's 60 schemes were used to annotate a small sample in CorpusTool[13]. Based on the data, for the second round of annotation, we added two more categories–*note* and *no reason given*–and prepared our own annotation guide with Wikipedia-based examples, resulting in revisions to the guide and recoding of the sample. Overall argument prevalence (RQ1) was estimated from the second round of annotation, and to scope the further annotation, we revised the annotation guide to comprise 17 categories as shown in Table 1. First, we selected the subset of 14 argumentation schemes that appeared more than 2% of the time. Besides these argumentation schemes, we had three additional categories: *Note* was used for standardized, templated notes used for routine notices. *No reason given* was used for messages that indicate a position without stating an argument. *No argument* was used for messages that do not state an obvious argument. Examples of all 17 classifications are given in Table 1.

Restricting to the most prevalent argumentation schemes, we tested annotation consistency and the annotation guide, in the third round, which used two independent coders. Annotators were an upper-level undergraduate and a graduate student familiar with the corpus from previous annotation tasks with a different categorization on the same corpus [30]. Before the third round of coding, annotators had an initial training meeting with the principal investigator to discuss the annotation guide and tools; during the meeting we independently coded a test sample from a sample corpus and then compared codings. Following discussion and collaborative coding, in the third round, we tested the clarity of the guide by having the two assistants spend 2-3 hours independently coding sample debates from a second, sample corpus[14], in order to surface problems with the annotation guidelines and examples of hard-to-categorize messages. Subsequently, we met to discuss the annotation scheme and suggest refinements. The principal investigator reviewed the annotated test corpus, examining the argumentation schemes within each category, and listing the messages with discrepancies between the two annotators to provide them with further feedback.

For the fourth round of annotation, an updated manual was prepared, providing further guidance about the categories, based on feedback on the annotation and discriminating examples. Then the same two assistants annotated the original corpus with the final annotation manual, spending about 10 hours on this task. Examples from the manual are shown in Table 1. Interannotator agreement was strong, considering the extreme difficulty inherent in the task, due to the number of categories (17) and the complex analysis involved in determining and categorizing the main argument. Overall, interannotator agreement statistics are shown in Table 2.

To prepare text files for annotation, each debate was downloaded as a single HTML file, then HTML was stripped out

[13]http://www.wagsoft.com/CorpusTool/

[14]Drawn from debates discussed on March 1, 2012 http://en.wikipedia.org/wiki/Wikipedia:Articles_for_deletion/Log/2012_March_1

Issues (RQ3)	Argumention Scheme	Definition	Rough example from Wikipedia	Example from 2012-03-01 corpus
⚠	Argument from Analogy	Based on a similar case.	Articles like X are not notable enough for their own standalone articles.	The test is not for just the combination of those two items, but for the notability of it as a topic. For example, if there are articles on "cars", and "trailers" that doesn't necessarily mean that there should be an article on "cars with trailers" even if that combination of words is common in a google search. That's the question here. I don't know the answer.
	Argument from Bias	Bias suspected.	Reads like an advertisement.	Delete as nothing more than promotional guff by a clearly problematic editor who seems hell-bent on spamming his business and products across Wikipedia.
⚠	Argument from Cause to Effect	Using cause and effect.	Given what's here, it's reasonable to assume that other sources mention X.	Given the vast amount of coverage Apple gets for its product launches I'm sure they will be covered in business courses in the years to come as a good way to do business and get large amounts of attention towards your products.
	Argument from Composition	From the parts to the whole.	Mostly about already discussed at X.	The article is largely surplus to requirements given the information already contained in Battle of Stalingrad and the associated Axis order of battle at the Battle of Stalingrad and Red Army order of battle at the Battle of Stalingrad .
	Argument from Evidence to Hypothesis	Providing evidence.	Source X isn't good enough because... // Here are the sources, which tell us...	Weak keep. Here is some coverage in Publishers Weekly that backs up the "500,000 copies in print" assertion[35]. A writeup in School Library Journal[36]. And some newspaper reviews[37][38][39][40]: the reviewers aren't Michiko Kakutani, but taken together I'd be inclined to keep--preferably as one consolidated article for all the books.
⚠	Argument from Ignorance	Assumption when no supporting evidence can be found.	No search results.	A seemingly unnotable website and blog. It has no references that would support any sort of notability. Searching around only gives results of personal pages (facebook, twitter, etc), thus it fails WP:RS .
	Argument from Need for Help	Help should be provided when possible.	If the article can be fixed through normal editing, then it is not a good candidate for AfD.	Keep - this article needs extensive development and lots of citations, but it is unquestionably notable. It does need some expert attention to select and paraphrase good review articles (i.e. secondary sources) from the thousands of papers on immunity and inflammatory diseases.
	Argument from Position to Know	Personal knowledge.	I grew up in that area & had never heard of her.	Keep: Like Clarityfiend, I know zilch about modern art. But I've actually heard of this guy.
	Argument from Precedent	Based on past decisions.	We've had this same debate for numerous articles, and decided...	Comment by previous closing admin: The deletion requests for this article reminds me of Wikipedia:Articles for deletion/Corn soup. LED-embedded glass is, like corn soup but obviously to a much lesser extent, something almost inherent to any modern metropolitan resident's daily life, hence there is likely to be lots of Google hits but not many of them useful as encyclopedic citations. That said, Google Books did yield some useful results: Popular science magazine, 1986 Structural glass textbook, 2011 Building materials textbook, 2010 and Gizmodo how-to guide As the closing admin of last month's AfD, I don't think it's appropriate for me to !vote here, but as an engineer myself I just want to flag up a few things that may be relevant to this discussion that aren't discussed on the article or the previous AfD.
	Argument from Rules	Rule-based argument.	Fails <guideline>.	Delete . Fails WP:FOOTYN and WP:GNG .
⚠	Argumentation from Values	Evaluate with value judgments.	It's a useful search term, so make it a redirect.	Delete per nom. A list of tallest buildings for a place without any especially tall buildings is pointless and even kind of insulting.
	Argument from Verbal Classification	Definitional arguments.	The current title is misleading.	The concept of immune-mediated inflammatory diseases is not widely recognised within the medical community. Despite what the article says, it is very difficult to group together the widely divergent diseases listed. The fact that they're all treated with immunosuppression is about the only thing. Searching the term as a text word on Pubmed yields 45 references, none of which address the concept in itself. I think deletion is the best step here.
⚠	Argument from Waste	Avoid wasted work.	Merge to save the work. // Delete to save time	This article has been created and then deleted at least three times in the last 12 months. On each occasion it has appeared in a similar format and without much difficulty established that it was self-promotional. On this occasion the author has admitted working for the subject corporation from the get-go. At least they're being honest but this the reliable, independent, standard we aspire too. The article needs to go.
⚠	Practical Reasoning	Actions towards a goal.		Merge with Ledglass, noting that the latter article says "may also be described as LED Glass or LED embedded Glass", and also that the single reference given for this (LED-embedded glass) article doesn't seem to use that phrase but only "Light-emitting diode (LED) illuminated glass".
	No reason given	Vote without explanation.	Per nominator.	Delete per above.
	Note	Non-argumentative note; only templated messages	Note: This debate has been included in the list...	Note: This debate has been included in the list of Arts-related deletion discussions.
	No argument	Non-templated; meta-arguments	Officially withdrawing nomination. I didn't know if the above statement brought notice as far as withdrawing the nomination went, but I'm posting this just in case.	Comment. The same article appears to have been discussed a month and a half ago under a different title: Wikipedia:Articles for deletion/Transparent LED-embedded glass. That discussion resulted in 'keep'.

Table 1. The 17 argumentation schemes annotated in round 4, with examples taken from our annotation manual. Argumentation schemes that can be problematic are marked; these are further discussed in RQ3 results.

Cohen's Kappa	.48
Kappa Maximum	.75
Kappa Std Err	.01
weighted Kappa	50
Percent Agreement	54%
Chance Agreement	12%

Table 2. Inter-annotator agreement for Round 4 annotation

with a standard parser, finally regular expressions were used to trim excess page content (including the consensus result and archiving notices) and to add linebreaks at the timestamps (providing a visual indication of message boundaries).

Identifying Novices

After classifying arguments in the entire 72-debate corpus as described above[15], we identified participants, establishing novices as those with either low overall edit count[16] (< 105) or no edits to deletion discussions prior to the observation period. We culled participants from user Talk page links in the HTML, then used the API to retrieve their contribution histories prior to January 14, 2011, the start of the first debate. Novices were confirmed manually. 22 double-novices[17] met both the low edit count and low discussion participation criteria. A further 6 participants met only one criterion (3 wiki novices had low edit count and 3 deletion novices had no previous participation in deletion discussions). The debates which included contributions from these 28 novices formed a subcorpus of 28 articles that was used to determine how an arguer's experience affects the arguments they give (RQ2).

RESULTS

We present results for each of the research questions in turn.

Argumentation Schemes Used (RQ1)

Our core corpus of 72 debates yielded 1213 arguments in 741 messages. The most common argumentation schemes (RQ1) are shown in Table 3; each of these 14 schemes is used in at least 2% of arguments. Two non-argumentative categories, Note, and No Reason Given, also each comprise more than 2% of messages, as shown in Table 3.

Certain schemes are more prevalent compared to a general argument corpus: five of Wikipedia's top third most common deletion arguments–Arguments from Rules, Values, Bias, Precedent, and Waste–are not in the top two-thirds of the most commonly used arguments (pers. communication, Snaith) in the only widely-available informal argument corpus, the Araucaria corpus [21]. This shows Wikipedia's focus on precedent and rules, and the tendency to discuss articles in terms of both values or community norms and article contributors or supporters. Certain common schemes have no relevance to debates: for instance Fear Appeal and Distress were not observed, and Popularity was rare.

Differences in Argumentation: Novices vs. Experts (RQ2)

We next examined whether a participant's arguments depend on their experience with Wikipedia editing or the Wikipedia deletion process. We focused on a subset of our core corpus, using only the 28 debates in which novices participated. We found 555 arguments, including 93 arguments in 46 comments from novices. This subset corpus showing novices' participation is further analyzed in Table 3, which shows how often novices, compared to everyone (novices+experts) used a particular argumentation scheme.

Argumentation schemes used by novices and experienced users are different (RQ2); statistically significant differences are given in bold in Table 3. Experience leads to more Arguments from Precedent and, unsurprisingly, more contributions of non-argumentative, administrative notes. Novices are more likely to give arguments which can have underlying flaws, using schemes such as Argumentation from Values, Argument from Cause to Effect, and Argument from Analogy, as will be detailed in RQ3 results.

The volume of participation is markedly different between novices and experts. In our corpus, only 6 novices made more than one comment, and only 3 novices participated in more than one debate (2,6,8 debates)(debates avg 2.2, stddev 1.9). By comparison, only 2 experts commented in just one of the 72 debates in our sample; overall, experts averaged 5.4 comments in 3.6 articles (stddev 10.1 for comments and 6.6 for articles). While the two largest number of comments (99 comments in 62 articles and 32 comments in 24 articles) were due to administrative notes and debate closing decisions, three experts participated in 11 to 20 debates and seven experts made 10 to 20 comments.

While regulars may read all debates, or all debates on a topic, novices are attracted to a debate by their knowledge of a topic, or by their desire to become more active in the community (for instance to support a nomination for adminship). Novices may be interested parties – creators or subjects – who may argue to keep an article without sufficiently understanding the criteria to be applied. Cases which attract many novices can become contentious, causing challenges unless there is strong policy to be applied [24]. In our sample, 'no consensus' discussions either lacked significant discussion (2) or involved discussions with a novice creator (2). Discussions with article creators showed strong emotion in five out of six cases, as indicated by the use of high sentiment words.

Novices arguing for deletion of an article are more likely to be participating in multiple arguments, and are more likely to cite policy correctly. Our sample showed a clear difference in the rhetoric of keep and delete comments, for example, in the ten comments left by IP users. Keep (6) comments exhibited emotional involvement and indicated confusion about polices, especially on notability, original research, and verifiability. Delete comments (4) used standard formatting and supporting resources. While further research is needed, this provides deeper insight on Lam et al.'s earlier findings that Keep outcomes involving novices are more likely to be overturned [24].

Experience with deletion has some effect on the skill and rhetoric with which people argue a case. In Wikipedia, policy knowledge is a particular stumbling block for novices. The difference between real-world importance and Wikipedia-

[15]Novice classification took place after the second round of annotation; the third and fourth rounds of annotation was conducted by student annotators who were unaware of the classification.

[16]This was chosen based on a natural breakpoint in the contribution count of our user sample; previous research has indicated that about 100 edits is a moderately low edit count.

[17]Including 9 of 10 IP address 'users'; the tenth, though a wiki novice, contributed to 16 previous debates starting in October 2010.

RQ2 More often given by	RQ3 Can be prob.	Argumentation Scheme	RQ1 Full corpus 72 debates (novices & experts)	RQ2 Subcorpus 28 debates (novices & experts)	RQ2 Subcorpus 28 debates (novices only)	RQ2 χ^2	RQ2 Sig. level
		Argument from Evidence to Hypothesis	19.29%	20.65%	21.51%		
		Argument from Rules	16.90%	18.66%	12.90%		
Experts		**Note**	**13.69%**	**10.14%**	**0.00%**	χ^2=3.66	$p < .05$
Novices	⚠	**Argumentation from Values**	**4.20%**	**4.17%**	**9.68%**	χ^2=5.13	$p < .05$
		Argument from Need for Help	4.12%	3.62%	2.15%		
		Argument from Bias	3.87%	4.53%	6.45%		
		No reason given	3.22%	3.62%	5.38%		
		Argument from Position to Know	3.05%	2.36%	4.30%		
Experts		**Argument from Precedent**	**3.05%**	**3.80%**	**0.00%**	χ^2=3.66	$p < .1$
	⚠	Argument from Ignorance	2.97%	3.08%	4.30%		
		Argument from Composition	2.56%	2.54%	2.15%		
Novices	⚠	**Argument from Cause to Effect**	**2.31%**	**2.72%**	**7.53%**	χ^2=5.59	$p < .02$
Novices	⚠	**Argument from Analogy**	**2.23%**	**2.36%**	**8.60%**	χ^2=9.86	$p < .05$
	⚠	Argument from Waste	2.23%	2.54%	1.08%		
	⚠	Practical Reasoning	2.23%	2.72%	3.23%		
		Arg. from Verbal Classification	2.06%	1.45%	2.15%		

Table 3. The most common argumentation schemes, sorted by prevalence in our full corpus. Prevalence in the the subcorpus of 28 debates to which novices contributed is also shown, both for novices and everyone (novices & experts). Statistically significant differences between novices and experts' argumentation (based on Round 2 annotation) are noted in bold. For definitions and examples, see Table 2.

importance (notability) is quite confusing to newcomers; this newcomer asks

> *Why an article on Juvenile Justice System Rules prevelant (sic) in the largest province of Punjab having population of more than 90 million people including juveniles is not Notable?*

Among novices, confusion about reliable sources (RS) is particularly prominent–for instance claiming that a self-published biographical website counts as a source for a biography, or providing insufficient detail (e.g. *I see notability and RS*, without specifying the reliable sources). Verifiability, which is of particular importance for avoiding bias, can also be misunderstood; this newcomer wants to rely on plausibility instead:

> *if you folks had been around actively working on the Web in 2000, you would know when the Dot Com Bubble burst, many, many companies went out of business. Servers with information about me... were taken off line.*

We further discuss problematic arguments next, looking at novices' and experts' arguments that are not compelling.

Which Arguments are (not) Accepted (RQ3)

Newcomers are particularly likely to use certain common, but problematic, arguments, which are enshrined in policy and in essays such as Arguments to Avoid.[18] We describe some common problematic arguments, along with its Wikipedia nickname and its Walton scheme in Table 4.

Novices

Argumentation from Values is the second most common argument given by novices; this is unfortunate since it is problematic when it is used to argue from individual (rather than accepted community values). Hence novice arguers sometimes provide uncompelling arguments, based on ignorance of community standards, e.g. to keep an article because it is *obviously of interest to the public in general.*

Similar problems with Argumentation from Values are found in the AfD for Emsworth Cricket Club. With 17 messages, Emsworth Cricket Club is one of the longest debates in our sample, yet could have been quickly decided. All four novices–two IP users and two with newly created accounts–advocate keeping, while experienced participants argue unanimously for deletion. While one novice argues well, pointing to the British Newspaper Library (though not specifically to any individual references), the other novices' comments are largely uncompelling, arguing from personal, but not shared Wikipedian values (e.g. *Why just because it is a small team and not major does it not deserve it's own page on here?*). Delete comments, however, cite specific notability policies and the need for reliable secondary sources. The novices have not sufficiently understood the criteria to be applied, or the possible counterarguments. Such discussions can escalate into heated discussions which increase effort and may alienate participants, unless diffused by skillful arguing backed by strong policy.

In this case there is strong policy, but perhaps a lack of tact. The final word goes to an experienced participant who urges reading the policy, saying *This speicalness* (sic) *argument is getting lame.* Socializing newcomers involves not only informing them about policy, but also taking an encouraging tone; in this case, warning away inexperienced (and hence presumably non-valuable) contributors takes priority over socializing them.

[18]http://en.wikipedia.org/wiki/Wikipedia:Arguments_to_avoid

Potentially problematic argument	Typical Argumentation Schemes	Wikipedia terminology
Personal preference	Argumentation from Values	ILIKEIT
Few search engine results	Argument from Ignorance	Google test
Large number of search engine hits	Argument from Cause to Effect	Google test
Requesting a favor	Argumentation from Values, Argument from Waste, or Practical Reasoning	PLEASEDONT
Analogy to other cases	Argument from Analogy	OTHER
No harm in keeping an article	Argumentation from Values or Argument from Waste	NOHARM
Topic will be notable in the future	Practical Reasoning	CRYSTALBALL

Table 4. Some common problematic arguments, along the Walton scheme and the Wikipedia acronym.

In good outcomes, novice creators learn policies and get mentoring on improving an article during the process: these fueled the No Consensus decisions in our sample[19]. Yet in other cases, novices who do not know the rules do not get mentored; they leave with the article deleted and no more insight into why the sources or notability were insufficient, with unanswered questions such as *If this page is deleted can it be added again once it has reliable sources?* In cases where experienced users are unanimous, there may be a particular incentive to ignore the voices of newcomers: this retains decision quality and minimizes effort at the expense of alienating participants.

In our corpus, the most severe conceptual errors were demonstrated by novices. Novices' comments may indicate lack of clarity on what a reliable source is (2); confusion about the relationship between reliable sources and notability (2); or failure to understand that reliable sources are needed for verification of a topic's existence (2). By comparison, experts tend to be familiar with policies and guidelines.

Experts

The problems demonstrated among experienced users, were significantly less severe. Sometimes such vagueness or rhetorical mistakes attract counter arguments. For instance *This article is inside WP:BIO*[20] *and should be kept* attracts a reply asking

> *...which part of WP:BIO is met....actually providing some rationale would be more helpful than a WP:VAGUEWAVE*[21].

In other cases, unchallenged arguments fail to be convincing. For example, a statement such as *It is an important historical part of Hamburg and I believe it deserves mention here.* would be decisive with sources. Such lack of justification or insufficient detail is common, yet detracts from arguments.

Even very frequent participants may make boilerplate arguments that lack enough detail to be convincing. For instance, out of 20 messages by one experienced user in our corpus, 15 say only *Delete – notability not demonstrated in a reliable secondary source.* This expert's 5 remaining messages argue for keeping an article (1); name what concept is not notable (1); and mention a second, additional concern (1); but only one provides an explanation of the problem (*I can't tell if any of this is notable stuff, because no sources tell us.*). The lack of justification is troubling because the argument that there are no reliable sources is an Argument from Ignorance: one key critical question is whether a given search for sources was sufficiently thorough.

Among experienced users, there can be disagreements, for instance, about what "good sourcing" means or whether given sources are sufficient to establish notability. Counting sources is not sufficient: understanding what makes coverage appropriate is also needed. The fact that sources are used both to verify information and to establish a topic's importance complicates some arguments even amongst experienced commenters (e.g. *The reliability of the sources is not being questioned, nor is it an issue as far as this AfD is concerned. The issue is, and remains, notability.*).

Experts also make strategic errors in arguing: Four experts in our corpus present arguments based on an objection to policy (e.g. *Frankly, the basis of my disagreement with you here is that I don't agree with the guideline*), but these are uncompelling and do not carry the debate. One administrator's closing justification notes this pointedly, admonishing: "do not make up rationales contrary to policy and guidelines on individual AfDs"; rather, as the administrator notes, polices are to be developed on discussion pages. Essentially, the experts have made an error of jurisdiction.

DISCUSSION & CONCLUSIONS

Supporting Novices

Wikipedia policies are complex [14], and for novices, this poses problems of both learning and understanding the guidelines and policies. Newcomers would benefit from support in finding their way through the vast, dispersed information [4]. The deletion process can be confusing, and sometimes discouraging, especially to newcomers, who may become disillusioned or frustrated when content they contributed is deleted for reasons they don't always understand: Wikipedia's notability[22] policy, the main reason for up to 28% of deletions [25], is especially likely to be misunderstood by newcomers. Helping new arguers ground arguments in policy could be helpful, since rules and policy indicate the main consensus values; by contrast, statements grounded in personal values, such as *obviously of interest to the public in general* do not make a significant contribution to the outcome of a debate. Since users don't read instructions [6], to maintain quality in user-generated content without disillusioning users, summarizing content policies and presenting them in task-based contexts seems essential.

We also suggest increased sensitivity and attention to support involved parties–page creators and those who edited a page

[19]See [30] for detailed examples.

[20]http://en.wikipedia.org/wiki/Wikipedia:Notability_(people)

[21]http://en.wikipedia.org/wiki/Wikipedia:Arguments_to_avoid_in_deletion_discussions#Just_pointing_at_a_policy_or_guideline

[22]http://en.wikipedia.org/wiki/WP:Notability

before it was nominated for deletion. The emotional attachment of this group adds complication, especially when they are new to the deletion discussion process. Based on our corpus, newcomers are more likely to take the process personally, making statements such as *I know wikipedia* (sic) *has a dislike for all things [article topic].* In contrast, experienced Wikipedians' contributions do not typically show high levels of emotional involvement. Rather, experienced Wikipedians appear to use personal pronouns to report on actions they have taken (e.g. changes made to the article), to suggest new policies, to mark uncertainty (e.g. *I would say*), or to show a personal opinion that may difference from the consensus view (e.g. *I don't expect my saying that to alter the outcome of this AfD*). Statistical analysis of the use of sentiment and personal pronouns could provide further evidence for the differences in personal engagement we see. Yet we think that these differences are sufficiently clear to warrant immediate community response in attending skillfully to newcomers.

The emotional tenor of discussions can change dramatically based on the skillfulness and sensitivity of the responses newcomers receive. For example, one newcomer from our corpus, now a prolific contributor, was initially frustrated when their first article was nominated for deletion, commenting: *To be honest it's been a real turn off adding articles to WP and I don't think I will add articles again. So smile and enjoy.* It appears that the support and co-editing from other editors during the deletion process tempered this frustration. Balancing emotion and detachment seems helpful, as exemplified by this quote, from another novice editor finally accepting that deletion is the right outcome: *I believe that (much as it would break my heart based on the no of hours I have put in over the years working on the article) it is perhaps sensible that the piece is deleted.* Understanding the process and what made it *sensible*, following extensive iterative discussion with more experienced editors, appears to have tempered the emotion for this editor. Feedback and mentoring during the AfD can impact the outcome for editors, potentially mediating the negative emotional impact. Existing work on values expressions in Wikipedia discussions [26] and on language use for mediation [3] may provide some guidance; further work, more specific to deletion, is needed. For instance, a small fraction of new editors do continue editing after an article they created was deleted; further investigation of their motivations and experience could be helpful.

Supporting All Participants

In future work we are developing experimental interventions for deletion discussions in hopes of defusing contentious conversations while also supporting newcomers in learning the relevant policies and rhetoric. For instance, extracting discussion topics could help focus the discussion on the disputed points. People often explicitly identify what they believe the issues to be, in attempts to focus the discussion. Standardized, easily detected phrases may be used, such as, 'the real issue is:' or 'I haven't heard any arguments yet which refute that point. In addition, coordination, social, and instructional messages can also appear in discussions, for instance to thank someone else; to point out a change a user just made; or to provide instructional content. We would like to test whether these interventions matter to newcomers' ongoing community participation as well as to the community satisfaction with the decision.

To develop future support mechanisms, focusing on argument structure could also be helpful. Walton's schemes can be construed as one approach to quality measurement, allowing arguments to be weighed against one another, and their strengths compared. In particular, each argumentation scheme indicates the critical questions that attack the argument; this can help to decide which argument prevails. To structure argumentation based on community standards, community-specific templates based partially instantiating the most common argumentation schemes could be used. Use of argument templates might simplify the structure of typical debates while aiding participants in making appropriate arguments, potentially bring both rigor and ease.

Studying Social Sensitivity in Online Ad-Hoc Task Groups

While there is existing research on dedicated arbitration in text-based arguments [3], further research is needed on the collective intelligence of online *ad-hoc* task groups. For in-person task groups, collective intelligence correlates with the average social sensitivity of a group [35]; if similar phenomena operate online, techniques for increasing the social sensitivity of ad-hoc online task groups would be helpful.

Social sensitivity and neutrality may also help counter the fatigue of ongoing participation in contentious activities such as deletion. A taxonomy of the emotional triggers and the associated needs discussants are trying to address (e.g. 'understand why this article was deleted', 'provide further information about a point that was not taken into consideration', 'vent about policy and bureaucratic challenges') could help suggest ways to meet participants' needs while defusing emotional debates, and might suggest likely subproblems that could be fruitfully addressed.

Reusing Argumentations Analysis Methods

The analysis techniques we describe can also be reused. This process is intensive and difficult to apply, yet it is appropriate to and transferrable to any textual discussion or online system where it would be valuable to understand the argumentation at a high level of detail. This would allow a comparison of the reasoning patterns and argumentation used.

Understanding the argumentation used in online discussions throughout the Web is also important. Towards a deeper understanding of persuasive and acceptable argumentation in online fora, Walton's argumentation schemes–which he acknowledges are not exhaustive–should be customized to particular domains (e.g. online reviews, open source bug reports) and fora (e.g. Wikipedia deletion discussions, W3C standardization discussions). This would enable support for newcomers, an understanding of common fallacies in different genres of Web conversations, and a comparison of the rhetoric. For instance, online fora make different uses of policy: In the context of Wikipedia, appropriate rhetoric and good use of policy are closely connected to successful arguments. We expect different results in communities with a less well-developed policy sphere. Application of the analysis techniques used in this paper is a first step towards that deeper understanding.

Acknowledgements

This work was supported by Science Foundation Ireland under Grant No. SFI/09/CE/I1380 (Líon2). Thanks to the Wikipedia community, especially those we informally interviewed about deletion, and its researcher community. We are particularly grateful to Bernie Hogan, for pointing out that deletion is of wider interest than article discussions. For annotation work, we thank Laura O'Connor and Lyndia Peters. We thank Mark Snaith for data on argument prevalence and Adam Wyner for conversations on argumentation. We also thankfully acknowledge the anonymous reviewers for several rounds of valuable feedback starting with the 2012 revise and resubmit process, and comments from Luigina Ciolfi, David Randall, and Trevor Bench-Capon on an early draft.

REFERENCES

1. J. Antin and C. Cheshire. Readers are not free-riders. In *CSCW '10*.
2. F. Barcellini, F. Détienne, and J.-M. Burkhardt. Participation in online interaction spaces. *Int'l Journal of Industrial Ergonomics*, 39(3):533–540, 2009.
3. M. Billings and L. A. Watts. Understanding dispute resolution online. In *CHI '10*.
4. S. L. Bryant, A. Forte, and A. Bruckman. Becoming Wikipedian. In *GROUP '05*.
5. B. Butler, E. Joyce, and J. Pike. Don't look now, but we've created a bureaucracy. In *CHI '08*.
6. J. M. Carroll and R. L. Mack. Human-computer interaction. In *Learning to use a word processor: by doing, by thinking, and by knowing*, pages 698–717. Morgan Kaufmann, 1995.
7. P. K. Chilana, A. J. Ko, and J. O. Wobbrock. Understanding expressions of unwanted behaviors in open bug reporting. In *IEEE VL/HCC '10*.
8. B. Choi, K. Alexander, R. E. Kraut, and J. M. Levine. Socialization tactics in Wikipedia and their effects. In *CSCW '10*.
9. K. Crowston, Q. Li, K. Wei, U. Y. Eseryel, and J. Howison. Self-organization of teams for free/libre open source software development. *Information and Software Technology*, 49(6):564–575, June 2007.
10. W. Emigh and S. C. Herring. Collaborative authoring on the web. In *HICSS'05*.
11. S. Farnham, H. R. Chesley, D. E. McGhee, R. Kawal, and J. Landau. Structured online interactions. In *CSCW '00*.
12. R. Farzan, R. Kraut, A. Pal, and J. Konstan. Socializing volunteers in an online community. In *CSCW '12*.
13. A. Forte, N. Kittur, V. Larco, H. Zhu, A. Bruckman, and R. E. Kraut. Coordination and beyond. In *CSCW '12*.
14. A. Forte, V. Larco, and A. Bruckman. Decentralization in Wikipedia governance. *Journal of Management Information Systems*, 26(1):49–72, 2009.
15. R. S. Geiger and H. Ford. Participation in Wikipedia's article deletion processes. In *WikiSym '11*.
16. R. S. Geiger, A. Halfaker, M. Pinchuk, and S. Walling. Defense mechanism or socialization tactic? *ICWSM '12*.
17. A. Halfaker, R. S. Geiger, J. Morgan, and J. Riedl. The rise and decline of an open collaboration system. *American Behavioral Scientist*, In Press.
18. E. Hovy. Annotation tutorial. In *ACL '10*.
19. M. Huysman, C. Steinfield, C.-Y. Y. Jang, K. David, M. H. I. N. T. Veld, J. Poot, and I. Mulder. Virtual teams and the appropriation of communication technology. *CSCW*, 12(4):411–436, 2003.
20. E. Joyce, B. Butler, and J. Pike. Handling flammable materials. *iConference '11*.
21. J. Katzav, C. A. Reed, and G. W. A. Rowe. Argument research corpus. *Practical Applications in Language and Computers '03*, pages 229–239.
22. S. W. Kozlowski and D. R. Ilgen. Enhancing the effectiveness of work groups and teams. *Psychological Science in the Public Interest*, 7(3):77–124, 2006.
23. R. Kraut, M. Burke, J. Riedl, and S. Drenner. "Dealing with newcomers". In *Evidence-based social design*. MIT Press, 2010.
24. S. K. Lam, J. Karim, and J. Riedl. The effects of group composition on decision quality in a social production community. In *GROUP '10*.
25. S. T. K. Lam and J. Riedl. Is Wikipedia growing a longer tail? In *GROUP '09*.
26. J. T. Morgan, R. M. Mason, and K. Nahon. Lifting the veil: the expression of values in online communities. In *iConference '11*.
27. K. Nemoto, P. Gloor, and R. Laubacher. Social capital increases efficiency of collaboration among Wikipedia editors. In *HyperText '11*.
28. I. Rahwan. Mass argumentation and the semantic web. *Web Semantics*, 6(1):29–37, 2008.
29. C. Reed. Walton's theory of argument and its impact on computational models. In C. Reed and C. W. Tindale, editors, *Dialectics, Dialogue and Argumentation*. College Publications, London, 2010.
30. J. Schneider, A. Passant, and S. Decker. Deletion discussions in Wikipedia: Decision factors and outcomes. In *WikiSym '12*.
31. B. Suh, G. Convertino, E. H. Chi, and P. Pirolli. The singularity is not near. In *WikiSym '09*.
32. D. Taraborelli and G. L. Ciampaglia. Beyond notability. In *IEEE SASOW '10*.
33. D. Walton. *Argumentation Schemes for Presumptive Reasoning*. Routledge, 1995.
34. D. Walton, C. Reed, and F. Macagno. *Argumentation Schemes*. Cambridge, 2008.
35. A. W. Woolley, C. F. Chabris, A. Pentland, N. Hashmi, and T. W. Malone. Evidence for a collective intelligence factor in the performance of human groups. *Science*, 330(6004):686, 2010.

Keeping Eyes on the Prize: Officially Sanctioned Rule Breaking in Mass Collaboration Systems

Elisabeth Joyce
Edinboro University of Pennsylvania
Department of English
ejoyce@edinboro.edu

Jacqueline Pike
Duquesne University
Palumbo Donahue School of Business
pikej@duq.edu

Brian Butler
University of Maryland
Robert H. Smith School of Business
bsbutler@umd.edu

ABSTRACT
Mass collaboration systems are often characterized as unstructured organizations lacking rule and order. However, examination of Wikipedia reveals that it contains a complex policy and rule structure that supports the organization. Bureaucratic organizations adopt workarounds to adjust rules more accurately to the context of use. Rather than resorting to these potentially dangerous exceptions, Wikipedia has created officially sanctioned rule breaking. The use and impact of the official rule breaking policy within Wikipedia is examined to test its impact on the outcomes of requests to delete articles in from the encyclopedia. The results demonstrate that officially sanctioned rule breaking and the Ignore all rules (IAR) policy are meaningful influences on deliberation outcomes, and rather than wreaking havoc, the IAR policy in Wikipedia has been adopted as a positive, functional governance mechanism.

Author Keywords
Governance; Wikipedia; wikis; mass collaboration; policies; rules; rule breaking

ACM Classification Keywords
K.4.3 [Organizational Impacts]: Computer-supported Collaborative Work

INTRODUCTION
Mass collaboration systems are efforts to mobilize large groups of people to create valuable artifacts [29, 44]. Central to these efforts is the use of information technology to capitalize on otherwise lost time and resources. Individuals make small contributions, separately not amounting to much, and the information technology aggregates these contributions to accomplish meaningful work. These initiatives are possible because of new technologies, such as wikis.

One of the most visible examples of technology-enabled mass collaboration is Wikipedia. Individuals contribute and modify short articles on various topics to provide the basis for an encyclopedia that serves as a major source of information for many Internet users. Started in January 2001, this online, open source encyclopedia has grown to include over 20 million articles in over 270 different languages with over 30 million participants [53]. Wikipedia is important for the focus of a study because it creates a useful artifact that is increasingly reliable and credible, and it does so through unique self-governance and dispersed community effort. It consistently appears on the top-level of Internet searches and handles large numbers of visitors [15]. While focusing attention on successful cases can be problematic, especially in online contexts where the proportion of collective groups that become sustainable is low, a growing body of literature asks how Wikipedia has become a successful mass collaboration effort and seeks to identify lessons that can be learned from it [6, 9, 10, 17, 35, 50, 56].

Both academic and popular writings have argued that successful mass collaboration systems are distinctive because of their openness to and reliance on voluntary action. Wikipedia and other mass collaboration systems are often portrayed as being free-form, emergent, uncontrolled, unstructured, egalitarian collections of amateur volunteers [e.g., 29, 44]. On one level, this characterization is simply descriptive. As in other online communities, individuals participating in Wikipedia also do the work of managing the community, organizing the materials, and aggregating small individual efforts to produce content that is more searchable and accessible [4, 36, 48, 50]. The English Wikipedia relies on more than 15 million individuals, who voluntarily perform article construction, content maintenance, and participant management tasks. In this sense, like open source software projects, Wikipedia is distinctive because it is a reasonably high quality resource [47] that is created and maintained by self-selected and unpaid people.

Yet, on a different level the characterization of mass collaboration systems as emergent, collaborative groups of engaged volunteers is an attempt to assert that these structures are new ways of organizing work that are fundamentally different than the corporate organizational forms that are currently dominant [47]. From this perspective, the idea of unconstrained action by anyone who wishes to participate is presented as a core principle that underlies the success of open mass collaboration efforts, including open source software development and Wikipedia. Both the popular press and some scholars argue that these systems are a new way of organizing, a new way of doing work, or a high-profile example of the power of mass collaboration and the wisdom of crowds [20, 27, 44, 48]. In this view, Wikipedia and other mass collaboration successes represent examples of collectives and collective actions that are successful, largely because of their greater support for the individual freedom to act and the absence of control structures typically found in traditional formal organizations.

In response to these assertions, researchers have begun to examine the claim that mass collaboration systems are fundamentally different from traditional organizations by looking more specifically at these differences. These studies have found that mass collaboration efforts retain many features and structures of formal organizations [38]: formal or official areas of jurisdiction, hierarchical authority, coordinated filing structures, separation of personal and official identities, special identification of particular management skills, and systems of rules that define accepted, standard procedure [as summarized in 19, 23, 51]. For example, Wikipedia has roles with specific responsibilities which participants occupy and has established carefully outlined selection procedures for filling those roles. The community of Wikipedia editors and administrators maintains a phalanx of policies, guidelines, and rules; it has developed a full-scale system of governance on the basis of those rules; it incorporates features of a complex organization through multiple subgroups (formal and informal); and it has devised explicit forms of behavior which are embedded in standard operating procedures [11]. Thus, in spite of the claims made by some commentators, Wikipedia and other mass collaboration systems have the elements of a Weberian bureaucracy, the prototype of traditional formal organizations [2, 52].

Rules lay out routines for behavior in an organization so that participants are guided in their pursuit of the common goals of the organization. Rules, however, do not always fully match each context that arises. In response, members of organizations often develop workarounds or exceptions that are not formally accepted or approved. These informal adjustments to rules can be critical for workers in "getting the job done," as when a nurse goes ahead and gives a patient a drug now because of immediate need, but formal procedure requires lengthy and complicated bureaucratic measures that might delay administration of the medicine and threaten the patient's life.

While workarounds can promote organizational efficiency and can better match rules to contexts of use, in their unofficial capacity and in their informal and singular development, they can be harmful to organizations as well as to individuals. As they are in essence rule violations, they can be motivated by personal goals as opposed to group goals; as they are unsanctioned, they may entail unintended and possibly negative consequences.

Wikipedia avoids these potential threats by officially sanctioning workaround behavior through the Ignore all rules policy (IAR). Officially Sanctioned Rule Breaking (OSRB) is not only the explicit recognition on the part of the organization that situated cognition can be used to resolve cases in which the rules do not suit the details of the context [13, 19, 22, 46], but the controlled and purposeful application of workarounds to protect the interests and goals of the organization.

In this paper we examine the role and impact of OSRB in a successful mass collaboration effort. The research questions we seek to address are: Does OSRB actually affect decision outcomes? Does OSRB affect outcomes of decisions when it is being used in disalignment with the proposal and existing policy? And does OSRB affect outcomes when it is being used to thwart individual policies or particular policy domains? We begin with a discussion of rules in organizations, why rules are broken, and the positive and negative implications of rule violations. We then consider Wikipedia's novel approach to rule inadequacy, Officially Sanctioned Rule Breaking, as embodied in its Ignore all rules policy. Using data from Wikipedia governance and deliberation archives, we test hypotheses about the impact of OSRB in Wikipedia. We then conclude with a discussion of how OSRB might explain and support successful mass collaboration efforts in other contexts.

THEORETICAL BACKGROUND

Rules

Organizations use rules to increase efficiency, quality, coordination and transparency. Rules provide direction for behavior [12, 14, 37, 39], and facilitate the use of information to make high quality decisions efficiently [25, 32]. Rules generalize across contexts so that they can last over time and operate well over multiple situations [21]. Rules set up routines [43] and create institutional memory [2] so that individuals do not have to recreate procedures or processes each time they are required. The coordination function of rules relates closely to their role in bureaucracies identified by Max Weber. As rational coordination mechanisms, they improve the operation of the organization [8, 33] by preventing groups and individuals from having to recreate processes anew on every occasion, and in doing so, rules reduce effort and increase standardization. A rule-oriented organization sets out precedents clearly and explicitly describes procedures. Once individuals have been socialized into an organization, they are able to understand, explain, and perform necessary activities with significantly less effort.

Another, less commonly considered, aspect of rules is their role in transparency and fairness. Rules set up "transparent motives" and "legible behavior" [31], thereby increasing efficiency, fairness [24] and predictability [46]. While the coordination and fairness aspects of rules may conflict, they typically exist and operate simultaneously, and hence, they are complementary rather than competing theories of rules and their impact.

Examination of the administrative structures of Wikipedia reveals a comparably complex structure of rules, processes, policies, and roles.[1] There are 52 wiki pages in the "Wikipedia Official Policy" category as of May 2012. There are 147 wiki pages categorized as "Wikipedia guidelines," which are organized into seven subcategories. In addition, these do not seem to be sufficient, since there are 107 pending proposals and 441 rejected proposals for guidelines and policies. Likewise, in spite of the fact that bureaucracy and formal organization are regularly (and loudly) disparaged in discussions within Wikipedia, the reality is that Wikipedia and other mass collaboration efforts contain large and complex rule and policy structures which are inextricably integrated into their ongoing activities and practices [42].

Informal Rule Breaking

Rule-making is dependent on the ability to generalize across situations. At the same time, rules may not be sufficient for supporting organizational goal attainment because they are too general; they may not account for all situations requiring procedures or particular types of behavior. Individuals faced with general rules often find that even in the best cases, they match the needs of the situation imperfectly, while in the worst ones, they lead to nonsensical, dysfunctional outcomes [26]. Overly general rules or polices fail because they do not account for relevant aspects of the situation [14]. If rules fail to match the context of use, they can transform too rigidly into absolutes [41] and can lead to stagnation and decline [18].

In response to mismatches between formal rules and specific contexts, organizations may create new rules or modify existing rules in order to record exceptions and alternatives to the existing policies and procedures [49]. Yet, each of these solutions leads to greater complexity of the rule set, and neither fully eliminates the problem of a completely accurate policy system. Rules that are too specific overwhelm the capacity of individuals and groups to apply them without providing the intended efficiency and consistency benefits. Creating more and more rules cannot address all contexts of use. In the worst case, the complexity of the rule system itself can impose significant costs [40].

Evidence of both expansion of the policy system and greater internal complexity of each policy is seen in Wikipedia where the rule set has grown from the 12 policies in 2002 to the 50 plus policies in 2012. As the rule set has grown, so too have the texts of the rules themselves. Biographies of living persons, for instance, grew from its first version of 12 words to the current 5289 words [1]; from one sentence to 24 sentences with greatly expanded notes and supporting materials.

Many organizations turn to a third solution for balancing generalization and specific application of rules: tolerance of 'appropriate' rule breaking. Scholars have developed many euphemisms for unofficial yet permitted rule violations, indicating their prevalence in traditional organizations: "substantive rationality" [46], "indulgency pattern" [22], "service orientation" as opposed to "procedural orientation" [19], "toleration of illicit practices" [7], "latent particularism" [13], "discretion" [21], and "management by exception" [30]. In each case, the term refers to the ability of a bureaucracy to tolerate decisions by individuals to respond to a given situation in a way that is not consistent with the prescriptions of the formal policies and procedures – and in doing so, to allow for better outcomes and organizational learning [14] without jeopardizing the integrity of the system as a whole.

However, workarounds and exceptions may be enacted with either the goals of the organization or the goals of the individual in mind. Sometimes rule exceptions really are rule violations, disregarding both the 'letter' and the 'spirit' of the policies and as a result potentially harming the institution. They can include intentional errors and manipulations of data, as well as other forms of corruption [16, 37]. Rule violations can lead to "higher turnover, lower job satisfaction, lower trust, [and] weaker performance" [45, 49]. Other times, individuals feel justified in breaking rules in support of their own goals without malicious intent. In most cases, these actions are not criminal in nature, but threaten the organization's collective goals nonetheless.

Officially Sanctioned Rule Breaking

The question is, therefore, how policies within a mass collaboration system can be managed to be general enough to be widely applicable, specific enough to address the context of use, and still keep the overall goal attainment effort as the focus. Healthy organizations try to avoid rule inaccuracy and mismatch and workarounds by adjusting rules constantly over time, but this organizational learning is time-consuming and can be difficult to accomplish within a mass collaboration system.

Officially Sanctioned Rule Breaking (OSRB) is an explicit statement on the part of the organization that individuals may disregard one or more of the written policies [7, 13, 19, 22, 46]. By formally encouraging individuals to reconsider the rule set in light of the organization's goals, OSRB has the potential to protect the organization, enable greater efficiency, and bridge the inevitable gaps between the written rules and the context of the moment.

[1] We do not distinguish between rules and policies, particularly since Wikipedia itself uses the word "rule" to refer to policy in IAR. Wikipedia does distinguish between policies and guidelines: "Our policies are considered standards that should be followed, whereas our guidelines are more advisory in nature."

Within Wikipedia rule breaking appears to be officially and openly sanctioned in the Ignore all rules (IAR) policy which states: "If a rule prevents you from improving or maintaining Wikipedia, ignore it" [55]. Not only is rule breaking tolerated, it is formally sanctioned within the Wikipedia policy system and prominently highlighted in the community. IAR is in Wikipedia's central area reserved for materials focused on Wikipedia itself (i.e., Wikipedia namespace), is listed on the Wikipedia List of Policies page above all the other policies outside of the policy categories, and is included in the Wikipedia policy template (i.e., a predetermined box of links that can be added to a page to provide streamlined access to critical policies and rules).

Although related to rule-specific exceptions, IAR is more general and appears to be less constrained. However, a careful reading of it shows that it describes a particular class of situations in rules that can be broken acceptably, that is, only in cases where following the rules would harm or hinder the organization. By keeping the editor's focus on the goals of the organization, IAR ensures that the rule breaking will not create harmfully low morale or behavioral problems and will, in fact, support organizational learning and positive approaches to decision-making. Although the policy of IAR itself does not require that an editor indicate which policy is being ignored, in many situations this information is provided. This suggests that IAR, which might appear to be universal permission to break all rules all the time, is in fact formal acceptance of the need for some rules to be violated under some conditions. Furthermore, the IAR policy does not grow in complexity, remaining general and overarching. While its size does fluctuate over time, it returns always to its concise form, and it has not morphed into a ream of attendant essays or guidelines. This persistence suggests a collective will to bound complexity and specificity and to maintain the policy's strong OSRB status.

Deliberation is a mechanism by which many open mass collaboration efforts determine how the rules apply to a situation. In Wikipedia deliberations, editors are encouraged to cite the policies that support their proposals or votes (e.g., Figure 1). For example, the Articles for Deletion (AfD) policy states, "AfDs are a place for rational discussion of whether an article is able to meet Wikipedia's article guidelines and policies," suggesting that the policy set is the metric against which proposed actions are to be judged.

If IAR is functioning as OSRB in Wikipedia, we predict that when it is cited within a deliberation in support of a particular outcome, that outcome will be more likely to occur. If deliberations about the application of rules encounter problems trying to apply the rules because they are underspecified or contain contradictions, an organization faces potential paralysis. It is in those cases that OSRB will come into play in conjunction with the idea that the problem will be resolved in a way that will break one or several rules in order to permit the desired outcome. If the use of IAR significantly affects the outcome of a meaningful decision within Wikipedia (i.e., IAR citation increases the likelihood of a particular decision arising from the deliberation), it suggests that OSRB is a functional, acceptable part of the governance system.

Hypothesis 1: Explicit use of officially sanctioned rule breaking in favor of an outcome within a deliberation increases the likelihood of that outcome.

Another way that OSRB might contribute to the functioning of the rule system in an open mass collaboration is by providing a mechanism to resolve the problems that arise from unanticipated interaction of multiple rules and the details of a particular context. If IAR is functioning as OSRB it must be the case that citation of it in a deliberation has some impact on the resulting decisions (Hypothesis 1). It should also be the case that IAR has a greater likelihood of impacting these outcomes when the difficulty of reconciling the rule system and the immediate situation is greater. Therefore, it is expected that IAR will have a greater effect on deliberation outcomes when the proposal that started the deliberation cites multiple policies.

Hypothesis 2: Explicit use of officially sanctioned rule breaking in favor of an outcome within a deliberation increases the likelihood of that outcome more when the proposal cites more than one policy.

Additionally, if the policy cited in the proposal for a deliberation matches the policy cited in conjunction with IAR, it indicates that there is some agreement within the community about which policy is potentially relevant to the context of the moment. However, since the policy cited in the initiating proposal is the one being ignored when IAR is cited in the deliberation, it is expected that IAR will increase the likelihood of the outcome going against the

- Whether or not its fame allows us to, WP:IGNORE certainly does. I'm trying to maintain the quality of WP by defending viable articles from someone who wants to eliminate them for no particular reason. I'm in no way intending to make this a personal attack, but what do you so severely hate about "Family Guy"? Why not nominate every single "Simpsons" episode, every single "Futurama" episode, List of I Love Lucy episodes, the section of The Office (UK TV series) dealing with episode summaries... need I go on? If we deleted these articles, we would literally have to delete thousands of articles. And there's no reason for that just because you have some vendetta. You make the point that you would never find episode guides in an Encyclopedia Britannica, but you know what? That's why the first thing listed in WP:NOT is that WP is not paper. -- Kicking222 23:40, 31 May 2006 (UTC)

Figure 1 – Excerpt from a Deliberation That Contains Reference to IAR Policy

proposal. Thus, deliberations with a match between the policy cited in the proposal for the deliberation and the policy cited in tandem with IAR are more likely to conclude with a decision or action that is counter to the initiating proposal.

Hypothesis 3: Explicit use of officially sanctioned rule breaking to override the proposal's policy citation reduces the proposal's likelihood of success.

The Wikipedia policy set is organized into seven categories: Content, Conduct, Deletion, Enforcement, Legal, Procedural and Other. If the category of the policy cited in tandem with IAR matches the category of the policy cited in tandem with the proposal for the deliberation, there is evidence that the policy set is inadequate at addressing the given situation and potentially even contains conflicting guidelines. Thus, the citation of IAR will further impact the outcome of the deliberation, or increase the likelihood of a keep outcome as in H3.

Hypothesis 4: Explicit use of officially sanctioned rule breaking in the same policy domain as the proposal's negates the proposal's success.

Beyond predicting the power of IAR to alter outcomes, OSRB also suggests that the effects of IAR will change as the rules and the rule system develop. Specifically, as the rule system develops and more specific rules are created, the impact of a general rule breaking provision will increase as it is needed to account for the nuances not covered in the newly generated rules. Thus, IAR is needed to fend off these new rules, and invoking it is more likely to affect outcomes. Hence, we predict that citing IAR when there are more rules will be more likely to lead to an outcome in line with the IAR-citing argument. In other words, IAR's use for rule breaking will be more effective when there are more rules in the Wikipedia policy set.

Hypothesis 5: Explicit use of officially sanctioned rule breaking in favor of an outcome within a deliberation when there are more rules in the rule system increases the likelihood of that outcome.

As the sophistication of the policy set and policy making process increases, the "damage" done by ignoring the rules seems to increase. This perspective is reflected in many calls for elimination of IAR. Furthermore, attempts to eliminate or limit IAR have been justified with arguments stating "policies can be changed" and "rules can be changed." However, IAR should be more necessary (and hence more effective), the more complex the rules. As the number of noted exceptions and explicitly defined details and particulars increases, so too do the chances that the complexity might interfere with efficient execution of desirable activities. An increase of the cognitive burden on those trying to apply the rules leads to an increased acceptance of OSRB as a mechanism for avoiding cognitive burden and the greater use of IAR in deliberations. As a result, the impact of invoking IAR will increase the greater the complexity of the rules.

Hypothesis 6: Explicit use of officially sanctioned rule breaking in favor of an outcome within a deliberation when there is greater rule system complexity increases the likelihood of that outcome.

METHODOLOGY AND CONTEXT

Rules are important in Wikipedia in many situations and contexts. Some rules govern group decision-making and how to assess consensus and guide group deliberation. Others, such as the Civility policy, set standards for behavior that might be left more implicit in a face-to-face community. One area that is critical to the ongoing success, survival, identity, and effectiveness of Wikipedia as a knowledge source and a community is the Articles for Deletion (AfD) policy. The AfD process in Wikipedia is important because it structures debate about whether an article merits inclusion in the encyclopedia. The outcome of AfD debates, retention or deletion of articles, determines whether or not materials are included in the encyclopedia. Wikipedia policy explicitly lays out the procedure for article deletion [54]. Editors volunteer articles for deletion, but it is only under unusual circumstances that anyone other than an administrator can actually remove an article. AfD proposals include specific reasons, such as the violation of a particular Wikipedia policy, as to why a page is being proposed for deletion. Interested parties, like the original authors of the page, are often alerted about the AfD action. Deliberation about the reasonableness of the deletion proposals ensues, with individuals proposing and advocating alternative strategies for dealing with the article (e.g., keep, delete, merge, etc.). After seven days for discussion, the AfD is closed by an administrator who decides the outcome, not strictly on the basis of vote counts, but based on his or her assessment of consensus.

Inconclusive debate leads, by default, to keeping the article. The AfD proposals are quite active; the number of articles recommended for deletion varies, but averages between 80 and 90 per day. Debate about each article also varies widely, from the open-and-shut cases with few remarks and solid consensus to those provoking wide-ranging, highly emotional, and inconclusive discussions.

The AfD deliberations are a place where many policies come into play. Proposals indicate specific reasons for deleting an article. During AfD debates, editors suggest ways of handling each case and cite policies as rationales for their recommendations. As such, AfD is a context in which issues and questions about what policies mean and how they should be applied arise. Editors may also advocate disregarding an existing policy, often citing the IAR policy as a rationale. The IAR policy is a tool that can be used to argue for or against a position. So, AfD is expected to be a place where OSRB regularly arises as the Wikipedia community works to reconcile the general intent of its policies with the details of particular applications. It is in this context, the AfD process, that we will test the proposed hypotheses.

Sample

To construct a suitable dataset, disproportionate stratified random sampling was used. This method is "appropriate whenever an important subpopulation is likely to be underrepresented in a simple random sample or in a stratified random sample" [5]. While AfD proposals are fairly common, explicit citations of the Ignore all rules Policy appear in only a subset of the AfD proposals. AfDs with explicit citations of the IAR policy are an important subpopulation for this study, and a disproportionate number of these debates are included in the final sample to reflect this.

Two strata were created: 1.) AfD proposals that explicitly cited the IAR policy and 2.) AfD proposals that did not explicitly cite the IAR policy. The AfD proposals for the first stratum, or those explicitly citing IAR, were collected from a list of all AfD discussions that cited IAR between April 2005 and October 2008 downloaded from Wikipedia. This resulted in a list of 295 AfD discussions that cited the IAR policy.

The AfD proposals for the second stratum, or those that did not explicitly cite IAR, included all AfD proposals between April 2005 and October 2008 not included in the first stratum. To allow for controlled comparison of IAR-citing AfDs and non-IAR-citing AfDs, a matched sample of AfD discussions not citing IAR was constructed. For each IAR-citing AfD discussion in the first stratum, a non-IAR citing AfD proposal from the second stratum was randomly selected from the same date. The samples were constructed using this procedure to control for possible impacts of changes in AfD debate participants, large-scale policy changes, and other factors that might have changed as Wikipedia evolved. The result of this procedure was a total sample of 588 AfD deliberations comprised of 16,000 utterances by Wikipedia editors.

Data and Measures

The raw data downloaded from Wikipedia consisted of archived AfD deliberations, all policy documents, and their histories. Each AfD deliberation included the initial proposal, individual recommendations/votes for strategies for handling the article, and the conclusion reached by the closing administrator. The archived policy documents and their histories included all policies created in Wikipedia, their prior versions, and the date of the first appearance of the policy. This raw data, which was gathered for all of the sampled AfD discussions, served as the foundation for the analysis dataset.

The analysis dataset, which contains measures used to operationalize the key constructs in each of the hypotheses, was constructed manually based on the raw data. *Deliberation Outcome,* the dependent variable, was measured by recording the outcome of the AfD deliberation (0=delete, 1=keep). The outcome of the AfD deliberation is determined at the end of the debate period by an administrator based on his or her view of the consensus and it is explicitly recorded at the top of the AfD deliberation archive. AfD deliberations that did not result in a clear delete or keep consensus or where the IAR policy was not cited in a delete or keep vote (33 cases) were dropped, leaving a dataset of 555 AfD deliberations in the analysis dataset.

Measure Name	*Definition*	*H 1*	*H 2*	*H 3*	*H 4*	*H 5*	*H 6*
Outcome	Outcome of the discussion (0 = article deleted, 1 = article kept)	D	D	D	D	D	D
Total Delete Votes	Total number of delete votes in the AfD	I	I	I	I	I	I
Total Keep Votes	Total number of keep votes in the AfD	I	I	I	I	I	I
Delete Votes with IAR	Total number of delete votes that cite the IAR policy in the AfD	I				I	I
Keep Votes with IAR	Total number of keep votes that cite the IAR policy in the AfD	I	I	I	I	I	I
Multiple Policy Citations	No. of policy cites in the AfD proposal (1=>1 cite.; 0=1 or 0 cite.)		I				
Policy Match	Comparison of policy cited in AfD proposal and IAR citation (1=the same policy cited in both; 0=different policies cited in each)			I			
Policy Category Match	Comparison of policy category cited in AfD proposal and IAR citation (1=policies from the same category were cited in both;				I		

	0=policies from different categories were cited in each)						
Rule System Size	Number of policies in the rule structure					I	
Rules System Complexity	Word count of policies in the rule structure						I
Date of the AfD	Control – date the AfD started	C	C	C	C	C	C
Number of Delete Votes	Control – Number of delete votes in the AfD	C	C	C	C	C	C
Number of Keep Votes	Control – Number of keep votes in the AfD	C	C	C	C	C	C

Table 1: Measures

Variable	*Model 1 (controls)*	*Model 2 (H1)*	*Model 3 (H2)*	*Model 4 (H3)*	*Model 5 (H4)*	*Model 6 (H5)*	*Model 7 (H6)*
Date of AfD	0.006 (0.000)	-0.016 (0.000)	-0.053 (0.000)	-0.091† (0.000)	-2.090* (0.000)	0.004 (0.000)	0.004 (0.000)
Number of Delete Votes	-0.535** (0.002)	-0.524** (0.002)	-0.561** (0.003)	-0.552** (0.003)	-0.553** (0.003)	-0.520** (0.002)	-0.520** (0.002)
Number of Keep Votes	0.752** (0.002)	0.682** (0.002)	0.662** (0.002)	0.667** (0.002)	0.676** (0.002)	0.682** (0.002)	0.682** (0.002)
IAR Delete		0.040 (0.036)				0.744* (0.418)	1.226* (0.664)
IAR Keep		0.173** (0.037)	0.153** (0.052)	0.248** (0.061)	0.294** (0.067)	0.895 (0.602)	1.315** (0.932)
Multiple Policy Citations			-0.113* (0.068)				
IAR Keep X Multiple Policy Citations			0.105† (0.099)				
Policy Match				0.080 (0.067)			
IAR Keep X Policy Match				-0.100 (0.090)			
Policy Category Match					0.121† (0.063)		
IAR Keep X Policy Category Match					-0.164* (0.088)		
Number of Policies						0.024 (0.008)	
IAR Delete X Number of Policies						-0.705† (0.011)	
IAR Keep X Number of Policies						-0.729 (0.015)	
Number of Policy Words							0.027 (0.000)
IAR Delete X Number of Policy Words							-1.186* (0.000)
IAR Keep X Number of Policy Words							-1.149 (0.000)
R^2	0.493	0.513	0.523	0.514	0.519	0.515	0.515
**: p<0.01 *: p<0.05 †: p<0.10 DV: Deliberation Outcome	F(3, 551) = 180.414 (p<0.000)	F (5, 549) = 117.927 (p<0.000)	F (5, 259) = 49.352 (p<0.000)	F (6, 243) = 44.891 (p<0.000)	F (6, 243) = 45.845 (p<0.000)	F(8, 546) = 74.559 (p<0.000)	F (8, 546) = 74.665 (p<0.000)

Table 2. IAR Citation, Policy Citation, and AfD Deliberation Outcomes

Instances of OSRB, or *Rule Breaking*, were measured by noting the citation of the IAR policy in each AfD deliberation. The IAR policy can be cited in either a vote for deleting the article (IAR Delete) or a vote for keeping the article (IAR Keep). *IAR Delete* records when the IAR policy was cited in favor of deleting an article (1=IAR cited in favor of delete, 0=IAR cited in favor of not deleting), and *IAR Keep* was used to record when the IAR policy was cited in favor of keeping the article (1=IAR cited in favor of keep, 0=IAR cited in favor of not keeping). In cases where IAR was not cited at all, both IAR Delete and IAR Keep were set to 0. The *Multiple Policy Citations* measure indicates whether multiple policy citations were present in the AfD proposal (1=two or more policy citations in the AfD proposal, 0=less than two policy citations in the AfD proposal).

In AfDs with a citation of IAR, policies cited alongside it and policies cited in the proposal of the AfD were noted. These two values were used to determine whether there was a *Policy Match* (1=the same policy was cited with IAR and in the AfD proposal, 0=different policies were cited with IAR and in the AfD proposal). Further, the category to which each of these policies belonged was noted and these two categories were analyzed to determine *Policy Category Match* (1= policies from the same category were cited with IAR and in the AfD proposal, 0=policies from difference categories were cited with IAR and in the AfD proposal).

Rule System Size was captured by counting the number of policies. The number of policies was determined by counting how many policies were in existence in Wikipedia on the date each AfD deliberation began. *Rule System Complexity* is measured with the word count of all of the policies. The word count of all of the policies was determined by obtaining the word count of each policy and summing the word count of the policies that existed on the date each AfD deliberation began.

Other factors may affect the outcome of an AfD deliberation. To control for these, the following variables were collected in addition to those used to test the hypotheses: the date the AfD deliberation begins (*Date of AfD*), the number of delete votes cast during the deliberation (*Number of Delete Votes*), and the number of keep votes cast during the deliberation (*Number of Keep Votes*).

Analysis and Results

Linear probability models were used to test for the hypothesized relationships in the collected data. While logit and probit models are more commonly used when the dependent variable is dichotomous, linear probability models were chosen for this study due to issues and problems [3, 28] associated with interpretation of interaction effects in logic and probit models. All hypotheses involved interpretation of interaction effects. Linear probability models avoid the problems put forth by the logit and probit models because only linear terms are included in the interactions. All models were estimated using OLS regression in SPSS v20. For all of the models reported, the variance inflation factors (VIFs) are low and multicollinearity was not an issue.

Models testing Hypotheses 1, 2, 3, and 4 are presented in Table 2, with models 1 and 2 using the full dataset, model 3 using all IAR-citing AfDs, and models 4 and 5 using all IAR-citing AfDs that also cited another policy. Model 3 only used the data regarding IAR-citing AfDs because it is examining the role of no or few vs. multiple policy citations in an IAR-citing AfD. Models 4 and 5 only use a subset of IAR-citing AfDs because they examine only those AfDs that cite other policies. Model 1 is the baseline model and included the controls: Date of the AfD, Number of Delete Votes, and Number of Keep Votes. Model 2 included the baseline model with independent variables IAR Delete and IAR Keep. Models testing Hypotheses 5 and 6 are presented in Table 2, with both models based on the full dataset.

H1 states that explicitly using OSRB in favor of an outcome within a deliberation increases the likelihood of that outcome, that is, citing IAR in a vote will increase the likelihood of the AfD resulting in that vote's recommended outcome. Hence, it is expected that an AfD deliberation containing a delete vote that cites IAR will be more likely to result in the article being deleted and an AfD that includes a keep vote that cites IAR will be more likely to result in the article being kept. To test this hypothesis, we ran Model 2 shown in Table 2. H1 was supported (Table 2: Model 2, $\beta=0.173$, $p<0.01$) for the IAR Keep measure. This indicates that an AfD is significantly more likely to result in a keep outcome if an editor cites IAR in a vote for keep. However, the relationship between the presence of an IAR-citing delete vote in the AfD discussion and a deletion outcome is not statistically significant. That is, an AfD is not more likely to result in a delete outcome if an editor cites IAR in favor of a delete recommendation. H2 states that explicitly using OSRB will have a greater effect on the deliberation outcome when the initiating proposal relies on the policy system. In other words, citing IAR in a vote when the AfD proposal cites multiple policies will have a greater impact on the likelihood of the AfD resulting in that vote's recommended outcome. Model 3 examines this hypothesis. The results support H2 with the marginally significant IAR Keep and Multiple Policy Citations interaction measure (Table 2: Model 3, $\beta=0.105$, $p<0.10$). This indicates that an AfD deliberation is significantly more likely to result in a keep outcome if an editor cites IAR and the AfD proposal cites multiple policies.

H3 states that explicitly using OSRB when citing a policy that is also cited in the deliberation-initiating proposal increases the likelihood of that outcome. To examine this hypothesis, we ran Model 4. Neither the main effect for Policy Match nor the interaction of Policy Match and IAR citation was significant. Hence, H3 was not supported. H4 states that explicitly using OSRB with a policy category citation that is also cited in the deliberation initiating proposal increases the likelihood of that outcome. To examine this, Model 5 was run. The results do not support H4. Unexpectedly, the interaction between IAR Keep and Policy Category Match is significant but negative. (Table 2: Model 5, β=-0.164, $p<0.05$). This indicates that an AfD deliberation is significantly more likely to result in a delete outcome if an editor cites IAR in a keep vote with a policy in a category that matches the policy category cited in the initiating AfD proposal.

H5 predicts that the explicit use of OSRB in favor of an outcome within a deliberation will have a greater impact on the deliberation outcome when there are more rules in the rule system. Based on the results, H5 is supported for delete votes with IAR citations (Table 2: Model 6, β= -0.705, $p<0.10$). This indicates that citing IAR in a delete vote is significantly more likely to result in a delete outcome when more policies are present in the overall rule system.

H6 predicts that the explicit use of OSRB in favor of an outcome within a deliberation will have greater impact on the likelihood of that outcome when the overall rule system complexity is higher. Based on the results, H6 is supported for delete votes with IAR citations (Table 2: Model 7, β= -1.186, $p<0.05$). This indicates that an AfD deliberation is significantly more likely to result in a delete outcome if an editor cites IAR in a delete vote when the rule system is more complex.

DISCUSSION

Open mass collaboration systems, such as Wikipedia, rely on rule and policy systems. Policies are focused on the survival of the collaborative effort as a whole as mass collaboration systems seek to aggregate individual efforts to create and maintain complex artifacts [34]. Scholars and practitioners interested in mass collaboration systems must understand how to develop and manage rule systems which can maintain a balance between the generalized abstractions and the details of particular contexts.

In this paper, we argue that Officially Sanctioned Rule Breaking can be a meaningful part of a successful mass collaboration rule system. Drawing on existing theories of rules, we hypothesized that OSRB could enable mass collaboration systems to achieve collective goals of creating a common artifact even when its rules and policies fail to adequately address the needs of the particular situation. We then tested six hypotheses about the impact of OSRB with data regarding the use and impact of the Ignore all rules (IAR) policy in Wikipedia's Articles for Deletion (AfD) deliberations. The results demonstrate that there is a relationship between whether or not officially sanctioned rule breaking occurs and the outcome of a deliberation. In particular, there is a relationship between whether the Ignore all rules policy is cited and the outcome of an Article for Deletion decision in Wikipedia. Referencing the IAR policy as a basis for keeping an article even though keeping it breaks established rules increases the likelihood of an article being kept. The results of the analyses suggest that Wikipedia has been able to adopt a form of officially sanctioned rule breaking as a positive, functional governance mechanism.

Hypotheses 2, 3, and 4 examined different conditions under which OSRB logic suggests that IAR should have greater impact on deliberation outcomes. H2 and H4 were supported, implying that IAR can be thought of as an instantiation of OSRB. The results indicate that OSRB provides individuals a greater ability to influence deliberation outcomes in situations where application of the rules is more complex and problematic. This reflects the nature of IAR as a collaborative workaround. Examination of the different conditions demonstrates that citation of IAR is not equally influential in all situations, but instead is most influential when the there is sufficient complexity in rule application and some agreement about the category of rules that might be relevant (and hence might be ignored).

However, and unexpectedly, the interaction between a citation of IAR in a vote to keep an article and a policy citation in a category that matches that of the proposal to delete the article correlates significantly with the deletion of the article. This finding suggests that in cases in deliberations to delete articles where an editor tries to use OSRB to undermine the proposal for deletion's rationale, the community prevents the rules from being broken unreasonably and where potential damage to the organization might occur. For example, if a proposal for deletion cited the Notability guideline in arguing that a subject of an article is not sufficiently notable for inclusion in an encyclopedia, an editor who would like to have the article kept, but is unable to produce adequate support to validate an acceptable degree of notability, is likely to vote to keep the article in violation of Notability. The Wikipedia community is equally likely to respond negatively to this incitement to break this rule, to ensure that only articles that meet encyclopedia standards will be retained.

Hypotheses 5 and 6 examined the relative impact of IAR as the size and complexity of the overall policy system changes. As expected by OSRB logic, citation of IAR had greater impact on deliberation outcomes when the rule system was larger and more complex.

Taken together, these results suggest that, while it may not be the only function of IAR, officially sanctioned rule breaking is a meaningful aspect of what this distinctive policy adds to the Wikipedia policy system. Referencing IAR in AfD deliberations allows individuals to influence the outcomes of those deliberations, particularly when many rules are potentially applicable and the overall rule system is larger and more complex. Given the challenges that any mass collaboration is likely to face with aligning its rule system to the particulars of the context of use, these results suggest that IAR-like policies which instantiate OSRB may be an effective way to harness the "wisdom of the crowd" to apply and maintain a rule system.

Beyond suggesting that mass collaboration system designers consider OSRB as a governance mechanism, the findings suggest that IAR may also be useful as an indicator of where the rule system fails to address the needs of particular situations. The conditions described in H2 and H4 (citation of multiple policies in an AfD proposal with IAR and a match between the category of the policy cited with IAR and the category of the policy cited in the AfD proposal) suggest that the policies cited in conjunction with the use of IAR are potential indicators of where participants in the deliberation believe the mismatch between the rule system and particular context lies. Additional study is needed to determine if and when mass collaboration participants recognize these indicators of the potential need to change formal policies. However, the OSRB logic developed here suggests that the use of OSRB policies, such as IAR, may be a useful way to make explicit the beliefs that participants hold about the relevance and appropriateness of existing rules and policies.

While the hypotheses correctly predicted that IAR would affect the deliberation outcomes, they were only partially supported. The reported results found that when the IAR policy is cited in a vote for keep, the article is significantly more likely to be kept, but when the IAR policy is cited in a vote for delete, the article is not significantly more likely to be deleted. While on the surface this partial support might be seen as casting doubt on the OSRB interpretation of IAR, closer examination of the AfD process suggests otherwise. The AfD process begins when an individual proposes that an article be deleted. While it is not strictly required, the vast majority of AfD proposals cite existing policies to justify why the identified article should be removed from Wikipedia. As such, each AfD proposal can be seen as an attempt by a single individual to apply the rule system of Wikipedia to a particular case. The AfD deliberation is the community's response to that application of the existing written rules. Wikipedians either indicate agreement (by recommending that the article be deleted) or disagreement (by voting that the article be kept). And while the statements of their opinions seem to be an assessment of the article, they are in fact an assessment of the proposed application of the rule system. This interpretation of an AfD deliberation makes clear why IAR/OSRB would have an asymmetrical impact on deliberation outcomes. An individual recommending article deletion is agreeing that the proposed application of the existing rule system is appropriate, and hence the article under consideration should be removed. In this case, the recommended course of action does not contradict the written rules, and hence OSRB is not needed. This is reflected in the lack of a significant impact of IAR on delete outcomes in AfD deliberations. On the other hand, an individual recommending that an article be kept is indicating that the proposed application of the rules in this case is not appropriate. OSRB allows both an individual and the community to make the judgment that the existing written rules are not adequate for a particular case. It is under these conditions that IAR/OSRB is most needed to, and in fact does, allow an individual to influence the deliberation outcomes. Therefore, the "partial" support for the hypothesis is actually further confirmation that, at least within the AfD process, IAR is acting as officially sanctioned rule breaking.

Qualitative examination of the Wikipedia policy system corroborates the results, suggesting that the Ignore all rules policy sets up the concept of formally sanctioned rule breaking as one of the core values of Wikipedia, since, as noted earlier, the Ignore all rules policy has a primary position in the policy list and is one of the Five Pillars (i.e., the standards for Wikipedia's value system). When editors cite IAR to disregard an established policy or to resolve a conflict between a written policy and the needs of a particular situation, they explicitly recognize that certain principles under certain circumstances run counter to the shared goals of the mass collaboration system. Officially sanctioned rule breaking and the IAR policy are meaningful influences on deliberation outcomes. Wikipedia, a successful mass collaboration, also recognizes officially sanctioned rule breaking as important. This further suggests that officially sanctioned rule breaking can be incorporated into and have an impact on mass collaboration systems.

CONCLUSION

Wikipedia has evolved into a successful mass collaboration community with an extensive rule system but with the unusual feature of incorporated officially sanctioned rule breaking, providing adjustments "on the fly" to the policy system to ensure continued support for collective goal attainment in context. Despite fears to the contrary, the presence of OSRB in the form of the IAR policy has not led to the downfall of Wikipedia. Rather, it is a meaningful part of the functioning governance system for a large-scale, open mass collaboration system. While the results of this study cannot conclusively tell us whether OSRB is critical to the success of mass collaboration efforts, they do raise the issue of what might be lost if IAR or some other form of OSRB were absent. Is OSRB essential to the long term functioning of large-scale, open mass collaboration systems? If so, does this mean that these systems are fundamentally incompatible with the control-oriented authority structures found in most traditional organizations? If not, what are the boundary conditions for the effective use of OSRB within mass collaboration efforts? What function might OSRB fulfill in rule systems, particularly in rule system flexibility and adaptability? For researchers and practitioners interested in understanding and modeling mass collaboration efforts, the arguments presented here can serve as a starting point from which we can better understand the interplay of individual choice and formal rule structures in these new technology-enabled organizational forms.

REFERENCES

1. *Wikipedia: Biographies of living persons.* en.wikipedia.org/wiki/Wikipedia:Biographies_of_living_persons
2. Adler, P. S. The sociological ambivalence of bureaucracy: From Weber via Gouldner to Marx. *Organization Science 23*, 1 (2012), 244-266.
3. Ai, C. and Norton, E. C. Interaction terms in logit and probit models. *Economic Letters 80* (2003), 123-129.
4. Anthony, D., Smith, S. W. and Williamson, T. Reputation and reliability in collective goods: The case of the online encylopedia Wikipedia. *Rationality and Society 21*, 3 (2009), 1-24.
5. Bernard, H. R. *Social Research Methods.* SAGE Publications, Thousand Oaks, CA, 2000.
6. Beschastnikh, I., Kriplean, T. and McDonald, D. W. Wikipedia self-governance in action: Motivating the policy lens. In *Proc. 2008 AAAI Int'l Conf. Weblogs and Social Media (ICWSM '08)* (2008).
7. Blau, P. M. *The dynamics of bureaucracy: A study of interpersonal relations in two government agencies.* University of Chicago Press, Chicago, IL, 1963.
8. Breton, A. and Wintrobe, R. *The logic of bureaucratic conduct.* Cambridge University Press, New York, 1982.
9. Bryant, S. L., Forte, A. and Bruckman, A. Becoming Wikipedian: Transformation of participation in a collaborative online encyclopedia. *GROUP '05*, ACM Press (2005), 1-10.
10. Burke, M. and Kraut, R. *Mopping up: Modeling Wikipedia promotion decisions. CSCW '08,* ACM Press (2008), 27-36.
11. Butler, B., Joyce, E. and Pike, J. *Don't look now, but we've created a bureaucracy: The nature and roles of policies and rules in Wikipedia. CHI '08.* ACM Press (2008), 1101-1110.
12. Cyert, R. and March, J. *Behavioral theory of the firm.* Blackwell, Oxford, 1963.
13. Danet, B. *'Giving the underdog a break': Latent particularism among customs officials.* Basic Books, New York, 1973.
14. Desai, V. M. Rule violations and organizational search: A review and extension. *International Journal of Management Reviews 12*, 2 (2010), 184-200.
15. Fallis, D. Toward an epistemology of Wikipedia. *Journal of the American Society of Information Science 59* (2008), 1662-1674.
16. Ferneley, E. H. and Sobreperez, P. Resist, comply or workaround? An examination of different facets of user engagement with information systems. *European Journal of Information Systems 15* (2006), 345-356.
17. Forte, A. and Bruckman, A. Why do people write for Wikipedia? Incentives to contribute to open-content publishing. *Workshop on Sustaining Community: The Role and Design of Incentive Mechanisms in Online Systems, ACM Group* (2005).
18. Foster, J. L. and Jones, J. H. Rule orientation and bureaucratic reform. *American Journal of Political Science 22*, 2 (1978), 348-363.
19. Francis, R. G. and Stone, R. C. *Service and procedure in bureaucracy: A case study.* University of Minnesota Press, Minneapolis, 1956.
20. Frishauf, P. Are traditional peer-reviewed medical articles obsolete? A pitch for the Wikipedia oncept. *Medscape General Medicine 8*, 1 (2006), 5.
21. Goldfeld, S. M. Rules, discretion, and reality. *American Economic Review 72*, 2 (1982), 361-366.
22. Gouldner, A. W. *Patterns of industrial bureaucracy.* Free Press, Glencoe, IL, 1954.
23. Hall, R. H. The concept of bureaucracy: An empirical assessment. *American Journal of Sociology 69*, 1 (1963), 32-40.
24. Hammond, T. H. and Miller, G. J. A social choice perspective on expertise and authority in bureaucracy. *American Journal of Political Science 29*, 1 (1985), 1-28.
25. Heimer, C. A. Cases and biographies: An essay on routinization and the nature of comparison. *Annual Review of Sociology 27* (2001), 47-76.
26. Heller, J. *Catch-22.* Simon & Schuster, New York, NY, 1961.
27. Hendry, A. Who's behind Wikipedia? *ComputerWorld* (February 6, 2008). www.computerworld.com.au/article/205180/who_behind_wikipedia/
28. Hoetker, G. The use of Logit and Probit Models in strategic management research: Critical issues. *Strategic Management Journal 28* (2007), 331-343.
29. Hof, R. Wikipedia: Maybe it's Democratic after all. *BusinessWeek*, (September 4, 2006). www.businessweek.com/the_thread/techbeat/archives/2006/09/lately_some_ske.html
30. Howell, J. M. and Hall-Merenda, K. E. The ties that bind: The impact of leader-member exchange, transformational and transactional leadership, and distance on predicting follower performance. *Journal of Applied Psychology 84*, 5 (1999), 680-694.
31. Kallinikos, J. The social foundations of the bureaucratic order. *Organization 11*, 1 (2004), 13-36.
32. Karami, N. and Iijima, J. A logical approach for impementing dynamic business rules. *Contemporary Management Research 6*, 1 (2010), 29-52.
33. Kellogg, K. C., Orlikowski, W. J. and Yates, J. Life in the trading zone: Structuring coordination across boundaries in postbureaucratic organizations. *Organization Science 17*, 1 (2006), 22-44.
34. Kim, A. J. *Community building on the Web: Secret strategies for successful online communities.* Peachpit Press, Berkeley, CA, 2000.
35. Kittur, A., Suh, B., Pendleton, B. A. and Chi, E. He says, she says: Conflict and coordination in Wikipedia. In *Proc. of CHI '07,* ACM Press, 453-462.

36. Kriplean, T., Beschastnikh, I., McDonald, D. W. and Golder, S. A. *Community, consensus, coercion, control: CS*W or how policy mediates mass participation. GROUP* 2007, ACM Press (2007), 167-176.
37. Lehman, D. W. and Ramanujam, R. Selectivity in organizational rule violations. *Academy of Management 34*, 4 (2009), 643-657.
38. Loubser, M. and den Besten, M. *Wikipedia Admins and Templates: The organizational capabilities of a peer production effort*. (2008). Available at SSRN: http//ssrn.com/abstract=1116171
39. March, J. *Decisions and organizations*. Basil Blackwell, Oxford, 1988.
40. March, J. G., Schulz, M. and Zhou, X. *The Dynamics of rules: Change in written organizational codes*. Stanford University Press, Stanford, CA, 2000.
41. Merton, R. Bureaucratic structure and personality. *Social Forces 18* (1940), 560-568.
42. O'Mahony, S. and Ferraro, F. The emergence of governance in an open source community. *Academy of Management Journal 50*, 5 (2007), 1079-1106.
43. Pentland, B. T. and Rueter, H. H. Organizational routines as grammars of action. *Administrative Science Quarterly 39* (1994), 484-510.
44. Pfaff, C. and Hasan, H. *Democratising organisational knowledge: The potential of the corporate Wiki. ICIS 2007 Proc.* (2007). Paper 144.
45. Robinson, S. and Bennett, R. Workplace deviance: Its definition, its manifestations and its causes. *Research on Negotiations in Organizations 6* (1997), 3-27.
46. Rothschild-Whitt, J. The collectivist organization: An alternative to rational-bureaucratic models. *American Sociological Review 44*, (1979): 509-527.
47. Shirky, C. *Here comes everybody: The power of organizing without organizations*. Penguin, New York, 2008.
48. Tapscott, D. and Williams, A. D. *Wikinomics: How mass collaboration changes everything*. Portfolio, New York, NY, 2008.
49. Vaughan, D. The dark side of organizations: Mistake, misconduct and disaster. *Annual Review of Sociology 25*, (1999): 271-305.
50. Viégas, F. B., Wattenberg, M., Kriss, J. and van Ham, F. *Talk before you type: Coordination in Wikipedia. HICSS-40* (2007).
51. Weber, M. *Essays in Sociology*. Oxford University Press, New York, 1958.
52. Weber, M. *The theory of social and economic organization*. Free Press, New York, NY, 1964.
53. *Wikipedia*. http://www.wikipedia.org
54. *Wikipedia: Articles for Deletion*. en.wikipedia.org/wiki/Wikipedia:Deletion_policy
55. *Wikipedia: Ignore All Rules*. en.wikipedia.org/wiki/Wikipedia:Ignore_all_rules
56. Zhang, X. M. and Zhu, F. Intrinsic motivation of open content contributors: The case of Wikipedia. *Workshop Info. Sys. and Econ.* (2006).

Designing Collaboration: Comparing Cases Exploring Cultural Probes as Boundary-Negotiating Objects

Megan K. Halpern
Department of Communication
Cornell University
mkh46@cornell.edu

Ingrid Erickson
Department of Library & Information Science
Rutgers University
ime7@rutgerrs.edu

Laura Forlano
Institute of Design
Illinois Institute of Technology
lforlano@id.iit.edu

Geri Gay
Departments of Communication and Information Science
Cornell University
gkg1@cornell.edu

ABSTRACT

This paper examines the use of cultural probes as a method for fostering collaboration within groups of diverse experts working on creative projects. Using two case examples, we show that probes—short, oblique, and at times whimsical sets of activity prompts—have boundary object properties that can jumpstart interdisciplinary and cross-functional exchange. The first case explores how social scientists and designers used a smartphone-based scavenger hunt activity to gather insights for a workshop on organizational innovation. The second case examines how artist/scientist pairs utilized probe-like prompts to develop short performances for an arts festival. Drawing together theoretical views on boundary objects and cultural probes, we suggest that designed experiences such as probes can create opportunities for both boundary work and the establishment of common ground, which is increasingly vital in the highly collaborative contexts that define work today.

Author Keywords

Designing collaboration, boundary work, cultural probes, boundary objects

ACM Classification Keywords

H.5.m. Information interfaces and presentation (e.g., HCI): Miscellaneous

INTRODUCTION

Collaboration among diverse groups of specialists has become the *de facto* way of working in the 21st century. We are in an era where creative projects—that is, projects directed toward making something new for a specific purpose—are key and innovation is highly valued. With an emphasis on making and doing, we are turning increasingly to new forms of organization to inspire and accelerate this creative practice. Groups, teams and virtual organizations, in both formal and informal situations, are working across temporal, cultural, structural and expertise boundaries. In theory, it is expected that such collaborations will benefit from this mixture of expertise, knowledge, and methodological insight. In reality, however, this level of heterogeneity often results in conceptual and social islands that sometimes prove challenging to bridge.

Given both the rise in and challenge of collaboration, it makes sense that we see a parallel interest in understanding how interdisciplinary and cross-functional creative work might be most effectively structured and/or facilitated. Like many organizational experiences, a successful collaboration is a combination of social, psychological, cultural, temporal, and structural considerations [12,14]. Tools, routines, protocols and collaborative environments also help to supply scaffolding for pushing beyond common interpersonal barriers and encouraging interaction. While there is no one magic formula for spurring substantive engagement among a set of diverse individuals, some findings suggest certain approaches are more generative than others [4,19,20].

These insights can be applied in ways that showcase collaboration as a designed experience, one that cannot be strictly controlled but that can nevertheless be channeled purposively via particular structures and/or activities. In this sense, effective or substantive interdisciplinary collaboration can be seen as a multiplex design challenge, to which a spirit of design thinking and experimentation can be readily applied. We have approached the question in such a way and report in this paper how the use of a set of tool-based activities that prompt rapid, lightweight engagement among individuals can be a way of enabling them to bridge their differences and begin building synthesis as a group.

THEORETICAL ORIENTATION

Challenge of Diversity

Diversity within collaborations is positively correlated with the notion that varied inputs will be more effective in surfacing new ideas or identifying potential solutions than information drawn from a more homogenous set of individuals. Being able to see a particular problem or issue from more than one angle or approach increases the likelihood that one of those angles or approaches will yield a

CSCW '13, February 23–27, 2013, San Antonio, Texas, USA.

successful solution. This is the logic that underlies crowdsourcing at a large scale as well as interdisciplinary teamwork on a smaller scale [22,25].

For all of the potential insights and solutions that teams of diverse collaborators promise, interdisciplinary collaboration is often fraught with conflict, much of which stems from epistemological clashes surrounding disciplinary vocabularies, levels of analytical thinking, and valued areas of emphasis. Although greater diversity of disciplinary knowledge within a collaboration can increase the potential for original discoveries, it also increases the functional distances that separate collaborators and reduces their technical overlap, which in turn impairs interpersonal interaction [15]. Disciplines have distinct vocabularies, assumptions, methodologies, and intellectual goals—in short, epistemological frames—that facilitate work within but impede communication, trust, and understanding between disciplines [3,6]. Epistemological frames are defined as implicit beliefs about the nature of knowledge [21], which play an influential and conditioning role on an individual's thinking and learning [13,27], academic persistence [7], and ability to cope with ill-structured problems [16].

Practitioners from different fields often engage in boundary work as a way to protect and defend the legitimacy of their respective epistemological frames. In the sciences, for example, Gieryn writes that boundary work serves to expand or monopolize authority or to protect autonomy [9,10,11]. Since professionalization practices tend to reinforce, rather than lessen epistemological frames, we should expect evidence of some type of boundary work to be present any time that professionals from different disciplines work together.

One way of overcoming the potential debilitations associated with boundary work is to establish common ground collectively as a group. Common ground, in this sense, can be a common vocabulary, a working understanding of means and purposes, or a shared foundation of reciprocal trust and respect [15,23]. These qualities are sometimes established by recognizing shared similarities, i.e. shared gender, culture, theoretical orientation, etc., but more often common ground is the outcome of some effort on the part of the members of the group or team.

A method that often facilitates the establishment of common ground is to use an artifact, concept, or other type of 'object' that is flexible enough in meaning or presentation that it supports the variety of interpretations present within a diverse group. Star and Griesemer [24] famously dubbed these methodological tools 'boundary objects'. According to their conceptualization, true 'boundary objects' possess clear, symbolic representations of meaning, weak global structures, and the ability to support common identification. They are effective in lending themselves to multiple, overlapping interpretations so that actors can see beyond their respective epistemologies to find a kernel of shared understanding. Star and Griesemer's ur-example of a boundary object is a map of the state of California, which administrators, volunteers, and scientists at a museum at the University of California, Berkeley successfully used to outline their differentiated, yet integrated, work.

Following on the work of Star and Griesemer, Lee [17] introduced 'boundary-negotiating objects' to the discourse on collaboration. She acknowledges that robust boundary objects are rarely used to initiate conversations among interdisciplinary or cross-functional collaborators. More often, teams employ less fully formed objects like a spreadsheet or a sketch to initiate engagement with one another. In her work at a large natural history museum, Lee discerns that there are five types of boundary-negotiating objects, which together are used to "record, organize, explore and share ideas; introduce concepts and techniques; create alliances; create a venue for the exchange of information; augment brokering activities; and create shared understanding about specific design problems" [13:403].

In distinction to boundary objects, boundary-negotiating objects allow teammates to quickly take a snapshot of an individual thought and transfer it in a lightweight fashion among the other members of the group. The lightweight character of negotiating objects assists in de-emphasizing their epistemological qualities, while at the same time their malleability encourages alteration and improvement by those with alternate points of view. As such, these objects become mechanisms for destabilizing and pushing against extant boundaries, and in this constant negotiation and re-negotiation groups begin to build a common base of reference. In sum, by offering a way for individuals with multiple epistemological perspectives to come together and begin negotiating the boundaries that separate them, boundary objects and boundary-negotiating objects can be useful in bolstering the integrative potential of interdisciplinary collaborations.

Cultural Probes for Boundary Work

Cultural probes [2,7,8] have been identified by many designers as effective ways to jumpstart ad hoc collaboration—that is, short term or rapid types of engagement. Traditionally, the focus on engagement was on ways of involving users or constituents as part of the design process, as can be seen in the definition by Boehner et al. [2]: probes are "designed objects, physical packets containing open-ended, provocative and oblique tasks to support early participant engagement with the design process" [2:1077]. For example, Gaver's original probes included disposable cameras, maps, and postcards, each of which came with instructions, or prompts, for creative use. Gaver widely documented the use of cultural probes in his research for The EU Presence Project, in which probes were used as a method for designing ways to increase the presence of the elderly in three European cities. Attempting to create an experience with a playful spirit, the design team left probes with groups of elderly participants to complete on their own and return back to the design team. This method had multiple aims in mind: to better understand the wants and needs of this group, to learn about the community, and to elicit a dialogue between themselves as designers and the seniors. Gaver explains, "Trying to establish a role as provocateurs, we shaped the probes as interventions that would affect the elders while eliciting informative responses from them" [7:25].

Since Gaver's work with the elderly communities, there have been many permutations of cultural probes, mainly in the field of human computer interaction. As in the EU project, most implementations of probes are not directly observed, but elicit and gather evidence from constituents on their own time and in their own manner. The purpose of probes has been highly contested over the years, particularly their use as a sort of "discount ethnography" [2,5] in which researchers substitute time spent observing people with time spent analyzing information gleaned from cultural probes. Traditionally, ethnography as a method involves not only qualitative forms of observation, but participation with a community such that the 'emic', or native, perspective is represented completely and holistically. Gaver, and others, explicitly say that probes should not be used as a method for collecting data, but rather as a way to interact with and inspire/be inspired by users.

We suggest that one of the parallel uses for probes is—in tandem with Gaver's spirit of provocation—to spark collaborative work. In this sense, we believe cultural probes can assist in the rapid generation of new boundary objects. We do not suggest that these objects, created quickly, will easily bridge boundaries and create harmonious collaboration, Rather, the collective action of completing the probe provides opportunities to develop the kind of trust and overlapping knowledge and interests usually developed through the collaborative work in which the groups are engaged. The two cases we describe below articulate the way that probes can serve as methods for encouraging positive engagement amongst individuals with different epistemological frameworks. Notably, these probes appear to accomplish this work not by way of their common artifactual nature, but rather for their ability to prompt activities in which multiple perspectives are valuable.

CASE DESCRIPTIONS

The two case studies we showcase here are similar in that they both detail incidents in which it is important for a set of individuals with distinct background, expertise and methodological orientations to work together to accomplish some specified end. The cases differ in the amount of time each group had to work together, the use of the product they were asked to produce, and the context in which their probe-based activity was situated. Our comparison focuses on how the probe was deployed and taken up by participants, with consideration for the differing contexts in which they were deployed.

Case 1: Open Design for Organizational Innovation Workshop

In November 2011, author C organized and led a one-day workshop in Brooklyn, New York in collaboration with a project called *Amplifying Creative Communities,* a Rockefeller Foundation-funded initiative to document and foster urban activism in New York City, which is based at the DESIS Lab at Parsons The New School for Design. The Open Design for Organizational Innovation (ODOI) workshop was organized around the principle that a set of diverse constituents—designers, academics, students, and urban activists, among others—can build on and shape successful community practices by joining forces. Part of the Amplify model is that designers and community leaders co-design new scenarios and service concepts that solve issues pertaining their everyday life in their specific communities by connecting with existing action and networks.

The workshop was attended by over 30 designers and social scientists, the bulk of whom were from the greater New York City area, but also included participants from as far away as Australia and Italy. The goal of the day was to deploy open design methods to assist a long-standing community organization improve their structure, internal and external communication practices, and overall engagement with the community. Open design is a form design practice based on open source methods and creative commons principles whereby ideas are generated to be widely shared and used [1]. In this workshop, designers, non-designers and various other stakeholders were all brought together to encourage interdisciplinary, multi-perspectival dialogue that could seed accessible, available and sharable design ideas for the client organization. The ultimate aim of the ideas generated at the workshop was to improve the organization's capacity to engage the local community.

The agenda for the workshop was centered on a set of hands-on activities. The morning was dedicated to orienting participants to the design task, understanding the client, and developing a sense of the constraints and opportunities for design. In the afternoon, the group broke into four separate teams to brainstorm and prototype ideas focused on the following four themes: Telling Our Story, Staying Connected, Finding and Mobilizing Resources, and Engaging End-Users. Workshop activities were documented by dedicated observers, who took notes, captured photographs, recorded audio and video, and collected the artifacts produced by participants.

Designing the Scavenger Hunt

Gaining an understanding of the context, specifically the neighborhood, in which the community organization did its work was an important first step for workshop participants. As a provocative way of saturating them in this complex situation quickly, we designed an activity that would be introductory in a fun and lightweight way, but also required small teams to produce a collective understanding of key local issues to benefit the larger group in its afternoon activities.

Given their diversity, we knew the workshop participants would represent multiple points of view and would have little existing common ground to draw on as collaborators. As such, we designed an activity that would have the properties of boundary-negotiating object, namely one that would allow teammates to record and share ideas, showcase individual perspectives, and build social bonds with one another. Through this activity, we hypothesized that groups would create a common base of knowledge that would also act as common ground for their subsequent integrative collaboration. The exercise was also intended to be easy enough so that anyone could participate.

The activity we ultimately decided on was a cultural probe fashioned as a scavenger hunt. Our initial impulse had been to allow individuals a block of time for unbounded ethnographic observation, but we elected to use a group scavenger hunt activity instead because of the flexible, but constrained, directions it provided for the participants.

To put a focus on the contextual factors of the client organization, we decided to ask participants to photograph aspects of the neighborhood. To orient them toward the organization during this exercise, we drew inspiration from the organization's webpage regarding their mission and vision, specifically regarding five areas of active engagement: home, family, economic development, community, and opportunity. We believed that these themes were broad enough to invite interpretation and creative thinking, but focused enough to point the participants toward the kinds of themes with which they would work in the afternoon design session.

Workshop participants were given one hour to work in small teams of 2-4 people. One member of the team needed to have a smartphone with a camera to execute the following instructions:

"The aim of this exercise is to begin thinking about the mission and vision of [community organization], and how that might be embodied in parts of the neighborhood . . . While exploring the neighborhood, pairs should take pictures, and post them to Twitter with the hashtag identified in each picture and the hashtag #odoi11. There is no need to complete these in order, and multiple photos can be uploaded with the same hashtags.

- *Take a picture of something that represents family (post it with #family and #odoi11).*
- *Take a picture of something that represents a home (post it with #home and #odoi11).*
- *Take a picture of something that represents economic development (post it with #development and #odoi11).*
- *Take a picture of something that represents opportunity (post it with #opportunity and #odoi11).*
- *Take a picture of something that represents culture (post it with #culture and #odoi11).*
- *Take a picture of community, post it with #community and #odoi11.*
- *Take a picture of sustainability, post it with #sustainability and #odoi11.*

Describe the community:

- *As you walk around the neighborhood, tweet a list of words that describe the kind of community you see, please include the hashtag #odoi11.*
- *Tweet a description of the character of the community with the hashtag #odoi11."*

In all, the small teams collectively posted 46 photographs based on the cultural probe directions. Posted tweets all included one or more of the hashtags suggested in the prompt, and some also incorporated original hashtags, for example, the tag "#ornamentalparanoia" attached to Figure 1. Participants also produced several textual tweets, as well as dozens of additional photographs that were not uploaded via Twitter due to technical or time limitations.

Observing the Scavenger Hunt

During the scavenger hunt, observers followed and videotaped the groups as they made their way through the neighborhood. Observers also wrote detailed notes; two observers were also interviewed by one of the authors of this paper. The following details derive from these data in aggregate.

Toward the beginning of the walk, we noticed that groups were focused primarily on following instructions—so they restricted their attention to discovering artifacts and incidents that represented home, family, opportunity, community, and culture as directed. However, as they walked about the urban streets of Brooklyn completing their task, they also began to ask one another questions about their backgrounds, current work, and various other personal details. With these details quickly out of the way, we observed a noticeable shift in conversation that occurred soon afterward: teammates began to ask about and offer up their own expert insights related to the neighborhood and the design tasks at hand. For example, one group member who lived in a nearby neighborhood described the culture surrounding the neighborhood bodegas. In another group, toward the end of scavenger hunt activity, one group member asked another, a landscape architect, to explain the design for buildings he deemed "unattractive."

Later in the activity, group members started to shift away from the scripted instructions and began looking for examples the reflected some of the collective conversation that had sprung up within the team. Groups began to capture specific images centered on their own themes. As the interviewed observer noted in her debrief: "they were very investigative" at the beginning of the exercise, yet as the groups continued to chat and wander their conversations became "less investigative and more analysis-based."

Figure 1. Photo tagged #odoi11 #home #ornamentalparanoia

Figure 2. A photo of a fenced and locked community garden. Participants appreciated the irony of the juxtaposed words "community" and "open to public" on the sign.

One of the self-selected themes that emerged as teams shifted from an investigative to an analytical stance was 'juxtaposition'—particularly the juxtaposition of locks, gates, and bars with 'community' areas. At first, groups began taking images like the one shown in Figure 2, which showcases a garden, complete with a sign advertising 'Open To Public', behind chain link fencing. As teams progressed through the probe activity, they began to record instances of locks on doors and gates, bars on windows, and 'Keep Out' signs. Their conversation shifted in parallel to reflect on the meaning of these symbols in the context of the community and in turn discuss the significance of an open/closed narrative in the neighborhood on residents as well as for the work of the client organization.

Similar conversation sprung up between the juxtaposition of new and old in the neighborhood; however, we do not have space to discuss this analysis at length herein. Suffice to say that groups were able to use the probe scavenger hunts as tools to build common ground with one another, and having established this were then able to collectively generate new interests and interpretations about the neighborhood based on their own direct observations as individual teams.

Using the Scavenger Hunt

In addition to serving as a way to jumpstart collaboration within the workshop's creative teams, the aggregate data compiled by all teams during the activity was meant to have utility for the second half of the workshop. In specific, we hoped that the multiple, but targeted, views collected by the teams would produce a sensible constellation of the client organization's community context that could be used to inform any potential design solutions produced by the workshop teams. Thus, as workshop participants were returning back from their wanderings and settling in to lunch, we posted the Twitter feed (with accompanying photographs) on one of the walls in our meeting room so that everyone could see the aggregation of images and tweets from all groups and begin to establish a comprehensive view of the themes and issues salient to the client organization.

In the afternoon, workshop participants broke into four groups of approximately 8-10 people that were organized around the themes mentioned in the workshop description. Groups were asked to brainstorm and produce prototypes that addressed the theme outlined in their design challenge. During the brainstorming phase, we observed individual groups turning to the photographic Twitter feed for reference and also sharing images with one another that had not be officially tweeted. These early collaborative exchanges revealed that the teams entered into the afternoon activities with an existing experience of common ground and understanding of one another's' areas of expertise. The scavenger hunt gave them all a common body of knowledge—the local neighborhood—that they could then leverage to negotiate the nuances of different brainstorms and design solutions as they arose. Groups were able to unpack their expert understandings without contentious boundary work because they had developed a rapport with one another and a common body of knowledge via the execution of the cultural probe. While none of the final presentations overtly referenced the scavenger hunt activity, we suggest that it was a vital preliminary step that launched a day of successful collaboration. The probe was both a shared experience, which resulted in a body of common knowledge, as well as a grounded activity that could be used as a reference when negotiating the ideation and production of prototype design solutions.

Case 2: Across the Great Divide

The second case that we discuss with regard to cultural probes, *Across the Great Divide*, was a performance project developed by author A in which 4 artist/scientist pairs were asked to collaborate to develop 10 minute performances for an art and science festival held in upstate New York. For this paper, we will call the pairs H and S, L and J, M and I, and T and J. Each pair met three times over the course of several months to develop their project, and then once more to for a dress rehearsal the day before the final performance. Author

A acted as a facilitator as well as a participant observer for each of the pairs. She designed the meetings so that each was a bit less structured than the last. The first meeting comprised a probe-like activity (discussed in greater detail below); the second began with a review of the first meeting and moved into open discussion and development of the performance; and the third meeting provided a chance for the pairs to refine and practice their performances.

Designing the Cultural Probe

The probe provided at the first meeting was designed to encourage creativity and provoke discussion between the pairs as they developed their performances. It consisted of eight activity prompts. Each prompt was contained inside its own envelope, and markers and paper were left on the table (Figure 3). It included prompts that suggested discussion, as well as prompts that suggested activities like drawing and writing. Most topics focused on either each individual's work, or on the broader theme of art and science. The final prompt asked them to write a mission statement for the piece they would like to create. Author A designed the probes with four goals in mind 1) to help the pairs develop a rapport and working relationship, 2) to inspire creativity and meaningful conversation as they thought about what they wanted to do for their performance, 3) to serve as a kind of interview that each pair would answer collaboratively rather than individually, and 4) to serve as a tool for planning and executing the rest of the experience. To achieve these goals, the probe needed to have specific goals embedded, but not specific outcomes. By this, we mean that the process for each prompt needed to have its own arc, but that the direction in which the pairs took the task and the way they knew they were finished had to be their own.

The prompts given are listed here; however, in the activity, each was provided in a separate envelope with any additional materials, like the quotes and images provided in prompts 4 and 5.

1. *"I begin each day of my life with a ritual: I wake up at 5:30 AM, put on my workout clothes, my legwarmers, my sweatshirts, and my hat. I walk outside my Manhattan home, hail a taxi, and tell the driver to take me to the pumping iron gym at 91st street and First Avenue, where I work out for two hours. The ritual is not the stretching and weight training I put my body through each morning at the gym; the ritual is the cab. the moment I tell the driver where to go, I have completed the ritual." -Twyla Tharp What rituals begin your work? Take us through them. Write them down or draw them. At what moment are your rituals complete? At what moment do you begin your work?*

Figure 3: The aftermath of the cultural probe activity. Each envelope contained a prompt and any additional materials necessary for the pairs to complete the prompt.

2. *Find 5 things you have in common.*
3. *Draw an Artist or Performer. What words or phrases do you use to describe artists and performers? Draw a scientist. What words or phrases do you use to describe scientists?*
4. *Respond in any way you see fit to each of the following. (several quotes were provided).*
5. *Is this art or science? What does it mean? If you had to write one sentence together that would capture the meaning of this image, what would it be? (several images were provided).*
6. *Write the history of your career in Newspaper Headlines. Tell each other your histories. How are they different? How are they the same? Would your stories be in the same papers?*
7. *Draw where you work. Draw your favorite thing about your work. Draw your least favorite thing about your work*
8. *Write a mission statement for the piece you will create. What will it do? What do you want the audience to think about?*

Observing the Cultural Probe

This initial meeting became the crucible of the collaboration not only because the pairs set a direction with their "mission statement", but also because they had developed a kind of partnership that might be described as rapport, but it went beyond a simple "friendly relationship." The relationship developed between the pairs also contained their understanding of one another's views on the relationship between science and art, on the nature of science and of art, and on their perceptions of their own role within their field. This, in turn, provided rich qualitative data for the participant observer about the participants' beliefs regarding art and science, as well as their approaches to collaboration and brainstorming.

As the pairs moved through the eight prompts in the probe, some adhered more closely to them than others. For example, L and J diverged from the prompts quickly, using them more as a point of departure from which to engage in their own conversations, while M and I adhered strictly to the probes.

The pairs also engaged in much boundary work while completing the probes, but, as Halpern [10] argues, boundary work, under certain circumstances, can become a way to negotiate and establish new roles in interdisciplinary activities. There was some indication that this is what happened.

Using the Cultural Probe

Each pair left with a mission statement for their performance, but they also incorporated their work on the other prompts into their scripts. At the second meeting, the pairs were given their notes and sketches from the probe, along with transcripts from their first meeting for reference. At this point, each pair developed along a different trajectory. One pair, M and I (a physicist and a dancer), found similarities in the process of creating a dance and of creating new knowledge in physics. During the first meeting, they began to develop a model to describe this process. They spent the second meeting refining this model and trying to develop a way to speak to an audience about it. Another pair, L and J (a poet and a physicist) found that during the probe, one of them would respond to a prompt, and, in doing so, would spark a memory or idea from the other. The pair found that they greatly enjoyed these mutual springboards and aimed to develop a performance that could display this process. Each instance of interacting or negotiating, then, resulted in a different way to use these interactions in the final performance.

DISCUSSION

The scenarios for cultural probes we outline herein are based on a pair of different collaborative experiences, marked in particular by different temporal features (i.e., one day versus several months) and different technical features (i.e., an aggregated Twitter feed versus interaction with physical objects). These distinctions provide ample basis for comparison and synthesis. To distinguish probes used to facilitate boundary work from traditional cultural probes or boundary objects, we use the term 'boundary probes'. We make three arguments about the nature of these probes in the following section.

Exogeneity

The first key element that spans both of these two cases is the function of a probe as an 'exogenous shock' [26] to the small organizational system that is the team, working group, or other social structure. The exogenous nature of the probe—the fact that it is inserted from the outside into a collaborative situation in an attempt to provoke some type of response—renders it different in many ways from the traditional conceptualization of a boundary object or boundary-spanning object, which is typically conceived as an inductively recognized tool developed by a group of collaborators over a period of time. When Star and Griesemer [24] speak to the plasticity of the map of California as a boundary object for zoological researchers and their collaborators, they underscore that the bridging work being done by the tool is an outcome of previous trial and error; the object is not an input. The map comes to be recognized for its ability to span disciplinary epistemologies, methods, specialized language, power differentials, social homogeneity, etc., but does not start out with these affordances.

In many situations in which unfamiliar and diverse groups of people must learn to collaborate quickly, however, there is no time for such recognition around objects or artifacts to develop. In these cases—such as those articulated in this paper—a probe becomes an initiating mechanism for collaboration. It is an outside interruption to normal practice that requires immediate adjustment, and it is that intentional disrupting effect that endows the probe with its utility. The activity required by the probe's directives engenders boundary spanning. Individuals with disparate perspectives come together through their joint action, and it is through this work that they find common meaning, purpose or direction. The activity becomes codified in a recognizable way—it takes on the affordances of plasticity and multiplex commonality that we understand in the more material conceptualization of boundary objects. The activity brings people together, but goes beyond more than just breaking the ice by being plastic enough to incorporate multiple perspectives. A boundary-spanning probe in this case acts as a scaffold, not a prescription; it is a coherent and enticing alternative for collaboration, not a step-by-step recipe.

When thinking beyond these empirical cases toward a more generalizable theory of boundary probes, we would suggest designers build on the exogenous shock value of activities that intervene to push people beyond their normal routines and practices. When they must engage in an activity that is totally new and equally unsettling for all, people can legitimately start afresh without the need for the extensive impression management that complicates so many interdisciplinary collaborations. It is this leveling of the social landscape that gives the probe its boundary spanning affordance.

Scaffolding

In addition to their external orientation, probes provide a recognizable structure for people to act upon. This structure is elemental for engendering productive boundary work—work that serves as a way for each team to become familiar with one another, establish a group identity, and collectively orient toward project goals. In response to a specific set of direct questions and a directed technological methodology, small teams on the scavenger hunt, for example, were able to move beyond the specifics of the task to develop a kind of 'question and answer' rapport in which different group members specifically asked one another for input related to their respective expertise. The probe's instructions—the recognizable scaffold—nudged groups to begin joint work together as outlined above, but soon these limits gave way to make room for more endogenous forms of collaboration like creating new themes for documentation. As time moved on, we also saw a pattern of inquiry and analysis emerge within groups, as in the example of teammates querying a peer about architecture having come to recognize the relevance of her expertise over the course of the activity.

In the Across the Great Divide case, probes provided a different type of scaffolding. Here, the prompts were divided into several kinds of activities: activities in which participants shared their professional experiences (e.g., prompt 6: your career in headlines; or prompt 2: finding things you have in common); activities specifically designed to bring the subject of art and science into conversation (e.g., prompt 5: looking at images and deciphering whether they were art or science; prompt 6: responding to quotations about the relationship between art and science); and activities designed to spark conversation about what their collaboration would look like (e.g., prompt 8: design a mission statement for the piece you will create). Because of this directed design strategy, pairs engaged in very direct forms of boundary work and then collaboration: they first learned about one another's professions, then with that conversation in mind, they used that knowledge to help them draw boundaries between and around their work, and finally to use those boundaries to help them develop a narrative. As a result, their eventual collaboration took on a constructive nature in which teams were able to negotiate with interest and respect, and ultimately create artifacts that had collective meaning in the context of their larger festival agenda. For example, a physicist and dancer described a similar cycle of observation, synthesis, creation, and presentation in their work. They used this cycle as the basis for their performance, highlighting the ways science and art were similar. Part of their comfort level in doing so stemmed from the safety they found in the boundaries they had designated between art and science.

Again, drawing out the generalizability of boundary probes, we see that they need to be designed with enough specificity to guide an initial set of actions in a mutual direction (i.e., collection of tagged, neighborhood photographs; production of festival artifacts). Tasks need to be recognizably salient to the context in which they're found, but they also need to be easily understood in a way that compels directed engagement. In the cases presented above, it was precisely the recognizably relevant, yet plastic, nature of these activities that encouraged engagement by everyone and facilitated open discussion and exchange. Their lightweight, almost informal, structure was also significant: there was little pressure on the teams to come to a specific conclusion or consensus by argumentation, rather the mandate to explore together necessitated a style of interaction that eventually encouraged genuine collaboration, including synthesis and/or the production of a collective point of view. Directed, but unbounded, tasks like those articulated here appear to be valuable in de-emphasizing behaviors that amplify epistemological differences, while yielding a social environment in which diversity can be channeled profitably and lightheartedly.

Improved by Diversity

Both of the cases presented here showcase the third important feature of a boundary probe: its ability not only to encourage joint participation within diverse communities, but also to be improved by that diversity. For example, in Across the Great Divide, there were several task prompts that required participants to answer questions about themselves and their work (e.g., prompts 2 and 6). The result of this complexity might have been an overt conflict or a collaboration breakdown. Instead, because the task scaffolded activity toward a cumulative project in which broad thinking was required—the production of a mission statement—the probe enabled the group to find direct value in their diverse viewpoints.

The scavenger hunt too benefitted from the multiple eyes and diverse perspectives of its participants. The probe's prompt to look for local evidence of community, family, etc., was by definition one that needed to be considered from varying perspectives. Urban planners and designers took pictures that incorporated their knowledge of built structures and the social landscape of the city, while social scientists and designers saw different aspects of the environment. In each case, the scaffolded nature of the probe's tasks acted as a funnel for diverse inputs to become collective insights. An effective boundary probe allows each participant to offer insights based on his or her area of expertise, but simultaneously transforms that diversity—usually by providing a change of conceptual frame—into something salient for the work the group must do together.

In summary, we underscore the fact that many of the practices common to cultural probes are also important in the creation of boundary probes. Oblique tasks that invite interpretation and meaning making have the most potential to spark creative discussions. Good probes often require the use of varied media and modes of thinking. For example, they use prompts with photography, drawing and mapping to encourage visual thinking, as well as different kinds of written prompts, such as phrases, poems, and, as in Across the Great Divide, newspaper headlines.

Boundary probes differ, however, in their structured ability to start conversations. Whereas Gaver's classic probes are meant to be completed alone and mailed back to the researcher/designers, boundary probes are group tasks—which, on some occasions, are observed by the researchers or designers. The most important point to bear in mind when conceiving of boundary probes is that there is no standard design; there is no template for engendering joint engagement. Rather, each probe must be salient enough to make sense within the larger context of the project, recognizable enough to prompt immediate understanding, robust enough to improve with diverse inputs, and scaffolded enough in its task design to converge toward a joint outcome.

ROLE OF IT IN BOUNDARY PROBES

Each of the examples we present herein involve a fair amount of co-located activity, which prompts the question: what is the role of information technology in boundary probes? The challenges of distributed collaboration, which are many and well documented, often revolve around a lack of common ground and, thus, trust. These issues fall well within the scope of boundary probes, which could easily be adapted to these distributed settings. Given that we do not yet have extensive empirical data from which to draw grounded conclusions, we take this opportunity to speculate on the affordances that networked tools and/or mediated interactions might provide for provoking successful collaboration at a distance.

In the case of the neighborhood scavenger hunt, which involved both distributed and co-located interaction, Twitter and its companion application, TwitPic, enabled unknown collaborators to move beyond their individual viewpoints toward nascent collective understanding. The mobile app allowed individuals to spread out across a large distance to take advantage of spatial distribution as well as personal perspective. The use of hashtags allowed for folksonomic cataloging of photographs and provided a lightweight form of organizing that both allowed individuals to formalize insights (i.e., the creation of new tags) while insuring proper aggregation (i.e., use of provided hashtags). Finally, TwitPics' display of each uploaded picture—ordered by time—emphasized the democracy of the task as well as the equality of each input—a key element of a boundary probe as articulated above. By using a simple social media tool like Twitter, the task was transformed automatically from one of personalized presentation to one of crowdsourcing and collective intelligence.

This efficacy of Twitter in this case hints at additional features that could extend Twitter or a similar crowdsourcing tool to support the same task with groups who are completely distributed. Photo and textual input could remain the same (i.e., uploading files with hashtags and other metadata), however the design of the interface that assembled and displayed these aggregated inputs would need to engender an interaction space that supported collective sensemaking. In the spirit of a digital light table, clusters of images could be automatically organized into thematic groups by hashtag, but the tool would also need to provide users an easy way to perpetually revise organizational schemes as they negotiated together to understand the meaning of the data. During this sensemaking process, the tool might also provide ways for collaborators to hear the thinking aloud of fellow team members as they draw inferences and make associations—an affordance that is currently built into other collaborative task spaces like massive multi-player online games.

Boundary probes in distributed collaboration could also support extended activity in a way that is impossible in face-to-face situations. Probe activities could be designed so that their exogenous shock value lies less in an immediate, re-ordering intervention and more in the gradual recognition of collective value. The most obvious precedent for such a tool is a casual social game like Farmville. If a boundary probe were designed as a game, distributed collaborators could engage in a set of scaffolded activities over a period of months, occasionally checking in to track their progress. Per the design of the probe, the group might build on and revisit their collective insights at successive phases, leveling up at certain points to meet new challenges that result in greater collaborative outcomes.

Whether groups are wholly co-located, totally distributed, or somewhere in between, the opportunity to design and implement boundary probes affords design researchers the opportunity to discover more about the socio-technical bases that allow people to work and play well together. Our future work will explore how issues such as probe type (i.e., challenge, game), situational context (i.e., workplace, neighborhood street, online), and timing (i.e., rapid, longitudinal) effect group dynamics and collaborative outcomes. We believe that this perspective on collaborative interaction will yield discoveries and insights that will benefit the CSCW community.

CONCLUSION

The two boundary probes described in this paper were each designed as sets of structured activities that would engage diverse participants in directed work that could build on epistemological differences in an aggregative instead of homogenizing way. The design of these probes drew on insights from boundary objects [17,24] and cultural probes [7,8] as mechanisms for facilitating new insights and interactions. In both cases, we saw teams use the activities comprising the probe to share ideas, create alliances, exchange information, and develop shared understanding.

To understand what made these activities successful, we go back to their design. Although each probe activity was tailored to the project in which it was situated via specific prompts, the expected outcomes were unbounded and even ambiguous. In other words, the open-endedness of the goal created space for expertise and personal discovery, while the focused nature of the prompts guided this diversity in a way that allowed collective brokering and sensemaking to support the establishment of common ground. While these two case studies are exploratory in nature, they show great promise for future collaborative work, both on and offline.

ACKNOWLEDGMENTS

We would like to thank the participants in both the workshop and the performance, the Cornell Interaction Design Lab, and Lara Penin and Eduardo Staszowski at Parsons The New School for Design. This work is supported in part by the National Science Foundation (OCI 1025498).

REFERENCES

1. Abel, B., Klaassen, R., Evers, L., and Troxler, P. *Open Design Now: Why design cannot remain exclusive*. BIS Publishers, Amsterdam, 2011.
2. Boehner, K., Vertesi, J., Sengers, P., and Dourish, P. How HCI interprets the probes. *Proceedings of the SIGCHI conference on Human factors in computing systems*, ACM (2007), 1077–1086.
3. Cetina, K.K. *Epistemic Cultures: How the Sciences Make Knowledge*. Harvard University Press, 1999.
4. Cramton, C.D. The Mutual Knowledge Problem and Its Consequences for Dispersed Collaboration. *Organization Science 12*, 3 (2001), 346–371.
5. Dourish, P. Implications for design. *Proceedings of the SIGCHI conference on Human Factors in computing systems*, ACM (2006), 541–550.
6. Galison, P.L. *Image and Logic: A Material Culture of Microphysics*. University Of Chicago Press, 1997.
7. Gaver, B., Dunne, T., and Pacenti, E. Design: Cultural probes. *interactions 6*, 1 (1999), 21–29.
8. Gaver, W.W., Boucher, A., Pennington, S., and Walker, B. Cultural probes and the value of uncertainty. *interactions 11*, 5 (2004), 53–56.
9. Gieryn, T.F. Boundary-Work and the Demarcation of Science from Non-Science: Strains and Interests in Professional Ideologies of Scientists. *American Sociological Review 48*, 6 (1983), 781–795.
10. Halpern, M.K. Across the great divide: Boundaries and boundary objects in art and science. *Public Understanding of Science*, (2011).
11. Hilgartner, S. The Dominant View of Popularization: Conceptual Problems, Political Uses. *Social Studies of Science 20*, 3 (1990), 519–539.
12. Hinds, P.J. and Bailey, D.E. Out of Sight, Out of Sync: Understanding Conflict in Distributed Teams. *Organization Science 14*, 6 (2003), 615–632.
13. Hofer, B.K. and Pintrich, P.R. The Development of Epistemological Theories: Beliefs About Knowledge and Knowing and Their Relation to Learning. *Review of Educational Research 67*, 1 (1997), 88–140.
14. Jehn, K. A Multimethod Examination of the Benefits and Detriments of Intragroup Conflict. *Administrative Science Quarterly 40*, (1995), 256–282.
15. Kraut, R., Patterson, M., Lundmark, V., Kiesler, S., Mukopadhyay, T., and Scherlis, W. Internet paradox. A social technology that reduces social involvement and psychological well-being? *The American Psychologist 53*, 9 (1998), 1017–1031.
16. Kuhn, T. *The structure of scientific revolutions*. Chicago, IL□: University of Chicago Press., 1996.
17. Lee, C.P. Between chaos and routine: boundary negotiating artifacts in collaboration. *Proceedings of the ninth conference on European Conference on Computer Supported Cooperative Work*, Springer-Verlag New York, Inc. (2005), 387–406.
18. Livengood, J.M. Students' Motivational Goals and Beliefs about Effort and Ability as They Relate to College Academic Success. *Research in Higher Education 33*, 2 (1992), 247–61.
19. Mortensen, M. From Teams to Recombinant Collaboration: Understanding the Evolution of Organizational Work. *SSRN eLibrary*, (2012).
20. Poltrock, S. and Handel, M. Modeling Collaborative Behavior: Foundations for Collaboration Technologies. *System Sciences, 2009. HICSS '09. 42nd Hawaii International Conference on*, (2009), 1 –10.
21. Schommer, M. Synthesizing epistemological belief research: Tentative understandings and provocative confusions. *Educational Psychology Review 6*, 4 (1994), 293–319.
22. Shirky, C. *Here Comes Everybody: The Power of Organizing Without Organizations*. Penguin Press, 2008.
23. Somerville, M.A. and Rapport, D.J. *Transdisciplinarity: ReCreating Integrated Knowledge*. McGill-Queens, 2002.
24. Star, S.L. and Griesemer, J.R. Institutional Ecology, `Translations' and Boundary Objects: Amateurs and Professionals in Berkeley's Museum of Vertebrate Zoology, 1907-39. *Social Studies of Science 19*, 3 (1989), 387–420.
25. Surowiecki, J. *The Wisdom of Crowds: Why the Many Are Smarter Than the Few and How Collective Wisdom Shapes Business, Economies, Societies and Nations*. Doubleday, 2004.
26. Tolbert, P.S. and Zucker, L.G. Institutional Sources of Change in the Formal Structure of Organizations: The Diffusion of Civil Service Reform, 1880-1935. *Administrative Science Quarterly 28*, 1 (1983), 22–39.
27. Wineburg, S.S. Historical Problem Solving: A Study of the Cognitive Processes Used in the Evaluation of Documentary and Pictorial Evidence. *Journal of Educational Psychology 83*, 1 (1991), 73–87.

Medication Management in the Making: On Ethnography-Design Relations

Tariq Osman Andersen
Dept. of Computer Science – University of Copenhagen
Njalsgade 128 bldg. 24 5th floor, 2400 Copenhagen S, Denmark
tariq@diku.dk

ABSTRACT

The relation between ethnography and design is often discussed in terms of being direct or indirect. The debate on using ethnography in design, models the problem as a matter of mediating between users and designers. This fails to take 'use' serious and renders the problem epistemic i.e. a matter of creating a better understanding or description of the user. Inspired by later developments in Science and Technology Studies I engage an ontological reconceptualization and turn to consider and practice the relation as performative – thus making ethnography, design and users' practices converge. I show this by the case of how the concept of 'medication management' has been performed differently on a combined CSCW and participatory design project in healthcare. It is suggested that through design interventions with working prototypes; prospective analysis and participatory design can be fruitfully assembled in situations of use.

Author Keywords

Ethnography; participatory design; design intervention; design-in-use; prospective analysis; performative ontology; ontological convergence; medication management.

ACM Classification Keywords

D.2.2; H.5.3; J.3; J.4

INTRODUCTION

CSCW may be viewed as a response to the challenge of designing 'better' or more useful computer systems. Sociologists and anthropologist, in particular, have radically reformulated this challenge as being a matter of better understanding the broader social and organizational context of cooperate activities. However, in Schmidt and Bannon's [38] programmatic call for CSCW they advocate a reorientation of social science and emphasize that if CSCW is to be taken seriously, CSCW research should not be descriptive but "constructive". They suggest investigating exactly how insights from studies of cooperative work might be applied in the design of useful computer systems: *"[T]he objective of social science contributions to CSCW should not be to cash in on the new wave and do what they have always done but rather to explore exactly how insights springing from studies of cooperative work relations might be applied and exploited in the design of useful CSCW systems."* [ibid.]

A response to this call can be found in the long-standing debate on the role of ethnography in systems design. Some argue for the analytic purchase of ethnography while others are more critical and argue that *"designers do not need ethnography to do what they wish to do"* [5]. Either way, the logic of the debate models the problem as being about user-designer relations. This, I argue, is unproductive because it essentially fails to take an interest in use and because it renders the ethnography-design relation to be a matter of creating representations (such as analytic descriptions).

In this paper I draw on Science and Technology Studies (STS) to engage an *ontological reconceptualization* [25] of the problem of how to mobilize ethnography in design. I suggest working towards what could be termed 'ontological convergence' by creating situations where ethnography, design and users' practices can be performed as mutually constitutive. By a short review of the status of the debate on the relationship between ethnography and design, I make the case of medication-management to show how it has been performed differently throughout a research and development project in healthcare; as ethnographic practices, as participatory design practices, and finally as actualized simultaneously in interdisciplinary practices.

ETHNOGRAPHY-DESIGN RELATIONS

The use of ethnography in systems design can be grouped into approaches that a) employ ethnography strategically as a way to inform design *directly* and into approaches that b) inform design *indirectly* by developing conceptual and theoretical foundations in CSCW [e.g. 36, 37].

Indirect Relation

The makings of theory and analytical concepts have been central to the development of CSCW. This line of work has its roots in workplace studies where a commitment to analysis as a component of ethnography is prevalent [29, 37]. These studies are typically naturalistic, ethnographic studies, of complex cooperative environments, where people are considered inseparable from the situated and contingent unfolding of activities in which tools and technologies are used. Generally, it is agreed that workplace ethnographies and the making of analytical concepts are "critical" and they have had, and continue to have, a profound impact on CSCW systems design [15, 33, 37]. However, this is not in the form of a direct relationship such as requirement specifications but in indirect and more diffuse forms, which makes it difficult to demonstrate explicitly [36]. For example Suchman's influential study and coining of 'situated action' have enlightened and attuned designers in many ways [ibid.]. However, the histories of the trails of this impact remain mostly implicit in papers reporting on findings [37]. The principal motivation behind the analytical and conceptual development in CSCW is therefore the long-term contribution to the reshaping of how we conceive everyday social actions and interactions in the workplace [29, 37] – and not the direct impact this may have on systems design.

Direct Relation

However, ethnography has also been employed much more strategically as a way to mediate directly between users and designers. In CSCW and HCI, the term 'ethnography' has become shorthand for fieldwork investigations that to some extend are in situ, qualitative, or open-ended. It includes a wide range of specialized methods, such as Contextual Inquiry [24], which most often do not aspire to following the principles of what is considered traditional ethnography.

Proponents of more traditional versions of ethnography have been critical of this "misconception" of the term and have argued for the value of keeping to the classic approaches and principles [5, 14, 15, 18]. Ethnomethodologists in particular [e.g. 10, 35] have claimed that ethnography can provide access to users' needs and make visible the relevant action and interaction of a workplace through detailed analyses. Here, ethnography is typically operated in a hierarchical mode as a *subordination-service* [6] to design where analytical insights are made available through a process of translation, thus maintaining the principled ethnographic approach. Approaches to bridge the gap [33] between users' context and designers' activities include iterative incorporation of fieldwork analysis into a "requirements capture process" [35] and securing ways of effective communication: "*Our purpose is to inform systems designers – i.e., those parties who are actively involved in the development of computing systems and applications [...]*" [14].

The most common form of translating analytical points to inform design is through the development of design principles, rules, or guidelines [36]. In CSCW and HCI, this approach is widespread and is particularly visible in papers in which a section on 'implications for design' is included. However, as workplace ethnographies (with no ambition of informing design directly) are considered "critical", approaches that employ ethnography to mediate directly between users and designers are considered "problematic" by many [5, 9, 15, 35-37].

Anderson [5], for example, calls it a misunderstanding to use ethnography as a method for accessing information about users and as a method to capture requirements. He reminds us that "*[w]ithin the social sciences, ethnography is a form of reportage and not a form of data collection*" and "*[a]t bottom, ethnography is a literacy practice: an analytic strategy that deploys certain modes of representation.*" He argues that the failure to appreciate ethnography's analytic aspirations misconstrues the character of ethnography and consistently subverts the analytic component of ethnography. Dourish [15] revisits Anderson's argument in a critique of the approach of "implications for design" and argues that translating analytical insights to design implications does not succeed in utilizing the potential of ethnography in systems design: "*... a bullet list of design implications formulated by an ethnographer is not the most effective or appropriate method*" [ibid.]. The sympathy for the merits of traditional ethnography and the critical position towards the 'misuse' of the social scientific heritage is also visible in the labeling of remodeled fieldwork methods such as *quick-and-dirty ethnography* [35], *scenic fieldwork* [10], or *quasi-ethnographic work* [18].

THE PERFORMATIVE TURN

Whether traditional ethnography is considered well or ill suited for the purpose at hand – the logic, of which the discussion is turning, is epistemic. What is discussed is essentially whether or not ethnography is a fruitful approach to *mediate between users and designers*. The ethnography-design debate is about "user-designer relations", as Hartswood et al. [22] calls it and the challenge of designing useful systems is framed as a matter of better understanding the users. It is "endemic", as Rogers [36] calls it, that social scientists are seen as being in a much better position of understanding and articulating the users' concerns.

This logic of problematization introduces a set of problems, which in this paper, I propose ways to overcome. The first problem is the construction of a separation between design and use. Focusing on the user-designer relation suggests a design process where design happens away from users and situations of use and where designers, as a consequence of being distant, need some kind of representations of users and their situational context to do their work. It suggests that "*once we get an accurate representation, we will solve [the users'] problem*" [8]. This stands in stark contrast to a process "*where the design practice and the designed-for practice are not separated in time or space.*" [ibid.] Creating useful systems by focusing on creating good representations of users and their problems (such as ethnographic descriptions) has limitations - particularly because it installs a separation of design and use (see [8, 22, 23] for a similar critique).

The second problem is related to the first. It is the conceptualization of the relationship between ethnography and design as an ontological gap to be bridged. That is, to some researchers, ethnography is basically a literacy practice that does not suit the purpose of design, whereas to others, ethnography is considered useful if just we can find effective ways of translating and bridging the gap between a descriptive and prescriptive practice i.e. *in what ways can representations of ethnography (theory, concepts, description) be useful for design.* For these reasons, the debate has considered the relationship in terms of direct or indirect and that ethnography, at heart, is an epistemic practice that works by creating representational descriptions of the world. It therefore becomes troublesome to mobilize the critical value of ethnography since it, ontologically, is depicted as entirely different from design. Instead of positioning ethnography on a par with design in the work of designing useful systems, the ethnography-design relation is framed as a problem of managing ontological differences. However, attempts to "challenge divisions" [34] have been made and to come "full circle" [7] by performative ethnography and participatory design in situations of use [e.g. 9, 21, 23, 26, 40].

Design Interventions and Co-Realization

In the early studies at Xerox Park Suchman, Blomberg, Orr, Trigg, and others [40] have suggested *design interventions* as a work-oriented and cooperative strategy for novel technology production. Through this disciplinary interworking they propose a research strategy that *"establish relations with specific work settings and to use those as sites for cooperative applications design"* [40]. With a similar ambition, Karasti [26] suggests the projection of design suggestions into the users' lived experience of the future practice, thus simulating *technology-in-use.* Büscher, Gill, Mogensen, and Shapiro [9] propose a *bricolage approach* as a way to develop the relationship between ethnographic and participatory approaches to design. By empirical examples they propose this as *"developing CSCW 'in practice'"* through *situated experimentation* and *"careful attunement to the circumstances of work".*

Hartswood et al. [23] acknowledge the fundamental problem of letting ethnomethodologists act as a "proxy" for users i.e. making visible the detailed aspects of a workplace as an informational input and as part of requirements capturing. They suggest overcoming these troublesome user-designer relations by creating a "shared practice" between users and IT professionals that is grounded in the lived experiences of users. *Co-realization,* they call it.

ONTOLOGICAL RECONCEPTUALIZATION

As a way to explore how the critical value of ethnography in design could be otherwise, I engage in *ontological reconceptualization* [25]. Instead of framing the problem of the ethnography-design relation as being a matter of representing the user, I frame the problem as being a matter of how ethnography and design can be *performed* simultaneously in situations of use. Basically, this is a turn to away from considering the problem as epistemic. By a performative ontology users' needs are not considered to be *"out there waiting to revealed"* [20] or described and re-presented. Rather, users' needs are continually in the making and *emerge* as effects of interworking ethnography and participatory design.

To make this case I present an approach where we (design researchers) work deliberately to overcome the disciplinary boundary between ethnography and participatory design. In many ways our approach resembles the methods presented above, where a reflexive relationship between ethnographic researching and in-situ appropriation of technologies in situations of use engages in co-realization. However, in other ways I suggest a more radical mobilization of ethnography and design. I want to suggest a shift in thinking and practicing ethnography-design relations as an orientation towards *effecting ontological change* [6]. By this I mean to give up on the ontological differences and to begin making ethnography, design, and users' practices mutually constitutive as interdisciplinary practices. That is, to start considering participatory design practice as ethnographic practice and vice versa.

To enable an investigation of the ways in which ethnography and design have methodologically converged in our project, I turn to later developments in Science and Technology Studies (STS) where 'performativity' has been highly developed [28, 30]. Central to this philosophical shift is moving focus away from depicting ethnography as only producing representations (theory, concepts, descriptions) towards a concern with the actual physical encounter, the practice, and the real time action and activity of ethnography. Law [28] argues that (ethnographic) methods in practice *"not only describe but help to produce the reality that they understand."* Callon explains this as: *"Scientific theories, models, and statements are not constative; they are performative"* [12]. Turning to performativity, then, also has methodological consequences for design where representations (sketches, models, prototypes) are also no longer considered the ultimate product, but rather as equal actors in the practical making of ethnography, design and use.

This ontological reconceptualization means that ethnography should not be about acquiring knowledge in an epistemological way – as a matter of creating valid descriptions – but rather as a matter of attending to the multiple ways that objects are performed [30]. In her book, *The Body Multiple: Ontology in Medical Practice*, Mol [30] makes the argument that the illness of atherosclerosis is not singular, but multiple. According to Mol, there are *multiple* atherosclerosis i.e. each site produces its own version of atherosclerosis: At home, the patient experiences it as pain in the lower leg; in the radiology department atherosclerosis emerges as a relation between the body, the x-ray machine, and other artifacts; in the doctor's office atherosclerosis emerges as a relation between the desk, the chairs, the doctor and the letter from the radiology department. In short, practices produce 'atherosclerosis' differently. The performativity and multiplicity of reality has methodological implications for experiments, where ethnography and design are deliberately brought together in situations of use. Mol, Law and others' work signify a shift in investigating the doing, the being, and the ways in which objects emerge – or said otherwise; how objects are continuously *in the making*. For the project of this paper, I make the case of medication management in the making by describing an experiment of how ethnography and design have been performed in situations of use. To do this I examine the emergence of the concept of 'medication management' (as one among many concepts) on a research and development project in healthcare by asking the question: *How is mediation management performed differently, where, with what tools, and by what practices?* By investigating how medication management emerges *relationally* between practices of design, ethnography, patients, and clinicians, it is made possible to illustrate how methods in later phases of the project have converged.

The analysis is divided into three figurative stages to foreground the transformation of methods and techniques from traditionally different disciplines and to show the consequences of their convergence. In the first stage I highlight how the concept of 'medication management' emerges as an object of ethnography in a more traditional sense. In the second stage I do the same and look at how practices of participatory design perform medication management. In the last stage, I illustrate how it gets performed as ontological effects between ethnography, participatory design, and patients' and clinicians' practices.

'MEDICATION MANAGEMENT' IN THE MAKING

Co-constructing IT and Healthcare (CITH) is a combined CSCW and participatory design project in healthcare. CITH has engaged distributed healthcare actors in treatment of heart failure patients with an ICD (advanced pacemaker) in the Copenhagen Region, Denmark. The first period of the project, 2008-2011, has involved an interdisciplinary project group consisting of 11 researchers with backgrounds in e.g. Cardiology, Computer Science, and Sociology. The sub-project I report on here [see 31 for the other sub-project] involved 4 CSCW/participatory design researchers, more than 50 patients and their relatives, as well as a heterogeneous group of health professionals; 4 nurses, 4 bioanalysts, 5 Secretaries, and 7 cardiologists. The care for ICD patients is distributed according to specialty; medical care is carried out at local hospitals, whereas ICD device-centered care is carried out at the Heart Centre at the Copenhagen University Hospital. Initially, the project was open-ended with no technological solution imagined but as the project moved through various stages of experimental, explorative and interventionist design research, six consecutive prototypes of a web-based personal health record was developed and used as an actual part of the participants' health care.

Ethnographic Practices

In the first stage of the project we carried out ethnography in a more traditional sense. This involved fieldwork; *in situ* observations and interviews at the participating hospitals and in patients' homes. Focus was on getting access to field sites and creating a shared understanding of the distributed treatment organization and practices of heart patients with an ICD. By fieldwork investigation and analytical activities we established insights that proved to be vital for the development of what came to be a web-based prototype of a personal health record. In this work, a relatively mundane fieldwork tool, the patient interview guide, became useful also for project collaboration when preparing for and conducting field visits. The interview guide was most often accompanied by an audio recorder, a notebook, and a camera. An early version of the document shows an interest in patients' management of medication: *"How is medication managed? Which medicine? What are your experiences from taking the medicine?"*

Cooperative Activities; Sharing Symptom Experiences

Through initial field trips to ICD patient homes, we quickly found that the management of medication is an innate part of their everyday practices. Consider an extract from an early field trip to Hans' home (an invented name of a participating patient. All names in quotes and stories are anonymized).

> *Well into the interview, the Design researcher asks Hans: "Is there any medication you take every day?" Hans: "Oh, yes. I have to take 14 pills a day. Something called Dimitone [heart medicine; beta blocker], I have to raise the dosage every day – right. I need to reach 25 mg twice a day, but I have a hard time doing it, because I get so dizzy." Design researcher: "How do you get a hold of the medicine – do you need a prescription?" Hans: "Well, I call my own doctor and he rings the pharmacy." Design researcher: "And then you go to the pharmacy?" Hans: "Oh no, then my friend fetches it. Or... yes, sometimes I take the bus down there. Completely helpless, I'm not yet." (Transcription from audio recording, November 2008)*

From this interview and others, we learned that the majority of the patients take a variety of pills at different times every day. The individual act of pouring a glass of water and swallowing the pills is just a minor part managing medication. The work of keeping track of how many pills are left and getting the medication home is a collaborative activity. Hans needs to contact his GP to prescribe the medicine and sometimes relatives or friends help by going to the pharmacy in opening hours and collecting medicine to Hans.

Medication management is also about careful leveling of dosage. As with Hans, experienced symptoms and side effects have crucial consequences for everyday life such as dealing with side effect of dizziness and being tired. Experienced symptoms and side effects are fundamental to the practice of medication management: *Can I cope with taking the high dosage of Dimitone today as the doctor has prescribed? Maybe I won't experiment tomorrow when I leave the house to go shopping.* Moreover, such experiences are not only relevant for Hans' and other patients' practices of medication management at home. Experiences become essential information in the cooperation with cardiologists in medical treatment. This is highlighted in the following extract from an early observation of medical treatment – a cardiologist-patient consultation, in a regional hospital of Copenhagen.

> *Not long into the conversation, Kurt says: "I'm a bit more worried about my diet situation - I've lost five kilos in 2-2 ½ months. I was so proud when I reached 70 kilos, now I'm down to 65. It's obvious, because the food runs straight through me". The cardiologist says: "Hmm.... do you have any idea which of the pills we've given you makes the problem?" Kurt and the cardiologist discuss back and forth about Kurt's experiences and settle on a drug called Selo-Zok. Then they discuss whether or not Kurt should stick to the high dose. Kurt explains that after the increase in dose he is able to walk to the third floor without any problems. But now he has trouble with his stomach. Nonetheless, the cardiologist insists that he sticks to the high dosage. (Transcription from audio recording, June 2009)*

From this extract we see that Kurt has correlated the increase in dose of Selo-Zok with improvements in his physical condition. Living on the third floor is no longer a problem because he feels the symptoms of shortness of breath are disappearing. This is crucial information for the cardiologist since it reaffirms that the medicine is working. However, Kurt expresses his concern about the possible side effects; poor appetite and diarrhea. He indicates that he has kept track of his weight and that he lost five kg. This information, as well as Kurt's request of a prescription, makes the cardiologist write, stamp and sign a prescription for a different but related drug with supposedly fewer side effects. Fundamental to Kurt's successful medication management is therefore to monitor, and importantly, share why, when and where, symptoms and side effects are experienced. Medication management is inherently cooperative and involves good memory that is very often supported by conversations with relatives and writing down (on paper) symptoms, side effects, and questions. Successful medication management, then, is also about successful information management.

Reproducing the User-Designer Model

At this stage, Hans' and Kurt's ways of managing medication are left relatively untouched. The interviews and observations have had very little, perhaps no effect on the way they manage medication. Nonetheless, the field visits had affected our (design researchers') work on the project. To a large extent, we had been doing ethnography as practiced in CSCW; reviewing the literature on patient work; doing fieldwork observations and interviews; writing naturalistic descriptions and analyses; and documenting design implications. What I have just presented is a compressed version of what we mean by 'traditional' ethnography and according to Mol's [30] philosophy of multiplicity it exemplifies how ethnographic work (using audio recorders, interview guides, writing analytic working papers etc.) has *performed* medication management so far.

Collage 1. Ethnographic Practices [clockwise]: Interview about medication management in patient's home; collaborative analysis; writing up analysis; working papers;

An epistemic mode of practicing ethnography is reproduced and to a large extent it *keeps patients and health professionals and design researchers' practices apart* [For a similar critique, see 17]. The product of research is mostly materialized as text in digital documents and performed at sites away from the ones studied. The ethnography-design relation has so far reproduced the modeling of the problem as a matter of user-designer relations (see collage 1). The ontological differences have been sustained. So far we had employed ethnography as a subordination-service to design [6], using it as a proxy to provide access and insights about 'the user'.

Participatory Design Practices

With similar design interventionist intentions as Suchman et al. [40], Karasti [26], Büscher et al. [9], Hartswood et al. [23], and Halse et al. [20] we turned to Participatory Design and cooperative prototyping to look for methods, tools and techniques that could make the project more change oriented. Essentially, we wanted to not just think, write and discuss medication management, but also to simultaneously design and actualize an improved form of medication management. As we shall see, the project therefore came to include co-design workshops and sessions, web-page sketching and cooperative prototyping of a patient-centered web-application and we began to put more effort into promoting the project (i.e. making graphically inspiring invitations to workshops and making sure participants felt empowered through participating in the project).

Design Game

To begin a transition towards actualizing design and ethnography as part of a use situation, we carried out what we called a situation-card workshop. We arranged a workshop to co-explore and validate insights from the ethnographic activities and to enable co-design of solutions to experienced problems. Inspired by design games methods in Participatory Design, we developed a game board and twenty 'situation cards' divided into four themes (e.g. 'Medication' and 'Capturing Symptom Experiences') with an introductory text and a selection of related questions. Through the design game workshop, it became clear that the patients have medicine prescribed from various institutions and that it is the prescribing institution's responsibility to follow up on the specific drug. The format also provided for discussions of the idea of having one's own medicine list written down; for example on the computer or as a homemade list of medicine to fit the wallet (see collage 2). The participating patients agreed that an online patient-centered platform potentially could be a tool to support them in managing medication.

Collage 2. Participatory Design Practices [clockwise]: Design game; a patient's homemade medicine list; co-design workshop at university; co-design session in patient's home; design intervention at the Heart Centre

Now, medication management had been performed at the university with a cardboard game prompting discussions of the different ways patients keep track of medicine. It could be said that the interview guide from fieldwork activities had translated and materialized into a cardboard game and instead of asking about previous experiences it had been supporting the envisionment of different ways of managing medication. The design game reproduces more future-oriented tradition of Participatory Design [39].

Prototyping: Towards Design-in-Use

As part of prototyping and having interventionist ambitions, we decided that we needed to begin prototyping if we were to get answers on the real value of the ideas that were emerging. We were interested in working towards the integration of ethnography and design in situations of use i.e. *design-in-use* [16, 23]. We commenced an iterative development approach and made the first version of the web-based personal health record, the prototype, work as a combination of a tool for doing design research and a diary-like tool for patients to keep track of symptom experiences. The first version was a relatively simple web-application built on an open-source content management system. It had three features where patients could make different kind of text entries. The first prototype was therefore flexible in terms of the functionality it stipulated, leaving room for patients' own interpretative of use. Within four months we had employed a PhP web developer and sketched, implemented, and held two launch workshops at which we provided twelve patients and relatives with a login to their own profile in the prototype. We asked them to use it to write about symptom experiences and to prepare for medical consultations by e.g. noting down questions.

The twelve patients who signed up to use the first version wrote various things, including experienced symptoms, questions in relation to their ICD, summaries of consultations, and other diary entries. The majority wrote about their medication and one patient entered his own complete version of a medicine list. The list reveals how a participant (or 'user') performs medication management by explicating at what time a number of pills should be taken (morning, evening), their intended effect (e.g. diuretic, rhythm stabilizing, anticoagulant), how many milligrams, and the name of the generic drug name (e.g. Cordan):

> *"Morning Evening For:*
> *Selo-Zok (metopolosuccinat) 1A Pharma 50mg 1 rhythm-stabilizing*
> *Spiron 25mg 1 diuretic*
> *Trandolapril 0.5 mg 2 strengthens the heart*
> *Aspirin 75mg 1 against thrombosis*
> *Furix 40mg 1 diuretic*
> *Kaleorid 1 750mg potassium supplements*
> *Cordarone (Cordan) 200mg 1 rhythm-stabilizing*
> *Simvastatin 40mg 1 cholesterol-lowering*
> *Marevan 2.5 mg Agreement* anticoagulant"*
> (Transcription from a patient's writing in the Experience Diary feature of the first prototype [translated from Danish])

As a way to qualify what the participating patients had written, we arranged for co-design sessions in patients' homes. In this way, we could combine elicitation studies (discussing patient-generated information) with co-designing features of the second version of the prototype. The result of these co-design sessions was a collective decision to include a Medication Profile feature in the second version of the prototype. To aid sketching the Medication Profile web-page (and two other web-pages), we arranged another co-design workshop with patients at the university, as well as several co-design workshops with cardiologists and bioanalysts from the participating hospitals (see collage 2). After debriefing sessions, mini-workshops, and co-sketching of web-page features, the web-developer would take time to sit, either at home or in his office on the fifth floor at the university, to program the second version of the web-based prototype. Soon after, the second version of the prototype was launched in collaboration with 23 patients – now with the possibility to communicate with clinicians using a web-module developed for clinicians to view selected patient profiles.

At this stage, the project had moved from focus on creating an understanding of medication management (among other concepts) towards the participatory design of it. A shift in research mode had engaged a range of activities that are different from those of ethnography. Nonetheless, these types of activities are part the participatory design methods-tools-and-techniques catalogue and are in this respect not very exotic. But, in an STS-framing where activities and tools are foregrounded, it becomes apparent that some of the activities had provided for situations where ethnographic practices and the practices of design started to converge. Particularly though patients' use of the prototype and in co-design sessions in patients' homes where it started to become difficult to separate ethnographic inquiry from participatory design as moments of *design-in-use* [23]. The methods had started to converge in situations of use.

Interdisciplinary Practices

The second version of the prototype included features that made it possible to trial it as a collaborative tool and as an integrated part of health care. In this way, the ethnographic studies of the prototype in situations of use changed radically because the boundaries between ethnography, design, and use were severely blurred. It was no longer fruitful to characterize method activities as belonging to one or the other discipline. By employing *Design interventions* [4], we succeeded to create moments where multiple practices were performed simultaneously (see collage 3). Situations of trialing the prototype as e.g. part of a medical consultation, were not just moments where we could apply our ethnographic curiosity and proactively experiment with situations of use i.e. inquiring into other ways of performing medication management with the prototype. Design interventions were also situations where the participants and we could intervene and cooperatively re-design or suggest new features in the prototype etc.

By critically analyzing the design interventions with the working prototype, we realized that we had introduced a new category of invisible patient work [3]. With the prototype installed in use, the concept of 'medication management' was expanded, introducing expectations of active patient participation [2]. Patients now needed to log in to the prototype from home and write about their experienced symptoms, side effects and medicine list. They were asked to approve the medication profile they had entered, as a way to inform clinicians remotely. The integration of an analytical dimension (ethnographic reflexivity) in design interventions led to the discovery of new ways of relating ethnography and design. The prototype had become useful, not only in performing a newly designed and possibly better way of managing medication (e.g. letting patients easily share symptom experiences and side effects with cardiologists through the prototype and improving their overview by a keeping self-maintained medication list in the prototype). The prototype had also become a 'research device' [13] capable of making critical questions performative and thus operationalizing ethnographic inquiry in quite different ways than the interview guide and audio recorder. In Law and Callons' [12, 28] philosophy, the participants and we could create what we want to study. We could engage the ethnography-design relation in other ways than direct or indirect and instead work towards a convergence of the methods. The prototype features installed in use could support *proactive analysis* [41] of medication management *in the making* [11]. That is, we could explore and experiment with emergent forms of medication management instead of working to make a descriptive, retrospective analysis of (current forms of) medication management. Our approach provided for ways in which analysis could be proactively performed on par with participatory design [see also 27].

Prospective Analysis

To experiment with proactive analysis, we sketched and implemented a feature in the third version of the prototype called Tasks.

Collage 3. Interdisciplinary Practices [clockwise]: Sketching the Medication Profile feature; prototype module for clinicians; prototype of the personal health record's Tasks feature; design intervention at the Heart Centre;

It was designed to support collaboration in-between meetings by enabling clinicians to give patients taks in their personal health record (the prototype). This could be keeping track of side effects or writing down symptom experiences for the cardiologist to read when in need of the information. With the new feature, we could try out possibly better ways of collaboratively managing medication With Tasks we could also proactively perform ethnographic concepts such as *'diagnostic agency'*, *'invisible work'* [32] and *'homework'* [19], which accentuates implications of increased patient responsibility (see [1] for related use in CSCW). In the following extract, a third version of the prototype was launched and a patient, Karl, agreed to prepare for an upcoming medical consultation. He used the prototype to communicate his medication profile, symptom experiences, and side effects, and in turn, the cardiologist used the prototype and Karl's writing as support for his own preparation. However, neither the cardiologist nor the patient had been introduced to the new feature, Tasks, prior to the design intervention.

The design researcher arrives at the outpatient clinic with the patient and his wife and agrees with the cardiologist to follow him to his office to collect various documents and prepare for the medical consultation. It is the first time they have met, so the design researcher hands over a printed version of Karl's preparation and explains in very brief terms what the project is about and reads the first couple of lines from Karl's summary (5 lines in total). The cardiologist mumbles and reads through the rest of the notes and Karl's medication profile. Then, he collects various documents and test results and call in Karl and his wife to start the consultation. The cardiologist says: "You have completed this [printout from the prototype], and it was actually very helpful because you've explained very well what we really need to talk about ... precisely as you have written .... three weeks have now past and we have to find out what the plan should be by you telling how you feel". Karl replies: "I've been really ill... air ... and sadness. I've not been able to pull myself together".

They talk through the various symptoms and questions using the prototype printout and at one point Karl's wife interrupts: "But Karl, if I may say something, it's also been worse now that your stomach is bigger". Karl says: "Well, see it's a bit complicated. Now, down here [looking down an pointing to his stomach], I was usually fit and I could see my penis and all the funny parts but dammit, now I can't any more. It means that I have either air or water in my stomach". The cardiologist agrees. Karl continues: "Look, something like that also affects the air in the stomach [pointing at the prototype medication profile]" They are both sitting bent over, looking at the printout. The cardiologist: "Yes it does. You get out of breath more, your appetite gets poorer and so on and so on - if you've got water in the stomach. And the things you've mentioned here... [pointing at the prototype printout]... I think what we do is: We wait and see how things are going in a couple of weeks. You have to exercise and use your body, we increase Furix [the diuretic medicine] because it forces the water out of your stomach ..." [the design researcher takes note of this for use shortly after]

They continue the discussion back and forth about how much they should increase the diuretic medicine, Furix. After that they spend quite some time talking about side effects and whether Karl should try to decrease another drug; Cordan. They consult the medication profile in the prototype printout several times for the amount of quantities taken. (Transcription from audio recording, October 2010)

Now, the part of medication management, which involves meeting clinicians and discussing symptoms and side effects, has been reconfigured. First of all, the cardiologist encourages Karl to be an active participant i.e. he values getting Karl's notes and medication profile before the meeting. In addition, a new actor – the prototype – has found its place, supporting the discussion around medication. They both use the prototype several times to guide the conversation and get reassurance about certain things. It is not only Karl's explanation that counts; it is also the prototype and what is printed on it. What is interesting in terms of the ethnography-design relation, is that when Karl or the cardiologist point at the prototype, talk about it, or use it to guide the conversation, they at once mobilize earlier ethnographic practices (the interview guide, the working papers, the implications for design where 'medication management' was made 'visible') and participatory design practices (the cardboard game, the home-made laminated medicine card with a medicine list, the patient's written medicine list from using the first prototype and the web developer's PhP code). However, in the situation, these two disciplines come together. One is not without the other. In the design intervention, medication management is different than it was without the prototype.

Performing Ethnography-Design Relations in Use

So far so good. Now, on to the engagement of prospective analysis and participatory design as it happened in the design intervention. At this point in time, the Tasks feature and the related ethnographic discourse on patient work has not been connected to medication management in any situation of use. 'Homework' is still (only) an analytical category that has not yet been realized in situations of use. Then, after almost an hour, the consultation comes to an end and the cardiologist stands up while talking.

The design researcher sees his chance and speaks for the first time: "There is one more thing. We've created something we call 'Tasks', which are a little experimental, but in your discussion with Karl you indirectly ask him to do some tasks – that he must keep an eye on this and that – so, what should he enter in the prototype for your next meeting?" The cardiologist quickly gets the idea and immediately asks Karl to write down (in the prototype), everyday if possible, how far he can walk. This would be helpful in relation to his breathing. The design researcher: "And then there was something in relation to the medication – something with Furix?" and the cardiologist says: *"Yes, the weight, walking distance, and blood pressure. Clearly it would be a great help to have your experiences on that next time we meet".*

They end the conversation and shake hands, and Karl and his wife leave. The cardiologist sits down and says he just needs to finish off and dictate a summary for the medical record. He picks up the tape recorder and dictates: "Memorandum to Karl.... Meets for medical consultation. Full stop. See the above. New line. Since the last meeting. Colon. [the cardiologist looks at the prototype printout] Complaints of oppression, unpleasant upper abdomen [almost exactly as the first line of Karl's writing]... We try RECIPE CRESENDO [prescription, gradually increase] tablet FURIX to 40 mg x 2 plus KALEROID 40 mg x 2. Daily weight measurement and assessment of walking distance a few times a week. Full stop. Signed [cardiologist name]".

In these last minutes, the design researcher intervenes and connects Karl's and the cardiologist's discussion around Furix (bloated stomach) to an experiment of participatory design and performative ethnography: *Could Karl and the cardiologist possibly want to collaborate in new ways? Do they like this feature at all? What are the consequences of increasingly extending patient responsibility and active participation? How could homework make sense for both patients and cardiologists?* By the design interventionist move of suggesting using the prototype to collaboratively monitor the increase in Furix, the toolbox of participatory design is performed and in one and the same moment, proactive analysis is performed. It goes a bit further because what happens is that the cardiologist agrees with Karl to try to monitor his weight, since it is highly related to the increase in the dose of Furix. And as the cardiologist says: *"Clearly it would be a great help to have"*. The *"Daily weight measurement"*-agreement or the feature Tasks moreover materializes in the hospital's medical health record through the cardiologist dictating it. And later, which is out of the scope of this paper, it materializes in the prototype by Karl's self-monitoring and prototype use. By design interventions with the prototype, the ethnography-design relation is blurred and a transcended, proactive way of interdisciplinary practice has taken place. The original problem of modeling the ethnography-design relation as a matter of mediating between users and designers (directly or indirectly) is shifted to become a matter of engaging performative ethnography and participatory design, simultaneously, in situations of use.

CONCLUSION

The methodological problem, which is the point of departure for this paper, concerns the much-debated relation between ethnography and design. I frame the problem as failing to take an interest in use and as considering the ethnography-design relation as epistemic. That is, debating in terms of a direct and indirect relationship and modeling the problem as a matter of bridging the gap between users and designers. Some argue for employing ethnography as traditionally practiced [e.g. 5, 14], thus creating ontological differences, while others suggest to engage in co-realization [23] and employ design interventions [40] to make reflexive relations between understanding and designing. We have gone similar ways by critically integrating performative ethnography and participatory design as part of situations of use in healthcare. Inspired by later developments in STS I have engaged an ontological reconceptualization and shown how ethnography and design can become co-constituents together with users' practices in the collaborative making of 'medication management'. Using the prototype as a research device enables ethnography to be performed prospectively as participatory design and by installing ethnographic concepts in the prototype, ethnography becomes a way of doing participatory design.

By our empirical case I suggest the fruitfulness of turning to performativity and consider ethnography and design as mutually constitutive. I advocate an ontological shift, as is happening in broader lines of social science [6], and to engage ethnography-design relations in proactive ways, making for *ontological convergence*. Working towards performative ethnography and participatory design in situations of use is a novel direction for exploring Schmidt and Bannon's [38] programmatic call.

ACKNOWLEDGMENTS

I am grateful for the valuable collaboration with the patients and health professionals at the Heart Centre at Copenhagen University Hospital. I thank Finn Kensing and especially Jonas Moll for significant discussions and for the valuable collaboration on making the empirical basis of this paper. CITH is a 4-year project funded by the Danish Council for Strategic Research grant #2106-07-0017.

REFERENCES

1. Aarhus, R., Ballegaard, S. and Riisgaard, T. The eDiary: Bridging Home and Hospital through Healthcare Technology. In *Proc. ECSCW 2009*, Springer (2009).
2. Andersen, T. The participatory patient. In *Proc. PDC 2010*, ACM (2010), 151-154.
3. Andersen, T., Bjørn, P., Kensing, F. and Moll, J. Designing for collaborative interpretation in telemonitoring: Re-introducing patients as diagnostic agents. *International Journal of Medical Informatics,* 80, 8, (2011), e112-e126.
4. Andersen, T., Halse, J & Moll, J. Design Interventions as Multiple Becomings of Healthcare. In *Proc. Nordes 2011*, (2011).
5. Anderson, R. J. Representations and requirements: the value of ethnography in system design. *Human-Computer Interaction,* 9, 3, (1994), 151-182.
6. Barry, A., Born, G. and Weszkalnys, G. Logics of interdisciplinarity. *Economy and Society,* 37, 1, (2008), 20-49.
7. Berg, M. The politics of technology: On bringing social theory into technological design. *Science, technology & human values,* 23, 4, (1998), 456-490.

8. Bowers, J. M. The Janus faces of design: Some critical questions for CSCW. in *Studies in Computer Supported Cooperative Work.* Ed. by J. M. Bowers and S. D. Benford, Elsevier Science Publishers (1991).
9. Büscher, M., Gill, S., Mogensen, P. and Shapiro, D. Landscapes of Practice: Bricolage as a Method for Situated Design. *CSCW,* 10, 1, (2001), 1-28.
10. Button, G. The ethnographic tradition and design. *Design Studies,* 21, 4, (2000), 319-332.
11. Callon, M. Society in the making: the study of technology as a tool for sociological analysis. *The social construction of technological systems: New directions in the sociology and history of technology*, (1987), 83-103.
12. Callon, M. What Does it Mean to Say That Economics Is Performative? in *Do Economics Make Markets? On the Performativity of Economics.* Ed. by D. MacKenzie, F. Muniesa and L. Siu, Princeton University Press (2007).
13. Collins, R. Why the social sciences won't become high-consensus, rapid-discovery science. *Sociological Forum,* 9, 2, (1994), 155-177.
14. Crabtree, A., Rodden, T., Tolmie, P. and Button, G. Ethnography considered harmful. In *Proc. CHI 2009*, ACM (2009), 879-888.
15. Dourish, P. Implications for design. In *Proc. CHI 2006*, ACM (2006), 541-550.
16. Ehn, P. Participation in design things. In *Proc. PDC 2008*, Indiana University (2008), 92-101.
17. Fitzpatrick, G. and Ellingsen, G. A Review of 25 Years of CSCW Research in Healthcare: Contributions, Challenges and Future Agendas. *CSCW*, (2012), 1-57.
18. Forsythe, D. E. "It's Just a Matter of Common Sense": Ethnography as Invisible Work. *CSCW,* 8, 1, (1999), 127-145.
19. Grøn, L., Mattingly, C. and Meinert, L. Kronisk hjemmearbejde - Sociale håb, dilemmaer og konflikter i hjemmearbejdsnarrativer i Uganda, Danmark og USA. *Tidsskrift for Forskning i Sygdom og Samfund [Journal for research on illness and society],* 9, (2008).
20. Halse, J., Brandt, E., Clark, B. and Binder, T. *Rehearsing the future.* The Danish Design School Press (2010).
21. Halse, J. and Clark, B. Design rituals and performative ethnography. In *Proc. EPIC 2008*, (2008), 128-145.
22. Hartswood, M., Procter, R., Rouchy, P., Rouncefield, M., Slack, R. and Voss, A. Working IT out in medical practice: IT systems design and development as co-realisation. *Methods of Information in Medicine,* 42, 4, (2003), 392-397.
23. Hartswood, M., Procter, R., Slack, R., Voß, A., Büscher, M., Rouncefield, M. and Rouchy, P. Co-realization: Toward a principled synthesis of ethnomethodology and participatory design. in *Resources, Co-Evolution and artifacts: Theory in CSCW.* Ed. by M. S. Ackerman, C. A. Halverson, T. Erickson and W. A. Kellogg, Springer London, (2008).
24. Holtzblatt, K. and Jones, S. Contextual inquiry: A participatory technique for system design. in *Participatory design: Principles and practice.* Ed. by D. Schuler and A. Namioka, (1993).
25. Jensen, C. B. CSCW design reconceptualised through science studies. *AI & Society,* 15, 3, (2001), 200-215.
26. Karasti, H. Bridging Work Practice and System Design: Integrating Systemic Analysis, Appreciative Intervention and Practitioner Participation. *CSCW,* 10, 2, (2001), 211-246.
27. Kimbell, L. Closing Keynote Address - Reassembling the visual. *EPIC '08,* 2008, 1, (2008), 316-324.
28. Law, J. *After method: Mess in social science research.* Psychology Press (2004).
29. Luff, P., Hindmarsh, J. and Heath, C. *Workplace studies: Recovering work practice and informing system design.* Cambridge Univ Press, (2000).
30. Mol, A. *The body multiple: Ontology in medical practice.* DUKE (2010).
31. Mønsted, T., Reddy, M. C. and Bansler, J. P. The Use of Narratives in Medical Work: A Field Study of Physician-Patient Consultations. In *Proc. ECSCW 2011*, Springer (2011), 81-100.
32. Oudshoorn, N. Diagnosis at a distance: the invisible work of patients and healthcare professionals in cardiac telemonitoring technology. *Sociology of Health & Illness,* 30, 2, (2008), 272-288.
33. Plowman, L., Rogers, Y. and Ramage, M. What are workplace studies for? In *Proc. ECSCW 1995*, Kluwer Academic Publishers (1995), 309-324.
34. Pors, J. K., Henriksen, D., Winthereik, B. R. and Berg, M. Challenging divisions. *SJIS,* 14, 2, (2002), 3-7.
35. Randall, D., Harper, R. and Rouncefield, M. *Fieldwork for design: theory and practice.* Springer-Verlag New York Inc (2007).
36. Rogers, Y. Reconfiguring the social scientist: Shifting from telling designers what to do to getting more involved. in *Social Science, Technical Systems, and Cooperative Work - Beyond the Great Divide.* Ed. by G. C. Bowker, S. L. Star, W. Turner and L. Gasser, Lawrence Erlbaum Associates Publishers (1997).
37. Schmidt, K. The critical role of workplace studies in CSCW. in *Workplace studies: recovering work practice and informing system design.* Ed. by P. Luff, J. Hindmarsh and C. Heath, Cambridge Univ Pr (2000).
38. Schmidt, K. and Bannon, L. Taking CSCW seriously. *CSCW,* 1, 1, (1992), 7-40.
39. Simonsen, J. and Robertson, T. *Routledge International Handbook of Participatory Design.* Routledge, (2012).
40. Suchman, L., Blomberg, J., Orr, J. and Trigg, R. Reconstructing technologies as social practice. *The American Behavioral Scientist,* 43, 3, (1998).
41. Vikkelsø, S. Description as Intervention: Engagement and Resistance in Actor-Network Analyses. *Science as Culture,* 16, 3, (2007), 297-309.

Why CSCW Needs Science Policy (and Vice Versa)

Steven J. Jackson
Cornell University
Department of Information Science
sjj54@cornell.edu

Stephanie B. Steinhardt
Cornell University
Department of Communication
sbg94@cornell.edu

Ayse Buyuktur
University of Michigan
School of Information
abuyuktu@umich.edu

ABSTRACT
This paper explores the relationship between CSCW studies of scientific collaboration and the larger worlds of science practice and policy they are embedded in. We argue that CSCW has much to learn from debates in science policy, including questions around the changing nature of science and science-society relations that are partly but obliquely referenced in technology- or data-centered accounts of scientific change. At the same time, science policy has much to learn from CSCW – about design, infrastructure, and the organizational complexities of distributed collaborative practice. We conclude with recommendations for a better integration of the CSCW and science policy literatures around collaboration and new infrastructure development in the sciences, and speculation around what a post-normal cyberinfrastructure – and post-normal CSCW – might look like.

Author Keywords
science; collaboration; policy; collaborative tools; cyberinfrastructure; e-research

ACM Classification Keywords
A.m. Miscellaneous.

I. INTRODUCTION

Can CSCW research shape science policy? Should it? In her Athena Lecture at the 2012 CSCW Conference, Judy Olson challenged the field to think in new and creative ways about how and where the insights of CSCW might be brought to bear on real-world practices and problems. As Olson describes, the impacts of thirty-odd years of work in CSCW are in many ways impressive. The field has generated theory and findings that have changed the way researchers across several fields have approached questions of computational development and social change: HCI, computer, and information science, but also (albeit more modestly) psychology, sociology, organizational science, and science and technology studies. CSCW has shaped the education of large numbers of students at the doctoral, professional Masters, and undergraduate levels, many of whom have gone on to positions in research or industry that draw heavily on CSCW concepts and methods. Academic and industry-based CSCW researchers have helped shape the design and deployment of products and services at IT firms ranging from Microsoft, IBM, and Intel to Google and Facebook. And leading CSCW researchers have authored or contributed to key documents [8, 24, 36] that have been read and acted on by decision makers, managers, and participants in new collaborative projects in industry, academia, and the non-profit world.

At the same time, argues Olson, CSCW has not done all it might to achieve or extend impact, especially in light of the activist or social change leanings that led many participants to the field in the first place. CSCW has not yet done enough to translate its theoretical knowledge into forms and instruments (assessment tools, templates, toolkits, etc.) usable by the wider communities who might act on its findings. While the field has sometimes engaged in forms of action research with clear and measurable impacts on specific communities and areas of concern (e.g. [21, 30]), in other cases it has failed to engage communities in a sustained and meaningful way. And while individual researchers have made contributions to science and technology policy debates, the field's efforts in this space have been more limited than in the traditional CSCW heartlands of design; compare for example the near canonical status of 'implications for design' [11] versus the general neglect of 'implications for policy' in CSCW discussion sections. In all these ways, much work remains to be done to realize and extend the field's long-standing ambitions of impact.

This paper addresses the problem of CSCW impact in a contemporary policy debate of considerable importance: namely, the funding and development of new collaborative infrastructures in the sciences (the crux of today's cyberinfrastructure or e-research development efforts). It argues that while CSCW work has made important contributions along several key dimensions [8, 9, 17, 32, 37, 39] it has often struggled to connect its work to scholarship and practice in the wider science policy world. This is important for at least two reasons: first, because science policy is increasingly built and predicated (sometimes naively) around questions of collaboration and

CSCW '13, February 23–27, 2013, San Antonio, Texas, USA.

infrastructure that CSCW research has legitimate expertise in answering; second, because many of the challenges confronting CSCW researchers around scientific collaboration in fact flow from dynamics that live at the policy level – about which CSCW, in turn, may be naive. Better understanding of these dynamics can help CSCW to do its traditional work better, and move towards new sites of analysis and intervention that can expand the range and impact of the field.

This paper represents one theoretical and empirical step in that direction. Building on U.S. examples, it draws out CSCW contributions to science and cyberinfrastructure policy debates to date, and points to additional questions on which CSCW research has remained largely silent (or failed to connect to parallel debates going on in science policy research and practice). It draws in key frameworks from the science policy world – notably concepts of 'post-normal,' 'mode-2' and 'Pasteur's Quadrant' science – that can help explain the shaping, dynamics, and limits of contemporary cyberinfrastructure or e-research development efforts. It outlines ways in which CSCW-level discourses and practices nevertheless can and should feed back into more general science policy debate and analysis. Drawing on original ethnographic research into policy processes surrounding key infrastructure projects in ecology and water science, it speculates on the distinctive challenges attending the development of infrastructure under post-normal or mode-2 conditions. And it concludes by asking what this might mean for CSCW itself, as a collaborative, contextualized, and even post-normal endeavor.

II. WHY CSCW NEEDS SCIENCE POLICY

II.I. CSCW and scientific collaboration

For CSCW researchers, the study of scientific collaboration has always carried distinct intellectual and institutional advantages. Scientific researchers occupy a partially shared world with academic CSCW scholars, building useful forms of connection and understanding (common service on university committees, overlapping social networks, parallel work rhythms and calendars, shared institutional concerns around teaching and advising, research funding, promotion and review, etc.). Research in (some) academic science may be comparatively free of concerns around commercial competition, trade secrets, intellectual property, or national security that can produce pressures towards secrecy or closure in other contexts. In many instances, academic scientists engaged in collaborative research projects lack dedicated managerial or IT support and experience, making the organizational and design insights of CSCW researchers of immediate practical interest and benefit. Relationships between CSCW researchers and formal cyberinfrastructure development projects have in some cases been actively brokered or encouraged by science funders, building powerful incentives towards access. And CSCW studies of scientific collaboration have been historically well funded in their own right, giving important local support and legitimacy to faculty and doctoral research in this space.

For all these reasons, scientific collaboration has long functioned as a crucial site for the development and testing of CSCW theories, methodologies and technologies. Work by Star & Ruhleder [41] in the 1990s on the WORM Community System led to the development of core CSCW theory around the characteristics and tensions of infrastructure and its function within distributed collaborative communities. Research on scientific collaboration has also fueled the development of more general CSCW theories around distributed work (see for example the contributions to Hinds and Kiesler [23]). The early conceptualization of the "collaboratory" as a "center without walls, in which the nation's researchers can perform their research without regard to geographical location" [46] was an important precursor to subsequent generations of CSCW work around virtual teams [9], infrastructure design [13], and groupware [36].

This work has been extended in recent years through growing investments in scientific cyberinfrastructure (or 'e-research') among government funders in the U.S., Europe, and elsewhere. In 2003, the NSF published its Blue Ribbon Panel report, "Revolutionizing Science and Engineering Through Cyberinfrastructure" (aka the 'Atkins Report') [1], describing a "new age" in science and engineering research "pushed by continuing progress in computing, information and communication technology, and pulled by the expanding complexity, scope, and scale of today's challenges." Coming initially out of the Computer and Information Science and Engineering (CISE) Directorate and a longer history of NSF reports and activities in this space,[1] the Atkins Report described the hardware, software, and organizational possibilities embedded in a new suite of scientific communication, computation, and storage tools. In 2007 this vision was updated and extended under the NSF's "Cyberinfrastructure Vision for 21st Century Discovery," emphasizing the development of high performance computing, data visualization and analysis tools, virtual organizations, and new modes of workforce training and development as key opportunities and drivers of scientific change [44]. The report also emphasizes the cultural nature of the envisioned change: for example, NSF Director Arden Bement's claim that "at the heart of the cyberinfrastructure vision is the development of a cultural

---

[1] In rough order, the Lax [31], Branscomb [35], and Hayes [21] reports in 1982, 1993, and 1995; the NSF supercomputer centers and Advanced Scientific Computing Program of the 1980s; and the National Partnership for Advanced Computational Infrastructure (NPACI), High-Performance Computing (HPC), and NSF 'collaboratory' initiatives of the 1990s.

community" built around "distributed knowledge communities that collaborate and communicate across disciplines, distances, and cultures." [44] This broad vision drove the 2005 formation of the NSF Office of Cyberinfrastructure and a new suite of funding programs (though never the $1 billion the original Atkins Report called for) dedicated to the design, construction, and analysis of transformative cyberinfrastructure.[2] Many of these programs have become important sources of support for ongoing CSCW research in this space.

Activities at the NSF have been broadly paralleled by programs at other funding agencies in the U.S., Europe, and elsewhere. In 2000, the U.K. Director General of Research Councils from the Office of Science and Technology, coined the term "e-Science" to describe infrastructures supporting distributed and interdisciplinary collaborations. This was followed in 2001 by a report from De Roure et. al. [10] articulating a plan and agenda for the development of e-Science tools and infrastructure built around the principles of service-oriented architecture and the semantic grid. Other European initiatives soon followed, including the Netherlands e-Science Center, European Grid Infrastructure, the Danish e-Science Center in Copenhagen, and a range of activities sponsored under the Ministry of Science and Innovation (MSI) in Germany. In Asia similar initiatives have recently been launched, driven in part through collaborations and partnerships involving U.S. and European researchers and institutions – for example, the Academia Sinica Grid Centre (ASGC) in Taiwan associated with the European Enabling Grid in e-Science (EGEE).

Other important institutional actors, including many located at industrial research firms like Microsoft, have pursued questions of scientific transformation with a principal focus on data – and the potential that new and extended forms of data collection, storage, processing, and analysis can bring. Such advocates point to an emerging "4th paradigm" of science, in which tailored but interoperable algorithms, software, data analysis, and information management tools emerge to manage and accelerate forms of learning and collaboration built on the new torrents of data produced by increasingly massive systems of scientific instrumentation and monitoring. The same rough principle finds its dystopian counterpart in fears around the 'data deluge': namely, that our proliferation of data has become so intense that it overwhelms our ability to keep up and make sense of it at all. [12]

---

[2] For example, interdirectorate programs in Human and Social Dynamics (HSD); Cyber-Enabled Discovery and Innovation (CDI); Virtual Organizations as Sociotechnical Systems (VOSS); and changes to a host of existing programs and mechanisms (including the MREFC instrument described below) that sought to realize and extend the NSF's cyberinfrastructure vision.

The explosion of activity and support in these areas has fed new generations of CSCW research. Lee et. al. [32] have explored "the human infrastructure of cyberinfrastructure," calling attention to human and organizational actors integral to the function of cyberinfrastructure that are often obscured in prevailing tool- or technology-centered accounts. Other researchers have emphasized temporal dimensions and challenges of infrastructure development in the sciences, examining tensions between short and long term orientations [28, 38], and the more general problem of aligning collaborative rhythms [25]. Other researchers have explored behavioral motivations towards collaboration and data sharing, emphasizing individual and institutional incentives that might support or undermine patterns of scientific sharing and collaboration [3, 4]. Others have sought to tie such patterns to systems of scientific credit and reward, including the crucial but fuzzy concept of authorship [2]. Still others have focused on thorny questions around data production [45], curation [28], ontologies [33], metadata [14], and reuse [16].

II.ii. Cyberinfrastructure and the policy gap

Many of the above questions relate to questions of science policy, at least in the loose sense of relating to problem areas (for example, data) that contemporary policymakers have sometimes sought and struggled to address. Other CSCW work has attempted to make this link more direct, pointing to features of the policy world that can impact local practices of collaboration.

The 2007 Understanding Infrastructure workshop and report [13, 24] explored tensions and dynamics surrounding the development of large-scale infrastructure, pointing to issues around sustaining funding, the differing practices of funding agencies across initiatives, and the influence of publishing on the research and development process. The report locates the development of cyberinfrastructure in a wider political economy shaped by the pairing and discrepancies of public and private sector interest, the shifting interests of funding agencies, the emergent properties of plan and planning, and the institutional norms and cultures that bear on the practice of scientific work in lab, field, and classroom. Some of these themes are taken up and extended in Ribes & Finholt [38], which locates cyberinfrastructure development and practice in a wider and multi-scalar frame, including a series of macro-level tensions that operate at the institutional level of funders like the NSF. Kee [29] makes a similar point, linking challenges and discrepancies in scientific collaboration to a series of "dialectical tensions" in the funding of cyberinfrastructure. Cummings and Kiesler's [9] analysis of NSF ITR grants from the 1990s has revealed the significant coordination costs imposed by the inter-institutional organization of academic research teams.

Other CSCW work has approached questions of policy through the medium of data. Work by Borgman [4] has explored the links and frequent discrepancies between the everyday data practices of scientists and the data sharing guidelines and mandates of institutional funders like the NSF, NIH, and European funding bodies (including key centers like the UK Wellcome Trust and Digital Curation Center). Vertesi and Dourish [45] have emphasized the political economy of data production, exploring the significance and diversity of local and institutional contexts of data production, and arguing against simplified and commodified visions of data economies and the one-size-fits-all approaches to regulation and policy they can produce. Howison & Herbsleb [22] have pursued broadly parallel questions around the provision, circulation and maintenance of software in the biology and physics communities, pointing to the interaction of funding structures, systems of academic credit and reward, and software licensing practices as constraints and shapers of collaborative practice in these worlds.

In all these ways, CSCW as a field has approached but not fully tackled the broader questions of science policy that frame and shape efforts at cyberinfrastructure and collaborative scientific development. Institutional and policy constraints have been acknowledged as an outer ring of CSCW concern, but rarely thematized as a topic of CSCW research per se. In their introduction to the special issue on cyberinfrastructure of the Journal of CSCW, Ribes & Lee [40] note the project-level and short-term inclinations of the field, and argue for a more holistic examination of cyberinfrastructure as "something sorely needed in the field" (pp. 240). Karasti et. al. [27, 28] applaud CSCW's insight into the short-term and design-sensitive analysis of distributed collective practice, but urge it to think longer and broader – a recommendation that includes attention to questions and phenomena like institutions, laws, and policies that live on a different scale. CSCW has in some instances become good at speaking back to the people who practice, manage, and build cyberinfrastructure, but the main practical import of its lessons tend to be posed and absorbed at the level of project management, such as best practice guides on how to build and support collaborative science projects under current operating conditions. It has rarely turned its attention to larger questions around the mechanisms and broad policy choices that set those conditions, or engaged in a deeper sense how policy-level shifts and dynamics can advance or retard, enable or undermine, the collaborative concerns, issues, and possibilities we care about. This is a world that CSCW researchers who care about scientific collaboration can and need to connect to. But to make this bridge, we need new ideas and approaches. Science policy can help.

III. CHANGING SCIENCE: THE VIEW FROM SCIENCE POLICY

In the immediate aftermath of World War II, the U.S. scientific establishment faced a question: what to do with the resources of the nation's science community recently mobilized by war? An early and influential answer was offered by Vannevar Bush, head of the Office of Scientific Research and Development (OSRD) that had overseen the unprecedented national organization and expansion of scientific research funding during the war. In his influential 1945 report *Science: The Endless Frontier* [6] delivered to President Truman and his more popular July 1945 Atlantic Magazine essay, "As We May Think," [7] Bush supplied a framework that would shape U.S. (and in smaller measure western European) science policy thinking and practice through most of the ensuing decades. At its core was a call for a National Research Foundation that would carry on some of the funding and leadership activities of the erstwhile OSRD, organized now under civilian auspices. The new foundation would continue the wartime pattern of public support for basic scientific research (arguably the most significant and enduring invention of the war), ensuring the continuity of the massive research explosion stimulated by conflict while directing these to new and peaceful ends (basic discovery, economic growth, etc.). In Bush's proposal, the new foundation was to be science-run and science-led, with minimal interference from Congress or indeed the broader public.[3]

In 1950, this vision was realized (with modification) by presidential advisor John Steelman in the form of the National Science Foundation Act [42]. At the core of the model was a central trade-off or compromise. Science would be supplied the kind of resources, discretion, and autonomy called for by Bush. In exchange, it was expected to deliver findings, insights, and eventually applications that would feed national economic growth and global competitiveness, quality of life, and improved public decisions around matters of common concern. Investments at the new NSF would be targeted towards "basic" research, whose findings were expected (but only later) to feed into downstream forms of application and products that would produce the payback on public investment. This basic trade-off came to be called America's "social contract with science."

At the heart of this vision lay a distinctly linear imagination of scientific research and impact, which was likened to a pipeline. Suitably primed, the pump of science would produce breakthroughs and discoveries that would flow through (more or less automatically) into applications, products, and other goods of clear public value. As a model

[3] While space allows us to focus only on features of the U.S. model, some of these principles were replicated in different forms in the systems of postwar science funding emerging in Western Europe and later East Asia.

of innovation, this represented a science-push stance that argued for the course of scientific discovery as best and most reliably guided by the native curiosities and standards of scientists themselves. Efforts to tie programs of research to distinct social or national goals or subject them to popular or Congressional scrutiny were, beyond a certain very general point, regarded as unhelpful and more likely to dry up the pipeline than to focus or direct it in any successful way. From the standpoint of policymakers and the general public, science was to operate as a black and somewhat magical box: funding would go in, and some time later (through means radically underspecified in the model) useful results or products would come out. Above all, the whole process was to be driven, evaluated, and run by scientists [20].

This postwar "social contract" did important things for the organization of science. It established the standing of universities alongside industrial and government research labs as leading recipients of federal research dollars and sites for scientific research in general. It established key institutional principles and mechanisms, including the process and centrality of peer review, by which quality was to be assessed and resources allocated. It set up the unique system of NSF "rotators", in which practicing scientists would spend periods of time at the NSF in functional roles ranging from Program Officer to Assistant Director. In its directorate and program structures, it established divisions and fixed boundaries between what were then often still nascent disciplinary identities and divides (though made less nascent as the effects of institutionalization set in). It established, in fact, the principle of organizing the funding of American civilian science around disciplinary principles at all. (Imagine for example how different the world of science policy and infrastructure might look today had Bush and Steelman chosen to organize the civilian science effort around *problems* rather than 'fields.') Above all, it drew a bright red line down the center of the science/society relationship, and established the terms of exchange on each side: society, in the form of taxpayer dollars and cultural consent funneled through the NSF and similar bodies, would provide the dollars and an extraordinary degree of autonomy and generalized trust; science would pursue its work guided by its own internal lights, and eventually, as basic research filtered through to applied insights and products, supply the goods. These general principles constituted the starting point for how we would approach questions of science and science policy for the next half-century, and arguably still dominates the imagination – and in some quarters, the practice – of science policy today.

III.i. Post-normal science

While the postwar pipeline model was not without critics from day one, it took until the 1970s before alternative principles began to emerge in the science policy literature. An early and important example of this came in Funtowicz and Ravetz's [18] arguments around the changing nature and policy implications of "post-normal" science. As Funtowicz and Ravetz describe, the emergence and recognition of post-normal science rests on the growing realization that "the new problems facing our industrial civilization, although requiring scientific inputs for their resolution, involve a problem-solving activity that is different in character from the kind that we have previously taken for granted." Citing the increasing social salience of risk and the demonstrated failure of predictive risk assessment techniques, post-normal science emphasizes the experience and growing prominence of fields like nuclear and environmental regulation, where "facts are uncertain, values in dispute, stakes high, and decisions urgent." Under such conditions, the "puzzle-solving" orientation of normal science breaks down, and new forms and strategies may be required: "extended stakeholder dialogues," "extended peer review," and even "extended facts" built on inputs and participants (e.g. communities affected by environmental decision-making) beyond the usual scientific set. Such fields thus encounter and ultimately depend on a degree of epistemic pluralism unaccounted for under the pipeline model: both at the intersection of previously distinct and self-governing disciplines, and the more radical and sometimes fractious break between scientific and broader public means of assessing knowledge and risk around matters of common interest and concern.

Beyond the difficulties of adjudicating competing knowledge claims in regulatory and other decision contexts, post-normal science may have implications for the kinds of knowledge infrastructures we seek to build and support as a matter of policy. To begin, the increasingly blended quality of the problems that large-scale infrastructures are called upon to solve point to earlier and more complex disciplinary integrations at the level of research; the kinds of conflicts and disputes noted by Funtowicz and Ravetz as a feature of the regulatory arena are thereby pushed back into the infrastructure of the research process itself. The same blended and extended quality produces both arguments and a constituency for earlier and more substantive engagement with concerned but non-credentialed publics, seen for example in popular epidemiology [5] or patient group activism [15]. These groups, too, are being pushed back into the infrastructure in ways unanticipated and awkwardly accommodated under pipeline models of the research process.

III.ii: Mode-2 Science

Over the past 20 years, a loose collective of European science policy scholars [19, 34] have offered an alternative take on science policy reform. Like Funtowicz and Ravetz, their prescriptions follow from a fundamentally different take on the relation between science and society: not the separate, arms-length and linear relation imagined under the post-war social contract, but a more complex, intimate, and dynamic one in which society enters into the making and shaping of science, and vice versa, from day one. This relationship extends from the definition of problems of interest, to the public negotiation of scientific fact, to the entry of non-credentialed experts into the high-stakes game of scientific expertise and decision-making.

In all these ways, argue Nowotny et. al. [34], scientific knowledge finds itself increasingly "contextualized": whether the "weak" contextualization of CERN and the particle physics community (in which the autonomy of internal science decisions continues to weigh heavily against the social claims and rationales for investment); or the "strong" contextualization of contemporary environmental research programs (in which scientific autonomy and internal shaping may be outweighed by specific claims of social or public interest). In such a "mode-2" world, both the justification and autonomy of science have become less automatic than under the Endless Frontier ("mode-1") vision. Science retains enormous importance and cachet; indeed, its reach into the details of social life is arguably intensified and expanded. But it is also expected to provide a better and more specific account of its activities, and to operate within a more pluralistic universe of knowledge and values, in which it remains a crucial but no longer necessarily dominant player. These effects are strongest where mode-2 conditions of uncertainty, pluralism, and deep social values most apply.

In Nowotny et. al.'s wide-ranging discussion, mode-2 science is characterized by a number of additional traits: the increasing social distribution of expertise and broader appreciation for the values and contributions of more distributed knowledge forms; the heightened importance and permeability of key knowledge-making institutions, like industrial and government research labs, research councils, and universities; and a shift from certainty and reliability to "socially robust knowledge" as a value and marker of effective scientific work. These features have implications for the internal organization of research (a line which is indeed increasingly difficult to demarcate). Thus, pluralism is recreated and celebrated in the form of interdisciplinarity, as the disciplinary organization of "basic" research is replaced by a more "applied" focus on problems, around which disciplinary structures and interests are left to sort themselves out. Science funders are increasingly insistent on measures and rationales of impact; more stringent around questions of project management and reporting; more directive in channeling scientific work towards socially identified goals and objectives (e.g. the numerous "grand challenge" frameworks issued by national academies and federal funders in recent years); and insistent on the transformational quality of publicly-supported research. In these and other ways, mode-2 approaches look to balance the competing claims of scientific autonomy and social accountability in ways fundamentally different than under the postwar social contract.

III.iii. Pasteur's Quadrant

A leading example of post-pipeline approaches in U.S. science policy scholarship comes from Donald Stokes [43] and his emphasis on the importance of "use-inspired basic science" as a form and model of scientific research. Drawing on leading historical scientists as exemplars, Stokes divides the world of research into four basic quadrants defined by orientation towards the quest for fundamental understanding on one hand, and considerations of use on the other. These span the spectrum from forms of pure research conducted with no consideration for downstream use or impact (personified by physicist Niels Bohr's work on the atom), to the highly applied forms of research exemplified in Thomas Edison's invention of the phonograph. But Stokes' true interest lies in a third form that combines the best features of each: "use-inspired basic research" as exemplified in the work of Louis Pasteur.

Work in "Pasteur's Quadrant" exhibits features that mark it as a particularly promising target for public investment. It requires no faith in the magical efficacy of the pipeline, as considerations of use enter into the framing of research in its early stages. It fits well with the political realities of science funding, including popular expectations that scientific research will feed into matters of public concern in more direct ways. In training the efforts of the scientific community in particular directions, it may improve the strength and efficacy of the science-technology link, while providing constraints and scaffolding that in fact focus and inspire rather than restrict path-breaking forms of research. And it may provide a more accurate description of how research works in the world, while building deeper and more generative relations between forms and sites of work – for example, academic and industrial research labs – that tend to get separated and/or mystified under the basic/applied split central to Bush's model. In all these ways, work in Pasteur's Quadrant shows better hope of modifying, renewing and sustaining the social compact with science under the conditions of a globalizing and post-Cold War world.

III.iv. Discussion

Taken collectively, the post-normal, mode-2 and Pasteur's Quadrant frameworks provide a useful extension to the simplified assumptions of the post-war social contract ideal. As each of these models suggest, the basic relationship between science and society may be undergoing profound change, both politically and institutionally. It is not clear, as debates from stem cell research to climate change suggest, that scientific experts now or will ever again possess the kind of unassailable public respect and authority granted them under the postwar social contract. Nor is it clear that the dominant post-war mechanisms of science funding and evaluation championed by Bush – single or small-team PI-driven research awarded on a project basis and vetted through discipline-centered forms of peer review – are adequate to the increasingly mode-2 problems we encounter. Instead, we are likely to see interdisciplinary and translational mechanisms and mandates expand, along with new efforts to link academic research with sites and actors that would have once looked distinctly and suspiciously 'applied' – practitioners, commercializers, etc. Many of these challenges only intensify as we turn to the emergent, integrative, and fast-moving areas of science that cyberinfrastructure developers have targeted as particularly promising sites of impact and transformation. These conditions tend to magnify rather than reduce the types of uncertainties, collisions, and combinations noted above as features of a post-normal, mode-2 or Pasteur's Quadrant world.

All of these points are borne out when we turn to the forms of cyberinfrastructure development being pursued at the NSF and other funders today. Beyond the enabling role of tools and technologies, the shifting social conditions of science provide the single best explanation for why we need many of the things that cyberinfrastructure promises to deliver – collaboration, interdisciplinarity, larger and multiple perspectives on problems of public import, etc. In this regard, cyberinfrastructure is as much a child of science policy and shifts in science-society relations as it is of technology per se. But as the brief empirical vignette that follows illustrates, these same features pose distinct challenges to design, governance and practice that CSCW scholars need to take into account.

IV. EMPIRICAL DISCUSSION: POST-NORMAL TENSIONS IN THE DEVELOPMENT OF CYBERINFRASTRUCTURE[4]

In 1995, the National Science Foundation established its first agency-wide account for the regularized funding of major science and engineering infrastructure. Subsequently renamed the Major Research Equipment and Facilities Construction (MREFC) Account, the new category was designed to support the planning and construction of crucial large-scale infrastructure whose costs (typically in the hundreds of millions of dollars) exceeded and sometimes dwarfed the budget capacities of individual NSF directorates. Candidate projects were required to go through an intensive multi-year planning and review process modeled after project management techniques drawn from the defense sector and mission science agencies like NASA and the Department of Energy. The process proceeded through a series of structured steps culminating in National Science Board, Office of Management and Budget, and Congressional review.

In comparison to the PI-driven research programs dominating most other activities of the Foundation (often referred to as 'R&RA' activities, for 'Research and Related Accounts'), prospective MREFC projects are subject to an unusually detailed and complex set of demands. To pass muster with peer and internal NSF and National Science Board reviews, MREFC planners must articulate a basic research program around a unified set of science questions that meet the standards of traditional and usually discipline-based peer review. At the same time, NSF, White House and Congressional leaders – who ultimately approve or disapprove projects as annual line items in the Presidential and Congressional budgets – must be convinced of the broad public merit of the requested investment, usually by promoting the project's ability to provide new and crucial findings that help solve problems of identified national interest and need. This intense political engagement can erode the autonomy scientists have traditionally enjoyed, and departs from the insulated pipeline model characteristic of the post-war era. In many of the cases we've studied, it also sets up a series of difficult-to-resolve challenges and tensions that lie at the intersection of mode-1 and mode-2 expectations and concerns.

One MREFC project for which this clash proved problematic was the Water and Environmental Research Systems (WATERS) Network, a proposed $400 million effort to create a national network of observatories and cyberinfrastructure for water-related research in the U.S. that arose in the early 2000s and ended in most respects with the failure to secure ongoing MREFC support in 2010. In the broadest terms, the WATERS effort brought together three distinct groups: a consortium of hydrologic scientists intending to develop new infrastructure and support tools for hydrology; a parallel and initially separate group of environmental engineers seeking to develop similar infrastructure for environmental field facilities; and somewhat later teams of social science researchers working on questions of human and social consumption. The union between the first two groups was often characterized by our informants as a "shotgun marriage" necessitated by the fact that leaders at the NSF and in Congress were unlikely to fund two separate and expensive infrastructure projects in the broad water space.

---

[4] This section draws on ethnographic work conducted by the first and third authors between May 2009 and December 2010. During this period we conducted 26 semi-structured interviews with WATERS project leaders and participants, NSF officials, and members of the Congressional and White House science policy staffs. Each interview took 1-2 hours in length, and was transcribed and coded according to grounded theory principles. We also participated in several workshops dedicated to the planning and evaluation of WATERS and other large-scale science projects, and reviewed documents and reports coming out of the WATERS planning effort, official project reviews and meeting notes, workshop reports, technical reports associated with WATERS and related network initiatives, and several policy reports associated with the construction and funding of large-scale science infrastructure. Fuller analysis of the WATERS case appears in separate work currently under review.

Almost from day one, the WATERS effort faced major challenges in aligning the worldviews of its two (later three) constituent fields: as described to us, on one hand the curiosity-driven nature of hydrologic science, and on the other the problem-solving nature of engineering. The difficulty of this alignment showed up most clearly when it came time to articulate the science questions that would drive and justify the new network. As numerous informants and the members of the National Science Board that reviewed and ultimately panned the WATERS proposal recounted, the proposal lacked a compelling and unified set of concerns that would unite and justify the work from a 'pure science' point of view.

WATERS also faced challenges around the shifting composition and nature of NSF management and advocacy around the project. High turnover rates among NSF rotators from the program officer up to the Assistant Director levels led to shifting waves of interest and enthusiasm as key supporters and senses of priority came and went. Finally, the distinctly linear style of MREFC development produced endemic problems of currency and timeliness. Under the terms of the MREFC, the design of infrastructural components is to be blueprinted early in the process in an attempt to build accountability and freeze costs. This becomes problematic in areas where the infrastructure in question lacks the one-time capital equipment quality of an accelerator or telescope (the models after which the MREFC was originally imagined) and where technological advances tend to be rapid. A fixed design runs the risk of becoming obsolete by the time the technical infrastructure components are actually built and implemented, posing deep challenges to more incremental and adaptive development models. The extent to which the timeline was truly fixed – and indeed, what could count as infrastructure at all – was also subject to disagreement and evolution by the various actors involved, including the different directorate constituencies at NSF.

Issues like these raise questions around the crucial interaction between policy-level entities like funding categories and the forms of design and collaborative practice more commonly addressed in CSCW research. They also raise questions around whether emergent and collaborative research networks can be effectively built through the MREFC mechanism in fields not previously organized around large equipment investments (e.g. physics and astronomy), and whether the MREFC mechanism itself may need to be rethought or applied differently for problem areas that draw in fields and research communities traditionally organized along decentralized and small science lines. Here again, CSCW expertise around infrastructure, coordination, and collaborative practice may have central contributions to make.

There are however important counter-examples to the WATERS experience. Running through the MREFC milestones just ahead of the WATERS planning effort was the National Ecological Observatory Network (NEON), a distributed and national scale ecological research platform that ultimately overcame the problems and controversies that scuttled the WATERS initiative and in summer 2011 officially moved into construction. On the face of it, NEON bears certain resemblances to WATERS. Like WATERS, it sought to organize a community of work with a fairly limited prior history of centralization, big infrastructure, or large-scale collaboration. Like WATERS, it faced the challenge of matching an expansive and distributed suite of infrastructure investment against the need for a coherent but potentially evolving set of science questions. And like WATERS, it was required to satisfy internal criteria of scientific legitimacy and review while making a compelling case for impact and national priority at the policy and wider public levels. At the same time, as informants at both WATERS and NEON noted, there were important features that set the two networks apart. First, through most of its planning history NEON retained high-level champions within the NSF whose support was maintained and transferred through successive rounds of rotation and turnover. Second, whereas WATERS was a multidisciplinary and multi-directorate effort (spread between the Biological Sciences, Engineering, and Social Behavioral and Economic Sciences respectively), NEON came out of a single directorate (Biological Sciences) and was thus spared some of the larger institutional and disciplinary translation problems that afflicted the WATERS effort.

As the extremely truncated stories of the MREFC, WATERS, and NEON begin to suggest, efforts to develop collaborative infrastructure in the sciences are likely to confront significant barriers and challenges at the policy level, many of which live in the tension between a mode-1 and mode-2 world. We have seen, for example, how projects such as WATERS can get caught in the middle between problem and discipline-centered framings and expectations of infrastructure, and how this plays out in the uncertain politics of peer and wider Congressional and administrative review. Normal versus post-normal orientations may also work their way into the complicated politics of scale and rhythm that attend the development of new collaborative infrastructures in the sciences. There is debate, for example, around the relative merits of centralist vs. distributed funding models, the big push vs. the long tail (or what we've identified elsewhere as the question of Networks vs. networks). The former lives easily in a mode-1 world (recall that the orienting metaphor for large-scale infrastructure projects under the MREFC remains the ships and telescopes of established research communities), and has many of the virtues that scale and stability bring. The latter is less certain, and doesn't look necessarily like *either* the large capital projects traditionally funded as infrastructure at the NSF or the short term and one-off tradition of the investigator-led project. The same general discrepancy may attend key questions around time and rhythm that shape the development and practice of collaborative infrastructure in the sciences [25].

Finally, transitions and legacies between earlier and contemporary moments of science policy may be reflected in the somewhat complicated institutional dynamics and limitations that surround the efforts of agencies like the NSF. In many key respects, the NSF today looks different than the agency founded in 1950. The work the foundation supports, the problems it seeks to address, its mechanisms for intra-agency brokering and coordination, and the relations it maintains to government and the broader public have all shifted, in lesser and greater ways. But in other key structural and perhaps cultural regards, the institution looks uncannily the same. With minor adjustments for content and certain efforts at foundation-wide integration, the NSF's basic structure and operation remain unchanged from its early post-war manifestations. The agency still follows the same basic principles around peer review, rotation, and evaluation championed in The Endless Frontier. If the ghost of Vannevar Bush were to return to the NSF today, he would almost certainly find the place recognizable. But this raises deep questions about the relationship between institutional stasis and the kinds of flexibility and innovation better associated with creative and forward-looking work in the science policy space. In the language offered here, the NSF circa 2012 may be a normal institution trying to do post-normal things. Nowhere are these tensions more evident than in the complex and emergent world of new infrastructure development and collaboration in the sciences.

VI. CONCLUSION: WHY SCIENCE POLICY NEEDS CSCW

We have now discussed possibilities and challenges confronting the development of collaborative scientific infrastructure in the distinctly post-pipeline world of contemporary science policy. As the discussions of MREFC funding and the more specific challenges of projects like WATERS and NEON make clear, collaborative science efforts today must navigate a more complex policy world than the one described and partially built by Vannevar Bush. Contemporary collaborative science projects like WATERS, NEON, and other efforts studied by CSCW researchers are both children and victims of this new environment. The trends toward contextualized, problem-centered and translational research account for many of their most distinctive features, and in fact help explain the more interdisciplinary and collaborative models of work at their core. But they also present projects like WATERS and NEON with some of their thorniest problems: challenges of interdisciplinarity, conflicts between scientific autonomy and social responsiveness, etc. Many of these tensions and uncertainties stem from the messy intersection of mode-1 and mode-2 expectations and realities. It is this intersection, rather than the neat description of either, that defines the making and doing of large-scale collaborative science today.

In such a world, it turns out, science policy has much to learn from CSCW. The first and most obvious contribution concerns design and the role of tools and infrastructure as avenues or drivers of change. It is striking, for example, that neither the post-normal, mode-2, nor Pasteur's Quadrant frameworks pay much attention to computational development as a source of change in their models (a rather shocking absence, given the dynamism of changes in this sector. If fourth paradigm and other data or tool-centric accounts make too much of computing as a driver of scientific change, the broader science policy literature almost certainly makes too little. In failing to engage design in a specific sense, science policy loses the chance to draw more specific lessons: for example, the rather important one of how different modes and approaches to infrastructure development might impact the world of science and broader science-society relations differently. Science policy frameworks have tended to emphasize sociological or natural drivers of change to the general neglect of the crucial relationship between tools and everyday practices of work – something CSCW has a great deal to say about.

Second, CSCW research has much to say about the human and organizational dimensions of distributed collaborative forms. Where science policy struggles to understand the effects of individual users and the ties and forms of exchange that bind them into more and less loosely bound collaborations, CSCW has developed rich theoretical and methodological traditions around these questions that science policy has for the most part failed to grasp.

Third and finally, common CSCW approaches and sensibilities around the iterative nature of planning and development might help change the way we think about the relationship between planning and practice in the science and wider policy communities. As evidenced in the above discussion of the MREFC planning process, science policy mechanisms and debates may be uncomfortably stuck in a view of the world that unreasonably divorces planning from downstream action, undermining necessary principles of flexibility, adaptation, and the opportunities for learning and correction they provide. CSCW design approaches built around different principles – iteration, interactivity, prototyping, etc. – may have important contributions to make in opening up this world. For these and many other reasons, science policy needs CSCW.

Ironically, such an engagement may raise distinctly mode-2 questions for CSCW itself. Can CSCW think towards new modes and aspirations for engagement, above and beyond its usual forms and sites of work (and can the insights of scholars like Nowotny, Funtcowicz and Ravetz, and Stokes help get us there)? What might such a move do to our own 'internal' practices of knowledge making (and how should we respond)? Is there such a thing as post-normal CSCW? And should there be?

The question as framed is misleading. In many key regards, CSCW was born post-normal, an example (even a poster-child!) of the sorts of disciplinary mixing and science/society reconfigurations that post-normal and mode-2 scholars have emphasized. The concerns around impact that opened this paper, for example, are recognizably mode-2 concerns and would be largely foreign to the researchers of a pipeline world (in which impact is taken as a matter of faith, or as someone else's business.)

But as illustrated above, the conditions and tensions associated with post-normalism, Pasteur's Quadrant, etc. also pose distinct difficulties and challenges, some of which we would expect to see in the form of tensions and divisions within the CSCW community. These map in predictable ways the ones noted above: for example, tensions around evaluation (how to judge quality across methodological and disciplinary divides?); credit (how to weigh contributions of 'service' and impact versus old-fashioned journal and conference publications?); constituencies (who do we want to engage with our work, and what kind of relationships do we want to have with them?); and support (what kind of work should funders and we as a research community put our dollars behind, and what kind of efforts do we want to support in this space?).

One response to the uncertainties above – let's call them mode 2 anxieties – is a retreat or nostalgia towards established disciplinary norms and practices, including more traditional or externally certified standards of quality and rigor. For first generation CSCW scholars who grew up in other academic homelands, some of these will be the disciplinary traditions we came from. This may account for at least some of the methodological anxieties that haunt the margins of scholarship in CSCW, information science, and related fields. Many of us find ourselves longing for worlds in which statistics are more rigorously practiced and understood, experiments are more precisely conducted, or higher and deeper standards of ethnographic work prevail (take your disciplinary pick). We may also long to see our students trained with the same depth and care that we received in our own core areas of work. Such concerns run deep and real, and must be taken into account under any serious engagement with the practice and politics of interdisciplinarity. One natural reflex under mode 2 conditions is thus to move or look backwards, escaping uncertainty and the epistemological tensions and anxieties it occasions by retreating to older or more settled systems for the production and validation of knowledge.

Another response, however, is to move forward – to make CSCW, in effect, 'post-normaler'. Under this model, CSCW would get less comfortable, and push forward into modes of work that the field has been less inclined to prioritize and reward to date. CSCW scholars would continue the trend toward deeper and more sustained engagement with cyberinfrastructure practice at the project level, with or without the near-term promise of publication. But they would also strengthen their efforts at higher levels of engagement, bringing CSCW insight to the shaping of science policy itself. This could take multiple forms: contribution to high level reports and science advisory activities (for examples to date, see [8, 24]); extended service at the NSF or other federal funders; and heightened participation in broader science policy processes in Washington, including at the White House (e.g. Office of Science and Technology Policy) and Congressional levels. Such engagements are best supported by modes of CSCW research that understand and embrace the policy world, building better bridges from CSCW's traditional interests in design, organization, and collaborative practice to broader policy questions around institutions, publics and governance that the field would do well to embrace.

REFERENCES

1. Atkins, D.E., Droegemeier, K.K., Feldman, S.I., et al. Revolutionizing Science and Engineering Through Cyberinfrastructure: Report of the National Science Foundation Blue-Ribbon Advisory Panel on Cyberinfrastructure. *Report of the National Science Foundation blue-ribbon advisory panel on cyberinfrastructure*, (2003).
2. Birnholtz, J. What does it mean to be an author? The intersection of credit, contribution, and collaboration in science. *Journal of the American Society for Information Science 57*, 13 (2006), 1758–1770
3. Birnholtz, J.P. and Bietz, M.J. Data at work: supporting sharing in science and engineering. *Proceedings of the 2003 International ACM SIGGROUP Conference on Supporting Group Work*, ACM (2003), 339–348.
4. Borgman, C.L. The conundrum of sharing research data. *Journal of the American Society for Information Science and Technology*, (2011), 1–40.
5. Brown, P., Mikkelsen, E.J. No safe place: toxic waste, leukemia, and community action. University of California Press, Berkeley and Los Angeles, CA, 1997.
6. Bush, V. *Science: The Endless Frontier: A Report to the President on a Program for Postwar Scientific Research.* National Science Foundation, Washington, DC, 1945.
7. Bush, V. As we may think. *The Atlantic Monthly*, 176, 101-108.
8. Cummings, J., Finholt, T., Foster, I., Kesselman, C., and Lawrence, K.A. *Beyond being there: A blueprint for advancing the design, development, and evaluation of virtual organizations*. NSF, 2008.
9. Cummings, J. and Kiesler, S. Coordination costs and project outcomes in multi-university collaborations. *Research Policy 36*, 10 (2007), 1620–1634.

10. De Roure, D., Jennings, N., and Shadbolt, N. Research agenda for the Semantic Grid: a future e-science infrastructure. *Commissioned for EPSRC/DTI Core e-Science*, December (2001).

11. Dourish, P. Implications for design. *Proceedings of the SIGCHI conference on Human Factors in Computing Systems*, (2006), 541.

12. The Economist. The Data Deluge, 2010. Retrieved December 7, 2012 from the Economist: http://www.economist.com/printedition/2010-02-27

13. Edwards, P.N., Jackson, S.J., Bowker, G.C., and Knobel, C.P. Report of a Workshop on "History & Theory of Infrastructure: Lessons for New Scientific Cyberinfrastructures", January 2007. Available at: http://hdl.handle.net/2027.42/49353.

14. Edwards, P., Mayernik, M.S., Batcheller, A., Bowker, G., and Borgman, C. Science Friction: Data, Metadata, and Collaboration. *Social Studies of Science*, (2011).

15. Epstein, S. Impure Science: AIDS, activism and the politics of knowledge, University of California Press, Berkeley and Los Angeles, 1996.

16. Faniel, I.M. and Jacobsen, T.E. Reusing Scientific Data: How Earthquake Engineering Researchers Assess the Reusability of Colleagues' Data. *Computer Supported Cooperative Work, 19*, 3-4 (2010), 355–375.

17. Finholt, T.A. and Olson, G.M. From Laboratories to Collaboratories: A New Organizational Form for Scientific Collaboration. *Psychological Science 8*, 1 (1997), 28–36.

18. Funtowicz, S. O., and Ravetz, J.R. The emergence of post-normal science. in von Schomberg R. ed. Science, politics, and morality: Scientific uncertainty and decision making , Kluwer Academic Publishers, Dordrecht, 1993, 85-123.

19. Gibbons, M., Limoges, C., Nowotny, H., Schwartzman, S., Scott, and P., Trow, M. *The New Production of Knowledge: The Dynamics of Science and Research in Contemporary Societies*, Sage Publications, Thousand Oaks, 1994.

20. Guston, D.H. Between politics and science: Assuring the Integrity and Productivity of Research. Cambridge University Press, Cambridge, 2007.

21. Hayes, E.F., Bemet, A.L., Hennessy, J., Ingram, J., Pitts, N., Young, P.R., Kollman, P.A., Vernon, M.K., White, A.B., and Wulf, W.A. (1995) Report of the Task Force on the Future of the NSF Supercomputer Centers Program.

22. Howison, J. and Herbsleb, J.D. Scientific software production: incentives and collaboration. *Proceedings of the ACM 2011 Conference on Computer Supported Cooperative Work*, (2011), 513–522.

23. Hinds, P. J., & Kiesler, S. *Distributed Work*. MIT Press, Cambridge, 1-145, 2002.

24. Jackson, S.J., Edwards, P.N., Bowker, G.C., and Knobel, C.P. Understanding Infrastructure: History, Heuristics, and Cyberinfrastructure Policy. *First Monday, 12*(6), 2007, 1–9.

25. Jackson, S.J., Ribes, D., Buyuktur, A., and Bowker, G.C. Collaborative rhythm: temporal dissonance and alignment in collaborative scientific work. *Proceedings of the ACM 2011 Conference on Computer Supported Cooperative Work*, ACM (2011), 245–254.

26. Jasanoff, S. Science and Public Reason (The Earthscan Science in Society Series). Routledge, New York, NY, 2012.

27. Karasti, H., Baker, K.S., and Halkola, E. Enriching the Notion of Data Curation in E-Science: Data Managing and Information Infrastructuring in the Long Term Ecological Research (LTER) Network. *Computer Supported Cooperative Work, 15*, 4 (2006), 321–358.

28. Karasti, H., Baker, K.S., and Millerand, F. Infrastructure Time: Long-term Matters in Collaborative Development. *Computer Supported Cooperative Work, 19*, 3-4 (2010), 377–415.

29. Kee, K.F. and Browning, L.D. The Dialectical Tensions in the Funding Infrastructure of Cyberinfrastructure. *Computer Supported Cooperative Work, 19*, 3-4 (2010), 283–308.

30. Kolko, B.E., Hope, A., Brunette, W., et al. Adapting collaborative radiological practice to low-resource environments. *Proceedings of the ACM 2012 conference on Computer Supported Cooperative Work - CSCW '12*, (2012), 97.

31. Lax, P.D. Report on the Panel of Large-scale computing in Science and Engineering. DOD, NSF, DOE, NASA, 1982.

32. Lee, C.P., Dourish, P., and Mark, G. The human infrastructure of cyberinfrastructure. *Proceedings of the 2006 20th Anniversary Conference on Computer Supported Cooperative Work*, (2006), 483.

33. Millerand, F., and Bowker, G. C. Metadata standard: Trajectories and enactment in the life of an ontology. In M. Lampland & S. L. Star ed. *Standards and their stories. How quantifying, classifying, and formalizing practices shape everyday life*. Cornell University Press, Ithaca, 2009, 149–165.

34. Nowotny, H., Scott, P., and Gibbons, M. *Re-Thinking Science: Knowledge and the Public in an Age of Uncertainty*. Polity, Cambridge, 2001.

35. NSF-CISE. From Desktop To Teraflop: Exploiting the U.S. Lead in High Performance Computing, Report. NSF Blue Ribbon Panel on High Performance Computing, 2003.

36. Olson, G.M. The next generation of science collaboratories. *2009 International Symposium on Collaborative Technologies and Systems*, December 1999 (2009), xv–xvi.

37. Olson, G. M., Zimmerman, A., & Bos, N. *Scientific Collaboration on the Internet (Acting with Technology)*, MIT Press, Cambridge, 2008.

38. Ribes, D. and Finholt, T.A. The Long Now of Technology Infrastructure: Articulating Tensions in Development. *Journal of the Association for Information Systems, 10*, 5 (2009), 375–398.

39. Ribes, D., Jackson, S.J, Geiger, S., Burton, M., and Finholt, T. A. "Artifacts That Organize: Delegation in the Distributed Organization." Information and Organization (forthcoming).

40. Ribes, D. and Lee, C.P. Sociotechnical Studies of Cyberinfrastructure and e-Research: Current Themes and Future Trajectories. *Computer Supported Cooperative Work, 19*, 3-4 (2010), 231–244.

41. Star, S.L. and Ruhleder, K. Steps Toward an Ecology of Infrastructure: Design and Access for Large Information Spaces. *Information Systems Research 7*, 1 (1996), 111–134.

42. Steelman, J.R. *Science and Public Policy.* Government Printing Office, Washington, D.C., 1947.

43. Stokes, D. *Pasteur's Quadrant: Basic Science and Technological Innovation.* Brookings Institution Press, Washington, D.C., 1997.

44. U.S. National Science Foundation. Cyberinfrastructure Vision for 21st Century Discovery, 2007.

45. Vertesi, J. and Dourish, P. The Value of Data : Considering the Context of Production in Data Economies. *Proceedings of the ACM 2011 Conference on Computer Supported Collaborative Work*, (2011), 533–542.

46. Wulf, W. A. The collaboratory opportunity. *Science, 261*, 5123 (1993), 854–5.

What is a File?

Richard Harper[1], Eno Thereska[1], Siân Lindley[1], Richard Banks[1], Phil Gosset[1], William Odom[2], Gavin Smyth[1], Eryn Whitworth[3]

[1]Microsoft Research Cambridge
7 JJ Thomson Avenue
Cambridge, CB3 0FB, UK
Email: intialsur-name@microsoft.com
Except r.harper@

[2]Carnegie Mellon University
Human-Computer Interaction Institute
Pittsburgh, PA, USA
Email wo@willodom.com

[3]The University of Texas at Austin School of Information
1616 Guadalupe
Austin, TX 78701-1213
Email
eryn@mail.ischoolutexas.edu

ABSTRACT
For over 40 years the notion of the *file*, as devised by pioneers in the field of computing, has been the subject of much contention. Some have wanted to abandon the term altogether on the grounds that metaphors about files can confuse users and designers alike. More recently, the emergence of the 'cloud' has led some to suggest that the term is simply obsolescent. In this paper we want to suggest that, despite all these conceptual debates and changes in technology, the term file still remains central to systems architectures and to the concerns of users. Notwithstanding profound changes in what users do and technologies afford, we suggest that files continue to act as a cohering concept, something like a 'boundary object' between computer engineers and users. However, the effectiveness of this boundary object is now waning. There are increasing signs of slippage and muddle. Instead of throwing away the notion altogether, we propose that the definition of and use of files as a boundary object be reconstituted. New abstractions are needed, ones which reflect what users seek to do with their digital data, and which allow engineers to solve the networking, storage and data management problems that ensue when files move from the PC on to the networked world of today.

Author Keywords
File; file systems; databases; cloud computing; grammar of action; metadata; generic object; ownership, possession; command; social networking; consumer devices.

ACM Classification Keywords
H.5.m. Information interfaces and presentation (e.g., HCI): Miscellaneous.

INTRODUCTION
As long ago as 1981, Frank Halasz and Tom Moran argued that the term file was harmful to good HCI [5]. In their view, users have some kind of mental model or 'internal picture' of files, and this is necessarily different from the 'abstract conceptual model' that is embedded in a computer. When the term is used to conjure 'literary metaphors' [p. 385] in, say, the design of interfaces, muddles inevitably result. For the model that ends up being presented to the user will never 'fit' the actual system – it can never do so, in their view. The two are fundamentally irreconcilable; the metaphorical model and the 'real' model embedded in the system.

This view certainly seems cogent and doubtlessly is one that many in HCI would accept. After all it turns around a basic premise in much of the psychology used in HCI. This holds that the external world needs to be represented in some kind of internal form or 'qualia' in the human mind and good design ensures that there is a fit between this internal model and the external. Since there is unlikely to ever be a 'good internal model' of computer files, then Halasz and Moran's case is that it would be unwise to try and design towards that model; it is best to design on the basis of the 'real thing' even though that prohibits certain types of metaphor – like those associated with the term file.

But today, as new applications and technologies confront the user, the apparent cogency of Halasz and Moran's case seems to be weakening. For it turns out that it is not clear what the entities that users deal with might be from anyone's point of view – the users *or* the engineers. What a file might be is becoming muddled, lost perhaps; certainly confused.

For example, one of Microsoft's products is *OneNote*. To a user, a OneNote *Notebook* looks very much like the thing produced in word processing applications – a document of sorts; one might even suggest a file-like thing. One of the appeals of OneNote is that it is somewhat more flexible than typical word processing applications, such as Microsoft's own *Word*. Users can easily add images and pictures, cut and paste from the Web, even add their own scribbles to a Notebook which the system can convert through OCR to typescript. All this can be brought together as a single thing. The application treats the thing that a user thus creates in a particular way. A Notebook is not a single entity; it is not, as it were, a single file. It is a collection of files – and indeed this is how the engineers who designed and built One-Note think of it: as a thing that consists of a number of 'read-write objects'. The important point to understand, however, is that, in OneNote, it is 'Sections' that define what a 'file' is. A user creates Sections within OneNote (although they may also interact with a Page, which they may think of as components of a Section).

Thus far, so good; in this scenario what a file is from the user's and the system engineer's point of view is pretty close; there is some correspondence between the 'mental model' and the 'real model'. However, when a user tries to save a Notebook on to a cloud service, like *SkyDrive* (as it happens also a Microsoft product), something else comes into play: namely, a different understanding of what are the file entities that makes a Notebook. In SkyDrive – to put it in simple terms – instead of a Section being a file (irrespective of how many pages it consists of), a file is sometimes redefined by the cloud storage application itself, one result of this being that on occasion a Section will be stored as several files. The cloud system stores its data in terms of the file abstractions, as bundles of files, but these don't correspond to the originating application's way of doing so: in one, 'files' take a different form to another.

That the cloud system defines files in its own way would not matter to the user as long as conversion back again is consistent. However, it does become an issue if a user's attempt to save to SkyDrive is interrupted (as often happens when accessing cloud services). For when they go back to SkyDrive after the interruption, they might find a version of their Notebook already there. This version will, though, be partial; incomplete in some respects and reflecting not their own understanding of the structure of their 'thing' nor the view of the file structure that developers of OneNote had in mind but something else: what the engineers behind SkyDrive conceived of as the file entities constitutive of a Notebook. It is this vision that will have determined which entities (files) were copied over before the interruption began.

At first glance, this would seem to confirm Halasz and Moran's fear: don't expect the user's mental model to fit systems. But this is not all that is going on here. What this scenario illustrates is that computer scientists don't have a common understanding of files *either*. This issue, this divergence of basic concepts, is not so much new, as it is one that comes to be highlighted with the massively networked, distributed world we are coming to where differences in basic concepts in applications start clashing when brought together.

This is not the only change that needs to be borne in mind, however. If the examples above evoke the PC and how it works, there are now other devices that are becoming almost as common and these have no files at all. The iPad, for example, has no equivalent to the Windows File Explorer for the simple reason that it has no files to view. It is file-less. Or at least this is what some would have us believe. For underneath the hood of this [see 7] and similar devices – like the more advanced smart phones – there are things that get called files although this is a label for 'abstractions' that allow the systems in question to run efficiently – address book information can be re-used in various applications, for example, as can user identity information. Unfortunately, it turns out just what these abstractions are and how they might be used is far from fixed or agreed. Attempts to ensure that new application developers avoid some of the difficulties that these ambiguities produce through, for example, sandboxing their applications (and hence hiding any abstractions from the developers' grasp), cause considerable complaint and besides, the boundaries of the sandpits are routinely broken by developers who find ways to illicitly access file stores via the OS.

A Way Forward

So what is one to make of this all? We don't think that the way forward in the current context is to abandon the term files altogether. We think that the term – and related ones such as 'to file' and 'filing'– can be linked in a way that can allow computer scientists and users to orient to a shared object or set of objects, even though the tasks they have in mind are in many respects quite distinct. In this regard, we think that the term can label what Star and Greisemer called in 1989 a 'boundary object' [18, see also Star's revised and more nuanced view, 17]: a device of sorts that can, amongst other things, allow two or more distinct communities to interact around a mutually comprehended and agreed 'object' and which can, at the same time, bring them together through focused arrangements and processes of action. In this view, files are not merely the neutral ground between users and engineers but a label for a space of organised collaboration.

Our argument will not be that the term file is already a boundary object of sorts however (it might well have been – but historical questions are not our main interest), so much as that it can become an *effective* one if it is given renewed meaning and vitality. A new set of definitions for the term file is required: ones that will allow computer scientists to engineer what users require, that will provide a meaningful base for those users to act upon and which can enable an evolving interaction of design and practice to emerge.

More than this, however: our goal is not only to propose how a refined definition of the term, a renewed boundary object, can enable these two sides to collaborate. It can also be, in our view (and consequent on this), part of a larger effort to define a new *grammar of action* for an HCI of the 21st century. This will be of concern to users and engineers.

It seems to us that the practices of users are now profoundly more social in nature than they were when the term 'file' was first coined by computer scientists and the first digital 'file' presented to users. Today, users don't just want to create and store files. They also want to share those files with friends and buddies on social networks. Sometimes they want to give those files to their friends, and sometimes they want to keep ownership or possession of them, even while their buddies view them. And all of this might happen in ways that make the question of where a file is stored sometimes relevant and sometimes not. At the same time, the tasks that computer scientists have to attend to given this evolution in user practice, the diversity of devices that engineers need to ensure run efficiently as the bedrock for these new practices, and the need to enable interaction between applications both between devices and on occasion processed remotely on the web, requires that from their view, a revived and invigorated notion of files needs to be deployed that can allow them to engineer in effective and hopefully novel ways.

Overview of the Paper

Our goals are then quite bold, albeit our topic might seem prosaic, almost obsolescent if some commentators are to be believed. Given this, we will structure the paper as follows. First, we want to remark on something that might seem orthogonal to our main goal, though as the paper unfolds we hope that this will be seen to be not the case.

We commence with the question of how words are to be understood. If one were to believe Halasz and Moran, words label things; thus the thing labelled by the word file in the outside world is (or ought to be) mapped into a representation of that thing (i.e., a qualia) in the mental world. But we think words are best understood as performative, as ways of doing things as well as sometimes labels for things. If this is so, we argue that when we approach the problem of what files 'are' (or might be – we shall assume it for the purposes of argument) we need to be sensitive to how the word itself is used and as we shall see, that use is quite diverse. It is important we do not muddle up uses as we try to plan a way forward for future use; rather we need to see what are the kinds of action that maps across and binds some uses while distinguishing others. These actions can be the basis of the grammar of action we will want to propose later on.

Having set the conceptual scene, we then turn to the more substantive topic of what files do (or did) in early computer system design. We remark on how the role of files has evolved and altered over the years. Though only a sketch, we will look at early attempts to move away from file systems to, for instance, database systems. The latter can be seen as emphasising relationships among files, rather than the file and its location within a folder or file hierarchy, in that the unit of most interest was the type of relationship itself. We then remark, again in passing, on attempts to design interfaces (primarily for the desktop) that sought to move away from the file metaphor or which sought to reinvigorate it, claiming that it has some cognitive value, Halasz and Moran notwithstanding. We will note that many of these papers did not attend to the question (or the role) of files from the engineer's point of view and so don't effectively comment on files as a boundary object. Nevertheless, this research does point towards new user practices.

We shall then turn to the technologies of the current time: to the world of cloud storage, social networks and applications like Facebook and Flickr, as well as to a world in which users have multiple devices and access points to a file. Building on examples such as provided above with regard to OneNote, we further illustrate some of the many difficulties that the old file abstraction has and is creating in this new world. We argue that these difficulties attest not to an 'incorrect model' of a file, so much as to the stresses that emerge when engineers and users try to orientate to what they think is the 'same model', when so many changes and dynamics are afoot that the model (or models) in question are made muddled, hybrid not to say contradictory. Besides, we go on to argue that the technology is changing, what applications allow users to do is changing, what users themselves want to do is also altering and this is begging the question of not so much what files are as what they ought to be or could be. The role of a file as a boundary object in the current context is thus losing its efficacy, we suggest, but if reinvigorated could lead us to inquire into new possibilities. It needs to be made more than simply a term used in common (or simply used by one side) obviously; it needs to be a label for some thing and for some practices that bind and enable, that direct and constrain, and that facilitate coherent innovation.

We then outline what we think might be a way forward, a path that allows designers to offer systems that reflect what users are seeking to do and which can be engineered so that the prosaic but neverthcless essential concerns about where data-as-files might be stored, and how it (they) might be accessed, copied, moved, made secure and so on, are thus dealt with effectively. But here we don't offer technological descriptions, say, as illustrative of where a new file abstraction might come to play a role, or recommendations for the design of a data store that combines file entities with other data types, such as graph relations (something that is required in many web-based application experiences [see 19]). Rather, we offer what we think ought to be the foundation of all such considerations: more nuanced vocabulary about what a system needs to enable and allow. This can be achieved, we believe, only in part by redefining what is meant by the word file and the doings associated with that usage; what is also required, and this is the rub of our paper, is a new grammar of action: a grammar for both users and engineers that provides the common ground of cohering their plans, their doings, their goals, around files and the other things they want to do in the age of the cloud.

WORDS AND MEANING: FILES AS A PERFORMATIVE CATEGORY

When one reads papers like Halasz and Moran's 'Analogy Considered Harmful' one is led to thinking of language as being a kind of tool, one that when used properly labels things. From this point of view, one of the troubles that HCI has to contend with is that users don't always know how to deploy language terms properly; there are infelicitous in their use and their understanding. Experts, meanwhile, technicians, computer scientists, HCI professionals and so forth, don't suffer from this egregious practice: their training ensures they use words correctly.

This is not the only way of approaching the general relationship between the use of terms in everyday life and in specialist or expert contexts, however. Other approaches treat user understandings as distinct from the technical but not as competitors to one another, with the user model often seeming weak or fallible in the way evoked by Halasz and Moran. Here, philosophers like Hanfling [6], following Wittgenstein [22], suggest that everyday language terms are not, as is often claimed by some (most notoriously the Churchlands [2]), part of 'common sense' attempts to do science – bad science to boot. Everyday terms do have a use, a purpose if you like; but in this view scientific usages have another.

The moral from this is that one ought to allow and assume this diversity. Nor should one rush to judge the former by their applicability to the latter. Terms are to be assessed by what they are used to do in the places in which those terms do 'work'. The term file and its various uses in everyday and technical contexts illustrates this kind of diversity and workload; it highlights too the broad distinctions between the everyday and the technical action with language.

In ordinary life, words like 'file' are often used to label things. In this respect there is an empirical referent at issue, one that subdivides the world into things that can be filed and those that cannot. But the ways in which the term is used are more nuanced than this. Thus, a letter from the Bank might be called a file but a love letter not so. The term implies, that is to say, something about its contents. Further, the term is also deployed to highlight particular relationships, between a 'file' and a person, for example. When this happens what is being pointed towards is accountability; the onus that someone might have to look after something is being emphasised. These usages (and doubtless others), which are commonplace in everyday life, are glossed over by the language of empirical reference.

In computer science, meanwhile, the term file is used to label the minimal digital entity that can be 'persisted'. A file is a label for a bundle of data, that is to say, but what that bundle consists in (i.e., what the binary data represent) doesn't really matter nor is it implied in the use of the term. A love letter and correspondence from the Bank are the same. And while the computer scientist does worry about accountability, in their case, they are concerned not with how an individual needs to look after a file but how a system does. The engineer seeks to answer questions like 'where does the file system put a bundle?', 'how does it name it?', 'retrieve' and 'make that file secure?' As it happens, some of these bundles can themselves be bundled into larger entities, and these start to look like the things that users 'see' when they interact with digital objects like Microsoft Word 'files'. Hence the term files is often labelled an *abstraction* in computer science, both because it labels a category that is a step higher than digital bytes, and because it can encompass various types of associations, bundles that look like 'user files' from above, from the users' point of view.

The point of these remarks is to allow us to assert the claim that, if and when language is understood as being made up of terms that are used in diverse and rich ways (as is the case with the term files), then one should not necessarily reject attempts to make linkages between instances of language use just because the empirical referent in question is diverse or complex, or because one use is empirical and another is not. Rather, one needs to approach the possibility of connection between uses of words carefully. Perhaps linkages of some kind are useful, perhaps they are not; it depends on what similarity (or otherwise) in actions are implied in each case.

Files as a *Way* of Bundling

This is illustrated when discussions about the cloud beg questions about what is the stuff that users want backed up and how it might be that computer scientists can engineer systems that are secure, economic and pliable with regard to this stuff. In these discussions one will find that computer scientists (if one can treat them as a single group for the moment) use the word file to label things that need to be dealt with quite carefully, and the doings that they are thinking of when they use the word are themselves quite particular and specialised. We have begun to remark on what those details are. Let us push that further. We have seen that computer scientists need to bundle the stuff they store. They need to put it somewhere and know where it is – though they care little for what it is. But at the same time, they do care that, whatever it is, it 'survives'. And this is an issue for computer scientists – not because they are neglectful in their design. Far from it. The problem is that the stuff they deal with, the stuff that comes in the form of bits and bytes, exists in an environment where that stuff (leaving aside what it consists of) can disappear.

Computer scientists need to cater for the practical reality that computer systems fail. They fail in part and they fail in totality; disk sectors can develop defects as a case in point (and this may mean that part of the digital store for a file is faulty) and sometimes disks can fail altogether (in which case remote back-up is required). Given this, computer scientists engineer computer systems (all systems, not only the flaky PC but also cloud storage systems and servers) to store data in such a fashion (or arrangement) that if part of the data is destroyed or even the whole, this event does not catastrophically affect the system's functioning, its utility. For the architecture duplicates data, so that if some is lost (as it is assumed will happen), then a copy will be available (somewhere or other) and can thus be used as a replacement. This in turn means that there has to be a system element to manage these duplications and stores: this keeps these versions up to date after changes are made, for example, and knows where they are stored. In this view, a 'file' is *not* the stuff stored, *it is a way of bundling that stuff* into identifiable materials that in turn can be managed, stored, retrieved, duplicated, preserved and so on, by the computer system and its component applications.

Some of the actions done with this abstraction, these things called files and the systems of which they are a part, are mirrored in the things that users can see (and do) and some are not. For example, with the abstraction in hand, a system can allow a file to be 'read' – and thus seen by the user, to put it crudely, even though the system also has the task of bringing together the thing-as-seen by the user from the various parts stored in different places. Likewise, when a user 'saves', the system 'writes' that data (i.e., the elements constituted at an abstract level as 'a file') somewhere and this means the system stores that data. Or to put this another way (though still simply), when a user 'saves', the system 'writes', when the user 'opens' a file, the system 'reads' that file, and so forth (See Fig. 1).

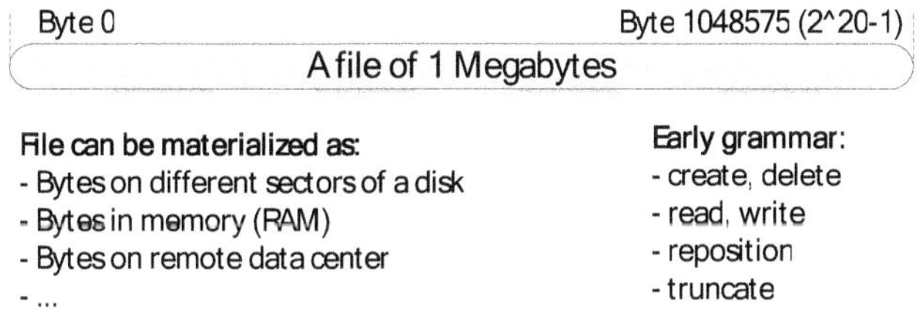

Figure 1: operating system view of a file abstraction as a consecutive, uninterrupted range of bytes [14, pp. 372-372]. The abstraction relieves users from understanding how the bytes that make up a file are scattered across memory or disk, giving them a simple logical object to operate on.

It is important to bear in mind that all of this work, all these doings, are not necessarily seen or understood by users – though these doings allow users to get their doings done whatever they might be. Questions of where bytes are stored are systematically hidden from the user's view.

Files as Boundary Objects

The point is that the term abstraction does label how computer scientists view the issues at hand, the issue of what a file is for both them and the user. One might say that users have a different abstraction, one that reflects what they think of as the properties of a thing that is a file as constituted in everyday life, while the computer scientist has another. It is in fact more complicated than that, however; it is not two abstractions. They are distinct yet bound in various ways. One element that coheres both views is that the thing itself – the OneNote file, say – is *at the point of use* for both the user and the computer scientist effectively a unitary object, a single entity, not a composite. So although a file may be made up of bits brought together from other files – and again, those other files might not be singular – those bits are brought together in real time when the user 'engages' with them. Never mind what a file system does with the entities constitutive of this file; the point is that *at the moment of interaction*, at the interface between the user and the system and thus, to put it crudely, *at the interface as understood by HCI*, what the user sees and what the computer scientist sees is the same thing, though how this gets assembled, what 'it' (i.e., the file) is going to become and where it came from, is different. The talent of the designers of early systems is reflected in the fact that despite these differences in orientation, the interaction that is undertaken nevertheless succeeds: users by and large get what they want, a file that can be handled as they understand it and a system that can function efficiently and effectively. Things get read and saved, users can act, the system can function.

This description is obviously a simplification of file systems design just as the one above was of the orientations of everyday life. But it is sufficient, we hope, to convey the claim that one might think of the word file – or rather the concept 'file' – as something like a boundary object [18; see also 17]. Without wishing to make any historical claims at this point, this object would appear to stand in the middle ground between the user and the computer scientist in a complex and delicate way, foreshadowing certain moments of cohesion while allowing differentiated paths of activity. It links and binds computer scientists (and their abstraction) and the user's point of view (and all that implies). The user can orient to digital content as if that content had properties similar to a corporeal file, being an object that can persist, that can be changed, kept and destroyed; and the computer scientist can architect systems that allow them to store the data constitutive of the file-as-seen-by-the-user wherever they wish, and to ensure that system errors do not destroy or corrupt data irretrievably.

Previous Attempts to Reconstitute Files

We have suggested that in being an abstraction, a boundary object, there is a profoundly complex yet binding differentiation between the everyday use of the term 'file' and the use of the same word with regard to systems. Over the years many attempts have been made to alter the form of this differentiation, and crudely speaking to bring these different orientations to files, the user's and the computer scientist's, closer together, or at least to alter this connection so that it is better able to allow users to do what they want and engineers to support those doings more effectively. In this regard one might say that there have been attempts to reconstitute the boundary object.

More particularly, and until recently, there have been three major and related themes of inquiry on this topic: the first concerning how to make documents on computers seem more like documents from the everyday human point of view; the second focusing on how to rethink the storage of a file in a way that gets away from treating a file as an entity in a hierarchical order, and moves towards distributed systems where a file can be an entity in more than one place and with more than one relationship to other files (superordinate or otherwise). The latter can be interpreted as a way of realising the former, and so oftentimes the arguments seem to blur into one another.

Beginning with the first theme: documents. There have been numerous attempts to redesign computer file systems to reflect the ways that people use and understand documents. Xerox PARC's *placeless documents* research project, at the end of the last century, was perhaps the most ambitious and well thought out of these efforts, reflected in subsequent years by other similar efforts. In Dourish *et al.'s* view [4], the placeless documents paradigm can be contrasted with a hierarchical file system. This latter approach typically puts a file in only one place in a hierarchy, irrespective of the fact that users might come to a document from different points of view and concerns (there are exceptions to this with 'multiple directory entry' points being allowed on some systems, for example, and with 'shortcuts' in Windows, as another exception).

For example, a document concerning travel plans might be relevant for budgeting and scheduling. These are distinct concerns. But the nuance of these distinctions cannot be represented if the file is only in one place and where the relationship is always superordinate – where a file must be in either one or other structural order but not both; either a budget representation or a scheduling one. Hence, a hierarchical system is too constrained, the Xerox researchers argue; a more human point of view more subtle. So management of documents becomes conflated in hierarchical systems: a file can be retrieved according to one criterion, as against the multitude of criteria users might apply; the hierarchical location of a file is used to determine back-up, not its salience to a user. One could go on.

The placeless documents system, in contrast, made paramount the user orientations to documents. So, for example, since users tend to associate all sorts of apparently ad hoc properties to their documents, the system would similarly allow any property to be associated in the 'file system' (leaving aside what 'a file' is for the moment) when representing a document. Hence, any categorisation the users prefer would be acceptable to the system; any way of collating and bundling would be acceptable too. Furthermore, these properties might be related to a specific user, and so the system ought to allow this too. This is important because the person who uses a document may not be who first created it – and this may be as important as what constitutes the use itself. Metadata that allow and govern access and interaction should reflect this.

All of these arguments can be seen to turn around the idea of getting away from things in fixed places to relationships that link things and doings with those things, from a system that stores a file to databases that create links between entities, some of which may be file-like. Such a view permits the heterogeneity highlighted above, and supports the position that not all files are equal while moving away from the notion of a hierarchy. In this view, documents are the objects in the PARC system, and metadata the material that allows for the searching, collating and use of those documents.

This leads us to the second theme: a more general interest in the relationship between hierarchical systems (documents being one instance of things in a hierarchy) and databases, where the latter was to replace the former. This interest was common in computer science research at the time of Dourish *et al.*'s efforts. It still is. Some of the titles of well-regarded papers on the topic, such as Seltzer and Murphy's 'Hierarchical File Systems are Dead' [13], say it all. Much of the research turned around the idea of treating the things represented by a file as an object that exists within a database. Thus configured, the argument went, such an object can be associated and bundled and accessed in all sorts of more complex ways.

This was the view that drove the WinFS effort in Microsoft, as an example, undertaken at the start of the last decade [21]. In the case of WinFS, treating a file in this fashion would allow users to access a file according to a multitude of criteria, to associate that file with other files in equally diverse ways, and to render a file and its relations, graphically, in manners that reflected this diversity.

Though there was much hyperbole at the time, for a variety of reasons this way of treating files did not get released. However, various efforts that resonate with the aspirations behind WinFS have since appeared, at least within the research community. Jones *et al.'s* 'Don't take my Folders away' of 2005 [8] explored some of the cognitive muddles that went with folders and file hierarchies, for example, and pointed towards ways that current file directories prohibit multiple locations of file instances, though users themselves would prefer that such hybridity was allowed. Such possibilities needed to be met without negating the importance of place in the mental furniture of the mind. Jones *et al.* did not make any suggestion as to how to engineer such a system, however. Cutrell *et al.* [3] proposed a system that combined web-functionality with the PC with their *Phlat* system, allowing rich searching and browsing through augmenting PC files with the kinds of metadata hitherto associated with websites. Meanwhile, Voida *et al.* [20] sought to devise a desktop interface that reframed the entities engaged with (such as a Word document or an email) around semantically defined activities – thus evoking Bellotti *et al.'s* email threading paper of 2003 [1]. Like Jones *et al.*, none of these attempted to address the design of data stores, focusing instead on the interface.

More recently, Oleksik *et al.* [10] have presented a system that enables a form of threading and association between digital entities. Users create this through a tagging system. These tags hide the precise provenance or location of a digital object – a PowerPoint file, a Website (URL) or a Word file say – and instead present the user with a collage of thumbnails bundled together into a 'cloudlet' or similar graphical representation. These concepts are expressly designed with the technical affordances of multiple devices and cloud infrastructures in mind, and while the research leaves aside strong claims about engineering, it would appear that this new mode of interaction would further distance the connection between the user and file entities storing data. The abstractions would consist of metadata and, though looking similar to the user, being all represented as thumbnails, these metadata would actually point to different locations and entities from the system point of view. Some of these indicators would be files to which the system could read and write, while others would be to the capacity of the system to request copies and/or viewing rights from content actually stored on a webserver.

What these studies all affirm, however, is the merits of reconsidering the basic concept of files. This is especially the case as knowledge work develops beyond the production of documents, to hybrid and heterogeneous interactions around multiple digital entity types, which themselves have complex relations to devices and locations. In the view of these papers, files are only one of the abstractions that might cohere interfaces between the user and the systems engineer.

A File as a Leaky Abstraction

That this is so reflects how it is that, in recent years, there has been an increasing proliferation of devices and computers: heterogeneity certainly seems to be a word for labelling this new world. When Xerox were looking at their systems, most people (even in PARC) only had access to one device, the machine that sat in front of them, linked via a local network to other identical machines. But over the past ten years or so, this singularity has been replaced by a plurality of devices. People have become used to having many more devices than ever before, and technologies with distinctly new properties. These changes have had consequences for the abstraction that is a file in the digital world, which have further ramifications for users and computer scientists alike.

The important point that derives from this change has to do with the fact that these devices are not copies of one another; people have different devices doing different things. They will have a laptop for example, supporting many of the office and work-related tasks that the original Xerox machines were designed to support all those years ago: the creation of texts, reports, memoranda, spread sheets. They may also have music players, cameras, flash drives (or memory sticks in common parlance), and so on.

Bound up with this change are two further shifts. Firstly, people are dealing with an increasing range of file types, encompassing music (e.g., MP3s), image (e.g., JPEGs), and movie (e.g., SWFs), to name but a few. Secondly, people are encountering their data in a number of contexts, some of which render them in ways that are less 'file-like' than hierarchical systems typically did. The implicit linking of file with application in operating systems such as Apple's iOS, where the underlying file structure is hidden from the user, would appear to be a case in point.

However as Harter *et al.* note [7], the emergence of this complexity and diversity can disguise the persistence of the term and function of files in computer architectures. They find on the Apple desktop that the relationship between different types of digital entities (such as word processing and graphical objects) most often turns around file type definitions and abstractions, though these are ragged and inconsistent, with users thinking one thing and the system treating file types in another way. Besides, Harter *et al.* also note that the architecture often breaks down when the OS operates upon different data types since there is no consistency between the apps and the OS. This is all the more startling when one considers the hyperbole given to Apple's new data store, the iCloud.

For if it is the case that users are confronted with more data types, they are also increasingly encountering a new term, one describing a raft of services and technologies all of which were meant to let them 'back up' these 'things', these 'files' the cloud. This technology, if single technology it might be, was introduced to the user as offering them new ways of storing their digital stuff and of accessing programs to create that stuff. The cloud was also claimed to offer new ways of connecting those same people to those with whom they might want to share their stuff with. In much of this discussion the term file was used. And here lies the rub: was this new arrangement of limitless back up and continuous connectivity to be achieved around that same concept of a file as had been critiqued, say, by the Xerox researchers? Or, in the same way that WinFS prioritised relationships, was the cloud being designed to support complex connections across data, now distributed across different people and different places? If we consider WinFS as one way of underpinning a collection of files that are hybrid and diverse, albeit a way that is ill-equipped for now, we might hope that the bundle of services and applications constitutive of both the cloud and the things the cloud will link to, through their common use of the concept of a file, could offer a way of cohering this diversity.

However, if it was once the case that computer scientists were of a mind that file architectures were a way of dealing with hardware fallibility and that there was a time, somewhat later, when they began to think that database systems provided a way forward, now the world that was being engineered could not be so easily described, however much the word file was used. If one might have said that users are rather capricious in their use of the term file, then any examination of systems encompassed by the desktop PC and the cloud would say that computer scientists were coming to be lax in a different way. When they used the term, they were evoking not just an abstraction but several, each slightly different; they were designing for a range of devices too, each of which affected what that abstraction stood for. Following Spolsky [16], we might suggest that the abstraction is 'leaky'. The concept of file is an abstraction of certain details that are central to systems design. Mismatch in how those details are abstracted introduce problems. The problems that began to arise in this period (when the cloud first started being mentioned) arose not because the abstraction was altered; it was rather that it became muddled up and mixed: what a file came to stand for was the problem.

The Elusive "Smallest Allotment"

It may be unsurprising to a HCI audience that what users think of as a file could differ from what engineers devise their file abstractions to allow. Indeed, that this is so may be of little importance; as long as the user can use a file sensibly and the engineer design systems that are effective, what is the issue? As we have seen however, issues surrounding what a file means in regard to computers, though often subtle, are leading to solecisms more problematic than the distinction between what a file 'is' from the user's point of view and what the system 'writes as a set of data when abstracted as a file'. They are leading to muddles that cut across what it means to save one type of file as opposed to another, and highlight sensitivities regarding whether certain types of object that we might consider file-like, can be 'saved' at all.

"...From a user's perspective, a file is the smallest allotment of logical secondary storage; that is, data cannot be written to secondary storage unless they are within a file." [14, p. 372]

The term 'users' in the above statement probably refers to fellow engineers, and in this case the abstraction places much emphasis on a file describing a single unit of data. But the example that we presented at the outset, of how OneNote constructs its file storage system, illustrates how the very same application can have different underlying structures. Let us take another example to show what a smallest unit – the file – could be. Like all of the products in Microsoft's productivity suite, Word uses a file system to store a file. But what a file is within this system, how a .DOC file can be treated and managed as a result, and, relatedly, how that links to or is understood by users of a Word file, is quite particular, special to Word.

At first glance it would appear that a Word file as conceived of in the application (and the OS) is quite close in its abstraction to the way the user understands it. When a user creates a Word file, the application creates a single file too; when a user saves a file, after making some changes, the application saves pretty much the same thing as the user understands as well. The addressable object, to put it in more technical terms, is close if not identical for both the application and the user. But things start to show some delicate differences when crashes occur. In actuality, Word periodically writes to a hidden temporary file as the user makes edits; when the user saves the document, Word 'commits' the changes by manipulating the original and temporary file to make it seem like the original file has been updated. If the system crashes before the user selects save, however, then any changes that a user has made since the last save are not flushed to the original file. This can muddle the user: sometimes the crash loses changes; sometimes it does not.

Be that as it may, one can imagine that a typical user might find any of these particularities, the smallest allotment being a Word file, curious if they found out about them, but not necessarily consequential. The only time they might find these differences consequential is when things do not go as expected during an operation like copy or move. The user's expectation is that their commands operate on the unit as a whole (atomically, as computer scientists say), but the file system operates on a different, lower unit. It is then likely that during a crash, or when things go wrong, the user might puzzle on how the unit ends up being divided, with some parts of it updated, but some not.

Implications for a Grammar of Action

What this example (and the OneNote example from the introduction) shows is that the particular concept of a file and the associated assumptions that go with it are not universal, reflecting some common agreement amongst those who design applications. To coin a phrase from the philosopher Oswald Hanfling, the 'grammar of action' associated with the use of the concept can be and often is different in different instances [6]. The differences in grammar turn around what is understood by the term file, and relatedly, what action is meant when the terms 'create' and 'save' are used. Systems designers have come up with different ways of enabling these actions in different applications.

One needs to consider these complexities not only when they manifest themselves when new technologies, like the cloud, are being introduced. One ought to also consider them when one tries to understand what motivated earlier attempts to design actions around a file, undertaken when file systems were less complex and less diverse. The development of Xerox Star [22], for example, was predicated on the notion of *generic objects*. These objects could be treated the same way throughout the OS, being manipulated through a set of *generic commands* (move, copy, delete, etc.) that were designed into the system, each performing *"the same way regardless of the type of object selected"*. Smith *et al.* [15] continue, *"They strip away extraneous application specific semantics to get at the underlying principles, and embody fundamental computer science concepts and are consequently widely applicable. This simplicity is desirable in itself..."* [p. 523].

The point that Smith *et al.* make highlights the importance of the slippage we have described. These differences are significant to engineers who try to link applications like Word to cloud services, and for those who are trying to design cloud services for this and other types of user orientated applications: the grammar that each is relying on is different, this simplicity is compromised, and this is because the generic nature of the objects, some of which are files, that are central to systems can no longer be taken for granted. The function of the concept 'file' as a boundary object is failing; it is no longer an intermediary that binds alternative views, but one that muddles them by dint of only seeming to bind.

Let us return to examples relating to the Xerox Star system. Smith *et al.* note an additional *"subtle advantage"* of the simplicity of utilising generic objects mentioned above: *"it makes it easy for users to form a model of the system"* [p. 523]. Implicit here is the assumption that users understand the nature of systems and of the doings that these enable: a consistent grammar aids understanding of what actions are available. These actions pertain to the things the system provides, such as 'a file'. The set of generic actions that can be imposed on a file reinforce the perception of that thing, that file as a generic object, as an instance of 'a file'. When the doings that are bound up with files lose this consistency, confusion is likely to ensue: users lose confidence that what they have at hand is 'a file'; engineers too begin to wonder what abstraction they are working to.

A WAY FORWARD

To this point we have put forward the argument that the term file is fundamental to user experience as well as serving as a central concept for computer scientists. It has acted as a boundary object. But as increasingly diverse applications and networked services have emerged, so the reliance on the term file has begun to break down. This stretching shows itself in the grammar of actions associated with various digital objects, some of which are file-like and some not. For example, it is no longer always clear what it means 'to save' – the term can mean something different across applications and even within the same application; it can mean different things with different types of data entities; and all of these and other distinctions are compounded by questions to do with when 'saving' is done to different locations: one's own computer or the cloud, for example. Does one save to the cloud, or does one save first to one's PC? If one is a back-up of the other, does synching solve the riddle of what version was saved most recently?

At first glance this might simply suggest a need for increased consistency, in service of the engineering community as well as to support users in understanding these systems. But though laudable, this would be to ignore the fact that users are likely to want to have files and *other* digital types, things which are not file-like. Indeed, looking at the way that new social networking services have been adopted in particular demonstrates that there are now a range of data types that people produce, share and engage with, and these things go alongside what may be thought of as file-like. Given this, reworking the abstraction of a file is only one part of what might be developed, but nevertheless, changes even as regards this apparently partial component of the current world opens up an opportunity for something much bolder. A reconstitution of what a file is could be a *necessary part* of a new grammar of actions. In allowing file-like behaviours, other behaviours become possible through being distinct. It will allow users to navigate and appropriate as they see fit and in ways that suit the current landscape. It will allow users to separate what are postings, say, from what are action records (such as likings and playlists), and those digital phenomena that they have an especial relationship with, those objects that are file-like, but somehow present and shared in the networked, multi-device, collaborative tagging world of today.

Towards an Abstraction that Encompasses Metadata

"...A file has certain other attributes, which vary from one operating system to another, but typically consist of...[a] name, ...[a] type, ...[a] size, ...access-control information, ...[a] time, data and user identification..." [14, p. 372]

The first suggestion for a way forward is perhaps the most obvious: it entails rethinking the role of metadata. This is becoming central not only to applications such as OneNote, but also to current technological ecosystems, including recent offerings by Apple, Google and Microsoft, where the application is represented as being bound up with the file. But metadata is also now becoming central to what users understand as a file, though they might not always think of tags, comments, playlist information and so forth as metadata. For what a file is *is* now often bound up with the things added to it, not only by the originating user but by others too.

Consider for example, behaviours reported by Odom *et al.* [11]. In their study of teenagers and their virtual possessions, participants reported that part of the value of photos posted on Facebook was the metadata associated with them: comments and 'likes' were so pertinent that they were reported to be printed out and pasted into scrapbooks alongside photos. This materialisation of the digital is indicative of a difficulty associated with the current technological landscape.

It is not clear how one would digitally export a Facebook photo in order to view it alongside this metadata – the tags and comments – with another computer program or application, and this remains so despite recent innovations in the Facebook service. Yet it is not surprising that users should want to treat these entities in the way they treat a file. If they can upload their photos to Facebook, and given that they do so the photos are file-like objects, why can they not download them again, while retaining the value they have accrued, but still with the benefits of file-like properties? Although it is now easier for users to export their data from

Facebook, these exports, once represented simply as 'a file' on a hard disk, lose their potency. They are disconnected from the social life they were bound up with; they are the bare bones of the thing that the original file became when it was posted on Facebook.

An analogy might be helpful. If in the past a file was a single entity to the user, but the system broke the file up into blocks and bytes when it came to storage, the value of social networking is to make what starts as a single entity become a 'network of stuff', a composite of the file and the metadata accreted through use on the social network. Hence, when a creator of the original file wants to download the thing that it has become on Facebook, they want to download not the single thing that was the file, but the various objects constitutive of the stuff (entities) that have derived from the social discourse around it. They send up a single entity, and want the system to send back a bundle of bits, whether these be pointers to data of various types, stored in various places, or a large entity, originally called the file but now lined with tags of various kinds. This bundle, this new 'file' type, is not merely a complex data type; the important thing from the users' point of view is that it is a mirror of the social life that the file enables.

Rethinking the Grammar of Copy

This suggests much more than an extension of the scope of the thing 'copied' or downloaded, however. The shift that we describe above, towards an abstraction encompassing metadata, which in itself reflects the social life of the object in question, has a number of implications.

For the sake of simplicity, let us continue with examples taken from actions related to Facebook (and disregarding the variety of actions that are supported by different social networking services). Things like the 'author' and 'place' tags, as well as the 'likes' and 'comments' that can be appended to images and other posts, create rich layers of data on an originating file, which can imbue this file with greater meaning. Reflecting on this, we have suggested that it is sensible for a user to be able to interact in file-like ways with this combination in order to retain this value.

However, this immediately raises complexities. For instance, images posted to Facebook might be copied not only by the person who posted them, but also by others. In these circumstances, should these others be able to copy the metadata, the tags as well as the thing-itself? If so, what of the rights of the owner or, if you prefer, the maker of the initial file (see also [9])? When people copy an originating file, would they be creating a new file or would their new entity be a version of the original one? Is there an order of precedence that we are proposing and ought this to be reflected in the concept of a file that might apply?

It seems to us that there is a distinction that ought to be made between things that are put on the web, which the originator wants to have file-like properties (even as that thing develops a social life once on the web), and those things that are posted that the user does not want to have file-like properties. The properties we are thinking of have to do with questions like whether 'making a copy' means making a duplicate, or having and owning (as it were) the originating thing itself and keeping traces of when copies as somehow distinct 'lesser' entities are produced. Each type of 'copy' has implications for the ensuing social life of the digital entity in question.

The issue here is what grammars of action are implied for these related but evidently distinct objects, some file-like and some not, and how this spills out in terms of the actions possible that mediate the social relations in question. There are evidently subtleties here. We have begun to point out some; it is to others we now turn.

Rethinking the Grammar of Delete

Consider this quote, from interviews reported in [12],on the discontinuities between people's expectations about what they can do with their digital material and what they can in fact do when they place it on social networking sites.

"I guess I can delete them (photos on my computer)... online, well I can try to delete something but who knows? Who deletes the deleted? Where does it go when I delete it? I don't know but I don't think it disappears and that way it feels like I don't have control over it..."

What is implied here is the possibility, conceived from this user's point of view, that a digital object is something that can be done away with. At least, this is their understanding of what seems to happen when they interact with things – certainly this is their understanding of what happens when they interact with their PC (notwithstanding the subtleties of this for the moment).

This individual is making a contrast however, between interacting with their PC and when they venture elsewhere, onto Facebook (or Flickr, say, for want of another illustrative context). Though only one person's account, it seems to us that this can be taken as representative of the view held in common. After all with a computer, the abstraction representative of a file has for some years now allowed a user to treat a file in this way: as something that can be done away with. Never mind that most computer systems have not been designed so that a file is truly eviscerated when the 'delete' command is selected (instead simply re-addressing the digital space used by the file in question). For the purposes of the user, this is sufficient for them to get on with their doings: for their practical intentions, their delete action does way with the file.

How different the situation is as both regards this basic interaction and the essential status of the thing filed and-or deleted when the 'place' that this interaction is occurring on is remote, on some server, either the cloud or on some social networking service. It is in this sense that the doubts that this interviewee expressed, though tentative, are accurate. They are right to ask, albeit rhetorically, 'just what does happen when delete is selected?' 'What is implied here?' They are asking, 'What is left unstated but necessarily relied upon when I press delete?' Their understanding, as represented in this single quote, is not naïve so much as too knowledgeable: just as they understand that on a computer, to delete doesn't mean to completely eviscerate or destroy a file, so now they worry that same will apply in this new landscape.

It is precisely because of issues such as these that the grammar of action that was devised for the PC cannot be the solution that is applicable for the current multiple device, cloud-linked, multiple file type, social networking world we have now. Something more is required than was true in the past if one is to copy or delete in this new context. The grammar must imply more.

What is needed is not only a file abstraction through which the user's desire to hold on to the metadata that makes their files meaningful can be encompassed, when a file gains what one might say is its 'social life'. It is that, in addition, this thing, distributed as it is, can nevertheless be done away with, removed, taken out of play, ended. A boundary object needs to be developed that can bridge the abstraction of the user and the one of the engineer, who needs to worry about this thing that keeps growing and changing, and where the locale of storage changes too, such that when a user says 'delete', the thing whatever it is and wherever the entities constitutive of it are, are indeed, done away with.

Expanding the Grammar of Action: to Own

These examples of the thing that is a file, of the copying of that thing and, last of all, the deleting of a file, show how reconstituting a file abstraction needs to be done mindfully. Nevertheless, one might say that these are still actions that resonate with the world that existed when engineers at Xerox were developing the Star. But the world is much more different than is suggested by the continuing applicability of these terms. Numerous technological shifts are already underpinning various actions that were not possible then: 'synching' and 'streaming' are amongst this novel set of behaviours. Devising a new file abstraction also requires that some actions implied but not stated in the original concept of 'a file' now require explicit attention in ways that would have startled the Xerox engineers more than the introduction of the concept of 'synching' would.

Take the following two quotes, from two different participants (from [12]), as illustrative here:

"the more I talk about it, the more the idea of owning something online seems lost in translation."

"it feels like there is this illusion that they are mine, that I own them. But they could disappear at any moment."

These quotes are suggesting that the relationship a user can have to digital stuff can be one where *ownership* is applicable. At first reading one might think they are alluding to digital rights management. But further reflection brings this into doubt. They appear to be thinking of something that they had been able to take for granted hitherto, something that went hand in hand with their understanding of what a file is.

Later on in these same interviews, these participants talk about how it used to be that they knew where a file was. They stated that they used to have a desire to put a file *"on a CD"* so that *"it could be safe"*. But they go on to say that they find that this is hard to do in the context of cloud storage. The reasons why they wanted to do this (before we remark on the difficulties) were that, for them, where a file is could act as an instrument of ownership. Being *"here"*, *"on their PC"*, or *"in a CD"*, could make it *"theirs"*. That they can see *"it is here"* could assure them that their ownership has not been violated.

What is being pointed towards is a set of assumptions, relating to the functioning of a file on a computer that harks back to the discussion of deletion above. The thing that can be a file, and hence the thing deleted or in this case owned, is treated as if it has a physical locale, a knowable place where it lives. This somewhere used to be (of course) *"there"*, in a particular machine, on their desk at home or at work. But when it comes to the current world, where this 'there' might be is no longer clear; there is often no knowing where a file is, certainly from a user's point of view.

What follows on from this is the possibility that what once was taken for granted can no longer be. In the UK, where this research was conducted, one's ownership of digital data was manifest in the physical presence of the devices that housed that data. Now that proxy relationship no longer applies. And users are right to wonder about what ownership means in this new context. Amazon's continuing efforts to specify how Kindle users can lend each other (whose?) books highlight the complexities in this space; it certainly doesn't offer a way forward and out of them.

We think that a new concept of what a file might be does, and further, that unpacking such a concept presents an occasion for rethinking what ownership might look like. Translating what was once a relationship between a user and a physical thing into one between a user and a digital thing is not simply a matter of replication and, even if it were, the reinforcing of one model of possession would mean disregarding other ways in which ownership is accomplished. Expanding the grammar of action to encompass possession means considering how to enable the doings that underpin what ownership looks like in the many parts of the world where file infrastructures are used. It means acknowledging the complexities that are associated with this concept and designing for a diverse range of actions. And it opens up the possibility that cloud computing could enable new kinds of practices to emerge, which change ideas about how individuals relate to 'their' data, and to each other via it.

CONCLUSION

Whatever future work does need undertaking – and there are obviously plenty of opportunities here – these examples have been presented to assert our view that users sometimes want a particular type of digital entity. This entity needs to let them do certain things, a particular job. A new version of what users think of as a file can let them do this, we have proposed. But we are also proposing that this new entity needs to be engineerable, too. The thing that will result may well not look a file as conceived of in file architectures; nor will it have quite the same assembly of interactional features, the same grammar of action as we have put it, as a file on a computer.

We have noted that the devising of a new abstraction needs to be done in a way that is cognizant of the grammar of action that it will imply. Enduring actions, such as copy and delete, need to be re-thought, and new actions may be needed, for example to provide a sense of ownership of data. A new abstraction might allow users to *eradicate* a file that is stored in the cloud, or *withdraw* one from a social network. It might allow them to knowingly *place* a file in a particular location, one that is tied to a physical locale. It might resolve issues surrounding the *loaning* of digital media or enable a sense of shared ownership. Although we conclude with these suggestions, we make them tentatively. A new abstraction, and a new associated grammar of action, will require a good deal of thought and experimentation. In this case, diligent HCI research is warranted more than ever.

ACKNOWLEDGMENTS

Many thanks to reviewers and to colleagues in SDS.

REFERENCES

1. Bellotti, V., Ducheneaut, N., Hoard, M. and Smith, L. 2003. Taking email to task: the design and evaluation of a task management centred email tool. In *Proc. CHI 2003*, ACM Press, 345-352.
2. Churchland, P. and Churchland P. 1995. *The Engine of Reason, The Seat of the Soul: A Philosophical Journey into the Brain.* Boston: MIT Press.
3. Cutrell, E., Robbins, D., Dumais, S. and Sarin, R. 2006. Fast, flexible filtering with Phlat. In *Proc. CHI 2006*, ACM Press, 261-270.
4. Dourish, P., Edwards, W. K., LaMarca, A., Lamping, J., Petersen, K., Salisbury, M., Terry, D. B. and Thornton, J. 2000. Extending document management systems with user-specific active properties. *ACM Trans. Inf. Syst. 18*, 2 (2000), 140-170.
5. Halasz, F. and Moran, P. 1981. Analogy considered harmful. In *Proc. CHI 1981*, ACM Press, 383-386.
6. Hanfling, O. 2000. *Philosophy and Ordinary Language: The Bent and Genius of Our Tongue*. London: Routledge.
7. Harter, T. Dragga, C., Vaughn, Arpaci-Dusseau, A. and Arpaci-Dusseau, R. 2011. A file is not a file: understanding the I/O behaviour of Apple desktop applications. In *Proc. SOSP 2011*, ACM Press, 71-83.
8. Jones, W., Phuwanartnurak, J., Gill, R. and Bruce, H. 2005. Don't take my folders away!: organizing personal information to get things done. *CHI '05 Extended Abstracts*, ACM Press, 1505-1508.
9. Marshall, C., McCown, F. and Nelson, M. 2007. Evaluating personal archiving strategies for internet-based information. In *Proc. IS&T Archiving 2007*, 151-156.
10. Oleksik, G., Wilson, M., Tashman, C., Rodrigues, M., Kazai, G., Smyth, G. Milic-Frayling, N. and Jones, R. 2009. Lightweight tagging expands information and activity management practices, In *Proc. CHI 2009*, ACM Press, 279-288.
11. Odom, W., Zimmerman, J., Forlizzi, J. 2011. Teenagers and their virtual possessions. In *Proc. CHI 2011*, ACM Press, 1491-1500.
12. Odom, W., Harper R., Sellen. A., Thereska. E. 2012. Lost in translation: understanding the possession of digital things in the cloud. In *Proc. CHI 2012*, ACM Press, 781-790.
13. Seltzer, M. and Murphy, N. 2009 Hierarchical file systems are dead. In *Proc. HotOS 2009*, USENIX Association, 1-1.
14. Silberschatz, A, Galvin P.B and Gagne G. (2002) *Operating System Concepts, (6th Ed)*. New York: Wiley.
15. Smith, D.C., Irby, C., Kimball, R. and Harlsem, E. 1982. The Star user interface: an overview. In *Proc. AFIPS 1982*, ACM Press, 515-528.
16. Spolsky, J. 2004. *Joel on Software*. Berkeley: Apress.
17. Star, S.L. 2010. This is not a boundary object: reflections on the origin of a concept. *Science Technology & Human Values 35*, 5 (2010), 601-617.
18. Star, S.L and Greisemer, J.R. 1989. The structure of ill-structured solutions: boundary objects and heterogeneous problem solving. In L. Gasser and M.N. Huhns (Eds.) *Distributed Artificial Intelligence: Vol. 2*. San Francisco: Morgan Kaufmann, 37-54.
19. Thereska, E., Gosset, P. and Harper, R., 2012. Multi-structured redundancy. Presented at *HotStorage 2012*, June 2012, Boston, MA. https://www.usenix.org/system/files/conference/hotstorage12/hotstorage12-final6.pdf
20. Voida, S., Mynatt, E.D. and Edwards, W.K. Re-framing the desktop interface around the activities of knowledge work. In *Proc. UIST 2008*, ACM Press, 211-220.
21. WinFS. Wikipedia, accessed 23 August 2012. http://en.wikipedia.org/wiki/WinFS
22. Wittgenstein, L. 1953. *Philosophical Investigations*. Trans. A.N. Anscombe. Oxford: Blackwell.
23. Xerox Star. Wikipedia, accessed 23 August 2012. http://en.wikipedia.org/wiki/Xerox_Star.

Supporting a Sense of Connectedness: Meaningful Things in the Lives of New University Students

Elizabeth Bales
University of California, San Diego
9500 Gilman Drive
La Jolla, California 92093
ebales@cs.ucsd.edu

Siân E. Lindley
Microsoft Research Cambridge
7 JJ Thomson Avenue,
Cambridge, CB3 0FB, UK
sianl@microsoft.com

ABSTRACT
We report findings from interviews with new undergraduate students, in which they identified particular items as supporting a sense of connectedness with home. We characterize ways in which artifacts underpinned a sense of connection, including by conveying the character of the parental home, supporting a sense of continuity with it, and enabling a physical presence to be maintained there. We then consider how simple affordances offered by these artifacts, such as being able to move, position and sort them, enabled participants to reinforce the meanings that were associated with them. Such actions are normally taken for granted, but we describe how they are compromised for social media especially, due to functional limitations and questions of ownership. We highlight design opportunities for making the transition from home more gradual, and supporting the archiving and display of social media.

Author Keywords
Cherished object, memento, virtual possession, ownership, residential mobility, transition, cloud, physical, digital.

ACM Classification Keywords
H.5.2. User Interfaces: User-centered design

INTRODUCTION
The importance of cherished objects is well recognized in HCI. Researchers have tried to understand how it is that objects come to be cherished, the roles they play within family life [11], and why it is that participants rarely highlight the digital when talking about their cherished possessions, despite an increasing abundance of digital mementos, including video, photos, and emails [20]. These studies tend to explore established 'family archives' [e.g. 11, 20, 21], but less is known about how these archives are formed and curated over time, or the events that prompt people to consciously shape them, discarding things once considered precious, and keeping others, in a reaffirmation of their status as important.

Yet there are clear trigger points that cause people to take stock of their belongings and consciously engage with them. Transition points, such as moving, are an excellent example of this. These periods of transition create moments when people are forced to make decisions about what to bring with them, decisions that will shape the way that they can connect with the past, and continue to reminisce in the future. In this paper, we focus on a specific type of transition: that of moving away from home for the first time to go to university. The move to university is especially interesting because students often simultaneously maintain a space at home whilst creating a new space for themselves at university. This echoes social changes that also occur in the lives of students at this time. They may wish to balance the maintenance of ties with their childhood friends and family with the forging of a new identity for themselves in their new environment.

New university students are also an interesting group because they, generally speaking, belong to a generation of so-called 'digital natives'. While HCI researchers have struggled to get participants to identify the digital when pointing to things that are cherished, work with teenagers has revealed a more complex set of practices surrounding what Odom et al. [19] describe as 'virtual possessions'. These practices include making virtual possessions physical, for example by printing them, and combining media to create new, personalized digital artifacts. We might expect digital things to also fall under the rubric of cherished possessions for university students and, while virtual possessions are not subject to the same sort of constraints as physical things, the psychological and social nature of the transition to university may nevertheless prompt their curation. This may especially so for content on social network sites, which play an inherent role in interactions with (new) others.

In this paper, we report findings from interviews with ten new university students about their meaningful things after moving to a new hall of residence, placing particular emphasis on how these items support a sense of connectedness to home. We show how this was underpinned by a variety of artifacts, and consider how the affordances that they offered enabled participants to reinforce the meanings associated with them. We note that this was compromised with social media especially, which nevertheless served as a key source of content for our

CSCW '13, February 23–27, 2013, San Antonio, Texas, USA.

participants. We suggest opportunities for design that relate to supporting the personal archiving and display of social media content, and a transition from home that is gradual.

RELATED WORK

Research on transitioning to university has explored how technologies play a role in supporting communication between college students and their parents as well as how new technologies might be designed to support a sense of connectedness to home. Chen and Katz [3] focus on the fundamental role that the mobile phone plays in supporting communication between college students and their parents, and Dey and de Guzman [6] highlight the importance of objects such as photographs and gifts, that can be peripherally displayed and that cue memories associated with friends and family. Smith et al. [25] illustrate a more complex relationship with home: in their research, the use of technologies by college freshmen was seen as mediating both closeness with, and independence from, parents. Smith et al.'s work in particular underlines how the nature of going to university entails something of a balance between staying connected and moving on. Yet, this circumstance is not unique to students. Shklovski et al.'s [23] research on residential mobility more generally suggests the need, initially at least, to keep in touch with a prior location, be this through following local news or checking the weather. Such practices not only support a sense of connectedness, but also serve as a social vehicle for conversations with friends who still live there. Shklovski et al.'s later work [24] examines in more detail how technology is implicated in keeping in touch following a residential move. They highlight the role of communications such as emails, which can be understood as both communication act and tangible good, and which serve as an unobtrusive reminder of a relationship as they persist in the inbox.

However, and as Shklovski et al. [23] note, an essential part of settling into a new home is overcoming the tension between the old and the new by leaving aspects of the old behind. Marcoux [13] has demonstrated how this tension is sometimes tackled head-on; the act of sorting through one's possessions can serve as a means to re-evaluate relationships and "reshuffle memories", enabling the opportunity to leave things behind. On the flip side of this, of course, possessions that survive a move and become integrated into new living spaces and practices can serve as a point of continuity with the past. Petrelli and Whittaker [20] argue that homes are designed to express and reinforce memories, with mementos being integrated into familiar spaces and everyday practices. Kirk and Sellen [11] build on this point, noting that the 'archiving' of cherished objects entails their being enmeshed in and constitutive of the material fabric of the home. They note that artifacts on display support a form of "ready reminiscence" by dint of their being continually present. In other cases, sentimental objects (such as a grandmother's ladle) are stored in such a way as to support functional use, while a third category of artifacts are placed in 'deep storage', where they might be encountered serendipitously but otherwise need to be consciously sought out. Kirk and Sellen suggest that through being embedded in the home, objects play a role in defining the self, honoring those that are cared about, connecting with the past, framing the family, fulfilling duty, and enabling forgetting. Durrant et al. [7] also observe how the display of photos at home is curated to present a unifying image of family.

This integration of material objects in home life offers a contrast to the ways in which virtual possessions are stored and used. While family members in the studies described above could readily identify physical objects as sentimental or cherished, they found it difficult to do the same for their virtual possessions. Petrelli and Whittaker [20] suggest that the digital mementos that their participants did eventually identify, such as photos and communications, did not initially spring to mind because of the ways in which they are stored; they are simply not located in places where they are persistently encountered. Related to this, Petrelli et al. [21] note that the periodic sorting and distilling of personal belongings is important in sustaining a compact collection that one can meaningfully engage with, a process that is atypical with digital content [e.g. 14]. Additional reasons highlighted in various studies include that digital media is not really experienced as an 'object' [8], that it is perceived as transient and inexpressive [20], and that it conveys simple and representative meanings, rather than these being abstract and esoteric [21]. In an exploration of the attributes of physical and digital things, Banks [2] also notes that the former offer qualities such as uniqueness and the acquisition of patina, which are difficult to meaningfully replicate with digital materials.

Nevertheless, other researchers have argued that virtual possessions are valued artifacts. Indeed, Banks [2] also notes that digital artifacts have their own set of attributes, such as the ability to underpin serendipitous encounters, which offer opportunities for design, and Golsteijn et al. [8] highlight how the *crafting* of digital artifacts such as websites can add to their perceived value. Furthermore, work with teenagers has highlighted text messages as gifts that can embody memories, and has shown how practices develop around preserving those that are deemed particularly special [26]. In a more recent study, Odom et al. [19] demonstrate how some of the unique qualities of digital media, such as the accrual of metadata and the placelessness of data stored online, support a unique set of meanings and uses. Metadata was found to provide a platform for users to collaboratively and individually personalize digital media, as well as to link different types of content together. The collaborative tagging of and commenting upon Facebook photos was felt to create a more authentic representation of an event and to reinforce affiliations amongst friends, whilst the giving and receiving of musical playlists often incorporated modified metadata, such as photos instead of album artwork. The placelessness of content in the cloud also enabled teenagers to draw on their virtual possessions across contexts. Interestingly though, they also amplified the material presence of their digital things, by keeping their computers, mobile phones and media devices always on and connected to their virtual collections, and in some cases by printing them out to create physical collages.

Odom et al.'s [19] findings illustrate how teenagers find ways to integrate their virtual possessions into their environments, whilst also highlighting the collaborative and essentially placeless nature of these artifacts. These qualities are of interest in the context of transitioning to university and maintaining a connection to home. Text messages, emails and social media might all be understood as virtual possessions that, as Shklovski et al. [24] note, serve as reminders of relationships but, more than that, might be consciously integrated into student bedrooms to underpin a sense of connectedness.

Yet the nature of content stored in the cloud has been found to have other implications for how virtual possessions are understood. Odom et al. [17] have argued that simple concepts such as that of 'possession' become weakened when one does not really know *where* one's content is. We might wonder if this sense of ownership might be compromised further by the collective quality of social media, yet Marshall and Shipman have demonstrated through surveys that people do feel they have the right to save and reuse photos [16] and tweets [15] that are shared online. Thus it seems that the ways in which people conceptualize these new types of 'virtual possession' are complex and perhaps even contradictory: a sense of ownership over one's own content is diluted, but also extended to embrace that which is generated by others.

RESEARCH AIMS

Given this mix of physical objects, virtual possessions stored on one's own devices, digital content in the cloud, and digital content posted online by others, we sought to explore how new university students would conceptualize their meaningful 'things' and, further, the ways in which these would support a sense of connectedness with home. We expected that, due to their recent transition to university, it would be important to new students to retain a sense of connectedness to home [3, 25], and that they would be sensitized to the notion of selecting and curating their belongings to support this. Indeed, if homes are understood to be curated [7], or even designed to reinforce memories [20], then we might expect new students to do something similar with the bedrooms that represent the first step in their transition from the parental home.

During our interviews, we focused especially on what attributes of these objects (both physical and digital) facilitated feelings of connection, and whether this was with the notion of home as a place, or with the people who live there. Our aim was to draw on these observations to underpin recommendations for design.

We also aimed to unpack the potential value of social metadata such as comments and tags, and to explore how issues of ownership come into play when considering cherished possessions. In particular, we wondered whether digital artifacts that have a collaborative quality (such as the Facebook photos described by Odom et al. [19]) would be valued differently to personal archives that are hosted online (such as webmail archives), and whether these in turn would take on different meanings to digital content that is stored on one's own personal devices and, perhaps, associated with a stronger sense of 'possession'. We anticipated that, like the teenagers that Odom et al. [19] describe, university students would have a range of meaningful virtual possessions, and that these might be stored or hosted in a number of places including the cloud and on social network sites. Indeed, we wondered whether the small amount of space allocated to students in halls of residence might lead to a greater emphasis on digital content when discussing their possessions.

In the following sections we describe how items identified by the participants supported a sense of connectedness, and how the different qualities of these things, being physical, digital, stored in the cloud, or hosted in shared spaces such as social network sites, affected the ways in which participants viewed them as meaningful. We begin by describing our approach in more detail.

METHOD

Participants

We recruited and interviewed ten first-year university students (five female, five male) within the first two months of their moving away from home for the first time (October of 2011). Participants were all between 18 and 21 years old. We selected for students who came from homes located at least 40 miles (~64 km) distant, and who did not personally own a vehicle. Due to the practicalities of the move, each participant had only been able to take a single carload of possessions with them to university, and therefore had to be selective about what they chose to bring. Participants were recruited through a combination of fliers and advertising in a weekly university email bulletin, and were compensated with a gift voucher to an online retailer for participation in the study. Each participant had a personal computer, and half of those computers had been purchased recently, specifically for university. All ten also had cell phones; three had two cell phones. Two had cameras, seven had iPods, and other digital devices that participants had brought with them to university included an iPad, a digital photo frame, a digivice, a Gameboy, and a Kindle. Additionally all participants regularly accessed their personal webmail and Facebook accounts.

Interviews

We conducted semi-structured interviews situated in the participants' personal bedrooms. The university where we conducted the interviews provides each first-year student with their own private room, so the bedroom spaces consisted only of items the participants had brought, along with some university provided furniture.

The interview began with general questions about what participants had brought with them to university that was important to them and made them feel connected to home. Often this question prompted descriptions of physical objects, and so we also explicitly asked questions about digital items, both stored on computers and hosted in the cloud, to allow us to understand if, and if so, why (or why not) these other types of content were also seen as meaningful. We designed several of our questions based on those asked by Csikszentmihalyi and Rochberg-Halton [5] in their work on meaningful things, adapting them as needed to include digital objects. We were concerned that asking unaltered questions such as, "If the building were on fire what three items would you save?" might skew students towards considering only physical items, so we added additional questions that focused on purely digital content, such as, "If you could save only three digital things what would you save?" We also asked questions relating specifically to identifying objects both digital and physical which supported feelings of connectedness with home, such as "can you show me something on your computer that reminds you of home, family, or friends?" The interviews were audio recorded and transcribed. All objects were photographed at the end of each interview.

ANALYSIS

Transcripts of the interviews were analyzed using grounded theory techniques [4], so as to allow themes to emerge from the data in a bottom-up manner. This approach was adopted because of the broad nature of the research questions. Initial data analyses comprised of ascribing open codes before undertaking axial coding and developing higher-level categories. We did a first pass at this after conducting five interviews in order to inform the focus of the remaining data collection. After a further five interviews we undertook a second pass of coding, iterating the development of categories until we the judged that the major categories showed sufficient depth and breadth and we considered sufficient sampling to have occurred.

FINDINGS

In this section we first discuss the different ways in which the objects that participants identified underpinned a sense of connectedness with home. We then consider how the attributes of these things supported this sense of connection.

Supporting a Sense of Connectedness

The artifacts that participants pointed to supported a sense of connectedness with home for numerous reasons that resonate with prior work. They were, for example, previously owned by, created by, or received as gifts from, family and friends. We will not re-articulate these values here, focusing instead on the transition to university and how connectedness is supported in this context. We focus on five non-mutually exclusive themes: integrating representations of friends and family; conveying the unique character of home-life; supporting continuity with home; maintaining a sense of home *at* home; and visiting digital spaces to connect with home.

Integrating representations of friends and family

Our participants' bedrooms featured content that was carefully curated, and in some cases especially created, in order to integrate representations of friends and family from home into this new space. This was done by placing framed photos around the room to highlight particular individuals such as boyfriends and girlfriends, as well as by building larger collages to represent groups of friends and family. Where montages of printed photos were assembled, care was taken to include everyone, even if this meant including pictures that were less favored, as 7M describes:

"I was trying to kind of go through and work out which friends I wanted to be reminded of in particular. Went roughly on that and then I found there's some people like there just aren't any photos of them that I have, so I kind of, that's why some of the photos are just massive group ones."

Similarly, where participants had brought with them a selection of their belongings, such as only a fraction of their books, they had been careful to include those that represented friends and family. For example, 2F kept a book that had been written by a friend with a small collection of others that she had brought with her:

".. it's a novel that a friend of mine wrote, and I love the friend dearly, but it's a terrible novel, it's really awful, but I love the person so it's there."

Although 2F did not enjoy reading the book, she kept it with others that were important to her, a collection that also included a copy of Shakespeare that had been owned by her mother and grandfather, and a first edition copy of an Oscar Wilde book gifted from a boyfriend. Through grouping these together, she was able to emphasize their significance. This type of enmeshing is easier with physical objects, although participants did do something similar with digital content when creating collages. Here photos printed from friends' Facebook pages were combined with those printed from the participants' own collections, and with older photos from the family film camera.

In rare cases, content was displayed in its digital format. This was mainly achieved by setting computer desktop wallpaper to display a particular photo. Like the framed photos we saw, these were often of a significant other rather than representing a scrolling collection or a randomly generated slideshow. In contrast, the only digital photo frame that we encountered in the study, which would have offered a slideshow experience, was switched off.

In summary, the ways in which artifacts were integrated into participants' bedrooms was undertaken to highlight relationships with boyfriends and girlfriends, to group together friends and family and to encompass objects that connected the participants with others into more general collections of meaningful objects. This integration supported a sense of connectedness with home.

Conveying the unique character of home-life

While artifacts identified in the previous section were notable for their associations with people, be these particular individuals or entire groups of friends, other objects were notable for the ways in which they highlighted the qualities of home-life more generally, and its idiosyncrasies in particular. These often reflected in-jokes that were associated with family or particular groups of close friends, meanings that could not be understood by others. Nevertheless, these objects were often prominently displayed. As an example, 4F described how a pipe (see Figure 1) that was positioned by her window represented "*a running joke I had with my dad about how I'd like to be a gent*" (4F). The pipe supports the telling of a humorous tale that highlights something of the character of 4F and ties this to her relationship with her family (4F being a woman who wishes to be a pipe-smoking English gentleman). Other items on display also had the potential to support this type of storytelling, for example 3F described how a printed copy of a digitally-drawn picture of herself and her closest friends, which was pinned to her notice board, incorporated various in-jokes that only made sense to them, and M8 pointed out a glass vase that made him feel connected to his parents:

"Um, you see that glass thing there? That's sort of what I suppose that's um an example of a habit my parents have. I really like going and looking around charity shops and car boot sales and stuff, um and that's sort of a habit they have. I actually unashamedly enjoy doing that with them so that was something I got here."

Such objects enable participants to reveal (or choose not to reveal) aspects of their character to new-found friends. In this way they can serve as social vehicles for conveying how identity is bound up with home.

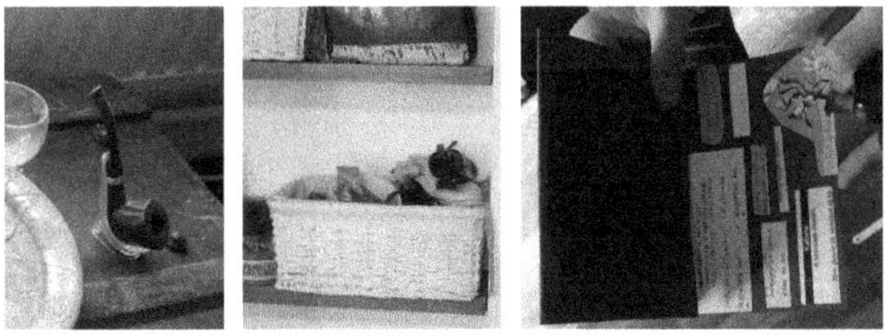

Figure 1. Objects highlighted by participants: a pipe, baskets taken from home, and a photo frame with hidden mementos.

Supporting continuity with home

Another value associated with objects that supported a sense of connectedness with home was bound up with continuity. These artifacts had either been part of the home environment, or somehow echoed aspects of that space. These objects might be practical or precious, and cherished for themselves or appreciated for the practices they enabled. For example, 4F described how she had had the opportunity to buy new items for her room at university but had decided to bring her existing storage baskets instead:

".. originally I was thinking maybe I should just leave them at home, and then just get new stuff, but then I thought it was quite nice just to have a little bit of continuity, and I knew they'd look good. It's quite nice as well just to have some bits from your old room, sort of scattered about so it's not a completely separate place."

Practical objects of this type had not been brought primarily for reasons of nostalgia or sentiment, but nonetheless were noted for supporting connectedness through their use. 4F also described how a dressing gown she had brought to university simply because did not have one of her own, and chiefly appreciated because she now found herself using a communal bathroom, also had more subtle qualities that reminded her of home:

".. she [my mother] was sort of saying before I left you know you have to have a proper dressing gown and I was like naw don't worry I'll just sort of put on a jumper, but she was like no have a dressing gown [...] it also has a slight smell of one of her perfumes which actually I didn't realize 'til I got here and I was like, Oh!"

Such everyday items often supported feelings of connectedness in addition to fulfilling immediate needs. In other cases, objects were brought to university purely out of sentiment. 3F commented upon a stuffed toy seal that provided a sense of connection with her life at home:

"[seal is] a constant factor that has been there for my whole life. And that's quite nice when you've like moved somewhere completely new with completely new people, and then it's just like one thing constant, that I can always like hug and pretend like I'm at home still, which is nice occasionally."

In 3F's case her stuffed seal represented a bridge between her new life and her old. The continuity with home that seal provided was a welcome comfort as she adjusted to living away from her family for the first time.

Finally, a sense of continuity with home was underpinned by objects that were duplicates of, or otherwise mirrored, those at home. When 1F described a wedding portrait of her parents that was positioned in her room, she also noted that "*we have a larger one at home on the shelf*". Similarly, 2F had a decorative bird shaped candleholder that was twinned with another "*at home hanging in the window*".

Maintaining a sense of home at home

A fourth value that emerged relates not so much to the bringing of belongings to university, but the leaving of them behind. By not bringing every meaningful item with them, students were able to maintain a sense that their space at home was intact, to be returned to. Most participants still retained their childhood bedroom, and did not want to empty this of their possessions, as stated by 4F:

"I wanted to leave like a fair amount of stuff at home just to um so that my room didn't look too bare when I got back".

Home was also seen as a safe place for precious possessions. Several participants described items that they chose to leave behind out of fear of loss or damage to them:

"..for my 18th I got like a photo album of my last kind of 18 years that I left at home purposely [...] cos it's valuable to me and it would probably be safer at home" (10M).

By keeping these meaningful items at home students were able to protect them, whilst also retaining a presence in their home space while they were away.

Visiting digital spaces to connect with home

As a final point, some participants spoke about practices that involved visiting websites and social network sites or perusing digital archives in order to feel connected with home, friends and family.

The visiting of websites associated with home was often a newly developed practice, which centered around previous schools, sports teams and other groups participants had belonged to. 3F described how she visited various websites that reminded her of home:

"I sort of go on my old school and sixth form website and see what's happening there sometimes. Which is quite nice, sort of stalk them a little bit."

In other cases, participants described how they revisited old text messages or reminisced by visiting Facebook:

"I do go back [on Facebook] and look at old photos and yeah sometimes, I don't know just for no particular reason really" (1F).

Unlike visits to the websites, this type of activity tended to be something that participants would get sidetracked into after going to Facebook to chat with friends, check for notifications and read recent news feeds. Similarly, the perusal of old text messages was something that participants engaged in while killing time or got sucked into during the larger activity of sorting out their inboxes. For our sample, reminiscing through Facebook seemed to be encouraged by a now retired Facebook feature, which highlighted old photos and conversations in the side bar, increasing the likelihood that users would encounter older content.

In discussing the advantages of socially networked content, participants noted that the comments attributed to photos posted on Facebook could enhance their meaningfulness:

"I think it's more just like people's character coming through, so you, cos they're quite chatty, so, it gives the photos a bit more life I suppose" (6F).

Further, this type of content was also noted for supporting a very strong sense of connection by providing a platform for joint action. 1F described how she and her friends from home would comment on the same Facebook photos:

"I like it, and then, I mean I know I'm not the only person that does this, you get notifications from friends on photos from like three years ago leaving some soppy comment, and that's cool and then everyone goes back, and everyone is looking at all their old photos at the same time, and that's nice, it's like you're having a mass reunion even though you're all really far away from each other."

The experience of interacting around an old photo enabled joint reminiscing, offering the experience of being in the same place, at the same time, together.

Nevertheless, comments and metadata were not always perceived as a reliable way of identifying meaningful content online. 3F noted that no metadata could "*reference the enjoyment I got out of it*", and 1F noted how online content often failed to depict her own "*emotional*" reactions to content. Thus, while commenting provided a vehicle for social interaction and thus could convey the character of others, it was not seen as accurately capturing one's own feelings towards digital content.

In summary, digital spaces were implicated in new practices that enabled participants to feel connected to home. Unlike in the prior themes, the artifacts highlighted by our participants here were valued for the exploration they supported; participants became immersed in reading text messages, or got sidetracked into looking at Facebook photos and, occasionally, into conversing around them.

Reinforcing the Meaning of Things

Having described how artifacts, both digital and physical, were found to support a sense of connectedness with home, we now analyze in more detail how the meanings associated with them were reinforced through their material qualities and the actions that they consequently permitted.

We focus in particular on how participants were able to interact with these artifacts because, while it is true to say that some of the objects identified were highlighted because of some inherent quality, such as the lingering scent of a mother's perfume on a dressing gown, in most cases their meanings were intrinsically linked to the choices that participants made and the actions they took in relation to them. This difference was perhaps most evident when we looked at participants' descriptions of photos, a medium that existed prominently in both the physical and digital realm. In many cases, printed photos identified by participants as important were also available in digital format, either stored locally or on social network sites. However, when asked about meaningful content stored digitally, these same photos were never highlighted (indeed, participants found it difficult to pinpoint any photos that they particularly valued within their digital archives). We use this example to highlight how, while the image is the same, the affordances that these digital and physical photos offer clearly had implications for how they were able to underpin a sense of connectedness to home. In what follows, we highlight three themes that relate to attributes of artifacts identified by participants, and consider how these were important in reinforcing the meanings they were associated with.

Moving and choosing

The first set of actions we wish to highlight in this paper relate to being able to move artifacts from one place to another. For example, as we have already seen, participants left objects at home as a means of maintaining a physical presence there, selected items that represented their friends and family for their new bedrooms, and included artifacts that echoed or otherwise represented continuity with home.

This sense of *moving* things from one space to another was largely lacking for digital things, and only in cases where digital media had been carefully embodied was there a sense that it had been deliberately placed in a particular location. For example, 1F described how she left her USB sticks containing precious digital media at home, encased in a cardboard box that was taped shut. However, this type of example was very rare in our data. In general participants brought all of their digital content with them, copying indiscriminately from the family computer if they had recently acquired a new laptop (half of our sample owned new computers). Further, this duplication of digital content was not seen as echoing other spaces in the same way that duplicates of physical things were, and while maintaining a physical space at home was important, maintaining a digital presence at home was simply not reflected upon. Indeed, participants often had very little idea of what digital content they had stored in different places, either locally or remote, or how content was duplicated across these locations.

Rather, going to university was found to encourage participants to *create* new artifacts, such as collages, out of digital media. For example, the printed photo montages that participants pointed out had often been downloaded from Facebook or copied from the family computer. Instead of necessitating the choosing of which digital artifacts to bring to university, the transition seemed to trigger the crafting of virtual-made-material displays.

Positioning and grouping

Of course, moving things from one location to another was only one aspect of how objects were acted upon. Their specific positioning within the participants' bedrooms, be that apart from others, or as part of an important collection (such as in the case of the "terrible" novel), was also essential in reinforcing the meanings associated with them. For example, 5M described a framed photo that his long-distance girlfriend had given to him before he left for university (see Figure 1):

"It's a picture of us and inside there are some um, things that remind me of the things that we have done together. Disney World, airplane ticket to Miami, things like that."

The frame was designed so that only the photo was visible to an observer, whilst hidden inside was a selection of mementos. The singular status of this photo frame was made evident through it being set apart from other things, an emphasis that was also lent to desktop wallpapers that featured images of significant others or depicted special occasions, such as a picture of a picnic with a boyfriend:

"That (current desktop photo) was the night before I left, we went out and had a night-time picnic on the cliffs" (2F).

The positioning of collages was also done mindfully, in order to separate out different types of relationship and to support encounters with them. For example, 6F had two notice boards in her room featuring photos printed from her digital collection, one focusing on family and one on friends. The family board was prioritized in terms of its location *"cos you know, I probably miss them more"* (see Figure 2). 7M also described how he positioned his photos above his desk in order to support encounters with them:

"...I put them there so it was like the ones that I really wanted up. [...] I just look at them and kind of smile [...] If I've been working a lot all day and you just turn, it kind of reminds you that you're not always working".

Figure 2. Favorite photos positioned above desk; Photos of family placed on a separate board in a more central location.

When asked about meaningful content on their laptops or on Facebook, neither of these participants mentioned these same images. In contrast, the printed versions had had their meaningfulness reinforced from the context of the room, where they had been organized into collections and made glanceable from specific viewpoints.

Sorting, gathering and deleting

In contrast to artifacts that were brought to university from home, participants also had to manage assemblies of digital content that continued to grow and require managing after the move. These included inboxes of emails and text messages, and content hosted on social network sites. These archives were spaces that participants could visit, explore and get sucked into as a way of feeling connected to home.

That these archives underpinned this type of exploration was related to the ways in which they were managed. For example, 1F told us, *"I don't save all my old texts, just the ones I like"*, and 9M put every email from his parents in the same webmail folder:

"I'm kind of making a family archive, sort of every email I get from my parents or whatever so I can remember it. So that sort of reminds me of home."

These approaches are very different: while 1F maintains a small, selective collection of text messages that she wants to keep, 9M creates a resource of every single email he receives from his family. Indeed, he noted how he adopts a similar strategy with his new phone:

"on my old phone I did delete every text after, pretty much after I'd read it, [...] whereas my new phone I've kept all my texts cos it does it in sort of a conversationy thing, with bubbles and stuff. I don't think I'd want to delete them cos it's sort of memories and stuff."

Here the structure of the data affects the perceived value of the messages. 9M's webmail allowed him to create structure, while his old phone neither provided by default, nor supported the creation of, a structure for his texts.

In addition to these personal archives, content hosted on social network sites was also noted for supporting a sense of connectedness. However, websites like Facebook were not generally seen as hosting content that could be managed and curated, and this was the case even when that content was one's own. Put simply, participants did not feel fully in control of the content that they and their friends posted online. Some of the reasons for this were straightforward; for example, participants noted the difficulty of being able to 'keep' content that is not really their own:

"I guess it makes it, you know, more difficult for me to keep them cause since they are not my pictures they can always get deleted from one day to the other" (5M).

But in other cases the reasoning was more subtle. Participants described how what they posted and what they removed was done with a wider view to the social nature of Facebook. They described how they would post content to "*elicit a conversation*" (2M), and then "*just delete it .. if it doesn't have very many 'likes'*" (1F). Further, they were sometimes explicitly asked to remove content because it was, for example, deemed unflattering: "*they'll be like oh please take it down it's not nice*" (4F).

The social quality of Facebook meant that photos were posted for social ends and edited with regard to the views of others, rather than to emphasize one's own set of meanings. Consequently and, as noted earlier, participants felt that there was little on the site in terms of comments or metadata to illustrate which images were most enjoyable *to them*, or had triggered emotional reactions *for themselves*. Instead the collection was seen as "*pretty generic*" and "*nice to have*" (4F) rather than essential to keep. This is particularly striking, given that only two of our participants owned their own cameras, and only a further two knew how to download photos off their camera phones. Thus despite this ambivalence, Facebook represented a primary source of photos. As 7M commented about his printed photos:

"they're virtually all from Facebook, um there's a couple that are actually from like my [family's] camera or someone else's camera where I got an email and I copied, but at least three quarters are from Facebook".

DISCUSSION

In this paper we have considered how physical and digital artifacts support a sense of connectedness with home for new university students, and have reflected on how the affordances they offer enable the meanings associated with them to be reinforced through action. In the discussion, we consider opportunities for the design of technologies to support connectedness for new students, before considering whether our findings can generalize beyond this group.

Opportunities for Design

Our findings suggest a number of opportunities for design, including creating archives that can be browsed and explored [20], designing digital materials that can be persistently encountered [20] and kept in 'functional' storage [11] rather than hidden away in computers, enabling digital 'gifts' [8] and supporting happy coincidences [1] through interactions around content. Some of our observations suggest ways in which these might be realized, for example, the now-retired Facebook feature that enabled 'mass reunions' around old photos was a good example of how digital media can be more persistently encountered, and in doing so, support interactions with old friends. In general though, these findings resonate with prior work. Therefore, in this section we focus on three opportunities that relate to supporting connectedness in the circumstance of transitioning to university, and where the predominance of social media means that virtual possessions are often collectively, rather than personally, owned.

Integrating the digital into physical space

Physical artifacts were an important part of making the transition to university; they supported the notion that participants still had a place at the parental home, allowed this presence to be gradually withdrawn, reinforced the idea of home as a safe place, and allowed for a sense of continuity with it. Opportunities for the design of technology include supporting ways of storing digital content that can be prominently displayed (a good example here is George Guo's hard disk robot [9]), so that it can be integrated into the fabric of both old and new locations. Content stored on such devices would, of course, need to be deeply secure, and this could be reinforced if it could only be accessed from certain locations, for example one's bedroom at home and one's bedroom at university. The notion of twinning locations also suggests a second possibility. Location-sensitive desktop wallpapers might be displayed only in one's bedroom, be this either at university or at home. Both suggestions could underpin a sense of continuity, emphasizing a connection across the two spaces.

Curation of archives that are collectively owned

Curation was a way of reinforcing the meanings of digital materials, be this by maintaining small selective archives of text messages, or by developing webmail folders to emphasize the importance of certain relationships. Yet the curation of digital materials is notoriously difficult [14], and we found it to be especially complex when it comes to content hosted on social network sites. This complexity has both technical and social elements. Firstly, content hosted on social network sites spans users. Thus the collection of photos that one is tagged in, or that one can browse, is unlikely to be the same as that which one has rights to edit. Secondly and importantly, even if the technical means were available for users to edit photos within this collection, the social nature of the site makes it difficult for them to do so. Indeed, we found that participants did not feel in control of their *own* content because of the implications that editing it had for others. This extends prior work on the concept of ownership, suggesting that while users do feel able to *download* and reuse social media [16], they do not feel a real sense that they can do with it as they will while it is hosted *online*. Further, their sense of control is not only compromised by a lack of certainty regarding *where* content is [17], but more strongly by the simple fact that it is hosted in a space where their actions have implications for others.

This suggests an opportunity for social network sites to provide a means for users to privately 'archive' this collective content. Enabling a way of doing this that is not disclosed to the wider network is essential if such an archive is not to become compromised by concerns over self-presentation and the management of social relationships. Further, users would only be likely to invest in such a feature if there was no risk that content would then be withdrawn; such a feature would only be compelling if it enabled one to 'keep' content through the process of 'archiving' it. Implicated here is the management of digital rights to images posted online, and who can do what with them. Actions such as tagging may offer a natural way for users to extend permissions to specific others, enabling them to copy or even 'keep' content.

Creating digital displays that acknowledge provenance

Golsteijn et al. [8] suggest craft as a means of making digital objects more cherishable, and here we found that the move to university was a significant motivator for the creation of new artifacts out of digital materials. Furthermore, these materials were often owned by others, many having been printed off from Facebook. Making the provenance of these materials visible could be one way of supporting connectedness, in the same way that physical artifacts previously owned by others, such as the dressing gown and copy of Shakespeare, underpinned this. This suggests an opportunity for the creation of dynamic photo displays that acknowledge origin whilst also supporting personalization.

In designing for such displays we could draw inspiration from ancient Chinese art, where in addition to the artist leaving his seal on the painting, prominent owners would leave their own seal and add additional colophons, recording their thoughts about the piece in beautiful calligraphy [12]. Similarly, digital materials could be designed to become more unique through making their provenance visible whilst also allowing them to be tailored by the person who crafts their display. Such displays could be created using e-paper, and could show favorite photos along with visual indicators that show the heritage of the photo, such as an image of who the photo was taken by. This kind of digital patina can complement other existing sources of digital personalization, such as photo comments on a social network, and digital photo filters such as those provided by services like Instagram [10], allowing for the creation of unique digital objects that hold their own value.

Limitations and Future Work

Our decision to interview first year university students for this study was taken because we expected them to be sensitive to the process of choosing which items to bring to university to help them feel connected to home. Additionally, we expected them to have a wealth of virtual possessions, thus supporting a discussion about valued digital things. The advantages of using such a sample can be balanced against the limitations, as follows.

Firstly, our findings offered insights into the importance of maintaining a space at the parental home when transitioning to university. This is a unique circumstance that does not typically generalize to residential mobility, where people leave a location behind. Nevertheless, it does suggest possibilities for future work. One group worth exploring further may be children of divorced parents. Prior research [18] has indicated how the shift from living in one parental home to residing across two might be eased by the integration of personal things into new spaces. Our own findings raise questions regarding whether supporting presence in absence could also be valued, and how this can be achieved through virtual possessions, which are known to be meaningful for teenagers in particular [19].

Secondly, our participants were interesting because of the type of digital content that they owned or had access to. Only two owned cameras and, while all ten had a camera phone, only two could easily extract photos from them. Instead photos were taken from social network sites and family computers. The fact that many of our participants did not own their own cameras, or relied on photos posted online by others, is not out of kilter with other work (see e.g. [7, 27]), and offers an interesting contrast to prior work on cherished objects that has largely focused on parents and their own content [11, 20, 21]. We believe our findings point to the importance of an emerging issue, that of being able to archive content that is 'collectively' owned and hosted on social network sites.

CONCLUSION

We have reported findings from an in-bedroom interview study conducted with first year undergraduate students within two months of moving away from home for the first time. Participants derived a sense of connectedness with home through displaying and interacting with a variety of artifacts, including those that represented others, conveyed the character of home-life, and supported a sense of continuity with home. Further, while physical items allowed participants to maintain a presence at their parental home, digital spaces became the focus of new practices. We consider how the affordances offered by these artifacts enabled participants to reinforce the meanings associated with them, and note that this was compromised for social media especially. A first set of reasons for this were technical, in that there is a lack of functionality for storing and organizing social media, especially when this has been uploaded by someone else. A second set of reasons were social, because any actions taken in relation to social media are performed in a public space, and thus have ramifications for others, as well as possibly triggering or influencing interactions with them. Opportunities for design include providing a means for the personal archiving and display of social media content. We believe that the current requirement to download and print off social media content in order to make it one's 'own' could be improved upon by providing new possibilities for interacting with it both online and through the creation of new digital displays. Doing so could result in artifacts that encompass values currently associated with either digital or physical media, but not with both.

ACKNOWLEDGMENTS

Our thanks go to the participants and to members of the SDS group at Microsoft Research Cambridge.

REFERENCES

1. Ashkanasy, S., Benda, P. and Vetere, F. Happy coincidences in designing for social connectedness and play through opportunistic image capture. In *Proc. DUX 2007*, Article 4.
2. Banks, R. 2011. *The Future of Looking Back*. Microsoft Press, Redmond.
3. Chen, Y.-F. and Katz, J.E. 2009. Extending family to school life: college students' use of the mobile phone. *Int. J. Human-Computer Studies 67*, 179-191.
4. Corbin, J. and Strauss, A. 2008. *Basics of Qualitative Research (3rd ed)*. Sage Publications, London.
5. Csikszentmihalyi, M., and Rochberg-Halton, E. 1981. *The Meaning of Things*. Cambridge University Press, Cambridge.
6. Dey, A.K. and de Guzman, E. 2006. From awareness to connectedness: The design and deployment of presence displays. In *Proc. CHI 2006*, 899-908.
7. Durrant, A., Frohlich, D., Sellen, A. and Lyons, E. Home curation versus teenage photography: Photo displays in the family home. *Int. J. Human-Computer Studies 67*, 12, 1005-1023.
8. Golsteijn, C, van den Hoven, E., Frohlich, D. and Sellen, A. 2011. Towards a more cherishable digital object. In *Proc. DIS 2012*, 655-664.
9. Guo, G. Hard disk robot. CGHub. http://cghub.com/images/view/90512/
10. Instagram. http://instagram.com/
11. Kirk, D., and Sellen, A. 2010. On human remains: values and practice in the home archiving of cherished objects. *ACM Trans. Comput.-Hum. Interact. 17*, 1-43.
12. Lee, S. 1964. *A History of Far Eastern Art*. Abrams, New York.
13. Marcoux, J.-S. The refurbishment of memory. In D. Miller (Ed.), *Home possessions*, 2001. Berg, Oxford.
14. Marshall, C.C. How people manage digital information over a lifetime. In W. Jones and J. Teevan (Eds.), *Personal Information Management*, 2007. University of Washington Press, Seattle.
15. Marshall, C.C. and Shipman, F.M. 2011. Social media ownership: using Twitter as a window onto current attitudes and beliefs. In *Proc. CHI 2011*, 1081-1090.
16. Marshall, C.C. and Shipman, F.M. 2011. The ownership and reuse of visual media. In *Proc. JCDL 2011*, 157-166.
17. Odom, W., Sellen, A., Harper, R. and Thereska, E. 2012. Lost in translation: understanding the possession of digital things in the cloud. In *Proc. CHI 2012*, 781-790.
18. Odom, W., Zimmerman, J. and Forlizzi, J. 2010. Designing for dynamic family structures: Divorced families and interactive systems. In *Proc. DIS 2010*, 151-160.
19. Odom, W., Zimmerman, J. and Forlizzi, J. 2011. Teenagers and their virtual possessions: design opportunities and issues. In *Proc. 2011*, 1491-1500.
20. Petrelli, D. and Whittaker, S. 2010. Family memories in the home: contrasting physical and digital mementos. *Pers. Ubiquit. Comput. 14*, 153-169.
21. Petrelli, D., Whittaker, S., and Brockmeier, J. 2008. AutoTopography: What can physical mementos tell us about digital memories? In *Proc. CHI 2008*, 53-62.
22. Reid, J., Hull, R., Cater, K., & Fleuriot, C. (2005). Magic moments in situated mediascapes. In *Proc. ACE 2005*, 290-293.
23. Shklovski, I.A. and Mainwaring, S.D. 2005. Exploring technology adoption and use through the lens of residential mobility. In *Proc. CHI 2005*, 621-630.
24. Shklovski, I., Kraut, R. and Cummings, J. 2008. Keeping in touch by technology: Maintaining friendships after a residential move. In *Proc. CHI 2008*, 807-816.
25. Smith, M.E., Nguyen, D.T., Lai, C., Leshed, G. and Baumer, E.P.S. Going to college and staying connected: Communication between college freshmen and their parents. In *Proc. CSCW 2012*, 789-798.
26. Taylor, A. and Harper, R. 2003. The gift of the gab? A design oriented sociology of young people's use of mobiles. *Computer Supported Cooperative Work 12*, 3, 367-396.
27. Van House, N.A. Collocated photo sharing, story-telling, and the performance of self. *International Journal of Human-Computer Studies 67*, 12, 1073-1086.

An Exploration on Long-distance Communication between Left-behind Children and Their Parents in China

Lu Pan[1], Feng Tian[1, 2*], Fei Lu[1], Xiaolong Zhang[3], Ying Liu[4], Wenxin Feng[5], Guozhong Dai[1, 2] and Hongan Wang[1, 2]

[1] Intelligence Engineering Lab, Institute of Software, Chinese Academy of Sciences, China
{panlu, tf, lvfei, dgz, wha}@iel.iscas.ac.cn
[2] State Key Lab. of Computer Science, Institute of Software, Chinese Academy of Sciences, China
[*]Corresponding author: tf@iel.iscas.ac.cn

[3] Pennsylvania State University, USA
lzhang@ist.psu.edu
[4] Intel Corporation, China
ying.s.liu@intel.com
[5] Computer Science Department, Boston University, USA
wenxinf@bu.edu

ABSTRACT
In China, hundreds of millions of migrant workers have moved to cities or coastal regions for more or better-paid jobs and have left their children behind at their rural homes. Separated by thousands of kilometers, these "left-behind" children and their migrant parents use mobile phones as their primary—and often only—method of maintaining family connections. To better understand the use of technology in this long-distance communication, we conducted a multi-phased study using interviews and surveys in three different Chinese rural areas. In this paper, we report our findings on how these children communicate with their migrant parents and what information they exchange. We also discuss design implications derived from these findings that may improve communication between left-behind children and their parents.

Author Keywords
Long-distance communication; left-behind children; mobile mediated contact.

ACM Classification Keywords
H.5.m [Information interfaces and presentation]: Miscellaneous.

INTRODUCTION
The rapid economic development in China is associated with a massive migration of workers from the countryside to cities and coastal regions, as well as a huge number of children who are left at home by their migrant parents. According to official reports, there are more than 140 million migrant workers [1, 27] and 58 million "left-behind" children [27] in China. Growing up with grandparents or other relatives instead of their parents, these children often face challenges in their daily lives, education, and personal development [10, 27].

On average, migrant workers can only return home about once every two years. To maintain family connections and keep communication open while separated by hundreds or even thousands of kilometers, migrant workers and their children rely on mobile phones, which are widely available in rural China [11]. By using mobile phones, migrant workers can talk with their children regularly.

Considering the huge number of left-behind children in China, we believe it is important to investigate how they and their migrant parents communicate and how technology can help them. However, little research has been done to study this matter. Existing studies on left-behind children are largely in an international context, often looking at transnational issues; these issues are not directly applicable to Chinese left-behind children, whose migrant parents stay in China. Also, while there are studies on social-level issues concerning phone-based communication between left-behind children and their migrant parents, few studies examine the issues from a behavioral perspective, such as how left-behind children communicate with their parents, what information is exchanged between them, and whether current phone technologies meet their needs.

To understand these matters, we conducted research on the use of mobile phones between left-behind children and their parents in China. We wanted to first understand the current status of the communication between them, and then with that knowledge, further explore what new designs and tools on mobile phones are needed to support their needs.

The research is a three-phased investigation in three Chinese provinces involving left-behind children, their parents, and their school teachers. In the first phase, we used semi-structured interviews to gather information about the daily life of left-behind children in Henan and Anhui, two of the 10 provinces with the greatest numbers of left-behind children [27]. The goal of the research in this phase was to identify the major problems left-behind children may have encountered. In the second phase, we first developed a questionnaire based on the information we gathered in the first phase, and then conducted a survey study in a school in Chongqing, a municipality in Southwest China where many left-behind children can be found. The research in the third phase was semi-structured interviews with left-behind children and their migrant parents. The interviews helped us better interpret the answers to the questionnaire with information from multiple perspectives.

This paper presents a first step toward understanding long-distance communication between left-behind children and their parents in China. In this paper, we first provide the context of this study, showing the scale of the issues concerning left-behind children. Then, we review related research. Next, we describe our method and present the findings of our research, and some design implications to help migrant workers and left-behind children. Finally, we discuss the limitations of our research and future research directions.

CONTEXT

One of the driving forces behind the rapid Chinese economic growth in the past three decades is migrant workers. "Migrant workers" here refers to those people who move from poor regions to cities or more developed regions outside their hometown for more or better-paid jobs and stay there for at least 6 months. According to official reports, there were about 140 million migrant workers in 2008 [27]; in 2011 this number reached about 159 million [1]. Among these workers, more than half (50.3%) crossed the border of provinces. Almost sixty percent (58.2%) of migrant workers are married.

Most migrant workers live in conditions not suitable for families. About half (49.9%) get housing support from their employers, but they usually share apartments with others or live in temporary houses on work sites. Those who do not get housing support from employers (about 41%) spend about 16% of their monthly income on rent. Only 14.3% rent apartments independently. The number of those who can purchase their own house is a mere 0.7% [1].

In addition to poor housing, other factors also contribute to the decision to leave their children at home. For example, migrant workers have strenuous work schedules: almost 9 hours per day and 25 days per month. Furthermore, the school systems in China are largely designed for local residents, and cannot easily absorb children of migrant workers.

The combination of factors such as these has led to a huge number of children left home by their migrant parents. There are an estimated 58 million left-behind children [27] in China, with 52% of these children concentrated in six provinces: Sichuan, Anhui, Henan, Hunan, Jiangxi, and Guangdong. For more than half of these children, both parents are migrant workers, and so the children usually stay with grandparents or relatives. For example, for children from 0 to 5 years old, about 40% are with grandparents; for children from 6 to 11 years old, this number is 38% [1].

News media and government agencies have recently begun to pay greater attention to issues facing left-behind children, such as family intimacy, physical and psychological well-being, education guardianship, and personal security. For example, although more than 80% of left-behind children were in school, most of their grandparents (about 80%) do not have formal education beyond elementary school. In a culture in which deep family involvement in a child's education is critical, this educational gap becomes a huge concern of both migrant parents and society at large.

Some of these challenges are similar to those faced by left-behind children in other countries (e.g., the Philippines) [21]. Like the parents in those cultures, Chinese migrant parents try to use technology to shorten the physical and psychological distances between them and their children, and to offer remote parenting using mobile phones.

RELATED WORK

Migrant workers and related social issues are a world-wide concern [4]. Research has been done to understand various aspects of migrant workers, such as related economics [26] and its impacts on family [14]. Considering the focus of this research, which is the use of technology by migrant workers and their left-behind children to maintain family ties, we narrow our review down to the areas of the impact of migrant workers on their left-behind children, the communication between children and parents, and technical designs to enhance communication between children and parents who are separated physically.

Impacts of Migrant Workers on Left-Behind Children

Relationships between migrant workers and their left-behind children have drawn interest from researchers [14, 29]. Often researchers have taken a transnational perspective to examine how parents and children, who live in two different countries, interact with each other and organize their work and life. An example of such studies is by Parreñas [21], who studied how Filipino migrant mothers and their young adult children overcame international distance to achieve family intimacy.

Various studies have examined the impacts of parents' absence on left-behind children from the perspectives of education, health, and psychological development. For education, Bryant's review on existing research related to the Philippines [3] indicated mixed findings: while the remittances from migrant parents can help children perform better in school, the absence of parents may also have negative impact on educational achievement.

The impact of migration on children's health is complicated. On one hand, the remittance from migrant parents allows left-behind children to access better healthcare facilities [5]. On the other hand, the absence of parents may lead to health risks such as less preventive care [17].

Left-behind children may also face risks in their psychological development. Children may see migration as a path they would follow, and so become less interested in school work [18]. In some countries, children of migrant workers become the victims of social discrimination because of the prejudices the society has against migrant workers [20].

These studies offer a larger context in which to examine the problems associated with left-behind children. A recent report [9] echoed the concerns raised by researchers, outlining some risks in the psychological development of Chinese left-behind children, including anxiety over their studies and difficulty in social interactions.

Communication between Children and Parents

Studies have found that frequent and regular communication between migrant parents and left-behind children can help to address certain problems left-behind children may face. It has been found that phone calls from Filipino migrant mothers can help the lives of their children in various ways [21]. It should be noted that the perceived effectiveness of such remote parenting on family intimacy may vary. As the same research shows, while Filipino mothers enjoyed remote parenting, their children sometimes felt such phone calls could be interrupting and caused anxiety.

Not surprisingly, parents and children often disagree on how and what they should communicate. For example, it has been found [31] that while parents often prefer synchronous or asynchronous communication methods, children strongly prefer face-to-face communication. Dalsgaard et al. [7] partially attributed such disagreements to the unequal relationship between parents and children.

Tools for Distant Family Communication

Studies have been done to explore new designs to support long-distance family communication. Some designs focused on systems to support family activities. Efforts have also been made to create a common place in which distant family members can work and play together [12, 15, 30]. For example, Pokaboo [24] now offers a network-based toy that distant family members can play with together. Odom et al. [20] examined communication practices in divorced families, especially between the children and their distant parent, and suggested that designs must consider the cultures of two families.

Some studies argued that video chatting is helpful to family communication [2]. Video-based systems have been designed for children. For example, Raffle et al. [23] developed a storytelling system to let distant grandparents read stories to their grandchildren; Follmer et al. [10] improved such systems by adding activity sharing, such as games played by multiple people.

Some systems go beyond sharing space and playing games together and try to support more complex family activities, such as experience sharing. Globetoddler [19] is a system that supports children and their traveling parents to share information and experiences. Parents can upload pictures or audio clips to the system, and the children can download them with a doll. eKiss [6] allows children to upload their phone pictures to a weblog so that their distant parents can share their experiences.

To make family-oriented games or systems succeed, Davis et al. [8] suggested that designers focus on four things concerning the interaction between children and parents: unity, inequality, reciprocity, and play. They also offered a game, Virtual Box, as an example.

Designs targeting left-behind children are rare. One exception is by Wong-Villacres and Bardzell [28], who investigated left-behind children in Ecuador and suggested that designs enable more experience sharing and encourage children to take more initiative in communicating.

In summary, many studies have been done on migrant workers and their children. It has been found that regular communication between them can help to ease the problems children may face. However, these studies usually focused on the level of society, and did not examine the behavioral issues related to communication between left-behind children and their parents. At the same time, although there are many studies on the use of technology to support the communication between children and their distant family members, little research has been done to examine the needs and practices of left-behind children.

METHOD

To better understand the situations of left-behind children and their communication with their parents, we took a multi-phased approach. The work in the first phase was preliminary interviews. We visited two schools where many left-behind children studied and interviewed some left-behind children as well as their teachers and school principals. The information we gathered in this phase focused on their daily life and how they communicated with their parents. Research in Phase Two was a survey study. Based on the information gathered in Phase One, we designed a questionnaire focusing on gaining information about the status of the communication between left-behind children and their parents. The questionnaire was distributed to left-behind children in a third school. The third phase was semi-structured interviews with both left-behind children and their migrant parents. The interviewees were chosen randomly from questionnaire participants. Our meetings with children were face-to-face, and we asked them to elaborate their answers to the questionnaire. Our interviews with parents were phone-based.

The research works in these three phases are interwoven. The information gathered in the first phase lays the foundations for the questionnaire design. The answers to the questionnaire guide the design of interview questions in Phase Three. The data from Phase Three not only helps us gain deeper and more detailed information about the communication between children and their parents, but also allows us to validate the answers from Phase Two and have a more comprehensive understanding of the matter by taking inputs from both sides.

Phase I: Interviewing Left-behind Children

We interviewed four children at two schools. The first school was Youji Middle School in Lingbi County, Anhui Province. The second was Beiguan Primary School in Xin'an County, Henan Province. These two provinces are among those where left-behind children are most highly concentrated [27]. In Youji Middle School, more than 70% of its students are classified as left-behind children. Most of these students are boarders.

Our investigation in Youji Middle School involved two left-behind students, four school teachers, and the school principal. With the help of the principal, we randomly selected two students—a boy and a girl, both around 11 to 12 years old. One student lived with grandparents, and the other was taken care of by the child's aunt. We also met four school teachers. Two of them taught in school, and interacted with these two students mostly in the classroom. The other two were in charge of boarding matters, and had more contacts with the students outside the classroom.

We used semi-structured interviews and each interview lasted between 30 to 45 minutes (Figure 1). For the left-behind children, our interview had 28 questions covering:

- basic information about the family and the guardians;
- status of both family life and school life;
- communication status with migrant parents; and
- digital tools for long-distance communication, such as a mobile phone or a compute

Figure 1. Interview with a student at Youji Middle School.

In our meetings with the school teachers and the principal, we focused on obtaining information concerning the family and school life of the students, as well as the digital tools they may possess. Such information could help us to verify the data we collected from students.

Our investigation in Beiguan Primary School was similar to that in Youji Middle School, except that we selected two younger students (also one male and one female), both aged from 7 to 9, to interview. We did so for the purpose of collecting data from more diverse samples. Both students were under the custody of their grandparents. Our interviews in this school were conducted in the same way as that in the other school, except that we did not involve teachers who were in charge of boarding life of their students, because this school is not a boarding school.

No	Gender	Age	Guardian	Father's Occupation	Mother's Occupation
1	F	11	Grandmother	Driver	Cleaner
2	M	11	Aunt	Warehouse Keeper	Factory Worker
3	M	11	Other relative	Cloth Seller	Cloth Seller
4	M	11	Other relative	Machine Repairer	Shoe Maker
5	F	10	Other relative	Driver	Cloth Seller
6	F	11	Grandfather	Factory Worker	Factory Worker
7	M	12	Grandmother	Factory Worker	Factory Worker
8	M	12	Grandfather	Factory Worker	Waitress
9	M	12	Other relative	Machine Repairer	Repairman
10	M	12	Other relative	Waiter	N/A
11	M	12	Grandfather	Miner	Watch Repairer
12	M	13	Grandparents	Factory Worker	N/A
13	M	12	Grandfather	N/A	N/A
14	F	11	Grandmother	N/A	N/A
15	F	11	Grandmother	N/A	N/A

Table 1: Background information of left-behind children interviewed.

From the interviews, we found students had a feeling of being alienated from their parents. Although they enjoyed their school life very much and had good relationship with their classmates and their teachers, they felt a psychological distance between them and their parents, who were physically far away. This feeling was observed from students in both schools.

Three issues may contribute to this problem. First, most of these children's parents came home only once every year or two. They did not have sufficient time to communicate with their children face-to-face. Second, the parents called their children at most once a week, a frequency much lower than what their children expected. Third, due to the feeling of alienation and the nature of phone calls, the children tended to focus on superficial issues that could be discussed quickly, such as their daily lives and what grades they earned, rather than more serious matters that are difficult to dig into over the phone, such as the hurdles they encounter in their studies, or the emotional and psychological needs they have. The lack of the discussion of these deep issues may make the children feel more alienated from their parents.

These children communicated with their parents primarily through mobile phones, and rarely used other devices (e.g., computers). All these children could easily access mobile phones: they either had one themselves, or could use the phone of their guardians. Although computer-based communication methods (e.g., IM, social networks) are popular among urban Chinese children, these rural, left-behind children do not use computers for communication purposes. Students in Youji Middle School could access school computers during programming courses, but the use of the computers was strictly limited to programming purposes. Beiguan Primary School has no computer at all. None of these students had a computer at home.

Students also reported some other issues in school, such as popularity contests and peer pressure to get good clothes and phones; these issues were confirmed by school teachers. Compared with the feeling of alienation from their parents, however, these issues were regarded by students as less serious. Thus, we did not focus on them in our works in Phases Two and Three.

Phase II: Survey Study

With the basic information about the live of left-behind children and their communication with their parents, we conducted a survey study. Our survey focused on the status of communication between left-behind children and their parents. We designed our questionnaire by focusing the investigation on:

- the work situation of the left-behind children's parents;
- the manner and frequency of communication between left-behind children and their parents;
- the topics of communication expected by children;
- the use of communication devices;
- the comments on the communication methods by left-behind children; and
- the expectations for mobile apps by left-behind children and their parents.

Following the guidelines for questionnaire design [25], we developed a questionnaire. Some of the questions included were:

- Where do your parents work?
- Who are your guardians at home?
- How often do your parents come back home?
- How often do your parents contact you?
- What topics do you usually talk about with your parents?
- Do you have a mobile phone? If not, do your guardians have one?
- What do you usually do with the mobile phone?
- Do you have a computer? If not, do your guardians have one?
- Do you play games on the phone or the computer?
- If you do play games, what kind of games do you like?
- Are you online with the mobile phone or computer?
- What do you do usually when you are online?

We distributed the questionnaire to left-behind students in Baishixiang Central Primary School in Chongqing, which is a municipality in Southwest China where many left-behind children can be found. We chose this school largely because of our access to the school's students.

We identified 46 students as eligible participants, all left-behind children and all between the ages of 10 to 13 when our study was conducted. We distributed the questionnaire to all 46 students and got back 41.

Phase III: Interviews with Children and Parents

After collecting the questionnaires, we conducted in-depth, semi-structured interviews with both the children and their parents. Our goals here were two-fold: first, we wanted to verify the answers from the students; and second, we hoped to uncover the communication behaviors and expectations of left-behind children and their parents that could not be captured by the questionnaire.

We interviewed 15 randomly selected children from among those who returned our questionnaire. The interviews were face-to-face. Each interview took about half an hour. We started our conversation with questions about their general background. We then encouraged them to tell us about their experiences communicating with their parents. Next, we talked about the communication tools they currently used, and asked them to elaborate how they used them and what features they liked.

Table 1 shows the background information of the 15 left-behind children we interviewed. Some of the children could not provide us with complete information.

We also told these students that we wanted to talk to their parents over the phone with the students present. They were all happy to provide us with a phone number to reach their parents. We could only reach the parents of 8 students. For each parent, we conducted a half-hour long, semi-structured interview. The procedure and questions were the same as those in our interviews with students. Because the students were present, our conversations with the parents also often involved the students.

We audiotaped all of our interview sessions, and transcribed and coded all of the interviews. Statements of interest were extracted from each interview and grouped together by themes that emerged in the process of interviewing.

RESULTS

Basic Information of Left-Behind Children

Our survey data reveals that those students who answered our questionnaire had at least one parent who is a migrant worker: 43% indicated that both parents were migrant workers, 37% said that their father was a migrant worker, and 20% pointed to their mother. In terms of their guardians, 51% of them had a parent as the guardian, 44% had grandparents, and 5% had other relatives (e.g., aunt).

The physical distances between left-behind children and their parents varied. Among those students we interviewed, nearly half of their migrant parents worked in Southern China, such as Shenzhen, Guangdong Province, a city almost 2000 km away from their children. About one-fifth of parents worked in neighboring counties or provinces, such as Chongqing, which is about 300 km in driving, and Chengdu, Sichuan Province, a city at a driving distance of around 600 km. Because of the different distances, parents went home with different frequencies: from once every other week to once a year or more. Figure 2, generated from the questionnaire, shows the distribution of the homecoming frequency by migrant parents. As shown, the majority of migrant parents came home once a year or more. One child said that his parents had not been home for nearly four years.

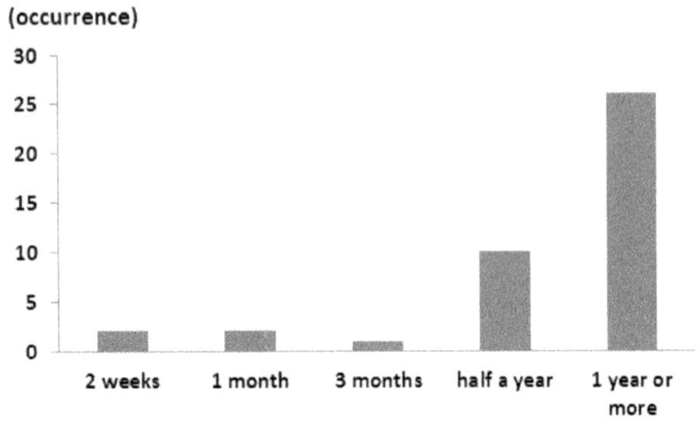

Figure 2. The distribution of the homecoming frequency by migrant parents.

Communication Channels and Devices

Communication Channels

Few left-behind children and their parents communicated via letters. They considered this method old and slow. They only used mail for packages, such as toys for children.

They preferred mobile phones for the convenience. Although phone calls were not cheap, migrant parents believed that the importance of the communication with their children could justify the expense of phone calls, as some parents indicated:

> *"I don't care how much it costs if my child would like to talk to me."*
>
> *"Communication costs are not a problem."*

Mobile Phone Use

The survey result shows that only 20% of left-behind children had their own mobile phones, but for those without a phone, they could use the phones of their guardians. According to the questionnaire, children tended to use mobile phones of their guardians. Most of the phones they used were simple feature phones, not smartphones.

Figure 3 also comes from the questionnaire and shows the distribution of the commonly used functions of mobile phones by left-behind children. As shown, they mostly used mobile phones to contact people, but equally important, they also played games on mobile phones. Our interviews with children confirmed the high frequency of playing games on phones. The most popular games include jigsaws, shooting-type games, and Mahjong. Some students also used mobile phones to play music, and only a few did Internet surfing with mobile phones. In comparison, most migrant parents only used mobile phones to make phone calls. Games, music, and internet surfing are the functions they rarely touched. This may be related to their limited leisure time and technical skills.

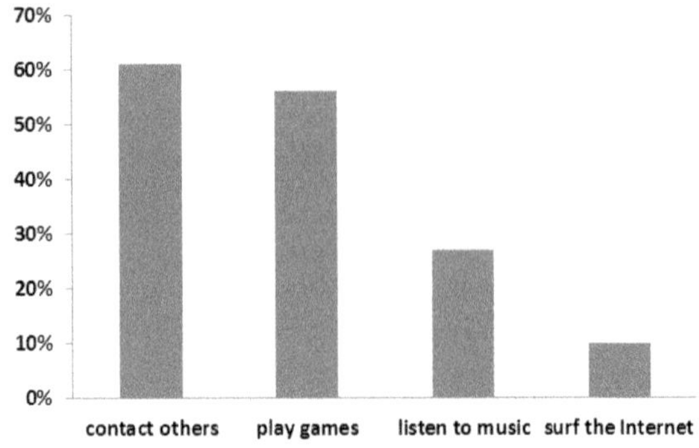

Figure 3. The distribution of main phone functions used by left-behind children.

Personal Computer Use

The use of personal computers among left-behind children is fairly low. From the survey, we know that only one child had a computer. Our interview data shows that it is hard for migrant workers to afford a computer. Although Baishixiang Central Primary School has a classroom equipped with computers, the computers are for course-related work only. Thus, the left-behind children's exposure to computers is very limited.

Furthermore, nearly all the parents said that they know little about computers. They usually had a negative attitude toward computers because of their association with computer games, which are regarded as a distraction from school work by most Chinese parents. As one parent said:

> *"I will not play computer games. Neither will my daughter."*

Communication between Children and Migrant Parents

Because left-behind children and their migrant parents can rarely meet, phone calls have become the most important method of communication. We examined various aspects of their phone calls, including the frequency, the topics, and the depth of communication.

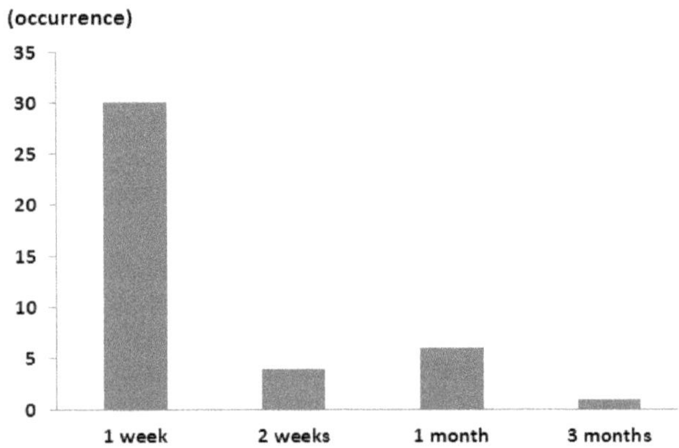

Figure 4. The distribution of the frequency of phone calls between children and their parents.

Frequency of Communication

From the questionnaire, we got the frequency of phone calls, as shown in Figure 4. As we can see, most children talked to their parents once a week, while we also found one child who had such communication once every three months.

Having a phone call once a week seems low, considering the need to maintain communication from both sides and the wide availability of mobile phones, so we asked the children and parents to explain why they could not talk more often. As we have learned, this is primarily due to the busy work schedules of migrant parents: after they get off the work every day, it has already past their children's bedtime. Thus, the weekend is the only time good for both. It should be noted that many migrant workers work six days a week, so they only have one day off per week.

All children, including the child who communicated with parents once every three months, wanted more communication time with their parents. Some hoped to have daily conversations, although they knew their parents were not able to do so.

Although children were eager to communicate with their parents more, they usually did not initiate phone calls. Only 14% of the students in our study would initiate phone calls to their parents. The majority, 54%, would wait for the calls from parents. The rest, about 32%, would talk to their parents after their guardians called the parents to discuss various issues concerning the children.

These asymmetric roles of parents and left-behind children in phone call initiation could be explained by the unequal social relationship between them [7]. While parents bear more family responsibilities and feel the need to pay attention to their children's development, children depend on their parents and may not see the need to report their every move to them. In our case, the feeling of alienation by left-behind children may further reduce the feeling of dependence on their parents and make it even less likely for children to initiate phone calls to share their emotions with parents. Another factor that prevents children from initiating phone calls could be the lack of having their own mobile phones.

Topics of Communication

We also investigated the topics involved in phone conversations. Based on data from the interviews, we identified three major topics: education, health, and work. These topics account for more than 90% of the conversation (Figure 5) (The data comes from the interview and means the percentage of people who ever discussed that topic in their calls.). The children's education is the topic discussed most (about 38% of the time). They also talked about issues concerning the health of both the children and the parents (about 28% of the time), and the work of the parents (25% of the time). There were also other topics of conversation, such as what the cities the parents work in look like.

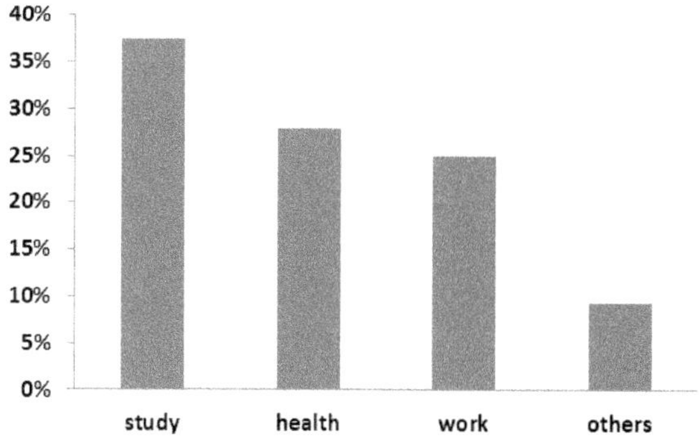

Figure 5. The distribution of topics in phone calls between left-behind children and migrant parents.

We asked both children and parents what information they wanted to know about the other party. Children were interested in knowing about the life, work, and health of their parents. As some children put it:

> *"I want to know whether they had a good meal or whether the work is hard."*

> *"I want to know what my parents' work is like, and I also want to go where they are."*

What migrant parents wanted from their children was almost the same:

> *"I want to know everything, whether it is good or not."*

> *"I want to see more photos of my children."*

We also asked them what kinds of things they would *not* share with the other party. For parents, this question was hard to answer. They tended to emphasize the positive side of their life as migrant workers, and hid from the children the difficulties and challenges they faced in their work and life. As one parent said:

> *"Some things cannot be said. Some things I can say, but when they ask, I'll only tell them the positive aspects."*

The children apparently understood fully the situations of their parents and the sacrifice their parents made. Thus, to live up to the expectation for them by their parents, they did not want to share such negative things as poor school grades and difficulties in study and living, which would make their parents disappointed and worried.

Depth of Communication

To know more about what they talked about over the phone, we asked children and parents to elaborate on the conversations they had. More than half of the children told us that they would love to share with their parents events at school and at home. However, what types of events to share vary from child to child. Some children liked to tell their parents only pleasant things, not sharing the problems they had, such as poor grades or bad school experiences. As some students put it:

> *"I don't want to talk about school and life problems. I don't want them to worry."*

> *"I'm embarrassed to tell them that I have been bullied."*
>
> *"When I get a good grade, say, 90, I really want to show my exam paper to my parents."*

Such attitudes were confirmed by their parents. One parent told us that:

> *"The kid usually talks about something happy."*

Some students, however, indeed opened up to their parents about the issues they had. One student said:

> *"I want to tell him [father] that I was disciplined by my teacher today, and also scolded by grandpa."*

While these children may just want to seek comfort and sympathy from their parents, parents sometimes overlooked such needs. Some parents had a negative response to such information:

> *"(He) will not talk about fun things, just arguments or conflicts with teachers at school."*

In addition to exchanging information about events in school and at home, some children, although a minority, would discuss with their parents their deep emotions and feelings, such as their desire for normal family life. One student, both of whose parents were migrant workers, said that in a phone conversation with his father, he told him:

> *"I feel very sad when my mother cannot take care of me, (and feel even more upset) when I saw other mothers with their own kids."*

Most children were too shy to say that they were eager to communicate with their parents about their innermost feelings and emotions in our interview, but when asked with specific questions like "Would you like your parents to know you miss them?" and "Would you like to know whether your parents miss you?", they all gave positive answers. One explanation to this phenomenon, according to Dalsgaard et al. [7], is that emotional bounding between children and parents often goes beyond words.

However, some students seldom or never talked about inner thoughts with parents. On the contrary, they would either share their feeling with their guardians or hide their emotions from others totally. Sometimes, parents did not sense such reservations of their children, and thought their children would share their emotions and feeling with them, although in reality, it is not the case. One parent believed that his child would talk with him about her inner thoughts:

> *"She would tell me about any thoughts like that."*

However, the child told us another story:

> *"I would only talk about those thoughts with my grandpa and grandma."*

This kind of misunderstanding could be caused by several reasons. First, the generation gap may contribute to the unwillingness of children to share their inner thoughts with parents. As one child said:

> *"There is no common language with them (parents)."*

This phenomenon that these Chinese children resist deep communication with their parents seems similar to findings from other research on western children [13, 16]. In addition to the generation gap, we believe that the physical distance between left-behind children and their migrant parents may also lead to psychological distance that further impedes the openness between children and parents.

Beyond Phone Calls: Doing Things Together

In our interviews, both children and parents expressed a strong desire to be together physically. Children often recalled what they had done previously with their parents when they were home and hoped to do that again:

> *"My father took me fishing. We caught a lot of fish."*
>
> *"I made dumplings (with my parents). I feel very happy even though they said my dumplings were ugly."*

For parents, they indicated that if they could be home, they would help their children with their school work, play with them, and do anything that could "benefit their growth," as one parent put it.

Certainly, children also knew that having their parents around was more a dream than a reality. Thus, some of them offered an idea to stay "closer" to their parents with technology—playing games on mobile phones together with distant parents. One child told us he would "love to play [mobile] games with my father." More than half of the children had played various games (e.g., badminton, chess) physically together with their parents, and they saw the games on mobile phones as natural extensions of those games.

However, migrant parents were not as enthusiastic about mobile games as their children and did not play such games. Also, it seems that from their point of view, such games distract children from school work. The benefits of playing games together with children for the enhancement of family ties may not justify the perceived negative impact of these games on their children's education in the long run.

Many children indicated that although they preferred to do things together with their parents, they would still love to just be with their parents even if they would not be able to play with them. This finding echoed the discoveries by Dalsgaard et al. [7], Raffle et al. [24], and Follmeret et al. [10]: being with their parents is the most important thing to children.

Communication and Interactions between Left-behind Children and Guardians

To gain a more comprehensive understanding of the life of left-behind children, we also asked children how they communicated and interacted with their guardians. Our data shows that the majority of children, about 60%, would discuss their studies, school life, and daily life with their guardians regularly. However, the conversions were often limited to day-to-day events, such as:

"I talked about family expenses with grandpa when I was free."

"I talked about school with grandpa: we had a test today or I made a mistake on a question."

In terms of their deepest thoughts and emotions, most children chose not to discuss with their guardians. Sometimes, they even did not want express their emotions at all. As one student said:

"My grandpa always asks me about school. I don't want to talk about fun things that happened in school."

Of course, there are some exceptions. As we described early, one student was closer to her guardians—her grandparents—than to her parents, and would only share her innermost thoughts with grandparents, not parents.

Although to what extend children wanted to share their thoughts with their guardians varied, they all said that they wanted to do things together with their guardians, such as house work, farm work, and watching TV, and really enjoyed such experiences. This may indicate that left-behind children have a strong desire for family intimacy, and love to be with and interact with people on whom they can depend.

DESIGN IMPLICATIONS

Based on our findings, we identified some design implications for long-distance communication between left-behind children and their parents. The main communication tool in China for left-behind children and their parents is mobile phones. Our study shows that Chinese left-behind children rarely have a computer at home, and school computers, if there are any, are limited to educational purposes only. Design suggestions such as video phones and complicated experience-sharing tools are therefore inapplicable, and so our focus was on designs for mobile phones.

New designs should encourage children to initiate phone calls to their parents. Our research indicates that several factors may contribute to the lack of willingness by children to take initiative on phone calls, such as superficial conversation topics on school activities and academic grades, and the feeling of alienation by children. We also learned that children were eager to discuss interesting topics such as the life in the cities where their parents are, showing their school achievements with methods beyond phone conversations, and playing mobile games with their parents. These findings indicate that to encourage more communication between left-behind children and migrant parents, new designs should aim at uniting children and parents through topics and content of common interest.

Following this direction, we believe that designs that can support rich media sharing on simple feature phones will benefit left-behind children and their migrant parents greatly. Although many apps for smartphone users are available for video and picture sharing, these apps are not appropriate for left-behind children and their parents, because 1) children and parents usually do not have smartphones, and 2) rural areas often do not have the infrastructures for data transmission required by these apps. New designs should target low-end phones, consume as little bandwidth as possible, and be easy to use by both children and migrant workers.

Furthermore, new designs should also consider tools that can recommend content for children and parents to share. Such tools can examine content available in the phone (e.g., pictures) and then provide suggestions on what might be interesting.

Mobile games that could offer educational benefits would also be useful. Children love to play games with their parents, but parents have concerns with the potential negative impact of games. One way to narrow down this gap of perception is to design educational games involving both children and parents, such as collaborative jigsaw puzzles, or team Sudoku. Again, these games should consider the technology infrastructure in rural areas and the usability on simple feature phones.

Our study shows that although children mostly avoid negative things, parents really want to know anything about their children's study and life, positive or negative, and even like to talk to the teachers and guardians of the children. Thus, one way to deepen the communications between children and parents is to build a system that involves not only children and parents, but also teachers and guardians. One possible design is to build a system that allows the teachers, parents, and guardians to follow the progress of a child's schoolwork. This system can integrate services on PCs and mobile devices and supports synchronous and asynchronous communications among involved parties.

When using this system, the four parties can decide what information (e.g., exam grades, homework assignments, etc.), should be shared; among whom (e.g., parents only, parents and guardians, etc.); how frequently to share (e.g., once a day, once a week, etc.); and in what ways (e.g., email, short message, picture message, etc.). With this system, parents will be more informed about their children's schoolwork. Having a fuller picture about their children's studies may promote greater communication, further improving the relationship between parents and children.

CONCLUSION

How to help the left-behind children of migrant workers in China has drawn attention from government, media, and academia. We conducted a multi-phased study and used interviews and surveys to study phone-based communications between these children and their parents. Our study identified some communication needs of left-behind children and some potential new designs that may help to improve long-distance communication. To our knowledge, our research is the first of its kind to examine the behaviors of left-behind children in communicating with their migrant parents in eastern countries.

We recognize some limitations of methods. First, our survey sample size was small, making our findings less conclusive. Second, the locations of our interviews, which were the schools the children attended, may implicitly make children provide biased answers that are more socially acceptable. Furthermore, phone-based interviews with parents made it difficult to capture certain subtle but important information from parents.

In the future, based on our design implications, we will explore new designs and implement multi-channel platforms on mobile phones to help left-behind children better connect with their migrant parents. With such designs, we will also conduct long-term field studies on the effectiveness of such technologies.

ACKNOWLEDGEMENT

This research is supported by National Key Basic Research and Development Program of China (Award 2013CB329305), National Natural Science Foundation of China (Award 61232013, 61170182 and 61100151), and Nokia Research China.

REFERENCES

1. 2011 survey and monitoring report of China's migrant workers. http://www.stats.gov.cn/tjfx/fxbg/t20120427_402801903.htm
2. Ames, M.G., Go, J., Kaye, J.'J.', Spasojevic, M. Making Love in the Network Closet: The Benefits and Work of Family Videochat. *Proc. CSCW'10,* ACM(2010) , 145-154.
3. Bryant, J. "Children of International Migrants in Indonesia, Thailand and the Philippines: A Review of Evidence and Policies". *Innocenti Working Paper No. 2005-05,* UNICEF Innocenti Research Centre: Florence, (2005).
4. Cortés, R. Children and Women Left Behind in Labor Sending Countries: An Appraisal of Social Risks. *Global Report on Migration and Children.* A report submitted to UNICEF, (2007).
5. Cortés, R. Remittances and children's Rights: an overview of Academic and policy Literature. *Division of Policy and Planning Working Papers,* Unicef: New York, (2007).
6. Dalsgaard, T., Skov, M.B., and Thomassen, B.R. eKiss: Sharing Experiences in Families Through a Picture Blog. *Proc. British HCI,* (2007), 67-75.
7. Dalsgaard, T., Skov, M.B., Stougaard, M., and Thomassen, B. Mediated intimacy in families: understanding the relation between children and parents. *Proc. IDC'06,* ACM (2006), 145-152.
8. Davis, H., Skov, M.B., Stougaard, M., and Vetere, F. Virtual box: supporting mediated family intimacy through virtual and physical play. *Proc. OZCHI'07,* ACM (2007), 151-159.
9. "First report of "left-behind children's health and personality" was released, exposing worrisome defects". http://news.xinhuanet.com/health/2012-07/08/c_123384791.htm.
10. Follmer, S., Raffle, H., Go, J., Ballagas, R., and Ishii, H. Video play: playful interactions in video conferencing for long-distance families with young children. *Proc. IDC'10,* ACM (2010), 49-58.
11. Internet Development in Rural China 2009 Survey Report. China Internet Network Information Center. http://www.cnnic.net.cn/dtygg/dtgg/201004/t20100415_13712.html.
12. Judge, T.K., Neustaedter, C., Harrison, S., and Blose, A. Family Portals: Connecting Families Through a Multifamily Media Space. *Proc. CHI'11,* ACM (2011), 1205-1214.
13. Kasesniemi, E., Rautiainen, P. Mobile Culture of Children and Teenagers in Finland. Perpetual Contact (2002), 170-192.
14. Levitt, P. & Glick Schiller, N. Conceptualizing simultaneity: A transnational social field perspective on society, *International Migration Review 38,* 3 (2004): 1002-1039.
15. Lindley, S.E., Harper, R., and Sellen, A. Designing a technological playground: a field study of the emergence of play in household messaging. Proc. CHI'10, ACM (2010), 2351-2360.
16. Ling, R. Yttri, B. Control, Emancipation and Status: The Mobile Telephone in the Teen's Parental and Peer Group Control Relationships. In Kruat, R., et al., (Eds.), Computers, Phones and the Internet: Domesticating Information Technology (2006).
17. McKenzie, D. Beyond Remittances: The Effects of Migration on Mexican Households. http://web.worldbank.org/. (2006).
18. Moctezuma, M. "Redes sociales, comunidades filiales, familias y clubes de migrantes. El circuito migrante Sain Alto, Zac.-Oakland, Ca." *TesisDoctoral, El Colegio de la Frontera,* (1999).
19. Modlitba, P.L. *Globetoddler: Enhancing the experience of remote interaction for preschool children and their traveling parents.* Masters Thesis. Media Laboratory. MIT. (2008).
20. Odom, W., Zimmerman, J. and Forlizzi, J. Designing for Dynamic Family Structures: Divorced Families and Interactive Systems. *Proc. DIS'10,* ACM (2010), 151-160.
21. Parreñas, R. Long distance intimacy: class, gender and intergenerational relations between mothers and children in Filipino transnational families. *Global Networks.* 10 (2005), 317-336.
22. Pribilsky, J. "Nervios and Modern Childhood. Migration and shifting contexts of child life in the Ecuadorian Andes". *Childhood, 8,* 2 (2001), 251-273.Norte, diciembre de 1999.
23. Raffle, H., Ballagas, R., Revelle, G., Horii, H., Follmer, S., Go, J., Reardon, E., Mori, K., Kaye, J.J., Spasojevic, M. Family Story Play: Reading with Young Children (and Elmo) Over a Distance. *Proc. CHI'10,* ACM (2010), 1583-1592.
24. Raffle, H., Mori, K., Ballagas, R., Spasojevic, M., Rd, P.M., and Ca, P.A. Pokaboo: A Networked Toy for Distance Communication and Play. *Proc. IDC'11,* 201-204.
25. Schwarz, N. Self- reports: How the questions shape the answers. *American Psychologist.* 54(1999):93-105.
26. Taylor, E. "The new economics of labor migration and the role of remittances in the migration process". *International Migration, 37,* 1 (1999), 63-88.
27. The report of left-behind children status in rural China. http://www.women.org.cn/allnews/02/1985.html.
28. Wong-Villacres, M., Bardzell, S. Technology-Mediated Parent-Child Intimacy: Designing for Ecuadorian Families Separated by Migration. *Proc. CHI'11,* ACM (2011), 2215-2220.
29. Yang, D. International Migration, Remittances and Household Investment: Evidence from Philippine Migrants' exchange rate shocks, *Working Paper 12324,* in http://www.nber.org/papers/w12325. (2006)
30. Yarosh, S., Cuzzort, S., Mueller, H., and Abowd, G.D. Developing a media space for remote synchronous parent-child interaction. *Proc. IDC'09,* ACM (2009), 97-105.
31. Yarosh, S., Abowd, G.D. Mediated Parent-Child Contact in Work-Separated Families. *Proc. CHI'11,* ACM (2011), 1185-119.

Revisiting the Relationship between Reunion and Technology-Mediated Separation in Periodically Transitioning Families

Konstantinos Kazakos
Dept. of Computing and Information Systems
The University of Melbourne
kazakosk@unimelb.edu.au

Steve Howard
Dept. of Computing and Information Systems
The University of Melbourne
showard@unimelb.edu.au

Frank Vetere
Dept. of Computing and Information Systems
The University of Melbourne
f.vetere@unimelb.edu.au

ABSTRACT

Reunion is one of the most important facets in the lives of periodically transitioning families - families who experience repeated transitions between being together and apart due to work-related or personal reasons. Even though the role of technology in mediating essential family interactions has been a l ongstanding focus within HCI and CSCW, the experience of periodic family reunion and its relationship with technology use while apart is little explored. To address this gap, we conducted a f ield study with nine families from two different professional backgrounds - defence and academic. Through a comparison between the two cohorts, our findings generate a qualitative understanding of the experience of reunion and describe specific aspects of this experience that are influenced by technology-use while apart. We discuss the complexity of this relationship and reflect on the role of technology in shaping the experience of periodic family reunion.

Author Keywords

Periodically transitioning families, family reunion, computer-mediated communication, separation, parent-child interaction

ACM Classification Keywords

H.5.3. **[Information Interfaces and Presentation (e.g. HCI)]**: Group and Organization Interfaces.

INTRODUCTION

Reunion is the process of people coming together after time apart that *"encompasses a flow of past memories, present reality and the future"* [16]. One of the main characteristics of the contemporary family life is the periodic transitions between reunion and time apart due to work-related and personal reasons [17]. In the presence of young children, these transitions may weaken the parent-child bonds and jeopardize the family wellbeing [5,21].

Recent research has explored the role of technology in mediating family interactions [1,10,11,13,23]. Early research investigated the relationship between online and offline interactions across different settings, including domestic, creating different views on the nature of these relationships [2]. More relevant to our work, studies have focused on understanding the life of dynamic or 'atypical' family structures – be they divorce related or work-separation – as an effort to map opportunities for designing technologies that are appropriated to the life of the families' communication needs [5,9,12,13]. Even though all of these works investigate the complicated interaction between being physically together and apart they only address the experience of reunion superficially. We fill this gap by asking, how does technology-mediated separation in families affect the experience of *reunion*?

Through a field study with nine families, we generate a qualitative understanding of the experience of periodic family reunion and its current relationship with technology use while apart. Our findings suggest that specific aspects of the reunion experience are influenced by the nature of technologies and the interaction mediated when families are physically dispersed. This work builds on the recent work of Turkle who mentioned that even though parents and children might be physically *together* they might feel *alone* [22]. Our contribution in this paper is twofold. Firstly, we present empirical findings that lead to a qualitative understanding of the experience of reunion with defence and academic families. Secondly, we use this understanding to provide a rich account of the current nature of the relationship between the experience of reunion and that of technology-use while apart.

In the remainder of this paper, we review the current work on reunion and mediated communication as well as present our field study findings. We discuss those findings and reflect on the role of technology in shaping the experience of reunion.

RELATED WORK

Reunion and periodically transitioning families

Studies within sociology and psychology have identified single instance reunion as a prescheduled meeting of family members who have been physically dispersed and is associated with annual familial or cultural events (e.g. family gatherings over Christmas dinner, annual family coming togethers) [19]. The basic attribute of single-instance reunion is its annual periodicity alongside the ritualistic and celebratory nature of interactions amongst the reunited family members. Examples of rituals in reunion include the exchange of gifts, the planning and enjoyment of the first family dinner and the sharing of experiences that occurred while family members were apart.

Periodic-reunion, which is the focus of this paper, refers to the cyclic family event that follows some type of physical separation particularly due to work-related or personal reasons [3]. In this paper, we call these families 'periodically transitioning families'. This type of reunion occurs across families of different professional backgrounds (defence, mining, business etc.) as well as immigrants, divorced and incarcerated families. Wood et al. [24] explored the role of reunion within defence families and showed the importance of narrative, play and reflection in enriching the family bonds when in reunion.

Moreover, in a comparative study between mining and defence families Kaczmarek et al. [12] highlighted the role of reunion in fostering the family togetherness after a separation. They noted that even in cases where reunion was surrounded with negative sentiments – mainly due to the unwillingness of the returning parent to engage in conversations – the physical presence of all the family members was a positive element that assisted in the resolution of these differences. Campos et al. [3], conducted a naturalistic observation study of dual-earner families focusing on what occurs when the family reunites at the end of a day. This is an extreme facet of periodic reunion that, however, manifested the different aspects of this experience in the contemporary family life. Works within the transnational context as [14,20] have, also, provided insights on the challenges that the parent-child reunion faces when it occurs periodically and potential solutions aligning with the use of narrative and collective engagement to enrich collocated family activities during reunion.

Periodic family reunion in HCI and CSCW

Outside of the sociological and psychological research context there has been little attention on periodic family reunion. Most of the recent work has focused on mediating essential parent-child interactions [10] through the use of synchronous or asynchronous tools to support closeness, intimacy, play as well as awareness [1,10,11,13,23]. However, recently there has been a shift in better understanding the role of technology within families who periodically separate due to work-related or divorce reasons, where reunion was recognized as an important finding [15,18,25,26].

In their work with travelling parents, Modlitba and Schmandt conducted a series of interviews with toddlers and their parents in order to identify potential design opportunities that support separation [19]. This work depicted the need for future systems to take into account the asymmetry of needs for communication technologies among parents and children. At the same time they found that many of the children would anticipate the eventual return of their parent even when keeping in touch at a distance. Following on this work, Yarosh and Abowd explored the perceptions and strategies employed by parents and children of work-separated families for coping with periodic separation [25]. They suggested that different facets of work-related separation should be taken into account when designing technologies to support separation and identified challenges for designing technologies for specific 'atypical' families (e.g. defence). Relating to reunion their findings suggested that collocated children anticipated the eventual reunion; a finding closely aligned with Modlitba and Schmandt [15].

Within divorce-related separation, Yarosh et al. explored the role of technology in supporting parent-child communication [26]. They underlined the importance of technologies that could enrich closeness and take into account the tensions arising within this type of family. Even though reunion was not explicitly noted in this work, the authors highlighted the tensions arising between the divorced parents for the attention of the child while it was transitioning between the households. In another study of divorced families, Odom et al. investigated the design space of technologies that might support the complicated nature of co-parenting in divorced families [18]. Amongst other findings, they highlighted the challenge on behalf of children to construct and maintain their identity when travelling between households and, thus, reuniting with their separated parent.

Relationship between mediated and physical interactions

The relationship between the physical interactions – that constitute a major part of reunion - and the online ones has been central to CMC studies. Baym, in her recent account of this relationship, revisited the context of personal connections in the digital age through a series of reflections that lead to the formulation of key concepts based on which we can build an understanding of how mediated separation influences personal interactions [2].

Moreover, Turkle presented numerous field studies over a period of two decades that depicted her concern in relation to being 'alone together' [22]. She mentioned the need to revisit the relationship between mediated separation and co-located interactions, in order to address the gap between the technological and the physical with the aim of enriching face-to-face interactions. Alongside those findings were the ones also from Hollan and Stornetta who noted the need to design communication tools that "go beyond being there" and add richer value to the physical interactions to a point that "people will want to use them even when they are co-located" [8]. These works provided the necessary context for understanding the relationship between physical interaction and CMC tools. Yet, they only touched the surface of the experience of reunion within periodically transitioning families.

Summary

The work within the current literature has outlined different perceptions relating to the relationship between physical interactions and technology use while in separation. Works within HCI have focused on understanding how to design for separation and why is that important. More recent research lines commence to highlight the different threads of reunion within the contemporary family life. However, there is little understanding of the interplay between the experience of reunion and the one of technology-mediated separation. Providing support for family separation does not necessarily mean that reunion is addressed within periodically transitioning families. In order to fill this gap, we answer the following question:

> *What aspects of the reunion experience are influenced by technology-mediated separation in periodically transitioning families?*

APPROACH

We conducted a series of qualitative, semi-structured interviews interwoven with observations from our site visits with nine periodically transitioning families (N=9).

Participant Information

The recruited families fulfilled the following criteria:

- Families experienced some type of periodic reunion due to work-related reasons over the last 12 months.
- At least one parent was away for duration of two weeks or more at a time.
- The frequency of separation was at least once every two months.
- All families had children aged between 5 and 11 years old.

We drew participants from two cohorts: academic and defence. Academic families are those who have at least one parent working in an academic environment (e.g. a university) and residing away from their familial home. Defence families are those who have at least one parent in the military and are subject to frequent deployments. In the case of defence families, separation signifies not only the absence of a parent but also the commencement of a persistent concern about his or her safety of wellbeing [24]. On the other hand, academic separation occurs due to reasons that relate to the different responsibilities of an academic. Examples of this might be the continuous trips for fieldwork or in most cases the fact that an academic might find a position in a country different to the one of his or her origin where the rest of the family (e.g. mother and children) decide not to follow for their own personal reasons. In that case, academic separation resembles to business traveling or mining ones with the difference that it might occur for longer periods of time, which is the type of separation that this research is focused on [12,17].

The reason we chose to recruit defence and academic families was due to the fact that even though they both go through periodic transitions between collocation and separation, the nature of the transition as well as the use of technology while apart is different. By doing so our aim was to be open to exploration of different themes that sourced from both of the families and could provide an account of the experience of reunion and its relationship with technology mediated separation. In all families the father was the person who was separated from the rest of the family. In the case of defence families, the fathers were in active combat deployments. Table 1 summarizes the family members interviewed, the durations of separation and reunion, and the most common communication technologies used whilst separated.

Data Collection

We conducted a series of semi-structured interviews (N=27) with parents and children from the four defence and five academic families following a s imilar approach as [18,25,26]. We interviewed the distant and the home based parent as well as one of the children – selected by the parents - from each family. The families were recruited by advertising at a local university campus and with the help of a local Defence Support Organization. The one-hour interviews were conducted either in the families' houses or online using communication software (e.g. Skype).

Each participant (including children) was interviewed alone without the presence of the other family members. The only exception was the child of family 8, who was interviewed with his mother due to his very young age. Initially, we asked each participant to give us a general account of how they perceived the current life of their family. Then, we focused the discussion on the aspects of separation and reunion. Questions covered the feelings of the interviewee on the separation of their loved one, the manner with which they kept in touch while separated as well as their perception of reunion and the role of separation – including technology use - on reunion. In the instances where we visited the families' home we also observed the children's rooms and asked to see any gifts that they might have received from their father upon reunion. With our questions we intended to understand the experience of reunion and deepen our understanding on its relationship with technology-use while apart. All family members shared their experiences of separation and reunion, their reflections on the periodic transitions between the two as well as how they used communication technologies to keep in touch whilst separated. As a token of appreciation all participants received a book voucher.

#	Interviewees (Father/Mother/ Child: Age in years)	Professional Background	Frequency of separation	Duration of Separation	Duration of Reunion	Communication technologies while separated			
						Mobile phone	Landline phone	Email	Skype Video
1	F: 34, M: 32, C: 7	Defence	Twice per year	6 months	2 months			✔	
2	F: 43, M: 40, C: 8	Defence	Three per year	4 months	1 month		✔	✔	
3	F: 48, M: 45, C: 7	Defence	Twice per year	3 months	2 months		✔	✔	
4	F: 42, M: 40, C: 9	Defence	Twice per year	7 months	1 month	✔	✔		
5	F: 41, M: 38, C: 11	Academic	Approx. four per year	3 months	2 weeks- 2 months	✔			✔
6	F: 52, M: 40, C: 11	Academic	Approx. four per year	4 months	2 weeks- 3 months	✔		✔	✔
7	F: 34, M: 32, C: 10	Academic	At least five per year	2 months	2 weeks	✔		✔	✔
8	F: 41, M: 38, C: 5	Academic	Twice per year	6 months	2-3 weeks	✔			✔
9	F: 38, M: 34, C: 10	Academic	At least six per year	1 month	2 weeks	✔		✔	✔

Table 1. Participant characteristics (F: father, M: mother, C: child).

Data Analysis

The data collected from the interviews was analyzed using a grounded theory approach [4]. Once the interviews were completed, they were transcribed and analyzed using the NVivo software package. The initial transcripts were analyzed and coded. While analyzing the data, we focused on the duration of separation, access to communication technologies while separated, the frequency of keeping in touch, type of technology used, the influence of time-zone differences and the sensitivity of the environment (e.g. life-threatening versus 'normal' conditions). The codes were then analyzed and categories emerged (focused coding). This iterative analysis, upon saturation, resulted in a stable theme set (theoretical coding). Integrated with the qualitative memos, the final themes were extracted and organized. We felt that we reached saturation after iterating the passing of the data multiple times and ensuring that no new evidence emerged. This analysis provided us with a series of themes that described the relationship between the experience of reunion and technology use while apart in the two cohorts.

FINDINGS

In this paper we ask what aspects of the reunion experience are influenced by technology-mediated separation in periodically transitioning families. Through the answer to this question, this paper contributes to understanding better the relationship between the experience of reunion and technology-mediated separation within the domestic domain. We chose to construct the findings around the three phases of the reunion process: pre-reunion, upon-reunion and post-reunion. Pre-reunion is the phase that occurs just before the physical interaction between the family members (e.g. days before the eventual reunion). Upon-reunion is the moment of reunion when the family members come physically together. Post-reunion is the phase that follows the initial moment of reunion up to yet another separation. We have to note that different sections of the interview transcripts are used to illustrate the themes. These are attributed by the number of the family followed by the acronym of the family member. For example, 4F means family 4 – father; 4M family 4 – mother and 4C family 4 – child. With that in mind we present our findings. Figure 1 depicts the basic themes raised from our interviews through the analysis.

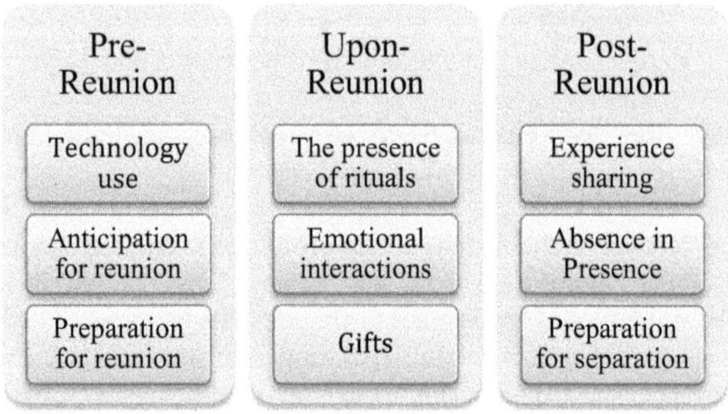

Figure 1. Themes raised in each reunion phase.

Pre-reunion

In this phase of reunion, family members are not physically together but very close to the eventual reunion. When questioned about the actual time boundaries of pre-reunion all of the family members gave a time range between a week and hours before reunion. We take this into account in describing the basic themes emerging from the first phase of reunion.

Technology use

Defence and academic families used different types of communication technologies to mediate their interactions while in separation. As table 1 shows, most of the defence families used landline phones and emails to keep in touch with their family while separated. The nature of the profession alongside the cumbersome access to other types of technologies – apart from landline phone and email - was apparent within the defence families. While in the pre-reunion phase, defence family members noted that they would increase the frequency of communication with their separated loved one. As the mother and child of family three note:

> *"Yes I'd say that while waiting for him to come we uhm try to communicate more often.if that is possible..To make sure that he is ok and that he will be finally coming the date that he told us" [3M]*

At the same time, the defence fathers felt more 'agitated' to harvest any available technology to communicate with their loved ones in order to ensure their mental and physical wellbeing prior to the upcoming reunion. On the other hand, four of the academic family members did not use technology differently while in pre-reunion. As the child of family six states:

> *"Well, yeah I would be in touch with dad throughout while he's away so it does not really make a gr eat difference when it is coming closer to him coming back" [6C]*

The mother from academic family seven described what happens while in pre-reunion in regards to the use of technology:

> *"Well, I would not say that that we talk more often. We know that he is safe and it does not really matter if he texts us or not more often as long as he comes back the day that he promised [laughs]..there are many things waiting to be dealt with here." [7M]*

This asymmetry in the frequency of technology use, as families went closer to the eventual reunion, was due to the nature of the profession and the access to technology throughout separation. It seemed that the at-home academic family members seemed more 'secure' about their loved one compared to the defence families' ones.

Anticipation for reunion

Another theme, aligned with the previous one, was the anticipation to the eventual reunion. The talks between the at-home defence family members would be around the eventual return of the separated father.

> *"we would be always talking about him coming back in three or two or one more sleeps.we are really want him to be back" [2M]*
>
> *"I would be thinking of him in so many uhmm random moments..especially uhmm when it w ill be like some days that he returns" [4C]*

The eventual return of the separated father is anticipated with anxiety from the defence family members, as they are concerned about his safe return. The defence fathers would also be looking forward to their reunion with their wives and children. Three of the fathers depicted this anticipation as a continuous thought of their loved ones, which interweaves with fear of not being able to seeing them again. They noted that regardless of how many times they reunite, the anticipation and 'longing' to be with their family once more was always present. In the case of academic families, anticipation was regarded in a different way. All of the at-home mothers stated that they would be happy for the eventual reunion with their husband but as academic mother five noted:

> *"Anticipation, especially after so many years of experiencing this, is slowly deteriorating..i think"[5M]*
>
> *"I might feel anticipation but literally minutes or hours before seeing them" [7F]*

Along the same lines as academic mother, the at-home children would anticipate for the return of their father but mainly for gifts – as will be discussed in the upon-reunion section. Finally, the academic fathers would anticipate for the upcoming reunion but would do so only in the final moments before the actual reunion. For example when they are in the plane or when arrive at the airport.

Preparation for reunion

Between the two family cohorts different practices were used to prepare for reunion, while in the pre-reunion phase. Defence mothers noted that there was a 'preparation procedure' days before the actual reunion took place:

> *"We would meet days before he comes back with his mom and dad and with the kids would prepare something for him. And then the dinner is fantastic!" [4M]*

At the same time, defence fathers would spend time preparing for the upcoming reunion by choosing gifts for their at-home loved ones and by

> *"[..] dreaming of how the moment that I would hold them once more in my hands will be like"[2F]*

Academic family members noted that no real preparation for reunion occurred:

> *"I would make a special dinner for him.and the kids might help but it would be probably for a big occasion like if we missed his birthday"[9M]*

However, when academic family members were asked to reflect on the first time that they were waiting for the upcoming reunion they said that some sort of preparation was done but as it happened again and again:

> *"we simply stopped preparing for it as there is no point for preparing any more..I am worring that this not might be good."[6M]*

This hints that the periodical nature of the transitions between separation and reunion influences the preparation for the upcoming reunion, which was reflected upon as a negative aspect of the family's life.

Upon Reunion

This is the phase of reunion that describes the physical coming together between the family members. We present the themes emerging from the interviews with family members in regards to the 'upon-reunion' phase.

Rituals

Within defence families, the moment of reunion was regarded as a moment of excitement and a celebration of family unity. Defence family members said that every time that their loved one came back they would be waiting in the airport where they would have prepared a welcoming banner or would have brought with them the favorite cake or sweet of their loved one. Unfortunately we could not access a welcoming ceremony for defence families but a short online search depicts the importance of this ritualistic aspect of the upon reunion phase. In academic families, three out of five families noted that upon the return of their loved ones would not pick them up from the airport or wait with the children for their arrival home:

> *"Most of the times we would meet in the house..Of course we are happy for him to be here, but there are so many things that the kids and I have to do."[9M]*

In that sense, academic families would depict a different aspect of the nature of a ritual upon reunion. It seemed that each of the academic families appropriated the rituals to their personal experience as different reunions were experienced. For example, two of the academic families noted that in the first reunion some sort of rituals would occur.

> *"it is not only that we have been experiencing that for many years now, but also that in the first time we did not have any uhmm good contact with technology while away..we do have that now and I think this has changed something..not sure what it is"[7M]*

Apart from the physical interaction (hug etc.) there would be someone waiting at the airport, children would have had a drawing ready for their father but as more reunions were experienced these rituals faded away.

Emotional Interactions

Within defence families, the moment of reunion was interwoven with positive sentiments, acts of affection and intense physical interactions between family members.

> *"We would hug and cry and just be so excited and happy that he is back!"[1M]*

All defence families perceived reunion as an experience that signified the coming together of the family. On many occasions defence families saw the moment of reunion as the event where the family can finally start to 'recuperate' from the painful and stressful experience of separation.

> *"For me [the moment of reunion] is all about being together again in our home. Doing all those activities that we have not done for some time now. Together" [3M]*
>
> *"blah blah..[reunion] is very similar to being part of the family again. It is physical and i t is important to be physical"[1F]*

In defence family four, the child expressed his pride and happiness in seeing his father once more:

> *"It is cool to see him in the uniform and he is here with us. My friends are jealous! "[4C]*

Four of the academic families noted that in many cases the children would show modest interest in the return of the father, and the children were aware of this:

> *"He will return and the kids will just be upstairs carrying on with their stuff. Still not know why this happens.."[6M]*
>
> *"Well dad m ight be back, but we will be playing with [name] and I might not go and hug him or stuff. I will see him later anyways."[5C]*

According to the academic mothers, the children exhibited less interest in the event of reunion because of the numerous activities that they were involved in, and the fact that they already felt connected with their father due to their keeping in touch whilst previously separated.

Gifts

It was common for the absent father to bring gifts on his return. For defence children the return of the father signified not only the return of a loved one but also the anticipation of gifts. Similarly, both defence and academic children said that the first thing they do once their father is back is to search for a gift in his luggage. They expressed their expectation and certainty that their beloved father would have some sort of present for them:

> *"Daddy will come back and yeah I will go through his stuff and search for gifts. I like that."[4C]*

It was evident from the interviews with the children that the gift played a very important role in building anticipation prior to the return of the father.

> *"I am so happy that he is back especially when he shows me the gift. That makes me so happy. I don't care which gift he brings me. Well I think!"[6C]*

The absent parent would pick the gift based either on the personality of their child or because they would expect the gift to mediate a nice experience that they had while in travel. In both cohorts, family members noted that gifts were important since they were associated the reunion of the whole family. The parents felt that, in some occasions, their bond with children was reinvigorated through the process of gift-exchange upon reunion.

Post Reunion

In this phase family members are physically together until the upcoming separation. This is the most important phase of the reunion process, which is primarily characterized by the different practices that each family employs in order to 'recuperate' from the physical separation. These practices are centralized around the sharing of experiences and the mechanics of feeling connected again. However, both families experienced those practices in a different manner.

Experience sharing

When all family members are physically together after time apart, it is necessary that they reconstruct their family bonds in order to enrich their relationships. This occurs primarily through the sharing of experiences, which can have different interpretations for different families and for different family members. Technology played an important role in being used as a platform for sharing of experiences. In the case of defence families it was common that they would share photographs at reunion. They would reflect on experiences that were not possible to be mediated through technology (they named those 'lost experiences') but would do so through a protocol. The location of where the sharing occurred played an important role. For instance, all of the families who shared physical (printed on card or paper) photos chose the first family dinner or after the dinner in the family living room:

> *"After the dinner we will just sit down and talk with the kids about things that happened. Then [name] would have some photos and the kids would be happy to see where dad was.." [4M]*

The younger and older members of the family would engage in some form of discussion and on many occasions the father would ask the children to reflect on their life at school or other important elements of their life that had occurred whilst separated. However, this sharing of experiences was not bidirectional since in most cases the fathers did not disclose many details of their life while in deployment for fear of traumatizing their children. Across defence families the concept of 'lost' experiences arose. Six out of eight parents felt that reunion was an opportunity to address issues that had occurred while the family members were apart and could not be mediated through the communication technologies used:

> *"The fact that we do not really talk a lot while away makes this [the coming together] even more important. We can now talk about things." [2M]*

These experiences often occurred between the two parents, though in cases with the active participation of the children. Nevertheless, the children's participation was mostly around clarifications of details. Academic families, on the other hand, stated that they would rarely use technology while in post reunion, to share their experiences of separation:

> *"When dad is back we do not really see photos or things like that, uhmm, we might talk about it but no photos or videos." [5C]*
>
> *"Well, I don't think that we would share photos or anything like that. What might happen is for [child's name] to show some of his drawings."[8M]*

When asked to elaborate more on why they do not use technology to reflect on past experiences, academic family members noted that:

> *"We keep on talking daily. Especially through skype so when we come together we are already up to date with each other..not sure if that is a good thing or not though"[6F]*

The experience sharing, in the case of academic families, was mostly a momentous process and it did not involve the practices that were used by defence families. Academic family members did not feel the need to share 'stuff' when reunited but as the extract from the interview with the father of family six shows, that does not mean that they were feeling comfortable with that neither.

Absence in presence

Related to the lack of experience sharing within the academic family members another theme that arose was the feelings of absence in (co) presence. This theme is best described by the following transcript extracts:

> *"When he comes back to the house it is as if he was never gone. It is the same every time. He will come back and then leave again for so many times that we are getting used to it. It is as if he is absent while he is also present.." [6M]*
>
> *"For sure I enjoy that my father is here..But still many times it is very plain.it is like he is back and we just say hi and nothing more" [7C]*

This feeling of being absent even though the family should all be (co) present was apparent in three out of five academic families. The mothers of these families felt responsible for stimulating the interest of their children and their partners in engaging both parties at some form of discussion:

> *"I feel many times that I am trying to provoke conversation when the family comes together. I do understand that since we are talking every day when [name] is away uhmm but still I would like the family to talk more. Maybe I am asking too much." [7M]*

As the mother of academic family seven notes, the lack of discussion among the family members in post reunion was perceived as an issue of concern for the whole family. Fathers of these families would care mostly about the family issues that had to be coordinated upon their arrival back to the household. In some cases, this would result in tensions among themselves and their partners since academic mothers expressed their hope to see their partners and their children engaged in more interaction. Another mother from family nine noted that:

> *"It is as if we are together but struggle to really be together. We struggle to feel connected again."[9M]*

When the fathers of these families were asked about the absence that their partners felt while in reunion they stated that the continuous use of technology while apart and the fact that they have been experiencing reunion for many times now was partly due to blame. As the father of family seven said:

> *"This [reunion] has been happening for a lot time now and uhmm we always keep in touch while I am away. We use skype all the time and it would seem redundant to go over the same things when we come together. It has become a routine [reunion]. I am not sure that this is a good thing" [7F]*

In these families (the three out of the five academic) it was clear that meaningful interactions in post-reunion would be essential for the whole family. Engaging in what each family would consider as meaningful per their values, was of upmost importance. In the case of defence families there existed only some instances of this absence, primarily when defence fathers did not want to share their experiences while apart due to the sensitivity of the nature of their profession:

> *"I would not like for the kids to hear what it is like to be in Afghanistan; .in a war environment. So I just tell them the one part of the story. The beautiful one [laughing]" [1F]*

Defence family members noted that they did not feel the kind of absence that is described by academic ones. Their main goal was to assist their loved one in being part of the family once more and focus on this as a family unit. For this reason they would use each day of reunion as a new and different one where they would employ all essential practices for the family to be really connected again.

Preparation for the next separation

Another important theme that emerged in the post-reunion phase was the fact that all families felt the need that they should somehow prepare for the next separation. However, the practical activities that would address this need were not implemented in the same manner from both families. In defence families, preparation for the next separation associated with continuous use of reunion as a ground for enriching the family bonds. The anxiety of being separate once more and all the dangers involved in deployment alongside the lack of ways to mediate essential interactions while apart were key reasons for:

> *"preparing for the next separation is more than really preparing. It is about thinking of how you would make use of everyday when you are together and r eally bring the family together..Be really prepared for the next deployment" [2M]*

Defence family members would prepare for the next separation by discussing of the critical issues associated with deployment and by reflecting on ways with which they could address issues that arose in previous deployments:

> *"even though I do not like discussing about it, yeah we go through of what might happen while I am away, what we did wrong in previous deployments and of ways we can use to keep connected"[3F]*

Preparing for next separation became also planning for next separation and becoming aware of what it entails within the defence families. A different perception of preparing for next separation was encountered in academic families. All of the academic family members felt more secure in regards to the upcoming separation with their loved one. This security arose, mainly, from the fact that they could use technology to keep connected while apart and of the lack of sensitivity of the profession:

> *"preparing for another separation is not, I think, one of the main goals of this family while in reunion. Well, apart from the practical stuff.."[8M]*

However, when asked to reflect on the importance of preparing for another separation all of the academic family members depicted their concern on the fact that they had not though of this before. For academic families it seemed as if reunion and separation were closely aligned with each other:

> *"Yes it is really strange but we would not really talk about the next separation, we might do so a couple of days before but we should have. We take for granted many things you know"[8F]*

There was no need to prepare for the next separation yet there was a deep concern, primarily from the parents, that they were not using reunion as a time of enriching their bonds between themselves and their children. The access to technology while in separation resulted in parents and children feeling more secure about their communication while apart. Yet, even though they were feeling secure, it was clear that sadness and remorse was apparent not only for separating once more but also for not having used reunion as a ground for strengthening the parent-child bonds.

DISCUSSION

Comparing the experience of reunion between the two cohorts

For both academic and defence families the experience of reunion was a three-phase process: pre-reunion, upon-reunion and post-reunion. However, when comparing the main themes across the two cohorts we can highlight many differences. In pre-reunion, defence families would endeavor to harvest different communication resources - that in many cases were limited and simple - and ensure that the family members were aware of the safe return of the deployed parent. The anticipation to reunite increased closer to the reunion date due in part to the life-threatening context of the deployment and the limited access to communication technologies while deployed. It was manifested with the increased frequency of technology use, which served as a way of preparing for the forthcoming reunion. Similar work in defence family studies depicts the significant role of email and landline phones in not only communicating an awareness of the physical and mental wellbeing of the deployed parent but also preparing the deployed and at-home family members for reunion [12,24]. On the other hand, in academic families, the at-home family members would not demonstrate different uses of technology during pre-reunion. For instance, they would have positive sentiments of current technologies used to mediate separation and not increase their use of those technologies. For academic families, the anticipation of reunion was evident but in a scarcer manner compared to defence. They would anticipate reuniting but this would have an instant character, happening primarily minutes or hours before meeting. In terms of preparation for reunion, academic family members rarely prepared for reunion, in part due to the continuous use of technology whilst in separation and the non-sensitive context of the profession compared to the dangers of the defence sector.

When reunion occurred defence families regarded it a s a pivotal event interwoven with rituals and emotional interaction. For instance, at-home family members would be waiting at the airport or preparing the first dinner as a family. Academic families did not regard the moment of reunion with the same gravity. The rituals of academic families had a more 'routine-like' manner that was still important for the family wellbeing but different to defence. This aligns with previous work on business related travelling and dual-earner families, which outlined the routine-like experience of reunion [3,17,21]. In the moment of reunion the emotional connection between the returning parent and the child was evidenced by a hug or a kiss. These actions were, of course, meaningful but not in the same way or with the same intensity as defence reunions. Parents and children were happy to be together yet the periodic nature of reunion and the different communication technologies used altered the way in which the moment of reunion was experienced. In all cases the families exchanged gifts upon reunion. The close relation of gift and reunion was evident in the reactions of the children. In many cases, children would search for a gift, which took on the characteristics of a 'hide and seek' game, a playful activity for both parents and children.

While in post-reunion, defence families would engage in different practices of experience sharing. Defence family members had the need to reinvigorate their bonds and did so through discussion and shared family activities. Defence parents reflected on what they called 'lost experiences', those that were hard to share whilst apart due to the cumbersome use of technology. Throughout post-reunion defence families would organize family activities where all members (including the extended family) would participate. Digital artifacts had a central role in the post-reunion phase of defence families in not only facilitating experience sharing but also in informing all family members and preparing them for the next separation. The benefits of the collocated use of technology that we observed in defence families have been documented extensively elsewhere in photo sharing, the collocated use of displays for experience sharing and the role of collocated technology generally [6,9]. However, within academic families the collocated use of technology for experience sharing was not apparent. Family members would not engage in extensive reflection about their time apart, either through photos or other types of technology. They felt that the increased frequency and access to technology whilst apart – in particular through video-mediated tools - was successful in keeping in touch with absent family members. Therefore, in most of the academic families a sentiment of 'absence in presence' would be evident that depicted a lack of engagement in post-reunion collocated family activities (e.g. through dialogue). This absence of collocated interaction also resulted in a lack of preparation for forthcoming separation. We understand these differences, particularly during post reunion, to be due to the nature of experiences mediated by technology whilst in separation, as well as the periodicity of the transition between reunion and separation. There exist other reasons (e.g. threatening professional context and nature of existing family bonds as [12] underlines) but for the purposes of this paper we confine our discussion to periodicity and the nature of mediated interactions.

Periodicity not only relates to the frequency of separation and reunion but to the broader temporal aspects of reunion and separation. Since we are focused on reunion and inspired by previous work on the temporal aspects of usability [7], we frame the periodicity of reunion as being defined by the duration, location and frequency of the reunion event. The duration of reunion refers to the actual duration of the family members being together prior to another separation. The location of reunion is when the reunion happened in relation to other events (birthdays, Christmas, funerals etc.) and the frequency is how often reunion occurred. The nature of experiences mediated whilst separated depends on the type and frequency of use of the specific technologies. Most academic families – as table 1 shows – had continuous access to synchronous technologies (mobile phones and Video Mediated Communication tools as well as in some cases access to social media) that they were content to use, whereas defence families sporadic access to asynchronous ones (e.g. email). Academic families were able to mediate their essential interactions through easy access to technology. Despite different technologies that enable family members to enrich their collocated interactions [9] academic family members would not use them since they felt that they had little more to share and most importantly no creative ways in which they could engage in the reunion prior to another separation. This was manifested in different aspects of the post-reunion phase that were attributed to concerns about the strength of the family bonds by the academic parents.

What aspects of reunion are influenced by technology-mediated separation?

Recent sociological research has depicted the opportunities that reunion provides to families to enrich their the quality of their relationship through collocated parent-child activities [5,12,14,17,20,24]. However, returning to our original study question, we have identified a series of aspects of the reunion experience that are influenced by technology-mediated separation during both pre- and post-reunion.

The anticipation to reunite was one of the threads of the reunion experience influenced by technology use whilst apart. The sentiment of anticipation has been mentioned within the previous work on work-related separation and 'atypical' family structures [15,25]. In all of those studies children anticipated the eventual reunion. In fact as [25] describes, in most cases, children would prefer to not engage with their separated parent through communication tools but would wait for the eventual physical reunion. We found similar practices by the younger family members in the case of defence families but not with academic families. In the latter case, children would look forward to the eventual reunion not only because the family was together once more but also because of the gift that awaited them. In that case, the anticipation to reunite was embodied in the 'artifact' that the parent would bring along upon his return. In the case of preparation for another separation research on work-related and divorce separation [15,18,25,26] is the separation anxiety that family members feel approach the separation event. Our study found similar results but academic families felt more secure about the separation due to the less-sensitive professional context and the different types of technology-use whilst separated.

However, a contradiction was apparent. Even though it seemed that technology was achieving the purpose of ensuring the continued connectedness and closeness of physically separated parents and children [1,11,13], academic parents felt that it was also responsible for the lack of interaction amongst family members during reunion. Academic families experienced a feeling of *absence in presence* (an inversion of the more commonly used phrase 'presence in absence') relating to a lack of engagement felt in collocated family activities during reunion. This finding aligns with the work of Turkle, who in addition to accounts of the role of technology in the everyday life, refers to the thin line between feeling alone and together even though one might be collocated with the significant other [22]. Throughout her research she extracted observations from a series of interviews that she conducted with children and adults over a ten-year period. Her main claim is that even though technology is omnipresent with the purpose of enriching our essential interactions whilst apart, in many cases it is technology that makes us feel alone even if we are collocated.

This view might be regarded as a dystopian one by many researchers; however, it was apparent within the academic families. As stated above, our purpose is not to take a stance in favor of technology use while apart or during reunion. We do not argue against the use of technologies that mediate separation or against having contact when separated. The main message of this paper is that there exist specific attributes of reunion that are influenced by technology-mediated separation and that it is important to consider those aspects when designing for transitioning families.

Our work does have certain limitations (e.g. in all cases it was the father that was separated from the family). In future work we intend to further explore opportunities for informing the design of communication technologies that do not only mediate family interactions but also help them appreciate and reflect on the importance of reunion. Inspired by Hollan and Stornetta [8], we envision technologies that go "beyond being there" and balance mediating essential interactions whilst separated with adding value to reunion.

CONCLUSION

The relationship between reunion and technology-mediated separation is important and complex. This paper investigates the nature of this relationship, within two diverse family cohorts, in order to map the different aspects of reunion that are influenced by technology-use whilst apart. We found that the nature of family interactions mediated through different communication channels does influence certain aspects of the reunion experience. These aspects are centered on the post-reunion phase and associate with the sharing of experiences when the family members are physically together but in preparation for yet another separation. The lack of experience sharing leads to a sentiment of *absence in presence* that was a concern for academic families. Our work extends current literature in that it provides empirical findings, which suggest there is a need to design technologies that not only support separation but also add value to reunion within periodically transitioning families.

ACKNOWLEDGEMENTS

We are deeply grateful to all the participating families. This work was supported by an Institute for Broadband Enabled Society (IBES) PhD top up scholarship.

REFERENCES

1. Ames, M.G., Go, J., Jofish' Kaye, J., and Spasojevic, M. Making love in the network closet: the benefits and work of family videochat. *Proceedings of the 2010 ACM conference on Computer supported cooperative work*, ACM (2010), 145–154.
2. Baym, N.K. *Personal connections in the digital age.* Polity, Cambridge,UK, 2010.
3. Campos, B., Graesch, A.P., Repetti, R., Bradbury, T., and Ochs, E. Opportunity for interaction? A naturalistic observation study of dual-earner families after work and school. *Journal of Family Psychology 23*, 6 (2009), 798–807.
4. Charmaz, K. *Constructing Grounded Theory: A Practical Guide through Qualitative Analysis.* Sage Publications Ltd, 2006.
5. Davies, H. Affinities, seeing and feeling like family: Exploring why children value face-to-face contact. *Childhood 19*, 1 (2012), 8–23.
6. Durrant, A., Taylor, A.S., Frohlich, D., Sellen, A., and Uzzell, D. Photo displays and intergenerational relationships in the family home. *Proceedings of the 23rd British HCI Group Annual Conference on People and Computers: Celebrating People and Technology*, British Computer Society (2009), 10–19.
7. Fabre, J. and Howard, S. Introduction to the Special Issue on Temporal Aspects of Usability. *Interacting with Computers 11*, 1.
8. Hollan, J. and Stornetta, S. Beyond being there. *Proceedings of the SIGCHI conference on Human factors in computing systems*, ACM (1992), 119–125.
9. Van House, N.A. Collocated photo sharing, story-telling, and the performance of self. *International Journal of Human-Computer Studies 67*, 12 (2009), 1073–1086.
10. Isola, S. and Fails, J.A. Family and design in the IDC and CHI communities. *Proceedings of the 11th International Conference on Interaction Design and Children*, ACM (2012), 40–49.
11. Judge, T.K., Neustaedter, C., Harrison, S., and Blose, A. Family portals: connecting families through a multifamily media space. *Proceedings of the 2011 annual conference on Human factors in computing systems*, ACM (2011), 1205–1214.
12. Kaczmarek, E.A. and Sibbel, A.M. The psychosocial well-being of children from Australian military and fly-in/fly-out (FIFO) mining families. *Community, Work & Family 11*, 3 (2008), 297–312.
13. Kirk, D.S., Sellen, A., and Cao, X. Home video communication: mediating 'closeness'. *Proceedings of the 2010 ACM conference on Computer supported cooperative work*, ACM (2010), 135–144.

14. Mazzucato, V. and Schans, D. Transnational Families and the Well-Being of Children: Conceptual and Methodological Challenges. *Journal of Marriage and Family 73*, 4 (2011), 704–712.

15. Modlitba, P.L. and Schmandt, C. Globetoddler: designing for remote interaction between preschoolers and their traveling parents. *CHI '08 extended abstracts on Human factors in computing systems*, (2008), 3057–3062.

16. Moss, M.S. and Moss, S.Z. Reunion Between Elderly Parents and Their Distant Children. *American Behavioral Scientist 31*, 6 (1988), 654–668.

17. Nicholas, H. and McDowall, A. When work keeps us apart: a thematic analysis of the experience of business travellers. *Community, Work & Family 15*, 3 (2012), 335–355.

18. Odom, W., Zimmerman, J., and Forlizzi, J. Designing for dynamic family structures: divorced families and interactive systems. *Proceedings of the 8th ACM Conference on Designing Interactive Systems*, ACM (2010), 151–160.

19. Peterson, J.S. Reunion. *The Family Journal 14*, 1 (2006), 85–87.

20. Ramirez, M., Skrbiš, Z., and Emmison, M. Transnational Family Reunions as a Lived Experience: Narrating a Salvadoran Autoethnography. *Identities 14*, 4 (2007), 411–431.

21. Thomas, M. and Bailey, N. Out of Time: Work, Temporal Synchrony and Families. *Sociology 43*, 4 (2009), 613–630.

22. Turkle, S. *Alone Together: Why We Expect More from Technology and Less from Each Other*. Basic Books, New York, New York, USA, 2011.

23. Vetere, F., Gibbs, M.R., Kjeldskov, J., et al. Mediating intimacy: designing technologies to support strong-tie relationships. *Proceedings of the SIGCHI conference on Human factors in computing systems*, ACM (2005), 471–480.

24. Wood, S., Scarville, J., and Gravino, K.S. Waiting Wives: Separation and Reunion among Army Wives. *Armed Forces & Society 21*, 2 (1995), 217–236.

25. Yarosh, S. and Abowd, G.D. Mediated parent-child contact in work-separated families. *Proceedings of the 2011 annual conference on Human factors in computing systems*, ACM (2011), 1185–1194.

26. Yarosh, S., Denise Chew, Y.C., and Abowd, G.D. Supporting parent–child communication in divorced families. *International Journal of Human-Computer Studies 67*, 2 (2009), 192–203.

Exploring Remembrance and Social Support Behavior in an Online Bereavement Support Group

Michael Massimi
Microsoft Research Cambridge
mmassimi@microsoft.com

ABSTRACT
Designing interactive systems that sensitively engage with end of life issues is a key challenge for CSCW as more and more people turn to the Internet to grapple with the realities of death. However, there are few studies that document how specific remembrance or support features of bereavement websites are used in a real-world setting. This paper describes Besupp, a website where bereaved individuals can participate in online support groups. Three support groups used Besupp in a ten-week long deployment study. Based on this study, I describe how participants perceived and used the remembrance and social support features of the site. These results form the basis for a set of implications regarding the design of technologies for remembrance, social support, and bereavement more generally.

Author Keywords
Bereavement; remembrance; social support; support groups; thanatosensitive design; grief.

ACM Classification Keywords
H.5.m. Information interfaces and presentation (e.g., HCI): Miscellaneous.

INTRODUCTION
The death of a loved one is a challenge that we all encounter in our lives. Following such a loss, families face a wide array of challenges; dealing with finances, handling possessions and property, organizing memorial services, and consoling one another. Underscoring all of these activities is the grief that each individual endures as they struggle to adjust to a life without their loved one. For some people, talking with compassionate peers can be a helpful way to find strength, knowledge, and comfort. Support groups are a common setting where these needs can be met.

This paper describes the design of a website called Besupp that allows bereaved individuals to meet in online support groups. Working in conjunction with a community bereavement support centre, Besupp was built to support two primary functions. First, it supports remembrance about the deceased by offering a place to host and share digital mementos. Second, it allows users to create profiles, share background stories, and converse with peers in an effort to create a social support environment.

Besupp was deployed in a ten-week long deployment study. It was used by three different support groups for bereaved parents, spouses/partners, and young adults. The ways in which participants used the remembrance and social support features of the website were explored through analysis of participant interviews and system logs. These revealed usage scenarios that speak to the relative merits of particular system features. Based on these results, I then share a set of implications for design. These implications contribute to ongoing discussions in three important topics of concern to CSCW and HCI: digital mementos and remembrance, online social support, and technology design for the end of life.

RELATED WORK
Recent work in HCI and CSCW has begun to focus on how technology plays a role at the end of life. The term "thanatosensitive design" has been used to describe a design process that actively engages with issues pertaining to death and dying as part of the design concept [25]. I now turn to pertinent literature on online social support and remembrance.

Internet-Based Social Support in Bereavement
Using the Internet for social support is a well-established practice. Much of the work examining social support has focused on health conditions such as cancer [2,31], caring for high-risk infants [22], or improving physical fitness [6]. While bereavement is not a health condition, it is also a life-altering occurrence. In the case of bereavement, online interaction can potentially impact five of Barrera *et al.*'s six forms of social support: behavioral assistance, intimate interaction, guidance, feedback, and positive social interaction [1]. In a survey of bereaved respondents, Lehman *et al.* found that contact with similar others, opportunities to vent, and expressions of concern were rated the three most helpful gestures during grief [16]. All of these opportunities can be found online [33]. Crafting and sharing narratives is a key part of these exchanges – "[t]hrough the use of storytelling, [participants] begin to

make sense of their malaise, to take control of events formerly beyond their power of influence" (p. 391) [3].

However, support groups (whether online or face-to-face) are not necessarily effective for all bereaved people. In a systematic review of the literature on bereavement treatments, Forte *et al.* found that interpersonal support groups were not effective in a systematic review of the literature [8]. For example, Levy *et al.* found that levels of depression, anger, and stress for support group participants were not significantly different 18 months following the loss of a spouse from those who did not attend a group [18]. Indeed, Levy and Derby found that those who join such support groups report higher levels of depression, anger, anxiety, and stress, but are not significantly different from non-joiners in terms of perceived social support [19]. Picton *et al.* suggest that such groups are most effective for those with poor family support and within three months of the loss, but that the perceived need for support persists irrespective of time elapsed since the death [29]. Regardless of their efficacy, support groups remain a common and well-established platform for finding peer support.

Technology and Remembrance of the Deceased

One survey and interview study found that technology frequently plays a role in how the bereaved remember the deceased [23]. Other work has shown that one of the key ways in which we mediate our relationships with the deceased is through objects [12]. In a series of home tours with bereaved individuals, Odom et al. present a rich description of how inherited items – both physical and digital – help supplement (or confuse) the relationship between the living and deceased [26]. Recent work has also questioned how we may support older adults in organizing their possessions to ease the bequeathal process [21]. For some, safeguarding symbolic objects indicative of the relationship with the deceased is of key concern – Volkan terms these special items "linking objects" [35].

Social networking sites are a primary platform for communication with the deceased and mourning. Drawing on continuing bonds theory [15], Getty *et al.* report on how Facebook users write on profiles of the deceased to keep their relationship "alive," and to visibly perform activities associated with mourning such as remembering, sharing, and consoling [10]. In a larger-scale study of deceased MySpace users' profiles, Brubaker and Hayes report similar findings and point out how these activities become part of larger, temporally-recurring rituals of remembrance, reflection, and socialization [4].

Photos play a clear role in remembering the deceased – scanning and organizing photos for a memorial service is a common task [23]. Increasingly, digital photos reside on both desktops and in the cloud; even so, using these photos for memorial purposes requires a great deal of "photowork" [13]. Using interactive devices to share these photos across time and distance is an increasingly common occurrence as well and often helps to support storytelling [9]. In an examination of how older adults arrange their living spaces, photos of the deceased were frequently displayed in all parts of the home [17]. Photos play a key role in novel interactive devices designed to support remembrance, such as ThanatoFenestra [34].

COMMUNITY-BASED DESIGN

Since 2009, I have worked closely with BFO – a non-profit community organization that offers support groups to bereaved individuals. My involvement with BFO shares some similarities with action research, which involves "a circle of planning, action, and fact-finding about the result of the action" [20]. In this tradition, I seek not to make claims regarding the efficacy or wide applicability of the software we co-designed, but rather document the decisions that we made, why we made them, and how they played out in a real-world deployment. In order to unpack and critically examine this process, it is important to share three of BFO's key organizational values[1]:

1. *Like-loss membership.* Multiple groups run simultaneously, and are organized based on the type of loss. Examples of recurring groups include: parents who have lost an infant, parents who have lost a young or adult child, individuals who have lost a spouse or partner, and young adults (ages 18-30) who have lost a parent or sibling. All members of a group – including the trained facilitator – must have experienced the same kind of loss. This value stems from the acknowledgment that those best suited to provide support must have experienced the loss themselves.
2. *Peer support.* The facilitators of the group are trained by BFO to ensure safety and respect among group members. Importantly, the facilitators are not professionals (*e.g.*, psychologists, counselors, social workers). There is an emphasis placed on "not fixing:" the facilitators are only there to help start and guide discussion, not to prescribe actions or treatment for dealing with grief.
3. *One-on-one screenings.* Before attending a support group, each potential member must first complete a one-on-one interview with a BFO facilitator. During this session, the moderator judges whether the individual would be able to participate in a group effectively. The time between the death and the one-on-one varies from person to person, as does the time between the one-on-one and the beginning of the support group. This reflects BFO's understanding that we all grieve differently, and on different timelines.

Support groups consist of 10 weekly sessions of 2 hours each. Each week has a pre-determined discussion topic,

[1] See www.bfotoronto.ca for more information about the organization and its values.

such as discussing the memorial service or funeral, and how to deal with friends and family members. Groups range in size from 5-12 people. As an organization, BFO maintains strict policies surrounding confidentiality and privacy. For this reason, observing support group sessions was not permitted. Instead, a series of focus groups were held with previous support group participants who responded to an ad placed in the BFO newsletter. These focus groups yielded a number of insights and considerations for design [24].

In order to build and maintain relationships with BFO, I also redesigned BFO's website, and in so doing, learned a about organizational values and procedures through monthly meetings with their board of directors and communications team. Second, I conducted 4 one-on-one design sessions with BFO's directors and volunteers. Potential design options were discussed, including a mobile phone application for "support anywhere" and a domestic ambient display that offered messages of support to residents who passed by it. These early participants were recruited through word-of-mouth and convenience, and were not part of the deployment study discussed below.

Feedback from BFO directors and volunteers resulted in the following design suggestions.

- The system should be a separate space away from Facebook, email, and other existing platforms. Participants wanted a "safe" place where feelings of grief could be expressed openly, without spilling over into their existing social networks.
- A website was considered the most appropriate form of technology. The rationale was that a website could serve the largest number of BFO clients because the web is an established technology that participants can integrate easily into their lives.
- The system should follow from the values established at BFO (outlined above). Groups should be organized according to like-loss membership and consist solely of peers (i.e., no "professional advice"). They should be moderated by a trained support group leader, and members should be screened to ensure they were emotionally ready to participate.

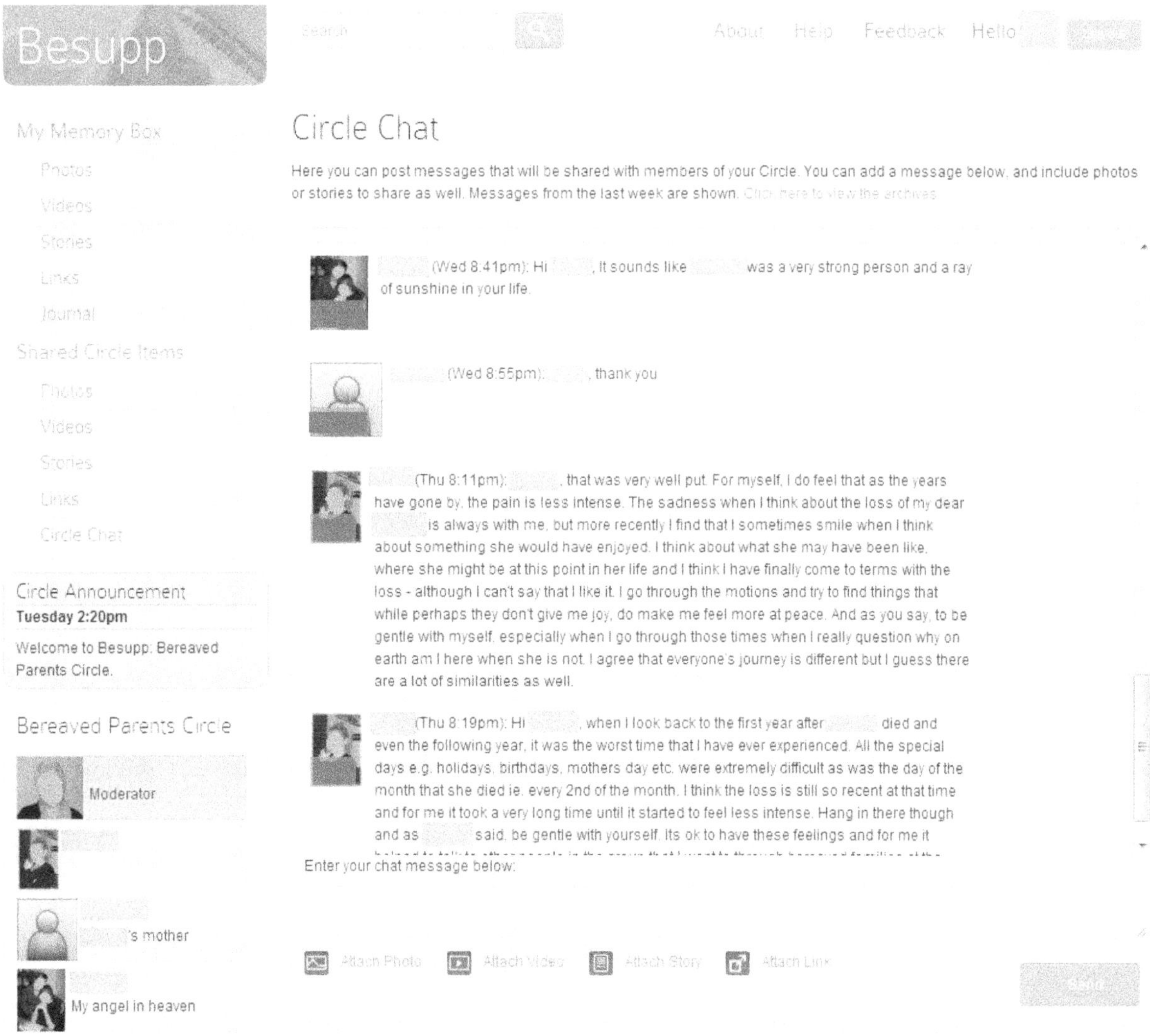

Figure 1. Besupp interface showing Circle Chat room (center) and main menu (left column).

- The system should support common group activities based on current weekly sessions. These activities retelling the story of the loss, sharing mementos, and suggesting resources they have found personally helpful (e.g., books, websites, activity suggestions).

SYSTEM DESIGN: BESUPP

Based on the design suggestions above, Besupp (short for "bereavement support") was developed. Besupp is a custom website designed specifically for bereaved individuals seeking an online support group experience similar to the format offered by BFO (Figure 1). Key to the concept for Besupp is the notion of a "memento-based" social support group, where digital mementos can be included to augment or prompt discussion. Digital mementos are often valued for not only sentimental reasons, but because they serve an important role in communication [26,28]. Besupp's functionality is divided into two corresponding feature sets: the Memory Box, and the Circle.

Memory Box

The Memory Box serves as a user's private space on the website. Inspired by bereaved individuals who keep physical memory boxes and bring them to support group meetings, it provides a virtual container for mementos related to the individual's loss. In order to share mementos, they must first be uploaded to the Memory Box.

Users can include five major types of mementos in their Memory Boxes: photos, videos, stories, links, and journal entries. Photos can be uploaded from the user's computer or imported from an existing URL (e.g., from Facebook or Flickr). Videos cannot be uploaded due to technical constraints, but users can provide a link to the YouTube URL in order to import a video into the Memory Box. This also provides a method for users to include music in their Memory Box by linking to a YouTube video of a song. In the Memory Box, stories are comprised of a title and story text, and can be sorted according to creation date and title. Users can further include links to other resources on the web that they find meaningful or helpful; for example, creating a link to a website containing poetry. Finally, the Memory Box provides a private journal in which the user can record his or her thoughts. All of the mementos in the Memory Box can be edited or deleted at any time, and captions can be provided for photos and videos.

The Circle

The Circle is the shared part of Besupp. All items in the Memory Box, with the exception of journal entries, can be shared or unshared with members of the Circle. Users can then browse the collection of shared photos, videos, stories, and links. The Circle mirrors the Memory Box in terms of presentation and functionality for photos, videos, stories, and links.

Each user is assigned to one thematic Circle (e.g., bereaved parents), and can view a listing of the other people in the Circle. Each user has a profile that is visible to all members of the Circle. If they so choose, users can provide a profile photo and basic background information (name, age, gender, email). Users can also set a brief "role" tag in their profile, such as "bereaved mom." Finally, the profile contains a field for the user to enter their own background story.

Each Circle can contain one or more users designated as a moderator. Moderators are authorized by the site administrator to help monitor and guide members of the Circle. Unlike normal users, moderator messages appear in a highlighted color in the chat. Further, they can set a Circle Announcement that appears on each page in order to demarcate current topics the Circle is discussing.

The Circle Chat is, in many ways, the heart of the site. Circle Chat is a custom asynchronous, persistent chat system where users can post messages to all members of their Circle. Messages are displayed on the Circle Chat page for seven days before being moved to an archive page. When sending a message, users can attach items from their Memory Boxes; these attached items are automatically shared and displayed in line with the sent chat message.

DEPLOYMENT STUDY

Given this design, a deployment study was conducted to answer the research question: "How do bereaved participants perceive, use, and value the remembrance and social support features in the system?"

Working with coordinators at BFO, we determined that the audience for such a website would be individuals who had previously completed a support group (and therefore had been screened in a previous one-on-one interview), but desired ongoing, long-term support. Three types of groups were identified as representative of BFO's offerings:

- **Young Adult (YA):** youth between the ages of 18 and 30 who experienced the loss of a parent or sibling;
- **Bereaved Parents (BP):** individuals of any age who had experienced the loss of an infant or adult child, or of a child who was not carried to term;
- **Spousal and Partner Loss (SP):** individuals of any age who have lost a spouse or romantic partner.

BFO coordinators circulated a recruitment email to their database of YA, BP, and SP members with an original limit of 5 years since the loss. The initial response rate did not yield enough participants to meet BFO's minimum support group size of at least 5 members. As such, the limit of 5 years was lifted and the recruitment advertisement was circulated a second time, yielding enough to conduct 3 simultaneous support groups using Besupp. Each group had a facilitator who completed BFO's intensive facilitator training process and had moderated previous face-to-face groups. Coincidentally, all participants were female. In total, 19 participants used Besupp (Table 1). The number of

Group	Size	Photos Shared/Total	Stories Shared/Total	Messages sent
YA	7	12/16	0/1	62
BP	7	7/11	6/8	180
SP	5	6/6	5/5	39
Total	19	25/33	11/14	281

Table 1. Besupp usage statistics by group. Links and journal were very rarely used and omitted from the table.

years since the loss occurred varied among participants. The most recent loss occurred 5 months before the study, while the most distant was 19 years ago. Twelve of the 19 participants endured the loss less than 5 years ago.

Method

A ten-week long deployment study was conducted, with each of the three support groups (YA, BP, and SP). At the beginning of the study, all members of each group were invited to an in-person meeting, where they had the opportunity to meet one another and the researcher. After obtaining consent, each participant was given a demonstration of Besupp and provided with a set of instructions and a username and password.

Following the initial introduction to the site, each participant completed individual semi-structured interviews at the beginning, middle, and end of the 10 weeks. This resulted in a total of 56 individual interviews with the 19 participants that lasted between 30 and 60 minutes each (approximately 42 hours of interviews in total). Participants were asked to use the site in as realistic a manner as possible, and were compensated $10 per week.

The semi-structured interviews collected responses to the two major functions of the system: remembrance (as supported by the Memory Box) and social support (as supported by the Circle). Using remembrance and social support as guiding constructs, a thematic analysis of the interview transcripts was conducted. In the rest of this paper, I focus on the interview data concerning these two themes, and then report on other emergent results.

RESULTS: REMEMBRANCE

In Besupp, the Memory Box was intended to help individuals reminisce on their own and share mementos with peers. Most participants thought the Memory Box made good use of an existing mental model regarding storage of loss-related mementos.

"I like the term 'Memory Box.' I liked the idea...and the analogy of the physical box with pictures and notes. That totally makes sense." - SP1, final interview

While all participants found the site accessible and appreciated its design elements, there were more profound concerns regarding the inclusion of reminiscence as part of the system concept. While the early design work and literature suggested that having a digital space for bereavement-related assets and activities would be valuable, participants' low usage rate and attitudes conveyed a different story.

"I look at it more as a sharing tool. Like what I put in there, stories or something like that, I always share with other people. I don't think I'd just put stuff in there just for me. The only reason I put stuff in there was the way to get it into the shared part... On my own drive, I have a folder of poems I like and stuff like that. A folder of [my son's] stuff. I have that already in Word so I don't know, if I have that on my computer already, why would I put it on here?... I don't know if the site will run forever in reality. I know this will close, but if I were on a site like this I have no guarantee that it'd always be there. The only reason is to share it with other people." - BP6, final interview

As reflected by this quote, the Memory Box was subservient to the functions of social support, rather than a standalone tool for reminiscing. As a result, the Memory Box imposed an extra step when users wanted to directly share assets with other members of the Circle. Even then, including journals and links inside of the Memory Box revealed some confusion and a blurring of the distinction between talking about the loss, and talking about grief.

"A lot of times when we're talking in the groups or even chatting, what is important is the emotions and the grief journey that the bereaved person is on... Memory Box puts that emphasis on the person that you lost, which is important, but... the journal would be about what is going on for you right now. That's not about memories. That's about me, and not about [my partner] at all." - BP1, final interview

In other words, some of the assets participants chose to include in the Memory Box were not actually mementos. Instead, they were resources or artifacts that arose in response to the loss (*e.g.*, a link to a website for widows). Furthermore, participants were concerned about sharing aspects of a deceased loved one's life in a group context:

"I'd do the sharing cautiously because you have this memory and I don't want to just put it out there. [My husband] was still a private individual. Though I am happy to share my grief...I don't want to just throw him out there as exhibit A. These are my relationships, not his." -- SP4, final interview

These quotes illustrate the distinction between the creation and maintenance of current relationships with members of the support group as part of the grieving process, and the private nature of mementos that come from the loss itself. The Memory Box prompted rumination about the loss rather than acting as a mechanism for coping.

"Personally I am ready to start talking about the future... grief and loss are different things. If we're meeting to talk

*about the loss, then that's the past, what they were like then. Grief is **now**. It's what we're doing now and what we will be doing for the rest of our lives." - YA4, final interview, her emphasis*

Because participants wanted to focus on coping and sharing supportive messages, relatively few mementos were uploaded. Seventeen of the 19 participants said that they would include the Memory Box in future versions of the site. SP2 (whose loss occurred 1 year ago) disagreed, and found it too difficult to work with mementos due to the freshness of her loss:

"I find it difficult. To put a memory or photos into the box you have to go through the pictures and all. Some things I don't know if it's too soon, or I'm still in the grieving stage or whatever. I just can't seem to look at pictures right now... I can't even look at them let alone upload them. I chalk it up to being that it's still pretty raw for me... I thought I could do it when I started. I thought it would help me, but can't even do simple things. It's just not good." - SP2, final interview

As shown here, the emphasis on working with digital assets was not always welcome. However, for some, uploading content to the Memory Box was a positive experience. YA2 described that going through her photos and stories gave her an opportunity to *"focus on the good times,"* while BP9 enjoyed the ability to *"do stuff"* and *"create something new."* Indeed, stories and photos were the most frequently created mementos, and were often shared to ground and enrich these types of exchanges.

Stories

As Table 1 shows, only 11 stories were shared in total, and no stories were shared in the YA group. However, all 19 participants wrote a "background story" as part of their user profile. In this context, stories served multiple functions. First, background stories helped participants get to know each other, and to recall the details of others' losses.

"Some of the stories are quite brave. What people have gone through. Yeah, I think you can certainly identify with the losses." - BP3, final interview

Identifying with these losses was a key way that participants achieved a sense of normalcy about what they were experiencing during their grief (a common goal of grief support [5,7]). While no Memory Box stories were shared in the YA group, the moderator offered some explanation regarding her personal experience with them:

"I wish people would have used [stories] more... but at the same time... anything I wanted to make public I put on the chat, so I didn't use the stories...I think there's a place for telling stories and we use those in the face-to-face groups as well. But the deeper connection comes when it opens up to a conversation. That is what facilitates the deeper connection with people." - YA1, final interview

As YA1 points out, the goal of writing stories was to share them with other people. In other words, the stories that were told had audiences. In Besupp, stories in the Memory Box contained thoughts and questions, rather than narratives. For example, one participant in the SP group had a child with a man who died after they had split, and wrote a "story" to ask advice about her circumstances:

"We are quickly approaching [his] 'death day' and I am never sure what to do. How do I mark that day? Is it time to take our 4 year old to the cemetery, or is she still too young? Do I send flowers to his parents or is a phone call a better idea?" - excerpt from a story written by SP5 on Week 2

Posing these kinds of questions in a story then led to a conversation in the Circle Chat, as the group moderator explained:

"It started discussion. When [SP5] shared her story, it was about the anniversary of the day her partner died. So that started a bit of a discussion on what to do in an anniversary." - SP1, final interview

This reveals something about one type of storytelling in bereavement support groups. In the lay sense, storytelling often refers to a narrative with a start, end, plot, characters, and so on. In this system, the stories were also used as ways to convey current or ongoing thoughts or experiences, with a goal of receiving feedback from the Circle -- something resembling a letter to an "advice column" more so than a "story." Being able to link to a story directly from the Circle Chat appeared to help with this as well:

"I think it makes sense if it's the kind of story where you want other people to comment on it, or you want to start discussion... a link you wanna say `Hey this is interesting because...' and comment on it in some way." - SP1, final interview

Summarily, the background stories opened up opportunities for participants to introduce themselves and relate to one another. However, the storytelling that occurred is better characterized as unfolding in conversation rather than as a form of closed-ended narrative. While blogs and forums are not necessarily designed with grieving people in mind, their capacity for open-ended textual expression (e.g., a blog or forum post) is supported by participant feedback.

Photos

Photos were the most commonly used type of digital memento in Besupp. Overall, participants shared 25 photos out of the 33 that were uploaded to the Memory Box (Table 1). Like stories, photos were used as a form of visual storytelling and as a way to share with the group.

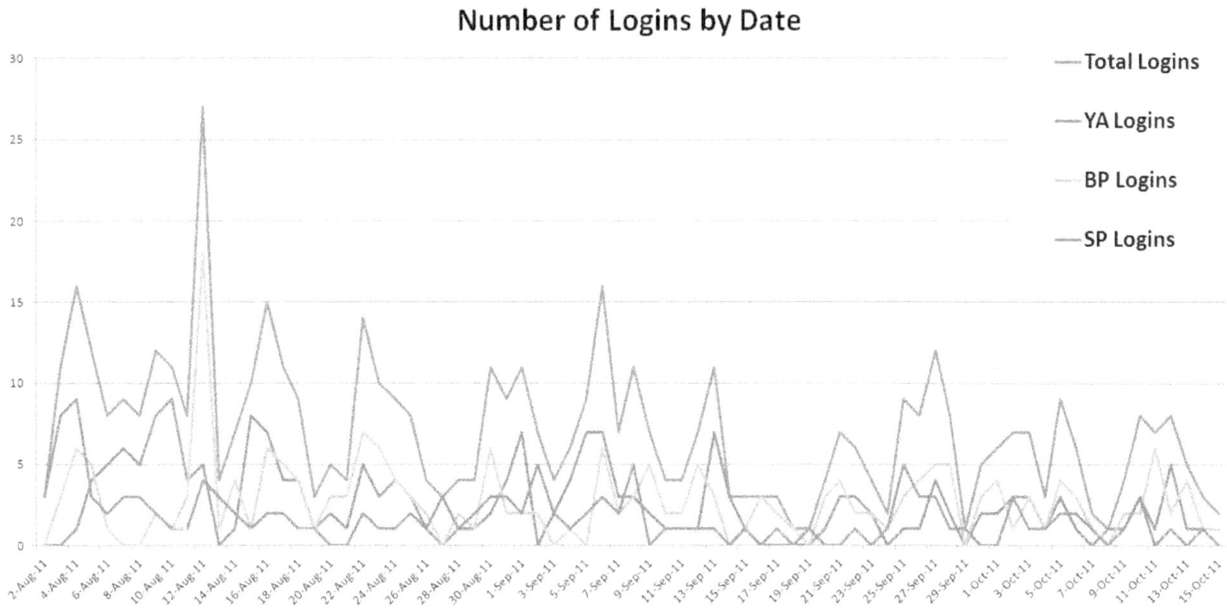

Figure 2. Number of logins per day over the 10 weeks of the study.

"Yeah I mean the first thought was to put no picture. I liked the anonymity of it all. I felt quite guilty that I didn't have a photo of my mom or stepmom to share, so I thought that I should put ***something****. The second thought was to put a picture of myself, but I felt silly doing that since the site is about more than just me... it didn't share enough of my story." - YA1, interim interview (her emphasis)*

One of the main ways that this story was told was by uploading photos showing the user with the deceased person, foregrounding the nature of their relationship. In the Circle, 5 participants selected photos that showed themselves with their loved one, 4 chose photos of their loved one only, and 2 chose photos only showing themselves. In total, 9 of the 11 profile photos showed the deceased loved one. By saying that the site is about *"more than just me,"* YA1 suggests that the personal relationship she had with her mother and step-mother are important to share with others in order to successfully exchange support, and photos were a key way to expose this.

In performing this "visual storytelling," several participants chose photos of only "happy memories." Here, BP1 describes why she chose to upload two photos, one for each of her two sons who died:

"It's a picture I really like because he's got such a devilish grin on his face. Even going through treatment [Son1] was such a happy child... I'm not especially fond of that one either but because [Son2] looks sad, his eyes are so sad, he looks a little hopeful." - BP1, interim interview

As noted in previous work concerning photos [14,27], BP1 consciously avoided photos where her loved one was frail, or sickly, and instead used photos to tell a particular kind of happy story. Indeed, photos needed to stand on their own as forms of storytelling. As SP5 put it, looking at others' photos sometimes felt *"one-sided"* because of a lack of context.

Summarily, even though mementos like stories and photos could be shared with the Circle, the results suggest that they should be interwoven more fluidly into a supportive exchange (e.g., uploading a photo to a Facebook wall), rather than standing alone in a separate part of the site. In turn, these exchanges can leverage how well stories and photos provide carefully-selected background information, and set the stage for more in-depth social support.

RESULTS: SOCIAL SUPPORT

Besupp provided a space for expressing emotions that was separate from existing relationships such as friends, family, or Facebook. Participants valued the ability to log on and "vent" to sympathetic others when they felt their needed to:

"It was really late at night and it's not like I can call anybody. I don't want to bug anyone but I just needed to vent. So this was a way to just put it down somewhere. It felt like somebody was listening, could hear my frustrations because I wasn't going to bug anyone else with this." - SP4, interim interview

While Besupp provided a place to express these emotions, the lack of a timely response to these thoughts became problematic. Participants noted that the amount of activity on the site was less than they had expected and lower than a face-to-face group. Figure 2 demonstrates a pattern of use where a large number of logins occurred roughly once per week, followed by a period of relative inactivity.

Participants attributed this low rate of exchange to a range of factors. This included busy lifestyles, travel, and technical difficulties. Participants also thought that the group was not big enough to keep discussion flowing (even though these numbers were on par with numbers in face-to-face groups). The following exchange occurred in the BP Circle Chat during Week 7:

BP1 (moderator) (Tue 9:31am)*: I've also been thinking about this website and how different it is from the groups. I think if we could try and check in once a day, it would help. Otherwise when someone makes a post, it is kind of left hanging, particularly if it directed at someone specific, and that person doesn't check in for awhile. What does everyone think?*

BP9 (Tue 12:51pm)*: Maybe we could meet once a week with a selected topic like the group did.*

This led to the BP group using Besupp to schedule a chat session where three of the members logged into Besupp at a pre-determined time. This real-time chat explains the relatively large number of messages sent by the BP group (180) in comparison to the YA (62) and SP (39) groups. In the follow-up interviews, participants reflected upon the real-time chat favourably:

"The one day that we did make a date to go online and talk there were only 3 of us, but we did do the chatting for about an hour. That was really good. It was kind of like being in a group." - BP2, final interview

Participants suggested a range of alterations to the system that might support more conversation: meetings might be more scheduled, or more participants might be involved in the group. Others thought that the chat system might support availability notifications and instant messaging.

In addition, participants wanted moderators to take more prominent roles in stimulating and directing conversation. Generally, the presence of a moderator in the Circle was seen as critical by both non-moderators and moderators alike. Moderators were primarily valued as safeguards against inappropriate or harmful behavior, but were most valued by participants when they took a direct role in structuring the discussion. Participants frequently remarked that the moderators should choose a conversation topic and ensure that people contributed to the discussion.

"A lot to do with interaction from an admin. Someone to keep the conversation going. In this type of environment either creating a type of structure that everything follows, the way BFO does with Week 1 is Topic A, Week 2 is Topic B. And a topic list of 15 things or something for your admin. Then, every time the conversation died down then you can introduce something new to keep things going.." - YA3, final interview

The Circle Announcements were intended to help moderators create discussion topics. While the moderators were the three most active individuals on Besupp, there remained an inability to create and maintain a discussion.

Self-Editing

Like many face-to-face support groups, sharing stories and emotions was a large part of the experience on Besupp. Choosing what to tell and share became a deliberated process. In interviews, participants frequently reported revising what they were about to say before sending it to the chat room.

"In the face-to-face groups they were very careful to keep things moving... With the chat room people can dwell on whatever they choose to...I think it gives you a chance to work things through in more detail maybe than in face-to-face...You respond to your own stuff too in addition to other people." - BP9, interim interview

In an online support group, the bereaved can carefully craft the image that they wish to convey to others. Unlike a face-to-face group where physical behaviors and expression can belie raw grief, a computer-mediated communication channel can hide, disguise, or alter these emotions by offering "hyperpersonal" methods of communication [36]. At the same time, using all of the available communication methods may result in "burn-out." Whether this ability to more carefully control the way that one responds to prompts in the support group is beneficial for particular types of grievers or purposes remains an open question.

Helping Behaviors

While many of the activities concerning mementos were not heavily used, the Circle Chat offered a form of "something to do" that was more successful. Participants used the Circle Chat to offer support and give back, with little desire to "receive" it. For example, BP5 lost her son 16 years ago, and has since become an active member of BFO, volunteering to conduct one-on-ones. She saw Besupp as a place to share the wisdom of her experience:

"I always thought the site would be good to share. Because talking and sharing helps you with your grieving process and helps others with the grieving process. It shows them they are not alone. That their feelings are similar. Many people think that their loss is so unique... I thought sharing would make the people understand that others have gone through this and they are better off after a certain period of time." - BP5, final interview

The moderator of the BP group similarly described her motivation for volunteering as a moderator both in Besupp and in BFO groups:

"Comes out of a feeling of being able to help others. I have been through so many of these things that I can show them that you can carry on, it's possible. With my experience, and it makes my experience meaningful." - BP1, final interview

This form of group activity allows the bereaved to draw on their experiences within a safe environment. Designers developing social support systems might think about how to support this type of use case more fully.

EMERGENT RESULTS

In this section, I remark on results that emerged during interviews that refer to more general aspects of the system and/or study.

The Effort of Addressing Grief Online

The relatively low usage rate led to interesting conversations with participants about its efficacy, and how their grief - and need for support - fluctuated. Despite a perceived need for support, a barrier identified by participants was the large amount of emotional effort required to use Besupp. For some participants, this left them feeling drained and brought back negative emotions:

"It was very hard for me emotionally and way harder than I thought it would be after hearing everyone's story. I felt like... pretty upset about it truthfully. It was hard for me to come back...hearing all the sad stories again was really hard for me to take because I'm in a different place now... people using it seem to be getting a lot out of it but for me I'm just a bit heartbroken." - YA4, interim interview

In a way, this highlights the benefits of a weekly 2-hour support group: it limits the time that participants are exposed to thoughts and emotions of grief. The constant availability of Besupp shifted the onus of managing exposure onto the user, making it more difficult to disengage from these emotions.

Additionally, while the creation of a separate space for bereavement activities was initially met with enthusiasm, participants remarked on how the website made social support seem more formal than it is in face-to-face groups. For example, YA4 felt she could not share certain items she associated with her brother because they were not somber enough for a bereavement website:

"There are some songs he liked from the 90s, like `Mambo Number Five' by Lou Bega. I thought about uploading that from YouTube, but I didn't know how seriously to take it. That's the problem with grief... I laugh a lot when I talk to his friends and we talk about happy memories. It's not sad but there's something about when you call it `grief support online' that you should be doing your `grief work.' And I'm not sure if Lou Bega has anything to do with grief work." - YA4, final interview

YA4's hesitation to include a "fun" link in Besupp could be a result of participation in a study, but at the same time, it shows that the inability to monitor the reactions of others in real time makes it difficult to interpret the appropriateness of particular statements in a grief context. While the dearth of social cues in online systems is well-established, in this context it results in a flattening of the complicated emotions that the bereaved may feel. Systems for the bereaved must acknowledge that grief, while painful, is not the sole emotion to be felt or shared.

ID	Years since Loss	Number of Logins
BP7	1	28
SP2	1	12
YA4	2	23
YA8	3	48
SP4	3	7
BP6	4	57
YA7	4	36
BP9	4	35
SP5	4	32
YA3	4	22
YA6	5	4
BP2	6	37
YA1	7	45
SP6	7	22
SP1	11	57
YA2	11	16
BP1	12	39
BP5	16	5
BP3	20	6

Table 2. Number of logins per participant and number of years since loss. (BP1, SP1, and YA1 are moderators.)

Timing of the Study

Most participants experienced their losses 2 or more years ago (Table 2). For this group of participants, Besupp was seen as a potentially useful tool, but not for them at the current stage of their grief journey. Rather, they believed it would be much more helpful closer to the time of the loss.

"I like the idea to have it as an option again, given that I'm 4 years into grieving my mom. I don't know that it would be as necessary for me, but... I'm thinking 4 years back I was searching desperately in the middle of the night and everyone was asleep. And I was online trying to find something... so I think it's a necessary tool to have, but more for people who are freshly grieving. But again there are times where I'm like `Who do I talk to?' and it'd be nice to know that it's there, but I don't know that I'd use it." - YA2, final interview

Many participants believed that they would have garnered greater benefit from Besupp if they had participated within 6 months to 2 years following the loss. Of the two participants who were within a year of their losses, one preferred face-to-face groups and the other had difficulty finding any group at all from which she could derive value. The correlation coefficient between the number of logins and the number of years since loss was -0.45 (with moderators excluded), indicating there was a moderate negative relationship (Table 2). This medium correlation suggests that users with fresher losses logged in more frequently, and supports the idea that online support groups would be best applied within the first year after the loss.

IMPLICATIONS AND CONCLUSIONS

Based on the results presented above, I conclude with a series of implications for the design of systems for social support, remembrance, and bereavement more generally.

The value of digital mementos changes over time. In Besupp, participants valued photos and stories for their ability to share common experiences and build trust. Following this initial "getting to know you" period, digital mementos became less useful resources in a support setting. Conversation in the Circle Chat replaced photos and written stories. This deployment study raises issues about audience, timing, and instrumental usage of mementos for HCI and CSCW researchers.

This shift towards conversation highlights the need for designers to more carefully *consider distinctions between loss and grief.* As participants pointed out, mementos helped to convey the loss, but can dredge up painful emotions. This runs counter to the purpose of social support – to find ways to cope with grief. To paraphrase YA4, loss was **then**, but grief is **now**. Systems for the bereaved (such as Besupp or online memorials) may inadvertently intermingle the two. Future systems should carefully consider how these two processes of remembrance and coping impact one another.

At the same time, *people who have learned to cope can find value in offering support to those with fresher losses.* For those further along in their grief, Besupp offered an opportunity to proffer compassion and experience to a group of receptive others. This raises a question of audience. When we design for the bereaved, we need not simply design for those who are currently in need, but also for those who have the compassion and desire to share their time and experience.

The study also showed that *systems should be designed for intermittent use.* While participants valued Besupp as a place to meet their support needs, engaging with the collective grief of the Circle was emotionally draining. Besupp was a place to unload thoughts and feelings, log out, recharge for a few days, and then revisit later. Indeed, what participants perceived as a low usage rate seemed to actually be a reflection of this cycle. As designers, we might consider what this means for the success of the systems we build. A low rate of adoption or usage is not necessarily a sign of poor design; on the contrary, it may simply be part of working within an ongoing coping process and journey towards self-support. Besupp is an example of an application where value stems not from frequent use, but from the comfort of knowing it is available if needed. This is similar to other social networking sites, such as MySpace or Facebook [11,30].

In contest with this point, designers might *consider ways to mitigate burnout.* Because Besupp was always available, the onus for managing exposure to the Circle's grief was placed on the participant. Designers might consider systems that are available only for brief amounts of time (e.g., once a week) or only in specific circumstances (e.g., while at home). Building these restraints into a system can limit emotional drain, and potentially ameliorate additional burnout from low rates of participation and conversation.

Finally, it is important to bear in mind that *technology operates among a rich set of supports.* At the outset, some participants saw Besupp as a potential replacement for a face-to-face support group, and were dismayed when the depth of perceived connection was less than in a face-to-face setting. The results support the idea that technology is not a way to replace face-to-face support groups. Rather, it is a complementary, optional component of a richer, more comprehensive set of practices and places for experiencing grief. Designers should consider how their system fits into an ecology of grief supports, including family, friends, peers, clergy, and counselors.

Overall, the design and deployment study presented in this paper contributes to a fuller understanding of the value, limits, and opportunities that technology presents in the context of bereavement. By shedding light on these topics, the CSCW community may be better able to address the needs of the bereaved, and those seeking social support in an online community more widely.

ACKNOWLEDGEMENTS

Thanks to the study participants, Bereaved Families of Ontario – Toronto, the GRAND NCE, Ronald Baecker, Garry Ing, Carrie Demmans Epp, and Karyn Moffatt.

REFERENCES

1. Barrera, M. and Ainlay, S.L. The structure of social support: A Conceptual and empirical analysis. *J. Comm Psych 11*, (1983), 133–143.
2. Bender, J.L., Jimenez-Marroquin, M.-C., and Jadad, A.R. Seeking support on Facebook: a content analysis of breast cancer groups. *J. Med Internet Res 13*, 1 (2011), e16.
3. Bosticco, C. and Thompson, T.L. An examination of the role of narratives and storytelling in bereavement. In L.M. Harter, P.M. Japp and C.S. Beck, eds., *Narratives, Health, and Healing: Communication Theory, Research, and Practice*. Routledge, 2005, 391–412.
4. Brubaker, J.R. and Hayes, G.R. "We will never forget you [online]": an empirical investigation of post-

mortem MySpace comments. *Proc. CSCW 2011*, ACM (2011), 123–132.
5. Buckle, J.L. and Fleming, S. *Parenting after the Death of a Child: A Practitioner's Guide*. Routledge, 2010.
6. Consolvo, S., Everitt, K., Smith, I., and Landay, J.A. Design requirements for technologies that encourage physical activity. *Proc. CHI 2006*, ACM (2006), 457–466.
7. Dominick, S.A., Irvine, B.A., Beauchamp, N., et al. An internet tool to normalize grief. *Omega 60*, 1 (2009), 71–87.
8. Forte, A., Hill, M., Pazder, R., and Feudtner, C. Bereavement care interventions: a systematic review. *BMC Palliative Care 3*, 1 (2004), 3.
9. Frohlich, D., Kuchinsky, A., Pering, C., Don, A., and Ariss, S. Requirements for photoware. *Proc. CSCW 2002*, ACM (2002), 166–175.
10. Getty, E., Cobb, J., Gabeler, M., Nelson, C., Weng, E., and Hancock, J. I said your name in an empty room: grieving and continuing bonds on Facebook. *Proc. CHI 2011*, ACM (2011), 997–1000.
11. Graves, K.E. Social Networking Sites and Grief: An Exploratory Investigation of Potential Benefits. 2009. https://dspace.iup.edu/handle/2069/215.
12. Hallam, E. and Hockey, J. *Death, Memory and Material Culture*. Berg Publishers, 2001.
13. Kirk, D., Sellen, A., Rother, C., and Wood, K. Understanding photowork. *Proc. CHI 2006*, ACM Press (2006), 761–770.
14. Kirk, D.S. and Sellen, A. On human remains: Values and practice in the home archiving of cherished objects. *ACM Trans. Comput.-Hum. Interact. 17*, 3 (2010), 1–43.
15. Klass, D., Silverman, P., and Nickman, S. *Continuing Bonds: New Understandings Of Grief*. Taylor & Francis, 1996.
16. Lehman, D.R., Ellard, J.H., and Wortman, C.B. Social support for the bereaved: Recipients' and providers' perspectives on what is helpful. *J Consult Clin Psych 54*, 4 (1986), 438–446.
17. Leonardi, C., Mennecozzi, C., Not, E., et al. Knocking on elders' door: investigating the functional and emotional geography of their domestic space. *Proc. CHI 2009*, ACM (2009), 1703–1712.
18. Levy, L.H., Derby, J.F., and Martinkowski, K.S. Effects of membership in bereavement support groups on adaptation to conjugal bereavement. *Am J Comm Psych 21*, (1993), 361–381.
19. Levy, L.H. and Derby, J.F. Bereavement support groups: Who joins; who does not; and why. *Am J Comm Psych 20*, 5 (1992), 649–662.
20. Lewin, K. Group decision and social change. In E. Maccoby, T. Newcomb and E. Hartley, eds., *Readings in Social Psychology*. Holt, Rinehart, and Winston, 1958, 197–211.
21. Lindley, S. Passing on memories in later life. *Proc. CHI 2011 Workshop on Bridging Practices, Theories, and Technologies to Support Reminiscence*, (2011).
22. Liu, L.S., Hirano, S.H., Tentori, M., et al. Improving communication and social support for caregivers of high-risk infants through mobile technologies. *Proc. CSCW 2011*, ACM (2011), 475–484.
23. Massimi, M. and Baecker, R.M. A death in the family: opportunities for designing technologies for the bereaved. *Proc. CHI 2010*, ACM (2010), 1821–1830.
24. Massimi, M. and Baecker, R.M. Dealing with death in design: developing systems for the bereaved. *Proc. CHI 2011*, ACM (2011), 1001–1010.
25. Massimi, M. and Charise, A. Dying, death, and mortality: towards thanatosensitivity in HCI. *Proc. CHI 2009 Extended Abstracts*, ACM (2009), 2459–2468.
26. Odom, W., Harper, R., Sellen, A., Kirk, D., and Banks, R. Passing on & putting to rest: understanding bereavement in the context of interactive technologies. *Proc. CHI 2010*, ACM (2010), 1831–1840.
27. Odom, W., Pierce, J., Stolterman, E., and Blevis, E. Understanding why we preserve some things and discard others in the context of interaction design. *Proc. CHI 2009*, ACM (2009), 1053–1062.
28. Petrelli, D. and Whittaker, S. Family memories in the home: contrasting physical and digital mementos. *Personal Ubiquitous Comput. 14*, 2 (2010), 153–169.
29. Picton, C., Cooper, B., Close, D., and Tobin, J. Bereavement support groups: Timing of participation and reasons for joining. *Omega: Journal of Death and Dying 43*, 3 (2001), 247–258.
30. Roberts, P. '2 people like this': Mourning according to format. *Bereavement Care 31*, 2 (2012), 55–61.
31. Skeels, M.M., Unruh, K.T., Powell, C., and Pratt, W. Catalyzing social support for breast cancer patients. *Proc. CHI 2010*, ACM (2010), 173–182.
32. Sofka, C., Cupit, I.N., and Gilbert, K.R. *Dying, Death, and Grief in an Online Universe: For Counselors and Educators*. Springer Publishing Company, 2012.
33. Sofka, C. Adolescents, technology, and the internet: Coping with loss in the digital world. In D. Balk and C. Corr, eds., *Adolescent Encounters with Death, Bereavement, and Coping*. Springer, New York, 2009, 155–174.
34. Uriu, D. and Okude, N. ThanatoFenestra: photographic family altar supporting a ritual to pray for the deceased. *Proc. DIS 2010*, ACM (2010), 422–425.
35. Volkan, V.D. The Linking Objects of Pathological Mourners. *Arch Gen Psychiatry 27*, 2 (1972), 215–221.
36. Walther, J.B. Computer-Mediated Communication Impersonal, Interpersonal, and Hyperpersonal Interaction. *Communication Research 23*, 1 (1996), 3–43.

Collaborative Search Revisited

Meredith Ringel Morris
Microsoft Research
Redmond, WA, USA
merrie@microsoft.com

ABSTRACT

Despite recent innovations in technologies supporting collaborative web search [11, 13, 25, 34, 35, 37], the features of the primary tools for digital information seeking (web browsers and search engines) continue to reflect a presumption that search is a single-user activity. In this paper, we present the findings of a survey of 167 diverse users' collaborative web search practices, including the prevalence and frequency of such activities, the information needs motivating collaboration, the methods and tools employed in such tasks, and users' satisfaction with the status quo. We find an increased prevalence and frequency of collaborative search, particularly by younger users, and an appropriation of "old" technologies like e-mail as well as "new" technologies like smartphones and social networking sites, rather than the use of dedicated collaborative search tools. We reflect on how and why collaborative search practices have changed in the six years since the first survey detailing this phenomenon was conducted [22], and synthesize our findings to offer suggestions for the design of future collaborative search technologies.

Author Keywords

Web search, collaborative search, social search, CSCW.

ACM Classification Keywords

H.5.m. Information interfaces and presentation (e.g., HCI): Miscellaneous.

INTRODUCTION

Information-seeking technologies and collaboration technologies are the two most popular online tools; a 2011 Pew Research survey [32] found that 92% of online American adults use search engines, and a similar proportion use email. However, this compartmentalization of practices as either search or collaboration is tenuous. Although web search is often considered a *de facto* solo activity, and nearly all mainstream search technologies are designed for single-user scenarios, a growing body of research suggests that active collaboration on search tasks among users with shared information needs is relatively commonplace [13, 22, 25].

Our 2006[1] survey of 204 Microsoft employees [22] provided data regarding the prevalence of collaborative web search, the tasks motivating such practices, and the methods used to enable such collaborations. In the six years since we conducted that survey, the technology landscape has undergone significant changes, particularly the rise of social networking sites (only 16% of Americans had social networking profiles in 2006, compared with 66% in 2012 [4]) and the growing ubiquity of smartphones (46% of American adults owned smartphones as of February 2012 [36]) and other powerful portable technologies (e.g., tablet computers). The intervening six years have also seen a flurry of research and commercial technologies for collaborative search support, though none have had mainstream success.

In light of this changed landscape, we reassess status quo collaborative search practices through a survey of 167 American adults. Our results provide insight into the evolution of collaborative and social search practices; for instance, we find an increase in the prevalence and frequency of collaborative web search, as well as appropriation of new technologies like social networking sites and smartphones to support this phenomenon. We also find that users continue to piece together general purpose technologies to facilitate collaborative information seeking, rather than taking advantage of systems designed specifically for such experiences. In light of these findings, we reflect on barriers to adoption of collaborative information seeking tools, and identify key research directions moving forward.

RELATED WORK

The term *social search* is used to refer to a broad spectrum of information seeking behaviors, ranging from behaviors which are *implicitly* social (e.g., search over socially-generated data sets) to those that are *explicitly* social (e.g., interacting with other people during various stages of the search process) [13]. Evans and Chi [7] described the types

CSCW '13, February 23–27, 2013, San Antonio, Texas, USA.

[1] Though published in 2008, the survey data was collected in November 2006. We refer to it (and other surveys discussed) by the year of data-gathering rather than the year of publication, when known, since the former more accurately represents the socio-technical context of the findings given the rapid evolution of technologies and practices.

of social engagements possible at different stages of the Web search process.

Collaborative search [11, 13, 25, 34] is a subset of social search in which participants work together to satisfy an information need. The collaborative nature of search tasks in pre-web scenarios (e.g., in libraries and paper-driven offices) has a long history of scholarship (e.g., [9, 38]). Academic investigation of the challenges and practices associated with collaborative *web* search is a more recent phenomenon, usually associated with the 2007 introduction of the SearchTogether [24] system, whose design was informed by a survey of collaborative web search practices conducted in 2006 (but not published until 2008) [22]. Collaborative search has many benefits, including enabling participants to achieve synergic effects such as greater recall [31, 35], offering the potential to improve search skills through exposure to others' behavior [20, 21], and providing an opportunity to strengthen social connections [27, 28]. Note that the investigation of collaborative web search differs from prior work on collaborative web browsers (e.g., [12]) in that its focus is not on general-purpose web browsing, but specifically on the use of the web for information-seeking tasks.

In [22], we reported the results of a November 2006 survey of 204 Microsoft employees' collaborative web search practices. It is unclear how representative this demographic's behavior was, as respondents differed in many ways from the general population, primarily on the basis of their technical expertise, as well as along other demographic dimensions that were also non-typical (e.g., 80.4% of respondents were male). However, [22] presents the most complete picture available of the prevalence and characteristics of the collaborative search phenomenon; it found that, despite the lack of any tools designed to explicitly support collaborative web search, 53.4% of those surveyed had engaged in such activities by using the *bottom-up* [41] approach of appropriating existing technologies (e.g., email, instant messaging, etc.) to supplement the web browser. A smaller, diary-based study of 20 Microsoft employees [2] conducted in 2007[2] provided additional insights into the specific scenario of co-located collaborative search. More recently, several studies have characterized the *asymmetric* collaborative search scenario (in which participants have different roles and/or motivations [25]) of using social networking sites to engage contacts in various stages of an information-seeking task [6, 17, 27, 29].

In the intervening six years since our survey [22], a number of research prototypes supporting collaborative search have been introduced. Some innovations have proposed algorithmic techniques to enhance the collaborative search experience, including role-specific weightings of input [31], group personalization of results [26], expertise-matching of potential collaborators [16], and agents that use context from social network Q&A exchanges to suggest relevant links [15]. Others have proposed user interface enhancements, such as enhancing collaborators' awareness of each other's search process [20, 24], enabling distribution of control in co-located settings [1], supporting collaborative search among users with asymmetric access to devices [42], and supporting collaborative search on emerging technologies such as large touch surfaces [23].

Some commercial technologies have also included features supportive of specific subsets of collaborative search activities. Examples include Aardvark (a service to match users with experts to support their information-seeking; 2007), Flock (a web browser that incorporated social networking as a first-class feature in its design; 2008), HeyStaks (which uses feedback from communities of users with common interests to re-rank search results; 2008), Pinterest (a shared bulletin board for collections of web imagery; 2010), SearchTeam (a tool whose features are highly reminiscent of SearchTogether [24], 2011), and So.cl (a social network based around sharing collections of search results [8]; 2011). None of these commercial tools has achieved mainstream adoption – some, like Aardvark and Flock, have already become defunct; others, like Pinterest and So.cl, are still in limited, invitation-only beta stages.

This paper adds to this body of work on collaborative web search by presenting survey results that give an updated and more complete view of the current state of practice. Our survey reports on the collaborative search practices of a more representative sample of the general public (as opposed to highly technical knowledge workers, e.g., [22]), and reflects recent changes in the technological landscape (such as the growing prevalence of social networking [4] and smartphone use [36]).

SURVEY

We conducted an online survey over a one week period in March 2012 to assess current practices regarding collaborative information seeking. The survey consisted of both open-ended and multiple-choice questions. Respondents were asked whether they had ever collaborated with other people to search the Web; if they answered affirmatively, they were asked to describe their most recent collaborative search experience and to answer a series of questions about that specific search incident (a critical-incident approach [7, 10]). Additional survey questions addressed demographics and use of specific search and collaboration technologies.

The survey was advertised as a questionnaire on "Information Seeking Practices" via the Survey Monkey Audience recruiting service[3] to 1,025 adult American

[2] Data gathered in 2007; published in 2009.

[3] http://www.surveymonkey.com/mp/audience/

participants; 167 completed the entire survey, yielding a 16% response rate.

RESULTS

We first characterize the demographic details of our 167 respondents. We then report our findings regarding the prevalence of collaborative search and the nature of such searches. We also report findings on the use of specific technologies for collaborative information seeking, including smartphones, social networks, and Q&A tools.

Note that we use non-parametric statistical tests when analyzing Likert responses, due to the subjective and potentially non-linear interpretations of the "spacing" between adjacent items on such scales.

Demographics

Our 167 survey respondents were all residents of the United States; 40 of the 50 states were covered by our sample. 56% of respondents were female. 38% of respondents were aged 18 – 29; 24% were aged 30 – 44; 27% were aged 45 – 60; and 11% were older than 60 years. 5% had a high school diploma or less, 57% had completed some college, 29% had a college degree, and 9% had a graduate degree.

Occupations were varied, with students making up the largest single group at 25% of respondents. An additional 8% of the group was comprised of retirees. The remaining 67% of respondents had diverse vocations including sales person, customer service representative, teacher, nurse, school counselor, homemaker, mortgage broker, physician, stock analyst, insurance adjuster, cosmetologist, accountant, software engineer, dentist, paralegal, copy editor, and heavy equipment operator.

Respondents used search engines frequently; most (79.9%) reported using a major search engine (Ask, Bing, Google, or Yahoo!) several times per day, and nearly all (94.1%) reported doing so at least once per day.

Collaborative Search

All respondents were asked "Have you ever collaborated with other people to search the Web?" If they answered negatively, they skipped ahead to the questions about specific technologies (see the "Beyond 'Traditional' Search Engines" section) and demographics. However, the 109 respondents (65.3%) who answered affirmatively were asked several follow-up questions about their experiences with collaborative search.

Finding that 65.3% of respondents had engaged in collaborative search indicates an increased prevalence of collaborative search behavior – our 2006 survey [22] found the prevalence of collaborative search to be only 53.4% (and that was with a more "tech-savvy" audience, Microsoft employees, whom one would assume might be more likely to appropriate technologies in novel ways than the more diverse audience of the current survey). The prevalence of collaboration we found differs significantly from the

	2006	2012
Daily	0.9%	11.0%
Weekly	25.7%	38.5%
Monthly	48.6%	15.6%
Less Often	24.8%	34.8%

Table 1. Percent of respondents reporting collaboratively searching at various frequencies. 2006 numbers are taken from Table 2 of [22].

hypothesized proportions based on the 2006 survey, $\chi^2(1, N = 167) = 9.62, p = .002$).

Age was significantly negatively correlated with the likelihood of engaging in collaborative search (e.g., younger respondents were more likely to engage in this behavior), $r = -.26, p = .001$.

Note that percentages given in the remainder of this section ("Collaborative Search") and its sub-sections are out of the 109 people who indicated that they had searched collaboratively rather than out of the full 167 survey respondents.

11% of respondents who had searched collaboratively reported doing so on a daily basis, and an additional 38.5% report searching collaboratively at least once per week. This is a marked increase over the self-reported frequency of collaborative searching in 2006 [22], as illustrated in Table 1, $\chi^2(3, N = 108) = 155.26, p < .001$).

After indicating whether they had ever searched the Web collaboratively and how often they did so, participants who had searched collaboratively were asked to engage in a recent critical-incident self-report [7, 10]. They were asked in a free-text question to "think about the most recent time you collaborated with others to search the web," and then to "describe the nature of the information need that prompted this incident." They were then asked several follow-up questions about that specific incident. The following four sub-sections ("Topics," "Group Configurations," "Methods and Tools," and "Satisfaction") are based on the follow-up questions about the respondents' most recent collaborative search incident.

Topics

In addition to describing the information need prompting their most recent collaborative search in a free-response question, we also asked respondents to classify the nature of the information need they investigated collaboratively by selecting one or more topics from a list. The list of topic choices was created by combining the topics reported as prompting collaborative searches in [22] and the list of topics reported as likely and unlikely to prompt requests for search help from members of one's social network in [27].

Topic	# of Respondents	Example Task Description
professional	26	"we split up research for software development, searching individually for coding issues, gui design, and what would be appealing to our audience"
health/medicine	21	"we needed to find information about iron deficiency and hypokalemia"
news/current events	19	"looking for reference footage and images for a school project"
technology	18	"looking for printer parts for our business operation"
travel	16	"we were planning a trip to Alaska and all the details that go into it for a group of 10 of us"
shopping	15	"looking for a used car"
entertainment	14	"searching for music on YouTube and lyrics"
home/family	11	"genealogy"
finance	11	"we were researching different kinds of e-portfolios"
restaurants	10	"find local restaurants"
social events	10	"planning a wedding"

Table 2. The most common topics motivating respondents' recent collaborative Web searches.

Table 2 shows the most popular topics (those which 10 or more respondents said described their most recent collaboratively-investigated information need), and gives examples from respondents' free-form descriptions of their most recent search incident.

Group Configurations

Small-group collaboration was more common than larger groups. Pairs were the most common configuration (31.2%). Triads were also fairly common (22.9%), as were quartets (23.9%). Groups larger than four members were infrequent – 9.2% reported working in groups of five, 4.6% in groups of six, and 8.3% in groups having seven or more members.

Our 2006 survey [22] also found that smaller group sizes were more common than larger ones, though that survey found much smaller group sizes, reporting that 80.7% collaborated in pairs and 19.3% in groups of three or four, with no larger groups at all. Comparing our frequencies of pairs, groups of three or four, and larger groups to this earlier finding shows a significant change in group sizes, $\chi^2(2, N = 109) = 610, p < .001$. Our 2007 diary study of co-located collaborative search [2] also found smaller group sizes than our current study, with 85.7% collaborating in pairs and 9.5% in groups of three or four.

We also asked respondents to characterize their relationship with their collaborators on their search task. 55.0% reported collaborating with colleagues or classmates. Family was the next most common type of collaborator relationship, at 25.7%, followed by close friends (19.3%), and then casual acquaintances (11.0%). Collaboration with strangers or professionals (e.g., librarians) was rare, at 5.5%. Note that these values total to greater than 100%, as some respondents indicated that they worked with a group comprised of multiple relationship types.

Synchronous collaboration was more common than asynchronous, comprising roughly two-thirds of the incidents (64.2%). Remote collaboration was more common than co-located, characterizing 61.5% of the described searches. This is in contrast to the 2006 survey [22], which found a slight prevalence of co-located search configurations, although their question was phrased differently (asking respondents which of the following behaviors they had ever engaged in, versus asking them to describe a single recent critical incident as we do here), making direct comparisons difficult.

Methods and Tools

Participants used a checklist to indicate what tools they employed in their most recent collaborative search incident (they could check as many items as applied). The use of search engines was common (67.9% of respondents used them in their most recent collaborative search task), but other methods of online information-seeking were also employed, such as using a social networking site (19.3%) or Q&A site (6.4%). We explore the use of these latter two technologies in further detail in the "Beyond 'Traditional' Search Engines" section.

Devices: "Traditional" devices like laptops (61.5%) and PCs (39.4%) were the most common devices used in the

	Very Dissatisfied	Dissatisfied	Neutral	Satisfied	Very Satisfied
quality of answer found	2.8%	1.8%	12.8%	55.0%	27.5%
ease of working with others	1.8%	2.8%	16.5%	42.1%	35.8%

Table 3. Respondents' satisfaction with the informational and social aspects of their most recent collaborative search incident.

course of collaborative information seeking. Newer device types were also common, with 30.3% of the searches involving a smartphone and 11% involving a tablet. Technologies that might facilitate public sharing such as TVs and projectors were rarely employed, in only 1.8% and 0.9% of the searches, respectively. Non-digital tools were also an important part of collaborative search processes; for instance, 11% of respondents reported using paper to support their collaborative search task.

Communication: Since mainstream web browsers and search engines don't incorporate communication tools (which are important for facilitating remote collaborative search [24]), respondents often employed out-of-band communication channels. Email was the most common communication tool, involved in 46.8% of the searches. Other communication channels used were talking on the phone (27.5%), text messaging/SMS (30.3%), and instant messaging (12.8%). Videoconferencing was rare; only one participant reported employing it as a communications channel during a collaborative search.

Satisfaction

Responents used a five-point Likert scale to rate their level of satisfaction with both the informational (quality of answer found) and social (ease of working collaboratively) aspects of their most recent collaborative search. Table 3 summarizes those results. 82.5% reported satisfaction with the informational outcome and 77.9% reported satisfaction with the ease of collaboration. Though positive overall, these figures still indicate that there is room for improvement of both the informational and social aspects of the collaborative search experience.

Respondents were also given space to compose a free-form response regarding suggestions for how their collaborative search experience could have been improved. The most common response (7 people) was for facilities to make it easier to share the products of search with group members and increase group awareness of mutual activities (two issues that systems like SearchTogether [24], Coagmento [35], and WeSearch [23] sought to address). For example, one respondent said, "It might have helped if we had some sort of online bulletin board on which to post our findings…" Another noted that he would have liked "an easier way for the rest of the group members to access the information each of us found separately," and one person desired the ability to have "real-time comparisons between mine and my colleagues' information." Redundant work [22] remained problematic, with one respondent noting that "if there was a better way to communicate where one person had already looked it would have prevented overlap of seeking for information," and another observing that it would be helpful to have "a database that tracks collaborators' searches in a private group, so that you can see which papers others have already found."

	Daily	Weekly	Monthly	Less than once per month	Never
% of smartphone owners	36.1%	24.7%	21.6%	10.3%	7.2%
% of co-located searchers	38.9%	26.7%	23.3%	11.1%	N/A

Table 4. The reported frequency of engaging co-located multi-party smartphone searches among all smartphone owners in our sample (97 participants), and among those who reported engaging in this behavior at least occasionally (90 participants).

Beyond "Traditional" Search Engines

Although the questions surrounding respondents' most recent collaborative search incident were asked only to the 109 respondents who indicated that they had engaged in collaborative Web search, all 167 respondents were asked a series of questions about their use of several specific technologies, independent of the critical incident inquiry. In particular, we were interested in investigating the collaborative use of information-seeking technologies other than the traditional "using a search engine in a PC web browser." Our questions focused on three kinds of tools that have experienced significant changes or growth since 2006 – smartphones, social networking sites, and Q&A sites.

Smartphones

Though smartphones (which permit browsing the web and running third-party applications) existed in 2006, the capabilities and adoption of smartphones changed dramatically in 2007 with the introduction of Apple's iPhone, whose Safari browser provided the ability to view and interact with "real" web pages (rather than special mobile versions). By early 2012, 46% of American adults owned a smartphone [36]. Recent work suggests that mobile local searches (i.e., searching for businesses or services near a user's current geo-location) are often undertaken in a social setting, but does not offer detailed insight into multi-phone collaborative search practices [39].

In our survey sample, 58.1% of respondents reported owning a smartphone. Of these 97 smartphone-owning respondents, 48.5% had Android devices, 34.0% had iOS (Apple) devices, and the remainder had devices running the

	Facebook	Twitter	Google+	LinkedIn
have accounts	139 (83.2%)	49 (29.3%)	42 (25.1%)	50 (29.9%)
have ever asked a question	50.0%	33.3%	24.6%	24.6%
ask questions at least once per week	15.4%	9.5%	9.8%	4.6%
lurk (read content but never post)	4.3%	8.8%	12.5%	15.9%

Table 5. The first row reports how many of the 167 respondents had accounts on each social networking site. Additional rows report the percentage of those account-holders engaging in specific behaviors.

Palm, RIM (Blackberry), or Windows operating systems. Smartphone ownership was not significantly correlated with any demographic factors.

Although they may not have previously self-identified as having engaged in collaborative search, nearly all of the smartphone owners (92.8%) reported using their phones to engage in co-located collaborative searches in which several people simultaneously used their smartphones to look up information (Table 4). This behavior was surprisingly frequent – of the 90 respondents who reported engaging in this behavior, 38.9% reported doing so at least once per day, and 65.6% at least a few times per week. Younger respondents engaged in co-located multi-phone searches more frequently than older respondents ($r = -.26$, $p = .01$). These initial findings suggest that studying co-located collaborative smartphone search may be a rich area for further investigation to answer questions beyond the scope of our current survey, such as exploring what role specialized "apps" might play in such scenarios.

Social Networking Sites

Social networking sites were used by only 16% of Americans in 2006 (the year in which Facebook opened enrollment to the general public rather than merely to students at selected universities); by 2012, 66% had an account [4]. Social networking sites have taken on an increasingly prominent role in asymmetric collaborative information seeking [25], through mechanisms such as posting search results directly to social network feeds (e.g., Bing and Ping [5] or So.cl [8]), using socially embedded search engines (e.g., SearchBuddies [15]), or asking questions via status messages [6, 17, 27, 29]. For instance, a 2009[4] survey of Microsoft employees [27] found that 50.6% had posted questions to Facebook or Twitter.

[4] Survey conducted in 2009; published in 2010.

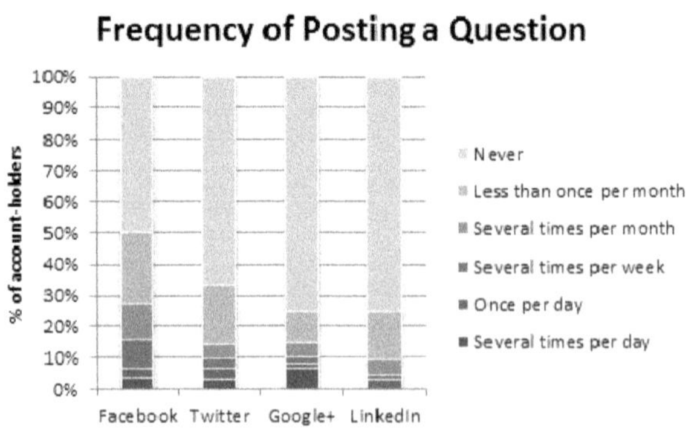

Figure 1. Self-reported frequency of posting a question as a status update, a form of asymmetric collaborative search, by account-holders on each social network.

87.4% of our survey respondents reported having social networking accounts, with Facebook being by far the most popular, distantly followed by Twitter, LinkedIn, and Google+ (Table 5). Other networks like MySpace, Orkut, Tumblr, and Yammer had negligible representation. Younger respondents were more likely to have social networking accounts than older ones ($r = -.27$, $p < .001$).

Asking questions on these social networking sites was common. 50.0% of those with Facebook accounts reported having used that network to ask a question, as did 33.3% of those with Twitter accounts, and 24.6% of those with LinkedIn and Google+ accounts. Our finding that half of Facebook users have engaged in status-message question asking is similar to the findings of a survey we conducted in 2009 [27], despite the fact that the 2009 survey audience was comprised of Microsoft employees while our current survey draws from a more diverse demographic. However, it conflicts with the findings of a survey by Lampe *et al.* conducted in 2011[5] [17] that found that most Facebook users in their sample did not view Facebook as an appropriate venue for information-seeking (i.e., via status message Q&A). The Lampe survey's audience consisted of employees at a U.S. university, who were less diverse (e.g., more educated, more female, older) than our sample population, which may explain this difference.

While prevalent, this behavior appears to be relatively infrequent (frequency of social network Q&A was not reported in prior surveys such as [27], which focused primarily on prevalence, motivations, and topics associated with this phenomenon). Only 15.4% of the Facebook users, 9.8% of Google+ users, 9.5% of Twitter users, and 4.6% of LinkedIn users reported asking questions at least once per week. The low use of LinkedIn for question-asking may reflect competition from other professional forums, such as internal enterprise SNS sites [40]. Figure 1 shows the reported frequency of question-asking by respondents holding accounts on each of those social networking sites.

[5] Survey conducted in 2011; published in 2012.

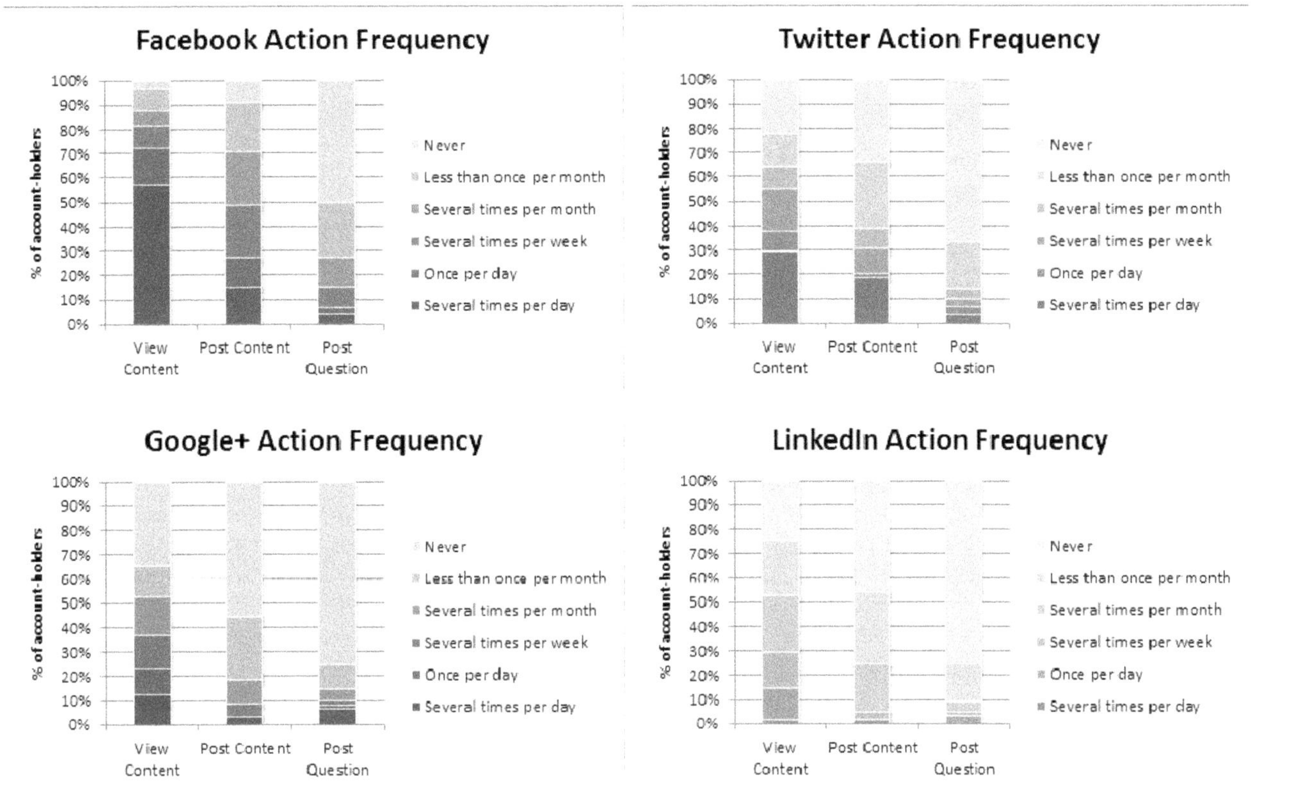

Figure 2. Frequencies of viewing content, posting content, and posting questions by account-holders on four social networks. The higher frequency of lurking (users who view but never post content) on Google+ and LinkedIn may contribute to their being viewed as less useful venues for getting questions answered.

On all of these social networks, viewing content is more common than posting content, which is more common than posting questions. "Lurking" (having an account and logging in to view content, but never posting any content yourself) was relatively uncommon. Only 4.3% of respondents with Facebook accounts were lurkers. Lurking on Twitter was more common, at 8.8% (note that this figure only includes respondents with Twitter accounts; many additional people likely read Twitter without having accounts at all). The lurking rates for Google+ and LinkedIn were higher still, at 12.5% and 15.9%, respectively. The lurking rate is strongly negatively correlated (r = -.94) with the rate of question-asking on each service, perhaps because it relates to the likelihood that someone who views a question will chime in with an answer. Figure 2 shows the frequency of different interactions on each social network.

The frequency of question asking on the three less popular social networks was significantly correlated ($p < .01$) (Twitter/Google+: r = .36; Twitter/LinkedIn, r = .34, Google+/LinkedIn: r = .44), perhaps representing a clique of "hard-core" askers who try many social venues in pursuit of an information need. In contrast, the frequency of asking on Facebook (a more popular activity overall), was not correlated significantly with asking on LinkedIn (the least popular venue for question asking), and had relatively weak correlations with asking frequency on Google+ and Twitter (r = .19, $p = .03$).

Demographic factors correlated weakly with the frequency of question asking on certain social networks. Younger respondents were more likely to ask questions on LinkedIn frequently (r = -.24, $p < .01$), as were respondents with lower education levels (r = -.18, p = .03). Among Facebook users, women reported asking questions more often than men (r = -.18, p - .03).

Q&A Sites

Q&A sites provide an alternative method of online information seeking than traditional Web search. These forums allow users to post questions for answering by either the general Web population (e.g., Yahoo! Answers, Mahalo Answers, Ask MetaFilter [14]), paid staffers (e.g., ChaCha, kgb), or self-identified topical experts (e.g., Quora [30]). Such sites typically archive past questions and answers, which are browseable and/or searchable by other users.

The past few years have seen an increase in the prominence of tools that form social structure around non-anonymous Q&A exchanges (e.g., Quora [33], founded in 2009) and of those that operate on a paid-staffer model, which is a modern-day analog of the reference librarian, (e.g., ChaCha, founded in 2006, whose answer volume surpassed that of Yahoo! Answers in 2011 [18]). Use of such "next-generation" Q&A sites could be construed as a form of asymmetric collaborative search [25].

We asked all respondents how often they posted questions to a variety of Q&A sites. Most respondents reported that they had never posted a question to Ask MetaFilter (97.3%), ChaCha (93.2%), kgb (98.6%), Mahalo Answers (100%), or Quora (99.3%). The only Q&A site in our survey that was occasionally used was Yahoo! Answers – 24% of respondents had posted a question at least once, though this behavior was infrequent (only 4.8% reported posting a question at least once a week).

The frequency of posting questions to Yahoo! Answers was not significantly correlated with demographic factors (age, gender, or education). There was, however, a significant negative correlation between the frequency of posting to Yahoo! Answers and the frequency of posting questions to some of the less popular social networking sites (Google+: $r = -.30$, $p < .01$; LinkedIn: $r = -.17$, $p = .04$). This might indicate that users employ two distinct "backup" strategies for seeking answers to difficult questions – either posting to a Q&A site or posting to a "secondary" social network.

We also asked whether respondents perused the archives of these Q&A sites for answers, even if they did not post a question themselves. 48.6% of respondents reported using Yahoo! Answers in this manner at least once, and 11% reported using ChaCha in this manner. The use of archived answers from Ask Metafilter, kgb, Mahalo, and Quora was negligible. Reusing answers was a more frequent behavior than posting new questions; 1.4% of respondents used the ChaCha archives at least once per week, and 11.7% did so for Yahoo! Answers (a Wilcoxon test comparing the frequency of posting vs. perusing Yahoo! Answers found that the latter was significantly more frequent, $z = -5.41$, $p < .001$). Reusing existing answers on Yahoo and ChaCha was significantly inversely correlated with age – younger users were more likely to engage in this behavior frequently (Yahoo! Answers: $r = -.41$, $p < .01$; ChaCha: $r = -.23$, $p < .01$).

DISCUSSION

In this section, we reflect on our survey findings. First, we compare and contrast our results with those of prior studies of collaborative search behavior, and discuss possible causes of differences. We then discuss the implications of our findings for the design of technical solutions supporting collaborative search.

Comparison with Prior Findings

Compared to six years ago [22], we found that more people are engaging in collaborative web search, and that they are doing so with greater frequency. 65.3% of our respondents reported having collaborated on web search, with 49.5% of those collaborative searchers engaging in such activities at least once per week. When asked about specific behaviors (such as engaging in co-located smartphone searches), even higher prevalence and frequencies were reported, suggesting that the 65.3% number may be an underestimate, perhaps due to the generic nature of the question ("have you ever collaborated with other people to search the web?").

The typical group size involved in such collaborations has increased, as well, likely due to the adoption of technologies that facilitate simultaneous interaction of larger groups of users for remote collaboration (e.g., social networking sites), and technologies that support larger group engagement in co-located collaboration by providing each group member with their own input device (e.g., smartphones). Despite the considerable press attention some emerging social information seeking solutions have received (e.g., Quora [33]), community Q&A sites do not appear to be part of a typical user's collaborative search repertoire.

We found that younger users were more likely to engage in collaborative searches. It is unclear whether the observed increase in collaborative search activities is due primarily to the coming-of-age of a new generation of technology users who are more comfortable pushing the bounds of a tool's intended use and/or have differing attitudes toward collaboration, or whether it is due to the invention and adoption of new technologies (smartphones, social networking, etc.). It is likely that both of these factors played a role in shaping our findings.

The tendency of respondents to appropriate existing communications technologies to create de facto collaborative search solutions (rather than using increasingly available dedicated collaborative tools) remains similar to six years ago. Consequently, respondents reported many of the same frustrations with collaborative search (lack of awareness, wasted duplication of effort) as in our earlier survey [22].

Our findings suggest that the meaning of the term "collaborative search" has evolved (or should evolve!). Our initial conception of collaborative search in our survey [22] and SearchTogether prototype [24] involved the synchronous or asynchronous use of search engines by multiple parties with a shared information need. However, our survey findings indicate that collaborative search now occurs beyond the search engine (e.g., in apps on smartphones, in questions on social networking sites, etc.).

Limitations

The reader should note that differences between our findings and prior work (particularly [22]) are difficult to attribute to a single cause. Differences may be due to social and technological changes occurring between 2006 and 2012, which is our primary hypothesis. Other sources of differential findings may be in the survey audience (highly technical respondents in [22] versus the more general population we reached with this survey), or in the nature of the questions themselves (the "have you ever" approach employed in [22] versus the recent critical-incident approach [7, 10] employed in the current work).

To explore whether our findings were due to audience background rather than sociotechnical changes occurring between 2006 and 2012, we issued the same survey to 250 randomly selected U.S.-based Microsoft employees in July 2012; 63 completed the survey (25% response rate). The results from this group were very similar to the results of the more diverse 2012 audience discussed in this paper – for instance, 61.9% of the 2012 Microsoft employee respondents reported having engaged in collaborative Web search, which is not significantly different than the 65.3% figure for the diverse group ($\chi^2(1, N=63) = .279, p = .597$). Similarly, of the 2012 Microsoft employees who searched collaboratively, 49.5% reported doing so at least once per week, which is quite similar to the 47.3% of our more diverse sample that collaboratively searched at least weekly. The similarity between the diverse and tech audiences' responses increased our confidence that differences in audience background between our survey and the 2006 survey are *not* the primary source of the differences in our findings.

Additionally, the reader should bear in mind the inherent limits of all self-report studies, such as potential inaccuracies in participants' memory or biases in what they choose to report (for more detail on the pros and cons of retrospective self-report methods, see [19]). It is also unclear whether these findings extend to other demographics, such as children or people outside the United States (e.g., staffed Q&A sites are reportedly a popular form of asymmetric collaborative search amongst Korean teenagers [18]). Combining our survey findings with other approaches, such as interview or observational methods, would provide a richer understanding of this phenomenon, and is a suggested direction for further study.

Challenges for Collaborative Search Solutions

Despite the increasing availability of tools designed specifically to support collaborative web search (e.g., free online tools including Coagmento [35], HeyStaks [37], SearchTogether [24], and So.cl [8]), none of our respondents utilized such technologies. General-purpose tools that could provide rich collaborative experiences, such as videoconferencing or projection technologies, were also rarely used. Instead, respondents repurposed simpler communications technologies that were part of their everyday routines (e-mail, texting, instant messaging, phone calls, and social networking) as a way to supplement status quo web browser and search engine technologies and enable collaborative information seeking. This suggests that technologies for collaborative web search must be sufficiently *lightweight* compared with status quo ad hoc solutions. One of our survey respondents articulated this well, observing, "It might have helped if we had some sort of online bulletin board on which to post our findings – but only if posting something to the bulletin board was faster and required fewer mouse clicks than copying a link into an e-mail message." The tension between dedicated, "top down" solutions versus ad hoc "bottom up" solutions is not unique to collaborative search; lessons learned about similar issues in areas like cyberinfrastructure development [41] may be applicable. Reflecting on our survey findings in light of this related work suggests that rather than creating dedicated tools for collaborative search, creating "glue" systems that offer integration, tighter coupling, and symbiotic functionality between existing social and information-seeking technologies might be a more promising approach.

Despite the challenge of striking a proper balance between having a low barrier to entry and offering rich collaboration support, there appears to be an unmet need for technologies supporting collaborative web search, as evidenced by the increasing prevalence and frequency of such activities. Our finding that collaborative search is more common among younger demographics suggests that its prevalence might continue to increase as a new generation of users with different attitudes about collaboration and technology emerges into the marketplace.

Our results suggest that systems that address users' frustrations regarding lack of awareness of collaborators' activities and the resulting redundant work that occurs would be particularly valued; these findings reinforce similar findings from prior work [22, 24], indicating a need that has continued to go unmet by technical advances. Solutions that can enhance common scenarios, such as the use of social networks for Q&A activities or the use of several smartphones for synchronous co-located searching, may be a particularly promising direction for research and development.

Shortly after the completion of our survey, Microsoft introduced collaborative search support into its Bing search engine with the "sidebar" feature [3], which enables a user to start a conversation with social network contacts around a query and a set of curated search results. The introduction of collaborative features into a mainstream search engine could potentially significantly alter the status quo reliance on bottom-up solutions. Revisiting the state of collaborative search practice in a few years seems prudent given the rapid evolution of technologies and attitudes in the social search space.

CONCLUSION

In this paper, we added to the growing body of knowledge about collaborative web search by presenting survey data about 167 diverse users' status quo collaborative search practices. We found that collaborative search has become an increasingly common type of information-seeking experience (and that the notion of what constitutes a "collaborative search" has evolved to include technologies beyond search engines, such as smartphones and social networking sites). We also found that ad hoc combinations of everyday technologies are used to support such collaborations, rather than dedicated solutions designed specifically for collaborative information seeking.

By contrasting our findings with earlier work, we identified changes in the prevalence of this practice and in the technologies employed. We also identified important challenges that remain to be addressed by designers of collaborative web search technologies. Our results indicate that there is great potential for technological innovation to enhance the surprisingly commonplace practice of collaborative information seeking in the digital era.

REFERENCES

1. Amershi, S. and Morris, M.R. CoSearch: A System for Co-located Collaborative Web Search. *Proceedings of CHI 2008*, 1647-1656.
2. Amershi, S. and Morris, M.R. Co-located Collaborative Web Search: Understanding Status Quo Practices. *CHI 2009 Extended Abstracts*, 3637-3642.
3. Bing Team. Introducing the New Bing: Spend Less Time Searching, More Time Doing. *Bing Search Blog*, May 10, 2012.
4. Brenner, J. Social Networking. *Pew Internet and American Life Project*, March 29, 2012.
5. Dybwad, B. Bing and Ping: Share Search Results on Facebook and Twitter. *Mashable*, Sept. 3, 2009.
6. Efron, M. and Winget, M. Questions are Content: A Taxonomy of Questions in a Microblogging Environment. *Proceedings of ASIS&T 2010.*
7. Evans, B. and Chi, E. Towards a Model of Understanding Social Search. *Proceedings of CSCW 2008*, 485-494.
8. Farnham, S.D., Lahav, M., Raskino, D., Cheng, L., Ickman, T., and Laird-McConnell, T. So.cl: An Interest Network for Informal Learning. *Proceedings of ICWSM 2012.*
9. Fidel, R., Bruce, H., Pejtersen, A.M., Dumais, S.T., Grudin, J., and Poltrock, S. Collaborative Information Retrieval. *The New Review of Information Behaviour Research,* 2000, volume 1, 235-247.
10. Flanagan, J. The critical incident technique. *Psychological Bulletin*, 51:327-358, 1954.
11. Foster, J. Collaborative Information Behavior: User Engagement and Communication Sharing. *IGI Global*, June 2010.
12. Greenberg, S. and Roseman, M. GroupWeb: A WWW Browser as Real Time Groupware. *Proceedings of the CHI 1996 Conference Companion*, 271-272.
13. Golovchinksy, G., Morris, M.R., and Pickens, J. Introduction to the special issue. *Information Processing & Management, Special Issue on Collaborative Information Seeking,* 46(6), November 2010.
14. Harper, F., Moy, D., and Konstan, J. Facts or friends? Distinguishing informational and conversational questions in social Q&A sites. *Proceedings of CHI 2009*, 759-768.
15. Hecht, B., Teevan, J., Morris, M.R., and Liebling, D. SearchBuddies: Bringing Search Engines into the Conversation. *Proceedings of ICWSM 2012.*
16. Horowitz, D. and Kamvar, S.D. The Anatomy of a Large-Scale Social Search Engine. *Proceedings of WWW 2010*, 431-440.
17. Lampe, C., Vitak, J., Gray, R., & Ellison, N. Perceptions of Facebook's Value as an Information Source. *Proceedings of CHI 2012*, 3195-3204.
18. Lee, U. Kang, H. Yi, E., Yi, M.Y., Kantola, J. Understanding Mobile Q&A Usage: An Exploratory Study. *Proceedings of CHI 2012*, 3215-3224.
19. Metts, S., Sprecher, S., and Cupach, W.R. Retrospective Self-Reports. In *Studying Interpersonal Interaction* (Montgomery, B.M. and Duck, S., eds.). The Guilford Press: 1991.
20. Moraveji, N., Morris, M.R., Morris, D., Czerwinski, M., and Riche, N. ClassSearch: Facilitating the Development of Web Search Skills through Social Learning. *Proceedings of CHI 2011*, 1797-1806.
21. Morris, M.R. Interfaces for Collaborative Exploratory Web Search: Motivations and Directions for Multi-User Designs. *CHI 2007 Workshop on Exploratory Search and HCI.*
22. Morris, M.R. A Survey of Collaborative Web Search Practices. *Proceedings of CHI 2008*, 1657-1660.
23. Morris, M.R., Fisher, D., and Wigdor, D. Search on Surfaces: Exploring the Potential of Interactive Tabletops for Collaborative Search Tasks. *Information Processing and Management*, 46(6), November 2010.
24. Morris, M.R. and Horvitz, E. SearchTogether; An Interface for Collaborative Web Search. *Proceedings of UIST 2007*, 3-12.
25. Morris, M.R. and Teevan, J. Collaborative Web Search: Who, What, Where, When, and Why? *Morgan & Claypool*, 2010.
26. Morris, M.R., Teevan, J., and Bush, S. Enhancing Collaborative Web Search with Personalization: Groupization, Smart Splitting, and Group Hit-Highlighting. *Proceedings of CSCW 2008*, 481-484.
27. Morris, M.R., Teevan, J., and Panovich, K. What Do People Ask Their Social Networks, and Why? A Survey Study of Status Message Q&A Behavior. *Proceedings of CHI 2010*, 1739-1748.
28. Morris, M.R., Teevan, J., and Panovich, K. A Comparison of Information Seeking Using Search Engines and Social Networks. *Proceedings of ICWSM 2010.*

29. Paul, S.A., Hong, L., and Chi, E.H. Is Twitter a Good Place for Asking Questions? A Characterization Study. *Proceedings of ICWSM 2011*.

30. Paul, S.A., Hong, L., and Chi, E.H. Who is Authoritative? Understanding Reputation Mechanisms in Quora. *Proceedings of Collective Intelligence 2012*.

31. Pickens, J., Golovchinsky, G., Shah, C., Qvarfordt, P., and Back, M. Algorithmic Mediation for Collaborative Exploratory Search. *Proceedings of SIGIR 2008*, 315-322.

32. Purcell, K. Search and email still top the list of most popular online activities. *Pew Internet &American Life Project*, August 9, 2011.

33. Rivlin, G. Does Quora Really Have All the Answers? *Wired*, May 2011.

34. Shah, C. Collaborative Information Seeking: The Art and Science of Making the Whole Greater than the Sum of All. *The Information Retrieval Series, Springer*, 2012.

35. Shah, C. and Gonzalez-Ibanez, R. Evaluating the Synergic Effect of Collaboration in Information Seeking. *Proceedings of SIGIR 2011*, 913-922.

36. Smith, A. Nearly half of American adults are smartphone owners. *Pew Internet & American Life Project*, March 1, 2012.

37. Smyth, B., Briggs, P., Coyle, M., and O'Mahoney, M. Google Shared: A Case Study in Social Search. *Proceedings of UMAP 2009*.

38. Taylor, R.S. Question-Negotiation and Information-Seeking in Libraries. *College & Research Libraries*, 29(3), 1968, 178-194.

39. Teevan, J., Karlson, A., Amini, S., Brush, A.J.B., and Krumm, J. Understanding the Importance of Location, Time, and People in Mobile Local Search Behavior. *Proceedings of Mobile HCI 2011*.

40. Thom, J., Helsley, S.Y., Matthews, T.L., Daly, E.M., Millen, D.R. What Are You Working On? Status Message Q&A within an Enterprise SNS. *Proceedings of ECSCW 2011*.

41. Twidale, M.B. and Floyd, I.R. Infrastructures from the Bottom-Up and Top-Down: Can They Meet in the Middle? *Proceedings of PDC 2008*, 238-241.

42. Wiltse, H. and Nichols, J. PlayByPlay: Collaborative Web Browsing for Desktop and Mobile Devices. *Proceedings of CHI 2009*, 1781-1790.

Online Silk Road: Nurturing Social Search through Knowledge Bartering

Yuqing Mao
National Center for Biotechnology Information
National Library of Medicine
National Institutes of Health
Bethesda, MD, USA
yuqing.mao@nih.gov

Haifeng Shen
School of Computer Science, Engineering and Mathematics
Flinders University
Australia
haifeng.shen@flinders.edu.au

Chengzheng Sun
School of Computer Engineering
Nanyang Technological University
Singapore
czsun@ntu.edu.sg

ABSTRACT
Social search empowers seekers to help each other find the information they need by sharing their domain knowledge and search efforts. Current social search activities are primarily voluntary, acted on the goodwill to help others or the purpose for self-promotion and the contributed content is mostly retrievable free of charge to the public. However, the voluntary nature of social search compromises its long-term sustainability as participants are not offered intrinsic incentives to contribute and share information, and free information presents intricate ramifications on the its quality. In this paper, we present the idea of knowledge bartering, where one can barter a knowledge item they have for another item they wish to have. To make the idea viable, we propose the online silk road solution to automate a knowledge bartering process that can maximise the social welfare within a community.

Author Keywords
Social search; question-and-answer system; knowledge market; incentive; knowledge bartering

ACM Classification Keywords
H.3.5 Information Storage and Retrieval: Online Information Services—*Data sharing, Web-based services*; H.5.3 Group and Organisation Interfaces: [Web-based interaction]; K.4.3 Computers and Society: [Computer Supported Collaborative Work]

INTRODUCTION
The participatory Web 2.0, especially through the ever-growing user-generated content (UGC) published in social media, has changed online information seeking from traditionally a solitary activity to a social behaviour, referred to as *social search* [7, 22], which empowers seekers to help each other find the information they want by sharing their domain knowledge and search experiences, processes, or results. The rationale behind this technology is the so-called "wisdom of crowds" [30], where large groups of cognitively and socially diverse individuals have proven superior than the elite few in solving problems, fostering innovations, or making decisions. Current social search systems are exemplified by social tagging [3] systems like *Faviki*, human-powered search engines like *Aardvark* [12], and question-and-answer (QnA) systems like *Yahoo!Answer*. These social search activities are mostly voluntary, acted on the goodwill to help others or the purpose to promote themselves, and the content contributed by the participants in a social search community are mostly retrievable free of charge to the general public.

While some contributions might seem trivial, e.g., sharing the queries they used to retrieve or the tags they used to annotate relevant results with their peers, some other contributions contain intimate knowledge and are made by investing tremendous time and great efforts in analysing information requirements, gathering relevant information, and organising and presenting the content, such as the epistemologies in the *Baijia* social search system [20] and some of the answers in QnA systems. For example, information on a cost-effective way of touring Europe from US, including cheap flights, discounted hotels, recommended tours, a not-to-do list, and so on, has to be gathered from effortful online searches, numerous queries to travel agents, valuable tips from friends, and personal experiences. As such, the contributor may not be willing to voluntarily share them for free. Therefore, to make social search sustainable in a long term, participants must be offered intrinsic incentives to contribute and share their knowledge. In addition, free information presents intricate ramifications on the its quality, possibly for the reasons below:

- If one does not expect any return by voluntarily sharing one's contributions for free, one may not be motivated to spend adequate time improving the quality of the contributions.
- If one contributes free content just for fun, one may not be serious about the quality of the contributions.

- If one does not intend to claim the ownership of one's contributions, e.g., anonymous or using a fake identity, one is unlikely to bear the responsibility for the trustworthiness of one's advises, leaving the consequences to whoever that has followed them.

A mainstream remunerative incentive mechanism is the so-called *virtual (or cyber) currency*, widely adopted in social media, virtual worlds, or online games, which can used to purchase virtual goods like avatars, digital supplies, virtual friends, or just information. For example, in *Yahoo! Answer*, one is rewarded points for their answer acknowledged by the asker and one can redeem accumulated points to post their own questions. Virtual currency may have partially tackled the quantity issue by incentivising participants to earn more "virtual money" through making more contributions, but its impact on the information quality is questionable because participants can accumulate virtual wealth through easy ways such as collusions or sockpuppets rather than through the hard work of improving the quality of their contributed information.

In this paper, we present the idea of *knowledge bartering*, where one can barter a knowledge item they have for another item they wish to have, as an alternative incentive mechanism for social search. This mechanism can address not only the quantity issue (the more knowledge items one can supply to others, the more knowledge items one can get from others through bartering) but also the quality issue (the higher quality a knowledge item has, the more likely it is accepted as a barter). Knowledge bartering is not prone to the problems encountered monetary [32] or barter markets, and escapes the traps of the modern economics in general [15]. To make the idea viable, we propose the *online silk road* solution to automate a knowledge bartering process that can maximise the social welfare within a social search community. We conducted a set of experiments to validate the knowledge bartering idea and test the feasibility and performance of the online silk road solution using a real-world dataset collected from *Yahoo!Answer*. We also demonstrated the application of knowledge bartering in a prototype social search system.

The rest of the paper is organised as follows. We first introduce work related to our research. We then present knowledge bartering followed by the online silk road solution that realises the idea. After that, we describe the methodology of the experiments conducted to validate our solution followed by the discussions on the experimental results. Finally, we conclude the paper with a summary of major contributions and future work.

RELATED WORK

It has long been advocated that *"Information wants to be free"* [31], but there is a growing trend for paid information. For example, all online newspapers used to be free (most of them still are) because it is believed that they can make profit from online advertising. However, the revenues from online advertising turn out to be even not enough to cover the cost of a tiny news operation incurred from hiring reporters and editors to gather, process, and edit the news. Since late 2010, *News Corporation* has erected a *"paywall"* service around its UK newspaper titles including *The Times* and *The Sunday Times*, in which readers are charged for accessing online articles. More recently, the *New York Times* has gained profit from its paywall service launched in March 2011 and now has 324,000 paid digital subscribers.

Although the intent to end free information on the Internet remains controversial, the paywall service does show that people are willing to pay for the quality of information. However, it is unreasonable to charge users for accessing UGC because no central authority exists to ensure the quality of UGC. On the other hand, the Internet is flooded by excessive UGC, but knowledge – true and reliable information which people like to have or need to solve their problems – is relatively small as it has to be created through skilled labour and hard work. From economics point of view, as knowledge has value, Internet should be not only a platform for people to create and acquire knowledge but also a *knowledge market* for people to trade their knowledge, i.e., sell the knowledge they have and buy the knowledge they need.

Knowledge market is based on the social exchange theory, i.e., the knowledge movement in the information society is powered by market forces. Davenport and Prusak proposed a mechanism for supporting and facilitating the sharing or exchange of knowledge among users, where organisational actors are defined as knowledge buyers or sellers within a marketplace [8]. Knowledge buyers are individuals who try to solve a complex issue that precludes an easy answer and knowledge sellers are those who have a reputation for their substantial knowledge about a subject or process. Knowledge trading in knowledge markets is established on the belief that both knowledge buyers and sellers can benefit from exchanging their intellectual properties [21].

The effective operation of knowledge markets has brought the knowledge flowing inside the knowledge net and realised the sharing of knowledge [14]. To improve business processes, knowledge management can be used to increase productivity. For example, Merx-Chermin and Nijhof analysed different quality management methods for knowledge marketplaces and discussed the commonalities and differences between traditional knowledge management systems and knowledge markets. Compared to trading physical goods, knowledge trading is more convenient on the Web. In addition, computer-based actors, e.g. software agents that enact buyers and sellers, can be used to automate knowledge trading processes in Internet-based knowledge markets [28]. Zhang and Jasimuddin proposed a mathematical model for investigating the working mechanism behind an online knowledge market, i.e., the pricing strategies of users and the company administrating the market [33]. But no existing work has focused on the prerequisites for the market behaviour, especially the incentives driving the exchange of knowledge for social search.

As a representative example of online knowledge markets, Web-based QnA systems currently predominate in the social search arena and are still growing rapidly. QnA systems can be categorised into community QnA services (CQA) and payment QnA services. CQA services, including general-purpose CQA like *Yahoo! Answer*, domain-specific CQA like *Stack Overflow*, network-specific CQA like *Facebook Question*, adopt a free trading model that only offers an increase of reputation or points to contributors. As a pioneer of payment QnA service, *Google Answers* adopted a monetary trading model, allowing askers to offer bounties to the experts who have provide good answers to their questions. Its successor *Uclue* has inherited the same model, where customers need to pay via *PayPal* when they post a question. *ChaCha* developed another payment QnA model, which offers a subsidised knowledge market where askers are given free answers through interactions and conversations with the answerers who are paid to do the job.

In past years, much research has been done on CQA, including search of high-quality answers or questions [4], models for retrieving CQA archives [29], CQA interfaces and user experience studies [19], collaboration and social network analysis in CQA [24]. In particular, there has been intensive research on expert locating in CQA, as it can direct questions to those who are best positioned to answer them [1]. For example, Bouguessa used network analysis algorithms such as *InDegree* to characterise user activities and identify users with high expertise in *Yahoo! Answers* [5]. Pal and Konstan proposed a method for identifying experts by modelling the bias involved in selecting questions to answer [23]. Users are ranked based on their expertise scores without using an explicit indicator of who should be considered as an expert. While answering is not subsidised in CQA, incentive mechanisms based on social psychology and game theory are used to encourage users to generate high-quality content [9], e.g., Jain proposed a game-theoretic model with the approval-voting and proportional-share scoring rules for *Yahoo! Answers* [16].

In contrast, not much work has been done on payment QnA services. Some research in economics has studied how to improve the quality of contributions in payment QnA services through economic incentives such as helping behaviour, pricing discrimination, quantity of money, and reciprocity [26]. Hsieh studied *Mahalo Answers*, a paid QnA service where users providing good answers are rewarded with *Mahalo Dollars*, and found that askers are willing to pay for fact-based questions and pay more for difficult questions [13]. Harper found that payment QnA services typically provide higher quality answers than CQA services do and paying more generally leads to better outcomes [11]. The more recent QnA system *Quora* has implemented a monetary trading model, where credit, a kind of virtual currency, can be earned by answering questions or getting answers up-voted. People can also use credits to get others to follow their questions, or directly send their questions to the best experts. Since questions and answers can be updated, followed and voted, it is possible to generate higher-quality content and make it more reusable.

KNOWLEDGE BARTERING ON THE ONLINE SILK ROAD

Knowledge Bartering

Bartering was the mechanism with which ancient people trade their goods before the introduction of common monetary currencies. Barter markets escape most of the traps in modern economics such as inflation and still exist in our modern economy, but to a very limited extent because of its own problems. However, thanks to the essential differences between virtual and physical goods, these problems either do not exist or can be solved altogether in our knowledge bartering approach.

First, the absence of common measure of value in a barter market makes it difficult to trade different kinds of goods. For example, how many sheep would one offer in exchange for a ship? This is a critical problem in the trading of physical goods because once the transaction is done, one would lose one's own goods and one would be disadvantaged if what one exchanged for were not worth what one offered. In contrast, the same problem appears rather insignificant when it comes to the virtual goods – knowledge – because both trading parties get new goods while still possessing their own goods after the transaction is done. Therefore, it is reasonable to assume all knowledge items in a barter market have the same value.

Second, bartering of physical goods usually requires both trading parties to bring their own goods to the same marketplace, where they exchange their goods on the spot. A transaction would not be possible if they could not bring their goods along with them and meet at the same place at the same time. The problem does not exist in the Internet-based knowledge markets because the virtual goods can be accessed anywhere anytime by anyone authorised and neither trading party is required to be personally and physically present for the transaction to occur.

Last, a barter transaction usually involves only two trading parties. If more than two parties were required, it would be difficult to identify parties whose supplies and demands match each other and even if a match were found, it would still be difficult to make the transaction successful because the more parties are involved, the more complex a barter process would be, e.g., the first two problems would be exacerbated. For example, if participant P_a supplies the goods participant P_b demands, but P_b does not supply the goods P_a demands, at least one more participant P_c must be identified who not only supplies the goods P_a demands but also demands the goods P_b supplies. The problem also exists in knowledge bartering, but we propose the following online silk road solution to address it.

Online Silk Road

Knowledge bartering is inspired by the inter-regional trading activities on the ancient *Silk Road*. Along the silk road routes, China traded their silk and porcelain for precious stones with India and India traded the silk and porcelain they got from China for gold and silver with the Roman Empire. All these transactions were performed based on the item-to-item bartering, as the foreign currency exchange did not exist at that time.

We want to model a knowledge bartering process using the idea of online silk road. For example, assume participant P_a supplies a knowledge item in history and demands a knowledge item in computing, participant P_b supplies the knowledge P_a demands but demands a knowledge item in medicine, while participant P_c supplies the knowledge P_b demands but demands the knowledge P_a supplies. As such, a match can be found involving parties P_a, P_b, and P_c. An knowledge bartering online silk road consists of matches involving the maximum number of parties in order to maximise the social welfare, that is to get as many parties as possible benefited from the barter transactions.

Knowledge bartering can be modelled as a directed graph $G = (V, E)$, where a vertex in V represents a participant and a weighted edge e_{ij} from vertex v_i to vertex v_j in E expresses that participant v_i can supply the knowledge item demanded by participant v_j. The weight $w_{e_{ij}}$ is assigned to e_{ij} according to the gain v_j can get from the knowledge item supplied by v_i. The weight takes a number of factors, e.g., the TF-IDF relevance [17] between the demand and supply knowledge items, the trustworthiness of the supplier, and the preferences of the requester. For the sake of simplicity, the current model only takes the TF-IDF relevance into account, but other considerations can be factored in later.

We first consider the case of Single-Supply-Single-Demand (SSSD), where each participant is allowed to supply and/or demand only one knowledge item. The case of Multiple-Supply-Multiple-Demand (MSMD) will be discussed later. A possible barter transaction is represented as a cycle in the graph, with each participant obtaining the knowledge item supplied by the next one in the cycle. If a cycle c contain m edges, namely e_1, $\cdots$, e_m, the cycle's weight w_c is the sum of all edge weights in the cycle:

$$w_c = \sum_{i=1}^{m} w_{e_i} \text{ , where}$$

$m \geq 2$. A knowledge bartering online silk road is a collection of cycles with the maximum cardinality, i.e., it contains the most number of vertices in order to benefit the most number of participants.

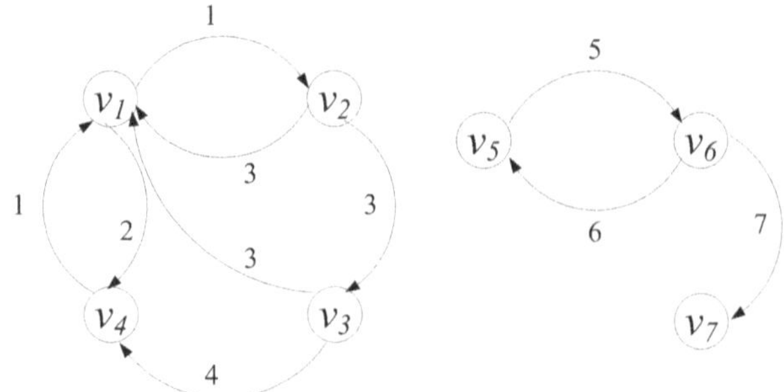

Figure 1. Knowledge bartering graph

Figure 1 illustrates a knowledge bartering process involving 7 users $\{v_1, v_2, \cdots, v_7\}$, where all edges are labeled with some weights. Five cycles exist in the graph, namely $c_1 = \{v_1, v_2\}$, $c_2 = \{v_1, v_2, v_3\}$, $c_3 = \{v_1, v_2, v_3, v_4\}$, $c_4 = \{v_1, v_4\}$, and $c_5 = \{v_5, v_6\}$. Obviously, v_7 is not included in any of the cycles probably because nobody has demanded the knowledge item supplied by v_7. Two knowledge bartering online silk roads, namely $sr_1 = \{c_2, c_4, c_5\}$ and $sr_2 = \{c_3, c_5\}$, can be discovered and each consists of a collection of cycles that cover the most number of vertices in the graph.

In the current model, cycles are edge-disjoint, i.e., no two cycles share a common edge, but not vertex-disjoint, i.e., a vertex can appear in more than one cycle. This is to allow one to barter the same item with more than one other party, which is one of the unique characteristics of knowledge bartering but strictly prohibited in item-to-item bartering of physical goods. As George Bernard Shaw said, *"If you have an apple and I have an apple and we exchange apples then you and I will still each have one apple. But if you have an idea and I have an idea and we exchange these ideas, then each of us will have two ideas."* Nevertheless, the model can be easily adapted to suit other bartering requirements, e.g., vertex-disjoint for the sake of facilitating item-to-item bartering of physical goods.

Social Welfare Maximisation

If a knowledge bartering online silk road sr contains n cycles, namely c_1, $\cdots$, c_n, the weight of the silk road w_{sr} is the sum of the weights of all cycles it contains:

$$w_{sr} = \sum_{i=1}^{n} w_{c_i} \text{ , where}$$

$n \geq 1$. The silk road with the maximum weight has achieved the maximum social welfare, which means if knowledge items are bartered along this route, the most of number of participants will be benefited from the barter transaction. For the example in Figure 1, sr_1 has achieved the maximum social welfare because its weight $w_{sr_1} = (1+3+3)+(1+2)+(5+6) = 21$, which is greater than $w_{sr_2} = (1+3+4+1)+(5+6) = 20$.

However, identification of the knowledge bartering online silk road with the maximum social welfare must consider a critical constraint: cycle length, i.e. the maximum number of edges a cycle is allowed to include. First, generally speaking, the shorter the cycle is, the more efficient the barter transaction would be. A shorter cycle means fewer parties are involved in the transaction, essentially reducing the overhead in waiting for the approval by all parties, e.g., not all parties are simultaneously online and some may be in different time zones. Second, if the transaction fails, e.g., because one party declines, a shorter cycle means fewer parties would be affected by this unsuccessful transaction. Last, trust is a natural element in any barter transaction because one must be confident with the authenticity and trustworthiness of the person one is going to barter with. A shorter cycle means less time would be spent on authentication of all parties involved in the transaction. In item-to-item bartering of physical goods, the cycle length constraint is also strictly applied, for example, in *Swap Market*, where people can barter goods like books, CDs, DVDs, and video games, a transaction can only involve up to four parties.

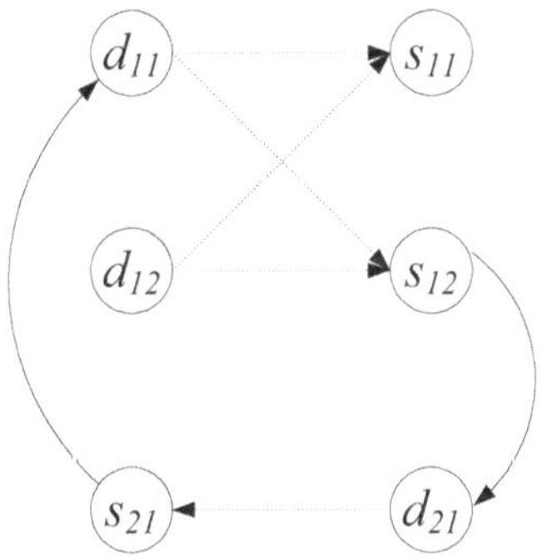

Figure 2. An example of MSMD

Therefore, the problem is to find the maximum-weight online silk road (MWOSR) consisting of cycles whose length is under a constraint K. The MWOSR problem is a variant of the *Cycle Covering Problem (CCP)* [27] in graph theory. Similar to the *traveling salesman* problem, where the goal is to find a Hamiltonian cycle with a minimum or maximum weight, or other variants of CCP such as the constrained version of the *Chinese Postman Problem* [10], the MWOSR problem is also NP-complete. Therefore, approaches based on approximation are generally applied to solve the problem. However, in order to avoid dissatisfaction of barter opportunities caused by the loss of optimality, we aim at an optimal solution based on an *Integer Linear Programming (ILP)* formulation, which is the technique for the optimisation of a linear objective function. ILP formulation allows one to add additional constraints to the problem, and to model a number of variations on the objectives. For example, long cycles can be given lighter weights if participants prefer short to long cycles when they decide to approve the certain transactions.

The MSMD case can actually be handled in a way similar to the SSSD case. As shown in Figure 2, vertex s_{ij} represents the jth knowledge supply from participant i and vertex d_{ij} represents the jth knowledge demand by participant i. A zero-weight edge, depicted as a dashed line, is added from d_{ij} to every s_{ik}. A barter transaction between participants i and j is likely to happen if there exists a cycle that covers both participants' supply and demand vertices, e.g., $c = \{d_{11}, s_{12}, d_{21}, s_{21}\}$.

Cycle Formulation

When the cycle length constraint is set to 2, the MWOSR problem can be converted into the classical *assignment problem* [6], which is to find a maximum-weight matching in a weighted bipartite graph and can be solved by a reduction to the perfect matching in the graph. For example, for the knowledge bartering graph $G = (V, E)$ in Figure 1, a new graph G' on V, as shown in Figure 3, can be constructed by creating an edge to represent each cycle of length 2 in the original graph and the edge's weight is the cycle's weight. As such, each matching in G' corresponds to a cycle cover by those cycles of length 2 in G. Therefore, the MWOSR problem under the constraint $K = 2$ can be solved by finding a maximum-weight matching with a polynomial time complexity.

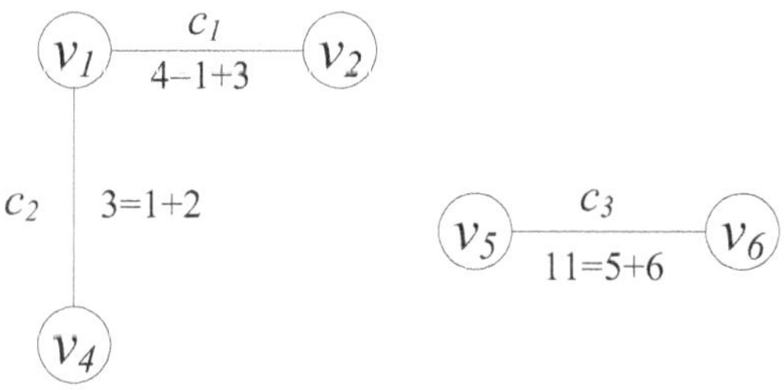

Figure 3. Cycle formulation under constraint K=2

The solution can be generalised to allow an arbitrary K. Let $\Gamma_K = \{c_1, \cdots, c_n\}$ represent the set of all edge-disjoint cycles whose length is no more than K. Variable x_c is used to indicate whether cycle c is selected to be part of the cycle cover:

$$x_c = \begin{cases} 0 & \text{if c is not selected} \\ 1 & \text{if c is selected} \end{cases}$$

Variable a_c^e is used to indicate whether edge e is included in cycle c:

$$a_c^e = \begin{cases} 0 & \text{if e is not included in c} \\ 1 & \text{if e is included in c} \end{cases}$$

Then the maximum-weight cycle cover by cycles in Γ_K can be solved with the following ILP:

$$max \sum_{c \in \Gamma_k} w_c x_c \text{ , subject to}$$

$$\sum_{c \in \Gamma_k} a_c^e x_c \leq 1 \text{ , } \forall e \in E \text{ , with}$$

$$x_c \in \{0,1\} \ , \forall c \in \Gamma_k$$

An ILP problem can be efficiently solved using tree search techniques, such as *branch-and-bound*, *branch-and-cut*, and other branching algorithms. We choose the branch-and-bound algorithm to solve the MWOSR problem as it tends to perform better than other alternatives. A performance comparison will be given in the next section. The branch-and-bound MWOSR algorithm is given in Algorithm 1.

ALGORITHM 1: The branch-and-bound MWOSR algorithm

1. Initialise a list of problems (P) to solve. The first problem to be included in the list is the root problem. It is the linear programming relaxation, which is a linear program that replaces the constraint in the ILP, i.e., each variable must be either 0 or 1, by a weaker constraint, i.e., each variable belongs to [0, 1].
2. If $P = \emptyset$, the best known feasible solution is optimal; otherwise, choose a problem p from P and delete it from the list P.
3. Solve the linear relaxation of p.
   - If the solution is integral, update the best known integral solution and eventually the best known solution value and then return to *Step 2*.
   - If the value of the objective function exceeds that of the best known feasible solution, return to *Step 2*.
   - Otherwise, partition problem p into two new problems using some linear inequality, e.g., first choosing a variable with a current fractional value $\overline{x_{ij}}$ and then imposing $x_{ij} \geq 1$ in one problem and $x_{ij} \leq 0$ in the other. Consequently, all feasible solutions to p will be contained in the union of the feasible (integral) solutions to each of the two problems. Add the two new problems into the list P and return to *Step 2*.

EXPERIMENTAL VALIDATION

The primary goal of conducting experiments is to validate the knowledge bartering idea and test the feasibility and performance of the online silk road solution using a real-world dataset.

Data Collection

To best simulate the environment where participants interact as a social search community, our experimental dataset was collected from *Yahoo!Answers New Zealand*. We used its API to retrieve the questions and answers in different categories. There were 92,112 questions in total with at least one answer in the period from April 2008 to March 2011.

It is worth clarifying that *Yahoo!Answers* adopts a points-based incentive mechanism built on the free trading model rather than knowledge bartering on the online silk road. Our experiments were intended to testify that exchange of questions and answers can actually be done differently using knowledge bartering. To that end, we need to construct the knowledge bartering graph from the collected dataset. To help find matches between supplies and demands based on the TF-IDF relevance, every participant needs to make an abridgement or snippet of each of their knowledge supplies (not the full knowledge item; otherwise anyone can get it for free rather than through bartering) publicly available.

We first find supply-demand matches based on the categories of the supplies and demands. If one asked a question in a category and another provided an answer in the same category, an edge of weight 1 between the two participants would be created. This is based on the hypothesis that if one offers an answer in a category, one is likely to be an expert in the field concerned and probably able to provide the answers to other questions in the category. Further to that, if the TF-IDF relevance score between the question and the answer is high, the edge weight would be increased to 2. By applying these two rules to the collected dataset, we have obtained 109,027 supply-demand pairs. By further filtering out participants who either only asked questions but did not answer any question or only answered some questions but did not ask any question as they would not be involved in any knowledge bartering process, we have obtained 1,430 participants and 23,210 questions.

Experimental Results

Table 1 shows some characteristics of the constructed knowledge bartering graph. More than 2,200 cycles exist in the graph if the cycle length is capped by 2 ($K = 2$) and more than 3,800 cycles would be found if the cycle length is capped by 8 ($K = 8$). This result has confirmed the feasibility of knowledge bartering on the online silk road.

Table 1. Characteristics of the constructed knowledge bartering graph

Length of cycles	Number of cycles	Average weight of maximum-weight cycle covers	Coverage
K = 2	2275	324.2	13.1%
K = 3	2618	360.9	14.4%
K = 4	2939	383.6	15.3%
K = 5	3287	402.7	15.9%
K = 6	3506	413.3	16.2%
K = 7	3718	420.7	16.4%
K = 8	3841	426.5	16.5%

Apart from the positive validation of the proposed solution, Table 1 also shows that the coverage of the maximum-weight cycle covers was noticeably low in the dataset, e.g., only 13.1% knowledge supplies and demands would be included in the maximum-weight cycle covers if only the two-way knowledge bartering, i.e., a transaction only involves two parties, were permitted ($K = 2$). This phenomenon is partially attributed to the fact that the points-based incentive mechanism built on the free trading model is not good enough to incentivise participants to contribute answers in *Yahoo!Answers*. The supplies and demands are rather unbalanced in the knowledge market in that on average each participant asks a lot more questions than the number of answers they have actually provided to others, resulting in few vertices in the knowledge bartering graph to be included in the maximum-weight cycle covers. We would conjecture a much higher coverage of maximum-weight cycle covers if the knowledge bartering approach were adopted by the system.

To further address the low coverage problem, we can extend the online silk road solution to allow iterative knowledge bartering, i.e., a user can iteratively barter a knowledge item they have got from an online silk road transaction for a new item through another transaction until they have eventually got the item they exactly want, which is similar to the legendary *"from one paperclip to a house"* barter story [18]. The knowledge bartering based on the participants' original knowledge items is not the end of an online silk road. If one does not have the right knowledge item to barter for what one really wants, one can first barter it for whatever one can get and then barter the bartered item iteratively until a satisfactory item is obtained. In a social search system that adopts iterative knowledge bartering, participants only need to specify their final search targets and provide their knowledge items for bartering, and the system can automatically generate the multiple online silk road transactions.

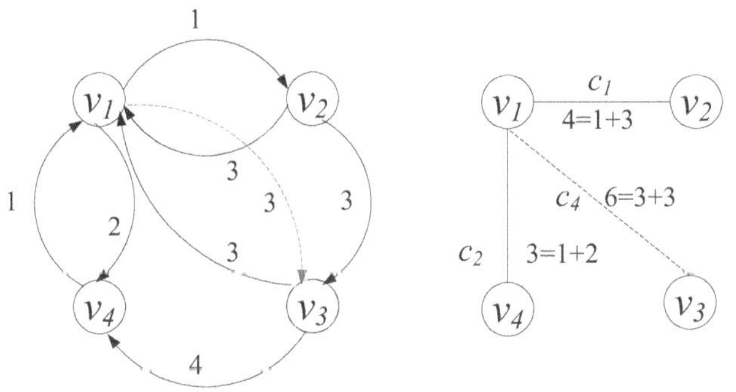

Figure 4. Iterative knowledge bartering example

After each transaction, some participants change their roles from requesters to suppliers, leading to more cycles and a better coverage in a knowledge bartering graph. For example, v_3 in Figure 1 is not covered by the cycles in Figure 3. Assume after the transaction in Figure 3, v_1 has got a knowledge item that v_3 wants from v_2 and consequently changed from a requester to a supplier, i.e., supply to v_3 as shown in Figure 4 (left). At the next online silk road transaction shown in Figure 4 (right), v_3 would be included in the coverage. Table 2 shows the results of iterative online silk road transactions performed on the knowledge bartering graph with the cycle length capped to 5 (K = 5). The coverage has been significantly improved against that in Table 1.

Performance Study

To measure the performance of the proposed branch-and-bound MWOSR algorithm, we compared it with two other algorithms. One was a lowest-first branch-and-cut procedure, where the LP relaxation is initialised by taking all the constraints in the last LP solved at the parent node to each node of the branching tree [2]. The other was a local search algorithm, which wanders through the space of feasible solutions, moving from one feasible solution to another nearby measured by *Hamming distance* at each step [25]. The experiments were carried out on a Dell Precision Workstation T3400, which has an Intel Core2 Quad CPU Q9450 @ 2.66GHz and 8 GB RAM, and runs Windows XP Professional.

Table 2. Iterative knowledge bartering

Iteration times	Number of cycles	Coverage
N = 1	3287	15.9%
N = 2	4625	18.6%
N = 3	5481	21.2%
N = 4	6224	23.1%
N = 5	6958	24.6%
N = 6	7555	26.1%

Table 1 further shows that the average weight of maximum-weight cycle covers with the cycle length capped to 5 ($K = 5$) is not much different from that with the cycle length capped to 8 ($K = 8$), suggesting the maximum social welfare gained under the two constraints are actually comparable. Therefore, to compromise between the computational cost (referring to Table 3) and the social welfare gain, it is reasonable to cap the cycle length to 5 ($K = 5$), while still approximating the optimal social welfare.

Table 3. Computation costs of the three algorithms

Length of cycles	Branch and bound	Branch and cut	Local search
K = 2	9.2	15.2	53.7
K = 3	14.5	25.4	92.0
K = 4	23.8	35.1	149.2
K = 5	36.4	50.6	197.1
K = 6	49.7	79.3	240.8
K = 7	70.1	110.8	312.3
K = 8	93.9	158.4	398.7

Table 3 shows the computation costs in terms of CPU time in seconds incurred by the three algorithms under the seven constraints, i.e., $K = 2, \cdots, 8$. It is clear that the branch-and-bound algorithm we used significantly outperforms the other two. It is also noticeable that when K, i.e. the cycle length cap, increases, the computation cost increases dramatically. For example, when $K = 5$, the branch-and-bound algorithm needs 36.4 seconds to solve the MWOSR problem, but when $K = 8$, the computation time drastically increases to 93.9 seconds. Even for $K = 5$, the time of 36.4 seconds is still not short, although it is partially attributed to the limited computation power of the workstation we used to conduct the experiments. Therefore it is worth further exploring advanced heuristic techniques and parallel computing algorithms in order to improve the efficiency of solving the MWOSR problem.

CONCLUSIONS AND FUTURE WORK

QnA systems currently predominate in the social search arena, however, analysis on a dataset we collected from a commercial QnA system has discovered a significant imbalance between the number of people who seek help and the number of volunteers who offer help. Most people have asked a lot of questions but offered few or no answers to the questions asked by others and on average each participant asks a lot more questions than the number of answers they have actually provided to others. This discovery suggests that the points-based incentive mechanism built on the free trading model adopted by the QnA system is not good enough to incentivise participants to contribute their answers.

In this paper, we have contributed the idea of knowledge bartering as an alternative incentive mechanism for social search systems. This mechanism can motivate people to not only contribute more because the more they can offer to others, the more they can get from others but also improve the quality of their contributions because the higher quality a contribution has, the more likely it is accepted as a barter. A key issue in a bartering process is to discover participants who can supply each other's demand so that a barter transaction is made successful among these participants. We have also contributed a novel online silk road solution that can not only discover the barter parties automatically but also achieve maximum social welfare. Experiments using the dataset collected from *Yahoo!Answers* has validated the knowledge bartering idea and tested the feasibility and performance of the online silk road solution.

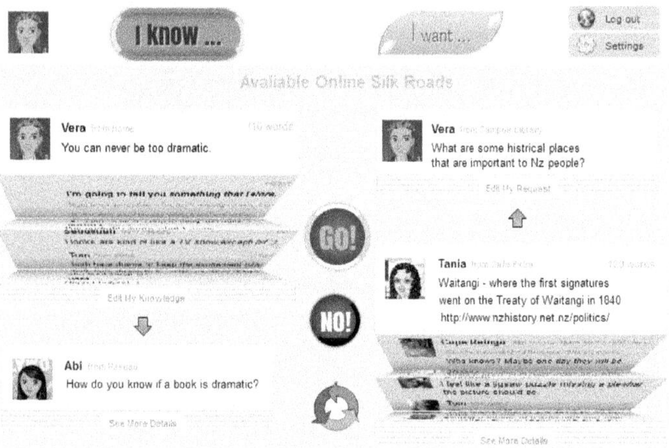

Figure 5. Knowledge bartering in social search

It is worth clarifying that although we used a dataset collected from a commercial QnA system to test the feasibility and performance of our solution, it does not suggest that our solution can only be used in QnA systems. Therefore, we have also developed a rudimentary prototype system to demonstrate its application in a social search system. As shown in Figure 5, users submit their knowledge supplies (I know) and requests (I want) to the system, and the system will automatically generate relevant online silk roads for them to choose which transactions they like to happen. The intellectual property of a knowledge item is protected by making only a fraction of its content available to the public and the full content only available to those involved in an online silk road transaction.

We are conscious that our experiments have only testified the feasibility of using the knowledge bartering incentive mechanism for QnA systems. By no means have they testified that this new incentive mechanism can attract more and better contributions. An imminent future work is to improve the prototype system so that we can then conduct usability testings to measure the balance (or imbalance) between the supplies and demands and testify whether this mechanism encourages more and better contributions compared to the mechanisms adopted by existing systems.

ACKNOWLEDGMENTS

The work was partially supported by an establishment grant (36426) from Flinders University, Australia. The authors would like to thank anonymous reviews for their comments that helped improve the paper.

REFERENCES

1. L. A. Adamic, J. Zhang, E. Bakshy, and M. S. Ackerman. Knowledge sharing and yahoo answers: everyone knows something. In *Proceedings of the International Conference on World Wide Web*, pages 665–674, 2008.
2. N. Ascheuer, M. Jünger, and G. Reinelt. A branch & cut algorithm for the asymmetric traveling salesman problem with precedence constraints. *Computational Optimization and Applications*, 17(1):61–84, 2000.
3. S. Bao, X. Wu, B. Fei, G. Xue, Z. Su, and Y. Yu. Optimizing web search using social annotation. In *WWW'07*, pages 501–510, 2007.
4. J. Bian, Y. Liu, E. Agichtein, and H. Zha. Finding the right facts in the crowd: factoid question answering over social media. In *Proceedings of the International Conference on World Wide Web*, pages 467–476, 2008.
5. M. Bouguessa, B. Dumoulin, and S. Wang. Identifying authoritative actors in question-answering forums: the case of yahoo! answers. In *Proceedings of the ACM SIGKDD International Conference on Knowledge Discovery and Data Mining*, pages 866–874, 2008.
6. R. Burkard, M. Dell'Amico, and S. Martello. *Assignment Problems*. SIAM, 2009.
7. E. H. Chi. Information seeking can be social. *Computer*, 42(3):42–46, 2009.

8. T. H. Davenport and L. Prusak. *Working Knowledge: How Organizations Manage What They Know*. Harvard Business Press Books, 1997.
9. A. Ghosh and P. McAfee. Incentivizing high-quality user-generated content. In *Proceedings of the International Conference on World Wide Web*, pages 137–146, 2011.
10. M. Guan. Graphic programming using odd and even points. *Chinese Mathematics*, 1(3):273–277, 1962.
11. F. M. Harper, D. Raban, S. Rafaeli, and J. A. Konstan. Predictors of answer quality in online q&a sites. In *Proceedings of the ACM Conferece on Human Factors in Computing Systems*, pages 865–874, 2008.
12. D. Horowitz and S. D. Kamvar. The anatomy of a large-scale social search engine. In *Proceedings of the International Conference on World Wide Web*, pages 431–440, 2010.
13. G. Hsieh, R. E. Kraut, and S. E. Hudson. Why pay?: exploring how financial incentives are used for question & answer. In *Proceedings of the ACM Conference on Human Factors in Computing Systems*, pages 305–314, 2010.
14. R. Hugginsa, A. Johnstona, and R. Steffensonb. Universities, knowledge networks and regional policy. *Cambridge Journal of Regions, Economy and Society*, 1(2):321–340, 2008.
15. D. Irwin, J. Chase, L. Grit, and A. Yumerefendi. Self-recharging virtual currency. In *Proceedings of the ACM SIGCOMM workshop on Economics of peer-to-peer systems*, pages 93–98, 2005.
16. S. Jain, Y. Chen, and D. C. Parkes. Designing incentives for online question and answer forums. In *Proceedings of the ACM Conference on Electronic Commerce*, pages 129–138, 2009.
17. Karen Spärck Jones. A statistical interpretation of term specificity and its application in retrieval. *Journal of Documentation*, pages 132–142, 1972.
18. K. Macdonald. *One Red Paperclip: How a Small Piece of Stationery Turned into a Great Big Adventure*. Ebury Press, 2007.
19. L. Mamykina, B. Manoim, M. Mittal, G. Hripcsak, and B. Hartmann. Design lessons from the fastest q&a site in the west. In *Proceedings of the ACM Conference on Human Factors in Computing Systems*, pages 2857–2866, 2011.
20. Y. Mao, H. Shen, and C. Sun. Supporting exploratory information seeking by epistemology-based social search. In *Proceedings of the 15th ACM Conference on Intelligent User Interfaces*, pages 36–39, 2010.
21. M. Merx-Chermin and W. J. Nijhof. Factors influencing knowledge creation and innovation in an organisation. *Journal of European Industrial Training*, 29(2):135–147, 2005.
22. M. R. Morris. A survey of collaborative web search practices. In *CHI'08*, pages 1657–1660, 2008.
23. A. Pal and J. A. Konstan. Expert identification in community question answering: exploring question selection bias. In *Proceedings of the ACM International Conference on Information and Knowledge Management*, pages 1505–1508, 2010.
24. K. Panovich, R. Miller, and D. Karger. Tie strength in question & answer on social network sites. In *Proceedings of the ACM Conference on Computer Supported Cooperative Work*, pages 1057–1066, 2012.
25. C. H. Papadimitriou and K. Steiglitz. On the complexity of local search for the traveling salesman problem. *SIAM Journal on Computing*, 6(1):76–83, 1977.
26. S. Rafaeli, D. R. Raban, and G. Ravid. How social motivation enhances economic activity and incentives in the google answers knowledge sharing market. *International Journal of Knowledge and Learning*, 3(1):1–11, 2007.
27. S. Sahni and T. Gonzalez. P-complete approximation problems. *Journal of the ACM*, 23(3):555–565, 1976.
28. D. H. Shin. Understanding purchasing behaviors in a virtual economy: Consumer behavior involving virtual currency in web 2.0 communities. *Interacting with Computers*, 20(4-5):433–446, 2008.
29. A. Shtok, G. Dror, Y. Maarek, and I. Szpektor. Learning from the past: answering new questions with past answers. In *Proceedings of the 21st international conference on World Wide Web*, pages 759–768, 2012.
30. J. Surowiecki. *The wisdom of crowds: why the many are smarter than the few and how collective wisdom shapes business, economies, societies and nations*. Little, Brown & Company, 2004.
31. R. P. Wagner. Information wants to be free: Intellectual property and the mythologies of control. *Columbia Law Review*, 103, may 2003.
32. J. Yang, M. S. Ackerman, and L. A. Adamic. Virtual Gifts and Guanxi: Supporting Social Exchange in a Chinese Online Community. In *CSCW'11*, pages 45–54, 2011.
33. Z. Zhang and S. M. Jasimuddin. Pricing strategy of online knowledge market: The analysis of google answers. *International Journal of E-Business Research*, 4(1):55–68, 2008.

Real-Time Crowd Labeling for Deployable Activity Recognition

Walter S. Lasecki, Young Chol Song, Henry Kautz, and Jeffrey P. Bigham
University of Rochester Computer Science
{wlasecki, ysong, kautz, jbigham}@cs.rochester.edu

ABSTRACT
Systems that automatically recognize human activities offer the potential of timely, task-relevant information and support. For example, prompting systems can help keep people with cognitive disabilities on track and surveillance systems can warn of activities of concern. Current automatic systems are difficult to deploy because they cannot identify novel activities, and, instead, must be trained in advance to recognize important activities. Identifying and labeling these events is time consuming and thus not suitable for real-time support of already-deployed activity recognition systems. In this paper, we introduce Legion:AR, a system that provides robust, deployable activity recognition by supplementing existing recognition systems with on-demand, real-time activity identification using input from the crowd.

Legion:AR uses activity labels collected from crowd workers to train an automatic activity recognition system online to automatically recognize future occurrences. To enable the crowd to keep up with real-time activities, Legion:AR intelligently merges input from multiple workers into a single ordered label set. We validate Legion:AR across multiple domains and crowds and discuss features that allow appropriate privacy and accuracy tradeoffs.

Author Keywords
Activity Recognition; Crowdsourcing; Human Computation

ACM Classification Keywords
H.4.m Information interfaces and presentation: Misc.

INTRODUCTION
Automatically recognizing human activities offers the potential for timely, task-relevant information and support in diverse domains, such as prompting systems that keep people with cognitive disabilities on track [34], smart homes that detect when to summon help so that older adults can live independently longer [29], and surveillance systems that detect troublesome behavior in busy environments [21]. Unfortunately, recognizing activities in the real world is difficult. The same high-level activity may be performed in very different ways by different people, with different tools, or in different contexts. As a result, identifying activities robustly can require both commonsense knowledge and high-level reasoning. Due to this, automatic approaches to recognizing these activities remain brittle, with the performance of systems highly dependent on the particular instances of an activity and context in which a system has been trained. People are able to recognize these activities well, but are generally not able to supply labels quickly or consistently enough to use in a real system. Moreover, monitoring services that employ trained human workers are prohibitively expensive and introduce privacy concerns. As a result, activity recognition systems are expensive to deploy and difficult to scale.

In this paper, we introduce Legion:AR, a system that combines the benefits of automatic and human activity labeling for more robust, deployable activity recognition. Legion:AR uses an active learning approach [34] in which automatic activity recognition is augmented with on-demand activity labels from the crowd when an observed activity cannot be confidently classified. In contrast to prior systems that have used human labelers to train activity recognition systems offline, Legion:AR is designed to work on-demand and in real-time, allowing the human labels to be integrated directly into the deployed system. By engaging a group of people (*the crowd*), Legion:AR is able to label activities as they occur more reliably than a single person can, especially in complex domains with multiple actors performing activities quickly.

Involving humans in activity recognition naturally raises privacy and confidentiality concerns. In addition to the crowd being a source of anonymous workers who can be completely unknown to the user, Legion:AR includes two features to provide application designers flexibility when choosing how to address these concerns. First, Legion:AR can automatically detect people and veil them by showing only a colored silhouette (Figure 1). We show that, in some common settings, hiding visual details does not significantly affect the quality of the labels generated by human workers. Second, Legion:AR allows designers to provide application users the ability to cancel crowd labeling of activities if they respond within a specified time window, e.g. opt-out via a prompt on a mobile device. Finally, in some domains, people may be willing to give up some privacy to receive the benefits of the system. For instance, older adults may make privacy sacrifices in order to independently live in their homes longer [20]. Because the crowd can be engaged only when automatic activity recognition fails, many of the privacy benefits of a fully-automated system are maintained using Legion:AR.

Figure 1. Worker view of a multi-actor scene from the monitoring domain in which people have been automatically identified and veiled in separate colors to preserve privacy. These veils can cover only the face (as seen in the left two panels), or the entire silhouette of the user ('red' user in the right most panel). Our experiments show that this veiling does not decrease workers' ability to accurately label the activities they are performing.

We explore Legion:AR in the context of two systems that use activity recognition. The first is a prompting system designed to help people with cognitive disabilities keep on track while performing activities of daily living, e.g. making dinner [8]. We test Legion:AR on a set of eight routine tasks in a home environment by training separate Hidden Markov Models (HMMs) using crowd labels generated in real-time and expert labels generated offline. We show that the crowd can outperform single users and that using the labels suggested by the HMM, crowd workers more quickly and accurately converge to consistent labels. The second is a surveillance system that uses a Microsoft Kinect 3D camera to gather visual data from self-service snack store in our department. We then used Legion:AR to label the activities of people near the store, e.g. choosing a snack, buying a snack, walking past. With this example, we demonstrate both that Legion:AR is able to label the activities of multiple actors simultaneously, and that the system can label activities accurately even when people are veiled in a colored silhouette to conceal their identity. We then show that workers are able to jointly generate accurate labels at different hierarchical levels, allowing Legion:AR to collect a richer sets of tags than even trained labelers.

Our contributions are the following:

- We introduce a system that enables the crowd to collectively label activities on-demand in real-time, and performs active learning from crowd-generated labels.
- We demonstrate that groups of workers (even anonymous web workers) are able to reliably generate *consistent* labels, in real-time, that are more accurate and complete than that of a single worker with the help of our system.
- We articulate the idea for creating more deployable activity recognition systems by supplementing automatic approaches with on-demand crowd labeling.
- We present features that application designers can employ to appropriately balance privacy and functionality in systems that use activity recognition.
- We demonstrate that workers can label activities of desired individual actors in scene containing multiple people, with varying granularity, even while preserving the privacy of users by automatically veiling people in video.

THE CROWD

We identify users as people whose activities are being identified and workers as members of the crowd helping to generate label data. We define *the crowd* as a dynamic pool of possibly anonymous workers of varying reliability that can be recruited on-demand. Because the pool is dynamic, workers come and go, and no specific worker can be relied upon to be available at a given time or to continue working on a job for a set amount of time. Workers cannot be relied upon to provide high-quality work of the type one might expect from a traditional employee for various reasons including misunderstanding of task directives, laziness, or even maliciousness. Finally, workers may experience delays that are beyond their control, such as network bandwidth variability.

For enabling real-time activity recognition, the dimensions of the crowd that are most relevant are (i) the time each recruited worker continues working on the task and (ii) the quality of the worker's output. These can be measured empirically for a specific crowd source, but are expected to be task-dependent [30]. A related dimension is the latency required to recruit workers to a particular job. Our system builds on prior work that has shown workers can reliably be recruited in seconds by using pre-recruiting and retainer pools [3, 4].

In this paper, we run experiments using pools of workers drawn both from local study participants and from Amazon's Mechanical Turk. For some applications that require real-time activity recognition, companies may find value in offering vetted pools of workers [2]; in others, family members or other trusted individuals may form the crowd. As a web-based framework, Legion:AR is compatible with diverse worker pools, and users may select the types of crowds that will power the system. Even when workers are trusted, Legion:AR is still a benefit because it allows workers the flexibility to come and go, and allows the group to collectively provide better and more complete labels than the average constituent labeling individually.

RELATED WORK

Legion:AR builds on work in both activity recognition and real-time human computation. In recent years, the development of small unobtrusive sensors has made it practical to create smart environments that can both recognize our ac-

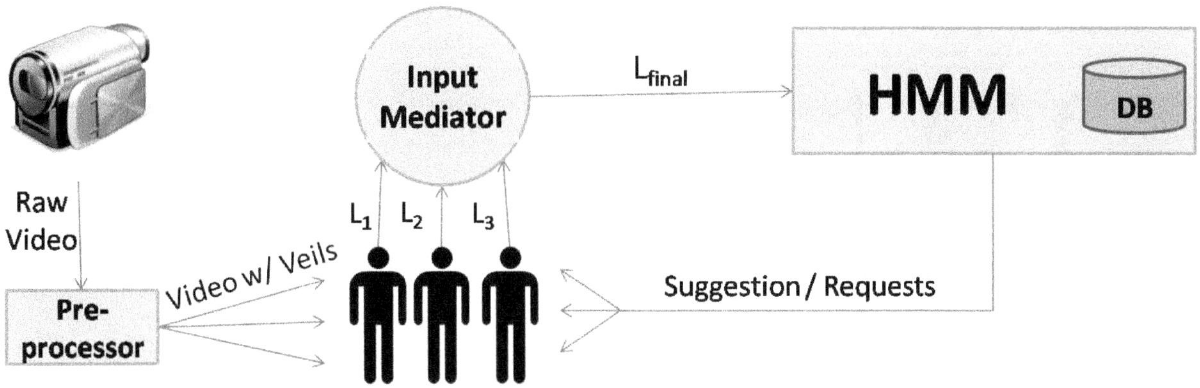

Figure 2. The Legion:AR system. When the automatic system (HMM) is unconfident about an activity label, it requests labels from the crowd. Crowd workers are able to see the system's predicted activity label and either validate it or propose a new label of their own. The labels from the crowd workers (L_i) are sent back to Legion:AR, which then determines a final label and uses it and the associated segment of sensor data to train the HMM. The HMM adds this to its model in order to identify the activity later and forward that prediction back to the crowd.

tions and act to improve our experience in the environment. The importance of these environments has emerged especially in the area of automated health monitoring, where there is tremendous need to promote aging in place and improve quality of life for the elderly [19]. However, accurate detection of activities in the home is challenging because of the wide range of possible activities. Crucial events in health monitoring, such as user errors, and critical actions, such as falling, occur randomly and are rarely observed. While an automated activity recognition system may perform accurately in well-trained situations, it is impossible to train all possible activities ahead of time in a deployed system. Legion:AR fills in the gap left by automated systems by leveraging the crowd.

Prior work in activity recognition has addressed the need to gather instances of activities in diverse contexts by engaging groups of people. A common use of human effort in activity recognition is for offline labeling, in which people label the activities in a video and this data is used to inform the learning model [34, 35]. These approaches have shown that both small controlled crowds and larger ones, such as Amazon's Mechanical Turk, are capable of providing effective training data. Another common approach is to ask users to perform and annotate activities in the contexts in which they want them to be recognized [1]. Crowdsourcing has been used to gather labels from many users, associate new users with existing personas, and then allow individuals to correct mislabeling of their activities [13]. In contrast to these approaches, Legion:AR enables the crowd to label activities in real-time, allowing it to correctly label novel events on their first occurrence. For home monitoring, this means that potentially harmful events, such as an individual cutting oneself with a knife, can be identified the first time they happen. Likewise, for public monitoring domains, criminal acts, fires, or other dangerous events can be correctly reported even if the system was not trained specifically for the event. To our knowledge, Legion:AR is the first system to employ the crowd in real-time to augment activity recognition systems so that they can respond interactively to novel activities and contexts.

Legion:AR is an example of human computation: integrating people into computational processes to solve problems too difficult for computers. Human computation has been shown useful in a variety of domains, e.g. writing and editing [6], image description and interpretation [3, 31], and protein folding [9]. Most work in human computation has focused on obtaining quality work from an unreliable pool of workers, and has generally introduced redundancy and layering into tasks so that multiple workers contribute and verify results at each stage. For instance, guaranteeing reliability through answer agreement [31] or the find-fix-verify pattern of Soylent [6]. Unfortunately, these approaches take time, making them less well-suited to real-time tasks such as activity recognition.

Several systems have explored how to make human computation interactive. As an example, VizWiz [3] answers visual questions for blind people quickly. It uses quikTurkit to pre-queue workers on Amazon's Mechanical Turk so that they will be available when needed. Adrenaline uses a retainer model to recruit workers in just a few seconds to enable real-time photography assistance [4]. The Legion system enables real-time collaborative control of an existing user interface by allowing the crowd to collectively act as a single operator [15]. Individual crowd workers input suggestions as to what commands should be executed next, and the Legion system uses an 'input mediator' to intelligently choose which to forward to the actual interface based on such metrics as "crowd agreement." Legion:AR builds on this framework and workflow, and introduces the idea of forwarding not only select single inputs, but also sequences of inputs that are generated by merging multiple different workers contributions. This effectively expands the model introduced in Legion to handle situations in which the problem is not only the reliability of individual workers, but also the inability to provide answers at a sufficient rate, such as providing natural language activity, action, and object labels for complex actions. Legion:AR includes an HMM to learn from those labels, and introduces a number of other features specific to this domain, e.g. those features included specifically to address privacy concerns.

Prior work has looked into using multiple camera angles to allow automatic systems to use silhouettes in addition to RFID tags to recognize activities while preserving the anonymity of users in a home activity domain [22]. Other systems have

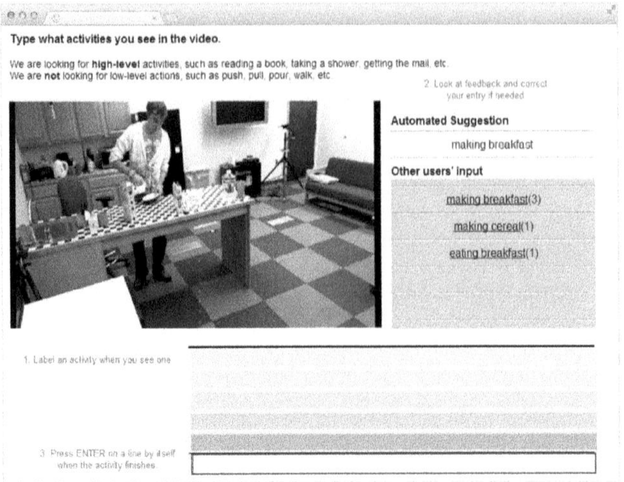

Figure 3. The Legion:AR worker interface. Workers watch live video of an activity and enter open-ended text labels into the text field below. They can see labels from other workers and the learning model (HMM) on the right, and can agree with them by clicking on them. Workers also indicate when activities have ended in order to segment the video.

used simple anonymous sensors such as motion detectors and pressure mats along with RFID tags to maintain a certain amount of privacy when detecting activities in the home [32]. We use a similar approach with Legion:AR, using RFID tags and automatically generating privacy veils to cover each user. Since people are able to gain more information from context, we show that it is not always necessary to use multiple cameras at different angles (though improvement could still be seen when more are available). Reducing the amount of information introduces a tradeoff between levels of privacy and activity awareness. Some of these tradeoffs have been explored in a workplace setting by [12].

Legion:AR

Legion:AR consists of three primary components (Figure 2): (i) the worker interface for displaying data and collecting real-time labels, (ii) an input mediator that collects inputs from multiple crowd workers and merges them into a final activity segment and label set, and (iii) an automatic activity recognition system that uses an HMM to identify activities. Applications using Legion:AR for activity recognition provide a data stream that is used by the HMM to generate an activity label. If it cannot confidently derive a label from the stream, then it asks the crowd to label the activity. Currently, it uses a variant of quikTurkit [3] to recruit crowd workers within a few seconds. Crowd workers see the worker interface (Figure 3) and either type the activities they see in the included video or agree with activity labels provided by others. These labels are sent back to Legion:AR, which merges the input of multiple workers by associating overlapping labels and inserting new ones into an ordered stream. Legion:AR then forwards the labels and corresponding segmentation to the HMM to be used for training so that the activity can be recognized later.

Requesters begin by starting the Legion:AR application and providing a data stream. Our current implementation of Legion:AR uses a HMM that can be trained using either video and RFID data, or visual data from a Microsoft Kinect. RFID data is collected from a powered, wrist-mounted RFID reader worn by users. The visual data is collected via cameras mounted in the area in which activities are to be observed.

These sensors provide a fine-grained context for recognizing individuals and their activities. RFID tags provide a rich source of context information through object interactions. Activity recognition using RFIDs are shown to be extremely accurate if users and environments are correctly instrumented [24]. However, in some situation this may be difficult and accuracy can fall due to some interactions not being picked up [17]. The tradeoffs involved in selecting a source of feature data for the automated system when using Legion:AR are the same as in traditional AR. In our kitchen lab environment, multiple RFID tags are instrumented on each object, and each RFID tag is uniquely identified for the object it is attached. Users then wore an RFID sensor on their wrists. We also use a Kinect, which is capable of detecting distinct individuals via its capability to differentiate multiple people from the background, making it possible to easily create separate per-user streams for each individual in the scene. User tracking is provided by the Kinect, which enables us to easily distinguish each person in the scene and veil their silhouettes accordingly. In our current system, we focus on indoor activities with relatively few ($n \leq 6$) people. However, our method of real-time crowd labeling can also be extended to outdoor activities and crowded environments using different sensors such as video cameras [11], accelerometers [1] and GPS [26].

Hidden Markov models and their variations have previously been successfully used for accurately modeling activities for recognition, and has been shown effective for modeling high-level activities such as the ones recognized in this paper [25]. Given sensor data from RFID tags or from the Kinect, and the activity from the previous time step, we try to classify what the current activity is. In this task, we use a HMM where each activity is represented as a single state. While this model is sufficient for our evaluations, we can also easily extend the model to recognize more complex activities [10, 24]. A simplified state diagram of our model is shown in Figure 4.

Generating Tasks

Legion:AR uses active learning to increase its knowledge of potential actions. Using multiple annotators who remain present for the entire task for active learning has shown to be effective [33]. However, prior work has not yet investigated this problem when workers are dynamic and change from moment to moment, meaning that the "best" worker to ask a specific question cannot be learned in most cases.

When Legion:AR does not recognize an activity that is being performed, it streams video to be labeled by the crowd. The stream is first fed through a pre-processor (custom for each input type) then identifies the number of actors visible in a scene and adds privacy veils when appropriate (discussed below). If multiple actors are detected in the scene, each one is marked using a different colored outline on the video to differentiate them for workers, then an individual labeling task is generated for each. This way, workers never have to focus on

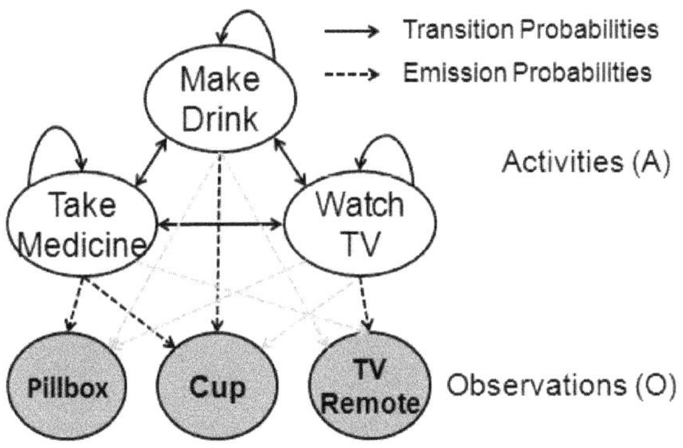

Figure 4. State Diagram of a single state per-activity HMM.

more than one user's actions and coordination between multiple crowd workers is easier, keeping the task simple enough for workers from sources such as Mechanical Turk to complete for a low price (under 10 cents per 90 second segment in our experiments). In this paper, we perform this segmentation using the Kinect SDK to reliably isolate each user.

Legion:AR begins to recruit workers into a waiting pool when started, so that workers can be ready on-demand. Workers can be recruited from any source of participants, but in this paper we considered only local volunteers and workers from Mechanical Turk. Once workers enter the waiting pool, they are paid a small amount of money to play a simple game. This game keeps workers focused on the current window, reducing the time needed to begin labeling once a task is issued. When the HMM encounters an activity it does not recognize with sufficient confidence, it makes a request to issue a new task.

Worker Interface

Once a task is generated, workers are immediately forwarded from the waiting screen to the labeling interface (Figure 3) which contains a video stream, text box, history of previous labels, and a field which displays the recent input of other workers performing the task and the HMM's best guess. Workers can either choose to enter a new label for the activity if the correct one has not yet been proposed, or they may select a previous answer proposed by another worker.

Once workers enter a label it is displayed in the current options viewer, making it visible to the other workers completing the task. Workers can change their answers at any time before the end of an activity in an attempt to agree with the best one. This style of interface provides two benefits: i) providing examples encourages workers to use similar phrasing in their answers, and ii) people are generally able to identify correct answers better than they can generate them [28]. Thus, this interface helps promote consistent labels that allow for more reliable learning from multiple sessions, and gives workers a better chance to be accurate. When a worker believes the current activity has ended, they signal this by submitting a blank label, or selecting 'Activity Complete'. The worker's input is then sent to Legion:AR's input mediator.

Combining Input

In order to recombine the input from participating workers, we assume workers each submit ordered, but incomplete, sets of labels for a task. These labels may correspond to slightly different definitions of a task with different beginning and ending times, and may be time shifted by varying amounts, so we cannot simply associate tags based on timing data.

Instead, we match labels entered by a single worker with the similar inputs from others in the same time window (we use 15 seconds). We use the label viewer on the worker interface to encourage workers to use similar terms, then use a relaxed measure of equality based on the Damerau-Levenshtein distance (similar to edit distance) which measures how many corrections must be made to a word or phrase to match another to account for typos. We set a dynamic cutoff of approximately 1 error per 5 letters typed, then consider any two words within this distance as equivalent. A structured language corpus such as WordNet [18] could also be used to consider semantic similarity between terms.

Worker labels and their equivalents are then merged into single nodes in a graph, given one is not already an ancestor of the others. This prevents cycles in the graph and leverages the proper-ordering assumption we made earlier. As nodes are added and merged, a directed acyclic graph is formed (shown in Figure 5). The nodes are weighted with the number of matched inputs they contain, and edges are weighted using the number of inputs in both the parent and child that were generated sequentially by the same user. For example, if 8 workers said "making coffee" (parent node), 6 workers said "making breakfast" (child node), and 3 of those workers said both in a row, then "making coffee" (weight 8) is linked to "making breakfast" (weight 6) by an edge of weight 3. As multiple partial sequences are aligned, we can use a most-likely traversal to recreate the original (correct) sequence of labels. Based on the tuning parameters of this traversal, more complete or more accurate label sequences can be recovered. Furthermore, since the algorithm works even when we limit the size of the current graph to only recent events, Legion:AR can be used to label video streams of unbounded length.

The power of this approach is that it runs fast enough to combine input without adding any additional delay (few milliseconds), and branches can be merged to increase the total recall of the final output. This can be done using a statistical model of actions that is learned over time, so as more activities are seen by the system, the better it becomes at predicting the order of actions. Alternatively, the graph can be greedily traversed to find the best sequence of labels to use. This approach scales better, but cannot account for ambiguity in the graph created by worker's input as well. After the sequence is reconstructed, it is then paired with the feature data recorded during the segment by either the RFID sensor or Kinect, and used to train the HMM on new activities, in real-time.

Multiple Actors

To label activities in scenes with multiple users, such as public spaces, we can use the same process described above, but with a separate crowd, task, and input mediator instance for each user in the scene. Users are made identifiable by coloring the veil that hides their identity, then asking workers to provide labels for the user of a specific color. Individual sets of labels can then be provided by workers for each individual.

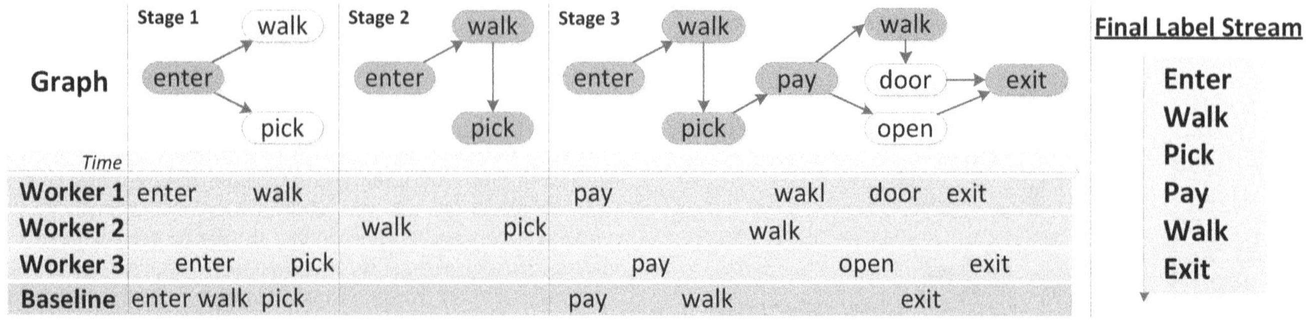

Figure 5. An example of the graph created by the input mediator. Green nodes represent sufficient agreement between multiple workers (here $N = 2$). The final sequence is correct despite overly-specific submissions by 2 out of the 3 workers, and a spelling error by one worker on the word 'walk'.

The system can also select a subset of users that it is unsure of the activities of rather than all of them, which helps to reduce cost. For instance, in the case where Legion:AR is being used to monitor an entire public square, there may potentially be hundreds of actors, but if only a single one is performing an unknown activity, we would only generate one task.

Complex Labels

Using multiple sets of workers each belonging to a different task can also independently label a different aspect of the activity such as the objects being used, the fine-grained actions being performed, or the effect of the current action. This can then be used to build (from a pre-defined set of relations) a more complex label consisting of each of these aspects being described at every point in time. For instance, we can label what agents, objects, and actions a given activity consists of by using sets of workers to each gather agent, object, action and activity labels. Providing the relationships between the data (and thus between the labels provided by workers) allows us to automatically recombine the labels to generate tags of a specific form. This works because in our tests, we found that workers were able to divide tasks into consistent segments given the same instructions, even if their labels differed when no special measures were taken.

Training the Learning Model

The HMM is given a sequence of labels and time segmentation intervals generated by the workers, and a stream of RFID tags recorded from the RFID reader on the user's wrist. Each interval has a matching label and a set of RFID tags that the HMM can train. Legion:AR is capable of training the HMM online, by using the sequence of labels and corresponding tags just as they would be if provided by an expert, as they are finalized by workers. Additionally, the learning model can be modified to provide feedback to Legion:AR such as its prediction of the current action, which is then forwarded to workers as a suggestion which they can agree with if correct. Using the underlying model to suggest answers can greatly reduce the amount of effort that volunteer workers will have to put in for actions that have already been learned (but still have low confidence) by the system.

Privacy Protection

In activity recognition, privacy is always a key topic. This is especially true in the case of Legion:AR since it can potentially be used to stream live video of a person's home or specific public location to a work force comprised of anonymous people on the web. Since some level of information must be exposed to workers in order to allow them to accurately label activities, users must use discretion in their use of the system and system developers must make users aware of the trade-off between privacy versus recognition accuracy. We discuss some of the ways Legion:AR tries to help mitigate potential privacy concerns below.

Video Adjustments

To help obfuscates the identities of users, Legion:AR automatically hides their face (or even whole body) with a virtual *veil* (shown in Figure 1). However, this is does not preserve the anonymity of the surroundings in applications such as the home monitoring domain. To prevent detailed information from sources such as bills or other paperwork being forwarded to the crowd, we can use a low video resolution between 300×200 and 640×480. In initial tests, workers showed no difference in their ability to identify actions if given a higher resolution video. Legion:AR can also ensure no single worker from the crowd stays longer than a short period of time to prevent any one worker from collecting too much information about a person's routine or surroundings.

While our results indicate that veils and low resolution do not significantly reduce the recognition quality, it's clear that there is still a tradeoff. For example, if a user wants to hide their race, gender, or clothing from workers, covering their entire silhouette with a veil would be effective. However, to hide information such as height or weight, the system could veil the user entirely with an ambiguous shape (i.e. circle or rectangle). However, we expect this would have a significant impact on workers' ability to identify what action is being performed since little more than position would be available.

Opt-In/Out System

Legion:AR also uses a mobile app to prompt users before displaying video to the crowd, instead of letting the system decide by itself. When Legion:AR identifies a segment of actions it does not recognize, an alert to use the crowd to label the segment of video is sent to the user's phone or other mobile device. These alerts can be set to either opt-in, which may be useful when privacy is the primary focus, or op-out which is better suited to monitoring for critical events such as accidents in the home, where the user may not be able to answer the alert afterwards. In public setting where many users might be present, the system is not able to use opt-in feature.

Future implementations could use facial recognition to allow the ability for users opt-out of content being forwarded to the crowd by contacting the system with an image of themselves. This registration can be done once, and the system would remember their preferences when it recognizes them again later.

EXPERIMENTS

Legion:AR is capable of training activity recognition systems online. To validate this, we show that groups of workers can accurately generate labels in real-time, even while preserving the privacy of the actors in the scene. We then demonstrate that the system is able to automatically generate tasks that are manageable for single workers on crowd markets such as Amazon's Mechanical Turk, and that workers will label the correct aspect of the scene (the actions of the individual actor they were assigned to). Finally, we extend the idea of assigning groups of crowd workers to different sub-tasks, and demonstrate that, using Legion:AR, workers can label tasks at even fine granularities, allowing the system to collect more detailed activity labels than would be possible for a single worker to generate in real-time.

Real-time Activity Label Generation

To test the ability of groups of workers to generate labels for activities in real-time, we ran Legion:AR on a video stream of a person performing various household tasks in our lab, which is configured as a kitchen and living room. This recreates a scene which may be observed when monitoring elderly or cognitively disabled individuals to ensure they are performing necessary activities such as eating, taking medicine, toileting, and to monitor for situations where they may need assistance, such as a medical emergency.

Our crowd was composed of volunteers who had no prior experience with the system and were given a brief verbal description of how to label the data. In a real use-case, members of the crowd would differ from day to day, and having different workers at different times will likely effect the terminology used to label the same activities from one session to the next. We recreated these factors by scheduling tests on different days, with workers selected at random from the available set of 30 volunteers. Trials were not excluded for workers who misunderstood the directions or had connectivity issues, as this is expected in the real-world case. We ran 8 tests, each with 5 of the 8 different activities performed in them. Each of these activities was deliberately performed quickly (on the order of 10-30 seconds) in order to test the ability of the 5-worker group to agree in a short period of time. As activity times get longer, there is more time for the workers to converge on an answer and agreement becomes easier. We compared the results gathered from both a group of workers collaborating in real-time via our system and a single worker, to an expert labeling by training an HMM using the approach and comparing the resulting performance.

We conducted a leave-one-out cross validation of 8 activity sequences. The HMM was first trained online with worker generated labels and RFID observations from the training set, and then tested using the RFID sensor data from the test set. The output of the automated system was then compared with

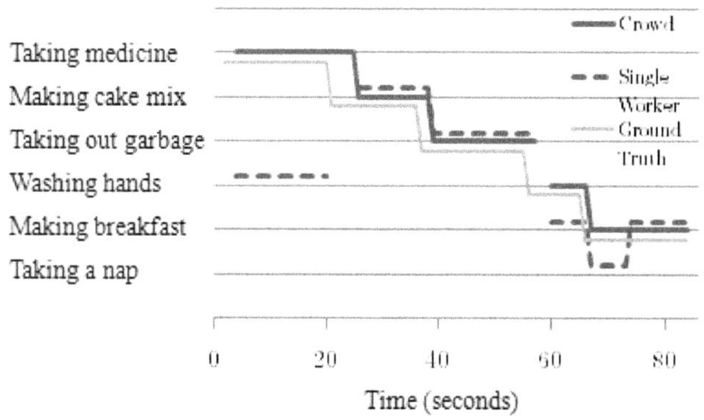

Figure 6. Automated recognition results. Inference results for a single activity sequence trained from crowd-generated labels (thick solid line) compared with the single worker labels (dotted line) and ground truth (thin solid line). Crowd-generated labels are more complete, allowing the automated system to do better when trained on them.

labels from the expert. However, since the expert labels differ from crowd generated labels, we manually associated each crowd label with a corresponding expert label for comparison. Our results show that the automated recognition system trained from crowd generated labels was able to achieve high average precision (90.2%) and was also able to recall all of the conducted activities, while the system trained from individual workers provided relatively noisy results (66.7% and 78% average precision and recall, respectively).

These labels were also highly consistent over multiple labels for the same actions, generating 8 unique labels for the activities shown. Since the system would automatically propose a label for actions it had seen already, the crowd was able to see previous best answers and agree with them, rather than generating a new name for each occurrence. This consistency is a key element of the labels produced by Legion:AR because it allows the system to accurately associate repeated events when it sees them again later, possibly performed in a slightly different way. For examples, without strong agreement the HMM might think that 'preparing breakfast' and 'making breakfast' are different activities, increasing the difficulty of the learning problem. The labels were also generated quickly enough to forward back to the system within seconds – fast enough to respond to critical events effectively.

Automatic Suggestions

We also tested what effect having the system propose possible answers as if it were an additional worker would have on the overall task performance, and the amount of effort required from the workers. We ran a new test with a different set of workers using the home monitoring data, and a system trained on each trial collected from the first run except for the one being tested on. The HMM constantly provided its prediction of what the current action was, and workers could accept this prediction if they agreed it was correct. While the results of the segmentation did not improve significantly, 80% of workers mentioned that using automatic suggestions made it easier to quickly agree with others on a shared label for the task being observed (between multiple runs). This is because it reduces the amount of search that must be done for an appropriate label.

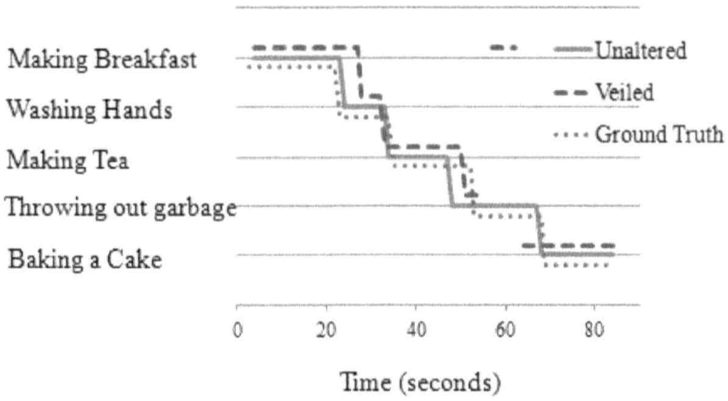

Figure 7. Crowd labeling results for a single activity sequence with veiled user (dashed red line) compared with labels of workers viewing the original unaltered video (solid line) and ground truth (thin dotted line).

Privacy

Since Legion:AR's automatically generated privacy veils obscure part of the video image, potentially making it more difficult for some activities to be identified, we ran tests to confirm that workers were still able to identify activities in the augmented video.

We re-ran a set of trials from the initial tests, again with 5 new workers. The results are shown in Figure 7. Only one label was missed due to the obfuscation of the user. This was caused by the veil generation on basic video being more imprecise than it was with the Kinect, resulting in covering all of the objects in front of a user, instead of being able to identify and cover only a person's body, or, if desired, even just their head and face. These findings agree with previous work using blur and pixelation filters that showed hiding identity in video clips could be done without having a detrimental effect on people's ability to identify properties of the scene such as position, number of actors, and level of activity [7].

Multi-actor Scenes

Next, we looked at how Legion:AR could be used in a more complex environment with multiple actors and activities occurring on at once. We mounted a Kinect near our department snack store to monitor people using this public space and watch for critical events such as theft, or accidents.

Because public space monitoring occurs on a much larger scale than home monitoring, there is a smaller group of concerned potential volunteers relative to the number of observed domains. As such it is important to show that other work forces beyond just volunteers, can effectively generate labels such as these.

We first evaluated the ability of workers recruited from Mechanical Turk to label specific workers based on their veil color. The results showed that over 11 trials, workers got on average 85% correct. There was no significant correlation between the number of actors in the scene and the quality of the labels generated by workers.

Complex Labels

In many domains, it is useful to have more fine grained labels including specific actions and what objects are being used. To produce these complex labels, we extend the procedure used to label scenes with multiple actors by using multiple crowds

Entering	Stealing	Purchasing
walking	going back	counting money
standing	picking up	paying
walking into the room	walking	removing purse
leaving	grabbing something	pays for item

Figure 8. Activities and corresponding worker labels excerpts from the multi-actor scene.

Watching TV	*Actions*	Placing, Clicking, Pointing, Carrying, Watching
	Objects	TV, Television, Remote, Controller, Couch
Making Tea	*Actions*	Making, Drinking, Holding, Opening, Picking up
	Objects	Tea, Mug, Cup, Packet, Kettle
Taking Medicine	*Actions*	Sipping, Swallowing, Drinking, Taking, Opening
	Objects	Pills, Bottle, Medicine, Water, Cup

Figure 9. Selected subset of action and object tags generated by five workers for three activities.

instead of just one. By first defining the structure of a label, then dividing it into smaller labeling tasks, multiple groups of workers can provide independent sets of labels that can then be automatically merged.

We tested this by using two groups of volunteer workers. One group was instructed to label the actions being performed at each step, and the other was asked to list the objects being used in the current action. There were 25 actions and 28 objects that the user interacted with in two video sequences. Figure 9 shows the results from 5 workers generating tags.

As a baseline, we used an expert labeler who was experienced in annotating video for activity recognition. They were allowed to label and segment the video entirely offline and could replay and pause the video at will.

Individually, workers labeled an average of 48% of the objects used in the videos, while 5 workers were able to identify 90% (Figure 10). Additionally, workers correctly identified 12 unique objects that did not appear in the expert-labeled baseline. For actions, individual workers labeled an average of 32% of the actions used in the video, while 5 workers were able to identify 66%, with 24 unique actions that were not included in our baseline. For example, the crowd correctly identified both 'picking up' and 'clicking' on the remote, where the expert labeler only included 'picking up'.

The results can then be combined with the activity data using the timestamps, resulting in statements of the form:

`(clicking)` using `(remote control)` as part of `(watching TV)`

Using this type of fine grained labeling, we can provide a system trying to reason about the actions with more detailed information, such as hierarchical structure and the roles of different objects. We can also forward RFID data to workers to allow them to select which objects being read by the scanner rather than enter new labels which must be associated with the tags. Providing this information may also reduce the number of workers required to obtain high-quality results.

DISCUSSION

The results described in the previous section demonstrate that crowds of workers, both volunteer and paid, can accomplish the task of real-time label generation faster and more effec-

Figure 10. Average number of objects and actions correctly labeled by worker groups of different sizes over two different activity sequences. As the group size increases, more objects and actions are labeled.

tively than an individual could. In the fine-grained tests, even when compared to our experienced labeler (who generated labels offline), workers were able to find additional actions that had been overlooked in our baseline. This improvement demonstrates the potential for crowds to generate labels that are more comprehensive, as well as available quicker.

Collaborative Label Generation

We observed that users of Legion:AR seemed more comfortable in their task than those working alone. Exit interviews revealed that this was in large part because they received validation from the system, through either the automatic AR system or other workers, that they were providing the correct types of answers. Additionally, since each worker is required to do less work on average to contribute a single label, we can reduce the number of workers that are needed to attain agreement on every segment label.

Interface Improvements

Worker feedback also showed that most workers were able to quickly learn and easily use the labeling UI, but many found the change in modality between proposing a label using the keyboard and agree with a label using the mouse to be a hinderance. Because of this, several workers just retyped the content they saw in the label set from other workers, which the system then counted as a vote. In future versions we will address this issue by providing a optional number-based selection scheme that can quickly and easily be operated via keyboard, or adding auto-complete to reduce the worker's required effort. Some workers also noted that the positioning of the answer box relative to the video display made it more difficult to view the responses of other while still paying attention to the video. This can be addressed by relocating the suggestion list directly below the video so that the content is more in-line with the label entry and selection fields.

FUTURE WORK

Legion:AR enables a wide range of interactive applications and collaborative tasks that could benefit from activity recognition. For example, in game playing, a system may want to interact with a human player by observing their the actions, without having to first learn a set of actions before being functional. Streaming video of a video game or other desktop application instead of a camera is supported by Legion:AR— all that needs to be defined is a method for the HMM to receive feature data from the environment. Other applications such as public virtual assistants may seek to leverage knowledge about the user's actions even during one-off interactions.

Intent Recognition and Modeling Failed Attempts

Prior work has presented models of intent recognition by using a model that looks at both movement and interactions with other actors in the scene [26], and that modeling failures can improve classification accuracy when using specific learning models [27]. We plan to explore how the crowd can work collaboratively with the system to leverage these models by labeling subtle events, such as when two actors interact or when a user fails to complete an attempted action, then letting the system use the labels to infer actions. This could enable models that are able to identify suspicious actions before they occur, even before fully trained — further reducing response times and even helping prevent critical events.

Merging Crowd Input

Many tasks require special skills to complete, even if no special knowledge is required. In most cases, specially trained individuals exist who can perform these tasks, such as a professional captionist hired to transcribe audio to text in real-time. However, due to the requisite skill and training involved, these individuals are rare and come at a high cost.

In this work, we use a general framework for allowing groups of non-expert workers to collectively generate complete input even when no individual member of the group is capable of doing so individually. This is done by intelligently merging the input of all contributing workers. We used this approach in two forms: in the first, we averaged the workers' segment boundary times, and in the other we merged their labels.

Future systems using this framework need only to define the answer stream they want from the system, then present appropriate information to workers. For example, Legion:Scribe is a system that enables groups of non-expert workers recruited from local sources [16] or the crowd [14] to caption audio in real-time. Scribe builds of off of the same basic model as Legion:AR, but uses a fully automated approach to synthesize worker input into a single caption stream based on implicit agreement. On the other hand, in cases where there is no shared 'true' answer as there is with captioning, we have shown that the answers generated by groups of workers on more open-ended problems can be made consistent between sessions by displaying the group's answer proposals along the way. This makes the training process more tractable for the underlying learning model.

CONCLUSION

In this paper, we outlined a framework for using groups of non-expert workers to contribute information that would usually need to be generated by a trained expert. We demonstrated the utility of this approach using Legion:AR, a system for training an arbitrary activity recognition system in real-time using a crowd of workers. Legion:AR enables workers to collectively provide labels even in situations where a single user cannot, allowing systems to be trained online even in complex domains, thus avoiding the risk of missing an important event that requires immediate response the first time it is observed. We have shown that groups of workers can successfully label tasks in real-time using Legion:AR, even when no individual worker provides completely correct input. Furthermore, we found that the labels generated by groups of workers can outperform any single online worker, and even generate correct tags that were missed by an expert offline labeler. We also demonstrated methods for dividing complex tasks into forms that workers from multiple types of crowds, such as those available from micro-task marketplaces including Mechanical Turk, can accomplish collectively. Legion:AR provides the foundations for systems that can be deployed in a wide range of real-world setting with no prior training, and enables new applications of AR in situations where identifying user actions with only one-off observations is important.

REFERENCES

1. L. Bao and S. S. Intille Activity Recognition from User-Annotated Acceleration Data. *In Proc. of Pervasive 2004*, v. 3001/2004, pp. 1-17, 2004.
2. J.P. Bigham, R.E. Ladner, and Y. Borodin. The Design of the Human-Backed Access Technology. *In Proc. of the ACM Intl. Conf. on Computers and Accessibility (ASSETS 2011)*, pp. 3-10, 2011.
3. J.P Bigham, C. Jayant, H. Ji, G. Little, A. Miller, R.C. Miller, R. Miller, A. Tatrowicz, B. White, S. White, and T. Yeh. VizWiz: Nearly Real-time Answers to Visual Questions. *Proc. of the ACM Symp. on User Interface Software and Technology (UIST 2010)*, pp. 333-342, 2010.
4. Michael S. Bernstein, Joel R. Brandt, Robert C. Miller, and David R. Karger. Crowds in two seconds: Enabling realtime crowd-powered interfaces. In *Proc. of the 24th Symp. on User Interface Software and Technology (UIST 2011)*, 2011.
5. M. S. Bernstein, D. R. Karger, R. C. Miller, and J. Brandt. Analytic methods for optimizing realtime crowdsourcing. In *Proc. of Collective Intelligence (CI 2012)*, To Appear, 2012.
6. M. S. Bernstein, G. Little, R. C. Miller, B. Hartmann, M. S. Ackerman, D. R. Karger, D. Crowell, and K. Panovich. Soylent: a word processor with a crowd inside. *Proc. of the ACM Sypm. on User Interface Software and Tech. (UIST 2010)*, pp. 313–322, 2010.
7. M. Boyle, C. Edwards, and S. Greenberg. The effects of filtered video on awareness and privacy. *Proceedings of the 2000 ACM conference on Computer supported cooperative work*, pp. 1–10, 2000.
8. Y. Chu, Y.C. Song, H. Kautz, and R. Levinson. When Did You Start Doing That Thing That You Do? Interactive Activity Recognition and Prompting. *AAAI 2011 Workshop on Artificial Intelligence and Smarter Living*. 2011.
9. S. Cooper, F. Khatib, A. Treuille, J. Barbero, J. Lee, M. Beenen, A. Leaver-Fay, D. Baker, Z. Popovic, and FoldIt Players. Predicting protein structures with a multiplayer online game. *Nature*, 466(7307):756–760, 2010.
10. T. Duong, H. Bui, D. Phung, and S. Venkatesh. Activity Recognition and Abnormality Detection with the Switching Hidden Semi-Markov Model. *Proc. IEEE Conf. Computer Vision and Pattern Recognition, vol. 1*, pp. 838–845, 2005.
11. L. Fiore, D. Fehr, R. Bodor, A. Drenner, G. Somasundaram, and N. Papanikolopoulos. Multi-camera human activity monitoring. *Journal of Intelligent and Robotic Systems, vol. 52*, pp. 5-43, 2008.
12. S. Hudson, and I. Smith. Techniques for addressing fundamental privacy and disruption tradeoffs in awareness support systems. *Proceedings of the 1996 ACM conference on Computer supported cooperative work*, pp. 248–257, 1996.
13. N. Lane, Y. Xu, H. Lu, S. Hu, T. Choudhury, A. Campbell, and F. Zhao. Enabling Large-scale Human Activity Inference on Smartphones using Community Similarity Networks *Proc. of Ubicomp 2011*, 2011.
14. W.S. Lasecki, J.P. Bigham. Online Quality Control for Real-time Crowd Captioning. In *Proc. of the ACM International Conference on Computers and Accessibility (ASSETS 2012)*, pp. 143-150, 2012.
15. W.S. Lasecki, K.I. Murray, S. White, R.C. Miller, J.P. Bigham. Real-Time Crowd Control of Existing Interfaces. In *Proc. of the ACM Symp. on User Interface Software and Technology (UIST 2011)*, pp. 23-32, 2011.
16. W.S. Lasecki, C.D. Miller, A. Sadilek, A. Abumoussa, D. Borrello, R. Kushalnagar, J.P. Bigham. Real-Time Captioning by Groups of Non-Experts. In *Proc. of the ACM Symp. on User Interface Software and Technology (UIST 2012)*, pp. 23-34, 2012.
17. B. Logan, J. Healey, M. Philipose, E. Tapia, and S. Intille. A Long-term Evaluation of Sensing Modalities for Activity Recognition. *Proceedings of the 9th international conference on Ubiquitous computing*, pp. 483–500, 2007.
18. G. Miller. Wordnet: A lexical database for English. *Comm. ACM 38, 11*. pp. 3941, 1995.
19. J. Modayil, R. Levinson, C. Harman, D. Halper, and H. Kautz. Integrating Sensing and Cueing for more effective Activity Reminders. *Proc. of the AAAI Fall 2008 Symp. on AI in Eldercare: New Solutions to Old Problems*. pp. 60-66, 2008.
20. E.D. Mynatt, A.S. Melenhorst, A. D. Fisk, W. A. Rogers Aware technologies for aging in place: understanding user needs and attitudes. *Pervasive Computing, IEEE*, v3-2, pp. 36-41, 2004.
21. W. Niu, J. Long, D. Han, and Y-F. Wang. Human activity detection and recognition for video surveillance. *Proc. of ICME 2004*, pp. 719-722, 2005.
22. S. Park and H. Kautz Privacy-Preserving Recognition of Activities in Daily Living From Multi-View Silhouettes and RFID-Based Training. *AAAI Symp. on AI in Eldercare: New Solutions to Old Problems*. 2008.
23. A. Shinsel, T. Kulesza, M. Burnett, W. Curran, A. Groce, S. Stumpf, and W-K. Wong. Mini-Crowdsourcing End-User Assessment of Intelligent Assistants: A Cost-Benefit Study. *Proc. of the IEEE Symposium on Visual Languages and Human-Centric Computing (VL/HCC '11)*. pp. 47-54, 2011.
24. D. Patterson, D. Fox, H. Kautz, M. Philipose. Finegrained activity recognition by aggregating abstract object usage. *In ISWC 05: Proceedings of the Ninth IEEE International Symposium on Wearable Computers*. pp. 4451. 2005.
25. W. Pentney, et al. Sensor-based Understanding of Daily Life via Large-Scale Use of Common Sense. *Proceedings of AAAI*. 2006.
26. A. Sadilek, and H. Kautz. Recognizing Multi-Agent Activities from GPS Data. In *24th AAAI Conference on Artificial Intelligence (AAAI 2010)*. 2010.
27. A. Sadilek, and H. Kautz. Modeling and Reasoning about Success, Failure, and Intent of Multi-Agent Activities. In *Proc. of UbiComp 2010*.
28. Y. Sun, S. Roy, G. Little. Beyond Independent Agreement: A Tournament Selection Approach for Quality Assurance of Human Computation Tasks. *AAAI Workshop on Human Computation*. 2011.
29. E. Tapia, S. Intille, and K. Larson. Activity Recognition in the Home Using Simple and Ubiquitous Sensors. *Pervasive Computing*, pp. 158-175, 2004.
30. M. Toomim, T. Kriplean, C. Prtner, and J. A. Landay. Utility of human-computer interactions: Toward a science of preference measurement. In *Proc. of the ACM Conf. on Human Factors in Computing Systems (CHI 2011)*, pp. 2275-2284, 2011.
31. L. von Ahn, and L. Dabbish. Labeling images with a computer game. *Proc. of the Conf. on Human Factors in Computing Systems (CHI 2004)*, pp. 319–326, 2004.
32. D. Wilson, and C. Atkeson. Simultaneous tracking and activity recognition (STAR) using many anonymous, binary sensors. *Proc. of PERVASIVE 2005*, pp. 62-79. 2005.
33. Y. Yan, R. Romer, F. Glenn, and D. Jennifer. Active Learning from Crowds. *Proceedings of the 28th International Conference on Machine Learning (ICML-11)*, pp. 1161–1168, 2011.
34. L. Zhao, G. Sukthankar, and R. Sukthankar. Robust Active Learning Using Crowdsourced Annotations for Activity Recognition. *AAAI 2011 Workshop on Human Computation*. pp. 74-79, 2011.
35. L. Zhao, G. Sukthankar, and R. Sukthankar. Incremental Relabeling for Active Learning with Noisy Crowdsourced Annotations. *IEEE Intl. Conf. on Social Computing*. 2011.

Who Wants to Know? Question-asking and Answering Practices among Facebook Users

Rebecca Gray[1]
College of Communication Arts and Sciences
Michigan State University
409 CommArts Building
East Lansing, MI 48824
grayreb2@msu.edu

Nicole B. Ellison[2], **Cliff Lampe**[4]
School of Information
University of Michigan
105 S. State St
Ann Arbor, MI 48109
{enicole, cacl}@umich.edu

Jessica Vitak[3]
College of Information Studies
University of Maryland
Room 4105 Hornbake Bldg, South Wing
College Park, MD
jvitak@umd.edu

ABSTRACT

Research has identified a link between Facebook use and bridging social capital, which speaks to the informational resources provided by a diverse network of connections. In order to explicate the mechanism through which Facebook may help individuals mobilize these embedded informational and support resources, this study explores the role of bridging social capital, question type, and relational closeness on the perceived utility and satisfaction of information obtained through questions posed to one's network of Facebook Friends through the status update feature. Employing a mixed-method approach, we utilize survey data collected from a sample of non-academic university staff (N=666), as well as actual Facebook question examples and responses collected during a follow-up lab session from a subset of this sample (N=71). Results indicate that question-askers' bridging social capital positively predicts the utility of responses received on SNS, while useful responses are more likely to be received from weaker ties.

Author Keywords

Social network sites; social search; Q&A; Facebook; social capital; information seeking.

ACM Classification Keywords

H.5.3 **[Group and Organization Interfaces]**: Web-based interaction.

INTRODUCTION

Originally used primarily for relationship maintenance purposes, social network sites (SNSs) like Facebook are gaining increasing attention as venues for a variety of information exchanges between individuals, ranging from the quotidian to the substantive. Research suggests this is a relatively common practice [20], and SNS scholars point to specific technical and social affordances that make SNSs useful sites for information gathering and sharing [15]. Through these information-sharing practices, individuals attempt to harness the latent resources of their personal connections by asking questions and requesting other kinds of assistance, such as social and instrumental support, from their SNS connections. These forms of support are captured in the concept of social capital [3], and activities like posing a question to one's network via a SNS can be viewed as a distinct attempt to mobilize, or enact, one's social capital. In this paper, we propose that asking a question on Facebook is an explicit action enacted by users in order to convert the social relationships maintained on the site into actionable information and other social capital outcomes. In order to gain insight into social capital processes on the site, we focus on one particular instance of social capital conversion: questions posed via status updates.

There are many social and technical affordances of SNSs—and Facebook in particular—that make them an appropriate forum for asking questions. For instance, SNSs enable users to communicate with a potentially large audience through a single post [5]. On Facebook, status updates are presented to one's network via the News Feed, an aggregated collection of content presented in reverse chronological order. This broadcasting feature, a key component of most SNSs, allows users to distribute content, including requests for informational or emotional support, to their network. This feature is especially useful when seeking information because it enables users to broadcast inquiries to a wide set of ties at a minimal cost in terms of time and effort expended [20]. The ability to broadcast is also helpful when one does not know which specific person in a larger group holds the needed information or when the information is held by weak ties only available through Facebook.

Past research on question-asking in this context reveals that individuals who use SNSs to pose questions to their social networks predominately report two motivations for seeking information: a) trust in their online contacts and b) the expectation of subjective relevance regarding the answers provided by their contacts [20]. These motivations highlight the unique advantages of posing questions on SNSs compared to more generic Q&A sites and echo patterns identified by research on information seeking which suggests that certain information needs, such as those revolving around quotidian occurrences, are more commonly sought from individuals one already knows [25], as opposed to other formal sources such as organizations. Johnson [14] found that turning to known individuals to solve an information need as compared to turning to organizations or other media sources (e.g., newspapers and television) resulted in more successful and satisfying outcomes. Likewise, Nardi and O'Day [21] argue that members of one's social network are valuable in the information seeking process because they have context-based information about the question-asker and can tailor responses accordingly. In short, when seeking information, it is advantageous to turn to one's social network, because you know (and presumably trust) your network, and they know you.

A number of studies have identified a positive relationship between individuals' reported use of SNSs such as Facebook and their perceptions of social capital (e.g., [5, 10, 12]), and the research presented here extends this investigation by focusing on instances of informational exchanges between users connected on Facebook and by examining the relationship between perceived bridging social capital and question-asking outcomes. In contrast to much of the existing work on social capital and SNS use [9,10,11], this study utilizes actual examples of broadcasted questions posed by participants on Facebook (as captured on the site itself), enabling us to empirically assess *naturally occurring instances of social capital conversion in action.* Thus we believe this line of inquiry – focusing on specific, "in the wild" examples of Facebook-enacted question-asking – can productively complement other work that employs more general perceptual measures of social capital (e.g., [10]) and can shed insight into the relationship between these perceptual measures of bridging social capital and other components of social capital, such as the utility of information received via SNS contexts.

Additionally, we explore whether the relationship between the question-asker and answerer impacts the kinds of responses one receives in an SNS. Recent research examining online social information seeking behavior has examined the relationship between relationship strength (between information-seeker and responder) and the utility or quality of information received. Examining instances of question-asking on Facebook, Panovich, Miller and Karger [22] found that responses from close ties were rated as contributing more to participants' overall knowledge than weak ties. Additional research by Burke and Kraut [4] found that after losing a job, communication with individuals' strong ties was more instrumental to finding new employment within 90 days. These findings are somewhat unexpected given support for the theoretical framework proposed by Granovetter [13], which argues that weaker ties will be more instrumental for accessing novel information. This framework, known as the "Strength of Weak Ties," has been empirically supported in a wide range of contexts [4, 19, 22, 25]. We extend this literature through an empirical assessment of how relational closeness affects the perceived utility and satisfaction of information obtained through questions posed on Facebook. Lastly, we explore how these patterns change when the *kinds* of information and *types* of assistance requested vary.

RELATED WORK

Question-asking on SNS

Research on question-asking in SNS contexts, which confirms individuals are repurposing SNSs for information seeking purposes, has documented how and to what ends this practice is occurring and examined the perceived utility and quality of responses to broadcasted questions. Morris et al. [20] found that 94% of participants believed the questions they posted were answered promptly, and roughly 70% rated the responses as helpful. Exploring the effectiveness of asking questions on SNSs, Teevan, Morris and Panovich [26] found that characteristics of the question itself predicted the quality, quantity, and speed of responses. In particular, a concise style of question-asking, a defined scope (or audience), and the inclusion of a question mark were associated with more and higher quality responses within shorter periods of time [26]. Likewise, research on Twitter found that two-thirds of questions received responses within 30 minutes and 84% of responses were deemed "relevant" to the question [23]. Across the various question *types*, responses to rhetorical questions were deemed least useful, probably because answers to these questions are either not expected at all or are not truly expected to be useful [20].

Bridging social capital and access to novel information

As described above, we view question-asking as an activity meant to enact an episode of social capital conversion. Emerging from the sociological tradition but now employed by a range of disciplines, social capital theory has been used to study outcomes such as educational outcomes and civic participation [3, 6, 7, 18, 24]. The construct of social capital captures the benefits associated with one's network: these benefits can be in the form of access to information (which is the focus of this study), provisions of social support, exposure to different world views, or other outcomes. For the questions this study addresses, bridging social capital is most useful as it speaks to the informational benefits associated with one's social network [24].

Putnam [24] defines bridging social capital as being associated with exposure to heterogeneous networks. Coming into contact with diverse kinds of people is productive for information seeking purposes, in that different groups of individuals can broker access to distinct perspectives, worldviews, and information. Exposure to diverse opinions can result in broader horizons, more open-mindedness, feelings of being connected to a wider community, and a willingness to try new things [6, 27]. Burt's [6] work demonstrates that those in bridging positions (connecting two clusters of people) are typically more successful in meeting certain information and communication goals, in part because they have access to information from multiple clusters and control the flow of information between these clusters. A long line of research on homophily reinforces the fact that "Similarity breeds connection" [19]. These "birds of a feather" are more likely to have access to the same stores of information as one another. Conversely, weaker ties are associated with diverse and novel information, and thus in some situations (such as looking for an employment opportunity) information-seekers find ideas or information from weaker ties to be more useful than information generated from their closer ties [13].

Social capital measures assess the extent to which individuals feel they have access to diverse individuals within their network who expose them to different kinds of worldviews and information. Thus, we expect to see a relationship between those with higher levels of bridging social capital and more useful responses, as the type of network associated with bridging social capital is also associated with question-askers' ability to obtain useful answers to their questions in a SNS setting.

H1: Bridging social capital will be positively related to perceived usefulness of responses to a question posed on Facebook.

Strength of ties and knowledge transfer

As suggested by the work on bridging social capital reviewed above, tie strength (the degree of relational closeness between two individuals) is related to the extent to which these individuals are likely to provide novel (and thus useful) information. One of the most important investigations of the role of tie strength on information exchange is Granovetter's [13] work on "The Strength of Weak Ties." This work emphasized the significance of weak ties (e.g., those with whom one is not in frequent contact) in one's network in gathering novel information.

Contrary to findings about the role of weak ties in accessing novel information and resources, there is increasing evidence that close ties play a role in the acquisition of new information and levels of bridging social capital. Past research has pointed to the superiority of strong ties in knowledge exchange [11, 12]. Some researchers maintain that these strong ties may be more likely to ensure that the information they provide is understood and capable of being implemented effectively [11, 15]. Krackhardt [14] in particular argued the importance of strong ties in transferring tacit, complex knowledge within organizations, particularly because they are usually more accessible and willing to help. Additionally, in a recent investigation of information flow in white-collar, professional e-mail networks, Aral and Van Alstyne [1] advanced the argument for the strength of close ties by considering the dynamic environments in which knowledge transfer occurs. When looking at the utility of ties *per unit time*, close ties are more instrumental to knowledge exchange, as individuals are likely to target others they know can help with their information needs, as opposed to reaching out to more distant connections in their network with whose knowledge bases they may not be as familiar.

Looking specifically at question-asking in SNSs, where these information needs can be broadcast to multiple ties at once, Panovich et al. [22] also found support for close ties being more instrumental to knowledge contribution. Responses received from close ties were more highly valued than those from weak ties and were less likely to provide information the question-asker already knew. Similarly, recent research by Burke and Kraut found that communication with *strong* ties was concurrently predictive of greater feelings of stress, but most importantly, predictive of finding employment in three months following the loss of a job whereas weak ties were not as instrumental to this end. These findings are in contrast with the "strength of weak ties" argument made by Granovetter [13]. One possible explanation offered for this was the notion of information *personalization* in SNS information seeking [22]. Close ties may be better able to tailor their responses to the information-seeker than weak ties, making their responses more useful. Depending on the type of question asked, weak ties or strong ties may be more likely to provide a useful answer.

Given the discrepancy between the theoretical predictions of tie strength and the empirical findings above, we pose the following research question regarding the relationship between tie strength and information utility:

RQ1: What is the relationship between tie strength and usefulness of responses to questions posed on Facebook?

Responses to questions in SNSs serve multiple goals, sometimes simultaneously. Although in many cases, commenters may be motivated by an altruistic desire to help by providing useful information, Ellison et al. [12] note that the lack of non-verbal attention cues (such as eye contact) in SNSs may create an additional layer of motivation for responding to a query from a SNS "Friend" – signaling attention to components of one's network and engaging in social grooming with these ties. Responses to questions may perform a relationship maintenance function, serving as intrinsically satisfying or meaningful to the receiver – even if they do not explicitly answer the question posed. For instance, an old friend posting "Congratulations!" to a question about what to wear to one's graduation may not provide *useful* information, but it may still be *satisfying* and meaningful because it provides another resource, i.e., social support. One possible reason for why an answer might be satisfying but not useful to a question-asker is based on his or her relationship to the answerer. Panovich et al. [22] reported that information provided by close ties in SNS Q&A was more highly *valued* than information from weak ties; however, the literature does not speak to how the closeness of a relationship may impact one's *satisfaction* with a question response. Thus, we additionally ask:

RQ2: What is the relationship between tie strength and satisfaction with responses received to a question posed on Facebook?

Question Types and Response Quality

Morris, Teevan, and Panovich [20] surveyed Microsoft employees about SNS question-asking and answering practices and found that half of the respondents reported using Facebook or Twitter to pose a diverse set of questions to their social network, with the most common categories of questions being recommendations (29%), opinions (22%), and factual knowledge (17%). Subsequent research by Paul, Hong, and Chi [23] analyzed 1.2 million tweets to identify questions being asked on Twitter and develop categories of the types of questions users asked through the site. They found that, somewhat in contrast to Facebook, the majority of question-based tweets were rhetorical questions (42%), requests for factual knowledge (16%), and polls (15%).

Although many kinds of SNS-hosted questions may elicit answers that have the potential to be useful to the question-asker, not all questions are attempts to solicit actual information or action. Some may be attempts to initiate conversation, communicate a need for social support, or achieve other interpersonal goals. For example, Harper et al. [14] identified "conversational questions," while Morris et al. [20] labeled these questions as "rhetorical" and defined them as "aimed at prompting discussion rather than eliciting practical answers" (p. 1743). Consequently, in their study, Morris et al. [20] found that response usefulness was impacted by question type. Specifically, responses to rhetorical questions were rated as having a significantly smaller percentage of helpful responses than non-helpful responses. In our study, we anticipate that responses to rhetorical questions will be, on average, rated less useful by the question-asker than responses that are aimed at soliciting practical or informational responses.

H2: Responses to rhetorical questions will be rated as less useful than responses to non-rhetorical questions.

Within an SNS context, it is possible that some information requests are more successful or satisfying than others. Those asking questions of their Friend networks may perceive that responses to recommendation questions are more satisfying than social invitations, and so on. Given the lack of literature on this topic that might provide a basis for predicting which questions result in more satisfying responses, we pose the following research question:

RQ3: Are responses to certain question types perceived as more satisfying than others?

Past research has not attempted to distinguish between the 'usefulness' of an answer (presumably based on the quality of the information and its ability to address the information needs of the asker) and the 'satisfaction' one feels with the answer, perhaps based on the fact that a particular person took the time and effort to post a visible response. We are curious as to whether "non-useful" answers can still be considered satisfying or whether these two attributions are always linked.

Similarly, RQs 2 and 3 investigate whether tie strength and question type play a role in the relationship between the usefulness of and satisfaction with responses received to questions on SNS. If, in fact, tie strength and question types do correlate with usefulness of and satisfaction with responses, it may be that this changes the way usefulness and satisfaction relate to one another. Thus, we pose the following three final research questions:

RQ4: What is the relationship between the reported usefulness of an answer and one's level of satisfaction with it?

RQ5: Does the relationship between usefulness and satisfaction of responses vary based on the relationship between the question-asker and answerer?

RQ6: Does the relationship between usefulness and satisfaction of responses vary by question type?

METHOD

Data presented here were collected as part of a larger data collection effort examining the role of SNSs in information seeking processes among adults. Non-academic staff at a large Midwestern university were invited in fall 2010 and

Figure 1: Sample question with responses from dataset

spring 2011 to participate in an online survey about their use of online communication tools, including their use of Facebook and their attitudes about the site in general and as a useful place to get information. Of the 3,150 staff members invited to take the survey, 666 staff members completed the survey, and 106 of these respondents participated in a follow-up lab session.

Criteria for participation in the lab selection were based on responses to three survey items regarding their propensity to perform information seeking behaviors on Facebook: "How often do you… (1) ask questions of your Facebook friends? (2) respond to questions from your Facebook friends? (3) coordinate with your Facebook friends?" In the fall, the participants invited to lab sessions were those who reported asking their Facebook friends questions "often" (22 participants), "very often" (11 participants), or "sometimes" (37 participants). We also included in the lab sessions three participants who reported "rarely" asking questions of their Facebook friends but reported high levels of question-answering behaviors. Similar selection criteria were utilized in the spring 2011 data collection. During this phase, participants included those who reported asking their Facebook friends questions "often" (26 participants), "very often" (4 participants) and "sometimes" (as well as reporting engagement in the other behaviors listed above "sometimes" or more frequently; 81 participants). A total of 184 respondents were invited to participate in a lab session in either the fall or spring, and 106 attended a lab session. All participants invited to participate were offered an incentive of an Amazon gift card ranging from $10-$15[1].

During the lab sessions, participants first completed a semi-structured interview with one of three research assistants, during which they were asked general questions about their use of Facebook and their propensity to use Facebook to ask questions. Participants were then asked to go through their Facebook history and locate the most recent example of a status update that met two criteria: (1) the goal of the update was to seek information or feedback from their Facebook Friends and (2) they had received at least two comments from two Friends on the update (in order to capture examples of both question-asking and the variety of responses that network members might provide through the site). (See Figure 1 for an example of a question and its responses from our dataset.) In cases where participants could not locate an example of question-asking in their Facebook history, we used the most recent status update with two or more responders. Examples that were not questions were excluded from the analyses presented here. Of the 106 participants, we were unable to collect usable data for approximately 25% of them (i.e., some of these participants could not locate any examples of status updates at all and reported during the interview that they had never used the feature), leaving us with a total of 71 question examples and 420 response ratings to analyze. Of the participants that could find adequate examples, the majority were female (71%), White (81%), and highly educated, with over 85% of the sample having acquired at least a bachelors degree. The average participant age was 41 years old (SD = 9.50).

[1] All participants received a minimum of $10 for participating in the lab session, with some receiving more based on participation in a separate task.

Question Type	Number of Instances (% of Total)
Suggestion/Recommendation	9 (13%)
Factual knowledge	2 (2.9%)
Social coordination/invitation	4 (5.7%)
Request/favor	13 (18.6%)
Opinion/poll	12 (17.1%)
Rhetorical	17 (24.3%)
Non-questions	13 (18.6%)

Table 1: Distribution of question categories

Participants received a median of 5 responses (M = 5.89, min = 2, max = 16) to their questions. The participants were asked to rate each response to their question in terms of its usefulness and their satisfaction with it on a 10-point scale in response to the prompts: "How useful was this response?" (1 = Not at all useful, 10 = Extremely useful; M = 6.01, SD = 3.36) and "How satisfied were you with this response?" 1 = Not at all satisfied, 10 = Extremely satisfied; M = 7.52, SD = 2.98). Participants did not rate their own comments, if any were included in the comment stream. Upon completion of the response-rating task, participants rated their perceived level of closeness and relationship type (e.g., former classmate, close friend, etc.) with each responder. Participants also answered two final questions about the overall utility of Facebook for getting their question answered ("On a scale of 1 to 10, how useful was Facebook in getting this question answered?"; M= 6.83, SD = 2.77) as well as their likelihood of using Facebook for similar questions in the future ("On a scale of 1 to 10, how likely are you to use Facebook to ask a similar question in the future?"; M= 8.88, SD = 1.57).

Measures

Perceived closeness. Perceived closeness of the participant to the respondent was measured using Aron, Aron, and Smollan's [2] Inclusion of Other in Self (IOS) scale. This one item, pictorial measure of relational closeness utilizes a scale of seven images of two circles with increasing degrees of overlap conveying increasing degrees of connectedness or closeness. Aron et al. [2] demonstrated that this measure shows convergent validity with other established multi-item scales of relational closeness. The average reported degree of closeness to question-answerers was 3.07 (SD = 1.68).

Question examples were rated using an adaptation of the question typology created by Morris et al. [20]. The categories used were: *suggestion/recommendation, factual knowledge, social coordination/invitation, request/favor, opinion/poll, rhetorical questions,* and *non-questions.* See Table 1 for distribution of question categories.

Facebook-specific bridging social capital. This measure (10 items, alpha = .82, M = 3.84, SD = 0.49) was adapted from earlier research [27] to reflect the resources associated with bridging social capital – such as access to diverse information – that individuals perceive are available via members of their Facebook networks. Example items include: "Interacting with people in my Facebook network reminds me that everyone in the world is connected" and "Interacting with people in my Facebook network makes me want to try new things." Responses employed a 5-point Likert scale (1 = Strongly disagree, 5 = Strongly agree).

Frequency of using Facebook to ask questions. This one-item measure (M = 3.62, SD = 0.83) reflects how often individuals use Facebook to ask others in their networks for information. Individuals responded on a scale of frequency ranging from 1 to 5, in which 1 = Never and 5 = Very often.

Facebook information seeking behaviors. This measure (4 items, alpha = .82, M= 3.42, SD = 0.61) captures the extent to which individuals use Facebook to seek information. Sample items include "I use Facebook to get business referrals" and "I use Facebook to get advice about something I want to buy." Individuals responded with their level of agreement on a 5-point Likert scale (1 = Strongly disagree, 5 = Strongly agree).

RESULTS

Research questions and hypotheses were investigated utilizing both univariate and hierarchical statistical analyses. The following analyses did not include non-question examples.

To examine the relationship between bridging social capital and the perceived usefulness of responses (*H1*), we used hierarchical linear modeling (HLM) as we were using two levels of data: question-askers (i.e., participants) and responders. HLM is an ideal type of analysis for evaluating multilevel data where level-2 variables – in this case the bridging social capital of the question-asker – are used to explain between-group variance in the level-1 variables – here, the utility of responses of question-responders. Also entered into the model as fixed predictors of response utility were *Facebook information seeking behaviors* and *frequency of asking questions on Facebook,* which served as controls for the question-asking behaviors of the participants. The model using bridging social capital, Facebook information seeking behaviors, and frequency of asking questions to predict usefulness was a good fit, $\chi2$ = 341.85, p < .001; thus H1 was supported. The level of perceived bridging social capital positively predicted the perceived usefulness of responses from the commenters.

To examine the relationship between tie strength and perceived usefulness of responses (*RQ1*), a simple Pearson correlation demonstrated an inverse relationship between the variables, $r(239)$ = -.20, p < .001. When removing rhetorical questions – hypothesized to differ from the other question categories in terms of useful acquired answers – the correlation became slightly stronger while remaining negative, $r(182)$ = -.24, p < .001. For information needs and other non-rhetorical questions, responses received from weaker ties were rated as more useful than responses received from closer ties. Another question posed in this study was whether or not responses from network members would be perceived as more or less satisfying dependent on the strength of tie or closeness of the relationship (*RQ2*). There was no significant relationship between perceived closeness and satisfaction with question response, indicating that participants perceived responses to be equally satisfying, regardless of their perceived relational closeness with the responder..

Our second hypothesis predicted that rhetorical questions would receive less useful responses than other question types (*H2*). A one-way ANOVA using question category to predict usefulness of the answer indicated a significant difference between question types on the response usefulness, $F(339)$ = 9.981, p < .001, η^2 = .105, but post-hoc comparisons using Tukey's procedure at p < .05 showed that although usefulness of responses varied by question type, rhetorical questions did *not* result in the least useful responses on average, as predicted by H2 (see Table 2). In other words, question-askers were just as likely to mark answers to rhetorical questions as useful as they were to mark responses to other kinds of questions as useful.

Although we did not predict a relationship between

Question Type	Usefulness
Social coordination/ Invitation	3.88_a (3.34)
Suggestion/ Recommendation	4.66_{ab} (3.23)
Rhetorical	5.96_{bc} (3.43)
Favor/ Request	6.86_c (3.37)
Opinion/ Poll	7.39_c (2.99)

Note: Means having no letter in common in their subscripts differ significantly at p < .05 according to Tukey's procedure. Standard deviations are reported in parentheses.

Table 2: Mean usefulness scores as a function of question type

question type and how satisfying responses were, we wanted to explore whether the satisfaction with responses varied by question category (*RQ3*) and found that satisfaction did vary significantly by category, $F(336) = 14.490$, $p < .001$, $\eta^2 = .147$. Using Tukey's post-hoc comparison, we found that *requests/favors* ($M = 8.18_a$, $SD = 2.75$), *opinions/polls* ($M = 8.68_a$, $SD = 2.13$), and *rhetorical* questions ($M = 8.24_a$, $SD = 2.85$) were considered more satisfying than responses to *suggestion/recommendation* questions ($M = 5.63_b$, $SD = 3.32$) and *social coordination/invitation* questions ($M = 6.17_b$, $SD = 3.24$).

Our next research question asked about the relationship between the rated usefulness of a response and how satisfying it was (*RQ4*). There was a strong, positive correlation between usefulness and satisfaction, $r(348) = .661$, $p < .001$. To examine how the relationship changed between satisfaction and usefulness ratings by tie strength (*RQ5*) and question type (*RQ6*), we used the absolute value of the difference between the two ratings – or "discrepancy" – for each comment. For tie strength, there was a small, significant correlation between this discrepancy value and strength of ties, $r(234) = .161$, $p < .05$. Closer ties' responses were more likely to have a greater difference between their satisfaction and usefulness ratings than weaker ties' responses. There was no significant change in the relationship between usefulness and satisfaction by question type.

DISCUSSION

Research suggests SNSs are used for interpersonal purposes, such as maintaining distant relationships and "checking out" (or socially surveilling) proximate and distant others [12], these interpersonal activities are well-aligned with popular beliefs about the purpose of these sites. More recently, scholars have identified other uses of SNSs, which are increasingly being used for information-gathering and question-asking, in organizational [8] and educational contexts [17]. We believe these two sets of activities – relationship maintenance and question-asking – are inextricably and intimately related to one another when viewed through the lens of social capital, and this paper emphasizes the implications for social capital conversion in the latter.

These information-based uses are important to study because instances of question-asking are *explicit instances of social capital in action*. Studying these instances in a SNS context offers insight into the ways these tools are changing the fabric of everyday life for their users, not only helping them to achieve interpersonal goals but also to get things done—solve problems, get advice, share opinions and information, learn about new opportunities, and participate in sundry other activities that help day-to-day life go more smoothly. The present study examines organic examples of individuals mining their Facebook networks for informational resources and examines the outcomes of these requests in light of the individuals' perceived bridging social capital. In doing so, we can take the first steps toward linking *perceptions of bridging social capital* as utilized in SNS scholarship with *concrete outcomes* – the responses our participants received when they posted questions to their Facebook networks. Additionally, we identify and analyze the specific types of questions in an attempt to gain a sense of how the type of information solicited might be related to the quality of responses and relationships with responders. Our findings complement and extend our knowledge of information seeking in SNSs and how it relates to bridging social capital in several ways.

A consistent stream of research has identified a link between perceptions of social capital and Facebook use among undergraduate student and adult users of the site [5, 10, 12]. However, less research examines the specific mechanisms behind these associations. Asking questions of one's network using the broadcasting features of Facebook is an observable, explicit instance of social capital conversion. In our study, we found that bridging social capital was positively related to the reported usefulness of the responses (or "answers") received in response to the question they posed to their Facebook network. As access to useful – and especially novel – information is an important component of bridging social capital, this is unsurprising. However, this finding is important because it helps to validate social capital scales that assess perceptions of access. This is one of the first studies to demonstrate a robust relationship between Williams' [27] social capital scales and one component of the construct – access to information – measured using specific behavioral data contributed by users' networks and users' retrospective rating of these responses.

Past research has shown that other behaviors on SNSs, such as receiving messages from friends [5] and signaling attention to others via "Happy Birthday" posts and other methods [16] are associated with increased bridging social capital. One possibility is that asking a question acts as an invitation for a social exchange that may not happen on its own. In other words, answering a question on Facebook gives individuals an excuse to interact and to signal they are paying attention to their ties on the site. This is more likely to be important for weak ties, who may be critical for bridging social capital outcomes. In this way, these interactions serve to support the entire lifecycle of social capital, as individuals extract benefits, put themselves in debt to others (and thus helping to cultivate future interactions due to reciprocity norms), and contribute to the strength and longevity of their network connections through their interactions.

In contrast to findings by Panovich et al. [22] that strong ties provide more useful answers and contribute more to overall knowledge, we find that *weak* ties are more associated with response utility. This is consistent with the Strength of Weak Ties perspective and early work on SNSs that predicted that the "technologies that expand one's social network will primarily result in an increase in available information and opportunities – the benefits of a large, heterogeneous network" (p. 80) [9]. Closer connections within our social networks are typically more similar to us, with access to similar, redundant information or viewpoints, while connections that are weaker likely share fewer mutual contacts and offer exposure to new and different ideas. This finding also differs, however, from Burke and Kraut's [4] recent discovery that communication with strong ties is more useful than communication with weak ties in terms of gaining employment after a job loss. Future research should explore this question further to help determine whether these inconsistencies are due to different measures, participant population, or the type of question asked. For example, the respondents in Panovich et al.'s [22] study were instructed to ask technology-focused questions, whereas in this study, participants found an example from their past history. Although our method did not include qualitative analysis of our participants' questions and responses, in reading through them it was clear that many of the questions identified by our respondents had affective components as well as purely informational one. This could mean that a "useful" answer was emotionally supportive in addition to, or rather than, informative, which changes the nature of the exchange.

Although weak ties were more likely to supply useful responses, we found no significant role between reported *satisfaction* with responses and tie strength. Regardless of the responder's relationship to the question-asker, comments were equally as likely to be seen as satisfying when they were provided by a close tie as when contributed by a weak tie. Additionally, the mean satisfaction rating was relatively high (7.67/10). A participant's "satisfaction" with the response may be associated with other factors we did not measure (such as time since last interaction), but our findings suggest that tie strength did not have a uniform relationship with satisfaction valence. We believe that one's "satisfaction" with responses to a posted question may be more closely linked to the emotional investment signaled by a response, such that any response will be satisfying, regardless of who posted it, because it signals that someone paid attention to the utterance and made the effort to respond. Future research should explore other methods of assessing the relational maintenance functions of question-answering on Facebook. It may be that any response – useful or not – is satisfying in that a comment or other visible activity trace is the only way to know with certainty that someone not only saw the post (which isn't clear with the News Feed filtering algorithm), but took the time to acknowledge it and in doing so invest in the social connection.

In addition to examining relationships of bridging social capital and strength of ties with question-asking outcomes, we sought to learn more about differences in outcomes inherent to the various types of questions identified. Our analysis found that rhetorical questions did not result in fewer useful responses than non-rhetorical questions, as found by [20], which is surprising. However, responses did vary in their overall usefulness by question type. Responses to opinion and favor/request questions had the highest usefulness ratings, while social coordination/invitation had the lowest. Our method – in which we asked participants to retrospectively rate the usefulness of responses – may have contributed to this finding, in that social coordination and other time-sensitive invitations have a more limited "shelf life" than other kinds of questions, and thus our method may have been biased against them in terms of their retrospectively perceived usefulness. Solicitations for opinions were rated highly, which may result from their being no "wrong" answer possible for this type of question, or they may also be solicitations for emotional support, which comments could provide regardless of the extent to which they include objective, "useful" information.

In terms of satisfaction, opinion/poll questions had the most satisfying responses while suggestion/recommendation questions had the least. We suspect that in some of these cases, even if the askers are not getting useful answers, the process of requesting help and getting some response may still be important for meeting relational goals. As Ellison et al. [11] note, responses to questions may constitute a form of social grooming – signaling attention in a context in which attention is not apparent unless explicitly signaled. The reciprocal nature of social capital may also come into play here, in that responses may be satisfying because they signal a continued pattern of interaction between two parties. Finally, the usefulness of a comment was strongly correlated with how satisfying an individual rated it.

Tie strength was positively related to the discrepancy between usefulness and satisfaction ratings. In essence, participants gave answers from weak ties more similar ratings for usefulness and satisfaction than they rated those from closer ties. Given that we found tie strength negatively relates to usefulness, with weak ties providing more useful responses, and that reported satisfaction does not vary by tie strength, we can interpret that weak ties are providing responses that are rated more closely on useful *and* satisfying dimensions, while comments from close ties are rated as slightly less useful than they are satisfying. This supports the idea that close ties may be more likely to be commenting to signal attention or convey interest as a form of relational maintenance and not always providing useful or novel information as homogenous ties are typically associated with redundant information [10]. When looking at the relationship between usefulness and satisfaction by question type, we found no significant difference, indicating that there were no specific question types that were more likely than others to have responses that were not useful but still satisfying. If we had found that responses to rhetorical questions were rated as significantly less useful than responses to non-rhetorical questions (i.e., findings similar to the findings of Panovich et al. [20]), we likely would have seen that rhetorical questions had comments with greater usefulness-satisfaction discrepancy.

One curious aspect of our data collection worth considering is the gap between those participants who indicated they asked questions on Facebook (by responding to the question "How often do you use Facebook to ask questions of your Facebook friends?" with a response of at least "sometimes") but then were unable to find any instances of question-asking in their News Feed in the lab – approximately 25% of our participants said they asked questions of their network but were unable to find an example. This suggests that either participants have a faulty ability to self-report this behavior or perhaps are gaining information on Facebook through channels other than the status update. Although past literature and an affordance-based consideration of SNSs suggest the status update is well-suited for broadcasting informational requests to a wide network with one action, perhaps users are encountering useful information through other activities on the site, such as browsing others' updates, or perhaps are gaining information even through responses to updates that are not "questions." Future work should use other methods to explore these issues, such as interviews or analysis of server-level data to identity instances of resource mobilization that do not take the form of a question.

Limitations

SNS activities leave behavioral traces that can be used as a source of data and as user prompts during lab studies or interviews, potentially leading to perceptual data that is more accurate than purely self-report. However, our method also has some limitations that should be considered when reviewing our findings. We asked participants to retrospectively rate aspects of their post and its responses, which may have led to biased responses due to difficulties remembering details about the incident, the fact that relationships may have changed between the original posting and the lab appointment, or other factors. The collection of naturalistic question examples from individuals' feeds also led to some limitations in terms of analysis that could be performed; specifically, we were unable to investigate differences in usefulness or satisfaction of responses within *factual knowledge* questions in analysis of variance, because of the low occurrence of this question type (N=2). Although asking participants to rate responses and relationship characteristics as they occurred would have ameliorated this concern, we felt this was a better compromise than asking participants to rate an artificial stimulus or have to contend with the intrusive nature of a real-time rating application. As mentioned by Panovich et al. [20], the number of responses per person could bias ratings (in that those with more responses may have been rated more useful, regardless of the content of their contribution). Finally, we only considered instances in which a question received more than two responses, so questions with only one or zero responses were not considered in this analysis. There is more we can learn from unanswered, broadcasted questions and future research should explore these instances as well as information seeking through Facebook channels other than the status update (e.g., private messages). Future research needs to further delineate the nuanced relationship between relational closeness, type of information need, and utility of information received, as well as to identify whether or not bridging social capital is more instrumental for certain information needs over others.

CONCLUSION

Question-asking within SNS settings is an increasingly prevalent activity performed by individuals to satiate a variety of interpersonal goals and information needs. In this study, we've looked at individuals' performance of broadcasting questions via the status update feature on Facebook, which allows users to seek information among an entire network of strong and weak ties at once, in order to connect perceptual measures of bridging social capital with concrete outcomes in a naturalistic setting. Ultimately, perceived bridging social capital *was* significantly positively associated with obtaining useful responses to questions broadcasted on Facebook, supporting the notion that information exchanges on SNSs can serve as a form of social capital conversion.

Information exchanges in SNS may be different than what is found between users and search engines like Google, or even in social search services like Quora or Yahoo! Answers. Our findings suggest that SNS questions and answers may contain multiple agendas, including requests for emotional support and feedback, and responding can be motivated by more than just wanting to share a correct answer. Question exchanges in SNSs may help maintain relationships by signaling attention and reciprocity, as well as provide a context for weak ties to interact in a socially acceptable manner. As the extant research suggests, SNSs are well suited to foster information exchanges and thus can be a valuable source of knowledge sharing among users. When viewed through a social capital lens, we see that receiving responses to questions in this social context can serve not only to exchange useful information or support but also to facilitate conversation and maintain relationships with close and weak ties, suggesting that relationship maintenance and question-asking activities are intimately related and should not be studied in isolation.

In this study, we have only started to unpack the complexity of knowledge exchange within this online social context, as it is bound up in messy entanglements of interpersonal relationships, attention signaling, information exchanges, norms of reciprocity, and social capital processes. We believe that SNSs have the potential to lower barriers to information sharing, make potential resources in our networks more visible, and reshape networks. However, even beyond their purely information value, these types of exchanges in social network sites may be ways in which users are connecting with and strengthening their bonds with others. In other words, question-asking is a means, not an end.

ACKNOWLEDGMENTS
This work was supported in part by the National Science Foundation (HCC 0916019). The authors would also like to thank Brandon Brooks for his help with data collection and Andrea Parker for her help with data analysis.

REFERENCES
1. Aral, S. and Van Alstyne, M. The diversity-bandwidth trade-off. *American Journal of Sociology*, *117* (1). 90-171.
2. Aron, A., Aron, E.N. and Smollan, D. Inclusion of other in the self scale and the structure of interpersonal closeness. *Journal of Personality and Social Psychology*, *63*. 596-612.
3. Bourdieu, P. Forms of Capital. in Richardson, J.G. ed. *Handbook of Theory and Research for the Sociology of Education*, Greenwood Press, New York, 1983.
4. Burke, M. and Kraut, R., Using Facebook after losing a job: Differential benefits of strong and weak ties. . in *2013 ACM Conference on Computer Supported Cooperative Work. (CSCW)*, (San Antonio, TX, 2013), ACM.
5. Burke, M., Kraut, R. and Marlow, C. Social capital on facebook: differentiating uses and users *Proceedings of the 2011 annual conference on Human factors in computing systems*, ACM, Vancouver, BC, Canada, 2011, 571-580.
6. Burt, R.S. *Structural Holes*. Harvard University Press, Cambridge, MA, 1992.
7. Coleman, J.S. Social Capital in the Creation of Human Capital. *American Journal of Sociology*, *94*. S95-S120.
8. DiMicco, J., Millen, D.R., Geyer, W., Dugan, C., Brownholtz, B. and Muller, M. Motivations for social networking at work *Proceedings of the ACM 2008 conference on Computer supported cooperative work*, ACM, San Diego, CA, USA, 2008.
9. Donath, J. and Boyd, D. Public Displays of Connection. *BT Technology Journal*, *22* (4). 71-82.
10. Ellison, N., Steinfield, C. and Lampe, C. The benefits of Facebook "friends:" Social capital and college students' use of online social network sites. *Journal of Computer Mediated Communication*, *12* (4). article 1.
11. Ellison, N., Vitak, J., Gray, R., Lampe, C, & Brooks, B. Cultivating Social Resources on Facebook: Signals of Relational Investment and their Role in Social Capital Processes *iCS-OII 2011 "A Decade in Internet Time" Symposium.* , Oxford, UK, 2011.
12. Ellison, N.B., Steinfield, C. and Lampe, C. Connection Strategies: Social Capital Implications of Facebook-enabled Communication Practices. *New Media & Society*, *13*. 873-892.
13. Granovetter, M.S. The Strength of Weak Ties. *Amerian Economic Review*, *78* (6). 1360-1480.
14. Harper, F.M., Moy, D. and Konstan, J.A., Fact or friendship?: Distinguising informational and conversational questions in social Q&A sites. in *Proceedings of the 27th international conference on Human factors in computing systems.*, (2009), 759-768.
15. Krackhardt, D. The strength of strong ties. . in Nohria, N. and Eccles, R.G. eds. *Networks and organizations: Structure, form and action*, Harvard Business School Press, Boston, 1992, 216-239.
16. Lampe, C., Vitak, J., Gray, R. and Ellison, N., Perceptions of Facebook's Value as an Information Source in *30th International Conference on Human Factors in Computing Systems (CHI)*, (Austin, TX, 2012), ACM Press.
17. Lampe, C., Wohn, D.Y., Vitak, J., Ellison, N.B. and Wash, R. Student use of Facebook for organizing collaborative classroom activities. *International Journal of Computer-Supported Cooperative Learning*, *6* (3). 329-347.
18. Lin, N. *Social Capital: A Theory of Social Structure and Action*. Cambridge University Press, New York, NY, 2001.
19. McPherson, M., Smith-Lovin, L. and Cook, J.M. Birds of a Feather: Homophily in Social Networks. *Annual Review of Sociology*, *27*. 415-444.
20. Morris, M.R., Teevan, J. and Panovich, K. What do people ask their social networks, and why?: a survey study of status message q&a behavior *Proceedings of the 28th international conference on Human factors in computing systems*, ACM, Atlanta, Georgia, USA, 2010.
21. Nardi, B.A. and O'Day, V.L. *Information Ecologies: Using Technology with Heart*. MIT Press, Cambridge, MA, 1999.
22. Panovich, K., Miller, R. and Karger, D. Tie strength in question & answer on social network sites *Proceedings of the ACM 2012 conference on Computer Supported Cooperative Work*, ACM, Seattle, Washington, USA, 2012, 1057-1066.
23. Paul, S.A., Hong, L. and Chi, E.H., Is Twitter a Good Place for Asking Questions? A Characterization Study. in *ICWSM - International Conference on Weblogs and Social Media*, (Barcelona, Spain, 2011).
24. Putnam, R.D. *Bowling Alone*. Simon & Schuster, New York, 2000.

25. Savolainen, R. Everyday life information seeking: Approaching information seeking in the context of "way of life". *Library & Information Science Research*, *17* (3). 259-294.

26. Teevan, J., Morris, M.R. and Panovich, K., Factors Affecting Response Quantity, Quality, and Speed for Questions Asked via Social Network Status Messages. in *ICWSM - International Conference on Weblogs and Social Media*, (Barcelona, Spain, 2011).

27. Williams, D. On and Off the 'Net: Scales for Social Capital in an Online Era *Journal of Computer Mediated Communication*, *11* (2).

Investigating the Appropriateness of Social Network Question Asking as a Resource for Blind Users

Erin Brady[1], Yu Zhong[1], Meredith Ringel Morris[2], Jeffrey P. Bigham[1]
[1]University of Rochester
Rochester, NY, USA
{brady, zyu, jbigham}@cs.rochester.edu
[2]Microsoft Research
Redmond, WA, USA
merrie@microsoft.com

ABSTRACT
Recent work has shown the potential of having remote humans answer visual questions that blind users have. On the surface social networking sites (SNSs) offer an attractive free source of human-powered answers that can be personalized to the user. In this paper, we explore the potential of blind users asking visual questions to their social networks. We present the first formal study of how blind people use social networking sites via a survey of 191 blind adults. We also explore whether blind users find SNSs an appropriate venue for Q&A through a log analysis of questions asked using VizWiz Social, an iPhone app with over 5,000 users, which lets blind users ask questions to either the crowd or friends. We then report findings of a field experiment with 23 blind VizWiz Social users, which explored question asking on VizWiz Social in the presence of monetary costs for non-social sources. We find that blind people have a large presence on social networking sites, but do not see them as an appropriate venue for asking questions due to high perceived social costs.

Author Keywords
Social networks; Q&A; blind users; visual impairment; friendsourcing.

ACM Classification Keywords
H.5.m: Information interfaces and presentation (e.g., HCI): Miscellaneous.

INTRODUCTION
Popular social networking sites (SNSs) like Facebook and Twitter allow users to post short status messages and to view and reply to their contacts' posts. Such services are extremely popular – a February 2012 survey found that 66% of online American adults use SNSs [10]. While the use of social networks by some populations with disabilities has been studied (e.g., the autism community [8, 17]), the use of social networking tools by blind people has been largely ignored in the academic literature.

SNSs are used not only as forums for socializing, but also as a venue for information seeking, such as by posting a question in one's status update in order to receive high-quality, personalized, and trusted responses from friends [22, 23, 31]. The use of social network contacts to accomplish productivity tasks such as Q&A is sometimes referred to as *friendsourcing* [5] (in contrast to *crowdsourcing*, in which strangers such as those on Amazon's Mechanical Turk service accomplish tasks in exchange for pay).

Blind people often recruit assistance from their family and friends in order to overcome accessibility problems in the physical world. Some call their contacts to look up information for them while away from home, while others prefer to run errands outside the house only if a sighted companion can join them [19]. Since blind people already rely on family or friends for information access, making their entire social network available to them while mobile may increase their feelings of independence and security outside of their homes [1].

We hypothesize that friendsourced Q&A has the potential to offer significant benefits to blind users, as this demographic often encounters questions about their environment that they are unable to answer when not in the presence of a sighted companion. For example, blind users found great value in the original VizWiz application [6], which allowed users to send photographs with accompanying audio questions from their smartphones to Mechanical Turk and receive speedy answers. They asked questions like "What denomination is this bill?" and "What kind of drink does this can hold?".

Friendsourcing, rather than crowdsourcing, might improve upon the VizWiz experience by removing the financial cost of the service (which is currently absorbed by our organization) and by improving the quality and trustworthiness of the answers received [23]. Friends may be better able to answer questions because they know the question asker. For instance, fashion questions may be best answered by those who know the user's style. Answerers who frequent the same locations as the user might be able to draw on outside knowledge in constructing an answer. Another potential advantage of friendsourcing is that users can get social value in addition to informational value from their Q&A exchange [22, 23]. But, asking friends can also have drawbacks. Users may appear or feel less independent.

CSCW '13, February 23–27, 2013, San Antonio, Texas, USA.

Imagine, for instance, a blind user asking friends who a letter is from, only to discover it is from an embarrassing source such as a debt collector or medical professional. Users may also create real or perceived social debts; they may not want to feel like a burden or for their friends to feel pressured to answer.

In this paper, we explore the potential of social networking sites as a mechanism for answering visual questions for blind users. The goal of this paper is to better understand the appropriateness of social network question asking for blind people, which may differ from the general population due to such reasons as blind users' increased need for the information, heightened awareness of privacy, and wanting not to appear needy or dependent on others.

We first present survey results on the use of social networks by 191 blind adults and their current practices and attitudes regarding social network Q&A. We then introduce VizWiz Social, a publicly available iPhone app with over 5,000 users, which enables blind users to send photographs and accompanying audio questions to either crowdsourced or friendsourced services. We add to our insights on blind users' attitudes toward friendsourcing through a log analysis of questions asked with VizWiz Social, and through a field experiment with 23 blind VizWiz Social users that varied the pricing of crowdsourced answers on VizWiz Social.

Our results indicate that blind users have a large presence on social networking sites (particularly Twitter). However, despite the availability of personalized answers from friendsourcing and the reduced cost in comparison to crowdsourcing, blind people are extremely reluctant to post questions to their social networks due to high perceived social costs. Their smaller-than-average network sizes may also reduce the quality of their SNS Q&A experiences, further biasing them against viewing their online social networks as an information source.

RELATED WORK

In this section, we discuss related work on the use of social networks by people with disabilities, the original VizWiz application, social network Q&A, and social costs associated with SNS use.

Social Networking and Disabilities

Online social forums like SNSs can be particularly valuable to people with disabilities. For example, the site PatientsLikeMe [patientslikeme.com] enables members to establish connections with others sharing similar medical diagnoses, providing a space for both social/emotional support and information-sharing regarding treatment options, medications, etc. The ASL-STEM Forum [11] is a social network for deaf students, designed to promote a shared awareness of invented sign language representations of scientific and mathematical terminology encountered in advanced courses. Burke et al. [8] identified opportunities and challenges associated with SNS use for adults on the autism spectrum. The SocialMirror [17] is part of a social networking tool for young adults with autism and their caregivers, designed as a safe space to practice life skills.

The World Health Organization estimates that 285 million people are visually impaired, 39 million of whom are blind [37]. Relatively little is known about how blind users interact with mainstream social networking technologies. A few social networking sites specifically for blind users exist, most notably Inclusive Planet [inclusiveplanet.com], but in general blind people use the same SNSs as everyone else. An informal 2009 poll of 62 blind people [2] by the American Foundation for the Blind found that about a half used Facebook, a third used Twitter, and a quarter used LinkedIn and MySpace. In a 2010 study, Wentz and Lazar [35] found that Facebook's web site was more difficult for blind users to navigate than Facebook's mobile phone application. The accessibility of various SNSs may impact frequency of use, and some interfaces specifically designed to be more accessible exist for specific sites, e.g. EasyChirp for Twitter [easychirp.com].

In this paper, we add to the knowledge of social networking use by people with disabilities by presenting findings from the first formal survey on blind users' social networking habits, as well as presenting log and experimental data that illustrate how blind users use social networks for Q&A.

VizWiz

VizWiz is a mobile phone application for blind users that allows them to take a picture of their environment, record an audio question about something in the picture, and then have answers read aloud by the phone's screen-reading software [6]. In a pilot study of the application, answers were collected from members of the Amazon Mechanical Turk service [mturk.com]. Mechanical Turk is an online marketplace of Human Intelligence Tasks (HITs) that workers can complete for small amounts of money. Answers took about two-and-a-half minutes to arrive.

Though answers were received quickly and members of the original pilot study found the service useful, there were some drawbacks to the initial design. The VizWiz team spent seven cents for each answer from Mechanical Turk. While this cost was not prohibitive for individual questions, it could add up with frequent use. More importantly, the Mechanical Turk workers were different for almost every question, so no contextual information from previous questions was used to answer new questions, and the workers did not know anything about the question-asker that could allow their responses to be customized to a specific user's needs.

In response to these concerns, we developed VizWiz Social, an iPhone application that allows blind people to choose where their questions should be sent – options include both crowdsourcing (Mechanical Turk, IQ Engines) and friendsourcing (using Twitter, Facebook, or email), or a combination of the two. In this paper, we report on differential use of these crowd- and friend-based options to understand the utility of social network Q&A for the blind.

The original paper describing VizWiz [6] only had a small test deployment with 11 users. In contrast, VizWiz Social has been deployed on the iTunes store for over a year, and we report large-scale and long-term log data from the users to provide insight into ecologically valid use.

Social Network Question Asking

66% of online American adults used social networking sites as of February 2012 [10]. Such sites are commonly used for their namesake purpose of socializing [28], although recent research indicates that many people turn to their social network as a way to "friendsource" [5] their information needs through the practice of social network Q&A, in which users post a question in their social network status update and receive replies from their network contacts.

Morris et al. [22] conducted a survey of Microsoft employees' use of Facebook and Twitter for Q&A, finding that half of respondents had used their status messages to ask questions of their friends. A classification of a sample of questions asked found that subjective questions seeking recommendations and opinions were quite common (51% of questions), followed by those seeking factual knowledge (17% of questions). Answers received from social networks are typically personalized and highly trusted [23]. Social network Q&A is more effective when the asker and answerer know each other well [24, 25], and when the asker has a large network [23, 30]. The practice of social network Q&A appears to extend to a variety of networks, including Facebook [20, 22, 25], Twitter [13, 26], Google+ and LinkedIn [21], enterprise networks [31], and sites popular in Asian countries (e.g., Weibo) [38]. Lampe et al. found that users are more likely to engage in information-seeking on Facebook if they are younger and have larger network sizes [20].

Due to their inability to process information visually, blind users often have an unmet need for Q&A with regard to explicating such visual content [6]; this paper explores whether social network Q&A might be a viable option to fulfill this need. While the aforementioned prior work has studied the use of social networking sites for question-asking by general populations, we explore the new concerns, challenges, and use cases that arise when blind users engage in social network question asking. Though the field experiment performed dealt with photograph-based Q&A, our survey of blind people's use of social networks for Q&A did not specify the type of Q&A that would be performed, so we could compare the results to general perceptions of social network Q&A.

Social Costs

Bonding social capital represents the benefits of the emotional support and companionship from close relationships with family and friends, while bridging social capital refers to the benefits of new information or opportunities that can be provided by a diverse group of acquaintances [7]. Burke et al. found that higher engagement on Facebook was associated with increased bonding social capital and greater overall well-being [9], and that users with higher frequencies of direct communication with specific individuals also had higher bridging social capital [7]. However, these benefits came primarily from directed communication, and there was no effect of broadcasted communication such as Facebook statuses on bridging social capital. Burke et al.'s studies did not address the impact of asking or answering status message questions on social capital. Lampe et al. [20] found that users with more bridging social capital were more likely to seek information using Facebook.

Previous psychology research has found that people might not always be willing to ask members of their social network for help, due to the psychological costs that can arise for both the asker and person asked. People can be reluctant to ask for help if it will incur costs to the person asked or to the asker themselves, or if they think the question they have should be easy to solve [12]. The person asked may develop a lesser opinion of the asker after helping them with their question [36]. These costs may discourage the use of social networks for question-asking, as the questions will be seen by all the users' friends and contacts and the user may feel that they are being judged.

Morris et al. found that users were reluctant to post revisions to their questions on Facebook, due to concerns about spamming friends' news feeds with too many posts [23]. However, a study by André et al. [3] found that tweets asking questions of one's followers were among the types of content that readers found more interesting, suggesting that users' perceptions of the social costs of status message Q&A may not align with those of their networks.

The "norm of reciprocity" may also influence users' likelihood of engaging in social network Q&A, as social scientists have found that people are averse to "over benefiting" from social interactions [32]; this may translate into limiting the number of questions asked to network connections.

These prior investigations of the social costs and benefits of SNS technologies motivated our investigation of the perceived social costs of question asking by blind users of SNSs. Because of their disability, blind users may have less opportunity to build social capital (e.g., by reciprocating in Q&A exchanges), and may be more acutely aware of social costs, and more likely to try to avoid them.

SURVEY OF SOCIAL NETWORK USE BY THE BLIND

In order to learn more about blind people's use of SNSs and their impression of such sites as a potential source of information, we conducted a survey of blind internet users. We created an accessible online survey, which was available for a three-week period in January-February 2012. We advertised the survey via email to North American organizations for the blind (e.g., the National Federation of the Blind, the American Foundation for the Blind, the Canadian Council of the Blind), and raffled a gift card as an incentive. Our recruiting e-mail requested people not share

frequency (Facebook)	log in (read content)	status update	ask a question
several times / day	28.9%	5.9%	2.0%
once / day	28.9%	19.1%	1.3%
weekly	23.0%	27.0%	8.6%
monthly	7.2%	12.5%	10.5%
less than once / month	11.8%	35.5%	77.6%

Table 1. The frequency with which the 152 blind adults with Facebook accounts in our survey sample engaged in various behaviors on that network. Q&A is relatively rare.

frequency (Twitter)	log in (read content)	tweet	ask a question
several times / day	41.4%	25.3%	3.0%
once / day	8.1%	13.1%	9.1%
weekly	12.1%	12.1%	14.1%
monthly	8.1%	9.1%	13.1%
less than once / month	30.3%	40.4%	60.6%

Table 2. The frequency with which the 99 blind adults with Twitter accounts in our survey sample engaged in various behaviors on that network. Q&A is relatively infrequent, though it is more common on Twitter than on Facebook for this demographic.

the survey link through social media (so that our survey sample wouldn't be biased toward social media users).

203 people completed the survey; however, 12 self-reported that they did not consider themselves blind (perhaps identifying with other impairments such as low vision), so their results were discarded. Our analysis includes only the 191 surveys from blind respondents.

Respondents were generally experienced internet users (73% reported using the internet for 10 years or more, and only one reported having less than a year of internet experience). 56% of respondents were female. 19.3% were under age 30, 36.7% were aged 30 – 49, and 44% were 50 or older. The age distribution of our sample likely reflects that fact that many people lose their vision as they age. Note that this means our sample is older than the typical SNS user – a 2012 Pew survey found that 86% of those under 30 had SNS accounts, decreasing to 72% of those age 30 – 49, and down to 50% of those age 50 – 64 [10].

General Use of Social Networking Sites

The use of social networking sites was quite common among our blind respondents – 92% reported using one or more social networking sites. This is an extremely high adoption rate; for comparison, a February 2012 Pew survey found that 66% of online U.S. adults used social networking sites [10], and the proportion decreased with age, which makes this high rate of adoption particularly surprising given the older age skew of our sample. The SNS use rate in our sample is significantly higher than the proportions predicted by the Pew finding, $\chi^2(1, N=191) = 55.88$, $p < .001$ (the adoption rate of SNS in each age bracket is also significantly higher than the Pew proportions, at the $p < .001$ level).

The highest participation was on Facebook (80%) and Twitter (52%). Other, less-frequently-used SNSs included LinkedIn (40%), Google Plus (15%), MySpace (4%), Yammer (3%), Inclusive Planet (3%), and Orkut (1%). Since 85% of respondents used at least one of Facebook or Twitter, we focus the rest of our analysis on their use of those two sites. The high penetration of Twitter, at 52% of our respondents, was surprising, since Twitter is much less popular in the general population (15% of online adults had accounts as of February 2012 [29]); this likely reflects the accessibility of Twitter's simple, text-based interface.

Respondents with Facebook accounts used them actively. 81% reported logging in at least once per week. However, respondents seem to tend towards "lurking" rather than posting; only 52% reported posting a status message at least once per week. 62% of the Twitter users reported logging in at least once per week, while only 51% authored tweets with that frequency. Tables 1 and 2 provide more detail about the frequency of various actions by blind account-holders on Facebook and Twitter.

Network size seems to be smaller than average. Blind Facebook users' median network size was 100, whereas a recent Pew survey found that median network size was 111 [16], and Facebook's own statistics page recently reported a figure of 130 [14]. On Twitter, our sample of blind account-holders reported having a median of 45 followers; finding accurate comparison numbers for the general population has been difficult - a 2009 article reported that users have 126 followers on average [4], though it is not clear whether this average is a median or mean.

Network composition varied between the two services. Those with Facebook accounts reported having networks comprised primarily of friends and family (72%), followed by colleagues (24%). In contrast, only 32% of the Twitter users reported having networks composed primarily of friends and family, and 27% had networks comprised mostly of colleagues; instead, 42% of the Twitter users in our sample reported that the majority of their followers were people they had met on Twitter itself. A Wilcoxon test was used to evaluate whether reported network composition differed significantly between the two services; the proportion of networks comprised mostly of colleagues was similar, whereas Facebook had a higher proportion of networks comprised primarily of family and friends ($z = -4.37$, $p < .001$) and Twitter had a higher proportion of networks comprised of contacts met on the service itself ($z = -5.11$, $p < .001$).

Social Network Q&A

In addition to asking respondents about their general use of social networking sites, we also asked about their current practices regarding using such sites to ask questions of their online social networks. When asked about SNS Q&A in general ("Do you think questioning on a social network site is an effective way to get answers?"), only 55% of respondents answered positively, indicating that they perceived this approach could be either "very" or "somewhat" effective (on a five-point Likert scale ranging from very effective to very ineffective). Our questions did not specify any particular method of Q&A (eg. textual or image-based).

Status message Q&A ("How frequently do you post questions in your [statuses on Facebook/tweets on Twitter]?") was relatively infrequent, particularly on Facebook, where only 12% of account-holders reported asking questions at least once per week (Table 1). In contrast, 26% of Twitter users reported asking questions at least once per week (Table 2). A Wilcoxon test (used due to the non-parametric nature of Likert scale responses) found that the reported differences in the frequency of posting questions to these two networks was significantly different ($z = -2.16$, $p = .03$). As a point of reference, a recent survey of sighted users status message Q&A habits [21] found that a similar proportion of Facebook users (15.4% compared with 12% in this survey) asked questions at least once per week, but only 9.5% of Twitter users did so with similar frequency (as compared with 26% in our survey).

Of those who asked questions on Facebook, only 34% reported that many or all of their questions received answers; this number was 33% for the Twitter users. This appears to be a low response rate in comparison to other studies – for example, Morris et al. reported that over 90% or those posting a question to Facebook or Twitter received answers [22], while a controlled experiment by Teevan et al. [30] found that over 75% of questions posted on Facebook received answers. (Paul et al. [26] reported a response rate of 18.7% in a study of questions on Twitter, but that study included a high proportion of rhetorical questions, which presumably would not elicit an answer, and may account for the low answer rate they found.)

On a five-point Likert scale ranging from "very comfortable" to "very uncomfortable," only 37% of the Facebook users reported feeling "very" or "somewhat" comfortable with posting questions to Facebook. In contrast, 54% of the Twitter users indicated a similar level of comfort with the concept of posting question tweets (though this difference was not statistically significant).

Motivations for Limiting SNS Q&A

To better understand the concerns that blind people associate with SNS Q&A, we also asked whether those with SNS accounts had ever intentionally limited the number of questions they post to such sites, and, if so, to explain why in a free-text response. 16.4% of the Facebook users and 17.0% of the Twitter users reported having actively limited the number of questions they ask in these venues. We categorized their free-text explanations of this behavior using a grounded theory approach [15] with a two-pass process; in the first pass, we developed a labeling scheme based on common themes in the responses, and in the second pass we applied a label to each response.

The most common reason for limiting Q&A for both Facebook and Twitter users was *social costs* (mentioned by 10 users and 5 users, respectively). Explanations illustrating concerns about social capital included a respondent's statement that he limited his question asking because, "my followers' time is important and I don't want to waste it on something I could figure out myself." Another noted, "People will not respond to too many questions asked at a go." A third observed, "I think it's annoying to post too many questions without also helping other tweeters along the way. Karma, reciprocity, etc."

Usability and accessibility issues were another source of question-limiting on both Facebook (7 users) and Twitter (3 users), with users stating that "Facebook is very difficult to use as a blind person," and "[it's] slower with a screen reader."

As suggested by the response to our earlier survey question about comfort levels surrounding asking personal questions on SNSs, *discomfort with public question-asking* was another theme in participants' responses (6 Facebook users and 3 Twitter users). For example, one user said, "I will only ask people who I am close to privately." Another said, "I am not sure the network is the place to post questions I can get answered by an e-mail."

Poor response rates were also discussed by 2 of the Facebook users and 1 Twitter user, who indicated they limited questions for reasons such as "lack of response from prior questions."

Three Twitter users also cited the *short format of tweets* as a deterrent to engaging in Q&A on that site, noting discouragement due to the "limited number of characters."

Discussion of Survey Results

Our survey findings represent the first formal study of the use of social networking sites by the blind. The high adoption rate of these technologies, with 92% of our 191 respondents using SNSs, is quite surprising, particularly in light of the challenges of using such sites with a screen reader [34, 35] and in light of the relatively advanced age of our audience. Perhaps the ability to interact asynchronously, at a comfortable pace, increases the appeal of SNSs to blind people (CMC theory suggests that selective self-presentation is a benefit of asynchronous communication for general users [33]; this effect may be heightened for users with disabilities). The ability to connect with physically distant contacts may also be particularly appealing to this population, given the restricted mobility and travel challenges that can accompany blindness. The use of social networks to reach out and meet other members of the visually impaired community may be another factor driving high adoption rates – our findings regarding network composition suggest, however, that users' networks consist mostly of friends, family, and colleagues, rather than of new contacts met online.

The adoption rate of Twitter in this population was also unusually high. This may reflect the fact that Twitter's simple, text-based interface is more accessible to screen readers than the rich visual and multimedia experience of using Facebook. Twitter also fared better in blind users' perceptions as a venue for Q&A than did Facebook. This preference might also reflect fundamental accessibility issues. Another explanation may be due to the differing network compositions of our respondents on each service, combined with this demographic's concerns about social costs – since Twitter users were more likely to have networks comprised of contacts met online (as opposed to family or colleagues), they may have felt more comfortable "bothering" these weaker ties with their questions.

Overall, however, social network Q&A by blind people appears to be much less common than among more general populations [22, 26, 31, 38]. Concerns about social costs may account for some of this, as many users reported actively limiting the number of questions they asked due to such concerns. The smaller-than-average network sizes of blind users may also factor into their negative view of SNS Q&A – for example, the low reported response rates to questions asked may be due to having a smaller network, as past studies have found that network size impacts the number and speed of responses received to questions on Facebook [23, 30].

When interpreting this survey data, readers should bear in mind the inherent accuracy limits of self-report. Readers should also bear in mind that, while we have compared and contrasted our findings of blind users' SNS habits with findings from studies of SNS use by general populations, such comparisons must be interpreted critically due to the fact that demographic factors are not controlled across the different studies and due to variations in the methodologies across the studies. Additionally, it is possible that our sample of the blind community is non-representative (i.e., it is possible that people who subscribe to the mailing lists of the organizations we contacted may be more technologically savvy, better educated, or differ in some other systematic way from the "average" blind person).

Our survey provides background information about blind people's use and views of social networking sites, which provides helpful context for interpreting our findings on how they used them in practice via the VizWiz Social app.

VIZWIZ SOCIAL

We have created a variant of the VizWiz concept [6], which we call VizWiz Social. VizWiz Social was released to the public on May 31st, 2011 as a free app for the iPhone and has been installed by 5,392 people since its release. Every day, an average of 74 questions are asked by 36 users.

VizWiz Social's design is optimized for use with Apple's built-in VoiceOver screen reader technology. Using the phone's built-in camera, VizWiz Social prompts users to photograph the object about which they have a question (a challenging, but accomplishable task for the blind [18]). Users then record an audio caption that asks a question about the contents of the photo (Figures 1, 3a, 3b). Users are then prompted to select from among the available answer sources (and may choose as many as they wish) (Figure 3c). The main difference between VizWiz Social and the original VizWiz is the addition of new answer sources (crowdsourcing via "web workers" was the only answer source in the original VizWiz, whereas VizWiz Social also offers "friendsourcing" via social sources). When an answer arrives, users receive a notification, and the responses can be read via VoiceOver (Figure 3e).

There are two types of answer sources available for VizWiz Social questions: anonymous crowdsourced sources and social friendsourced sources. In the current version of VizWiz Social, all questions can be sent to any source free of charge (all financial costs, such as fees for Mechanical Turk workers, are absorbed by our organization). The response time and quality of the answers received depends on the selected source(s).

Anonymous (Crowdsourced) Sources

VizWiz Social offers two sources of crowdsourced, anonymous answers: *web workers* and *IQ Engines*.

The *web workers* source sends HITs to Mechanical Turk. Using an on-demand workforce to speed crowdsourcing [6], answers take a median of 98 seconds to arrive. However, the workers are given no contextual information about the user besides the question itself, so answers are not personalized. The VizWiz Social team pays workers five cents for each HIT answered.

The *IQ Engines* source uses a human-backed image recognition product offered by VisionIQ [iqengines.com]. If the vision algorithm cannot recognize the image, it falls back to human workers who manually identify the object. IQ Engines can recognize barcodes and commercial products quickly, but cannot answer more complex non-identification questions. The VizWiz Social team pays a monthly subscription fee to this service, which averages to about one cent per question.

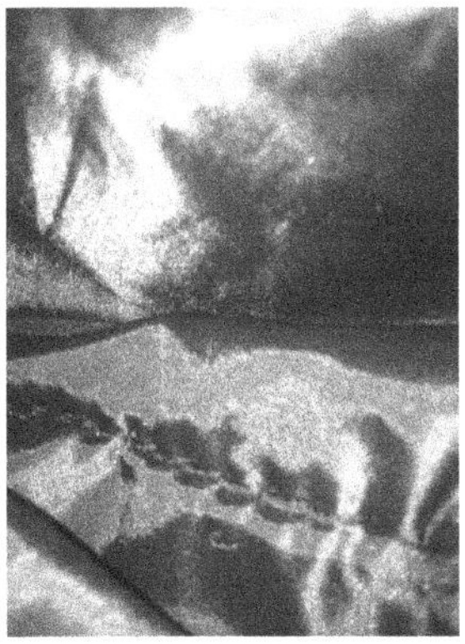

Figure 1: A photograph submitted by a VizWiz Social user. The accompanying audio question was: "What color is this sleeping bag?" Answers received from Facebook included "black," and "It looks navy blue to me."

Social (Friendsourced) Sources

VizWiz Social offers three sources of friendsourced answers from a user's own social circle. Questions can be sent to a specific friend via e-mail, or can be posted to social network contacts via a Facebook or Twitter status update (Figures 1 & 2). All posting is done by the VizWiz Social service (once the user has initialized this option by providing necessary account names and passwords), and the answers are also pulled from the social network and reported back using our accessible interface, so there are no additional technical or accessibility barriers to using social networks in this way. There is no cost for access to the Facebook or Twitter APIs, so these services are free to the VizWiz team.

While the user's social network provides a free source of answers that may hold greater personal significance, response rates and speeds are dependent on the user's contacts. If a user has a small network, their question may receive few (or slow) answers. Time of day may also impact response rate and timing, such as if a question is asked while contacts are generally asleep or at work.

Types of Questions Asked

In the first year since VizWiz Social was released, over 40,000 questions have been asked. In order to learn about the scenarios prompting question-asking by VizWiz Social users, we developed a categorization scheme for the questions. We randomly sampled 500 queries (5 were excluded from analysis due to image or audio quality issues). Four researchers were provided with the resulting set of the 495 image and transcription pairs, and clustered similar queries together to create a bottom-up affinity diagram. Queries could be similar in terms of image content, question content, or both. The researchers then refined the clustered queries into 22 groups, and formed four overarching query categories to encompass all the groups. These four categories were:

Identification questions (44%), which asked for an object to be identified by name or type. Examples included "What is this?"; "What kind of pizza rolls are these?"; and "Please identify this ready-meal package."

Figure 2: The answering interface for a VizWiz user's Facebook friends. The question ("what color are these flowers?") appears embedded as a video on the friends' news feed and on the user's profile page. Responses are entered as comments on the Facebook post.

Description questions (26%), which asked for a description of a visual or physical property of an object. Examples included "Is there a picture of something? [on a piece of paper]"; "What color is this shirt?"; and "Can you please describe in detail what's on the [TV] screen?"

Reading questions (23%), which asked for text to be read from an object or electronic display. Examples included "What does this package say?"; "What's the expiration date?"; and "I need to determine the CAPTCHA code in this image."

Unanswerable questions (7%), such as when the photo did not include the information required to generate an answer.

The makeup of the questions indicates the complexity of the questions asked and the usefulness of having human workers to answer questions, since less than half of questions were simple *Identification* questions.

Use of Social Sources

The use of social sources has been somewhat limited. In the month before our user study, 702 users asked a total of 3116 queries, for an average of 4.44 questions per user in a month (median 2). Only 15% of users ever tried any social source (this drops to 10.7% if e-mail is not counted).

Of the 3116 questions from that month-long period, only 156 (5%) were sent to social sources (with 94 sent to Twitter, 47 to email, and 26 to Facebook). Only three of the questions sent to Facebook and Twitter received answers, with a median response time of two hours and fifty-five minutes. In contrast, nearly all crowdsourced questions were answered: web workers had a 100% response rate with a median response time of 98 seconds, and IQ Engines had a 96.4% response rate with a median response time of 15 minutes, 46 seconds. There was no significant pattern in the distribution of question types (identification, description, or reading) to crowdsourced vs. social sources.

Our field experiment was designed to examine why social sources were so infrequently used, and if their value as a free source of answers to VizWiz users might increase if the true costs of crowdsourced answers were not absorbed by the VizWiz team.

VIZWIZ SOCIAL FIELD EXPERIMENT

In order to further explore the question asking behavior of blind users, we designed a field experiment. We recruited active users of VizWiz Social to participate, and placed financial restrictions on the anonymous answer sources in the service. These financial restrictions mirrored the cost of the Mechanical Turk and IQ Engine services (currently absorbed by the VizWiz team), and were implemented to see the value of each source to the users. We then examined their question-asking behaviors under these new conditions, and gave a post-study questionnaire to better understand their motivations in choosing whether to send a question to their social network or use the anonymous answer sources. A key goal of this experiment was to understand whether the low adoption of friendsourcing we observed in our log data analysis was a by-product of the artificial economics of VizWiz Social (in which the costs of crowdsourcing were absorbed by our organization rather than end users), or whether other factors were preventing blind users from successfully harnessing the benefits of friendsourcing.

Study Design

We hypothesized that the relatively low use of the social sources identified in our log analysis could be explained in part by the fact that participants did not pay the true costs associated with the anonymous answer sources (*web workers* and *IQ Engines).* In order to see how VizWiz Social users weighed the social costs of asking questions to members of their social networks under more realistic circumstances, we associated a financial cost with sending questions to the anonymous sources.

At the beginning of the month-long study, each participant was given a balance of $25 to spend on VizWiz Social questions. To enhance the validity of the economic decision-making process, users were told that they would receive a gift card containing the unused portion of this balance at the completion of the study (in addition to a baseline participation gratuity of $10).

Users were placed into one of two conditions: the *cheap* condition, where questions sent to web workers cost five cents each and those sent to IQ Engines cost one cent each; or the *expensive* condition, where questions sent to web workers cost twenty-five cents each and those sent to IQ Engines cost five cents each (Figure 3c,d).

The costs in the cheap condition were based on the approximate costs of the current VizWiz Social service (which until this point had been paid by our organization). Users were able to send each question to as many of the available answer sources as they desired, as long as their available cash balance permitted it. $25 was chosen as the starting account balance in order to make it possible for users who relied on the service to continue to ask questions at their normal rate for the one-month study period (our most active user asks about 100 questions per month).

The study ran for one month starting in April 2012. We also compared the behavior of users in the experiment to their usage in the previous month as a control.

Recruitment

Potential participants were chosen from the set of active VizWiz Social users in the month preceding the study. Users were eligible if they had asked at least four questions in the last month. The study was limited to this set of users so that their question-asking behaviors in the experimental month could be accurately compared to their previous question-asking behaviors. We released an update to the application that identified potential participants and presented them with an invitation to join the study. If they accepted, they were randomly assigned to the cheap or expensive condition and began participating in the study immediately.

A sample size of 30 participants was chosen for the study. 207 VizWiz users had asked at least four questions in a month-long period from March to April 2012, so they were eligible to join the study. Once the recruitment period began, any of these 207 users who had installed the latest version of VizWiz would be presented with an invitation to join the study. Of those 207 users, 60 were active during the recruitment period and received the study invitation; 30 agreed to join the study (participation was not mandatory, since many people rely on VizWiz Social for daily activities, and we did not want to force a modified experience upon them). 23 of the 30 asked at least one question during the course of the month-long study (11 in the cheap condition and 12 in the expensive condition). We first present the pre-study behaviors of these 23 users, and then discuss their behaviors during the study and their responses to a post-study questionnaire.

Pre-Study User Behaviors

We analyzed the pre-study question-asking behavior of the 23 active study participants. During the month before the study, these 23 participants asked a total of 217 questions, with an average of 9.86 questions per user. Users in the cheap condition asked an average of 9.1 questions, while users in the expensive condition asked an average of 10.8.

The majority of these 23 users' questions in the pre-study period were sent to web workers (81%) and IQ Engines (93%) (note that percentages total to greater than 100% since a single question may be federated to multiple answer sources). 14% of the questions were sent to social sources, with 21 (10%) going to Facebook, 7 (3%) going to Twitter, and 2 (1%) going to email. However, the majority of the socially-directed questions were asked by two users – 20 of the 21 questions sent to Facebook were asked by the same user (cheap condition), and all 7 of the questions sent to Twitter were asked by another user (expensive condition).

In-Study User Behaviors

The 23 active study participants asked a total of 170 questions, with an average of 7.3 questions per user (stdev 7.6) during the month of the study. The 11 participants in the cheap condition asked a total of 95 questions, while the 12 in the expensive condition asked a total of 75 questions. The number of questions asked by participants dropped during the month of the study for both the cheap and expensive conditions. However, these numbers were not significantly different than the number of questions asked in the pre-study period. Users in the cheap condition asked an average of 7.8 questions, while users in the expensive condition asked an average of 6.8 questions; the difference between questions asked in each condition was not significant.

141 of the questions were sent to web workers (83%) and 76 were sent to IQ Engines (45%). 47 of the questions were sent to both web workers and IQ Engines. Only 2 of the questions, both asked by the same user (in the expensive condition), were sent to friendsourced sources (Facebook), but both were also sent to at least one crowdsourced source.

Despite the monetary incentive to send questions to SNSs, these results highlight a strong reluctance to use social networking sites for question-asking, but do not provide any insight into the reasons for the limited number of questions that were friendsourced. In order to learn more about our participants' motivations to use (or not use) crowd- and friendsourcing, we sent out a questionnaire to the active participants after the completion of the study period.

Post-Study Questionnaire

We asked participants in our field experiment to complete a questionnaire about the types of questions they did and didn't ask with VizWiz Social, the sources that they used and preferred, and general demographic information. Twelve participants completed the entire questionnaire. Seven were male and five were female. Six were aged 30-39, while four were 20-29 and two were 50-59. Almost all (83%) had used the internet for more than 10 years. 75% of were members of Facebook, with an average network size of 176.1 (median 184.5), and 67% were members of Twitter, with an average network size of 245.5 (median 102.5). Network sizes were self-reported, and may be rounded or estimates.

Responses

Though all of the participants in the questionnaire reported being members of at least one social networking site, most were reluctant to use the sites for question-asking.

Users reported strongly preferring the crowdsourced answer sources. When asked to choose a single preferred source, all respondents chose crowdsourced sources (with ten choosing web workers, and two choosing IQ Engines). Given a chance to elaborate via free-form text response, one participant explained that their preference for using web workers stemmed from the availability of human answers that weren't necessarily contextualized by accessibility:

"Humans are much more reliable, in my opinion, and Web workers are entirely anonymous. They might necessarily not even know that they're dealing with an accessibility application if Amazon Turkit [sic] is involved."

9 of the 12 respondents reported that they "much preferred" to send their questions to web workers, while 1 "somewhat

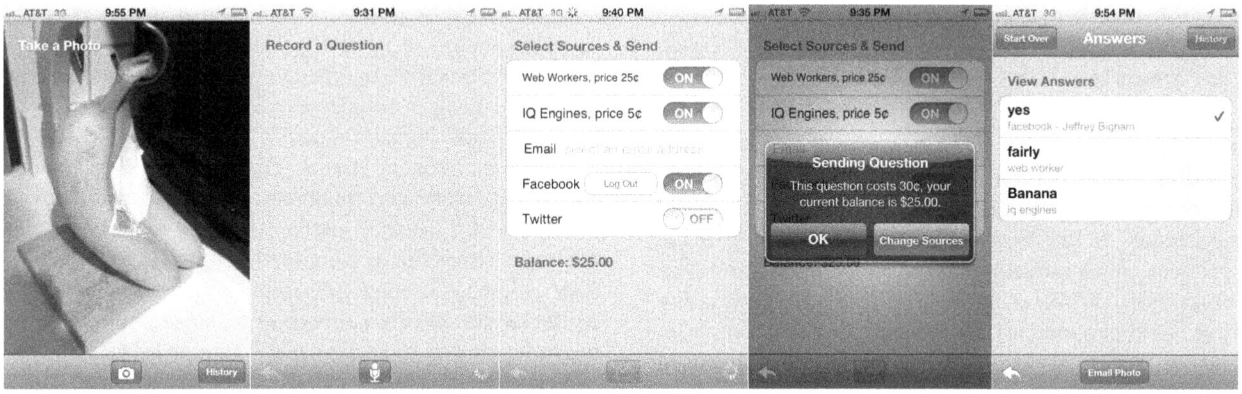

(a) (b) (c) (d) (e)

Figure 3: A participant in the "expensive" condition (a) takes a photograph, (b) records their question ("are these bananas ripe?"), (c) selects the sources they want to send the question to, (d) confirms the cost of the question and gets their current balance, and (e) waits for answers. All instructions and buttons can be navigated with the iPhone's built-in screen reader.

preferred" web workers over friendsourcing, and 2 had no preference. Respondents were allowed to fill in a free-form response section indicating why they preferred to ask questions via crowdsourcing over friendsourcing, and were able to give as many reasons as they wanted. The 10 respondents who preferred crowdsourcing mentioned its technical advantages, such as the speed of response (3 participants), accuracy and quality of responses (4), or the photograph-taking feedback the web workers gave when a picture was not focused on the correct object (1). The availability of web workers is important for contextual or time-sensitive questions, as mentioned by one participant:

"[I preferred web workers] because there's no guarantee that a facebook or twitter post would get you an immediate answer. When I need something identified like a can or TV Dinner I am going to use it now, not whenever my friends get around to telling me what it is. :)"

Others preferred to send their questions to crowdsourced answer sources specifically to avoid friendsourced response sources: either they wanted their questions to be anonymous (2), didn't want to broadcast the question to a large group (1), or didn't like using social networking sites in general (1). The user who had earlier preferred the web workers source overall for not drawing attention to the accessibility aspect of the questions voiced similar reasons for preferring it more than friendsourced sources:

Web-workers are completely anonymous, and there is sometimes no reason to think they are actually assisting with a disability related question.

In addition to preferring crowdsourced sources, respondents were also more likely to restrict themselves from asking questions to social sources. 8 of the 12 respondents reported choosing not to ask at least one question to friendsourced sources, while only 4 respondents reported the same for crowdsourced sources. When asked why they did not want to send questions to Facebook or Twitter, some users mentioned the social costs of asking questions on the sites. One responded,

"Not my friend's job to tell me that stuff. Plus it clutters up people's timelinesand [sic] they might not like it."

DISCUSSION

Our survey of blind users' social networking habits and attitudes, combined with our log analysis and experimental manipulations of the VizWiz Social application, provide perspectives on the potential of friendsourcing as a resource for blind users. While each of these methods (survey, log analysis, field experiment) has limitations, our intention in combining them is to create a more rich, nuanced understanding of the possibilities and challenges in harnessing the power of friendsourcing for the blind community. In addition to offering insights into this scenario, our findings also raise new questions, suggesting directions for future inquiry.

Both the survey findings and our experiences with the VizWiz Social app indicate that sending questions to Facebook and Twitter for answers is viewed as undesirable by blind people. This result is in spite of the fact that friendsourcing could be a valuable supplement to existing Q&A services for blind users that rely on crowdsourcing (e.g., [6]) by reducing costs, increasing answer quality, and offering social in addition to informational value [23].

Our finding that blind users have smaller than typical social networks may contribute to this negative attitude, as prior work has shown that answer speed and quantity are dependent on network size [23, 30]. The poor speed and response rates of social sources in VizWiz Social seems to justify this concern. Poor response speed seems particularly problematic for this audience in light of our log analysis of the type of questions asked with VizWiz Social, which suggests that most questions reflect an immediate need (e.g., an object that needs to be identified for immediate use or decision making). Smaller networks may also indicate reduced social capital [9] among this demographic, which can also reduce the likelihood of trying SNS Q&A [20].

Perceived social costs play a role, as well. Participants' comments in our survey and experiment indicated that they were reluctant to "bother" their networks with questions. A desire to appear independent, despite disability, may be heightening this concern, since disabled people understandably do not wish to give an impression of being helpless [27]. Blind users' reduced ability to reciprocate in SNS Q&A exchanges may also lead to concerns about incurring unpayable social debts; prior work shows that this concern is not be unfounded, as anticipated reciprocation is a key motivating factor in SNS Q&A [22, 38] (indeed, people are hesitant to violate norms of reciprocation in a variety of social scenarios [32]).

Our findings also suggest next steps for further exploring the potential of SNS Q&A as a resource for the blind. Interview studies could provide more nuanced understanding of the factors shaping this group's aversion to harnessing the power of their social networks. Further experimentation using the paradigm explored in our field experiment (such as by changing the costs associated with non-social answer sources or altering users' starting cash balance) could perhaps quantify the perceived social costs of Q&A in financial terms. Different technical solutions might also make this potentially valuable resource more palatable – for instance, perhaps framing requests to friends not as questions but as a competition or game would reduce their stigma, or perhaps routing questions only to a particular subset of a network (e.g., close family members) might be viewed more favorably. Exploring ways in which friendsourced answers could be produced more quickly would also be particularly important for enhancing the informational value of SNSes to the blind community, whose information needs are more immediate than the more general SNS Q&A examples discussed in prior work (e.g., [22]).

CONCLUSION

In this paper, we synthesize survey, log, and experimental data to gain insight into the suitability of social network question-asking as a tool for blind users. The contributions of this work include:

- a survey study of the general social networking habits of 191 blind adults, with a particular focus on their habits and concerns regarding social network Q&A;
- an introduction of the VizWiz Social system, a freely-available iPhone application that allows blind users to send audio-visual questions to either crowdsourced or friendsourced answer sources;
- a log analysis of the types of questions asked on VizWiz Social and the use of the social Q&A features "in the wild";
- an experimental study in which the price of crowdsourced answers was manipulated in order to see how pricing impacted blind uses' motivations to use social Q&A

Our findings indicate that despite the financial, personalization, and social benefits from friendsourced answers, the blind people who participated in our surveys and study were reluctant to use social networking sites to get answers to their questions. This seems to be due to a combination of objective challenges (e.g., inaccessible design of some social networking sites, low response rates due to small network sizes, and slow response times for real-time information needs) as well as some subjective challenges (e.g., concerns about imbalances in the potential or reciprocating, appearing overly dependent due to one's disability, and privacy).

These findings can help shape the design of future accessibility technologies that utilize social networking infrastructure. For example, blind users could trade access to each other's social networks for more private, but high quality, question-answering. Another avenue for future work is experimentation with signaling the urgency of a question, either explicitly or implicitly through careful wording, as this may be an avenue for understanding how to make SNSes more responsive to the particular types of Q&A exchanges that blind users engage in.

REFERENCES

1. Abascal, J. and Civit, A. Mobile communication for people with disabilities and older people: New opportunities for autonomous life. *Proceedings of the 6th ERCIM Workshop 2000*, 255-268.
2. American Foundation for the Blind. Survey Results on Social Networking. *AccessWorld* 10(3), May 2009. http://www.afb.org/afbpress/pub.asp?DocID=aw100306
3. André, P., Bernstein, M., and Luther, K. Who gives a tweet? Evaluating microblog content value. *Proceedings of CSCW 2012*, 471-474.
4. Arthur, C. Average Twitter User has 126 Followers, and Only 20% of Users go via Website. *The Guardian Technology Blog*, June 29, 2009.
5. Bernstein, M.S., Tan, D., Smith, G., Czerwinski, M., and Horvitz, E. Personalization vs. Friendsourcing. *ACM Transactions on Computer-Human Interaction*, 17(2), May 2010.
6. Bigham, J.P., Jayant, C., Ji, H., Little, G., Miller, A., Miller, R.C., Miller, R., Tatarowicz, A., White, B., White, S., and Yeh, T. VizWiz: Nearly Real-Time Answers to Visual Questions. *Proceedings of UIST 2010, 333-342.*
7. Burke, M., Kraut, R., and Marlow, C. Social Capital on Facebook: Differentiating Uses and Users. *Proceedings of CHI 2011*, 571-580.
8. Burke, M., Kraut, R., and Williams, D. Social Use of Computer-Mediated Communication by Adults on the Autism Spectrum. *Proceedings of CSCW 2010, 425-434.*
9. Burke, M., Marlow, C., and Lento, T. Social Network Activity and Social Well-Being. Proceedings of *CHI 2010, 1909-1912.*
10. Brenner, J. Social Networking. *Pew Internet & American Life Project*, March 29, 2012.
11. Cavender, A.C., Otero, D.S., Bigham, J.P., and Ladner, R.E. ASL-STEMForum: Enabling Sign Language to Grow Through Online Collaboration. *Proceedings of CHI 2010, 2075-2078.*
12. DePaulo, B.M. and Fisher, J.D. "The Costs of Asking for Help," *Basic and Applied Social Psychology* (1980), 37-41.
13. Efron, M. and Winget, M. Questions are Content: A Taxonomy of Questions in a Microblogging Environment. *Proceedings of ASIS&T 2010, Article 27.*
14. Facebook Official Statistics Page. Retrieved Sept. 12, 2009. http://facebook.com/press/info.php?statistics.
15. Glaser, B.G. and Strauss, A.L. The Discovery of Grounded Theory: Strategies for Qualitative Research. *Aldine Transaction*. 1977.
16. Hampton, K., Goulet, L.S., Marlow, C., and Rainie, L. Why Most Facebook Users Get More Than They Give. *Pew Internet & American Life Project*, February 3, 2012.
17. Hong, H., Kim, J.G., Abowd, G.D., and Arriaga, R.I. Designing a Social Network to Support the Independence of Young Adults with Autism. *Proceedings of CSCW 2012*, 627-636.
18. Jayant, C., Ji, H., White, S., and Bigham, J. Supporting Blind Photography. *Proceedings of ASSETS 2011, 203-210.*
19. Kane, S., Jayant, C., Wobbrock, J., and Ladner, R. Freedom to Roam: A Study of Mobile Device

Adoption and Accessibility for People with Visual and Motor Disabilities. *Proceedings of ASSETS 2009, 115-122.*

20. Lampe, C., Vitak, J., Gray, R., and Ellison, N. Perceptions of Facebook's value as an information source. *Proceedings of CHI 2012*, 3195-3204.
21. Morris, M.R. Collaborative Search Revisited. *Proceedings of CSCW 2013.*
22. Morris, M.R., Teevan, J., and Panovich, K. What Do People Ask Their Social Networks, and Why? A Survey Study of Status Message Q&A Behavior. *Proceedings of CHI 2010*, 1739-1748.
23. Morris, M.R., Teevan, J., and Panovich, K. A Comparison of Information Seeking Using Search Engines and Social Networks. *Proceedings of ICWSM 2010.*
24. Nichols, J. and Kang, J-H. Asking questions of targeted strangers on social networks. *Proceedings of CSCW 2012, 999-1002.*
25. Panovich, K., Miller, R., and Karger, D. Tie strength in question & answer on social network sites. *Proceedings of CSCW 2012*, 1057-1066.
26. Paul, S.A., Hong, L., and Chi, E.H. Is Twitter a Good Place for Asking Questions? A Characterization Study. *Proceedings of ICWSM 2011.*
27. Shinohara, K. and Wobbrock, J.O. In the Shadow of Misperception: Assistive Technology Use and Social Interactions. *Proceedings of CHI 2011*, 705-714.
28. Smith, A. Why Americans Use Social Media. *Pew Internet & American Life Project*, November 15, 2011.
29. Smith, A. and Brenner, J. Twitter Use 2012. *Pew Internet & American Life Project*, May 31, 2012.
30. Teevan, J., Morris, M.R., and Panovich, K. Factors Affecting Response Quantity, Quality, and Speed for Questions Asked via Social Network Status Messages. *Proceedings of ICWSM 2011.*
31. Thom, J., Helsley, S.Y., Matthews, T.L., Daly, E.M., Millen, D.R. What Are You Working On? Status Message Q&A within an Enterprise SNS. *Proceedings of ECSCW 2011.*
32. Uehara, E. Reciprocity Reconsidered: Gouldner's "Moral Norm of Reciprocity" and Social Support. *Journal of Social and Personal Relationships*, 12(4), 1995, 483-502.
33. Walther, J.B. Selective self-presentation in computer-mediated communication: Hyperpersonal dimensions of technology, language, and cognition. *Computers in Human Behavior*, 23(5), September 2007, 2538-2557.
34. Web Accessibility in Mind. WebAIM Screen Reader User Survey #4. May 2012. http://webaim.org/projects/screenreadersurvey4/
35. Wentz, B. and Lazar, J. Are separate interfaces inherently unequal? An evaluation with blind users of the usability of two interfaces for a social networking platform. *Proceedings of iConference 2011*, 91-97.
36. Wills, T.A. Perceptual Consequences of Helping Another Person. *84th Annual Convention of the American Psychological Association,* 1976.
37. World Health Organization. Fact Sheet #282: Visual Impairment and Blindness. October 2011.
38. Yang, J., Morris, M.R., Teevan, J., Adamic, L., and Ackerman, M. Culture Matters: A Survey Study of Social Q&A Behavior. *Proceedings of ICWSM 2011.*

Contributor Profiles, their Dynamics, and their Importance in Five Q&A Sites

Adabriand Furtado, Nazareno Andrade, Nigini Oliveira, Francisco Brasileiro
Systems and Computing Department
Universidade Federal de Campina Grande – Brazil
{adabriand, nigini}@lsd.ufcg.edu.br, {nazareno, fubica}@computacao.ufcg.edu.br

ABSTRACT
Q&A sites currently enable large numbers of contributors to collectively build valuable knowledge bases. Naturally, these sites are the product of contributors acting in different ways – creating questions, answers or comments and voting in these –, contributing in diverse amounts, and creating content of varying quality. This paper advances present knowledge about Q&A sites using a multifaceted view of contributors that accounts for diversity of behavior, motivation and expertise to characterize their profiles in five sites. This characterization resulted in the definition of ten behavioral profiles that group users according to the quality and quantity of their contributions. Using these profiles, we find that the five sites have remarkably similar distributions of contributor profiles. We also conduct a longitudinal study of contributor profiles in one of the sites, identifying common profile transitions, and finding that although users change profiles with some frequency, the site composition is mostly stable over time.

Author Keywords
Q&A sites; Empirical Methods, Quantitative; Datamining and machine learning; Studies of Wikipedia/Web

ACM Classification Keywords
H.5.3 [Information Interfaces]: Group and Organization Interfaces – Computer-supported cooperative work

INTRODUCTION
Question and Answer (Q&A) sites are currently useful for thousands of people each day. In their archetypical form, these sites enable users to post questions, answers, and comments, and to provide feedback on the quality of these posts to collectively identify good questions, adequate answers and valuable comments. Sites such as Yahoo! Answers and StackOverflow have shown the potential to leverage massive numbers of voluntary contributors to create valuable and dynamic knowledge bases [1,16,18].

It is only natural that the contributors of Q&A sites are diverse and behave accordingly. For example, users have different motivations to contribute [18,8,25], spend varying amounts of time contributing [16,18], possess diverse expertise [21,19], and ultimately have different preferences on what they would like to contribute [1,18].

As in any organizational context, examining the diversity in contributor behavior in Q&A sites is central for interpreting how these sites work internally. This interpretation can, in turn, help managing a site, inform the design of task allocation mechanisms, guide the development of personalized interfaces, and ultimately lead participants to better understand Q&A sites.

This paper contributes to the understanding of how contributors collectively produce knowledge in Q&A sites by examining the typical behaviors of these contributors. For that, we use historical data from five sites of the Stack Exchange Q&A platform, and devise a set of profiles that describes contributor behavior both in long- and short-term perspectives. In the long-term analysis, we leverage these profiles to compare contributor behavior in the five sites, and identify a number of regularities both in the composition of the sites, as well as in the aggregate contribution of groups of users from each profile. For the short-term analysis, we perform a longitudinal study in the most active of the five sites and investigate how user behavior changes over time. This analysis again reveals a noted stability on the composition of the site, and exposes the profiles that are most stable, as well as those associated with users that end up abandoning the site.

Our study advances previous knowledge in two major aspects. First, it considers a multifaceted characterization of contributors. The profiles we encounter are multivariate descriptions of contributors that simultaneously account for the quantity and quality of their questions, answers, and comments. Second, we investigate how stable user behavior is over time and the distribution of user profiles in a site changes over time.

CONTRIBUTOR PROFILES IN Q&A CONTEXTS
In the context of online communities, the analysis of contributor profiles has been largely done in two perspectives: to identify archetypical roles assumed by users, or to examine contributors which assume one profile known *a priori*, such as moderators or lurkers. In both cases, the overall goal is most often to help the interpretation of collective behavior or to inform the

development of task allocation strategies or mechanisms to promote or inhibit certain behaviors.

Characterizing contributors' behavior

In the first perspective, there is a large body of work examining historical usage data or conducting observational fieldwork to identify salient contributor profiles (or roles) in online communities. Studies along these lines have been conducted in varied contexts, including newsgroups (e.g. Usenet [29,26,6,30,10]), Wikipedia [28,5,15] and other wikis (e.g. Cyclopath [23]), content-sharing communities [7,4], movie recommendation sites [8], and Q&A sites (e.g. Yahoo! Answers [1], Naver Knowledge-iN [18] and StackOverflow [16]). Although the profiles that best define contributors are contingent of the community's context and the analysts' purpose, some regularities that are relevant for this work are discussed in the following. In doing so, we refer to contributors that provide high volumes of contributions as *highly active*, and dub contributors that provide highly valued contributions as *expert* contributors.

From the perspective of how much contributors act, studies in several systems have generally found a majority of less active contributors collaborating with a small proportion of highly active contributors [16,18,30,23,15,7]. In the context of Q&A sites, highly active contributors have been found to represent 1% of registered users but to account for 22-28% of all answers in different sites [16,18].

A second part of the literature shows that contributions are often also skewed in their distribution over time. The level of activity of a contributor over time has been reported to typically display an initially burst in their level of activity followed by a marked drop in more than one system [15,23,11]. For Q&A systems, Mamykina et al. [16] and Nam et al. [18] found an intermittent behavior marked by inactive periods in the posting and answering behavior in different communities. Moreover, Nam et al. also observed that the time contributors are active is positively correlated with the quality of their answers. Regarding the dynamics of group behavior, Kittur et al. [15] found that the bulk of contributions in Wikipedia and the social bookmarking site delicious are gradually shifting from being provided by the highly active users to a product of the acts of less active contributors.

Differentiating types of contribution, it is possible to identify groups of users that are highly active and/or experts only in certain types of contribution. Identifying the existing user groups in this perspective can, in turn, help managing the community and coordinating contributors. Usenet has been thoroughly studied with varying methods, and the resulting literature consistently points to a description of newsgroup participants that includes *answer persons*, *question persons*, *trolls*, and *lurkers* [29,26,6,10]. In the context of Wikipedia, distinct contributors of different profiles are chiefly responsible for certain types of contributions [28], and inexperienced and experienced users have been observed to contribute differently [5]. Welser et al. [28] also show that none of these profiles is formed by a large majority of experienced users. This observation suggests that the community does not depend heavily on experienced users for the service provided by editors in any of the profiles.

Specifically looking at Q&A sites, Nam et al. [18] suggested that, as in Usenet, contributors could be clearly separated in *askers* and *answerers* in Naver Knowledge-iN. Adamic et al. [1] also found these two profiles in Yahoo! Answers, but observed as an additional prominent profile the *discussion person,* which is a user who is highly active in asking and answering questions.

Examining or identifying experts and elite contributors

A different strand of research focuses on users from a specific profile. This research typically either examines such users closely or aims at deriving heuristics to predict which users will act according to the profile. The most popular profile considered in this approach is the highly active expert, sometimes named the "elite" contributor. Understanding how such users behave and automatically identifying them can again improve task scheduling or recommendation, and direct community efforts to fostering the participation of highly productive contributors.

Studies have shown that in some contexts elite contributors have a consistent behavior from their start in the system [23,22]. Also, several algorithms have been devised to identify experts or authorities in certain themes in the community [20,2].

When looking at Q&A sites, most attention has been given to predicting which users are likely to be experts in certain themes. For example, Riahi et al. [24] and Hamrahan et al. [12] explore automatic means for identifying the most adequate experts for a question. Pal et al. showed that it is possible to predict which users will be highly active experts using data from their first weeks of activity [21,19]. Looking at the dynamics of expert behavior, Pal et al. [19] report that experts are either consistently active, initially inactive and later active, or the opposite.

Our contribution

This work advances present knowledge about contributor profiles in Q&A sites in two main directions. First, it analyzes usage data from multiple Q&A sites to characterize contributors' behavioral profiles using multivariate analysis techniques. Each profile found in this characterization describes a common co-occurrence of values in a set of metrics that describes the quantity and quality of a contributor's activity for multiple contribution types. By accounting for the multiple contribution types and their quantity and quality dimensions, this characterization enables us to investigate, for example, whether expert contributors are also highly active, and hence create large volumes of answers, questions or comments. Such a richer picture can enable deeper understanding of different contributor skills, goals and needs in Q&A sites (as also suggested before by Gazan [9]), and inform community management, experts' characterization, and task allocation.

Second, our analysis contributes to expand present knowledge about how contributors' behavior changes over time. Our present understanding of Q&A sites does not describe how the quantity *and* quality of different types of contribution by a user change over time, or how the site structurally evolves with respect to its contributors' profiles. This analysis is necessary to identify prominent trends in contributor behavior, which again have implications for community management, experts' identification and task allocation mechanisms.

SITES STUDIED

Our analysis uses data from five sites of the Stack Exchange Q&A platform. This section describes how this platform works, the sites studied, and the data used.

The Stack Exchange platform

Stack Exchange is a platform that allows the creation and hosting of Q&A sites. At the time of writing, the platform hosted 83 sites focused on topics varying from computer programming and theoretical computer science to culinary and photography.

Each of the sites operates independently and similarly to the Q&A model of sites like Yahoo! Answers and Quora. The typical course of events for a question posted in the site is: (i) a user posts a question; (ii) other users visualize the question and may vote its utility up or down, or favorite it; (iii) one or more users post answers or comments associated with the question, which can themselves be visualized and voted up or down; and (iv) the user who posted the question may at any point select one answer as the best answer. As a result of this process, each question, answer and comment has a voting balance, based on the positive and negative votes received, and questions also have a favorite count.

Chosen sites

The five sites studied are described in Table 1. It is important to note that our site selection is not random and does not aim at providing a representative sample of all Q&A sites in Stack Exchange. Instead, we purposefully select a set of Q&A sites that are mature and popular, have the sizes of their user bases in the same order of magnitude, deal with reasonably related topics, and have existed for a similar timespan. Our intent is to, on the one hand, find profiles that are not specific of a single site, and on the other hand limit the effect of factors other than the user population on the contributor profiles we find.

Notably, we exclude from our sample the most popular among Stack Exchange sites, StackOverflow. The main reason for this decision is that this site was the original instance from which Stack Exchange was generalized. As a result, it has a much longer and peculiar history compared to the selected sites. Such differences render a comparison of its contributors to those in other sites out of the scope of this work.

Table 1: Description of the five sites studied as of August 2011.

Site	Topic	Contrib.	Posts	Creation
Super User	Computer power use	43,775	278K	2009-07
Server Fault	System administration and support	37,649	246K	2009-04
Ask Ubuntu	Ubuntu	9,904	92K	2010-09
Programmers	Software development	13,927	54K	2010-07
Mathematics	Mathematics	6,568	56K	2010-07

Data used

We use the historical data of the five sites studied from their beginning until August 31st, 2011, as published by the Stack Exchange administrators. Stack Exchange periodically releases datasets describing the activity log of all registered users since the beginning of each site[1]. We processed this data and extracted the following two groups of metrics for each user, considering a period of activity:

Motivation metrics:

- *Number of questions* posted;
- *Number of answers* posted;
- *Number of comments* posted; and
- *Activity duration*, defined as the number of days in which the user was active.

Ability metrics:

- *Mean utility of questions (MUQuestions)*: gauges how the community perceived the quality of the user's questions. The quality of each question is measured as the sum of the number of favorites and its voting balance. A user's MUQuestions is the average utility of all questions posted by this user.
- *Mean utility of answers (MUAnswers):* measures the ability of the user in answering a question compared to that of competing answerers. For each answer that a user provided to a question, and for which there are competitive answers, the utility of this user's answer is calculated by standardizing its voting balance compared to all other competing answers in that question (i.e. we calculate its z-score), or is set to zero, if none of the answers have votes. A user's

[1] http://blog.stackoverflow.com/category/cc-wiki-dump/

MUAnswers is the average utility of the answers posted by this user that had competing alternatives, or zero, if none of the user's answers had competition.

- *Mean utility of comments (MUComments)*, which evaluates how useful the community finds the comments a user makes in questions that were created by other users. It is calculated analogously to MUAnswers but considering the voting balance of comments posted by a user on other users' questions and answers.

CONTRIBUTOR PROFILES IN THE FIVE SITES

The first part of our analysis focuses on exploring salient contributor profiles in the five sites analyzed.

Method

The problem of finding contributor profiles is analogous to identifying a set of groups of contributors with similar behavior. We use clustering analysis [3] to approach this problem. Clustering methods aim at finding a grouping solution that maximizes simultaneously in-group homogeneity and intergroup heterogeneity.

For this analysis, we use the set of motivation and ability metrics we defined and calculate these metrics considering the complete activity of each user (we later revisit this procedure with a different timeframe). Contributors that were not active before the last month in the dataset are excluded due to the small amount of information available about their behavior. To prevent a bias towards behaviors most present in sites with larger user bases, we use a random sample of same size from users in each community. The number of active contributors in the smallest community, Mathematics, limits the size of this random sample. The resulting number of contributors taken from all communities is 32,840.

To define the space of similarity among users, we use the standardized values (z-scores) of the seven metrics considered to describe contributor behavior. Because the scales of the metrics in the different communities may differ, the standardization is performed by site. The similarity between the behaviors of two contributors is then the Euclidian distance between the contributors in the space defined by the standardized metrics.

Clustering algorithm

We employ a combination of hierarchical and nonhierarchical clustering algorithms to identify contributor profiles in our data. On the one hand, hierarchical clustering algorithms have the advantages of being independent of initial parameters and allowing the analyst to investigate a range of clustering solutions produced through iterative optimal cluster joining or splitting. Nonhierarchical clustering algorithms, on the other hand, optimize for the global solution and provide solutions that are more robust to outliers than those of hierarchical methods [17], but whose quality depends on an initial seed of cluster centers, and presumes a known suitable number of clusters to be discovered.

Our analysis combines these two approaches by first using the Ward hierarchical clustering algorithm [27] to explore a wide range of solutions with different numbers of clusters. The results of this exploration then inform a suitable number of clusters and their centers, which are in turn used to seed cluster centers in the k-means nonhierarchical algorithm [13]. We note that both the Ward algorithm and k-means are hard clustering techniques. Thus each contributor is present in exactly one cluster in our results.

Defining the number of clusters

Figure 1 displays the average within-cluster distances in a range of solutions that result from running the Ward algorithm in our data. It is notable that solutions with more than 11 clusters have little homogeneity gain compared to the 11-cluster solution. Examining the 10 and 11-cluster solutions closer, we identify that in the 11-cluster solution, two of the resulting clusters are very similar, with their distinction being a little variation on contributor behavior. On the other hand, a highly descriptive cluster present in the 11-cluster solution is absent in the 10-cluster solution.

Informed by this exploration, we opt to use the k-means algorithm to identify ten clusters, and to seed the algorithm with the centers of the ten most relevant clusters identified in the 11-cluster solution of the hierarchical algorithm. The resulting clusters are similar to the most relevant in the hierarchical solution, and are described in Figure 2. Table 4 in Appendix A also compares their centers using the unstandardized metric values.

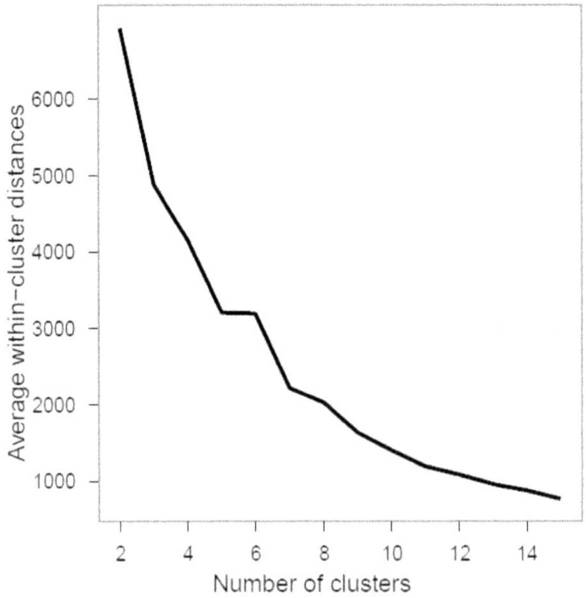

Figure 1. Analysis of the heterogeneity obtained in each cluster solution.

Labeling the contributor profiles

Given the selected set of clusters, the next step in the analysis is to make sense of them in the context of Q&A sites. Our labeling of the ten identified profiles and their marked characteristics are as follows:

1. *Low-activity*: contributors with infrequent participation in the site, and below-average motivation and skills.
2. *Occasional*: users that contribute moderately, and mainly questions, over an above-average activity time. Their questions tend to be considered useful.

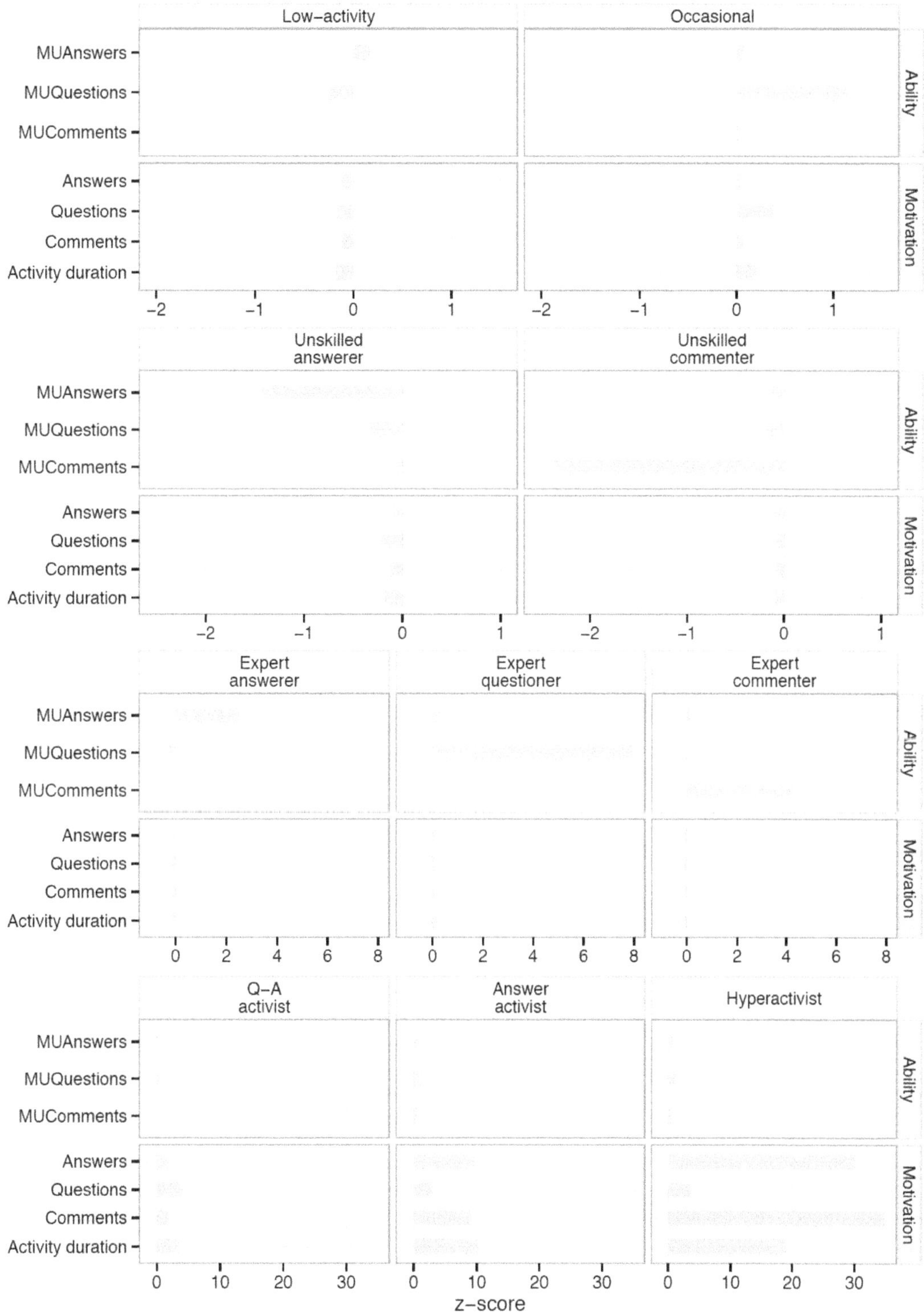

Figure 2. Cluster centers that describe the ten profiles in the analysis. Note that the horizontal axis is the z-score of a metric, and that the scales in the four groups of graphs vary.

3. *Unskilled answerer*: contributors of poorly evaluated answers, usually with low activity time. These users hadn't demonstrated any skill in providing answers.
4. *Unskilled commenter*: contributors that had comments rated substantially below those of other users commenting in the same questions.
5. *Expert answerer*: users whose numbers of postings are not pronounced, but whose answers are consistently well evaluated.
6. *Expert questioner*: contributors whose questions the community recognizes as important, and who are slightly more active than expert answerers.
7. *Expert commenter*: users with little activity, but who produce valuable comments in the eyes of other users.
8. *Q-A activist*: contributors who are highly active in the site, chiefly creating questions, and whose answering skills are slightly below average.
9. *Answer activist*: users with a long activity time and high numbers of postings, specially answers. Moreover, with generally well evaluated answers.
10. *Hyperactivist*: contributors with a profile similar to answer activists, but who contributed a disproportionate number of answers and comments to the site, and have the longest activity time among all profiles.

Discussion

The cluster analysis considering aspects of quantity and quality in users' contributions unveiled ten contributor profiles in the five Q&A sites studied. These profiles unveil the most common combination of activity level and skill among users. There are marked profiles defined by low to average, high and extreme activity levels. Among the less active profiles (all but activists and hyperactivists), we observe users that provide contributions of average quality, experts in one of each of the contribution types, and contributors that provide poorly evaluated answers or comments. Highly and extremely active users, in turn, are less marked by their ability than by their volume of contribution. Figure 3 summarizes this view. Notably, experts and highly active contributors are typically disjoint groups in our results.

The distinction between highly active contributors and experts is relevant for understanding where the expertise is located in the site, and has implications for task allocation mechanisms. First, it suggests the need to examine whether present methods developed for identifying highly active experts (e.g. [21,19,24,12]) can accurately recognize the experts in our results. Second, it seems promising to use task allocation mechanisms to direct experts to primarily answer difficult questions when they contribute to the system. Finally, because of their low activity levels, task allocation mechanisms should consider suggesting a same question to multiple experts, or to a combination of experts and highly active users to increase the chances of obtaining an answer in a reasonable time.

From the management standpoint, observing that experts are typically less active contributors shows the need for further understanding the motivations of the highly skilled users. On the one hand, fostering the participation of these users will likely have a positive impact on the service provided in the community. On the other hand, it seems necessary to understand to which degree these users are perceived as experts because they are very selective in the questions answered. It is not obvious that increasing the volume in their contribution will necessarily lead to mostly high quality contributions.

The salience of unskilled contributor profiles that our analysis identifies is also of interest to site designers and administrators. The absence of a distinct group of highly active unskilled users suggests that the design of Stack Exchange inhibits the continued contribution of content perceived as poor. Further examining which mechanisms have this effect can generalize good practices for Q&A sites. Nevertheless, in spite of the absence of highly active unskilled users, our results still point to marked profiles with consistently poorly evaluated contributions. This calls for an investigation of the necessary means to reduce the potentially negative effect such contributions may have in the sites.

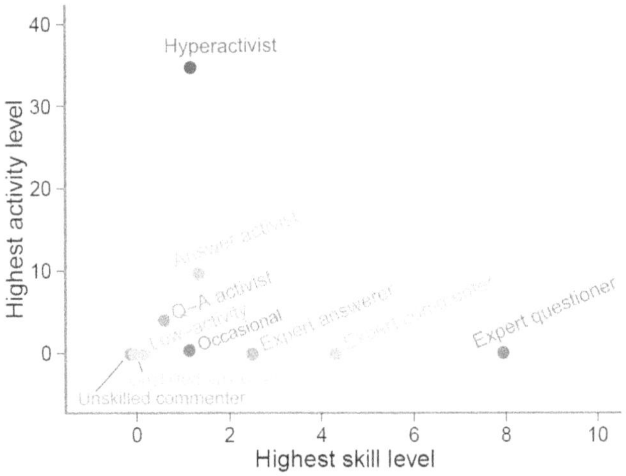

Figure 3 - Scatter plot of the highest skill and activity levels that define the centroids of the clusters found. Note that the points for unskilled answerer and unskilled commenter nearly coincide.

Focusing on the highly active users, we see profiles that distinguish themselves mostly by providing more questions than the average (Q-A activists), for answering notably more than the average (Answer activists), and for an exceedingly high contribution volume in general (hyperactivists). Identifying such users is relevant for allocating tasks in the community, as these are the contributors with the highest chance of providing a timely response to a request or suggestion. Also, a closer inspection at the hyperactivists highlights that these users are not only contributing content, but also concerned with the community functioning. An examination of the 2011 election for moderators in the largest of the sites studied – Super User – shows that one in six of the hyperactivists in that site nominated himself as a candidate. This number is orders of magnitude higher than probability of any other profile volunteering in the election. Identifying hyperactivists can thus help community managers in finding users that can contribute to moderate the site.

In general, our results are in consonance with previous analyses of Q&A that looked into profiles according to contributors' activity levels [1,18]. Previous research also identified question- and answer-oriented profiles. Our results complement this picture considering quality and quantity dimensions together, highlighting a more diverse set of profiles. Moreover, our analysis uncovers the unskilled profiles, which have not received much attention in the context of Q&A systems.

SITE COMPOSITION AND PROFILE PRODUCTIVITY

In this section we use the contributor profiles uncovered in the cluster analysis to examine the distribution of contributors among profiles in the five sites studied. Our goal is to investigate the prevalence of contributors in each profile, whether the five sites have similar compositions with respect to their contributors' profiles, and the role of user groups from each profile in producing knowledge in the different sites.

Finding all contributors' profiles

To analyze the contributor population in the five sites, it is necessary to find the profile of all users that were absent in the sample considered for the cluster analysis. For that, we train an artificial neural network (ANN) to classify users in profiles according to their motivation and ability metrics. The training data for the ANN is a sample of users whose profiles were identified in the cluster analysis. To facilitate the convergence of the ANN, this sample contains fewer cases from the more frequent profiles, and thus a higher proportion of the less represented ones. We find that the classifier has difficulties in distinguishing answer activists and hyperactivists, but considering these two profiles as one, the ANN achieves a 95% or higher detection precision for all profiles. We thus separate these classes in a second classification step, where a decision tree was trained only with data related to these two profiles in the training set. In this step the classifier achieves 95% or higher detection precision. Nevertheless, in the following analyses, we consider answer activists and hyperactivists together mostly because they seem to have the same impact on the sites.

Sites' composition

Figure 4 compares the distribution of contributors in profiles for the different sites. Generally, slightly more than half of the contributors in each of the sites fit in the low-activity profile. All sites also display similar proportions of occasional contributors (10-15%) and unskilled answerers (15-20%). Considering these three profiles, it is possible to note that the contributors of the five sites are typically composed by 80-90% of users with low to average activity and unskilled answerers.

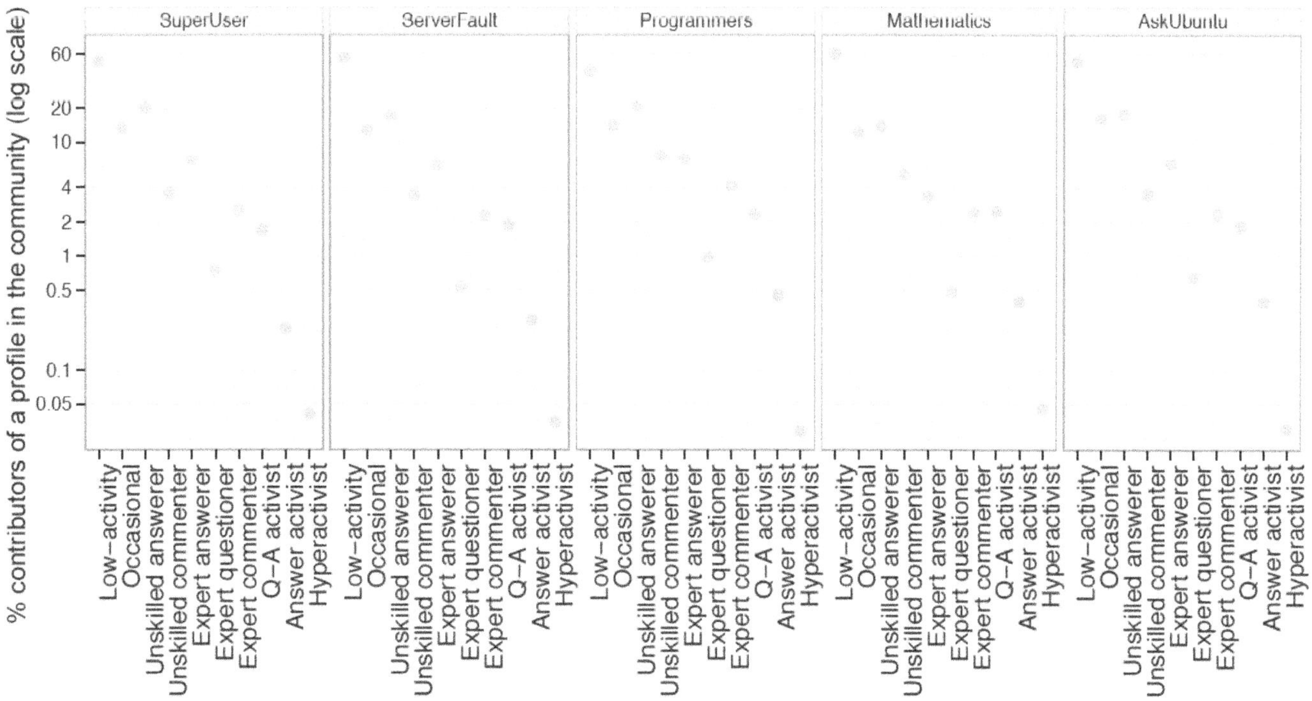

Figure 4. Distribution of the contributor profiles in the five communities.

Among the remainder contributors, the most common profile is the expert answerer. Comparing experts and activists, we see that expert answerers and commenters generally occur more frequently than expert questioners or activists of any type.

Overall, it is not surprising that expert and high-activity profiles are less common than those demanding less effort or skill. However, it is remarkable that, in spite of some peculiarities, the five sites exhibit the observed regularity in their composition.

Profile productivity

Figure 5 contrasts the quantity and quality of contributions from users of each profile in the five sites. For quantity, we consider how many questions, answers, and comments were produced by contributors from each profile. For quality, we consider the number of positive votes received in answers, questions and comments by the contributors. In this analysis we refer to low-activity and occasional users together as contributors with no marked skill.

In all sites, both unskilled and expert users aggregately produce a small amount of contributions and receive a small proportion of the positive quality assessments in the site. Users with no marked skills and activists create the large majority of content. Furthermore, highly active contributors are responsible for the largest part of answers and comments, and also receive most of the votes in these two types of contributions. Conversely, users with no marked skills contribute most of the questions, and receive more votes in their questions than the activists.

Overall, there is a visible regularity when comparing the results for the different sites. The noticeable exception is the Mathematics community, where activity and votes seem to be more concentrated on activists. This peculiarity may be related to the topic of the community, which may restrict more markedly the contribution of less dedicated users.

Considering the regularities, our analysis portraits the five sites as a combination of a larger base of contributors that act sporadically and collectively create most questions, and a smaller, more active nucleus of contributors that provides most of the answers to existing questions. These answers are complemented by contributors with no marked skill or unskilled, which still provide a sizeable proportion of all answers and receives a significant portion of votes in answers. Experts are of limited importance for the sheer number of contributions or votes received in contributions.

Regarding how answers are produced, our results are similar to those by Mamykina et al. [16]. They have found highly active and low-activity contributors to have similar importance in answer production. Our results show how this pattern occurs also for questions and comments, and is mostly regular across the five sites we consider.

Finally, this characterization indicates that community managers should cater not only for activists, but also for low-activity and occasional users to keep the site productive. Contributors with no marked skills are particularly important for providing questions. Also, our results point that the volume of content created by unskilled users is limited, but non-negligible. Mechanisms that help controlling the quality of contributions from these users may thus have a noticeable impact in these communities.

PROFILE DYNAMICS

Our analysis so far describes profiles and site compositions considering how the profile of a contributor is defined from the whole history of the contributor's activity. We now turn our attention towards a shorter-term characterization of profiles, investigating how the behavior of a contributor changes over time. Our goal is to examine the dynamics of contributor behavior and of sites' structural properties. For that, we use the largest of the five sites studied, Super User, and conduct a longitudinal version of our analysis in its historical data.

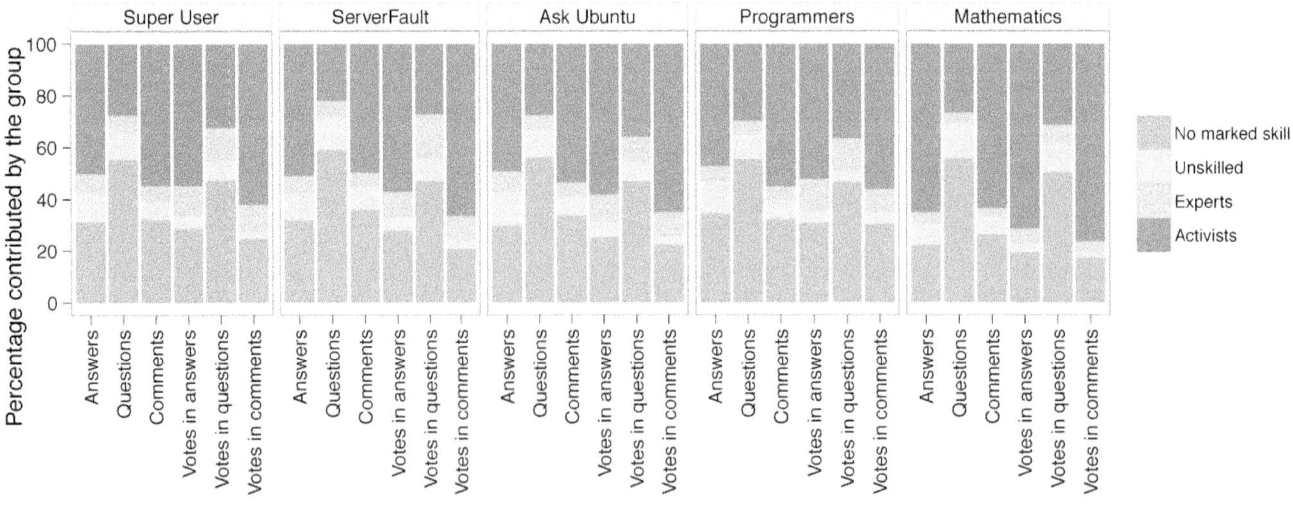

Figure 5. Parcel of the aggregate contribution for users in different profiles in the five communities. Profiles are grouped for readability, and the *no marked skill* label refers to low-activity and occasional contributors.

Method

The data for Super User encompasses a trace of 26 months of its activity. The mean (resp. median) time between the first and last seen contributions of users who start their activity in the first year of the trace is five (resp. eight) months. To avoid a bias towards identifying users departure from the system, even though they may contribute again in the following months, we exclude the last six months of the trace from the analysis. This period is only used to check if a user will still be active later than a given point in the trace. Using the remainder period in the trace, our analysis discretizes the data in ten two-month time windows. The size of the time window is chosen so that the activity of many contributors spans more than one unit of analysis.

A contributor is considered active in a time window if he or she contributes a question, an answer or a comment in the first month of that time window. Excluding contributors whose activity in the site start towards the end of a time window prevents us from underestimating the contributor's activity due to a too-short period of observation. Before performing any analysis, we also standardize contributors' motivation and ability metrics considering the activity of other contributors in the same time window.

After this preprocessing, we conduct a cluster analysis of active contributors using the same combination of hierarchical and nonhierarchical methods employed in the analysis of contributor behavior in the five sites.

Profile identification

The results of the cluster analysis for contributor activity considering 2-month time windows are remarkably similar to those of the analysis of the whole timespan of the site. The same ten profiles that characterized long-term contributor behavior are well suited to describe their short-term activity (Appendix B details the same results presented in the five sites analysis). It is worthwhile to note that identifying the same profiles in such different time windows and in different groups of contributors suggests the generalizability of the characterization results.

Structural dynamics of contributor profiles

The cluster analysis considering 2-month time windows informs us what was the distribution of contributor profiles over time in Super User. Figure 6 depicts how the proportion of contributors in each profile changes over time. The proportion of users in most profiles is stable over time. The noticeable exceptions to this stability are the proportion of low-activity users and expert answerers, and to a lesser extent, expert commenters, and unskilled commenters. Low-activity contributors increase in 10% in the second year of our data, while the experts mentioned consistently decrease over this period, with a sharper decrease for expert answerers. Unskilled commenters have a noticeable decrease in their proportion in the first year of the community.

Further examination shows that these trends are closely related to tendencies in the newcomers that the site attracts over time. Figure 7 shows the probability that a new contributor joining the community in different periods of its activity behaves according to the profiles whose probability change mostly in Figure 6. Over time, and more noticeably after the 6th time window, contributors that arrive in the community are to be more prone to behave as low-activity contributors, and less as the other profiles. Moreover, this trend starts one time window after the community begins to receive much higher numbers of new contributors than before (Figure 8).

The observation that the sustained high number of new contributors arriving in the community is correlated with a change in the profiles most often assumed by newcomers is of interest to community managers and merits further investigation. It is possible that Super User has started to attract a different type of public over time. However, it is also possible that the high number of arriving users has made it more difficult for new contributors to provide high-quality answers or comments, leading to the lower proportions of expert answerers and commenters in the community. Related to this result, it has been reported that Wikipedia has displayed a steady increase in the number of low-activity contributors over time [15].

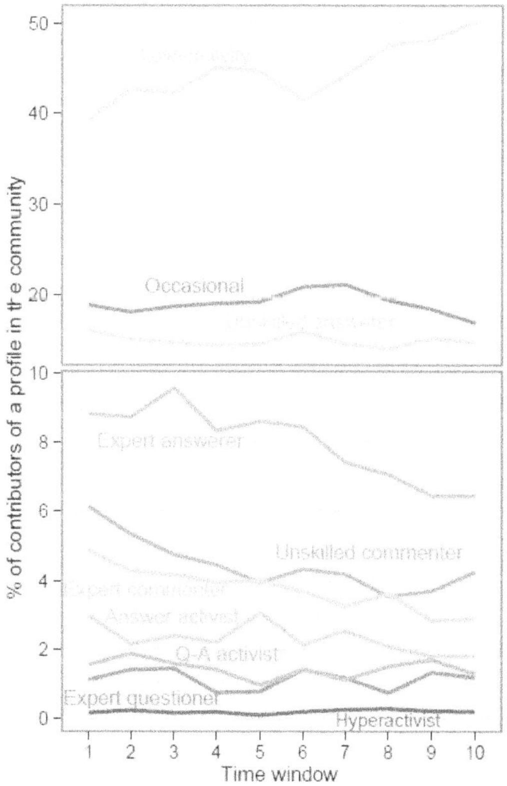

Figure 6: Composition of the population of active contributors in Super User over time. Note the scales are different in the two parts of the vertical axis.

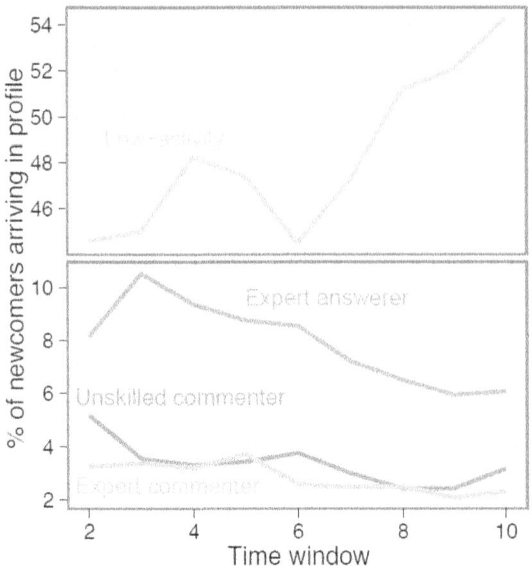

Figure 7: Percentage of newcomers in each window behaving according to the four profiles whose proportion change significantly over time in the community. Scales are different in the two parts of the plot.

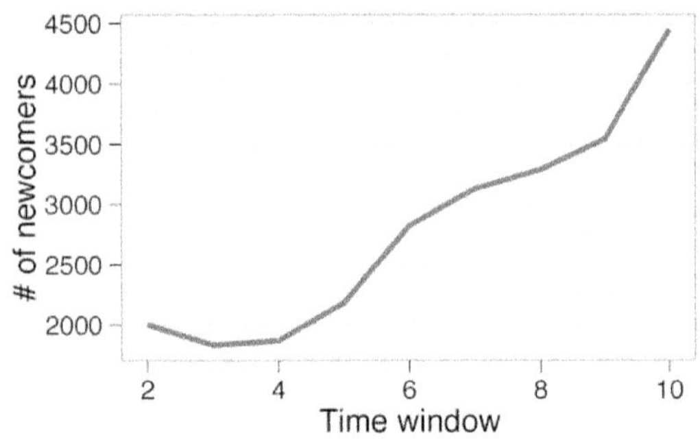

Figure 8: Number of newcomer contributors joining Super User over time.

Dynamics of individual contributor profiles

After examining the dynamics of site composition, we investigate the dynamics of each contributor's profile.

Our first experiment in this analysis is to measure the probability that a contributor transitions between any two profiles in two consecutive time windows. In this process, we also compute the probability that a contributor becomes inactive in the next time window, or abandons the site. A contributor is said to have abandoned the site if there is no contribution by that contributor neither in future time windows nor in the last six months of the dataset that are not analyzed as time windows. Inactive contributors are those that created no answers, questions or comments in a time window, but have not abandoned the system.

The transition probabilities between profiles, and from each profile to an inactive state or to abandoning the community are shown in Table 2. A contributor that is, at a moment in time, in any profile except activist or hyperactivist has a large tendency to reduce his or her activity in the following time window. Most of these contributors become inactive, low-activity or occasional contributors. Differently, activists and hyperactivists are the most stable profiles, and frequently maintain their behavioral profile in consecutive time windows. This observation is evidence that not only the proportion of highly active contributors is constant over time, but also that there is limited renovation among those behaving according to these profiles.

Also, this result reinforces previous analyses of the dynamics of activity in Q&A sites, which have consistently reported that some of the highly active contributors have a steady behavior, while most contributors have bursts of activity followed by inactive periods [16,18,19].

Further analyzing the highly active profiles, we see that hyperactivists and answer activists are closely related. There is a significant probability that hyperactivists turn into answer activists, and answer activists have the highest chance among all profiles of turning into hyperactivists. The dynamics of Q-A activists, on the other hand, are markedly different. There is little chance of a transition in either direction between this profile and answer activists or hyperactivists. Q-A activists are more likely to become occasional contributors, which indicates that activists that are not primarily concerned with answering and commenting have a more localized activity in time.

Considering again the overall picture, we see that besides having significant chance of becoming inactive for a complete time window, contributors are highly likely to remain in this state for consecutive periods. Among those returning to activity, most act moderately in the following time window, and low activity users, in turn, are likely to abandon the community.

Interestingly, the expert profiles show little stability. Moreover, expert answerers display a relatively high probability of abandoning the site. Similarly to the experts, contributors fitting in unskilled profiles are unlikely to remain acting in the same profile over time. Unskilled answerers show the highest chance of abandoning the site, and other unskilled contributors typically become low-activity or occasional users.

Taken together, our results point that expert profiles are not only more prevalent among less active users, but also that these experts tend to act during localized periods in the community's lifetime. Furthermore, expert answerers tend to act for a short period and abandon the community. This result indicates the need to further investigate how to increase the loyalty of such contributors. Also, the relatively short period of activity before abandoning the community implies that algorithms to identify experts should be able to locate these users early in their activity.

The observation that unskilled answerers have a high chance of abandoning the community suggests that providing poorly evaluated answers is demotivating to a significant proportion of contributors. On the one hand, this

Table 2: Probabilities of transitioning from profile X (row) to Y (column). As such, the sum of each row is 1. The CA column contains the probabilities of abandoning the community. Users that do not act in one time window are included as Inactive.

Profile	H	AA	QAA	EA	EQ	EC	UA	UC	O	LA	INA	CA
Hyperactivist (H)	.50	.37	.01	.01	.01	.00	.01	.03	.01	.01	.03	.00
Answer activist (AA)	.03	.47	.01	.06	.01	.03	.04	.04	.08	.18	.04	.01
Q-A activist (QAA)	.00	.04	.31	.02	.00	.02	.03	.01	.36	.14	.04	.02
Expert answerer (EA)	.00	.01	.00	.05	.00	.03	.05	.03	.07	.16	.28	.31
Expert questioner (EQ)	.00	.02	.01	.03	.01	.01	.05	.04	.11	.19	.28	.24
Expert commenter (EC)	.00	.01	.00	.07	.01	.06	.06	.05	.08	.20	.28	.18
Unskilled answerer (UA)	.00	.00	.00	.03	.00	.02	.06	.03	.06	.12	.23	.45
Unskilled commenter (UC)	.00	.01	.01	.05	.01	.04	.08	.05	.08	.20	.28	.19
Occasional (O)	.00	.01	.02	.03	.01	.02	.05	.02	.16	.20	.25	.24
Low-activity (LA)	.00	.01	.00	.03	.00	.02	.04	.02	.06	.16	.28	.38
Inactive (INA)	.00	.00	.00	.02	.00	.01	.04	.02	.06	.17	.66	-

Table 3: Results from a Pearson's chi-square test for association between being a newcomer or experienced contributor and the profile of the contributor. Hyperactivists and answer activists are considered together, to meet the assumptions of the test. Cells in bold denote the proportion found in the sample was significantly different from the proportion that would be expected if there was no association between the variables ($p < .05$).

Chi-square		H + AA	QAA	EA	EQ	EC	UA	UC	O	LA
Newcomer	Observed percentage	**1.37**	**0.90**	7.68	1.09	2.47	**18.29**	**3.02**	17.99	47.21
	Std residual	**-2.82**	**-2.01**	-0.44	0.01	-1.91	**2.26**	**-2.20**	-1.21	1.41
Experienced	Observed percentage	**4.17**	**2.50**	8.63	1.08	**4.90**	**10.88**	**6.13**	**22.01**	**39.71**
	Std residual	**9.05**	**6.45**	1.41	-0.03	**6.12**	**-7.26**	**7.05**	**3.87**	**-4.53**

phenomenon may limit the amount of content produced that does not meet the community standards. However, given the high proportion of unskilled answerers often present in the community (Figure 6), our results also indicate that Super User could benefit from improved mechanisms to educate its answerers. Preventing poorly evaluated answers may increase the retention of users willing to contribute to the site.

Newcomer vs. experienced contributor profiles

Our final experiment examines how the probability that a contributor behaves according to a given profile varies if the contributor is a newcomer or an experienced user. For the newcomer behavior, we examine the first profile assumed by all contributors. For the experienced contributor behavior, we use the fifth active profile of contributors that are active in at least five time windows. To test if there is an association between whether the contributor is a newcomer or not and the likelihood this contributor will behave according to a profile, we perform a Pearson's chi-square test. Table 3 shows the results of the comparison. Note that due to their small absolute number, hyperactivists were combined with answer activists to meet the assumptions of the chi-square test.

There is a significant association between being experienced or newcomer and the profile contributors display ($X^2(8)=330.0$, $p < 1e\text{-}10$). Experienced users are more likely to be on more active profiles compared to newcomers. Their chance of behaving as answer activists/hyperactivists and Q-A activists are significantly higher, and they are more likely to behave as occasional and less likely to behave as low-activity contributors.

Considering the expert profiles, it is interesting that experienced contributors only have a significantly higher chance than newcomers to behave as expert commenters. This does not happen for expert answerers or questioners. Newcomers are, however, significantly more likely to act as unskilled answerers.

Surprisingly, experienced contributors are significantly more likely to behave as unskilled commenters than newcomers. This seems to be a side effect of their higher likelihood to comment on posts. During time windows in which these users concentrate their activity on commenting, they have a higher chance of adding accessory comments in discussions where other users add valuable comments than the newcomers. This explanation is reinforced by the fact that experienced users are also more likely than newcomers to act as expert commenters.

These results bear some similarity to observations by Welser et al. [28] on Wikipedia. However, while Welser et al. found that Wikipedia does not seem to depend on experienced users for any role, we see that in Super User some profiles are more tightly related with experience.

Finally, the fact that newcomers are both as likely to act as expert answerers as experienced users, and more likely to act as unskilled answerers than the latter is also of interest. This result suggests that providing further guidance for newcomers in their first answers may increase retention in the community and lower the number of poorly evaluated content created.

DISCUSSION AND FUTURE WORK

This work provides a characterization of contributor behavior in five Q&A sites based on how much and how well users contribute different types of content over time. Building on this characterization, we analyze the composition and productivity of the sites, and examine the dynamics of contributor behavior over time in the largest of the five sites.

The ten profiles found in the characterization enrich our understanding of how Q&A communities work. Realizing that users that consistently provide high-quality contributions are not the highly active users is of particular interest. The knowledge that activists and experts are complementary profiles is useful for the development of task allocation mechanisms, expert identification and community management.

Regarding site composition, our study points to a high similarity in the occurrence of contributor profiles in the five sites. Moreover, the productivity of groups of users from the different profiles is also remarkably similar among sites. Although it is not possible to generalize these results for arbitrary Q&A sites, the regularities increase the chance that our findings are not specific of a site or context.

The analysis of composition and productivity also shows that unskilled answerers are a common occurrence in the communities. Adequately providing guidance and increasing the quality their contributions can thus have a significant effect on these sites. On a similar note, our results show that users with no marked ability produce a sizeable fraction of the content and receive a large proportion of the positive evaluations in the sites. This observation indicates that catering for such users has also a potential for the communities we study.

In the dynamic perspective, our work describe Super User, the largest among the sites studied, as a combination of a stable and highly active nucleus of contributors, a more volatile contingent of experts and unskilled users, and a large mass of low-activity contributors. This mass of low-activity contributors, in turn, includes at any time large proportions of the user that in other periods had a more marked activity. This result supports and complements multiple previous studies that report that the activity of contributors in Q&A sites happens in bursts.

Observing composition over time, we identify a trend in the increase of low-activity users combined with a decrease in expert answerers. Our analysis indicates that this tendency is linked to a change in the behavior of newcomer contributors, what merits further investigation.

Looking at the dynamics of behavior for individual contributors, we see that both unskilled answerers and the various expert profiles tend to abandon the community soon. This result reinforces the impression that there is an opportunity in identifying how to increase the retention of contributors likely to behave as experts, and how to better integrate the unskilled contributors.

Finally, our comparison of profile occurrence among newcomer and experienced contributors reveals that the community seems to depend on experienced users for behaving as activists. Interestingly, however, experienced users do not have a higher chance of acting as experts. This suggests that experts behave as such from their start in the system, but activists are likely to develop over time.

Future work should focus on deepening several aspects of our results. Investigating the motivations of users that fit in the expert profiles is of particular importance, but a qualitative understanding of all profiles unveiled in this analysis could help creating a clearer and richer picture of contributor behavior in Q&A systems.

A second line in which our results need further experimentation is on the evaluation of its generalizability. It is not clear if and how our results hold for Q&A sites of different themes and in different platforms. Finally, it may be fruitful to examine the dynamics of behavior in the different classes of contributors which we identify with a finer granularity. A longitudinal study of individuals in a contributor profile could also investigate the effect of system events on their productivity, and thus inform system designers and operators of risks for site productivity.

REFERENCES

1. Adamic, L. A., Zhang, J., Bakshy, E., and Ackerman, M. S. Knowledge sharing and yahoo answers: everyone knows something. *Proceeding of the 17th international conference on World Wide Beijing, C* (2008), 665-674.
2. Agarwal, N., Liu, H., Tang, L., and Yu, P. S. Identifying the influential bloggers in a community. In *Proceedings of the international conference on Web search and web data mining*, WSDM '08, ACM (2008), 207–218.
3. Aldenderfer, M. S., and Blashfield, R. K. *Cluster Analysis*, vol. 07-044 of *Sage University Paper Series on Quantitative Applications in the Social Sciences*. Sage, 1984.
4. Andrade, N., Santos-Neto, E., Brasileiro, F., and Ripeanu, M. Resource demand and supply in BitTorrent content-sharing communities. *Comput. Netw. 53*, 4 (Mar. 2009), 515–527.

5. Bryant, S. L., Forte, A., and Bruckman, A. Becoming Wikipedian: transformation of participation in a collaborative online encyclopedia. In *Human Factors*, vol. 6 of *Net communities*, ACM (2005), 1–10.
6. Fisher, D., Smith, M., and Welser, H. T. You Are Who You Talk To: Detecting Roles in Usenet Newsgroups. *Proceedings of the 39th Annual Hawaii International Conference on System Sciences HICSS06 00*, C (2006), 59b–59b.
7. Font, F., Roma, G., Herrera, P., and Serra, X. Characterization of the Freesound Online Community. In *Third International Workshop on Cognitive Information Processing* (Baiona, Spain, 2012).
8. Fugelstad, P., Dwyer, P., Filson Moses, J., Kim, J., Mannino, C. A., Terveen, L., and Snyder, M. What Makes Users Rate (Share , Tag , Edit ...)? Predicting Patterns of Participation in Online Communities. In *Communities*, CSCW '12, ACM(2012), 969–978.
9. Gazan, R. Social Q&A. *Journal of the American Society for Information Science and Technology 62*, 12 (2011), 2301–2312.
10. Golder, S. A., and Donath, J. Social roles in electronic communities. *Internet Research 5* (2004), 1–25.
11. Guo, L., Tan, E., Chen, S., Zhang, X., and Zhao, Y. E. Analyzing patterns of user content generation in online social networks. In *Proceedings of the 15th ACM SIGKDD international conference on Knowledge discovery and data mining*, KDD '09, ACM (2009), 369–378.
12. Hanrahan, B. V., Convertino, G., and Nelson, L. Modeling problem difficulty and expertise in stackoverflow. In *Proceedings of the ACM 2012 conference on Computer Supported Cooperative Work Companion*, CSCW '12, ACM (2012), 91–94.
13. Hartigan, J. A., and Wong, M. A. A K-Means Clustering Algorithm. *Applied Statistics 28*, 1 (1979), 100–108.
14. Kang, M., and Kim, B. Understanding the Effect of Social Networks on User Behaviors in Community-Driven Knowledge Services. *Journal of the American Society for Information Science and Technology 62*, 6 (2011), 1066–1074.
15. Kittur, A., Chi, E., Pendleton, B. A., Suh, B., and Mytkowicz, T. Power of the few vs. wisdom of the crowd: Wikipedia and the rise of the bourgeoisie. *Algorithmica 1*, 2 (2007), 1–9.
16. Mamykina, L., Manoim, B., Mittal, M., Hripcsak, G., and Hartmann, B. Design Lessons from the Fastest Q & A Site in the West. In *Human Factors*, CHI '11, ACM Press (2011), 2857–2866.
17. Milligan, G. W. An examination of the effect of six types of error perturbation on fifteen clustering algorithms. *Psychometrika 45*, 3 (1980), 325–342.
18. Nam, K., Ackerman, M. S., and Adamic, L. Questions in, knowledge in?: a study of naver's question answering community. *CHI* (2009), 779–788.
19. Pal, A., Chang, S., and Konstan, J. A. Evolution of Experts in Question Answering Communities. In *6th AAAI International Conference on Weblogs and Social Media*, ICWSM '12, The AAAI Press (2012), 274–281.
20. Pal, A., and Counts, S. Identifying topical authorities in microblogs. In *Proceedings of the fourth ACM international conference on Web search and data mining*, WSDM '11, ACM (2011), 45–54.
21. Pal, A., Farzan, R., Konstan, J. A., and Kraut, R. E. Early Detection of Potential Experts in Question Answering Communities. *Human-Computer Interaction* (2011), 231–242.
22. Panciera, K., Halfaker, A., and Terveen, L. Wikipedians are born, not made: a study of power editors on Wikipedia. In *Proceedings of the ACM 2009 international conference on Supporting group work*, GROUP '09, ACM (2009), 51–60.
23. Panciera, K., Priedhorsky, R., Erickson, T., and Terveen, L. Lurking? cyclopaths?: a quantitative lifecycle analysis of user behavior in a geowiki. In *Human Factors*, CHI '10, ACM (2010), 1917–1926.
24. Riahi, F., Zolaktaf, Z., Shafiei, M., and Milios, E. Finding expert users in community question answering. In *Proceedings of the 21st international conference companion on World Wide Web*, WWW '12 Companion, ACM (2012), 791–798.
25. Tausczik, Y. R., and Pennebaker, J. W. Participation in an online mathematics community: differentiating motivations to add. In *Proceedings of the ACM 2012 conference on Computer Supported Cooperative Work*, CSCW '12, ACM (2012), 207–216.
26. Turner, T. C., Smith, M. A., Fisher, D., and Welser, H. T. Picturing Usenet: Mapping Computer-Mediated Collective Action. *Journal of ComputerMediated Communication 10*, 4 (2005), 0.
27. Ward, J. H. Hierarchical grouping to optimize an objective function. *Journal of the American Statistical Association 58*, 301 (1963), 236–244.
28. Welser, H. T., Cosley, D., Kossinets, G., Lin, A., Dokshin, F., Gay, G., and Smith, M. Finding social roles in Wikipedia. In *Methods*, vol. 48 of *iConference* '11, ACM (2011), 122–129.
29. Welser, H. T., Gleave, E., Fisher, D., and Smith, M. Visualizing the Signatures of Social Roles in Online Discussion Groups. *Journal of Social Structure 8*, 2 (2007), 1–32.
30. Whittaker, S., Terveen, L., Hill, W., and Cherny, L. The dynamics of mass interaction. In *Proceedings of the 1998 ACM conference on Computer supported cooperative work*, CSCW '98, ACM (1998), 257–264.

APPENDIX A: UNSTANDARDIZED CLUSTER CENTERS FOR THE FIVE SITES STUDIED

Table 4: Unstandardized cluster centers for the profiles identified in the five sites studied.

Profile	Answers	Questions	Comments	Activity Duration	MUAnswers	MUQuestions	MUComments
Low-activity	1.14	1.06	1.47	2.73	0.00	0.87	0.01
Occasional	5.77	3.72	13.84	9.96	-0.05	7.46	0.02
Unskilled answerer	1.64	0.76	0.78	2.75	-0.84	0.47	-0.01
Unskilled commenter	1.62	1.47	3.50	4.23	-0.16	1.13	-0.70
Expert answerer	1.46	0.81	1.79	3.34	1.22	0.94	0.00
Expert questioner	6.94	2.26	15.23	9.16	0.05	39.73	0.01
Expert commenter	2.53	1.49	4.65	5.31	-0.03	1.78	1.29
Q-A activist	58.06	21.68	140.48	70.67	-0.11	4.86	0.04
Answer activist	299.49	16.91	668.80	199.42	0.20	8.41	0.16
Hyperactivist	921.81	19.61	2491.63	362.46	0.32	7.62	0.18

APPENDIX B: RESULTS OF THE CLUSTERING ANALYSIS OF THE TEN TIME WINDOWS IN SUPER USER

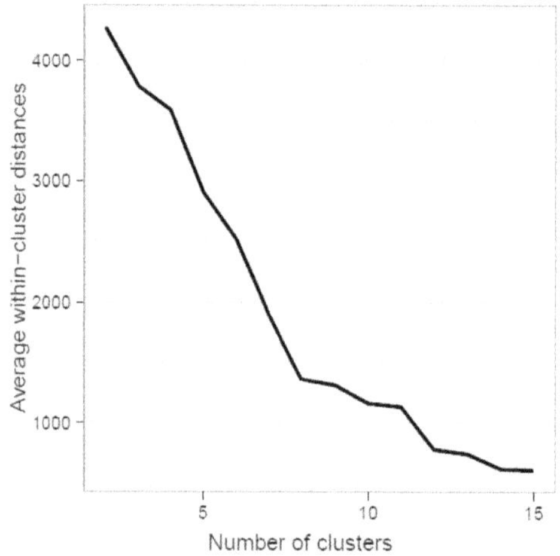

Figure 9: Analysis of the heterogeneity in the iterative cluster solutions in the hierarchical method applied to the ten time windows in Super User.

Table 5: Unstandardized cluster centers in the profiles identified for the ten time windows in Super User.

Profile	Answers	Questions	Comments	Activity Duration	MUAnswers	MUQuestions	MUComments
Low-activity	0.35	0.39	0.55	1.06	0.01	0.06	0.00
Occasional	0.65	1.72	2.66	2.70	-0.02	2.66	0.00
Unskilled answerer	1.00	0.09	0.33	1.13	-0.68	0.00	0.00
Unskilled commenter	1.13	0.30	1.78	2.06	-0.05	0.20	-0.57
Expert answerer	1.11	0.17	0.94	1.62	0.96	0.13	0.00
Expert questioner	0.98	0.88	2.81	2.11	0.03	12.90	0.01
Expert commenter	1.12	0.26	1.64	2.18	0.06	0.19	1.02
Q-A activist	4.36	11.88	18.23	12.70	-0.12	1.55	-0.04
Answer activist	33.58	1.42	41.79	23.43	0.10	1.18	0.09
Hyperactivist	166.81	2.06	238.12	44.02	0.16	2.74	0.09

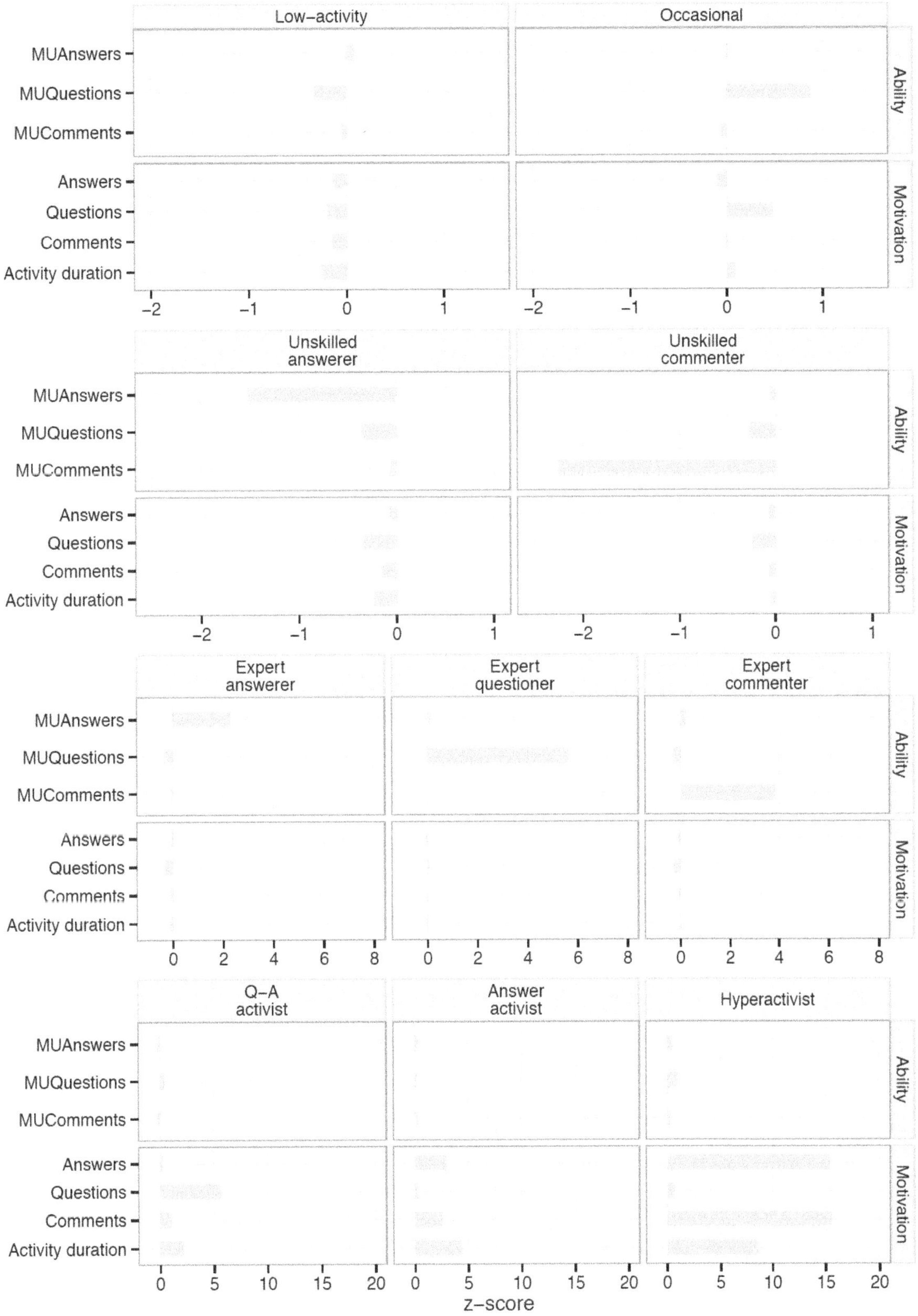

Figure 10: Centers of the clusters identified in the ten time windows for Super User.

To Answer or Not: What non-QA Social Activities Can Tell

Yingxin Pan, Lin Luo, Changyan Chi, Qinying Liao
IBM Research China, Bldg. 19, Zhongguancun Software Park, Beijing, P.R. China, 100193
{panyingx, luolin, chicy, liaoqy}@cn.ibm.com

ABSTRACT
Various methods have been proposed to help find answerers for a question in QA communities, but almost all work heavily depends on users' QA history. In this paper we seek to investigate the feasibility of leveraging users' non-QA social activities as a way of gaining insight into their question answering behavior. We collected data of 4,484 users on a QA community in an enterprise and examined the relationship of their QA behaviors and non-QA activities supported by other social tools. We found that the two sets of behavioral indicators are significantly correlated. The top user group for non-QA activities outperformed lower groups in both number and quality of the answers. Regression analysis showed involvement in personal blog, microblog and forum and replying and recommending behaviors in non-QA communities were predictive of a user's likelihood of answering questions. Online observations provided a qualitative understanding. Design implications and future work were discussed.

Author Keywords
Community Question Answering; social media; enterprise

ACM Classification Keywords
H.5.3 Groups & Organization Interfaces—collaborative computing, computer-supported cooperative work

INTRODUCTION

Community Question Answering (CQA) sites have emerged as an increasingly popular venue of sharing knowledge and seeking information. Users ask questions on SQA sites and anyone can answer them. These sites manifest strong social features, such as allowing users to discuss with one another, enabling users to follow others and providing tagging and rating functions, etc. Examples of the CQA sites include Yahoo! Answer, Baidu Zhidao (in China) and Quora.

In recent years, however, the efficiency of such QA services has been challenged due to the fast growth of the questions posted [4]. Users may not be able to obtain a satisfying answer to their questions within a short time [1]. To address this problem, a number of approaches of answerer recommendation have been proposed and developed [1, 4, 5, 10, 11, 15, 16, 20]. By doing this, potential answerers can be identified and recommended for a question raised in the community with the aim of improving answer speed and quality (e.g., Quora). These approaches have taken into consideration a wide variety of features such as question-related attributes (e.g., question length), user history (e.g., #answers), and user-user (e.g., #replies to the asker) and user-question interactions (e.g., topic relevance).

Nevertheless, almost all analysis is limited within a QA community and based on users' past QA history. There arises a risk of losing the potential contribution of those who have very few data available for such recommendation including new comers. This cold-start problem applies to the case of newly-launched CQA sites as well. Some researchers have studied the similar issue concerning newly-joined users. For example, Pal et al. [15] proposed methods to identify experts at the early stage of user participation in CQA sites, as the primary problem lies in the lack of strong markers to indicate user expertise.

We take an alternative approach to address the cold-start problem. In the era of Web2.0, people are adopting multiple social media tools at the same time; for example, they post opinions in Twitter, update status in Facebook, join discussions on Tianya (a top-tier Chinese forum) and ask questions on Quora. In Quora, many users attach their Twitter and Facebook links on their profile pages. People can easily know more about the person beyond the QA community if interested. On Baidu Zhidao, which is hosted on a comprehensive Baidu platform including Baidu forum (TieBa), Baidu Space (blog), and Baidu Document, etc., users are able to check all the activities of one user/ID across different social applications. The open social web has made it possible to turn to a broader context for user understanding and potential answerer identification.

In this paper, we seek to explore the feasibility of leveraging non-QA social activities to gain insight into users' answering behaviors in a CQA site within an organizational setting. In this enterprise, employees are provided with IBM Connections (IC) [8] that consists of various types of social applications including forum, blog, micro-blog and community. They can also post questions and receive answers on an internal CQA site called Answers@Tap, all using their unique intranet IDs. We hypothesize that the enriched social activities on IC are correlated with and have an impact on how users answer questions on Answers@TAP, because users' non-QA social activities tend to reveal their important personal characteristics that are of much value to finding appropriate answerers, such as willingness to contribute and trustworthiness.

To the best of our knowledge, this is the first in-depth work on investigating the relationship between question answering and non-QA social activities. The results will benefit the HCI community by adding a distinct and complementary perspective in finding answerers and help solve the cold-start problem by expanding the answerer group to users with a limited QA history. Though our study is conducted within a large IT corporation, we believe that our findings can extend beyond the enterprise. Because the usage of social tools and QA communities is similar to that in internet settings and user behaviors are often topic neutral, we believe our findings can be used in other web contexts.

The rest of the paper is structured as follows. We start by presenting related work on answerer recommendation using various features. We then give a brief introduction of IBM Connections and Answers@Tap where employees make social interactions, and describe the data and analysis used in our study before we report the results. Finally we discuss implications of our findings.

RELATED WORK

Our work aims to help identify potential answerers by taking advantage of their enriched social data. By and large, it falls into the research area of community answerer recommendation. A large body of answerer recommendation research has been done to recommend a user who is likely to answer a question, using various features extracted from his/her usage history. In general, there are three major threads of work in this area.

First, a lot of work focuses on matching the content of a question to the expertise and knowledge that a candidate answerer has by using text similarity or topic modeling [5, 11, 16]. In the social-network-based Aardvark CQA service, Horowitz et al. [7] modeled users by extracting topics from their existing online profiles, homepages and blogs, and computing users' social proximity and similarities from their social network connections. Richardson et al. [17] created user profiles by crawling and indexing email archives of internal mailing lists. They both emphasized content similarity but did not touch upon users' behavioral indicators such as activeness and trustworthiness reflected in other social tools.

In addition, many researchers have considered question-relevant contextual information such as question-user interactions (experts' bias on question difficulty level), user-user interactions (social connections, previous asker-answerer relationship), and time factor [1, 10, 20].

Another research area in answerer recommendation has investigated how to model users' personal characteristics and motivations for accepting to answer a question routed to them [15 , 21]. The work provides an important angle in answerer recommendation because a user of low motivation may just ignore a routed question even if he/she is capable of answering. A recent study by Morris et al. [13] discussed motivations of answering questions raised in one's social networks. Altruism (willingness to help) was cited as the top one reason, and a desire to connect socially and earn social capital were another two main reasons. Some researchers exploited users' answering history in CQA communities to model their personal characteristics in terms of willingness to contribute, ability and trustworthiness, etc. Pal et al. [15] proposed to use past answering behaviors to model motivation and ability factors for identifying expert answerers in an early stage. Basically, all approaches in this school of work heavily rely on users' past CQA information.

Our work seeks to provide a new but complementary perspective for finding answerers. As discussed earlier, a user's online social behavior is often an embodiment of his/her inner characteristics such as kindness to help, sense of obligation and reputation. For example, in Muller's paper, a user's lurking or contributing actions in online communities are partly driven by his/her personal trait [14]. Following this logic, in this paper we target to study whether and how enriched social activities can imply users' question answering behaviors.

In particular, our study aims to answer the following questions:

- Are users' non-QA social behaviors associated with their question answering? How do different participation levels of non-QA activities impact answering performance?
- What non-QA social behavioral indicators are able to predict the likelihood of answering?
- More specifically, in what ways can users' non-QA social activities help understand their answering behaviors?

STUDY OVERVIEW

We now introduce social tools adopted in the large global technology company, including a QA community called Answers@TAP and IBM Connections, a platform which offers a variety of social software features such as communities, blog, micro-blog, forum and personal profile page. And then we will describe the data and methods used in our study.

Answers@TAP

Answers@TAP is a social question-and-answer website in the enterprise under study and has achieved a regular adoption since March 2011. Any employee of the company can browse the site, but he/she must log in with his/her intranet user ID before asking, answering, commenting on and voting for a question/answer.

Answers@TAP provides a set of social features similar to popular CQA websites, including tagging a question, accepting, voting, and commenting on a question/answer. Users can also earn reputation points based on their past contributions on the site. The homepage of Answers@TAP presents a list of the most recent questions asked. The site allows users to browse via multiple views, such as viewing unanswered questions, checking questions by tag, or viewing all users sorted by their earned reputation points.

Till April in 2012, there had been 4,872 registered users, comprised of 1,732 askers and 1,091 answerers who had asked or answered at least one question. The rest of the users may either had made a comment or vote, or just browsed without any traceable record. Altogether Answers@TAP had received 2,892 questions and 4,207 answers.

IBM Connections (IC)

IBM Connections [8] is an enterprise social software application suite that was introduced in 2007. It is aimed to create a connected and collaborative workforce and employees are encouraged to use it in their daily work. At present, IC has been the only dominant social media adopted in the enterprise, offering all kinds of non-QA social capabilities to employees.

IC consists of various types of social applications including blog, micro-blog on personal profile pages, wiki, forum, file sharing, social bookmarking, and online community, etc. When a user logs in, the homepage displays what is happening on IC in the user's social network through a consolidated, customizable overview of it.

All the applications have similar structures to other familiar ones on the internet except communities and personal profile pages. **Communities** are created as containers of built-in social tools for exchanging and sharing information with other members of similar interests. The communities are set either for public or private use. The owner of a community can customize the built-in social tools by selecting from the social features IC provides, such as forum, blog, wiki, etc. Here forums can only be enabled in a community instead of being an independent application for personal use. The **profile page** in IC contains a personal photo and personal information in the company and shows an articulated social network in the form of reciprocal friend connections. A profile page also contains an embedded micro-blogging feature - users can post messages or make comments on their own or others' micro-blog board. Profile pages with the micro-blogging function are most analogous to current social networking services. So far, there have been over 150,000 blog posts, 880,000 forum posts and 550,000 micro-bloggings. Over 100,000 communities have been created on diverse topics.

Among these social applications, in our study we only focus on IC blog, micro-blog on profile pages, and public community blog and forum, which are popular in internet environment as well. While Answers@TAP is a separate application from IC, it enables users to switch to an employee's IC profile page by just clicking a link right beside his/her user name displayed on Answers@TAP.

Datasets

We collected data of the 4,872 registered users on Answers@TAP until the end of April, 2012 via the RESTful APIs provided by the development team. All the 2,892 questions and 4,207 answers were collected as well.

We then crawled all these 4,872 users' profile pages and their activity logs in personal blogs, public community blogs and forums on IC from 11, March 2008 till 24, April 2012 and found 4,484 users were valid. A user was considered invalid when he or she did not have any viewable data from both sites, that is, the number of every single behavioral indicator is zero. They just registered for the two sites but did not make any contribution. Our following analysis is conducted on the 4,484 users.

Of the 4,484 users on Answers@TAP, there are three user types: 1,091 answerers (24.3%) who provided at least one answer, 539 pure commenters (12%) who did not answer any question but made at least one comment on a question. The rest 2,854 (63.7%) users did not provide any answer or comment, of whom 1,335 users only asked questions. For each of the 4,484 users on Answers@TAP, the data consists of the number of answers provided, the number of accepted answers, the number of votes to their answers and the number of comments they provided. They can be interpreted in two dimensions. The number of answers and comments show the user's ***willingness to answer a question***. Though some users did not give an answer, they commented with an intention to clarify a question or offer a clue to help. The number of accepted answers and votes are a straightforward indicator of ***answerers' trustworthiness,*** which is reflected by their answer quality. Accepting or voting up an answer suggests user satisfaction and trust by the question askers and viewers. On Answers@TAP, users can either vote up or vote down an answer, and vote-down will result in negative points.

From IC, we collected a broad coverage of data of the 4,484 users on their personal blogs and micro-blogs, community blogs and forums, ranging from the number of their posts, replies and recommendations to others, to the number of replies and visits by others, the number of communities they joined and the number of tags added by others, to the number of people they interacted with. It resulted in a total of thirty variables. To streamline the many variables, we categorized them into three dimensions for further analysis (Table 1): activeness, influence and connectivity. We referred to literature on users' motivations to participate in online communities to construct the dimensions. According to Lampe and colleagues [9], there are six categories of benefits of participating: getting information, giving information, reputation building, relationship development, recreation, and self discovery. In our case, activeness addresses "giving information", influence relies on "reputation building" and connectivity is a measure of "relationship development".

Activeness: How much does a user contribute in terms of non-QA social activities? To indicate activeness, we calculated the number of posts a user published, the number of replies and recommendations a user made to other posts and the number of communities a user joined. The numbers measure the participation level of a user in enterprise social activities.

Influence: How well do other members respond to a user's non-QA online contributions? This dimension tells how much a user's impact spreads in online communities and how others think of it. So we calculated the number of replies/comments others made to a user's posts, the number of visits to the posts, the number of recommendations of a user's posts, the number of tags others gave to a user, and the number of posts others left on a user's micro-blog board. The recommendation function is specially designed for blog entries as a way to show readers' preference. A user can tag any other members on their profile pages. The tags assigned to a user represent the perception by others. We count the number of such social tags as influence because tagging behavior itself is a sign of how others recognize a user's social identity in online communities. It's the similar case for others to post on a user's board.

Connectivity: How connective is a user with other members in his or her non-QA social activities? This dimension addresses the openness of a user's social interactions with others. We decomposed it into two aspects: connectivity link-out referring to the number of people with whom a user takes the initiative to interact. In contrast, link-in is the number of people who come in to interact with a user. We counted link-out and link-in in personal and community blogs, micro-blogs and forums. The number of friends in a user's social network was also included in connectivity.

Methods

We used SPSS V19.0 to investigate the relationship of the two datasets from Answers@TAP and IC. As introduced above, we defined key aspects of a variety of behavioral variables for the two sites. In Answers@TAP, we studied two dimensions for question answering. The first one is *willingness to answer questions* represented by the sum of the number of answers and comments. The other dimension is *answerers' trustworthiness* measured by the sum of the number of accepted answers and votes. For non-QA social activities in IC, we added up values of all the variables under each category for an indicator to represent *activeness*, *influence* and *connectivity*.

We then carried out correlation analysis to verify our assumption on their relevance between the two sets of social behaviors. Difference tests were conducted to see whether different levels of participation in non-QA social activities mean distinct answering performance. In order to predict whether a user is likely to answer questions based on their past non-QA activities, we further ran a logistics regression on the non-QA behavioral indicators. Prior to that, we implemented factor analysis of the 30 variables to reduce dimensions so as to avoid problems with collinearity in the subsequent regression analysis. Finally, we employed online observations to acquire a more qualitative understanding of how non-QA social activities informed users' Q&A behaviors.

Non-QA Social Behavior Indicators		Description	Social Applications on IC
Activeness	#communities	number of communities the user has joined	community
	#selfPosts	number of posts the user has published	blog, micro-blog, community blog & forum
	#repliesTo	number of replies the user has made to others on his/her board	blog, micro-blog, community blog & forum
	#recommendationsTo	number of recommendations the user has made on others' blog entries	blog and community blog
Influence	#repliesBy	number of replies/comments others have made to the user	blog, micro-blog, community blog & forum
	#visits	number of visits others have made to the user's blog entries	blog and community blog
	#recommendationsBy	number of recommendations others have made to the user's blog entries	blog and community blog
	#others@me	number of post by others on the user's board	micro-blog
	#tags	number of tags assigned to the user by others	profile page
Connectivity	#friends	number of friends in the user's social network	profile page
	#linkIn	number of unique people the user has come out to interact with	blog, micro-blog, community blog & forum
	#linkOut	number of unique people who have come in to interact with the user	blog, micro-blog, community blog & forum

Table 1 Data collected on non-QA social activities of 4484 users (30 variables in total across all applications)

RESULTS

We first describe the general statistics of answering performance on Answers@TAP and that of users' non-QA social activities on IC respectively. Then we focus on exploring the relationship between the two sets of behaviors on the CQA site and non-QA social tools. We use regression analysis to identify predictive variables for the likelihood of answering. Results of qualitative observations are reported as well.

General Statistics

To understand the general performance of the CQA site, we looked at answer rate, acceptance rate and the speed to receive the first answer and to get an answer accepted on Answer@TAP. The average time for a question to receive its first answer is around 4 hours, while the average time taken for an answer to be accepted is about 5 hours. The server log data shows that 82.8% questions received at least one answer, and 38% of questions received multiple answers. The average acceptance rate (i.e., the ratio of questions that received an accepted answer) for all the questions that have been answered is 53.1%.

As shown in Figure 1, users of less contribution are the majority and the number of more active and capable users drops exponentially. It follows power-law distribution as is the case with most online Q&A communities [12]. A large proportion of the answers on Answers@TAP are contributed by a small set of users: the most active user himself contributed 228 answers with 86 of them accepted, and 20% of the 1,091 answerers provided 74% answers. If we count in the overall community population, the ratio of major contributors is even much lower. In this sense, expanding the user base of potential question answerers to those users with insufficient reference attributes by incorporating new social indicators will be valuable.

We then analyzed all data with a descriptive analysis in SPSS. Descriptive statistics appear in Table 2. The distributions of the two datasets were both strongly asymmetric. On Answers@TAP, medians of the number of answers, accepted answers, comments and votes were all zero for the entire community population (N=4,484) and the median of answer numbers was one when we only computed the 1,091 answerers. For non-QA social activities supported by IC, here we simply aggregated the variables and calculated

	Behavioral Indicators	Min	Max	Median
Answer@TAP	#Answers	0	228	0
	#Comments	0	227	0
	#Accepted answers	0	86	0
	#Votes received	-4	185	0
IC	Activeness	0	7063	32
	Influence	0	42255	485
	Connectivity	0	3711	17

Table 2 Descriptive statistics of two sets of variables on Answers@TAP and IC respectively.

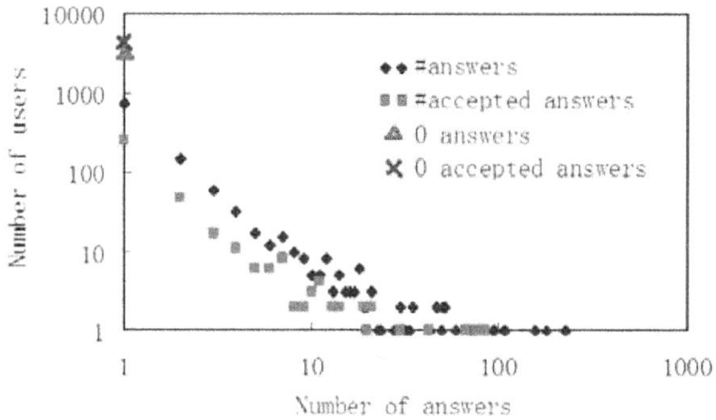

Figure 1 User contribution on Answers@TAP (numbers of users with 0 answers and 0 accepted answers are marked as isolated points to adapt to the log scales)

their means under each category for an overall indicator to represent activeness, influence and connectivity. We used non-parametric methods for our analysis considering the data skewness.

Correlation Analysis

To support our hypothesis of using non-QA social activities to infer answering behavior, first of all, we need to verify that users' non-QA social activities are associated with their answering behaviors in a general sense. Hence we implemented correlation analysis to determine whether and how well the two sets of behavioral variables were related. We used Spearman correlation analysis, a non-parametric measure of statistical dependence between two variables. As we found a strongest correlation between the number of accepted answers and acceptance rate (ratio of accepted answers/answers) (Spearman rho = .997, p<.001), which indicated the high similarity of the two, we didn't include acceptance rate into the following analysis.

The results in Table 3 showed that users' answering behaviors reflecting users' willingness to answer and trustworthiness on Answers@TAP were all positively correlated with their non-QA social activities in IC at a significant level (Spearman rho= .147 ~ .301, p<.001). The finding supports our assumption that a user's participation across different social applications is interrelated in the enterprise. The positive correlation suggests that a higher degree of user activeness, greater influence and more connectivity in non-QA social activities tend to imply the user's stronger willingness to answer questions and better answer quality provided.

We directly added the correlation coefficients of the variables of non-QA social behaviors in each of the three categories with the four answering behaviors and then calculated their means to represent the three dimensions, in that there are as many as thirty variables which display a substantial inter-correlation themselves. As shown in Table 3, a user's non-QA social behavioral indicators had the weakest relation with the number of comments a user posted while the coefficients were all greater than 0.2 for other answering behaviors.

Answering Behavioral Indicators		Non-QA Social Behavioral Indicators		
		Activeness	Influence	Connectivity
Willingness to answer	#Answers	.238*	.220*	.236*
	#Comments	.153*	.150*	.161*
Trustwor-thiness	#Accepted answers	.215*	.210*	.216*
	#Votes	.229*	.225*	.238*

Table 3 Spearman Correlation of two sets of variables on Answers@TAP and IC respectively (*p< .001)

Though the correlations were not strong on the whole, we are still interested to know what non-QA variables are more potent in respect of relationship with the answering behavioral indicators under research. We sorted out the top ten variables out of the thirty which are correlated with of the two dimensions of a user's question answering behaviors: willingness to answer measured by the sum of the number of answers and comments, and trustworthiness measured by adding the number of accepted answers and votes.

Table 4 presents the top non-QA behavioral variables that have a strongest correlation with a user's willingness to answer and trustworthiness in Answers@TAP. With regard to willingness to answer, users' active replies to others' blog entries and forum posts rank high. It makes sense because replying to others is very much like a Q&A interaction - contributing by addressing a specific request. For answer trustworthiness, actively replying to others in various social tools are also strong indicators. Connectivity was found to be important factors. It represents the extensity of a user's latent social network formed in online interactions. Greater connectivity directly implies the degree of how much the user interact with others, which is essential during the course of finding and answering questions. The number of influence indicators in the top list is smaller compared with the other two, with only one indicator listed out of the total 11 ones in that category. We believe the result is reasonable since how others respond to one's contribution in large-scale communities is often affected by many undesigned reasons. On the contrary, users are able to contribute and interact with others as much as they would like to.

Difference Tests

We have drawn conclusion on the significant correlation of answering behaviors on Answers@TAP and non-QA social activities on IC. In this section, we further look at how different levels of participation of non-QA social activities impact answering behaviors. Similar to our previous analysis, we used activeness, influence and connectivity to represent the three dimensions of a user's activities on social tools. Also we adopted the two answering indicators including willingness to answer and trustworthiness, measured by the sum of numbers of answers and comments, and the sum of numbers of accepted answers and votes, respectively.

		Willingness to Answer	Trustworthiness
Non-QA Behavioral Indicators	Activeness	P_blog-repliesTo mcrblog-selfPost C_forum-repliesTo C_forum-selfPost	mcrblog-selfPost mcrblog-repliesTo P_blog-repliesTo C_forum-repliesTo C_blog-repliesTo
	Influence	mcrblog-repliesBy	mcrblog-repliesBy
	Connectivity	P_blog-linkOut mcrblog-linkOut mcrblog-linkIn C_forum-linkOut C_forum- linkIn	P_blog-linkOut mcrblog-linkOut mcrblog-linkIn C_forum-linkOut

Table 4 Top non-QA variables correlated with Answering indicators (P_blog – personal blog, mcrblog – microblog, C_blog – community blog, C_forum – community forum)

We first sorted the users from the highest to the lowest according to the values indicating activeness, influence and connectivity respectively. Then we cut the top 30% of the users as the top group, the bottom 30% as the bottom group and the rest as the middle group. Due to many identical values, the final grouping line was slightly adjusted to make sure the same value is in the same group. As a result, there were top, middle and bottom groups for each of the above three aspects describing users' non-QA social activities (see Table 5). Finally, we carried out Kruskal-Wallis tests (K-W test), a non parametric method to compare independent samples, to explore whether different user groups exhibited different answering behaviors.

We found significant differences across the three users groups for both willingness to answer and trustworthiness (K-W test, $p<.001$). It suggested that the level of participation in non-QA social activities had an effect on user answering performance in a CQA site.

We further ran pair-wise post-hoc tests to identify specific differences between these groups. The results showed very similar patterns when using the three different grouping variables.

The top user group demonstrated a significantly higher level of willingness to provide answers than both the middle group and the bottom group (both $p < .001$), regardless of being divided by activeness, influence or connectivity in

Grouping Variables	Top Group	Middle Group	Bottom Group
Activeness	1347(30.0%)	1776(39.6%)	1361(30.4%)
Influence	1340(29.9%)	1378(30.7%)	1766(39.4%)
Connectivity	1353(30.2%)	2038(45.5%)	1093(24.5%)

Table 5. Number of people (percentage) in top, middle and bottom groups (total n=4484))

their non-QA social activities. In regard to answer trustworthiness, the top user group outperformed the other two groups at a significantly level as well (both $p < .001$). However, comparing the middle group and bottom group, we found no significant difference for the two answering indicators. The findings indicate that the top users actively engaged in non-QA social tools have great potential to provide answers which are often of good quality in a CQA site they register, compared with common users. They comprise the key user base to whom questions can be routed, especially when users don't have an even participation in QA communities and other social tools.

Factor Analysis and Logistic Regression

Previous analysis and results indicated that a higher level of engagement in non-QA social activities implied a higher level of a user's willingness to answer and their trustworthiness in terms of answer quality in QA communities. To make better sense of the results, we decided to build a regression model for predicting a user's likelihood of answering a question, as a function of his/her non-QA activities.

	Factor 1 Involvement in Personal Blog	Factor 2 Networking	Factor 3 Involvement in Community Blog	Factor 4 Involvement in Community Forum	Factor 5 Sharing
Proportion of variance	30.191	20.854	18.185	10.066	7.870
	Factor Loadings				
#P_blog-recommendationsBy	.873	.325	.028	.072	-.016
#P_blog-selfposts	.760	.202	.072	.066	.123
#P_blog-visits	.825	.214	-.008	.075	-.018
#P_blog-repliesTo	.760	.273	.352	.084	.316
#C_blog-repliesTo	.511	.068	.509	.191	.493
#P_blog-repliesBy	.876	.395	.014	.109	.010
#P_blog-linkIn	.846	.379	.025	.146	-.037
#P_blog-linkOut	.753	.260	.208	.054	.317
#C_blog-linkOut	.587	.144	.420	.182	.424
#mcrblog-selfposts	.309	.704	.235	.192	.123
#mcrblog-repliesBy	.312	.863	.091	.135	.196
#mcrblog-repliesTo	.457	.781	.222	.123	.067
#mcrblog-others@me	.384	.833	.049	.160	.101
#profile-tags	.268	.538	.122	.231	.100
#friends	.160	.753	.204	.202	.075
#mcrblog-linkin	.361	.808	.229	.193	.078
#mcrblog-linkout	.393	.844	.100	.185	.178
#C_blog-recommendationsBy	.036	-.038	.644	.173	.251
#C_blog-visits	.051	.167	.899	.166	-.026
#C_blog-selfposts	.138	.085	.728	.142	-.059
#C_blog-repliesBy	.065	.149	.937	.165	.041
#C_blog-linkIn	.078	.202	.854	.166	-.052
#communities	.079	.174	.126	.274	.114
#C_forum-selfposts	.112	.063	.160	.697	.007
#C_forum-repliesTo	.152	.250	.245	.755	.206
#C_forum-repliesBy	.050	.139	.114	.881	-.040
#C_forum-linkIn	.099	.288	.299	.792	.011
#C_forum-linkOut	.226	.269	.238	.549	.225
#C_blog-recommendationsTo	.089	.288	-.009	.030	.726
#P_blog-recommendationsTo	.163	.604	-.099	.057	.563

Table 6 Loadings of the 30 non-QA behavioral variables on the five factors. (P_blog – personal blog, mcrblog – microblog, C_blog – community blog, C_forum – community forum, n=4484)

We chose the binary logistic regression. It is a type of regression that is used to describe the relationship between one or more independent variables and a binary response variable (answer or not). One assumption for this regression analysis is that the input variables are not highly correlated. According to our correlation results, the rho coefficients of the three aspects of activeness, influence and connectivity were all above 0.8 (p<.001). We then decomposed them and calculated the correlations between each two of the 30 variables, many of which are of very strong correlations (rho .4~ .999). To avoid collinearity problem, we first performed a factor analysis on the 30 variables to identify the underlying dimensions of these non-QA social behaviors.

Using principal component factor analysis, we extracted five factors that explained 87.2% of the total variance; each of these factors had an Eigenvalue greater than 1. Table 6 presents the loadings of the 30 non-QA behavioral indicators with respect to the five factors. The result suggested that these 30 variables could be clustered under five factors.

Factor 1 included the items mainly about personal blog activities, such as publishing personal blog, replying to other's blog, and being replied by others, so it can be interpreted as "involvement in personal blog". The items loading principally on factor 2 were all related with profile pages, which function as SNS and where users update their status to their network friends. So we interpreted factor 2 as "Networking". Factor 3 dealt with one's community blog activities including posting blog and being replied in a community. It can be interpreted as "involvement in community blog". Similar to factor 1, involvement here not only meant a user's personal contribution representing his/her activeness, but also indicated a user's influence in terms of feedback received from others. We interpreted factor 4 as "contribution in community forum" as it mainly addressed how much a user contributed in a forum by making a post or replying to other posts. Factor 5 indicated how much a user recommended content to others, which could be interpreted as "sharing".

We then used the 5 factors as input to logistic regression to predict whether a user would answer a question on Answers@TAP. We performed a ten-fold cross-validation to obtain prediction accuracy, with a 50% probability as the baseline. In our study, of the 4484 cases, 1091 users answered at least one question while the rest 3393 users logged on the QA site without answering any question. Given this skewed distribution, we used an under-sampling technique to construct a balanced set of users who had or had not answered a question [19].

The overall logistic regression model resulted in classification accuracy of 63.8%. It showed that prediction of a user's likelihood of answering questions can be improved to some extent by adopting users' non-QA social activities.

Table 7 reports the statistics of the five factors in our regression model. Four factors were found to be significant predictors. Factor 1 "involvement in Personal Blog" indicated a strong willingness to share personal opinions and experience. Two items describing how much a user replied to other posts and people in community blog were included in factor 1 as well, which also represented a user's inclination of interaction. Factor 2 also achieved significance in prediction. This networking factor included the items related to one's social networking activities on their profile pages, where micro-blog is the most prominent feature. Among all the social applications on IC, micro-blog is the most ready-to-use in daily communication. Active interactions tend to reveal users' desire to socialize with others and attract attention. Factor 4 was mainly about forum involvement. Forum has actually served as an older way of questioning and answering, where users made discussions by replying to each others. The significance meant that forum behaviors should be considered as good predictive references in recommending an answerer. The last significant predictor was factor 5. It described a user's recommending behaviors. Sharing good content by recommending could be regarded as a reflection of altruism [13], which was a top reason why a user would like to answer a question. In summary, more involvement in personal blog and forum, and a higher tendency of replying to and sharing with others in communities would predict the higher likelihood of answering a question.

In contrast, only factor 3 didn't achieve a significant level in prediction. Factor 3 was all about community blogging. As we observed, IC communities are often created for projects or common interests. Writing community blog may be more driven by assignment, compared with personal sharing. It is noteworthy that replying and recommending to others in community blog were actually included in significant factors respectively. It demonstrated the predictive strength of these two behavioral indicators.

Online Observations

So far, we found a positive correlation between users' answering willingness and trustworthiness with their non-QA activities in other social tools. And the top users of non-QA social tools demonstrated great potential to answer questions in a CQA site. What's more, regression analysis identified four factors that were predictive of whether a user would like to answer a question. Now we further made a qualitative observation to understand in what ways users' non-QA social activities can imply their question answering.

	B	df	Sig.	Exp(B)
F1: Involvement in Personal Blog	.288	1	.001	1.334
F2: Networking	.539	1	.000	1.715
F3: Involvement in Community Blog	.057	1	.360	1.059
F4: Involvement in Community Forum	.397	1	.000	1.488
F5: Sharing	.302	1	.000	1.353
Constant	-.003	1	.946	.997

Table 7: Predicting whether to answer or not (n= 2034)

We looked at the QA profiles on Answers@TAP and the IC social activity summary of over 10 representative users from the top group and observed a few interesting manifestations which clearly displayed consistence between the two sets of social behaviors. To concentrate on an in-depth description of users' activities, here we only cited data from two users for illustration: user A is a software engineer from the consulting department in the enterprise. Most of his answers are for solution-seeking questions. User B is a relationship manager in chief information officer department. He provided quite a few answers to the questions about corporation internal knowledge.

Relevance in interest and expertise. We found that users show coherent interests in different social applications including the QA site and other communities. For user A, he has answered 12 questions related to "firefox" on Answers@TAP, e.g. "Is there a fix for memory usage issues with Firefox ESR" and "How to get WWER to launch in Firefox". When we looked up the communities he joined, there was one named "Firefox Champion" with such a community description as "ensure a successful deployment and adoption of modern browsers life Firefox". We also browsed his IC profile page and noticed that he was tagged "firefox" by other members twice. It could be regarded as a recognition of his expert identity in "firefox". In addition, user A published three blogs toward the topic of firefox, e.g. "Firefox Search Plugin for intranet Search Showdown". After reading his blog posts, we learned that user A was very expert in firefox related topics and he provided good suggestions on many common issues about firefox.

Consistence in social participation. As our regression results showed, some users were very active to answer questions on non QA social applications as well, especially in forums. User B interacted with community members and was very ready to reply to questions posted in forums. The questions he answered included "How to add 2D barcode to appear on the connections profile" and "What technologies are just emerging in 2012 that will become very important to our company over the next 25-30 years". User A also provided answers to others by replying to posts in community forums. It was also consistent with our earlier findings as well that actions of replying to others, especially to answer a question, in non-QA communities was a strong indicator for question answering potential in a CQA site. Likewise, we argue that the inclination of sharing good content in social communities tends to show a user's willingness to help. On his micro-blog board, we noticed that user B was fond of sharing resources and disseminating news which aroused active feedback in terms of comments. For example, he posted messages like: "I just saw a cool innovation for laptop. Have a look" and "w3Inviter is closing end of May. You can comment the bad news".

The observations echoed our previous results. Understanding of users' non-QA social activities sheds light on their question answering behaviors to a great extent. The non-QA social activities reflecting their interest and expertise serve as good indicators for an answerer's trustworthiness. At the same time, a user who is active in interacting with others and glad to share information can be very willing to answer questions routed to them.

DISCUSSION, CONCLUSION AND FUTURE WORK

Our research attempted to explore the feasibility of leveraging non-QA social activities to gain insight into their answering behaviors. We discovered significant correlation between the two sets of behaviors. Moreover, the top users who are most active in non-QA social applications were found to have better answering performance in terms of answer number and quality. Particularly, four significant factors were identified in predicting whether a user is likely to answer. The findings offer a novel angle in solving answerer cold-start issue by incorporating enriched social data to be used in answerer sense-making and recommendation rather than purely relying on their CQA history. Especially for users who display an imbalanced participation pattern with high involvement in non-QA social activities but low participation in CQA sites, our work suggests that they are very likely to be good answerers, resulting in an enlarged potential answerer base.

The factor analysis revealed an inner construct centered on social applications and user social behaviors. Our subsequent regression analysis revealed that involvement in personal blog, micro-blog, community forum and behaviors of replying to and proactive sharing with others are strong predictors for determining the possibility of answering a question. Personal blog is a typical social venue of sharing personal opinions and experience. It represents a user's willingness to share through composing posts and commenting on each other. A greater engagement in social networking activities predicts a higher possibility of answering as well. The networking factor includes one item describing the number of tags posed to a user. Tag is a representation of one's online identity. As our online observations suggested, a user's identity which is gradually built via activities in different non-QA social tools is also consistent in the CQA site they participated. The identity tends to reflect the user's interest, preference and expertise, which is of value for answerer recommendation. Interaction in forum is another predictor. We think the reason lies in the strong interactive nature of forum itself. Forum is mainly designed for generating discussions with community members and often involves many replying actions. Likewise, our online observation showed that active answerers asked and answered on community forums as well. Items describing replying to others were all incorporated in significant predictors. The result makes much sense because this particular behavior is very analogous to question answering. Recommending could be a reflection of altruism if interpreted from a personality perspective.

By performing the regression model, we also found that non-QA activities could predict a user's answering possibility with an accuracy of 63.8%, as compared with the baseline of 50%. There is one important factor that determines whether a user will answer a question or not: the correspondence of a user's expertise and interest with the question topic [5]. It implies good potential for further improvement in prediction accuracy if common content-related features are included.

Our work provides several important implications for future CQA system design. First of all, the significant predictors of non-QA activities identified in this study should be taken into consideration when designing back-end algorithms for recommending candidate answerers in a CQA site. It will complement current feature selection and enhance the overall prediction accuracy. Secondly, in recommending answerers to question askers, better explanation can be provided in two ways, leading to quicker and better-informed selections: 1) displaying the recommendation rationale supported by relevant non-QA social behaviors; for example, hyperlinks can be provided to take the asker to the non-QA contribution of a candidate for more information. 2) Providing prediction accuracy index (e.g., likelihood of answering, trustworthiness or expertise), so an asker can pick answerers they want to ask based on their specific needs. For example, for some general questions which don't require in-depth technical knowledge, candidates with a higher estimation on likelihood to answer may be more preferable.

Future work can be carried out in the following aspects. The users under research have all registered on the enterprise CQA site. However, we argue that the potential answerer base could extend beyond a specific CQA site for question routing (over tens of thousands employees in this entire enterprise), because top users for non-QA activities who have never logged on a CQA site, can be more willing to answer a question if they are invited. The future work can investigate its viability in a broader context. Another piece of future work can focus on combining a user's QA history with his/her non-QA activities and investigate if there is any interactive effect and how they together help improve recommender system performance. Temporal factor can also be one aspect for future work.

ACKNOWLEDGEMENTS

We would like to thank Michelle Zhou, Jeffrey Nichols and our anonymous reviewers for their insightful suggestions on this work. We would also like to thank Daniel Rucci and Ling Zhang for providing help on the data crawling APIs.

REFERENCES

1. Dror, G., Koren, Y., Maarek, Y., and Szpektor, I., I want to answer, who has a question? Yahoo! Answers recommender system. KDD'11, 1109-1117.
2. Dugan, C., Geyer, W., and Millen, D. R., Lessons learned from Blog Muse: andience-based inspiration for bloggers, CHI'10, 1965-1974.
3. Ehrlich, K., Lin, C., and Griffiths-Fisher, V., Searching for experts in the enterprise: combining text and social network analysis. Group'07, 117-126.
4. Gazan, R. Social Q&A. Journal of the American Society for Information Science & Technology, Advances in Information Science, 2011
5. Guo, J., Xu, S., Bao, S., and Yu, Y., Tapping on the potential of Q&A community by recommending answer providers. CIKM '08, 921-930.
6. Guy, I., Zwerdling, N., Ronen, I., Carmel, D., and Uiel, E., Social media recommendation based on people and tags, SIGIR'10, 194-201.
7. Horowitz, E., and Kamvar, S. D., The anatomy of a large-scale social search engine. WWW'10, 431-440.
8. IBM Connections, http://www-01.ibm.com/software/lotus/products/connections/
9. Lampe, C., Wash, R., Velasquez, A., and Ozkaya, E.. Motivations to participate in online communities. CHI'10, 1927–1936.
10. Liu, Q., and Agichtein, E., Modeling answerer behavior in collaborative question answering systems. ECIR'01, 67-79.
11. Liu, X., Croft, W. B., and Koll, M., Finding experts in community-based question-answering services, CIKM'05, 315-316.
12. Mamykina, L., Manoim, B., Mittal, M., Hripcsak, G., and Hartmann, B., Design lessons from the fastest Q&A site in the West, CHI '11
13. Morris, M. R., Teevan, J., and Panovich, K., What do people ask their social networks, and why? A survey study of status message Q&A behavior, CHI'10, 1739-1748.
14. Muller, M. Lurking as personal trait or situational disposition? Lurking and contributing in enterprise social media, CSCW'12, 253-256
15. Pal, A., Farzan, R., Konstan, J. A., and Kraut, R. E., Early detection of potential experts in question answering communities, UMAP'11, 231-242.
16. Qu, M., Qiu, G., He, X., Zhang, C., Wu, H., Bu, J., and Chen, C.. Probabilistic question recommendation for question answering communities. WWW '09, 1229-1230.
17. Richardson, M., and White, R. W., Supporting synchronous social Q&A throughout the question lifecycle, WWW'01, 755-764.
18. Thom, J., Helsley, S. Y., Matthews, T. L., Daly, E. M., and Millen, D. R., What are you working on? status message Q&A in an enterprise SNS, ECSCW2011
19. Weiss, G. M., McCarthy, K., and Zabar, B., Cost-sensitive learning vs. sampling: which is best for handling unbalanced classes with unequal error costs. Int. Conf. on Data Mining, 2007.
20. Zhang, J., Ackerman, M. S., Adamic, L., and Nam, K. K., QuME: a mechanism to support expertise finding in online help-seeking communities, UIST'07, 111-114.
21. Zhou, Z. M., Lan, M., Niu, Z. Y., and Yu, Y., Exploiting user profile information for answer ranking in cQA, WWW2012 companion.

Factors Influencing the Response Rate in Social Question &Answering Behavior

Zhe Liu and Bernard J. Jansen
College of Information Sciences and Technology
The Pennsylvania State University
University Park, Pennsylvania 16802
zul112@ist.psu.edu, jjansen@acm.org

ABSTRACT
With the increasing growth and popularity of social networking sites, social question and answering has become a venue for individuals to seek and share information. This study evaluates eleven extrinsic factors that may influence the response rate in social question and answering. These factors include the number of followers, the frequency of posting, the number of at-mentioned recipients, whether or not a question contains any at-mentioned verified account, unverified account, hashtag, emoticon, expression of gratitude, repeated punctuation and interjections, as well as the topic and the posting time period of a question. We collected and analyzed over 10,000 questions from Sina Weibo. Eight out of all eleven features were found to significantly predict the number of responses received. We believe that our study is of significant value in providing insights for the design and development of future social question and answering tools, as well as enhancing the collaboration among social network users in supporting social information seeking activities.

Author Keywords
Social search; Social Q&A; Social network; Information seeking; Weibo

ACM Classification Keywords
H.5.3

INTRODUCTION
Social networking sites (SNS), such as Facebook, Twitter, and Google+ have become popular in the recent decade. With their unique design, SNS have grown rapidly and become an important medium for people to build or maintain their social relationships. Daily, hundreds of millions of new pieces of content are posted by SNS users and shared with both their immediate networks and the larger Web community [1, 20]. This makes SNS remarkable resources for the real-time information seeking. Social search is the process of finding information online with the assistance of social resources [9]. Among various ways of conducting social search (e.g., reference help online, post questions on Q & A sites or forums etc.), posting questions to one's friends or followers on SNS attracts much researcher attention due to the popularity, simplicity and convenience of SNS. Also, besides relying on traditional information seeking resources, including search engines, online catalogs, IMs or emails, people have begun increasingly using SNS to satisfy their information needs. They accustomed to asking and answering questions on SNS. This information seeking process is known as social question and answering (Q&A). Examples include: *Does anybody know who won the NBA playoff game last night? Where can I find a tattoo artist that's good at 3D tattoos? Any recommendation for the cheapest place to get Polaroid 600 film?*, etc.

CSCW '13, February 23–27, 2013, San Antonio, Texas, USA.

Although social Q&A has a number of advantages, especially in terms of time and effort, it also has the defect of no guaranteed responses. In general, only 23% of questions posted on Twitter receive a response [5], which is only 1/3 of the response rate of professional Q&A sites. This might be due to multiple reasons, including the fairly casual nature of SNS and the huge volume of data being posted every second, as well as SNS's unique design of real-time updates. All of these may lead to some of the interrogative posts to be buried in a sea of updated comment streams.

Our research aim is to investigate possible ways of increasing the social response rate. In this work, our research question is: *What are the extrinsic factors that influence individuals to share their knowledge by replying others' questions posted on SNS?*

We limit our scope to extrinsic factors, given the existence of literature focusing on factors from both social and cognitive perspectives in knowledge sharing [19, 22]. In this work, we evaluated eleven factors via hypothesis testing in order to understand whether or not these factors impact the number of answers received. By understanding factors that underlie people's willingness to share their knowledge, our results can provide useful design implications for future social Q&A tools and can improve the low response rate in SNS. The data we use in this study are question posts collected from Sina Weibo, which is the most popular micro-blogging site in China at the time of the study. We analyzed the relationships among all eleven factors and the question response rate by conducting a multiple regression. We found eight of the eleven features have either positive or negative effect on a question's response rate.

Although a number of works have been done on the topic of social search [6, 7, 8, 9, 10, 11], few of them have focused on the perspective of response rate. This is also one of the first published studies of social Q&A on the Chinese site, Weibo, although we also expect our findings to inform behaviors on other social network mediums too. Based on our findings, design implications can be developed to improve SNS and to enhance human collaboration when using SNS to address their information needs.

In the rest of this paper, we provide a brief review of related major studies that have been done previously. In section 3, we introduce our research questions and hypotheses. Following, in section 4, we explain our analysis method, including data collection, pre-processing, and modeling process. We then present our data analysis results, including a detailed explanation of factors that are significantly related to the response rate of an interrogative post. Finally, we conclude our work with discussion on our findings and design implications based on our results in Section 6.

RELATED WORK

Given that social search combines the characteristics of both social network and professional Q&A, studies from those two areas are relevant to our work. Next, we will introduce those related works from the perspectives of both question asking and question answering.

Question Asking

As an emerged concept, the expectation is that social search has potential as an alternative to traditional information seeking tools (e.g. search engines, online catalogs, and professional question-and-answering sites). A number of studies have been conducted from the question asker's perspective exploring the motivations and patterns of current social Q&A experience.

Morris et al. [9] surveyed 624 social network users concerning their reasons for choosing social networks as the platform for Q&A. The results indicated that people search socially primarily due to their trust in friends over trust in strangers. Other than that, specific audience, weak beliefs on search engine performances, and non-urgent information needs also accounted for the reasons people turn to social networks to seek information. To further examine the factors that influence users' adoption of social search, the researchers also conducted another user study [10] and confirmed that seeking information on social networks can provide more personalized answers with higher response quality.

In addition to motivations, other research has been conducted to understand the taxonomy of questions asked on SNS. Through their analysis of 100 question tweets, Efron and Winget [7] found that Twitter users use their social network to satisfy their information needs by asking both factual and impersonal opinion questions to their friends online. Based on their findings, the authors proposed a taxonomy of questions asked under the microblogging environment. Evans and Chi [8] conducted their study using Broder's [12] proposed taxonomy of traditional search (transactional, navigational, and informational). The authors presented a social search model of user activities before, during, and after search and proved the value of social interactions in information seeking tasks. Utilizing naturally collected tweets from Twitter, Paul et al. [11] assessed whether or not Twitter is a good place for asking questions. By analyzing question tweets, the authors found that rhetorical questions were the most popular form of questions asked, followed by questions seeking for factual knowledge.

Question Answering

Although social search has been studied from the perspective of the question asker, limited work has been done from the standpoint of the answerer. Given the low response rate demonstrated in social search [5], many researchers turned their research focus to professional and other Q&A sites to explore the secret of high quality and high quantity response. Adamic et al. [14] in their work used Yahoo! Answer to understand patterns demonstrated in knowledge sharing activities. By clustering forum categories according to their content characteristics, the authors found a strong association between user's entropy (the broadness of user's focus) and the rating of the answers. Harper et al. [15] conducted field experiments utilizing multiple online Q&A sites and found that fee-driven sites, such as Google Answers received higher quality answers than other online but free sites. They also conclude in another study [18] that answer quality can be affected by both intrinsic factors and extrinsic factors, such as perceived ownership of information and reputation. Besides studies targeting on the answers, there are also other works studying the quality of responses by identifying the answerer's level of expertise in certain area [16, 17].

In addition to studies investigating answer qualities, there are also a few works focusing on the perspective of response quantity. Teevan et al. [13] conducted a user study in which participants are asked to search the Web while simultaneously posing a question on the same topic to their social network. By comparing the differences between traditional search and social search, the authors found that about half of the subjects received responses from their network before completing their search, which demonstrate the feasibility of using SNS for information seeking.. By performing statistical analysis based on real tweets, Paul et al. [11] noted that the majority of questions received no response on Twitter. They also found that among those few interrogative tweets with answers, the response rate is strongly related with some of the characteristics of the question askers, such as the size of their networks.

Although studies exploring response qualities on social search are insightful, there are even more basic issues that need to be addressed before we could move to that stage. Despite findings from Teevan et al.'s [19] and Paul et al.'s [11] studies, we still know very little about what happens when SNS users see their friend's or follower's questions online. What drives them to provide their response for knowledge sharing purpose? What deters them from responding? Given the very low response rate of Q&A on SNS currently [11], we believe that without a more comprehensive evaluation of factors affecting whether or not a question will be answered, SNS's power in social information seeking may never be achieved.

VARIABLES AND RESEARCH MODEL

To answer those research questions, we establish a framework on the basis of our own experience and previous literatures. We address eleven factors in our proposed model, with each variable associated with a hypothesis, testing its influence on the response rate under the social Q&A context. For better understanding of features covered in this study, we proceed with a detailed description of all eleven factors for later analysis.

1. Number of followers

One's "number of followers" has long been investigated as a possible indictor of the person's influence in spreading information to effective readers [23]. Given that questions posted on one's SNS can only be seen by his/her followers/friends, we assume that the more followers a questioner has the more responses he/she could expect to receive. Consistent with our assumption, Paul et al. [11] concluded in their study that the probability of receiving a response is intrinsically associated with the questioner's number of followers. Souza et al. [39] further supported such a significant relationship through their computational investigation. Based on the results from these studies, we therefore propose our first hypothesis:

Hypothesis 1. *The number of responses will be higher for questioners with more followers.*

2. Frequency of posting (per day)

Besides a large number of followers, a high posting frequency can also to some extent identify an online influencer [33]. Thus, it might have positive impact on the response rate of social Q&A as well. However, based on our own experience and past literatures, posting too much mundane information on one's social network may cause negative physiological consequences to audience and result in an information fatigue syndrome [34]. People may become uninterested in reading the messages posted by followees who disclose too much information [35]. Both Sibona et al. [31] and Kwak et al. [32] also demonstrated in their studies that people "unfriend" those who post too frequently about unimportant topics or mundane details of their lives. All the above arguments lead to the following hypothesis:

Hypothesis 2. *The number of responses will be lower for questioners with higher frequency of posting.*

3. Number of at-mentions

The at-mention feature of SNS enables users to directly reference others by putting an @ symbol before their screen names. According to Huberman et al. [45], this feature is widely adopted by Twitter users, with about 25.4% of all daily tweets being directed ones. At-mention has been proved as a strong predictor of information diffusion [37], as well as a significant factor in enlarging the visibility of a post and helping initiate responses and conversations [36]. The presence of such an effect was shown in both Comarela et al. [38] and de Souza et al.'s [39] studies. This leads to the following hypothesis:

Hypothesis 3. *The number of responses will be higher for questions with higher number of at-mentions.*

4. At-mention verified account

Verified account in SNS allows highly sought individuals or organizations in diversified areas to be verified as high-quality sources of information. Contrary to those general users, verified accounts tend to have more followers and thus be more influential on information diffusion and persuasion [21]. After at-mention those verified accounts, questioners would expect to get their questions retweeted by those influencers to receive more answers. To examine the effect of the verified account under the social Q&A context, the following hypothesis is set:

Hypothesis 4. *The number of responses will be higher for questions with verified account at-mentioned.*

5. At-mention general account

General accounts are the users not being verified by SNS services. Compared to directing messages to verified accounts, at-mentioning general accounts usually express some kind of close or familiar relationships and can be treated as an indicator of mutual trust [40]. Given the mutual familiarity, direct question to one's general followers/friends guarantees the visibility of the question, and even the probability of getting a response. Thus we propose hypothesis 5:

Hypothesis 5. *The number of responses will be higher for questions with general account at-mentioned.*

6. Hashtag

Hashtags is the way SNS categorize posts according to specific keywords or topics. Hashtag's values in grouping conversations and information diffusion [27] have been well studied. Rossi et al. [24] investigated the hashtag-based conversations and found that the adoption of hashtags breakthrough the restriction of the social network structure and made conversations based on non-reciprocal following relationships possible. Based on their findings, we suppose users can enlarge the visibility of their questions with the adoption of hashtrags, and thus get a higher possibility of getting responses. The following hypothesis is formulated:

Hypothesis 6. *The number of responses will be higher for questions that include hashtag.*

7. Emoticon

Emoticons are graphic representations of facial expressions that SNS users can embed in their post. Previous literature [41, 42] suggested that in compensation of the lack of social nonverbal cues, people tend to use more emoticons in computer-mediated communications. In that way they can better maintain their social presence and therefore be more engaged in social interactions. Besides, emoticons can also be used to draw the attentions from the recipients [25]. So we propose our hypothesis 7

Hypothesis 7. *The number of responses will be higher for questions that include emoticon.*

8. Repeated punctuations and interjections

As mentioned in [43, 26], repetition regardless of length limitations indicates the important role it plays in communicating one's social meanings to the others. Without adding any verbal information to the message, repeated punctuation and interjections are considered more often as an emphasis of the communicated emotion. Therefore, we expect a positive relationship between it and the response rate:

Hypothesis 8. *The number of responses will be higher for questions that include repeated punctuations and interjections*

9. Expression of gratitude

As a well-studied motivation behind prosocial behaviors, many literatures [44, 2] have affirmed the significant effect of gratitude expressions on social exchange. It is believed that through both agentic and communal mechanisms, gratitude expressions can enhance the helper's feelings of self-efficacy and social worth, and thus encourage them to engage in prosocial behaviors [57]. So our hypothesis 9 is phrased as follows:

Hypothesis 9. *The number of responses will be higher for questions that include expression of gratitude.*

10. Topical category

Given that expertise is usually context dependent. We naturally assume that the response rate for questions can be different across various topical categories. Several literatures support our assumption. Both focusing on the topical categorization of interrogative tweets, [7,9] presented significant differences on the number of questions posted across categories. Another study [3] proved such topical variance in people's knowledge sharing behavior, indicating that certain categories tend to attract more answers than the others. To examine this assumption, the following hypothesis is set:

Hypothesis 10. *Questions within certain topical categories will receive higher number of response than the others.*

11. Posting time period

Several previous studies, in both traditional search [28] and social Q&A [29], addressed significant changes in SNS post volumes along the day. Beitzel et al. [28] indicated in their work a significant variance in the frequency of information seeking across different time period of a day. Paul et al. [11] later showed the influence of posting time on Social Q&A response rate, given that tweets posted during peak hours can easily get buried in a sea of Twitter streams after a while. This lead us to believe that picking the right time to ask one's question may be important to getting a high response rate. So we hypothesize that:

Hypothesis 11. *Questions posted within certain time period of a day will receive higher number of responses than the others.*

METHODS

Data Set

In this study, we collected data from China's largest microblogging site, Sina Weibo. Launched in 2009, Weibo attracted nearly 30 million users within only three years, with a current average of 10 million Weibo statuses published every day [30], at the time of the study. Weibo essentially adopts the same operating concept and provides very similar functions to its users as Twitter.

The main reason to select Sina Weibo over Twitter as the data source in our study is because of its more user-friendly replying mechanism. Rather than mixing the replying tweets to different topics all together, Weibo's threaded comment feature obviously makes the responding process not only simpler, but it si also more organized. It can be seen in Figure 1, with Weibo user's replying and displaying actions all done in one section. Weibo's reply function makes the social feedback process much easier for its users, and thus could be a better source for studies focusing on the behaviors of social response.

In addition, another consideration that we chose Weibo in this study is because of its richer content. Due to the fact that Chinese characters are logograms rather than phonograms, the same number of Chinese characters can convey more information than English letters. Therefore, with the same 140-character limit, Weibo users can post much more elaborated questions and answers compared to Twitter users.

Using Weibo Search API, we collected 15,000 Weibo questions (published between September 1st 2011 and April 10th 2012), together with all their replies in a ten-day period from April 20th 2011. In this process, we adopted keywords with information seeking purpose, including "anybody know"(有没有人知道), "anybody can tell" (有没有人能告诉) and "almighty Weibo" (万能的微博, a well-known Weibo terminology, used to express one's desperate needs for help and information), plus question mark (？). Modified snowball sampling method was conducted to identify those above keywords used for the task of question extraction.

Criterion Variable

As we indicated in our hypotheses, the dependent variable is the response rate of each question. To control the effect of the time available to response on our dependent variable, we intentionally left a ten-day period (April 10th 2012 to April 20th 2012) for collecting the responses. Given the ten days gap and 97% of the replies to question tweets happen within an hour [3], we believed varied response time would not impact the number of replies collected. In addition, given the conversational nature of Weibo interactions, in this study we only counted replies made by distinct answerers. In other words, only one response would be counted even though an answerer might comment more than once regarding the same question.

Figure 1: Layout of Weibo Replying

Predictor Variables

Number of follower, Frequency of posting. Both features are from the perspective of the questioners. Number of follower can be directly derived from the Weibo API returns, whereas posting frequency needs to be calculated by dividing the total number of posts by the total number of days on Weibo from the first day of registration. We eliminated cases with zero number of followers or followees, given considerations of Weibo spammer bots.

Number of at-mentions, At-mention verified account, At-mention general account, Hashtag. All four features were extracted using regular expressions that matched the occurrence of Weibo specific symbols (e.g., @, #). Identities of the users being at-mentioned were verified through Weibo's User Search API. Besides the number of at-mentions, the other three variables were all binary coded, with the presence of the feature coded as 1, and the absence of it coded as 0.

Emoticon, Repeated punctuation and interjections, Gratitude expression. We extracted all three variables based on predefined patterns and coded in a binary manner (presence or absence). A full list of official Weibo emoticons was first derived from the Weibo API and was then used to match each of the collected questions. The remaining two features were both extracted in the similar manner, with the former using a defined list consisting of repeated punctuation (e.g., !!!!, ????, ……, etc.) and Chinese interjections, including "啊", "呀", "哇", "吧" (all have no actual meaning) and "急" (means urgent), and the latter using a list of gratitude words and phrases. All predefined patterns identified above were based on our observed frequencies of their occurrence based on analysis of user behavior on Weibo.

Topical category. We employed a categorization method by automatically submitting each of the collected questions into Baidu Zhidao (http://zhidao.baidu.com/) and retrieving their returned classifications. As the most famous professional Q&A site, Baidu Zhidao has a comprehensive hierarchical taxonomy of 14 main categories and a number of corresponding sub-categories within each main category (Figure 2). The most frequently occurred main category on the first returned page would be assigned to the question as its topic.

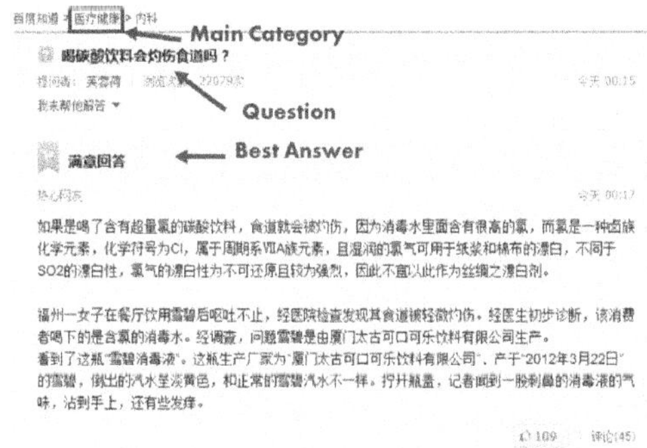

Figure 2: Layout of Baidu Zhidao

Among all 14 categories defined by Baidu Zhidao, we found that only 9 of them occurred quite often in our dataset, covering more than 92% of the interrogative posts crawled. Given the infrequency of questions from the other 5 categories, we discarded that data, reserving for future analysis. We didn't want those special cases to affect our prediction results. Also, even if we keep those infrequently asked questions, given their small percentage of occurrence, our results could not be impactful. We then dummy coded this category feature into nine dummy variables.

Posting time period. Posting timestamp can also be directly derived from the API returned results. W divided the posting timestamp into four categories of equal durations, including: nights (0:01AM - 6:00AM), morning (06:01AM – 12:00PM), afternoon (12:01PM – 6:00PM) and evening (6:01PM – 12:00AM), as inspired by findings from previous studies [46, 47]. As a categorical predictor, posting time period is also dummy coded for later analysis.

Data Analysis

Given the criterion variables for all of our eleven hypotheses, we adopted a multiple linear regression analysis to test all hypotheses simultaneously. Before we conducted the regression analysis, multicollinearity was checked by examining the bivariate correlations across all predictor variables. As none of the values in the bivariate correlation matrix exceeded the recommended value of 0.7 [4], our data suggested a lack of multicollinearity among independent variables in the multiple linear regression models. Given the highly skewed distribution of all our numerical variables, we used a log-transformation to normalize the data. All categorical predictor variables were dummy coded. We employed SPSS for the analysis. The p-value was set at 0.05 to be statistically significant.

RESULTS

Descriptive Statistics

Descriptive statistics for all variables in this study are reported in Table 1. Overall, the 13,818 interrogative Weibo posts that we used in this study generated 30,705 responses, receiving on average 2.22 unique replies from distinct respondents. 33.3% of the Weibo questions get responses from at least one answerer, and 2.0% of them received 10 or more replies. In general, approximately 84.0% of the total questions got responses of 5 or less, which forms the 'long tail' in the dataset as shown in Figure 3.

Multiple Regression Model

Results of our multiple regression analysis are listed in Table 2. The overall model of question response rate on Weibo is significantly predicted ($F_{20,\ 13797} = 157.33$, $p < .001$). All eleven proposed predictor variables, taken together, accounted for roughly 19% of the total variance. Although R-square value is not high, the significance F-value and the results of the beta-coefficients all indicate that our propose predictor variables have significant relevance with the question response rate on Weibo. Given that all eleven features studied in this work are all extrinsic factors that may have impact on people's social Q&A behavior. Without inclusion of any intrinsic determinant, we believed a relatively lower R-square value in our model is reasonable.

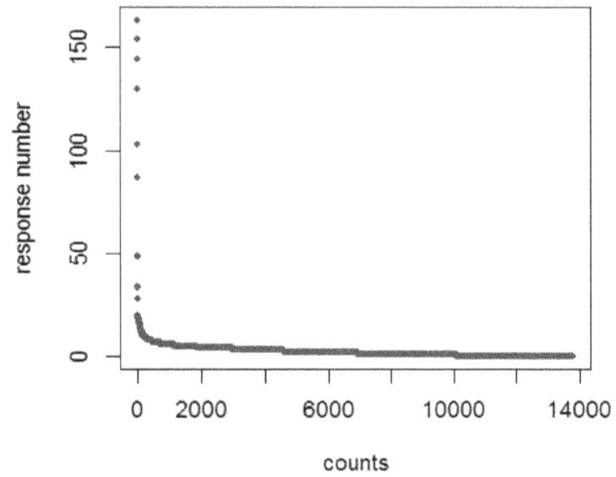

Figure 3: Distribution of response numbers

In addition to an overall assessment of the prediction model, we also tested our proposed hypotheses by examining the p-values and the beta-coefficients associated with each of the predictor variables. We found no statistical evidence to support Hypothesis 5, 8 and 9, with their p-values greater than .05, which indicated that both the adoption of at-mentions on general accounts, the usage of repeated punctuations, interjections, and gratitude expression in one's question could not significantly affect its response rate on Weibo.

Although Hypotheses 4 and 6 demonstrated significant statistical correlation between the response rate and the at-mention of verified account and the usage of hashtag, they still can not be accepted given that the sign of their coefficient is the opposite of what we have hypothesized. Therefore, we concluded that among all eleven assumptions, only hypotheses 1 (number of followers), 2 (frequency of posting), 3 (number of at-mentions), 7 (emoticons), 10 (topical category), and 11 (posting time period) are supported given our results.

Variable	Mean	Median	Standard Deviation
Number of followers	1882.39	408.00	13543.012
Frequency of posting	5.31	3.00	16.091
Number of @mentions	0.47	0.01	1.402
Number of responses	2.22	2.00	3.398

Variable	Frequency	Percent
@mention verified account		
Yes. (=1)	1793	12.98%
No. (=0)	12025	87.02%
@mention general account		
Yes. (=1)	1462	10.58%
No. (=0)	12356	89.42%
Hashtag		
Yes. (=1)	878	6.35%
No. (=0)	12940	93.65%
Emoticon		
Yes. (=1)	4522	32.73%
No. (=0)	9296	67.27%
Repeated punc and interj		
Yes. (=1)	2446	17.70%
No. (=0)	11372	82.30%
Gratitude expression		
Yes. (=1)	6510	47.11%
No. (=0)	7308	52.89%
Topical category		
Region. (=0)	2683	19.42%
Life. (=1)	2076	15.02%
Entertainment. (=2)	2424	17.54%
Society. (=3)	453	3.28%
Health. (=4)	1662	12.03%
Education. (=5)	1520	11.00%
Computer. (=6)	1783	12.90%
Commerce. (=7)	511	3.70%
Electronics. (=8)	706	5.11%
Posting time		
0:00 AM – 06:00 AM (= 1)	2132	15.43%
06:01 AM – 12:00 PM(= 2)	3711	26.86%
12:01 PM – 18:00 PM (= 3)	3779	27.35%
18:01 PM – 23:59 PM (= 0)	4196	30.37%

Table 1: Descriptive statistics for predictor and criterion variables

Features Impacting the Response Rate

Through the analysis of multiple regression, we successfully tested our proposed hypotheses and determined features with significant impact on the response rate. It only provides us general indication of their associations. To better understand those associations, more in-depth analyses was then conducted for each individual feature. Relevant patterns were documented and are further discussed in the following section.

Feature	Coefficient	P-value
Constant	- .19	< .001*
Number of follower	.21	< .001*
Frequency of posting	- .14	< .001*
Number of @mention	.20	< .001*
@mention verified account	- .33	< .001*
@mention general account	.03	< .39
Hashtag	- .184	< .001*
Emoticon	.10	< .001*
Repeated punc and interj	.03	.06
Gratitude expression	.01	.19
Topical category	–	–
Life - Region	-.0366	< .001*
Entertainment - Region	- .626	< .001*
Society - Region	- .37	.574
Health - Region	- .432	< .001*
Education - Region	- .609	< .001*
Computer - Region	- .226	.029*
Commerce - Region	- .135	.132
Electronics - Region	-.083	.170
Posting time		
0:00-06:00AM - 18:01–23:59PM	–	–
06:01-12:00PM - 18:01–23:59PM	- .139	.018*
	.002	.963
12:01-18:00PM - 18:01–23:59PM	.060	.217
$F_{20, 13797}$ = 157.33		< .001*
R^2 = .186		
Adjusted R^2 = .185		

Table 2: Multiple Regression Model Results

Number of followers. To further investigate the effect of the number of followers on the response rate, we first selected a subset of our collection generated by questioners with less than or equal to 1,000 followers. We chose 1,000 followers to represent most of Weibo users (Median = 408). By grouping questioners with every 100 followers into a bucket, we then plotted the average response rate versus each category, representing a particular range of follower numbers. As can be seen form Figure 4, response rate increases as the number of followers becomes larger.

Posting frequency. Regarding to the negative relationship between the two variables, we wanted to investigate under what posting frequencies Weibo users start becoming uninterested in following one's updates, and in turn stopping to provide their responses. To accomplish that, we put questioners into groups based on their daily frequencies of posting according an interval of 5 posts a day. Given 5 as the average posting frequency of Weibo users, we would like to see how response rate would change as the questioners double, triple, or even quadruple their daily posts.

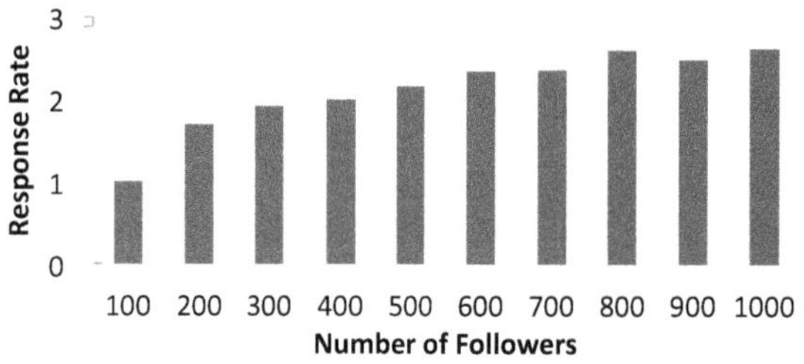

Figure 4: Response rate and the number of followers

Shown in Figure 5, we see that questioners with either very low or very high posting frequencies tend to receive less responses as compare to those who post somewhere in the middle. To be more specific, we first observed an increase in the number of responses when the posting frequency is doubled, up to 9 posts per day (2.40). However, we next detected continuous decrease as the posting frequency is tripled (2.06), quadrupled (1.94), and quintupled (1.80) (we stop at 24 posts per day, given that higher frequency is not common). We believe this decrease is due to Weibo user's syndrome of information fatigue that happens when someone keep on posting mundane information.

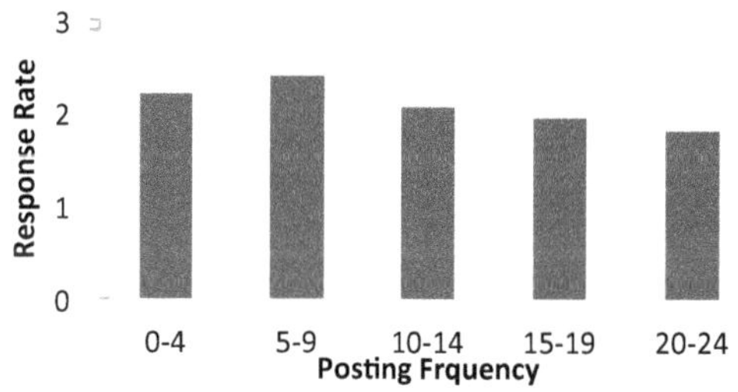

Figure 5: Distribution of response rate and the posting frequency

Number of at-mentions. In our dataset, about 80% of the questions were posted without at-mentioning any account. 11.5% of the questions at-mentioned one account for direct reference. Among the remaining 8% of questions, the number of at-mentions adopted varied largely from 2 to 22. We grouped questions included different number of at-mentions. From Figure 6, we see a general increase in the response rate along with more at-mentions adopted in each question, even though the increasing trend is not that significant due to the large variance.

At-mention verified account. Among all 13,818 Weibo questions that we collected, 1,793 (13.0%) of them contained at-mentions to at least one verified account. The mean response rate for those questions is 1.93, which is a little lower than that of questions not at-mentioning any verified account (2.27 replies per question).

While analyzing all the verified accounts being at-mentioned in our dataset, we noticed one potential bottleneck which might impedes Weibo from become the optimal place for question asking and answering. We found that questioners sometimes do not know whom to ask given Weibo's current lack of assisting services (e.g., expert recommender, or question routing mechanism). Without knowing who the experts in the field are, questioners randomly direct their questions to a large amount of varied recipients. This lead to the circumstances that among a total number of 1,975 verified recipients, only one of them has been mentioned in more than half of the directly asked questions, while the rest being at-mentioned only once or twice.

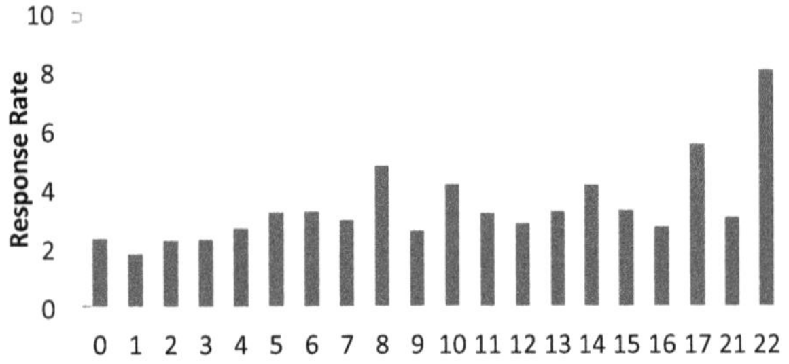

Figure 6: Distribution of response rate and the number of at-mentions

Given questioner's trust in that one verified account, we did some further analysis on it to assess its helpfulness. The account being at-mentioned the most (1,036 times) is @wangxiaoshan (@王小山), who is well known at the time of the study for his enthusiasm for answering others' questions. We extracted all the questions at-mentioned him and their corresponding replies. We plotted the actual response rates of questions being retweeted and replied by @wangxiaoshan (represented with red dots in figure 7) and those without his contribution (represented with blue dots).

From Figure 5, we see the significant effect of "celebrity endorsement". Questions replied and retweeted by @wangxiaoshan received much higher total number of responses than those without his help. Although this demonstrated the value of authorities in social Q&A, given their limited energy, most of the Weibo questioners still cannot benefit from their at-mention behaviors (i.e., only 6.6% of all the questions being directed have been replied by @wangxiaoshan).

Hashtag. Similar as our findings on at-mentioned verified accounts, given no set rules for hashtag creation, the frequency of Weibo hashtag usage followed a relatively long tail distribution, with 97% of the hashtags appeared only once or twice. 874 of all 13,818 total questions contained hashtag and 22.3% (195) of them got at least two replies. In contrast, 34.0% of the questions without hashtags received the same rate of replies. This indicated hashtag's negative impact on response rate, which is consistent with our previous findings in the multiple regression analysis. Given hashtags' heavy usage in spam posts [42], we surmised the negative impact of hashtag usage on question response rate might be due to the fact that using hashtags can sometimes annoy some readers and lead them to skip one's questions without leaving their response.

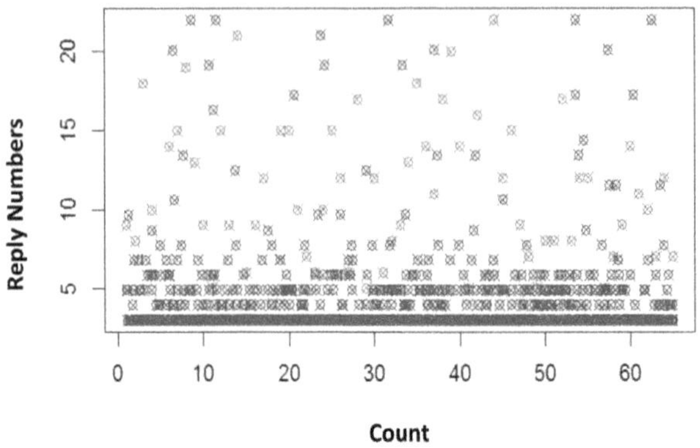

Figure 7: Distribution of response rate for questions replied and retweeted by @wangxiaoshan and without

Topical category. As shown in Table 1, the number of questions asked by Weibo users varied largely among all nine categories returned by Baidu Zhidao. The topic asked the most on Weibo was region (2,683, 19.42%). This can be easily understood giving the increasing number of mobile Weibo users in China and the current popularity of location-based search. In contrast, the topic that received the least questions was society (453, 3.28%), as shown in Figure 8.

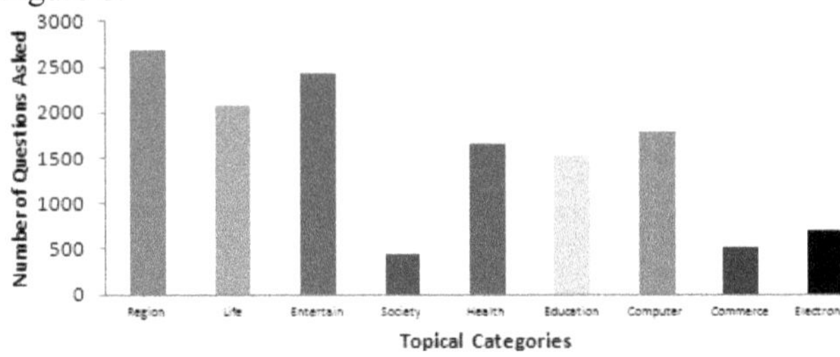

Figure 8: Distribution of number of questions asked and the question's topical category

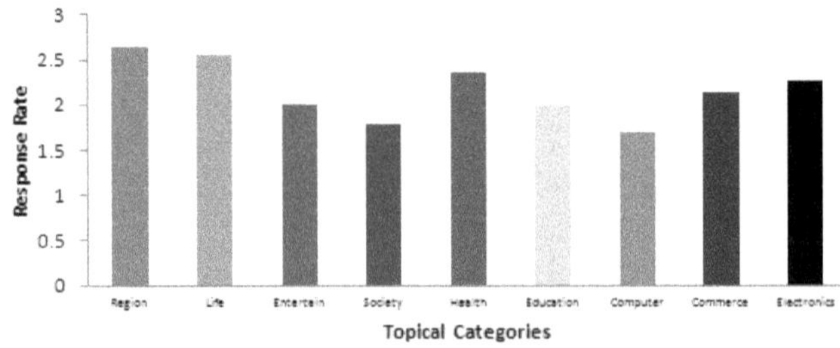

Figure 9: Distribution of response rate and the question's topical category

From Figure 9, we further indicated that although the number of questions asked varied significantly across categories, the question response rate did not show huge differences, except certain categories with specific background requirements (such as education and computer). In that sense, again we believe that any mechanism that can direct a Weibo questioner's post to the right field expertise could be very beneficial in the social Q&A context.

Posting time of the question. We conducted an analysis on the temporal effect on social Q&A behaviors. As can be seen from Figure 10, consistent with previous studies [28], we found that people asked the most questions on Weibo between 18:01 PM and 23:59 PM and the least questions from midnight to the early morning. Different from question posting, the response rate failed to show significant difference among the other three time periods, except 0:00AM – 6:00AM, which received the least average number of replies (2.00), as shown in Figure 11.

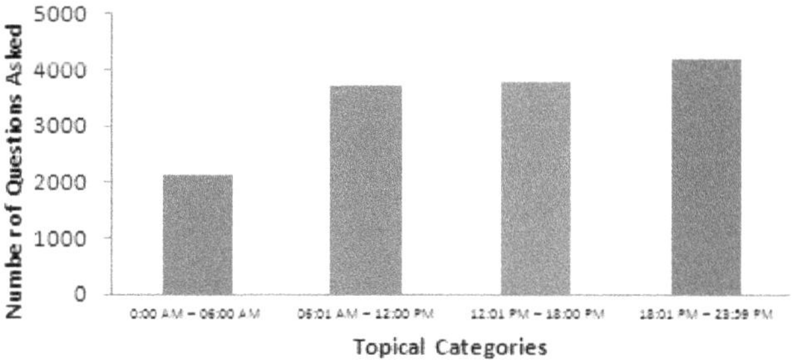

Figure 10: Distribution of questions asked across time periods

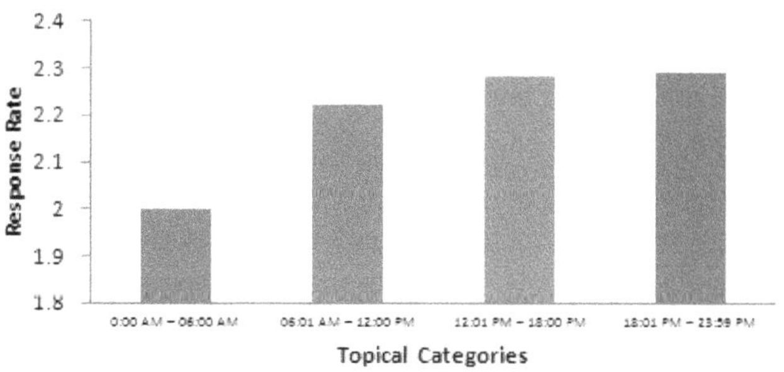

Figure 11: Distribution of response rate across time periods

DISCUSSION AND IMPLICATIONS

Our work presented in this paper is valuable to people in the field of social information seeking, ranging from social scientists to social network users. Given the lack of studies focusing on the response quantity of social Q&A, our predictive model can be adopted as the foundation for future studies with the related focus. Social technologists could also benefit from our study by understanding user's behaviors toward various features when they decide to interact and help others by responding to questions. Taking advantage of our findings and suggestions can help social technologists know the bottlenecks of current systems in the social Q&A environment so that they can develop new tools to support user's questioning and answering behaviors on SNS. When asking questions on SNS, users can utilize the results of our study to match their conditions, checking to see if their question has the potential to receive an ideal number of replies. In summary, our work is of good value to the research community. We aim to continue with it to eventually build some tools, such as an expert recommender, or a question routing mechanism, to make the social Q&A process easy for users to use.

Limitations of our current work include the keyword method of extracting interrogative posts. Although those questions are representative given their high frequency of occurrence, only focusing on them would affect the generalizability of work, especially when facing uncommonly asked questions. As we discussed earlier, with only extrinsic features considered the current model may not achieve high prediction. Adding more intrinsic and social predictors into the model will increase its predictability. The investigations on the relationships between social predictors and the response behavior could be one possible direction for later work.

CONCLUSION

With the objective to enhance user interactions and cooperation in social Q&A context, we performed an analysis on the relationships between eleven extrinsic features and the question response rate. Using Weibo as data source and multiple regression as statistical method, we found in this study that eight out of our eleven features have significant impacts on the response rate. Those features include: the questioner's number of followers, frequency of posting, the number of at-mentions adopted in a question, whether or not a question include any at-mention to any verified account, hashtag, emoticon, as well as the topic and posing time of the questionThe adoption of at-mention verified account and hashtag both have negative influences on the received number of replies, just opposite to our hypothesis. Although posting frequency also negatively associated with the criterion variable, it was expected given previous literatures [31-35].

Through our further analysis of those predictors, we noticed the design problems from two perspectives that may impact the usability of social Q&A. Since there are no official rules of hashtag usage from major SNS providers, hashtag might not be beneficial in the context of social Q&A given that it cannot increase the visibility of the question. The value of verified account in social Q&A was small in our study as compared to their important function in the process of information diffusion. This may be due to the fact that users cannot properly target the "right" expert and the verified users do not have a lot of energy to answer all the questions. Based on the present situation, development of corresponding tools and mechanisms, such as interrogative hashtag vocabularies, expert authentication, recommendation, and compensation, could make the user's expert seeking process easier and the experts more willing to share knowledge with others.

Based on these possible implications proposed, we believe that our study offers valuable insights into the future development of social search systems or tools that can make good use of those features as introduced in this study.

REFERENCES

1. Twitter.numbers. http://blog.twitter.com/2011/03/numbers.html.
2. Tsang, J. –A., Gratitude and prosocial behaviour: An experimental test of gratitude. *Cognition & Emotion (2006)*, *20*, 138–148.
3. Yang, J., & Wei, X. Seeking and offering expertise across categories: A sustainable mechanism works for baidu knows. *Proceeding of ICWSM* (2009).
4. Slinker, B. K., & Glantz, S. A. Multiple regression for physiological data analysis: the problem of multicollinearity. *American Journal of Physiology-Regulatory*, Integrative and Comparative Physiology (1985), 249(1), R1-R12.
5. Sysomos. Replies and Retweets on Twitter. http://sysomos.com/insidetwitter/engagement/
6. Dent, K., & Paul, S. Through the twitter glass: Detecting questions in micro-text. In *Workshop on Analyzing Microtext at the 25th AAAI Conference on Artificial Intelligence* (2011).
7. Efron, M., & Winget, M. Questions are content: a taxonomy of questions in a microblogging environment. *Proceedings of the American Society for Information Science and Technology* (2010), 47(1), 1-10.
8. Evans, B. M., & Chi, E. H. Towards a model of understanding social search. In *Proceedings of the 2008 ACM conference on Computer supported cooperative work* (2008), pp. 485-494. ACM.
9. Morris, M. R., Teevan, J., & Panovich, K. What do people ask their social networks, and why?: a survey study of status message q&a behavior. In *Proceedings of the 28th international conference on Human factors in computing systems* (2010), pp. 1739-1748. ACM.
10. Morris, M. R., Teevan, J., & Panovich, K. A comparison of information seeking using search engines and social networks. In *Proceedings of the Fourth International AAAI Conference on Weblogs and Social Media* (2010).
11. Paul, S. A., Hong, L., & Chi, E. H. Is twitter a good place for asking questions? a characterization study. In *Proceedings of ICWSM'11* (2011).
12. Broder, A. A taxonomy of web search. *In ACM Sigir forum* (2012), 36(2), pp. 3-10. ACM.
13. Teevan, J., Morris, M. R., & Panovich, K. Factors Affecting Response Quantity, Quality, and Speed for Questions Asked via Social Network Status Messages. In *Proceedings of ICWSM'11*(2011).
14. Adamic, L. A., Zhang, J., Bakshy, E., & Ackerman, M. S. Knowledge sharing and yahoo answers: everyone knows something. In *Proceedings of the 17th international conference on World Wide Web* (2008), pp. 665-674. ACM.
15. Harper, F. M., Raban, D., Rafaeli, S., & Konstan, J. A. Predictors of answer quality in online Q&A sites. In *Proceeding of the twenty-sixth annual SIGCHI conference on Human factors in computing systems (2008),* pp. 865-874. ACM.
16. Kleinberg, J. M. Authoritative sources in a hyperlinked environment. *Journal of the ACM (JACM)* (1999), 46(5), 604-632.
17. Guo, J., Xu, S., Bao, S., & Yu, Y. Tapping on the potential of q&a community by recommending answer providers. In *Proceedings of the 17th ACM conference on Information and knowledge management* (2008), pp. 921-930. ACM.
18. Raban, D., & Harper, F. Motivations for answering questions online. *New Media and Innovative Technologies* (2008).
19. Chow, W. S., & Chan, L. S. Social network, social trust and shared goals in organizational knowledge sharing. *Information & Management* (2008), 45(7), 458-465.
20. Jansen, B. J., Zhang, M., Sobel, K., & Chowdury, A. Twitter power: Tweets as electronic word of mouth. *Journal of the American society for information science and technology* (2009), 60(11), 2169-2188.
21. Bentwood, J. Distributed Influence: Quantifying the Impact of Social Media. *Hentet den* (2008), *15*.
22. Lin, M. J. J., Hung, S. W., & Chen, C. J. Fostering the determinants of knowledge sharing in professional virtual communities. *Computers in Human Behavior* (2009), 25(4), 929-939.
23. Cha, M., Haddadi, H., Benevenuto, F., & Gummadi, K. P. Measuring user influence in twitter: The million follower fallacy. In *Proceeding of 4th international aaai conference on weblogs and social media* (2010), 14(1), p8.
24. Rossi, L., & Magnani, M. Conversation Practices and Network Structure in Twitter. *In Sixth International AAAI Conference on Weblogs and Social Media* (2012).
25. Kriplean, T., Toomim, M., Morgan, J., Borning, A., & Ko, A. Is this what you meant?: promoting listening on the web with reflect. In *Proceedings of the 2012 ACM annual conference on Human Factors in Computing Systems (2012)*, pp. 1559-1568. ACM.
26. Suh, B., Hong, L., Pirolli, P., & Chi, E. H. Want to be retweeted? large scale analytics on factors impacting retweet in twitter network. In *Proceeding of IEEE Second International Conference on Social Computing* (2010), pp. 177-184. IEEE.
27. Huang, J., Thornton, K. M., & Efthimiadis, E. N..Conversational tagging in twitter. In *Proceedings of the 21st ACM conference on Hypertext and hypermedia* (2010), pp. 173-178. ACM.
28. Beitzel, S. M., Jensen, E. C., Chowdhury, A., Frieder, O., & Grossman, D. Temporal analysis of a very large topically categorized web query log. *Journal of the American Society for Information Science and Technology* (2007), *58*(2), 166-178.
29. PCOline, Sina Weibo Statistics http://pcedu.pconline.com.cn/softnews/yejie/1205/2782402.html
30. Granovetter, M. S. The strength of weak ties. *American journal of sociology* (1973), 1360-1380.
31. Sibona, C., & Walczak, S. Unfriending on Facebook: Friend request and online/offline behavior analysis. In *Proceeding of 44th Hawaii International Conference* (2011), pp. 1-10. IEEE.
32. Kwak, H., Chun, H., & Moon, S. Fragile online relationship: a first look at unfollow dynamics in twitter. In *Proceedings of the 2011 annual conference on Human factors in computing systems* (2011), pp. 1091-1100. ACM.

33. Reynolds, W. N., Weber, M. S., Farber, R. M., Corley, C., Cowell, A. J., & Gregory, M. Social media and social reality. In *Proceeding of 2010 IEEE International Conference on Intelligence and Security Informatics* (2010), pp. 221-226. IEEE
34. Gelter, H. Friluftsliv as slow and peak experiences in the transmodern society. In *Proceedings from Ibsen Jubliee Friluftsliv Conference* (2009). North Trøndelag University College.
35. Oulasvirta, A., Lehtonen, E., Kurvinen, E., & Raento, M. Making the ordinary visible in microblogs. *Personal and ubiquitous computing* (2010), 14(3), 237-249.
36. Vega, E., Parthasarathy, R., & Torres, J. Where are my tweeps?: Twitter Usage at Conferences. Paper, Personal Information Management class, Virginia Polytechnic Institute and State University (2010).
37. Yang, J., & Counts, S. Predicting the speed, scale, and range of information diffusion in twitter. *In Proceeding of ICWSM* (201).
38. Comarela, G., Crovella, M., Almeida, V., & Benevenuto, F. Understanding factors that affect response rates in twitter. *In Proceedings of the 23rd ACM conference on Hypertext and social media* (2012) pp. 123-132. ACM
39. de Souza, C., de Magalhães, J., de Costa, E., & Fechine, J. Predicting potential responders in twitter: a query routing algorithm. *Computational Science and Its Applications–ICCSA* (2012), pp714-729.
40. Lumbreras, A., and Gavalda, R. Applying trust metrics based on user interactions to recommendation in social networks. *In Social Knowledge Discovery and Utilization Workshop* (2012).
41. Lo, S. K. (2008). The nonverbal communication functions of emoticons in computer-mediated communication. CyberPsychology & Behavior, 11(5), 595-597
42. Walther, J. B., & D'Addario, K. P. The impacts of emoticons on message interpretation in computer-mediated communication. *Social Science Computer Review* (2001), *19*(3), 324-347
43. Kalman, Y. M., & Gergle, D., CMC Cues Enrich Lean Online Communication: The Case of Letter and Punctuation Mark Repetitions, (2010).
44. Bartlett, M. Y., & DeSteno, D. (2006). Gratitude and Prosocial Behavior Helping When It Costs You. *Psychological Science*, 17(4), 319-325.
45. Huberman, B. A., Romero, D. M., & Wu, F. Social networks that matter: Twitter under the microscope. *First Monday*, 14(1). (2008).
46. Demirbas, M., Bayir, M. A., Akcora, C. G., Yilmaz, Y. S., & Ferhatosmanoglu, H. Crowd-sourced sensing and collaboration using twitter. In *Proceeding of 2010 IEEE International Symposium on World of Wireless Mobile and Multimedia Networks* (2010), pp. 1-9. IEEE.
47. Wakamiya, S., Lee, R., & Sumiya, K. Crowd-based urban characterization: extracting crowd behavioral patterns in urban areas from twitter. In *Proceedings of the 3rd ACM SIGSPATIAL International Workshop on Location-Based Social Networks* (2011), p10. ACM.

Crowd vs. Crowd: Large-Scale Cooperative Design through Open Team Competition

Cheong Ha Park, KyoungHee Son, Joon Hyub Lee, Seok-Hyung Bae
I²DEA Lab, Department of Industrial Design, KAIST
291 Daehak-ro, Yuseong-gu, Daejeon 305-701, Republic of Korea
cheongha.park | kyounghee.son | joonhyub.lee | seokhyung.bae @kaist.ac.kr

ABSTRACT

Following the recent remarkable successes of crowdsourcing, there have been attempts to apply it to design. However a design problem is often too complex and difficult to break down into simpler, distributable tasks as required by the conventional crowdsourcing model. In this paper, we present Crowd vs. Crowd (CvC), a novel design crowdsourcing method, where several design teams made up of designers and crowd compete with each other. In each team, a designer coordinates effective communication between the crowd members and takes responsibility for the final design output, and the crowd contributes at different stages of design. We conducted an initial evaluation of CvC in comparison with other collaborative design methods, and found that: CvC can attract more people to participate; the crowd can make useful contribution in CvC; CvC can produce competent design outputs. We then applied CvC to two real-life design problems: first, designing a new logo for a university department; second, for a small tech company. With quantitative and qualitative analyses on these applications, we observed that the elements of competition and collaboration helped to sustain the crowd's motivation to participate, and to produce quality design outcomes with higher level of satisfaction for the stakeholders.

Author Keywords
Design process; crowdsourcing; competition; collaboration

ACM Classification Keywords
H.5.3 [Group and Organization Interfaces]: Collaborative computing.

General Terms
Design.

INTRODUCTION

Traditionally, industrial design processes focused on creating aesthetically pleasing products, and were conducted only by professional designers. However, industrial design has expanded to include design of systems, interfaces, services and user experiences, and newly emerging design methodologies are inviting various stakeholders including end users to take part in the design process to meet their various needs and wants. Notable open methods include: 'user centered design' that emphasizes the actual conditions and needs of users; 'participatory design' in which users equally participate as designers [11]; 'co-design' that lets users customize a design [20]; 'non-intentional design' that draws design inspirations from users' unconventional use of everyday objects [3]. Active participation of non-professionals is becoming a main stream in design with its expanded scope.

Building on such an inclusive trend, there are attempts to crowdsource the design process itself, in the hope that a large number of non-designers will participate and collaborate to solve a design problem better than any single designer or a design team can. Crowdsourcing has been particularly effective in generating volume and diversity, and previous attempts to crowdsource design have shown that large-scale crowdsourcing can be beneficial at separate stages of design process such as data collection [23], user study [12], and design evaluation [27].

However, it is more challenging to crowdsource the entire design process, as it requires analysis of the design problem, insight on the design context and integration of creative solutions at a deeper level. Such an oversight is difficult to achieve with the simple crowdsourcing model, which breaks down a problem into small pieces, distributes them, and collects and combines individual solutions mechanically. In addition, a non-designer individual without the appropriate design skills and expertise will not be able to visualize, develop and finalize a design, no matter how small a piece it may be. Moreover, such a design crowdsourcing would benefit from the crowd keeping track of the design process in progress, but it is difficult to sustain the level of motivation and enthusiasm required for them to do so.

In this paper, we suggest a new method to effectively crowdsource the entire design process. We begin with the acknowledgement that designers and non-designers can contribute in different ways, and develop a way for them to effectively collaborate. In doing so, we pay special attention on different characteristics of various phases within a design process, on utilizing designers' expertise to visualize, develop and finalize a design, and also on sustaining the level of motivation of the crowd. Finally, we show that our new method can be applied to a real design problem to produce satisfactory design output.

CSCW '13, February 23–27, 2013, San Antonio, Texas, USA.

RELATED WORK

Crowdsourcing Simple Tasks

There are many successful cases of crowdsourcing in various fields. Representative works are: 'Be a Martian' by NASA that organizes and analyzes hundreds of thousands of pictures taken from Mars [1, 10]; 'RECAPCHA' that prevents automated string input on a website by asking the user to type characters from a scanned image of a document which cannot be recognized with OCR [21]; an online game 'FoldIt' that predicts folded structures of proteins [5]; 'eBird' that watches birds through networking local volunteers [24]; and 'The Johnny Cash Project' that creates new music videos by having Johnny Cash's fans redraw still-cut frames of the original music video [26]. Online labor markets such as MTurk of Amazon reduced the cost and effort required to construct the necessary infrastructure, and inspired new crowdsourcing possibilities.

One characteristic of these cases is that they crowdsource by providing participants with micro tasks, which are easy enough for each participant to conduct for a small amount of cash or out of personal interest. Another characteristic is that a large number of partial results can be accumulated into a meaningful solution, often requiring quantity more than quality of work.

Crowdsourcing Complex and Creative Tasks

There are recent crowdsourcing projects that deal with more complex and creative tasks. Lakhani et al. claimed that modularization through task decomposition is essential in solving these tasks [17]. Early attempts relied on multitudinous trials. An example is an algorithm which asks people on MTurk to interpret badly written handwritings repeatedly until the match rate improves [18]. The focus shifted to proper distribution of tasks among crowd with a predefined format or workflow, for example, in writing an article [14], translating English text into Latin [13], and summarizing a video [25]. More recent studies explore ways for crowdsourcing operators to interactively modify the workflow based on the participation trend or feedback from the crowd [7, 15, 16].

Capturing the interests and therefore the devotion of the proper kind of crowd is also important. Heimerl et al. showed that installing a physical kiosk at the target-specific location and giving out proper reward results in high participation rate and task performance [8].

Crowdsourcing to Solve Design Problems

Design processes are increasingly conducted by a team of different experts rather than by an individual designer. This trend of expansion combined with social network infrastructure implies a possibility of large-scale crowd collaboration. Previous web-based design crowdsourcing studies involve crowd in various isolated stages of design process: data collection [23]; user research [12]; and evaluation of the final design [27].

More recently, Yu & Nickerson proposed an iterative design process of idea generation and evaluation to design a chair for children [28]. They showed that crowd can generate creative and diverse ideas through combining and mutating the previous generation of design ideas. However, their method did not produce a design output at the level of quality required for real-life application. We think that this is due to the fact that their non-designer crowd lacked the necessary design skills and expertise such as graphical visualization and consideration of user scenario and manufacture needed to mature and finalize a design.

On the other hand, online design competitions such as '99 Designs' [29] implement the conventional design contest on the web. Because they accept only finalized designs, non-designer crowd cannot actively participate.

Many previous studies have shown the benefits and potentials of crowdsourcing, but crowdsourcing the entire design process remains largely unattempted. We assume that if crowd understands the whole design process in which ideas diverge and converge, and shares the design context with professional designers, the crowd will become better motivated and generate more relevant, higher quality ideas during different stages of design process.

CONSIDERATIONS FOR DESIGN CROWDSOURCING

To effectively crowdsource the entire design process, it is important to understand it. Thus, in this section, we explain the nature of the design process, and categorize design working styles to search for a new opportunity area on which to build a new design crowdsourcing method.

Iterative Nature of Design Process

In a design process, concept generation and controlled convergence repeat, and design ideas gradually converge to a final concept. During the initial stage divergent exploration is important; during the more mature stages, convergent decision-making is. Designers tend to collaborate to explore multitudes of ideas during the more open, divergent phases, while they tend to compete in the decision-making, convergent phases. In such an iterative process, rationales for decision-making [4] need to be shared explicitly for effective communication and contribution.

Collaborative Nature of Design Process

Designers cooperate in a design process to collect information and share ideas. Evaluation and selection of these ideas follow. During the course of these activies, a leader plays a significant role in coordinating the design communciation and finalizing the design concept [9]. The leadership is especially important in an online collaboration, since there is no face-to-face interaction and the communication channel is limited to text and figures [6, 19].

Competitive Nature of Design Process

In terms of aesthetics and style, there is no single absolute standard; design process is about searching for the most acceptable solution within given constraints. This requires numerous decisions to be made in a design process and an unavoidable competition among designers for their design to be selected. According to a study on innovation contests [2], adding competitors increases "the likelihood of emergence of an extreme-value solution" and enhances the "overall performance for high-uncertainty problems". Similar dynamics may be applicable to design problem solving, which is one form of innovation.

Existing Working Styles in Design Process

To properly combine the two elements of design process, collaboration and competition, we have categorized and placed different design working styles on a graph of which the axes are collaboration and competition (**Figure 1**). We attempted to find the space of new opportunity by analyzing the graph.

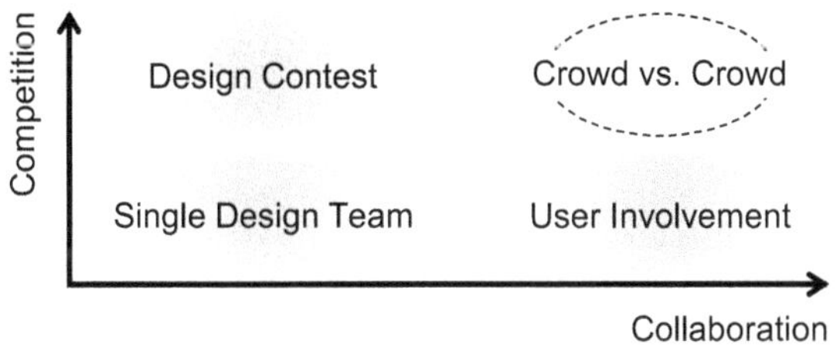

Figure 1. Design working styles categorized by the levels of collaboration and competition to find areas of new opportunity.

- Single design team: A single body is responsible for all design activities. An individual designer or an internally collaborating group of designers fall under this category. With this working style, there is no external competition or collaboration. Crowd is not involved.
- Design contest (Multiple design teams): Multiple, independent bodies externally compete to win. A large number of contestants may compete for a big prize, but there is no collaboration between the contestants.
- User involvement: A single design team may externally collaborate by involving users. A typical example of user involvement is user centered design, using surveys to collect users' opinions and needs.

Opportunity Area for Crowdsourcing in Design Process

With existing working styles, either collaboration or competition dominates, or both occur at a small-scale in a single design team. No large-scale collaborative style includes both elements. By plotting existing working styles on the graph, we found out that a working style including both collaboration and competition at large-scale remains unexplored.

CROWD VS. CROWD

We propose a method for crowd participation in design, Crowd vs. Crowd (CvC) which is applicable to design tasks that require complicated and creative solutions. In CvC, a crowd of people are motivated to actively participate in design on an open platform, where they form several competing teams.

Procedure

The procedure of CvC is as follows (**Figure 2**).

① System construction: A system where designers will deliver intermediate and final design results and crowd will participate and communicate with each other and the designers in a design process is built. The system can either be online or offline. In case of an online system, the system may utilize an interactive webpage or a social network service.

② Designer recruitment: Designers are recruited to lead teams of crowd. Each designer is responsible for making important decisions within the team and for the quality of the final design outcome of the team.

③ Proposal and promotion: Initial proposals of designers are released and full promotion initiates. Crowd who are interested in the design problem gathers and the attractiveness of the proposals affects them in deciding to participate. For active participation of crowd, appropriate vitalization in this initial stage is crucial.

④ Team formation: At the early stage of design, each crowd participant freely chooses one or more teams. Even without any dividing wall, some participants start to settle in specific teams. Based on positive experiences of good communication and advancing design activities, participants begin to recognize themselves as the design team members.

⑤ Design development: Each designer continues to lead the crowd in each team, and develops design with the feedbacks and suggestions from the crowd members. In this stage cooperation in group boosts the design process and at the same time, competition among teams develops. At the end of this stage, each team selects and submits one design from the generated alternatives.

⑥ Design selection: The best design among the candidates is selected. Selection can take different forms, including: vote by end-users; selection by the highest decision maker; evaluation by experts.

⑦ Reward: After the final design is chosen, the winning team shares the reward. The reward is divided based on each participant's quantitative and qualitative contribution to the design. The reward can be non-financial: for example, recognition and honor within the community.

Roles of Participants

Designer

In the actual design process, the quality of the final outcome is as important as its innovativeness. Thus, the designers, who have the skills to finalize designs, are given the responsibility of ensuring the final design quality. Such

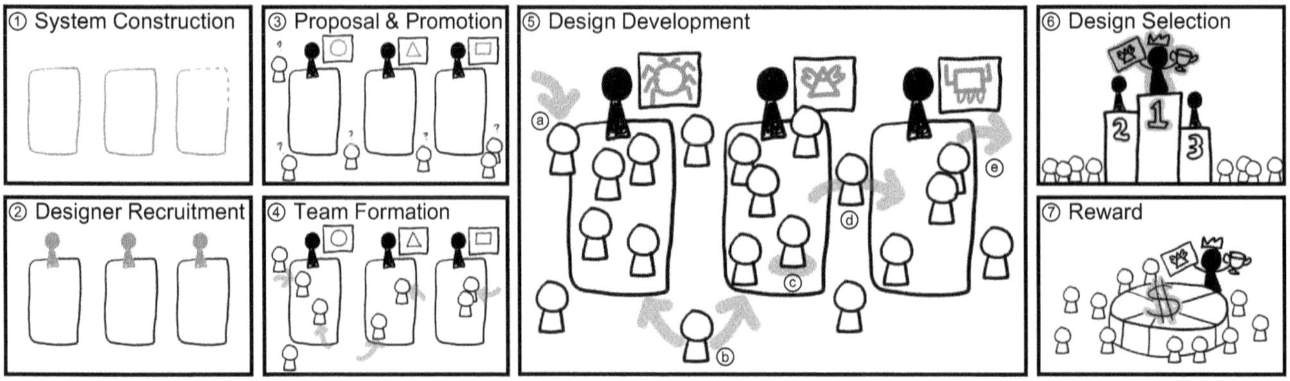

Figure 2. Conceptual overview of the Crowd vs. Crowd (CvC) design method.

a quality-control is missing in the current design crowdsourcing attempts. Without the designers' support in visualizing and finalizing ideas generated by the crowd, participation would become, in general, more demanding and less interesting. In addition, there is a risk that even when everybody is interested, nobody takes on the laborious job of finalizing designs, resulting in unfinished work.

With our CvC method, the designers give feedbacks to the crowd's comments or visualize their ideas using graphical tools, and take the responsibility of developing alternative ideas and finalizing them. Moreover, the designers also decide whether to adopt an idea of the crowd or not. Through such activities, the designers can save the time and effort required to collect relevant information, generate ideas based on them, and to gather opinions on design alternatives. The designers' expertise safeguards the quality of the final design in addition to aiding effective communication between the crowd.

Crowd

The main role of the crowd is to support the designers in various ways. The crowd members may contribute in different ways. During the early stage, the crowd can share personal experiences to inform the designers about the design context. The crowd can also search for relavant information, designs, or images and share them with the designers. During the developmental stage, the crowd may generate creative solutions with different perspectives, drawing inspiration from the designers' works in progress. Near the final stage, preferential opinions of the crowd can be used to simulate evaluation by clients, helping the designers make decisions.

At the beginning of the CvC design process, Each participant is motivated extrinsically to join (**Figure 2**ⓐ), for example by financial reward [22], and may take part in several teams concurrently (**Figure 2**ⓑ). However, as the process progresses, each participant tends to feel more attached to the design team in which his or her ideas have been responded to, and reflected in the work. Along with such attachments, factors such as the sense of connection among teammates, and the sense of loyalty may induce each participant to settle in one team (**Figure 2**ⓒ). In this process, individual traits such as sociality and interest for fun activities motivate participants intrinsically [22]. Each participant freely chooses and switches teams (**Figure 2**ⓓ), simply by preference, or out of the interest of being in the winning team and receiving the reward. A participant can also choose to opt out at any point (**Figure 2**ⓔ).

EVALUATION

Goals

Following hypotheses are to be verified.

- In comparison with other collaborative design methods, CvC should be able to attract a larger number of participants, with its collaborative and competitive elements triggering crowd's extrinsic and intrinsic motivations.
- CvC should be useful for designers in developing design alternatives during the design process.
- The level of competence of design outputs produced by CvC should be at least equal to those produced by other design methods, with the same time frame.

Evaluation Design

To evaluate the effectiveness of CvC, we compared it with design contest and user centered design utilizing survey (user involvement). Among the design working styles shown in **Figure 1**, the single design team case was excluded from the comparison, because it does not require crowd. Design contest and survey, on the other hand, require crowd participation and include elements of collaboration and competition. To fairly compare the methods, the same design task was given, on the same website. Crowd motivation and the design quality were directly compared. On the other hand, the usefulness of CvC, which was not directly comparable, was evaluated through designer interviews.

The design topic selected was a camera interaction technique specialized for taking self-pictures (**Figure 3**). In the absence of real stakeholders, a design topic which was interesting and could be easily visualized was selected as we needed to encourage participation from a crowd of people who were mostly unfamiliar with product design.

Figure 3. Evaluation design topic: to design a camera interaction technique that enables the user to take better self-pictures.

Evaluation was carried out for 8 days for all three methods. For the survey method, the actual survey was completed in 5 days so that the designer could have 3 days to finalize the product based on the collected information.

4 professional designers with industrial design major were recruited to gather data from crowds, and support development and finalization of designs. Each designer was paid \$100 as the front money. 3 of them were assigned to use CvC and 1 to utilize the survey method. To promote participation, we advertised the event online and offline through: notifications around the campus; social network services such as Facebook and other online communities; QR code promotions. We did not collect private information apart from what was needed to transfer rewards. Participants were able to freely access all the design drafts at the CvC website and participate in the survey. In contrast, the design contest was for submission only.

For evaluation, the crowds participating in the CvC method, design contest, and survey were informed that \$250 of reward in total will be distributed as follows. When a proposed CvC design is selected as the best design, each participant of the winning team will receive portions of the reward depending on his or her participation, influence on the final design, and contribution evaluated by the team's designer. When a design produced by the design contest is selected as the best design, the winner takes all the reward. When a design produced by the survey method is selected, the designer takes all the reward. In addition, every participant of the survey receives an online credit worth \$0.5, with no extra rewards, even when the survey contributed greatly in the developing the winning design.

Evaluation 1: Comparison of Crowd Participation
To confirm that CvC can attract more participants compared to other design methods, we counted the number of participants for each method and also analyzed the page views.

Results
We used the number of page views as an indication of crowd participation, and compared it for the 5 pages (**Figure 4**): one for survey, one for design contest, and three for CvC. The percentage exceeded 90% for CvC, showing that most of the people who visited the website were interested in the design process of CvC.

Figure 4. Number of page views (T#: CvC Team #, C: Design contest, S: Survey).

The numbers of people participated in CvC, design contest, and survey are given in **Figure 5**. More than two thirds of the total participants applied for CvC, showing CvC's lower entry barrier.

Figure 5. Number of participants (S: Survey, C: Design contest).

Evaluation 2: Helpfulness of Crowd in CvC
To verify the helpfulness of crowd in CvC, we analyzed how the crowd's comments were reflected in the design process and also devised a survey to measure designers' satisfaction with CvC.

Reflection of Crowd's Opinions
With CvC, the crowd raised a wide variety of opinions about the designers' drafts and their developments. Such opinions were reflected in the design process by influencing the designer's decision making, with some opinions even directly affecting the final concept. For example, the ideas from the crowd include: the protection cap of the 2nd draft of Team 1; the use of multiple cameras and panoramic view in the 3rd draft of Team 1; and the material mimicking a gecko's feet in the 3rd draft of Team 2 (**Figure 6**).

Designer Satisfaction
We asked the designers to evaluate CvC in 5 aspects. Full credit for each was 7 points. Designers were overall satisfied with the collaboration (average: 5.0), suggesting that the crowd was supportive. Designer 2 highly appreciated the creativity of the crowd, but was negative about the ideas which he chose not to reflect in the final product. Designer 3 was the most satisfied, with the average score of 6.

Evaluation 3: Design Quality of CvC
Because this is a virtual design problem without real stakeholders, we conducted an expert evaluation for the 5 final designs produced by CvC, design contest and survey. The evaluators were 13 design experts, industrial design majors with at least 6 years of professional design trainings.

The evaluation was carried out in two ways. First, each design was ranked from the 1st to 5th. Second, scores were given on Likert scale, according to the evaluation criteria of *Concept Design Section* of *Red Dot Award,* one of the internationally renowned design competitions (**Figure 7**).

Results
For the relative ranks, we used χ^2 analysis on the frequency of each design selected as the best. Team 1's design from CvC was the best, regarded as the best design by 58.3% of all evaluators. The result regarding the frequency of selection was statistically valid (χ^2=14.038, df=4, p<0.05).

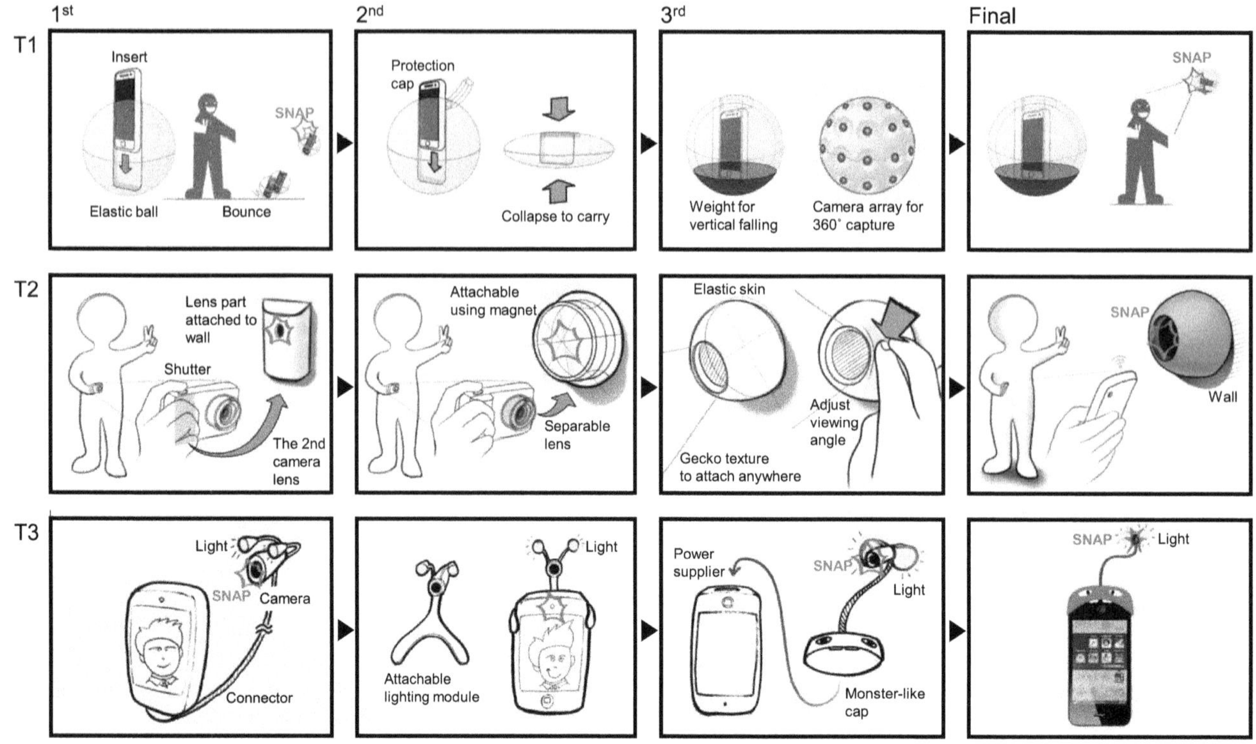

Figure 6. Design progress in each team in CvC (T#: CvC Team #).

For the scores, according to repeatedly-measured ANOVA, the design of Team 1 was also selected as the most prominent and showed excellence in degree of innovation ($F=4.65$, $df=2$, $p<0.05$), aesthetic quality ($F=11.88$, $df=2$, $p<0.05$) and emotional content ($F=8.27$, $df=2$, $p<0.05$) among the seven criteria.

Based on the result of the evaluation, the reward was distributed to the 22 participants of Team 1. The portion of the prize that each received was decided based on the number of comments and on the designer's evaluation of the level of contribution. In comparison with the design contest method, the reward of CvC was relatively small, but participating as crowd would be much easier than trying to win a contest. In addition, the smallest amount granted to a participant in Team 1 was $1.5, still three times larger than the reward for the survey participation, $0.5. The most active participant was granted $62.25 which was 25% of the total amount, $250. The top 6 active participants (27% of participants of Team 1) received $171.5, which amounted to 70% of the total reward.

APPLICATION TO TWO REAL DESIGN PROBLEMS

We applied CvC to two logo design projects, to evaluate CvC's usefulness and effectiveness in a situation where the real needs of the users and the stakeholders are present. In Application 1, we analyzed crowd participation qualitatively, and in Application 2, quantitatively.

With the two real-life applications, we were able to com-

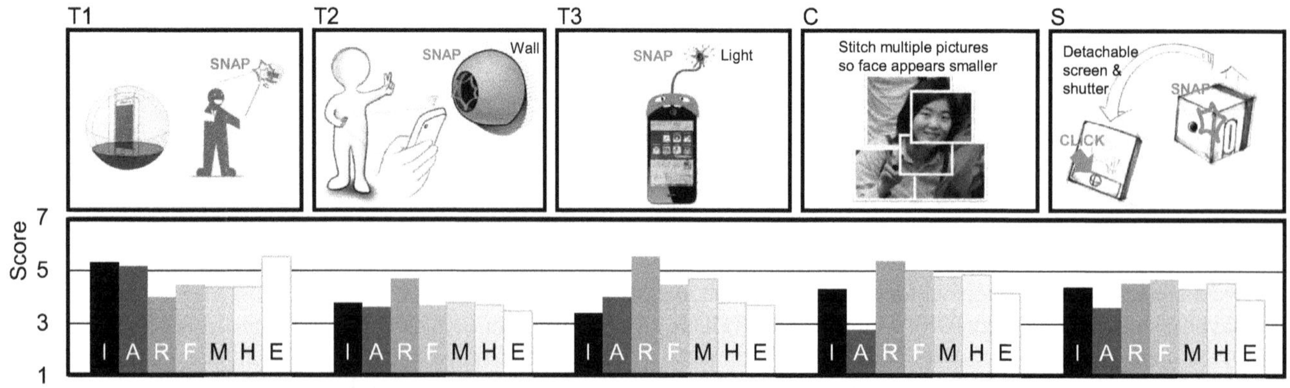

Figure 7. Evaluation of designs produced (T#: CvC Team #, C: Design contest, S: Survey) in terms of degree of innovation (I), aesthetic quality (A), realization possibility (R), functionality and usefulness (F), manufacturing efficiency and cost of manufacturing (M), ergonomics and human interface (H), and emotional content (E).

pare CvC with other design methods mapped on Figure 1. In Application 1, we compared CvC with an open design contest. In Application 2, we compared CvC to design work performed on a contractual basis, by a design company, i.e. single design team.

Application 1: Logo Design of a Chemistry Department

We tried to apply CvC to solve an actual design problem where the stakeholders and their needs were real and well-defined. The selected topic was a logo design for the department of chemistry in a university.

CvC was carried out concurrently with a design contest which had started a week earlier. CvC lasted for 9 days, and 3 additional days were given for each team's designer to finalize the logo design. To select the best design, a departmental poll was held for 5 days.

Since the logo needed to reflect the characteristics of a chemistry department, one designer and one chemistry department student were assigned to lead each team and receive supports from the crowd. All members of the department including the professors, graduate students, undergraduate students, and staffs were asked to participate as crowd because they were the actual users of the final design. The crowd was able to view the design processes of all designers and their supporters.

The front money for each designer was \$100. The total reward was \$500. If a design from the design contest won, the winner could take the entire prize. If a design from CvC won, the designer of the team could receive \$200 with the team members sharing the other \$300 depending on participation and contribution as evaluated by the team designer.

A departmental poll was held to determine the final logo design. There were 8 candidates to vote for: 4 designs from the 4 CvC teams and 4 designs selected from the design contest. The department administration team selected those 4 designs from the contest. The voters were asked to choose one logo design and evaluate it in terms of satisfaction, on a 100 point scale.

Results

4 CvC teams successfully finalized their designs. In addition, 30 designs were submitted to design contest in total, and 4 were selected (**Figure 8**). 306 people from the department voted. Among them, 211 people voted for the designs from CvC, accounting for 72.2% of votes casted (**Figure 9**). The selected final logo was one from Team 2 which received 86 votes (28.1%) and 83.9 points for satisfaction out of 100. The logo design by Team 1 took the 2nd place, which received 80 votes (26.1%) and 86 points.

Observations

We observed the public participating through both collaboration and competition in an actual design problem solving. The designer and the crowd played the roles we expected them to. We also noticed a few interesting events as follows.

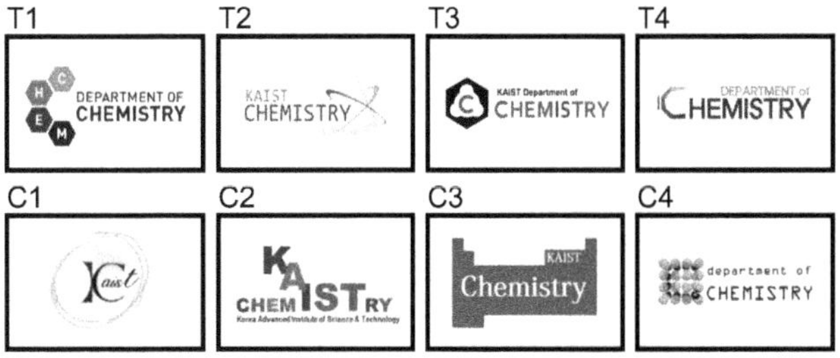

Figure 8. Results of the department logo design (T#: CvC Team #, C#: Contestant #).

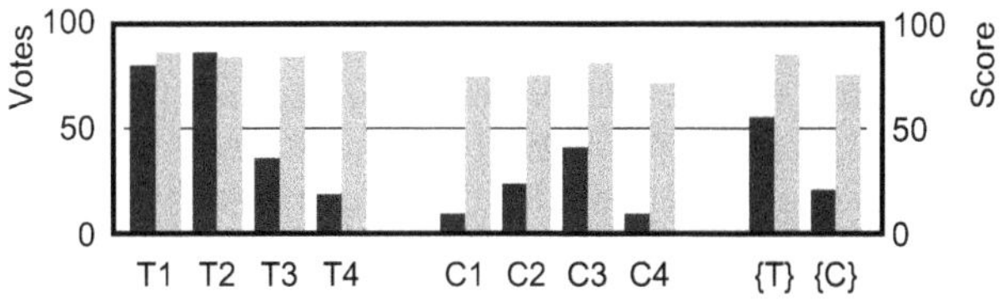

Figure 9. Votes and satisfaction level for each candidate (T#: CvC Team #, C#: Contestant #, {T}: Average of all CvC teams, {C}: Average of design contestants).

When ideas diverged, the crowd provided a rich source of opinions on how to develop the design. One example was suggestion of colors and motifs for logo design. For example, use of blue color signifying stability and motifs of steroids and double-bonds were proposed by the chemistry-savy crowd. In addition, various information voluntarily collected by the crowd allowed the designers to expand their thoughts and diversify their design ideas.

The crowd also contributed in convergence of ideas, helping the designers make design decisions. The designers referred to the crowd's opinions in deciding whether to pick up certain ideas or not. The crowd also gave feedbacks from the viewpoints of stakeholders: they exhibited preferences on design alternatives and made choices.

An unexpected event was the emergence of a self-promoted designer. Initially the design process had started with 4 design teams. However a crowd participant actively uploaded design ideas on one of the designer's page and called out for attention. We granted him the status of a designer, and gave him his own page to form a new team.

This newly emergent team, however, dropped out prematurely and did not submit the final design. One of his crowd alerted others that the logo design uploaded by the new designer very much resembled a logo from the web. Many comments suspecting plagiarism followed. This incident seemed to have played a critical role in the designer's resignation. In CvC, crowd does not only play a passible, supporting role but also checks on designer's mistakes.

Even though CvC was carried out anonimously, some members were aware of the identities of some other members because the majority of the crowd was of the same department. This drew interest within the department, and competition heated up between some design teams. Competition was particularly intense between two teams to the very last moment of the poll. These were the two teams that took the first and the second place in the final poll. Such a competition seemed to induce attention and participation of the crowd, positively enhancing the design process and also the final outcome.

Application 2: Logo Design of a Small Tech Company

CvC was applied to design a logo for a company that produces sound and vibration measurement instruments. The company had already worked with a design company for 6 weeks, and received 8 logo candidates to choose from. We produced 6 additional candidates using CvC, to compare them against the logos produced by the design company, i.e. single design team, on a contractual basis.

We conducted CvC for 8 working days; designers updated for 4 days consecutively, took a break for 2 days during the weekend, and updated again for the following 4 days. Such half-periods enabled us to make chronological comparisons. The final design candidates were submitted on the last day, with a company-wide poll conducted on the next morning.

3 industrial designers were recruited. Similar to the case of logo design for the chemistry department, one designer and one employee from the company (the 'teammate') were assigned to lead each team and receive support from the crowd. All 15 employees of the company participated. In addition, the company sent out promotion e-mails to its business partners so that they could also take part. Only the company employees were asked to provide private information, for analysis purposes only. CvC was conducted anonymously.

The total sum of reward was \$2,100. The front money for the 3 teams was \$900: 3 × (designer \$200 + teammate \$100). The winning design team could receive \$600: designer \$400 + teammate \$200, with one-day paid leave. The winning team's crowd shared \$600. A participant in the winning team received 1 point for each comment contributed to the winning team, with additional 5 points if the designer evaluated it as a valuable comment. The \$600 was distributed proportionally according to the points earned.

There were 15 design candidates: The present logo + 8 design candidates produced by the design company + 6 design candidates produced by CvC, 2 each from the 3 teams. In addition, we conducted a company-wide survey, and asked the employees to evaluate each design candidate in terms of aesthetics and expressiveness of the company identity, on 7 points Likert scales. Employees could write a short comment for each design candidate, and choose one design he or she liked the most. Lastly, the president of the company gave each design candidate a satisfaction score out of 100 points, and also wrote a comment for each. He considered the employees' opinions by referring to the survey result, and chose one final logo design.

Results

The 15 design candidates are shown in **Figure 10**.

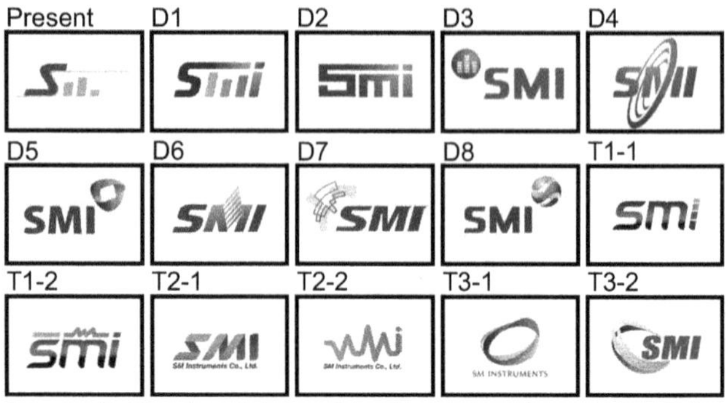

Figure 10. Results of the small tech company logo design (D#: Design # by the design company, T#-1&2: Team #'s two designs).

13 out of 15 employees completed the survey. T3-2, a design candidate produced by CvC, scored the highest overall, when evaluated in terms of aesthetics and expressiveness of the company identity on 7 point Likert scale. The average score of CvC candidates (identity 4.2, aesthetics 4.0) were higher than that of candidates produced (identity 3.3, aesthetic 3.0) by a design company on a contractual basis.

In addition, we asked the 13 employees about the design candidate he or she liked the most. The result organized by design methods is shown in **Figure 11**. CvC designs won 9 votes (69%), showing the employees' satisfaction with the designs they contributed in making. T3-2, in particular, received 4 votes (23%).

The president gave 90 points, the highest, to T3-2, while giving 78 points for the 15 design candidates on the average, and 80 points for the present logo. He commented that the T3-2 candidate "expresses the high levels of sophistication and creativity the company strives for," and that "the candidate would make a fine logo with minor changes on the font type and colors." This logo design was attained with CvC effectively at about 10% of the price the company paid to the design company.

18 people contributed to Team 3, and shared the \$600 reward in accordance with their contribution levels. The smallest amount granted was \$4, and the highest \$210. Top 5 contributors took 82% of the entire award.

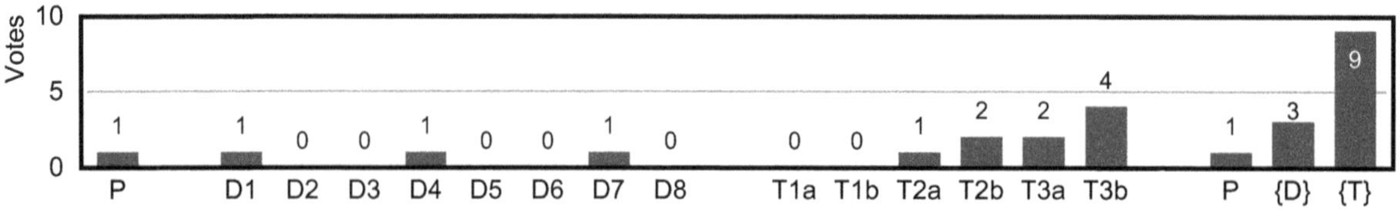

Figure 11. Votes for each design candidate (P: Present logo, D#: Design # by the design company, T#-1&2: CvC Team #'s two designs, {D}: All designs by the design company, {T}: All designs by the CvC teams).

Analysis on Crowd's Behaviors

To quantitatively analyze the interaction between the designers and the crowd, we analyzed the number of comments written by the designer and the crowd of each team, for each day. There was a positive correlation between the numbers of comments (Pearson's r=0.725, n=24, p=0.0005, one-tailed). This result shows that the more active the designer is in engaging the crowd, the more responsive and communicative the crowd is.

Figure 12 visualizes the number of unique visitors and the number of comments throughout the CvC period. Both were higher during 1st half of the period, and lower during in the 2nd half of the period, with statistical significance ($t=2.253$, $df=6$, $p<0.05$ for the number of unique visitors, and $t=2.845$, $df=3.056$, $p<0.05$ for the number of comments). There was no statistically meaningful deviation from Day 5 to Day 8. One additional observation is that the peak for the number of unique visitors was on Day 2, whereas it was on Day 3 for the number of comments. This may be because the crowd spectated on the website until they found the process interesting enough to participate.

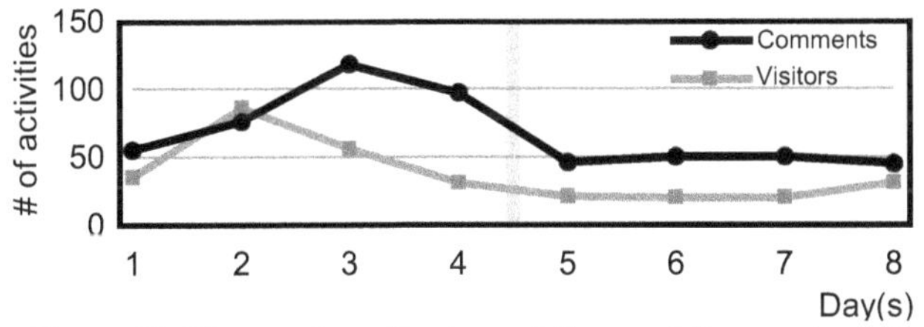

Figure 12. The number of unique visitors and the number of comments throughout the CvC period.

We also observed that each crowd member contributed in a fewer number of teams, when we compared the 2nd half of the period to the 1st half of the period (mean=-0.353, $t=-1.852$, $df=16$, $p<0.05$). This result shows the settling behavior, which we expected from the earlier evaluation and application.

CONCLUSION AND FUTURE WORK

In this paper, we first analyzed existing design working styles in terms of competition and collaboration, and discovered an opportunity area on which to develop a new design crowdsourcing method. Then we proposed the CvC method where open competition of multiple teams motivates the crowd to participate and collaborate actively. We quantitatively and qualitatively examined the feasibility of CvC through an initial evaluation case and two real-life application cases. Our findings are:

- CvC can crowdsource the entire design process, to solve a complex and creative design problem.
- CvC is easy to understand and is engaging for non-designer crowd. The crowd intuitively finds various ways to contribute during different phases of design process under the leading designers' appropriate coordination and technical assistance. Intrinsic and extrinsic motivations arising from elements of competition and collaboration sustain the crowd's participation.
- CvC is useful for designers, as the crowd helps the designers collect valuable design materials, explore a wide range of ideas during the divergent phases, and also make decisions during the convergent phases. The designers are better supported when they respond to the crowd's feedbacks and opinions faithfully.
- CvC produces competent design outputs by holding the designers responsible and leveraging on their expertise for development and finalization of design.
- CvC is particularly effective when the stakeholders of design participate as the crowd. They are eager to help design what is meaningful to them, actively contribute by sharing their community-specific knowledge, and find such an activity fulfilling. They tend to be more satisfied with the design they helped to create, meaning that CvC can be applied to resolving various public design issues.
- CvC is cost competitive and transparent.

As future work, we will explore interfaces to assist crowd activity. We will also study application of CvC at a much larger scale, which would highlight more practical issues. In addition, approaches of computational social science will be used to analyze social dynamics within CvC.

ACKNOWLEDGEMENT

We thank: Jeong-Ro Yoon, Youn-Kyung Lim, the members of I²DEA Lab, and the reviewers for their invaluable comments and assistance; Young-Key Kim (SM Instruments, Inc.) and Sang Kyu Kim (Department of Chemistry, KAIST) for cooperating with us in CvC application; all the designers and crowd members for participating in CvC.

REFERENCES

1. Be a Martian, http://beamartian.jpl.nasa.gov/
2. Boudreau, K., Lacetera, N., and Lakhani, K. (2011). Incentives and problem uncertainty in innovation contests: an empirical analysis. *Management Science 57*, 5, 843–863.
3. Brandes, U., Stich, S., and Wender, M. (2008). *Design by Use: The Everyday Metamorphosis of Things*, Birkhäuser.
4. Buxton, B. (2007). *Sketching User Experiences: Getting the Design Right and the Right Design*, Morgan Kaufmann.
5. Cooper, S., Khatib, F., Treuille, A., Barbero, J., Lee, J., Beenen, M., Leaver-Fay, A., Baker, D., and Popović, Z. (2010). Predicting protein structures with a multiplayer online game. *Nature 466*, 7307, 756-760.
6. Cranshaw, J. and Kittur, A. (2011). The polymath project: lessons from a successful online collaboration in mathematics. In *Proc.CHI 2011*, 1865-1874.
7. Dow, S., Kulkarni, A. Klemmer, S., and Hartmann, B. (2012). Shepherding the crowd yields better work. *In Proc. CSCW 2012*, 1013-1022.

8. Heimerl, K., Gawalt, B., Chen, K., Parikh, T., and Hartmann, B. (2012). CommunitySourcing: engaging local crowds to perform expert work via physical kiosks. In *Proc.CHI 2012*, 1539-1548.
9. Joseph, M. and Reagle, J. (2007). Do as I do: authorial leadership in wikipedia. In *Proc. WikiSym 2007*, 143-156.
10. Kanefsky, B., Barlow, N., and Gulick, V. (2000). Can distributed volunteers accomplish massive data analysis tasks? *Lunar and Planetary Science 32*, 1272.
11. Kensing, F. and Blomberg, J. (1998). Participatory design: issues and concerns. *Computer Supported Cooperative Work 7*, 3, 167-185.
12. Kittur, A., E. H. Chi., and Suh, B. (2007). Crowdsourcing user studies with Mechanical Turk. In *Proc.CHI 2008*, 453-456.
13. Kittur, A. (2010). Crowdsourcing, collaboration and creativity. *XRDS 17*, 2, 22-26.
14. Kittur, A., Smus, B., Khamkar, S., and Kraut, R. (2011). CrowdForge: crowdsourcing complex work. In *Proc.UIST 2011*, 43-52.
15. Kittur, A., Khamkar, S., André, P., and Kraut, R. (2012). CrowdWeaver: visually managing complex crowd work. In *Proc.CSCW 2012*, 1033-1036.
16. Kulkarni, A., Cam, M., and Hartmann, B. (2012). Collaboratively crowdsourcing workflows with turkomatic. In *Proc.CSCW 2012*, 1003-1012.
17. Lakhani, K., Hila, L., and Tushman, M. (2012). Open innovation and organizational boundaries: the impact of task decomposition and knowledge distribution on the locus of innovation. *HBS Working Paper 12-057*, 1-53.
18. Little, G., Chilton, L., Goldman, M., and Miller, R. (2009). TurKit: tools for iterative tasks on mechanical Turk. In *Proc.HCOMP 2009,* 29-30.
19. Luther, K. and Bruckman, A. (2008). Leadership in online creative collaboration. In *Proc.CSCW 2008*, 343-352.
20. Piller, F., Schubert, P., Koch, M., and Möslein, K. (2005). Overcoming mass confusion: collaborative customer co-design in online communities. *Journal of Computer-Mediated Communication 10*, 4, 1-25.
21. RECAPCHA System, http://recaptcha.net/
22. Ryan, R. and Deci, E. (2000). Intrinsic and extrinsic motivations: classic definitions and new directions. *Contemporary Educational Psychology 25*, 1, 54-67.
23. Salganik, M. and Levy, K. (2012). Wiki surveys: Open and quantifiable social data collection, *ArXiv e-prints.* 1-29. http://arxiv.org/abs/1202.0500/
24. Sullivan, B, Wood, C., Iliff, M., Bonney, R., Fink, D., and Kelling, S. (2009). eBird: A citizen-based bird observation network in the biological sciences. *Biological Conservation 142*, 10, 2282-2292.
25. Tang, A. and Boring, S. (2012). #EpicPlay: crowd-sourcing sports video highlights. In *Proc. CHI 2012*, 1569-1572.
26. The Johnny Cash Project, http://www.thejohnnycashproject.com/
27. Xu, A. and Bailey, B. (2012). What do you think?: a case study of benefit, expectation, and interaction in a large online critique community. In *Proc. CSCW 2012*, 295-304.
28. Yu, L. and Nickerson, J. (2011). Cooks or cobblers?: crowd creativity through combination. In *Proc.CHI 2011*, 1393-1402.
29. 99 Designs, http://99designs.com/

Co-Worker Transparency in a Microtask Marketplace

Peter Kinnaird, Laura Dabbish, Sara Kiesler, Haakon Faste
HCI Institute and Heinz College
Carnegie Mellon University
Pittsburgh, PA 15213
{kinnaird, dabbish, kiesler, hfaste}@cs.cmu.edu

ABSTRACT

Workers in microtask work environments such as Mechanical Turk typically do not know if or how they fit into a workflow. The research question we posed here was whether displaying information about the number of other workers doing the same task would motivate better or poorer work quality. In experiment 1, we varied the information about co-workers presented to the worker and the number of his or her co-workers: "you" or "you alone" are doing a task, or "you" plus 5, 15, or 50 co-workers. We compared these conditions with a no-social information control. In experiment 2, we crossed the number of co-workers (5 vs. 50) with the type of incentive (individual or group). Results show that visual presentations of co-workers changed workers' perceptions of co-workers, and that the more co-workers participants perceived, the lower their work quality. We suggest future work to determine the kinds of co-worker information that will reduce or increase work quality in microtask settings.

Categories and Subject Descriptors

H5.m. Information interfaces and presentation (e.g., HCI): Miscellaneous.

General Terms

Human Factors

Keywords

Crowdsourcing, group size, co-workers, workflow, CSCW, work motivation, productivity, entitativity

INTRODUCTION

Employers and researchers are increasingly using microtask platforms such as Amazon's Mechanical Turk (MTurk) to accomplish work that can be separated into discrete tasks and distributed to a number of people. However, fully leveraging these systems remains challenging. Work quality is generally low on such platforms, in part because workers have a fleeting relationship with the employer and low pay [3,15,23]. Furthermore, many crowdsourced tasks are routine, repetitive or boring, requiring little creativity or variety, forcing employers to motivate the work entirely through pay [20].

MTurk amplifies these threats to motivation through design decisions such as automatic task approval, the absence of a strong reputation management system, and impersonal persistent identifiers. Jobs can employ dozens or hundreds of interchangeable, anonymous workers. If workers perceive they are tiny cogs in a large machine, they potentially feel less accountable for their contributions, that their task lacks meaningfulness, and that their effort does not count for much. Lack of identifiability and the interchangeability of workers reduce trust and motivation and increase free riding [6] and social loafing (reduced individual effort that sometimes occurs in group settings) [5,12,21].

Employers using microtask platforms can mitigate the effect of poor worker motivation on the final product of crowdsourced work with workflows featuring high task redundancy and internal checks to redress low worker quality [1,16,18]. MTurk's best practices guide suggests asking multiple workers to complete each posted task (HIT). Some schemes apply complex incentives including threats of nonpayment for poor or incomplete work (e.g.[3,9,20,22]).

Another approach is to use social transparency to increase worker motivation [14]. Social transparency, in this context, means creating or increasing the visibility of the social aspects of an online setting to the people in that setting [11,24]. Almost all crowdsourced tasks present the worker with information only about their own small task even when it is embedded within a larger workflow and may be interdependent with others' work. For example, workers may be asked to search for information. Their search task might be simultaneously assigned to many other workers in order to replicate and check on their quality of work [2,12,13]. Workers typically do not know how many other workers are also working on the same task or how their work may influence or be influenced by other tasks.

Employers on microtask platforms have the option of informing their workers that there are others doing the same task, but we do not understand how this information

Figure 1. Co-worker information in MTurk Experiment 1.

influences motivation and work quality. In this paper, we describe two experiments in which MTurk workers were shown an image displaying whether or not they had co-workers (see Figure 1).

The effect of co-worker information on worker motivation must be carefully tested. On the one hand, if workers learn they have some co-workers, they might become more motivated because they feel like part of a social entity. Common identity engenders loyalty and social feelings among members [10,12]. A worker learning he has co-workers might feel good that he has compatriots, and is sharing their fate. A recent study in which MTurk workers were shown where they stood in a workflow suggests this is a possibility [14]. On the other hand, information about co-workers could backfire if workers receiving this information feel their work is redundant and they are a small part of a large, impersonal process.

How many co-workers?

A related research question is whether employers should inform workers about the number of their co-workers. What if this number is large? We propose that too many co-workers will undermine worker motivation. Research on the group size shows that small groups of fewer than 10 people are more cohesive than larger groups whereas people in larger groups also feel less effective and tend to contribute less [2,8]. In one study of helping conducted in three cities, a large crowd of bystanders was less likely to help someone who dropped coins or pencils than a small group of bystanders, suggesting diffusion of responsibility in larger crowds [19]. Larger numbers of co-workers could also suggest to workers that they are redundant, meaning their work is less valuable to the final product. Studies show that perceived redundancy reduces worker effort and motivation [7,8]

TWO EXPERIMENTS ON CO-WORKER VISIBILITY

We conducted two between-subjects experiments on co-worker visibility in Mechanical Turk. We drew on the literature above to pose the following hypotheses:

H1: Workers informed they have a small number of coworkers will perform better quality work than those not informed about the existence of co-workers.

H2: Workers informed they have a small number of coworkers will perform better quality work than those informed they have more coworkers.

Experiment 1: Method

Participants were paid 25 cents for completing a HIT in MTurk. Workers were recruited between 2 PM EST on April 10, 2012 and 8 AM EST on April 12, 2012. In the HIT, we presented participants with a list of 18 statements made in the past year by prominent politicians in the U.S., evenly split between Democrats and Republicans and displayed in random order. For example, one statement was, "Health care is something that the American people need, and they need it for everyone, not just a few people who are rich." (Harry Reid, Senate majority leader.) The worker's task was to identify the speaker of each statement by selecting the correct politician from a dropdown box with 11 choices.

We limited participation to the United States to reduce the impact of language understanding on the results. Workers could participate in just one of the experiments. After participants accepted the HIT and completed the minimum required work they advanced to a brief survey. Participants were only required to try to identify the speaker of one of the statements.

Independent variable – co-worker information

Participants in experiment 1 were randomly placed into one of six conditions in a 1 x 6 experimental design as shown in Figure 1. Participants in the control group were shown no information about co-workers. Participants in the no-coworker condition were shown a simple cartoon image of a worker ("you") and a caption explaining they were doing the task. After pretesting, we discovered many participants in the no co-worker condition assumed that they had co-workers, so we added the "Alone" condition to emphasize that they had no co-workers and were doing the task alone. The participants in the other three conditions were shown a cartoon with a caption to emphasize the number of their co-workers. The purpose of the brief text and simple drawings was to make the number of co-workers visually salient (see [4,25].)

Dependent measures

Our primary dependent measure was work quality, accurately identifying the correct speaker as a percent of the total speaker identifications attempted. (This total did not differ across conditions). We were mainly concerned with accuracy because selecting choices randomly would be valueless for an employer. We used a log score to normalize these data but the results are in the same direction without the transformation.

We also measured perceived number of co-workers. On the post-task survey we asked participants how many other Turkers were working on their task. We did this to determine whether coworker information influenced perceptions of co-workers. In the analyses, we truncated the number of perceived co-workers to a range of 0 to 101 because a few participants estimated 1000 or 2000 co-workers, which would have biased the data. We then normalized responses using a log score. This technique is suitable to prevent very high scores from distorting the results.

Experiment 1: Results

One hundred seventy-seven participants completed the HIT, with 28 to 31 per condition. The post-task survey

Experimental Conditions	N	Mean Number Co-Workers Reported* (*SE*)	Mean Number Items Completed (*SE*) (n.s.)
"You Alone"	25	6.2^{a} (*5.2*)	12.6 (*1.3*)
"You"	30	17.8^{abc} (*5.0*)	11.4 (*1.3*)
"You and 5 others"	28	7.6^{ab} (*5.2*)	12.7 (*1.3*)
"You and 15 others"	32	21.4^{bc} (*4.9*)	11.1 (*1.2*)
"You and 50 others"	31	37.4^{d} (*5.0*)	13.8 (*1.2*)
Control – No Information	28	29.4^{cd} (*5.2*)	13.9 (*1.3*)

Table 1. Experiment 1 mean number of co-workers reported and items completed by condition.

**Conditions with unique superscripts are significantly different at $p < .05$ based on a Student's t test. There are no differences in the number of items completed across conditions.*

showed that the manipulations differentially affected the perceived number of co-workers ($F [5, 171] = 5.7$, $p < .0001$). Control participants, who were not informed they had co-workers, nevertheless estimated they had almost 30 co-workers. This number fell in between the "50 co-workers" and "15 co-workers" conditions. The lowest estimate was in the "You alone" condition; evidently the single word "alone" made it clear to most participants they were not working with others (Figure 2).

Although the images altered the perceptions of coworkers differentially, it is evident from Figure 2 that some participants ignored or did not believe the coworker information. About 26% of the participants reported a larger or smaller number of perceived co-workers than the intended number. This inattention (or disbelief) was associated with lower work quality and mitigated the direct effect of the coworker information. Thus the direct effect of the manipulations did not significantly change the quality of work. Instead, the perceived number of co-workers (driven by the manipulations) influenced work quality. We checked for selection bias problems with a chi-squared test on whether co-worker information resulted in a higher dropout rate. We discovered no difference in dropout rate across conditions ($p = .96$) and no difference in accuracy between those who completed the HIT and those who dropped out mid-way through the task ($p = .69$).

When participants perceived they had more co-workers, their quality of work declined, as predicted in Hypothesis 2 ($F [5, 158] = 5.7$, $p = .01$; Figure 3). This result holds whether or not we control for the number of items

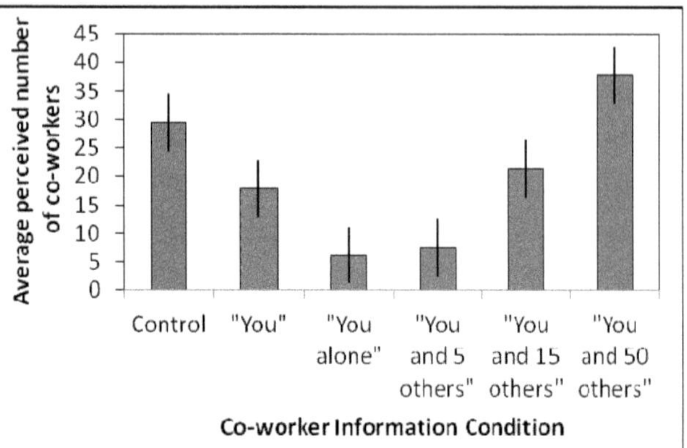

Figure 2. Reported number of co-workers in experimental conditions of Experiment 1.

completed or condition. This result suggests that, without other interventions creating group identity or other feelings of similarity or common bonds with other workers, simply having more co-workers leads to more social loafing or free riding, and poorer work quality. We found no evidence to support Hypothesis 1, that simply having co-workers would increase work quality.

In summary, our results show that increasing the number of displayed coworkers positively influences perceived coworkers, which in turn reduces work quality.

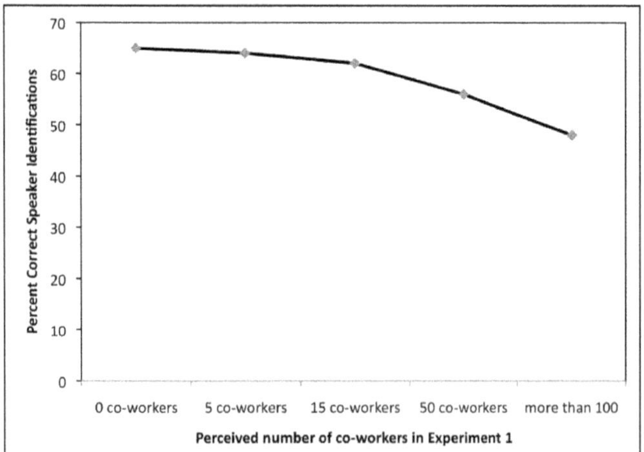

Figure 3. Perceived number of co-workers negatively affects work quality (Experiment 1).

Experiment 2: Method

We conducted Experiment 2 to investigate whether adding interdependence with other workers would change the negative effects of perceiving co-workers, found in Experiment 1. Workers were again recruited only from the United States and were recruited between 1 PM EST on May 20, 2012 and 10 AM EST on May 21, 2012. The design was a 2 x 2 between-groups experiment, with two levels of co-worker number (5 vs. 50 co-workers, as in Figure 1) and the control no coworker information condition. The second independent variable was individual versus group incentive. In the individual incentive condition, the HIT had a 4-cent bonus, plus an addition 2-cent bonus for a correct answer, and one cent off the bonus for each incorrect answer. In the group incentive condition, participants had some level of outcome interdependence with their co-workers, earning a 2-cent bonus for each correct answer that they and the majority of others answered, and losing 1 cent for each quote they and the majority of others got wrong.

The method was identical to that in Experiment 1 except participants were given 36 statements and 20 speaker options (rather than 18 statements and 11 options as in Experiment 1), increasing the possible total amount of work and reducing the chances of getting a correct answer by guessing.

Experiment 2: Results

There were 186 participants who completed the HIT and the survey. As in Experiment 1, the coworker information changed how participants perceived the work environment. In the control condition, they estimated, on average, they had 20 (SE = 3.95) co-workers; in the "5 other workers" condition, they estimated they had 16.2 (SE = 2.8) co-workers and in the "50 other workers" condition, they estimated they had 44.4 (SE = 2.9) co-workers ($F [2, 179] = 26$, $p < .0001$). (These averages use the truncated distributions so as not to bias the results with estimates

Experimental Conditions	N	Mean Number Co-Workers Reported* (*SE*)	Mean Number Items Completed (*SE*) (n.s.)
Five Co-workers	77	16.2[a] (*2.8*)	28.4 (*1.9*)
Fifty Co-workers	70	44.4[b] (*2.9*)	30.3 (*1.4*)
Control – No Information	39	7.6[a] (*3.9*)	28.8 (*1.3*)

Table 2. Experiment 2 mean number of co-workers reported and items completed by condition.

**Conditions with unique superscripts are significantly different at p < .05, based on a Student's t test. There are no differences in the number of items completed across conditions.*

over 100.) We checked for selection bias problems with a chi-squared test on whether either co-worker information or incentive condition resulted in a higher dropout rate. We discovered no difference in dropout rate across conditions ($p = .61$) and no difference in accuracy between those who completed the HIT and those who dropped out mid-way through the task ($p = .13$).

Overall, the results replicated those of Experiment 1 even more strongly. For those who completed the HIT and survey, there were no direct effects of co-worker information or incentive, but the perceived number of co-workers significantly affected work quality. Those who perceived more co-workers did poorer quality work ($F [1,181] = 2.9$, $p = 0.08$). This result held whether or not we controlled for number of items completed. The accuracy rates were 78% correct when no co-workers were reported, 76% when 5 co-workers were reported, 58% when 50 co-workers were reported, and only 38% correct when more than 100 co-workers were reported. Given that the control group who saw no co-worker information may have just been guessing about the number of co-workers, we conducted one further ANOVA excluding their data. In the rest of the conditions, workers who reported larger numbers of co-workers performed poorer quality work ($F [1, 140] = 7.7$, $p = .006$).

Interestingly, outcome interdependence appeared to increase attention to the number of co-workers. Workers in the group incentive condition perceived significantly more co-workers (34) than those in the individual condition (23) ($F [1,137] = 5$, $p =.03$). The group incentive also tended to reduce work quality (60% correct versus 65% in the individual incentive condition) but there was no interaction between incentive and displayed or perceived number of co-workers.

DISCUSSION

Our results suggest that co-worker information in the task environment in microtask marketplaces can significantly influence worker motivation and work quality. This influence is not always positive, as our results indicate. Information about other workers increased the number of others perceived to be doing the same task, which ultimately reduced work quality. We believe that the coworker information we presented heightened workers awareness that they were simply one of many, potentially reducing feelings of task significance and work importance. Workers may have felt they were interchangeable with others and that the outputs of their many co-workers would be combined to account for any mistakes in their work, and thus less accountable for the output of their work. This result contradicts other recent work suggesting workflow information does in some cases have a positive influence on motivation. Future research should examine the boundary conditions of our result.

It is important to note that participants may have gotten cues about coworkers from other areas on MTurk. In both experiments, multiple HITs from the same requestor were available at the same time. It is possible that the number of HITs available could suggest a particular number of coworkers to a given participant. On the other hand, the prominent image of coworkers within the HIT coupled with the common practice of including slightly different tasks in a single group of HITs suggests it is unlikely the number of HITs influenced perceived coworkers. In addition, by describing other workers as coworkers on a task" we intended to decouple the manipulation of coworker information from the number of HITs available in the group.

The strong correlation between the coworker information in the condition and participants' perceived number of coworkers suggests our manipulation was successful. It may be that under certain conditions larger numbers of co-workers can have a positive influence on motivation and work quality and it is important to identify those conditions. In particular the nature of the attachment among co-workers (bonds or common identity) and the nature of interdependence may change the influence of perceived group size. For example, if workers felt more strongly connected to their co-workers, especially if they felt accountable to one another, through a common social identity such as an organizational affiliation, as suggested by Kraut and Resnick [17], co-workers could increase their motivation according to collective effort theory. In addition, if their work output was transmitted to a larger rather than a smaller set of co-workers, meaning those workers were dependent on them, this consequence could enhance perceived task significance.

One implication of our result is that task designers should make it clear to workers when they are posting individual tasks. Knowing that one is working alone improved work quality in our studies.

Our work suggests that we must be careful in presenting workflow information in microtask marketplaces. In some cases this information can reduce motivation and work quality. Further research is needed to identify the social and task structures that impact how individuals perceive social transparency.

ACKNOWLEDGEMENTS

This research is supported by the Center for the Future of Work at Carnegie Mellon University's Heinz College and a National Science Foundation grant, CNS-1040801.

REFERENCES

1. Bernstein, M.S., Little, G., Miller, R.C., et al. Soylent: a word processor with a crowd inside. *Proceedings of the 23nd annual ACM symposium on User interface software and technology*, ACM (2010), 313–322.

2. Brewer, M.B. and Kramer, R.M. Choice behavior in social dilemmas: Effects of social identity, group size, and decision framing. *Journal of Personality and Social Psychology 50*, 3 (1986), 543–549.
3. Downs, J.S., Holbrook, M.B., Sheng, S., and Cranor, L.F. Are Your Participants Gaming the System□? Screening Mechanical Turk Workers. *Science*, (2010), 2399–2402.
4. Fekete, J.-D., Wijk, J.J., Stasko, J.T., and North, C. Information Visualization. In A. Kerren, J.T. Stasko, J.-D. Fekete and C. North, eds., Springer-Verlag, Berlin, Heidelberg, 2008, 1–18.
5. George, J.M. Extrinsic and Intrinsic Origins of Perceived Social Loafing in Organizations. *The Academy of Management Journal 35*, 1 (1992), 191–202.
6. Granovetter, M.S. The Impact of Social Structure on Economic Outcomes. *Journal of Economic Perspectives 19*, 1 (2005), 33–50.
7. Hackman, J.R. and Oldham, G.R. Motivation through the design of work: test of a theory. *Organizational Behavior and Human Performance 16*, 2 (1976), 250–279.
8. Huberman, B.A., Romero, D.M., and Wu, F. Crowdsourcing, attention and productivity . *Journal of Information Science 35* , 6 (2009), 758–765.
9. Ipeirotis, P.G. and Paritosh, P.K. Managing crowdsourced human computation: a tutorial. *Proceedings of the 20th international conference companion on World wide web*, ACM (2011), 287–288.
10. Jans, L., Postmes, T., and Van Der Zee, K.I. The induction of shared identity: The positive role of individual distinctiveness for groups. *Personality social psychology bulletin 37*, 8 (2011), 1130–1141.
11. Jones, G.R. Task Visibility, Free Riding, and Shirking: Explaining the Effect of Structure and Technology on Employee Behavior. *The Academy of Management Review 9*, 4 (1984), 684–695.
12. Karau, S.J. and Williams, K.D. Social Loafing: A Meta-Analytic Review and Theoretical Integration. *Journal of Personality and Social Psychology 65*, 4 (1993), 681–706.
13. Kerr, N.L. Illusions of efficacy: The effects of group-size on perceived efficacy in social dilemmas. *Journal of Experimental Social Psychology 25*, 4 (1989), 287–313.
14. Kinnaird, P., Dabbish, L., and Kiesler, S. The Impact of a Transparent Workflow in Mechanical Turk. *GROUP*, ACM (2012).
15. Kittur, A., Chi, E.H., and Suh, B. Crowdsourcing user studies with Mechanical Turk. *Proceeding of the twentysixth annual CHI conference on Human factors in computing systems CHI 08 08*, April 5-10 (2008), 453.
16. Kittur, A., Smus, B., and Kraut, R.E. CrowdForge□: Crowdsourcing Complex Work. *Human-Computer Interaction*, (2011), 1801–1806.
17. Kraut, R.E., Resnick, P., Kiesler, S., et al. *Building Successful Online Communities: Evidence-Based Social Design*. MIT, Boston, MA, 2012.
18. Kulkarni, A., Can, M., and Hartmann, B. Collaboratively crowdsourcing workflows with turkomatic. *Proceedings of the ACM 2012 conference on Computer Supported Cooperative Work*, ACM (2012), 1003–1012.
19. Latane, B. and Dabbs Jr., J.M. Sex, Group Size and Helping in Three Cities. *Sociometry 38*, 2 (1975), 180–194.
20. Mason, W. and Watts, D.J. Financial incentives and the "performance of crowds."*ACM SIGKDD Explorations Newsletter 11*, 2 (2010), 100.
21. Roland E. Kidwell, J. and Bennett, N. Employee Propensity to Withhold Effort: A Conceptual Model to Intersect Three Avenues of Research. *The Academy of Management Review 18*, 3 (1993), 429–456.
22. Shaw, A.D., Horton, J.J., and Chen, D.L. Designing Incentives for Inexpert Human Raters. *CSCW*, (2011), 1–8.
23. Snow, R., O'Connor, B., Jurafsky, D., and Ng, A.Y. Cheap and Fast — But is it Good□? Evaluating Non-Expert Annotations for Natural Language Tasks. *Proceedings of the Conference on Empirical Methods in Natural Language Processing 254*, October (2008), 254–263.
24. Stuart, H.C., Dabbish, L., Kiesler, S., Kinnaird, P., and Kang, R. Social transparency in networked information exchange: a theoretical framework. *Proceedings of the ACM 2012 conference on Computer Supported Cooperative Work*, ACM (2012), 451–460.
25. Ware, C. *Information visualization: perception for design*. Morgan Kaufmann Publishers Inc., San Francisco, CA, USA, 2000.

EmailValet: Managing Email Overload through Private, Accountable Crowdsourcing

Nicolas Kokkalis, Thomas Köhn, Carl Pfeiffer, Dima Chornyi,
Michael S. Bernstein, Scott R. Klemmer
Stanford University HCI Group
Computer Science Department, 353 Serra Mall, Stanford, CA
{nicolas, thomasko, carlp87, chornyi, msb, srk}@cs.stanford.edu

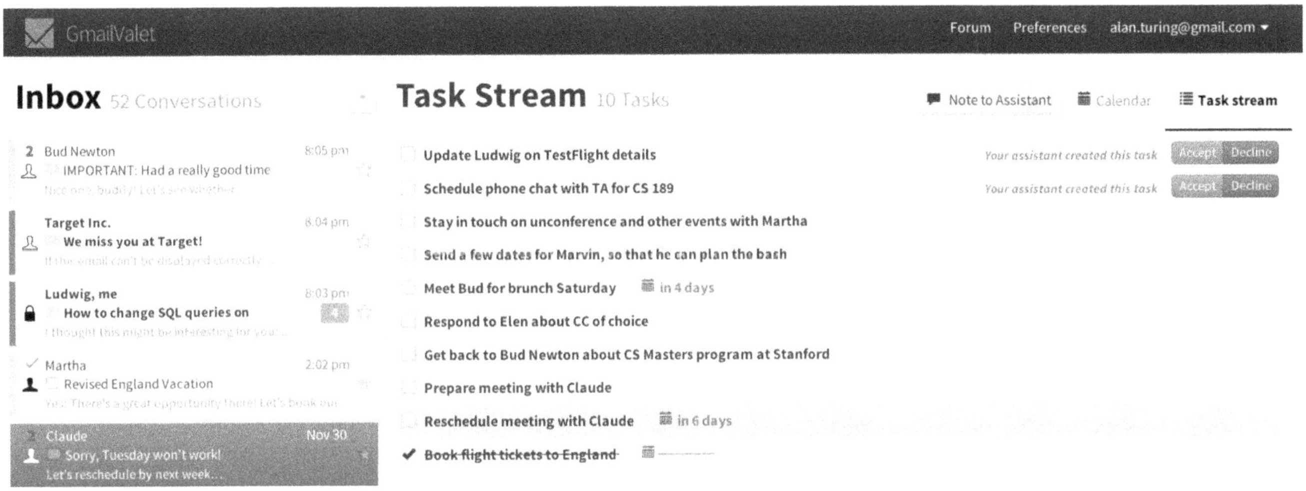

Figure 1. The EmailValet email client draws on crowdsourced expert assistants to transform a cluttered inbox into an organized task stream. Assistants are given limited, accountable access to the user's inbox so that they may extract tasks from each email.

ABSTRACT

This paper introduces privacy and accountability techniques for crowd-powered systems. We focus on email task management: tasks are an implicit part of every inbox, but the overwhelming volume of incoming email can bury important requests. We present *EmailValet*, an email client that recruits remote assistants from an expert crowdsourcing marketplace. By annotating each email with its implicit tasks, EmailValet's assistants create a task list that is automatically populated from emails in the user's inbox. The system is an example of a *valet* approach to crowdsourcing, which aims for parsimony and transparency in access control for the crowd. To maintain privacy, users specify rules that define a sliding-window subset of their inbox that they are willing to share with assistants. To support accountability, EmailValet displays the actions that the assistant has taken on each email. In a weeklong field study, participants completed twice as many of their email-based tasks when they had access to crowdsourced assistants, and they became increasingly comfortable sharing their inbox with assistants over time.

Author Keywords

Crowdsourcing; Email Overload; Human Assistants; Task Management; Access Control.

ACM Classification Keywords

K.4.3 [Organizational Impacts]: Computer-supported collaborative work.

General Terms

Design; Human Factors.

INTRODUCTION

Email management means triaging a never-ending tide of incoming requests. New messages push important requests out of view, and those requests can be unintentionally missed [26, 38]. To avoid overlooking important messages, people spend large amounts of time carefully processing their inbox or triage by focusing only on high priority messages [6, 18, 35]. However, people often keep unfinished tasks in their inbox [38], and triaging is error-prone [35]. As a result, tasks are often mixed with other emails, get pushed down by new messages, become hard to find, and forgotten.

Current approaches for handling email-based tasks are limited and/or expensive. Integrating task management directly into the email client [3, 8] or asking communicators to structure their requests [39] requires significant manual effort. Automatic techniques have shown some promise in identifying tasks in emails [12, 16, 19, 25], but they are not yet fully reliable [25] and require heavy-handed user interaction [12] and training [19]. Finally, while privileged individuals have long relied on personal assistants to help with email, their integration into the email client is limited and the cost can be prohibitive.

In this paper, we combine the accuracy and oversight advantages of personal assistants with the large-scale availability and affordability of crowdsourced experts. We recruit workers from expert crowdsourcing platforms to help extract tasks, and share these assistants across multiple people. This multiplexing increases employment for assistants and affordability for users. To present these task-organized messages, we introduce the *EmailValet* mail client. EmailValet's task list (Figure 1) condenses an inbox to actionable items, makes tasks more prominent and easier to track, increases efficiency through task-oriented interactions (rather than coopting general email primitives, like marking as unread), and focuses attention on the most important emails.

To explore the potential for crowdsourced solutions, we conducted a formative survey finding that people feel a tension recruiting remote assistants for managing complex, personal information: they want help, but have reasonable concerns about giving strangers unfettered access. To address this tension, this paper introduces the *valet* crowdsourcing approach. Like a valet key, valet interfaces seek a dual objective of parsimony and transparency. First, they parsimoniously give assistants just enough access to help with most of the work. Second, they make access boundaries transparent so users have an accurate model of what the assistant can and cannot do, and they cause transgressions to leave fingerprints. Achieving these dual objectives provides peace-of-mind for users and limits liability for assistants.

We illustrate this approach through EmailValet. For parsimony, EmailValet's access control shares a limited window of the inbox (by default, the 100 most recent messages), and limits assistants' actions (to creating tasks). Users author a whitelist and blacklist of messages to be shared, and for transparency, each message presents its access status with glanceable icons. Furthermore, EmailValet provides a viewable log of all assistants' actions.

We hypothesize that EmailValet helps people manage the tasks in their inbox, while maintaining acceptable privacy

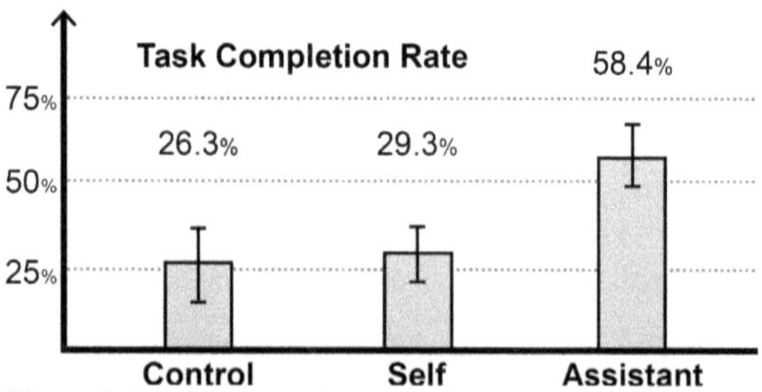

Figure 2. Participant task completion rates were significantly higher when assistants auto-extracted tasks for them.

and accountability practices. A field experiment compared participants' task completion rates when they did not use EmailValet's task functionality (*Control* condition) to when they extracted tasks themselves (*Self* condition) and to when they took advantage of crowdsourced expert task extraction (*Assistance* condition). With crowdsourced task assistance, people completed twice as many email-based tasks than with either standard email or EmailValet's task interface without assistants (Figure 2). Participants grew more comfortable sharing their inbox with assistants as the study progressed.

This work contributes:

- The first use of crowdsourced expert assistants to support personal information management.
- The valet approach for privacy and accountability, which seeks parsimonious, transparent sharing.
- The EmailValet system for email task management, which introduces crowd assistants, richer sharing filters, and icons summarizing assistants' activity.
- A task-integrated feedback interface. This lightweight feedback structure helps users negotiate common ground so assistants can personalize their support. These conversations are shared with all assistants helping that user.
- Empirical results that crowdsourced assistants manage information accurately, enabling EmailValet users to accomplish more tasks.

RELATED WORK

EmailValet extends work on email overload, automated email management, and task extraction. It contributes the valet approach, crowdsourcing these goals to an expert assistant who is multiplexed across many users.

Email overload is an enduring challenge [18, 38]. While email has many positive impacts on organizations [13], frequent email interruptions can decrease productivity and large volumes can create information overload [21, 22, 36].

Data mining, categorization, and metadata extraction can help users organize their email. These approaches ease email filing [2, 7, 11, 23, 31, 32, 33], detect important emails [2, 11, 20, 33], summarize messages [29], forward and reply to messages [21], and filter spam [30]. For example, Gmail's Priority Inbox identifies and highlights emails that the user is likely to want to read and respond to. Other work shares EmailValet's goal of detecting action items and tasks in emails [9, 12, 19, 33] or even automating their execution (*e.g.*, booking a meeting room) [19]. However, these machine learning approaches often suffer from false positives [12] that a professional assistant would not make [15]. Consequently, EmailValet reaches out to human assistants.

Information workers manage many of their tasks using their email clients [25, 38]. Common mail clients (*e.g.*, Outlook, Gmail) allow people to mark a message as a task and set a due date [3, 4]. Taskmaster grouped message threads by task and allowed users to customize these groupings [8]. TimeStore-TaskView is an email interface that is centered around the relationship between messages, with the focus on managing future tasks [20]. EmailValet, like TaskView and Taskmaster, foregrounds tasks rather than messages. It differs from this prior work by integrating human assistants into the loop to lower users' organization burden. EmailValet's inbox interface also adds iconic cues that reflect assistants' activity.

Executive assistants help stem the tide of email overload, focusing their principal's attention on important messages, shielding them from unimportant ones, and handling simple tasks autonomously [15]. Reflecting this, mail clients such as Microsoft Outlook allow users to delegate limited inbox access to assistants [1, 5]. This paper generalizes and extends these relationships to a large class of new users and assistants. To do so, we introduce techniques for an assistant to support multiple users, and focus on building common ground and maintaining transparency with remote assistants.We hypothesize that the manual effort of user-controlled systems and low accuracy of automated systems have yielded low adoption in practice. Our intuition was that paid crowd assistants could be a high-accuracy, low-effort, and affordable solution, but that user trust would be a main concern. Previous crowd-powered systems (*e.g.*, [10]) have largely sidestepped the challenges of sharing private data with crowd workers.

FORMATIVE SURVEY AND INTERVIEWS: CONCERNS WITH CROWD ASSISTANTS

We combined a large-scale online survey with semi-structured interviews to establish current email privacy and security concerns. We began with an online survey on Amazon Mechanical Turk with 585 U.S. residents (59% female; 36% aged 18–25 and 33% aged 26–35). It offered a $0.01 payment, which reduced the incentive to spam and selected for workers with intrinsic interest in the subject.

We followed up with 48 semi-structured interviews (32 male). We recruited participants through email lists at our university and from our professional networks. Thirty-three participants were MBA students; 15 had technical backgrounds, five of whom were at the manager level, six were students, and four were researchers. Seventeen interviews were conducted in-person; 31 were online. The interviews discussed specific concerns and opportunities with crowd-powered inbox assistants.

We combined the interview and survey data inductively. We clustered themes from the interviews and matched them with quantitative survey results. Several authors then collaborated to code interview notes and transcripts with those themes.

Results

Respondents expressed strong concerns about sharing their inbox with a crowdsourced assistant. However, they also resonated with the goal of better task management in email and raised design opportunities around filters, whitelists, and accountability.

Task Management in Email

Forty-eight percent of respondents reported using emails to manage tasks. Of those, 77% sent email reminders to themselves, 47% used their inbox as a to-do list, and 41% stated that they would use an online service that helps better manage tasks in email. Survey participants offered a glimpse into their day-to-day email triage: for example, "I want to be able to add little notes to every email in my inbox. I would isolate the exact action I need to take on each email." Another participant shared: "The biggest pain point is that for each email for which I need to take action, I have a specific action I want to take, but I cannot record it anywhere for the email. Every time I see the email, I go into it and rethink about what the action is, and then I decide if I have time to do the action. I do this an average of 2-3 times per email. It kills me."

Participants were interested in having crowdsourced assistants support inbox triage. One manager wanted an assistant to filter the inbox and "automatically archive all messages that do not require me specifically to take some action." Another participant, familiar with Priority Inbox, said: "I want an affordable [...] human alternative to applying my rules to emails, *i.e.*, what to escalate to me immediately, respond to quickly with a canned response, flag for my review quickly, flag for my response immediately, distill the action I need to take, delete, etc."

Privacy and Security

The responses indicate that privacy concerns were the major roadblock to adopting a system like EmailValet. More than two thirds of respondents cited major concerns: they were only willing to share a few messages manually (35.4%) or share nothing at all (38.1%). Roughly one quarter (26.2%) were comfortable with an automatic solution via email rules; only a few (4.1%) were ready to share their entire inbox.

Participants who were only willing to hand-pick emails that an assistant could see acknowledged that this might neutralize any time savings the assistant might offer: "Unfortunately, the only way I'd feel totally comfortable is if I could pre-screen messages beforehand, but even the act of forwarding certain messages to an assistant [...] feels too time-consuming."

Respondents who were willing to share parts of their inbox wanted strict access restrictions. They viewed historic inbox data as unnecessary: "[Historical access] would make me nervous about finding something I didn't remember was in there." Most participants also wanted the inbox automatically filtered to remove personal emails and financial information and passwords; and the ability to revoke permission when a sensitive email slips through.

The more freedom the assistant has to take actions, such as write replies or archive emails, the more participants felt the need for monitoring. A manager said: "I do not mind sharing, as long as I can verify exactly how my information is used." This phenomenon has been noted previously with shared inboxes [24].

Trust was the critical concern: to share their inbox, respondents needed to feel they could rely on the assistants. Some suggested that they would want to "talk to them personally", get to "know them somewhat well" or "vet them myself". Furthermore, respondents wanted confidentiality assurance: "I'd want some liability insurance for what a rogue assistant might do with my information."

In summary, despite improvements in email clients, information workers still spend significant effort managing tasks in email. Respondents desired human assistance, but listed trust and privacy as core concerns, requiring mechanisms to limit potential damage. Designing for privacy concerns is important. At the same time, people's real-world practices often differ from their pre-usage estimates. Consequently, it is important to observe actual usage and not rely exclusively on survey data.

EMAILVALET

EmailValet (Figure 1) is a task-based email client that enables collaboration with crowdsourced assistants. The current prototype shares a sliding-window history of a user's inbox with assistants who annotate messages with tasks. In principle, this approach could support other delegated tasks such as summarizing messages, negotiating meeting times, or drafting/sending replies. EmailValet makes all assistant actions visible to the user. Icons clearly identify when messages have been processed by assistants or contain tasks (Figure 3a). Actions performed on each email are displayed along with the email headers (Figure 3c). A complete log is also available to establish peace of mind (Figure 5). Our prototype is integrated with Gmail and is available at https://www.gmailvalet.com.

In the EmailValet inbox, the left column displays email threads (Figure 3). On the right, the system presents a stream of all tasks that the user or assistant created from messages. To view an email, a user either clicks on the thread (in the inbox) or the task (in the task stream). When viewing or composing email, the message consumes the right pane; its related tasks are shown at the top (Figure 3b).

Assistants log in to a limited, 'valet' view of each inbox that they have support. They can read emails and create tasks associated with those emails.

Creating and Viewing Tasks

To lower the friction for task creation, assistants and users can create a task by entering its title at the top of the email (Figure 3b). In the other direction, clicking a task shows its originating email. Icons in the inbox indicate whether an assistant can or has viewed the message, and also whether its tasks are completed (Figure 3a).

The right-hand task stream (Figure 1) gives users an at-a-glance overview of their tasks. Our vision is that users can treat this task stream as an action-oriented view of their email, facilitating efficient message handling. By default, tasks are ordered by recency; users can reorder them by priority.

A calendar view provides users with an overview of when tasks are due. If possible, due dates are automatically extracted using Natural Language Processing (NLP); they can also be manually edited.

Accountability and Access Control

Survey respondents were concerned about limiting assistants' access and monitoring their actions. Consequently, EmailValet introduces facilities for accountability and access control.

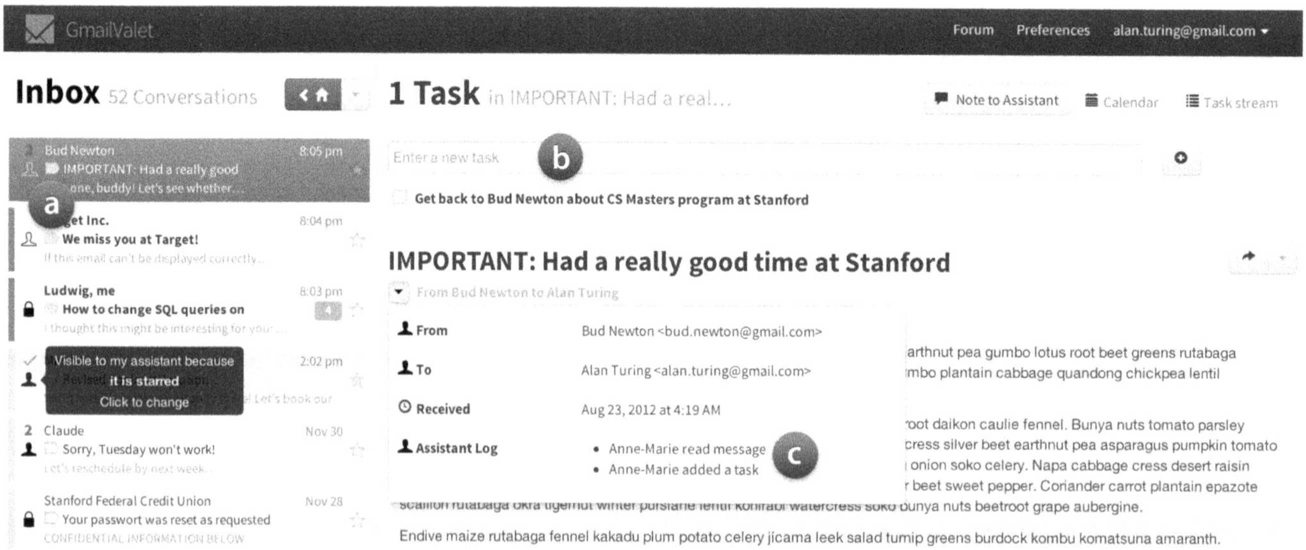

Figure 3. a) Icons to the left of the message summary indicate whether an assistant can or has viewed the message, as well as how many open tasks remain. Hovering reveals the system's reason for the current visibility setting. Clicking opens the email on the right and displays its associated tasks. Users can also add a task (b) and view actions the assistant has taken with this message (c).

Accountability

EmailValet offers three monitoring techniques. First, inbox icons show whether the assistant has processed an email and extracted a task (Figure 3a). Second, the detailed message view lists all logged activities for that email: for example, opening an email, sending a response, or creating a task (Figure 3c). Third, a user can view a complete chronological log of all an assistant's actions (Figure 6). Logging doesn't prevent abuse, but does leave "fingerprints" [37]. We anticipate this log's primary benefit to be deterrence and peace of mind — like a security camera — rather than frequent monitoring by users.

Access Control

Assistants can only view a user's mail through EmailValet. EmailValet, by default, restricts the assistant to a sliding window of the most recent 100 messages and search is disabled. Users can provide whitelist and blacklist filtering for finer-grained control. Whitelist filters restrict the assistant's view to particular labels or folders, such as starred messages, Gmail's Priority Inbox, or messages sent to oneself. Furthermore, users can provide blacklist filters to exclude sensitive messages, such as emails from family, passwords, or financial information (Figure 4).

These restrictions attempt to balance the assistants' need to understand contextual connections with the user's desire not to expose their whole history to the crowd. Assistants' actions are also limited; EmailValet's current policy prevents assistants from deleting messages.

Finally, EmailValet also integrates with automatic approaches. To illustrate this, with the EmailValet prototype, users can restrict assistant-visible emails to Gmail's Priority Inbox.

Feedback and Learning

The tasks that assistants create may not always be the tasks that users want. Tasks mean different things to different users: this is one reason automated approaches often fail [19]. To provide assistants feedback, the simplest way for a user to remove a task is to decline it (Figure 1). EmailValet shows assistants which tasks were accepted or declined, and encourages users to add an explanatory comment to the assistant (Figure 5). To help assistants learn what they missed, they can see tasks that users create themselves.

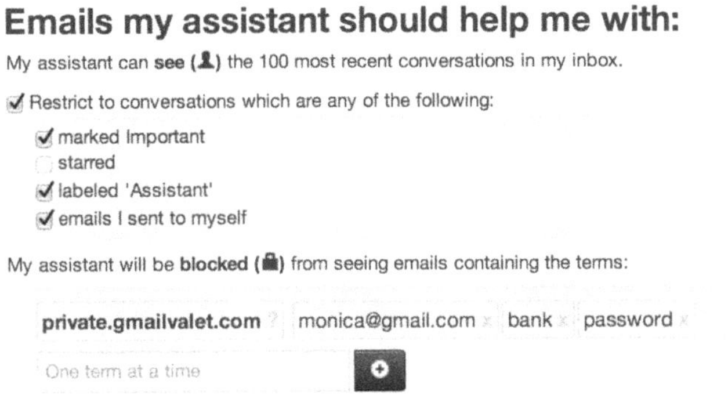

Figure 4. For privacy, users can specify rules for which emails will be visible to their assistant.

To frame discussions, users can leave an introductory note about their preferences. This note is especially helpful for providing new assistants with context and user-specific heuristics. For example, users may want to emphasize certain senders or ask the assistant to apply labels to their tasks (*e.g.*, "put [Event] in front of every event").

Assistants and users can also open a chat window to clarify any confusion. While a few crowdsourcing systems provide limited interactive feedback with requesters [14], we are unaware of other crowd-powered systems that support interactive worker conversation with end users. We have found that chat helps efficiently achieve common ground:

Assistant: *Do you want me to create tasks from [name]?*
User: *Yes, please.*
Assistant: *Ok I will, I made one and it got declined so I just wanted to make sure.*

Multiple Users per Assistant

Assistants can help many users simultaneously, increasing affordability for users and labor opportunities for assistants. To provide easy access to multiple accounts, assistants can switch between users with a drop-down menu. Awareness indicators on this menu show users with unread messages.

FIELD STUDY

A weeklong field study investigated whether EmailValet helps users complete tasks and whether its privacy and accountability features satisfy users' concerns. We found that EmailValet accurately extracted tasks from email, that users found value in the system for their task management, and that users became increasingly comfortable with EmailValet's privacy tradeoffs.

Method

We deployed EmailValet in a one week field study, recruiting twenty-eight participants using mailing lists at our university. Six were MBA students and twenty-two were university students of other majors, mostly technical. We offered participants a $50 gift certificate. We hired three online assistants through the oDesk crowdsourcing marketplace: one from Illinois, two from California. Two were work-at-home mothers. Assistants were compensated at $8 per hour to process all shared emails during the study.

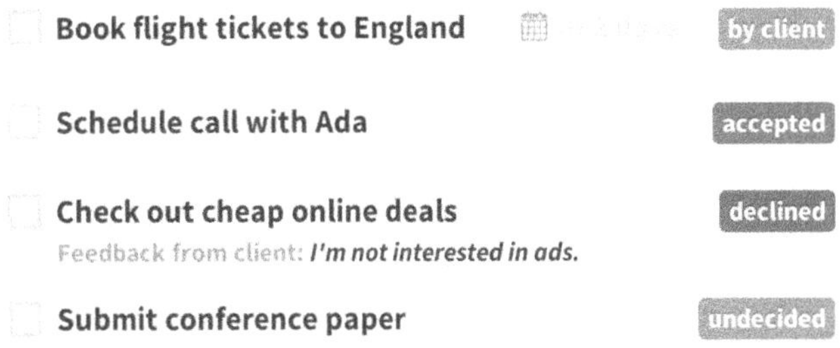

Figure 5. The assistant's view of the task stream. Feedback helps the assistant to learn the user's intentions: accepted and rejected tasks, freeform text, and user-created tasks.

Action	Task	Message	Assistant	Time
Read message	—	[#VWJ-824-43394]: Explanation from Stanford U.	Ludwig	6 min ago
Created task	Set up unconference meeting with Martha	MyGSB Digest for the week of from MyGSB Digest	Ludwig	6 min ago
Read message	—	MyGSB Digest for the week of from MyGSB Digest	Ludwig	16 min ago

Figure 6. The log supports accountability by showing all of the assistant's activities to the user.

Participants began by authoring whitelists and blacklists that determined the assistants' access control. Each participant was instructed to use EmailValet at least twice each day to process their new emails and tasks. At the conclusion of the study, participants completed a survey focused on EmailValet's qualitative usefulness, privacy, and assistant quality.

We ran a within-subjects experiment to investigate whether EmailValet helps users complete the tasks in their email. Participants rotated through three interface conditions. Following a one-day warm-up, each participant spent two consecutive business days in each condition:

- *Control:* Participants could not see assistant-created tasks or create their own tasks.
- *Self:* Participants could not see assistant-created tasks. However, they could create their own tasks.
- *Assistance:* Participants could see assistant-created tasks and create their own tasks. Participants could give task feedback to their assistant.

The order of conditions was randomized for each participant, in a Latin square manner. Participants could always read and write email. The assistant extracted tasks from emails in all three conditions. However, in the Control and Self conditions, the assistant did not receive feedback on tasks from the participant because the participant could not see their extracted tasks. At the end of each condition, participants saw any previously-hidden tasks that the assistant created. To produce ground truth, participants then accepted or rejected these tasks, gave feedback, created any tasks the assistant missed, and marked whether or not they had completed each task.

We measured the percentage of new tasks that the user marked completed while each condition was in effect. This metric combines the tasks that the assistant authored and the user accepted with the tasks that the user authored themselves. If the assistant's tasks were hidden during the condition (e.g., Self or Control), we counted tasks that were accepted during the end-of-condition review. We manually merged any duplicate tasks that the user and assistant both created. Users and assistants may make extraction mistakes, so this metric may not represent every task in the inbox.

We hypothesized that users would complete more email-based tasks with EmailValet's task extraction than when they must extract tasks on their own (Assistance > Self) or cannot extract any tasks (Assistance > Control). We further hypothesized that the discipline of self-managed task management would still produce some benefit: Self > Control.

Results

Of the 28 participants who filled out the final survey, 16 consistently and successfully participated in all three conditions and thus had measurable task completion rates. In this section, we analyze qualitatively and quantitatively: 1) the assistants' accuracy at extracting tasks, 2) users' behavior and feedback regarding EmailValet as a task support tool, and 3) users' feedback to the privacy concerns and functionality in EmailValet. Table 1 displays examples of assistant-extracted tasks.

Assistants' Accuracy

We measured the *precision* and *recall* of assistant-created tasks so that we could better understand how accurate the assistants were at extracting important tasks for users.

Precision measures the percentage of assistant-created tasks that participants accepted. On average, users accepted 71.6% of the tasks extracted by assistants. This ratio was very similar across all three assistants (σ=3.5%). Precision rose throughout the study, starting at 62.1% on the first day and ending with 84.8% on the last day. The rise in precision is most likely due to participants' feedback regarding tasks and to the assistants learning more about their users. One assistant noted, "it has become easier to extract good and accurate tasks from my clients' emails over time. I feel I have gotten to known my clients better and understand the conversations better".

The final survey asked, a free-response question: were the assistants' tasks relevant, or just busywork? About two thirds of participants (19 of 28) found assistant-created tasks to be of value and worth completing. Notably, four of these participants praised the assistants' creations as being on the same level as their own; one thought the assistant was even better than themselves ("they used more detail than I did") and three lauded the assistants for extracting

- *Schedule to meet first week of September with Priya*
- *Complete flyer by the end of the week*
- *Print out flight information*
- *Send International Student Advisor a scan of my I-20*
- *Review Emily's ideas and if possible add onto it*
- *Lunch with Al*

Table 1. Tasks extracted by assistants during the study.

more tasks and events than they would have done ("made the week easier"). However, some participants felt that the assistants were overeager, complaining that assistants created tasks from irrelevant mailing lists, created tasks that were too ambiguous or missed tasks completely. On the other hand, a participant explicitly called their assistant "too conservative" and would have preferred to receive more tasks. Users typically did not mind false positives: as a participant wrote, "Deleting [tasks] was easier than creating."

Recall measures how many tasks the assistant missed: the number of accepted tasks that the assistant authored divided by the number of accepted tasks that either the user or the assistant authored. This measure only includes tasks created during the Assistant condition because this is the only time that users could see the assistants' tasks in real time and add any missing tasks. By this calculation, recall was 68.6%. Often, the user logged in before the assistant had time to process the new email, so eventual recall may be higher.

We asked users a free-response question: were they confident that their assistants would not miss important tasks? We coded their responses and found that more than half of participants (17 of 28) felt they could fully or almost fully rely on their assistant, five participants had mixed feelings, and six had negative impressions. Participants praised assistants' consistency ("after the first few days they established that they could keep track of impt [sic] details"). Missing contextual knowledge was the most common cause of missed tasks: "Many important tasks (that are not obvious) are not extracted."

EmailValet's Usefulness

Users found the assistants to be generally accurate, but did the system help those users manage their tasks? We compare the percentage of tasks completed in each condition and supplement the results with qualitative feedback.

Of the sixteen participants who consistently used EmailValet through all study conditions, users completed a significantly higher percentage of tasks in the Assistance condition (M=58.4%, SD=34.4%) than in the Self condition (M=29.3%, SD=28.7%) or Control condition (M=26.3%, SD=34.5%). We performed a repeated-measures ANOVA with condition as independent variable and task completion rate as the dependent variable. We found a significant effect of condition, $F(2,30)=4.483$, $p<.05$. Posthoc pairwise t-tests with false discovery rate (FDR) correction found a significant difference between Assistance and Control, $t(15) = 2.89$, $p<.05$, and between Assistance and Self, $t(15)=2.49$, $p<.05$. No difference was found between Self and Control $t(15) = 0.24$, *n.s.* So, participants completed more tasks in the Assistance condition than in the Self or Control condition.

Participants were enthusiastic about the positive impact EmailValet had on their task management. When asked if they would like to continue using EmailValet, one participant replied, "any help in making sure everything gets done would be greatly appreciated." Another insisted that they would like to use it only with the assistant: "What I need is an extra pair of eyes." A third participant praised the assistant's work because their tasks were "like magic": "very convenient and much easier than doing it myself." For users who didn't feel that assistants supported their task management, they still found that the task-centric interface kept them aware of incomplete tasks. Roughly 40% of the participants wanted to use EmailValet as their main task list following the study (12 of 29), and several continued using it voluntarily the week after the study concluded. Those who were uninterested in continuing felt that it needed deeper integration with other PIM tools for them to fully integrate it into their workflow.

Privacy Concerns and Trust

We asked our participants which emails they made available to assistants and which they blocked. Only two participants opted to manually whitelist individual emails for the assistant to see. Most participants shared everything or whitelisted a set of filters (*e.g.,* priority messages, starred messages, school, work). Those who filtered for privacy blacklisted patterns such as passwords, banking information and more intimate contacts. As one participant put it: "I thought the only way for the service to be most helpful would be to ensure they could look at everything." Some participants loosened their settings over time: as one put it, "Originally I did not share emails from my boyfriend [name], but I changed that after realizing he sent me emails with tasks for me to do".

A majority of participants (18 of 28) initially felt somewhat uncomfortable entrusting an assistant with their emails. However, over half of those with concerns (10 of 18) and over a third of all participants (11 of 28) reported that they felt more comfortable with the service over time, while no one reported a decrease in comfort. Reasons for the increased trust were diverse: One participant named the first task extractions ("I felt more optimistic and was pleasantly surprised [...] it was surprisingly useful and effective"). Another one found the assistant biography helpful ("my assistant was a mother"). A third simply got accustomed to what she called a "slight breech [sic] of privacy": "In the beginning, it felt weird that my assistant was reading personal emails from my family and then creating a task for me to do based on it, but I didn't really feel strongly enough about it to change my privacy settings... I just kind of went with it."

Assistants shared the discomfort, as they were initially not at ease with going through their users' emails and occasionally stumbling upon sensitive information: "Some emails I felt like I was invading their privacy because it was emails between my clients and their family, but I didn't react anyway because it's a job I have to do". Similar to users, assistants became more comfortable over time.

Despite of this increased level of comfort, almost two thirds of participants (19 of 28) said the assistant did not care for them personally but was simply "doing their job," and only one participant felt the assistant personally cared. This was not necessarily bad: four participants explicitly stated that they did not want to get to know their assistant. However, seven other participants suggested more communication with the assistant so that they could feel more like the assistant personally cared. Similarly, opinions were split on whether knowing the assistant made it more or less comfortable share your inbox.

Assistant Economics

The assistants recorded 70 hours of work during the study. They processed 12,321 messages—8,679 for the 28 participants and the rest for 10 existing users of the system who did not take part in the study—and created 779 tasks. On average, each assistant processed 2.94 messages per minute. This rate would extrapolate to 1,408 messages in an eight-hour workday if the assistant were fully occupied. On average, assistants created 6.32 tasks per 100 emails they read. Participants received 38.8 messages per day on average, fewer than recent studies have reported [18].

At this rate, one assistant could support 36 users simultaneously in an eight-hour workday. Such support would cost each user $1.78 per day. However, in our deployment, each assistant was assigned 12 users on average. We asked the assistants to tell us how many users they felt they could support. They generally felt that they had additional bandwidth. For example, one said, "[I have] 10 current clients, it's pretty easy to keep track of the clients, […] so ideal would be probably 20 to keep me busy more".

Limitations

This study has several limitations. First, the sample is not fully representative: the participants are largely young, technology-literate, and self-selecting to participate in a study that shares their private emails with assistants. In addition, the study's short duration capures the first days of usage, but usage patterns may evolve. A longitudinal evaluation with a broad population is a clear next step.

DISCUSSION

EmailValet extends crowdsourcing to tasks that require access to private or sensitive data. In this section, we reflect on the implications of this decision, the importance of context and common ground, and on a future vision of massively multiplexed crowd assistants.

Adaptation to the Privacy Breach

Fully 70% of the formative survey respondents reported they would be unwilling to share significant fractions of their inbox. Yet, after a week of use, only 10% of participants cited privacy as a reason that someone might abandon EmailValet. Even accounting for sampling differences, this is a major shift. Furthermore, participants rarely used EmailValet's accountability features: the features were more useful as a security blanket than as functionality. While engineers and designers often describe privacy as a property—a system either has privacy or it does not—in practice, privacy is dynamic [28]. When the benefit exceeds the invasion, we share information that we previously considered private.

The Assistants' Lack of Context

Traditional crowdsourcing systems focus on context-free micro-tasks (*e.g.*, [10]). However, supporting personal and private tasks requires rich context [15]. There were several situations where EmailValet assistants lacked this context and produced incorrect tasks. The assistants recognized this challenge: in the future, they asked for a short fact file about each user, including their profession and place of residence. We are eager to let assistants flag messages that they find useful for understanding each user, and to allow them to write or share notes between each other. These notes institutionalize assistant knowledge, which would enable a smooth "changing of the guard" as assistants begin and end their work. Companies can also lessen the context and privacy problems by adapting a model midway between EmailValet's distributed experts and in-house administrative assistants.

Tasks and Busywork

Users completed more tasks in the Assistance condition, but is this because EmailValet focused them on unimportant busywork? There is some evidence that this may be happening: one participant explained that they accepted "tasks or events I didn't necessarily plan to do [...] because it was still good to have it there [as] a reminder, whereas I wouldn't have bothered to make note of that task myself." These tasks were likely middle priority: not as unimportant as busywork, but not important enough to be the top priority. In general, however, it is up to the user to decide whether an assistant-created task is important or busywork. The framing for this decision can be communicated to the assistant, helping them adapt to each user's needs.

From Personal to Massively Multiplexed Assistants

Online assistants may be affordable enough for most information workers to use in small amounts. Likewise, assistants can multiplex their services across multiple users. Are we seeing the beginnings of democratized access to executive assistants? Not yet: several issues remain and demand workable solutions. First, as our formative work revealed, people are reluctant to entrust online assistants with access to their sensitive data. As systems like EmailValet establish trust and produce high-quality work, these concerns may lessen. Second, the quality of an online assistant may not compare to that of an executive assistant entirely dedicated to one person. Users of EmailValet-style systems thus face a trade-off between cost and quality. However, collective intelligence of multiple assistants may produce higher quality than any dedicated assistant. Third, as we saw, missing context remains a major struggle for many assistants.

CONCLUSION & FUTURE WORK

This paper introduces *valet* techniques that preserve privacy and accountability for sharing private data with crowdsourced assistants. These techniques take shape in EmailValet, an email client that recruits crowdsourced human assistants to extract tasks from each email in the inbox. As a valet interface, EmailValet focuses on: 1) parsimony, providing just enough access for assistants to extract tasks and giving users rich controls to limit assistants' permissions; and 2) visibility, surfacing all assistant actions within the interface. In a one-week evaluation, EmailValet users completed about twice as many tasks when they had access to the assistants' help.

Crowdsourced assistants could support many additional personal information management activities. For example, email assistants could crate action plans for tasks [24], identify meeting requests, link references to other threads, mark priorities and write personal reminders. These extensions create an opportunity to design alternative consumption methods for the inbox, for example a compact, glanceable stream of events. The assistant could also support other personal information management tools, curating the user's calendar, maintaining a contacts list or organizing appointments. More ambitiously, assistants could execute tasks such as booking a flight or reserving a conference room. Finally, by formalizing the assistant's actions, we can train machine learning systems and improve the automatic approaches to task extraction.

Additional materials about this research are available at http://hci.st/valet.

ACKNOWLEDGEMENTS

The authors thank Greg Little for thoughtful discussions; oDesk for sponsoring the oDesk workers; Ryan Globus, Thomas Bridges-Lyman, and Arun Prasad for their contributions during their Summer internship; and Ludwig Schubert for work on the figures and video. This research was sponsored in part by NSF POMI 2020 Grant No. CNS-0832820.

REFERENCES

1. Allow Someone Else to Manage Your Mail and Calendar. http://office.microsoft.com/en-us/outlook-help/allow-someone-else-to-manage-your-mail-and-calendar-HA010355554.aspx.
2. ClearContext tames Outlook. http://news.cnet.com/8301-17939_109-9947065-2.html.
3. Create Tasks and To-Do Items. http://office.microsoft.com/en-us/outlook-help/create-tasks-and-to-do-items-HA001229302.aspx.
4. New in Labs: Tasks. http://gmailblog.blogspot.com/2008/12/new-in-labs-tasks.html.
5. Set up Mail Delegation. http://support.google.com/mail/bin/answer.py?hl=en&answer=138350.
6. Barley, S.R., D. Meyerson, and S. Grodal. E-mail as a Source and Symbol of Stress. *Organization Science 22*, 4. 2011.
7. Bekkerman, R., A. McCallum, and G. Huang. Automatic Categorization of Email into Folders: Benchmark Experiments on Enron and SRI Corpora. *Technical Report IR-418*. 2004.
8. Bellotti, V., N. Ducheneaut, M. Howard, and I. Smith. Taking Email to Task: The Design and Evaluation of a Task Management Centered Email Tool. *Proc. CHI 2003*. 2003.
9. Bennett, P.N. and J. Carbonell. Detecting Action-Items in E-mail. *Proc. SIGIR 2005*. 2005.
10. Bernstein, M.S., G. Little, R.C. Miller, B. Hartmann, M.S. Ackerman, D.R. Karger, D. Crowell, and K. Panovich. Soylent: A Word Processor with a Crowd Inside. *Proc. UIST 2010*. 2010.
11. Boone, G. Concept Features in Re:Agent, an Intelligent Email Agent. *Proc. AAMAS 1998*. 1998.
12. Corston-Oliver, S., E. Ringger, M. Gamon and R. Campbell. Task-focused summarization of email. *ACL 2004 Workshop: Text Summarization Branches Out*. 2004.
13. Crawford, A.B. Corporate Electronic Mail — A Communication-Intensive Application of Information Technology. *MIS Quarterly 6*, 3. 1982.
14. Dow. S., A. Kulkarni, S.R. Klemmer, and B. Hartmann. Shepherding the Crowd Yields Better Work. *Proc. CSCW 2012*. 2012.
15. Erickson, T., C. Davis, W. Kellogg, and M. Helander. Assistance: The Work Practices of Human Administrative Assistants and their Implications for IT and Organizations. *Proc. CSCW 2008*. 2008.
16. Faulring, A., B. Myers, K. Mohnkern, B. Schmerl, A. Steinfeld, J. Zimmerman, A. Smailagic, J. Hansen, and D. Siewiorek. Agent-assisted task management that reduces email overload. *Proc. IUI 2010*. 2010.
17. Feldman, M.S. Constraints on Communication and Electronic Mail. *Proc. CSCW 1986*. 1986.
18. Fisher, D., A.J. Brush, E. Gleave, M.A. Smith. Revisiting Whittaker & Sidner's "email overload" ten years later. *Proc. CSCW 2006*. 2006.
19. Freed, M., J. Carbonell, G. Gordon, J. Hayes, B. Myers, D. Siewiorek, S. Smith, A. Steinfeld, and A. Tomasic. RADAR: A Personal Assistant that Learns to Reduce Email Overload. *In Proc. AAAI 2008*. 2008.
20. Gwizdka, J. TaskView – Design and Evaluation of a Task-based Email Interface. *Proc. CASCON 2002*. 2002.
21. Horvitz, E., A. Jacobs, D. Hovel. Attention-sensitive alerting. *Proc. UAI 1999*. 1999.
22. Jackson, T., R. Dawson, and D. Wilson. The Cost of Email Interruption. *Journal of Systems and Information Technology 5*, 1. 2001.
23. Kiritchenko, S. and Matwin, S. Email Classification with Co-Training. *Proc. CASCON 2001*. 2001.

24. Kokkalis, N., T. Köhn, J. Huebner, M. Lee, F. Schulze, S.R. Klemmer. TaskGenies: Automatically Providing Action Plans Helps People Complete Tasks. *Technical Report* CSTR 2012-04. 2012.
25. Lampert, A., R. Dale, C. Paris. Detecting Emails Containing Requests for Action. *Proc. ACL 2010*. 2010.
26. Mackay, W. E. More than Just a Communication System: Diversity in the Use of Electronic Mail. *Proc. CSCW 1988*. 1988.
27. Muller, M. J., and Gruen, D. M. Working Together Inside an Emailbox. *Proc. ECSCW 2005*. 2005.
28. Palen, L., and P. Dourish. Unpacking "Privacy" for a Networked World. *Proc. CHI 2003*. 2003.
29. Rambow, O., L. Shrestha, J. Chen, and C. Lauridsen. Summarizing Email Threads. *Proc. HLT-NAACL 2004*. 2004.
30. Sahami, M., S. Dumais, D. Heckerman, and E. Horvitz. A Bayesian Approach to Filtering Junk E-mail. *AAAI Workshop: Learning for Text Categorization*. 1998.
31. Samiei, M., J. Dill, and A. Kirkpatrick. EzMail: Using Information Visualization Techniques to Help Manage Email. *Proc. IV 2004*. 2004.
32. Segal, R.B. and Kephart, J.O. MailCat: An Intelligent Assistant for Organizing E-Mail. *Proc. AAMAS 1999*. 1999.
33. Shen, J., L. Li, T.G. Dietterich, and J.L. Herlocker. A Hybrid Learning System for Recognizing User Tasks from Desktop Activities and Email Messages. *Proc. IUI 2006*. 2006.
34. Takkinen, J. and N. Shahmehri. CAFE: A Conceptual Model for Managing Information in Electronic Mail. *Proc. HICSS 1998*. 1998.
35. Venolia, G., L. Dabbish, J.J. Cadiz, and A. Goopta. Supporting email workflow. *Technical Report MSR-TR-2001–88*. 2001.
36. Weber, R. The Grim Reaper: The Curse of E-Mail. *MIS Quarterly 28*, 3. 2004.
37. Weiser, M. The Computer for the 21st Century. *Scientific American*. 1991.
38. Whittaker, S. and C. Sidner. Email Overload: Exploring Personal Information Management of Email. *Proc. CHI 1996*. 1996.
39. Winograd, T., and F. Flores. *Understanding Computers and Cognition: A New Foundation for Design*. Ablex, 1986.

The Future of Crowd Work

Aniket Kittur[1], Jeffrey V. Nickerson[2], Michael S. Bernstein[3], Elizabeth M. Gerber[4], Aaron Shaw[4], John Zimmerman[1], Matthew Lease[5], and John J. Horton[6]

[1]Carnegie Mellon University, [2]Stevens Institute of Technology, [3]Stanford University, [4]Northwestern University, [5]University of Texas at Austin, [6]oDesk
{nkittur, johnz}@cs.cmu.edu, jnickerson@stevens.edu, msb@cs.stanford.edu, {egerber, aaronshaw}@northwestern.edu, ml@ischool.utexas.edu, john_horton@odesk.com

ABSTRACT
Paid crowd work offers remarkable opportunities for improving productivity, social mobility, and the global economy by engaging a geographically distributed workforce to complete complex tasks on demand and at scale. But it is also possible that crowd work will fail to achieve its potential, focusing on assembly-line piecework. Can we foresee a future crowd workplace in which we would want our children to participate? This paper frames the major challenges that stand in the way of this goal. Drawing on theory from organizational behavior and distributed computing, as well as direct feedback from workers, we outline a framework that will enable crowd work that is complex, collaborative, and sustainable. The framework lays out research challenges in twelve major areas: workflow, task assignment, hierarchy, real-time response, synchronous collaboration, quality control, crowds guiding AIs, AIs guiding crowds, platforms, job design, reputation, and motivation.

Author Keywords
Crowdsourcing; crowd work; organization design; research vision

ACM Classification Keywords
H.5; K.4.3

INTRODUCTION
Crowdsourcing rapidly mobilizes large numbers of people to accomplish tasks on a global scale. For example, volunteer-based collective projects such as Wikipedia owe their success and longevity to the ongoing efforts of thousands of individual contributors around the world.

Complementing volunteer-based crowdsourcing, a paying *crowd work* industry is now quickly growing in scope and ambition. Crowd work today spans a wide range of skill and pay levels, with commercial vendors providing access to a range of workers and focused support for various task. For example, anyone with access to the Internet can perform *micro*-tasks on the order of seconds using platforms such as Amazon's Mechanical Turk, while more skilled workers can complete multi-hour tasks on professional online marketplaces such as oDesk or work for months to solve R&D challenges on open innovation platforms (e.g. Innocentive). Incentives and work structures also vary tremendously, ranging from crowdsourcing contests awarding prizes to winners (e.g. programming tasks on Topcoder) to micro-labor platforms that pay workers per task.

While not all jobs are amenable to being sent down a wire, there are portions of almost any job that can be performed by the crowd [63]. We foresee a world in which crowd work continues to expand, unlocking an incredible number of opportunities for careers and skilled work in online marketplaces. However, we also foresee a serious risk that crowd work will fall into an intellectual framing focused on low-cost results and exploitative labor. With diminished visibility and communication channels vis-a-vis traditional workplaces, workers may be treated as exchangeable and untrustworthy, having low or static skill sets and strong motivations to shirk. Workers may become equally cynical, having fewer bonds, enforceable contracts, and power than with traditional workplaces [130]. Such concerns may grow ever sharper unless this trajectory is somehow altered.

This work originally emerged from the question: "*Can we foresee a future crowd workplace in which we would want our children to participate?*" We suggest that this question has a number of attractive properties as a banner around which to rally research, as well as serving as an anchor to ground speculation. It is simple enough to convey concisely, involving an evaluative component that everyone, with or without children, can make. We intentionally keep the "we" ambiguous so that readers with different values and cultural contexts may "try on" the question, providing a conceptual lens easily refocused, and encourage discussion regarding the challenges this question poses to deciding what is valuable and pride-worthy work. What new services, systems or features are needed for a future of crowd work that the reader would be proud to see

CSCW '13, February 23–27, 2013, San Antonio, Texas, USA.

his or her children take on as their livelihood? Is this a desirable path for the next generation?

Looking toward that positive future, in this paper we contribute an analytic framework for research in crowd work. We lay out a vision for a possible future for crowd work that entails:

- **Worker considerations**, such as motivation, feedback, and pay. These may be addressed by mechanisms to maintain reputation, provide better interaction with requesters, and increase motivation.
- **Requester considerations,** such as coordination, task decomposition, and quality control. These may be addressed through workflow mechanisms including electronically mediated collaboration.

Our analytic framework is organized around a multidisciplinary survey of the literature that speaks to these challenges and helps to envision a positive future. We also include specific comments from crowd workers we surveyed in order to elicit their thoughts and suggestions. We translate our findings into a set of pragmatic design considerations that we believe are crucial in guiding design and motivating research in this field. We are following in the tradition of a set of research contributions which delineated design principles as part of a call for action [69,98,102,114,123].

Crowd Work

A variety of terminology is currently used in regard to crowds, e.g. crowdsourcing, collective intelligence, human computation, serious games, peer production, and citizen science [2,12,90,105]. We focus this paper on *paid, online crowd work*, which we define here as the performance of tasks online by distributed *crowd workers* who are financially compensated by *requesters* (individuals, groups, or organizations). In this sense, crowd work is a *socio-technical work system* constituted through a set of relationships that connect organizations, individuals, technologies and work activities [142]. Online crowd work takes place in marketplaces that allow requesters to seek workers and support workers in finding work. For this paper, we surveyed a number of contemporary, popular crowd work platforms. These platforms include general-purpose marketplaces (e.g., Mechanical Turk, oDesk, Freelancer, Crowdflower, MobileWorks, ManPower) as well as markets for specific expertise (e.g., TopCoder, uTest, 99Designs). While these platforms are intended for legitimate tasks, these and other platforms are sometimes appropriated for illegal or nefarious purposes (e.g., gold farming, CAPTCHA solving, and crowdturfing) [35].

Through our definition, we necessarily omit a wide range of voluntary crowd work, such as wikis [22], games with a purpose [2], captchas [3], and citizen science [31,106,122]. Much has already been written about these systems (e.g., [12,108]). However, not only is paid work the cornerstone of our existing economy and labor markets, but even volunteers typically engage in some form of paying work in order to sustain themselves. Moreover, we believe there will always be some forms of work needed by society which are not amenable to gamification and volunteering, and for which demand will outstrip supply via unpaid channels. As such, we are interested in developing a future of paid crowd work that extends paid work into the online environment. In addition, we exclude offline crowd work, such as day labor, as it does not possess the same opportunities for distribution and global scalability as online work. For the remainder of the paper, we will use the term *crowd work* to refer to the performance of online tasks by crowd workers who are financially compensated by requesters.

We intentionally focus coverage on areas that may be of greater interest to the CSCW community, especially issues related to computer science, psychology, and organization science. We also draw on other important areas where appropriate (e.g., labor economics, ethics, law) and acknowledge these as critical to the future economy. Many aspects of these issues lie beyond the traditional purview of scientists or designers (e.g., labor regulations); however, we recognize that addressing them will be necessary for a positive future of crowd work.

Pros and Cons

Crowd work has the potential to support a flexible workforce and mitigate challenges such as shortages of experts in specific areas (e.g., IT work) or geographical locations. For individuals, crowd work also creates new opportunities for income and social mobility in regions of the world where local economies may be stagnant and local governmental structures discourage investment.

However, crowd work can be a double-edged sword, equally capable of enhancing or diminishing the quality of workers' lives. We may see echoes of past labor abuses in globally distributed crowd work: extremely low pay for labor, with marketplaces such as Amazon's Mechanical Turk reported to effectively pay an average of $2/hour [65][126] with no benefits or worker protections. The per-task payment structure used in most crowd work markets is akin to piecework compensation in manufacturing [118], and can offer an invitation for gaming behavior which can negatively influence quality [78]. Moreover, crowds can be deployed in the service of questionable goals: to break captchas, to mine gold in games, and even, potentially, to locate dissidents [158]. The recent film "In Time" (2011) provided a pop culture depiction of how such a society might function where continual performance of menial tasks was literally required for worker survival. Many writers have painted similarly bleak pictures [40,136,137].

Crowd work may also displace current workers and has the potential to replace some forms of skilled labor with unskilled labor as tasks are decomposed into smaller and smaller pieces. Tasks such as speech transcription and copyediting are increasingly being accomplished with crowd labor, and researchers have found that even some complex and expert tasks such as writing, product design, or translation may be amenable to novice crowd workers with appropriate process design and technological support [75,77,152,153].

This displacement is coupled to a new form of Taylorism [88,141], in which organizations optimize cognitive efficiency [157] at the expense of education and skill development. Taylorism yielded to more enlightened job design after several decades (and protracted struggles by workers), but given the short time commitment between crowd worker and requester, it is easy to imagine heightened exploitation and dehumanization.

As scientists, engineers, and designers, we can propose and evaluate new structures for crowd work and help imagine and bring about more positive futures. We can do so both through the intentional creation of desirable work environments as well as the cultivation of increased demand for work and workers. In particular, we suggest a role for researchers in conceptualizing and prototyping new forms of crowd work that go beyond the simple, independent, and deskilled tasks that are common today, with the goal of blazing a trail for organizations and platforms that will form the foundation of future crowd work.

ENVISIONING FUTURE CROWD WORK

How can we move towards a future of crowd work that is more attractive for both requesters and workers than existing systems? Even more ambitiously, can we design a future of crowd work that is more attractive and more effective than traditional labor systems?

Current crowd work typically consists of small, independent, and homogenous tasks, as shown in Figure 1. Workers are paired with an instance of each task to produce an output. Such simple, small-scale work has engendered low-pay, piece rate reward structures, in part due to the perception that workers are homogenous and unskilled. The current model is also insufficient to support the complexity, creativity, and skills that are needed for many kinds of professional work that take place today. Nor can it drive factors that will lead to increased worker satisfaction, such as improved pay, skill development, and complex work structures.

Theories of Organizational Behavior and Distributed Computing

Much professional work consists of complex sets of interdependent tasks that need to be coordinated across individuals with different expertise and capabilities [89]. For example, producing a book, an academic paper, or a new car all may involve many individuals working in structured teams, each with different skills and roles, collaborating on a shared output. To address these more complex goals we draw on concepts from both the organizational behavior [89,97,143,148] and the distributed computing literatures [9,132]. We propose that

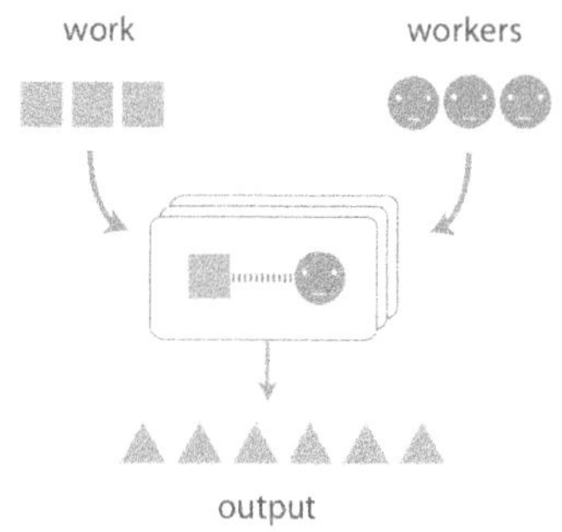

Figure 1: Current crowd work processes.

crowdsourced labor markets can be viewed as large distributed systems in which each person, such as a worker on Mechanical Turk, is analogous to a processor that can solve a task requiring human intelligence. In this way a crowdsourcing market could be seen as a loosely coupled distributed computing system [9]. Fleshing out this analogy, we develop here the beginnings of a framework for the future of crowd work that integrates the human aspects of organizational behavior with the automation and scalability of the distributed computing literature.

Both distributed organizations and computing systems face many common fundamental challenges in accomplishing complex work. Key challenges in distributed computing include partitioning computations into tasks that can be done in parallel, mapping tasks to processors, and distributing data to and between processors [9,25,96,132]. Many of these challenges map to coordination dependencies identified by Malone & Crowston [89] that also apply to human organizations. Below we discuss two categories of overlap between coordination dependencies discussed in organizational science, their analogs in distributed computing, and their implications for the beginnings of a framework for the future of crowd work.

Managing shared resources

Whenever a limited resource needs to be shared, coordinating how that resource is allocated becomes important. Allocating a fixed pool of workers to multiple tasks that must be completed under a deadline is a classic example of managing shared resources. Malone & Crowston [89] suggest a number of examples of task allocation mechanisms, ranging from first come/first serve, to markets, to managerial decisions. In distributed computing systems, managing shared resources is of similarly vital importance. Tasks must be mapped to processors, requiring functions to govern task partitioning. Reorganization of this mapping must be possible as well, for example if a processor fails or takes a long time to return results (e.g., MapReduce [34]).

Managing producer/consumer and task/subtask relationships

In many situations, one activity produces something required as input for another activity. For example, the structure of an article needs to be decided on before the sections can be written. These same requirements exist in distributed computing, in which tasks need to be scheduled so that they can be completed in the correct sequence and in a timely manner, with data being transferred between computing elements appropriately. Deciding how to divide a task into subtasks and managing those subtasks is also a challenging problem, especially for complex and interdependent tasks [61,89]. This is true whether a manager in an organization is trying to plan a large project or a programmer is trying to parallelize a complex task. Furthermore, top-down approaches in which a single person (e.g., the task creator) specifies all subtasks a priori may not be possible, or subtasks may change as the task evolves.

Crowd-Specific Factors

Unlike traditional organizations in which workers possess job security and managers can closely supervise and appropriately reward or sanction workers, or distributed computing systems in which processors are usually highly reliable, crowd work poses unique challenges for both workers and requesters ranging from job satisfaction to direction-setting, coordination, and quality control. For example, organizations can maintain high quality work through management, worker incentives, and sanctions. While some of these methods are available in crowd work (e.g., how much to reward workers, whether to reject their work, or impose a reputation penalty) their power is attenuated due to factors such as lack of direct supervision and visibility into their work behavior, lack of nuanced and individualized rewards, and the difficulty of imposing stringent and lasting sanctions (since workers can leave with fewer repercussions than in traditional organizations, such as to reference letters or work histories). The worker's power is also limited: requesters do not make a long-term commitment to the worker, and endure few penalties if they renege on their agreement to pay for quality work. In distributed computing systems, by contrast, requesters (programmers) have fewer problems with motivating and directing their workers (computers). However, machines cannot match the complexity, creativity, and flexibility that human intelligence manifests. Combining ideas from human and computer organization theories may thus provide complementary benefits and address complementary weaknesses over using either alone.

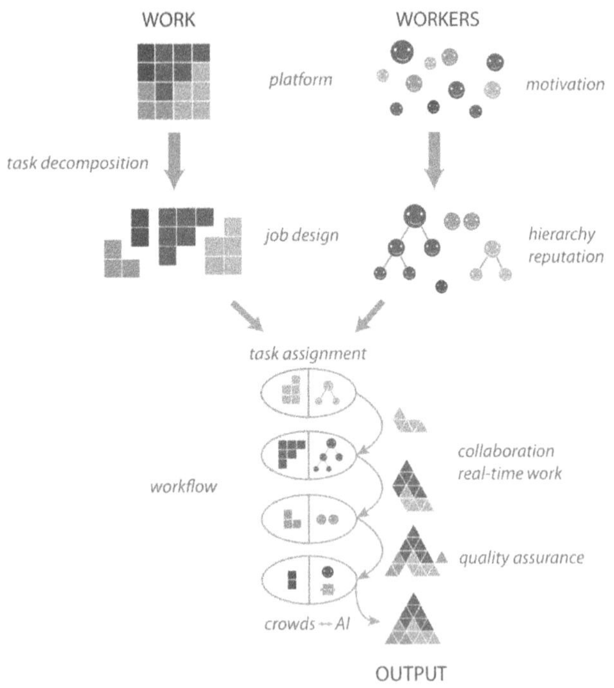

Figure 2: Proposed framework for future crowd work processes to support complex and interdependent work.

Framework

Figure 2 presents a framework that integrates the challenges posed by managing shared resources (such as assigning workers to appropriate tasks), managing producer-consumer relationships (such as decomposing tasks and assembling them into a workflow), and crowd-specific factors (such as motivation, rewards, and quality assurance). Many of its elements combine insights from organizational behavior and distributed computing: for example the task decomposition and task assignment functions use both human and computational processes.

The goal of this framework is to envision a future of crowd work that can support more complex, creative, and highly valued work. At the highest level, a **platform** is needed for managing pools of tasks and workers. Complex tasks must be **decomposed** into smaller subtasks, each **designed** with particular needs and characteristics which must be **assigned** to appropriate groups of workers who themselves must be properly **motivated**, selected (e.g., through **reputation**), and organized (e.g., through **hierarchy**). Tasks may be structured through multi-stage **workflows** in which workers may **collaborate** either synchronously or asynchronously. As part of this, **AI** may guide (and be guided by) crowd workers. Finally, **quality assurance** is needed to ensure each worker's output is of high quality and fits together.

Because we are concerned with issues of design – the technical and organizational mechanisms surrounding crowd work – we highlight in the process model twelve specific research foci (Figure 2) that we suggest are necessary for realizing such a future of crowd work. These foci are grouped into three key dimensions: foci relevant to the work process; the computation guiding, guided by, and underlying the work; and the workers themselves. Our 12 foci overlap each other in places. However, in total they provide a wide-ranging multidisciplinary view that covers current and prospective crowd work processes. For example, workflow techniques may be useful for handling the flow of documents through a set of tasks [111], but the effectiveness of these techniques can be amplified through clever job design that divides tasks and allocates incentives in a way that benefits both workers and requesters (cf. [62]).

Our model is based on empirical as well as theoretical input. In forming this model, we gathered feedback from both task requesters and workers. The authors of this paper have been requesters, have designed crowd workflows, and have worked for platform companies, and so requester and platform company issues are represented. We wished to also represent the voices of workers. We chose one popular crowdsourcing platform, Amazon Mechanical Turk, and asked questions of workers in the two countries with the largest number of crowd workers – the United States and India – who had completed and had approved more than 500 tasks (as enforced by the platform). Workers were paid USD $2 to comment on and add design suggestions for the 12 foci discussed below. Fifty-two workers responded from the US and 52 from India. Four of the responses were removed from the sample because of incomplete or inconsistent answers. Workers in India had a mean age of 27 (σ=6). Workers in the US had a mean age of 33 (σ=11). In India, 27% of workers were female, and in the US, 58% were female. In both countries responders had considerable experience: the mean total lifetime tasks were 6562 (σ=15292) and 9019 (σ=22460) for Indian and U.S. workers, respectively. The purpose of the survey was to provide workers a vehicle through which they could contribute their own insights. In general, the workers' responses were thorough and insightful, and we have integrated their ideas into this paper, quoting their answers where appropriate. Even though our survey is informal and relatively small in scale, we believe that it enriches this paper by providing a variety of workers' perspectives on the 12 topics we discuss next.

RESEARCH FOCI

In the sections below, we survey and analyze the 12 research foci that comprise our model. First, we consider the future of the work processes and how the work is organized and accomplished. Second, we consider the integration of crowd work and computation, including the symbiosis between human cognition, artificial intelligence (AI), and computationally-enabled crowd platforms. Finally, we consider crowd workers and how we can develop jobs, reputation systems, motivations, and incentives that will benefit them. In each subsection we state our motivation and goals, briefly review related work, and propose research issues and themes.

The Future of Crowd Work Processes

Increasing the value and meaning of crowd work will require that it move beyond simple deskilled tasks to complex professional work. In this section, we focus on the key challenges that must be met in order to enable complex crowd work processes: designing workflows, assigning tasks, supporting hierarchical structure, enabling real-time crowd work, supporting synchronous collaboration, and controlling quality.

Workflow

Motivation/Goals. Complex crowd work cannot be accomplished using the simple parallel approaches that are common today, such as aggregating multiple independent judgments through voting or majority rule. Complex tasks have dependencies, changing requirements, and require multiple types of expertise. Instead, *workflows* are needed that facilitate decomposing tasks into subtasks, managing the dependencies between subtasks, and assembling the results. While initial research has shown that enabling more complex workflows can result in large differences in output quality even with small differences in instructions, rewards, and task order [72,127], we have barely begun to understand the broader design space of crowd workflows.

Related Work. Traditional organizations have developed expertise in workflow design and management. The division of labor is a core tenet of task coordination; Adam Smith in his classic *The Nature and Causes of the Wealth of Nations* [133] described the associated efficacy benefits. Via division of labor, a greater pool of agents can work in parallel, specialize for the tasks they perform, and complete an assignment with less time lost to switching tasks [10]. Coordination is difficult among distributed workers, but organizational coordination techniques can be profitably applied to crowd work (e.g., [72,74,90,97,143]). Systems and formal languages support workflows in traditional firms [39], ranging from purely computational [151] to hybrid approaches where tasks are self-selected and then automatically routed onward [138].

In the context of crowds, workflow could involve a much larger scale of operation, and a much more heterogeneous set of actors. The design space ranges from massively redundant, independent tasks (e.g., contests that choose one entry [8,19,20]) to highly serial processes with work passed from one worker to the next (e.g., passing a task from worker to worker for improvements [87]). Recent systems and toolkits pursued a "flare and focus" approach for complex work by exploring a space of options and then drilling down to flesh out those options [15,75,87,150]. Crowd workers can guide workflows as well [1,75,80,154].

Research Proposal. Crowd workflows are still quite brittle, and are most successful with highly targeted tasks. To improve existing workflows, we must experiment and iterate on a large space of parameters, instructions, incentives and decompositions. Costs of doing so may be reduced through models of worker behavior [120] or by encapsulating and reusing proven design patterns [1][73]. Then, we must push crowd workflows toward more general tasks and wicked problems that have no clearly defined solution [112]. Rather than edit text, for example, crowd workflows should be able to support complex goals such as creativity and brainstorming, essay writing, music composition, or civic planning. Crowd workers reminded us in our survey responses that they also need help managing their own workflows as they juggle tasks from different requesters.

Task Assignment

Motivation/Goals. Sharing limited resources requires

coordination — allocating a fixed pool of workers to multiple tasks with deadlines is a classic example [117]. Ideally, requesters will see their tasks completed quickly, while workers are continuously employed with tasks that match their interests. In the worst case, workers are matched to tasks that are uninteresting or too difficult, and won't make the income they want or deserve.

Related Work. Management scientists have developed techniques such as first come/first serve task queues, markets, and managerial decisions [117]. Computer science research adds useful abstractions drawn from data partitioning, OS scheduling, and failover (e.g., [34]). Currently, workers are usually forced to sort queues by task volume and recency [29]. But some algorithms form teams dynamically based on expertise [5].

Research Proposal. Task assignment has typically involved either a first-come/first-served model (e.g., the ESP game, Galaxy Zoo [2,106]) or a market model (e.g., oDesk, Mechanical Turk). In either case, task designers must guess at the right combination of incentives and iterate until success. This process is both time-consuming and expensive. Better theoretical models, markets or automatic computational matching processes (e.g., [14]) could drastically reduce development costs and address search friction [4], an important issue in labor economics. The assignment of tasks in relation to individuals' abilities has also been studied as part of business workflow research [110,128]. Several workers in our survey complained that they spent too much energy finding appropriate tasks; one suggested that platforms provide automatic recommendations of possible next tasks based on workers' previous task choices. These comments suggest a research question: are the workers or the platforms better-suited to manage task assignment? That is, should tasks be pulled by workers or pushed by platforms?

Hierarchy

Motivation/Goal. Hierarchy has become the primary management strategy in traditional organizations. It benefits coordination, decision making, quality control, and assigns incentives and sanctions [30,92]. Hierarchies decompose large and complex tasks such as developing and manufacturing an automobile by clarifying legitimate authority and workflow across organizations. Hierarchies in crowd work could enable groups of workers to tackle new classes of complex work, increase efficiency, and support consistency and integration. Hierarchies may also allow workers to act more like teams, for example developing accountability standards, decision-making and conflict resolution processes, and review policies.

Related Work. Volunteer crowdsourcing platforms have evolved their own hierarchies and decision-making processes [104,156], appropriating techniques from other online communities where appropriate [101]. Most paid approaches have workers make hierarchical decisions collectively: for example, task decomposition and integration [75,80], quality oversight of each others' contributions [78,100], and leader elections to represent collective opinions [83]. oDesk and MobileWorks identify and empower workers to serve in leadership roles [79]. No comparative analyses of the effectiveness of these approaches exist yet.

Research Proposal. The fluid nature of crowd work opens the door to new kinds of hierarchy where workers transition between roles continuously. Crowd management could entail a layered tree made up of worker-leaders, requesters, machine learning systems, and algorithms. In such a setup, participants might be leaf nodes (workers) in one job but managers in another. Realizing this vision will require improvements to the platforms (e.g., oDesk teams) and the creation of systems that take advantage of it. Alternatively, organized groups of workers might begin applying to jobs as a single entity. But there may be resistance to hierarchy: one worker wrote, "I like the way it is. There does not seem to be a hierarchy. In fact, this is one of the most satisfying aspects of Mturk. Anyone can be their own boss." This comment suggests the value of further empirical study of the willingness of crowd members to manage or be managed by each other. Perhaps current forms of organizational structure will yield to new ones, in which the processes of managing and being managed will be more intertwined and are conceptually different than what we currently experience.

Realtime Crowd Work

Motivation/Goal. For work with tight completion-time constraints, we will need to create *flash crowds*: groups of individuals who arrive moments after a request and can work synchronously. Any application that wants to embed on-demand crowdsourcing (e.g., [15,17]) is limited by the problem of crowd latency, but current crowd tasks can take hours [15] or days [72].

Related Work. Fast recruitment has been the major research thrust in realtime crowdsourcing so far. Early attempts were motivated by time-limited tasks such as searching for a missing person [59] and timed "competitions" [99,140]. In paid crowdsourcing, researchers began e-mailing a set of workers the night before the study and announced a time for the experiment. Keeping workers busy with old tasks brought wait times down to a half minute to one minute [17], and paying workers a small wage to stay on call is enough to draw a crowd together roughly two to three seconds later [13,14]. This technique can be modeled using queuing theory and adapted to bring together crowds in as little as 500 milliseconds.

Research Proposal. The two core challenges for realtime crowdsourcing will be 1) scaling up to increased demand for realtime workers, and 2) making workers efficient enough to collectively generate results ahead of time deadlines. What happens as more tasks need such responses, and as the size of the crowd increases? Is it possible to support a large number of realtime crowdsourcing tasks competing for workers' attention [14]?

Workers who arrive quickly can still be slow at completing work [13]. It is possible to design algorithms and workflows to guide workers to complete synchronous tasks quickly. So far, these techniques are restricted to particular domains [13], but general approaches may be possible. What would it take to begin with a sketch on a napkin, find a designer to mock up interface alternatives, a usability analyst to test those prototypes, and a front-end engineer to implement the best one, all in a single afternoon? Workers seem interested in such tasks: one suggested providing "More communications options with the requester, something better than just emailing them, like some sort of immediate chat." Another wrote: "I'd like to see some sort of worker alert system on the dashboard for such events."

Synchronous Collaboration

Motivation/Goal. Many tasks worth completing require cooperation – yet crowdsourcing has largely focused on independent work. Distributed teams have always faced challenges in cultural differences and coordination [60], but crowd collaboration now must create rapport over much shorter timescales (e.g., one hour) and possibly wider cultural or socioeconomic gaps.

Related Work. Many attempts at collaborative crowd work highly structure the communication between participants. For example, crowds can solve distributed problems by observing the behavior of neighbors [91], letting the system choose which suggestions to focus on [13], continuously elect new leaders [83] and pass on knowledge to new members [84]. These techniques reduce the damage that a single poor or malicious crowd worker can do, while also limiting the types of collaboration possible. They also set up opportunities for feedback and learning [42].

Unstructured collaboration also shows promise, for example by giving workers a task and placing them in collaborative text authoring software [77]. These techniques draw on synchronous collaboration research (e.g., [53,66]).

Research Proposal. To shift from independent workers to teams of on-demand collaborators, we must revisit and extend traditional CSCW work on distributed teamwork. Short periods of intense crowd collaboration call for fast teambuilding and may require the automatic assignment of group members to maximize collective intelligence [5,149]. Finally, it will be a major research undertaking to invent and describe the tasks and techniques that succeed with synchronous collaboration.

Quality Control

Motivation/Goal. Quality problems are a serious challenge to the mass adoption of crowd work. The most appealing aspects of crowd work — such as high throughput, low transaction costs, and complex/subjective tasks — also make it susceptible to quality control issues. Workers *satisfice*, minimizing the amount of effort they expend, and in the extreme cheat or game the system. For example, 30% or more of submissions on Mechanical Turk may be low quality [15,72]. One worker warned us: "People collude to agree on wrong answers to trick the system." That is, quality filters based on consensus may be fooled by workers who agree to coordinate answers. Workers who have low expertise and requesters who provide unclear instructions also contribute to subpar responses. Problems arise even for workers who are highly motivated: these "eager beavers" often make well-intentioned but counterproductive contributions [15]. In our survey, workers saw quality control as a major issue that affected their compensation, and they expressed a dislike for their peers who lowered quality standards through misbehavior. However, many complained about requesters: one said: "Too often the job itself is badly designed or is messed up and there is a degree of misunderstanding between the worker and the job engineer."

Related Work. Of the research foci, quality control has arguably received the most attention so far. Approaches for quality control largely fall into two camps: up-front task design and post-hoc result analysis. Task design aims to design tasks that are resistant to low-quality work. For example, requesters can split work into fault-tolerant subtasks [15,75,103], apply peer-review or agreement filters [2,15,17,42,63,75], optimize instructions [43,72,127], and manipulate incentives [26,115,127].

Worker output approaches filter out poor quality work after results have been submitted. Workers' results can be compared to gold standard data on a pre-labeled set of the tasks [24,43,85]. Including gold standards can prevent workers' inherent biases from dominating the results [37]. However, authoring gold data can be burdensome, and gold standards may not be possible for subjective or generative tasks (e.g., writing an essay). Other common methods scale the influence of a submission according to how well that worker agrees with others [24,36,64,134] or according to the workers' votes. However, recruiting multiple workers costs more, agreement may not be possible for subjective or generative tasks, and the approach is susceptible to collusion [41]. False identities are increasingly being created as an attack on quality assurance methods.

A promising approach that addresses some worker output issues examines the way that workers do their work rather than the output itself, using machine learning and/or visualization to predict the quality of a worker's output from their behavior [119,120]. Similar but simpler approaches provide requesters more visibility into worker behavior, such as oDesk's Worker Diary which periodically takes snapshots of workers' computer screens. While powerful, such techniques must address privacy and autonomy concerns if widely deployed.

Research Proposal. While quality control is improving for tasks with a closed set of possible answers, we still have few techniques for open-ended work and highly skilled tasks. Is it possible to robustly gauge workers' skills at tasks such as audio engineering, art critique, or poetry? Should we rely on peer evaluation, or data mine low-level activity to predict output quality? Do quality metrics map well across different marketplaces?

In the long term, we must move from reducing poor quality work to scaffolding truly excellent work. To do so, we can optimize workflows for creativity, innovation, and discovery. This vision will involve recruiting experts; metrics that enable us to evaluate such factors; and reward structures that value high-quality artifacts.

The Future of Crowd Computation

Crowd labor is already mediated by computation. However, computation has the opportunity to step into a much more active role in helping recruit and manage workers as well as contribute directly to work processes. Hybrid human-computer systems could tap into the best of both human and machine intelligence. We structure our discussion around the potential for reciprocal benefits between crowd workers and computational systems. *Crowds guiding AIs* considers how crowd intelligence can help train, supervise, and supplement automation. *AIs guiding crowds* considers how machine intelligence can help make the crowd more efficient, skilled, and accurate. Finally, we also consider the design and evaluation of crowdsourcing platforms.

Crowds Guiding AIs

Motivation/Goal. In human computation, people act as computational components and perform the work that AI systems lack the skills to complete [2]. By tapping into crowd intelligence, computational systems can support a much broader set of tasks. It should be understood that this area, out of all areas, least excites crowd workers, and perhaps with good reason: crowd workers may end up training machines to replace them.

Related Work. Paid crowds have gathered large amounts of data to train algorithms. For example, crowds can: 1) match expert annotations on natural language processing tasks such as word sense disambiguation [23,134], 2) generate speech corpora for spoken language research [23,95], 3) annotate objects and people in images [135], and 4) help with graphics tasks such as identifying depth layers [51]. Crowds can also solve algorithmic problems such as graph coloring [68,91].

Research Proposal. While algorithms will continue to benefit from crowd-generated training data, there are opportunities to integrate crowds more deeply into algorithms. Rather than treating crowd data as ground truth labels, it may be profitable to understand and model the biases and intuitions that human cognition brings [147]. It may be possible to design machine learning algorithms that more deeply understand the human nature of these labels. Algorithms may also more directly model the tradeoff between cost and performance: for example, by using a combination of active learning and semi-supervised learning to collect the most informational labels [155].

AIs Guiding Crowds

Motivation/Goal. While large groups are increasingly adept at completing straightforward parallel tasks [54,139], they can struggle with complex work. Participants have varied skill levels, even well-intentioned contributions can introduce errors, and errors are amplified as they propagate through the crowd. It is possible to integrate crowds directly inside of software [15,17,46], and use the software to help guide crowd work; for example, a machine learning model can determine which work products may still be improved, and then assign workers most likely to make such improvements [32,33]. These systems may also be able to predict their expertise needs in advance, then train and adapt workers in an online fashion via automated tutoring [47,113] or peer learning [18].

Related Work. Computational approaches for designing and integrating workflow, incentive, and instruction patterns have shown promise [32,125], as well as techniques that trade off the strengths of crowds and artificial intelligence [67,146]. AIs could also serve as a reflective aids, encouraging the crowd to learn by pointing out what others have done in similar contexts (e.g., [109]).

Research Proposal. The research community should examine whether algorithmic management is an improvement over traditional organization management techniques. In an algorithmic organization crowds will need to be able to raise exceptions, as well as halt and restart processes. And AIs will need to know when then can proceed, when they need human help, and when they need to help the workers. In addition, workers should be able to modify their supporting AIs as needed. In the end, both workers and AIs should improve. To accomplish this, we will need to move from a setting where simple AIs completely determine a workflow to a richer, mixed-initiative setting where crowds and AIs jointly teach each other, and jointly control the work process.

Crowdsourcing Platforms

Motivation/Goal. Crowdsourcing platforms provide the central nexus between requesters and workers. As a result, platform design offers the opportunity to change our perceptions and understanding of crowd work in general, as well as shape the relationships and practical interactions between workers and requesters in practice. While several platforms already exist, limiting ourselves to existing platforms greatly restricts the scope and nature of change we can enact. By contrast, novel platforms can help drive the diffusion of new designs and techniques for crowd work.

Related Work. Platform research tends to optimize existing processes or reach out to new populations. For example, CrowdFlower experiments on its own gold standard metrics to minimize the number of times a question is asked [129].

Platforms may also manage a large number of real time requests or route tasks to ensure that all tasks have steady streams of incoming workers [14]. MobileWorks promotes its own workers to management positions based on their performance [79]. To find new populations, MobileWorks and mClerk engage with the developing world through specifically-tailored mobile phone interfaces [56,100]. Incentives can be used to recruit local experts as well: for example, a vending machine served up exam grading tasks and dispersed candy as a reward [58].

Research Proposal. While designing and building a new platform may seem daunting, examples like Brin and Page's Google [21] show that two graduate students can disrupt the commercial landscape and dramatically change the way people work. We challenge the community to similarly revolutionize our conception of what a crowdsourcing platform is and can achieve. Innovation should articulate a vision for crowd work that is effective, efficient, and fair. Beyond mere technology, negotiating the balance of power between interested parties is central to platforms and markets [11,130]. As crowd work already faces challenges related to power inequalities similar to those encountered in offline labor markets, future platforms may shape or be constrained by future regulatory intervention, on, for example, the use of independent contracting for regular, recurring work [45]. Beyond money, platforms might also support labor exchanged for virtual goods or performed in virtual environments, which raises additional policy issues [44]. Privacy is another issue: how can platforms disclose enough information to be trusted as a source of worker quality while also maintaining privacy? Experience with markets such as eBay and Amazon suggests that greater transparency may be helpful, but such mechanisms must be carefully managed to avoid abuse [38].

Security concerns will also continue to grow in importance. For example, recognition of trusted workers may lead to identity theft and fraudulent use of compromised accounts [41]. Security research must consider both new attacks on platforms and use of platforms for launching attacks [144].

The Future of Crowd Workers

Crowd work involves a partnership between requesters and workers. Thus, when designing the future of crowd work, it is important to develop tools to support not only the work itself but also those performing the work. Below we identify and discuss three important research challenges for supporting the crowd workers of the future: job design, reputation and credentials, and motivation and rewards.

Job Design

Motivation/Goals. Some tasks that need to be done are just dull. Motivating workers to accomplish such tasks can be challenging, and may lead to reduced engagement with the system: "It would be better if some of the task assignments weren't so monotonous…I don't see the long-term payoff and it discourages me." While dressing up such tasks as games may reduce boredom, entertainment represents a fairly superficial form of work satisfaction. We believe the future of crowd work depends on creating jobs that achieve both organizational performance and worker satisfaction.

Related Work. In traditional firms, when managers design jobs that provide skill variety, task identity, and task significance, workers find their jobs more meaningful [57]. When workers have autonomy in their jobs and receive feedback, they experience increased responsibility for and understanding of the impact of their work. Combined, these lead to increased performance for the firm and reduced employee problems such as absenteeism and turnover [57].

Unfortunately, many paid crowd work platforms do not provide as much skill variety, task identity, and task significance as volunteer platforms such as Wikipedia. There are direct payoffs when requesters convey the identity and significance of tasks to crowd workers [26,115]. Timely and task-specific feedback from peers and requesters, as well as opportunities for self-assessment, help workers to learn, persevere, and produce better results [42].

Research Proposal. An ideal crowd work system would allow workers to complete a whole and identifiable piece of work in a way that is satisfying and measurable (cf. [62]). The system would explain the significance of the job, offer peer-to-peer and expert feedback, and encourage self-assessment. These systems could offer a variety of ways to complete the task, and thereby not only provide autonomy for the worker, but also reduce errors [55]. Achieving this vision will require communication with workers about the scope and impact of their work, as well as verification that workers understand their impact.

Providing more context has tradeoffs, however. On the one hand, more context enables workers to better judge how the fruits of their effort will be used so they can make informed decisions about whether or not to perform work. On the other hand, reducing context may streamline work, leading to greater efficiencies for both requesters and workers. Moreover, requesters may not always want to fully disclose the context of work due to privacy, security, or intellectual property concerns. This suggests a need to balance distinct and competing concerns: how much information a worker needs before consenting to provide labor, how much information should be shared to motivate and retain workers, how to share context without introducing inefficiency and how much information may be legitimately withheld to protect interests of requesters.

Reputation and Credentials

Motivation/Goals. In traditional firms, reputation and credentials (e.g., letters of reference, certifications, work history) are critical to recruiting, creating lasting rewards and sanctions, and managing work quality. For example, institutions with brand names such as Google and Apple are likely to attract software engineers to apply for jobs, and, in turn, such names on the resumes of software engineers attract other prospective employers. However, many existing crowd work systems have only coarse reputation and credentialing systems. For example, a worker's history on Mechanical Turk primarily measures the percentage of work that has been approved. In contrast, traditional employers judge a prospective employee's education and work history through a variety of instruments, including interviews, transcripts, and references. Likewise, applicants can investigate employers' reputation (and crowd workers in our survey wanted better reputation rankings for employers to be established within the platform [130]).

Related Work. Robust mechanisms for supporting trust, assurance, and accountability can support volunteer-based crowds and collaboration online [28,76]. Likewise, in the context of monetary rewards, reputation can have serious financial consequences [111], motivating people to manipulate systems for their own benefit. For example, workers may build networks of Sybil identities — that is, create pseudonyms [41] — to enhance their reputations and to foil quality control methods. Workers may also boost their ratings by agreeing implicitly or explicitly to recommend each other reciprocally [38]. The design and evaluation of future crowd work reputation systems must address these issues.

Research Proposal. The core challenge with reputation is trading off the benefits of pseudonymous, low transaction cost hiring with the richer but higher transaction cost hiring decisions most firms make today. For example, employers know little about workers on Mechanical Turk, but such workers can be hired and engaged in work nearly instantaneously. Meanwhile, platforms such as oDesk with richer reputation systems incur correspondingly higher transaction costs in hiring workers, involving negotiation and handshakes between workers and employers.

To address this challenge reputation systems will need to be robust to cheating and gaming while preserving the benefits of pseudonymity and supporting low-transaction cost hiring. One possible solution would be to create a web of trust in which requesters and workers validate each other as trustworthy [79]. However, malicious workers and requesters can infiltrate the community and spread their own web of trust. Interfaces may support detection of bad actors: for example, by highlighting topology [121,144], statistical patterns [93] and behavior [120].

The creation of technical tools for sharing information about workers should be coupled with more robust systems for monitoring and reporting requester abuses [131]. Lastly, these initiatives towards enhanced reputation systems should be balanced with the need to preserve privacy, as well as the potential payoffs of anonymous collaboration for both workers and requesters [16].

Motivation and Rewards

Motivation/Goals. Requesters often envision crowd workers as either anonymous individuals who are motivated to complete piecework by small monetary rewards or highly-skilled professionals who work on large, higher-paid tasks without management oversight. However, crowd workers are a diverse and multifaceted population with a range of motives and experiences. Many workers in micro-task environments are ambitious individuals, desiring to be CEOs or top-rate school teachers [48]. Yet few researchers have grappled with the diversity and richness of the motives of the individuals comprising the crowd. One worker reminded us that requesters, as well as workers, need to be motivated:

> *We could definitely use more motivation, we perform task[s] for mere pennies. Mturk should encourage and reward requesters that provide clear instructions, quick payment, and higher pay. Rewarding them would create more worthwhile tasks that we would take more seriously and work hard on. Good, credible HITs are few and far between.*

Related Work. Research in psychology, sociology, management, and marketing provide insights into human motivation that are applicable to crowd work. Management research illustrates the challenge of clearly understanding, communicating, and rewarding desired behavior [70]. Workers seek to understand which activities are rewarded and then tend to do those activities to the virtual exclusion of others. Other studies find mixed results on the effect of financial incentives on the quality of workers' outputs, and underscore the performance and satisfaction benefits of harnessing intrinsic motivations in task design such as non-financial awards and recognition, meaningfulness of tasks, and the feeling of contributing towards the greater good [26,72,86,94,115,127].

Past research suggests requesters should (1) clearly understand and communicate desired behaviors, (2) understand and align worker motivations and incentives with these desired behaviors, and (3) design the requests and incentive structures in order to achieve both effective task completion and worker satisfaction. This also requires requesters to understand variations in crowd workers' motivations (e.g., [7,11,71,116]), for example in competence, enjoyment, connectedness, prosocial orientation, and autonomy [49].

Research Proposal. The future of crowd work requires that requesters and platform designers consider a broad set of motivations, not just financial incentives. We must create frameworks that acknowledge the dynamic nature of motivation and its dependence on context. For example, it is not clear that payment alone will be the optimal motivator for expert crowdsourcing markets. Such frameworks should enable us to move from analysis to design of new motivational schemes. Research should overcome the dichotomous emphases on dehumanizing piece-work and frictionless virtual collaboration in order to provide a more holistic framework within which to understand and build systems that support workers' diverse motivations (e.g., [22,50,52,81,82,107,124]).

NEXT STEPS

Many of the really difficult problems that workers and requesters face will require advances on multiple foci at the same time. Below we describe three design goals demonstrating how the integration of multiple foci can lead to concrete next steps and calls to actions that will create a better environment for crowd workers, and a better set of human resources for requesters.

Create Career Ladders - *[motivation, job design, reputation, hierarchy]*

Crowd work today is largely a dead-end job, offering few opportunities for career advancement and economic mobility. As workers demonstrate aptitude and diligence, it is to the advantage of both requesters and workers to recognize workers' potential to take on new tasks requiring greater knowledge, effectiveness, and responsibility. As all organizations benefit from making the best use of available talent and workers' diverse abilities, more skilled workers should be paid for their expertise, and encouraged to train less skilled workers: for example, MobileWorks promotes workers to management jobs based on performance [79].

As workers demonstrate proficiency, they might be invited to create gold labels for verifying the quality of work from other, less established workers, which could be used to build webs of trusted workers. Proficient, trusted workers could also manage other workers, respond to reported issues, and provide first-pass triage of new task designs (to catch problems or make suggestions before new tasks go live). Crowd workers could eventually become employees themselves, or develop the skills needed to launch their own business using crowd work. For example, a career trajectory might proceed as: 1) entry-level, untrusted worker; 2) trusted worker; 3) hourly contractor; 4) employee. First steps toward building such a ladder include studying worker *motivations* in order to develop better *job designs*; creating lasting and transferable mechanisms for *reputation and credentialing* for workers; and building greater support for *hierarchy* in the form of structured teams that provide training for novices by skilled workers.

Improve Task Design through Better Communication - *[quality assurance, job design, task assignment, realtime crowd work, synchronous collaboration, platform]*

There is a popular myth that the poor quality of some crowd work stems largely from workers being lazy, stupid, or deceitful. In practice, both we and our surveyed workers have observed many cases where poor quality work instead arises from poorly designed crowdsourcing tasks. For example, a requester might assume a task obvious to them should be equally obvious to everyone else. However, even highly-educated workers may have difficulty understanding exactly what the requester actually wants. Task instructions are often incomplete or ambiguous, do not address boundary cases, and do not provide clarifying input-output examples of what is expected. Task interfaces may be poorly designed or even have bugs that make it impossible to complete a task. Gold labels used as trap questions may be far more subjective than requesters realize, leading to mistaken rejection of work.

What might we do to address these problems? Designers can make it easier and faster for requesters to create effective tasks. For example, platforms might provide task templates showing examples of proven task designs [27] to encourage shared mental models and improve *quality assurance*. Platforms could also help educate requesters about the impact of *job design* and *task assignment* on resulting quality, best practices, and common errors to be avoided. Platforms might even offer a "first pass" service in which a set of trusted workers (known to the platform) test out the task and report any issues encountered.

Platforms might also provide a wider array of communication channels between requesters and workers supporting *synchronous collaboration* and *real-time crowd work*. Workers we surveyed were adamant that the perception of poor crowd work quality was due, at least in part, to unclear instructions and insufficient feedback, and that they need more guidance to better understand what is expected. They suggested instant chat with requesters to clarify jobs, though we note this would require the continual presence of requesters while work is being performed. They also requested feedback during or just after a task. Both would be consistent with the practices of good managers and workers in other labor contexts, and so more experimenting with channels of communication could potentially have a large effect on both worker satisfaction and job quality. As a first step, requesters might provide ways for workers to clarify tasks in real time – with the requester, or with a more experienced worker. And, when work is in progress, they might provide informal feedback through these same channels.

Facilitate Learning - *[quality assurance, AIs guiding crowds, crowds guiding AIs, task assignment, reputation and credentials, platform]*

Crowd work naturally involves learning and assessment. Workers may need to acquire new skills to perform unfamiliar tasks, before or in the midst of performing the actual work. Workers may also polish and refine existing skills while completing more familiar tasks. Requesters must continually engage in *quality assurance*. Such a training-assessment cycle of work offers potentially exciting synergies with online, education by-doing. For example, DuoLingo (duolingo.com) explores this direction for foreign language learning. This idea can be generalized much further; for example, content generation tasks could be designed to better assess and enhance writing skills. A self-sustaining cycle might involve *AIs guiding crowds* on which tasks to complete (*task assignment*) depending on the worker's and requester's skill development and quality assurance goals, and then using the crowd-generated data to automate some of the simpler tasks (*crowds guiding AIs*).

The potential of crowd work-based education is enormous and multi-faceted, benefiting all parties by producing more skilled and employable workers. Online tutoring systems, perhaps augmented with human tutoring, could provide a path toward delivering more scalable education to the public at large [6,146]. Moreover, tracking and mining of work history could support personalized instruction and feedback, as well as recommending new tasks and learning modules. As workers master new skills and are assessed, badges or *credentials* could document this proficiency so that others can recognize and utilize this enhanced skill set. *Platforms* themselves can also be an important element of learning: data from crowd work can reveal what kinds of requests attract talented workers, patterns of learning and skill building among workers over time, the valuation and interaction between extrinsic and intrinsic rewards, and which types of tasks are most appropriate for which types of workers.

CONCLUSION

Crowd work may take place in the scale of minutes, but the impact of crowd work may be felt for generations. We have asked: what will it take for us, the stakeholders in crowd work – including requesters, workers, researchers – to feel proud of our own children when they enter such a work force? Answering this question has led to a discussion of crowd work from a longer-term perspective.

Specifically, we have synthesized a framework for the future of crowd work based on theory from organizational behavior and distributed computing, and informed by the concerns of crowd work stakeholders. Our hope is that this framework and the corresponding research challenges will spur discussion, experiment, and further insight. In sum, we envision a future where many cognitively complex, large-scale tasks can be decomposed into workflows and executed by crowds consisting of novices, experts and algorithms, and that the crowd work environment can be designed in such a way that satisfies the needs of both workers and requesters. After identifying the twelve major research foci that constitute the framework, we probed their current state, identified gaps, and created a call for action demonstrating ways they can be profitably integrated.

Calls for action must be made responsibly. Crowd work marketplaces are complex socio-technical systems, composed of many people and a changing technical infrastructure, with emergent organizational forms, new incentives being offered, and shifting labor pools. As a result of this complexity, there is the possibility of unpredictable side effects. For example, innovations that effectively train workers through micro-tasks may have ramifications for the world's educational institutions, and thereby for society as a whole. Hybrid combinations of workers and artificial intelligence that seek to build collective intelligence may instead lead to mechanized workers or human-imitating machines.

Our call for action, then, calls for both exciting innovation and also close observation of its effects. In crowd work, we have two important affordances: an ability to constitute new forms of organization in short amounts of time, and an ability to situate these organizations in an experimental context. While organization science has been built slowly based on observation, the proliferation of crowd work makes large-scale organizational experiments comparing distinct management strategies and task designs possible. These comparisons will help us understand how to improve crowd platforms, workers' skills, and requesters' assignments. Perhaps instead of a hadron collider, the field of crowd work needs a "social collider" in which different forms of organization can be tested. The goal should be better systems, better requests, better work, and better experience. We hope the community's observational, experimental, design and technical skills will play a vital role in shaping the future of crowd work and the next generation of workers.

ACKNOWLEDGEMENTS

We thank all the participants in the CHI 2012 CrowdCamp Workshop for their suggestions, and in particular Paul Andre who spearheaded the effort. We are pleased to acknowledge the crowd workers of the present: for their opinions and creative suggestions in response to our queries, and, more generally, for their pioneering spirit. Finally, we acknowledge Ashima, the nascent inspiration for this paper.

This work was supported under National Science Foundation awards IIS-0968561, IIS-0855995, OCI-0943148, IIS-0968484, IIS-1111124, IIS-1149797, IIS-1217096, and IIS-1217559. This work was also supported by a DARPA Young Faculty Award N66001-12-1-4256, a Temple Fellowship, Northwestern University, and the Center for the Future of Work, Heinz College, Carnegie Mellon University.

Any opinions, findings, and conclusions or recommendations expressed in this publication are those of the authors and do not necessarily reflect the views of the funding agencies.

REFERENCES

1. Ahmad, S., Battle, A., Malkani, Z., and Kamvar, S. The jabberwocky programming environment for structured social computing. *Proc. UIST '11*, (2011).
2. Von Ahn, L. and Dabbish, L. Labeling images with a computer game. *Proceedings of the SIGCHI conference on Human factors in computing systems*, ACM (2004), 319–326.
3. Ahn, L.V., Blum, M., Hopper, N.J., and Langford, J. CAPTCHA: Using hard AI problems for security. *Proceedings of the 22nd international conference on Theory and applications of cryptographic techniques*, (2003), 294–311.
4. Albrecht, J. The 2011 Nobel Memorial Prize in Search Theory. *Department of Economics,*

Georgetown University.[http://www9. georgetown. edu/faculty/albrecht/SJE Survey. pdf], (2011).
5. Anagnostopoulos, A., Becchetti, L., Castillo, C., Gionis, A., and Leonardi, S. Online team formation in social networks. *Proceedings of the 21st international conference on World Wide Web*, ACM (2012), 839–848.
6. Anderson, M. Crowdsourcing Higher Education: A Design Proposal for Distributed Learning. *MERLOT Journal of Online Learning and Teaching 7*, 4 (2011), 576–590.
7. Antin, J. and Shaw, A. Social desirability bias and self-reports of motivation: a study of amazon mechanical turk in the US and India. *Proc. CHI '12*, (2012).
8. Archak, N. and Sundararajan, A. Optimal Design of Crowdsourcing Contests. *ICIS 2009 Proceedings*, (2009), 200.
9. Bal, H.E., Steiner, J.G., and Tanenbaum, A.S. Programming languages for distributed computing systems. *ACM Computing Surveys (CSUR) 21*, 3 (1989), 261–322.
10. Becker, G.S. and Murphy, K.M. The division of labor, coordination costs, and knowledge. *The Quarterly Journal of Economics 107*, 4 (1992), 1137–1160.
11. Bederson, B.B. and Quinn, A.J. Web workers unite! addressing challenges of online laborers. *Extended Abstracts CHI '11*, (2011).
12. Benkler, Y. *The wealth of networks: How social production transforms markets and freedom*. Yale Univ Pr, 2006.
13. Bernstein, M.S., Brandt, J., Miller, R.C., and Karger, D.R. Crowds in two seconds: Enabling realtime crowd-powered interfaces. *Proc. UIST '11*, (2011).
14. Bernstein, M.S., Karger, D.R., Miller, R.C., and Brandt, J. Analytic Methods for Optimizing Realtime Crowdsourcing. *Proc. Collective Intelligence 2012*, (2012).
15. Bernstein, M.S., Little, G., Miller, R.C., et al. Soylent: A Word Processor with a Crowd Inside. *Proc. UIST '10*, (2010).
16. Bernstein, M.S., Monroy-Hernández, A., Harry, D., André, P., Panovich, K., and Vargas, G. 4chan and /b/: An Analysis of Anonymity and Ephemerality in a Large Online Community. *Fifth International AAAI Conference on Weblogs and Social Media*, AAAI Publications (2011).
17. Bigham, J.P., Jayant, C., Ji, H., et al. VizWiz: Nearly Real-time Answers to Visual Questions. *Proc. UIST '10*, (2010).
18. Boud, D., Cohen, R., and Sampson, J. Peer learning and assessment. *Assessment & Evaluation in Higher Education 24*, 4 (1999), 413–426.
19. Boudreau, K.J., Lacetera, N., and Lakhani, K.R. Incentives and problem uncertainty in innovation contests: An empirical analysis. *Management Science 57*, 5 (2011), 843.
20. Brabham, D.C. Moving the crowd at iStockphoto: The composition of the crowd and motivations for participation in a crowdsourcing application. *First Monday 13*, 6 (2008), 1–22.
21. Brin, S. and Page, L. The anatomy of a large-scale hypertextual Web search engine. *Computer networks and ISDN systems 30*, 1-7 (1998), 107–117.
22. Bryant, S.L., Forte, A., and Bruckman, A. Becoming Wikipedian: transformation of participation in a collaborative online encyclopedia. *GROUP '05*, ACM Press (2005), 1–10.
23. Callison-Burch, C. and Dredze, M. Creating speech and language data with Amazon's Mechanical Turk. *Proceedings of the NAACL HLT 2010 Workshop on Creating Speech and Language Data with Amazon's Mechanical Turk*, Association for Computational Linguistics (2010), 1–12.
24. Callison-Burch, C. Fast, cheap, and creative: evaluating translation quality using Amazon's Mechanical Turk. *Proceedings of the 2009 Conference on Empirical Methods in Natural Language Processing: Volume 1-Volume 1*, (2009), 286–295.
25. Casavant, T.L., Braun, T.A., Kaliannan, S., Scheetz, T.E., Munn, K.J., and Birkett, C.L. A parallel/distributed architecture for hierarchically heterogeneous web-based cooperative applications. *Future Generation Computer Systems 17*, 6 (2001), 783–793.
26. Chandler, D. and Kapelner, A. Breaking monotony with meaning: Motivation in crowdsourcing markets. *University of Chicago mimeo*, (2010).
27. Chen, J.J., Menezes, N.J., and Bradley, A.D. Opportunities for Crowdsourcing Research on Amazon Mechanical Turk. *Interfaces 5*, (2011), 3.
28. Cheshire, C. Online Trust, Trustworthiness, or Assurance? *Daedalus 140*, 4 (2011), 49–58.
29. Chilton, L., Horton, J., Miller, R.C., and Azenkot, S. Task search in a human computation market. *Proc. HCOMP '10*, (2010).
30. Coase, R.H. The Nature of the Firm. *Economica 4*, 16 (1937), 386–405.
31. Cooper, S., Khatib, F., Treuille, A., et al. Predicting protein structures with a multiplayer online game. *Nature 466*, 7307 (2010), 756–760.
32. Dai, P., Mausam, and Weld, D. Decision-theoretic control of crowd-sourced workflows. *Proc. AAAI '10*, (2010).
33. Dai, P., Mausam, and Weld, D.S. Artificial intelligence for artificial artificial intelligence. *Twenty-Fifth AAAI Conference on Artificial Intelligence*, (2011).
34. Dean, J. and Ghemawat, S. MapReduce: Simplified Data Processing on Large Clusters. *To appear in OSDI*, (2004), 1.
35. Debeauvais, T., Nardi, B.A., Lopes, C.V., Yee, N.,

and Ducheneaut, N. 10,000 Gold for 20 Dollars: An exploratory study of World of Warcraft gold buyers. *Proceedings of the International Conference on the Foundations of Digital Games*, (2012), 105–112.
36. Dekel, O. and Shamir, O. Vox populi: Collecting high-quality labels from a crowd. *Proc. 22nd Annual Conference on Learning Theory*, (2009).
37. Della Penn, N. and Reid, M.D. Crowd & Prejudice: An Impossibility Theorem for Crowd Labelling without a Gold Standard. *Collective Intelligence*, (2012).
38. Dellarocas, C. Analyzing the economic efficiency of eBay-like online reputation reporting mechanisms. *Proceedings of the 3rd ACM Conference on Electronic Commerce*, (2001), 171–179.
39. Van Der Aalst, W.M.P., Ter Hofstede, A.H.M., Kiepuszewski, B., and Barros, A.P. Workflow patterns. *Distributed and parallel databases 14*, 1 (2003), 5–51.
40. Doctorow, C. *For the Win*. Voyager, 2010.
41. Douceur, J. The sybil attack. *Peer-to-peer Systems*, (2002), 251–260.
42. Dow, S., Kulkarni, A., Klemmer, S., and Hartmann, B. Shepherding the crowd yields better work. *Proc. CSCW '12*, (2012).
43. Downs, J.S., Holbrook, M.B., Sheng, S., and Cranor, L.F. Are your participants gaming the system?: screening mechanical turk workers. *Proceedings of the 28th international conference on Human factors in computing systems*, (2010), 2399–2402.
44. Felstiner, A. Sweatshop or Paper Route?: Child Labor Laws and In-Game Work. *Proceedings of CrowdConf*, (2010).
45. Felstiner, A. Working the Crowd: Employment and Labor Law in the Crowdsourcing Industry. *Berkeley J. Emp. & Lab. L. 32*, (2011), 143–143.
46. Franklin, M., Kossmann, D., Kraska, T., Ramesh, S., and Xin, R. CrowdDB: answering queries with crowdsourcing. *Proc. SIGMOD '11*, (2011).
47. Gal, Y., Yamangil, E., Shieber, S., Rubin, A., and Grosz, B. Towards collaborative intelligent tutors: Automated recognition of users' strategies. *Intelligent Tutoring Systems*, (2008), 162–172.
48. Gerber, E. and Dontcheva, M. *Career Aspirations for Crowdworkers*. In preparation.
49. Gerber, E., Hui, J., and Kuo, P. *Crowdfunding: Why creators and supporters participate*. Segal Design Institute, Evanston, IL, 2012.
50. Ghosh, R. and Glott, R. *Free/Libre and Open Source Software: Survey and Study*. European Commission, 2002.
51. Gingold, Y., Shamir, A., and Cohen-Or, D. Micro Perceptual Human Computation. *To appear in ACM Transactions on Graphics (TOG)*, (2012).
52. Glott, R., Ghosh, R., and Schmidt, P. *Wikipedia Survey*. UNU-MERIT, Maastricht, Netherlands, 2010.
53. Greenberg, S. and Bohnet, R. GroupSketch: A multi-user sketchpad for geographically-distributed small groups. *Proc. Graphics Interface'91*, (1991).
54. Grier, D.A. *When Computers Were Human*. Princeton University Press, 2005.
55. Grier, D.A. Error Identification and Correction in Human Computation: Lessons from the WPA. *Proc. HCOMP '11*, (2011).
56. Gupta, A., Thies, W., Cutrell, E., and Balakrishnan, R. mClerk: Enabling Mobile Crowdsourcing in Developing Regions. *Proc. CHI '12*, (2012).
57. Hackman, J.R. and Oldham, G.R. Motivation through the design of work: Test of a theory. *Organizational behavior and human performance 16*, 2 (1976), 250–279.
58. Heimerl, K., Gawalt, B., Chen, K., Parikh, T.S., and Hartmann, B. Communitysourcing: Engaging Local Crowds to Perform Expert Work Via Physical Kiosks. *Proc. CHI '12*, (2012).
59. Hellerstein, J.M. and Tennenhouse, D.L. Searching for Jim Gray: a technical overview. *Communcations of the ACM 54*, 7 (2011), 77–87.
60. Hinds, P. *Distributed work*. The MIT Press, 2002.
61. Von Hippel, E. Task partitioning: An innovation process variable. *Research policy 19*, 5 (1990), 407–418.
62. Holmstrom, B. and Milgrom, P. Multitask principal-agent analyses: Incentive contracts, asset ownership, and job design. *JL Econ. & Org. 7*, (1991), 24.
63. Horton, J.J. and Chilton, L.B. The labor economics of paid crowdsourcing. *Proceedings of the 11th ACM conference on Electronic commerce*, (2010), 209–218.
64. Ipeirotis, P.G., Provost, F., and Wang, J. Quality management on amazon mechanical turk. *Proc. HCOMP '10*, (2010).
65. Ipeirotis, P.G. *Mechanical Turk, Low Wages, and the Market for Lemons*. http://www.behind-the-enemy-lines.com/2010/07/mechanical-turk-low-wages-and-market.html, 2010.
66. Ishii, H. and Kobayashi, M. ClearBoard: a seamless medium for shared drawing and conversation with eye contact. *Proc. CHI '92*, (1992), 525–532.
67. Kamar, E., Hacker, S., and Horvitz, E. Combining Human and Machine Intelligence in Large-scale Crowdsourcing. *Proc. AAMAS '12*, (2012).
68. Kearns, M., Suri, S., and Montfort, N. An experimental study of the coloring problem on human subject networks. *Science 313*, 5788 (2006), 824–827.
69. Kensing, F. and Blomberg, J. Participatory Design: Issues and Concerns. *Computer Supported Cooperative Work (CSCW) 7*, 3 (1998), 167–185.
70. Kerr, S. On the folly of rewarding A, while hoping for B. *Academy of Management Journal*, (1975), 769–783.
71. Khanna, S., Ratan, A., Davis, J., and Thies, W.

Evaluating and improving the usability of Mechanical Turk for low-income workers in India. *Proc. ACM Symposium on Computing for Development '10*, (2010).
72. Kittur, A., Chi, E.H., and Suh, B. Crowdsourcing user studies with Mechanical Turk. *Proceedings of the twenty-sixth annual SIGCHI conference on Human factors in computing systems*, (2008), 453–456.
73. Kittur, A., Khamkar, S., André, P., and Kraut, R.E. CrowdWeaver: visually managing complex crowd work. *Proc. CSCW '12*, (2012).
74. Kittur, A., Lee, B., and Kraut, R.E. Coordination in collective intelligence: the role of team structure and task interdependence. *Proceedings of the 27th international conference on Human factors in computing systems*, (2009), 1495–1504.
75. Kittur, A., Smus, B., Khamkar, S., and Kraut, R.E. Crowdforge: Crowdsourcing complex work. *Proceedings of the 24th annual ACM symposium on User interface software and technology*, (2011), 43–52.
76. Kittur, A., Suh, B., and Chi, E.H. Can you ever trust a wiki?: impacting perceived trustworthiness in wikipedia. *Proceedings of the 2008 ACM conference on Computer supported cooperative work*, (2008), 477–480.
77. Kittur, A. Crowdsourcing, collaboration and creativity. *XRDS 17*, 2 (2010), 22–26.
78. Kochhar, S., Mazzocchi, S., and Paritosh, P. The anatomy of a large-scale human computation engine. *Proceedings of the ACM SIGKDD Workshop on Human Computation*, (2010), 10–17.
79. Kulkarni, A., Gutheim, P., Narula, P., Rolnitzky, D., Parikh, T.S., and Hartmann, B. MobileWorks: Designing for Quality in a Managed Crowdsourcing Architecture. *IEEE Internet Computing To appear*, 2012.
80. Kulkarni, A.P., Can, M., and Hartmann, B. Turkomatic: automatic recursive task and workflow design for mechanical turk. *Proceedings of the 2011 annual conference extended abstracts on Human factors in computing systems*, (2011), 2053–2058.
81. Kuznetsov, S. Motivations of contributors to Wikipedia. *SIGCAS Comput. Soc. 36*, 2 (2006), 1.
82. Lakhani, K. and Wolf, B. Why hackers do what they do: Understanding motivation and effort in free/open source software projects. In J. Feller, B. Fitzgerald, S.A. Hissam and K.R. Lakhani, eds., *Perspectives on Free and Open Source Software*. MIT Press, 2005, 3–22.
83. Lasecki, W.S., Murray, K.I., White, S., Miller, R.C., and Bigham, J.P. Real-time crowd control of existing interfaces. *Proc. UIST '11*, ACM Press (2011).
84. Lasecki, W.S., White, S.C., Murray, K.I., and Bigham, J.P. Crowd memory: Learning in the collective. *Proc. Collective Intelligence 2012*, (2012).
85. Le, J., Edmonds, A., Hester, V., and Biewald, L. Ensuring quality in crowdsourced search relevance evaluation: The effects of training question distribution. *Proc. SIGIR 2010 Workshop on Crowdsourcing for Search Evaluation*, (2010), 21–26.
86. Lewis, S., Dontcheva, M., and Gerber, E. Affective computational priming and creativity. *Proceedings of the 2011 annual conference on Human factors in computing systems*, (2011), 735–744.
87. Little, G., Chilton, L.B., Goldman, M., and Miller, R.C. Turkit: human computation algorithms on mechanical turk. *Proceedings of the 23nd annual ACM symposium on User interface software and technology*, (2010), 57–66.
88. Littler, C.R. Understanding Taylorism. *British Journal of Sociology*, (1978), 185–202.
89. Malone, T.W. and Crowston, K. The interdisciplinary study of coordination. *ACM Computing Surveys (CSUR) 26*, 1 (1994), 87–119.
90. Malone, T.W., Yates, J., and Benjamin, R.I. Electronic markets and electronic hierarchies. *Communications of the ACM 30*, 6 (1987), 484–497.
91. Mao, A., Parkes, D.C., Procaccia, A.D., and Zhang, H. Human Computation and Multiagent Systems: An Algorithmic Perspective. *Proc. AAAI '11*, (2011).
92. March, J.G. and Simon, H.A. Organizations. (1958).
93. Marcus, A., Karger, D.R., Madden, S., Miller, R.C., and Oh, S. Counting with the Crowd. *In Submission to VLDB*, (2012).
94. Mason, W. and Watts, D.J. Financial Incentives and the "Performance of Crowds". *Proc. HCOMP '09*, ACM Press (2009).
95. McGraw, I., Lee, C., Hetherington, L., Seneff, S., and Glass, J.R. Collecting voices from the cloud. *Proc. LREC*, (2010).
96. Milner, R. *Communicating and mobile systems: the [symbol for pi]-calculus*. Cambridge Univ Pr, 1999.
97. Mintzberg, H. An emerging strategy of" direct" research. *Administrative science quarterly 24*, 4 (1979), 582–589.
98. Moran, T.P. and Anderson, R.J. The workaday world as a paradigm for CSCW design. *Proceedings of the 1990 ACM Conference on Computer-supported Cooperative Work*, (1990), 381–393.
99. Nalimov, E.V., Wirth, C., Haworth, G.M.C., and Others. KQQKQQ and the Kasparov-World Game. *ICGA Journal 22*, 4 (1999), 195–212.
100. Narula, P., Gutheim1, P., Rolnitzky, D., Kulkarni, A., and Hartmann, B. MobileWorks: A Mobile Crowdsourcing Platform for Workers at the Bottom of the Pyramid. *Proc. HCOMP '11*, (2011).
101. Nickerson, J.V. and Monroy-Hernandez, A. Appropriation and creativity: User-Initiated contests in scratch. *System Sciences (HICSS), 2011 44th Hawaii International Conference on*, (2011), 1–10.
102. Norman, D.A. and Draper, S.W. *User centered*

system design; new perspectives on human-computer interaction. L. Erlbaum Associates Inc., 1986.
103. Noronha, J., Hysen, E., Zhang, H., and Gajos, K.Z. Platemate: crowdsourcing nutritional analysis from food photographs. *Proc. UIST '11*, (2011).
104. Preece, J. and Shneiderman, B. The Reader-to-Leader Framework: Motivating Technology-Mediated Social Participation. *AIS Transactions on Human-Computer Interaction 1*, 1 (2009), 13–32.
105. Quinn, A.J. and Bederson, B.B. Human computation: a survey and taxonomy of a growing field. *Proc. CHI '11*, (2011).
106. Raddick, J., Lintott, C., Bamford, S., et al. Galaxy Zoo: Motivations of Citizen Scientists. *Bulletin of the American Astronomical Society*, (2008), 240.
107. Rafaeli, S. and Ariel, Y. Online Motivational Factors: Incentives for Participation and Contribution in Wikipedia. In A. Barak, ed., *Psychological Aspects of Cyberspace*. Cambridge University Press, New York, NY, 2008.
108. Raymond, E. The cathedral and the bazaar. *Knowledge, Technology & Policy 12*, 3 (1999), 23–49.
109. Redmiles, D. and Nakakoji, K. Supporting reflective practitioners. *Software Engineering, 2004. ICSE 2004. Proceedings. 26th International Conference on*, (2004), 688–690.
110. Reijers, H., Jansen-Vullers, M., Zur Muehlen, M., and Appl, W. Workflow management systems+ swarm intelligence= dynamic task assignment for emergency management applications. *Business Process Management*, (2007), 125–140.
111. Resnick, P. and Zeckhauser, R. Trust among strangers in Internet transactions: Empirical analysis of eBay's reputation system. *Advances in Applied Microeconomics 11*, (2002), 127–157.
112. Rittel, H.W.J. and Webber, M.M. Dilemmas in a general theory of planning. *Policy sciences 4*, 2 (1973), 155–169.
113. Ritter, S., Anderson, J.R., Koedinger, K.R., and Corbett, A. Cognitive Tutor: Applied research in mathematics education. *Psychonomic bulletin & review 14*, 2 (2007), 249–255.
114. Rogers, Y. Exploring obstacles: integrating CSCW in evolving organisations. *Proceedings of the 1994 ACM conference on Computer supported cooperative work*, (1994), 67–77.
115. Rogstadius, J., Kostakos, V., Kittur, A., Smus, B., Laredo, J., and Vukovic, M. An Assessment of Intrinsic and Extrinsic Motivation on Task Performance in Crowdsourcing Markets. *Proceedings of the Fifth International AAAI Conference on Weblogs and Social Media: Barcelona, Spain*, (2011).
116. Ross, J., Irani, L., Silberman, M.S., Zaldivar, A., and Tomlinson, B. Who Are the Crowdworkers? Shifting Demographics in Amazon Mechanical Turk. *alt.chi '10*, ACM Press (2010).
117. Roth, A.E. The economist as engineer: Game theory, experimentation, and computation as tools for design economics. *Econometrica 70*, 4 (2002), 1341–1378.
118. Roy, D.F. Work satisfaction and social reward in quota achievement: An analysis of piecework incentive. *American Sociological Review 18*, 5 (1953), 507–514.
119. Rzeszotarski, J. and Kittur, A. CrowdScape: interactively visualizing user behavior and output. *Proceedings of the 25th annual ACM symposium on User interface software and technology*, (2012), 55–62.
120. Rzeszotarski, J.M. and Kittur, A. Instrumenting the crowd: using implicit behavioral measures to predict task performance. *Proc. UIST '11*, (2011).
121. Sadlon, E., Barrett, S., Sakamoto, Y., and Nickerson, J.V. The Karma of Digg: Reciprocity in Online Social Networks. Paris, December 2008. *Proceedings of the 18th Annual Workshop on Information Technologies and Systems (WITS)*, (2008).
122. Savage, N. Gaining wisdom from crowds. *Communications of the ACM 55*, 3 (2012), 13–15.
123. Schmidt, K. and Bannon, L. Taking CSCW seriously. *Computer Supported Cooperative Work (CSCW) 1*, 1 (1992), 7–40.
124. Schroer, J. and Hertel, G. Voluntary Engagement in an Open Web-Based Encyclopedia: Wikipedians and Why They Do It. *Media Psychology 12*, 1 (2009), 96.
125. Shahaf, D. and Horvitz, E. Generalized task markets for human and machine computation. (2010).
126. Shamir, B. and Salomon, I. Work-at-Home and the Quality of Working Life. *The Academy of Management Review 10*, 3 (1985), 455–464.
127. Shaw, A.D., Horton, J.J., and Chen, D.L. Designing incentives for inexpert human raters. *Proceedings of the ACM 2011 conference on Computer supported cooperative work*, (2011), 275–284.
128. Shen, M., Tzeng, G.H., and Liu, D.R. Multi-criteria task assignment in workflow management systems. *System Sciences, 2003. Proceedings of the 36th Annual Hawaii International Conference on Social Sciences*, (2003).
129. Sheng, V.S., Provost, F., and Ipeirotis, P.G. Get another label? improving data quality and data mining using multiple, noisy labelers. *Proc. KDD '08*, ACM (2008), 614——622.
130. Silberman, M.S., Irani, L., and Ross, J. Ethics and tactics of professional crowdwork. *XRDS 17*, 2 (2010), 39–43.
131. Silberman, M.S., Ross, J., Irani, L., and Tomlinson, B. Sellers' problems in human computation markets. *Proc. HCOMP '10*, (2010).
132. Skillicorn, D.B. and Talia, D. Models and languages for parallel computation. *ACM Computing Surveys (CSUR) 30*, 2 (1998), 123–169.

133. Smith, A. The Wealth of Nations (1776). *New York: Modern Library*, (1937), 740.
134. Snow, R., O'Connor, B., Jurafsky, D., and Ng, A.Y. Cheap and fast—but is it good?: evaluating non-expert annotations for natural language tasks. *Proc. ACL '08*, (2008).
135. Sorokin, A. and Forsyth, D. Utility data annotation with Amazon Mechanical Turk. *Proc. CVPR '08*, (2008).
136. Sterling, B. *A good old-fashioned future: stories*. Spectra, 1999.
137. Sterling, B. *Shaping things*. 2005.
138. Stohr, E.A. and Zhao, J.L. Workflow automation: Overview and research issues. *Information Systems Frontiers 3*, 3 (2001), 281–296.
139. Surowiecki, J. *The Wisdom of Crowds*. Random House, New York, 2005.
140. Tang, J.C., Cebrian, M., Giacobe, N.A., Kim, H.-W., Kim, T., and Wickert, D. "Beaker". Reflecting on the DARPA Red Balloon Challenge. *Communications of the ACM 54*, 4 (2011), 78.
141. Taylor, F.W. *The principles of scientific management*. Harper & Brothers, New York, 1911.
142. Trist, E.L. *The evolution of socio-technical systems: A conceptual framework and an action research program*. Ontario Quality of Working Life Center.
143. Van de Ven, A.H., Delbecq, A.L., and Koenig Jr, R. Determinants of coordination modes within organizations. *American sociological review*, (1976), 322–338.
144. Viswanath, B., Mondal, M., Clement, A., et al. Exploring the design space of social network-based Sybil defenses. *Proceedings of the 4th International Conference on Communication Systems and Network (COMSNETS'12)*, (2012).
145. Wang, G., Wilson, C., Zhao, X., et al. Serf and Turf: Crowdturfing for Fun and Profit. *Arxiv preprint arXiv:1111.5654*, (2011).
146. Weld, D.S., Adar, E., Chilton, L., Hoffmann, R., and Horvitz, E. Personalized Online Education—A Crowdsourcing Challenge. *Workshops at the Twenty-Sixth AAAI Conference on Artificial Intelligence*, (2012).
147. Welinder, P., Branson, S., Belongie, S., and Perona, P. The multidimensional wisdom of crowds. *Neural Information Processing Systems 6*, 7 (2010), 1—9.
148. Williamson, O.E. The economics of organization: The transaction cost approach. *American journal of sociology 87*, 3 (1981), 548–577.
149. Woolley, A.W., Chabris, C.F., Pentland, A., Hashmi, N., and Malone, T.W. Evidence for a collective intelligence factor in the performance of human groups. *science 330*, 6004 (2010), 686–688.
150. Yu, H., Estrin, D., and Govindan, R. A hierarchical proxy architecture for Internet-scale event services. *Enabling Technologies: Infrastructure for Collaborative Enterprises, 1999.(WET ICE'99) Proceedings. IEEE 8th International Workshops on*, (1999), 78–83.
151. Yu, J. and Buyya, R. A taxonomy of scientific workflow systems for grid computing. *ACM Sigmod Record 34*, 3 (2005), 44–49.
152. Yu, L. and Nickerson, J.V. Cooks or cobblers?: crowd creativity through combination. *Proceedings of the 2011 annual conference on Human factors in computing systems*, (2011), 1393–1402.
153. Yu, L. and Nickerson, J.V. An Intenet-Scale Idea Generation System. *ACM Transactions on interactive Intelligent Systems 3*, 1 (2013).
154. Zhang, H., Law, E., Miller, R.C., Gajos, K.Z., Parkes, D.C., and Horvitz, E. Human Computation Tasks with Global Constraints. *Proc. CHI '12*, (2012).
155. Zhao, L., Sukthankar, G., and Sukthankar, R. Robust Active Learning Using Crowdsourced Annotations for Activity Recognition. *Workshops at the Twenty-Fifth AAAI Conference on Artificial Intelligence*, (2011).
156. Zhu, H., Kraut, R.E., Wang, Y.-C., and Kittur, A. Identifying shared leadership in Wikipedia. *Proceedings of the 2011 annual conference on Human factors in computing systems*, ACM (2011), 3431–3434.
157. Zittrain, J. Ubiquitous human computing. *Philosophical Transactions of the Royal Society A 366*, (2008), 3813–3821.
158. Zittrain, J. Human Computing's Oppenheimer Question. *Proceedings of Collective Intelligence*, (2012).

Going Digital: Understanding Paper and Photo Documentation Practices in Early Childhood Education

Anne Marie Piper[1,2], Sarah D'Angelo[2], James D. Hollan[2]

[1]Northwestern University
2240 Campus Dr., Evanston, IL 60208, USA
ampiper@northwestern.edu

[2]University of California, San Diego
9500 Gilman Dr., La Jolla, CA, USA
{sdangelo, hollan}@ucsd.edu

ABSTRACT

Documentation of development is a critical aspect of the work of early childhood education teachers. Through field observations and interviews, we detail the process and tools used in documenting development for children age three months to five-years-old at one school. Teachers use paper forms and printed photos to record and analyze observations of development. The evolving final product is a paper portfolio of development. This practice relies heavily on the teacher's ability to objectively observe children *in situ*, create a record of the activity, and make salient the link between evidence and developmental milestones. We describe current paper and photo documentation practices in light of an online record keeping system that will be introduced at this school within the next year. The present analysis contributes to a growing literature on the role of paper and digital media in documentation.

Author Keywords

Documentation; Education; Paper; Photos; Preschool

ACM Classification Keywords

H.5.3 Information Interfaces and Presentation (e.g. HCI): Group and Organization Interfaces

INTRODUCTION

Much research within CSCW focuses on the transition from paper-based work practices to integration with a digital system. Organizations are often hopeful about the idea of going paperless, yet there are many unexpected consequences of this change, and paper rarely disappears entirely from the task [31, 11]. There are changes in how information is represented, stored, and disseminated. Metadata for paper (e.g., penmanship, margin notes) is different from metadata for digital documents (e.g., timestamps, file types). New policies may be required for who accesses digital information, when others may make changes, and how these changes propagate throughout the broader system [4].

One context in which extensive paper-based documentation occurs is early childhood education. The present research takes place at one early childhood education center affiliated with our university. We focus on the practice of completing the California Desired Results Developmental Profile (DRDP) for each child, a paper-based portfolio of development. Teachers and administrators at this school are enthusiastic about "going digital" with DRDPtech, a new web-based system for teachers and administrators to enter developmental ratings for children. The web interface replicates the paper-based DRDP rating forms teachers currently complete. All information fields, measures, and rating scales are the same as on paper. Administrators and teachers see many possible benefits from moving to a web-based system.

> *"DRDPtech...will be online and it should be pretty cool because we should be able to transfer the information from one classroom to another when the child moves up... Hopefully it will lessen a lot of this paper work... Eventually all the data that they put into the computer will automatically prepare these [overview sheets]." –School Administrator*

Teachers and administrators are enthusiastic about DRDPtech because it promises easy aggregation of data across children and over time. The system generates graphs to illustrate developmental trajectories and may help pinpoint areas for improvement. This optimistic view of the system highlights potential advantages but neglects the details of how teachers accomplish documentation work. We combine 10 months of classroom observations with detailed interview data to understand current documentation practices and potential challenges of this transition. Sellen and Harper [31] explain:

> It is only by looking carefully at people's interactions with paper artifacts, and with the digital technologies they have to hand, that we can hope to predict the circumstances under which they might be willing to give up paper.

Our analysis highlights the importance of both paper and digital media in documentation of early childhood development. Currently, observations of development are recorded on paper in a variety of ways, and throughout the documentation process observations are intertwined with photo data. A critical piece of this practice relies on the use of photos as an anchor for the teacher's memory of an episode as well as a way to more objectively represent the child's progress. Photos, often printed on paper, are pervasive throughout the documentation process and serve as a critical cognitive resource for teachers. Interestingly, DRDPtech does not support uploading or linking of digital photos or scanned documents.

We analyze current documentation practices in light of the online system that will be in place over the next year. While we discuss the opportunities and challenges for one specific context, our analysis contributes to the broader literature on transitioning from paper to digital records and highlights the needs and constraints of various actors in this context.

RELATED WORK

Much work examines how individuals and organizations keep records of activity, access and share this information, and transform it over time. Records serve as coordination mechanisms [29] and allow decisions and commitments made during the work to persist in time [7]. Goody [7] also notes that written artifacts can be brought into interaction to clarify ambiguities and settle disputes. Suchman [34] observes that standard procedures help workers understand what things should be part of the record, and not necessarily how or in what order they should arrive there. That is, people may go back and construct orderly records to demonstrate compliance with standard procedures in place.

Paper-based documentation practices are of particular relevance to the present research. In their seminal work, Sellen and Harper [31] detail the many affordances of paper including how it supports collaboration, information sharing, and communication. They highlight the goal of designing workflows through which paper and digital media work in concert with one another instead of trying to eradicate paper altogether. Paper documentation plays an important role in safety critical tasks such as airline flight operations [24, 27]. Heath and Luff [11] describe medical practitioners who use paper medical record cards in lieu or in addition to an electronic system. The use of paper medical cards is a socially organized practice and critical to physicians' reasoning processes. Ackerman and Halverson [1] examine the distributed nature of organizational memory of a telephone hotline, describing the changing states of information through mental, paper, and digital representations. Furthermore, there are different ways in which people share and collaborate through paper versus screen-based documentation [23].

The structure and format of the paper record, or its template, critically shapes documentation practices, and more importantly, it shapes how people reason about and accomplish the task at hand [11]. Such structures are instrumental in reducing the complexity of the work by providing constraints to the conduct of the actor [16]. In a similar vein regarding checklists, Norman [28] argues that "the fact that the preparation of the list is done prior to the action has an important impact upon performance because it allows the cognitive effort to be distributed across time and people." However, we note that such a checklist predetermines what should be considered part of the record. We observe many artifacts and cultural practices in the present research that help divide the task of documenting development among different people, various representational states, and over time [16].

Documentation in Educational Contexts

The central focus of this work is documentation practices within early childhood education. Early childhood education centers typically support children from birth to age 5 (or just before kindergarten). Seitz [30] states that, "the documenter is a researcher first, collecting as much information as possible to paint a picture of progress and outcomes." Here the *documenter* is most often a teacher, teaching assistant, or administrator. Documentation may include:

> Samples of a child's work at several different stages of completion: photographs showing work in progress; comments written by the teacher or other adults working with the children; transcriptions of children's discussions, comments, and explanations of intentions about the activity; and comments made by parents. [17]

In some educational communities, particularly early childhood education, there has been a pedagogical shift from measuring development through standardized tests to conducting observational reports that track development. As part of this pedagogy, classroom activities are initiated by the children and self-guided. This is central to the Reggio Emilia Approach [5, 13], which is a core philosophy of the school described within the present research. A unique contribution of the Reggio Emilia Approach to early childhood education is the use of documentation of children's experiences as a standard part of classroom practice [17].

While factors such as cost, effort, and time must be considered, there are many arguments for this style of assessment over standardized tests. In particular, this approach may produce more authentic evaluation of learning [35]. Documentation also allows teachers to reflect on and refine their instructional practices [21], thus enabling an evolving curriculum negotiated around children's needs [30]. Many early childhood educators document development and learning in a variety of ways, and most use this evidence to communicate with families [3]. The key, however, is to provide "authentic" evidence of the young learner's growing competencies [30]. The goal is to make learning visible, and Helm *et al* [12] refer to this as providing "windows on learning."

The current analysis focuses on the transition from paper to digital documentation, but the idea of maintaining an electronic portfolio of learning development is not new. For example, electronic portfolios such as the Progress Portfolio [22] and ePEARL [26] were designed to support students in planning and evaluating their own learning. Here we examine portfolios for teachers rather than student reflection.

Capture and Access Technologies

There is a growing use of digital media (photos, video, sensor data, etc) as mechanisms to document daily activity. As an extreme case, Bell and Gemmell [2] describe documenting years of activity using a variety of sensors and recording devices. There is evidence that revisiting collections of photos captured via a SenseCam can stimulate and rehabilitate autobiographical memory [14]. Marcu *et al* [25] examined wearable cameras worn by children with autism as a way to help parents understand the child's daily experiences and needs. Hayes *et al* [9, 10] also describe the design of capture and access technologies for understanding development of children with autism. Kientz *et al* [20] analyze family needs around record-keeping for health and wellness of children, and based on this they introduce KidCam [18] and Baby Steps [19] as capture and access technologies aimed at tracking development. While space precludes a full treatment of related work in this area, the analysis presented in this paper provides a foundation for developing future documentation systems within early childhood education classrooms.

METHOD

This research takes place at an early childhood education center affiliated with our university. The school applies the Reggio Emilia Approach, specifically by encouraging child-initiated exploration and measuring development through documenting experiences. It is a state subsidized center and provides care for 210 children age three months to just before kindergarten (five years old). The school has 38 teachers spread over 10 classrooms. Names of teachers are not disclosed, instead teachers are identified by a single initial and their classroom age group (as noted in quotes below). Photos of children's faces and names are blurred to protect their identities. The research team obtained IRB approval prior to this study.

Field Observations

Our research team has been present at this field site for 10 months conducting regular classroom observations. Most of our observations were conducted in one classroom for children age four to five, although we have made observations at each grade level within this school. Focusing on a single classroom allowed the research team to observe the daily activities of teaching staff, children, and parents within a focused setting. As participant observers, we worked with children during center time, including an arts and crafts table, a reading area, a computer center, and free play outside. In this capacity we observed many classroom practices, and most salient was the process of documenting development. Teachers wrote notes on clipboards and took photos of children with a digital camera. Some teachers annotated a child's artwork and filed it away as part of their development. Following these initial observations we initiated a deeper exploration of documentation practices more broadly within this school, specifically how teachers complete the California Desired Results Developmental Profile[1] (DRDP).

Interviews

Building on our field observations, we conducted 12 interviews with nine teachers and one supervisor at this early childhood education center. Interviews were conducted in a semi-structured fashion and focused on the process of completing the DRDP. Two teachers were interviewed twice to follow up on their process of photo documentation. Teachers were asked to select one child's portfolio that they were completing as part of their regular documentation practices. We interviewed teachers individually and had them walk us through the portfolio. Two researchers were present and took notes during the interviews. All interviews were video recorded and then later transcribed. Interviews lasted 20-45 minutes and were conducted at the school.

[1] http://www.wested.org/desiredresults/training/form_drdp.htm

Method of Analysis

We combine sustained *in situ* participant observations with teachers' detailed accounts of completing development portfolios. Our approach is informed by theories of distributed cognition [16, 15], in which we focus on the larger system of activity and attend to the transformation and propagation of information over time. All field notes, interview data, and photo and video records were reviewed in detail and then synthesized to develop themes. Our goal in this work is to understand how teachers accomplish the task of documenting development for young children and to identify opportunities and challenges in how they go about this practice, particularly with respect to the pending introduction of the online system.

RESULTS

Teachers and administrators at this early childhood education center are optimistic about a new online documentation system that will be introduced over the next year. This system will purportedly help teachers and administrators track developmental progress of individual children as well as analyze classroom- and school-wide data about development. Currently, however, the school uses predominantly paper-based methods to document development. This allows our research team to examine the details of the current paper-based recording system to anticipate challenges and opportunities for the online system. We present a detailed account of how teachers make observations of learning as well as document and share information regarding development.

Desired Results Developmental Profile (DRDP)

Documentation of development is only one aspect of a teacher's work at this school. Most classes have two to four teachers. Each teacher is assigned a group of three to eight students depending on the age group. Children are assigned to these groups upon entering the class. Among their many tasks, teachers are responsible for the specific needs of students, including observing development, completing the DRDP, leading parent conferences, and customizing curriculum based on student needs.

The DRDP is completed 60 days after the child has joined the class, then again in six months, and once more 60 days later if the child is still in the same classroom. Some students may have three assessment periods within a single classroom. The DRDP is state-mandated for children who receive subsidized tuition, although at this school teachers complete the DRDP for all students. It is the primary mechanism for documenting all aspects of development of children within this school. The state provides printable PDFs containing rating scales along 35 dimensions for infants and toddlers (birth to 36 months) and 43 dimensions for preschool children (age 3-5).

There are several audiences for the DRDP. At the highest-level, the state may audit DRDPs to ensure appropriate documentation is being maintained. School administrators also review individual portfolios. Administrators analyze results of the DRDP in aggregate to set curriculum goals. Teachers are the main creators of the portfolios, and they are also a primary audience for viewing this information. The assessments build on each other, or at least teachers suggest that

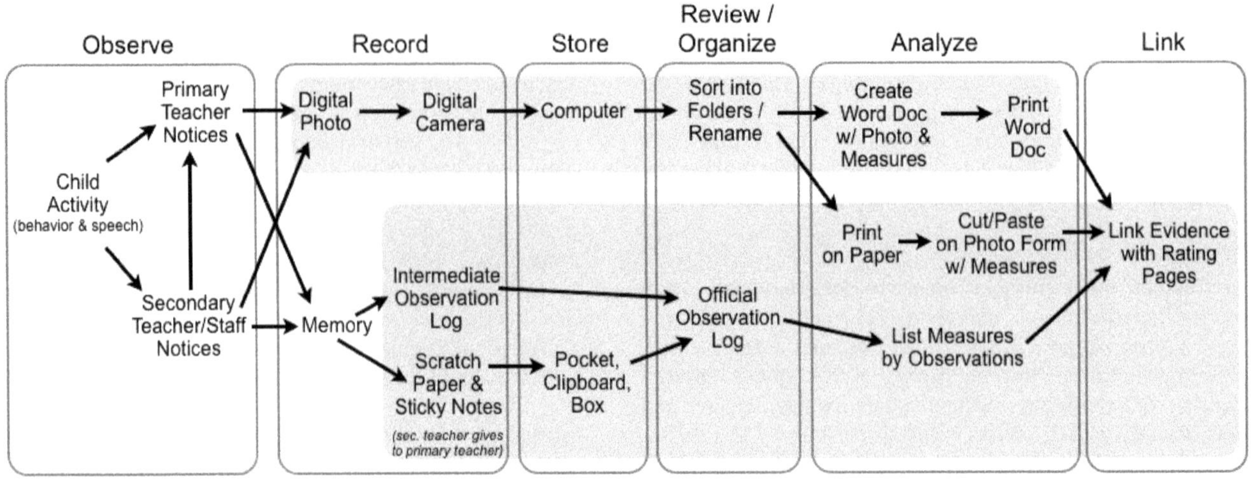

Figure 1. The process of transforming a child's behavior and speech into evidence that guides developmental ratings. The blue area highlights digital aspects and the green area highlights paper-based aspects of this process.

they should. A child's portfolio will evolve and continue to accumulate assessments over their time at the center, potentially containing five years of data. Finally, parents view their child's DRDP as part of parent-teacher conferences. Parents are rarely given access to the entire portfolio and are instead shown a high-level summary about development that is based on data in the portfolio.

Completing the DRDP is a multistep and continuous process. Teachers observe children's activity in the classroom area, record what they see and hear children do, store this information or evidence in various formats, review and organize the evidence, analyze the evidence against standard developmental measures, and finally develop interconnected paper trails that link pieces of evidence with various measures. At different points in this process, information is shared with other teachers, parents, and administrators. Figure 1 illustrates this process of transforming a child's behavior and speech into actionable evidence that drives assessment.

Observe: Gathering Evidence of Development

Gathering evidence of development is the foundation for this documentation practice and central to the ultimate product of a DRDP portfolio. Several teachers use the word "proof" to describe evidence of learning. Identifying proof is a skilled practice of looking [6] that requires training and experience. Teachers are constantly observing children in the classroom and documenting their interactions with other people and the environment. Much time and care is spent making and documenting observations of children.

> *"It's not something I like to say 'okay I'm going to observe you in a week and have all these answers' cause I want at least a month. It's important for me to get that longevity into it." –M, 2-3*

Types of Evidence

Teachers gather three primary types of evidence: written observations (behaviors and quotes), photos, and work samples. Observations are written on paper and describe what a child accomplished, their reaction to an event, or at times even adverse behaviors. Teachers often write down quotes from the children to elaborate and supplement written observations.

> *"[Quotes are] a really good way of presenting evidence... it comes directly from the child versus 'I think that Johnny enjoys dinosaurs'." –L, 4-5*

The most pervasive form of evidence is photo documentation. Each classroom has a digital camera that teachers use to document behaviors. Teachers may accumulate hundreds of digital photos for a single child. They described many benefits of photo documentation, particularly that they can easily take photos and then do not need written observations of an event. Several teachers report that photos are their preferred form of evidence.

> *"I take a lot of photos... I like photo observations the best because I think it captures certain things. Captures it better." –N, 2-3*

> *"We get a lot of the observations through pictures, which is really key... The pictures help so much." –M, 2-3*

Photos provide valuable evidence of development as well as serve as memory aids for the teachers completing the DRDP. Revisiting and analyzing the photos is an interesting part of the larger process. We describe the organization, manipulation, and analysis of photos in more detail below.

Samples of artwork and writing are additional evidence. We observed teachers in classrooms collecting artwork for this purpose. Teachers annotate these work samples, most commonly with the child's name and date. Quotes and commentary from children may be directly added to artwork, which then becomes additional data about that activity. Work samples are included less frequently than other forms of evidence. They are most prevalent in portfolios for children age four and older. Our analysis focuses primarily on the qualities of written observations and photo documentation that are pervasive throughout the age groups.

Learning to Make "Good" Observations

Teachers skillfully watch child interactions [6] for indicators of developmental progress. One teacher said that making observations *"just becomes part of our day."* A critical technique in how teachers make observations is by narrowing their focus to a small subset of children. Teachers indicate that focusing on a small group (3-8 children) helps them know the children better and attend to critical episodes of activity. Teachers also use concrete examples of behaviors (provided in the DRDP) that map to various measures and ratings as scaffolding while learning to observe. An example of the highest level of "shared use of space and materials" is "while coloring with crayons, offers a crayon to another child". Over time teachers learn to generalize beyond specific examples.

An administrator reported that one challenge is teaching teachers to make "objective" observations. Teachers receive training on how to make observations that clearly illustrate a behavior without a layer of interpretation, although such records are always inherently subject to one's interpretations formed by socially and culturally rooted practices of looking [6]. Teachers describe this learning process.

"The biggest thing that I had to learn... is not interpreting what you see, so I might see a child crying because they fell down or whatever... I don't want to interpret that... Sometimes I would write 'they were sad because they fell'." –A, 1-2

Teachers seek authentic observations that occur naturalistically within the classroom [30]. They do not want to setup an activity just to observe a particular aspect of development, which is central to the Reggio Emilia Approach [5, 13].

"I don't want to feed them something that they don't come up with on their own. I just don't think it's accurate." –M, 2-3

"I want it to be authentic. I never a tell a child 'oh here use the marker' so I can get a DRDP note." –A, 1-2

Another key component of good written observations is making a record shortly after the episode of interest. Teachers have many responsibilities outside documenting development: they are busy carrying out lesson plans, handling conflicts, and generally running the classroom. Documenting fleeting observations is a challenge. As soon as they get "off the floor" they write observations. Teachers describe relying on their memories of the activity whether they record it immediately following the event or later in the day. In addition, teachers express the value of photos in reestablishing context around a particular episode of activity.

"I'll see it and instead of writing it down to where later I gotta get more context, I just go take a photo of it... I don't have to leave the floor... I prefer to take a photo of it cause it's a lot easier to just come back to it later." –N, 2-3

"I try to pick a photo where I can really remember and it's really stuck in my mind what he's been doing." –C, 2-3

Record: Written Observations and Photos

Making a record of activity is a critical step in the larger process. Teachers do this by writing notes and taking photos.

Paper Observation Logs

Teachers systematically list observations and quotes from children on a paper observation sheet (Fig. 2). Observation sheets may be out in the classroom for easy access. Some teachers attach them to clipboards and carry them around the classroom. Teachers have created their own versions of the observation sheet, each with a similar format including the date, measure numbers, and the observation. Some teachers

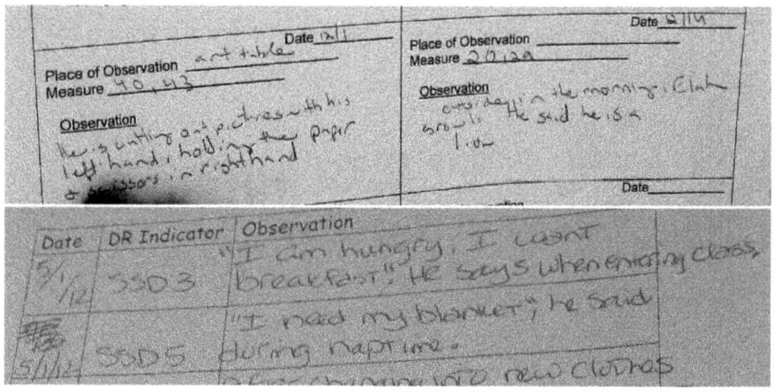

Figure 2. Excerpts from paper observation sheets.

keep observation sheets for each child and write directly on those logs. Other teachers keep a teacher-specific log sheet.

Scratch Paper and Sticky Notes

While some teachers record their observations directly onto a paper observation sheet, many teachers use scratch paper and sticky notes to record observations.

"I constantly make notes, either at the end of the day or just on scratch pieces of paper, that way I can add them when I have time... I have a little caddy of books so I might have a piece of paper in there." –M, 2-3

"If somebody mentions something, I'll write it down on a piece of paper and throw it in my box..." –N, 2-3

"I find myself writing on stickies and then putting them in my pocket or if I have a clipboard writing on there...but occasionally those papers get missed placed... I have a note somewhere but where did I put it? Why isn't it in the file? I should have put it in the file right away." -I, 3-4

The use of scratch paper as an intermediary before the official observation sheet helps preserve details of the interaction. This is an especially important step in remembering the details of what children say.

"If I'm not going to remember the words then I'll write it on a little stickum, then I'll put it in her folder and I'll write it in [the observation sheet] afterwards." –G, 4-5

"If I have a conversation with somebody, the second that it's over and they walk away... I write it down sort of like a script, like a movie script." –A, 1-2

With early language development, teachers note that it is important to preserve the characteristics of the child's speech, and they do this when making notes on paper. For example, if a child says "the wheels on the bus go wound and wound," they would write down "wound and wound" not "round and round."

Digital Photos as Observations

In addition to making written notes, teachers working in the classroom take photos of children engaged in various activities. Several teachers keep digital cameras with them throughout the day, others keep a shared camera on an easily accessible shelf in the classroom, and one teacher brings in her personal camera to ensure access when needed.

"I pretty much wait for the action to happen, okay grab the camera... It's usually on the desk right inside the door that leads from

the outside, so we can either reach around and get it or ask someone to get it." –M, 2-3

"I carry the camera around with me. We have a classroom camera and I also bring my own personal camera... because if [another teacher] is doing a project and she wants to take pictures of the kids and I'm outside with a group of kids and they're doing something really great, I want to capture that too. I don't want to let it go to waste, so I use two cameras sometimes." –A, 1-2

Teachers take multiple photos to highlight specifics like motor movement or the focus on a child's face as well as to illustrate the sequence of activity.

"I'll take pictures...so you see his whole body, so you know it's [child], and then I'll zoom in on his hand... I try not to just take a picture and then walk away. I keep going, so like a flip book...I try to make as many sequence shots as I can... Sometimes the camera doesn't work that fast..." –A, 1-2

"I wanted to demonstrate with the photo the problem solving skills. If you just had this [one photo] you could claim, you know, he's solving a problem...but with both photos it clearly shows he had a problem and how he solved it. Just makes it even clearer to the observer." –N, 2-3

Photo sequences capture the state of interaction over a period of time. Teachers note that this technique highlights the process rather than the product. For this reason, photos of the artwork creation process, especially with infants and toddlers, are often used instead of just the final artifact.

Review, Rewrite, Organize, and Manipulate

Teachers spend time reviewing, rewriting, and organizing their evidence. Observations written on scratch paper and sticky notes and even temporary observation logs must be transferred to an official observation sheet. Rewriting observations was described as "busy work" by one teacher, yet teachers seemed to value neatly written comments in portfolios that are ready to share with supervisors, other teachers, or possibly parents. Observations must be grouped by child so that the observation sheet can be filed into that student's portfolio. Teachers report that they are required to write up observations once per week per child. We found that several teachers rely on an accumulation of jotted notes throughout the week and then transfer them to the observation sheet in one sitting. They may do this on the weekend at home, as many teachers do not have sufficient time during the day to complete this part of the process.

At various points during the documentation procedure, but particularly when they begin to complete a child's DRDP, teachers manage, organize, and review their collection of digital photographs. This is a multistep process that involves loading photos onto the computer, deleting unwanted photos, organizing them by child and then perhaps further by date, selecting a subset of photos for a particular child, and printing them on paper or inserting them individually into Microsoft Word documents. The vast majority of teachers print out a collection of photos on paper, cut them up, and tape them into the portfolio. Teachers have one computer per classroom as well as a computer in several break rooms that they may use to upload and print photos. There is one centralized color printer available for use. All photos are printed in color with the date on them. We were surprised by the volume of photos teachers have for each child as well as the variation in how teachers organize and review their photos. Often we observed teachers with 100 to 200 photos per child that they accumulated over the past months from which they select a small subset (as few as four photos, but typically between 10 and 15) to include in the portfolio.

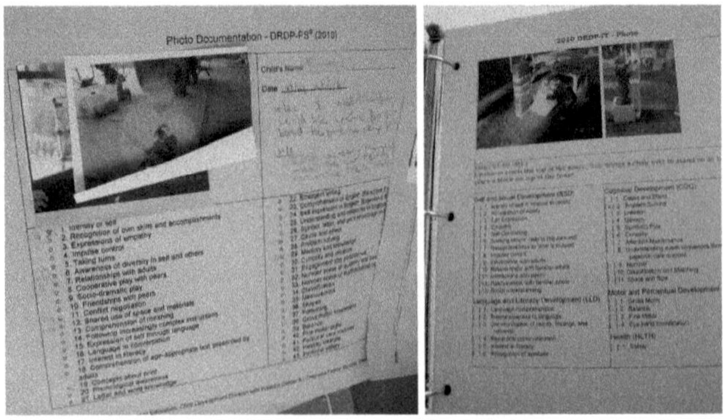

Figure 3. Paper photo documentation forms. *Left*: The standard DRDP photo documentation template. *Right*: Custom photo form created in Microsoft Word.

Select and Analyze Evidence

Teachers accumulate more data than they can include in the portfolio. They make decisions about which observations and photos to include as part of the assessment. This part of the process is completed using two standard format templates (one for observations and the other for photos); however, with both forms we observed custom variations created by teachers. These variations contained the same information fields but had a slightly different layout. These forms serve as boundary objects [33] and provide a common structure that is understandable by various stakeholders who may interact with the portfolio.

Observation Sheets

We found several formats of the observation sheet that appear in a child's folder. The vast majority of these observation sheets include a space to write measure numbers that could be satisfied by this observation. Teachers fill in the measure numbers at various times. Experienced teachers write down measure numbers from memory and only occasionally look up missing items.

Photo Documentation Form

Teachers select certain photos to include in each child's portfolio. Most teachers use a printed photo documentation form that is part of the DRDP. With this they cut up photos and tape them to the documentation page. We encountered two teachers, however, who create their own version of the form electronically with Microsoft Word (see Fig. 3, right).

"I like to do it this way because I have the pictures on the computer and I can just...take it from my folder of pictures and put it onto the Word document and then write my captions that go with it rather than cut and glue and or tape and all that..." –L, 4-5

In contrast to digital templates, working with paper photos allows teachers to lay out sequences of photos and then attach the group of photos (typically stapled together) to the page. We observed teachers quickly flipping through and organizing stacks of paper photos as they matched them with various measures of development.

When Written Observations are Better

Digital cameras provide an ease of capturing rich information about an activity, and photos are the preferred method of documentation by many teachers. However, photos are not optimal for all interactions or all times. Self and social development standards (e.g., relationships with adults, conflict negotiation) are particularly difficult to capture through photos because these tend to be more conversational or relationship-based. Teachers need to document when a child is part of a conflict yet they cannot leave the situation to get a camera. Instead they rely on after-the-fact written reports of the episode. Similarly, the teacher in the infant room is the sole person responsible for observing development in six babies (age 3-12 months). She reports that is it challenging to capture behaviors in this age group because infants may do certain actions infrequently. She is busy attending to the infants and cannot always get the camera. The opportunity may pass before she has time to document it through photos, so written observations from her memory of an event are valuable.

Link and Synthesize Evidence

Hand-written observations and photos are continuously gathered, organized, and analyzed in the classroom. The integration of evidence into a child's DRDP usually occurs during the weeks just before the portfolio is due. Central to the DRDP is rating children on various standards using a paper form (Fig. 4). Infants and toddlers (birth to 36 months old) are rated on 35 measures using a five-point scale (responding with reflexes, expanding responses, acting with purpose, discovering ideas, or developing ideas). Preschool children (age 3-5) are rated on 43 measures using a four-point scale (exploring, developing, building, or integrating). This is likely the point in the process where teachers would interface with DRDPtech. Before rating a child, teachers described reviewing all of their observations, quotes, work samples, and photos.

> *"I actually go through all the picture ones first and then I go through the written ones and then I kinda just decide on the things... I kinda go through, I'm looking at observations and I'm filling in bubbles based on where they are on specific standards." –N, 2-3*

Linking Evidence with Measures

For each measure, teachers must provide evidence of their rating. They do this by writing a note that redirects to a specific observation, a photo documentation page, or a work sample. The critical information in this linking is the type of evidence and the date. Figure 4 provides an example of this linking between multiple parts of the paper record. Teachers may have multiple pieces of evidence for a single measure, and also have multiple measures for a single piece of evidence. Through this process teachers create a web of interconnected pages, as illustrated in Figure 4.

Synthesis and Curriculum Planning

Teachers and school administrators calculate developmental progress for individuals, classes, age groups, and the school as a whole. They use these calculations to plan and tailor curriculum. Aggregating ratings from these paper forms and deriving new goals based on this data is a challenge for teachers and school administrators. Currently this is done on paper and then transferred to Microsoft Excel for further analysis. Teachers are responsible for contributing data on each of their children for the aggregate reports.

Communication and Information Sharing

Documenting development in this context is a seemingly independent process with one teacher held responsible for the portfolio. We observed, however, three themes around communication and information sharing involving DRDPs.

Sharing Among Teachers

Within each classroom teachers constantly discuss the children and their development. They do this informally as well as during scheduled weekly meetings. Teachers primarily focus observations on their own children but will call another teacher's attention to an activity or share data when the other teacher's child is involved an a joint activity. In terms of more direct support in gathering evidence, school administrators and teaching assistants occasionally provide teachers with observations and quotes.

> *"Occasionally our teacher assistants will be helpful enough to say 'oh here, here's what I caught from your children today' and they'll have time to do that for us... Recently we've had a teacher's aid in our class that handed me a piece of paper and said 'here's some quotes I got from your kid'." –M, 2-3*

Teachers also work together more directly to complete the DRDP if the child transitions between two primary teachers during the assessment or if the child's native language is different from the teacher's. Finally, teachers share digital photos (on the camera and computer) as well as printed photos. They are careful not to delete photos from a shared camera without checking with others in their classroom.

> *"I don't just print my kids' [photos]. I keep every single photo we have in the computer so that way if someone else wants one too, I can tell them 'oh yea go in my folder, you can print out some for your kids too'." –A, 1-2*

Information Sharing with Parents

Parents are a primary audience for the DRDP, although the full portfolio is not shared with them. Teachers state that the rating scales may be overwhelming or misinterpreted as grades by parents. Teachers make decisions about which information to present to parents and how to message their findings. After completing the assessments, teachers generate a summary report (either written by hand or in Microsoft Word) for each child. This summary is filed into the child's portfolio and shared with parents along with printed photos. Teachers pull out photos to illustrate points and even give parents photos during the conference. A goal of the conference is to have the parent agree on the summary report. Parents have a space to add their own goals for their child and to sign regarding the summary sheet. According to teachers, one difficult message

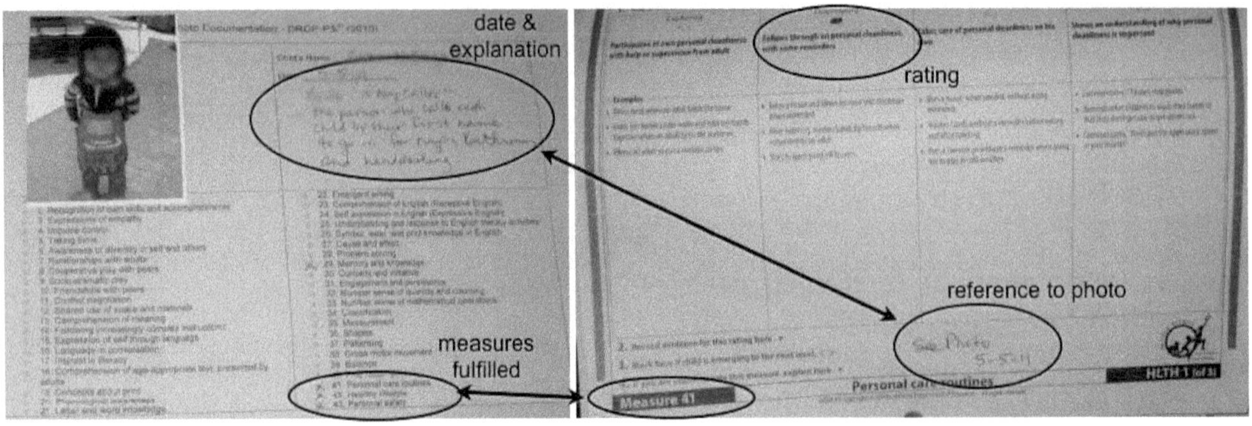

Figure 4. ***Left:*** **Photo documentation linked to measures.** ***Right*****: Measure with rating linked to photo documentation as evidence.**

to communicate with parents is when there may be a developmental delay with a particular child. Reviewing a portfolio can give clues about developmental delays or behavior problems [20], and teachers do this to look for patterns over time.

Accumulating and Sharing Information Over Time

At any point a school administrator or auditor may access the portfolios to ensure proper documentation is in place. Portfolios must remain in a condition where information is ready to share with outside observers. More interestingly, however, the portfolio is an evolving record of the child's development. Teachers add to the portfolio as the year goes on and as the child transitions to each new classroom. This record serves as a reference for teachers as a child moves throughout the school. With multiple teachers contributing to a single portfolio over time, there are challenges with consistency in documentation. Teachers say they may ignore previous evaluations if they differ greatly in format, are lacking in some way, or the ratings seem incorrect.

> *"Because everyone kind of thinks that they're doing the best that they can do and their own format and you know their own way, then it becomes a problem because then other people say 'well no that's not how I do it in my classroom' so therefore it's filed. It's tucked away... Why waste all this work and all this information that somebody worked so hard on..." –L, 4-5*

DISCUSSION

This is the first phase of a larger research project that studies the transition to an online documentation system. We now review our key findings and, in light of these, discuss implications of DRDPtech and design alternatives.

Needs and Constraints

The teacher's primary role is to interact with the children. There are many issues a teacher must attend to within a classroom in addition to watching for episodes of activity that signify a child meeting a developmental standard. Furthermore, their attention is spread among a group of children. They cannot easily leave to document an activity or manage a device that requires great attention. They lack time to learn or deal with more complex technology (even video cameras). Teachers strive to setup classrooms that promote exploration and self-guided learning. Similarly, in their documentation practices they aim to preserve the authenticity of child interaction with others and the environment. Quickly jotting notes on scratch paper that can be tucked away provide the necessary discreteness and immediacy. Documentation technologies should not take away from or disrupt the classroom.

Many teachers have developed strategies to quickly capture and preserve the details of interaction. Most often they do this by writing brief notes on paper or taking a photo. There are challenges in this, such as misplacing the paper note, misremembering details of the interaction, or the episode of interest ending before the teacher can get the camera. When possible, the use of digital photos helps address these challenges by providing a rich, detailed record that aids recall of an event. The digital camera itself is a key documentation tool for teachers. Digital cameras are small and portable devices that quickly capture valuable context and automatically timestamp observations. Teachers use photos (both digital and printed on paper) as reminders about an episode of activity. Sequences of photos illustrate the process a child engages in rather than just the final product. Teachers spend time printing and organizing hundreds of photos. In paper form, these photos are shared with and even given to parents and other people who review a child's portfolio. The photos act as conversational anchors [32] among teachers and parents. Paper photos afford spreading out on a surface, stacking, and annotating. The backs of paper photos may hold notes about the activity or relevant measures. Stacks of paper photos are organized into flip books illustrating an interaction sequence.

While photos are critical to documentation, certain measures that are more conversation-based are captured through a hand-written transcript. Teachers make written observations for many reasons (e.g., to capture a conversation, no access to a camera, document a memory of an event). The process of making, documenting, and analyzing written observations is lengthly and time consuming. Teachers need solutions that facilitate more efficient transitions between various steps.

A teacher can improve their efficiency by making observations that apply to multiple measures. Photos are particularly useful in this case because of the detail captured by an image. A single photo observation form may satisfy several measures. Building the connections between a piece of evidence and a measure is a challenging part of the process. Teachers spread out pages of paper documentation, pointing and highlighting the ways in which the data fit together. Some teachers, however, disregard prior evaluations if the portfolio has a different format than what they use, appears to be lacking in depth, or contains incorrect ratings (developmentally too advanced for the age). Much effort and data is wasted because of inconsistencies among classrooms.

Parents play a central role in monitoring and improving their child's development. Moreover, they want help recording information about development and need tools to assist with this [20]. While many parents are in constant communication with teachers about their child's progress, when it comes to the DRDP, parents only play a peripheral role and see a filtered view of the final product. There are interesting research opportunities in how to more effectively involve parents.

Implications of DRDPtech

While DRDPtech has yet to be formally introduced in this school, our analysis of the system indicates that it only directly supports the latter phase of the documentation process where teachers rate children on each measure and share information with supervisors or other teachers. Teachers go to great lengths to document development and establish clearly traceable steps in their evaluation process. These aspects of the process are not directly supported by the system, and teachers may need to continue their elaborate paper-based practices. "Going digital" may in the end conflict with and hide the richness and detail in documentation.

One salient concern is that DRDPtech does not support uploading of photos or scanned images, data that are central to this process. Simply including digital photos in DRDPtech is a natural next step; however, the affordances of photos printed on paper should not be overlooked. Another concern is that DRDPtech lacks a way to link multiple measures with a single piece of evidence and multiple pieces of evidence with a single measure. With DRDPtech, the work of linking evidence with measures must be done in preparation rather than by means of the online system, as Suchman [34] describes.

A natural question to ask is whether this school needs a new system at all when clearly this transition will present many challenges. One perceived value of DRDPtech is that it will help standardize certain aspects of documentation. Specifically, the system should improve timeliness of entries (or at least better awareness about late entries) and shared access to data over time. However, with this transition, many of the nuances in how teachers record and analyze evidence may remain but perhaps become hidden by the online system making it difficult to assess documentation quality [11]. A related question is how the technology may redistribute or create more work for the teachers. DRDPtech will certainly redistribute the work of lead teachers and administrators tasked with aggregating and visualizing data. Since the system will track the timeliness of entries, teachers will have harder deadlines for reporting and may be forced to complete the portfolios on their own time at home. Teachers also noted varying levels of technical ability among the staff. DRDPtech is likely to add more work for less tech savvy teachers, and several teachers described how much easier it was for them to create reports on paper than the computer.

Finally, it is unclear how DRDPtech will impact information sharing with parents. Parents do not have access to the system and teachers may ultimately still print out paper copies of the reports to share with parents. Teachers currently do not give parents full access to the portfolios because they do not want to overwhelm parents or make them feel as if their child is being graded. These challenges still exist with DRDPtech.

Design Alternatives

The richness of the documentation practices observed in the field generates many ideas for design. Although our team has yet to influence the design of DRDPtech specifically, we describe several technology-based solutions that could support teachers' needs and work in coordination with the system.

One promising solution involves a mobile application for a tablet or smart phone. This would allow teachers to take photos or videos of children and immediately tag children appearing in the scene (automatically with face recognition or manually), select relevant measures, and add text or audio annotations. They could also flag content for sharing with parents. Teachers would need to carry the device around with them as they do their digital camera, but this type of device may present an additional distraction to students.

Another design direction involves digital pens[2] that preserve the affordances of paper and provide the ability to easily upload data to digital environments. This has potential to help bridge between paper and digital recording practices. Certain digital pens[3] have the ability to link audio recordings with handwritten notes, enabling a teacher to capture what a child is saying in time with notes about its significance.

As another alternative, classrooms may be instrumented with cameras to selectively archive episodes of interest [9]; however, this may not provide the necessary resolution for fine-grain interactions. Wearable cameras as in [25] may provide better detail about a child's experiences. The fear of surveillance by teachers and students may interfere with the benefit of the evidence gathered [8], although some work has shown this to be relatively unfounded [9].

CONCLUSION

This research examines the documentation and information sharing practices of early childhood education teachers. We describe the ecology of tools used in this practice, including pervasive paper notes and digital photos. We seek a deeper understanding of how various media contribute to the documentation process. As an essential first step, we have begun by documenting teachers' practices in the many and varied activities involved in early childhood education. It is clear that there are many opportunities to improve the design of both paper and digital tools to augment this process and associated practices. We hope this analysis of the documentation process will serve others confronting the complexities of supporting activities involving paper and digital media.

[2]www.anoto.com

[3]www.livescribe.com

REFERENCES

1. Ackerman, M. S., and Halverson, C. Considering an organization's memory. In *Proc of CSCW* (1998), 39–48.
2. Bell, G., and Gemmell, J. *Total Recall: How the E-Memory Revolution Will Change Everything*. Penguin Books, 2009.
3. Brown-DuPaul, J., Keyes, T., and Segatti, L. Using documentation panels to communicate with families. *Childhood Education 77* (2001).
4. Brush, A. J. B., Bargeron, D., Grudin, J., and Gupta, A. Notification for shared annotation of digital documents. In *Proc of CHI* (2002), 89–96.
5. Cadwell, L. *Bringing Learning to Life: A Reggio Approach to Early Childhood Education*. Teachers College Press, New York, NY, 2002.
6. Goodwin, C. Professional vision. *American Anthropologist 96*, 3 (1994), 606.
7. Goody, J. *The Interface between the Written and the Oral*. Cambridge University Press, Cambridge, 1987.
8. Hayes, G. R., and Abowd, G. D. Tensions in designing capture technologies for an evidence-based care community. In *Proc of CHI* (2006), 937–946.
9. Hayes, G. R., Gardere, L. M., Abowd, G. D., and Truong, K. N. Carelog: a selective archiving tool for behavior management in schools. In *Proc of CHI* (2008), 685–694.
10. Hayes, G. R., Kientz, J. A., Truong, K. N., White, D. R., Abowd, G. D., and Pering, T. Designing capture applications to support the education of children with autism. In *Proc of Ubicomp* (2004), 161–178.
11. Heath, C., and Luff, P. Documents and professional practice: "bad" organisational reasons for "good" clinical records. In *Proc of CSCW* (1996), 354–363.
12. Helm, J., Beneke, S., and Steinheimer, K. *Windows on learning: Documenting young childrens work*. Teachers College Press, New York, 1998.
13. Hewett, V. Examining the reggio emilia approach to early childhood education. *Early Childhood Education 29* (2001).
14. Hodges, S., Berry, E., and Wood, K. Sensecam: A wearable camera which stimulates and rehabilitates autobiographical memory. *Memory* (2011).
15. Hollan, J., Hutchins, E., and Kirsh, D. Distributed cognition: toward a new foundation for human-computer interaction research. *ACM TOCHI 7*, 2 (2000), 174–196.
16. Hutchins, E. *Cognition in the Wild*. MIT Press, 1995.
17. Katz, L., and Chard, S. The contribution of documentation to the quality of early childhood education, 1996.
18. Kientz, J. A., and Abowd, G. D. Kidcam: Toward an effective technology for the capture of children's moments of interest. In *Proc of Pervasive* (2009), 115–132.
19. Kientz, J. A., Arriaga, R. I., and Abowd, G. D. Baby steps: evaluation of a system to support record-keeping for parents of young children. In *Proc of CHI* (2009), 1713–1722.
20. Kientz, J. A., Arriaga, R. I., Chetty, M., Hayes, G. R., Richardson, J., Patel, S. N., and Abowd, G. D. Grow and know: understanding record-keeping needs for tracking the development of young children. In *Proc of CHI* (2007), 1351–1360.
21. Kroeger, J., and Cardy, T. Documentation: A hard-to-reach place. *Early Child Educ. Jour. 33* (2006).
22. Loh, B., Radinsky, J., Reiser, B. J., Gomez, L. M., Edelson, D. C., and Russell, E. The progress portfolio: promoting reflective inquiry in complex investigation environments. In *Proc of CSCL* (1997).
23. Luff, P., Heath, C., and Greatbatch, D. Tasks-in-interaction: paper and screen based documentation in collaborative activity. In *Proc of CSCW* (1992), 163–170.
24. MacKay, W. Is paper safer? The role of paper flight strips in air traffic control. *TOCHI 6*, 4 (1999), 340.
25. Marcu, G., Dey, A., and Kiesler, S. Parent-driven use of wearable cameras for autism support: A field study with families. In *Proc of UBICOMP* (2012).
26. Meyer, E., Abrami, P., Wade, C., Aslan, O., and Deault, L. Improving literacy and metacognition with electronic portfolios: Teaching and learning with epearl. *Computers & Education 55* (2010).
27. Nomura, S., Hutchins, E., and Holder, B. The uses of paper in commercial airline flight operations. In *Proc of CSCW* (New York, USA, 2006), 249–258.
28. Norman, D. Cognitive artifacts. In *Designing interaction: Psychology at the human-computer interface*, J. Carroll, Ed., Cambridge University Press (New York, 1991).
29. Schmidt, K., and Simone, C. Coordination Mechanisms: Towards a Conceptual Foundation of CSCW Systems Design. *Computer Supported Cooperative Work 5* (1996).
30. Seitz, H. The power of documentation in the early childhood education classroom. *Young Children* (2008).
31. Sellen, A. J., and Harper, R. *The Myth of the Paperless Office*. MIT Press, November 2001.
32. Sit, R. Y., Hollan, J. D., and Griswold, W. G. Digital photos as conversational anchors. In *Proc of HICSS* (2005).
33. Star, S., and Griesemer, J. Institutional ecology, 'translations' and boundary objects: Amateurs and professionals in berkeley's museum of vertebrate zoology. *Social Studies of Science 19* (1989).
34. Suchman, L. Office procedures as practical action: Models of work and system design. *ACM Trans. on Office Information Systems* (1983).
35. Wiggins, G. The case of authentic assessment. *ERIC Digest* (1990).

Experiences2Go: Sharing Kids' Activities Outside the Home with Remote Family Members

Kori Inkpen[1], Brett Taylor[1,2], Sasa Junuzovic[1], John Tang[1], Gina Venolia[1]

[1]Microsoft Research
One Microsoft Way
Redmond, WA 98052 USA
{kori | sasajun | johntang | ginav}@microsoft.com

[2]University of Saskatchewan
110 Science Place
Saskatoon, SK S7N 5C9 Canada
brett.taylor@usask.ca

ABSTRACT

Video communication is moving beyond face-to-face discussions on desktop computers to sharing experiences out in the real world. We explored how mobile video could enable distributed family members to share experiences wherever they occurred – kids' sporting events, birthday parties, etc. We investigated how people used two technology probes to share activities outside the home: an iPad running Skype and our Experiences2Go prototype composed of a networked slate and a camcorder on a tripod. We observed their use in the field with nine families and explored the impact that their mobility, optical zoom, and multiple view features had on sharing the experience. We identified four sets of stakeholders in sharing experiences, the variety of sharing scenarios enabled, and reactions to the features that each probe offered, leading to design considerations for future mobile shared experience systems.

Author Keywords

Shared experiences; family; technology probe; CSCW.

ACM Classification Keywords

H.4.3 [Information Systems Applications]: Communications Applications – computer conferencing, teleconferencing, and videoconferencing.

INTRODUCTION

Grandma feels like she is missing out on her grandkids' soccer games, swim meets, and play activities, since they live 200 miles away. Sometimes her daughter will call her afterwards to tell her how it went, but Grandma still feels a little left out since she is not able to be there. They tried using Skype on her daughter's phone, but it did not provide an adequate view of the activity and it was tiring for her daughter to hold the phone up the whole time.

CSCW'13, February 23–27, 2013, San Antonio, Texas, USA.

Video chat is moving beyond just face-to-face discussion as people discover new ways to use video to socially connect with remote family members and close friends [2]. The previous narrative illustrates an increasingly popular type of social connection where family members remotely join an event that they cannot attend in person. Such situations occur frequently due to physical distance, availability (e.g., busy schedule), or ability (e.g., wheelchair accessibility). Many of these events occur outside the home, prompting people to use mobile video chat applications, such as Skype and FaceTime, to include remote family members.

Unfortunately, today's mobile technologies limit what types of activities people can easily share. Current mobile video chat tools are limited by the cameras on the devices, which typically do not offer sufficient zoom or depth of field to clearly capture events at a distance, such as a soccer game. Although mobile devices offer front- and rear-facing cameras, video chat applications require the local person to choose between the two cameras. As a result, the remote person can either see the event or chat face-to-face with the local person, making it hard to truly share the experience.

Our research explored how to enable sharing experiences over distance and identified what capabilities are important to provide that sense of sharing. We studied the use of two technology probes [4] in real-world situations to better understand problems with existing technologies and design opportunities for the future. We focused on kids' events that occur outside the home (e.g., park, school, gymnasium).

We studied the use of two systems for sharing experiences: 1) an iPad running Skype and 2) an Experiences2Go (E2G) prototype we built, consisting of a networked slate and

Figure 1. Mom remotely watches her daughter play together with Dad through the Experiences2Go prototype.

camcorder mounted on a tripod. The distinct capabilities of the two probes allowed us to test a variety of features. The iPad is highly mobile but can only transmit the front- or rear-facing camera view at a time. E2G can capture events at a distance using the camcorder's telephoto lens and provides the remote person with simultaneous views of the event and the local people. E2G's tripod mount allows it to stand without being held, but makes it less mobile.

We deployed the technology probes with nine families to understand their use in real-world settings, what types of activities they enable, and the current obstacles to providing engaging experiences. Our observations provided insights into the types of engagement made possible when people at a distance can share experiences together. Our experiences also showed that this scenario is more than streaming a live event – it is about socially connecting people.

This paper first presents related work. Then it describes a pilot study we conducted to make some initial design choices. It then presents the E2G prototype and results from our deployment with nine families. Finally, it provides insights into sharing experiences on the go and design considerations for technologies that enable them.

RELATED WORK

Traditional videoconferencing systems work well for face-to-face conversations but are limited in their ability to go beyond the talking heads experience. Specifically, they are not well suited for supporting many of the activities that naturally arise during a social interaction. Bly et al. highlighted the importance of both informal and task-specific interactions for organic, spontaneous collaborations [1]. Furthermore, Gaver et al. [3] found that talking heads did not provide adequate information about the remote environment, which is important when sharing an activity.

Despite the limitations of existing systems, people have used video in their homes for personal connections. Kirk et al. [7] surveyed home users and identified that a desire for social closeness motivated using video communication. Judge et al. [5] described how distributed family members used video to share experiences across distance. Brubaker et al. [2] found that people are exploring and experimenting with using video to share a diverse range of activities (e.g., watching movies together, cooking with mom, remote baby-sitting). People have also been using video outside the home to maintain personal connections. Juhlin et al. [6] analyzed how people use mobile technology to broadcast live video, enabling sharing experiences even when they are not at home. O'Hara et al. [10] found that over half of video calls made on mobile phones occurred outside the home or work settings, indicating the growing opportunities for video chat on the go. Peek-A-Boo [9] explored creating video connections from the home to a mobile phone.

Prior research has also investigated prototypes designed specifically for sharing experiences. Weisz et al. [15] created a system for sharing text messages while watching video together. Romero et al. [12] created a system for sharing awareness of daily activities through text and pictures among remote family members. Vutborg et al. [14] created a system designed for remote communication between grandparents and their grandchildren. They found that augmenting the video chat with other shared context was important. This finding was supported by Raffle et al. [11] who designed StoryVisit, which combines video communication with reading a book together. Others have also created video chat systems that provide a shared communication context. Yarosh et al. [16] created a system for children to have play dates over a distance using video communication and a shared task space, and Mueller et al. [8] enabled a shared jogging experience between remote joggers just through a live audio connection and spatialized sound to create a sense of jogging side-by-side.

These studies and prototypes demonstrate the desire to push the boundaries of existing technology for personal video communication. People want to share experiences using video communication, both at home and in mobile environments. Our work differs from prior work in two ways. First, we investigate the notion of using video to share experiences outside the home. Second, rather than focusing on a single system for sharing experiences, we studied two technology probes with fundamentally different features to get a wider range of insights into pain points and solutions for them when sharing experiences on the go.

PILOT STUDY

We began by exploring whether it is beneficial for remote users to be able to see the activity itself and interact with the local adult attending the event. However, it was not clear whether it was necessary to show views of the event and the local adult simultaneously, and if so, how to present these views to the remote attendee. We conducted a pilot study to help us understand the importance of multiple views and identify a good way to present them.

Methods & Setup

We recruited four groups consisting of two adults and multiple children. We looked for couples with kids or adults whose kids were friends with each other. Two groups were mother/father and two were mothers who were friends. We asked these groups to visit our lab and watch their children play Microsoft Xbox Kinect games.

The children played from a selection of Kinect games. One adult ("local adult") was seated on a sofa watching from behind as the kids played. A Microsoft LifeCam Studio webcam mounted behind the local adult captured a view of the children playing, similar to what the local adult saw. The second adult ("remote adult") was in an adjoining room watching the kids play via Skype on a 42" wall-mounted TV. Sound was transmitted using ClearOne USB speakerphones. The local adult always saw the remote adult on a Samsung 11" slate positioned on a table in front of the sofa, offset approximately 45 degrees to the right. This slate displays video captured by a webcam in the remote room. To capture video of the local adult, a second local webcam was mounted near the slate. We explored three arrangements for presenting the local video feeds to the remote adult.

In the *Swappable Views* condition (Figure 2), the remote adult could see on the TV either a view of the children playing Xbox or the local adult, but not both at the same time. Both adults could "swap" the views using a keyboard key. The local adult had an icon on their slate that indicated which view the remote adult was viewing. The remote adult was captured by a webcam centered under the TV.

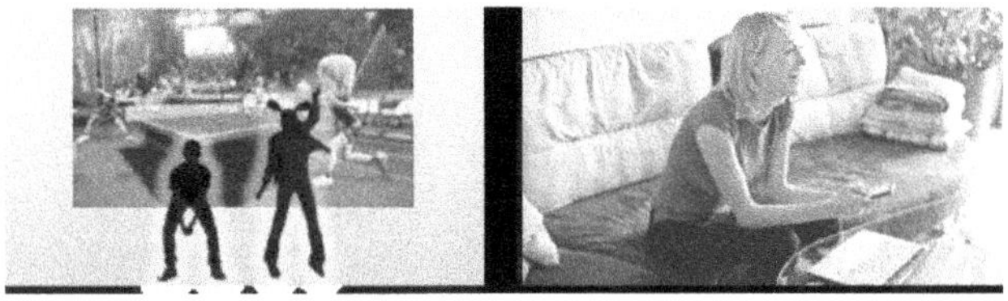

Figure 2. Swappable views condition (remote views).

In the *Picture-in-Picture* condition (Figure 3), the remote adult could see both the children and the local adult at the same time on the TV. A keyboard key was used to switch between having the children full-screen and the local adult in a small inset window, or vice versa. Similar to the first condition, the local adult knew which video view was enlarged by an icon that appeared on their slate. As before, a webcam centered under the TV captured the remote adult.

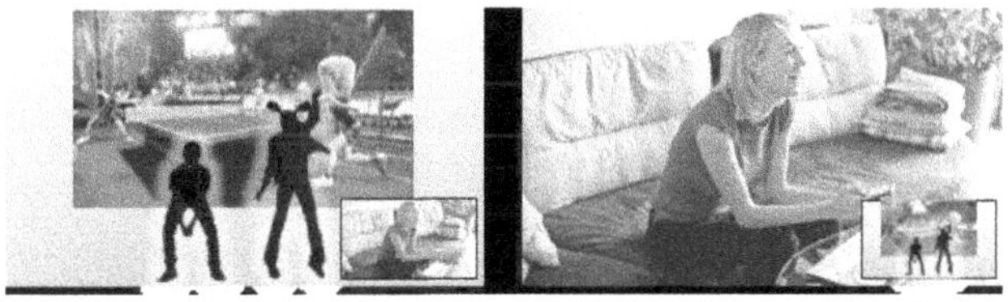

Figure 3. Picture-in-picture condition (remote views).

In the *Social Proxy* condition (Figure 4), we explored the use of a separate device to represent the local adult. The remote adult was provided with a separate screen (an 11" slate) to view the local adult, rather than having them appear on the TV. The slate was placed on the table directly in front of the participant, offset by approximately 45 degrees to the left. The webcam capturing the remote adult was placed directly above this slate to provide more accurate gaze information.

Figure 4. Social proxy condition (remote view).

We ran each condition for approximately 10 minutes and concluded the pilot study with a brief interview.

Results on Multiple Views

Swappable Views. People generally did not like swappable views. They did not like having to switch back and forth between the views and often lost track of what was happening in the other view. There was also some confusion as to who should swap the views. The local adult knew what was going on in the activity, but did not know exactly what the remote adult wanted to see.

Picture-in-Picture. People generally preferred picture-in-picture. It enabled them to see both views simultaneously without forcing the remote adult to attend to two separate screens. Views were switched (event large vs. local person large) less frequently than in the swappable views case.

Social Proxy. While some people preferred the social proxy, others found it distracting to attend to two screens. They did not like having to turn their heads back and forth. However, several local people liked that they could easily tell which screen their partner was attending to given the gaze feedback provided in this configuration.

During this pilot, we observed that socializing between the local and remote adults was an important part of the experience. The adults frequently talked with each other while watching the children. As a result, we developed a prototype design that provided simultaneous views of the local adult and the activity.

EXPERIENCES2GO (E2G) PROTOTYPE

Building on our pilot study results, we designed a prototype to explore mobile shared experiences with the following key design goals: 1) incorporate multiple simultaneous camera views; 2) use cameras that had pan, tilt, and zoom control and handled variable lighting conditions; and 3) work with standard Skype to leverage software with which our remote participants were already familiar.

Our E2G prototype utilized a Samsung 11" slate running Windows 7. We chose a slate, instead of the mobile phones used in earlier work, both to provide a comfortable size for viewing people over longer durations of interaction and provide a sufficiently powerful device to run our custom software described below. The front-facing camera on the slate provided the view of the local person. The built-in microphone and speakers on the slate were used for audio when possible; however, in many situations the ambient noise level was high, so the participants had to use a headset with a microphone.

Webcams are typically designed for near-field capture, which makes it difficult to capture events at a distance, especially since most webcams do not support optical zooming. Instead, we used a camcorder because its design affords capturing a wide range of activities. We utilized a Sony HDR-XR260V with a 30x optical zoom. Both the camera and the slate were mounted on a tripod to keep them steady without needing to be held (see Figure 5).

We streamed video from the camcorder to the slate using an EasyCap USB dongle, which converts a composite video signal to USB. We built a custom virtual webcam driver to produce a composite picture-in-picture image using the camcorder as the primary image and the front-facing camera on the slate as the secondary, smaller image.

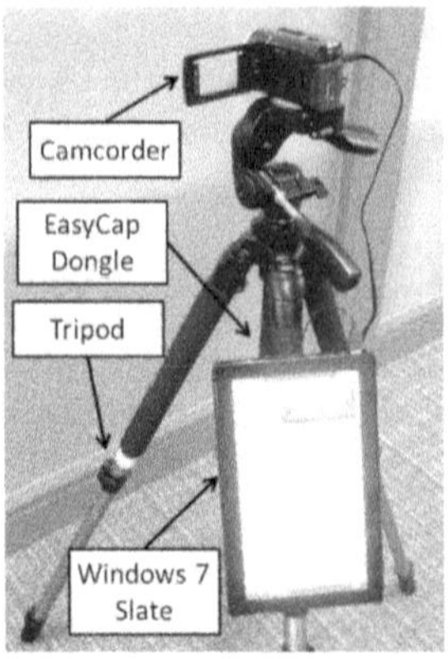

Figure 5. The E2G prototype enables a remote person to attend an event while also socializing with others at the event.

Skype was used for the audio and video connection. A Verizon 4G hotspot provided internet connectivity. Thus, our E2G prototype was completely wireless with approximately 100 minutes of battery life, allowing portable use almost anywhere.

FIELD STUDY

We deployed the two technology probes during real-life activities to explore their potential to share experiences with remote family or friends.

Methods

We recruited nine groups who were comfortable using Skype for video chat. Similar to our pilot, we recruited families with children who had a remote relative or close friend that wanted to watch an upcoming kids' activity. We provided suggestions but left it up to the parents to identify the event as well as the remote participant.

We wanted the experience to reflect real-life as much as possible, including the process of incorporating technology into an activity. Thus, we simply demonstrated how to use the devices, control the cameras, and made sure everything was working; otherwise, the participants did what they wanted and moved around with the devices as they liked.

After completing the study, we asked the local participant to complete a brief questionnaire and conducted a short semi-structured interview. The remote participant completed a similar questionnaire by email. We reviewed our interview and open-ended questionnaire response data for recurring themes and inductively compared specific instances of those themes across participants [13]. Our analysis focused on what features in the probes affected the participants' ability to share the experience over distance.

Results

We first describe the activities we observed. Because of the diverse activities and configuration of people involved, the insights gained varied across the sessions. We briefly summarize, illustrating with a photo, each of the nine sessions. We then follow up with more general results aggregated across the sessions. Seven of the groups used both devices, but due to technical issues, Group 1 used only the E2G prototype and Group 2 only the iPad.

Activities

The types of activities our participants chose for the study included watching children's sports events (swimming, gymnastics, soccer, and track and field), a birthday party, and play sessions (at the park and a local play center). Of the nine sessions, one involved remote grandparents, one a close friend, and the rest involved the other parent.

The activities can be clustered in terms of whether the adults were primarily spectators (i.e., just watching the activity), or if they were involved in the activity. Having the adults involved in the activity meant that 1) the local adult was interacting with both the children and the remote adult and 2) the children could also interact with the remote adult. We had three activities where the local parents were involved in the activities (a birthday party and two play sessions). The remaining activities were primarily spectator activities (sports) where the local and remote adults watched the activity together and talked with each other.

Group 1 - Fishing (local parent involved in the activity)

Our first session was a birthday party at a trout farm hatchery with two families and their five children. They connected with two grandparents who were located in different states. This group only used the E2G prototype. Although there was quite a lot of ambient noise from the pond (water pumps and a fountain), they did not use a headset since multiple people wanted to interact with the remote grandparents. However, using the internal speakers on the slate made it difficult for the local adult and kids to hear the grandparents unless they were very close to it.

Figure 6. Fishing with remote Grandmother and Grandfather.

The father was the primary person interacting with the E2G prototype and his parents (one at a time) were the remote participants. He spent a lot of time talking with his mother or father while watching the children. He gave his parents a tour of the facility and commentary about what the kids were doing. When one child caught a fish, remote Grandma was able to see this for herself from across the pond and became visibly excited: clapping and congratulating her grandson. From time to time, the grandkids would approach the E2G prototype and talk to their remote grandparents, even when neither of their parents were near it.

Both the father and the grandparents enjoyed interacting with the E2G prototype. They both also indicated that seeing each other was very important, as well as seeing the people and the activity at the same time.

When asked what they liked best about the experience, the father commented that *"having the [front-facing] and [rear-facing] video simultaneously is a great advantage.*" The grandfather explained that he liked "*the opportunity to talk one on one with your partner, while feeling a part of the activities.*" When asked what types of events the grandmother could imagine using a device like E2G, she replied, "*Watching my grandkids. At games, vacations. Feeling like I'm there with them.*"

Group 2 – Park (local parent involved in the activity)
The Group 2 session involved free play in a public park on a sunny day. The mother attended with her two children (ages 18 months and 3 years) while the father worked from home. Because of the loud noise of lawnmowers in the park, the mother had to use headphones. Due to technical problems she was unable to try the E2G prototype.

Figure 7. Playing in the park with remote Dad.

The mother had a difficult time managing the iPad while attending to her children. She struggled to carry one child while keeping up with their toddler who was running around the park with a friend. She tried balancing the iPad on her stroller to free her hands, but this did not capture the view she wanted (and the iPad eventually fell to the ground). Her attention was fragmented between what was going on with her kids in the local environment and her conversation with her husband.

The mother commented that she wanted ultra-mobility with "*a smaller device* [she] *could pull out of* [her] *pocket.*" For her, the iPad was bulky. The father commented that he liked the ability to "*be part of my kids' life while I am not able to be there physically*" even though he found the "*shaky camera image*" to be problematic. Neither parent felt that it was important to see each other.

Group 3 – Play Center (local parent involved in the activity)
For Group 3, the father took his daughter (21 months old) to an indoor play center while the mother attended from home. The play center had music playing in the background, so the father wore a headset to hear the mother. The headset tethered him to the device, limiting his movement. He first used the iPad and later used the E2G prototype.

The father started with a tour of the space after which he followed their daughter around as much as possible using the iPad. Apart from the initial greeting, he primarily used the rear-facing camera. There was no interaction between the remote mother and the daughter.

Figure 8. Play center with remote Mom.

After switching to the E2G prototype, the father struggled to keep up with his daughter, frequently moving and lifting the tripod. Eventually, he tried to position the tripod and engage in play with his daughter. He first positioned the camera so that the mother could see him push their daughter on a toy train, and later he aimed the camera to capture himself and his daughter playing with blocks on the floor. In both setups, he talked to the remote mother but did not seem to look at her on either the iPad or the E2G's slate. He commented that the "*[video of my wife] was not really that much important because I know her, I know where she is*".

The father felt that mobility was the most important feature, and therefore preferred the iPad setup, while the remote mother valued a zoomed in view of her daughter the most, and therefore preferred E2G. The mother also commented that she often had to ask her husband to adjust the camera to better capture their daughter and would therefore have liked "*to be in control of the zoom in and zoom out feature*" herself. The husband also agreed that it would be "*an amazing idea... I'm busy with her [daughter] playing around... and of course she [wife] would be interested in seeing more.*" Even though he was busy with the daughter and equipment, he said that "*I didn't really find it a big problem of like really concentrating on the conversation with my wife and with my child.*"

Group 4 – Swimming Lesson (local parent spectated)
In Group 4, a mother took her two sons (ages 8 and 13) to their swim lessons while a family friend (Jenny) connected from home via a laptop. Due to the noise in the pool area, the mother used a headset to hear Jenny better. She used the iPad first and then switched to the E2G prototype.

Figure 9. Swimming lesson with remote friend watching.

With the iPad, she stood at the edge of the pool to show the children swimming, primarily using the rear-facing camera. She had to be careful about getting splashed from the pool. She also wanted the children and Jenny to see each other, so she turned the iPad screen to the kids but struggled with displaying the correct (front-facing) camera.

When she switched to the E2G prototype, the mother sat down on a nearby bench to manipulate the camera. She was able to capture the children at any position in the pool while maintaining her conversation with Jenny.

During the interviews, both participants indicated that the interaction was very natural, especially when the remote person could see a zoomed in view of the event and the local person at the same time. Jenny said that "*it felt like I was sitting next to her when I could see her reactions and the kids swimming at the same time*". However, Jenny also reported that the view was choppier when it was zoomed in. This could be because the zoomed in view was disorienting to her when the mother panned and tilted the camera.

When asked what she liked best about the experience the mother explained "*it was wonderful to share my kids' activities real-time rather than just shooting video and emailing it later. It was fun to do.*" She also commented that she liked "*the immediacy of reaction with Jenny and her ability to ask questions and get answers real-time.*" Jenny also suggested improvements related to multiple views: "*I enjoyed the picture-in-picture but sometimes I wanted to be able to move it so I could see what it was covering up... or to turn that part off for a moment so I could see the whole picture of what the kids were doing.*"

Group 5 – Swim Team Practice (local parent spectated)
The Group 5 session involved a father watching his 12 year old daughter at her swim practice at a public pool, while the mother connected from home. Because of the noise in the pool area, the father had to use a headset to talk with his wife. He started with the iPad and primarily held it by balancing it on his knee. He periodically switched between the front- and rear-facing cameras on the iPad as he attempted to capture their daughter swimming but also engage in a conversation with his wife.

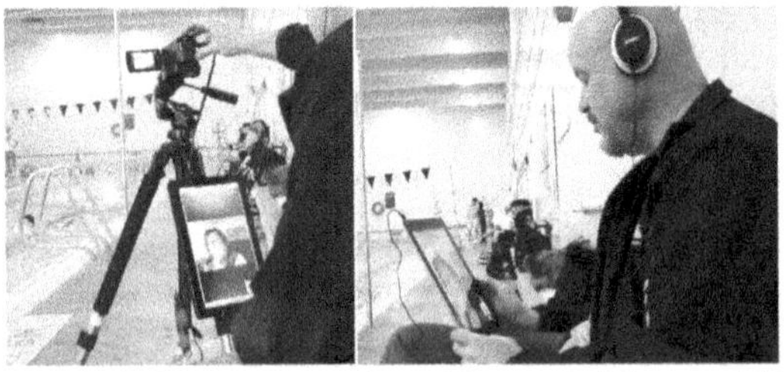

Figure 10. Swim team practice with remote Mom watching.

Next, he used the E2G prototype. He controlled the camera and zoomed into various shots of their daughter without difficulty. He and his wife conversed the whole time.

During the interview the father commented that he and his wife talked both about their daughter's swimming and general things related to their daily life. Both parents indicated that it was important to be able to see the other person as well as their daughter's swimming, and for this reason they liked the E2G system.

When asked what she liked best about the experience the remote mother commented: "*I liked being able to talk to my husband and also be able to see what was going on with my daughter.*" The father indicated that he liked being able to "*talk and show the event*". He also commented: "*the iPad is handy to just grab and go, making it portable. The camera + tripod takes a little more planning but would be great to capture special events where a loved one can't be there.*"

Group 6 – Gymnastics (local parent spectated)
For Group 6, a mother took her daughters (ages 7 and 9) to a gymnastics class while the father connected from home. The father was attending to both the gymnastics lesson and the dinner he was cooking. The mother wore a headset to hear the father over the noise of the gym. While she appeared to know several other parents at the gym, she interacted with them only once.

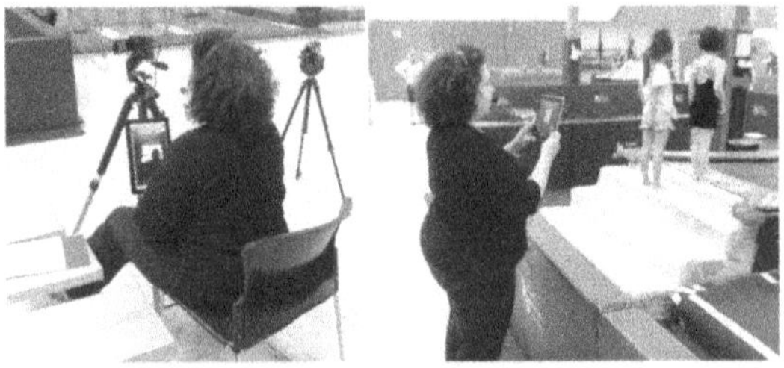

Figure 11. Gymnastics class with remote Dad.

They started with the E2G prototype and then used the iPad. With the E2G prototype, the mother sat on the benches and used the camcorder to zoom in, across the gym. With the iPad, she switched to the rear-camera and walked around the gym to get close to where her daughter was practicing. At times, she even removed her shoes and walked across the mats to capture a better shot. Throughout the session, the mother and father talked continuously. The video of the father was oversaturated because of a bright window behind him, making it difficult to see him. Also, due to technical problems, the iPad was unable to receive the father's video at times (the audio still worked fine).

When asked what they liked best about the experience, the mother commented that it was "*very cool to show my husband what the girls do at gymnastics. It felt like we were together.*" The father commented: "*I enjoyed the opportunity to watch my children's event. Being able to talk with them and see their event while preparing dinner from home was awesome.*" The mother also explained that she "*liked the clarity of the camera + tripod, but it limited motion*", and she "*liked the mobility of the iPad but it did not allow zoom/close-ups.*" The remote father felt that it was important to see both his wife as well as his daughters' activities, and hence he preferred the E2G system.

Group 7 – Outdoor Soccer (local parent spectated)
The Group 7 session involved a mother taking her 4-year old son to his soccer practice while the father connected from home. They first used the E2G prototype and then the iPad. Because the practice was at an outdoor field, the mother chose to have the tripod raised up high so she could

stand while both watching her son and talking to her husband. The mother would also occasionally talk to her son or the coach during the practice.

While using the E2G prototype, the mother frequently adjusted and zoomed the camera to keep their son in frame. During one water break, the son came over and wanted to talk to his father. When using the iPad, the mother primarily used the rear-facing camera and walked up and down the sideline, trying to keep her son in frame. In general, the parents talked throughout most of the session, often talking about their son's behavior during the soccer practice.

Figure 12. Outdoor soccer practice with remote Dad.

The mother felt that optical zoom was important because she could focus the camera on their son and talk to her husband. She preferred the simultaneous dual views of the E2G prototype "because I was able to interact with my husband at the same time as he was watching. With the iPad you either had to be flipping back and forth or you could only see one thing." Both parents felt that seeing each other was important as well as being able to see their son's soccer practice. Hence, both preferred the E2G prototype.

Group 8 – Indoor Soccer (local parent spectated)

For Group 8, the mother took her daughter (age 6) to her indoor soccer practice, while the father connected from his office. The mother used a headset to hear over the noise in the arena. They first used the E2G prototype followed by the iPad. The arrangement of the slate on the tripod made it difficult for the mother to sit, control the camera, and be face to face with her husband. Nevertheless, she felt that it was simply "*kind of a new thing that you've gotta get used to following someone around.*" During a water break, the daughter came over to her mother and her mother tried to get daughter to say hello to her father.

Figure 13. Indoor soccer practice with remote Dad.

With the iPad, the mother put a lot of effort into capturing a good view for her husband, walking everywhere to try to get close to her daughter. The mother stood to use the device but seemed to have to awkwardly look around the iPad to see what was going on for herself. "*I generally liked the freedom of moving the iPad around. I didn't like that you couldn't zoom in… I liked the freedom of being able to move around more and then switch from front to back.*"

Overall, this couple spent very little time talking, and primarily used the session as an opportunity for the father to watch his daughter. While the mother said it was somewhat important for her to see her husband, the father did not feel that it was important to see his wife's video.

Group 9 – Track Event (local parent spectated)

In Group 9, the father attended a district high school track and field event with his daughter (age 16) while the mother attended from home. The father wore a headset so that he could hear over the field announcements.

Figure 14. Track and field race with remote Mom.

The father was very comfortable using the camcorder mounted on the tripod. He first showed his wife the field and tried to find other kids they knew. He then zoomed in to where his daughter waited with her friends for her event. When the race started, he panned the camera to follow the event. Interestingly, the starting line for one race was on the other side of the track, which was difficult to see from the stands. The camcorder not only provided the remote mother with a view of her daughter, it also enabled the father to see his daughter at the starting line. "*What my wife liked is what she could see. It was like, 'Hey, I've never been able to see her get into her blocks'…being able to zoom way over there…she kept saying, 'Hey, this is kinda neat!'*"

When using the iPad, the father primarily used the rear-facing camera, even after his daughter's event was over and he returned to conversing with his wife. However, the mother was not able to see as much detail as she could with the E2G prototype.

The father commented that he liked being able to "*interact and share the activity*". He was very comfortable with the tripod and liked being able to zoom in with the E2G prototype. Unfortunately, the mother did not submit her questionnaire so we do not have her feedback.

Overall Preference

The goal of this study was not to compare the iPad to the E2G prototype, but instead look at the participants' overall preferences to provide insights into the importance of the features of each device. Of the seven groups that tried both devices, 12 participants expressed a preference (two remote participants did not complete these questions). In what follows, we represent a participant by their group number followed by L for local and R for remote person.

Looking at the absolute preferences, six participants preferred the iPad (3L, 4L, 6L, 8L, 4R, 8R). Preferring the iPad correlated with the importance of mobility for the event and not being concerned about seeing or socializing with the other adult. All three participants who expressed that they did not care whether they could see their partner favored the iPad (6L, 4R, 8R) as did the couple who did not socialize much and instead focused primarily on allowing the remote father to see the activity (8L, 8R).

The remaining six participants preferred the E2G prototype. Remote participants liked seeing both the local adult and the activity at the same time (5R, 3R, 6R), and local participants used the prototype in situations where mobility was either not critical or not possible (5L, 7L, 9L).

Engagement

One of the key goals of this study was to better understand how to support a feeling of *togetherness*, where families felt like they were experiencing the event together. The questionnaire posed three questions related to this aspect, "Compared to other forms of videoconferencing:"

1. it felt more like my partner and I were interacting naturally, as if we were together
2. it felt more like I was experiencing the activity with my partner
3. this experience was more engaging

Participants were asked to provide ratings for each of these questions on a seven point scale (1=strongly disagree; 7=strongly agree). For the 12 participants who provided ratings for both the E2G prototype and the iPad, we analyzed the responses using Wilcoxon Signed Ranks tests. Table 1 shows the mean and median results for each question, along with the number of people who gave each prototype the higher rating.

		E2G	iPad
Q1	# who gave higher rating	7	1
	mean (SD)	5.3 (1.2)	4.5 (1.6)
Q2	# who gave higher rating	8	1
	mean (SD)*	6.0 (1.2)	4.8 (1.7)
Q3	# who gave higher rating	7	2
	mean (SD)*	6.1 (1.0)	5.1 (1.6)

Table 1. Engagement ratings for E2G and iPad (*p<.05).

For all three questions, more participants rated the E2G prototype higher. For both Q2 and Q3, the difference in ratings was significantly different, Z=-2.35, p=.019 and Z=-2.0, p=.046 respectively, while the difference for Q1 was not statistically different, Z=-1.653, p=.098.

These results suggest the combined ability to zoom in on the action and for the local and remote person to see each other is important for the feeling of togetherness. The participants' comments offer further evidence of this. Several participants explicitly commented that they enjoyed the experience and felt very connected to their partner. 6L exclaimed: "*It felt like we were together. Personally, I loved the engagement I felt with my husband. Very cool!!*" 4R reported: "*I felt like I was sitting next to her when I could see her reactions and the kids swimming at the same time.*" 5R also commented that the shared context that multiple videos provided meant that "*I could sit and talk like I was next to him*".

Technology concerns

Several key concerns related to both the E2G prototype and the iPad were observed during the study.

Hands-Free Mobility

Mobility is important for the types of scenarios examined in this study. First, all of these activities took place outside the home, so any technology being used needs to be transported to the event. This was problematic for our current E2G prototype since it is relatively large and awkward. Several participants commented that this was the key drawback of the device. Second, if the local adult needed to move around during the activity (as was the case for the play sessions), mobility became even more critical. Third, holding a device in-hand for an extended period of time is inconvenient if the adult is participating in the activity and tiresome over long periods of time. Ideally, the local adult should have a device that is both mobile and hands free.

Video

The E2G prototype was better able to capture most of the kids' activities because it utilized a camcorder with 30X optical zoom. The lack of camera zoom was the biggest concern for most people using the iPad (7L: "*[I] liked the mobility of the iPad but it did not allow zoom/close-ups*"). The video from the iPad was reasonable when the local adult could get close enough to the activity, but the remote adult had a hard time following far away activities.

Unlike the iPad, the E2G prototype was able to simultaneously show the view of the local adult and the activity, and many of our participants expressed a strong desire for this feature. E2G shows both video streams to the remote adult using a picture-in-picture configuration. However, several remote adults felt that sometimes the picture-in-picture view obscured key areas of the video, so they wanted the ability to move and occasionally turn off the inset picture.

With both the E2G prototype and the iPad, the local adult framed the view for the remote adult. While this makes sense for coarse camera positioning, continual fine-grain adjustments were tedious. Several remote adults commented that they would like to be able to pan and zoom the camera themselves (3R: "*I also would have liked to be in control of the zoom in and zoom out feature*").

Audio

The audio in our experiment was problematic in most of the sessions. It was hard for the local and remote adult to hear each other given the ambient noise in the locations. As a result, the local adult in all but two of the sessions used a headset to improve audio quality. While the headset was beneficial in this regard, it also meant that only one person could talk to the remote adult, and the local adult was cutoff from conversations with other local people at the event. Furthermore, the headset prevented the remote adult from interacting with other local people (including the kids).

Framing

Keeping the children's activity in the camera frame was a challenge. In most cases, the E2G prototype provided better framing, but required the local adult to continuously adjust the camera pan, tilt, and zoom settings.

Another challenge related to framing was getting a reasonable view of the local adult. The positioning of the slate on the tripod often made it difficult for the slate camera to adequately capture the local adult, especially while they were operating the camcorder on the tripod.

Interestingly, in several of our sessions the children wanted to see the remote adult as well. For the E2G prototype, this worked if the child came around to the back side of the prototype (in front of the slate), but if the child interacted from the front of the prototype, they were able to talk to the remote adult, but could not actually see them. The same was true for the iPad, unless the local adult turned the iPad around and switched to the front-facing camera view.

DISCUSSION

The results of this study have several implications for the design of future video communication systems.

Going Beyond Talking Heads

At the highest level, our study shows that people want to share experiences outside the home with remote family and friends. These experiences go beyond talking heads on screens to configurations that enable remote users to feel like they are actually attending an event. Enhancing users' sense of presence is challenging, but as shown in our study, providing multiple camera views can help a remote user feel like they are watching the event *and* socializing with other people who are local to the event.

Designing for Multiple Stakeholders

The design of systems for shared mobile experiences must consider the needs of all stakeholders. When Grandma is remotely watching her grandson's baseball game, it is easy to envision Grandma as the main stakeholder (as depicted in our opening vignette). However, our observations identified four distinct types of stakeholders, and it is important to design for all of them.

One stakeholder is of course the remote observer, such as a parent, grandparent, or close friend, who benefits by being able to observe the local event live. The primary need of the remote observer is to see and hear the event. However, as we observed in this study, enabling the remote person to also socialize with other stakeholders is valuable.

A second stakeholder is the local observer who is sharing the local experience with the remote participant. The local observer has two key roles: streaming the activity to the remote observer and socializing with the remote observer. We observed many pairs talking and interacting with each other during the event. While some of this interaction was about the shared activity, it was often general discourse about daily life. This "small talk" (also found in [10]) is an important feature when people share activities in person, and mobile video extends opportunities for keeping socially in touch with remote people. For the local person, being able to socialize with a remote person can also make the activity more enjoyable by filling in dead time in the activity (e.g., time between kid's races, breaks).

A third set of stakeholders is the local participants engaged in the activity, such as the children in our study. Enabling remote people to attend the event means that it can feel like more people are joining to watch their activity. For instance, kids will feel like the local *and* remote adults are actually at their event, which is important to them. Many of the children in our study loved the fact that their remote family members could be at their activity, and we observed several kids waving to or trying to talk to the remote adult.

The fourth stakeholder is the social context around the shared activity. This social context is made up of the three sets of stakeholders already discussed and other people around the local observer (i.e., other people watching the activity). We observed that these people sometimes interacted with the local and remote observers. Such interactions are important for enhancing the remote attendee's feeling of being at the event. Also, the experience should not detract from the local participants' social interactions with others at the event. Therefore, it is important to consider the social context around the activity when designing systems to support shared activities.

Our findings complement those from studies of mobile video calls out in public [10], which identified issues around managing boundaries for privacy and distraction between the private video call and others in the surrounding area. Our goal was to *include* a remote person in the shared activity, enabled in part by the larger video window in either E2G or the iPad. Thus, our design implications include how to integrate the surrounding social context as a stakeholder, rather than maintain boundaries from it.

Supporting Diverse Scenarios

Our participants illustrated a diverse range of scenarios for sharing experiences in mobile environments. The variety of these events and the different needs of the stakeholders identify several important considerations when designing technology to support these activities.

One key consideration is the wide variation of motivations and goals for joining in the activity exhibited across our nine groups. One of the more compelling scenarios is including geographically remote participants who could not otherwise attend, like the grandparents in Group 1. This distance naturally provides motivation for enabling opportunities to participate in kids' events and socialize more with the local adult family members. However, it is interesting to reflect on the motivations of the remaining eight groups that chose to involve a spouse or a friend that was geographically local. These "nearby" participants were involved in other activities (cooking, working from home) or in settings that did not offer scheduling flexibility (working at the office). Remotely joining offered them more flexibility in terms of scheduling (avoiding travel time). Specifically, while doing other activities they could pay partial attention to the kids' event and socialize with adults at the event. While we did not initially envision these scenarios, our experiences suggest that if sharing mobile experiences becomes easy and satisfying, connecting nearby participants may become a more common scenario.

Another key factor is the degree of involvement of the local observer in the event. On one end of the spectrum, the local observer may only be a spectator, such as the father who watched swim practice from the pool side. At the other end of the spectrum, the local observer may be highly embedded in the activity, such as the father who helped his kids catch fish at the fish hatchery birthday party.

When the local observer is spectating, seeing the remote person may be important so that socializing is more natural and enjoyable. However, when the local observer is participating in the activity, it may be less important to see the remote person. In our study, we observed two activities where this requirement differed. In the fish hatchery scenario, the father divided his attention between helping his children fish and talking with his parents. Having a view of his parents was important when he or his kids were talking with them, but it was less critical when he was busy with his children. In contrast, during the play center scenario, the father was actively engaged in playing with his daughter and did not want to visually attend to the device. He also did not feel it was important to see his wife; therefore, an audio-only link may have been sufficient.

Another consideration is whether the local person is primarily stationary or moving around at the event. When moving around, it is important that the device is easy to carry or reposition. For example, the mother watching her daughter's soccer practice wanted to walk around to get a good view, which the small form factor of the iPad afforded. A counter example is the father watching his daughter's swimming lesson. He was primarily stationary, so he liked the hands-free nature of the E2G prototype, even though it was less portable than the iPad.

Another factor is whether the local person is close to or far away from the event. At one end of the spectrum, the local observer may be close to the event, or able to walk up close to the event, as with the mother at the gym with her children. On the other end of the spectrum, the local observer may be far from the event or physically prevented from coming close, as with the father watching his daughter's track and field event from the stands. When the parent is close to the activity, a typical webcam may be sufficient. However, when the parent is far away, a camera that supports optical zoom will likely be required, and may benefit both the local and the remote participant.

A further distinction is whether the people taking part in the activity (e.g., the children) or other local observers want to interact with the remote person. For example, the children in the fish hatchery session wanted to talk to their grandmother and show her the fish they caught. In order to support these auxiliary social exchanges it is important that everyone can see and talk to the remote person.

Providing Technological Support

We used the iPad and E2G to probe two points in a wide design space of possible systems to support mobile shared experiences. By observing the usage of two devices with different capabilities and limitations, we gained insight and understanding into the important capabilities for enabling mobile shared experiences. As our observations showed, neither the iPad nor the E2G prototype was optimal for all the activities we observed. In this section, we discuss some of the design implications open for future exploration.

Mobility

When the local participant is in a crowded space or wants to move around, having a smaller, more portable device, such as an iPad, is beneficial. At the same time, if the participant is involved in the activity, having to hold the device can be problematic. As we observed in Group 2, it was extremely difficult for the mother to hold the device while playing with her kids in the park, and it was not easy to set the iPad down and capture the event. Additionally, continually holding the device for long activities will get tiresome. More design exploration is needed for a compact yet hands-free devices, perhaps something that is wearable.

Pan-Tilt-Zoom

When the local participant is far from the event, having optical zoom capabilities is important. However, when high optical zoom is used, such as the 30X in our prototype, it is important to stabilize the video or else the remote experience will be unstable and jerky.

Who controls the pan-tilt-zoom is also important. In our study, the local observer controlled the pan-tilt-zoom, but several people commented that the remote observer should control the camera. This feature would provide the remote person with the freedom to choose the view they were most interested in and free up the local observer to enjoy the event and to socialize with others. These observations suggest that future systems should include powerful pan-tilt-zoom capabilities that can be controlled by both local and remote participants.

Seeing Both People and Activity Simultaneously

Many of the remote observers in our study expressed a strong desire to see both the local observer and the activity at the same time. The ability to see and hear each other can dramatically improve the social aspects of the experience. When providing remote observers with multiple video streams, it is also important to give them control over how each video appears on-screen. In the E2G prototype, the video of the local observer was fixed in size and inset into the video of the activity. Several remote adults expressed that sometimes the picture-in-picture view obscured key areas of the video. As a result, future systems should allow flexible positioning of concurrent multiple views.

Robust Audio

Ambient noise was often an issue in the shared experiences we observed. Using headsets can improve the quality of the audio between the local and remote person, but limits interaction with others. The local participants cannot easily talk to other local people at the event and interaction with the remote person is reduced since only the person with the headset can talk to them. A better solution may be to use microphones with ambient noise suppression and loud speakers. Of course, use of loud speakers may not be socially acceptable when there are strangers around. As is often the case with video communication, clear audio with appropriate volume control is crucial for a good experience.

CONCLUSION

Our goal was to gain a better understanding of the types of experiences outside the home that people want to share and the pain points they encounter when using existing technologies to accomplish this. We carried out a field study using two technology probes with distinctly different capabilities as a way to get a wider range of insights into these scenarios.

Our study produced several insights. First, the results show that people want to share experiences outside the home with remote and nearby family and friends. While they understand the limitations of existing technologies, they are willing to struggle through them to share the experience with a remote loved one. Second, besides the remote participant, there is a rich social context of other stakeholders that needs to be considered in designing mobile shared experiences. Third, there is a wide variety of sharing scenarios with different participant goals and requirements. Finally, we propose design implications for future systems around mobility, zoom, camera control, video views, and audio.

In the future, we plan to expand shared experiences beyond those involving kids at a particular location to events with a broader range such as a hike or a visit to a zoo. We will also continue to investigate whether audio between the local and remote observers is sufficient in certain circumstances if they have a shared view of the event. Finally, we plan to explore additional technology probes that combine the mobility and sleekness of the iPad with the zoom and multi video streaming capability of the E2G prototype.

ACKNOWLEDGEMENTS

We would like to thank our study participants for their time in sharing their experiences with us. In addition, we are grateful to Tom Blank and Kris Crews for helping us construct the E2G prototype.

REFERENCES

1. Bly, S., Harrison, S., Irwin, S. Media spaces: bringing people together in a video, audio, and computing environment. *CACM* 36, 1 (1993), 28-46.
2. Brubaker, J, Venolia, G., Tang, J. Focusing on shared experiences: Moving beyond the camera in video communication. *Proc. DIS 2012* (2012), 96-105.
3. Gaver, W., Sellen, A., Heath, C., Luff, P. One is not enough: multiple views in a media space. *Proc. CHI 1993,* 335-341.
4. Hutchinson, H., Mackay, W., Westerlund, B., Bederson, B., Druin, A., Plaisant, C., Beaudouin-Lafon, M., Conversy, S., Evans, H., Hansen, H., Roussel, N., Eiderbäck, B. Technology probes: Inspiring design for and with families. *Proc. CHI 2003*, 17-24.
5. Judge, T., Neustaedter, C. Sharing conversation and sharing life: video conferencing in the home. *Proc. CHI 2010,* 655-658.
6. Juhlin, O., Engström, A., Reponen, E. Mobile broadcasting: the whats and hows of live video as a social medium. *Proc. MobileHCI 2010,* 35-44.
7. Kirk, D., Sellen, A., Cao, X. Home video communication: mediating 'closeness'. *Proc. CSCW 2010,* 135-144.
8. Mueller, F., Vetere, F., Gibbs, M., Edge, D., Agramanolis, S., Sheridan, J., Heer, J. Balancing exertion experiences, *Proc. CHI 2012*, 1853-1862.
9. Neustaedter, C., Judge, T. Peek-A-Boo: The Design of a Mobile Family Media Space, *Ext. Abstracts Ubicomp 2010*, 449-450.
10. O'Hara, K., Black, A., Lipson, M. Everyday Practices with Mobile Video Telephony. *Proc. CHI 2006*, 871-880.
11. Raffle, H., Revelle, G., Mori, K., Ballagas, R., Buza, K., Horii, H., Kaye, J., Cook, K., Freed, N., Go, J., Spasojevic, M. Hello, is grandma there? let's read! StoryVisit: family video chat and connected e-books. *Proc. CHI 2011,* 1195-1204.
12. Romero, N., Markopoulos, P., van Baren, J., de Ruyter, B., IJsselsteijn, W., Farshchian, B. Connecting the family with awareness systems. *Personal and Ubiquitous Computing* 11, 4 (2007), 299-312.
13. Strauss, A., Corbin, J. Basics of Qualitative Research, Sage Publications (1998).
14. Vutborg, R., Kjeldskov, J., Pedell, S., Vetere, F. Family storytelling for grandparents and grandchildren living apart. *Proc. NordiCHI 2010,* 531-540.
15. Weisz, J., Kiesler, S., Zhang, H., Ren, Y., Kraut, R., Konstan, J. Watching together: integrating text chat with video. *Proc. CHI 2007,* 877-886.
16. Yarosh, S., Inkpen, K., Brush, A.J. Video playdate: Toward free play across distance. *Proc. CHI 2010,* 1251-1260.

Opportunities via Extended Networks for Teens' Informal Learning

Peyina Lin
The Information School
University of Washington
pl3@uw.edu

Shelly D. Farnham
FUSE Labs, Microsoft Research
One Microsoft Way, Redmond, WA 98052
shellyfa@microsoft.com

ABSTRACT
With the increasing use of the Internet and social media for knowledge and social connections, we might expect that people more easily expand their opportunities for new learning through social relationships online. Yet, this mixed methods study of teens' use of technologies (e.g. YouTube and social media) in informal learning contexts reveals that, in teens' preferred learning activities, few interact with new ties outside their *immediate networks* (school, family, and friends). Given the value of social interaction and weak ties for learning new knowledge, this research investigates teens' use of networked technologies with people and resources outside their immediate networks. Based on 23 semi-structured interviews, we describe teens' informal learning activities and technology practices, from which we identify design opportunities. To inform these, we examine teens' paths into extended networks, including the role of digital skills, technology access, intrinsic motivation, and sense of relatedness. We find that relatedness both motivated and inhibited teens to reach beyond immediate networks into *extended networks* for informal learning activities.

Author Keywords
Teens; social networks; ties; informal learning; social media; motivation; relatedness; mixed methods.

ACM Classification Keywords
H.5.m. Information interfaces and presentation (e.g., HCI): miscellaneous

General Terms
Human Factors

INTRODUCTION
Livy joined a community of vegan bloggers and one of fan video creators on YouTube. Through these communities, she made new friends and learned new skills: "*I use [the Internet] to learn different things and get involved in communities...*".

Shel, on the other hand, chose how to spend time based on her friends, to the point of missing out on developing other interests: *"I kinda want to do gymnastics, but they don't have that in school. So I feel I'm missing out... I could join a gymnastics team, but I just don't like doing things where I don't know anybody..."*

Livy and Shel both consider themselves to be advanced users of the Internet, and both rated themselves similarly on a series of technology skills. However, Livy expands her learning domains by connecting via technologies with her *extended networks*—people outside the networks of the family, friends, and school with whom the average teenager regularly interacts throughout the day. In contrast, Shel limits her learning activities based on what her friends do, thus restricting her connections within her *immediate networks*—people embedded in the average teenager's structured daily activities: school, family, and friends. This paper is primarily about these differences in teens' social and socio-technical behavior of *informal learning* in extracurricular activities. From their experiences, we draw some conceptual design implications aimed at encouraging teens to use technologies to interact with their extended networks for new informal learning opportunities. We use *technologies* to refer to interconnected, computerized tools such as social media, peer-production sites, and texting.

Reaching *extended networks* is important because learning new information is more likely to occur via *weak* and/or *new ties* [16]—people not deeply embedded in existing networks of social relationships. Those that reach extended networks will likely bridge networks that are otherwise disconnected. By spanning such structural holes [9] between networks, these people have "early access" to learn alternative ways of thinking, "which gives them a competitive advantage in seeing good ideas" [9].

Learning via *technologies* has individual and societal benefits. Individually, technologies help teens more easily reach out to their extended networks to access resources not available face-to-face. At the societal level, if people can conveniently reach extended networks, then they have the opportunity to contribute to social capital by acting as brokers between networks; e.g., transferring best practices, or synergizing elements beneficial across networks [9]. Thus, those who reach extended networks can contribute to learning, creativity and innovation in society [9, 11].

Teens are particularly poised to benefit from technologies that support learning from extended networks. Develop-

CSCW '13, February 23–27, 2013, San Antonio, Texas, USA.
Copyright 2013 ACM 978-1-4503-1331-5/13/02...$15.00.

mentally, teens are forming vocational interests and life-long learning patterns. These are shaped by teens' socio-cultural ecologies [28]. During the teenage period, these ecologies evolve to depend less on parents or peers [28]. Nowadays, embedded in teens' ecologies are technologies like Facebook, texting, and YouTube as teens are amongst their most frequent users [24]. So, through these technologies we have a design opportunity to support teens' development in ways that broaden their horizons with diversity, specialized knowledge, and social support.

Despite high levels of teen social media use [24] and the benefits of new knowledge via extended networks, we found in this study of teens (ages 13-17) that few interact with extended networks for informal learning. Therefore, our primary research question in this paper is: **why are some teens using technologies for informal learning via extended networks online while others are not**?

In the rest of the paper, we explore first the informal learning activities teens engage in; what contributes to their initiation and continuation; the role of technologies for informal learning, and the differences of technology use with immediate vs. extended networks. We identify design opportunities based on these differences, and delve into participants' social behavior to inform such space. We analyze how technology affordances may explain differences in use. Then, we propose pathways to reaching extended networks. First, we examine how digital skills, technology access, and motivational forces are related to informal learning behaviors. Then, we explore how *relatedness* (desire for belonging and connection) encourages and inhibits technology use with extended networks. Finally, we offer conceptual design recommendations to encourage teens to use their extended networks online for new learning opportunities.

BACKGROUND AND RELATED LITERATURE

Because we are interested in teens' development of sustainable life-long learning behaviors, we focus on the *informal learning* practices occurring in activities that are not required by the school. The social and learning processes occurring in such extracurricular activities are referred to as *informal learning behavior* [1, 4]. Focusing on informal learning is important because more than 80% of teens' waking hours consist of informal learning outside the classroom [1]. More importantly, when teens pursue extra-curricular activities of interest such as playing sports in a team, music apprenticeships, or producing and sharing videos with friends, they are more likely to build the social and personal supports needed to sustain their participation in these activities and to develop their formation as persons [4]. That is, in addition to developing expertise, these activity contexts support the development of feelings of competence and sense of belonging [4], which are central to a learner's motivation and well-being [32].

In line with informal learning practices, we take a broad perspective of *learning* as the practices and social interactions that support the development of interests and continued engagement in an activity. Rather than measuring changes in domain expertise or knowledge, we focus on occurrences that support the initiation and continuation in extracurricular learning activities.

Teens spend more time using technologies out of school than in school [2], which sets informal learning as a rich setting to study technology use. In the HCI/CSCW community and nationally, there has been widespread interest in computer-supported learning of technology development skills. Different approaches have been used to advance such learning, including improving the user interface to help learn programming logic [26, 27], learning through gamification [21, 26], tailoring learning to particular interests [8], or addressing social-psychological concerns like sense of community [7] and work attribution [27].

We deliberately chose to focus on teens' informal learning in *any* extracurricular activity rather than specifically on computer programming to prevent biasing against the technologically disadvantaged. To clarify, a digital divide exists, such that the economically disadvantaged cannot afford the resources to regularly access the technology, people, and specialized knowledge needed to succeed at technology development [33]. Furthermore, focusing on technology development can turn off learners who do not identify as computer people. Their social identification constrains their desire to learn about computers [10, 25].

The emerging prominence of social media across people with varying computer skills may provide new informal learning opportunities. This is especially of interest since, according to social constructivism [34], learning occurs through social interaction and the collaborative creation of shared meaning. For example, Bruckman[1] [7] shows that social interaction with community members is the basis for socio-technical support for children learning computer programming. Greenhow and Robelia [17] find that students receive social and academic support from friends through social network sites. Others study the socialization and feedback enabled by peer-content-production-and sharing [6, 27], conduct experiments to assess how virtual environments transform social interactions between teachers and learners [3], or develop social software to support formal learning [14]. Our research differs from this body of work as we focus on how interests develop and are sustained in informal learning contexts, and how technologies may support this.

Another related body of work focuses on social media for friendships, intimate relationships, and social capital. For example, research on digital youth [6, 19, 30] finds that teens largely interact with friends and rarely meet strangers online (which we add, exist in their extended networks) because it is risky and scary [6, 30]. We similarly explore teens' interactions with friends and strangers; however, we

[1] Technically, her stance is social *constructionism*, with an additional focus on object construction; though in both stances knowledge is built by the learner via interaction with an "other".

focus on pathways that facilitate reaching extended networks in areas of interest to enrich informal learning.

Immediate and extended networks

We carefully chose the terms *immediate networks* and *extended networks* after evaluating existing theories. No terminology fully fit our data, but Granovetter's seminal work on *strong* and *weak* ties [16] was most relevant.

Although Granovetter [16]'s work is popularly known, the terms *strong* and *weak* ties naturally lead people to think of the strength of ties at the expense of potentially overlooking two network *structural* characteristics, which he emphasizes: *network density* and the *bridging power* of weak ties. As he states: "one's weak ties which are not local bridges might as well be counted with the strong ties, to maximize separation of the dense from the less dense network sectors" [16]. (Local bridges are ties that directly connect people from socially distant networks [16].) Citing Epstein [13]'s "effective network," Granovetter explains that people in these dense networks are more likely to know each other, and thus more likely to diffuse redundant information that could be obtained from someone else in the network. In contrast, Epstein's "extended network" refers to the remainder of one's network—the non-densely connected and therefore less likely to know each other [13].

We preserved Epstein [13]'s use of *extended networks* rather than "weak ties" (in its structural sense) to refer to people not densely connected with one's network, who can bridge one to new connections regardless of tie strength. Although we do not measure tie strength or network density, conceptually, separating structural concepts from tie strength prevents us from the ambiguous placement of close-ties-that-bridge (and weak-ties-that-do-not-bridge). In other words, there may be people with whom a teen feels close, who *bridge* the teen to extended networks; e.g., a close friend who does not participate in the same activities and who has a distinct set of friends from the teen's. Under a *structural* view that forgoes tie-strength, these close-connections-that-bridge would be considered "weak ties" in extended networks because their networks are not densely connected with the teen's (the reason their ties do not overlap). In fact, "sparse" and "dense" ties rather than "weak" and "strong" ties would better capture density-structure independently from tie strength. Additionally, during Internet times, *extended networks* may include strangers (which could become ties); e.g., new social interactions on deviant art or YouTube.

Conversely, we use the term *immediate networks* to refer to *dense*-connections-of-strong-ties[2] and some weak-ties-that-do-not-bridge; e.g., classmates involved in similar activities. Furthermore, although *immediate networks* share structural meanings with "strong ties" or Epstein's "effective networks" by referring to *densely* connected people with whom teens interact intensely and regularly (i.e., teens' family and activity friends), our findings suggest that these networks are not always "effective." They may act as barriers for learners to reach new networks.

We clarify that both the person who reaches the extended network and the person in the extended network being reached may become local bridges [16] for their immediate networks. The bridge is formed by the link between them. Thus, as made evident in Burt [9], the bridging power of Granovetter [16]'s weak ties is explicitly related to the "vision advantage" in Burt [9]'s work on structural holes. Specifically, people who reach extended networks are positioned to synthesize ideas from otherwise disconnected networks or seemingly distinct ways of thinking; and thus are positioned to learn and generate new ideas.

MIXED METHODS STUDY

We performed a mixed methods study with 23 in-depth semi-structured interviews (120 minutes each) with teens aged 13 to 17. Given the interdisciplinary nature of the problem space, we adopted a mixed-method approach in which "the researcher mixes or combines quantitative and qualitative research techniques, methods..., or language into a single study" [22]. Our purpose is to answer our research questions through triangulation (corroborating results from quantitative and qualitative analysis) and complementarity (use qualitative data to clarify numeric findings) [22] where possible. We drew on literature to inform our data collection instrument and sensitize our analysis, but let the exploratory nature of studying teens' informal learning carry us to unexpected territories. For example, although we were initially vested in teens' learning communities on and offline, our conceptualization of immediate and extended networks arose as each interviewee led us to further probe on why only a few teens interacted with extended networks via technologies.

Our semi-structured interviews guided the direction of the interview, but let participants shape the flow of conversation based on their experiences [31]. The interview had various subsections, as described next.

Informal learning activities: We asked each participant to pick an extracurricular activity for which they "learned something *new*, were creative, and found enjoyment." We asked them to pick an activity that they could "delve into quite deeply", and left this open-ended to explore opportunities to engage teens around their interests. Participants also talked about activities they would have liked to learn but gave up.

Technology use: At the start of the interview, we asked participants about their technology usage and technology skills. After discussing their extracurricular activity, we asked: "What resources if any did you use during...?" their activity, including technologies, information, or people. Participants showed how they used these resources. When possible, they re-enacted what they had done in real-life.

Motivation: As motivation can play an important role in learning [32], we probed for motivational forces behind

[2] We emphasize the term dense rather than strong for network density enables us to know our strong ties' ties.

teens' activities. We drew on Self-Determined Theory (SDT) [32], a theory of motivation. Based on SDT, motivation has two broad categories: intrinsic and extrinsic. *Intrinsic motivation* is the inherent disposition a learner has towards activities for their enjoyment, satisfaction, novelty, and optimal challenge [32]. *Extrinsic motivation* refers to a learner's disposition towards activities which are done to fulfill expectations or achieve separable outcomes [32]. Extrinsic motivation can be internalized, and the degree of internalization falls along a continuum[3] [32].

Questions to get at motivation include: "how did you first get involved in...?" "Who or what inspired you to get involved?" In addition, we asked True/False questions adapted from [32]. Indicators of intrinsic motivation include: "is enjoyable; is interesting to explore; is positively challenging." Indicators of extrinsic motivation include: "because when completed someone will give you a price, reward, or other form of recognizing your accomplishment; to avoid feelings of guilt; to prove to others you can do it."

Relatedness: *Relatedness* refers to the need for belonging and connectedness. Skills, competence or autonomy on their own are insufficient to sustain a learner's engagement [32]. Motivation can become internalized when *relatedness,* autonomy and competence are supported over time.

Relatedness affects initial engagement because people "are prompted by others to whom they feel (or want to feel) attached or related" [32]. Thus, to get at *initial* influence, we derived from motivation questions such as "who inspired you". To get at the support for *continued* engagement, we asked: "Did you get any feedback on how you did in...? From whom? How?" "Did you feel like others valued your learning/participation in this activity?"

Digital and social digital skills, and technology access: As there is widespread interest in the role of digital skills or competencies in enabling life-long learning [18, 33], we sought to examine the relationship between digital skills, technology access, and using technologies with extended networks. We use the terms skills and competencies interchangeably. Because we were particularly interested in how teens initially reached extended networks, we separated the social skills for using communication technologies from other digital skills.

Thus *social digital skills* refer to the sense of competence towards communication and social media technologies. These skills include using email, social network sites, Twitter, creating/using group-tools like Facebook groups and forums, sharing information, and setting privacy (adapted from [18, 33]). *Digital skills* refer to the self-reported sense of competence on technologies that do not involve social interactions with others. Digital skills include using the web, producing websites, searching, altering photos, creating PDFs, audio and video production, and online security related items [18]. Participants self-rated their expertise on a scale (1 = novice, 5 = expert). Items were averaged to represent their overall skills score.

Technology access is also relevant to our study because it is associated with the strategic use of technologies [33]. Though *technology access* is a compound concept [12, 33], we adopted *usage access* or Internet use in hours per week, as a quick proxy during recruitment. Both when screening for participation and during the interviews participants provided basic demographic, technology access, digital, and social digital skills in a brief questionnaire.

PARTICIPANTS

We recruited participants of diverse ethnicity, socio-economic status, and varying levels of technology use. We balanced for gender and levels of Internet access.

We used 12 hours a week or less to categorize a participant as having low technology access. This cutoff point was based on the natural gap between frequent and infrequent Internet users. It was challenging to find participants at low and very high extremes of Internet use. Therefore we used diverse forms of recruiting on and offline. 15/23 participants responded to recruitment via outreach to youth groups, Craig's List, and Facebook. The remaining 8 were recruited from an internal database of people interested in participating in research who joined through a web form.

A total of 23 participants completed our interviews; 52% female, 48% male. 16 of our participants were Caucasian, 3 Asian, 2 Hispanic, and 2 African American. 9 had low technology access *(M = 6.4 hrs/week)*, and 14 had high technology access, *(M = 20 hrs/week)*. In terms of social technologies, those with low access reported spending 2.3 hours a week on Facebook, 6.7 texting, and 1.0 emailing. Those with high access reported spending 9.2 hours a week on Facebook, 18.9 texting, and 2.8 emailing. While some participants had lower levels of access in terms of hours spent online, 22/23 participants had access to the Internet at home. One used it via the library. In terms of self-reported Internet use experience, 9% were beginners, 48% intermediate, 35% advanced, and 9 % expert.

ANALYSIS

All interviews were transcribed. For open-ended questions, we used the constant comparative method, balancing systematic qualitative data coding with the constant reintegration of theoretical notions arising from new data [15]. In line with the notion of *sensitizing* concepts [5], when insights emerged from a participant's interview data, we iteratively reviewed previous interviews to examine whether the newly realized concept existed in previous participants, and/or how previous participants' experiences changed our initial interpretation of newly emerged concepts. We synthesized our qualitative coding with the close-ended survey questions, and found no contradictions. Through this process, we identified conceptual categories that co-occurred across participants, and evaluated the role of technologies in their activities and pathways to reaching extended networks. Two researchers independently rated

[3] This continuum includes 5 levels, which we used to rate teens' motivation. For simplicity, we only describe the extremes, and *extrinsic* is a composite of the two most external levels.

participants on their extent of a) technology use (see Levels of Mediated Sociality section) to reach people and information in extended networks (or Tech with Extended Networks) and b) internalized motivation for each activity. Large discrepancies between raters were discussed. Then, participants were re-rated, and these ratings averaged.

A VARIETY OF LEARNING ACTIVITIES

23 participants nominated 55 extracurricular activities (*M = 2.4*) for which they felt they were learning something new, being creative, and found enjoyment. Table 1 summarizes 47 activities which were discussed in-depth during the interviews, excluding activities that participants had given up. For short, we refer to these as *preferred learning activities*. These activities covered a wide range of topics.

Type of Activity	Name of Learning Activity		Num. Activities	Num. using Tech.
Team/crew sports	Track (3)* Baseball (3)* Swimming (2)* Martial arts (2)* Basketball (1)*	Football (1) Volleyball (1) Skiing (1) Breakdancing (1)*	15	6
Music	Piano (3)* Guitar (2)** Choir (1)	Violin (1) Clarinet (1)	8	3
Making/ building	Minecraft (2)** Building computers (1)* Carving (1)	Making things (1)* Faceplate painting (1)*	6	5
Video production	YouTube video production (4)**** General video production (1)*		5	5
Service/ personal development	Boy scout (1)* Girl scout (1) Business week (1) Foreign languages (1) Hanging out with friends (1)		5	1
Other content production	Blogging (1)* Poetry writing (1)* Story writing (1)		3	2
Cooking/ baking	Baking (2)** Cooking (1)		3	2
Art	Photography (1)* Painting (1)		2	1
Total			**47**	**25**

Table 1. Preferred learning activities.
***Number of asterisks = number of teens who used technologies for the activity. A teen may be counted twice if s/he discussed more than one activity in depth.**

Participants showed remarkable diversity in extracurricular areas of interest. Surprisingly, 32% of the preferred learning activities were team or group sports. Of the non-team activities, 17% were music; 13% were of the making/building type; and 10% were video production and service development each. The rest were on writing, cooking, and art/photography.

RELATEDNESS FOR INITIATION AND CONTINUATION

We examine how teens initiate and continue engaging in *any* new informal learning activities, whether technologically-mediated or not, to later draw implications for encouraging teens to initiate and continue reaching extended networks. We found that across all participants, *sense of relatedness*, or feelings of belonging and connection was key to their engagement. The majority of teens initiated new learning activities when prompted by people with whom teens felt a sense of *relatedness* (supporting self-determination theory [32]). For example, teens were most frequently prompted by friends (12 activities), moms (11), and dads (8). Group/teams only influenced the initial engagement of 2 activities. Yet, group/teams were the reason for continued engagement for 10 activities. For example, Kay started swimming to spend time with one friend (extrinsic motivation not influenced by group/team). Yet, her identification with the swim team influenced her decision to continue with swimming rather than soccer:

> "I chose swimming... Soccer is a lot of drama, and I could relate better to my swim mates… Swim team people are studious, not slackers. Soccer people are more like party, don't give a whatever people… I identified more with swim people" *(Kay[4])*.

Group identity affected both genders, and lack of group identity was usually followed by giving the activity up:

> "I wasn't socially included in my team though my coach liked me. That's how I decided to leave" *(Livy)*.

Of the 47 learning activities for which there was sufficient data to code on motivation, 42 (89%) were initiated by a desire for connection with close ones. In addition, many who had ongoing, continued engagement in the learning activity did not rely solely on intrinsic motivation. Rather in 35 (74%) activities, teens mentioned someone to whom they felt attached or related who supported the teens' continuation (see Table 2).

Type of Motivation at Interview	N	Percent (of Row) Prompted by Others to Initiate Activity	Percent (of Row) Relying on Others to Continue Activity
Extrinsic *only*	18	17 (94%)	16 (89%)
Intrinsic *only*	7	5 (71%)	3 (43%)
All activities	47	42 (89%)	35 (74%)

Table 2. Role of *relatedness* in initiating and sustaining engagement in activities by type of motivation. For simplicity, intermediate levels of motivation are not represented, but their values lie between the extrinsic and intrinsic values.

Table 2 shows encouraging data in light of current theory. To elaborate, according to [32], intrinsically motivated activities are more likely to be sustained over time. And, the internalization of motivation is more likely to occur when *relatedness* is supported. However, aiming for motivation internalization would be a challenging and uncertain task for a technologist. Our findings suggest that technology designers can contribute to initial and continued engagement in new learning activities by designing for increased sense of relatedness. As Table 2 shows, continued engagement in new activities is possible even when motiva-

[4] We use pseudonyms when quoting participants.

tion is not internalized: Although a higher percentage of extrinsically motivated activities relied on others to be initiated (94% vs. 71% of intrinsically motivated activities) a high percentage of these extrinsically motivated activities also relied on others to be continued (89%).

Given its importance, in later findings, we will continue to weigh the role of sense of relatedness in teens' engagement in informal learning activities.

ROLE OF TECHNOLOGY IN INFORMAL LEARNING

As there is value in reaching extended networks for learning, and technologies play a key role in reaching extended networks, we examine technology's role in teens' activities. 25/47 activities incorporated technologies; 100% of video production, 83% of making/building, 67% each of other content production and cooking/baking. Only 40% of sports and 20% of service/development activities included technology use, **suggesting areas for potential growth in use.** A counter argument to such potential growth is that some activities may be more suited to technology use than others. However, our data shows that across all activities, social support played a strong role in using technologies with extended networks, especially considering the high use of YouTube in sports—an activity some may assess to be less suited for technology use.

Online Resources as Learning Supplements

The role of technologies in teens' activities was varied. From the activities in Table 1, the most common purpose for which participants used technologies was to supplement face-to-face learning with people in immediate networks. 14 activities fit this purpose. That is, participants reported that their main learning source was a coach or regular practice. In such cases, YouTube was the most frequently used technology to consult experts and/or role models' performing the learning activity. For example:

> "I've spent a lot of time on YouTube watching people from the Olympics swim. Two days ago I watched a technique for kicking...and just kept that in my mind... In the pool, I just play that image in my head again and try to do that in the water" *(Kay).*

Comments on videos were also consulted for learning:

> "If I don't know a move, I look through a comment on YouTube to see if anybody comments about that move. If they do, I just look it up to see if that's what it's called. Then I find a 'how to' video ..." *(Quen).*

Not surprisingly, search engines were used by most teens to find information. Surprisingly, YouTube was used by some as the first search location:

> "I usually search on YouTube first. If I can't find it there, then I try Google" *(Dan).*

The general web and wiki's were less frequently mentioned as supplements to other types of learning.

Online as Main Learning Resource

For at least seven of the activities mentioned, technologies were the main source for learning. Here, activities that stood out involved searching for information as a step prior to performing the activity (e.g., baking, or how to modify a computer game). For these activities, participants tended to use the web or subject-specific wikis. One exception was Cat, who was learning piano primarily from YouTube:

> "I learn 80% from YouTube and 20% from my sister... I'm a slow learner... [With YouTube] I can replay over and over without having to ask [my sister] to repeat and frustrate [her]..." *(Cat).*

YouTube stood out for its approachability, its repeated access to lively, albeit not "live" role-models, and affording a sense of independence and social appropriateness.

Inspiring Creative Efforts in Informal Learning Activities

A few of the preferred learning activities were artistic: photography, poetry, and drawing. Participants primarily used the web to find inspiration; e.g., looking up images, synonyms, or samples to consult for their creation. Sites used include Poetry.com, Deviant Art, Lookbook.nu, and YouTube, as inspiration for video production.

Push Information and Participate in Communities

A few participants used technologies to push personal creations/productions to a wider community of people. Jan uses Tagged.com specifically to post poems and reach people who are not connected to her immediate networks. Her extended networks in Tagged.com enabled her to experiment freely with new expressions about her feelings and not risk judgment from her immediate networks:

> "What have I posted on here? More about how I'm actually feeling... I've got my parents on Facebook. So when there's something I wanna express but I don't want my parents to see it 'cause they'll freak out or something, then I'll put it on here" *(Jan).*

Livy uses it to spread her writing widely and participate in the blogging community:

> "With blogging, I know that I can reach a wider audience sooner than other people... I write openly and simply... so I don't intimidate people, and can reach friends and others in the blogging network" *(Livy).*

The use of blogs to reach others with similar abilities or interests and the popular use of YouTube to supplement face-to-face learning (albeit primarily for physical and step-by-step activities) raises the question: were some technologies used more frequently to reach extended networks than others? We address this in the next section.

LEVELS OF MEDIATED SOCIALITY: 4-TIER ANALYSIS

Given the possibility that some technologies facilitate reaching extended networks more than others, we delve deeper into the type of interaction with extended networks across learning activities. Presumably, direct and two-way social interaction is likely to provide different learning opportunities than one-way consumption of information. Therefore, we examined technology use in terms of level of interpersonal sociality with the source. Tier 1: No interpersonal sociality. Participant consumed information without regard for its authorship or potential interaction. Tier 2: Participant obtained information from an identified author with whom they illustrated socio-emotional connection, but did not interact. Tier 3: Participant pushed content as identified author, and exhibited socio-emotional connection from others' feedback. Tier 4: Two-way interaction. Social interaction is more involved at higher Tier Levels[5].

Tier 1: Get Info. (No Sociality)	Tier 2: Get Info. From People	Tier 3: Push Info. To People	Tier 4: 2-Way Interaction
	a. Technologies Used With *EXTENDED* Networks		
Web –17 Specific site –3 Wikis –2 Q&A sites –2 Minecraft lab –1	YouTube –13 Specific site –1 Twitter –1	Blogs –2 YouTube –2 Tagged.com –1	Blog –2 Twitter –1 FB Group –1 Tagged.com –1 Email –1
Total: 25 tech mentions	**Total: 15** tech mentions	**Total: 5** tech mentions	**Total: 7** tech mentions
20 activities, 20 participants	13 activities, 13 participants	5 activities, 5 participants	6 activities, 6 participants
	b. Technologies Used With *IMMEDIATE* Networks		
NA	FB –1	FB –1 Blog –1	FB[Ψ] –13 FB Group* –7 Texting –8 Blog –3 XBox –2 IM –2 Twitter –1 Email –1
Total: 0 tech mentions	**Total: 1** tech mentions	**Total: 2** tech mentions	**Total: 37** tech mentions
0 activities, 0 participants	1 activity, 1 participant	1 activity, 1 participant	30 activities, 22 participants

[Ψ]Includes FB private chat. *Includes the use of FB group chat.

Table 3. Technologies used with a) *extended* and b) *immediate networks*: 4-Tier analysis. Tier 1: no social or emotional connection. Tiers 2 and 3: no 2-way interaction, but involve socio-emotional connection. Number next to technology: number of participants using it for a learning activity. Info = information; FB = Facebook; IM = instant messaging.

On Table 3, we categorize participants' technology use with extended (3a) vs. immediate networks (3b). Based on our definition of extended networks as people outside the bounds of one's immediate networks, it would seem strange that watching a YouTube video is categorized as "people" (in Tiers 2 and 3). We clarify that although there is no direct social interaction in Tiers 2 or 3, in these Tiers, participants exhibited socio-emotional connection with others, such as affection, inspiration, and desire to emulate. Thus, Tiers 2 and 3 are of higher sociality than Tier 1, which does not involve any social or emotional connection. Despite not being part of participants' interpersonal networks, we placed Tier 1 alongside Tables 3a and 3b for easy comparison. We placed accessing web information next to Table 3a because such web sources reside outside our teens' immediate networks.

[5] We assume producing and sharing content as an identifiable author is a more involved process than obtaining content.

Most participants accessed information from the web. However, as the social interaction became more involved (higher Tier) the number of participants who reached extended networks via technologies drastically diminished. 20 participants used the web or other virtual worlds for information, without involving any social interaction (Tier 1). 13 used YouTube, Twitter, and content specific sites to get information from known individuals or role models (Tier 2). 5 used content production sites to push information to people (Tier 3), and only 6 used various technologies for 2-way social interaction with people in extended networks (Tier 4).

Many[6] participants used networked technologies for 2-way social interaction, but primarily with their *immediate networks* (Table 3b). As can be seen, with immediate networks, 30 activities involve 2-way social interaction (compared to 6 in Table 3a). Table 3 also shows that some technologies were used mainly for 2-way social interaction with immediate networks (e.g., Facebook, texting), while others were used mainly to learn from role models (e.g., one-way consumption on YouTube). We see the gaps in quantity and type of technologies used with immediate and extended networks, presented above, as **design opportunities for the CSCW community to support informal learning via extended networks** (Figure 1).

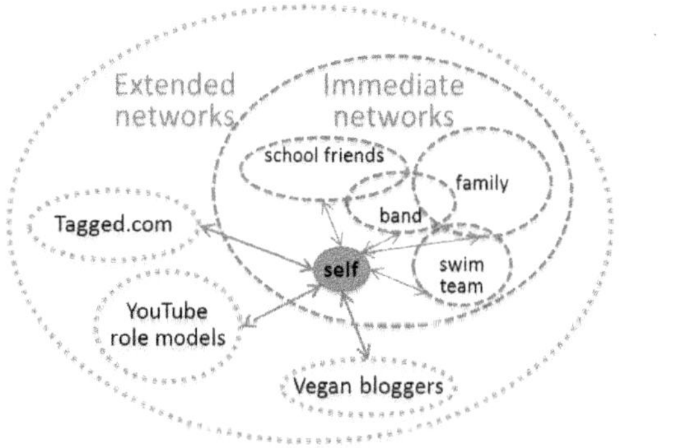

Figure 1. Illustration of informal learning opportunities via extended networks and related design opportunities. Lines = social connections. Red solid lines = design opportunities for interaction with extended networks; e.g., experts on YouTube, global Vegan Bloggers, or strangers on Tagged.com

Social media arguably enhance people's relatedness, yet they seldom help teens build learning relationships with *extended networks* the way Livy did on blogs. Synthesizing the identified design opportunities with findings on relatedness, we see room to **design for *sense of relatedness* with teen-learners' *extended networks.***

To inform such space, we further delve into participants' social behavior: how they used technologies with immediate and extended networks based on their affordances; and pathways to reaching extended networks.

[6] Likely, more teens used technologies in their activities. We report what teens voluntarily shared, which has validity because people tend to report relatively stable patterns of interaction [35].

USES BASED ON SOCIALITY AFFORDED

In this section we discuss differences in technology use with immediate vs. extended networks. We draw on technology affordances to explain such differences. We loosely adopt Norman [29]'s conceptualization of *affordance* as action possibilities that a technology offers and the user is able to perceive and enact. We posit that different technologies afford different *sociality* or relational qualities of interaction. Not all relational qualities may create a path to extended networks; yet, they provide insights for the gaps between uses with immediate and extended networks.

As mentioned, YouTube stood out as one of the most used technologies to reach extended networks. Interestingly, YouTube use with extended networks was mostly for one-way consumption, while Facebook and texting were used for two-way interaction with immediate networks. We found that the main difference existed due to the concern, care, and social validation that teens tend to seek *privately* from "insiders" in their immediate networks with a common history to the teens. For example, before every swimming practice, Jill and her swim-friends texted each other to send reminders or find out why someone is missing; e.g., "it's your event, where are you?" Kay used Facebook's live chat to get last minute advice from seniors in the swim team. Jan who posted her art publically in tagged.com emailed drafts of her poems to a group of close friends for feedback.

Thus we ask, while peer-production sites like YouTube support learning from role models, could they also provide social support in informal learning the way texting and Facebook's chat do? We found value in considering the power that teens' ability to affect others had on their level of engagement in informal learning activities.

In both technology-mediated and non-mediated activities, providing for others made teens feel worthy and encouraged them to sustain involvement in the new activity while providing social support to others. For example, as a mentor to new freshmen, Meg felt central to her school community. Eventually, she gave freshmen her cell phone number to be available as needed. Livy felt that through her blog, she was useful to other vegans in need of it (e.g., sharing vegan recipes and "things other [vegans] might not have access to"). As mentioned, she became avidly involved in the vegan blogging community, friending bloggers in person. Thus, we see opportunities **to design for continued engagement in new informal learning by supporting teens' contribution to the needs of others** in extended networks.

Furthermore, as contributing to the needs of others in extended networks may evolve into more personal interactions, and given the few teens who had personal interactions on peer-production sites, we also see opportunities to design **for more intimate relationships with extended networks in peer-production sites.**

PATHWAYS TO EXTENDED NETWORKS

Personal Factors: Digital Skills, Access, Motivation

We first evaluate simple associations (correlations): how personal factors like Digital Skills, Technology Access, Internalized Motivation, and Relatedness are associated with using technologies to reach extended networks for informal learning or Tech with Extended Networks. Our participants had intermediate levels of Digital Skills (M = 3.0, sd = .65, where 1 = novice and 5 = expert) and higher levels of Social Digital Skills (M = 3.5, sd = .68). Participants' Technology Access (Internet use) was also high (M = 14.97 hrs/week, sd = 8.5). However, we found overall intermediate levels of using Tech with Extended Networks (M = 4.97, sd = 2.6, where 1 = did not use at all, 10 = used frequently and intensely). In terms of motivation, participants had intermediate levels of internalized motivation (M = 4.7, sd = 1.57, where 1 = extrinsic and 7 = intrinsic), and sense of relatedness played a role in a high proportion of participants' involvement in informal learning activities (M =.75, where 0 = absent, and 1 = present).

	Digital Skills	Social Digital Skills	Internalized Motivation	Relatedness	Tech with Extended Networks
Tech Access	.31	.26	.24	.18	**.48**
Digital Skills		**.70**	.38	.17	**.46**
Social Digital Skills			.29	.06	.26
Internalized Motivation				-.18	.28
Relatedness					.31

Table 4. Correlations (Pearson) between concepts of interests. Bolded items are significant at $p < .05$ (2-tailed).

Not surprisingly, Digital Skills and Technology Access are significantly correlated with Tech with Extended Networks ($r = .46, p < .05$ and $r = .48, p < .05$ *respectively*). In other words, teens with higher Digital Skills scores were more likely than not to use Tech with Extended Networks; and teens who spent more time online were more likely than not to use Tech with Extended Networks (Table 4).

However, correlations did not fully capture the relationship between concepts of interest. For example, Relatedness also played a critical role in using Tech with Extended Networks, as suggested earlier. Yet, the correlation was not significant because Relatedness both encouraged and inhibited teens' use of Tech with Extended Networks (as described later). We also found that Internalized Motivation was not significantly correlated with Tech with Extended Networks because as reported, participants go online to learn because of Relatedness—they are prompted by others or seek out a sense of connection with others, not because they had an intrinsic desire to learn about the topic.

Table 4 also does not capture the ceiling effect in Social Digital Skills—that is, because these skills consisted of using communication and social media technologies, which most participants used frequently and were good at, a correlation with Tech with Extended Networks could not be observed. In comparison, Digital Skills included sophisticated technology skills on which participants tended to rate low, such as addressing computer malware, configuring a server, and building websites. Knowing these skills usually meant that the participant accessed non-regular school resources. We recognize that there may be more levels of sophistication to Social Digital Skills, and raise this as an area for future researchers to further address.

In short, we must consider the importance of basic Technology Access, Digital Skills, and Relatedness when designing for teens to reach extended networks.

Social Factors: Reaching Extended Networks or Not

For the most part, the social factors contributing to reaching extended networks pertain to relatedness—teens' desire for social validation and connection, as described below.

Pushed by Immediate Network

Despite existing research suggesting that teens mainly use technologies with existing ties [6, 19, 30], we were still surprised by teens' heavy reliance on friends and family for inspiration, information, and social support in informal learning contexts. Often, participants reached extended networks when pushed by someone in their immediate networks with whom they sought connection or social validation. For example, Brad is extrinsically motivated to be in Boy Scouts because he wants to earn his Eagle Scout, the highest rank in the Boy Scouts of America. He was one of the few who used technologies with people in extended networks. He emailed a chemist to evaluate his chemistry merit badge to be awarded the next ranking level. Brad was pushed by his immediate network—scouts—to reach expertise from extended networks.

Similarly, Pat's enjoyment of baseball is centered around friends (extrinsic motivation): "I went to baseball camp... to hang out with my friend." Pat observed baseball role models on YouTube (people in extended networks) at his coach's suggestion (pushed by immediate network).

Being pushed by immediate networks to reach extended resources occurred also for participants engaging in activities of internalized motivation. For instance, Pete who enjoyed video production in itself (internalized motivation) needed a push to try new unfamiliar resources. He had not used interest groups as resources for video production, but:

> "If someone suggested that I find interest groups online, I'd give it a try" *(Pete).*

Design can raise teens' awareness of friends' technology use with extended networks and reward the emulation of such behavior to *push* teens to reach extended networks.

Pulled by Extended Network

For some teens, encounters and exposure to specific communities of interest in social media (in their extended networks) further *pulled* them to *continue* engaging in completely new activities. For example, Livy shares:

> "I was taking an English class and thought that if I started blogging, I would practice my writing style... Veganism was something new to me... I learned more about it via others' blogs... I [too] started sharing [blogging] good vegan recipes I found" *(Livy).*

For some teens, regular exposure to content-sharing sites (YouTube, blogs) was followed by learning to create content for these media. Dan is one such example. He created his own YouTube video after watching videos from accounts he admired. From YouTube users he followed, he learned about Indy Mogul, where he learned video production tips for his video. Further feedback on YouTube encouraged him to produce more videos.

In Livy's case sharing content with the vegan community led to interacting with people in these extended networks. As Livy became more centrally embedded in this community, she also volunteered, and won a cooking contest. These interactions sustained her engagement:

> "Amy who runs a big vegan blog shared my blog. I didn't blog to get followers, but when others repost or follow, it feels good" *(Livy).*

As "reposts" were not triggers for teens' initial engagement with extended networks, there is room for design to increase the pull by extended networks by matching teens with similar interests across networks.

Lack of Support in Immediate Networks

Reaching extended networks may also occur due to lack of support from people in teens' immediate networks. For example, after learning video production from his cousin, Pete got interested in taking a video class at school. Then, one day, he faced the need to use a video resource online community because he exhausted his teacher's knowledge:

> "I wanted to do more things that my teacher didn't really know... He suggested I search online. So, I went online to search ... I learned how to make exploding text using a tutorial on *Video Copilot*" *(Pete).*

To add to the value of reaching extended networks, as a byproduct of needing to reach his extended networks, Pete mastered other digital skills: He admits to searching online more often now that he "can find stuff more easily."

We note that the "lack of support" in immediate networks may be informational, social, and/or emotional. For instance, we introduced Jan earlier, who used Tagged.com to connect with people that would not judge her creative expressions. For Cat, impatience from her sister/piano teacher led her to reach pianists on YouTube to learn piano.

While we expected to find that learners with internalized motivation were more likely to reach extended networks than not, neither our correlational nor qualitative data supported this expectation. For instance, while Pete had internalized motivation for video production and Cat had extrinsic motivation for piano (she wanted to play because her friends played at social gatherings), they both reached their extended networks due to lack of support from their immediate networks. In Pete's case, his teacher did not have the knowledge. In Cat's case, she did not have the social support from her sister. Thus, even without intrinsic motivation, if a learner's immediate networks cannot fulfill the teens' need, then s/he might reach extended networks.

While it would be unethical to purposefully make a teens' immediate network unavailable for support, design can heighten a teens' awareness about the additional and easily reachable expertise in extended networks.

Immediate Networks as Barriers

In previous sections, immediate networks were the triggers for some teens to reach extended networks. However, immediate networks also acted as barriers for some teens to reach into extended networks to support their informal learning activities, such as the case of Shel in the introduction. Mar, who used the Internet less than 3 hours a week, was also constrained by her immediate network:

> "Mom's paranoid tendencies about viruses have rubbed off on me… I tend to be on the computer fairly conservatively… that's how I avoid viruses…" *(Mar).*

While some teens may be reaching extended networks for pragmatic reasons (e.g., whether they can get the support they need in their immediate networks or not), our data suggests strongly that relatedness plays a key role in teens' initiation and engagement in informal learning activities. Additionally, if prompted, teens may try out reaching into extended networks. Furthermore, parents' attitudes matter. Thus, incorporating parents' concerns when designing to encourage reaching into extended networks for informal learning is a feasible (and worthwhile) challenge.

IMPLICATIONS & RECOMMENDATIONS

Based on teens' informal learning, we identified design spaces for engagement with extended networks. We provide conceptual design recommendations in such spaces.

1. Support relatedness: Enable the *pull by extended networks* by helping teens develop friendships with similar others in extended networks. Increase awareness of how friends reach extended networks as friends can *push* teens to do the same, and reward the adoption of these friends' behavior. While current social media do display recommendations for new connections, these are usually not purposefully contextualized within learning activities. Furthermore, support geographic collocation. While not stated earlier, for most teens, regular physical interaction and ease of face-to-face access were important conditions for continuation. Finally, support ways for teens to provide for others' needs because it increases their sense of belonging and consequently, their continued involvement.

2. Support mentoring structure: Make evident the existence of accessible expertise outside teens' immediate networks. Match learners with mentors who have the expertise sought in ways that encourage sustained relationships. One way to support continued engagement is to give learners the opportunity to play mentoring roles, especially since a mentoring structure, which rotates responsibilities, may also contribute to feelings of worth and inclusion.

3. Design private communication channels in peer-production sites: Blend private communication channels in peer production sites with other communication channels. We see opportunities for innovation where elements of social support, validation, mentoring, and private interactions are combined with YouTube affordances (lively video demonstrations, approachability, repeatability, and access to expertise world-wide). Here Isaacs et al. [20]'s channel blending study should also be consulted.

4. Technology as prompt: Embed peer or professionally created digital artifacts of diverse content and materiality in teens' socio-technical environments. Many teens initiated activities through encounters with artifacts, both digitally (e.g., Livy and blogs; Dan and YouTube videos) and in analog formats (a not yet described example is Mel being inspired to learn photography by photo displays at school).

5. Design for the learner's social ecology: This includes family and friends. Teens' immediate networks sometimes acted as barriers to reaching extended networks. As parents are influential in teens' technology and learning attitudes, systems need to support parent's changing roles in teens' development of self-directed learning. For example, provide parental "support" opportunities to let parents feel that the activity is beneficial. Design for parent-child or peers to use the technology *together* in collaboration.

LIMITATIONS

It should be noted that we do not have a representative sample that is generalizable to the population of teens. Our participants were selected for technological and demographic diversity to help carve design spaces. We also do not explicitly state how online safety can be addressed through design. Such focus would require a separate study. Additionally, learning via extended networks may not produce qualitatively better outcomes than learning via immediate networks. Our emphasis is on the opportunities for new learning and the synergy of ideas that are more likely to be offered by reaching extended networks.

CONCLUSIONS & CONTRIBUTIONS

Interacting with people in extended networks yields valuable informal learning opportunities. In a study of teens' informal learning in extracurricular activities, we found that few used technologies to interact with their extended networks. We found sense of relatedness to be such a strong motivator to engage in informal learning activities that sociality should be a primary consideration in designing informal learning systems for teens.

We observed that a higher percentage of teens used technologies with immediate networks vs. extended networks. In examining how teens used technologies with their social relationships, we found that technologies used with extended networks were not as often used for developing deeper interpersonal relationships in the way that technologies used with immediate networks were. By delving deeper into the reasons why teens' reach beyond their immediate networks we provide conceptual recommendations for how to encourage teens to reach extended networks online for informal learning, such as matching learners with similar interests, mentoring relationships, and co-learning.

We make four valuable contributions:

1. We identified the benefits of extended networks for informal learning, and **defined the term by clarifying structural concepts in Granovetter [16] and Burt [9].**
2. By exploring teens' informal learning in extracurricular contexts, **we uncovered new design opportunities** in the void of teens' interactions with extended networks.
3. We explored **pathways to reaching extended networks**, including the role of digital skills, technology access, and motivation, and most importantly the *desire for relatedness* both pushing and pulling them to new informal learning opportunities via extended networks.
4. We provided **design recommendations** that address relatedness, social inclusion, and inspirational prompts; and fill the gap between different affordances of technologies used with immediate and extended networks.

ACKNOWLEDGMENTS

Thanks to Jeff Huang, Gifford Cheung, David W. McDonald, and the reviewers for their constructive feedback.

REFERENCES

1. Atkins, D.E., Bennett, J., Brown, J.S., and Chopra, A. *Learning Powered by Technology*. Department of Education, 2010.
2. Arafeh, S., Levin, D., Lee, R., and Lenhart, A. *The Digital Disconnect: The Widening Gap between Internet-savvy Students and their Schools.* Pew Research Center, 2002.
3. Bailenson, J.N., Yee, N., Blascovich, J., and Beall, A.C., et al. The use of immersive virtual reality in the learning sciences: Digital transformations of teachers, students, and social context. *J Learn Sci*17, 1 (2008), 102–141.
4. Barron, B. Interest and self-sustained learning as catalysts of development: A learning ecology perspective. *Hum Dev 49, 4* (2006), 19.
5. Blumer, H. What is wrong with social theory? *Am Sociol Rev 19*, 1 (1954), 3–10.
6. boyd, danah. Friendship. In *Hanging Out, Messing Around, and Geeking Out: Kids Living and Learning with New Media.* The MIT Press, 2010, 79–115.
7. Bruckman, A. Community support for constructionist learning. *Computer Supported Cooperative Work* (CSCW) 7, 1 (1998), 47–86.
8. Buechley, L. and Hill, B.M. LilyPad in the wild: how hardware's long tail is supporting new engineering and design communities. In *Proc. DIS*, ACM Press (2010), 199–207.
9. Burt, R.S. Structural holes and good ideas. *Am J Sociol* 110, 2 (2004), 349–399.
10. Colley, A.M., Gale, M.T., and Harris, T.A. Effects of gender role identity and experience on computer attitude components. *J Educ Comput Res* 10, 2 (1994), 129–137.
11. Cross, J. *Informal Learning: Rediscovering the Natural Pathways that Inspire Innovation and Performance.* Pfeiffer, 2006.
12. DiMaggio, P., Hargittai, E., Neuman, W.R., and Robinson, J.P. Social implications of the Internet. *Annu Rev Soc*, (2001), 307–336.
13. Epstein, A.L. The network and urban social organization. In *Social Networks in Urban Situations*. 1969, 116–132.
14. Gillet, D., El Helou, S., Yu, C.M., and Salzmann, C. Turning web 2.0 social software into versatile collaborative learning solutions. *Adv Comput-Hum Int,* IEEE (2008), 170 –176.
15. Glaser, B.G. The constant comparative method of qualitative analysis. *Soc Probl 12*, 4 (1965), 436-445.
16. Granovetter, M.S. The strength of weak ties. *Am J Sociol,* (1973), 1360–1380.
17. Greenhow, C. and Robelia, B. Informal learning and identity formation in online social networks. *Learning, Media and Technology 34, 2* (2009), 119–140.
18. Hargittai, E. An update on survey measures of Web-oriented digital literacy. *Soc Sci Comput Rev 27, 1* (2009), 130.
19. Horst, H.A. Families. In *Hanging Out, Messing Around, and Geeking Out: Kids Living and Learning with New Media.* The MIT Press, 2010, 149–94.
20. Isaacs, E., Szymanski, M., Yamauchi, Y., Glasnapp, J., and Iwamoto, K. Integrating local and remote worlds through channel blending. In *Proc. CSCW*, ACM (2012), 617–626.
21. Ito, M. Gaming. In *Hanging Out, Messing Around, and Geeking Out: Kids Living and Learning with New Media.* The MIT Press, 2010, 195–242.
22. Johnson, R.B. and Onwuegbuzie, A.J. Mixed methods research: A research paradigm whose time has come. *Educ Researcher 33*, 7 (2004), 14–26.
23. Lange, P.G. Creative production. In *Hanging Out, Messing Around, and Geeking Out: Kids Living and Learning with New Media.* The MIT Press, 2010, 243–293
24. Lenhart, A., Madden, M., Smith, A., and Macgill, A.R. *Teens and social media: An overview.* Pew Internet 2009.
25. Lin, P. Information literacy barriers: language use and social structure. *Library Hi Tech* 28, 4 (2010), 548–568.
26. MacLaurin, M. Kodu: end-user programming and design for games. In *Proc. FDG 2009,* ACM Press (2009), 2.
27. Monroy-Hernández, A., Hill, B.M., Gonzalez-Rivero, J., and boyd, d. Computers can't give credit: how automatic attribution falls short in an online remixing community. In *Proc. CHI 2011,* ACM Press (2011), 3421–3430.
28. Muuss, R.E. Erik Erikson's Theory of identity development. In *Theories of adolescence.* McGraw-Hill New York, 1996, 42–57.
29. Norman, D.A. Affordance, conventions, and design. *Interactions* 6, 3 (1999), 38–43.
30. Pascoe, C.J. Intimacy. In *Hanging Out, Messing Around, and Geeking Out: Kids Living and Learning with New Media.* The MIT Press, 2010, 79–115
31. Patton, M.Q. *Qualitative Research and Evaluation Methods.* Sage Publications, Inc, 2002.
32. Ryan, R.M. and Deci, E.L. Self-determination theory and the facilitation of intrinsic motivation, social development, and well-being. *Am Psychol* 55, 1 (2000), 68–78.
33. van Dijk, J.A.G.M. *The Deepening Divide: Inequality in the Information Society*. SAGE, 2005.
34. Vygotsky, L.S. *Mind in Society: The Development of Higher Psychological Processes*. Harvard Univ Pr, 1978.
35. Wasserman, S. and Faust, K. *Social Network Analysis Methods and Applications (Structural Analysis in the Social Sciences)*. Cambridge University Press, 1994

I want to be Sachin Tendulkar! A Spoken English Cricket Game for Rural Students

Martha Larson[1] Nitendra Rajput[2] Abhigyan Singh[1] Saurabh Srivastava[2]

[1]Delft University of Technology
Delft, Netherlands
m.a.larson, a.singh@tudelft.nl

[2]IBM Research - India
Vasant Kunj, New Delhi
rnitendra, saurabhsrivastava@in.ibm.com

(Authors are in alphabetical order)

ABSTRACT

We present a mobile phone based cricket game for improving the spoken English pronunciation of school children designed and tested within a specific socio-cultural context in rural India, the Mewat district of Haryana State. The development of the game concept was informed by a field study, which identified cultural restrictions respected by the community as well as community interests and motivations. The game was accessible using a low-end mobile phone and evaluated with a group of 63 students from classes 4 and 5 of a rural school. The results suggest that the cricket game can be effectively used to engage students and to improve their spoken English skills in the given setting. Further, the game serves as an informative example of how factors impacting the acceptability and appropriation of a technology in a particular setting can be taken into account from the very beginning of the design process.

Author Keywords

Spoken English; mobile game; cricket; commentary; rural India; speech recognition; education.

ACM Classification Keywords

H.5.1 [Multimedia Information Systems]: Audio input/output;

INTRODUCTION

A good command of spoken English unlocks enormous opportunities in India for personal and economic improvement. In this paper, we take a broad perspective on English language learning and investigate three factors prevalent in India: an awareness of the importance of English, the lack of means to learn spoken English and the enormous popularity of the game of cricket. These three factors emerged from a field study, which revealed that their co-occurrence opened a previously unidentified possibility to support improvement of spoken English skills using a mobile phone based game.

How these factors interact to create the context for the game is better understood by examining each in turn. The importance of spoken English skills in India is well established, as reflected by studies that have been carried out across different communities. In [1], hourly wages of men were reported to be 34% higher in case they know English. In [10], observations are made on the sociolinguistic implications of English and its growth towards dominant social and administrative roles. Not only is English important, it is also widely perceived to be important. Due to this community awareness, school children, even in rural areas in India, are interested in learning spoken English.

Despite the awareness of the importance of English, there is widespread lack of a means and a motivational environment in which spoken English can be learned. Primary school education in India is impeded by a shortage of quality teachers, especially for the English language, and high drop out rates. In [9], the drop out rate is reported to be 39% with 37% of respondents to a drop out survey reporting that drop out was caused by the child not being interested in the studies. Clear potential exists for providing engaging learning contexts for spoken English that will leverage the underlying awareness of its importance.

The game of cricket in India enjoys a seemingly boundless power to engage and fascinate. The game's audience has been recorded to be more than 200 million in a particular tournament [14]. Most households followed this game either on television or on a radio. More recently, people have started to follow the radio commentary through their mobile phones. Most low-end mobile devices can receive radio signals. The importance of cricket in the Indian context is reflected in popular media, e.g., in the title of a recent book, "If cricket is a religion, Sachin is God" [17]. 'Sachin' is a reference to the widely admired cricket star Sachin Tendulkar. We include his name in the title of the

CSCW 2013, February 23–27, 2013, San Antonio, Texas, USA.

paper to emphasize the strength of the power of engagement of the game of cricket over fans, for whom Sachin serves as a role model in India. A priori, cricket, provides a good fit with a collaborative language learning scenario. Since it is a team game, students work together to score well for the team; however, as suggested by the existence of cricket idols, individuality is still preserved, and a single person responds at a time with the emphasis on improving their individual spoken English pronunciation skill.

The existence and importance of these three factors were established by a field study in Mewat, a district in north India. The study was open ended in that it was constrained only by the context of a highly abstract goal: to develop new applications for mobile speech that would support the efforts of underprivileged communities to achieve economic development and improvement of living conditions. The insights and findings of the field study gave rise to the design of the mobile phone based cricket game. The game provides students with spoken English words and asks them to speak them back over phone. Cricket commentary makes the game exciting and engaging. The quality of the students' pronunciations determines the scoring and the follow-up commentary.

This paper makes three contributions: First, we report on a field study that identified both challenges and opportunities for mobile phone applications in primary schools in rural India. The field study is carried out in Mewat, a district whose unique culture contributes to a set of specific restrictions and opportunities for designing applications that not only address community needs, but are also consistent with available technologies (i.e., low-end mobile phones). Second, based on the insights gained from the field study, we describe the design and implementation of a mobile phone based cricket game. The game is evaluated with a group of students at a rural school. Evaluation results demonstrate the ability of the game to engage the students and improve their spoken English pronunciation. Third, we provide an outlook on future design possibilities beyond the specific setting of Mewat in the form of a concise discussion on the possible generalization of our design insights. These insights could be expected to extend to other settings in which application design would stand to benefit if both socio-cultural limitations and community motivations could be taken into account from the very beginning of the design process.

The paper is structured as follows. After describing the study and reporting its results, we present the design of the cricket game, which was created on the basis of the findings of the study. We then present the evaluation of the game, conducted with 63 students at a rural school in Mewat, with the goal of determining if the game has the ability to engage students and improve their spoken English. Finally, we give an outlook on the generalization possibilities of our design insights to future work and summarize our conclusions.

RELATED WORK

Work related to our own falls into three categories: first, the potential of collaborative interaction with mobile devices for engaging learners, second, designing technology for children, and, third, the use of games in education.

The use of collaborative systems and mobile devices has clearly demonstrated potential in educational settings. The Mogslass system [20] provides a collaborative environment to help in understanding and ultimately also to support the creation of music through networked mobile devices for children. The *Meaning* [16] system uses mobile devices to capture children's activities in kindergartens and presents to parents, allowing increased communication within families. *LeafView* [19] system is a tablet PC application that aids in identification of botanical species, providing support for student field trips. Explore! [2] is a mobile-learning system that helps students acquire historical knowledge. These examples provide evidence that education in the Western world is undergoing a significant change in terms of the content and its delivery methods. There is a clear trend toward increased use of multimedia content and of engaging, collaborative interactions.

The space of technology design for children has been extensively researched in [4,5,8]. These studies have effectively utilized the creative skills of children in developing search interfaces [4], mobile storytelling [8] and their experiences in interacting with digital library [5]. Authors in [18] also emphasize the value in co-designing with children using a layered elaboration technique. Such interactive techniques clearly highlight the importance of an iterative design approach when building interfaces for children. In this paper, our design incorporates close interaction with children via both the initial field study and also the validation within the context of a tournament based on the theme of the dream, "I want to be Sachin Tendulkar!"

Other work has focused explicitly on the ability of games to support education. We adopt the guidelines for educational games of [13], which emphasize the importance of fun, flow, engagement, feedback, goals, problem solving, game balance and pacing, and fantasy narrative. For rural regions, authors in [11] propose the use of traditional rural games to design digital games and their study shows that if a digital game has the same game mechanics as a traditional game, then rural children are easily able to relate to it. The authors use these design guidelines to develop localized games on mobile devices to improve spoken English in [12]. The game design is centered on local themes such as trying to protect the crops from thieves and animals in a farm. Language learning is integrated into the game by displaying words and asking students to speak them. A speech recognition system drives the scoring, which is then translated to the game. This game differs from our own in that it needs a high-end mobile device, which can display rich visuals and also run speech recognition software.

SOCIO-CULTURAL SETTING

Mewat is a district located in the Haryana state in northern India with a population of approximately 1.1 million and is one the least developed districts of Haryana. Despite its proximity to the metropolitan area of New Delhi, a large percent of the population (ca. 88.6%) lives in utter poverty in rural areas. The rural areas of Mewat lack basic infrastructure, such as water supply, electricity, and sanitation. It is important to mention that the level of penetration of mobile phone infrastructure in Mewat is high. The contrast with the availability of other infrastructures is striking and the ubiquity of mobile phones served as one specific motivation to focus on this region.

Mewat enjoys a socio-cultural uniqueness, not only because it is the only Muslim population pocket in Haryana, but also because the historically the population has roots in Hindu culture, which are cherished and preserved. This unique ethnic group is commonly referred as 'Meos' or 'Meo Muslims'. The main motivation for the choice of the Mewat district was the observation that there is great potential for improvement in the educational system. The 2011 Census of India reports that Mewat's average literacy rate is 56.10%, while female-literacy remains very low at 37.1%. The people of Mewat speak in Mewati dialect, Hindi, Urdu and Haryanvi dialect. Arabic is spoken in 'Masjid' or Mosque for religious teaching of the Quran, but is not used for everyday communication. The students are taught English in school, but it is not used locally, making it difficult to acquire command of the spoken language.

Kanwarsika and Salaheri Villages

Two villages in Nuh block of Mewat district were chosen on the basis of their representativeness for the region. Kanwarsika Village (cf. Figure 1, left) is located just off Gurgaon-Alwar State Highway (SH-13) and it is one of the more urbanized villages in Mewat. The population of Kanwarsika is 1646 (848 male/798 female) with a total of 235 households. Kanwarsika School consists of two public (i.e., government) schools, a primary and a middle school, sharing the same campus, and is considered a model school in Mewat. Kanwarsika School has a total of 274 students (123 male/151 female) and 9 teachers (4 male/5 female), making the student-to-teacher ratio ca. 30:1.

Figure 1: Kanwarsika Village (left) & Salaheri Village (right).

Salaheri Village (cf. Figure 1, right) is ca. 3 km removed from the SH-13 and it is considered to be a 'remote' village. Salaheri is one of the lesser-developed villages of Mewat. The population of Salaheri is 5457 (2839 male, 2618 female) with a total of 713 households. Two public schools, a primary and a middle school, are located close to Salaheri, and have a total of 1559 students (818 male, 741 female) who are taught by 28 teachers (26 male, 2 female), making student-teacher ratio ca. 56:1.

FIELD STUDY

This section reports the setup of the field study and its findings, which provided the basis for the design of the mobile phone cricket game discussed in the next section. The use of a field study to inform the design process was motivated by our underlying appreciation that the intersection the culture and the availability of technology in a particular setting gives rise to constraints, motivations, opportunities, as well as user needs, that impact the acceptability and uptake of applications in that setting.

Field study background and methodology

The field study was conducted in February and March 2012 for duration of six weeks. The study was carried out by a male design researcher, who was able to communicate with local community members in Hindi, but was otherwise an outsider to the community and had no previous acquaintance with the community history or its social tradition.

The field study engaged a variety of local actors in the research. A total of 51 students (33 male/18 female) from Kanwarsika and Salaheri primary and middle school participated in 6 sessions (group interviews and brainstorming sessions). A total of 19 teachers from Kanwarsika and Salaheri School participated in 22 sessions (group interviews, in-depth interviews and brainstorming sessions). A total of 17 local villagers (14 male/3 female) participated in informal discussions on village life. It is worth mentioning that the gender and identity of the field-researcher (male and 'outsider') limited the possibility of engaging female members of the local community in the research. A total of 10 field-officials and program coordinators of a local NGO [Name Removed for Purposes of Anonymization] participated in 15 informal discussions on variety of issues relevant for the research.

The other important participants in the field-research are: a 'Maulavi' (a local religious teacher), a local historian, a local poet, two Radio Mewat officials, a Mewat Development Agency Official. The field-research also incorporated visits and informal discussions at 5 different local mobile phone shops in Kanwarsika, Salaheri and semi-urban center of Nuh.

A variety of methods were employed in the field study: group interviews, in-depth interviews, participant observation, village transect walks, resource map drawing exercises, and field-notes. The group interviews, in-depth interviews and informal discussions varied between 30 minutes to 3 hours of time duration.

Field study findings

The findings of the field study are reported organized around the major themes.

Mass media and ICTs. The Meo's cultural and religious identities are inter-twined and have a significant impact on their consumption and appropriation of mass media and ICTs. Traditionally, the local population respects strict restrictions on the use of photography, videography and digital editing. Many locals view photographs as the prime reason for religious objection to Hindi newspapers, which are read by a negligibly small portion of the population. Salaheri Village has only 25 televisions sets in total, most of which are installed in local tea or snack shops.

The orthodox locals and religious leaders raise serious objections to any image, sketch or photograph of any 'living' object. The local 'Maulavi' attributes this categorical opposition to their interpretation of Islam. He further added that there is no religious objection to visual representation of 'non-living' objects or in use of human voice in any application like a mobile or computer game. He explained that Nokia's popular mobile game 'Snake' is objectionable to the local community as the game entails a digital representation of snake, a 'living' object. If the game had been modelled as 'Rope' or any other 'non-living' object, the game would not violate religious sentiments and then had better possibility to be accepted by the local community. Restrictions on imagery provide a possible explanation for the immense popularity of the audio-only medium of radio in Mewat. It has a local FM Radio Station called Radio Mewat. Most people have radio sets at home; mobile phones are also popularly used to listen to FM radio.

Figure 2: Use of mobile technology young users Mewat (left) & A mobile shop in Kanwarsika Village (right).

An interesting recent development is huge penetration of mobile phones in Mewat (cf. Figure 2). The households, even in the remotest of villages, have multiple mobile phones. All the participants in the field study including students and teachers reported multiple mobile hand-sets in their individual households. The presence of various flourishing local mobile shops and businesses in villages and semi-urban centre of Nuh further confirms the popularity of mobile phones in Mewat. Many local villagers perceive mobile phone as 'neutral' and as a device that does not violate or challenge the local religio-cultural identity. Mobile phone use is asymmetric between the genders. The household's mobile phones are invariably 'owned' by the male members of the family and the female family-members 'borrow' them in order to use them. This gender disparity parallels a deeper gender asymmetry rooted in the traditional social set-up of Mewat.

Desire for spoken English language skills. There is an overwhelming desire amongst the students of Kanwarsika and Salaheri Schools to develop English language proficiency. Most of the participants including students, teachers, local villagers, local NGO officials, and religious leader voiced the need to focus on development of English language skills. The study participants consider English language skill to be important for improving the employment opportunities and self-esteem of the students.

The English language education starts from Class 1 in schools in Mewat but many of the schoolteachers acknowledged not having sufficient proficiency to teach English language skills. Some confirmed having problems in understanding even a basic letter or announcement published in English by the Education Ministry or in having a simple conversation in English. Further, students and teachers informed us that although written English is a focus of the curriculum, there is hardly any opportunity for students to learn and practice spoken English. One of the common issues that the students report is the lack of a conversational partner. Many of them report being very unsure of their English pronunciation and state this uncertainty also negatively impacts the self-esteem. A group of male students narrated how they experience low self-esteem and self-confidence when they visit Delhi or Gurgaon (highly urbanized centres) and see their city peers conversing in English. The schoolteachers point out that students need constant encouragement to overcome their inhibition to speak English.

A general awareness was observed regarding the potential of mobile phone technology for supporting English learning and the limitation of the currently available applications. Some students demonstrated mobile phone based applications, like a English-to-Hindi dictionary, which they have downloaded and installed. The students pointed out various limitations of these applications: lack of coherence of the content with English curriculum taught in school, lack of focus on spoken English and lack of possibility for structured language learning.

Popularity of cricket. In general sports are very popular amongst the students of Mewat. Recently, Salaheri School hosted a state-level wrestling competition. Also, teachers proudly mention the athletic meet held in the school compound few years ago and the huge support and participation of local community. Some of the more popular sports amongst students are cricket, *kabbadi*, *kho-kho*, track and field, volleyball, and wrestling. One unique aspect of cricket in Mewat is its huge popularity amongst both male and female students. Although female students are excluded from many other sports, it is not an uncommon sight to see female students playing cricket in the same sports compound as male students during lunch breaks.

All student participants of the field study reconfirmed the popularity of cricket. The traditional and still the most common way of following cricket matches is listening to live radio commentary. The local villagers are well attuned to the voice modality and nuances of cricket commentary.

GAME CONCEPT AND DESIGN

The field study provided us important insights that informed the development of the spoken English cricket game. The following are the key insights and the design choices that were derived from the study:

1. Input from teachers and observation of parents highlighted that students need a self-engaging mechanism to improve their education since most parents are not literate enough to help their children at home. *Therefore we realized that the application has to be engaging and motivating, which led to choosing a game as the application.*
2. The study clearly highlighted that cricket is a popular game among both male and female students while other sports, like wrestling, were not popular amongst female students. Further, the students are well aware of nuances of cricket and are accustomed to listening to cricket commentary on radio. *We therefore chose cricket as the game on which to model the application for the students.*
3. Interaction with teachers and students revealed that spoken English skills are in need and highly desired, but go unaddressed due to lack of English speaking teachers, parents and fellow students. *We therefore chose spoken English as the teaching material for the game.*
4. The field study documented high penetration of mobile phones even in the remotest of the villages of Mewat. Furthermore, the practice of listening to the radio, including cricket commentary, on mobile phones is very common. *Hence, we were assured that the mobile phone is a relevant platform for the application.*

The Spoken English Cricket Game Design

The game experience for students is set as an Interactive Voice Response (IVR) system implemented on a server. There are no visuals provided to the user. This ensures that the game can be accessed using any low-end phone device by dialing a phone number. The students hear commentary similar to the one that they would hear while following such a game on the radio.

In order to understand the game design, it is necessary to understand at least the basic structure and nomenclature of cricket. We supply a high-level description, for readers who might be unfamiliar with the game. Cricket is played between two teams as shown in Figure 3. Fielders and bowlers are from one team and batsmen are from the other team. Periodically, the team that bats (hits) and team bowls (pitches) switch roles. The action involves a bowler pitching the ball towards the batsman; batsman swings at the ball with the aim of hitting it and scoring as many runs as possible; fielders attempt to prevent runs by catching the ball. The action is an individual act between the bowler and the batsman and the team aspect involves the individual batsmen working to add to their team score.

Figure 3. A visual depiction of the player roles and the action in the game of cricket. Bowlers and fielders (in blue) form one team while the batsmen (in green) form the second team.

Our cricket game provides an audio realization of the basic action of the cricket game. Instead of the bowler pitching the ball, the system speaks a word to a student (batsman) and the student is supposed to hit it (speak the best pronunciation) in order to score maximum runs. The better the student pronounces a given word/phrase/sentence, the higher the score. The system speaks the result of the action in a commentary, which takes the same form as used in a real cricket broadcast, and keeps track of the score for the game. The action ("pitching" of the word by the system and "hitting" its answer by the user) is repeated multiple times.

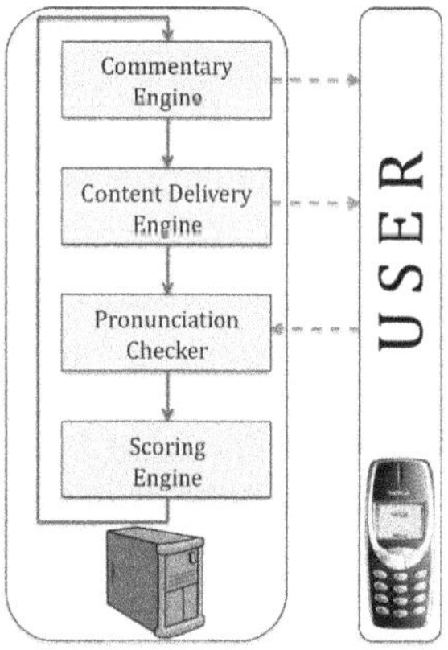

Figure 4. The components of the spoken English cricket game. Students access the game by a mobile phone. The game is deployed on the server.

A logical system diagram of the designed game is shown in Figure 4. It consists of four components: Commentary Engine, Content Delivery Engine, Pronunciation Checker and the Scoring Engine. The blue line shows the action flow while the green (dashed) line shows the interaction with the user.

Commentary Engine

The Commentary Engine provides the feedback to the user about the progress of the game. It takes the scoring input from the Scoring Engine and based on the score of the current hit by the user, it generates a relevant commentary in cricketing terms. In order to provide a realistic commentary, following sets of dialogs are provided:

- Feedback commentary: There are three categories of dialogs for providing the user with a feedback of her current hit (speech input). If the user does not provide any input, a dialog from the *no-input* set is played as the commentary. Dialogs in the *no-input* set are mostly of the type where the commentator says that the ball was a very good one and the batsman was not able to play any shot (i.e., did not swing or could not hit). If the users provide a completely incorrect pronunciation, for which the scoring engine returns a 0 value, then a dialog from the *no-match* set is played. The *no-match* dialogs mention that the user played a shot, but it was fielded by a fielder and so the batsman could not score any runs. If the Scoring Engine returns a value greater than 0, then an appropriate commentary is played, which mentions the number of runs scored by this ball along with a description of how the ball was played. In order to provide a realistic and a non-repetitive experience to the user, each set of dialogs has 10 variations and any one of them is played out at random. Specifically, the Commentary Engine has 10 dialogs for *no-input* situation, 10 dialogs for *no-match* situations and 40 *run* dialogs for the four situations of different runs (which in our game is 1, 2, 4 or 6 runs). The run dialogs include the sound of applause and cheering to provide a realistic commentary experience.
- Encouragement commentary: These are generic dialogs that mention how the team is performing. They are not played after every ball, but are randomly inserted after every few balls. One of the dialogs is chosen at random from a set of 6 dialogs.
- Ball commentary: Before a word is spoken to the user (for which the user has to speak back the pronunciation), the Commentary Engine explicitly prepares the user for the word by mentioning that the next ball is about to come. The specific dialog is also chosen randomly from a set of 10 such dialogs.
- Transition commentary: The game involves several transitions when different events happen. These events could be change of fielding positions, change of bowlers. To parallel the real commentary, like encouragement commentary, these are also played out randomly after a few balls. One of the dialogs is chosen at random from a set of 6 dialogs.
- Total score commentary: This commentary provides the total score of the team so far through a set of 10 sentences, one of which is randomly chosen each time.

All the commentary is provided in a male voice in the local language Hindi, as this is usually the case with the radio commentary, to which users are used to listening.

Content Delivery Engine

The content delivery engine consists of an English word/phrase/sentence that is spoken by the engine to the user. In order to clearly distinguish the content from the commentary, the content is spoken in a female voice. After the word is spoken, a beep sound prompts the user to respond back. Once the user responds, irrespective of the quality of the user response, the meaning of the word/phrase/sentence in Hindi and the spelling (only in case of words) is spoken back to the user.

The need for coherence of the content of the game with the English-language curriculum of the books was clearly established by the discussions with the students and the teachers. For the prototype of the game, we decided to select ten words each for 'easy', 'medium' and 'difficult' category. Similarly we selected ten phrases and ten sentences for the game. Therefore the game had a total of 50 pronunciation "balls". We selected the words, phrase and sentences randomly from the English curriculum books of classes 3, 4 and 5. The content presented to the user is changed based on the user performance in the game. If a user is performing well, the content category is changed from easy to medium and then to difficult words. On the other hand, if a user's performance in a given category is poor, then words from an easier category are presented. The content delivered to the user is therefore a function of the total score of the team in the game in a particular instance.

Pronunciation Checker

The Pronunciation Checker is a speech recognition system that captures the user input and passes it to Scoring Engine. The speech recognition system uses a fixed grammar of one word/phrase/sentence and performs a forced alignment [6] of the word with the user input and generates a probabilistic score p_{asr} and passes to the Scoring Engine.

Scoring Engine

The Scoring Engine translates the user input into a score formulated in cricketing terms. The probabilistic scores returned by a speech recognizer range from 0 to 1. We map these scores such that any value less than 0.5 is considered to be a *no-match* and therefore zero runs are provided to the user. Values from 0.5 to 1 are mapped to scores of 1, 2, 4 and 6 in the following manner:

$$0.5 \le p_{asr} < 0.6 \Rightarrow r = 1$$
$$0.6 \le p_{asr} < 0.8 \Rightarrow r = 2$$
$$0.8 \le p_{asr} < 0.92 \Rightarrow r = 4$$
$$0.92 \le p_{asr} \Rightarrow r = 6$$

p_{asr}. is the speech recognition score and r is the number of runs assigned by the Scoring Engine. Since scoring 6 runs in a ball is very rare in cricket, a higher threshold of 0.92 has been selected for the game.

Referring back to the previously mentioned design principles [12] concerning game features: *fun* and *engagement* are provided through the concept of increasing score and the excitement to score more runs; *feedback* is provided through the feedback commentary; the response to content forms the *problem-solving* aspect; *pacing* and *fantasy narrative* is covered through the running commentary. The collaborative aspect of the interaction is derived from the fact that students form teams and then collaboratively try to defeat other teams by scoring better.

EVALUATION EXPERIMENT

The evaluation experiment was conducted in three phases over a period of three weeks. Our goal was to investigate: (a) whether the game is engaging enough that students play it multiple times, and, (b) whether the game helps to improve the pronunciation skills of the students.

The first phase of the experiment involved recruiting 63 (41 male/22 female) students of Class 4 and Class 5 from Kanwarsika village. Students were aged from 8 to 11 years. We chose students from these classes because this is the level where most students drop out of school [9] and also because their pronunciation skills had sufficient scope for improvement. Then we conducted manual pronunciation test of the students by asking them to speak a total of 20 words, four from each category: easy, medium, difficult, phrases, sentences. Each user input was graded at three levels: zero marks were given for incorrect pronunciation, two for an exactly correct pronunciation and one for an acceptable pronunciation. While these scores do not map exactly to the scores provided by the game, they relate well to how the teachers measure the pronunciation at school. This score formed the baseline for evaluation.

We then asked the students to dial the spoken English cricket game using their families' phone from home for a period of one week. We informed the students that this call would be toll-free. We also mentioned that there would be a tournament in the upcoming weeks on this game and so they were asked to practice for it. We did not provide any specific training to any of the students on how to play the game. The practice session in the first phase did not involve any collaboration between players. We maintained system logs of the usage of the game by students during this period.

In the second phase, we returned back to the school after a period of one week and then conducted another round of manual pronunciation tests of the same students using the same set of words. We then announced that the tournament will be conducted in a week's time and asked students to form teams of six students each for the tournament. They were again asked to continue to practice during this phase, but in teams. System logs were captured in order to observe the usage of the game by students in this period as well.

The final phase involved conducting the tournament where each team of six students was asked to "play" 30 "balls", i.e., speak the pronunciations for 30 words. The interaction took place using a mobile phone that was connected to a speaker so that all members of the team could hear the commentary. Each student in the team would use the mobile phone to "play" one word or phrase and then pass the phone on to the next student, who would take the next turn. After six balls, the students repeat the same order – of course with different words each time. The team that that scored the most runs was declared the winner and the student who scored the most runs was declared "Sachin Tendulkar". After the tournament, we conducted one final round of manual pronunciation tests of the same words with the same students.

RESULTS

Figure 5 shows scores for the first manual pronunciation tests (solid line). This forms the baseline for our experiments. Of a maximum of 40 marks, the highest score was 30 and lowest was 0, which was observed for three students. The average score for the 63 students was 9.22 with a high standard deviation of 6.76.

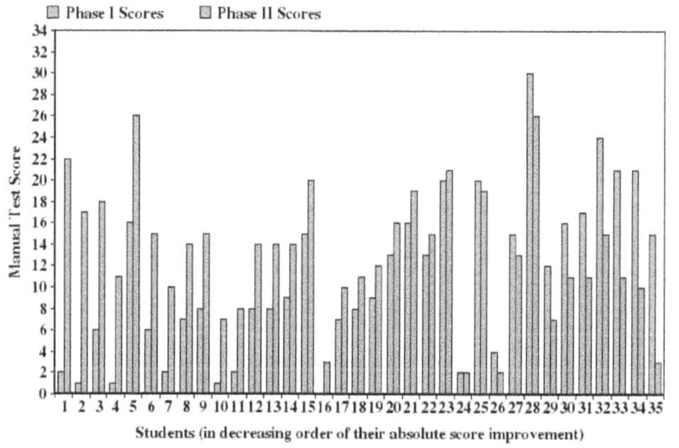

Figure 5: Changes in manual pronunciation scores of students over one week, in decreasing order of PhaseI – PhaseII scores.

After this manual test and after advertizing the game and the tournament to students, 46 of the 63 students tried the game at least once. Only five students tried the game more than five times, with most trying only once. A total of 554 balls were played by the students over the course of the week. On the average, each student played 12.04 balls, with a standard deviation of 5.4 balls.

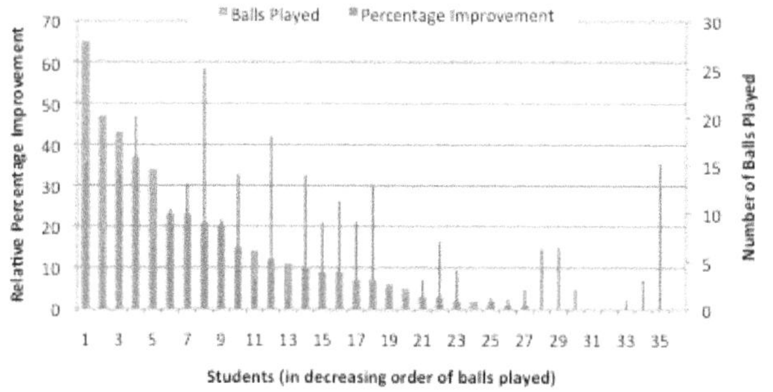

Figure 6: Correlation of number of balls played by a student with the relative percentage improvement in pronunciation.

In the second phase of the experiment, when we performed the manual pronunciation test, 27 of the original 63 students were not present. Out of the common 36 students that were present in the phase 1 and phase 2, a relative improvement of 20.53% was seen. We plot the relative percentage of improvement for each of these 36 students in relation to the number of balls that they had played on the game during the one-week period (Figure 6). The Pearson correlation of the improvement in pronunciation score with the number of balls played is 0.24.

The week in which the participants were asked to form teams for the tournament saw significant activity on the cricket game. A total of 2187 balls were played by the students in the third phase. When the final manual evaluations were conducted, of the 36 students common to both phase I and phase II, 26 were present for the phase III evaluations. These 26 students were part of the final tournament. They were joined by 28 other students (some of whom were part of the phase II evaluations) and out of this total of 54 students, 9 teams of six students each were formed for the tournament.

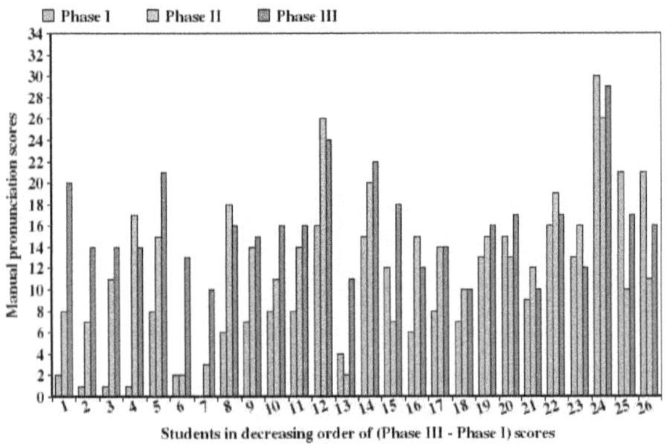

Figure 7: Manual pronunciation scores over the three phases, ordered by decreasing magnitude of improvement.

A comparison analysis of the 26 students that were common to all the three phases of the experiment is shown in Figure 7. The figure establishes that most bars (i.e., students) finish with their highest score being in the phase III, thus establishing that their pronunciation did improve through the process of practicing for the tournament and eventually participating in it.

The most significant evaluation of the game was to compare the manual performance of the pronunciation tests with the individual scores made by the students. The Pearson correlation between the individual scores in the tournament and the manual improvement made from phase I was 0.49 for these students.

Eventually the team that won the tournament also had the student that made the maximum score and hence was given the title "Sachin Tendulkar". The manual pronunciation test scores of this student in the three phases were 24, 28 and 29. The scores indicate that he had good English pronunciation already at the start of the tournament and therefore did not gain significantly from the game. However he did practice the game multiple times and had played 284 balls before the tournament.

The analysis of the experimental results revealed that (a) the students played the game multiple times and (b) the students' pronunciation improved as a result of playing the game. The improvement was reflected in both the manual evaluation of their pronunciation as well as in the pronunciation level as reflected in the scores that they achieved in the game. An important finding was that the pronunciation improvement found in the manual evaluation was reflected by parallel improvement in the game scores. Enthusiasm levels were high and game-play was observed. The game gave rise to collaborative interaction leading to team building. Players also were observed expressing frustration with other team members, in the context of high levels of excitement generated by the competition.

OBSERVATIONS AND DISCUSSION

In this section, we discuss in more depth additional observations made during the tournament. In total, 66 students were observed in action with the game.

Team Formation and Selection. When students were forming their teams, we observed that each team was built according to the current social circle of the captain. Later, all the teams got restructured in the process. We observed that the nominated captains tried and in few cases fought among themselves to form their teams consisting of students who regularly attended the school or who were supposedly good in the studies. A captain said, "*I won't let Ashima [another student] leave my team, she knows lot of English words and other team get benefits*" Another captain looked worried and told us, "*All of my friends are skipping school and I fear that they might not come on the day of tournament. I will make a new team.*"

Collaboration and Team Work. The competition was titled "Who wants to be Sachin Tendulkar?" and prizes were announced for both the "most valuable player" of series ("Sachin Tendulkar") and the winning team. During the final round, we noticed among all the teams, the major focus of each student was that their team wins. There were lot of giggles, applauses and pats when any team member answered correctly and the team scored. In case of a wrong answer, the team members reacted by sighs, holding their heads or demonstrating frustration. We also observed whispers and prompts to weaker team members on various occasions (cf. Figure 8, left). A loosing captain commented after the game, "*I told Anil [student] to practice more, it's due to him our team has suffered.*" While Anil complained, "*I got the harder words than the others*".

The team engagement and passion for the game continued beyond scoring: after some incorrect attempts by a team member, other members later spoke the correct answer, perhaps to establish that they knew the answer. The room in which the competition was held was surrounded by the other teams, who were interested to see and hear how the team was performing (cf. Figure 8, right). Many of the students were highly motivated and averred, "*No matter what happens, I will be Sachin Tendulkar.*"

Figure 8: Students whispering correct pronunciations (left) and students listening to the scores of other teams (right)

Gender and User Experience Several observations were made during the tournament concerning the students' user experience with the game from the perspective of gender. Because the evaluation did not focus on gender-specific aspects of the game, these observations are informal in nature and comprise a series of remarks, which we loosely structure according to the framework of Forlizzi & Battarbee [7]. This framework divides user experience in three parts: "experience" as related to users achieving their goals within the usage context, "an experience" as reflected in interactions and emotional or behavioral changes, and "co-experience", when shared with others in social context.

In terms of "experience", both male and female students were observed to achieve the goals of successful game play. Although the overall winning team was composed of male students, a female team won the competition at the level of class 4. The reactions of the students during play suggested a tendency of male students to assess goal achievement with respect to their individual success and react more strongly to their own individual failure. In terms of "an experience", teams of female students demonstrated reactions that could indicate the game gave them a different feeling of completion than experienced by teams of male students. A number of captains of the female teams that lost requested another chance or another tournament in the near future. In terms of "co-experience", observations suggested that the experience of the female teams was more inclusive than the male teams. Their attempts to answer were more collective, giggling and applause often ensued when any team member scored runs, and shared happiness with team success was more visibly externalized.

Phones and Phone Sharing. The mobile telephone as a platform was apparently appreciated by the students. They showed visible signs of enjoyment while interacting with the system. The average duration of a use session was in the range of 15-20 minutes. This observation was particularly gratifying in light of exploratory studies with other applications carried out in rural areas located in other parts of India, but sharing similarity with Mewat. During these studies, IVR systems are not well received by users, who experienced high levels of frustration with interacting with the system. In the case of the cricket game, the students did not demonstrate any evidence of facing similar usability or acceptability problems.

In rural regions of India, often the mobile phone is not a personal device but is readily shared amongst the family members. We observed that although most of the parents shared their mobile phones with the students, a few students could not practice for the tournament as their family members refrained from sharing their phones due to infrastructural issues. For instance, one student complained, "*My elder brother didn't give the phone to me. He said it will drain the battery and he can't charge as electrical supply is being short these days.*"

GENERALIZATION OF DESIGN INSIGHTS FOR FUTURE APPLICATIONS

As previously mentioned, the field study that led to the design of the cricket game was motivated by our underlying appreciation that the intersection of a local culture and technology reveals various constraints, motivations, needs and opportunities for the design of any application of technology. This perspective is shared, sometimes implicitly, across a wide range of design practices that focuses on specific socio-cultural settings. Best representative of our own perspective, is that of Dourish and Bell [3], as expressed by their statement, "*We start from the position that technology and social life are not easily separated – that social life is already entwined with technologies and technological practices of all kinds, and that technologies and their designs are embedded in social systems that they reflect, reproduce and transform.*" (p. 59). In order to allow future design efforts to make more optimal use of the lessons learned during the development of our cricket game, we include here a short discussion on the possible generalization of our design insights (as they are stated in the section "Game Conceptualization and Design") to future settings and applications.

First, the field study revealed that the application must be highly motivational in order to compensate for lack of opportunities within the community for students to engage in the interactions necessary to improve their spoken English. Generalizing this point, we can anticipate that engaging activities and practices that are already established in the community can provide a vehicle for extending motivations to domains that reach beyond capacity of the community.

Second, the field study identified cricket as the particular vehicle suited for Mewat because of its popularity and acceptability in the community. The most obvious generalization of this point is that the popularity of cricket extends to other parts of India and also other developing regions like Pakistan, Bangladesh and Sri Lanka. In cricket, the game scoring and the commentary track reinforce progress and success within the game. Users transfer their understanding and interest in the progress in a cricket game to their own progress in pronunciation improvement. The structure of the game encourages both collaboration and individual achievement. Further generalizing this insight, we expect that the effectiveness of cricket as a vehicle might extend to other learning goals beyond spoken English and also that the application could be based on other highly popular games, for example, soccer.

Third, the field study identified high motivation in the community for learning spoken English skills and acknowledgment of the lack of community resources to support this learning. We would like to highlight this point as an important aspect of the cricket game and one that was probably essential to the engagement of the users with the game. We must be careful when generalizing this point, since within our setting we only developed one application. However, we can state that we believe that by concentrating on a goal shared within the community and consistent with commonly held values, we were able to help to ensure that the resulting application faced a lower threshold for acceptance and appropriation, since in a sense it already "belonged" to the community from the beginning of the design process.

In this way, our work is related to the larger issue of how to design technologies that are "born appropriated". Here, we would like to specifically mention that a designer focusing on existing goals and motivations may be better able to avoid becoming an all-controlling *puppet master*, discussed by McGonigal [15], who dictates the goals of players in a game during the design process.

Fourth, the field study documented high penetration of low-end mobile phones in the area. Generalizing this point, we would like to emphasize the importance not only of the availability of the mobile phones, but also the importance of patterns of accessibility and use of mobile phones and voice modality. The students were "allowed" to play the game by their parents and in general the community response suggested that the game was welcome. The borrowing of mobile phones by the students needed to be negotiated within families, but in general this proved possible, even in the case of female student. The voice modality circumvented restrictions respected in the community on the use of images and the game could be accepted as an extension of listening to cricket on the radio, already a well-established and accepted pastime.

In sum, the success of the application in turn reflects the viability of an approach that allows the design of an application concept to be informed by a field study. The main design insights of the study show potential to generalize beyond the particular socio-cultural setting in Mewat, suggesting the conclusion that design processes can benefit if the design process begins with a field study that allows both socio-cultural limitations and community motivations to inform the design process.

CONCLUSION

This paper has presented a mobile phone based cricket game for improving the spoken English pronunciation of school children. The game was designed and tested within a specific socio-cultural context in rural India, the Mewat district of Haryana State of India. The paper reported on a field study that identified challenges, opportunities, and community needs for mobile phone applications in primary schools in this context. The field-study informed and shaped the design and implementation of the mobile phone based cricket game. The paper described the evaluation of the game with groups of students at a rural school in Mewat. The evaluation demonstrated the potential of the game to engage students and facilitate improvement in their spoken English pronunciation. Finally, the paper provided a discussion on future design possibilities beyond the specific socio-cultural setting of Mewat.

Our future work will involve investigating spoken English learning amongst students on a long-term basis. A possible approach is to run the game for duration of an academic year and simultaneously developing the game's content parallel to the English curriculum of the particular class of the school. This broader engagement will involve more extensive testing on aspects of learning and investigation into ways in which the mobile cricket game could be developed to complement education for schools in rural areas. For example, we noticed an increase in the competitive urge among the students as the tournament approached. We would like to gain a deeper understanding of the balance of competition and collaboration necessary to promote optimal learning and how our application can achieve this balance.

The mobile cricket game serves as an example of an application that helps to uncover the potential benefits of a design process that takes socio-cultural limitations and community motivations into account from the very beginning of the design process. In the future, we will explore similar mobile phone applications that make possible learning of subjects and skills that go beyond spoken English and that are based on games that go beyond cricket, to include other popular sports, such as soccer. We also will focus on extending the game beyond the specific social-cultural setting of Mewat. This extension will allow us to gain an even deeper understanding of how mobile phone applications and social life are entwined and how to design applications at the intersection of technology and local culture.

ACKNOWLEDGEMENTS

The authors would like to thank Dr. Suresh Reddy, SRF Foundation for establishing contacts with school staff and for providing support on the field throughout the study; STITPRO foundation for funding part of this research; teachers and students for actively participating in this research as subjects.

REFERENCES

1. Azam, M., Chin, A. and Prakash, N. *The Returns to English-Language Skills in India*. Institute for the Study of Labor (IZA), 2010. http://ideas.repec.org/p/iza/izadps/dp4802.html.
2. Costabile, M.F., De Angeli, A., Lanzilotti, R., Ardito, C., Buono, P. and Pederson, T. Explore! possibilities and challenges of mobile learning. In *Proc. CHI 2008*, ACM Press (2008), 145-154.
3. Dourish, P. and Bell, G. *Divining a Digital Future: Mess and Mythology in Ubiquitous Computing*. The MIT Press, 2011.
4. Druin, A., Foss, E., Hutchinson, H., Golub, E. and Hatley, L. Children's roles using keyword search interfaces at home. In *Proc. CHI 2010*, ACM Press (2010), 413-422.
5. Druin, A., Weeks, A., Massey, S. and Bederson, B.B. Children's interests and concerns when using the international children's digital library: a four-country case study. In *Proc. JCDL 2007*, ACM (2007), 167-176.
6. Finke, M. and Waibel, A. Speaking Mode Dependent Pronunciation Modeling In Large Vocabulary Conversational Speech Recognition. In *Proc. Eurospeech 1997*, (1997), 2379-2382.
7. Forlizzi, J. and Battarbee, K. Understanding experience in interactive systems. In *Proc. DIS 2004*, ACM Press (2004), 261-268.
8. Franckel, S., Bonsignore, E. and Druin, A. Designing for children's mobile storytelling. *International Journal of Mobile Human Computer Interaction 2*, 2 (2010), 19-36.
9. Jayachandran, U. How High Are Dropout Rates in India? *Economic and Political Weekly*, (2007). http://www.epw.in/discussion/how-high-are-dropout-rates-india.html.
10. Kachru, B.B. Indian English: a sociolinguistic profile of a transplanted language. In *Dimensions of Bilingualism: theory and case studies, Special Issue of Studies in Language Learning*. Urbana, IL: Unit for Foreign Language Study and Research, University of Illinois. (1976).
11. Kam, M., Mathur, A., Kumar, A. and Canny, J. Designing digital games for rural children: a study of traditional village games in India. In *Proc CHI 2009*, ACM Press (2009), 31-40.
12. Kumar, A., Reddy, P., Tewari, A., Agrawal, R. and Kam, M. Improving literacy in developing countries using speech recognition-supported games on mobile devices. In *Proc. CHI 2012*, ACM Press (2012), 1149-1158.
13. Linehan, C., Kirman, B., Lawson, S. and Chan, G. Practical, appropriate, empirically-validated guidelines for designing educational games. In *Proc. CHI 2011*, ACM Press (2011), 1979-1988.
14. Maurya, A. IPL: Birth of Cricketainment: A Case Study on Sports Marketing by Board of Control for Cricket in India. *SSRN eLibrary*, (2009). http://papers.ssrn.com/sol3/papers.cfm?abstract_id=1353725.
15. McGonigal, J. The Puppet Master Problem: Design for Real-World, Mission Based Gaming. In P. Harrigan and N. Wardrip-Fruin, eds., *Second person: role-playing and story in games and playable media*. MIT Press, 2007, 251-264.
16. Näsänen, J., Oulasvirta, A. and Lehmuskallio, A. Mobile media in the social fabric of a kindergarten. In *Proc. CHI 2009*, ACM Press (2009), 2167-2176.
17. Santhanam, V. and Balasubramanian, S. *If Cricket is a Religion, Sachin is God*. HarperCollins India, 2009.
18. Walsh, G., Druin, A., Guha, M.L., Foss, E., Golub, E., Hatley, L., Bonsignore, E. and Franckel, S. Layered elaboration: a new technique for co-design with children. In *Proc. CHI 2010*, ACM Press (2010), 1237-1240.
19. White, S.M., Marino, D. and Feiner, S. Designing a mobile user interface for automated species identification. In *Proc. CHI 2007*, ACM Press (2007), 291-294.
20. Zhou, Y., Percival, G., Wang, X., Wang, Y. and Zhao, S. MOGCLASS: evaluation of a collaborative system of mobile devices for classroom music education of young children. In *Proc. CHI 2011*, ACM Press (2011), 523-532.

Trend Makers and Trend Spotters in a Mobile Application

Xiaolan Sha
EURECOM
France
xiaolan.sha@eurecom.fr

Daniele Quercia*
Yahoo! Research Barcelona
Spain
dquercia@yahoo-inc.com

Matteo Dell'Amico
EURECOM
France
della@linux.it

Pietro Michiardi
EURECOM
France
pietro.michiardi@eurecom.fr

ABSTRACT
Media marketers and researchers have shown great interest in what becomes a trend within social media sites. Their interests have focused on analyzing the items that become trends, and done so in the context of Youtube, Twitter, and Foursquare. Here we move away from these three platforms and consider a new mobile social-networking application with which users share pictures of "cool" things they find in the real-world. Besides, we shift focus from items to people. Specifically, we focus on those who generate trends (trend makers) and those who spread them (trend spotters). We analyze the complete dataset of user interactions, and characterize trend makers (spotters) by activity, geographical, and demographic features. We find that there are key characteristics that distinguish them from typical users. Also, we provide statistical models that accurately identify who is a trend maker (spotter). These contributions not only expand current studies on trends in social media but also promise to inform the design of recommender systems, and new products.

ACM Classification Keywords
H.4.m Information Systems Applications: Miscellaneous

Author Keywords
Mobile, Social Marketing

INTRODUCTION
Marketers and researchers have shown great interest in being able to effectively identify trends [7, 2, 3, 19, 30]. That is because being able to identify them translates into effectively managing brands for marketers, and into explaining the general dynamics of opinion spreading for researchers.

*This work was done while at the Computer Laboratory of the University of Cambridge.

As we shall see in related work, there have been studies not only on trends but also on the individuals who create trends. This includes those who generate trends (defined in this paper as trend makers) and those who spread them (trend spotters). However, from these studies, it is not yet clear whether trend makers and trend spotters can be characterized by specific features, and whether these features can be used to easily identify them. To fill this gap, we examine a complete dataset of user interactions in the *iCoolhunt*[1] mobile social networking application and make two main contributions:

- We approach the analysis of who creates trends by defining two distinct classes of individuals: trend spotters and trend makers. We characterize them by combining multiple characteristics including their activity, content, network and geographical features. We find that trend spotters and trend makers differ from typical users, in that, they are more active, show interest in a variety of items, and attract social connections. We then study what differentiates trend spotters from trend makers. We learn that successful trend spotters are adult early adopters who hold interests in very diverse items, while successful trend makers are individuals of any age who focus on specific types of items.
- Using linear regression, we predict the extent to which one is a trend spotter or trend maker. Then, with an existing machine learning algorithm (SVM) and with a logistic regression, we perform a binary classification of whether one is likely to be a trend spotter (trend maker) or not. While linear regression has produced informative results, SVM and logistic regression have returned accurate predictions.

We conclude by discussing the theoretical implications of this work in the literature of opinion spreading, and its practical implications in designing recommender systems, and new products.

RELATED WORK
Previous studies of trends in social media have tried to answer two main questions: 1) what trends are; and 2) who creates trends.

What Trends Are. One way of extracting insights (e.g.,

[1] `http://www.icoolhunt.com`

predict large-scale events) from social media is to identify trends [3, 19, 30]. In the literature, there are two types of trends [7]. In a social media site, exogenous trends are those triggered by factors external to the site (e.g., reporting of a piece of news on TV). Endogenous trends are those created by internal factors (e.g., spreading of a piece of news within the site). Exogenous and endogenous trends can be distinguished based on statistical analyses. For example, the two types of trends are distinguishable based on simple temporal patterns in the video sharing site Youtube [7] and based on features that reflect content, interactions among users, and social network structure in Twitter [19].

Who Creates Trends. There are two different views on who creates trends. The first is that *trends are generated by influentials*, which are special kinds of individuals who: are able to spot trends early on [15, 12, 23]; are socially well connected [16]; are able to easily influence others [14]; are considered to be experts [25, 29]; or are celebrities [30]. The second view on who creates trends holds that *trends are generated by coincidences* and that anyone can be influential. As a result, what becomes popular in a network does not depend on the initiators and is thus an accidental process. Duncan Watts uses the terms "accidental influentials" as he considers social epidemics to be "mostly an accident of location and timing" [26], and ideas spread and ultimately become popular only if there is societal willingness to accept them. More recently, researchers have found that there are different classes of individuals who contribute to two parallel processes: early participants start contributing and thus create random seeding, and that contribution spreads then through low threshold individuals [1, 13]. This recent literature has focused on the two parallel processes, while we build upon that by focusing on the individuals who contribute to those processes.

Given what is known in the literature, it is still unclear whether those who generate trends by originally introducing them into social networks and those who spread trends are special individuals or not. To answer this question, we define trend makers (those who generate trends) and trend spotters (those who spread trends). We characterize them by their activity, content, network and geographical features, and quantitatively test whether they have special characteristics comparing to typical users. We show that these features can be used to predict who are trend spotters and trend makers. We do so by going beyond the widely-studied platform of Twitter: we examine a new mobile application, which is described next.

APPLICATION

The application under study is a social application with a mobile phone client in which users can share pictures of "cool items". Users upload photos of items that they encounter in the real world and consider "cool" (Figure 1). Upon submission, each photo must be tagged with a specific category selected among the five predefined categories (technology, lifestyle, music, design and fashion), and must be textually described. If one enables geolocation, one's photos are automatically geo-referenced with the locations in which they were uploaded. Users can vote others' photos with either a *like* or a *dislike* button. Every photo can receive limited-size comments from users, including the uploader. Every user is directly allowed to retrieve the list of popular pictures and latest uploads from any other user. In a way similar to what happens in Twitter, users of the application can follow each other. At the time of data collection, iCoolhunt didn't provide any "news-feed" of pictures uploaded by followed users: activities from social connections were only accessible by browsing their profile pages.

Figure 1. Screenshot of the mobile application.

We consider the *complete* dataset from February 2010 (the application's launch) to August 2010.[2] Within those first six months, 9,316 users uploaded 6,395 photos and submitted 13,893 votes.

The unique characteristics of this dataset fit particularly well our interest in characterizing trend spotters and trend makers. The dataset contains user demographic information, the follower-followee graph, votes, comments, and geographical location of the place where items are uploaded.

To better interpret the results of our data analysis and compare them to the findings in the literature (which are mainly about Twitter and, to a lesser degree, Foursquare), we spell out the similarities and differences between the mobile application and Twitter/Foursquare:

Similarities. In a way similar to Twitter, the mobile application's users can follow each other and, in a way similar to Foursquare, they can receive "honors" depending on how active they are (these honors are called "guru", "observer", "rookie", and "spotter" based on the number of followers one has and sum of votes his uploads have received).

Differences. There are two main differences with Twitter. The first is about social interactions. Twitter users can *reply*, *retweet* others' tweets, *mention* specific users, but cannot vote explicitly tweets (although similar information can be inferred from "favorites"). Instead, users of the mobile application can vote others' items with a "like" or "dislike", comment items, but can neither forward ("retweet") items

[2]The iCoolhunt web application was launched after the end of our study period and, as such, our dataset includes only mobile application users. The format of this dataset cannot be acquired via crawling but directly from the service providers. We did acquire data only until the end of August 2010.

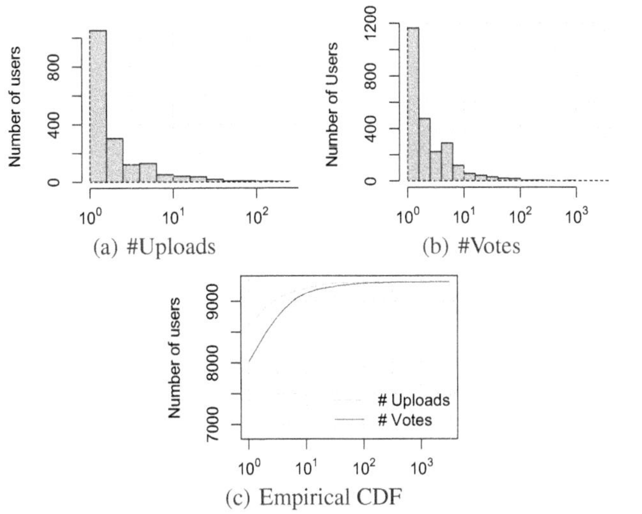

Figure 2. (a) Number of uploads per user; (b) Number of votes per user; (c) Distribution comparison on uploads and votes (log-scale on x-axis)

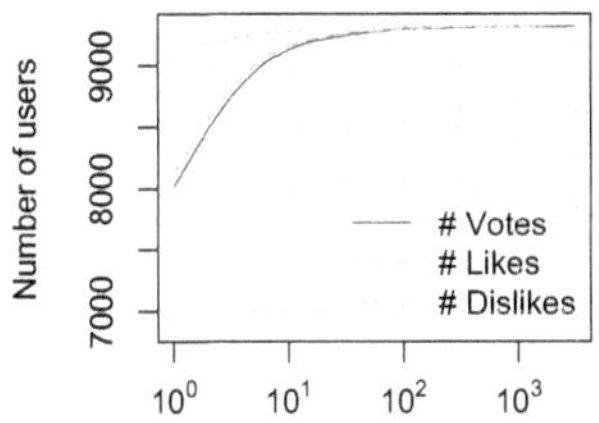

Figure 3. Empirical CDF of the number of votes, likes, and dislikes.

nor *mention* any other user. The second difference is about the user interface. Twitter users exchange status updates with each other, while the mobile application's users have no transparent way of being aware of what others are up to. We will discuss how these differences impact the effectiveness of our mobile application later on.

DATASET

The dataset includes 5,092 males and 4,224 females: 19% of males and 18% of females uploaded items and, out of a total of 13,893 votes, 69% of those were produced by males and 31% by females. This suggests that males are more active in voting than females. To understand how many users are actually using the application, we initially conduct a preliminary analysis of the behavior related to uploading, voting, and managing social relations.

Uploads and Votes

Uploading and voting pictures are the main activities in iCoolhunt, but, as one sees from the distributions in Figure 2(a) and Figure 2(b), only a small portion of the users are active in either uploading or voting. Out of the total 9,316 users, 1,761 (2,463) uploaded (voted) at least once and 710 (1,301) of them uploaded (voted) more than once. However, the minority who have uploaded more than once have contributed 83% pictures, while those who voted more than once have contributed 94% votes. That means that users prefer to vote pictures rather than to upload and, more importantly, that a minority of the users have contributed most of the content.

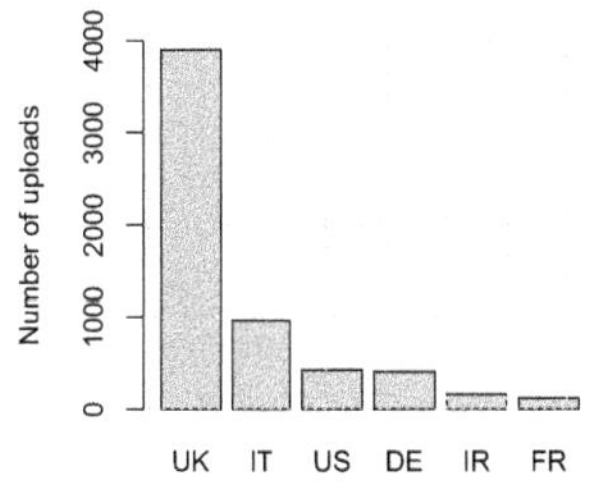

Figure 4. Number of uploads from each country (Top 6)

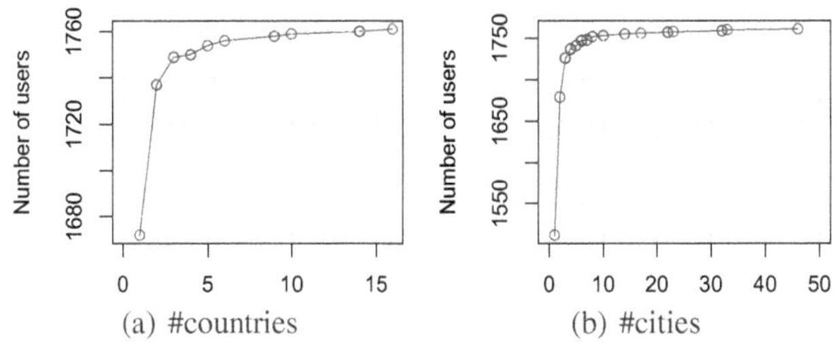

Figure 5. Empirical CDF of number of countries (cities) from where each user has uploaded, with y-axis representing the cumulative number of users.

Users are allowed to vote explicitly with a "like" or "dislike". Thus, to understand users' voting behavior, we separate votes into likes and dislikes and also consider any type of vote on aggregate. Figure 3 shows the distribution of the total number of votes per user and distinguishes "likes" from "dislikes": 584 registered users have submitted "dislike" votes, 2,349 have submitted "like" votes, and 2,463 have simply voted with either a "like" or "dislike". This suggests that iCoolhunt users are comfortable to express far more positive votes than negative ones.

Geography

Pictures are geographically tagged while they are uploaded. By tracing the locations of pictures, we are able to infer the number of places each user has been to. Using Google Maps, we are able to classify the coordinates into countries and cities/towns. The pictures have been uploaded from 57 different countries and regions. Among those there are only six countries with more than 100 uploads (Figure 4): United Kingdom (UK), Italy (IT), United States (US), Germany (DE), Ireland (IR) and France (FR). Also, each user could upload from multiple countries: among those who uploaded pictures, 89 users did so from more than one country (Figure 5(a)) and 249 users from at least two different cities/towns (Figure 5(b)).

Following

To cope with information overload, iCoolhunt users define lists of people they know or whose content they like. Each user then preferentially receives pictures from his/her own list of following, and eventually leaves comments and messages on those pictures. Figure 6 shows the number of followers/followees for each user - only few users follow other users, and even fewer users are followed. To then check whether users who upload more also have more followers/followees, we graph the scatter-plots of the number of

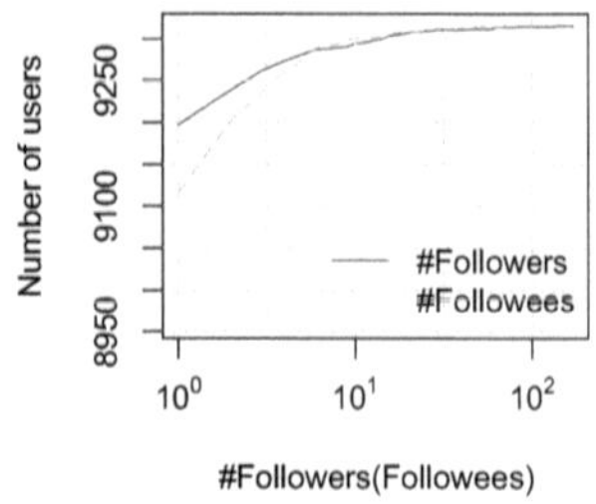

Figure 6. Empirical CDF of the number of followers and followees.

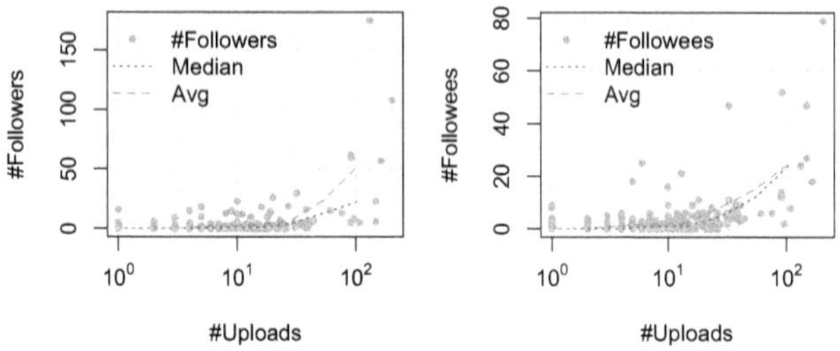

(a) Uploads vs. Followers (b) Uploads vs. Followees

Figure 7. Number of followers(followees) and number of uploads per user

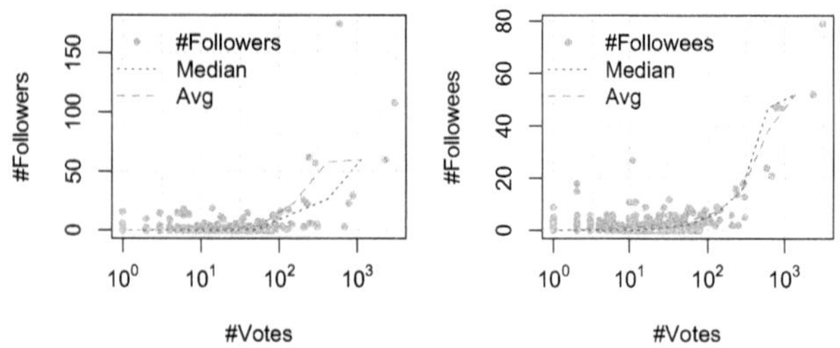

(a) Votes vs. Followers (b) Votes vs. Followees

Figure 8. Number of followers(followees) and number of votes per user

followers/followees (y-axis) as a function of the number of uploads and votes for each user. In a way similar to [17], we bin the number of uploads/votes on a log scale and show both of the mean and median of each bin. The relationships are clear: the number of followers increases with the number of uploads (Figure 7(a)) and number of votes (Figure 8(a)); so does the number of followees(Figures 7(b) and 8(b)). In short, people who contribute to the community get followed, those who lurk do not. This makes sense as lurkers are essentially invisible.

To sum up, as one expects, a minority of users have uploaded and voted most of the pictures. Since we cannot get hold of access logs, we are not able to identify lurkers (those who simply browse) among inactive users. What we are able to differentiate though is trend spotters (users who spread trends) from trend makers (those who upload trends), and we do so next.

TREND MAKERS AND SPOTTERS

Our analysis unfolds three steps: identify trend spotters and trend makers; characterize them by conducting a quantitative analysis based on selected features; and build a statistical

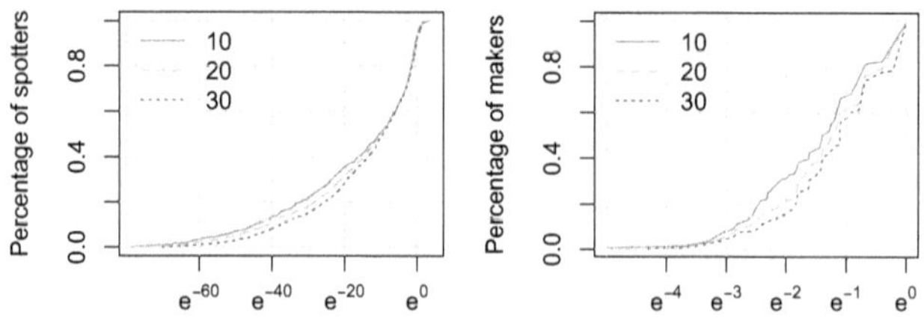

(a) Spotter Scores (b) Maker Scores

Figure 9. Empirical CDF of spotter (maker) scores (log-transformed) versus top-n ranked items.

model that identifies who is a trend spotter and who is a trend maker.

Defining Trend Spotters and Trend Makers

To identify trend spotters and trend makers, we need to define what a trend is first.

Trends. Trends differ from popular items, in that, they are not necessarily popular but they receive abrupt attention within a short period of time. To identify trends in the dataset, we define a "trend score" metric, which is derived from a simple burst detection algorithm proposed in [19]. At each time unit t (one-week window that incrementally slides every day), we assign to item i a $trendScore(i, t)$ that increases with the number of votes it receives:

$$trendScore(i, t) = \frac{|v_{i,t}| - \mu_i}{\sigma_i} \tag{1}$$

where $|v_{i,t}|$ is the number of votes item i has received within time unit t, μ_i is the mean number of votes it has received per time unit[3], and σ_i is the corresponding standard deviation. The higher the item's *trendScore*, the more votes it has received. For each time unit (each week), we sort items by their trend scores in descending order and select the top-n items to be trends. We have experimented with different $n \in \{10, 20, 30\}$ and found that spotter (maker) scores (defined later on) do not change very much (Figure 9) and, for $n = 10$, the resulting numbers of trend makers (140) and trend spotters (671) were sensible compared to the total number of users who voted (1,301) or uploaded (710) more than once. We thus report the results for $n = 10$.

Trend Spotters. Trend spotters are those who tend to vote items that, after a while, end up being trends. Not all trend spotters are equally good at voting trends. Considering a set of trending items, one's ability of voting trends depends on three factors: *how many* trending items one has voted, *how early* one has voted them, and *how popular* the voted items turned out to be.

We incorporate these three factors in a *spotterScore* for each user u by dividing the number of trends user u has voted

[3]The last time unit we consider is that in which the item received the last vote.

($\sum_{i \in \mathcal{I}_u} g_{u,i}$) by u's total number of votes (v_u):

$$spotterScore(u) = \frac{\sum_{i \in \mathcal{I}_u} g_{u,i}}{v_u} \quad (2)$$

In the numerator, $g_{u,i}$ is the gain user u acquires when voting on trending item i and incorporates the three factors of *how many*, *how early*, and *how popular*:

$$g_{u,i} = v_i \times \alpha^{-p_{u,i}} \quad (3)$$

where $\mathcal{I}_u$ is set of trends that u has voted ($\sum_{i \in \mathcal{I}_u}$ reflects the *how many*); v_i is total number of votes item i has received (which reflects the *how popular*), and α is a decay factor (which reflects the *how early*, $\alpha = 2$ in our experiments) whose exponent is the order with which u has voted item i ($p_{u,i}$ means that u is the pth user who voted i). A trend spotter is then anyone with trend spotter score greater than zero.

Trend Makers. Trend makers are those who tend to (not simply vote but) *upload* trending items. So the trend maker score of user u increases with the number of trends u has uploaded. The numerator of the score is $\sum_{i \in \mathcal{I}_u} I(i \text{ } is \text{ } a \text{ } trend)$, where $\mathcal{I}_u$ is the set of items u has uploaded, and I is the indicator function, which is 1, if the enclosed expression "*i is a trend*" is true; 0, otherwise. This numerator is then normalized by u's total number of uploads ($|\mathcal{I}_u|$) to account for those users who indiscriminately upload a large number of items without any quality control. A trend maker is then anyone with trend maker score greater than zero.

$$makerScore(u) = \frac{\sum_{i \in \mathcal{I}_u} I(i \text{ } is \text{ } a \text{ } trend)}{|\mathcal{I}_u|} \quad (4)$$

Typical users. If an active user (i.e., one who uploaded or voted more than once) is not a trend spotter or a trend maker, then he/she is considered to be a typical user. We discover that in our application, there were 1,705 typical users.

Characterizing Trend Spotters and Trend Makers

To characterize trend spotters and trend makers, we need to conduct a quantitative analysis that considers four types of features: activity, content, network, and geographical features.

Activity Features. The first activity feature we consider reflects how long an individual has been actively using the application. We call this feature "lifetime", and previous studies have identified it to be important as it conveniently identifies "early adopters" [10]. The literature recognizes that early adopters are a special interest group that heavily shapes usage of the application and ultimately determines the social norms within the application [8]. Once social norms are formed, changing them becomes very difficult and might backfire at times [9]. In addition to early adopters, we consider typical users as well. Their activity mainly consists of producing content (uploading pictures) and consuming it (voting pictures). Thus, we add two activity features to "lifetime": how frequently a user has been uploading pictures (*daily uploads*) and how many pictures the user has voted (*daily votes*).

Content Features. When users upload pictures, they are able to categorize them by selecting a proper category from the five predefined ones (technology, lifestyle, music, design and fashion). Previous studies on Twitter have linked category diversity to influence. According to [4] and [29], to become influential, one should "stay focused" – one tweet content in a specific category and become the "guru" in it. One may thus wonder whether our trend spotters and trend makers focus on specific categories of pictures, or, rather, whether they diversify consumption and production of content. To answer this question, we adopt a measure of categorical diversity from information theory called Shannon Index:

$$s = -\sum_{i \in \mathcal{C}} (f_i \ln f_i) \quad (5)$$

where $\mathcal{C}$ is the above set of five categories (echnology, lifestyle, music, design and fashion) and f_i is the fraction of items (out of the total number of items) that belong to i^{th} category. Using this expression, we measure three types of diversities for each user – *upload diversity*, *vote diversity*, *consumption diversity* (consumption translates into either voting or commenting pictures).

Network Features. Users of our application follow each other in a way similar to what happens in Twitter. Thus, the simplest network measures we could consider are in-degree (*number of followers*) and out-degree (*number of followees*). To then account for local network properties, we also consider the *clustering coefficient* [27] of a user, which is computed from the undirected graph whose nodes are users, and edges link users between whom there is at least one following relation. Clustering reflects the extent to which one's network is densely connected.

Geographical Features. Information propagation faces geographical constraints, caused by the decrease of the probability of a social tie between a pair of individuals with the increase of the geographical distance between the pair [5, 21]. In our application, when users upload pictures of items, these pictures are automatically geo-referenced – they report the longitude-latitude pairs of the items' positions. Thus, we can compute how often and how far users physically move (*wandering*), and we do so using the radius of gyration [6]:

$$r_u = \sqrt{\frac{1}{n} \sum_{i \in I_u} d^2_{l_i, c_u}} \quad (6)$$

where n is number of u's uploaded items, I_u is the set of u's uploaded items, c_u is user u's center of mass (which is the "average point" of all geographical locations of u's items), l_i is the location where item i has been uploaded, and d_{l_i, c_u} is the Euclidean distance between user u's center of mass and the location of each item i.

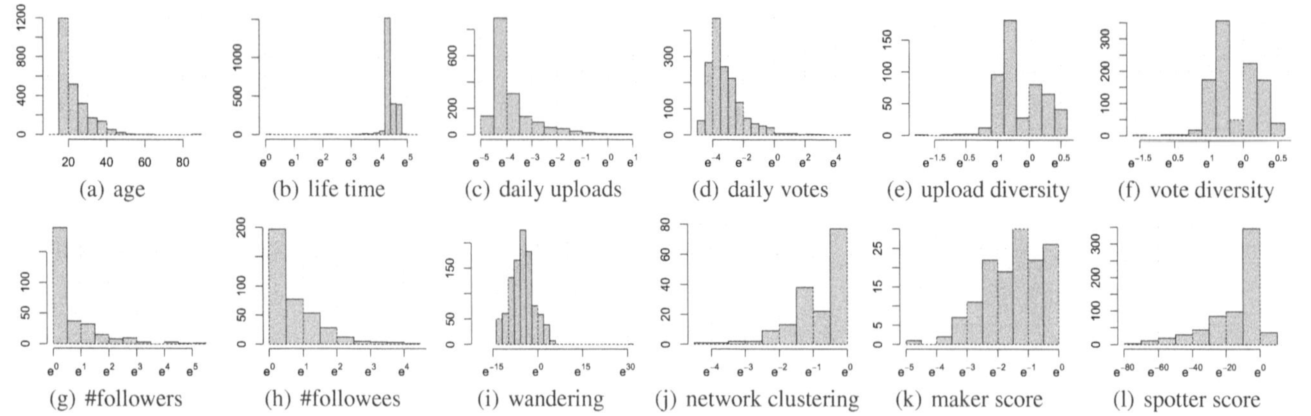

Figure 10. Distributions of features (a-j), trend maker (k) and trend spotter (l) scores with log-transformed values (except for the age feature). The x-axis represents the range of log-transformed features, and the y-axis represents the number of users.

	Content	Result
Spotters vs. Typical	H1.1 Trend spotters are more active than typical users.	√
	H1.2 Trend spotters tend to be more specialized than typical users in certain category of items.	×
	H1.3 Trend spotters attract more followers than typical users.	√
Makers vs. Typical	H2.1 Trend makers are more active than typical users.	√
	H2.2 Trend makers are more specialized than typical users in certain category of items.	×
	H2.3 Trend makers attract more followers than typical users.	√
Spotters vs. Makers	H3.1 Trend makers upload content more often than trend spotters.	√
	H3.2 Trend makers vote less often than spotters.	√
	H3.3 Trend spotters upload more diverse content than trend makers.	∗
	H3.4 Trend spotters vote less diverse content than trend makers.	×
	H3.5 Trend makers have more followers than trend spotters.	√

Table 1. Our Hypotheses (√: accept hypothesis; ×: accept the alternative hypothesis; ∗: unknown)

Feature (log-transformed)	S > T	M > T	M > S (if not shown otherwise)
Daily Uploads	**0.07** ∗	**0.45** ∗	**0.58** ∗
Daily Votes	**0.66** ∗	**0.18** ∗	**0.57** ∗ (M < S)
Upload Diversity	**0.31** ∗	**0.35** ∗	0.02 (M < S)
Vote Diversity	**0.31** ∗	**0.23** ∗	**0.27** ∗ (M < S)
#Followers	**0.06** ∗	**0.32** ∗	**0.26** ∗

Table 2. Summary of Kolmogorov-Smirnov test results of our hypotheses. D-values with significance level < 0.05 are highlighted and come with ∗. M, S and T stand for trend makers, trend spotters and typical users. We test a pair of distributions at a time - e.g., for S > T, we test whether the daily upload distribution for trend spotters is greater than that of typical users, and report the corresponding D-value.

Since locations are not only associated with pictures but also with users, we also compute the geographic span of a user's network [21]:

$$s_u = \frac{1}{m} \sum_{j \in \mathcal{F}_u} d_{u,j} \tag{7}$$

where m is number of u's followers, $\mathcal{F}_u$ is the list of u's followers, and $d_{u,j}$ is the distance between user u's center of mass and each follower j's center of mass.

We display the distribution of each feature in Figure 10. Since the distributions of the features are skewed, we show their log-transformed distributions.

Who trend spotters and trend makers are

Having all the features at hand, we are now able to run a comparative analysis. We compare trend spotters, trend makers, and typical users by testing hypotheses drawn from the literature, which Table 1 collates for convenience. We will now explain these hypotheses one-by-one.

1. Trend spotters (makers) vs. Typical users. Previous studies have shown that, compared to typical Twitter users, influentials tend to be more active, more specialized in specific categories, and be more popular (i.e., attract more followers) [24, 25, 4, 29, 30]. To draw parallels between Twitter influentials and trend spotters (makers), we hypothesize that, compared to typical users, trend spotters (makers) are more active (H1.1 and H2.1 in Table 1), specialized (H1.2 and H2.2), and popular (H1.3 and H2.3). To test these hypotheses, we run Kolmogorov-Smirnov tests (K-S tests [22]) and t-tests, and since both return the same results, we reported only K-S tests in Table 2. The idea is that we consider a pair of distributions, say, those of "daily uploads" for trend spotters (S) and for typical users (T) and compare them - we compare whether the mean of the distribution of trend spotters is greater than that of typical users (i.e., we test $S > T$). We find that, compared to typical users, both trend spotters and trend makers are more active (they upload and vote more) and are more popular (attract more followers). These results are statistically significant, that is, the corresponding p-values are below 0.05. Hence the four hypotheses H1.1, H1.3, H2.1 and H2.3 are confirmed. By contrast, hypotheses H1.2 and H2.2 are not confirmed. When consuming and producing content, trend spotters and trend makers neither focus on specific content categories nor diversify themselves more than what typical users do. However, by separating what users vote and what they upload, we find that the items voted by trend spotters are more diverse than those uploaded. This preliminary difference between trend spotters and trend makers opens up the way for dwelling on the similarities and differences between these two types of users.

2. Trend spotters vs. Trend makers. Since no previous study has compared the characteristics of trend spotters and trend makers, we need to start with some initial hypotheses based on our intuition. So we initially consider that trend makers tend to upload items, while trend spotters tend to vote items. More specifically, we hypothesize that, compared to trend spotters, trend makers upload more content (H3.1), vote less (H3.2), upload less diverse content (H3.3), vote more diverse content (H3.4), and are more popular (H3.5). After running Kolmogorov-Smirnov tests (Table 2), we find that trend makers *upload* more frequently than trend spotters who, by contrast, *vote* more frequently. That confirms both H3.1 and H3.2. By then considering what users upload/vote, we find that trend makers "stay focused" (i.e., they upload and vote items in specific categories), while trend spotters vote items belonging to a variety of categories. So trend makers act in a way similar to the content contributors discussed in [20, 18] who tended to have special care in producing quality content. In a similar way, our trend spotters tend to upload items in the few categories they are more familiar with, while they vote on items of different categories, suggesting a wide spectrum of interests. Finally, trend makers tend to be more popular (are followed more) than trend spotters. To recap, trend spotters preferentially engage in voting and do so across a broad range of categories, trend makers engage uploading within a limited number of categories. Both of them are popular, but trend makers are followed more than trend spotters.

PREDICTING TREND MAKERS AND SPOTTERS

By considering four types of features, we have been able to find statistically significant similarities and differences among trend spotters, trend makers, and typical users. Now we study to which extent these features are potential predictors of whether users are trend spotters (makers), and do so in two steps:

1. We model trend spotter (maker) score as a linear combination of the features.
2. We predict trend spotter (maker) using a logistic regression and a machine learning model: Support Vector Machines (SVM).

Upon the set of 140 trend makers, 671 trend spotters and 1,705 typical users (identified in the previous section), we now run our predictions.

Regression Models

Before running the regression, we compute the (Pearson) correlation coefficients between each pair of predictors (Table 5). As one expects, we find that different types of activities are correlated (i.e., high positive correlation between the *number of followees*, *daily uploads*, *daily votes*, and content diversity). Attracting followers is correlated more with uploading content (i.e., positive correlation between the *number of followers* and *daily uploads*) rather than voting content (i.e., no significant high correlation between the *number of followers* and *daily votes*).

(a) Logistic Regression

Features	$I(Score > 0)$ Spotters	$I(Score > 0)$ Makers
Age	2e-04	0.001
Life Time	**0.006** *	**0.001** *
Daily Votes (Daily Uploads)	**0.007** *	**0.16** *
Vote Diversity (Upload Diversity)	**0.38** *	**0.14** *
Wandering	-6e-15	-7e-15
#Followers	2e-05	**0.009** *
Network Clustering	0.08	**0.28** *

(b) Linear Regression

Features	$\log(Score)$ Spotters	$\log(Score)$ Makers
Age	**0.36** *	0.01
Life Time	**0.19** *	0.0001
Daily Votes (Daily Uploads)	0.16	**-1.03** *
Vote Diversity (Upload Diversity)	**7.28** *	**-1.09** *
Wandering	-2.1e-13	-1.4e-15
#Followers	-0.06	**0.01** *
Network Clustering	2.75	**-0.64** *
R^2	0.15	0.65
Adjusted R^2	0.14	0.64

Table 3. Coefficients of the linear regression. A correlation coefficient within 2 standard errors is considered statistically significant. We highlight and mark them with *.

Next, we perform both logistic and linear regressions on input of the following predictors that tend not to be strongly correlated with each other: *age*, *life time*, *daily votes*, *daily uploads*, *votes diversity*, *upload diversity*, *wandering*, *number of followers* and *network clustering*.

Regressions. We model trend spotter (maker) score as a combination of the features in two steps, as it is commonly done [11]. In the first, we use a logistic regression to model whether a user has trend spotter (maker) score greater than zero or not:

$$Pr(score_u > 0) = logit^{-1}(\alpha + \sum_{i \in \mathcal{V}} \beta_i \mathcal{U}_{u,i}). \quad (8)$$

In the second step, we take only those users with trend spotter (maker) scores greater than zero, and predict their scores with a linear regression of the form:

$$log(score_u) = \alpha' + \sum_{i \in \mathcal{V}} \beta'_i \mathcal{U}_{u,i}, \quad (9)$$

In Equation 8 and 9 , $\mathcal{V}$ is a set of predictors, and $\mathcal{U}_{u,i}$ refers to user u's value of predictor i.

The results of the logistic regression (coefficients in Table 2(a)) suggest that trend spotters tend to be early-adopters who vote often and are interested in diverse items, and trend makers tend to be early adopters who upload often and also upload items from different categories, moreover, they tend to attract followers and have a dense connected network.

Considering then only the users who have trend spotter (maker) score greater than zero, we focus on the features that can potentially predict how successful a trend spotter (maker) is. The results of the linear regression (β coefficients in Table 2(b)) suggest that successful trend spotters are adult early-adopters who vote items from various categories. By contrast, successful trend makers are users of any age who upload items belonging to specific categories (they "stay focused") and tend to attract social followers from different communities.

The goodness of fit of a linear regression model is indicated by R^2. In our case, the adjusted R^2 is very similar to R^2, which is 0.15 for trend spotter score and 0.65 for trend maker. So one is able to explain 15% variability in trend spotter score and 65% in trend maker score. The difference in these two results might be explained by either: 1) the idea that trend spotters might well be "accidental influentials" [26] and, as such, trend spotters are harder to identify than trend makers; or 2) the fact that our predictors simply encapsulate complex phenomena and, as such, their explanatory power is limited. Next, we test whether trend makers and trend spotters can be predicted by a machine learning model that has shown good performance in similar learning settings – that is, by SVM.

Support Vector Machines (SVM)

We formulate the task of predicting trend spotters (makers) as a binary classification problem, where the response variable is whether a user's trend spotter (maker) score is greater than or equal to zero. To our sample of 671 trend spotters and 140 trend makers, we add an equal number of typical users (those 1,705 users have been identified in the previous section). By construction, the resulting sample is balanced (the response variable is split 50-50), and interpreting the results becomes now easy as the accuracy of a random prediction model would be 50%.

We split randomly each set of samples into two subsets, 80% of them are used for training and 20% for testing. We apply SVM on the input of the same seven features previously used in the regressions to predict trend spotter and trend maker scores. We compare the results with those obtained by the previous logistic regression model. We compare prediction performance by ROC (Receiver Operating Characteristic) curve (Figure 11), AUC (area under the ROC curve), and accuracy (Table 4).

SVM and logistic regression show comparable performance (for both, $AUC = 0.77$; accuracy is 71.52% for the regression, and 71.85% for SVM). SVM only slightly outperforms the logistic regression in identifying trend makers. This suggests that one is able to effectively identify trend spotters and trend makers even with a simple logistic regression. Also, SVM might not have shown considerable prediction gain simply because of our (limited) dataset's size.

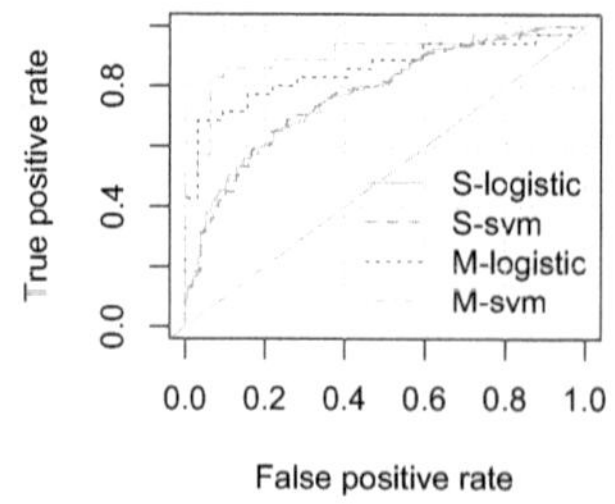

Figure 11. ROC curve of logistic regression and SVM model (S: trend spotters; M: trend makers).

	Spotters		Makers	
	AUC	Accuracy	AUC	Accuracy
Logistic	0.77	71.52%	0.85	82.09%
SVM	0.77	71.85%	0.90	88.06%

Table 4. AUC and best accuracy of each predictive model.

DISCUSSION

We have characterized trend spotters and trend makers based on four types of features (i.e., activity, content, network, and geographical features) and proposed a statistical model to accurately identify them. This work has both theoretical and practical implications.

Theoretical Implications

We show that trend spotters and trend makers are similar only to a certain extent. Compared to typical users, both of them: are more active in uploading/voting; attract more social connections; and upload/consume more diverse content. Yet, when they are compared not with typical users but with each other, differences emerge:

1. Trend spotters prefer voting more than uploading, and when they vote, they do so in very diverse categories. By contrast, trend makers act in a way similar to the content contributors in [18] who have special care in producing quality content and "stay focused" – they upload and vote items in very specific categories.
2. Successful trend spotters are early adopters who are attracted by diverse *items*, while successful trend makers attract diverse social *relations* (they tend to be followed by users from different social clusters).

These notable differences between trend spotters and trend makers would call for a rethink of current studies in opinion spreading.

In iCoolhunt, geographical features seem not to matter. That might suggest that, to be successful, trend spotters or trend makers do not necessarily need to move often or travel around. However, based on further analysis, we have learned that, while the application was originally designed to let users share items on the move, some users have started to assume unexpected behaviors – for example, some have started to post content (e.g., images from the Web) that was not explicitly related with the location from which it was uploaded. Given such behaviors, to make more grounded claims, a longitudinal analysis would be required.

	Age	Life Time	Daily Uploads	Daily Votes	Upload Diversity	Vote Diversity	Wandering	Follower Geo Span	#Followers	#Followees	
Life Time	0.21										
Daily Uploads	0.02	-0.12									
Daily Votes	0.05	-0.09	**0.47** *								
Upload Diversity	0.02	0.09	**0.40** *	0.08							
Vote Diversity	0.04	0.08	0.22	0.08	**0.42** *						
Wandering	0.004	0.13	0.16	0.11	0.06	0.05					
Follower Geo Span	0.05	0.12	0.16	0.10	0.12	0.11	0.23				
#Followers	0.03	0.23	**0.37** *	0.14	0.22	0.16	0.44	0.16			
#Followees	0.05	0.17	**0.52** *	**0.31** *	**0.29** *	0.22	**0.56** *	0.21	**0.64** *		
Network Clustering	0.03	0.13	0.22	0.04	0.24	0.23	-0.001	**0.27** *	0.08	0.22	
Spotter Score	0.07	0.18	0.03	0.01	0.05	0.10	0.04	0.07	0.13	0.11	0.15
Maker Score	0.07	0.10	0.06	0.01	0.07	0.06	0.02	0.12	0.12	0.09	0.10

Table 5. Pearson Correlation coefficients between each pair of predictors. Coefficients greater than ± 0.25 with statistical significant level < 0.05 are marked with a $*$.

Practical Implications

The ability of identifying trend spotters and trend makers has implications in designing recommender systems, marketing campaigns, new products, privacy tools, and user interfaces.

Recommender Systems. Every user has different interests and tastes and, as such, might well benefit from personalized suggestions of content. These suggestions are automatically produced by so-called "recommender systems". Typically, these systems produce recommendations people might like by *equally* weighting all user ratings. Given that trend spotters are effective social filters, one could imagine to weight their ratings more than those from typical users to construct a new recommender system.

New Products. Some web services (*e.g.*, 99designs[4]) provide a platform to crowd source design work, where clients submit their requests and designers try to fulfill them. Since trend spotters and trend makers are "fashion leaders", soliciting their early feedbacks might result into avoiding mistakes when designing new products. Often, at design stage, costs of correcting minor mistakes are negligible, while, at production stage, they become prohibitive.

User Interfaces. Trend spotters and trend makers do not connect to as many users as one would expect. That is likely because it is hard for iCoolhunt users to be aware of what others are up to. The user interface does not come with clear-cut "social features" that create a sense of connection and awareness among users as much as Facebook or Twitter sharing features do (as we have detailed in the Application section).

We are currently working on a recommender system that exploits the ability to distinguish between trend makers and trend spotters to suggest highly-dynamic content in a timely fashion.

[4]http://www.99designs.com

CONCLUSION

A community is an emergent system. It forms from the actions of its members who are reacting to each other's behavior. Here we have studied a specific community of individuals who are passionate about sharing pictures of items (mainly fashion and design items) using a mobile phone application. This community has a specific culture in which a set of habits, attitudes and beliefs guide how its members behave. In it, we have seen and quantified the importance of early adopters. In general, these individuals are those who initially set the unwritten rules that other community members learn (from observing those around them), internalize, and follow. In our case, early adopters tend to be successful trend spotters who like very diverse items. Trend makers, by contrast, tend to be highly organized individuals who focus on specific items. Understanding the characteristics of "the many" of regular individuals with specific interests (trend makers) connected to early adopters with very diverse interests (trend spotters) – turned out to be more important than trying to find the "special few". At least, it has been so for our social application, and for a variety of (more) complex networks [1, 13, 28].

ACKNOWLEDGEMENTS

The work was funded by the French National Research Agency (ANR) under the PROSE project (ANR-09-VERS-007), and by an industrial scholarship from PlayAdz [5].

REFERENCES

1. Aral, S. and Walker, D. Identifying Influential and Susceptible Members of Social Networks. *Science*, 337, 2012.

2. H. Becker, M. Naaman, and L. Gravano. Learning Similarity Metrics for Event Identification in Social Media. In *Proceedings of the* 3rd *International Conference on Web Search and Data Mining (WSDM)*, 2010.

[5]http://www.playadz.com

3. H. Becker, M. Naaman, and L. Gravano. Beyond Trending Topics: Real-world Event Identification on Twitter. In *Proceedings of the* 5th *International AAAI Conference on Weblogs and Social Media (ICWSM)*, 2011.

4. M. Cha, H. Haddadi, F. Benevenuto, and K. Gummadi. Measuring User Influence in Twitter: The Million Follower Fallacy. In *Proceedings of the* 4th *International AAAI Conference on Weblogs and Social Media (ICWSM)*, 2010.

5. Z. Cheng, J. Caverlee, and K. Lee. You are Where You Tweet: A Content-based Approach to Geo-locating Twitter Users. In *Proceedings of the* 19th *ACM International Conference on Information and Knowledge Management (CIKM)*, 2010.

6. Z. Cheng, J. Caverlee, K. Lee, and D. Sui. Exploring Millions of Footprints in Location Sharing Services. In *Proceedings of the* 5th *International AAAI Conference on Weblogs and Social Media (ICWSM)*, 2011.

7. R. Crane and D. Sornette. Robust Dynamic Classes Revealed by Measuring the Response Function of a Social System. In *Proceedings of the National Academy of Sciences of the United States of America (PNAS)*, volume 105, October 2008.

8. danah boyd. The Future of Privacy: How Privacy Norms Can Inform Regulation. Invited Talk at the 32nd International Conference of Data Protection and Privacy Commissioners, October 2010.

9. danah boyd. Designing for Social Norms (or How Not to Create Angry Mobs). http://www.zephoria.org/thoughts/archives/2011/08/05/design-social-norms.html, August 2011.

10. C. Droge, M. Stanko, and W. Pollitte. Lead Users and Early Adopters on the Web: The Role of New Technology Product Blogs. *Journal of Product Innovation Management*, 27(1), 2010.

11. A. Gelman and J. Hill. *Data Analysis Using Regression and Multilevel/Hierarchical Models*. Cambridge University Press, 2006.

12. M. Gladwell. *The Tipping Point: How Little Things Can Make a Big Difference*. Little, Brown and Company, 2000.

13. S. González-Bailón, J. Borge-Holthoefer, A. Rivero, and Y. Moreno. The Dynamics of Protest Recruitment through an Online Network. *Scientific reports*, 1, 2011.

14. A. Goyal, F. Bonchi, and L. V. Lakshmanan. Learning Influence Probabilities in Social Networks. In *Proceedings of the* 3rd *International Conference on Web Search and Data Mining (WSDM)*, 2010.

15. E. Katz and P. Lazarsfeld. Personal Influence: The Part Played by People in the Flow of Mass Communications. 1955.

16. D. Kempe, J. Kleinberg, and E. Tardos. Influential Nodes in a Diffusion Model for Social Networks. In *Automata, Languages and Programming*, volume 3580. Springer Berlin / Heidelberg, 2005.

17. H. Kwak, C. Lee, H. Park, and S. Moon. What is Twitter, a Social Network or a News Media? In *Proceedings of the* 19th *ACM Conference on World Wide Web (WWW)*, 2010.

18. M. Muller, N. S. Shami, D. R. Millen, and J. Feinberg. We are all Lurkers: Consuming Behaviors among Authors and Readers in an Enterprise File-Sharing Service. In *Proceedings of the* 16th *ACM International Conference on Supporting Group Work (GROUP)*, 2010.

19. M. Naaman, H. Becker, and L. Gravano. Hip and Trendy: Characterizing Emerging Trends on Twitter. *Journal of the American Society for Information Science and Technology*, 65, May 2011.

20. C. Neustaedter, A. Tang, and J. K. Tejinder. The Role of Community and Groupware in Geocache Creation and Maintenance. In *Proceedings of the* 28th *International Conference on Human Factors in Computing Systems (CHI)*, 2010.

21. J.-P. Onnela, S. Arbesman, M. C. González, A.-L. Barabási, and N. A. Christakis. Geographic Constraints on Social Network Groups. *PloS One*, 6, 2011.

22. M. Panik. *Advanced Statistics From an Elementary Point of View*. Academic Press, 2005.

23. D. Saez-Trumper, G. Comarela, V. Almeida, R. Baeza-Yates, and F. Benevenuto. Finding Trendsetters in Information Networks. In *Proceedings of the* 18th *ACM International Conference on Knowledge Discovery and Data Mining (KDD)*, 2012.

24. C. Steinfield, N. B. Ellison, and C. Lampe. Social Capital, Self-esteem, and Use of Online Social Network Sites: A Longitudinal Analysis. *Journal of Applied Developmental Psychology*, 29(6), 2008.

25. J. Tang, J. Sun, C. Wang, and Z. Yang. Social Influence Analysis in Large-scale Networks. In *Proceedings of the* 15th *International Conference on Knowledge Discovery and Data Mining (KDD)*, 2009.

26. D. Watts. Challenging the Influentials Hypothesis. *Measuring Word of Mouth*, 3, 2007.

27. D. Watts and S. Strogatz. Collective Dynamics of Small-world Networks. *Nature*, 393(6684), 1998.

28. D. J. Watts. *Everything Is Obvious: *Once You Know the Answer*. Crown Business, March 2011.

29. J. Weng, E.-P. Lim, J. Jiang, and Q. He. TwitterRank: Finding Topic-sensitive Influential Twitterers. In *Proceedings of the* 3rd *ACM International Conference on Web Search and Data Mining (WSDM)*, 2010.

30. L. Yu, S. Asur, and B. A. Huberman. What Trends in Chinese Social Media. *The* 5th *Workshop on Social Network Mining and Analysis (SNA-KDD)*, 2011.

I Need Someone to Help! A Taxonomy of Helper-Finding Activities in the Enterprise

Svetlana Yarosh
AT&T Research Labs
180 Park Ave,
Florham Park, NJ 07392, USA
lana@research.att.com

Tara Matthews, Michelle Zhou
IBM Research – Almaden
650 Harry Road,
San Jose, CA 95120, USA
{tlmatthe, mzhou}@us.ibm.com

Kate Ehrlich
IBM Research – Cambridge
One Rogers Street
Cambridge, MA 95120, USA
katee@us.ibm.com

ABSTRACT
Finding the right person to ask for help is a difficult task within a large enterprise. While there are a few studies detailing practices for finding an *expert* often in the context of an expertise locator system, there are fewer studies on workplace practices and challenges for finding a *person who can help*, especially independent of any particular technology. We conducted a two-part study of helper-finding activities with 36 enterprise workers, representing different job roles and levels of experience. First, we present a taxonomy of workplace helper-finding needs that involves *tasks*, *topics*, and *helper selection criteria*, developed by analyzing two weeks of participant diaries describing helper-finding problems. Second, we present the results of follow-up interviews with each participant, focusing on helper-finding challenges in the workplace. Finally, we present design implications for systems aimed at supporting helper-finding in the workplace.

Author Keywords
Social networking; expertise location; office; diary study.

ACM Classification Keywords
H.5.3. Information interfaces and presentation (e.g., HCI): Group and Organization Interfaces.

General Terms
Human Factors; Design; Measurement.

INTRODUCTION
Better person-to-person contact and communication help improve productivity of an organization [4,5,12,27]. While it may be feasible for employees in a small organization to easily find each other for help, this becomes more difficult in larger organizations [8]. Employees may have to rely increasingly on the help of well-connected individuals [19], weak ties [13], and strangers through online systems [6]. If we are to support enterprise employees in finding help from colleagues, we need to understand the nature of helper-finding in their jobs and the problems they typically face.

In this paper, we argue that prior literature on expertise location has focused on a narrower set of problems than exist in modern workplaces, and a new, broader definition of helper-finding is needed. Typically in the literature, an expert is defined narrowly as a person who has a measurable high level of domain knowledge and skills (e.g., see [1,9]). Based on empirical evidence, we define helper-finding to involve more factors about the person sought and the problem at hand. For example, a helper's accessibility may be more important than expertise if there will be a need to contact the person more than once. One's task—for example, an interest in collaborating—can affect the person sought—for example, someone who has the time and interest to collaborate for longer. A primary goal of this research is empirically determining the key factors involved in helper-finding in the workplace. As we articulate later in this paper, expert-finding is a subset of helper-finding, but it does not cover many of the relevant scenarios in which someone is looking for a person who may not be an expert.

While there are a few studies detailing practices for finding an *expert* [19] often in the context of an expertise locator system [9,16,25], there are fewer studies on workplace practices and challenges for finding a *person who can help*, especially independent of any particular technology. Current tools that are designed for expert-finding may not fulfill the requirements of helper-finding. Without an understanding of helper-finding needs and challenges, it is difficult to design and develop technologies that can directly address such needs. We thus conducted a study to explore the helper-finding needs within a large enterprise. Our study was driven by the following research questions:

1. What types of helper-finding situations do enterprise workers encounter (i.e., what workplace tasks and topics involve helper-finding)?
2. How do people find and select the right person to ask for help in the workplace?
3. What challenges do workers face when seeking the right colleague to ask for help?

To address these questions we conducted a two-part study with 36 employees of a large enterprise in diverse job roles. In the first part of the study, we asked the participants to keep daily diaries of their work-related helper-finding needs over the course of two weeks. In the second part of the study, we conducted 30-minute, semi-structured interviews with each participant to go over the diaries and ask about his or her helper-finding experiences.

The major contribution of this work is an empirically derived taxonomy of workplace helper-finding needs that involves *tasks*, *topics*, and *helper selection criteria*. We discuss how the combination of tasks, topics, and selection criteria is rarely considered together in tools, indicating that this conceptualization of helper-finding is novel and not obvious. Our study also shows that helper-finding tools were not effective for our participants. We discuss how helper-finding tools can be more effective if designed to consider tasks, topics, and selection criteria. A second contribution of this work is to identify a series of helper-finding challenges in an enterprise and suggest areas for possible design interventions. These contributions are of particular salience to those who design and evaluate technologies that support helper-finding in the workplace. We articulate specific directions for future design of helper-finding systems and provide a taxonomy of helper-finding query characteristics that can be used during a system evaluation to generate tasks that provide better coverage of typical queries.

We begin by presenting related work on how employees find help from others in the workplace. We then discuss our methods and give an overview of the diary and interview findings. Finally, we discuss our findings in the context of previous work and present implications for design.

RELATED WORK

First, we review the history of knowledge management systems in the organization, highlighting the shift in focus from finding an answer to a question, to finding an expert who can answer a question, to finding an appropriate person (not necessarily an expert) who is willing to help. Second, we discuss how our work relates to previous CSCW literature, highlighting how it contributes to our understanding of help-finding in the workplace.

From Knowledge Management to Expert-Finding

One approach to getting answers comes from research on knowledge management, which emphasizes the importance of people over stored repositories as sources of information [7]. The literature on knowledge management has identified successful knowledge transfer as a competitive advantage for an organization (e.g. [5,27]). However, knowledge transfer presents challenges due to the tacit and ambiguous nature of knowledge. For example, Allen [4] conducted a long-term ethnographic study examining the role of knowledge transfer in an engineering firm, finding distinct benefits to increased communication between project teams and disparate parts of the organization, but also showing that not all groups achieved this level of communication.

Research on CSCW and MIS have created a number of systems to help address the knowledge management needs of organizations. Early work focused on ways of organizing information in the workplace to make it easier for people to find what they need [3]. However, this approach soon garnered criticism due to the frequently static nature of such knowledge bases. The recognition that knowledge in an organization frequently resides with individuals [7, 15] led to a shift towards *expertise sharing systems* [1]. Some of these systems allowed users to post a question to a knowledge community where they would get a short answer [2]. Unfortunately, these systems have not been widely adopted in the workplace, largely due to organizational, cultural, and work barriers [18]. Instead, recent studies are pointing to new technologies for knowledge sharing such as forums [6], instant messaging [26], Q&A sites [17], and internal social networking sites [24]. Though these systems help users find quick answers, finding a person to help with something other than an isolated query remains an open problem. Today, employees find helpers in largely the same way they did in McDonald and Ackerman's 1996 ethnographic study, which showed that the primary strategy was to go through well-connected colleagues who they called *expertise concierges* [19].

In response to the early systems which allowed experts to self-identify (or "pull" questions to answer), Reichling and Veith [20] proposed that systems enable help-seekers "push" their questions to qualified experts. The emphasis on "pushing" questions is also followed in research on expertise location or recommender systems that provides a list of matched experts to a given inquiry. The information used to generate the list varies by system, including text analysis of documents and email [22], social connections [9], and analysis of a code base [26]. In all of these cases, the user relies on the system to recommend a list of experts, so that s/he can select one or more to contact. A major goal of these systems is to help the information seeker establish the *credibility and authority* of the suggested experts [1,9]. However, as we argue in the next section, this focus on expertise does not capture the variety of contexts that lead employees to search for a person who can help them.

From Expert-Finding to Helper-Finding

Prior research on expertise location in the enterprise has demonstrated that finding help, which involves several factors, is more nuanced than simply finding expertise. For example, the relationship (or lack of relationship) to a potential expert [21] and the strength of the relationship [13,17,22] influences the types of queries the expert receive. Seekers also consider many contextual factors, such as location and accessibility [29]. However, prior studies have not systematically explore the various factors involved in help-finding.

A focus on expertise also marginalizes certain help-finding needs such as the valuable work of administrative assistants, who rarely refer to their work as finding an expert [11]. Also, empirical work has shown that actionable knowledge (knowledge that can progress a current project) focuses not only on receiving a specific answer, but also on grooming strong-tie trusting relationships with information providers and on the co-construction of knowledge [7].

Cross and Sproull [7] found that these collaborations that can occur both inside and outside of an organizational unit and rarely included organizationally designated "experts."

To summarize, the terms "expertise location" and "expert finding" are too narrow to explain how workers actually look for help: primary factors other than expertise are considered, workers frequently do not describe what they do as finding an expert, and the person most helpful in constructing actionable knowledge is frequently not somebody identified by the organization as an authority or expert. Rather than broadening the definition of expert-finding—which could lead to confusion as to which definition is being used—we propose that expert-finding is just one type of a larger class of helper-finding problems. In this work, we investigate the diverse helper-finding problems faced by workers in one organization and discuss which are not well-supported by existing systems. Through this process, we hope to influence the design and evaluation of new helper-finding systems that more accurately reflect the variety of helper-finding tasks that occur in the workplace.

Tool-Centric Taxonomies Related to Helper-Finding

In our work, we develop a taxonomy of helper-finding scenarios. A number of studies have examined queries entered by employees into a particular organizational tool, such an expertise recommender system [10], a social Q&A tool [27], or a microblogging system [25]. These papers have resulted in tool-centric taxonomies of questions. Our study, on the other hand, takes a tool-agnostic approach in examining helper-finding needs. For example, Ehrlich and Shami [10] examined queries workers entered into an expertise recommender system and found four main types: ones seeking (1) a quick answer, (2) a longer discussion with an expert, (3) a general awareness of a topic, and (4) an appropriate person with whom to share some useful bit of information. Thom-Santelli et al. [25] examined questions posted through the status message on an internal company social networking site to identify seven types and nine topics of questions posed. However, requests entered through specific tools bias the requests to those the system can support. In contrast, our work focuses on investigating workplace helper-finding independent of any particular tool, thus exploring a fuller range of scenarios. Our goal is to provide a general taxonomy that captures helper-finding needs independent of tool use to identify issues that current systems may have failed to address. Unlike work which focuses on a broad organizational perspectives of why knowledge management systems succeed or fail (e.g., [18]), we focus on articulating the specific helper-finding tasks that may currently be left out of supporting software and provide specific suggestions for how these gaps may be addressed through design.

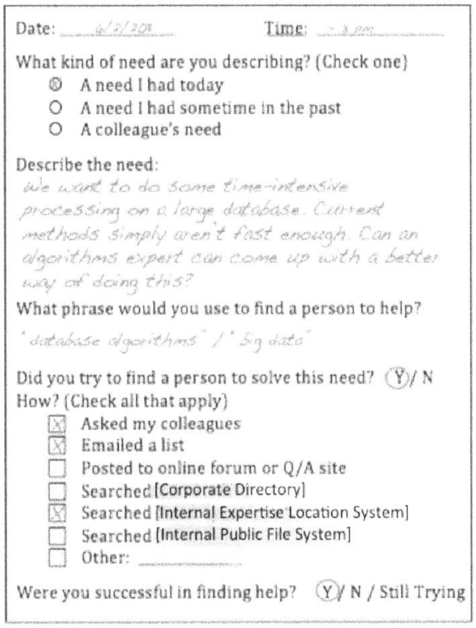
Date: 6/2/2011 Time: ~3 pm

What kind of need are you describing? (Check one)

- (●) A need I had today
- ○ A need I had sometime in the past
- ○ A colleague's need

Describe the need:

We want to do some time-intensive processing on a large database. Current methods simply aren't fast enough. Can an algorithms expert can come up with a better way of doing this?

What phrase would you use to find a person to help?

"database algorithms" / "big data"

Did you try to find a person to solve this need? (Y) / N

How? (Check all that apply)

- [X] Asked my colleagues
- [X] Emailed a list
- [ ] Posted to online forum or Q/A site
- [ ] Searched [Corporate Directory]
- [X] Searched [Internal Expertise Location System]
- [ ] Searched [Internal Public File System]
- [ ] Other: ______

Were you successful in finding help? (Y) / N / Still Trying

Figure 1. A sample paper diary as presented to participants.

METHOD

Our goal was to learn why and how participants sought colleagues for help in their jobs, and what challenges they faced. Here we describe our 36 participants, diary study method, and follow-up interviews.

Participants

Our study included 36 participants, all employees of a large, international company. Their professions included a variety of roles within the organization: research scientist (10 participants), manager (8), business/executive (5), engineer (3), administrative assistant (3), communications (2), HR (2), administrative staff (2), sales (1), and user experience (1). The "research scientist" job role included participants from multiple domains: Physics (2), Chemistry (1), Health Science (1), Computer Science (3), and HCI (3). We recruited for a wide variety of time working at the company, from 1 month to 30 years (M=11.8 years, SD=10.6 years). Since this was an exploratory study, our goal was to represent various levels of experience within the company and as many job roles as possible. Thus, we selectively recruited people whom we knew in each role and asked them to point us to others in that job role. To recruit participants who we may not have otherwise reached through our personal contacts, we also set up an information table outside the cafeteria. Overall, 26 were recruited through personal contacts (i.e., snowball sampling) and 10 at the information table.

Our participant population represents one potential limitation of this study. Since all participants were from the same company, our results may be skewed by the unique properties of that organization, including the nature of its business and organizational culture. However, the diverse nature of our participants' job roles may have helped to mitigate this limitation. We discuss the implications of our sample in the last sections of the paper.

Helper-Finding Systems at the Study Organization

Within the study organization, a number of helper-finding systems exist. The company has a corporate directory that includes basic information about employees: their name, job title, organization, reporting structure, location, and contact information. This directory serves as the basis for four separate helper-finding systems. To use all of these systems, employees could enter keywords and receive a list of people who match the keywords. (1) *Faces* is a research prototype that quickly searches the basic directory information. (2) *Profiles*[1] is a commercial corporate directory product enhanced with social features like tagging, friending, and microblogging. In addition to directory information, *Profiles* searches considered tags to return one or more names that match a query. (3) *SmallBlue Find* [16] is a state-of-the-art expertise recommender system and research prototype. In addition to directory information, SmallBlue Find searches consider public information within the company's intranet, such as forum posts, publicly shared presentations, and user-defined profiles, as well as personal communications, including emails and chats. (4) *Expertise Locator* is an internal system in which experts could opt to register by entering information about their expertise, which is considered in searches. The company also has multiple Q&A forums, where employees could ask a question and anyone in the company could post an answer asynchronously. These tools represent a range of the types of helper-finding systems discussed in the literature [6,9,16,24].

Procedure and Analysis

Our study started with a 10-minute introductory session, during which we explained the diary study (in-person for 33 participants, by phone for 3). We instructed participants to record at least one "helper-finding" need in a diary every day for two weeks (10 consecutive work days). Participants were given a paper (see Figure 1) and an online version of the diary that they could use to enter information. We also sent the participants daily email reminders with a link to the online version of diary. We instructed participants to record real helper-finding needs that they were experiencing. However, if no such need came up on a specific day, s/he could write about a need experienced in the past or that a colleague was currently facing similar to a need the participant might face (i.e., a common need of others in the same job role). We also asked what methods and tools participant used to find help and how effective these were.

After collecting the diaries (248 total), we analyzed them to identify the types and key properties of helper-finding needs in the workplace. We began with an open-coding pass through the diaries. New codes were added whenever we encountered an entry that did not fit into any previous codes. We then categorized our codes, discovering in this process that the codes described three separate attributes of helper-finding needs: the *task* the participant was trying to accomplish, the *topic* of the inquiry, and the *helper selection criteria* applied to the inquiry. After categorizing, we combined similar codes and developed concrete definitions for them, resulting in 18 codes across the three attributes.

Using these 18 codes, two investigators independently coded a portion of the participant diaries for task, topic, and helper selection criteria. For example, the diary entry "Talk to lawyer about copyright issues," involved the task "talk to," which was coded *gather information*; the topic "copyright issues," which was coded *domain knowledge*; and the selection criteria "lawyer," which was coded *role*. In some cases, one of the three attributes was implied in the participant's entry, but not explicitly stated. For example, in the diary entry "Looking for a couple of charts on key [location] projects for a high level overview by an [company name] exec," the selection criteria *location* is explicit, but *group* is implied, since only project group members would likely have the desired charts. Coders applied implied codes where it was reasonable to do so. The Cohen's Kappa of the inter-rater reliability was 0.848 (for 72 codes assigned to 23 diaries), which is classified as substantial agreement ($p < 0.001$). Once this agreement and process for coding was established, the lead author coded the other 225 diaries. If a particular helper-finding need in a diary could not be coded, it was marked for later discussion with the participant so that together we assigned appropriate codes to that entry.

After analyzing the diaries, we contacted each participant again for a 30-minute interview about his or her diaries and general helper-finding experiences. We conduced 34 interviews at the participant's office and 2 by phone. Each participant was presented with our coding of the diaries they had submitted and asked to correct any mistakes we might have made during the coding process. We also asked them the following questions: (1) Whether any of the tasks, topics or selection criteria were missing from their diaries or our list. (2) Whether the two-week time period of the diary study involved anything atypical of their job. (3) What methods they used to find help. (4) What kinds of information would be useful to have in order to decide whom to contact. (5) Whether any progress had been made so far on items marked as "still working on it" in the diaries.

All interviews were transcribed by the lead author and coded using a method recommended by Seidman [22]. The emerging themes from this analysis are presented in the results section. Additionally, each interview was coded for the tasks, topics, and helper selection criteria the participant reported experiencing in their job in the past (even if the particular task, topic, or criterion did not show up in the two-week diaries).

---

1 http://www.01.ibm.com/software/lotus/products/connections/profiles.html

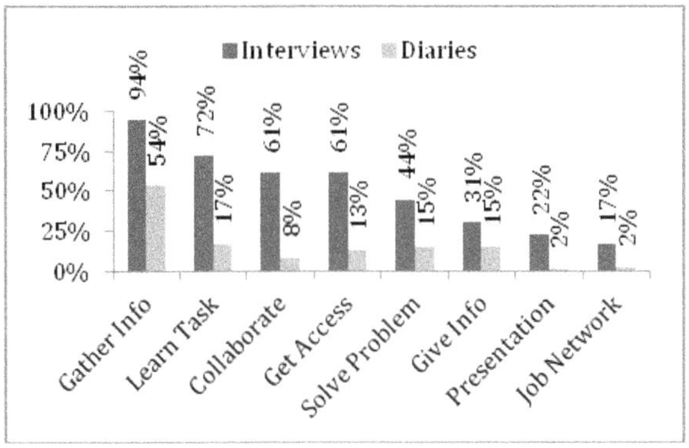

Figure 2. Helper-finding *tasks* according to the percent of participants who reported them in interviews and diaries.

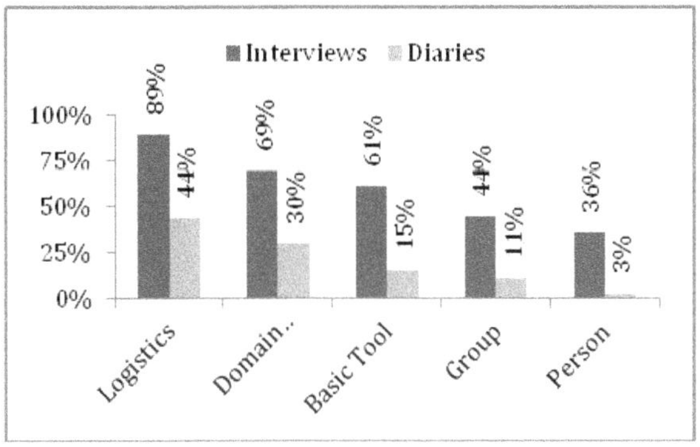

Figure 3. Helper-finding *topics* according to the percent of participants who reported them in interviews and diaries.

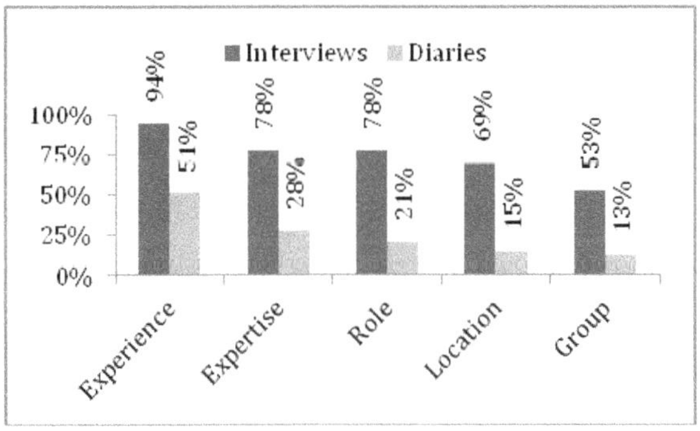

Figure 4. *Helper selection criteria* according to the percent of participants who reported them in the interviews and diaries.

FINDINGS

In this section, we present the descriptive statistics of the diary submissions, a three-dimensional taxonomy that characterizes helper-finding needs in the workplace, and five major themes emerging from the interview analysis.

Diary Statistics

Each helper-finding need entered is considered an entry in the diary. We collected 248 entries, with each participant submitting between 1 and 15 entries during the 10 workdays of the diary study (average of 6.89 diaries per participant). Of these entries, 163 (66%) described the participants' current needs, 60 (24%) described a past need, and 25 (10%) described a colleague's need typical of a need in the participant's job role. In 204 (82%) of entries, participants reported actually trying to find a person who could help answer the specific question.

Of these 204 entries, the methods used were as follows:

- Asked a colleague: 156 diaries (76%)
- Searched the company directory: 41 diaries (20%)
- Posted to email distribution list: 8 diaries (4%)
- Posted to forum or Q&A site: 5 diaries (2%)
- Searched an internal tool: <1% diary entries

Most often participants turned to their colleagues for help. We note the strikingly low use of technology, beyond the corporate directory, for helper-finding. We were intrigued to learn what, if any, properties of helper-finding tasks may have demotivated people from using tools.

At the time the diaries were submitted, just over half (150, 60.5%) of the needs were resolved, a third (83, 33.5%) were in progress, and a small minority of entries (15, 6%) were stuck. By the interviews (up to 2 weeks after finishing the diary study), participants reported that most (210, 85%) of the reported helper-finding needs had been resolved. However, this suggests that a relatively large portion of helper-finding needs in a large enterprise may remain unresolved for a fairly long period. We were interested to learn what challenges may have led to these unresolved needs.

Taxonomy of Helper-Finding Needs

From the diary analysis, we developed a taxonomy that characterizes helper-finding needs in this particular organization along three dimensions. All examples provided below are from the collected diaries.

The first dimension, *tasks*, concerns the main reason *why* a participant is seeking help. There are 8 task elements:

- *Collaborate* – find a person with whom to collaborate, work together, or form a general alliance (e.g., work on a grant proposal with a social analytics expert).
- *Learn a Task* – find a person who can teach you how to do a specific task (e.g., filing a patent at this company).
- *Presentation* – find a person to share his or her knowledge in a meeting or presentation (e.g., inviting a sustainability expert to speak at a seminar).
- *Job Network* – find a person who can help advance the seeker's career (e.g., finding a mentor at this location).
- *Solve a Problem* – find a person who can help solve a specific problem (e.g., debugging a piece of code).
- *Gather Information* – find a person who can share information on a certain subject (e.g., finding out about the components of a specific epidemiology model).
- *Get Access to a Resource* – find a person who can grant access to a specific physical or digital resource (e.g., getting a high resolution image of a project logo).

Task	Helper Criterion	Topic	#
Gather info about	-	logistics issue	65
-	Experience w/	logistics issue	64
Gather info from	X w/ experience	-	57
-	Expertise in	domain know.	48
Gather info about	-	domain know.	46
Gather info from	X w/ expertise	-	35
Gather info from	X in role	-	32
Learn task from	X w/ experience	-	30
-	Role	logistics issue	30
-	Location	logistics issue	27
-	Experience w/	basic tool	26
-	Experience w/	domain know.	26
Solve problem with	X w/ experience	-	25
Access resource for	-	logistics issue	23
Gather info about	-	group	21

Table 1. Fifteen most common pairings of tasks, topics, and helper selection criteria and the number of diaries with each pairing.

- *Give Information* – find a person who may be interested in hearing about a specific topic (e.g., tell a project manager about relevant new work in the space).

Figure 2 shows the frequencies of each task as reported in interviews and as observed in the diaries. Note that the percentage of participants reporting each particular task is larger for interviews than diaries. In interviews we asked about whether a particular helper-finding was an important part of the participant's help-finding needs (e.g., "How important is finding help in getting access to resources in you work?"), however the diaries only reflect the tasks that occurred during the two-week diary study. Thus, the interview findings are a better representation of the number of participants who experienced a particular task in their job, while the diary study is a better representation of the relative frequency of each task type.

The second dimension of the taxonomy, *topics*, concerns the subject or topic of a helper-finding need. There are 5 topic elements:

- *Logistics* – coordination or process-oriented tasks (e.g., applying for direct deposit).
- *Basic Tool* – a basic work tool or piece of basic equipment (e.g., setting up company email).
- *Group* – a specific group, project, department, or organization (e.g., learning about a company division).
- *Domain Knowledge* – specific domain knowledge of a scientific field, specialized technology, or method (e.g., learning about Dengue Fever transmission factors).
- *People Sense-Making* – learning more about a specific person (e.g., learning about the new division director).

Figure 3 shows the frequencies of each topic as reported in interviews and observed in the diaries.

The third dimension of the taxonomy, *helper selection criteria*, concerns the requirements that target helper must meet in order to be a relevant contact. There are 5 elements of this part of the taxonomy:

- *Location* – the person must be at a specific location (e.g., works in my building).
- *Expertise* – the person must possess certain knowledge on a specific topic (e.g., Dengue Fever transmission).
- *Experience* – the person has had some specific experience in the past (e.g., organized a certain conference).
- *Role* – the person is in a specific role within a group (e.g., is a Chief Architect).
- *Group* – the person is in a specific group, project, department, or organization (e.g., in research).

Figure 4 shows the frequencies of each helper selection criterion as reported in interviews and observed in diaries.

In addition, we identified and examined the most common pairings of the three dimensions. These represent perhaps the most typical helper-finding scenarios in a workplace, for which improved helper-finding technologies may provide the best value (Table 1).

We emphasize the importance of the taxonomy independent of the expression of or frequencies with which particular tasks, topics, and selection criteria occurred in our study. Tasks, topics and selection criteria should generally characterize helper-finding problems even if their expression might vary by audience or context. The value of this taxonomy is that it characterizes three key considerations for helper-finding tool designers. Our study found that helper-finding tools were not highly used and we argue that a major reason is their lack of consideration for a breadth of tasks, topics, and selection criteria. This point is elaborated in the next section presenting interview results.

Emergent Themes from Interviews

Five major themes pertaining to helper-finding in the enterprise emerged from the interview analysis: Aspects of our taxonomy of helper-finding problems were not well supported by existing tools, particularly (1) tasks requiring longer interactions, (2) certain helper-finding topics, (3) almost all helper selection criteria. (4) Our participants expressed a desire to specify selection criteria based on a similar person. (5) In general, helper-finding was difficult and tools rarely helped.

Helper-finding Tasks Often Require Longer Interactions

The opportunity for longer conversations, where the seeker could adequately explain the context of his or her needs, and that could potentially lead to future collaborations was an important aspect of helper-finding in the workplace. Participants preferred to go to their networks to find helpers for longer interactions, since existing tools were not seen as a good place to turn for longer-term needs. It is not clear that this perception was deserved, as some expertise recommenders, like SmallBlue Find, considered both social and expertise cues when recommending experts [21]. However, most expertise recommenders provided search results filled with strangers and Q&A systems focused on providing quick answers.

All of the three most frequently discussed tasks in our taxonomy—*gather information, learn a task,* and *collaborate*—can be time-intensive. At least five participants explicitly expressed in the interview that their main helper-finding goals could not be addressed with a quick exchange or answered with a single reply. For example, *gathering information* was not always a simple task involving a quick exchange. Oftentimes a longer conversation to adequately explain the context was necessary for the expert to be able to provide the answer:

> *In order to get a short answer, you need to have a long conversation. [Mechanical Engineer]*

When *gathering information,* participants wanted to take the time to build a personal connection, especially if the person had knowledge of relevance to one's work:

> *I'm not looking for an answer like '15' or an answer like 'check this website,' I want to be able to talk to the person if there is something that they're doing that parallels what we're doing so that we can leverage each other to be successful. So if you say 'gather information', well, certainly that's a part of it, but that may lead to a collaboration over long term... [Business Development Specialist]*

Some Helper-Finding Topics Are Not Well-Supported

This next interview theme illustrates the importance of explicitly considering different *topics* in helper-finding tool design. Most expertise recommenders typically focus on finding helpers with certain *domain knowledge*, but we found that other topics, in particular *logistics* for the population studied (expressed by 89% of participants in interviews), were challenging. In the company studied, *logistics* needs were largely about internal company processes, like how to submit an expense reimbursement form or enter into a contract with a client. Seven participants expressed frustration with a lack of helper-finding support for logistics.

> *Even though I've been here a long time, one of the things that happens is that everything changes constantly, so even if I knew how it worked the last time, it might not apply this time ... it's like rummaging around. That's the word I would use. It's not very technical, but it gives the feeling. [Manager]*

As shown in McDonald and Ackerman's study of expertise location in a workplace [18], our participants frequently turned to well-connected others to solve logistical problems. However, since these logistical problems are often not part of the go-to person's job description, it led to frustration on his or her part. One participant who became a go-to helper for logistical tasks, said:

> *They get frustrated using the system to look for that person, so the tendency is for them to come to me and as much as I would like to help them, I just don't have time to do all those tasks on a daily basis. [HR Professional]*

A focus on domain knowledge in helper-finding tools may have contributed to this lack of support for other helper-finding topics, most notably *logistics* for our participants.

Helper Selection Criteria Are Not Well Supported

Our taxonomy highlights how helper-finding requires selecting the right helper based on certain criteria. Our interviews revealed that existing tools had trouble conveying information about all criteria except *location*—this included *experience, role, group,* and *expertise*—a theme explicitly discussed by fourteen participants. Helper-finding tools have focused a great deal of effort on conveying *expertise*, and our interview results indicate that this is at the expense of other important selection criteria.

Regarding *experience*, what a helper *can do* is a composite of their rich work and educational history, which systems typically did not capture.

> *Well, I can probably think of a whole lot of things that I've worked on before that I'd know something about, but it would take a long time to make a list and it probably wouldn't be very complete because there would be something I didn't think about that maybe I did or something that seemed so obvious that I wouldn't list it... [Software Engineer]*

Regarding *role*, what a helper *actually does* cannot be easily summed up by a job title or group affiliation.

> *Sometimes, I know he's an expert in data mining or something, or sometimes I even know he's working for a project, let's say I know you're working for a project in [a particular] group, but I want to know the role. There are lots of different roles in one project. [Research Scientist – CS]*

Regarding *group*, it was difficult or impossible to determine with which groups a helper is affiliated, since existing tools did not do a good job representing all group affiliations. People noted that the main difficulty was that the corporate directory (upon which the company's helper-finding systems were based) represented an incomplete view of the organizational structure of the company. Like many other large companies, the company studied is a matrixed organization. This means that each helper will have one affiliation with a department, but may also have multiple affiliations with projects and initiatives that cut across departments. While departmental reporting structures are formally represented in the corporate directory, project/initiative structures were more mercurial and not represented in the directory or the company's helper-finding systems:

> *...For technical problems you may have to solve it with a couple of people and they may all be from different groups with different people managers, but for the problem there might be a different project manager. And that project manager in [the company directory] shows up to be far away from all the other people he's working with even though they're really working tightly together. [Technical Sales Specialist]*

Thus, people spent a great deal of effort attempting to glean *group* information:

I'm starting somewhere and then going up the management chain or down or over to see where are they ... Seeing where people fit in ... You know there's two or three people you're working with, what is their relationship to each other organizationally? [Manager]

Even *expertise*, for which tools have focused their support of helper selection, was not expressed in enough detail for seekers to determine what a helper *actually knows*.

I wanted to know someone that was working on social software for example in computer science, it doesn't necessarily say it by people's names in [the company directory] that they're working on social software or that someone is working on the centennial events at [our location]. Unless you know or unless you ask around, you really couldn't find this information on [company directory]. [Communications Specials]

Fundamentally, the problems described above are about the tools lacking the right information about key helper selection criteria from our taxonomy. A major contributor to this problem was that many of the helper-finding tools deployed within this company relied heavily on self-reported descriptions of one's expertise and did not even encourage a description of experience, role, and group. This is not an uncommon characteristic of helper-finding tools. In fact, participants commented that many people did not complete or update their self-reported information:

I actually feel more reliable if I know somebody and I ask the person than if I use these tools, because quite often these tools are not updated... [Manager]

Self-reported expertise were also problematic because some people distrusted them:

The people, who are good at things, don't bother putting them into the tool because everyone knows they're good at them. So what you get are people who are not good at them, but would like to be good at them. So, that makes those tools a great way to find someone who will spend a lot of time not answering your question. [Research Scientist – HCI]

In summary, participants found it difficult to assess key helper selection criteria from existing tools and self-reported expertise information compounded the problem since it was often inadequate or viewed as untrustworthy.

Specifying Selection Criteria Based on a Similar Person

A common need (discussed by eight participants) was to identify a helper based on a known person, with just one of the select criteria changed: *I want to find someone just like X, but with a different role, group, domain of expertise, etc.* This interview theme does not add dimensions to our taxonomy, but rather provides a useful way to leverage it, by pointing to people's desire to specify selection criteria based on a similar person. Some examples given by participants are as follows:

- A helper in the same *role*, different *location*:

  This is about finding the intern coordinator at [another location]. The [name removed] counterpart. [Communications Specialist]

- A helper in the same *role*, different *group*:

  I have a compensation person in [group name X] but I have all of these other areas, like [group name Y]. Who's my compensation person for [group name Y]? How do I find that? [HR Professional]

- A new helper in the same *role* (since job changes were common in a large company):

  If you start needing to find out 'Who has this job this time?' For example, we have people in Research who are taking the lead on various joint programs in terms of taking project proposals and working with groups, 'Who is the person this time?' [Manager]

This commonly expressed need of finding a helper similar along certain selection criteria is not supported by the company's existing helper-finding tools.

Helper-Finding is Difficult and Tools Rarely Help

In our diary study, we found that people most often turned to their colleagues and very rarely turned to technology for helper-finding, a seemingly dramatic failure for the helper-finding systems deployed within the company. The interviews have helped explain why people did not use tools for helper-finding: they did not do a good job of supporting the tasks, topics, and selection criteria that characterize workers' helper-finding needs. In general, the various issues outlined in the sub-sections above resulted in these tools often not providing good results:

I don't think these tools are perfect. At least, the answers I get are not perfect most of the time. So, it takes very long to solve very basic problems. [Technical Sales Specialist]

Right now, my searches for this are not very effective ... probably it's a 20% hit rate. [Business Development Specialist]

Even if participants did use a tool to get a pointer to a list of possible experts, a great deal of time was then spent learning more about each expert on the list to understand if they are indeed an appropriate person to approach:

I'm probably spending 5% of my [total time at work] trying to figure out who is the best person to go to. [Project Executive]

Facing these difficulties in using the tools, most of our participants turned to their social networks to solve helper-finding problems. However, participants told us (and the 15% of diary study needs that were still unresolved by the end of our study indicated) that colleagues did not necessarily return quicker or more accurate answers. One problem was that colleagues did not always know the right helper, requiring a few "hops" to find someone who could help. Another problem was that asking others took considerable time, since a requester would need to wait for a response via email or to try and find someone in person.

But, I found that I had to wait a couple of days to get the answer because I was using my friends or people who I know. [HR Professional]

Many times it just takes too long to get answers or you don't get answers and it just gets lost. [Technical Sales Specialist]

In short, our results within one company show that helper-finding was a common, challenging workplace need that was not well-supported by existing technology. Our results argue that a lack of consideration for tasks, topics, and selection criteria contributes to the problem.

DISCUSSION

Our study indicated that workers rarely turned to technology for helper-finding—a seemingly dramatic failure for the company's helper-finding systems, which represented a broad set of tools ranging from basic corporate directory search to state-of-the art, socially enhanced expertise recommenders. What demotivated people from using these tools? How can the tools be improved?

Taxonomy Support in Existing Helper-Finding Tools

Looking at the breadth of tasks, topics, and selection criteria needed by our participants, it is clear that existing tools are not designed to handle all of them. Examining different types of helper-finding tools, we can see their current strengths and what aspects of the taxonomy are neglected.

Expertise location systems—like Faces, Profiles, SmallBlue Find [16], and Expertise Locator, which were deployed within this company, and other research systems [2,21,25]—have narrowed their attention to tasks that revolve around expertise like *solving a problem* or *gathering information*, topics requiring *domain knowledge*, and have provided mainly limited selection information about *expertise*. Thus, they exclude explicit support for many of the other tasks, topics, and selection criteria workers experience. Knowledge community systems like forums and Q&A sites tend to encourage quick, one-off questions, since answerers must opt-in—lengthy, vague requests for information or discussion may not get a response. Also, forums tend to be focused on topics, but a seeker's topic needs may fall outside those supported by existing forums. Finally, social networking sites help seekers connect with others they know. These sites support the possibility of satisfying longer-term helper-finding tasks by building relationships and affording back-and-forth conversation [24]. However, they limit seekers to the topics and selection criteria found among the people they know, one of the major reason for creating expertise location system in the first place [1,7].

Overall, by making explicit the need to consider a range of tasks, topics, and selection criteria, our taxonomy and interview results highlight shortcomings in existing tools and helps designers determine ways to improve tools—or create new classes of tools—to fit a broader set of workers' needs. It also provides a framework for studying helper-finding needs in other organizational contexts. In the following subsections, we highlight and discuss key opportunities for future research on helper-finding systems.

Consider Helper Selection Criteria: Experience, Group Affiliation, and "Someone like X"

Our study revealed that existing systems did not make it easy to assess *helper selection criteria*, even though this assessment is an important step in the helper-finding process (and hence, also an important part in our taxonomy). Only very recently has helper selection garnered much attention from the research community, but one study has shown that making selection criteria visible in search results can significantly improve users' ability to select an appropriate expert [28]. The present study identifies the key classes of selection criteria to consider in future systems.

In particular, our results highlight the importance of *experience* as the most common selection criteria among our participants. *Experience* describes *what a helper has done*, and can be unrelated to their job role, self-described domain knowledge, publications or other information typically included in helper-finding systems. The focus in the previous research literature has been on *expertise* (e.g., [10,12,20]). But, our results encourage a new perspective on helper-finding in the workplace that looks beyond *expertise* and encourages researchers to find new ways to detect and present helper's *experience*.

Participants also discussed the challenges of assessing *group* affiliation during helper selection. Within a matrixed organization, it is difficult to understand a potential helper's collection of projects, relationships, and commitments. Previous systems have taken the approach of automatically inferring social connection from shared authorship of public documents [9] or of collecting social connections through a crowdsourced quiz game [14]. However, while these approaches help to generate an up-to-date social network for each individual in the company, they do little to specify how the people within that network are related or whether subsets of this network are associated with specific projects or initiatives—i.e., their various *group* affiliations. Gathering and presenting information helpful to assessing a potential helper's various *group* affiliations is an important opportunity for future social analytics research.

We have shown that helper selection criteria were hard to assess. Our interviews offered a practical insight that could help: participants commonly thought about helper selection criteria in terms of similarities and difference with another person. Systems that enabled users to "find someone like X" but with one of the selection criteria changed, would meet a major need and possibly ease the difficulties participants encountered in assessing selection criteria. Prior work has begun addressing the technical problem of finding similar experts [23]. Our work provides empirical evidence that further pursuit of this idea in the broader context of helper-finding is important.

Better Support for "Logistics" Helper-Finding Topics

Among all the topics in our taxonomy, *logistics* was the most common (experienced by 89% of the participants) and mostly ignored in helper-finding systems. While the studied company has a large collection of intranet pages aimed at logistics questions, these were often not adequate to address the needs of the participants in our study. Terveen and McDonald [23] describe two types of social matching systems that may be effective in resolving this problem: *Im-*

plicit social matching involves explicitly listing people who can help in knowledge management systems (such as the intranet pages with logistics information). *Opportunistic social matching* involves connecting the user with a potential helper based on a need inferred from their system activity. One of our participants described logistical needs as requiring a certain degree of "rummaging around." If this sort of activity could be detected, a system might be able to suggest a connection to an appropriate logistics expert. The advantage of both of these systems is that they would allow helpers to identify issues that are part of their job responsibilities. This would help avoid the "overworked expertise concierge" being approached with problems outside of the scope of his or her job responsibilities.

Support for Tasks Involving Longer Interactions

As our results show, the three most frequently discussed tasks in our taxonomy—*gather information, learn a task, and collaborate*—can be time-intensive. Participants described the importance of longer conversations and future collaborations in their helper-finding tasks. These results reinforce the importance of social recommender systems and systems that encourage interaction outside of the specific context of a single request. Many recent innovative systems for help-seeking in the workplace focus on automatically matching the seeker and the helper (e.g., IM-an-Expert [26]) or on allowing the expert to self-select (e.g., Stack Overflow [18]). These systems are effective at answering quick or specific questions, but often do not provide an opportunity for people to have a longer back-and-forth exchange or foster a relationship that may continue beyond the lifetime of a specific request. Likewise, expertise location systems that provide a list of strangers in response to a query may not be well-suited to support long-term interactions. However, our results indicated that in the enterprise, workers seeking help are often more interested in creating a relationship, than in getting a quick answer to a specific question. Designing systems to help users find others who are right for longer-term interactions would be beneficial for the most common helper-finding tasks.

Iterating on the Helper Selection Process

In this study, participants were asked to describe the kind of helper they needed for their work scenario. Because of this framing, they were more likely to discuss selection criteria that were necessary characteristics of the helper (e.g., *must* have expertise in Dengue Fever) rather than characteristics that might make one helper better than another for a specific purpose (e.g., somebody who can meet in person). In fact, there are sometimes multiple appropriate helpers and the decision to choose one over another is nuanced—there may be trade-offs in terms of the person's connections with other relevant experts, willingness to help, and more.

Inspired by this investigation, we continued our work on selection criteria in a follow-up study [28].[2] In the new study, we not only asked participants to *describe* the helper, but also to explicitly state the *types of information they would find useful* in assessing whether they would *contact* the helper. We found that the selection criteria of group, expertise, role, location, and experience are indeed in the top seven most important criteria considered by the users. Participants defined the type of detailed information that would help them assess different selection criteria. For example, about expertise and experience, participants wanted a mixture of both implicit evidence, like past projects or public document, and helper-specified descriptions. About role, participants wanted not only job title, but also time at that job and a listing of responsibilities. Participants also revealed two potentially new categories of helper selection criteria, which they ranked as less important than the criteria from the present study: (1) *likelihood of a response*, including the helper's willingness to respond to contact, approachability, and availability for meetings; and (2) *answer quality*, based on a history of that person's answers to other requests for help. In summary, the selection criteria presented in this paper are those deemed *necessary* qualities of a potential helper, but there are other qualities we have revealed in follow-up work that can help seekers decide who to contact amongst qualified helpers.

[2] [28] was chronologically conducted following this investigation and inspired by it, though the follow up results were published first.

Future Work

This study provides an exploratory investigation of helper-finding in the enterprise from the point of view of the help seeker. One limitation of this is that we could not know how complicated or time-consuming a particular task might be from the point of view of the helper. Getting help in the workplace involves both the help-seeker and the helper and may involve balancing the help-giving effort with the help-finding effort [15]. To gain a more complete understanding of how people find and help each other in the workplace, it would be prudent to conduct an analysis from the point of view of the helpers, particularly in terms of their perception of the types of queries that they may receive from colleagues. Also, we discovered that a non-negligible proportion (15%) of helper-finding needs remained unresolved for over two weeks. A future investigation may be able to more explicitly compare the characteristics of queries and the process taken by the information seeker that do and do not lead to a resolution. Lastly, this work is targeted towards system designers and evaluators. Its contributions can only be truly assessed once the presented implications for design and evaluation are put into practice.

CONCLUSION

We presented a tool-agnostic, empirical investigation of how and in what situations 36 participants with diverse job roles looked for help in a large enterprise, identifying challenges they encountered. Our work makes two contributions: (1) we presented a taxonomy that characterizes helper-finding problems in the enterprise in terms of tasks, topics, and selection criteria, and (2) we summarized the current helper-finding challenges in an enterprise and suggested areas for possible design interventions. These contributions can directly benefit the design and evaluation of technologies that support helper-finding in the workplace.

ACKNOWLEDGMENTS

We would like to thank our participants for their time and Tom Moran for his early guidance of this work.

REFERENCES

1. Ackerman, M.S. and Halverson, C. Sharing Expertise: The Next Step for Knowledge Management. In *Social Capital and Information Technology*. 2004, 273–299.
2. Ackerman, M.S. and Mcdonald, D.W. Answer Garden 2 : Merging Organizational Memory with Collaborative Help. *Proc. of CSCW*, (1996), 97–105.
3. Alavi, M. and Leidner, D.E. Review: Knowledge Management and Knowledge Management Systems: Conceptual Foundations and Research Issues. *MIS Quarterly 25*, 1 (2001).
4. Allen, T.J. *Managing the Flow of Technology*. MIT Press, Cambridge, 1977.
5. Argote, L. and Ingram, P. Knowledge Transfer: A Basis for Competitive Advantage in Firms. *Org. Behavior and Human Decision Processes 82*, 1 (2000), 150–169.
6. Constant, D., Sproull, L., and Kiesler, S. The Kindness of Strangers: The Usefulness of Electronic Weak Ties for Technical Advice. *Organizational Science 7*, 2 (1996), 119–135.
7. Cross, R. and Sproull, L. More Than an Answer: Information Relationships for Actionable Knowledge. *Organization Science 15*, 4 (2004), 446–462.
8. Dunbar, R.I.M. Neocortex size as a constraint on group size in primates. *Journal of Human Evolution 22*, 6 (1992), 469–493.
9. Ehrlich, K., Lin, C., and Griffiths-fisher, V. Searching for Experts in the Enterprise : Combining Text and Social Network Analysis. *Proc.GROUP*, (2007), 117–126.
10. Ehrlich, K. and Shami, N.S. Searching for expertise. *Proc. of CHI*, ACM Press (2008), 1093–1096.
11. Erickson, T., Danis, C.M., Kellogg, W.A., and Helander, M.E. Assistance : The Work Practices of Human Administrative Assistants and their Implications for IT and Organizations. *Proc. of CHI*, (2008), 609–618.
12. Faraj, S. and Sproull, L. Coordinating Expertise in Software Development Teams. *Management Science 46*, 12 (2000), 1554–1568.
13. Granovetter, M.S. The Strength of Weak Ties. *American Journal of Sociology 7*, 6 (1973), 1360–1380.
14. Guy, I., Perer, A., Daniel, T., et al. Guess Who? Enriching the Social Graph through a Crowdsourcing Game. *Proc. of CHI*, (2011), 1373–1382.
15. Hahn, J. and Subramani, M.R. A Framework of Knowledge Management Systems. *Proc. of ICIS*, (2000), 302–312.
16. Lin, C.-Y., Ehrlich, K., Griffiths-Fisher, V., and Desforges, C. SmallBlue: People Mining for Expertise Search. *IEEE Multimedia 15*, 1 (2008), pp. 78–84.
17. Malhotra, Y. Why Knowledge Management Systems Fail? In *Knowledge Management Lessons Learned: What Works and What Doesn't*. 2004, 87–112.
18. Mamykina, L., Manoim, B., Mittal, M., Hripcsak, G., and Hartmann, B. Design Lessons from the Fastest Q & A Site in the West. *Proc. of CHI*, (2011), 2857–2866.
19. McDonald, D.W. and Ackerman, M.S. Just Talk to Me : A Field Study of Expertise Location. *Proc. of CSCW*, (1998), 315–324.
20. Reichling, T. and Veith, M. Expertise Sharing in a Heterogeneous Organizational Environment. *Proc. of ECSCW*, (2005), 325–345.
21. Reichling, T. and Wulf, V. Expert Recommender Systems in Practice : Evaluating Semi-automatic Profile Generation. *Proc. of CHI*, (2009), 59–68.
22. Seidman, I. *Interviewing as Qualitative Research: A Guide for Researchers in Education And the Social Sciences*. Teachers College Press, New York, 1998.
23. Terveen, L. and Mcdonald, D.W. Social Matching : A Framework and Research Agenda. *ToCHI 12*, 3 (2005), 401–434.
24. Thom, J., Helsley, S.Y., Matthews, T.L., Daly, E.M., and Millen, D.R. What Are You Working On? Status Message Q & A in an Enterprise SNS. *Proc. of ECSCW*, (2011).
25. Vivacqua, A.S. Agents for Expertise Location Assisting the Help-Seeking Process. *AAAI Technical Report SS-99-03*, (1999).
26. White, R.W., Richardson, M., and Liu, Y. Effects of community size and contact rate in synchronous social q&a. *Proc. of CHI*, ACM Press (2011), 2837.
27. Wijk, R.V., Jansen, J.J.P., and Lyles, M.A. Inter- and Intra-Organizational Knowledge Transfer : A Meta-Analytic Review and Assessment of its Antecedents and Consequences. *Journal of Management Studies 45*, 4 (2008), 830–853.
28. Yarosh, S., Matthews, T., and Zhou, M. Asking the Right Person: Supporting Expertise Selection in the Enterprise. *Proc. of CHI*, (2012), 2247–2256.

Combining Social Information for Academic Networking

Tamara Heck
Heinrich-Heine-University Duesseldorf
Department of Information Science
Universitaetsstrasse 1, Duesseldorf, D-40225
tamara.heck@hhu.de

ABSTRACT

Researchers in almost all scientific disciplines rely heavily on the collaboration of their colleagues. Throughout his or her career, any researcher will build up a social academic network consisting of people with similar scientific interests. A recommendation system could facilitate the process of identifying and finding the right colleagues, as well as pointing out possible new collaborators. As a researcher's reputation is of great importance, the social information gleaned from citations and reference data can be used to cluster similar researchers. Web services, such as social bookmarking systems, provide new functionalities and a greater variety of social information – if exploited correctly, these could lead to better recommendations. The following chapter describes, by way of example, one approach to recommendation for social networking in academia.

Author Keywords

Social information; scientific collaboration; author recommendation; folksonomy; collaborative filtering; author co-citation; bibliographic coupling

ACM Classification Keywords

H.2.8 **[Database Management]:** Database Applications – Scientific databases. H.3.3 **[Information Storage and Retrieval]:** Information Search and Retrieval – Information filtering. H.3.5 **[Information Storage and Retrieval]:** Online Information Services – Web-based services.

General Terms

Measurement; Experimentation; Human Factors; Management

INTRODUCTION

Collaborations with scientific colleagues are essential for most researchers, forming an important aspect of their career. One of the most visible acts of collaboration is co-authorship, where two or more researchers contribute to a publication. Other than co-authorship, there are several other situations that call for collaboration, e.g. assembly of a (formal) working group in a large university department or company, gathering of researchers in order to prepare a project proposal for a research grant or searching for contributors to a conference, a congress or a workshop. Studies show [8, 14, 24] that there is a need for researchers, in academic circles as well as other knowledge-intensive organizations, to find qualified collaborators. In the expanding social Web a scientist can gather useful information about his or her potential partners. Social websites in particular offer new (and more varied) information about scientists, potentially improving the researcher's decision-making. Additionally to the classical information services as the Web of Science (WoS) or Scopus a new perspective can be considered – which is the users' perspective: Where in WoS and Scopus we have the publishing scientists, in bookmarking systems we have the users of the Web 2.0, who bookmark scientific articles and assign tags to them. The users contribute to the content of the social Web and may offer potential information which might help scientists in finding appropriate collaborators.

The following approach tries to help researchers in finding the right people and to recommend scientist for potential collaboration. It is assumed that combined social information, which derives from different perspectives either of users or of scientists, leads to better recommendations: To prove this assumption three different methods and datasets are analyzed and compared to each other. Hereby social information about a researcher and his or her partners is collected not only in multi-disciplinary information services such as WoS and Scopus, based on author co-citation analysis and bibliographic coupling of authors [23, 28]. But social information is also collected in the social bookmarking service CiteULike, using collaborative filtering methods to measure researcher similarity.

Ten "target researchers" took part in the study. They evaluated the recommended similar authors in a semi-structured interview, whereby they got lists of author names and additional visualized author networks to identify potential collaborators.

The approach tries to answer two basic research questions which are at the core of how to further develop an expert recommendation system:

1. Is the usage of social information from different sources more appropriate to help researchers in finding new potential collaboration partners?

2. In which way do the results based on diverse datasets and methods differ from each other and how can they be combined?

SOCIAL INFORMATION ABOUT RESEARCHERS

Similarity Measurements

It is an extremely difficult task to find serious collaborators – not just any who happen to be available but the "right" ones, proven experts with solid reputations [7]. A researcher's reputation grows with the number of publications he contributes to peer-reviewed journals, and with the frequency at which those publications are cited by others [8]. If a researcher wishes to know whether another scientist might be a good collaborator, he or she might look at the scientist's reputation and search for any relation between his or her work and the work of the scientist. He or she might ask: Who uses the same references in his or her publications like I do (bibliographic coupling measurement [19])? Or who is cited by the same authors like me (author co-citation analysis [39])? These two approaches measure the similarity between two authors. Similarity in both cases means that these scientists might be interested in the same research areas and topics due to the overlap in the citations of their works or in their usage of the same references. Similarity measurement is then used as an indicator for high collaboration potential. Of course an argument against this assumption is that researchers also search for "un-similar" collaborators who complement their own work. For example some of the ten physicist researchers, who took part in the following study, stated that they do computer simulations of physical processes. This does not mean that they only need collaborating colleagues, who also do simulations. But they might need physicists who set up experiments of their simulated processes. Another example is that a person who has established a theoretical concept might need a practitioner who can implement this concept into a real environment. The question is whether in these cases similarity measurement can be an indicator for high collaboration potential. When using bibliographic coupling and co-citation analysis as measurement method, it depends on the references and citations the authors use. If for example the theorists also cite researchers concerned with applied sciences in their published papers, these people could be recommended as potential collaborators. If they do not cite them, these people would not be retrieved in the following dataset of WoS and Scopus. Concerning the CiteULike dataset there might be a greater variety of related bookmarked papers and tags. This might lead to a greater variety of people who could be recommended to the target researcher. The next paragraph will talk about this new dataset in more detail.

In our study we gather social information based on author co-citation and bibliographic coupling in WoS and Scopus. The main aspect is in showing a target scientist new and unknown partners he or she has not recognized before. Therefore we only consider the implicit relations of author co-citation and bibliographic coupling and not the explicit relations of co-authorship and citations, for here it is certain that one author knows the other: of course one knows who one's co-authors are and, we can assume, the authors one

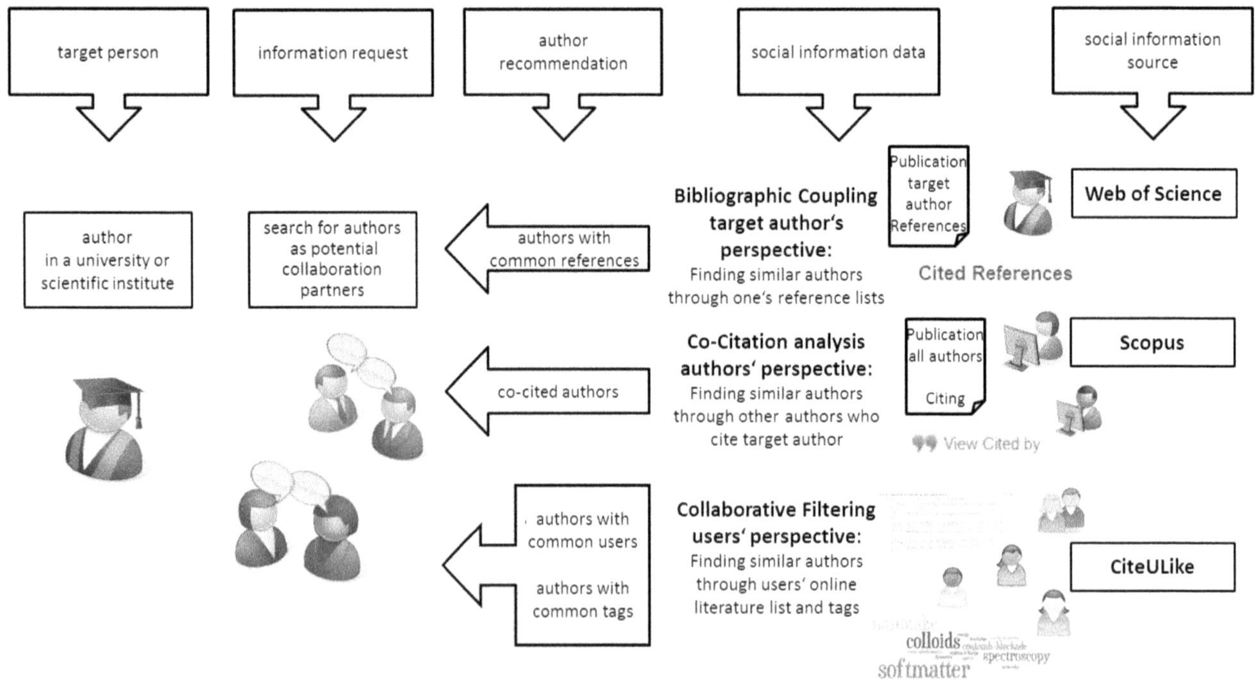

Figure 1: Concept of author recommendation based on different social information sources.

has cited. But additional social information about a researcher can be found in social bookmarking systems such as e.g. CiteULike. Here the users add social information about scientists to the services on the web. The advantage hereby is that the users' perspective is considered: Author co-citation only takes into account the perspective of a third researcher citing two other authors who might be similar. Bibliographic coupling only considers the perspectives of two authors, marked by their choice of references. Social information from web services also considers the users' perspective, as it takes into account the content they themselves have contributed to the services (Fig. 1). We thus have access to the perspectives of a large group of people. These people might be researchers themselves, but they might only be readers. That means we have the pure readers, i.e. readers who read and bookmark papers, but do not publish and hence do not cite [35]. Therefore we take into account the perspectives of people different to the publishing and citing authors in WoS and Scopus.

CiteULike is an online reference management system. The user can add article references and other Web-resource references to the system and save them as bookmarks on his or her profile. Tags, the keywords of a bookmarking system, can be assigned to references. They offer additional information and help the user sorting his or her references. The bookmark and tag lists of users are made public and are accessible by all other users, i.e. a user of CiteULike can search for a special paper or search for a special topic via the tags. The entries of the bookmarks show the resource, e.g. a scientific paper, the users who added the resource to their profile and the tags which were assigned to that resource. There is also the possibility to search for DOIs and authors of the bookmarked papers. In CiteULike users can also establish groups, e.g. open or closed research or project groups. Bookmarks added to the group's profile are then directly seen by the members of the group. As CiteULike offers a variety of functions there are different kind of users with different motivations to use this service: Users can be "common" readers, e.g. students or practitioners in a company, who use the service to manage their private references from any web-accessible device. They likewise might be scientists, who use CiteULike to manage their literature. Scientists might also be interested in distributing their own work while bookmarking their written papers. Or they are working on a project and establish a group in CiteULike to exchange potential important literature amongst their project colleagues. That means we might have those scientists in CiteULike, who might also be found in WoS and Scopus. But in CiteULike they have different motivations, i.e. here they might collect scientific papers they probably need for their work – also as papers' references, but not exclusively. So a scientist's bookmarking list might be much bigger than the reference lists of his or her published papers. Summarized we have a large group of users with different motivations; and the implicit or explicit relations between them, their bookmarks and their tags can be used to gather new social information about scientists and the relations between them.

Another aspect is that in CiteULike the researcher can get a more rapid response to his or her publications. The scientific papers can be bookmarked at the exact time when the paper is first published. When a user finds an interesting scientific article he or she can directly put it at the bookmarking list in CiteULike. This means even if a researcher's papers have not been cited yet, there might be social information about him or her in CiteULike, which leads to relations between him or her and other scientists. This aspect might particularly be important for young researchers who have only just started their academic career and have not built a scientific reputation for themselves yet. Blazek calls these "domain novice researchers", i.e. academics who enter a new domain and wish to use a collection of academic documents [4]. They face the cold start problem: Citation analysis can hardly be applied to novice researchers as long as they have little or no references and citations to their name. Furthermore, there is a time lag when measuring citations and author co-citations because an author's article will not be cited until several months after its publication, with differences in time span depending on the scientific discipline. This means that a researcher with a recently published article who might be a good collaboration partner simply will not be considered in author co-citation measurement. But if a user has bookmarked this article, the researcher can be considered when analyzing the CiteULike data.

Expert Recommender Systems

For a researcher in need of collaboration partners, a recommendation (or recommender) system could point out relevant individuals on the basis of various characteristics. Nowadays, recommender systems use different methods and algorithms for different items, e.g. products, movies, music, articles, etc., the goal being personalized recommendation [3] of items unknown, yet relevant, to the target user. The first question is where to find the best resources for a user and how to rank them according to their relevance [12]. One method is collaborative filtering (CF), which not only considers the ratings of a unique user, but also those of other users [a.o. 16, 30, 34]. One advantage of CF compared to the content-based method is that recommendations rely not only on the item's content, which may be insufficient for quality indication, but also on the evaluation of other users. When using CF to recommend potential collaborators to a target researcher, taking into account the users' perspective should yield new and more appropriate results. It is the principle of the Amazon-style recommendation. If, for instance, many users have added works by two certain authors to their online literature list in a social bookmarking system, this would be a further hint that these authors share similar research interests – assuming, of course, that the users are interested in a specific topic and also bookmark the relevant literature. This social relation is similar to author co-citation, but assigned to a social bookmarking service, with the difference that we don't necessarily have scientific authors, but users of the social web. The difference lies in the new dataset: Not only do we now have the opinion of more people, but this new user perspective may also expand a researcher's known social network and uncover new relations between researchers.

Recommender systems work by assigning user ratings to the items, a method called user-item response [12]. In our approach we use CiteULike, a social bookmarking and tagging system, where users are now also able to rate the bookmarked scientific articles. But instead of these ratings we consider the unary user-item response, which means that while a user has not rated an item, his purchase of or access to the item is interpreted as a positive response – and this response can be used for recommendations [15, 25].

There are several studies that investigate expert recommendation, e.g. for commercial enterprises [6, 32, 33]. Petry et al., for instance, have developed the expert recommendation system ICARE, meant to recommend experts within an organization [32]. In this system the primary spotlight is not directed onto an author's publications and citations, but rather on their organizational level, availability and reputation, among other aspects. Following a field study and interviews with employees, Reichling and Wulf explore the options of a recommender system to support their knowledge management [33]. In this system experts are defined via their collection of written documents, which have been analyzed automatically. The authors also used a post-integrated user profile with information about each individual's background and job description. The use of user profiles in bookmarking services might also improve the effectiveness of user recommendation.

In addition to user recommendation for commercial enterprises, several other approaches concentrate on Web 2.0 users and academics [10, 11]. Au Yeung et al. discuss the non-academic bookmarking system Del.icio.us and define an expert user as someone, who has deposited high-quality documents in their bookmark collection (many users who have high levels of expertise fulfill this criterion) and who tends to recognize useful documents well in advance of others (as seen in the timestamps on users' bookmarks) [1]. In contrast to the following approach, the "high-quality documents" in this experiment are the publications of the researcher to whom collaboration partners are meant to be recommended. Hence, it is vital for the purposes of recommendation that users bookmark at least one of the author's publications. Heck and Peters propose using social bookmarking systems for scientific literature such as BibSonomy, CiteULike and Connotea to recommend researchers unknown to the user, but who share the same interests and would thus be suitable partners for building a community of practice [14]. Users are recommended to each other when they have either bookmarks or tags in common. Ben Jabeur et al. [2] use social clues such as the connectivity of researchers and opportunities to meet in person, e.g. at scientific conferences, to improve the performance of the recommendation system. Nocera and Ursino focus on "social folksonomy", i.e. using information about user friendships and semantic information of tags [29] for their recommendations. What we consider in our approach are not the explicit relations between two researchers like in [2], but the indirect relations because we assume that they would provide more unknown potential collaboration partners for recommendation. Furthermore in our case a researcher does not need to be active in a social service, i.e. he or she does not have to bookmark his or her articles, but the users do this job. Nevertheless if a researcher bookmarked his or her own publications, this might increase the chance of other users also bookmarking these articles when they search for literature in the bookmarking system. This again would influence the relations between the researcher and other authors and might lead to new recommendations.

Another important aspect for recommender systems is their evaluation. Recommender systems should not only prove accurate and efficient, but must also detect the users' respective needs in order to be of use to them [17]. Several studies incorporate user evaluation in their investigation of the evaluation of model-based recommender systems [20, 26]. McNee et al. show the pitfalls of recommender systems in order to foster user acceptance and promote further usage of recommender systems as knowledge management tools [27]. The following example of a recommender system is also evaluated by the target researchers.

SOCIAL INFORMATION ABOUT RESEARCHERS

Collaborative Filtering in CiteULike

Unlike bookmarking systems such as Del.icio.us, CiteULike focuses on the management of academic literature. The basis for social recommendation is the service's folksonomy structure. A folksonomy [25, 31] is defined as a tuple F: = (U, T, R, Y), where U, T and R are finite sets with the elements of 'user name', 'tag' and 'resource' and Y is a ternary relation between them: $Y \subseteq U \times T \times R$ with the elements being called 'tag actions' or 'assignments'. To use this information for recommending authors to each other, we expand the folksonomy to FE:=(U, T, R, A, Y), where A is added as the finite set with the element 'authors' and $Y \subseteq U \times T \times R \times A$ is their relation.

In our experimental comparison, we want to cluster scientific authors with similar research interests. We are not interested in the networks and relations of the CiteULike users themselves but only in their bookmarks, i.e. the bookmarked publications of our target scientists, and the tags assigned to those bookmarks. Therefore we have two options for setting our database for author similarity measurement:

1. Searching for all users $u \in U$ who have at least one article by the target author a in their CiteULike bookmark list.

2. Searching for all resources $r \in R$ that have tags $t \in T$ in common with one bookmarked article $s \in R$ by our target author $a \in A$.

The disadvantage of the first method, for us, lies in the small number of users. Relying only on the users may not be enough to identify similarity [21]. The disadvantage of the second method is that users who have an article of target author a in their bookmark list, but have not tagged it, might get lost and not be in the dataset. But as many users tagged the articles of our target authors, we decided to use the second method (except of two cases: see experimental results): We searched for all resources which have been assigned the same tags as the resources of our target researcher. Resources (here: scientific papers) can be deemed similar if they have been assigned some shared tags. From here, we assume that the authors of these documents are also similar. Tags point to topical relations, i.e. authors connected via such relations regarding their research fields can be potential collaboration partners. Additionally, the more tags are shared by two documents, the more similar they are. In some cases, our target authors' articles were labeled with very general tags such as "nanotube" and "spectroscopy", so we decided to determine a minimum of two unique tags that a document must have in common with a target author's document.

To measure similarity we use the cosine coefficient. In our dataset we measure author similarity in two different ways: (A) Based on shared tags assigned to the resources of target author a and author b; (B) Based on shared users who have bookmarked the resources. The similarity between authors a and b is measured:

$$A) sim(a,b) := \frac{|T_a \cap T_b|}{\sqrt{|T_a| * |T_b|}} \qquad B) sim(a,b) := \frac{|U_a \cap U_b|}{\sqrt{|U_a| * |U_b|}} \qquad \text{Eq.(1)}$$

where T_a, respectively T_b, is the set of tags assigned to the scientific papers of target author a, respectively author b, and U_a, respectively U_b, is the amount of users having bookmarked scientific papers of a, respectively b.

Author Co-Citation in Scopus

Co-citations [22, 36, 37, 39] are undirected weighted linkages between two scientific papers, calculated via their fraction of co-citations. We then aggregate the data from the document level to the author level.

In Author Co-Citation (ACC), two authors a and b are linked if they are cited in the same documents. We cannot use WoS to mine author-co-citation data because only the first author of any cited document is listed in the reference section of its bibliographic entries, whereas we require a complete list of all authors [41]. Therefore we will mine this data from Scopus, for here we find more than one author of the cited literature. We perform an inclusive all-author co-citation, in which two authors are considered co-cited when another author cites a paper they co-authored [40].

In Scopus we search for all documents that cite at least one of the target author's articles. We analyze the references of these documents to find authors who are co-cited with our target researcher. For similarity measurement using the cosine coefficient we divide the number of documents co-citing the two authors by the product of both authors' citations (see Eq. (1)). We did not consider all authors who were co-cited with a target researcher. The main reason is the problem of ambiguous author names in the data (see paragraph about data limitations). To get a good quality of our dataset we searched for the co-cited authors and for their citations manually. Thus we limited the number of authors who are considered for similarity measurement: We ranked authors according to the total number of co-citations with our target researcher. Then we took those authors with a minimum number of x co-citations, where x determined the cutting point of the ranking. This number of co-citations may vary for each target scientist ($x >= 3$). By applying this procedure different numbers of authors are considered for similarity measurement for each of the ten target researchers (minimum 34, maximum 69 authors).

Bibliographic Coupling in WoS

BC is also an undirected weighted linkage between two scientific papers, calculated via their fraction of shared references. BC of authors means that two authors a and b are linked if they cite the same authors in their papers. We use WoS to mine data about bibliographic coupling, since this service allows searches for "related records", where relations are calculated via the number of references a certain document has in common with the source article [38].

Our assumption is: Two authors with one document each that share a high number of identical references are more similar than two authors with a large amount of shared references across many documents – the number of shared references per document being the vital quantity. For example: Let author a have 6 references in common with authors b and c. These 6 shared references are found in two unique documents by author a and author b respectively, but for author c they are distributed across 6 individual documents. In this scenario authors a and b are more similar than authors a and c, because the reference lists of a's and b's documents are more similar.

Therefore in WoS we searched for all related documents that share at least n references with any of the publications by target author a, where n may vary for each target scientist. We took the authors of these documents for the BC measurements. Authors of multiple documents in the dataset were summarized. After this step we searched for the number of authors with common references and their number of references in WoS manually to improve the quality of the dataset. Therefore we limited the number of authors who are considered for the similarity measurements: We ranked authors according to the total number of common references with our target researcher. Then we took those authors with a minimum number of y common references, where y determined the cutting point of the ranking. This number of common references may vary for each target scientist ($y >= 4$). By applying this procedure different numbers of authors are considered for similarity measurement for each of the ten target researchers (minimum 22, maximum 53 authors). We measure the similarity between these authors and our target scientist via the cosine coefficient and divide the amount of references shared by both authors by the product of the references of both authors (see Eq. (1)). Regarding the results of research literature, the best performance in terms of representing research activities is achieved by both methods, BC and ACC, in combination [5, 13].

Construction of Similarity Networks and Graphs

Applying the proposed three mined datasets and four similarity approaches, we are able to assemble four different networks of potential similar authors. One network is based on BC in WoS (BC-network), one is based on ACC in Scopus (ACC-network), one on CF of shared users in CiteULike (CULU-network), and the final network is based on CF of shared tags in CiteULike (CULT-network). We can now analyze those authors who, according to the cosine coefficient, are most similar to our target author, and evaluate the results. Also on the basis of the mined datasets we can measure the similarity between all authors of a network. These results are shown to the evaluators in visualizations, which we call graphs (example Fig. 3). Therefore, a visualized graph exists for each network and will likewise be evaluated. We used the Gephi software (www.gephi.org/) for network visualization. The size of the nodes (=author names) depends on number of relations of an author, the edges are sized according to the cosine weight. Note that the CiteULike graphs are much larger, since we cut off the list of related authors in WoS and Scopus. To get a clear graph arrangement for a better evaluation, we set thresholds based on the cosine coefficient when needed. Additionally, we left out author pairs with a similarity of 1 if they had only one user or tag (in the CiteULike dataset) in common, as this would have distorted the results.

Limitations of Data Collection

A good recommendation system highly depends upon the source dataset. Various problems arise while filtering information in the three information services. We will briefly discuss these problems: One of the main problems is the occurrence of ambiguous author names and different name spellings. We tried to identify unique authors mainly through co-authors and research field areas (e.g. subject areas in WoS). At best we could identify an author through his unique author-ID like in Scopus or at the website researcher-ID (www.researcherid.com: linked with an author's data in WoS and searchable in the service since 2012). Nevertheless author details in Scopus are not always correct. In CiteULike besides the diverse spellings of an author name, users might make mistakes and misspell the names and article titles. An all three sets we tried to detect the mistakes and corrected the author lists manually.

Furthermore in Scopus, we detected differences in the metadata: One and the same article may appear in several different ways, i.e. title and authors may be listed completely in one reference list but incompletely in the references of another article. In our case, several co-authors in the dataset went unmentioned and could not be considered for author co-citation analysis.

EVALUATION

Target Scientists and Interview Structure

We cooperated with the *Forschungszentrum Jülich, Germany*, and ask physicists to provide us their correct and complete publications lists. Ten researchers answered to be available for the interview. For those ten physicists we built individual networks and graphs. There were two phases of data collection and evaluation: One in May 2011 (evaluation by 6 authors) and one in May 2012. We limited the source for the dataset modeling to the authors' publications between 2006-2011, respectively in the second phase between 2006-2012, in order to make recommendations based on the physicists' actual research interests. While modeling the datasets, we found that one of the ten authors didn't have any users who bookmarked his articles in CiteULike. Some articles were found but they had been adjusted to the system by the CiteULike operators themselves, so the CiteULike networks couldn't be modeled for this scientist. Another researcher's articles were bookmarked, but not tagged. In this case we searched for all users who had bookmarked his articles (instead of all resources that have tags in common with his articles).

The main question the evaluators should answer was, if a recommended author is relevant for the evaluator's current research and if he or she could be a good collaborator. Another aspect, as we stated before, is that we want to recommend relevant, unknown potential partners the target researcher has not recognized before. The difficulty in this case is that a person cannot make a statement about another person's relevance if this person is unknown to him or her. The evaluator should at least know one or more scientific papers of the author he or she should evaluate. To evaluate the relevance of the recommended unknown people, one could have taken recent research papers written by these scientists. On the basis of the papers an interviewee could have made his or her opinion about the relevance of the authors of these papers. Due to lack of time during the interviews and the determined structure of those we did not consider this option, but will preserve it for further research.

For the interview we took the top ten most similar authors of all four measurements according to the cosine coefficient and listed them in alphabetical order (co-authors being eliminated). The evaluators should distinguish between two types of persons: First authors who were new and unknown to the evaluator (here the physicist was not able to make a statement about the relevance if this author and his or her appropriateness as a collaborator). Second authors the evaluator knows because he or she reads the author's papers or he or she is even personally acquainted to the author. Here the target researcher could make a statement about the author's relevance as a collaborator, although in some cases the evaluator stated that he or she doesn't know the author well enough and couldn't make a clear statement about the relevance. The target authors had to rank the known authors according to their relevance (rating from not important at all (1) to very important (10)). Note that only the known authors could be ranked. Additionally a target scientist could name authors who are not on the list, but are important for his or her current research.

The target scientists should also evaluate the graphs, the visualized networks with the relations between all authors based on the cosine coefficient. The graphs should be examined according to the right distribution of the authors and their relations to each other. Here a main aspect was the target author's own relations and the placement within the graphs' author network. Furthermore the interviewees should rate the graphs (rating from not important at all (1) to very important (10)) concerning the question whether a graph is helpful to find relevant partners, e.g. to organize a conference or workshop or for collaboration activities.

Relevance of Recommended Authors

For the recommended authors we have two groups, which could be distinguished: unknown authors and known authors. In almost all cases (except three) the number of unknown authors is higher than the number of known authors. The interviewees knew 211 recommended authors 166 recommended authors were unknown to the target researchers. It seems that senior scientists already have a huge collaboration network, as they also knew many authors personally. There were two reasons why the known authors would not be good collaborators: Either there was less topical overlap between the researcher's and the recommended author's work or the recommended author was rather a competitor than a collaborator.

On the first sight the relatively high number of unknown authors seems to be a good result as we want to recommend new potential collaborators to our target scientists. On the other hand the researchers stated that they are interested in new collaboration partners, but would prefer people of whom they at least know their scientific work. It seems that personal familiarity has a great influence on the decision whether a person is relevant to be a collaboration partner or not. This makes it difficult for a recommender system to choose the right people. Totally unknown people wouldn't likely be good collaborators, as the scientists couldn't evaluate their reputation and appropriateness of their work. Therefore a network only showing unknown authors would not be helpful for the scientists. To overcome this difficulty, links to a recommended author's published papers or web profile could help. With additional information about the author the target scientist could estimate his or her relevance in a better way. Another hint of good collaborators, which was claimed by the interviewees, is the relation of unknown people to relevant people who are known by the target author. Thus we decided to have a closer look at the identified relevant and important authors, who would be good collaborators.

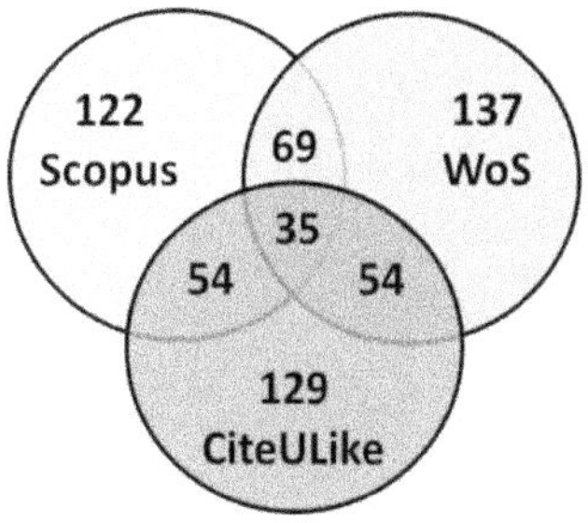

Figure 2: Distribution of important authors for all scientists.

To have a closer look at the important authors, we used the ratings the target researchers gave to the known authors: We defined important authors as authors with at least a rating of 5 who were deemed important by an interviewee, as well as all important authors added by the interviewee which were not on any network's Top 10 list. In general, our target authors named 18 till 55 people they regarded as important for their recent scientific work. Note that in some cases the target author changed his or her research field. Thus some known recommended authors were relevant collaborators in the past, but not appropriate for the current research. The general distribution of important authors in the three services is shown in Figure 2. It can be recognized that in all three datasets almost the same number of important authors is found, but that the overlapping is less, i.e. diverse important scientists are found using the diverse measurements in WoS, Scopus and CiteULike. Furthermore it is interesting to take a look at the important authors who were only found in the CiteULike networks: For example, 7 of the 35 important authors for target author *a2* are only found in the CiteULike-network, respectively 6 of the 29 important authors of *a3*. This approves our assumption that with the use of more diverse social information more relevant authors can be found. Thus a target researcher can get better recommendations.

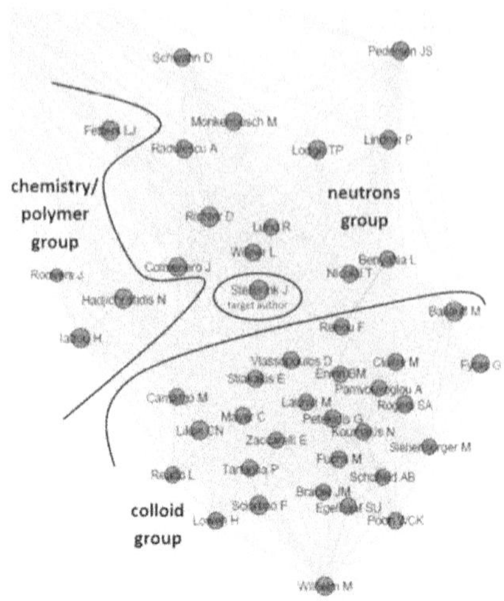

Figure 3: Extract of BC-graph with researcher groups detected by target author (in circle).

Relevance of Visualized Graphs

We assume from the statements of the evaluators that a network which shows known relevant authors and unknown people connected to the relevant ones would help an author to find new collaborators. To prove this we let the target scientists evaluate the graphs. The interviewees had to evaluate the graphs (from 1 till 10) concerning the question whether a graph is helpful to find relevant partners. The average graph relevance is:

- BC-graph: 7.95
- ACC-graph: 6.35
- CULT-graph: 4.81
- CULU-graph: 3.75

Six of the target authors claimed the BC-graph to be the best one. This ranking is not surprising since the interviewees stated to find good collaborators under the recommended, but already known authors. And with the BC method in WoS the most important authors were found. On the other hand the CULT-graph was claimed to be quite good. The authors suggested combining the BC- and the CULT-graph in order to be yielded all important authors and relevant research communities. The reason is that the BC-graph was said to show the main relevant authors, while the CULT-graph was said to reveal relations between authors of which the target scientists were not aware of before.

From the statements of the researchers we could detect two main aspects which influence the relevance of a graph. One aspect is the need of author recommendation: For the organization of e.g. a conference or workshop the scientists preferred rather bigger graphs with more unknown people. That means the CiteULike graphs could help them finding unrecognized scientists to be invited to a conference. In the BC- and ACC-graphs most interviewees stated that the authors in these two graphs were too obvious to be similar and said they were interested in bigger graphs featuring more potential collaborators. The graphs which only show relevant but already known authors might not be appropriate for recommendation, if there is a need for more unknown researchers to get new collaborators. On the other hand some interviewees said that a small network would be sufficient for them because they preferred to have a clear structure. This was the case when the researcher either does a lot of work on his or her own and is not in need of many new collaborators, or when the researcher has already built up a sufficient network and prefers the known scientists. Thus in a running recommendation system it would be good to enable users to choose between a smaller or bigger network (visualized graph). So they could decide either to stick with a smaller group of more known people or to widen their network to possibly find new collaborators. In any case the advantage of a visualized graph is that it shows the relations between the authors, which help the target scientist to recognize the relevance of a person. A simple list of recommended authors could not fulfill this aspect.

Looking at the graphs, all target authors remembered important colleagues that they had not thought of at first but whom they found very helpful. To give a clearer statement about new potential relevant authors unknown to the target researchers, the interviewees needed to have to look at their publications. But it may be assumed that if an unknown person is shown to be clearly connected to a known relevant research group, he or she probably does similar (and relevant) work. As the interviewees stated that the distribution of the researchers is shown correctly, it is likely, albeit not explicitly proven, that any unknown scientist would also be allocated correctly within the graph.

The second aspect which influences the graph rankings was the structure of the graphs themselves. At the beginning we assumed the novice researchers to suffer from the cold start problem. In fact it is a problem also by senior researchers. The coverage of the researchers' articles differs in Wos, Scopus and CiteULike, i.e. the data for the construction of the graphs also differs. It is surprising that CiteULike seems to have more articles from novice researchers and also more recent articles. To have a good structured graph the target authors' articles need to have users who bookmarked them and also assigned appropriate tags to them. If that's not the case, the huge CiteULike graphs get very unstructured and are thus not helpful for detecting collaborators and relationships among authors. If the graph had a clear structure which showed author communities and separated small groups, the researcher claimed the graph helpful in detecting author "hubs" and in finding new known and unknown collaborators. Then the target scientists could identify the important known authors and look at their relations to find unknown persons. If the graph was not well structured, which was the case if e.g. only a few tags were assigned to the target authors' articles in CiteULike, the identifications of important authors and groups was difficult. Then the interviewees claimed the graph not to be helpful in finding collaborators. Further categorizations, e.g. via tags or author keywords, might help to classify the scientists' work and avoid unclear distributions in a graph. During the graph evaluation the researchers already arranged author groups within the graph with the help of keywords (see Fig. 3). The tags assigned to the articles of the target authors were quite appropriate and could also be helpful to detect such author groups. Therefore it would be interesting to further analyze the quality of the users' tags.

To summarize the findings from the graph evaluation we could say that the BC and ACC graphs showed a quite good amount of potential collaborators which the target researchers found helpful. They stated that these graphs cover the core of their research field and showed many known people. On the other hand the CiteULike graphs, which were quite bigger, gave a wider overview of related research fields and their authors. CULU and CULT were thus more helpful if a researcher looks for many new collaborators, e.g. for a conference, or if the researcher has different research fields which should be covered in a graph. Two target authors stated that they are working in multidisciplinary research fields and none of the BC and ACC graphs covered all of the fields. Those scientists preferred the CiteULike graphs.

Discussing the Combination of Methods

Having discussed four different methods to help researchers find potential collaboration partners, there is the question if these methods should be combined in a recommendation system? One way is just to rank the recommended authors according to their similarity to the target author (cosine coefficient). For authors who are found in more than one network, one could sum up the cosine coefficients. But the difficulty is the great difference of the cosine values. In general, it can be seen that the cosine coefficient for BC is very low compared to that for ACC as well as similarity measurements in CiteULike. The highest cosine value for BC is 0.68, but in general the interval for a researcher is between 0.3 and 0.01. This is because some authors have a lot of references, which minimizes similarity. Additionally, similarity is comparatively high for measurements in CiteULike because the number of users and assigned tags related to the target authors' publications was relatively low. Here the maximum cosine value is 1. If we want to combine the results of the clusters, the summation and ranking of the cosine values would not be appropriate. For unique authors who were found in several networks we tried to normalize the cosine values (see example in table 1). The idea was that these authors should be ranked higher because it is assumed that an important author found in more than one dataset is highly relevant. That means e.g. if the target author's (BC), the other authors' (ACC) and the users' perspective (CF) brings together two authors through implicit relations, this indicates a high similarity between both. So the more implicit relations two authors have the more similar they are.

Important authors	norm Cos	rank mod Cos	cos ACC	rank ACC	cos BC	rank BC	cos CULU	rank CULU	cos CULT	rank CULT
Wales DJ	3.20	1	0.39	2	0.37	1	0.46	36	0.59	1
Wenzel W	1.92	3			0.02	47	0.87	2	0.51	3
Klenin K	1.86	4					0.87	1	0.51	2
Carr JM	1.83	5			0.22	2	0.71	3	0.24	89
Stock G	1.62	7	0.09	26	0.18	3	0.33	61	0.36	17
Derreumaux P	1.51	8	0.15	9	0.15	4	0.29	67	0.30	28
Klimov DK	1.48	9			0.09	30	0.50	11	0.39	7
Johnston RL	1.32	10					0.71	4	0.30	38
Nguyen PH	1.31	14	0.09	22			0.38	42	0.42	5
Miller MA	1.25	16					0.71	5	0.25	66
Caflisch A	1.15	25	0.05	59	0.12	9	0.22	124	0.29	44
Pande VS	1.12	30			0.13	7	0.32	64	0.24	93
Scheraga HA	1.00	44			0.09	32	0.26	99	0.27	47
Mu Y	0.84	62					0.35	47	0.25	67
Karplus M	0.82	64			0.10	21	0.17	191	0.21	143
Brooks CL	0.77	72			0.10	17	0.11	249	0.22	133

Table 1: Comparison: normalized cosine and cosine values and ranks for 16 important authors of one target scientist.

In the example the important authors got quite good ranks with the normalized and summated cosine values. On the other hand we showed that there are many important authors who are only found in one network (Fig. 2). The weakness of combining the datasets to only one big network is that these relevant people would not be found under the top ranks. Especially if a user is shown a rank list, he or she will probably not pay attention to the lower ranked authors. In a visualized graph all authors would appear and can be detected by the target researchers. However one challenge in a visualized graph, which shows results from all networks, will be the changing of the relations: That means that the relationships between authors and author groups will change. The target author might not be able to detect relevant persons and groups anymore. If the cosine values change, e.g. if an author-author-relation appears in more than one network and the different similarity cosine values are combined, the visualization of the network may change enormously. This will influence the perception of the target author concerning relevant persons and researcher groups. Therefore it should be evaluated if the relations of such a combined graph are still correct. Another great issue which should be considered when combining the networks is the problem of author ambiguity, which would be tough to handle when using different services with diverse spelling preferences. Thus it is arguable whether the combination of the methods, i.e. the cosine values, leads to any new advantages to the target author.

CONCLUSION

Regarding the need of a researcher to collaborate with his or her colleagues, social information can be used to build networks of researchers and to recommend similar people to each other. It is important for a service to recommend the right people in order to satisfy its users and be of advantage to them. For recommendations, the reputation of the potential partner is very important, hence citations and references should be considered. Our approach combined scientometric measurements with the CF-method and used data across three information services. We could show that user-generated social information in a bookmarking service complements author co-citation and bibliographic coupling measurements. All three measurements showed different results, i.e. different relevant authors were found and the number of relevant authors increased with the use of the three datasets. The graphs gave deeper insights into the usefulness of author recommendation: In the graphs the target researchers detected relevant collaborators whom they didn't recognize before. This aspect was found very helpful in finding new partners. On the other hand, the interviewees preferred networks with known relevant authors, who reveal other relations to unknown and potential knew collaborators. The relevant known authors function as orientation to find new relevant collaborators. A visualized network or graph is thus more helpful than a recommended author list because it doesn't only reveal author names, but also shows the relations between the authors. Nevertheless it also depends on the target researchers needs and preferences, which methods and graphs lead to good author recommendations.

In the following research we want to test our methods against other similarity measurements and methods to improve author recommendation. Besides other combinations of social information data can be tested. Further investigations testing the best algorithm for similarity measurement are required. The relations between user-based and tag-based similarity in a bookmarking system should also be considered, e.g. via a graph-based approach such as FolkRank [18] or user expertise analysis [1]. Aspects such as accuracy and efficiency should be tested in an operating recommendation system. Apart from technical aspects, the target users – for example, researchers – should be involved in the system's evaluation. If they don't see its benefits and don't trust its recommendations, the service won't be of any use.

ACKNOWLEDGMENTS

I would like to thank Wolfgang G. Stock, Isabella Peters and Oliver Hanraths for their contributions to the paper, and the physicists for their evaluation. The project was financed by a grant of the *Strategische Forschungsfonds* of the Heinrich-Heine-University Düsseldorf.

REFERENCES

1. Au Yeung, C. M., Noll, M., Gibbins, N., Meinel, C., and Shadbolt, N. On measuring expertise in collaborative tagging systems. In *Proc. Web Science Conference: Society On-Line.* (2009). Retrieved from http://journal.webscience.org/109.
2. Ben Jabeur, L., Tamine, L., and Boughanem, M. A social model for literature access: towards a weighted social network of authors. In *Proc. RIAO 2010,* ACM Press (2010), 32-39.
3. Berkovsky, S., Kuflik, T., and Ricci F. Mediation of user models for enhanced personalization in recommender systems. *User Modeling and User-Adapted Interaction, 18,* 3 (2007), 245-286.
4. Blazek, R. *Author-Statement Citation Analysis Applied as a Recommender System to Support Non-Domain-Expert Academic Research* (Doctoral Dissertation). Fort Lauderdale, FL: Nova Southeastern University (2007).
5. Boyack, K. W., and Klavans, R. Co-citation analysis, bibliographic coupling, and direct citation. Which citation approach represents the research front most accurately? *Journal of the American Society for Information Science and Technology, 61,* 12 (2010), 2389-2404.
6. Cai, X., Bain, M., Krzywicki, A., Wobcke, W., Kim, Y. S., Compton, P., and Mahidadia, A. Collaborative filtering for people to people recommendation in social networks. In J. Li (Ed.), *LNCS: Vol. 6464. Advances in Artificial Intelligence*, Berlin, Germany: Springer-Verlag (2011), 476-485.
7. Cronin, B. *The Citation Process. The role and significance of citations in scientific communication*. London, UK: Taylor Graham (1984).
8. Cronin, B., Shaw, D., & La Barre, K. A cast of thousands: Coauthorship and subauthorship collaboration in the 20th century as manifested in the scholarly journal literature of psychology and philosophy. *Journal of the American Society for Information Science and Technology, 54,* 9 (2003), 855-871.
9. Cruz, C. C. P., Motta, C. L. R., Santoro, F. M., and Elia, M. Applying reputation mechanisms in communities of practice. A case study. *Journal of Universal Computer Science, 15,* 9 (2009), 1886-1906.
10. De Meo, P., Nocera, A., Terracina, G., and Ursino, D. Recommendation of similar users, resources and social networks in a social internetworking scenario. *Information Sciences, 181* (2011), 1285-1305.
11. Deng, H., King, I., and Lyu, M.R. Formal Models for Expert Finding on DBLP Bibliography Data. In *Proc. ICDM 2008,* ACM Press (2008), 163-172.
12. Desrosiers, C., and Karypis, G. A comprehensive survey of neighborhood-based recommendation methods. In F. Ricci, L. Rokach, B. Shapira, & P.B. Kantor (Eds.), *Recommender Systems Handbook*. New York, NY: Springer-Verlag (2011), 107-144.
13. Gmur, M. Co-citation analysis and the search for invisible colleges. A methodological evaluation. *Scientometrics, 57,* 1 (2003), 27-57.
14. Heck, T., and Peters, I. Expert recommender systems: Establishing Communities of Practice based on social bookmarking systems. *Proc. I-Know 2010,* (2010), 458-464.

15. Heck, T., Peters, I., and Stock, W.G. Testing collaborative filtering against co-citation analysis and bibliographic coupling for academic author recommendation. In *Proc. RecSys'11 Workshop on Recommender Systems and the Social Web*. (2011). Retrieved from http://www.dcs.warwick.ac.uk/~ssanand/RSWeb11/index.htm.

16. Herlocker, J. L., Konstan, J. A., Borchers, A., and Riedl, J. (1999). An algorithmic framework for performing collaborative filtering. In *Proc. SIGIR 1999*, ACM Press (1999), 230-237.

17. Herlocker, J. L., Konstan, J. A., Terveen L. G., and Riedl, J. T. Evaluating collaborative filtering recommender systems. *ACM Transactions on Information Systems, 22,* 1 (2004), 5-53.

18. Hotho, A., Jäschke, R., Schmitz, C., and Stumme, G. Information retrieval in folksonomies: Search and ranking. In Y. Sure & J. Domingue (Eds.), *LNCS: Vol. 4011. The Semantic Web: Research and Applications*, Heidelberg, Germany: Springer-Verlag (2006), 411-426.

19. Kessler, M. M. Bibliographic coupling between scientific papers. *American Documentation, 14* (1963), 10-25.

20. Krohn-Grimberghe, A., Nanopoulos, A., and Schmidt-Thieme, L. A novel multidimensional framework for evaluating recommender systems. In *Proc. RecSys 2010 Workshop on User-Centric Evaluation of Recommender Systems and Their Interfaces*, (2010). Retrieved from http://ucersti.ieis.tue.nl/2010/program.html.

21. Lee, D. H., and Brusilovky, P. Social networks and interest similarity. The case of CiteULike. In *Proc. HT 2010,* ACM Press (2010), 151-155.

22. Leydesdorff, L. Similarity measures, author cocitation analysis, and information theory. *Journal of the American Society for Information Science and Technology, 56,* 7 (2005), 769-772.

23. Li, J., Burnham, J. F., Lemley, T., and Britton, R. M. Citation analysis. Comparison of Web of Science, Scopus, SciFinder, and Google Scholar. *Journal of Electronic Resources in Medical Libraries, 7,* 3 (2010), 196-217.

24. Luukkonen, T., Persson, O., and Sivertsen, G. Understanding Patterns of International Scientific Collaboration. *Science, Technology, & Human Values, 17,* 1 (1992), 101-126.

25. Marinho, L. B., Nanopoulos, A., Schmidt-Thieme, L., Jäschke, R., Hotho, A., Stumme, G., and Symeonidis, P. Social tagging recommenders systems. In F. Ricci, L. Rokach, B. Shapira & P.B. Kantor (Eds.), *Recommender Systems Handbook*. New York ,NY: Springer-Verlag (2011), 615-644.

26. McNee, S.M., Albert, I., Cosley, D., Gopalkrishnan, P., Lam, S.K., Rashid, A.M., Konstan, J.A., and Riedl, J. On the recommending of citations for research papers. In *Proc. CSCW 2002*, ACM Press (2002). 116-125.

27. McNee, S. M., Kapoor, N., and Konstan, J.A. Don't look stupid. Avoiding pitfalls when recommending research papers. In *Proc. CSCW 2006,* ACM Press (2006). 171-180.

28. Meho, L. I., and Sugimoto, C. R. Assessing the scholarly impact of information studies. A tale of two citation databases – Scopus and Web of Science. *Journal of the American Society for Information Science and Technology, 60,* 12 (2009), 2499-2508.

29. Nocera, A., and Ursino, D. An approach to provide a user with recommendations of similar users and potentially interesting resources. *Knowledge-Based Systems, 24,* 8 (2011), 1277–1296.

30. Parra, D., and Brusilovsky, P. Collaborative filtering for social tagging systems. An experiment with CiteULike. In *Proc. RecSys 2009,* ACM Press (2009), 237-240.

31. Peters, I. *Folksonomies. Indexing and Retrieval in Web 2.0.* Berlin, Germany: De Gruyter Saur (2009).

32. Petry, H., Tedesco, P., Vieira, V., and Salgado, A. C. ICARE. A context-sensitive expert recommendation system. In *Proc. Workshop on Recommender Systems on European Conf. on Artificial Intelligence*, (2008), 53-58.

33. Reichling, T., and Wulf, V. Expert recommender systems in practice. Evaluating semi-automatic profile generation. In *Proc. CHI 2009*, ACM Press (2009), 59-68.

34. Resnick, P., Iacovou, N., Suchak, M., Bergstrom, P., and Riedl, J. Grouplens: An open architecture for collaborative filtering of netnews. In *Proc. CSCW 1994,* ACM Press (1994), 175-186.

35. Rowlands, I., Nicholas, D. The missing link: journal usage metrics. In *Proc. Aslib, 59, 3* (2007), 222-228.

36. Schneider, J. W., and Borlund, P. Matrix Comparison, Part 1: Motivation and important issues for measuring the resemblance between proximity measures or ordination results. *Journal of the American Society for Information Science and Technology, 58,* 11 (2007), 1586-1595.

37. Schneider, J. W., and Borlund, P. Matrix Comparison, Part 2: Measuring the resemblance between proximity measures or ordination results by use of the Mantel and Procrustes statistics. *Journal of the American Society for Information Science and Technology, 58,* 11 (2007), 1596-1609.

38. Stock, W. G. Web of Science. Ein Netz wissenschaftlicher Informationen – gesponnen aus Fußnoten [Web of Science. A web of scientific information – cocooned from footnotes]. *Password, no. 7+8* (1999), 21-25.

39. White, H. D., and Griffith, B. C. Author cocitation: A literature measure of intellectual structure. *Journal of the American Society for Information Science*, *32*, 3 (1981), 163–171.

40. Zhao, D., and Strotmann, A. All-author vs. first author co-citation analysis of the Information Science field using Scopus. *Proceedings of the 70th Annual Meeting of the American Society for Information Science and Technology, 44,* 1 (2007), 1-12.

41. Zhao, D., and Strotmann, A. Counting first, last, or all authors in citation analysis. Collaborative stem cell research field. *Journal of the American Society for Information Science and Technology, 62,* 4 (2011), 654-676.

User-Centric Evaluation of a K-Furthest Neighbor Collaborative Filtering Recommender Algorithm

Alan Said
Technische Universität Berlin
alan@dai-lab.de

Ben Fields
Musicmetric (Semetric Ltd.)
me@benfields.net

Brijnesh J. Jain
Technische Universität Berlin
jain@dai-lab.de

Sahin Albayrak
Technische Universität Berlin
sahin@dai-lab.de

ABSTRACT
Collaborative filtering recommender systems often use nearest neighbor methods to identify candidate items. In this paper we present an inverted neighborhood model, k-*Furthest* Neighbors, to identify less ordinary neighborhoods for the purpose of creating more diverse recommendations. The approach is evaluated two-fold, once in a traditional information retrieval evaluation setting where the model is trained and validated on a split train/test set, and once through an online user study (N=132) to identify users' perceived quality of the recommender. A standard k-nearest neighbor recommender is used as a baseline in both evaluation settings. Our evaluation shows that even though the proposed furthest neighbor model is outperformed in the traditional evaluation setting, the perceived usefulness of the algorithm shows no significant difference in the results of the user study.

ACM Classification Keywords
H.3.3 Information Storage and Retrieval: Information Search and Retrieval - Information filtering, Retrieval models, Selection process; H.5.1 Multimedia Information Systems: Evaluation/methodology

General Terms
Algorithms, Design, Experimentation, Human Factors, Measurement

Author Keywords
Recommender Systems; Evaluation; Long Tail; Nearest Neighbors; Diversity; Usefulness; Collaborative Filtering; User-centric Evaluation

INTRODUCTION
In recent years the methods used in item-centric recommender systems have continued a steady increase in the accuracy of recommended items. Assuming the goal of a system is accurate prediction of ratings, this obviously represents progress. But it is worth asking, are we missing something? The way these systems are understood is explicitly defined via the way they are tested; focus on predictive accuracy can be sufficiently narrow as to miss the broader point. A system that recommends *items* to *users* needs to be tested to determine the rate of satisfaction of its users. Without measuring user satisfaction, there is no means to map the much more common automated measures (e.g. predictive accuracy) back to the users of an evaluated system [13].

CSCW '13, February 23–27, 2013, San Antonio, Texas, USA.

The most direct way to do this is via user study. Specifically, with the goal in mind of examining effects that may be lost to standard accuracy measures, this paper conducts a comparative user study looking at two distinct approaches to item-based recommendation. Both of these approaches come in the form of the neighborhood model. The first of the these two models is k-nearest neighbors (kNN), where *neighborhoods* of items are created based on item rating history. Each user's neighborhood is used as a basis to generate future recommendations. kNN is one of the most prevalent algorithms used in item-based recommender systems and has been explored in depth by e.g. [4, 6, 8, 25].

While kNN is widespread and understood, it is not without problems. Among these are: lack of *diverse* recommendations, the maximal distribution of recommended items across the space of all possible items, and of the *obviousness* of recommendations. These are all aspects which are not captured in standard recommender system evaluation measures. It is with these deficits in mind that the second algorithm has been selected. Starting with the core idea of kNN, that of a neighborhood of users, k-furtherest neighbors (kFN) pulls kNN inside-out; this approach creates neighbors of maximally dissimilar users and then recommends items that a user's neighbors are most likely to dislike [23]. It is hypothesized that this double-negative style of similarity-based recommender will perform better in terms of both novelty and obviousness, while maintaining an acceptable level of predictive accuracy. In order to evaluate the actual, *perceived*, quality of the recommendations, the user study focuses less on traditional evaluation metrics, and instead examines the algorithms from a *user-centric* perspective.

RELATED WORK

Two relevant channels of previous work provide background for this research. First, many existing approaches to increasing recommendation accuracy of recommender systems do so at the expense of diversity and novelty, and by increasing the computational cost of the resulting algorithms [12, 24]. Second, understanding the needs and opinions of your users (and how best to gather these) is critical to specifying an algorithm that adds significant value to a system from the user's perspective.

Accuracy vs. Diversity

One of the key reasons why lack of diversity, though long noticed in recommender systems, remains a problem, is tied to the observation that algorithms modified to increase diversity have as a byproduct lower predictive accuracy.

The broad justifications of the importance of diversity are outlined in [26]. Here diversity is held up in contrast to *similarity* as a counter aim of recommender systems. The paper proposes and evaluates some case-based reasoning (CBR) approaches to recommendation that emphasize diversity. While successful in its stated goals, the underlying CBR approach itself can be difficult to scale and quite complex. Further, the dichotomy set up in this work of similarity versus diversity can be seen as false if the task being considered is 'recommend the items a user will like'. The goal is neither to find items that are similar to each other or spread over the item space, rather to satisfy a user.

This idea of diversity tradeoffs not really being tradeoffs at all is furthered in [29]. In this work a *hybrid* of multiple algorithms is used to increase both predictive accuracy and diversity in a single system. While the output of such a system is excellent, it is not without cost. The effective complexity of such a system is quite high, being the combination of the underlying pieces of the hybrid model. However, this system does achieve its aims and in cases where the complexity is less important (e.g. domains with small datasets) it presents an effective solution.

Approaches which, like ours, try to raise the perceived values at the cost of standard accuracy metrics include [30] which defines the *intra-list similarity* metric as a means of measuring diversity in recommendations. Similarly [19] defines the metrics *unexpectedness* and *unexpectedness_r* for measuring the level of diversity a recommendation algorithm achieves. More recently, the Auralist framework [28], successfully creates a *serendipitous*, *diverse* and *novel* hybrid recommendation engine by combining several algorithms, similar to [29] the cost of this approach is the complicated underlying model.

There are of course multiple ways of considering diversity. While in the remainder of this paper we take diversity in terms of fixed-in-time snapshots of our dataset, diversity is considered via user ratings over time in [16]. The resulting model of diversity in time-ordered sequence highlights user-behavioral patterns of great interest when constructing a recommender system. The work reveals a number of insights into the effects of user behavior on recommended item diversity, such as an inverse relationship between profile size (i.e. items rated by a user) and the diversity of items recommended to a user.

User-Centricity and Satisfaction

When considering metrics for evaluation of a recommender system, keeping the user central and focusing on user satisfaction, is vital. Bringing people into the equation does complicate methods and evaluation though, and raises a number of issues.

One early way that recommender systems' users were explicitly considered was with regard to trust and privacy [15]. This work formalized various issues around trust in recommender systems especially concerning privacy in sharing preferences. Perhaps most relevantly, the paper considered how users may be prone to increase instances of explicit bias in the expression of ratings when they do not trust a recommender.

A means to increase a user's trust in a system is to optimize the utility or usefulness of the recommendations a system offers to a user. Previous research has concluded that the reliance on predictive accuracy as the most critical measure is detrimental to the overall utility of a recommender system [18]. Thus it makes a great deal of sense to consider a recommender using a more rich and diverse set of metrics, especially focused on the user.

This presents another problem though. If we give up a reliance on standard automatic measures, what evaluation should be done and why? The *ResQue* framework is one such solution [20]. This framework presents a unified and extremely rigorous approach to user-driven evaluation, though it is time intensive for participants and may be overly costly for focused hypothesis testing.

NEIGHBORHOOD MODELS

Commonly memory-based collaborative filtering models utilize the k-nearest neighbor approach to identify candidate items [7]. This approach uses a neighborhood of similar users to identify and recommend items to users. Neighborhoods are created by, for each user, finding users within a certain *similarity*. Each user's neighborhood contains the k users' who's similarity is highest, an abstract outline of the algorithm is shown in Algorithm 1. Recommendations are then created by iterating over all the items rated by the user's neighbors which have not been seen by the user, and estimating the preference of each item by averaging all neighbors' rating values for each item multiplied with each neighbor's similarity value. Ultimately, the highly rated items of the most similar neighbors are recommended. The similarity function for neighbor identification can be freely selected.

Algorithm 1: The k-nearest neighbor algorithm

Input: set $\mathcal{U}$ of users
Input: number k of neighbors
Output: k neighbors for each user $u \in \mathcal{U}$
foreach $u \in \mathcal{U}$ **do**
  foreach $u' \in \mathcal{U} \setminus \{u\}$ **do**
    $s_{u,u'}$ = similarity(u,u');
  select k neighbors $u' \neq u$ for u with largest $s_{u,u'}$

Common similarity measures used for neighborhood creation are cosine similarity and Pearson product-moment correlation coefficient, when working with data containing ratings.

The Person correlation is calculated by comparing the rating values of two users' co-rated items,

$$\mathcal{P}(u,v) = \frac{\sum\limits_{i \in \mathcal{I}_{uv}} (r_{ui} - \bar{r}_u)(r_{vi} - \bar{r}_v)}{\sqrt{\sum\limits_{i \in \mathcal{I}_{uv}} (r_{ui} - \bar{r}_u)^2} \sqrt{\sum\limits_{i \in \mathcal{I}_{uv}} (r_{vi} - \bar{r}_v)^2}} \quad (1)$$

where u and v are the two users, I_{uv} the intersection of user u's and v's rated items, and r the rating score, e.g. 4 on a scale from 1 to 5.

For binary co-occurrence data, common similarity measures include the Jaccard and Tanimoto coefficients [10, 11].

Nearest & Furthest Neighbors

Nearest neighborhood methods have been frequently used in information retrieval and information theory for many years [9], with satisfactory results. However, due to an inherent popularity bias in consumer-item interaction data [17], it is possible that nearest neighbor models recommend items which are merely popular and not explicitly personalized for the user [21,22]. Further, Bourke et al. found that the method of selecting nearest neighbors has little effect on the perceived quality of the recommender system itself [6].

Inverting the k-nearest neighbor algorithm into a k-furthest neighbor algorithm could serve as a means to mitigate the popularity bias and increase diversity, without adding more complexity (compared to a k-nearest neighbor algorithm) to a recommender system.

The motivation behind the k-furthest neighbor approach is simple. Due to the inherent bias towards popular items in the consumption patterns of people, and the positive rating bias of popular items [17,22], basic similarity measures can falsely create similarities solely based on popular items, instead of on actual taste [22]. In order to mitigate this effect, the furthest neighbor approach is used. The concept is based on an inverted similarity model, which finds items disliked by those least similar to a given user. This has the benefit of not being sensitive to bias induced by highly rated popular (i.e. obvious or non-novel) items. The approach first identifies the most dissimilar users to each user, to create *dissimilar* neighborhoods. In every neighborhood it then identifies the most disliked items and recommends these. This double negation creates a more diverse, yet personalized, set of recommendations.

Inverting Similarity Metrics

In order to create neighborhoods of the least similar users, a dissimilarity measure must be defined. Dissimilarity cannot simply be expressed by negating or inverting traditional similarity measures, as this would potentially create neighborhoods of completely unrelated, or disjoint, users. In order for a dissimilarity measure to work accurately, we propose the introduction of the following two constraints: (1) two users who share no co-rated items can be considered dissimilar by metrics such as the cosine similarity and the Pearson correlation. However, this dissimilarity is not based on an actual disagreement in taste, rather just on the two users not having an intersection of rated items. A similarity measure like this could result in extremely large neighborhoods of completely disjoint users. In order to circumvent these "false" dissimilarities, we propose a *minimum co-rated items* constraint. This constraint means that in order for two users to be considered dissimilar, they must both have co-interacted with a number of items. The constraint could be extended to treat popular items differently (e.g. lower weights for popular items). This, or similar, constraints are commonly used in kNN-based recommendation approaches as well in order to heighten (and strengthen) the level of similarity between prospective neighbors.
The second constraint, (2) the *opposed ratings* constraint, is introduced to secure an actual dissimilarity and is data-specific and relates to a rating scale. Consider this example:

Suppose that R is a set of ratings r_{ui} submitted by users $u \in U$ for items $i \in I$. Ratings may take values from the discrete set $\{1, 2, 3, 4, 5\}$ of rating scores. Typically, ratings are known only for few user-item pairs.
If u_a's set of rated items is (i_a, i_b, i_c, i_d) rated $(1, 3, 4, 1)$ respectively and u_b's set of rated items is (i_a, i_b, i_c, i_e) rated $(5, 3, 2, 2)$ respectively, then the intersection of items (i_a, i_b, i_c) creates a basis for a dissimilarity calculation. (i_a, i_c) are rated on the opposite end of the rating scale, i_b is however rated in the middle of the rating scale and has no antipode. This rating, as well as those for i_d and i_e, are thus not taken into consideration when calculating a dissimilarity.

Given this opposed ratings constraint, the minimum co-rated items constraint does not consider items rated with the middle value of the rating scale, as the rating cannot be inverted. This rating-based constraint should be modeled according to the rating scale used in the dataset or system. For a more precise dissimilarity, the matching of opposing ratings could be performed on a per-user level. This would be done by first identifying the personal rating scale of each user and subsequently matching this onto other users' personalized rating scales (e.g. some users may only use ratings from each end of the rating scale, others may predominantly use ratings from the middle, while others use the full rating scale meaning the matching of 2 to 4 might not be a true match for all users).

Applying this to the Pearson correlation as presented in Eq. (1), the similarity would be calculated as:

$$\acute{\mathcal{P}}(u,v) = \begin{cases} \mathcal{P}(u,v') & : \text{ if } |\mathcal{I}^*_{uv'}| \geq m \\ 0 & : \text{ otherwise} \end{cases}$$

where m is the number of minimum co-rated items, v' contains the inverted ratings of user v according to Eq. (2), and $\mathcal{I}^*_{uv'}$ is the list of co-rated items, excluding items rated with the "middle" score as specified by the opposed ratings constraint, i.e. (i_a, i_c) in the example above.

Each of user v's rating r_{vi} is inverted according to the following process

$$\acute{r}_{vi} = r_{max} - r_{vi} + r_{min} \quad (2)$$

where r_{max} is the highest possible score in the rating scale, r_{vi} is user v's rating on item i and r_{min} is the lowest possible score in the rating scale. In the example above u_b's ratings would be $r_{u_b,i_a} = 5 - 5 + 1 = 1$ and $r_{u_b,i_c} = 5 - 2 + 1 = 4$ turning the rating values 5 and 2 to 1 and 4 respectively.

A similar approach could be applied to many other recommendation scenarios, e.g. in a Singular Value Decomposition-based recommender [24], the ratings of the candidate user could be inverted prior to training the recommender, followed by recommending the items which, by the recommender, are deemed as least suitable for the user.

EXPERIMENTS & EVALUATION

To evaluate the quality of the furthest neighbor model, the Movielens[1] 10 million ratings dataset was used. Two sets of evaluation experiments were conducted: (1) a *traditional* setup using a portion of the ratings for training the model, and a portion used for validation, and (2) a *user-centric* evaluation method based on an online study evaluating the *perceived usefulness* of recommended items and users' overall satisfaction with the system.

Both the nearest neighbor and the furthest neighbor recommenders were implemented using the Apache Mahout[2] framework. Additionally, a random recommender, not taking the users' ratings into consideration when finding candidate items was also implemented using the same framework.

To create the neighborhoods, the Pearson correlation was used for the nearest neighbor approach. The furthest neighbor approach was created by inverting the Pearson correlation and applying the minimum co-rated and opposed ratings constraints as described in the previous section. The minimum co-rated items constraint was set to 5 based on small empirical experiments, as well as not to exclude users with few ratings. It should be noted that the higher this number is, the more the calculated dissimilarity accurately reflects the actual difference in taste, however it also minimizes the number of possible neighbors. In the nearest neighbor scenario, the minimum co-rated constraint was left to the default value set in the Mahout recommender library, 2. However, as the nearest neighbor approach requires two users to have *similar* taste, even a lower number should reflect some level of similarity.

The neighborhood size for both approaches was set to 30. Even though a larger neighborhood (up to approximately 100 neighbors [10]) can result in better performance in terms of accuracy metrics, the neighborhood size was kept low to minimize memory usage and keep the recommendation process fast for the survey.

An additional baseline recommender, a random recommender, not taking the users' ratings into consideration, was used as well. The baseline algorithm, a normal k-nearest neighbor algorithm, was chosen to show the duality of both approaches – thus showing the gain in diversity compared to a traditional recommendation setting. The random recommender was used to show that effect of the furthest neighbor algorithm were not random.

As mentioned in the previous section, similar inverted similarities could potentially be applied to other recommendation algorithm. Our choice of the k-nearest neighbor algorithm was based on it's illustrative qualities as well as on hardware limitations. Experiments with matrix factorization-based recommendation approaches required 5 to 7 minutes for retraining of the recommender. The participants in the study would need to wait for their recommendation for this period of time, which would likely have detrimental effects on the number of users who completed the study.

Dataset

The Movielens 10 million ratings dataset, provided by the Grouplens research group, contains 10, 000, 054 ratings by 69, 878 users on 10, 677 movies. The dataset additionally contains the titles and production years of movies.

Using the titles, additional information such as actors, directors, plot, etc., was collected from the Internet Movie Database[3]. This data was used to display additional information about the movies in the survey.

[1] http://www.grouplens.org/system/files/ml-10m-README.html

[2] http://mahout.apache.org/

[3] http://www.imdb.com

Traditional Evaluation

A traditional *offline* evaluation approach was used to assess the recommendation quality of the furthest neighbor approach. Offline in this sense meaning not interacting with users during evaluation, i.e. a data-centric or system-oriented evaluation. For this purpose, the above mentioned Movielens dataset was split into training and validation sets which were subsequently used to train and validate the furthest neighbor as well as the nearest neighbor model for comparative purposes.

For each user with at least $2 \times N$ ratings, precision and recall accuracy at N were evaluated for $N = \{5, 10, 100, 200\}$. In each of the cases 20% of the ratings of each user in the dataset were included. For the validation, only movies having been rated above each user's average rating plus 0.5 of the user's standard deviation of rating scores were considered. Thus making sure only positively rated items were treated as true positive recommendations. The remaining ratings were included in the training set.

User-Centric Evaluation: A Movie Recommendation Study

In order to make a real-life estimate of the perceived quality of the furthest neighbor approach, a user study was performed. The study consisted of two steps, first participants were asked to rate a minimum of 10 movies from a page showing 100 randomly selected movies out of the 500 most rated movies in the Movielens dataset, shown in Fig. 1. Due to the large number of movies in the dataset (more than 10,000), we chose randomly among the 500 most popular movies in order to show the participants movies which they would most likely be familiar with[4].

Having rated at least 10 movies, recommendations based on each participant's ratings were generated and a page containing the top 10 recommendations and a set of questions was shown, see Fig. 2. The recommender engine providing the survey with recommendations was similar to the one used in offline evaluation. The difference being that the complete Movielens dataset was used for training as this scenario did not include any offline evaluation. The time to generate recommendations for one user, using either of the neighborhood-based algorithms, was under one minute for users having rated a large portion of the 100 movies shown; this response time was considerably lower for those only having rated the minimum allowed number of movies (10). The random recommender did not need any noticeable time for generating recommendations, to create the illusion of personalized recommendations, one of the neighborhood-based algorithms was trained (but not used) in parallel to serve as a timer.

[4]In an earlier version of the survey, which was tested on a small number of users, random movies from the whole set of movies were shown instead. The vast majority of the reactions collected from these early testers were that most of the movies were completely unknown to them, thus we chose to present a random set from the 500 most popular movies instead.

Figure 1. The movie rating page where participants were asked to rate movies. The page contains a random selection of 100 of the 500 most popular movies in the Movielens dataset.

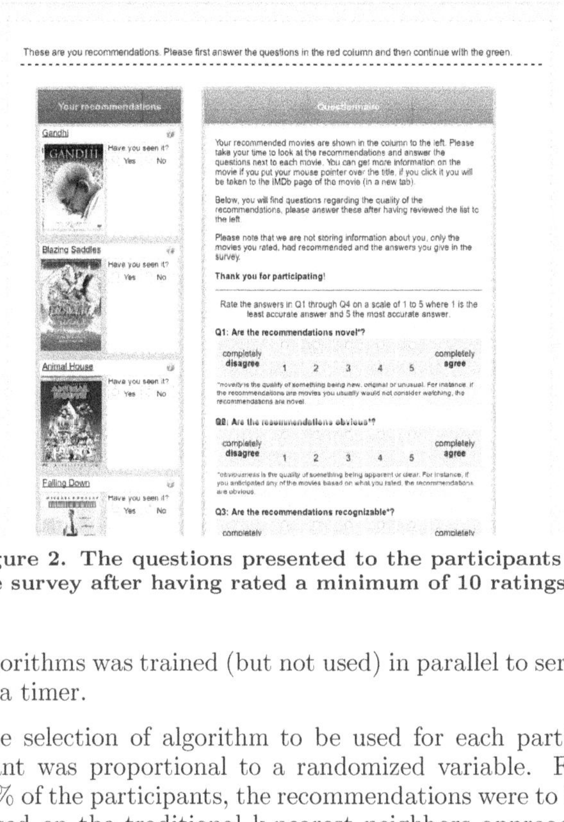

Figure 2. The questions presented to the participants of the survey after having rated a minimum of 10 ratings.

The selection of algorithm to be used for each participant was proportional to a randomized variable. For 40% of the participants, the recommendations were to be based on the traditional k-nearest neighbors approach. Another 40% of the participants were to be given recommendations based on the k-furthest neighbors approach, and finally 20% of the participants were to be presented with randomized recommendations, not taking their initial ratings into consideration.

Questionnaire

For each of the 10 recommended movies (shown in the leftmost column in Fig. 2), participants were asked to answer the following questions:

Have you seen the movie?

if Yes: Please rate it (5 star rating)

if No:

1. Are you familiar with it? (y/n)
2. Would you watch it? (y/n)

Additionally, participants were asked to answer a set of 8 question regarding the complete set of recommended items. The questions were:

1. Are the recommendations novel?
2. Are the recommendations obvious?
3. Are the recommendations recognizable?
4. Are the recommendations serendipitous?
5. Are the recommendations useful?
6. Pick the movie you consider the best recommendation
7. Pick the movie you consider the worst recommendation
8. Would you use this recommender again?

The participants were asked to answer question 1 through 5 by stating the level of agreement, from strongly disagree (1) to strongly agree (5). A short description was given for the terms *novel*, *obvious*, *recognizable* and *serendipitous* in order to mitigate erroneous answers based on misunderstanding of the question. Additionally a field for comments was placed on the bottom of the survey.

Submission of the answers was only possible after all questions had been answered.

The questionnaire was designed to create a truthful picture of users' perceived usefulness of the recommendations, considering aspects such as choice overload [5], construction of questions [13] and similar perception-related concepts [11,27].

The link to the survey was circulated on social media sites (e.g. Facebook, Twitter, Google+) during the last two weeks of March 2012. People from several professions (computer science professionals, lawyers, business management professionals) were asked to circulate the link in their networks in order to gain participants from several communities, thus attempting to minimize any biasing effects which could surface in answers from a homogeneous community. The data used in this paper was collected in early April 2012, by then a total of 132 participants had completed the survey.

Out of the 132 participants in the study, 47 (36%) were presented with recommendations based on the nearest neighbor model, 43 (33%) based on the furthest neighbor model and 42 (32%) based on the random recommender (due to the randomized seeding of the algorithm selection, the percentages are somewhat different from the intended 40%, 40%, 20% distribution).

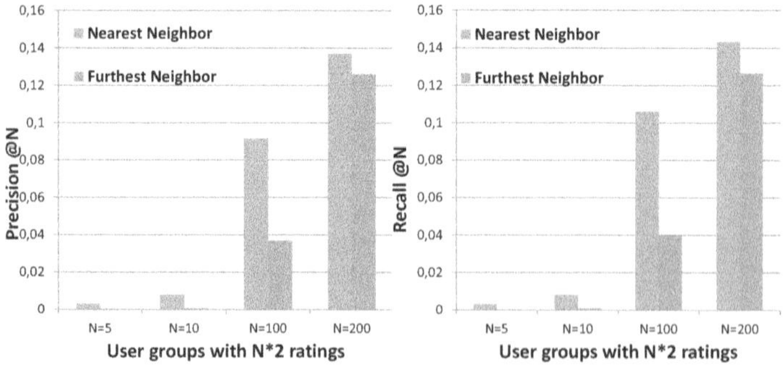

(a) Precision@N (b) Recall@N

Figure 3. The Precision@N and Recall@N values for users with $2 \times N$ ratings for the furthest and nearest neighbor models for the traditional offline evaluation approach.

Knijnenburg et al. claim that "at least 20 users" per condition should be adequate for being able to mine statistically sound data from a user study [14], indicating the amount of participants in our study should be sufficient.

No demographic data except for location (reverse lookup via IP address) was collected. The participants of the survey came from a total of 19 countries on 4 continents. Participants from Germany, Ireland and Sweden were most prominent, in descending order.

RESULTS & DISCUSSION

The furthest neighbor approach is outperformed by its nearest neighbor counterpart in terms of precision and recall when comparing the performance in an offline evaluation scenario. However, when comparing the results obtained from the user-centric evaluation, the outcomes are different.

Traditional Evaluation Results

For small values of N, nearest neighbor outperforms furthest by a factor of 8.4 in terms of precision(3.14×10^{-3} and 3.75×10^{-4} for $N = 5$ respectively). For larger values the difference in performance grows smaller, with the nearest neighbor approach outperforming the furthest neighbor approach by 8.6% at $N = 200$. Fig. 3(a) shows the values for all four evaluated Ns. Performance in terms of recall is almost identical to precision, as shown in Fig. 3(b). The results of the random recommender are not shown as they were several orders of magnitude lower than both neighborhood-based recommenders.

The nearest neighbor approach outperforms the furthest one in traditional information retrieval metrics. However, the recommenders seem to be almost entirely disjoint in terms of recommended items, as shown in Table 1, i.e. users get completely different items recommended from each of the neighborhood-based recommender algorithms.

	$N = 5$	$N = 10$	$N = 100$	$N = 200$
items	42	75	7,925	27,295
%	0.0013	0.0012	0.74	3.2

Table 1. The absolute number of intersecting items for the nearest and furthest neighbor recommender and the percentage of intersecting items from the whole set of recommended items (i.e. $N \times |U|$).

The almost complete orthogonality of recommended items indicates that both approaches are complementary, and if optimally combined into one, the resulting precision value would be the sum of the precision of both approaches. A recommender engine which would be able to create an ensemble recommender by estimating the true positive recommendations in each algorithm prior to recommendation would in this case serve as an optimal neighborhood algorithm. Ensembles are however commonly built by combining the intersecting items from both sets of recommendations, which becomes infeasible in this scenario.

User-Centric Results

As stated earlier, participants were presented with recommendations from either a nearest neighbor recommender, a furthest neighbor recommender, or a random recommender. The results of all three approaches are presented throughout this section. All t-test values presented are either for two-tailed t-tests (when only two distributions are compared), or ANOVA testing using two-tailed t-tests with Bonferroni correction ($n = 2$ for two comparisons) [2].

The results of the survey are either related to each of the movies which had been recommended, or to the whole list of recommended movies. Fig. 4 shows the results from the movie-related questions.

Considering whether the participants had seen the recommended movies or not, the ratio of seen vs. unseen was highest for the kNN approach, followed by the kFN, with the random recommender having the lowest ratio ($p < 0.1$), as shown in Fig. 4(a). Looking at this in the context of the ratings given to seen movies (Fig. 4(d)) per algorithm, we can conclude that the kFN algorithm indeed shows more unknown movies, whilst remaining an almost identical average rating score compared to kNN algorithm. This is interpreted as an indication of the kFN recommender being able to attain a comparable level of user satisfaction, with a higher level of diversity. The random recommender recommends more unseen movies, with the cost of a lower overall average rating.

Similar observations can be made for whether or not the participants were familiar (Fig. 4(b)) with the recommended movies ($p < 0.05$), and whether they would consider watching (Fig. 4(c)) the movie (showing a trend towards differences between both neighborhood approaches and random at $p < 0.1$).

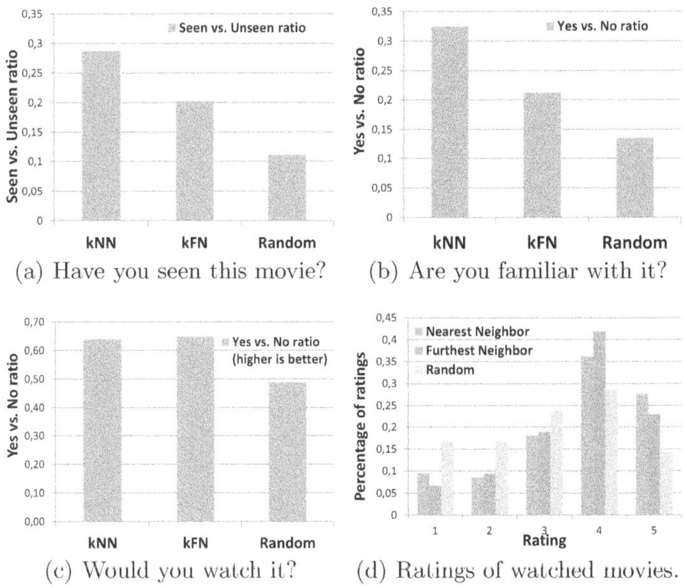

(a) Have you seen this movie? (b) Are you familiar with it? (c) Would you watch it? (d) Ratings of watched movies.

Figure 4. The ratio of yes versus no answers to the questions "Have you seen this movie?" (Fig. 4(a)) and "Are you familiar with it?" (Fig. 4(b)) both of which showing the diversity and non-obviousness of the recommended items. "Would you watch it?" (Fig. 4(c)), and the average ratings of recommended movies previously seen by the users (Fig. 4(d)) showing the general quality of the recommendations.

These observation, in conjunction with the the significance of tests (kNN/kFN vs. random $p < 0.05$, kFN vs. kNN $p > 0.1$ failing to reject the assumed null hypothesis of there not being a difference between the rating quality of both neighborhood-based recommenders) indicate that the overall quality of the kFN recommender seems to be on par with its kNN counterpart.

Looking at the results of the questions related to the full set of recommended movies (the leftmost column in Fig. 2), shown in Fig. 5, the trend continues. For instance, Fig. 5(a) shows that the perceived novelty of kFN matches that of kNN. Novelty, by it's nature implies new, or unheard of movies explaining the relatively high score of the random recommender. For obviousness, the distribution is almost opposite to that of novelty. The furthest neighbor model seems to be slightly less obvious than the nearest neighbor counterpart, high obviousness here being interpreted as something negative as obvious items could be found by the user without the help of a recommender system.

Generally, the differences between the neighborhood models and the random recommender show (at a minimum) trends towards being different, except for when it comes to serendipity (Fig. 5(c)) and novelty (Fig. 5(a)). We believe this is based on two factors: (1) the non-trivial meaning of the words (especially concerning serendipity for non-native English speakers[5], and (2) the

[5]In 2004 serendipity was voted the third most difficult English word to translate [3]

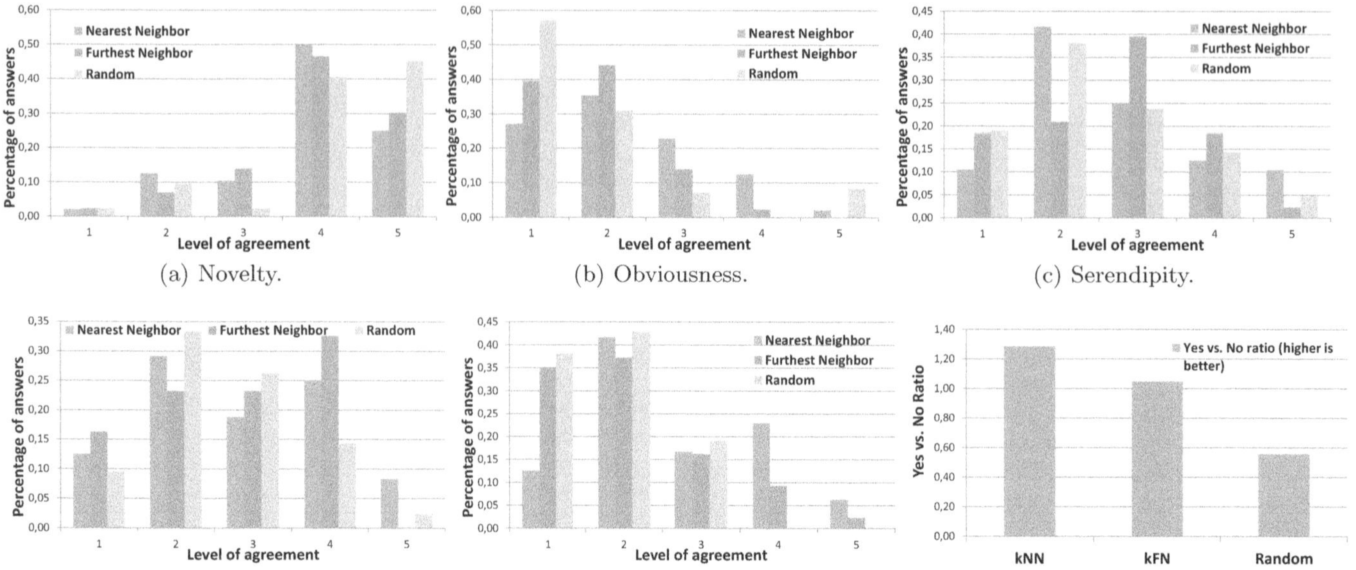

(a) Novelty. (b) Obviousness. (c) Serendipity.

(d) Usefulness. (e) Recognizability. (f) Would you use the system again?

Figure 5. The distributions of agreement levels of the non-movie related answers (i.e. those shown in the right column of Fig. 2) for each algorithm evaluated in the user study. In Fig. 5(a) to Fig. 5(e) the values $\{1, 2, 3, 4, 5\}$ correspond to $\{$*most disagree*, ..., *most agree*$\}$ respectively. In Fig. 5(f) the bars correspond to the ratio of yes vs. no answers.

Alg.	rating	novel	obvious	recogn.	serend.	useful
kNN	3.64	3.83	2.27	2.69	2.71	2.69
kFN	3.65	3.95	1.79	2.07	2.65	2.63
Rand.	3.07	4.17	1.64	1.81	2.48	2.24

Table 2. The average rating given by users for movies they had seen which were recommended by the different algorithms as well as the average of the agreement levels for novelty, obviousness, recognizability, serendipity and usefulness respectively.

inherent difficulty of rating. something which is not known (which both novelty and serendipity at least in part cover). Analogously, the assumed null hypothesis of there not being a difference between kNN and kFN fails to be rejected within significant levels of p.

Regarding the level of agreement on the usefulness (Fig. 5(d)) across all the algorithms, Table 2 shows both neighborhood models performing very similarly, t-test comparisons of the distributions show a p value close to one for comparison between neighborhood models and $p = 0.16$ for the comparisons between random and each of the neighborhood models.

However, recognizability is interpreted differently depending on the algorithm (two-tail t-tests give $p < 0.05$ between nearest and furthest, $p < 0.01$ between nearest and random, and a non-significant $p = 0.19$ between furthest and random). It seems the furthest neighbor recommender recommends less known items than the nearest neighbor does, which confirms the results shown in Fig. 4(b). We believe this provides, at least in part, an explanation to the lower precision values in offline evaluation, as less known items are less likely to have been seen by users, and are thus less likely to appear in the validation set.

Finally, on the question of whether the participants would use a recommender system like the one evaluated, there is a slight bias towards the nearest neighbor recommender, i.e. Fig. 5(f). However, this goes in line with users' natural bias towards known items as well trust-related aspects, e.g. before recommending unknown items a system should establish trust with the user [1, 11]. Establishing trust requires repetitive use of a system, which was not possible in the scope of the conducted study.

We believe that given the reported results, precision accuracy levels alone cannot be used to accurately evaluate an approach which is intended to recommend diverse items, e.g. items from the long tail. The results of the user study seem to confirm that even though the nearest neighbor approach outperforms the furthest neighbor approach in terms of traditional accuracy metrics, the general perceived usefulness of the recommenders by the users does not seem to differ substantially. Even though some of the reported t-test p-values show significance within a large error margin ($p > 0.1$), there is a definite trend pointing to similar perceived usefulness of both neighborhood approaches when considering all reported results in context.

Due to the fact that the nearest and furthest neighbor recommender are practically orthogonal in terms of recommended items, as shown in Table 1, this type of evaluation can have a higher positive effect than it would have had for two algorithms which recommend a similar set of items. In contrast, if comparing two recommendation algorithms that create less disjoint recommendation sets, i.e. by replacing the furthest neighbor approach with an algorithm recommending more "standard" items, it is reasonable to assume that the perceived usefulness would have a bias towards the algorithm that performs better (in terms of precision, recall, and similar metrics).

CONCLUSION

In this work we have presented an extensive analysis of the recommendation quality of both a nearest neighbor and a furthest neighbor algorithm. We evaluated the quality of these algorithms through traditional information retrieval metrics as well as through a user study in order to gain insight on the perceived usefulness of the algorithms. In terms of precision and recall, the nearest neighbor algorithm outperforms the furthest neighbor approach. The lists of recommended items are however almost completely disjoint due to the nature of the furthest neighbor approach, which recommends more non-obvious and diverse items. By analyzing the feedback obtained from a user study with more than 130 participants we have shown that a higher predictive accuracy of a recommender system, in this scenario, does not increase the perceived usefulness of the recommender system, from the users' perspective.

From the answers obtained in the study, we were able to recognize several aspects that point to the notion that *at least* similar satisfaction can be obtained with lower precision, e.g. proportionally the same amount of users claimed they would watch a movie recommended by the lower scoring furthest neighbor approach than a movie recommended by the nearest neighbor approach - Fig. 4(c). Similarly, the furthest neighbor recommender and nearest neighbor recommender received almost identical overall rating values, despite the differences in precision and recall, shown in Table 2.

ONGOING & FUTURE WORK

We believe that this model of evaluation of diverse and other non-obvious items needs to be analyzed in order to gain further insight on when traditional information retrieval accuracy metrics cannot express the quality of a recommender system accurately. For this purpose, we plan on extending the survey to include several more types of recommender algorithms and more questions. Specifically, we intend to study the perceived usefulness of similar algorithms (in terms of how recommendations are found), but which still perform differently in standard metrics. An extended study will be conducted within a multi-algorithm recommender system we have developed for user-centric evaluation. In this system we hope to mitigate any effects of the level of trust, or lack of trust, the users have towards the system by continuous interactions with the recommender system.

Furthermore, we believe that a similar approach could be applied to most recommendation algorithms in order to generate more diverse and non-obvious recommendations, i.e. by inverting the ratings of a user according to Eq. (2) and recommending the items found to be least likely to be liked by the user. This is however outside of the scope of this paper and left as a possible avenue for future work.

Additionally, we are investigating the possibilities of creating an ensemble recommender using both types of neighborhoods.

ACKNOWLEDGMENTS

The authors would like express their gratitude to all participants of the study and everyone who helped by distributing it in their communities, and to Bart Knijnenburg from UC Irvine and Michael Meder from TU Berlin for their help with conceptualization, implementation and evaluation of the user study.

REFERENCES

1. *FilmTrust: movie recommendations using trust in web-based social networks*, vol. 1 (2006).
2. Abdi, H. *Bonferroni and Sidak corrections for multiple comparisons.* Sage, 2007.
3. Avérous, Y. Untranslateable words - serendipity. *Journal of the Northern Californa Translators Association: Online Edition* (2005).
4. Bellogin, A., and Parapar, J. Using graph partitioning techniques for neighbour selection in user-based collaborative filtering. In *Proceedings of the sixth ACM conference on Recommender systems*, RecSys '12, ACM (New York, NY, USA, 2012), 213–216.
5. Bollen, D., Knijnenburg, B. P., Willemsen, M. C., and Graus, M. Understanding choice overload in recommender systems. In *Proceedings of the fourth ACM conference on Recommender systems*, RecSys '10, ACM (New York, NY, USA, 2010), 63–70.
6. Bourke, S., McCarthy, K., and Smyth, B. Power to the people: exploring neighbourhood formations in social recommender system. In *Proceedings of the fifth ACM conference on Recommender systems*, RecSys '11, ACM (New York, NY, USA, 2011), 337–340.
7. Breese, J. S., Heckerman, D., and Kadie, C. *Empirical analysis of predictive algorithms for collaborative filtering*, vol. 461. San Francisco, CA, 1998.
8. Candillier, L., Jack, K., Fessant, F., and Meyer, F. State-of-the-art recommender systems. *Collaborative and Social Information Retrieval and AccessTechniques for Improved User Modeling* (2009), 1–22.
9. Cover, T., and Hart, P. Nearest neighbor pattern classification. *Information Theory, IEEE Transactions on 13*, 1 (january 1967), 21 –27.

10. Herlocker, J., Konstan, J. A., and Riedl, J. An empirical analysis of design choices in neighborhood-based collaborative filtering algorithms. *Inf. Retr. 5*, 4 (Oct. 2002), 287–310.
11. Herlocker, J. L., Konstan, J. A., Terveen, L. G., and Riedl, J. T. Evaluating collaborative filtering recommender systems. *Trans. Inf. Syst. 22*, 1 (2004).
12. Karypis, G. Evaluation of item-based top-n recommendation algorithms. In *Proceedings of the tenth international conference on Information and knowledge management*, CIKM '01, ACM (New York, NY, USA, 2001), 247–254.
13. Knijnenburg, B., Willemsen, M., Gantner, Z., Soncu, H., and Newell, C. Explaining the user experience of recommender systems. *User Modeling and User-Adapted Interaction 22* (2012).
14. Knijnenburg, B. P., Willemsen, M. C., and Kobsa, A. A pragmatic procedure to support the user-centric evaluation of recommender systems. In *Proceedings of the fifth ACM conference on Recommender systems*, RecSys '11, ACM (New York, NY, USA, 2011), 321–324.
15. Lam, S., Frankowski, D., and Riedl, J. Do you trust your recommendations? an exploration of security and privacy issues in recommender systems. In *Emerging Trends in Information and Communication Security*, G. Müller, Ed., vol. 3995 of *Lecture Notes in Computer Science*. Springer Berlin / Heidelberg, 2006, 14–29.
16. Lathia, N., Hailes, S., Capra, L., and Amatriain, X. Temporal diversity in recommender systems. In *Proceedings of the 33rd international ACM SIGIR conference on Research and development in information retrieval*, SIGIR '10, ACM (New York, NY, USA, 2010), 210–217.
17. Marlin, B. M., and Zemel, R. S. Collaborative prediction and ranking with non-random missing data. In *Proceedings of the third ACM conference on Recommender systems*, RecSys '09, ACM (New York, NY, USA, 2009), 5–12.
18. McNee, S. M., Riedl, J., and Konstan, J. A. Being accurate is not enough: how accuracy metrics have hurt recommender systems. In *CHI '06 extended abstracts on Human factors in computing systems*, CHI EA '06, ACM (New York, NY, USA, 2006), 1097–1101.
19. Murakami, T., Mori, K., and Orihara, R. Metrics for evaluating the serendipity of recommendation lists. In *Proceedings of the 2007 conference on New frontiers in artificial intelligence*, JSAI'07, Springer-Verlag (Berlin, Heidelberg, 2008), 40–46.
20. Pu, P., Chen, L., and Hu, R. A user-centric evaluation framework for recommender systems. In *Proceedings of the fifth ACM conference on Recommender systems*, RecSys '11, ACM (New York, NY, USA, 2011), 157–164.
21. Rafter, R., O'Mahony, M. P., Hurley, N. J., and Smyth, B. What have the neighbours ever done for us? a collaborative filtering perspective. In *Proceedings of the 17th International Conference on User Modeling, Adaptation, and Personalization: formerly UM and AH*, UMAP '09, Springer-Verlag (Berlin, Heidelberg, 2009), 355–360.
22. Said, A., Jain, B. J., and Albayrak, S. Analyzing weighting schemes in collaborative filtering: Cold start, post cold start and power users. In *27th ACM Symposium On Applied Computing (SAC '12)*, ACM (New York, NY, USA, 2012).
23. Said, A., Kille, B., Jain, B. J., and Albayrak, S. Increasing diversity through furthest neighbor-based recommendation. In *Proceedings of the WSDM'12 Workshop on Diversity in Document Retrieval (DDR'12)* (2012).
24. Sarwar, B. M., Karypis, G., Konstan, J. A., and Riedl, J. T. Application of dimensionality reduction in recommender system – a case study. In *WebKDD Workshop at the ACM SIGKKD* (2000).
25. Schafer, J. B., Frankowski, D., Herlocker, J., and Sen, S. The adaptive web. Springer-Verlag, Berlin, Heidelberg, 2007, ch. Collaborative filtering recommender systems, 291–324.
26. Smyth, B., and McClave, P. Similarity vs. diversity. In *Case-Based Reasoning Research and Development*, D. Aha and I. Watson, Eds., vol. 2080 of *Lecture Notes in Computer Science*. Springer Berlin / Heidelberg, 2001, 347–361.
27. Swearingen, K., and Sinha, R. Beyond Algorithms: An HCI Perspective on Recommender Systems.
28. Zhang, Y. C., Séaghdha, D. O., Quercia, D., and Jambor, T. Auralist: introducing serendipity into music recommendation. In *Proceedings of the fifth ACM international conference on Web search and data mining*, WSDM '12, ACM (New York, NY, USA, 2012), 13–22.
29. Zhou, T., Kuscsik, Z., Wakeling, J.-G. L. M. M. J. R., and Zhang, Y.-C. Solving the apparent diversity-accuracy dilemma of recommender systems. *Proceedings of the National Acadamy of Sciences of the United States of America (PNAS) 107*, 10 (2010), 4511–4515.
30. Ziegler, C.-N., McNee, S. M., Konstan, J. A., and Lausen, G. Improving recommendation lists through topic diversification. In *Proceedings of the 14th international conference on World Wide Web*, WWW '05, ACM (New York, NY, USA, 2005), 22–32.

'On the Ground' in Sidi Bouzid: Investigating Social Media Use during the Tunisian Revolution

Volker Wulf[1,2], Kaoru Misaki[2], Meryem Atam[2], David Randall[1], Markus Rohde[1,2]

[1]Information Systems and New Media
University of Siegen, 57068 Siegen, Germany
[volker.wulf, dave.randall, markus.rohde]@uni-siegen.de

[2]International Institute for Socio Informatics (IISI)
Stiftsgasse 25, 53111 Bonn, Germany
misaki@iisi.de, meryem_atam@web.de

ABSTRACT
We present a study conducted in Sidi Bouzid, the Tunisian town where the Arab Revolution, also known as 'Arab Spring', started, and where the role of Web 2.0 and social media applications in the people's uprising have been much discussed. We identify four relevant phenomena: (1) the publication of classified materials via WikiLeaks challenged the regime's legitimacy, (2) Web 2.0 connected local activists with Arab satellite TV, (3) social media linked the young activists with actors in other cities in Tunisia, (4) social media allowed organizing resistance inside Sidi Bouzid. Methodologically, we question a too deterministic view of the role of the new media and the representativeness of investigative techniques that uniquely use the new media in order to assess their impact. At the same time, rigorous investigations 'on the ground' are extremely difficult. We present a modest and initial attempt to provide such an 'on the ground' approach, cognizant of necessary limitations. We compare our findings with studies which analyze data downloaded out of social media applications and suggest that studies of the kind we describe offer additional insight and play an essential role in better understanding political uses of social media.

Author Keywords
Arab Spring, social media, 'on the ground' studies

ACM Classification Keywords
H.5.m. Information interfaces and presentation (e.g., HCI): Miscellaneous.

INTRODUCTION
IT applications, and social media in particular, have become part of the everyday infrastructure for different aspects of life (Pipek and Wulf 2009; Wulf et al. 2011). Social media also appears to be where 'mobilization' of one kind or another takes place (see e.g. Starbird and Palen, 2011; Palen et al. 2010). Our specific interest here is the case of political activism and participation. Web 2.0 applications have important characteristics which arguably differentiate them from other (mass) media. In contrast to traditional communication channels, first they have the potential to reach large numbers of people quickly, second, equally important, offer two-way communication, and therefore provide opportunities for users to produce content and send news to the world. Users, as the research cited above attests, are not just passive recipients but can act as political organizers, commentators, or videographers.

In principle, then, the new media afford new prospects for activism. Some literature in recent years suggests we have seen an increasing density of IT usage in support of political activism (Diamond 2010) as well as a raised interest in the CSCW and CHI communities in these topics (Rohde 2004, Saeed et al. 2010 and 2012, Ben Ali et al. 2012; Kavanaugh et al. 2012). It looks like social media systems together with mobile phones may well play an increasing role in political uprisings such as the post-election protests in Iran in 2009 and the series of uprisings transforming the Arab world (the so-called 'Arab Spring') following the Tunisian revolution in January 2011. To the extent that this is true, these technologies go some way to meeting Amartya Sen's (1985) plea for new technology to focus on empowerment for choice and capability as an alternative to economistic and technological determinism. They may well bring with them new possibilities for engagement and participation (see e.g. Steyn and Johanson, 2011) and hold out a promise for addressing 'digital divide' issues (see e.g. Chen and Wellman, 2004).

Strong claims are sometimes made about the putative effects of these new affordances: *"The use of new technology as potent political communication, and mobilization tool was demonstrated in the Arab Spring that engulfs North Africa and Middle East since the beginning of 2011. In this case, a combination of social media including the mobile technology has increasingly empowered the people to be connected together. This connectivity enables the citizens to create communities engaged on single issue, and bounded together by a common goal, which has caused unparalleled political revolution that has consumed forces of undemocratic political hegemony in the Middle East."* (Olaore, 2011)

At the same time, some skepticism has been expressed concerning this role, and there are reasons to be cautious. Gladwell (2011), for instance, argues that the role of social media may have been rather overestimated by Western observers who did not have access to the events on the ground. Hassanpour (2011) even claims that sudden interruption of mass communication may accelerate revolutionary mobilization since it provides radicals with more effective venues for organization. Moreover, he argues that social media can act against grass root mobilization. It may discourage face-to-face communication and mass presence in the streets. Similar to more traditional and highly visible media, it creates greater awareness of risks involved in protests which in turn can discourage people from taking part in demonstrations. To formalize the dynamics of participation in political action, Hassanpour (2011) develops a graph theoretical threshold model. To support the plausibility of his model empirically, the author argues that the Egyptian uprising widened in participation and spread geographically after the Mubarak regime disrupted the Internet and the mobile communication for two days on February 28, 2011.

Even so, and as Anderson (2011) has pointed out, spontaneous eruptions of political protest across North Africa and the Middle East occurred in 1919 without the aid of such media. Further, the effects of this media role remain uncertain and will be contingent, at least to a degree, on local conditions, conditions which remain largely unexplored in research communities with a technological focus. As a Hansard report argues, while acknowledging the density of new media use: *"One must be careful not to overstate the role of social media; it is only a tool. The previous example was largely done face-to-face, not online, and what social media can achieve is down to alignment with social behaviour and its effective social appropriation."*(Hansard Society 2012)

There is, in sum, little doubt that the new media have been extensively used for mobilization during the Arab spring but we as yet have no convincing picture of how in detail they were and are used, nor of their effects. The contradictory findings and predictions described above require, we suggest, empirical investigations of a more traditional kind in order to supplement (but not replace) the e-research that typifies investigation at the moment. In the following, we present early results of such a study, which investigates 'on the ground' how social media was used in the uprising in Sidi Bouzid, Tunisia. In this paper we describe this from the perspective of those having participated in it. We were particularly interested in how activists in a provincial town made use of Web 2.0 and social media applications in: (1) supporting the uprising over a period of four weeks and (2) spreading the news to the rest of the country and beyond its borders.

The paper is structured as follows: We first summarize the state of the art on social media use during the Arab Spring. We then provide some historical and socio-economic information on Tunisia and its revolution. After describing our research methods, we present the empirical findings with regard to the local uprising, as well as to the use of social media in its support. Finally, we discuss our results and their limitations.

STATE OF THE ART

Most investigations of the role of the social media in the Arab Spring have relied on digital traces in one form or another Some kind of 'trace' ethnography or similar 'logging' methodology has been the main method by which data has been collected (Geiger and Ribes 2011). Examples include Ban Ani et al. (2012), who analyzed some 15.000 Egyptian blog entries which were posted in the period from 2004 to 2011 via an aggregator blog. Lotan et al. (2011) similarly examined Twitter usage in the Egyptian and Tunisian revolution. Looking for information flow of (nearly) duplicated tweets, they point out to the important role of both journalists and activists in disseminating news. Looking at data on the Egyptian revolution, Starbird and Palen (2012) confirm these findings. They analyzed Twitter data collected over a period of 13 days in February 2011. Looking at retweeting patterns, they speculate that information filtering and expressions of social solidarity can be meaningful for the social movement 'on the ground'.

Kavanaugh (2012) analyzed statistical data on social media usage during the Arab Spring and compared the findings with her own data of a survey among Egyptian students, collected in June 2011. Moreover, in January and February 2011 she collected Twitter data from Egypt and Tunisia. She argues that social media had an impact beyond its general adoption rates due to the age distribution of the user population, largely concentrated on the protesting youth. While quantitatively marginal, she suggests that Twitter users were most likely opinion leaders and therefore Twitter usage probably had a disproportionally larger social impact. As we have argued, however, there is a shortage of material that adequately describes how this media traffic actually translates into activity (political activism in practice). We know of no papers which investigate the role of the social media have played in enabling the Arab Spring 'on the ground'. The research reported here begins to fill that gap.

TUNISIA AND ITS REVOLUTION

After the independence from France, Tunisia was ruled by two presidents, Habib Bourguiba (1956 – 1987) and Zine el-Abidine Ben Ali (1987 – 2011) who impeached his predecessor in a bloodless coup d'état. Bourguiba's secular reform agenda included female emancipation, a state-run healthcare system, public education, fostering of literacy, administrative institution building, and attempts to a partial industrialization. Ben Ali mainly continued these politics, focusing on economic development, bolstering exports, foreign investment, and tourism. Throughout four decades, Tunisia managed to achieve an annual GDP growth of 4-5% (CIA World Factbook 2012).

While economic growth led to the emergence of a middle class, the Ben Ali regime was increasingly characterized by high levels of corruption and rising unemployment among young, often well-educated Tunisians. The political system was characterized by electoral fraud and a harsh suppression of the opposition, including people with an Islamist background. National radio and TV stations as well as newspapers were censored and under strict state control. However, since the 1990s satellite TV channels such as Al Jazeera, with its headquarters in Qatar, started to fundamentally change and influence the media landscape all over the Arab World. Most Tunisian households are able to receive satellite TV. While there are only 1.3 million telephone landlines, about 11 million cell phones are in use (of a population of 10.6 million inhabitants) (CIA World Factbook 2012). By the time of the Tunisian Revolution a significant proportion of these mobiles were smartphones with cameras and even internet access. At the end of 2010, Tunisia had one of the highest rates of Facebook usage among the Arab states (17.6%), which was strongly increasing during the months to follow (22.5% in April 2010). Young people made up 75% of the Facebook users. Twitter, in contrast, was only used by 0.34% of the population (Kavanaugh 2012).

In comparison with the coastal areas, the center of Tunisia, specifically the districts of Kef, Kasserine, Sidi Bouzid, and Gafsa, are economically disadvantaged. The standard of living is lower and the unemployment rate among young people is higher than in the coastal regions. Since 2008, these regions have already seen several local uprisings which were violently suppressed; specifically those in Gafsa in 2008 and in La Skhira in 2010 (cf. Bettaieb 2011).

Sidi Bouzid is a town of approximately 40,000 inhabitants, located inland about 200 km southwest of Tunis. The uprising in Sidi Bouzid started on December 17, 2010 when a street vendor named Mohamed Bouazizi immolated himself after a female policeman had humiliated him by accusing him of cheating his customers. The self-immolation happened in front of the governor's office after the governor had declined to meet Bouazizi. On the same day the self-immolation led to a spontaneous demonstration by Bouazizi's family members and other members of the Sidi Bouzid community. Three days later the demonstrations had reached neighboring villages (Mezzouna, Ouled Hafez) and districts (Kasserine, Gafsa, and Sfax). As suppression efforts by the police became more violent in Sidi Bouzid, the demonstrations reached the capital, Tunis, for the first time on December 27. Mohamed Bouazizi died on January 4. Two days later the first countrywide strike organized by the lawyers' association took place. Following a speech by Ben Ali on January 10, demonstrations spread throughout the country the next day. These demonstrations were subsequently suppressed by the Ben Ali regime. Allegedly, snipers and police forces killed hundreds of protesters. Ben Ali left the country on January 14, 2011 for Saudi Arabia, ending the first phase of the Tunisian revolution (cf. Bettaieb 2011).

RESEARCH METHODS

The data for this paper were collected in two phases. The central themes of this paper emerged from a 10-day visit to Tunisia from December 28, 2011 to January 8, 2012. In a second phase, we elaborated on our findings during a 7-day visit to Sidi Bouzid from August 14 to 21, 2012. At the time of the first anniversary of the Tunisian revolution, the first and second author travelled by means of public transportation from Tunis, the capital, along the coast south up to the island of Djerba. Later they visited districts in the center of the country: Tozeur, Gafsa, Sidi Bouzid and Kairouan. They spent two days in Sidi Bouzid. The findings of the first phase are mainly based on data collected at various occasions in Sidi Bouzid. A starting assumption was that the uprising in Sidi Bouzid was a contingent event, driven by the general dissatisfaction of local citizens and precipitated by the Bouazizi suicide. Therefore, we focused on interviewing citizens who were present during the uprising and participated in local activities contributing to the uprising.

We chose the small square in front of the governor's palace to come into contact with potential interviewees. The site of the self-immolation of Bouazizi was still a meeting point for citizens and political activists. During our first visit unemployed youths still maintained tents to remind the public of their problems and to show their dissatisfaction with the developments after the revolution. After their arrival in the city, the first two authors spent some 5 hours there conducting informal interviews. The interviews were conducted in the first instance with two persons who had taken part in the local uprising the year before. Subsequently, two small group discussions with people at the square took place. Later on, further informal interviews were conducted in the hotel, a local youth cafe, and during two long taxi rides. On the first and second day, two more activists were interviewed in front of the governor's palace. Overall, 12 interviews were conducted which lasted between 10 minutes and 2.5 hours. While the places for the interviews were chosen deliberately, the interviewees were selected on an opportunistic basis.

The interviews were non-structured and open ended. After some relationship and trust building between the interviewers and the interviewees, the local actors were typically asked to describe their personal background, how they perceived the last year's uprising, and which role they had taken in it. The interviews also dealt with the usage of the internet and social media applications. The interviews were conducted in French and English depending on the interviewees' foreign language capabilities and were not recorded.

Figure 1: Sidi Bouzid in front of the governor's palace (January 2012): Tents at the site of Bouazizi's self-immolation

Trust building turned out to be a real challenge. Locals typically assumed that the first author was a Western journalist of whom they had seen many during the last year. Certain actors distrusted Western visitors, specifically journalists. One actor, a translator by profession, expressed this attitude towards the second author – an Asiatic native. He mentioned that from his experience, Western media did not take local informants seriously. Their coverage follows, he argued, a Western political agenda, does not seriously reflect local voices, and focuses on facts about Sidi Bouzid which fit into such a world view.

Given the delicate political climate at the time of the uprising's first anniversary, we felt it inappropriate to write explicit field notes in front of the governor's palace. We also assumed that audio recording would have a negative impact on the interviewees' willingness to talk to us about these politically still sensitive issues. Still, in the course of the interviews, we wrote down some brief notes inside a travel guide book and took photos selectively with an iphone. However, we later found that using an iphone in public could put us in dangerous situations. In the evening, when the authors left a youth café, an attempt was made to forcibly remove the iphone from them. The resulting scuffle saw the first author falling to the street floor, shouting loudly for help. Given these circumstances, comprehensive summaries of the interviews, group discussions, and observations were only written in the evenings back at the hotel.

The results emerging from the interviews were extended and triangulated by findings from informal interviews conducted during the trip in other parts of Tunisia. The reliability of this information was also confirmed by an analysis of press reports and publications, specifically (Bettaieb 2011). Nevertheless, we were conscious that our empirical results were 'opportunistic' and perhaps lacked a certain robustness. Therefore, we collected additional empirical data in a second phase of the study. The third author who conducted the field research in September 2012 is a translator of Arabic and lecturer for intercultural communication. She conducted three semi-structured interviews based on guidelines emerging from the results of the first phase. The focus of the interviews was on social media use during the time of the uprising, by the local population in general, and, more specifically by the interviewees themselves.

In this second phase, interviewees were partly recruited via the third author's social network. She had worked before as a translator for a Tunisian businessman. One of the businessman's employees was from Sidi Bouzid and introduced her to local political activists: (1) a young member of the moderate Islamist El-Nahda Party who, however, had not been a member of the party at the time of the local uprising, (2) a 19-year-old Facebook user, (3) an internet "activist" to whom the author was introduced through the Facebook user; and who worked as a producer and cameraman for a local internet radio hub and web-based news platform. The notion "activist" implies here that this person attended some part of the local events in person.
The interview with the young member of the El-Nahda Party took place in the party's local premises, the one with the young Facebook user in the house of the contact person's family, while the interview with the internet activist and radio producer was conducted in a local street café. The fact that the third author was personally introduced to her interviewees played a crucial role in terms of trust and relationship building. Therefore, it was possible to audiotape all of these interviews. They lasted between one to three hours, one interview spanned two sessions. The interviews were partly translated from Arabic into English and transcribed by the third author.

As with the first phase of the study, the third author conducted additional informal interviews: in her hotel, during long bus rides, in a tea house, and when invited to the interviewees' families for "iftaar", the fast-breaking meal during Ramadan. She conducted a total of 15 informal interviews in Arabic which lasted between 10 minutes and 1 hour. Necessarily, interactions which involved - for instance - being invited to her contact person's and the young Facebook user's families entailed an 'observer as participant' role in discussions. Such an approach was both necessary and desirable since trust issues, as we had previously argued, were paramount. By trying to become friends, or at least, to be accepted by members of the community, she built trust so the target group did not feel threatened by her presence (Howell 1972). As an example, the third researcher adopted this 'observer as participant' role when joining the internet activist and local radio producer: in the evenings he and his friends would sit in a local street café drinking tea and smoking their water pipes. During some of these sessions the researcher preferred not to record any interviews but instead to adopt the very informal stance of attentively following the conversation around the table. These observations helped her to a better understanding the social context of the interviewees' media use.

SIDI BOUZID AND ITS UPRISING

The personal background of the interviewees reflected the economic problems Sidi Bouzid has to face. During the first phase of research conducted in front of the governor's palace the authors interviewed two young, well-educated adults aged between 20 and 30 who could not find proper jobs. One male interviewee went abroad for two years to work (illegally) in the Netherlands, Germany and China. Upon his return, he could not find an adequately paid job and by the time of the interview he depended on a low paid job in the building industry. Our first interviewee was a young mother with a university degree in biology who had not yet found a job either. She lived together with her husband who also had graduated from university and, like her, could not find an appropriate job. In order to make their living together with their three children, they had to depend on financial support from their families.

The interviewees also described how they experienced the suppression exerted by the Ben Ali regime. The male interviewee who had left Tunisia described how Tunisians living outside the "Zones Touristique" were controlled with regard to their contacts to foreigners. He said that the police registered these contacts. Media was strongly censored and critical reports were banned from publication. Therefore, accounts of local uprisings, like the one in Gafsa in 2008 which was similar to the one in Sidi Bouzid, were not widely known inside Tunisia, at least not during the time when these rebellions took place.

During the second phase of the research, the third author was referred to one interviewee, an 'internet junkie', whose pattern of life may explain why internet and Facebook play such an important role in this specific social environment. When invited by his mother on the occasion of the first day of the Eid el Fitr, the feast at the end of Ramadan, the third author witnessed this 19-year-old young man online continuously on his smartphone, for example when he walked with the author to his favorite tea house where he and his friends would hang out until late at night. At the family's home the mother pointed out that all through the evening her son was checking his Facebook account. At the time the interview was conducted the young man was about to finish school. The mother worked as a web designer on a freelance base, and her husband served in the medical sector. Both parents told us that they regularly record films and music from TV or the internet and are thus very comfortable with using all kinds of electronic devices.

There is little doubt that the new media are pervasive among this educated population. The mother smiled when explaining that "nowadays" young girls even meet their future husbands via Facebook. Young people in Sidi Bouzid otherwise seem to have rather limited choices regarding how to spend their free time which may also partly explain this usage density. Allied to the fact of the general economic situation, this kind of 'chat', either face-to-face or via Facebook, was - as the internet activist put it - "*the only pastime these youngsters have*". On the other hand the limited pastime opportunities for young people originate in the rather traditional and patriarchal family structures where sons and daughters stay with their families until they get married. Broadly, therefore, young men visit street cafés while young women are more likely to be at home. Both groups, however, actively use their Facebook accounts while engaging in these constrained forms of social interaction.

Figure 2: Sidi Bouzid, Monument of the Tunisian Revolution (January 2012): At the place where the police woman humiliated Bouazizi, the newly erected site represents his fruit stand and the chairs of Ben Ali's regime which were overthrown by the uprising.

Against this social background, the uprising in Sidi Bouzid lasted from December 17, 2010 until January 14, 2011 (the day of Ben Ali's resignation). According to the information given by the young El-Nahda member, in the beginning it was only individuals who took to the streets; the protest was not organized and took place in a spontaneous manner, he said. The demonstrations continued throughout the four weeks of the uprising. However, they seem to have differed in intensity. Soon after the beginning of the demonstrations the Ben Ali regime sent a large number of additional police forces into the city. Our interviewees spoke of about 3.000-4.000 additional policemen who had built up a provisional camp inside the town. Some of the police forces left Sidi Bouzid and moved to other towns when civil uprising began there. The policemen used barbed wire, tear gas, and rubber bullets. At some point, it seems, there were also snipers of the Presidential Guard in town. However, it seems that they used rubber bullets rather than real ones. One of our interviewees showed us a scar on his leg that he said resulted from a rubber bullet. Our interviewees reported that in Kasserine and towns closer by, live ammunition was used by the police and led to dozens of injuries and deaths. Several demonstrators died when climbing electricity poles to engage with the demonstrating crowd by shouting their support.

The extent to which these disturbances constituted a 'danger' very much depended on individual perspectives. One taxi driver reported that, for him, life continued 'more or less as normal' right through the events, while activists who took part in the demonstrations were adamant that they perceived their lives to be in danger.

The first two authors later talked to a hotel owner in Tunis who traveled by car through the centre of Tunisia on January 5-8 (Gabes, Tozeur, Gafsa, Kasseritne, and Sidi Bouzid). He said that most of these cities were still accessible to travelers at that time. However, he avoided going into Sidi Bouzid because the city was full of policemen and it did not seem safe to go to the center. According to the different accounts of our interviewees it seemed that the local actors themselves did not know until the very last moment whether or not the rebellion would finally be successful, nor how events on the ground were actually unfolding.

Figure 3: Sidi Bouzid, Monument of the Tunisian Revolution (January 2012): A young man appropriates the monument to pose for the photo.

THE ROLE OF SOCIAL MEDIA

At the time of the uprising, the internet was not widespread in the households of Sidi Bouzid, at least via PC-based hardware. It was available in five internet cafes, run by a start-up ('Publinet'). Some schools had internet access; they were later used by the protestors. Cell phones and smartphones were, in contrast, rather common in Tunisia. Besides camera functionality, some smartphones offered mobile access to the internet. The Ben Ali regime had blocked some www-sites for political reasons, but, significantly, not the ones of WikiLeaks.

According to the interviewees social media played a key role in promoting the people's uprising. Almost all interviewees regarded Facebook as important for the revolution, along with the Qatar satellite TV program Al Jazeera, and a number of other media resources. In a personal conversation, a newly appointed Tunisian minister (a member of El-Nahda, the moderate Islamist party, who had been a political prisoner for almost 20 years under the Ben Ali regime) called both Facebook and Al Jazeera '*heroes of the Tunisian revolution*'. The following effects were attributed by the interviewees to social networking systems.

Information disseminated via Wikileaks: The cables of the US embassies played a major role in preparing the uprising by delegitimizing the Ben Ali regime. According to our interviewees there were mainly two topics of importance in the cables of the US embassy in Tunisia: (1) The documents offered a detailed account of the corruption of the Ben Ali regime. The diplomats had described in detail the ways in which the presidential family was corrupt, especially the relatives of Ben Ali's second wife, Leïla Trabelsi. The relatives of Ben Ali's wife had controlled the important sectors of the Tunisian economy and taken bribes. (2) The cables also revealed the intense level of cooperation between Ben Ali and the State of Israel. Wikileaks showed that the Ben Ali regime had provided information to Israel to help in the murder of a Palestinian leader in Tunis. Moreover, the cables revealed that Ben Ali had business relationships with Israel. Even before this information had been revealed to the Tunisians, they knew that the regime was corrupt; however, our interviewees pointed out to the fact that the involvement in the assassination of the Palestinian leader clarified the huge discrepancy between pro-Palestinian rhetoric and the actual politics of the Ben Ali regime. The young mother stated, *"Despite all announcements of Arab solidarity, you could see who their real friends were."* We were also interested in how people in Sidi Bouzid were able to access this information. It looks like most of them did not access the WikiLeaks platform directly, but rather depended on satellite TV coverage. For example, the young El-Nahda member and the internet activist interviewed by the third author mentioned that they got these news mediated via satellite TV – Al Jazeera and France 24, the French government television channel for international news and current affairs.

Reaching international media: In contrast to Egypt, in Tunisia all terrestrial TV stations were strictly state controlled (see section 3) and did not report on the events in Sidi Bouzid. According to almost all of our informants, satellite TV played a key role in making the local protests known countrywide (see section 3, concerning satellite TV distribution) and provided them with a basis on which they could decide whether or not they would actively take part in the demonstrations. Al Jazeera was the first and most influential TV channel in reporting on the Tunisian Revolution (e.g. see the quote from the Tunisian minister).

Al Jazeera did not have a correspondent in Tunisia. The station had been banned by the Ben Ali regime. However, on the same day that the self-immolation of Mohamed Bouazizi took place, Al Jazeera broadcast the news on this event via Satellite TV. However, the video materials of the self-immolation itself were not released at that point in time.

When doing research on the ground we encountered conflicting accounts for how Al Jazeera became so rapidly informed of events. According to the local internet radio producer, the video that shows Mohamed Bouazizi setting himself on fire was taken by two eyewitnesses both of whom were filming with their mobile phones. One of the eyewitnesses was working for the ambulance and in charge of bringing the heavily injured person to the local hospital.

The other eyewitness happened to be on the scene by chance. The internet radio producer added that some other individuals also might have filmed Bouazizi's self-immolation. A third activist, it seems, subsequently uploaded the video material of the self-immolation to his public Facebook account. Then Ali Bouazizi (not one of Mohamed Bouazizi's relatives) as well as at least one other activist called Al Jazeera in Qatar to inform them of the event. This means that in this version of how the information flowed the traditional media (Al Jazeera) followed events on the new media (Facebook).

The young member of the El-Nahda Party disagreed with this version of the information flow, saying that the initiative to search for a person who could give a statement on the event came from an Al Jazeera journalist who was originally from Sidi Bouzid. According to the El-Nahda member, the Al Jazeera journalist was probably first called by someone from Sidi Bouzid and then tried to find a suitable person from Sidi Bouzid who could give a statement. This person was, according to the young El-Nahda member, Ali Bouazizi. In this alternative version, the traditional media played a more active critical journalistic role.

While we were not able to resolve the contradictions between the two versions, both agree the Facebook platform played an instrumental role in making the material accessible to Al Jazeera, the Qatar-based satellite TV station. Also, both interviewees' versions agree on the fact that it was by means of a telephone call that the broadcasting station's attention was drawn to the events in Sidi Bouzid.

What is not in doubt is that, in the course of the evolving uprising, people/citizens on the ground continued to take photos and videos of the demonstrations and upload them to the internet; in turn Al Jazeera continued to monitor and sort out those photos and videos from the internet to broadcast them more broadly over satellite TV. Many of the photos and videos of the demonstrations were recorded with mobile phones and then uploaded to Facebook. The internet activist was of the opinion that "95% of this information was true and provided evidence" of what was happening.

As far the role of international media is concerned, according to the receptionist of the only Western hotel in town, international journalists arrived in Sidi Bouzid on January 10, 2012, four days before Ben Ali's resignation (of course, they would not have known at that time that the resignation would come within this period). Specifically in the first phase of our study interviewees expressed their distrust towards Western mass media they claimed had not covered their uprising for a long time and reported on Tunisia in what they saw as a biased manner (see section 4). Al Jazeera, in contrast, was trusted for its perceived impartiality and quick response to events.

Reaching out to other cities in Tunisia: A significant number of activists used their network of friends, specifically those who had Facebook accounts, to make people outside of Sidi Bouzid aware of what was going on in the town. The young mother explained that she had uploaded photos of the demonstrations to her Facebook account and pointed out the existence and the extent of the rebellion in Sidi Bouzid to friends in other Tunisian cities.

Since Sidi Bouzid does not have a university, all young adults who want to receive university education leave the town. The young mother explained that during her time at university she built a network of acquaintances and friends in other parts of the country. Facebook, it seems, is widely used by young Tunisians to foster and maintain networks after university. These country-wide social networks seem to be one of the reasons why the news about the ongoing political activities in Sidi Bouzid started to circulate widely. Other cities followed rather soon with demonstrations (Kasserine, also Taba and Sfax). Specifically important were two places close by called Reguets and Barzem.

In an overall estimate of impact, the internet activist and producer of the Sidi Bouzid internet radio was even of the opinion that information spread via public Facebook accounts (especially through the "share" function) played a more important role in making the local events known to the Tunisian public than the satellite programs broadcast by Al Jazeera. The sheer speed with which information about the self-immolation went 'viral' was, he argued, unprecedented. The previous uprising of 2008 in Gafsa had failed, he said, because at that time there was no medium available to spread the news across the country. Instead, he explained, all the news concerning the uprising in Gafsa was able to be suppressed by the Ben Ali regime. While this judgment may be partial a result of this activist's overestimation, it makes clear how important the role attributed to Facebook in this context is.

Organizing resistance inside the city: According to our informants Facebook also played a major role in helping activists and others to organize the uprising. The organizers of the local demonstrations used Facebook to develop and communicate their strategies for the next day, such as where to gather or where to build barricades overnight. For example, one of the male interviewees with whom the first authors spoke was able to access the internet via his smartphone. He told us that he searched Facebook regularly to find out when the next planned demonstration would take place and where to meet. If he found some announcements, he distributed this information among other potential participants and acquaintances. The ones without internet access he called with his mobile phone. The young mother told us that even the building of barricades was planned and reported via Facebook. On Facebook the demonstrators also shared advice on how to deal with attacks by the police, e.g., "*for tear gas do not use water but milk*", or on "*how to build molotovs*".

The demonstration in Tunis was the first one with a nationwide call for participation and seemed to have been organized mainly via Facebook. The use of telephones and the internet was especially important during the days of curfew when the citizens were not allowed to leave their houses at night. At the same time, it should be stated that the effects of this curfew were intermittent - we were told that gatherings in street cafes continued to take place, albeit in relatively small numbers.

Dealing with the regime's suppression in the virtual world: Importantly, the police of Ben Ali did not seem to be completely aware of the importance of social media nor well enough equipped to deal with it technically. Champagne (2012) argues that the version of the internet surveillance software delivered to the Tunisian secret service by an Italian company was not yet fully functional. However, the local police authorities did act against social media users. It was possible for them to do so because the Facebook accounts that published information on the uprising were usually set to public access to reach the largest possible number of users, in Sidi Bouzid as well as in other Tunisian cities. The internet activist and local radio producer interviewed by the third author said that already during the first three days of the uprising a total of 200 persons, among them 60 young adults, were arrested on charges of having uploaded video materials, pictures and news of the local uprising to their Facebook accounts. The internet activist added that as a result, Facebook and internet users began to use nicknames instead of real names in order to protect themselves from prosecution. More experienced users connected to the internet via proxy servers, hot spots, and used other ways to hide their identities. In the words of another person we talked to the declared goal was to leave "zero trace". As soon as one Facebook account was shut down by the authorities, a new one was opened under another name. The most "effective" measure taken by the authorities to suppress and obstruct the information flow between local internet activists was, however, to reduce the speed of data transfer by manipulating and pressurizing the local provider. Thus, it took a long time to upload video materials to Facebook accounts. A solution sought by the internet activists was to send the material abroad via email in a low resolution, often to friends in France, and to ask them to upload it for public use.

DISCUSSION

Our empirical findings indicate the important role Web 2.0 and specifically social media played in (1) overcoming the limitations of a strictly censored national media system; (2) converting a network of friends into a base for political activism; and (3) organizing political action under harsh oppression. At the same time, we should be careful not to ascribe these outcomes to the new media alone. Their role was, without question, mediated by a number of factors. Firstly, the existence of a large class of well-educated but economically underprivileged young people with a great deal of time on their hands created both a politically aware class which actively sought information, offered in parts through WikiLeaks, and a Facebook culture through which information could be disseminated. There is little doubt that resentments caused by the association of high educational standards, including a degree of 'internationalisation', with low economic expectations created a climate that a Facebook generation was able to amplify. Again, a 'learning' process was engendered, such that privacy settings became used to maximize exposure of images and video; anonymous accounts and proxy servers were used by the technically competent, and their use disseminated to others.

Secondly, the role of the new media cannot be understood without understanding the way in which it was used by the mass media (notably Al Jazeera) and how 'word of mouth' acted to amplify these communications. What is especially interesting is the way in which social and mass media were mutually elaborative. Though national mass media were strictly censored in Tunisia, satellite provision was not. Ironically, it was the coverage by a French government-owned satellite channel of the Wikileaks' story that helped destabilize a regime that was for a long time a close ally of the West, especially France.

It is intriguing that citizens from a provincial town in Tunisia were able to reach the Qatar satellite TV channel Al Jazeera; and, in turn, how Al Jazeera was able to make use of a social media application (specifically Facebook) to cover a political uprising in a country in which it was not allowed to have journalists in place. Specifically among young Tunisians, openly accessible Facebook pages are appropriated in such a way that they almost function like a mass medium.

Thirdly, some part of the use of the new media was a function of the ineptitude of the regime. The amplifying effect of new media use was additionally facilitated by the relative technical incapability of the Ben Ali regime to fight for its interests in social media spaces (Champagne 2012). We have documented some of the strategies internet activists applied to overcome interventions by the government's security apparatus. However, we should remind ourselves that government behavior in cases such as Iran or Syria has been demonstrably different. There, social media spaces have been used for technologically sophisticated secret service activities. To better understand the role social media can play in political uprisings, more research is needed into governments' use of surveillance technologies, such as Deep Packet Inspection, and activists' counter-reactions.

To summarize, the events in Tunisia can be understood as being the consequence of a number of interlocking elements, of which the new media are one, albeit important, part. We agree with Kavanaugh (2012) that the Tunisian demographic, young people (aged 15-29) making up a large part of the total population, and their relatively intense appropriation of social media contributes to the political importance of these media. The young Tunisian peoples' high level of education and economic dissatisfaction created both an information seeking and an information disseminating network. A mutually elaborating amalgam of the new media and the more traditional mass media then facilitated and amplified these effects in specific ways. Taken together, they constitute an 'information ecology' which explains the patterns we describe.

We have alluded to the fact that 'on the ground' studies of the kind we advocate are, in circumstances such as these, difficult and occasionally dangerous to conduct. They place serious methodological limitations on investigation. The data presented were gathered between 12 to 18 months after the uprising took place in Sidi Bouzid. The mass media coverage may have influenced the interviewees' perceptions with regard to the importance of social media. Collecting the data was not easy due to the inaccessibility of interviewees, their attitude towards foreign investigators, the situational dynamics, and security concerns on the side the interviewees as well as on the side of the researchers. We, nevertheless, believe that this study led to relevant insights. Our data, collected from local interviewees, can be seen as complementary to data collected from (micro) blog sites (Kavanaugh 2012, Ban Ani et al. 2012). For understanding the role of social media usage in political uprisings, such as the Arab Spring, 'on the ground' studies seem to us desirable if not essential. Following the result of our investigation, there are at least three reasons why 'on the ground'-studies are required:

(1) They can relate social media usage to a broader understanding of the actors' political and social positions and practices, such as the motivational factors that illustrate their participation in discussions, demonstrations, or their engagement in political parties and trade unions.
(2) They allow understanding of how the usage of particular social media applications works as part of the (collective) information and communication ecology of citizens and political activists. This way it is possible to investigate how people perceive certain information (received via different applications), how actors switch among different social media applications, how they transfer data to tools for individual communication, and how they try to reach mass media.
(3) They may allow understanding (aspects of) secretive media usages that would typically not be found by traditional on-line data collection methods. Thus, the use of anonymous accounts, proxy servers, differing public and private Facebook settings, and so on, is largely invisible to online investigation. Investigations into usage data of social media applications can uncover interesting pattern of appropriation. By analyzing retweeting behavior, Starbird and Palen (2012) could, for example, reveal interactions between those who were "on the ground" in Cairo and those who were not. While this is an interesting phenomenon, its importance and relevance 'on the ground' remain unclear. We do not know what overall use density looks like in such cases without some kind of triangulation. Interestingly, Twitter usage was not mentioned in the interviewees' accounts from Sidi Bouzid while it seems to be the main social media application to be investigated in understanding the Arab Spring (Starbird and Palen 2012; Kavanaugh et al. 2012). Tweets can be rather easily downloaded by researchers far away from the events. However, Twitter may not be the most important social media, at least not for emerging uprisings starting in provincial towns. Accounts mainly based on tweets may not offer a differentiated enough picture of the events on the ground.

CONCLUSION

We believe that investigations of on-line materials needs to be complemented by 'on the ground' studies, such as this paper, even though on the ground approaches may have their own limitations. As we have already stated, we do not see such studies replacing 'trace' ethnographies or indeed any other form of online inquiry. Rather, such on the ground studies provide a useful method of triangulation or 'reality' testing.

Hassanpour's (2012) rather generic model, which argues that social media can impede grass root mobilization seems to be problematic. It does not take the historically grown differences in societies, the structure and the location of the uprising, and the variation of (social) media types into account in the ways we suggest. Once one does, we find that glosses on the 'Arab Spring' disguise local variation. In the case of Tunisia, Sidi Bouzid was a local focal point in which an uprising started in the countryside and spread to the rest of the country, including the capital. It shows a different appropriation of social media than one which is based on a central square in the capital – as it was the case with the Egypt uprising centered around Tahrir Square.

Our study is an exploration of the role social media played in enabling the Arab Spring in one context. The role of political organizations such as trade unions, the lawyers' association, or the Muslim Brothers should not be underestimated and needs further investigation. However, our data seem to indicate that social media, in conjunction with the more traditional media, performed an amplifying role for people who might otherwise have been content with a lower level of participation (Arnstein 1969).

While the role of new (social and mobile) media will continue to be mediated by local and contingent factors, our aim with this paper is to make a small contribution to that literature which includes aspects of e-governance, the 'digital divide' and participatory agendas. This discourse has as much importance to Western countries as to those in the Middle East, given the sometimes over-stated arguments about the determining role of the new media. Our research suggests that a nuanced view of real political and economic forces as well as online affordances is desirable to better understand the design and appropriation of social media in fostering social participation.

ACKNOWLEDGEMENTS

We thank Batya Friedman, University of Washington, and five anonymous reviewers for their insightful comments and support in developing this manuscript.

REFERENCES

1. Al-Ani, B.; Mark, G-; Chung, J.; Jones, J.: The Egyptian Blogosphere: A Counter-Narrative of the Revolution, in: Proceedings of ACM-CSCW 2012, ACM-Press 2012, 17-26
2. Anderson, L.: Demystifying the Arab Spring, in: Foreign Affairs, Vol. 90, No 3, 2011, 2 - 7
3. Arnstein, Sherry R.: A Ladder of Citizen Participation, in: Journal of the American Institute of Planning, Vol. 35, Nr. 4, 1969, 216-224
4. Bettaieb, V. (ed.): Dégage - La Revolution Tunesienne, Editions du Layeur, Tunis 2011
5. Champagne, A.: Netznutzer: Software für Diktatoren (Users of the Net: Software for Dictators), in: Le Monde Diplomatique (German Version), January 2012, p. 6
6. Chen, W., Wellman, B. 2004. The Global Digital Divide- within and between countries. IT and Society. 1 (7), 39-45
7. CIA (ed.): The World Factbook, (WWW-access on February 5, 2012)
8. Diamond, L.: Liberation Technology, in: Journal of Democracy, Vol. 21, No. 3, July 2010, 69-83.
9. Geiger, R.S., & Ribes, D.: Trace Ethnography: Following Coordination through Documentary Practices, in: Proceedings of HICSS-44, IEEE Computer Society 2011
10. Gladwell, M.: Why the revolution will not be tweeted. The New Yorker, 2010. Retrieved February 23, 2012. http://www.newyorker.com/reporting/2010/10/04/101004fa_fact_gladwell
11. Hassanpour, N.: Media Disruption Exacerbates Revolutionary Unrest: Evidence from Mubarak's Natural Experiment: in: American Political Science Association (APSA) Annual Meeting, September 2011, Seattle, WA.
12. Hansard Society: eDemocracy - Exploring the social and political impacts of technology http://hansardsociety.org.uk/blogs/edemocracy/archive/2011/04/19/social-media-and-the-new-arab-spring.aspx (down loaded on August 25, 2012)
13. Howell, Joseph T.: Hard Living on Clay Street: Portraits of Blue Collar Families, Prospect Heights, Illinois: Waveland Press 1972
14. Kavanaugh, A., et al.: Between a Rock and a Cell Phone: Communication and Information Use during the Egyptian Uprising, in: of Proceedings of the 9th International ISCRAM Conference – Vancouver, Canada, April 2012
15. Lotan, G., Graeff, E., Ananny, M., Gaffney, D., Pearce, I. & Boyd, d. 2011. The revolutions were tweeted: Information flows during the 2011 Tunisian and Egyptian revolutions. International Journal of Communication, 5 (2011), 1375-1405.
16. Olaore, O.: Politexting: Using Mobile Technology to Connect the Unconnected and Expanding the Scope of Political Communication. Proceedings of ISECON, Wilmington, N. Carolina 2011
17. Palen, L., Anderson, K. M., Mark, G., Martin, J., Sicker, D., Palmer, M., and Grunwald, D.: A vision for technology-mediated support for public participation and assistance in mass emergencies and disasters, in: Proceedings of the 2010 ACM-BCS Visions of Computer Science Conference, British Computer Society, Swinton, UK, 2010, 1-12
18. Pipek, V.; Wulf, V.: Infrastructuring: Towards an Integrated Perspective on the Design and Use of Information Technology, in: Journal of the Association of Information System (JAIS), Vol. 10, Issue 5, May 2009, 306-332
19. Rohde, M.: Find what binds. Building social capital in an Iranian NGO community system, in: Huysman, M., Wulf, V. (eds.): Social Capital and Information Technology, MIT Press, Cambridge MA 2004, 75-112
20. Saeed, S.; Rohde, M.; Pipek, V.; Wulf, V.: Managing Nomadic Knowledge: A Case Study of the European Social Forum, in: Proceedings of ACM Conference on Computer Human Interaction (CHI 2010), ACM-Press, New York 2010, 537-546
21. Saeed, S.; Rohde, M.; Wulf, V.: Analyzing Political Activists' Organization Practices: Findings from a Long Term Case Study of the European Social Forum, in: Computer Supported Cooperative Work (JCSCW), Vol. 20, No. 4-5, 2011, 265-304
22. Sen, A.: Commodities and Capabilities. Amsterdam: North Holland 1985
23. Starbird, K.; Palen, L.: (How) Will the Revolution be Retweeted? in: Proceedings of ACM-CSCW 2012, ACM-Press, 7 – 16
24. Steyn, J. and Johanson, G.: ICTs and Sustainable Solutions for the Digital Divide: Theory and Perspectives. IGI Global: Hershey. PA 2011
25. Wulf, V.; Rohde, M.; Pipek, V.; Stevens, G.: Engaging with practices: design case studies as a research framework in CSCW, in Proceedings of ACM-CSCW 2011, 505-512

Using Facebook after Losing a Job: Differential Benefits of Strong and Weak Ties

Moira Burke
Facebook
mburke@fb.com

Robert Kraut
Human-Computer Interaction Institute
Carnegie Mellon University
robert.kraut@cs.cmu.edu

ABSTRACT
Among those who have recently lost a job, social networks in general and online ones in particular may be useful to cope with stress and find new employment. This study focuses on the psychological and practical consequences of Facebook use following job loss. By pairing longitudinal surveys of Facebook users with logs of their online behavior, we examine how communication with different kinds of ties predicts improvements in stress, social support, bridging social capital, and whether they find new jobs. Losing a job is associated with increases in stress, while talking with strong ties is generally associated with improvements in stress and social support. Weak ties do not provide these benefits. Bridging social capital comes from both strong and weak ties. Surprisingly, individuals who have lost a job feel greater stress after talking with strong ties. Contrary to the "strength of weak ties" hypothesis, communication with strong ties is more predictive of finding employment within three months.

Author Keywords
Social network sites; tie strength; social capital; social support; job loss; stress; unemployment.

ACM Classification Keywords
H.5.3. Information interfaces and presentation [Information Interfaces]: Group and Organization Interfaces Collaborative computing, Web-based interaction, Computer-supported cooperative work

INTRODUCTION
Unemployment is at very high levels, reaching 8.1% in the United States in early 2012 and 10.8% across the EU [8,19]. Job loss leads to a multitude of psychological and physical problems, including headaches, stress, depression, and suicide [47]. Beyond the financial hardship imposed by losing a job, individuals also lose daily structure, social contact, and shared goals with coworkers [31]. These changes make job loss an acute stressor that can lead to psychological distress [45].

When individuals form relationships with others, they build networks of mutual trust and reciprocity that provide them benefits they would not otherwise have, a phenomenon known as social capital [6,16,36,44]. Social capital derives from one's position in a social network and the number and character of the ties one maintains [12,48]. One's connections differ in tie strength or closeness, from lovers to near-strangers. Granovetter defined tie strength as a "combination of the amount of time, the emotional intensity, the intimacy (mutual confiding), and the reciprocal services which characterize the tie" [23].

There is strong theoretical rationale and empirical evidence that social networks can buffer people from stress, with positive consequences for their health and well-being [29]. Social networks also play a key role in coping with job loss and finding new employment [23,47]. Therefore, technology that facilitates social networking may be especially important for those who have recently lost a job.

This work examines the psychological and practical implications of social network site use following the loss of a job, particularly communication with strong ties—close friends likely to provide emotional support—and weak ties—diverse connections who may know about new job opportunities. The focus of the present study is recent job loss rather than long-term unemployment, when the shock is still fresh and individuals are struggling to accommodate the change. The research pairs longitudinal surveys measuring social support, social capital, stress, and employment status of approximately 3000 Facebook users with three months' behavioral data from the site's servers. Drawing from theories of tie strength and social capital, we examine how communication online with strong and weak ties moderates the impact of job loss on stress, and how communication with these ties is linked to changes in social support, bridging social capital, and actually finding a new job.

Tie Strength and Finding New Employment
Empirical research has demonstrated that both weak and strong ties can be helpful when people are looking for jobs. Having a large network of diverse, weakly connected ties provides access to novel information about jobs and other topics [23]. People tend to have strong ties who are similar to themselves and each other, and get their news from the same sources. As a result, strong ties tend to produce redundant information [39].

CSCW'13, February 23-27, 2013, San Antonio, Texas, USA.

In contrast, having weak ties who travel in different social circles exposes people to new ideas and opportunities. Putnam [44] refers to this dimension of relationships as "bridging social capital." In the context of job loss, weak ties traveling in diverse social circles are likely to know of new job opportunities [23]. They also provide greater access to external resources, such as an "in" with a human resources department at a company that's hiring, and when individuals are connected to multiple disparate clusters, they are especially likely to gain from those connections [12,36]. Motivated job seekers who put more time and effort into the networking aspect of their job search—tapping their informal connections for information—are more likely to find a job and receive more offers [47]. Many job leads arise from "serendipity," simply talking to the right acquaintance at the right time [40].

However, in some circumstances, strong ties may be more beneficial for job-seekers. Granovetter [23] distinguishes between *information* and *influence* flowing through one's social network. While weak ties may provide more novel information about job openings, strong ties may be more willing to wield their influence on behalf of a close friend or relative. For example, in China, people tap their social connections to influence authorities who then assign jobs as favors, an act that requires the mutual trust inherent in strong-tie relationships [4]. In a time of recession, when there are more layoffs than openings, job-seekers may need to rely on their strong ties to create openings for them in the first place. Strong ties may also be more likely to transmit information about a job opening simply by being more frequent communication partners; weak ties with relevant information are useless if they never talk to each other [1].

Social Network Site Use and Social Capital

Social network sites (SNS) such as Facebook, Google+, and LinkedIn facilitate connections, potentially surfacing the bridging benefits of weak ties and providing a channel for social support from strong ties.

The Pew Internet and American Life Project documents the rapid growth of SNS from 8% of American internet users in 2005 to 65% in 2011 [37]. Facebook is not just for weak ties, either; Pew reports that 40% of SNS users have "friended" all of their close confidants, up from 29% in 2008 [24]. More than one billion people actively use Facebook, half of whom log on to the site on any given day [20]. While the widespread use may be reason enough to better understand the consequences of SNS use, the sites also have features that set them apart from earlier communication technology, and there is both theoretical and empirical evidence to suggest these features affect interpersonal relationships and social capital following the loss of a job.

Most social network sites provide an aggregated stream of social news about all of one's ties; this is known as the "News Feed" on Facebook. The feed contains a frequently updated stream of ties' recent activity, including their photos, favorite links, and conversations with other friends. These short updates allow individuals to keep tabs on many ties at once, without the purposeful effort of an email or phone call. Facebook users take advantage of the News Feed to observe much larger numbers of ties than the small cluster they actively communicate with [2,34]. Facebook's feed differs from similar "social awareness feeds" [41] elsewhere on the web in that it comes from ties with whom a relationship has been mutually agreed upon. In addition, Facebook is unique in its scale, with ties coming from a enormous user base, likely to contain one's closest friends and family [24].

Users of social network sites also maintain profiles listing their recent activity, current city, friend network, interests, and often, their employment history. Both the profile and News Feed facilitate lightweight interaction, allowing ties to "Like" or comment on each other's content with little effort. Site users can broadcast their own news through status updates and photo posts, reaching a wide audience of ties with little effort per audience member. In theory, contributing to and consuming from the News Feed may promote the serendipity and bridging social capital that facilitate reemployment.

Many studies have explored the connection between SNS use and social capital. Social network site users generally have higher levels of bridging social capital than non-users [17,25]. However, social capital on these sites is most strongly associated with active, one-on-one communication with ties—known as *directed communication* in this work—rather than more voyeuristic reading of ties' news—known as *passive consumption* [10,11] or one-to-many *broadcasts* to wider circles of ties. Though social network sites decrease the costs of keeping up with many ties at once, research suggests that you need to talk to your ties, not simply read their news or have them read yours, to extract resources from them. An important reason why passive consumption and broadcasting do not seem to generate social capital is that they do not provide what Ellison and colleagues refer as "signals of relational investment" [17]. People are never sure who has seen what. Explicit communication, such as commenting on a tie's news or writing on her wall, is required to notify a tie that her news was seen and mattered.

Therefore, the present work emphasizes the effect of directed communication with ties, rather than passive consumption or broadcasting. And while much of the computer-mediated communication literature examines the different effects of communicating with strong versus weak ties, the distinction has not been examined on social network sites, where profiles and dissemination of news may affect both feelings of tie strength and the likelihood of communicating with a given tie. Communication type and partner are often intertwined; the exchange of frequent, personalized messages is a characteristic of close-tie relationships [21], while generic broadcasts are a way to keep up with a large network of acquaintances [18].

However, with a large enough sample, communication type and partner can be examined separately. In particular, this work describes the different effects of one-on-one communication with strong ties—who may provide needed support and sympathy—and with weak ties—who may provide a bridge to new job.

Communicating online with strong ties can lead to improvements in well-being typically associated with emotional support (e.g., declines in depression symptoms), while communicating with strangers online does not deliver this benefit [3]. Adolescents who communicate with strong ties online are much happier than those who communicate with strangers [46]. Strong ties provide significantly more emotional aid, minor services, and companionship, as well as a broader array of social support than do weak ties [48], and so interacting with strong ties should be associated with greater increases in social support and reductions in stress than talking with weak ties.

H1. Directed communication with strong ties will be associated with reductions in stress, while directed communication with weak ties will not.

H2. Directed communication with strong ties will be associated with increases in social support, while directed communication with weak ties will not.

Tie Strength and Psychological Distress After Job Loss

Those who have recently lost a job feel greater levels of deprivation and anxiety about "getting by," and social support alleviates many of the psychological and physical responses to unemployment [22,47]. This form of emotional support typically comes from one's strong ties, including family and spouses, rather than weak ties, who are less invested in one's well-being [48]. Strong ties provide financial support, assist with moving, and lend a shoulder to cry on. The social support and companionship of strong ties is often a buffer, allowing an individual to cope with stress [30]. Moreover, the mere perception that others—even a single close tie—will provide aid when needed may have benefit in its own right. Perceived support is associated with lower levels of anxiety, distress, and depression [13].

However, strong ties can be inept at providing the right kind of support in a personal crisis, such as losing a job. Family members who haven't been directly affected by the crisis may make unhelpful statements, by pushing for recovery too quickly or aggressively offering unwanted advice, which elicits resentment from the receiver [35,50]. Gender differences in coping strategies cause mismatches in spouses, where husbands tend to hide problems, give unwanted advice, and be bothered by their wives' emotional expressivity [45]. Furthermore, strong ties may push a person to move on too quickly because they themselves are uncomfortable with their friend's distress [35]. Though strong ties are typically the providers of emotional support, it is unclear how they will affect individuals who recently lost a job.

Thus, while online communication with strong ties generally provides social capital benefits, it is not clear whether doing so provides the same benefits to individuals who have recently lost a job. Those strong ties may provide much-needed emotional support in a time of crisis, or may pressure an individual to find a new job quickly.

RQ1. How does job loss moderate the effect of strong-tie communication on stress and social support?

Although strong ties are associated with emotional support, weak ties on the internet seem to be especially valuable for getting informational support, such as finding resources before moving to a new location [27]. Weak ties provide novel information, connections to more diverse perspectives, and reminders of connections to a wider community [23]. Interacting with them should be linked with increases in bridging social capital [44]. Strong ties, with their redundant information and mutual, closed friendships, should not provide as great a bridging benefit.

H3. Directed communication with weak ties will be associated with greater increases in bridging social capital than will directed communication with strong ties.

However, when it comes to actually finding a new job in a recession, do the information benefits of weak ties trump the potential influence of strong ties? The reduced communication frequency inherent in weak-tie relationships may also result in a weak tie knowing of a relevant job opening, but not conveying it to a job-seeker. Strong ties may have less diverse information, but may be better able to transfer knowledge through their greater relational "bandwidth" [1]. For those who have lost a job, will talking with strong ties or weak ties be associated with a greater likelihood of finding a new job?

RQ2. Is directed communication on social network sites with strong or weak ties more predictive of finding a new job?

METHOD

To analyze the relationship between online communication, job loss, and stress, support, and social capital, we conducted a three-wave panel survey of Facebook users beginning in early June 2011, with follow-up waves in early July and August 2011. The survey contained measures of stress, social support, and bridging social capital, and questions about tie strength with a subset of respondents' Facebook friends. Survey responses were matched to the server logs of the participants' activity on Facebook beginning one month prior to the first survey and concluding on the date of the last survey.

Participants

Participants (*N* = 10,557, 54% female) were recruited through a combination of Facebook ads and email invitations. Recruiting was targeted at a random sample of English-speaking users around the world, aged 18 or older, who had been active on the site in the previous 30 days, stratified by gender and Facebook use (number of login days in the past month). After clicking on the survey link, respondents completed an online consent form, which invited them to participate and informed them about the nature of the research and that their questionnaires would be anonymously matched with their online behavior on Facebook in aggregate with the other participants.

A subset of participants, (n = 3,358, 59% female), who completed at least two consecutive waves, is included in the analysis. Compared to a random sample of Facebook users, survey respondents were older (M = 45.2 vs. 29.9, $p < 0.001$), and 11% more likely to be female (χ^2= 108.1, $p <$ 0.001). They were heavier Facebook users, with approximately 70 more friends than the average user, about twice the likelihood of logging in during the week prior to the survey. Dropouts were younger than returnees (M = 40.7 and 45.2 years, respectively, $p < 0.001$), had fewer online friends (M = 196 and 203, respectively, p = 0.04), and were 8% less likely to be female, (χ^2 =51.6, $p < 0.001$). There are no differences in communication volume with strong or weak ties or job status at Time 1. Survey participants came from 91 countries (48% from the US). Approximately 5% (183) reported losing a job during the three months of the study, and 13% (449) started a new job.

Behavioral Log Data: Independent Variables

Site activity was collected for the participants beginning one month prior to the first survey through the date of the final survey, three months later. All variables were aggregated from server logs and anonymized. All behavioral variables follow heavy-tailed distributions and have variances larger than their means (see Table 1). To control for skew, they were log-transformed (base 2, after adding 1) and then standardized by centering at the mean and dividing by the standard deviation. Activity variables were divided into three conceptual categories based on the nature of the interaction, described below. Within each category variables are highly correlated with each other and so are collapsed into a single composite scale representing the entire category.

Directed communication consists of targeted, one-on-one exchanges between a user and a friend, such as a private message, a wall post, or a comment (see Table 1 for complete list). The exchange may be visible by other people (e.g., a wall post), but is directed from one person to another, and the target receives a notification. Inbound and outbound directed communication are highly correlated (r = 0.89), and results are qualitatively similar using a measure combining inbound and outbound communication. Since the goal of this work is to understand the impact of one's network *on* a job seeker, inbound communication is used in the present analyses. Directed communication is further divided into communication with strong ties and communication with weak ties, to be described shortly.

Passive consumption is viewing and reading other friends' content, and includes counts of News Feed stories clicked

Facebook activity scales and items	Median	Mean	Std. Dev.	Correlation with scale
Directed communication from strong ties (scale alpha = 0.87)				
Comments received	2.0	14.1	34.6	0.87
Likes received	3.0	16.8	44.9	0.87
Messages received	2.0	9.5	36.0	0.79
Pokes received	0.0	4.3	28.3	0.49
Content friends saved on wall	0.0	0.4	1.8	0.57
Wall posts received	0.0	1.9	4.6	0.72
Photos tagged in	0.0	3.1	20.9	0.61
Distinct people user received direct communication from	4.0	8.1	10.6	0.88
Directed communication from weak ties (scale alpha = 0.86)				
Comments received	7.0	31.6	74.2	0.87
Likes received	7.0	33.8	94.5	0.86
Messages received	3.0	12.8	40.4	0.78
Pokes received	0.0	3.5	28.3	0.52
Content friends saved on wall	0.0	0.4	1.3	0.56
Wall posts received	0.0	3.3	13.3	0.65
Photos tagged in	0.0	9.7	34.8	0.66
Distinct people user received direct communication from	16.0	30.7	48.5	0.85
Passive consumption (scale alpha = 0.58)				
Profiles viewed	130.0	333.9	657.6	0.91
News feed stories clicked on	22.0	75.9	284.6	0.53
Photos viewed	0.0	73.4	302.8	0.55
Distinct people whose content user consumed	58.0	112.8	168.2	0.83
Broadcasting (scale alpha = 0.51)				
Photos posted	0.0	2.0	4.5	0.49
Content posted to own wall	1.0	6.6	21.3	0.83
Status updates	2.0	7.8	20.0	0.83

Table 1. Descriptive statistics for participant activities across one month. Composite scales were created for each section (e.g., "passive consumption") using log-transformed, standardized versions of these variables.

on, profiles visited, and photos viewed. This scale measures the extent to which a user consumes content, but does not communicate with the friend about it.

Broadcasting is the posting a user performs to a wider audience, including photo uploads and status updates. This scale includes anything that is not targeted at a single friend. While some users have privacy settings enabled so that their broadcasts go to a limited number of Facebook friends, these actions are still counted as broadcasting to distinguish them from the single-friend focus of directed communication.

Survey Content

Participants completed an online survey of validated scales described below. All measures were scored using the mean of 5-pt Likert scales.

Stress (10 items, scale alpha = 0.87) measures the degree to which situations in one's life are perceived as stressful [14]. Participants report how often they felt in the last month "Unable to control the important things in my life" and "Difficulties were piling up so high that I could not overcome them."

Social support (12 items, scale alpha = 0.88) is measured with the Interpersonal Support Evaluation List, assessing the functional components of social support [15]. The scale includes items such as "When I need suggestions on how to deal with a personal problem, I know someone I can turn to" and "If I needed some help in moving to a new house or apartment, I would have a hard time finding someone to help me." This scale is comparable to Putnam's concept of "bonding social capital" [44], and has been called that in previous work [10,11,18,49]. Social support is inversely correlated with stress (r = -0.49).

Bridging social capital (10 items, scale alpha = 0.87) measures the extent to which an individual is connected to a wide variety of people and feels part of a greater community [49]. Sample items include "Based on the people I interact with, it is easy for me to hear about new job opportunities" and "Interacting with people makes me interested in what people unlike me are thinking." Bridging social capital is moderately correlated with social support, r = 0.41, and inversely correlated with stress, r = -0.25.

Job status. Participants also reported whether any major life events had occurred in the previous month, derived from the Social Readjustment Rating Scale [28], including losing a job or getting a new one. Each was measured with a binary variable (checkbox) indicating whether the event occurred between survey waves.

Tie strength of communication partners. Responding to a prompt to identify "people you discuss important matters with, really enjoy socializing with, or anyone else you feel especially close to," participants selected up to six of their closest Facebook friends. Hampton and colleagues have demonstrated these "name generators" successfully elicit one's closest ties [38]. Participants selected a mean of 4.4 close friends. After participants selected close friends, the survey software randomly selected additional Facebook friends to bring the total to eight. For each of the eight friends, participants then evaluated "How close do you feel to [tie name]" on a 7-pt scale ranging from "Not at all close" to "Extremely close."

Participants' ratings of their eight ties were then used to train a model of tie strength across all of their ties on Facebook (see [9] for full details). Briefly, the model of tie strength is a multilevel linear regression at the dyad level, with independent variables coming from Facebook's server logs and users' profiles. For each dyad (whose members are referred to as 'ego' and 'alter'), tie strength is a linear combination of directed communication within the dyad (e.g., number of messages ego sent alter, number of comments alter left for ego), passive consumption by ego (e.g., ego's views of alter's profile or photos), static information about each person (e.g., age, gender) and static information about each dyad (e.g., number of days since the Facebook friendship was initiated, whether they live in the same city, whether they've stated that they're "in a relationship" together, number of mutual friends). In a held-out sample, predicted and self-reported tie strength were highly correlated (r = 0.66). The model was then applied to the participants in the present study, generating a tie strength rating for each of their Facebook friendships, approximately 2.4 million ties.

For the following analyses, tie strength was converted to a binary variable (strong versus weak) for each friend, with an estimate of 5 (out of the 7-point scale) as the strong-tie cutoff (inclusive). The cutoff was the average (both mean and median) estimated tie strength score for the ties participants selected as their very close friends. With this threshold, 39.4% of participants' ties were considered "strong" and the median user had 38 strong ties (M = 47). Directed communication actions were then counted separately, depending on whether they were exchanged with a strong or weak tie. Users received approximately half (52%) of their directed communication from strong ties according to this metric. This threshold may differ somewhat from Granovetter's, including more ties in the "strong" category, but is based on survey participants' empirical selections of people to whom they feel especially close. A binary threshold was used for mathematical simplicity in the regression models, and sensitivity tests with strong-tie cutoffs of 4 and 6 were also performed. They generally confirm the main analyses reported below and are discussed where appropriate.

Method of Analysis

To determine how site use relates to changes in stress, social support, and social capital, a linear multilevel model with a lagged dependent variable was used with the following form:

$$Y_t = \alpha Y_{t\text{-}30} + \beta_0 J_{(t..t\text{-}30)} + \beta_1 DCS_{(t..t\text{-}30)} + \beta_2 DCW_{(t..t\text{-}30)} + \beta_3 P_{(t..t\text{-}30)} + \beta_4 B_{(t..t\text{-}30)} [+\beta_5 JxDCS_{(t..t\text{-}30)} + \beta_6 JxDCW_{(t..t\text{-}30)}] + \varepsilon_t$$

Where:

Y =Dependent variable (Stress, Support, or Bridging capital)

J = Lost job

DCS = Directed communication with strong ties

DCW = Directed communication with weak ties

P = Passive consumption

B = Broadcasting

Because it includes a lagged dependent variable, the model therefore measures changes in the outcome (e.g., stress) associated with the activity variables (e.g., directed communication with strong or weak ties) that took place in the month between surveys. This form of autoregressive lagged model is common in econometrics and is appropriate when the dependent variable is stationary (the mean and variance do not change over time) and model residuals are not highly autocorrelated, as is the case here. Lagged independent variables (site activity the previous month) are not included because they are highly collinear, and thus would produce biased estimates [33]. All continuous independent variables are centered at their means and standardized.

Unlike cross-sectional models common in much research in this area, which simply correlate independent and dependent variables at a single time (e.g., [21]), this model is both more sensitive and less biased, in effect controlling for an individual's previous level of the outcome variable (e.g., stress) and all of the unmeasurable factors that contribute to it. This model then reveals the relationship between activity variables in the past month and changes in the outcome. While it is impossible to truly determine a causal relationship between the independent and dependent variables without a randomized assignment of participants—e.g., randomly preventing or encouraging Facebook users' friends to communicate with them for a month—this model is appropriate for observational studies.

For each participant, there are two or three observations of stress. As observations from the same participant are not independent of each other, the model was grouped at the individual level, treating participant as a random effect (not shown in the model above). Age and gender were included as controls (not shown). Country was not a significant predictor of any outcome and was excluded.

RESULTS AND DISCUSSION

Stress. First, we examine the relationship between Facebook use and stress. Table 2a presents influence of losing a job last month on stress, controlling for age, gender and stress the previous month. The intercept value of 2.37 is the stress level (out of 5) for the average person in the sample (a 45 year-old woman who felt the mean amount of stress last month and did the mean amount of directed communication, passive consumption, and broadcasting between surveys). Coefficients are additive. So, the coefficient on the lagged stress variable ($\beta = 0.77$) indicates that an otherwise identical woman whose stress last month was one point higher than average would have a current stress level of 3.14 (2.37 + 0.77). Participants who had just lost their jobs reported substantially higher stress levels, as expected, $\beta = 0.27, p < 0.001$.

Table 2b shows changes in stress associated with increases in the three classes of Facebook activities: directed communication with strong and weak ties, passive consumption, and broadcasting. Talking one-on-one with strong ties on Facebook is associated with reductions in stress, while talking with weak ties is not. Hypothesis 1 is supported. For every one-unit increase in directed communication with strong ties people participate in

	Table 2a. Stress		Table 2b. Stress		Table 2c. Stress	
	Beta	SE	Beta	SE	Beta	SE
Intercept	2.37 ***	0.01	2.37 ***	0.01	2.37 ***	0.01
Stress last month	0.77 ***	0.01	0.77 ***	0.01	0.77 ***	0.01
Lost job last month	0.27 ***	0.05	0.27 ***	0.05	0.26 ***	0.05
Facebook activity						
Directed communication from strong ties			-0.03 *	0.01	-0.03 *	0.01
Directed communication from weak ties			-0.02	0.02	-0.02	0.02
Passive consumption			0.02	0.01	0.02	0.01
Broadcasting			0.02	0.01	0.02	0.01
Interactions with job loss						
Lost job x Dir. communication with strong ties					0.20 *	0.09
Lost job x Dir. communication with weak ties					-0.02	0.08
*** $p < 0.001$ ** $p < 0.01$ * $p < 0.05$	$R^2 = 0.57$		$R^2 = 0.57$		$R^2 = 0.57$	

Number of observations: 5,285 Number of groups: 3,358 Age and gender included as controls (not shown).

Tables 2a-c. Changes in stress levels associated with losing a job and Facebook use. Directed communication with strong ties is associated with reductions in stress, but those who have recently lost a job feel increases in stress with strong-tie communication.

(approximately 40 additional comments and/or likes in the past month), their stress level declines by β = -0.03 points (p = 0.04). The effect does not come from talking generally, since it is not seen with directed conversation with weak ties (p = .27). Indeed passive communication and broadcast communication are associated with marginal increases in stress (p = .06 and .10 respectively).

Table 2c examines whether Facebook communication moderates the impact of job loss on stress. The interaction between losing a job and directed communication with strong ties shows that stress increases more with strong tie communication for those who have lost a job (β = 0.20, p = 0.02). Average people who lose a job and have one unit more directed communication with strong ties end up with more stress (2.37 + .77 +. 27 -.03 +. .20 = 3.31) than do comparable people with average communication with close ties (2.37 + .77 +. 27 = 3.14). In fact, the magnitude of this increase is about the same size as the stress incurred from losing a job in the first place (β = 0.26).

Why is communicating with strong ties so bad in this case? Strong ties often make the psychological distress of job loss worse by offering unhelpful advice and pushing for recovery too quickly [50]. Individuals may feel greater embarrassment or imposition from their strong ties (who know of the job loss and may be providing financial support offline) than weak ties (who are more peripheral, so are less likely to know), and so perhaps receiving contact from strong ties heightens that embarrassment and pressure to get a new job. They may feel their independence threatened, increasing resentment rather than relief [5]. Strong ties also experience anxiety about doing anything upsetting, which may cause them to switch to more "automatic" or "casual" modes of help-giving, making them less encouraging [35]. When prompted to describe whether Facebook made them feel better or worse about their lives, participants who had lost their jobs remarked,

"Worse . . . Everyone wants to know if I got a job already!"

"I feel worse about losing my job when using Facebook. I find it really hard to connect with people who care about me/my life. I get a lot of pity comments on Facebook"

Note that individuals who recently lost a job did not use Facebook differently than those who did not lose a job. There are no significant differences between the two groups on inbound or outbound directed communication with strong or weak ties, passive consumption, or broadcasting (p > 0.28 in all cases). Therefore, individuals who lost a job were not changing their communication habits online; rather, they are experiencing different outcomes from the same kinds of communication.

Social support. Table 3 shows that perceived social support improves with strong-tie communication, but does not change significantly with weak-tie communication. Hypothesis 2 is supported. Each one-unit increase in communication with strong ties is associated with a β =

	Social support	
	Beta	SE
Intercept	3.79 ***	0.01
Support last month	0.72 ***	0.01
Lost job last month	-0.07 ***	0.04
Facebook activity		
Directed communication from strong ties	0.05 ***	0.01
Directed communication from weak ties	0.03	0.01
Passive consumption	-0.02 *	0.01
Broadcasting	-0.02	0.01
Interactions with job loss		
Lost job x Dir. communication with strong ties	-0.09	0.09
Lost job x Dir. communication with weak ties	0.04	0.08
*** $p < 0.001$ ** $p < 0.01$ * $p < 0.05$		$R^2 = 0.56$

Number of observations: 5,285 Number of groups: 3,358
Age and gender included as controls (not shown).

Table 3. Social support increases with directed communication from strong ties but not from weak ties. Passive consumption is associated with decreases in support.

0.05 point increase in social support (p < 0.001). Weak-tie communication is associated with a non-significant increase in social support, β = 0.03, p = 0.06. This trend suggests that some support may come from ties at the higher end of the "weak tie" cutoff, and so we performed a sensitivity test (not shown) in which the cutoff to define a strong tie was lowered to 4. In this case, the distinction between strong- and weak-tie communication is magnified: communication with strong ties (those 4 or higher) is associated with a β = 0.06 increase in support (p < 0.001), while communication with weak ties is not (β = 0.00, p = 0.77). These results indicate that communicating with closer friends on Facebook activates feelings of support, a benefit not derived from weaker acquaintances. Furthermore, Table 3 also shows that, holding constant directed communication, passive consumption is associated with decreases in social support, (β = -0.02, p = 0.04). This finding is consistent with previous results suggesting that to benefit from ties, one must actively engage them, rather than simply read about their lives [10,17].

No significant interaction effect was found between job loss and strong- or weak-tie communication on perceived social support (p = 0.28 and p = 0.62, respectively). Combined, these results suggest that strong ties provide support generally, but that in the case of job loss, their presence may exacerbate feelings of embarrassment or distress, heightening stress levels. Weak ties, on the other hand, don't provide support, but neither do they aggravate the stress of unemployment.

Now we turn to the question of whether those weak ties provide bridging social capital and new jobs for the recently unemployed. Table 4 presents a model with bridging social capital as the outcome. It shows that bridging social capital increases with both strong-tie (β =

	Bridging social capital	
	Beta	SE
Intercept	3.76 ***	0.01
Bridging social capital last month	0.65 ***	0.01
Lost job last month	0.00	0.05
Facebook activity		
Directed communication from strong ties	0.04 **	0.01
Directed communication from weak ties	0.04 **	0.01
Passive consumption	-0.03 **	0.01
Broadcasting	0.01	0.01
Interactions with job loss		
Lost job x Dir. communication with strong ties	-0.10	0.08
Lost job x Dir. communication with weak ties	0.15 *	0.08
*** $p < 0.001$ ** $p < 0.01$ * $p < 0.05$	$R^2 = 0.46$	

Number of observations: 5,285 Number of groups: 3,358
Age and gender included as controls (not shown).

Table 4. Bridging social capital increases with directed communication on Facebook with both strong and weak ties. Those who have recently lost a job feel greater increases in bridging through weak-tie communication.

0.04, p = 0.003) and weak-tie (β = 0.04, p = 0.006) communication on Facebook. A sensitivity test raising the threshold for "strong tie" to 6 (not shown) provides similar results, with bridging still significantly associated with both strong and weak ties. Hypothesis 3 is partially supported. Passive consumption is again linked to decreases in bridging social capital, holding constant directed communication (β = -0.03, p = 0.002). Moreover the interaction effect shows that those who have recently lost a job feel greater increases in bridging social capital when talking with their weak ties (β = 0.15, p = 0.04). Given that those who have lost a job do not communicate in greater volumes with their weak ties, one interpretation is that job seekers approach those interactions with acquaintances with a different mindset, perceiving them as more useful in their job hunt, or that the content of their exchanges differ. That communication with weak ties is associated with increases in bridging social capital but not social support or stress reduction suggests that both strong ties and weak ties can provide bridging social capital, at least in the context of Facebook.

Getting a job. Finally, we examine whether Facebook use is associated with getting a new job, and find that it is. Table 5 presents a logistic regression on the subset of participants who reported losing a job in the first or second surveys (n = 169), with the outcome being whether they reported a new job by the third survey. The intercept of -1.68 indicates that those who lost their jobs had a 15.7% probability of finding a new one within three months. Those who spoke one unit more with their strong ties were roughly twice as likely to find a new job, with a 33.2% probability (p = 0.03). In contrast, weak-tie communication

	Found a new job	
	Beta	SE
Intercept	-1.68 ***	0.33
Age	-0.04 *	0.01
Male	0.58	0.39
Facebook activity		
Directed communication from strong ties	0.98 *	0.44
Directed communication from weak ties	-1.00	0.55
Passive consumption	0.32	0.37
Broadcasting	0.15	0.29
*** $p < 0.001$ ** $p < 0.01$ * $p < 0.05$ N = 169		$R^2 = 0.12$

Table 5. Directed communication with strong ties is associated with an increased likelihood of finding a new job within three months.

is marginally associated with a decline in the odds of finding a new job (p = .07). A post-hoc comparison confirms that the effect of talking with strong ties is greater than that of weak ties on finding a job (p = 0.02). Results are qualitatively similar for a regression containing all participants, not just those who reported losing a job, as some participants moved to or added new jobs without reporting losing a previous position. Talking to strong ties on Facebook is associated with an increased likelihood of finding a new job. Surprisingly, weak-tie communication is not.

General Discussion

In summary, this research demonstrates that Facebook communication predicts changes in the psychological and practical outcomes associated with losing a job. Directed communication with strong ties generally had positive effects, and was associated with overall reductions in stress, increases in perceived social support, increases in bridging social capital and the likelihood of finding a job. However, it was also associated with strong increases in stress among those who recently lost a job. Directed communication with weaker ties had weaker effects. Consistent with the idea that weak ties bring access to new information, communication with them was associated with increases in bridging social capital, and especially so among people who recently lost a job. However, inconsistent with Granovetter's strength of weak ties hypothesis, communication with weak ties was not associated with getting a new job.

By distinguishing communication partners, this work goes beyond previous studies that failed to find a connection between social network site use and improvements in social support [10]. By examining differences between strong and weak-tie partners, we see results consistent with other forms of computer-mediated communication literature, that emotional support comes from strong ties [3,46].

One limitation of this work is that we do not know exactly how participants reduced their stress, found support or found their new jobs—whether through a specific strong or weak tie, a combination of them, or through more formal channels. We simply correlate their communication in aggregate with strong and weak ties with their success. Furthermore, we do not analyze the content of those messages, but simply count the number of exchanges. This process ensures participant privacy but means that we do not know whether certain exchanges were higher in supportive language or job-relevant links. Strong ties may communicate more offline or via other channels, as well [26], and those interactions are not captured here. However, communication on Facebook is highly correlated with talking face-to-face, on the phone, and over email [9].

Although these results are consistent with a thesis that causal effects of interpersonal communication on psychological and practical outcomes depend on one's closeness to the communication partners, they do not identify the pathways producing these effects, assuming they exist. Below we speculate on some of the causal processes that could account for the patterns of results observed in this research.

The prior research literature on the psychological effects of interpersonal communication and social support suggest multiple routes by which communication with others in one's social network can reduce stress or have other positive benefits. Communication with others in one's social network can provide informational support (e.g., information about unemployment benefits or job prospects) [23], emotional support [42] such as expressions of concern or empathy, companionship and distraction to prevent rumination, or even the opportunity to offer support to others [7]. Moreover communication with others, especially close ties, provides opportunities to express one's emotions and cognitively process problems, and this self-expression has benefits independent of responses from others [43].

Literature on personal crises suggests that the most advantageous forms of support come from connecting people with others who are in similar circumstances and from allowing emotional expression [47,50]. Social network sites are perfect venues for that, and some users are taking advantage, such as laid-off coworkers who use Facebook to commiserate and share resumes. Wortman and colleagues [50] find that one of the most helpful responses to personal crises is providing people the ability to express their emotions. Participants reported that Facebook both hindered and helped this expression. Several participants reported that negative news does not belong in status updates—that they should be artificially cheery online:

"no one really shares sad or distressing stuff. They must have some concerns, but most of my contacts act as if they do not. So in comparison, I feel worse."

"Facebook has not made me feel better or worse about my new job. It did, however, make me feel worse when I was unemployed and I would regularly read newsfeed status updates celebrating personal successes."

And so those who have lost a job may feel constrained from sharing their true feelings. This may also account for the general reductions in well-being associated with passive consumption behavior. Consider two people, Alice and Brenda, who are identical in every way, including the amount of one-on-one conversation they have with friends on Facebook each month. Brenda, however, spends additional time looking at friends' profiles, photos, and status updates, but does not write to those friends. Despite viewing social news about a wide circle, Brenda feels less supported by and connected to them. One interpretation is that the content of the passive consumption matters, as does the relative state of the viewer—when individuals see news of their ties succeeding and they themselves do not feel successful, it aggravates feelings of distress or loneliness. These quotes are consistent with empirical work showing that people routinely assume their peers are having more fun than they are [32]. Future work should investigate the contexts under which passive consumption elicits social comparison and ways to mitigate negative consequences.

At the same time, respondents did feel support from ties on Facebook, especially when they found new jobs and posted the news:

"Felt a little better with supporting comments about losing my job. My friends gave me a better outlook on the situation."

"Better, I posted my new job (and upcoming move) on FB and I got so many nice comments"

Being able to connect with others in similar circumstances is a source of comfort after a crisis [35], and respondents frequently mentioned commiserating through the site.

"Yes, [I] am able to commiserate with other colleagues on losing our jobs (due to Bank failure) and getting prospects for new opportunities."

"Been able to share my worries, get help on Cvs, job hunting and general chit chat about whats happening to others."

"Much better it is way easier to stay connected when looking for employment t see what others found. If someone finds a lead they cannot use they pass it on in case anyone else can use it. We are finding jobs"

"It has made me feel a whole lot better - I have been able to share the ups and downs of my life with others who are in similar circumstances - and we have all been able to support each other emotionally."

Yet many of those who have recently lost a job do not know others in their network who are in the same situation, as people feel compelled to hold back negative personal news. If users had a way to discreetly identify that they were looking for work (such as a private setting in their profiles that was not visible to others), the site could automatically re prioritize content that would be more beneficial to them. Their news could be distributed more widely among ties who work for local companies that are hiring, increasing the likelihood of a fruitful match. The site could recommend resources such as online groups for the recently unemployed, or more targeted groups based on geographic region and educational background, so that individuals could sympathize with similar others and share job leads. Ads for local industries that are hiring could be targeted at the people who would be most likely to be a good match.

CONCLUSION

Unemployment is high across much of the United States and the European Union, and those who have recently lost a job are using social network sites just as much as their employed peers. Yet they experience different outcomes from the same kinds of actions, and the tool that can be so powerful for generating the connections they need to find a new job may also intensify stress when it provides unhelpful advice from strong ties. For those who have not recently lost a job we find that stress and support improve with communication from strong ties, while weak ties do not provide these psychological benefits. Finally, we find that passive consumption of ties' news is linked to decreases in social support and bridging social capital, and that to extract benefits from one's ties online, it is important to directly engage them. Social network sites provide great opportunities for those who have recently lost a job, but the effects depend on whom they talk to.

ACKNOWLEDGMENTS

The authors would like to thank Sara Kiesler, Justine Cassell, Sinan Aral, Cameron Marlow, Adam Kramer, and other members of the Facebook Data Science Team. This work was supported by NSF IIS-0808711, and graduate research fellowships from the NSF and Google.

REFERENCES

1. Aral, S. and Van Alstyne, M. The Diversity-Bandwidth Trade-off. *American Journal of Sociology 117*, 1 (2011), 90–171.
2. Backstrom, L., Bakshy, E., Kleinberg, J., Lento, T.M., and Rosenn, I. Center of attention: How facebook users allocate attention across friends. *Proc. 5th International Conference on Weblogs and Social Media*, (2011), 1–8.
3. Bessière, K., Kiesler, S., Kraut, R., and Boneva, B. Effects of internet use and social resources on changes in depression. *Information, Communication & Society 11*, 1 (2008), 47–70.
4. Bian, Y. Bringing strong ties back in: Indirect ties, network bridges, and job searches in China. *American Sociological Review*, (1997), 366–385.
5. Bolger, N., Zuckerman, A., and Kessler, R.C. Invisible support and adjustment to stress. *Journal of Personality and Social Psychology 79*, 6 (2000), 953.
6. Bourdieu, P. The forms of capital. *Readings in economic sociology*, (1986), 280–291.
7. Brown, S.L., Nesse, R.M., Vinokur, A.D., and Smith, D.M. Providing Social Support May Be More Beneficial Than Receiving It Results From a Prospective Study of Mortality. *Psychological Science 14*, 4 (2003), 320–327.
8. Bureau of Labor Statistics. *Employment Situation Summary*. 2011.
9. Burke, M. Reading, Writing, Relationships: The Impact of Social Network Sites on Relations and Well-Being. 2011. http://reports-archive.adm.cs.cmu.edu/anon/hcii/CMU-HCII-11-107.pdf.
10. Burke, M., Kraut, R.E., and Marlow, C. Social capital on Facebook: Differentiating uses and users. *Proceedings of the 29th international conference on human factors in computing systems (CHI '11)*, (2011), 571–580.
11. Burke, M., Marlow, C., and Lento, T. Social network activity and social well-being. *Proceedings of the 28th international conference on human factors in computing systems (CHI '10)*, (2010), 1909–1912.
12. Burt, R.S. *Structural holes: The social structure of competition*. Harvard Univ Press, 1995.
13. Cohen, S. and Wills, T.A. Stress, social support, and the buffering hypothesis. *Psychological Bulletin 98*, 2 (1985), 310.
14. Cohen, S., Kamarck, T., and Mermelstein, R. A global measure of perceived stress. *Journal of health and social behavior*, (1983), 385–396.
15. Cohen, S., Mermelstein, R., Kamarck, T., and Hoberman, H.M. Measuring the functional components of social support. In I.G. Sarason and B.R. Sarason, eds., Social Support: Theory, Research and Applications, 1985, 73–94.
16. Coleman, J.S. Social capital in the creation of human capital. *American Journal of Sociology*, (1988), 95–120.
17. Ellison, N., Vitak, J., Gray, R., Lampe, C. & Brooks, B. (2011). "Cultivating Social Resources on Facebook: Signals of Relational Investment and their Role in Social Capital Processes." Paper presented at the iCS-OII 2011 "A Decade in Internet Time" Symposium. Oxford, UK.
18. Ellison, N.B., Steinfield, C., and Lampe, C. The benefits of Facebook 'friends': Social capital and college students' use of online social network sites. *Journal of Computer-Mediated Communication 12*, 4 (2007), 1143–1168.
19. Eurostat. *Employment and Unemployment*. 2012.
20. Facebook. *Registration Statement*. United States Securities and Exchange Commission, 2012.
21. Gilbert, E. and Karahalios, K. Predicting tie strength with social media. *Proc. 27th international conference on Human factors in computing systems (CHI '09)*, (2009), 211–220.
22. Gore, S. The effect of social support in moderating

the health consequences of unemployment. *Journal of health and social behavior*, (1978), 157–165.
23. Granovetter, M.S. The strength of weak ties. *American Journal of Sociology 78*, 6 (1973), 1360–1380.
24. Hampton, K., Goulet, L.S., Rainie, L., and Purcell, K. *Social networking sites and our lives*. 2011.
25. Hampton, K.N., Sessions, L.F., Her, E.J., and Rainie, L. *Social isolation and new technology: How the Internet and mobile phones impact Americans' social networks*. Pew Internet & Internet Life Project, 2009.
26. Haythornthwaite, C. Social networks and Internet connectivity effects. *Information, Community & Society 8*, 2 (2005), 125–147.
27. Hiller, H.H. and Franz, T.M. New ties, old ties and lost ties: the use of the internet in diaspora. *New Media & Society 6*, 6 (2004), 731.
28. Holmes, T. and Rahe, R. The social readjustment rating scale. *Journal of psychosomatic research*, (1967).
29. House, J. and Landis, K. Social relationships and health. *Science*, (1988).
30. House, J.S., Kahn, R.L., McLeod, J.D., and Williams, D. Measures and concepts of social support. (1985).
31. Jahoda, M. Unemployed men at work. *Unemployed people: Social and psychological perspectives*, (1938).
32. Jordan, A.H., Monin, B., Dweck, C.S., Lovett, B.J., John, O.P., and Gross, J.J. Misery Has More Company Than People Think: Underestimating the Prevalence of Others' Negative Emotions. *Personality and Social Psychology Bulletin 37*, 1 (2011), 120.
33. Keele, L. and Kelly, N.J. Dynamic models for dynamic theories: The ins and outs of lagged dependent variables. *Political Analysis 14*, 2 (2006), 186.
34. Kluth, A. Primates on Facebook. *The Economist*, 2009. http://www.economist.com/node/13176775?story_id=13176775.
35. Lehman, D.R., Ellard, J.H., and Wortman, C.B. Social support for the bereaved: Recipients" and providers" perspectives on what is helpful. *Journal of Consulting and Clinical Psychology 54*, 4 (1986), 438.
36. Lin, N. *Social capital: A theory of social structure and action*. Cambridge Univ Pr, 2002.
37. Madden, M. and Zickuhr, K. *65% of online adults use social networking sites*. Pew Internet & American Life Project, 2011.
38. Marin, A. and Hampton, K.N. Simplifying the Personal Network Name Generator. *Field Methods 19*, 2 (2007), 163–193.
39. Marsden, P.V. Core discussion networks of Americans. *American Sociological Review*, (1987), 122–131.
40. McDonald, S. Right place, right time: serendipity and informal job matching. *Socio-Economic Review 8*, 2 (2010), 307.
41. Naaman, M., Boase, J., and Lai, C.H. Is it really about me?: message content in social awareness streams. *Proceedings of the 2010 ACM conference on Computer supported cooperative work*, (2010), 189–192.
42. Owen, J.E., Klapow, J.C., Roth, D.L., and Tucker, D.C. Use of the internet for information and support: Disclosure among persons with breast and prostate cancer. *Journal of Behavioral Medicine 27*, 5 (2004), 491–505.
43. Pennebaker, J.W. and Chung, C.K. Expressive writing, emotional upheavals, and health. *Handbook of health psychology*, (2007), 263–284.
44. Putnam, R.D. *Bowling alone: The collapse and revival of American community*. Simon and Schuster, New York, 2001.
45. Thoits, P.A. Stress, coping, and social support processes: Where are we? What next? *Journal of health and social behavior*, (1995), 53–79.
46. Valkenburg, P.M. and Peter, J. Preadolescents" and adolescents" online communication and their closeness to friends. *Developmental Psychology 43*, 2 (2007), 267.
47. Wanberg, C.R. Unemployment and Well-Being. *Annual Review of Psychology 63*, 1 (2011).
48. Wellman, B. and Wortley, S. Different Strokes from Different Folks: Community Ties and Social Support. *American Journal of Sociology 96*, 3 (1990), 558–588.
49. Williams, D. On and off the 'net: Scales for social capital in an online era. *Journal of Computer-Mediated Communication 11*, 2 (2006), 593–628.
50. Wortman, C.B. and Lehman, D.R. Reactions to victims of life crises: Support attempts that fail. *Social support: Theory, research and applications*, (1985), 463–489.

Major Life Changes and Behavioral Markers in Social Media: Case of Childbirth

Munmun De Choudhury **Scott Counts** **Eric Horvitz**
Microsoft Research, Redmond WA 98052
{munmund,counts,horvitz}@microsoft.com

ABSTRACT
We explore the harnessing of social media as a window on changes around major life events in individuals and larger populations. We specifically examine patterns of activity, emotional, and linguistic correlates for childbirth and postnatal course. After identifying childbirth events on Twitter, we analyze daily posting patterns and language usage before and after birth by new mothers, and make inferences about the status and dynamics of changes in emotions expressed following childbirth. We find that childbirth is associated with some changes for most new mothers, but approximately 15% of new mothers show significant changes in their online activity and emotional expression postpartum. We observe that these mothers can be distinguished by linguistic changes captured by shifts in a relatively small number of words in their social media posts. We introduce a greedy differencing procedure to identify the type of language that characterizes significant changes in these mothers during postpartum. We conclude with a discussion about how such characterizations might be applied to recognizing and understanding health and well-being in women following childbirth.

Author Keywords
childbirth; emotion; health; language; postpartum; social media; Twitter; wellness

ACM Classification Keywords
H5.3

INTRODUCTION
Social media platforms including Twitter and Facebook provide a window onto the thoughts and feelings of individuals and populations. Considerable recent research has focused on exploration and mining of such data in a variety of domains, ranging from financial markets to politics, public health, and crisis mitigation [3,28,37].

We explore the domain of personal health, specifically looking at the effects of a major life event on mood and behavior. To do so, we employ three social media-centric measures: (1) patterns of activity, (2) linguistic style, and (3) emotional expression. Patterns and levels of activity define interactions with others and overall engagement with the social landscape. Language has been shown to provide useful psychological markers [29], and prior research [36,38] has shown that usage of language has the potential to convey information about individuals' behavior, their social surroundings, contexts and crises they are in. Emotions are founded on interrelated patterns of cognitive processes, physiological arousal, and behavioral reactions [11]. They appear to serve to organize experiences and influence behavior by directing attention, and by influencing perceptions of self, others, and the interpretation and memories of events. All three of these—patterns of activity, linguistic expression, and emotion—have been used in a variety of ways to understand as well as to promote general wellness among individuals and encourage healthy behavior (e.g., [2,16,32]). Social media provides access to these dimensions of human behavior in a longitudinal manner, and thus may be an informative tool in the study of how people experience and respond to significant life events.

We use content from Twitter in our study. Twitter has a large user base, including many who have been using the service for years. The duration of periods of use allows for analyses at time scales long enough to include periods before and after one or more major life events. Furthermore, Twitter is often used to broadcast updates on daily life, as well as on external information of interest, with the goals of maintaining existing relationships with strong and weak ties, and at the same time building new ties [22]. Thus, Twitter is a natural medium for sharing news about important updates and happenings in peoples' lives, including such life-changing events as childbirth, marriage, and loss of a job, and such deeply traumatic experiences as death of a loved one, divorce, and a severe car accident.

We focus in this paper on the major life event of *childbirth*. We explore and present a number of measures of activity patterns, emotional expression, and linguistic style to detect changes in 85 new mothers in the postnatal phase (approximately the five months *following* childbirth), as compared to the prenatal period (approximately the five months *before* childbirth), based on Twitter postings. One contribution of the work is a method for identifying new mothers from Twitter data. We follow an iterative strategy to collect posts that are indicative of births in Twitter's Firehose stream, and then use crowdsourcing techniques to determine with high precision a set of new mothers.

Our analyses, both quantitative and qualitative, show that a percentage of new mothers in our dataset (~15%) in the postnatal phase undergo significant behavioral changes compared to other mothers, as well as to an average Twitter user. These changes include: reduced activity, reduced positive affect, heightened negative affect, and significant change in use of specific linguistic styles, including interpersonal pronouns. Furthermore, on identifying aspects of language in the Twitter posts that contribute to this change, we find that changes in usage of a narrow span of words (~1-10% of the entire language vocabulary characterizing the content of posts of the new mothers) distinguish new mothers who show significant changes across multiple measures compared to other new mothers. Such minimal yet discriminatory linguistic changes suggest that language-centric diagnostic tools might one day be developed to aid in the identification of potential postpartum disorders, thereby broadly helping to reduce non-invasively the stigma around temporary and persisting challenges with mood and mental illness.

We believe that the motivation, methodology, and direction of this research can be leveraged in a variety of areas. One scenario comprises better identification of forthcoming or new mothers who would benefit from support groups that encourage postpartum social support and provide wellness advice to prenatal and postnatal women. In essence, these groups can strive to provide a venue where new mothers can find each other, trade baby tips, and start up friendships. Broadly, through our proposed behavioral measures, we hope to introduce a line of research that will help promote health-related well-being, by reflecting and even forecasting reactions to a range of major life events, leveraging social media.

BACKGROUND LITERATURE

Understanding behavioral change has been a focus of attention for researchers in social, clinical, personality, and cognitive psychology [29,30,35,38], and more recently in the HCI [7] and social media communities [9,14]. Hence we draw upon insights from a variety of research areas on findings about behavioral patterns surrounding childbirth.

Behavior Analysis around Childbirth

Clinical and psychiatric studies around monitoring behavior of new mothers have been of interest to researchers for several decades including, for instance, the role of social support on the emotion, attitudes, and behavior of new mothers [30,34]. A considerable amount of research in this area has focused on *postpartum depression* (PPD), a type of clinical depression that affects a portion of mothers after childbirth [12,19]. For instance, Nielson et al. [24] examined demographic, obstetric, and psychosocial risk factors of postpartum depression, finding that psychological distress and perceived social isolation during pregnancy were both significant predictors of postpartum depression.

Research on psychological aspects of childbirth for mothers is challenged by the limitations of data availability and collection; obtaining relevant data can require collecting data about women from late pregnancy to months after childbirth. To date, studies have been based largely on self-reports that do not always scale to large populations, making it hard to generalize the findings about the behaviors of new mothers. To this end, social media and networking tools can provide a new window onto new mothers for studying behavioral changes at scale without necessarily requiring active engagement with the mothers.

Behavior Analysis in Psycholinguistics

Researchers in the psycholinguistics community have explored how utterances, written texts, or other expressions of language can be used to better understand human intentions, moods, competencies, and disorders. As examples, computerized analysis of written text has revealed cues and diagnostic markers about emotional closeness of individuals [17], neurotic tendencies, and depression and anxiety among other psychiatric disorders [27,29,38]. Oxman et al. [27] demonstrated that linguistic analysis of speech samples could reliably and accurately classify patients into diagnostic groups such as those suffering depression and paranoia. Along similar lines, Tellengen [35] investigated how the structures of emotional expression can be used to assess anxiety. However, studies of depression, anxiety, or other distinctive behavioral changes in these works have been explored without regard to the context of events in the lives of individuals. One exception is the work of Spera, Buhrfeind and Pennebaker [33], who examine how expressive writing may help people cope with job loss.

Behavior Analysis around Events via Social Media

There is an extensive body of work on using social media to understand and track the emotions and behavior of large populations [18]. While some of this work has focused on public events like collective crisis situations [36], the influence of major events in an individual's life (e.g., childbirth, death, job loss etc.) on expression in social media has not been explored in a rigorous manner. Along with the Spera et al. work [33] mentioned above, an exception is [5], where the authors used linguistic features to predict death related bereavement on the MySpace social network. On a similar note, the use of social media to enable the maintenance of friendships during personal moves has also been studied [31].

Social Media for Health and Wellness

Interest has been growing in opportunities to employ social media and networking and other Internet data to encourage and promote healthy behavior and well-being [1,16,20,32]. Bahr at al. [2] studied how social networks can be leveraged to help people combat obesity. Munson et al. [21] presented an application for Facebook that promotes health interventions. Jamison-Powell et al. [15] examined discussions around insomnia on Twitter.

The breadth of work aimed at the use of social media to promote physical and psychosocial health highlights the spectrum of opportunities for creating applications that can support and encourage health-related awareness and self-reflection. In many cases, these tools would benefit from methods for identifying users who most need them. Our hope is that the techniques and methodologies that we present here for measuring emotional and behavioral change around childbirth can be generalized to other health and wellness applications.

DATA

As we are interested in understanding behavioral change around the major life event of the birth of a child, our population of interest comprises new mothers: female Twitter users who are likely to have given birth to a child in a given timeframe. Although we have observed that many fathers post about the birth of a child soon after the birth, we focus maternally because it is well established that new mothers more consistently experience a significant change in their lifestyle and habits in the postnatal period, compared to the fathers (ref. [19,25]).

Identifying new mothers on social media based on their posts, and in the absence of self-reported gender, is a challenging problem. We follow a multistage approach involving (1) constructing a candidate set of likely new mothers based on filtering a large corpus of Twitter posts for birth announcement events, and (2) identifying with high confidence a set of new mothers using gender inference and ratings from crowdworkers recruited via Amazon's Mechanical Turk (AMT). We discuss these steps in the following subsections.

Identifying Birth Events

We first construct a list of several queries to search the Twitter Firehose stream (made available to us via a contract with Twitter) for candidate users likely to be posting about their childbirth—a proxy for announcement of a birth event. We focus on searching the Twitter stream over a fixed two-month period between May 1, 2011 and Jun 30, 2011 (English language posts only), roughly the midpoint of the Twitter data that we had available. This leaves us sufficient data before and after the period to compare the prenatal and postnatal behavior of the new mothers.

To obtain the queries, we examined archives of birth announcements in four local newspapers over a period of three years from 2009 to 2012 (The Beacon-News[1], Aurora News-Register[1], Crete News[1], and Gothenburg Times[1]). Based on independent manual inspection from two researchers, we formulated a lexicon of sets of keywords and phrases that typically characterized the newspaper birth announcements. The terms resonate with intuitions that parents announce the birth of their children in canonical ways, often including mention of the labor experience and reporting on the physical details of their newborn child, including gender, weight, and height. These phrases were considered as search terms to identify birth announcements, to find candidate sets of new mothers from the Twitter stream. Examples of these identifying queries are given in Table 1. This phase yielded a candidate set of 483 unique users, who were the authors of potential birth announcement Twitter posts.

(1) birth, weigh*, pounds/lbs, inches, length/long, baby/son/daughter/boy/girl
(2) announc*, birth of, son/daughter/brother/sister
(3) announc*, arrival of, son/daughter/brother/sister
(4) are the parents of, son/daughter/boy/girl/baby
(5) welcome* home by, brother/sister/sibling*
(6) is the proud big brother/sister
(7) after, labor, born
(8) it's a boy/girl, born

Table 1. List of queries for identifying birth events on Twitter.

Identifying New Mothers through Crowdsourcing

As we are interested in mothers, inferring the gender of the above constructed candidate user set is important. Twitter does not provide a facility for users to report on their gender. Thus, we relied on cues obtained from their self-declared first names to infer the gender of the users in our candidate set. To this end, we employed a lexicon-based approach that identifies matches of the first name of the Twitter user to a large dictionary of first names collated from the United States Census data, available for download (http://www.census.gov/genealogy/www/data/1990surnames/names_files.html), as well as a publicly available corpus of Facebook users' names and self-reported gender. Because of the cross-cultural nature of Facebook, crossing these two sources worked fairly well in inferring gender of the Twitter users. We tested the accuracy of this inference mechanism by randomly selecting 100 identified users and labeling their gender manually. The lexicon-driven gender inference mechanism yielded 83% accuracy. Following gender identification, we obtained a smaller set of likely new mothers comprising 177 users.

In the final step, we task crowdworkers at Mechanical Turk (https://www.mturk.com/mturk/) with reviewing the set of

[1] http://beaconnews.suntimes.com/, http://auroranewsregister.com/, http://cretenews.net/, http://gothenburgtimes.com/

likely new mother candidates and ruling out cases of false positives, in pursuit of a high precision dataset. We showed each crowdworker (min. 95% approval rating, English language proficient, and familiar with Twitter) a set of 10 Twitter posts from each user in our candidate set, such that five posts were posted right before the index childbirth post, and five after the post. Our goal was to provide crowdworkers with contextual cues to help them to judge whether the author of the posts was a legitimate new mother. Additionally, we also showed the Twitter profile bio, picture, and a link to the Twitter profile for each user. The specific question involved responding to a yes/no/maybe multiple-choice question per user, to evaluate if the user was a new mother. We thus collected five ratings per user from the crowdworkers, and used the majority rating as the correct label (Fleiss-Kappa was 0.69). For our final dataset, we considered the users with the "yes" label and this set consisted of 85 validated new mothers.

Finally, for each of these 85 assumed new mothers, we queried their Twitter timelines in the Firehose stream to collect all of their posts in two 5-month periods, corresponding to prenatal and postnatal phases around child-birth (Dec 1, 2010 – Apr 30, 2011 and Jul 1, 2011 – Nov 30, 2011, respectively). We note that these were public timelines. We discuss privacy and ethical considerations in the Discussion section.

BEHAVIORAL CHANGE MEASURES

We propose several measures to quantify the behavioral change of the new mothers.

Activity Measure. We characterize activity via a measure we refer to as *volume*, defined as the average normalized number of posts per day made by the new mothers, over the prenatal and postnatal periods.

Emotion Measures. We focus on four measures of emotional state. The first two measures, Positive Affect (PA) and Negative Affect (NA) were computed using the psycholinguistic lexicon LIWC (http://www.liwc.net/). LIWC's emotion categories are large in size, broad in usage and semantics, and have been scientifically validated to work on Internet language (see [29] for psychometric information), as well as for affect computation (see [14] for their usage in short text data, in the context of Twitter). For the third and fourth measures, activation and dominance, we utilized the ANEW lexicon [4]. This resource provides a set of normative emotional ratings for a large number of words in the English language. The approximately 2000 words in ANEW have ratings in terms of pleasure, arousal, and dominance (over a 1-10 scale); and can therefore be suitably used to measure activation and dominance measures of Twitter posts.

(1) *Positive Affect (PA).* We define a measure of *positive affect* (PA) of the new mothers, during the prenatal and postnatal periods respectively. We focus on the words in the positive emotion category of LIWC [14]. Given a post from a new mother posted during a certain day, we thereafter perform a regular expression match exercise to determine the fraction of words that match the words in LIWC's positive emotion category. This fraction gives the measure of PA per mother, per post.

(2) *Negative Affect (NA).* Like PA, we also define a measure of *negative affect* (NA) averaged over all mothers, during the prenatal and postnatal periods respectively. We again utilize LIWC for its negative affect categories: 'negative emotion', 'anger', 'anxiety', 'sadness' [14]. Based on the same word spotting technique, we measure NA per day, per mother.

(3) *Activation.* Our third emotion attribute is called *activation*. Activation measures the intensity of an emotion; hence it is an important dimension beyond PA and NA. As an example, while *frustrated* and *infuriated* are both negative emotions, *infuriated* is higher in activation. We adopt the ANEW lexicon [4] to determine the activation level of a given post for a mother, during the prenatal and postnatal periods. As with affect measurement, we follow a regular expression match exercise to spot for ANEW words in a post. Thereafter, using the corresponding activation values of each such word from ANEW, we determine a mean measure of activation per post, given a mother.

(4) *Dominance.* The fourth emotion-based behavioral attribute is called dominance. It represents the controlling and dominant aspect of an emotion. For instance while both *fear* and *anger* are negative emotions, *anger* is a dominant emotion, while *fear* is a submissive emotion. We again use the ANEW resource, and follow the same technique as activation measurement to determine the mean dominance of posts from each mother.

Linguistic Style Measures. We also introduce measures to characterize behavioral change, based on the use of linguistic styles in posts by mothers, during the prenatal and the postnatal periods. Linguistic styles capture how language is used by individuals and provide information about their behavioral characteristics subject to their social environment [29]. Typically researchers [27,29,33,38] have observed the usage of linguistic features, such as parts of speech that represent references and relationships in characterizing style [8].

We again use LIWC for determining 22 specific linguistic style markers including: articles, auxiliary verbs, conjunctions, adverbs, impersonal pronouns, personal pronouns, prepositions, functional words, fillers, assent, negation, certainty and quantifiers. To determine the usage of various linguistic styles, we again use a regular expression match exercise to find the proportion of each type of linguistic style words in a post from a mother. The mean value over all posts from a mother gives the final measure, per style.

PRENATAL—POSTNATAL COMPARISON

We now explore the behavioral differences of new mothers in the prenatal and postnatal periods, using the three categories of measures defined in the previous section.

Comparison with a Background Cohort

Our first study examines variations in behavior on Twitter by the new mothers compared to the average Twitter user. For this purpose, we sample a random set of 50,000 users from the Firehose stream over the same timeframe to ensure consistency in comparison. We collect all of the posts shared for each general user over the time period, and then compute the daily behavioral measures using the methods discussed in the previous section. We refer to this sample as the *background cohort*.

We now report trend analyses of the measures over the studied time frame, contrasting the new mothers with the background cohort. In the set of trend analyses displayed in Figure 1, blue lines within each panel show the demarcation between the prenatal and the postnatal time periods; beige lines represent trends of mothers while green lines show the trends for the background cohort. For brevity and clarity, for the linguistic style category, we show only the usage of 1st person pronoun and the 3rd person pronoun which have been found to be demonstrative of particular characteristics of human emotion, including depression [29].

To quantify comparisons of these trends, we report in Table 2 the difference of means of behavioral measures, for each of the following four comparisons: the difference in behavior of background cohort between the time periods *after* and *prior* to childbirth (BA-BP); the change of behavior of new mothers between the time periods *after* childbirth with respect to *prior* (MA-MP); the change of behavior of new mothers compared to that of background cohort during the time period *prior* to childbirth (MP-BP); and the change of behavior of new mothers compared to that of background cohort during the time period *after* to childbirth (MA-BA). To further illustrate our findings from a qualitative perspective, we report a set of randomly selected example posts in Table 3, for all of the cohorts—MA, MP and BP, BA together.

The trends and difference of means of behavioral measures in Table 2 show evident distinctions between the mothers and background cohort after childbirth (MA-BA), including drops in posting volume and in PA, and an increase in NA (see Table 3 for an example of high NA post; also see the posts from the background cohort). Use of 1st person pronouns increases, while that of 2nd and 3rd person pronouns falls off. For these measures, we find that the differences between the mothers and the background cohort after pregnancy are statistically significant via independent sample *t*-tests (see Table 2 for details).

The mothers also show changes in behavior after childbirth, with most MA-MP measures showing statistically significant change based on *t*-tests (again, for mean

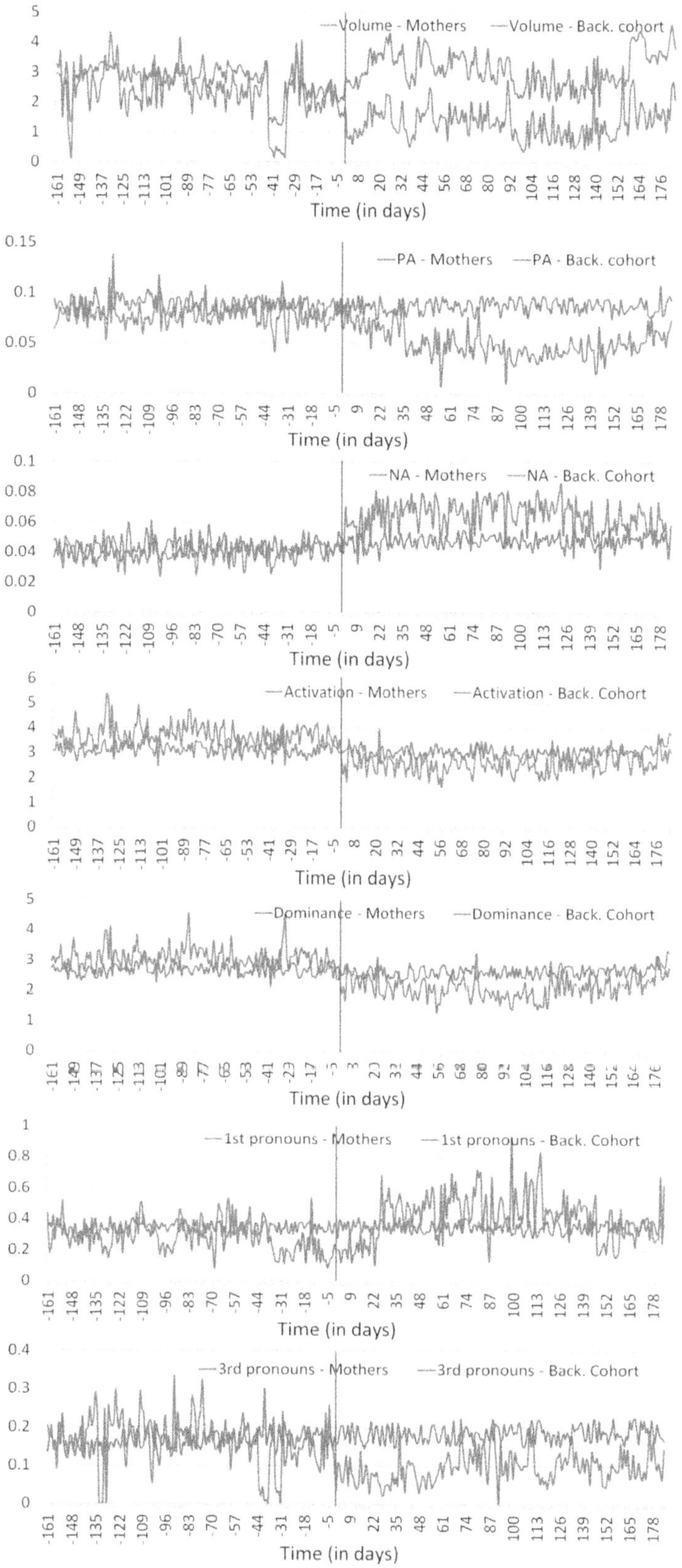

Figure 1. Comparison of behavioral measures between new mothers and the background cohort: volume (posts per day), Positive Affect (PA), Negative Affect (NA), Activation, Dominance, use of 1st person pronouns, use of 3rd person pronouns. Blue line represents the approximate time of childbirth.

amounts and directionality of change, see Table 2). The overall volumes of postings drops, indicating that women are posting less on average, suggesting a possible loss of social connectedness following childbirth. This may be expected given the time demands following the birth of a child, and the example posts in Table 3 (e.g. post (4)'s reference to lack of socialization) for the MA group supports this observation qualitatively as well. Within the content they do post, however, we see a drop in PA and increase in NA, a shift potentially attributable to the mother's physical, mental and emotional exhaustion [10], as well as the sleep deprivation typical of parenting a newborn. The NA trend (and to some extent the PA trend) for the mothers during the postnatal phase exhibits much higher variance, compared to that during the prenatal phase, possibly reflecting mood swings among the new mothers [13] as well as increased anxiety or being overwhelmed frequently but inconsistently. Post (2) indicating depressing feelings and helplessness attitudes, and post (3) in Table 3 for the MA group indicating anxiety and panic attacks, further bolster this observation.

Measures	BA-BP	MP-BP	MA-BA	MA-MP
Volume	0.053	-0.837	-1.5242***	-1.3958***
PA	0.001	-0.014	-0.0483***	-0.0294***
NA	0.002	0.008	0.0325**	0.0362**
Activation	0.049	0.575	-0.6924**	-1.6539**
Dominance	-0.025	0.592	-0.7249**	-1.3473**
1st pronouns	0.006	-0.062	0.1272**	0.1698***
3rd pronouns	-0.008	-0.026	-0.1993***	-0.1868***
2nd pronouns	0.023	0.041	-0.1267***	-0.1357***
Indefinite pronouns	0.007	-0.018	0.0324*	0.0215*
Articles	0.009	0.014	0.0984**	0.1486***
Verbs	0.010	-0.044*	-0.0443*	-0.0584**
Aux-verbs	-0.007	0.019	-0.0357*	-0.0311*
Adverbs	0.025	0.033	0.0526**	0.0942***
Tentative	-0.004	0.019	0.0115	0.0112
Func. Words	-0.006	0.007	0.0072	-0.0064
Negation	-0.008	0.078*	0.0891**	0.0954***
Inhibition	0.003	-0.007	0.0316*	0.022*
Assent	0.022	-0.031	-0.0521**	-0.0694**
Certainty	-0.023	-0.037	-0.0597**	-0.0647**
Conjunction	0.048	0.083*	0.0119**	0.1391***
Preposition	0.003	0.008	-0.0173	-0.0123
Inclusive	-0.002	-0.004	0.0073	0.0194*
Exclusive	0.002	-0.007	-0.0086	-0.0099
Swear	0.005	0.022	0.0618**	0.0777***
Quantifier	-0.013	-0.019	-0.0261	-0.0363
Non-fluency	0.043	0.062	0.0913*	0.1531**
Filler	-0.002	0.008	0.0294	0.0592*

*$p < 0.01$; **$p < .001$; ***$p < .0001$

Table 2. Difference of means computed over various behavioral measures comparing new mothers and background cohort. Note that the differences for each measure are on different scales. Each column corresponds to change of behavior between two sets: e.g., (MA-BA) implies change of MA with respect to BA. Here BP and BA represent the background cohort prior to and after the childbirth, while MP and MA represent new mothers prior to and after childbirth.

The activation and dominance measures also drop during the postnatal phase indicating a decrease in arousal, again potentially attributed physical and mental exhaustion or some form of "maternity/baby blues." Maternity blues typically exhibits as a heightened emotional state that can affect 80% or more of new mothers following the birth of a baby [25]. We conjecture that new mothers are likely to experience overwhelming fatigue from handling daily tasks around taking care of the baby and thus are more likely to express moods of low intensity (low activation) and more submission (low dominance). For instance, posts (1), (2) and (3) for the MA group in Table 3 (note words like "miserable," "frustrated," "disappointing") show that mothers are describing their perceived helplessness in caring for their babies, and consequently appear to be expressing negativity of low arousal and dominance.

Mothers after childbirth (MA)
1) `[high NA]` Ugh, my daughter hates her bassinet. I hate disappointing her. What a miserable day.
2) `[low activation]` My baby is only catnapping during the day. That's so sad and depressing. I feel helpless
3) `[low dominance]` Anxiety/panic attacks need to eff off!!!!!!!!!!!!!! I'm trying to lead a somewhat normal life with my baby!!!! #frustrated #miserable
4) `[high 1st person pronoun use]` No lie I fuckin miss all socializing..... my daughter keeps me occupied and exhausted. I have all my moments of the day
Mothers before childbirth (MP)
1) Derek & I sat on our screened in back porch listening to the thunderstorm & rain! So peaceful! Just to think in 35 hours we'll be parents!
2) Pregnant for the first time and I'm afraid I won't be able to stand the labor pain. Husband trying to reassure me, but he seems scared too. Thoughts????
3) I'm completely thrilled at the prospect of becoming a mother but the weight gain is bothering me :(:(. Do I just need to get over myself? Am I the only one :S
4) Days are getting busy!!! Need to start packing for the hospital, in case the baby is coming early!
Background cohort (BP, BA)
1) @some_user lol they would have called the police girl. ooh and ma make chicken and rice tonight. I was like oooh she is gonna be mad…
2) I've waited too long for that and I'm okay if I have to wait again for 1 or 2 weeks maybe. But please don't let me down.
3) Whenever someone tells me they're a fan of Lady Gaga, I smile and just go "Me too!" but in my mind I'm like <some_url>

Table 3. Example posts from MA, MP, BA and BP cohorts.

Similarly, the use of certain linguistic styles, particularly 1st person pronouns increases, while use of 3rd person pronouns drops, possibly reflecting the emotional distancing many new mothers go through after childbirth [19,30]. The sample post (4) in Table 3 for mothers after childbirth indicates this qualitatively as well. In this post, the particular mother appears to be experiencing exhaustion and pain, and exhibiting attention drawn to herself. She subsequently is found to use more first-person singular pronouns.

Though shown only in Table 2, we also observe increased use of articles, adverbs, conjunctions, swear, and negation style categories during postnatal phase for the set of assumed new mothers following childbirth with respect to the background cohort, as well as themselves before the birth of their child. Prior literature supports high usage of these styles with expression of negative emotion, or illness [6,29,38] that might correspond to the circumstances of some of the new mothers.

On the other hand, the difference of mean values of measures in Table 1, along with the example posts in Table 3, confirms an expected lack of change in the background cohort. Finally, the trends in Figure 1 reveal slight differences between the mothers and the background cohort *before* childbirth, suggesting an effect for pregnancy reflected in social media behavior (perhaps due to insomnia, exhaustion, physical discomfort etc.). In fact, these aspects are apparent in the posts for the MP group in Table 3, where mothers are discussing concerns around weight gain (post (3)), labor pain (post (2)), and preparations prior to the birth-related hospital trip (post (4)). In essence, pregnancy is likely to disrupt mothers' normal social media activities to some extent, explaining the seemingly minor differences with respect to the background cohort. However several of these differences are not found to be statistically significant (see Table 2), likely because the variance across the mothers is notably high (see, for example, the high variance in use of 3rd person pronouns in Figure 1).

In summary, we note that *t*-tests of means for various measures show statistically significant differences between pairs of cohorts. However, it is possible with our small sample size, that these significant effects could be a result of a handful of extreme-change mothers who have shown considerable behavioral anomaly, i.e., they changed more than others. Identifying these mothers specifically may have implications in terms of detecting potentially serious behavioral disorders and opportunities for intervention via development of new privacy-preserving services and applications. With such possibilities in mind, we focus more deeply on identifying individual level changes in our sample of new mothers in the following subsection.

Individual-level Comparison

To start, Figure 2 shows heat map visualizations of individual-level change for two measures: positive affect and activation. For brevity, we focus on these two measures as illustrative examples of variance in change across the

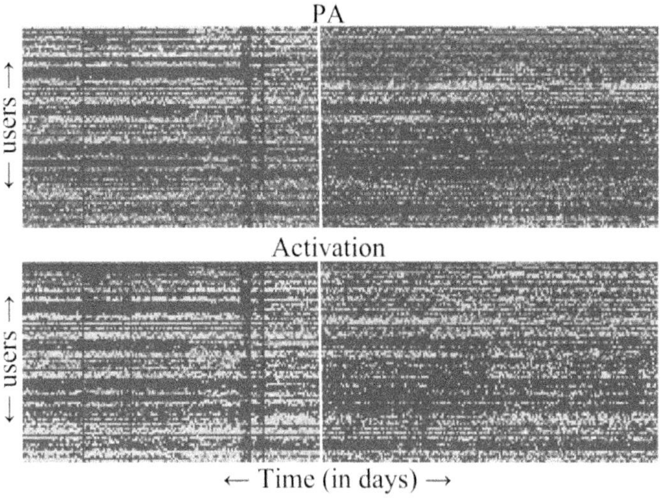

Figure 2. Heat-map visualizations show individual level changes for positive affect and activation in the postnatal period, in comparison to the prenatal phase. New mothers are represented in rows, time (in days) by columns. The colormap uses an RGB scale where red represents greater values and blue represents smaller values of each measure. The white line demarcation in each heat map shows the estimated time of childbirth.

new mothers, though we note that most measures showed similar patterns, as evidenced by the changes in the aggregated measures shown in Figure 1 and Table 2. The heat maps show decreases in PA and activation following childbirth for many mothers, but also give a sense of the variability across mothers, with some changing very little and some changing in the opposite direction of the majority.

Measure	Small effect	Medium effect	Large effect
Activity	38	29	*20*
Emotion	17	4	*12*
Style	43	3	*18*

Table 4. Effect sizes (based on Cohen's *d*) over the three types of measures. Numbers indicate the number of new mothers showing changes following childbirth of each effect size.

We formalize the individual-level differences across mothers by computing Cohen's *d*, per mother and per measure, in order to distinguish sets of mothers with small, medium and large effect sizes (considered as $d >= .2, .5.,$ and .8 respectively) . That is, for each mother individually, we computed the effect size of the change in their scores on the measures before and after childbirth in order to determine the extent to which they changed. We report the number of mothers with changes of the three effect sizes in each of the three measure categories in Table 2. In order for a mother to be included in an effect size category, she had to show change at that level across *all* measures within the category. Thus the numbers in Table 2 do not sum to our total number of 85 mothers, as some mothers did not show change even at small effect size amounts.

To summarize, from Table 2 we observe that, although there is a substantial number of mothers with large effect sizes for each measurement category, activity and linguistic style measures show relatively larger number of mothers with large effect size changes. While fewer mothers undergo such changes for the emotion measures, on combining across all measure types, it turns out that the 12 mothers who show large effect changes for emotion measures also show large effect changes for the activity and the style measures. This set of 12 mothers then is the set of mothers whose behavior changes the most in the postnatal period across all measures, and stands out as having changed more broadly and more substantially than the other mothers studied in our data. For comparison purposes, we perform the same exercise to determine the set of mothers who show small effects consistently across all measure types, which comes to 15 mothers.

SIGNIFICANT CHANGE POSTPARTUM

In this final section, we explore in depth, the behavioral change of the mothers showing large effects.

Mothers w/ small effects
1) I know some drs say it's ok to be on meds while breastfeeding but it kind of freaks me out cause it isn't proven longterm for baby's health.
2) Days are passing by as I watch my son grow! Can't wait for more and get together with the daddy!! Wish he was here
3) Just adjusting to having a new baby, new job and we just moved town. Need to calm down. Tips/suggestions on parenting, mothers??
4) Ugh... returning to work. I'm trying to enjoy these last few days with my baby...but all I can think about is that I will be leaving him for 10 hrs a day
5) I'm taking expressed breastmilk from the fridge on outings in the diaper bag and keeping it cool with an ice pack. Someone tried it?
Mothers w/ large effects
1) This is my first baby, feel so blessed!! But angry abt being sick all the time. I guess my hormones haven't taken nicely to this big change?
2) Starting to feel lost. I'm missing my love, my baby. Feel angry n disappointed in myself. Idk what to think or do....
3) My first time being alone with my baby and I cant stop crying. What is wrong with me? Am I depressed? Im just over here balling my eyes out
4) My DS doesnt sleep more than 3 hrs at a time and cries often and is so difficult to calm down. Cant remember when was the last time I slept
5) Feel like having a breakdown! ...like the WORST mother... feel so terribly that this poor child is stuck with this horrible monster mother..

Table 5. Randomly sampled posts from mothers with small and large effect sizes.

In the light of the two behaviorally distinct sets of mothers identified (large and small effect sizes), we first present a more rigorous examination of data characterizing the mothers with small and large effect sizes. We present randomly sampled example posts from the two cohorts in Table 5. A qualitative comparison of the nature of content shared by the two cohorts reveals that the mothers with large effects exhibit signals that are likely indicative of a lowered sense of social support ("Starting to feel lost.."), generally unhappy postings ("Feel angry n disappointed…", and even possible mental instability ("Feel like having a breakdown!", "balling my eyes out", "horrible monster mother"). Feelings expressed include anger, frustration and depression (posts (1), (3), (5)), lack of a sense of connectedness (posts (2), (3)), as well as physical discomfort and concerns about the baby (post (4)). On the other hand, the content from mothers with small effect sizes, although aligned with topics relating to bringing up the baby and expressing some sense of negativity ("Just adjusting…Need to calm down."), is less emotion-laden. For instance, we find that these mothers are using Twitter to invite comments and suggestions on their problems around typical adjustments to having a new baby–work-life balance, issues with breastfeeding and so on (posts (3), (5)).

Language Differences

Next, we quantify these seemingly qualitative differences through a comparison of the overall language change (change in usage of stop word eliminated unigrams) of the set of mothers with large effects, with respect to the set of mothers with small effects, as well as the background cohort. The goal is to be able to determine *what* language accounts for the distinctive change of behavior among the mothers with large effects.

To this end, we first use the Euclidian distance measure to compute a numerical distance score between the usage frequencies of unigrams in the two sets (one corresponding to the prenatal phase, the other to the postnatal period) for each group. (We experimented with other distance measures like cosine similarity and Janssen-Shannon divergence, which showed similar results.) The word usage distributions are then sorted by the absolute amount of change, regardless of direction as Euclidian distance is a symmetric measure. Table 6 lists the unigrams showing the most change in usage for each of the three groups in the postnatal period, compared to the prenatal phase. In order to get a sense of the directionality of change, we compare the relative volumes postpartum with respect to prenatal, and show the +ve or –ve direction of change as ↑ or ↓ respectively. Again, we note that these are relative changes, meaning that the top changing words for the background cohort do not necessarily change as much as those for the mothers with large effect changes.

We observe that the type of unigrams that change significantly vary substantially across the three groups. The background cohort's changes are mostly in words related to commonplace details of daily life (e.g., *tonight, here, morning, tomorrow*). For mothers with small effects, there is some evidence of going through the early childbirth phase (e.g., *fired, wait, days*). This reinforces our qualitative observation from Table 5 wherein we found these mothers using Twitter to seek support and feedback on their problems around typical baby upbringing issues. On the other hand, for the mothers with large effects, many words are emotional in nature (e.g., *aww, blessed, love*), again confirming the qualitative observations from Table 5 – see the usage of *blessed* in post (1) and the general affectionate postings (2) and (5) towards the baby.

Directionality of change in these words in Table 6 is critical. Considering the drops in PA and increases in NA shown earlier, along with the qualitative observations from Table 5, we are not surprised to see in Table 7, that many of the changes of the emotion words are in a negative direction for the mothers with large effects. For instance, use of *haha* and *lol*, frequently used terms of joviality expression in social media, are seen to drop sharply for mothers with large effect size. In fact, the example posts in Table 5, suggesting increased negativity and social isolation, make it further apparent why these mothers are not using these joviality words.

Background cohort	Mothers w/ small effects	Mothers w/ large effects
now (↓), shit (↑), back (↑), that (↑), day (↓), life (↑), time (↓), them (↑), me (↑), you (↑), fuck (↑), today (↓), sleep (↑), tonight (↓), love (↓), good (↓), here(↓), her (↓), morning (↑), tomorrow (↑), go (↑), know (↑), him (↓), people (↓)	#past (↑), duh (↑), people (↓), photo (↑), post (↑), decision (↓), reunite (↓), women (↑), story (↑), time (↑), asap (↓), do (↑), life (↓), wait (↑), fired (↑), days (↑), happy (↓)	haha (↓), blessed (↑), lol (↓), #lifecangetbetter (↑), awesome (↓), monthly (↑), fantastic (↓), cuddle (↑), home (↑), love (↓), sick (↑), aww (↑), scary (↑)

Table 6. Top unigrams showing the most change (in usage frequency) in the postnatal period, compared to the prenatal phase, for background cohort, mothers with small effects, and mothers with large effects.

Unigram Difference Analysis

Motivated by differences that we observed in language use among various groups, we explored the question of determining the number of unigrams whose change in usage frequencies actually renders the mothers with large effects significantly different from the background cohort and those with small effects. For the purpose, we introduce a greedy unigram elimination exercise for the mothers with large effects. Starting with unigrams exhibiting the most change (in usage frequency) in the postnatal as compared to prenatal phase, we eliminate in a greedy iterative manner unigrams from the lexicon of all unigrams for this group, computing the Euclidian distance at each elimination step, with respect to the other two groups. Naturally, as more

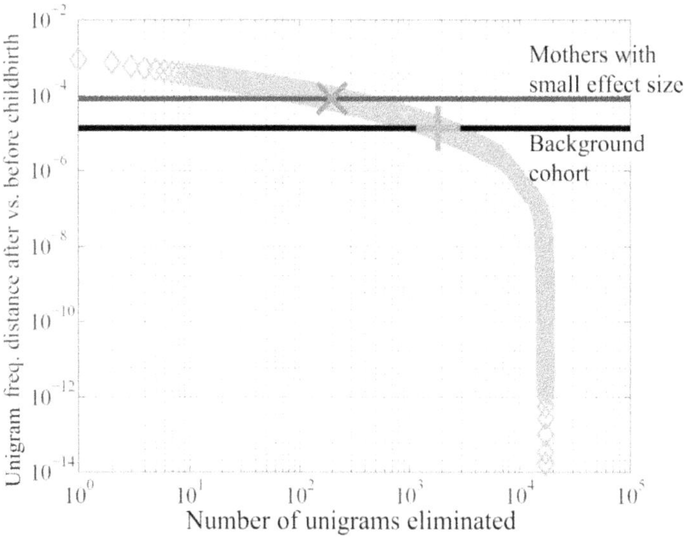

Figure 3. Unigram difference technique to determine empirical thresholds defining the language change corresponding to the mothers with large effects, with respect to those with small effects and the background cohort.

unigrams with big changes are eliminated, the Euclidian distance of language of the mothers with large effects consistently approaches that of the other two groups. The iteration(s) at which the distance becomes equal to that of the mothers with small effects (or the background cohort) can be taken as an indicator of language change in the postnatal period compared to the prenatal phase.

The results of this greedy unigram elimination exercise and the two unigram difference measures identified during this process are shown in Figure 3. The first difference measure is observed when, after the elimination of top 199 unigrams with biggest change, the distance of language usage frequencies of mothers with large effects becomes the same as that of those with small effects. Further, we also encounter a second difference measure following the elimination of the top 1837 unigrams with most change, wherein the language distance of the mothers with large effects becomes equal to that of the background cohort.

The two unigram difference measures suggest that the deviations observed for the mothers showing large effect size changes are captured by a rather small number of unigrams (merely 1.16% of entire unigram vocabulary compared to mothers with small effects; 10.73% with respect to background cohort), or in other words, *a narrow span of language*. This tells us that the changes in the activity, emotion, and style measures we observed earlier appear to be subject to big changes in the usage frequencies of a only few words. As a direction of research, we are interested in the feasibility of using these thresholds, as well as the unigrams that drive significant change, to forecast unusual behavioral changes in individuals over time.

DISCUSSION

Theoretical Implications

Through a case study around childbirth, we have demonstrated how the measurement of behavior in social media can help us analyze changes around important life events. We have found that, for a subset of mothers studied (14-15%), activity goes down, PA goes down, NA goes up, activation and dominance go down together, and the use of 1st person pronouns goes up, while that of 3rd person pronouns goes down. We also notice that some mothers consistently show these dynamics over the entire postnatal period of our analysis. In essence, we find that a portion of new mothers exhibit signs of decreased social interactions, as manifested through social media, along with a number of changes in emotional expression in a generally negative direction. These behavioral markers have been associated with depression of individuals in the psycholinguistic research literature [6]. In particular, isolation and loneliness are known risk factors for depression and lowered self-esteem.

An exciting implication and future direction is the possibility of leveraging social media for unobtrusive diagnostic measures of emotional disorders in new mothers, such as postpartum depression (PPD). We believe that there is opportunity to extend such modeling to make predictions in advance of birth about those mothers who are at the highest risk of suffering with an emotional disorder following childbirth. The detected group of approximately 15% of new mothers who showed broad and significant changes in behavioral and emotional expression following childbirth aligns with published reported rates of PPD in the United States [19]. We are interested in aligning these or similar social media-based measures with ground truth data on PPD. Establishing ground truth would also help address another diagnostic challenge: distinguishing actual depression from more common postpartum blues. Such maternity blues are considered more transitory and usually ebb within a couple of weeks after childbirth [25]. Since large effect changes among some mothers were observed over a longer period of time (PPD can last up to an year following childbirth [10,19]), we may be seeing evidence of mood changes that are more serious than those associated with maternity blues. We will need ground truth data to justify this observation. With additional study, the methods we outline could come to play a valuable role in public health via providing anonymized aggregate measurements of behavioral changes in new mothers. Such population-scale measurements can help inform governmental agencies, support groups, and the larger medical community about of PPD and postpartum blues.

Design Implications

Our approach and findings frame directions with implementation and design. These include the development of automated services and tools working on behalf of new mothers that can help monitor behavior and emotion in a nuanced manner, based on their social media activity. For instance, the tool could be a smartphone application that connects to the social sites the mother uses, and computes various measures over time to reveal trends in a private manner. On an individual level, monitoring some of these trends can serve as a self-narrative and help with self-understanding and reflection. Automated assessment could serve as an early warning mechanism to mothers showing significant behavioral change. This feedback could be especially valuable for mothers who are not aware of their risk of PPD. A monitoring application could log trends and serve as a diary-style data source to aid doctors or other trained professionals gain a deeper understanding of their patients. Emotional markers identified by such a tool could enable adjuvant diagnosis of postnatal disorders, and serve as a complement to survey based approaches, such as the Edinburgh Postnatal Depression Scale [25], and help with diagnosis or early intervention by caregivers (e.g., via psychotherapy treatments) aimed at promoting the health and wellness of women following childbirth.

Privacy and Ethical Considerations

Concerns regarding privacy and ethics may arise with analyses of social media as they ultimately leverage information that may be considered sensitive—even if publicly available [23]. We believe that the methodology we have described can be employed in a private manner. On the analysis of publicly available data, we believe that it is possible to harness public data to generate applications that are used in a private manner by individuals. As mentioned earlier, in our case, all data are public and, with the exception of the relatively benign Mechanical Turk task of verifying Twitter users as moms who had recently given birth, all analyses were conducted anonymously. As discussed earlier, the privacy of the user can be honored with user-centric design of applications that restrict the sharing of such information to the user herself and optionally to a trained medical practitioner or support group. Nevertheless, this type of research, and consequently the nature of the findings it generates, needs to be considered with caution, and we encourage continued discussion of the topic by the research and practitioner communities.

Limitations

We now discuss several limitations of our measures and the techniques and tools used to compute them. ANEW was used for arousal and dominance, while LIWC was used for valence, separated into positive and negative affect. We performed these analyses because, while LIWC is a promising resource used extensively for PA/NA computation [14], it does not support activation and dominance measures. The potential inconsistency of using two different lexica can be viewed as a limitation of the availability of linguistic tools. More generally, a lexicon-driven approach for determining emotions of users has some limitations. First, the methodology takes into account merely self-reported affective words, and it is not known how much they truly reflect the psychological state of the individual. Second, the approach does not take into account negation that could be used in conjunction affective words (e.g., "not happy"). In our context, we argue that while these limitations may add noise to the data, they do not invalidate the findings because: (1) we consider posts of a particular user over a long time period, and given the large numbers of posts (often in thousands), we observe reasonably accurate psychological reflections of the users; and (2) we perform comparisons across the prenatal and postnatal periods. Hence issues with a lexicon driven detection of emotion (e.g., use of negation) are likely to equally influence both prenatal and postnatal periods. Nevertheless, we believe that population-scale studies of behavioral changes around childbirth would benefit by more advanced techniques for detecting emotion.

We acknowledge the small size of the data sample of new mothers used in the study. As early research in this domain, we view our work as proof-of-concept; our purpose was to focus on a high-precision set of Twitter users with explicit evidence (on Twitter) of having given birth to a child. Our quantitative and qualitative findings on this sample align with observations in the psycholinguistic literature on behavioral changes around events (e.g., collective trauma [29]), which show promise in providing valuable signals in larger populations, and are likely not an artifact of the statistical methods that we used.

Moreover, while we find that the changes in behavior in certain new mothers are revealed as postnatal changes in a narrow range of words, we do not know the reasons behind the significant drop or rise in the use of these words. Hidden causes could include socio-economic factors, financial problems, and other variables that we cannot see. Availability of additional data about new mothers could shed light on factors that influence the behavioral changes.

Future Directions

Our studies show general promise in how activity patterns and language use in the social media posts of new mothers can reveal nuances of their behavioral and emotional change following a significant life event. Focusing on behavioral changes seen in new mothers, we attempted to lay the foundation for what we believe will be a rich line of research on harnessing signals from online social media activity to interpret, as well as predict and forecast behavioral changes in individuals and for populations. We hope that the work will lead to methods for providing new mothers with valuable advice and help.

We are interested in opportunities for using social media to both detect and explore the influence of other types of life events on people. These include loss of a job or financial instability (for understanding population scale unemployment dissatisfaction, or economic indicators); death-related grief and bereavement, and major physical and psychological trauma.

CONCLUSION

Social media tools provide unique platforms to individuals for personal expression, enabling them to share updates about their daily lives, including communicating about important life events. We conducted a case study on detecting behavioral changes of new mothers following childbirth, examining nearly a year of their posts on Twitter. After obtaining a list of 85 new mothers via identifying birth-indicative Twitter posts as well as leveraging crowdsourcing tools, we proposed three categories of measures—activity, emotion and linguistic style—to capture behavior of the mothers over the prenatal and postnatal periods. We observed that approximately 15% of the new mothers show significant change compared to other mothers and to a random set of Twitter users. By examining the types of words that best characterize the changes in language used on Twitter by new mothers, we were able to identify a small subset of 1-10% words that most contribute to the linguistic shift. These words define a distance measure that can be used to identify new mothers who show the largest linguistic divergence from the general population. We hope that the methods and results we have presented will frame new directions for promoting the health and wellbeing of new mothers.

REFERENCES

1. Anhoj, J., & Jensen, A-H. (2004). Using the Internet for life style changes in diet and physical activity: a feasibility study. In *J Med Internet Res* 8; 6(3):e28.
2. Bahr DB, Browning RC, Wyatt HR, Hill JO. (2009). Exploiting social networks to mitigate the obesity epidemic. *Obesity* 17: 723-728.
3. Bollen, J., Mao, H., & Pepe, A. (2011). Modeling Public Mood and Emotion: Twitter Sentiment and Socio-Economic Phenomena. In *Proc. ICWSM 2011*.
4. Bradley, M.M., & Lang, P.J. (1999). Affective norms for English words (ANEW). Gainesville, FL. *The NIMH Center for the Study of Emotion and Attention.*
5. Brubaker, J. R., Kivran-Swaine, F., Taber, L., and Hayes, G. R. (2012). Grief-Stricken in a Crowd: The language of bereavement and distress in social media. In *Proc. ICWSM 2012*, to appear.
6. Bucci W, Freedman N. (1981). The language of depression. *Bull. Menninger Clin.* 45:334–58.
7. Consolvo, Sunny, McDonald, David W. & Landay, James A. (2009). Theory-driven design strategies for technologies that support behavior change in everyday life. In *Proc. CHI 2009*. 405-414.
8. Danescu-Niculescu-Mizil, C., Lee, L., Pang, B. & Kleinberg, J. (2012). Echoes of power: Language effects and power differences in social interaction. In *Proc. WWW 2012*, to appear.
9. De Choudhury, M., Counts, S., & Gamon, M. (2012). Not All Moods are Created Equal! Exploring Human Emotional States in Social Media. In *Proc. ICWSM 2012*, to appear.

10. Edhborg, M., Lundh, W., Seimyr, L., & Widstrom, A-M. (2001). The long-term impact of postnatal depressed mood on mothers + child interaction: a preliminary study. In *Journal of Reproductive and Infant Psychology* 19: 61–71.

11. Ekman, P. (1973). Cross-cultural studies of facial expressions. In P. Ekman (Ed.), *Darwin and facial expression: A century of research in review* (pp. 169-229).

12. Fleming, A. S., Klein, E. and Corter, C. (1992). The Effects of a Social Support Group on Depression, Maternal Attitudes and Behavior in New Mothers. *Journal of Child Psychology and Psychiatry*, 33: 685–698.

13. Fleming, Alison S.; Ruble, Diane N.; Flett, Gordon L.; Shaul, David L. (1988). Postpartum adjustment in first-time mothers: Relations between mood, maternal attitudes, and mother-infant interactions. *Developmental Psychology*, vol 24(1), pp. 71-81.

14. Golder, S. A., & Macy, M. W. (2011). Diurnal and Seasonal Mood Vary with Work, Sleep and Daylength Across Diverse Cultures. *Science*. 30 Sep 2011.

15. Jamison-Powell, Sue, Linehan, Conor, Daley, Laura, Garbett, Andrew & Lawson, Shaun. (2012). "I can't get no sleep": discussing #insomnia on twitter. In *Proc. CHI 2012*. 1501-1510.

16. Kamal, Noreen, Fels, Sidney & Ho, Kendall. (2010). Online social networks for personal informatics to promote positive health behavior. In *Proc. WSM '10*.

17. Kapoor, A., Horvitz, E. & Basu, S. (2007). Selective Supervision: Guiding Supervised Learning with Decision-Theoretic Active Learning. In *Proc. IJCAI*.

18. Kramer, A. (2010). An Unobtrusive Behavioral Model of "Gross National Happiness". In *Proc. CHI 2010*.

19. Miller, Laura J. (2002). Postpartum Depression. *Journal of American Medical Association* (JAMA) 287 (6): 762–765.

20. Morris, Margaret E., Consolvo, Sunny, Munson, Sean, Patrick, Kevin, Tsai, Janice & Kramer, Adam D.I. (2011). Facebook for health: opportunities and challenges for driving behavior change. In *Proc. CHI EA 2011*. 443-446.

21. Munson SA, Lauterbach D, Newman, M, & Resnick P. (2010). Happier Together: Integrating a Wellness Application Into a Social Network Site. In *Proc. of Persuasive 2010*, Springer. 27-39.

22. Naaman, Mor, Boase, Jeff & Lai, Chih-Hui. (2010). Is it Really About Me? Message Content in Social Awareness Streams. In *Proc. CSCW 2010*.

23. Newman M, Lauterbach D, Munson SA, Resnick P., Morris, M. (2011). It's not that I don't have problems, I'm just not putting them on Facebook: Challenges and Opportunities in Using Online Social Networks for Health. In *Proc. CSCW 2011*.

24. Nielson, Forman D., Videbech, P., Hedegaard, M., Dalby Slavig, J. & Secher, N.J. (2000). Postnatal depression: identification of women at risk. *British Journal of Obstetrics and Gynaecology* (BJOG) 107 (10): 1210–1217.

25. O'Hara, M.W. (1995). Postpartum Depression: Causes and Consequences. *New York: Springer-Verlag*.

26. Ortony, A., & Turner, T. J. (1990). What's basic about basic emotions? *Psychological Review*, 97, 315-331.

27. Oxman T.E., Rosenberg S.D., & Tucker G.J. (1982). The language of paranoia. *American J. Psychiatry* 139:275–82.

28. Paul, M., & Dredze, M. (2011). You are what you tweet: Analyzing Twitter for public health. In *Proc. ICWSM 2011*.

29. Pennebaker, J.W., Mehl, M.R., and Niederhoffer, K.G. (2002). Pyschological aspects of natural language use: Our words, ourselves. *Annual Review of Psychology* 54: 547-477.

30. Scott KD, Klaus PH, Klaus MH.(1999). The obstetrical and postpartum benefits of continuous support during childbirth. *J Womens Health Gend Based Med*. vol 8(10):1257-64.

31. Shklovski, I., Kraut, R., & Cummings, J. (2008). Keeping In Touch By Technology: Maintaining friendships after a residential move. In *Proc. CHI 2008*.

32. Shyam Sundar, S., Oeldorf-Hirsch, Anne, Nussbaum, Jon & Behr, Richard. (2011). Retirees on Facebook: can online social networking enhance their health and wellness? In *Proc. CHI EA 2011*. 2287-2292.

33. Spera SP, Buhrfeind ED, Pennebaker JW. (1994). Expressive writing and coping with job loss. *Acad. Manag.* J. 37:722–33.

34. Tarkka, M.-T. & Paunonen, M. (1996). Social support and its impact on mothers'experiences of childbirth. *Journal of Advanced Nursing*, 23: 70–75.

35. Tellegen, A. (1985). Structures of mood and personality and their relevance to assessing anxiety, with an emphasis on self-report. In A. H. Tuma & J. D. Maser (Eds.*), Anxiety and the anxiety disorders* (pp. 681-706).

36. Verma, S., S. Vieweg, W.J. Corvey, L. Palen, J.H. Martin, M. Palmer, A. Schram, and K.M. Anderson. Natural Language Processing to the Rescue?: Extracting 'Situational Awareness' Tweets During Mass Emergency. In Proc. *ICWSM 2011*.

37. Vieweg, Sarah, Amanda L. Hughes, Kate Starbird, and Leysia Palen. (2010). A Comparison of Microblogging Behavior in Two Natural Hazards Events: What Twitter May Contribute to Situational Awareness. In *Proc. CHI 2010*. 1079-1088.

38. Weintraub W. (1981). Verbal Behavior: Adaptation and Psychopathology. New York: Springer.

The New War Correspondents: The Rise of Civic Media Curation in Urban Warfare

Andrés Monroy-Hernández **danah boyd** **Emre Kiciman**
Munmun De Choudhury **Scott Counts**

One Microsoft Way, Redmond WA 98052
{amh, dmb, emrek, munmund, counts}@microsoft.com

ABSTRACT

In this paper we examine the information sharing practices of people living in cities amid armed conflict. We describe the volume and frequency of microblogging activity on Twitter from four cities afflicted by the Mexican Drug War, showing how citizens use social media to alert one another and to comment on the violence that plagues their communities. We then investigate the emergence of civic media "curators," individuals who act as "war correspondents" by aggregating and disseminating information to large numbers of people on social media. We conclude by outlining the implications of our observations for the design of civic media systems in wartime.

Author Keywords
social media; social computing; civic media; crisis informatics; war; crowdsourcing; curation; news; microblogging; Twitter; Latin America; Mexico

ACM Classification Keywords
K.4.3 [Computers and Society]: Organizational Impacts–Computer-supported cooperative work. H.5.3 Groups & Organization Interfaces—collaborative computing, computer-supported cooperative work; K.4.2 Social Issues

INTRODUCTION
Since 2006, Mexico has been in the middle of a drug war as cartels engage in urban combat throughout the country. As of 2011, this ongoing, large-scale conflict has taken the lives of more than 60,000 people [10,44], and has displaced more than 230,000 people [43].

Frequent clashes among drug cartels, the military, and police forces take place in urban areas, inducing panic, cases of post-traumatic stress disorder [26], and, in some cases, taking the lives of innocent bystanders.

As drug war violence spreads and traditional news media weakens, frustrated citizens turn to the increasingly pervasive social media for "information and survival" [9]. Twitter in particular has become one of the principal sources of citizen-driven alerts in several Mexican cities; people often report, confirm, comment on, and disseminate information and alerts about the violence, typically as it unfolds. For example, the following Twitter message reports the time and location of blasts, along with a list of hashtags or keywords that both label and enable discovery of shared information resources:

> "There are reports of blasts on Venustiano Carranza Avenue #Shooting #RiskMty #MtyFollow."[1]

In the first part of this paper we examine a large corpus of messages like the one above, using observational and quantitative analyses, to understand how people living amid urban warfare in Mexico use microblogging to alert one another about frequent and often expected violent clashes. In the second part of this paper we examine, through quantitative and conversational techniques, the role of a small group of individuals who have a large audience and contribute a sizable amount of content related to acute events in specific cities.

This paper refines and extends the existing literature on crisis and emergency informatics by observing the longitudinal evolution of social media practices among people living in a setting where acute events cannot be temporally reduced to "uprisings" or "disasters," and where institutions are weakened.

PREVIOUS WORK
The phenomenon of people using social media during crisis is not new. Researchers have examined how people use social media in crises like floods [6,35] earthquakes [36], terrorist attacks [11], school shootings [29], and political uprisings [1,24]. Although all crises have attributes in common, those that occur as a result of warfare are qualitatively different: they are a part of everyday life, turning otherwise extraordinary events into ordinary ones.

Social Media in Wartime

CSCW '13, February 23–27, 2013, San Antonio, Texas, USA.
Copyright 2013 ACM 978-1-4503-1331-5/13/02...$15.00.

[1] Texts in Spanish are translated to English by the authors for exemplary purposes. To the extent possible, we maintain the style of the content translated from Spanish.

Research on social media use during the Iraqi war, for example, has described how blogs helped Iraqi citizens report events as they unfolded [2], maintain a routine [25], and enabled the discussion of topics that were socially unacceptable to discuss face-to-face. They even changed socialization practices, such as finding marriage partners [29]. Drawing on Powell's model of crises [30], Seeman and Mark [34] describe how people use social media differently depending on where they are in the crisis; they point out that war presents a special case for crisis informatics because people are experiencing several stages concurrently and, thus, using social media to serve different needs.

Government's Role in Emergencies

Another angle examined in the literature is the role of government officials. Typically, during crisis, governments attempt to play a helpful and central role in trying to restore normalcy, partly by brokering information. For example, in the United States, Public Information Officers (PIOs) are government officials "charged with coordinating communication activities and performing as spokespersons" during crises [22]. Researchers have found that with the advent of social media, the role of the PIO has changed: PIOs now can interact directly with the public on social media but also have to deal with fast-spreading misinformation on these new platforms [20].

Many government agencies leverage technology to inform the public, but what is provided is often incomplete or insufficient [18]. More troubling, some governments – such as China during the SARS epidemic [31] – use technology to purposefully misinform the public. In response to this, social media has also provided a venue to present a counter narrative to government-controlled media, as it was in the recent Egyptian revolution [1].

Yet, even with the increasing power of social media and other information technologies, in countries like the United States, PIOs and mainstream media are still the authoritative sources of information. However, in war zones, PIOs are weakened by conflict and are unable or unwilling to carry out their role. In such situations, government information is often unreliable [34]. As we will describe, this is the context in Mexico as the Drug War persists.

Social Media Curation

Twitter, Facebook, YouTube, and similar sites and services represent a genre of computer-mediated communication tools colloquially referred to as social media [12]. Social media enables participants to contribute content and share others' content. The resulting ecosystem of "user-generated content" is often contrasted with content produced by experts and pundits debating the merits of crowdsourced material. Yet, when people engage with this content, they help create a participatory culture surrounding what Henry Jenkins at al. [21] call "spreadable media." People take on numerous roles in this ecology, helping produce and disseminate content while also providing commentary and critique.

Often, for want of a better word, those who take an active role in spreading information through social media – with or without commentary – are colloquially identified as "social media curators." This term is fraught, given the precise roles that professional curators, librarians, archivists, and art collectors tend to play. Like other terms corrupted by social media (e.g., friend, social network), the concept of a social media curator metaphorically draws on, but is not equivalent to, the more precise term.

Social media curators seek to spread information to new audiences by selectively identifying and sharing content coming from the broader stream. These curators develop reputations with their audiences based on the perceived value of the information that they spread. Some curators simply pass on information posted by others, while other curators add commentary or insert their own interpretations or updates. While we recognize that this term is loaded, we use it throughout this paper to refer to those actors who position themselves as intermediaries in the flow of spreadable media.

Research on crisis informatics has started to examine decentralized efforts at news curation, such as those using systems like Ushahidi and wikis [23], where large numbers of somewhat homogenous participants collaborate to archive information about crises like the 9-11 terrorist attacks. As Sarcevic et al. [33] note, crises are inherently decentralized events, but social media and other networked technologies can play a crucial coordination role. Researchers have noted that during crises, mainstream media often invites citizens to share their reports via social media [20].

Weakening of Institutions in the Mexican Drug War

Like other armed conflicts, the Mexican Drug War is also a conflict over the control of information. Local news media organizations and governments have been forced into self-censorship and, as some claim, into collaborating directly with criminal groups.

Local news media organizations throughout the country have experienced extreme pressure not to report on the violence that engulfs the localities they serve. For example, a newspaper in Saltillo declared in an editorial [40] that due to the "threats on their editorial staff," they were "obligated, on occasion, to leave out information." Similarly, after several of their journalists were killed by drug gangs, a newspaper in Ciudad Juarez directed its front page headline to them, asking: "What do you want from us?" [39]. More recently, a newspaper office in Veracruz was burned down by criminal gangs [46]. Not surprisingly, a report [45] by the Committee to Protect Journalists ranked Mexico as the third most dangerous country for journalists. The result, according the foreign press [5], is a "near-complete news blackout" imposed by criminal organizations that "via daily telephone calls, e-mails and news releases" decide "what can and cannot be printed or aired."

Local governments, likewise, fail in public communication. For example, the foreign press reported how the mayor of a northern city "mysteriously disappears for days and refuses to discuss drug violence" [5]. Citizens' comments on social media and the comment sections of newspapers are filled with speculations on the reasons for this silence: fear of reprisals, collaboration with drug cartels, obliviousness, or an attempt to maintain an image of having everything under control.

Moreover, on those occasions when traditional news media or the government does report violence, the information is often published several hours later or even the day after the events take place. Hence citizens find these institutions ineffective at alerting them and helping them avoid violent clashes.

Social Media Usage in Mexico

Internet and social media use in Mexico have increased significantly in recent years, but neither is by any means universal. In order to situate our analysis of how social media is used to spread information, it is important to put social media usage in context. According to a report by the Mexican Internet Association [42], the number of people in the country with access to the Internet increased from 17.2% in 2000 to 34.9% in 2010. The report estimates that most of the 34 million people with Internet access are young: 37% are under 18, and 40% are between 18 and 34. The report also estimates that social media sites are used by 61% of people with Internet access and that of those, 39% use Facebook, 38% use YouTube, and 20% use Twitter. 53% of Twitter users reported using it at least once a day, from their home (39%), work (16%), and on mobile devices (18%). While Internet access in Mexico is neither universal nor uniformly distributed, social media does serve as an information channel that can reach a sizable percentage of the population. Furthermore, if Mexican citizens are anything like their American counterparts [32] younger citizens are more likely to turn to the Internet first for local news while older citizens are more likely to explore traditional media outlets first.

SOCIAL MEDIA USAGE IN THE MEXICAN DRUG WAR

In this section we describe how citizens are using social media as a resource for alerts of local violence in four cities embattled by the Mexican Drug War. There has been considerable attention in the media about Mexican citizens using Twitter to report violent events in their communities [7,9,14,27,38]. However, little is known concretely about the actual volume, content, or people involved. In this section, we provide a description and interpretation of the participation patterns in these cities over the course of sixteen months as manifested on the social media service Twitter. The choice of these quantitative metrics derives from aspects typically found to be of value in the crisis literature referenced in the previous section.

Methodology

We used a mix of observational, quantitative, and conversational techniques to understand how citizens are using Twitter to share information about the Mexican Drug War.

First, to get the lay of the land, we began our project by engaging in a variety of observational exercises involving the following processes:

a) *Searching and browsing Twitter*: Since early 2010, we have been informally monitoring Twitter for references of the violence occurring in Mexico. A key task of this step was to identify the types of hashtags that were being used by individuals in Mexico for violence reporting.

b) *Identifying co-occurring hashtags*: Once we identified a hashtag being used in tweets about violence, we started to search for others included in the same message. This was meant to improve the coverage of Twitter posts that are likely to contain information about events related to the Drug War.

c) *Monitoring trends*: Since mid-2011, we have been monitoring Twitter Trending Topics[2] in Mexico, which often are related to violence, through qualitative observations. When a trend related to violence would appear we would collect relevant data for further analysis.

d) *Reading news reports*: Once Twitter became known as a microblogging service where people were alerting each other, the news media started to report about this phenomenon and even use Twitter as the source for their articles related to the violence.

e) *Following high profile users*: Occasionally journalists, news media organizations, government officials, and public figures would amplify information from social media; this helped us to identify additional hashtags and gain a better sense of the ecosystem.

In collecting qualitative, observational data as a form of digital fieldwork, our goal was primarily to get an embedded sense of how digital media was being employed by citizens and understood by the media. This process benefited from our familiarity with the Spanish language, Mexico, Mexican media, and the Drug War.

City	Population	Hashtag	Tweets
Monterrey	4,000,000	#mtyfollow	211,278
Reynosa	600,000	#reynosafolllow	155,786
Saltillo	820,000	#saltillo	153,879
Veracruz	702,000	#verfollow	87,801

Table 1: Cities in the data set

Through our observations on Twitter, we identified a set of four cities central to discussions about the Mexican Drug

[2] Twitter's proprietary mechanism to demonstrate what type of topics are of high interest in a geographic region at a given point in time.

War: Monterrey, Reynosa, Saltillo, and Veracruz. For each of these cities, we identified a corresponding hashtag for analysis (see Table 1). We report their population size as a coarse comparative metric.

For each city, we identified the oldest and most commonly used hashtag in connection with violence reports for that city. Using the Twitter "firehose," available for use to our company through a contract with Twitter, we collected all public tweets containing the hashtags in Table 1 over the course of 16 months, from August 2010 to November 2011. This resulted in a corpus of 609,744 tweets for the four hashtags listed on Table 1.

Results

First, we found that, except for Reynosa, one third or more of the tweets (29.9% to 40%) were *retweets*, while a fifth were *mentions*, that is, tweets that included the name of another user (see Table 3). The high proportion of retweets over posting new content suggests that for those three Mexican cities, spreading information is the preferred mode of contributing to the discussion.

Second, we found that the number of daily tweets goes up and down constantly, spiking when violence erupts and decreasing when the city is calm (see Figure 1). The biggest spike in Monterrey (7,027 tweets) occurred on August 25, 2011, the day of an attack at a casino where 53 people were killed [3]. During this event people shared images of the attack and later on the names of missing people that family members presumed might have been at the casino. For Veracruz, the biggest spike (4,699 tweets) also happened on August 25, 2011, during a seemingly unrelated event, when rumors of school children being kidnapped spread on social media [29]. The biggest spike in Reynosa (2,745 tweets) happened on November 6, 2010 after intense clashes erupted due to the capture of a prominent drug lord [27]. For Saltillo, the biggest spike (4,637 tweets) occurred on October 12, 2011, also linked to clashes caused by the capture of a drug cartel leader [44].

City	Daily Median	Mentions	Retweets	Users
Monterrey	340	20.5%	40.1%	27,170
Reynosa	249	24.8%	15.9%	9,043
Saltillo	219	19.9%	29.9%	16,347
Veracruz	494	22.5%	35.3%	12,522

Table 3: Aggregate results of tweets per city

Third, doing a simple word (unigram) count and aggregation of the most common words by type (see Table 2), we found that the most common words are those used to refer to *places* in the city (such as the name of streets and neighborhoods), followed by words associated with *shootings*, followed by the verb "to report," followed by generic people references. Interestingly, the hashtag for a different city (Reynosa) is also one of the most common words in Monterrey.

Fourth, we found 65,082 unique posters across the four cities, who, on average, posted 9.4 tweets each. More specifically, those who posted new reports did so at a rate of 10.8 per person, those who spread tweets did so at a rate of 4.1 retweets per person, and those who referenced others did so at a rate of 5.5 per person. A few users contributed most of the content. For example, in the hashtag associated with Monterrey, half the people (52.8% or 14,898) tweeted only once, while a tiny fraction (0.03% or 9 people) tweeted more than a thousand times each. In the next section we analyze this activity difference in more detail.

Type of Words	Words (Spanish)
places	zona, san, sur, altura, garza, col., av.
shootings	#balacera, balacera, balazos, detonaciones
report	reportan
people	gente, alguien
city names	#reynosafollow

Table 2: Most common word types in Monterrey

Discussion

The popularity (i.e., high proportion) of retweets over posting new content suggests that for those Mexican cities, spreading information is the preferred mode of contributing to the discussion over interactions.

This would also explain the common use of Twitter for other purposes, including the search for blood donations, and even commercial purposes, which is often frowned upon by the community, as exemplified in this tweet:, "Sirs, I have created #mtyfollou so you can write your f*** stupidities there and stop misusing #mtyfollow."

As for Reynosa, the city with a bigger proportion of mentions, we find that for many people, Twitter is not only about alerts but also about interacting with others and creating bonds among those participating in the hashtags. For example, Reynosa tweets in the mornings are often about saying "good morning" to the members of a hashtag.

Our findings suggest that the adoption of Twitter did not happen simultaneously across the four cities. For example, Veracruz adopted this medium much later (see Figure 1). A likely explanation is that the practice spread as the violence spread. For example, we identified the first instance of the #verfollow where one person tells another of the possibility of using the hashtag #verfollow to find information about Veracruz: "you can find information about the state in verfollow or alertavera, messages should be short." Shortly after, another person sent a tweet to an influential/authoritative Twitter user informing that user of the new hashtag: "there is a new follow for Veracruz: #verfollow." It is interesting to note that the poster used the word follow as a noun.

Our data also suggests that, in the cities we examined, there is widespread adoption of Twitter. If we assume that each account represents a unique person, our data suggests that 1.48% of people living in the cities analyzed posted something on Twitter about the Mexican Drug War. Assuming these cities have similar Internet penetration as the rest of Mexico (34.9% of the population, as cited above), an average of 4.2% of the online population has posted something about the Drug War on Twitter. These estimates have many limitations because they assume that: 1) people tweeting with those hashtags live in the city associated with the hashtag, 2) Internet penetration is homogeneous, and 3) people have only one account. Conversely, not every person who uses the hashtags was analyzed. Additionally, Twitter's estimate that 40% of their active users sign in to "listen" [37], might also suggest that the percentage of the population reading tweets about the Drug War is higher

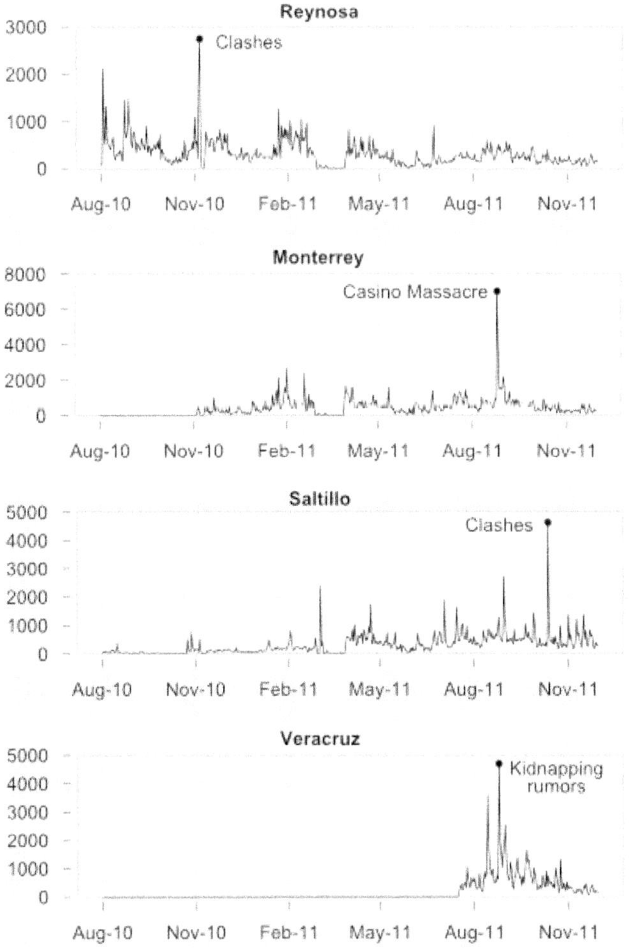

Figure 1: Tweets per day for each of the cities' hashtags

than those posting about them. Although it is almost impossible to tell precisely how many people are engaged in discussions surrounding the Drug War, it is not negligible.

THE EMERGENCE OF CURATORS

In the previous section, we saw how the volume of activity varied across different participants. In this section, we focus on those people who not only have significant contributions (i.e., tweet count), but also have a sizable audience (i.e., follower count).

Methodology

By analyzing each user's follower and tweet counts, we found distinct participation patterns. To better understand the distribution of participants, we present a scatter plot visualization depicting the relationship between tweet frequency and follower count (see Figure 2). First, a small number of highly-followed users – media organizations, celebrities, etc. – had contributed just a handful of tweets. For example, the account for "CNN en Español" has more than a million followers but had tweeted only once with the Monterrey hashtag. Meanwhile, a small number of users have a lot of followers and have contributed a lot of tweets (located towards the top right corner of the plots). We decided to examine those users.

In order to get a better understanding of curators' motivations and practices, we began reaching out to individuals who took on high profile curatorial roles on Twitter. As we found in our quantitative analysis, these curators often played a central role in helping spread information but they rarely provided their names on their profiles. As we learned through talking with them, the choice to protect their real identity is a conscious one.

We put together a list of the most active users in just the city of Monterrey by selecting those individually responsible for 1% or more of the city's tweets. This resulted in a list of ten users: one was responsible for posting 3% of all tweets, two were responsible for 2%, and the remaining seven were each responsible for 1% of the posts.

Initially, we had hoped to interview the various curators, but getting responses proved difficult. Although one coauthor approached a dozen of these users in Spanish as a researcher and Mexican national, they reasonably questioned the motives behind the project. Those who did respond (4 in total) often preferred not to talk outside of Twitter, so we began conversing with different curators in 140 character chunks, either publicly or through direct message. In some cases, we were able to transition our conversations to email or get them to respond to longer questions that we put up on a website. One curator agreed to be interviewed using a voice call on Skype.

It was clear during our recruitment and interviews that trust was a major issue. None of those willing to speak were willing to identify themselves and regularly refused to answer questions we asked. Still, the insights that we received proved valuable, shedding light on the found data collected through computational means.

Results

A closer look at the activity of those users with a high tweet *and* follower count over the course of the months we examined, shows that these people have taken the role of both aggregating and disseminating information to a large number of people in the city who follow them and who even send reports to them. These people, whom we call "curators," play a role akin to the PIOs in the United States, but through completely citizen-driven efforts.

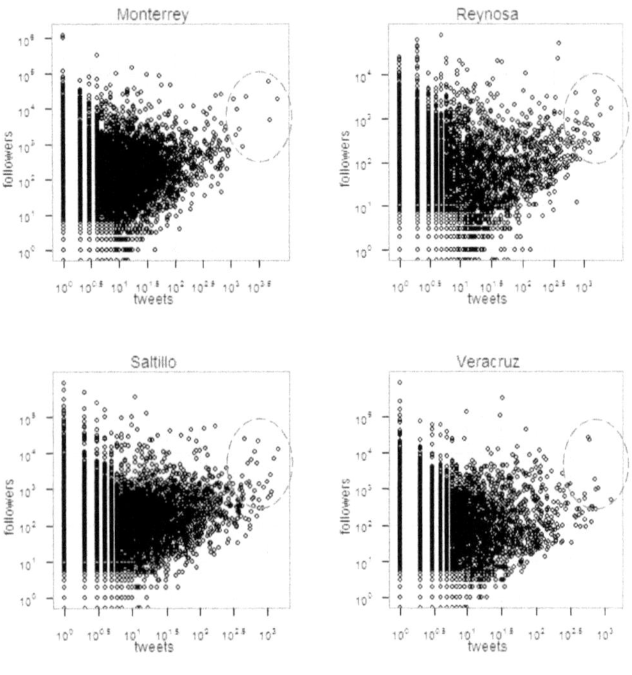

Figure 2: Followers and tweets for all users in each city. Curators region circled.

Some of those who posted frequently had few followers, while others had many followers (median: 9,305). Likewise, some accounts were regularly mentioned by others while others received few mentions (median: 303). The four accounts with more followers and mentions than the median all engaged in information curation, that is, receiving, responding to, and retweeting dozens of tweets from other accounts. Examining the dynamics of these accounts sheds light on the kinds of practices that are emerging in this ecosystem.

It is important to note that, besides these information curators, the other actors with a significant number of followers in the city are government officials (for example, the governor, the city police, and so on), news media (for example, newspapers and TV), and journalists. Together, four curators in Monterrey have 115,678 followers, almost three times the followers of the governor @RodrigoMedina (40,822) and almost as many as the most popular news media organization @Telediario (139,919).

Motivations: Altruism and Attention

Three of the accounts were created in 2009, the year when the violence in the city first spiked. Some joined mainly for personal reasons, or to follow celebrities. For example, "Angela," a woman in her early twenties, joined Twitter because a friend encouraged her to join, while "Claudia" started using Twitter because of the chance of interacting with celebrities: "I heard on the radio about how artists and celebrities would interact with their fans, so I got curious about it." All three of these curators identify themselves as women who want to do something to address the violent situation of their city. For example, "Claudia" described herself as "Praying for god to bless Monterrey," while "Alex" claims to be the "founder" of the concept of "city surveillance" and part of a "citizen network to protect and provide tips about civic safety, to avoid becoming victims of crime."

When asked, all of them mentioned feeling abandoned by their government and the media. "Angela" for example, when asked for her opinions on mainstream media, answered:

"…they forgot they have an obligation with the people… they started hiding information. Then, society started demanding information. This is when social networks took over."

When asked about their motivations, two of these curators cited *altruistic* reasons. "Angela" said "I always make clear that tweeting is an altruistic community service," before adding "it's like if I was a *news correspondent* on social networks of the war we are living." "Claudia" said that people tell her she is "like their angel for looking after them" to which she added: "that is one of the strongest motivations for me to continue tweeting daily!" Both of them mentioned being on top of their Twitter account throughout the day; "Angela" reported spending about 15 hours a day while "Claudia" just said "many hours."

The fourth account, *CIC* (which stands for Center for Civic Integration), emerged in 2011 and describes itself as a "network of trust, 100% driven by citizens that provides clear, reliable and authentic spaces for participation and to strengthen citizenship and quality of life." Unlike the other more organic, pseudonymous, and sometimes controversial curators, this account presents itself as a civic organization with a public presence in the media, staff, and offices. CIC also receives reports through e-mail, Facebook, and phone, and has staff that continuously checks these various communication channels and updates an online map mash-up. Although the organization was born out of citizens' frustration with the violence, CIC has expanded its reach to cover all sorts of urban issues such as problems with street signs and even psychological counseling for those suffering from the effects of the violence. Unlike the other three curators, this account maintains a more formal, serious, business-like presence online, while the other curators take a personable approach that implies that their posts come from passionate individuals.

Collaboration and Competition

Although there is certainly a fair amount of altruism in these people's participation, our conversations with curators gave us the impression that they are, in a way, competing with each other for attention. The one concern shared by most of the people we talked to was the issue of "tweet theft." As "Claudia" said, "I do not like that people often do not give credit in the retweets of my tweets," and when asked how this could be solved she replied, "it would be about the ability to be treated with importance, be given credibility, which would let more Twitter users know about you." Similarly, "Angela" complained that not only do others steal her tweets but they also change the timestamp she manually includes in many of her tweets to claim having scooped the news.

Being the first person to report on something is partly a matter of luck. "Angela" mentioned having her follower count increase significantly after one of her family members sent her the first photo of an event involving some people being hung from a bridge. The photo was gruesome but it spread quickly on Twitter, giving her a lot of followers. "Claudia" explained that most of her followers came from retweets that spread from friend to friend and through people searching for the relevant hashtags. Presumably, given the high volume of tweets and retweets from these curators, a search for the city hashtag would be likely to return tweets by some of these curators.

Lack of Trust among Curators

The second most striking issue mentioned by those we asked was the lack of trust and cooperation among curators. When asked why, one of the curators said: "I can't recommend anyone" and that "after what happened with @AnonCurator[3], I can't vouch for anybody, because I don't know who is behind that account. They are anonymous." This curator is one of the few that shows her face and has mentioned her real name publicly; the others go at lengths to maintain a high degree of anonymity. For example, "Alex" mentioned that "perhaps [the curator accounts use female names] to appear more trustworthy."

The scandal referenced by the curator was one reported on Blog del Narco [41] claiming that "military intelligence" had found evidence to suggest that @AnonCurator—one of the leading curators in the city—had been tricking citizens into "hawking" or reporting the location of the military convoys. Despite these and other suspicions, news agencies have been unable to validate whether cartels are using social media for that purpose [38].

Furthermore, even organizations like CIC are not immune to criticism; "Angela" mentioned that CIC is:

> "an association that presumes not having political objectives, but obviously, there are entrepreneurial-political interests. [...] not because they are in politics they are doing something wrong, not at all, that's great! But saying that it's from citizens for citizens, without political goals, I mean, don't say something you really are not."

Sources

Two of the people we spoke with said they had received most of the reports from their followers looking to amplify their messages, although "Claudia" acknowledged obtaining information from traditional media from time to time: "most of the information is through los tuiteros, my followers. In other cases it's the reporters on television, local news or newspapers." "Angela" on the other hand explained that she obtained most of the reports from offline sources, mostly from acquaintances or friends of friends:

> "[N]ot all the information comes in from Twitter, there's a lot of people I know, who know what I do, [people] have my phone and give me a call and they keep me informed, they are citizens, 100% citizens."

While trust regularly emerged as an issue for these curators, they often struggled to explain how they vetted their sources. When asked how to identify trusted tweets, "Claudia" simply replied "you use your instincts."

DISCUSSION

Nationally, there have been several efforts focused on curating information. One of the most popular is called "Blog del Narco," which has been the subject of much controversy for publishing gruesome drug war images and videos that traditional media does not publish [17]. The blog went through several challenges, claiming to be attacked by hackers and targeted for censorship by the government through Google's Blogger platform [13,16] until it eventually merged with Notirex, a lesser-known news website [4].

Although traditional journalists regularly serve as curators, both on Twitter and in the more mainstream media outlets, the rise of citizen curators suggests that existing outlets are not meeting public need. Both government officials and journalists have idiosyncratically engaged on Twitter, but much of the citizen curators' success in building an audience stems from their willingness to curate information even when government agencies, journalists, and other media outlets are not.

The rise of social media as an alternate information channel has enabled the emergence of civic media curators, some of which have turned into more institutionalized civic organizations. This nascent form of civic engagement is new in Mexico and has the potential of becoming an important force when traditional institutions are weak. Yet, this practice is not without controversy. Several journalists have raised skepticism about the potential for social media to spread fear and misinformation [15]. Indeed, the fear of

---

[3] Fictitious name

inaccurate information spreading has prompted government agencies to clamp down on citizen curators.

Citizen curators have been targeted both by governmental agencies and the cartels. For example, the government of Veracruz charged two people with "terrorism" for allegedly spreading misinformation on Twitter [19]; in Nuevo Laredo—one of Reynosa's neighboring cities—two bodies were found with visible signs of torture along with a placard that read: "This is going to happen to all the internet busybodies."

Yet, the popularity and prevalence of tweets related to the Drug War highlights that citizens are turning to Twitter to obtain and share information about the happenings in key cities where violence is occurring, as illustrated via our quantitative analyses.

Manuel Castells argues that insurgent communities of practice emerge in resistance to oppression when networked individualism and communalism collide [8]. These communities are constituted around a shared practice with a common set of beliefs. They are both individually motivated and committed to creating something of collective value. Citizen media curators and those contributing to popular hashtags are engaged in a shared project to inform, yet they are also driven by personal goals to gain status and attention. They are collectively engaged in resistance to both the flawed media ecosystem and the powerful role of the drug cartels; however, they are simultaneously mistrustful of each other. As an insurgent community of practice, they challenge media and governmental power by restructuring the networks through which information flows. Yet, in achieving networked power, they can both make themselves vulnerable to misinformation and also susceptible to de-anonymization, arrest, and even death.

Curators and others engaged in spreading information about the Mexican Drug War must balance between their desire to contribute to the public good, their personal interests in achieving attention or notoriety, and the vulnerabilities they face by becoming too visible or contributing too much. This tension shapes how people participate in this ecosystem.

CONCLUSIONS

We have presented how people use Twitter in the Mexican Drug War, an ongoing armed conflict in a country with significant Internet penetration and a highly visible presence of social media in public life. As we have described, for many Mexicans, social media has become a fluid and participatory information platform that augments and often replaces traditional news media and governmental institutions. Citizens in these localities are using social media as a resource for alerts and information dissemination.

As social media increasingly permeates society, its role in armed conflicts is poised to rise in prominence. From the Arab Spring to Occupy Wall Street, social media is one of the information platforms used in a wide range of movements. In this paper, we described how these technologies are currently used in war-like environments, and what their promises and challenges might be in the future. We illustrated the volume of activity and the number of people using social media to alert and connect with others during recurrent acute crises. We found that alerts containing location are among the most popular forms of participation. We then identified the small but influential role some users take as curators and presented their motivations and concerns.

In most crisis informatics work—and in many studies involving online communities—people are willing to trust strangers, either because the potential cost is minimal or simply because the potential gains (e.g., needed information, friendship) outweigh the costs. Yet, for those who are sharing information in an environment where doing so is risky, the potential cost of sharing is much higher. In many ways, what Mexican citizens are experiencing is the type of information ecosystem that is normally felt by criminals in an environment where they might get caught/punished. Yet, in a lawless warzone, the tables are turned.

Implications in Social Computing Research

This dynamic creates new challenges for designers. On the one hand, designers want to empower marginalized citizens to have a safe space in which to speak and share valuable information. On the other hand, the same tools that help oppressed people safely navigate information in a troubled society also serve as valuable tools for criminals in a lawful one. As a result, studies like ours reveal a design conundrum that raises serious questions about free speech, rights, freedoms, and protections in a digital ecosystem.

As designers grapple with this challenge, one intervention becomes apparent: there is a significant need for developing technical strategies to assess trust without revealing identity information. Most identity schemes focus on assessing whether or not someone is who they say they are. Indeed, Twitter has begun implementing "verified" identities. Verification, while valuable for certain types of interaction, is not necessarily what the curators we observed and interacted with need. While verification may be a decent proxy, all they really need to know is whether or not the information that is being presented is credible.

One way in which people seek to determine credibility of information is through reproducibility. Journalists, for example, check their sources by trying to see if other sources, disconnected from the original, have similar facts. It may be possible to simulate this in an online environment. For example, imagine that a user could see who else on Twitter posted a similar message and visually see the relationship between the posters. If information was only posted by people who were all connected to one another, it may be less reliable than if information was posted by a disparate collection of disconnected nodes. Other types of attributes of the Twitter interface have also been found to provide helpful proxies to evaluate credibility, such as profile pictures, as well as use of real names [28], or even links to external facing personal webpages of well-known individuals.

We have shown one context in which social media creates an alternate "user-generated" channel of communication that can address weaknesses in information flow. However, this new channel comes with its own credibility challenges such as issues of trust, reputation, and misinformation. Without having strong signals for interpreting the trustworthiness of the available information or the reputation of the people, viewers struggle to assess the quality of available information. This is not a new issue [18], but it becomes more salient in high stakes situations like the one described in this paper. Misinformation can have serious consequences, both for those who are consuming misinformation as well as those who are spreading it. Trust has a different valence when people fear for their safety. While more research is needed, based on our early observations of this armed conflict, we hope these insights be of value to system designers and crises responders.

REFERENCES

1. Al-Ani, B., Mark, G., Chung, J., and Jones, J. The Egyptian Blogosphere: A Counter-Narrative of the Revolution. *Proc. CSCW 2012*, (2012).
2. Al-Ani, B., Mark, G., and Semaan, B. Blogging in a region of conflict: supporting transition to recovery. *Proceedings of the 28th international conference on Human factors in computing systems*, ACM (2010), 1069–1078.
3. Benkler, Y. *The Wealth of Networks: How Social Production Transforms Markets and Freedom*. Yale University Press, New Haven, CT, 2006.
4. Bichara, L. Notirex le da la bienvenida a BlogdelNarco. *Notirex*, 2011. http://notirex.com/2011/11/notirex-le-da-la-bienvenida-a-blogdelnarco/.
5. Booth, W. In Mexico's Nuevo Laredo, drug cartels dictate media coverage. *The Washington Post*, 2010. http://www.washingtonpost.com/wp-dyn/content/article/2010/08/01/AR2010080103481.html.
6. Bruns, A., Burgess, J., Crawford, K., and Shaw, F. *#qldfloods and @QPSMedia: Crisis Communication on Twitter in the 2011 South East Queensland Floods*. Brisbane: ARC Centre of Excellence for Creative Industries and Innovation, Brisbane, Australia, 2012.
7. Calderón, V. 'Tuits' a prueba de balas. *El País*, 2011. http://www.elpais.com/articulo/internacional/Tuits/prueba/balas/elpepuint/20110826elpepuint_10/Tes.
8. Castells, M. *Communication Power*. Oxford University Press, USA, 2009.
9. Cave, D. Mexico Turns to Twitter and Facebook for Information and Survival. *The New York Times*, 2011. http://www.nytimes.com/2011/09/25/world/americas/mexico-turns-to-twitter-and-facebook-for-information-and-survival.html?_r=1.
10. Cave, D. Mexico Updates Drug War Death Toll, but Critics Dispute Data. *The New York Times*, 2012. http://www.nytimes.com/2012/01/12/world/americas/mexico-updates-drug-war-death-toll-but-critics-dispute-data.html.
11. Cheong, M. and Lee, V.C.S. A microblogging-based approach to terrorism informatics: Exploration and chronicling civilian sentiment and response to terrorism events via Twitter. *Information Systems Frontiers 13*, 1 (2010), 45–59.
12. Ellison, N.E. and boyd, danah. Sociality Through Social Network Sites. In W.H. Dutton, ed., *The Oxford Handbook of Internet Studies*. Oxford University Press, in press, 151–172.
13. Fabian, J.W. Google Kills Blog del Narco - Advantage Mexico News. 2011. http://www.advantagemexico.com/news/5064/google_kills_blog_del_narco.
14. Garza, X. Bloqueos en Monterrey: "Todo se vuelve inútil."*M Semanal*, 2010. http://www.msemanal.com/node/2811.
15. Gómez Leyva, C. Twitter nos quiere matar de miedo. *Milenio*, 2010. http://impreso.milenio.com/node/8725469.
16. Gómez Leyva, C. El exitoso Blog del Narco. 2010. http://impreso.milenio.com/node/8855061.
17. Gutierrez, R. Leaking secrets, leaking blood. *Boing Boing*, 2010. http://boingboing.net/2010/09/14/narco.html.
18. Hagar, C. and Haythornthwaite, C. Crisis, farming and community. *Journal of Community Informatics*, 3 (2005).
19. Hernandez, D. In Mexico, harsh charges over Twitter. *Los Angeles Times*, 2011. http://articles.latimes.com/2011/sep/05/world/la-fg-mexico-tweeters-20110906.
20. Hughes, A.L. and Palen, L. The Evolving Role of the Public Information Officer: An Examination of Social Media in Emergency Management. *Journal of Homeland Security and Emergency Management*, (2012).
21. Jenkins, H., Ford, S., and Green, J. *Spreadable Media: Creating Value and Meaning in a Networked Culture*. NYU Press, 2013.
22. Latonero, M. and Shklovski, I. 'Respectfully Yours in Safety and Service' - Emergency Management & Social Media Evangelism. *SSRN eLibrary*, (2010).
23. Liu, S.B. Trends in Distributed Curatorial Technology to Manage Data in a Networked World. *UPGRADE Journal: 2010 – Emerging Information Technologies (II), 11*, 3 (2010), 18–24.
24. Lotan, G., Graeff, E., Ananny, M., Gaffney, D., Pearce, I., and boyd, danah. The Revolutions Were Tweeted: Information Flows during the 2011 Tunisian and Egyptian Revolutions. *International Journal of Communication 5*, (2011).
25. Mark, G., Bagdouri, M., Palen, L., Martin, J., Al-Ani, B., and Anderson, K. Blogs as a Collective War Diary. *Proc. CSCW 2012*, (2012).

26. Menchaca, A. Dispara inseguridad estrés postraumático. *El Norte*, 2011.
27. Monroy-Hernández, A. Shouting Fire in a Crowded Hashtag: Narco Censorship & 'Twitteroristas' in Mexico's Drug Wars. *The New York Times*, 2011. http://www.nytimes.com/external/readwriteweb/2011/09/05/05readwriteweb-shouting-fire-in-a-crowded-hashtag-narco-ce-45910.html.
28. Morris, M.R., Counts, S., Roseway, A., Hoff, A., and Schwarz, J. Tweeting is believing?: understanding microblog credibility perceptions. *Proceedings of the ACM 2012 conference on Computer Supported Cooperative Work*, ACM (2012), 441–450.
29. Palen, L. and Vieweg, S. The emergence of online widescale interaction in unexpected events: assistance, alliance & retreat. *Proceedings of the 2008 ACM conference on Computer supported cooperative work*, ACM (2008), 117–126.
30. Powell, J.W. Baltimore: University of Maryland Disaster Research Project. In *An Introduction to the Natural History of Disaster. Baltimore*. 1954.
31. Qu, Y. SARS Epidemic. (2009).
32. Rosenstiel, T., Mitchell, A., Purcell, K., and Rainie, L. *How People Learn About their Local Community*. Pew Research Center's Project for Excellence in Journalism and the Pew Internet & American Life Project, 2011.
33. Sarcevic, A., Palen, L., White, J., Mossaab, B., Starbird, K., and Anderson, K.M. "Beacons of Hope" in Decentralized Coordination: Learning from On-the-Ground Medical Twitterers During the 2010 Haiti Earthquake. *Proceedings of the ACM Conference on Computer Supported Cooperative Work*, (2012).
34. Semaan, B. and Mark, G. 'Facebooking' Towards Crisis Recovery and Beyond: Disruption as an Opportunity. *Proceedings of the ACM conference on Computer supported cooperative work*, ACM (2012).
35. Starbird, K., Palen, L., Hughes, A.L., and Vieweg, S. Chatter on the red: what hazards threat reveals about the social life of microblogged information. *Proceedings of the 2010 ACM conference on Computer supported cooperative work*, ACM (2010), 241–250.
36. Starbird, K. and Palen, L. "Voluntweeters": self-organizing by digital volunteers in times of crisis. *Proceedings of the 2011 annual conference on Human factors in computing systems*, ACM (2011), 1071–1080.
37. Twitter. One hundred million voices. *Twitter Blog*. http://blog.twitter.com/2011/09/one-hundred-million-voices.html.
38. Valencia, N. Residents use social media to fight organized crime in Mexico. *CNN*, 2010. http://articles.cnn.com/2010-03-08/tech/mexico.crime.social.media_1_microblogging-cartels-social-media?_s=PM:TECH.
39. Mexico paper seeks cartel clarity. *BBC*, 2010. http://www.bbc.co.uk/news/world-latin-america-11370310.
40. Entre sombras. *Vanguardia*, 2010. http://www.vanguardia.com.mx/entresombras-589883-editorial.html.
41. Delincuencia organizada infiltrada en redes sociales. *BlogdelNarco.com*,2011. http://archivo.blogdelnarco.com/delincuencia-organizada-infiltrada-en-redes-sociales/.
42. *Redes Sociales en México y Latinoamérica*. Asociación Mexicana de Internet, Mexico, D.F., Mexico, 2011.
43. *Displacement due to criminal and communal violence*. Internal Displacement Monitoring Centre, 2011.
44. Quinto año de gobierno: 60 mil 420 ejecuciones. *Zeta*, 2011. http://www.zetatijuana.com/2011/12/12/quinto-ano-de-gobierno-60-mil-420-ejecuciones/.
45. *For journalists, coverage of political unrest proves deadly*. Committee to Protect Journalists, 2011.
46. Editor: Armed men attack Mexican newspaper office. *CNN*.http://articles.cnn.com/2011-11-06/americas/world_americas_mexico-violence_1_armed-men-newspaper-office-veracruz?_s=PM:AMERICAS.

Sensr: Evaluating a Flexible Framework for Authoring Mobile Data-Collection Tools for Citizen Science

Sunyoung Kim[1] **Jennifer Mankoff**[1] **Eric Paulos**[2]

[1]Human-computer Interaction Institute
Carnegie Mellon University
5000 Forbes Avenue, Pittsburgh, PA
{Sunyoung.kim, jmankoff}@cs.cmu.edu

[2]Electrical Engineering and Computer Sciences
University of California, Berkeley
Berkeley, CA 97420-1776
paulos@berkeley.edu

ABSTRACT

Across HCI and social computing platforms, mobile applications that support citizen science, empowering non-experts to explore, collect, and share data have emerged. While many of these efforts have been successful, it remains difficult to create citizen science applications without extensive programming expertise. To address this concern, we present Sensr, an authoring environment that enables people without programming skills to build mobile data collection and management tools for citizen science. We demonstrate how Sensr allows people without technical skills to create mobile applications. Findings from our case study demonstrate that our system successfully overcomes technical constraints and provides a simple way to create mobile data collection tools.

Author Keywords

Citizen science, mobile applications, sustainability.

ACM Classification Keywords

H.5.m. Information interfaces and presentation (e.g., HCI): Miscellaneous.

General Terms

Design

INTRODUCTION

Citizen science has a long history beginning as early as a century ago by the Audubon Society. They started the Christmas Bird Count, asking volunteers to count the number of bird species they observed during the winter holidays [24]. Since then, citizens' efforts to collect data for scientific work have been a great resource across a variety of domains.

There are currently over 15 million citizens watching or recording birds in the United States [3], and over 4,200 conservation organizations are listed in the National Wildlife Federation [25]. The domains to entail public participation become varied from traditional ecology and environmental conservation [37,7] to greater diversity including but not limited to astronomy [31], biology [10], archeology [40], and community monitoring [2].

This growth is facilitated by the increasing affordability, availability, and adoption rates of Internet-enabled and location-aware mobile devices. The Pew Internet Project reported that nearly half of all American adults (45%) and two-third of all young adults (66%) now own a smartphone as of Sep 2012 [36]. The proliferation of mobile computing technologies is making our urban environments rich in terms of sensing, providing diverse channels to scientists for data collection, and creating tremendous opportunities for everyday people to engage in scientific projects [16].

As such, mobile devices are well suited for spontaneous data collection by everyday people. However, under its guise of simplicity lies technical expertise and complex infrastructure. As a result, building such applications is a large investment that may limit smaller organizations.

Sensr, the primary contribution of this work, is an authoring tool that enables non-programmers to create mobile data collection tools for citizen science. It leverages the fact that the process and structure of data collection activities in citizen science are similar across domains despite their diversity [5]. Sensr combines a visual programing environment with a mobile application where people with limited technical expertise can build mobile data collection tools and manage data collectively. As illustrated in Figure 1, people seeking data can author a citizen science campaign on the Sensr website. The campaign is then deployed on the mobile Sensr application, and users of the mobile Sensr app can subscribe and contribute data to the campaign. Sensr radically simplifies the entire process of creating a mobile data collection tool for a wide range of citizen science domains. Authors only need to fill out a project description and design data-entry forms before launching their campaign within the mobile Sensr application for wide distribution. This frees authors from worrying about technical requirements and infrastructure constraints.

A secondary contribution of this paper is the analysis of design considerations for citizen science projects through a literature review and examination of online data about

CSCW '13, February 23–27, 2013, San Antonio, Texas, USA.
Copyright 2013 ACM 978-1-4503-1331-5/13/02...$15.00.

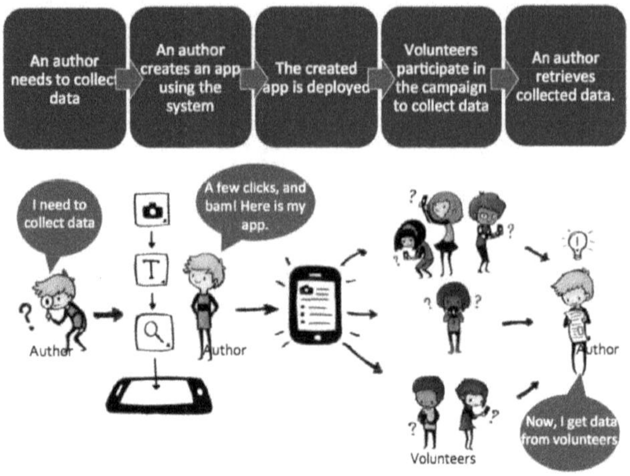

Figure 1. The process of using *Sensr*: an author creates a campaign → the created campaign is deployed on the mobile application → volunteers subscribe and collect data in the application → collected data is sent back to the author

existing digital citizen science projects, including both the authoring and volunteer experience. We discuss the current state of citizen science, particularly the use of mobile and computing technologies, and the roadblocks that inhibit digital citizen science's growth in order to develop design considerations to apply to Sensr as well as a reference for future citizen science research.

Our case study validates that authors without technical skills, in three separate organizations, successfully used Sensr to author mobile applications. Additionally, the study highlights real-world authoring issues such as translating existing campaigns into mobile-friendly reporting interfaces and the unexpected use of collected data.

Overview of Paper

We first provide our trend analysis of technology use in contemporary citizen science to elicit design considerations for digital citizen science. After explaining Sensr in detail, we employ a case study in which preexisting citizen science projects use our system. Finally, we discuss the implications this work has on the design of citizen science authoring technologies.

DESIGN CONSIDERATIONS FOR CITIZEN SCIENCE

In order to design a system that supports citizen science efforts, it is essential to understand the use of technology in contemporary citizen science. First, we review pre-existing projects to understand technology adoption, sensing, and distribution trends. Next, we explore three widely acknowledged user-acceptance factors in citizen science: data quality, privacy and motivation. Lastly, we review authoring technologies through a literature review. We will begin by defining citizen science.

Defining Citizen Science

Citizen science is a form of research collaboration between researchers and volunteers to address real-world problems [9]. Members of the public who volunteer for these collaborations participate in different phases of the research and in a variety of ways [8].

In the simplest case, the citizen science research process consists of three stages: designing a project, collecting data, and analyzing/interpreting collected data [4]. Several studies distinguish participation types and roles of volunteers [38]. Among those, Shirk *et al.* introduced five models on degree of participation: *contractual, contributory, collaborative, co-created, and collegial* [35]. In *contributory* projects, volunteers contribute to collecting data for the project designed by researchers. Projects that aim to produce data on a large geographic or temporal scale often fall under this model, and volunteers participate in the project both in person and remotely via internet [37]. In contrast, *co-created* projects occur when a group of individuals is deeply involved in most or all stages of the research process from designing a project to interpreting data. Community-based projects, like the collaborative monitoring of a neighborhood environment and local data interpretation, often fall under this model [41]. Volunteers participate in the project in person, sometimes utilizing digital collaboration tools such as Internet. *Collaborative* projects are activities for which volunteers are enlisted to help analyze and interpret scientific data. Scientific projects that require a vast quantity of data interpretation fall under this model [10,31], and volunteers can participate digitally.

Mobile devices and web technologies could easily facilitate citizen participation in *contributory, collaborative* and *co-created* projects. The *contractual* and *collegial* models lie at the far boundaries of the spectrum, so we did not explore them in this work.

Use of Technology in Citizen Science

We reviewed over 340 existing *contributory, collaborative* or *co-created* projects registered in an online citizen science repository[1] to understand the use of technology in citizen science.

Technology adoption

Only 39 projects (11%) provided companion mobile applications to facilitate data collection efforts. Compared to a wide adoption range of personal mobile devices, this shows how underrated the use of mobile devices is in citizen science. About 180 campaigns (53%) used websites as their primary point of data submission. These websites relied on custom servers or existing web services such as blogs, SurveyMonkey, Twitter, or Flickr.

Sensing

A common theme among the projects was the use of location meta-data associated with the data being sourced. Location data is both highly relevant to citizen science data collection and easily sensed with smartphone technologies. In the majority of these applications [2,7,23], GPS data was gathered and associated with other information, which varied by the type of observation and equipment used. Photos with accompanying text or numeric data were also common data sources.

[1] http://scistarter.com/

Distribution

The online citizen science repository was the only systemized distribution platform we found. Aside from this, they rely on word-of-mouth approaches such as neighborhood mailing lists and local newspapers for the distribution of their activities.

User Acceptance Factors in Citizen Science

There are several considerations in citizen science. Amongst, we explore three widely acknowledged user-acceptance factors: data quality, privacy and motivation.

Quality of Data

Citizen science relies on volunteers [8]. One potential issue in a system where the crowd becomes the source of data is quality of data [12]. Although data collected by amateurs can be of high quality (*e.g.*, [3,31]), amateur-collected data has potential for accidental submissions of bad data or malicious submissions of data [12]. This is arguably a fundamental issue for citizen science in general. A popular computational approach is redundancy where multiple workers repeat the same task [18]. A reputation model is another mechanism proposed to increase the reliability of citizen-collected data [17]. Meanwhile, Sheppard *et al.* showed that quality could be maintained by implementing a qualitative process, such as training users prior to participation [33] or providing standard data collection procedures to engage volunteers in data analysis [22]. We selected the latter approach for Sensr.

Privacy

Digital citizen science takes advantage of sensor-rich mobile phones and their extensive adoption, turning people from passive consumers to active producers of sensed data. Unavoidably, this raises privacy concerns, as people transfer a considerable amount of personal information when sensing [20]. Sensory data is our digital footprint, embedding details of everyday life. There is an inherent conflict between data sharing and privacy [15]. Location data is a fundamental part of the data being collected in citizen science applications, which when coupled with date and time data raises a number of additional concerns about privacy [39]. There exists an abundance of literature related to privacy concerns and possible solutions in citizen science [7]. Prevalent technological approaches include blurring or fuzzing information from original data [22]. Shilton *et al.* argues that participants should be engaged in the process of decision-making, claiming that urban sensing systems must allow people to negotiate social sharing for them [34]. Anonymizing data and selectively revealing information according to volunteer preference is another approach, which we used in Sensr [7].

Motivation for Participation

Attracting and retaining volunteers is crucial for designing technology-meditated science projects. Thus, motivational factors have to be addressed when building a tool [32]. Researchers have discovered that intrinsic and collective motivations like personal interests, enjoyment, following social norms, or acknowledgement are dominant factors, while reward motives are arguably less salient [26]. While important in citizen science, we did not consider this factor on the authoring side of citizen science in this work.

Authoring Technology for Citizen Science

Lack of technical expertise and resources are often the major obstacles to developing a mobile application. Many groups who wish to develop mobile citizen science applications are non-profits or local groups that lack the resources to hire experts or in-house technical staff to support such development. Beyond programming, managing data poses a significant challenge, as most of these communities do not possess server farms to manage collected data.

Distribution of the application presents another barrier. Current distribution models require financial and logistical coordination for an application to distribute with an application store. This model also results deployment delays and challenges volunteers to find existing applications.

To that end, approaches that support creating a mobile citizen science application have emerged, including participatory sensing, using existing infrastructure, and building a tool to lower technical barriers.

Participatory sensing is a computing paradigm that enables the collection of disseminated data by volunteers. It allows the increasing number of mobile phone users to share knowledge acquired by their sensor-equipped devices in diverse domains. As an example, the CENS group has designed mobile participatory sensing platforms in extensive domains for everyday people to systematically measure and share the world around them [6]. Two sample projects to mention include Campaignr, a software framework for mobile phones in which smartphone owners join data gathering campaigns for personal participatory sensing [19], and PEIR, a participatory sensing application which relies on location data sampled from mobile phones to calculate personalized estimates of environmental impact [23]. While many of the CENS systems have been tremendously successful in designing participatory sensing projects for particular needs, our efforts with Sensr lie in providing an authoring tool to support authoring mobile applications for citizen science.

Researchers have explored ways to use existing systems as an alternative platform to support citizen science. Twitter is one platform that can facilitate the distributed participation of everyday people [13]. While Twitter supports citizen activities in some aspects, it has several limitations: (1) there is little flexibility for customization, (2) it pollutes personal tweet threads, and (3) Twitter is better for announcing time-critical accidents such as disaster reports or rescue activities, less for reporting ordinary observation-type data. To maximize the capacity of mobile devices in citizen science, we claim there is a need to build a citizen science specific platform.

Table 1: Summary of authoring technology design considerations for citizen science

Authoring tool	Use of technology		User acceptance factors		Authoring type
	Sensing	Distribution	Quality assurance	Privacy	
Typical	Various	No support for distribution	Various	Various	Use a custom system or existing system (*e.g.*, Blog, Twitter, *etc.*)
Sensr	Locations/Photos/Text	Automatically launched in a web platform	Filtering/ Validation	Anonymity	Via web Forms
Ushahidi	Various	Automatically launched within an app	Various	Anonymity	xml, PHP and MySQL + custom s/w download or via web forms
Noah	Locations/Photos/Text	No support for distribution	Collection process	Social Negotiation	No support for authoring
Epicollect	Locations/Photos/Text	No support for distribution	Not specified	Not specified	Via web Forms

Recently, a small number of web platforms and tools that focus on simplifying the authoring process have emerged [1,19,21,28,30]. For example, Ushahidi is a web-based collaborative reporting environment that aggregates and shares information provided by citizens [21], and Open Data Kit (ODK) helps organizations author, field, and manage mobile data collection solutions [27]. While powerful and very flexible, most platforms require programming skills and/or infrastructure in some degree. Basic knowledge of xml, PHP, and MySQL is required to use ODK and Ushahidi. Authors need JSON for Pachubu, XML for Campaignr, and custom software download for Ushahidi. Most also require infrastructure.

Two platforms support authoring without programming: Project Noah and EpiCollect. Project Noah is a tool for citizens to explore and document wildlife [30], and EpiCollect allows people to collect and submit data to a central project from mobile phones [1]. Neither supports the variety or complexity that Sensr supports. Project Noah focuses on wildlife exploration, and EpiCollect supports application creation but not a distribution platform where volunteers find or subscribe to campaigns. Table 1 summarizes some of the design options applied to existing systems we observed.

Other Usability Factors

Studies of the data collection needs for mobile fieldworkers [29] reveal several usability factors to consider. First, when possible, a user's attention must be focused on the observation of the event or object, not on the interface. Also, a user should be able to enter data quickly and accurately across a variety of usage contexts, such as sitting, standing, or walking, and the interface needs high contrast colors for outdoor use. Finally, it should support a range of data fields to satisfy varying user needs.

Summary of Design Considerations

As summarized in Table 1, we applied the following design considerations, drawn from our literature reviews and field studies in designing Sensr to ensure usability in both *mobile* and *citizen science* applications.

Sensing: Photo and location data with a map and accompanying text inputs are essential in fieldwork type activities.

Distribution: A platform to share and review reported data among volunteers is needed but rarely provided.

Quality assurance: Simplifying the measuring and observing process is crucial to lowering the entry bar for amateurs' participation and to data quality

Privacy: Anonymizing data and selectively revealing information by volunteer preference reduces privacy threat.

Authoring type: Using web forms will make it easy to author a campaign.

SENSR: SYSTEM & IMPLEMENTATION

To take full advantage of mobile technologies, it must become easy to develop digital citizen science campaigns on mobile devices. Sensr aims to do precisely this, providing a transparent campaign-creation interface for people with limited technical skills to easily create campaigns to which users of the Sensr app can subscribe and contribute data. To clarify our work, we provide

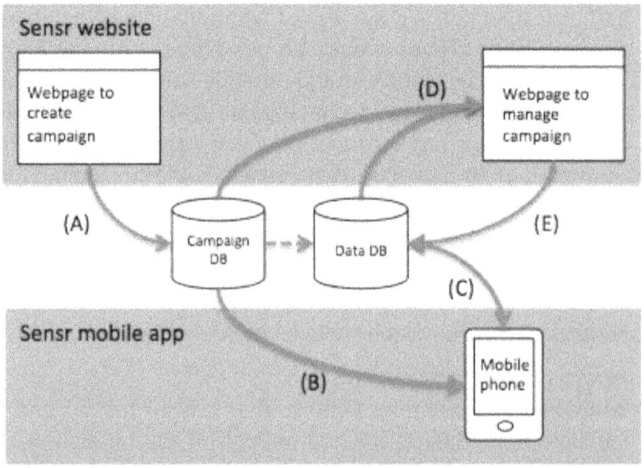

Figure 2. Functional architecture of Sensr; (a) campaign schema is saved to a server; (b) campaign schema retrieved to a mobile app; (c) reported data transfer between a server and a mobile app; (d) data retrieved to a web page; (e) discussion data saved to a server

several definitions: a mobile citizen science request for data collection is called *a campaign*, a person or organization who creates and manages the campaign is refereed to as *an author*, and an individual who contributes data to a campaign is *a volunteer*. As shown in Figure 2, Sensr system consists of two parts: (1) a website hosted through Amazon Web Services where authors create and manage campaigns, and where the public can access the list of active campaigns along with data visualizations, and (2) a mobile application with which volunteers can explore, subscribe to, and participate in campaigns.

For the server, we created two separate MySQL database tables: Campaign DB and Data DB. Campaign DB stores the basic schema of a campaign, including an interface structure, GUI components, and the general campaign information. Data DB stores data that volunteers report via the mobile application as well as discussion entries submitted from website. Then JSON serializes and transmits data over the network (see Figure 2). We used jQuery UI, Ajax, and PHP to build the interactive webpage where people can author a campaign. To build a mobile application running on iOS, we used objective-C with Apple's Cocoa API. We are planning to build a mobile app for Android in the near future.

Website experience

When designing the website, our main concern focused on accessibility for people without programming skills when authoring and managing campaigns. For that, we provide only two steps to create a campaign: (1) completing a general information page to describe the campaign, and (2) designing a data collection user interface using a simple drag and drop method.

Figure 3. Screenshots of mobile application creation from the website. Information entered in the html fields on the left automatically appears on a replica iPhone screen (top). An author can drag and drop widgets from a predefined set onto replica iPhone screen to design one's own application (bottom).

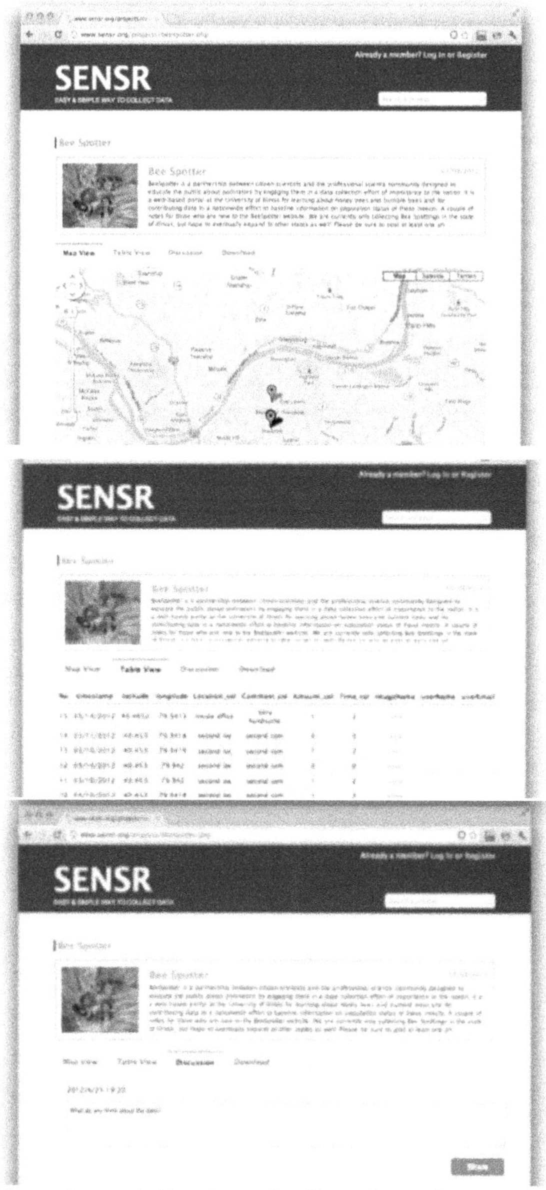

Figure 4. a website where all information and aggregated data for the campaign display. Collected data is displayed in two different formats: map and table (top and middle). People can discuss and share opinions about the campaign and relevant issues (bottom).

First, the author provides general information about the campaign, including a title, contact information, campaign description, a logo image, *etc*. The author's input is automatically displayed on a mock-up iPhone interface adjacent to the form. This page will be displayed on the mobile application when volunteers explore existing campaigns (See Figure 3 top).

Second, the author designs the data collection user interface by dragging and dropping widgets from a predefined pallet onto a simulated iPhone screen (See Figure 3 bottom). Following the guidelines for designing a mobile application we set in the previous section, widgets are selected from iOS user interface elements. Three different types of widgets are provided: photo, radio buttons (with two or three options), and a freeform text entry field. Currently, only one photo widget is allowed per report (a feature to submit multiple photos is to be added in the next version); however, multiple radio buttons and text entry fields can be added. Radio buttons are especially useful because they prevent users from struggling to type on the go.

On the mock-up iPhone screen, the author can rearrange the order of widgets, delete a widget, and edit the labels of widgets. Besides the widgets volunteers need to complete, the system automatically captures other sensor data such as a timestamp and GPS location. This page will be used as the mobile interface for volunteers to report data.

When satisfied with the design, the author submits the final campaign interface, which is then automatically converted into a version accessible by mobile application. a key feature of our system is that it avoids the technical burden, complexity, and cost of submitting apps to an app store for approval and distribution. Sensr uses an *in-app* subscription system to allow easy browsing, subscription, and removal of campaigns within the mobile application.

Once the campaign is created, the system automatically generates a hosting webpage to display all information and collected data for the campaign (See Figure 4). From this page, the author can modify campaign information, and view, filter, and operate aggregated data. This data is displayed in three different formats including a map-based visualization, a table view, and a downloadable file format. Additionally, the system provides a webpage where people can discuss and share opinions about the campaign. While the current discussion boards are primitive and lack novel features, we plan to expand its functionality to support collaborative discussion and analysis of the data in the final version [22,16]. The campaign's hosting page and data visualizations can be open to the public or shared among volunteers upon the author's setting.

Mobile application experience

On the mobile application, volunteers can subscribe to campaigns and collect, report and review data. The interface consists of three tabs: My Campaigns, My Data, and Settings (See Figure 5). The first tab, My Campaigns, lists all campaigns to which a volunteer is subscribed. When a volunteer wants to participate in other campaigns, he can visit the [add campaigns] page to explore campaigns by category or to search a particular one using a unique ID provided when a campaign is created. A volunteer clicks the [*participate*] button to subscribe. Then, the campaign is listed under My Campaigns. Clicking the title of each campaign leads to its main page where volunteers can explore existing data on a map or list view. A volunteer clicks the [*report*] button on this page to report data. The report page interface differs by campaign, according to the author's design. When connected to a network, volunteers can report data on the fly. Sensr also supports a critical citizen science feature of offline data collection by saving data locally and uploading it later when networked.

The second tab, My Data, stores data reported by the volunteer. Under the Settings tab, a volunteer can optionally set personal information including name, email, and place of residency. If a volunteer sets personal information to expose, it will be included with other report data when reported. Otherwise, personal information will not be included. Even when submitted, personal information is only visible to the author of the campaign.

Figure 5. Mobile application screenshots. From left to right, a list of campaigns a user added, a category to find and add a campaign, a campaign main page that can be viewed by map or list view, a repository of the data, and a customized form to report data

CASE STUDY

In this section, we describe a case study in which we presented Sensr to seven participants, who were interested in initiating mobile citizen science campaigns across three different organizations. Our objectives were to uncover how quickly and easily authors without technical skills could develop and maintain campaigns using Sensr, and to expose any system flaws before the application's launch. The method was as follows. First, managers from each organization gathered to discuss campaign organization issues in terms of volunteer recruitment and data collection. Next, we presented a working prototype of Sensr and explained its purpose. Managers browsed the interface before selecting one of their activities to deploy in Sensr. They created a mobile application using the Sensr website and tested the resulting mobile app in a separate room. Finally, the managers regrouped to discuss issues, benefits, and difficulties in using Sensr. All sessions were recorded and relevant portions have been transcribed.

Case Study 1: Air quality monitoring

Group Against Smog and Pollution (GASP, http://gasp-pgh.org) is a non-profit organization in Southwestern Pennsylvania working for a healthy, sustainable environment. Founded in 1969, GASP has been a diligent watchdog, educator, litigator, and policy-maker on environmental issues with a focus on air quality. GASP selected a diesel cleanup initiative to create a campaign.

Diesel Clean-Up Campaign

Diesel exhaust is one of the nation's most pervasive sources of toxic air pollution. Diesel engines, such as buses, trucks, trains, and construction equipment, are known for their durability, but older engines emit a toxic mixture of particles, metals, and gases including over 40 hazardous air pollutants as classified by EPA [14] unless properly maintained. While old diesel engines are known as a major source of diesel exhaust, it is relatively difficult to collect evidence because incidents are transient, and the exhaust disappears within several seconds. Distributed urban sensor nodes (*e.g.,* citizens equipped with smart phones) can be an appropriate medium to capture such incidents. GASP has sought ways to encourage everyday people to monitor neighborhood diesel emissions and share experiences with visual evidence like photos or videos. A photo of a fuming vehicle's license plate could be great evidence against companies with illegal emissions control. While aware that the use of a mobile application will facilitate their efforts, lack of software development skills has hindered GASP from developing a mobile application.

Creating a campaign

Three managers used Sensr to create a campaign, and they did not have any problems interacting with the web interface. Everyone easily figured out how to interact with the drag-and-drop interface and created a campaign with few mistakes. We did not find evidence for any usability issues when interacting with our system. The final interfaces were identical across managers: one photo and one comment field widget. We assume this is because the campaign is already underway, making the design of an interface for a mobile application obvious.

Issues and possible solutions

Data quality was of particular concern to this organization for several reasons. First, the party who contributes data is the error-prone general public. Also, a participant's data report could include photos containing inappropriate content, which would be detrimental to their reputation. However, the authors who tried Sensr felt that Sensr's mechanism for handling this issue addressed their concerns. Sensr provides a filtering process with which an author can confirm data before displaying it in public to ensure its quality. While this mechanism brought up a separate concern about extra time spent filtering data, they agreed to manage such commitment if it increased citizens' participation and the amount of useful data collected.

> *"There are always people who try strange things. We are the ones who officially organizes and runs this data collection activity. I am worried if people may think that our activities are full of useless incidents if the data quality is not decent."*

> *"Our logo will be put on top of all these data. We do not want to represent any junk data, and need ways to control its quality."*

While mostly satisfied with Sensr, they found it lacks the support for localization. Many grassroots activities are based in a particular area where locals monitor neighborhood environments. Because GASP runs activities solely for and within the Southern Pennsylvania region, they have no means to act upon data from outside the supported area. To prevent such wasted efforts, they suggested a feature to author a campaign by region.

> *"It won't hurt if someone in California reports us a picture of diesel emission there. But we can do nothing about it. Then that person's effort becomes useless... It would be nice if we can specify a locational boundary."*

Case Study 2. Watershed monitoring

The Mountain Watershed Association (MTWatershed, http://www.mtwatershed.org) focuses on the conservation, restoration, and protection of watersheds in Pennsylvania. They aim to remediate abandoned mine discharges, develop community awareness, promote cooperative community efforts for remediation, and encourage sound environmental practices. MTWatershed selected a Marcellus visual assessment program for a campaign.

Marcellus Visual Assessment Program

Marcellus shale is a rock formation that underlies approximately two-thirds of Pennsylvania and the adjacent area. The shale is believed to hold trillions of cubic feet of natural gas. Recently developed drilling technology makes extracting natural gas from the formation more feasible. The drilling process relies on a mixture of chemicals and a large amount of water, ranging from 3 to 7 million gallons, which may be illegally dumped afterwards, causing serious water and environmental pollution. MTWatershed offers a basic training course, called the Marcellus Visual Assessment program that instructs how to monitor Marcellus drilling sites. People learn to use their sight, hearing, and smell to identify potential issues resulting from drilling operations on site. Then they go into the field, observe sites, and come back home to report data via an online form in the website. Since location information is critical, MTWatershed wants to develop a mobile application to automatically capture geo codes. However, their limited resources and technical skills have hindered them from developing a mobile application.

Creating a campaign
Two managers created a campaign on our system and did not have any problems interacting with the web interface. Everyone easily figured out how to interact with the drag-and-drop interface, creating a campaign with few mistakes. While we did not find evidence for usability issues, we saw a disparity in the final two interfaces: one interface was almost identical to the online form currently used by the organization, and another interface modified the current form with an additional photo widget and fewer data fields. (The preexisting form consisted of seven selection fields and eight text-entry fields to report.) They explained that one manager simply copied the existing form to a mobile campaign while the other tried to adapt the existing format for the mobile interface. Even though an existing campaign was converted, the result conflicts with the finding from the previous case where the final interfaces were identical across managers. This finding reveals that the complexity of the preexisting form influences the mobile application design. The form in the previous case had only two data fields, which made it easy to translate to the mobile version, while the form in this case had fifteen data fields.

Issues and possible solutions
The discrepancy between the interfaces reflects a possible difficulty when creating a mobile version of existing campaigns. The current data entry form was not applicable to a mobile interface because it was lengthy and complex. In such cases, modifying an existing form is necessary to sustain mobile usability, which in turn causes the disparity in the formats of data collected from different media. Since the activity was already underway, the managers were hesitant to generate a separate module for a mobile version. This suggests the need to build in prompts to guide authors toward mobile-friendly interfaces. Through discussion, they optimized the form suitable for a mobile platform.

"I know that it cannot be the same from a web form to a mobile one. But I don't want to have two different sets for the same activity. We can merge a few questions to reduce the number of fields, and add a photo to remove some."

"Our current format is somewhat complicated as it needs to measure data using sensors we lend. If we can make it simple to fit into this system, we will have more people participate in it."

They raised another concern about the possibility of malicious data use. Public access to the data has both benefits and disadvantages: the aggregated data show volunteers where popular monitoring sites are and where more data is needed, but it also tells companies which locations are rarely monitored and thus, would be ideal for illegal dumping sites. The managers did not come up with any specific solution, but all agreed that more citizen participation would cover more sites and lessen the chance for such ill-purposed use cases.

"We monitor illegal wastewater dumping. If companies know where people are monitoring, they could use that information to find a site where no one monitors so that they can go dumping wastewater there."

Case Study 3. Local Parks Conservation
The Pittsburgh Parks Conservancy (http://www.pittsburghparks.org) was founded two decades ago by a group of citizens concerned with the deteriorating conditions of Pittsburgh's parks. The Conservancy participates in all aspects of park management to improve parks and thus, boost quality of life for the people of Pittsburgh. They conduct projects with environmental sensitivity, respect for the parks' historic landscape design, and an appreciation for the recreational needs of modern users. The Conservancy selected to create a campaign for an invasive species management program.

Invasive Species Management Program
Although many plant species are introduced to the United States from other countries without causing ecological damage, the small percentage of non-native plants that become invasive can have a devastating impact. Left unchecked, invasive species can completely take over sections of parkland, killing a wide variety of native vegetation and destroying the biological diversity that creates habitat for wildlife and keeps an ecosystem functioning. The Conservancy has been working to monitor and control the spread of invasive species in the parks. Volunteers can help by simply comparing plants in the wild with a provided list of invasive plants and reporting suspicious plants to the Conservancy. Currently, this program is only devoted to educating community members about invasive species and the proper way to remove them. Since school children partake in a variety of extracurricular activities at parks, the Conservancy has sought ways to encourage these children to participate in the program using mobile phones. However, lack of technical skills has been an obstacle.

Creating a campaign
Two managers used Sensr to create a campaign. While we did not find evidence for usability issues in interacting with our system, both managers struggled to create a campaign from the provided widgets alone. They wanted to create an extra page to display pictures of invasive species that the system does not provide. Setting this aside, both managers came up with similar interfaces consisting of one photo widget and a couple text and selection fields for extra information about the photo. After a discussion between the managers and researchers, they decided to create a web page to display pictures of invasive species, and link it to the campaign's mobile page to fulfill their needs.

Issues and possible solutions'
We did not find any usability issues from the case study with this organization, but they demonstrated a strong intent to use Sensr as a tool to reach broader populations.

The Conservancy has sought ways to promote youth participation in their conservation activities. The manager said that it was particularly difficult to make students interested in the activity. The managers appreciated the ease with which Sensr allowed them to operate a mobile application since the use of mobile devices would more easily allow and excite younger participants.

> *"It is hard to reach out younger population. Having a simple mobile application like this, we can attract high school kids!"*

IMPLICATIONS

The case study with three organizations highlighted several design implications for the authoring interfaces of mobile data collection tools for citizen science.

A guide to manage data collection from various platforms is needed

Sensor-equipped mobile devices are an apt platform for citizen science data collection but not the only platform an organization may use. Many campaigns are already designed for and executed on other platforms, such as paper or a website. This raises the issue of modifying pre-existing forms designed for other platforms to suit mobile devices. A mobile interface should be simpler than a paper or web form because of its screen size. However, pre-existing campaigns are often long and complex. This suggests the need for deeper considerations to help authors make a rational decision in transfering existing forms designed for various platforms to the mobile interface. Tools that could support the integration of data across platforms would be of value. Furthermore, as data collection platforms become varied, guidelines to manage data collection efforts for a campaign through various platforms need to be explored.

Location information is crucial for privacy and beyond

We learned from a literature review that location is crucial to interpreting data and protecting privacy and will work will need to continue in addressing this issue [7]. Our case studies also confirmed the essential nature of location data. Our participants were interested in a broader use of location than has been reported in the past. For example, participants wanted to know more about gaps in where data had been gathered to improve volunteer participation in a targeted way. Automated identification of "data quality gaps" could be a valuable area for future work.

Expert review ensures data quality and a feeling of control

Past work has pointed to data quality as an area requiring careful attention in citizen science campaigns (*e.g.*, [3,31]). Our study shows that many experts still doubt the quality of amateur-collected data. Sensr provides a filtering option that allows a campaign author to confirm collected data before displaying it publicly. This review step relieved authors' concern about amateur participation in scientific work. Future work could include tools that learn from author confirmation and eventually predict problems and highlight them automatically to campaign authors.

Mobile applications further increase public engagement and education in citizen science

Citizen science plays an important role in improving the public's scientific literacy [4]. While the direct effects of public participation may not be visible, volunteers learn to identify relevant phenomena and generate local knowledge, which can result in an active citizen advocacy [38]. All authors from the case study emphasized their belief that mobile applications would further promote public engagement, increase awareness of their activities, and provide volunteers with informal science education. In particular, mobile devices can be an effective medium to increase youth interest in participation. While usability and usefulness were our main considerations when designing Sensr, perhaps entertainment and enjoyment should also be considered to further increase engagement and educational aspects of citizen science.

CONCLUSION

The proliferation of mobile devices in our everyday lives has provided a rich sensor environment for citizens to observe, measure, and evaluate their world. However, technical barriers have prevented people from taking full advantage of the opportunities of these sensor rich mobile data collection platforms coupled with crowd sourcing..

This work has two major contributions to the fields of HCI and social computing for the proliferation of citizen science. Our primary contribution is Sensr, an authoring tool that overcomes the technical barriers in developing mobile applications for citizen science. We validated Sensr in a case study with seven participants at three local organizations. Our findings point towards a promising potential for digital citizen science on mobile technologies to expand participatory data collection efforts. In the future, we will deploy Sensr for further studies focusing on the volunteer use.

Through a case study, we validated that Sensr successfully helped people without technical skills author mobile citizen science applications. Furthermore, it revealed real-world issues in authoring mobile citizen science applications such as difficulties translating existing campaigns to mobile-friendly reporting interfaces and the unexpected uses of collected data.

While this paper focuses on the authoring side of Sensr, a secondary contribution is a broader exploration of design considerations for technologically enhanced citizen science projects for both authoring and volunteering.

Technologically enhaced citizen science has the potential to expand participatory data collection efforts, increasing the public engagement in problems that directly relate to everyday lives, health, and environmental issues. We hope to further this work and inspire others to contribute towards the emerging field of citizen science.

ACKNOWLEDGEMENT

We appreciate the valuable input of our anonymous reviewers. We also would like to thank all the study participants and users of our system. This work was supported by Heinz Endowments and NSF IIS-1211047.

REFERENCES

1. Aanensen, D. M., et al. (2009). EpiCollect: linking smartphones to web applications for epidemiology, ecology and community data collection. PloS one, 4(9), e6968.
2. Aoki, P. M., Honicky, R. J., Mainwaring, A., Myers, C., Paulos, E., Subramanian, S., Woodruff, A. (2009). A vehicle for research: using street sweepers to explore the landscape of environmental community action. In Proc. of CHI
3. Bhattacharjee, Y. (2005). Ornithology: a half-century of interaction with bird watchers has evolved into a robust and growing collaboration between volunteers and a leading ornithology lab. Science, 308, 1402–1403.
4. Bonney, R., Cooper, C. B., Dickinson, J., Kelling, S., Phillips, T., Rosenberg, K. V., & Shirk, J. (2009). Citizen Science: A Developing Tool for Expanding Science Knowledge and Scientific Literacy. BioScience, 59(11), 977–984
5. Burke, J., Estrin, D., Hansen, M., Parker, A., Ramanathan, N., Reddy, S., Srivastava, M.B. (2006). Participatory sensing. In ACM Sensys WSW Workshop
6. CENS, http://urban.cens.ucla.edu/
7. Cohen, J.E. (2008). Privacy, Visibility, Transparency, and Exposure. Univ. of Chicago Law Review, 75(1).
8. Cohn, J.P. (2008). Citizen science: can volunteers do real research? Bioscience 58, 192–197
9. Cooper, C. B., Dickinson, J., Phillips, T. B. Bonney, R. (2007). Citizen science as a tool for conservation in residential ecosystems. Ecology and Society 12(2): 11.
10. Cooper, S. et al. (2010). Predicting protein structures with a multiplayer online game. Nature, 466:7307,. 756–760.
11. Cornwall, A. (2008). Unpacking 'participation': Models, meanings, and practices. Community Development Journal, 43(3). 269–283.
12. Cuff, D., Hansen, M. and J. King (2008). Urban Sensing: Out of the Woods, Communications of the ACM, Volume 51
13. Demirbas, M.A., Bayir, C. G. Akcora, Y. S. Yilmaz, H. Ferhatosmanoglu, Crowd-sourced sensing and collaboration using twitter, IEEE International Symposium on A World of Wireless, Mobile and Multimedia Networks, 2010
14. EPA, http://www.epa.gov/diesel/
15. Erickson, T. and Kellogg, W.A. (2000). Social translucence: an approach to designing systems that support social processes, ACM Transactions on CHI
16. Estrin, D. (2010). Participatory Sensing: citizen science, scientific citizens, computational thinking
17. Huang, K., Kanhere, S., Hu, W. (2010). Are You Contributing Trustworthy Data?: The Case for a Reputation System in Participatory Sensing, In Proc. of MSWiM
18. Ipeirotis, P.G., Provost, F., & Wang, J (2010). Quality management on Amazon Mechanical Turk. HCOMP'10.
19. Joki, A., Burke, J., Estrin, D. (2007). Campaignr - a framework for participatory data collection on mobile phones. Technical report, CENS, UCLA, 2007.
20. Krontiris, I. and Maisonneuve, M. (2011). Participatory Sensing: The Tension Between Social Translucence and Privacy, In Trustworthy Internet, pp. 159–170.
21. Liu, S. Iacucci, A.A., & Meier, P. Ushahidi Haiti & Chile: Next Generation Crisis Mapping. American Congress on Surveying and Mapping, August 2010.
22. Luther, K., Counts, S. Stecher, K., Hoff, A. Johns, P. (2009). Pathfinder: an online collaboration environment for citizen scientists. In Proc. of CHI
23. Mun, M., et al. (2009). PEIR, the personal environmental impact report, as a platform for participatory sensing systems research. In Proc. of Mobisys '09
24. National Audubon Society (2010). Christmas Bird Count. http://birds.audubon.org/history-christmas-bird-count
25. National Wildlife Federation, http://www.nwf.org/
26. Nov, O., Arazy, O., Anderson, D. (2011). Technology-mediated citizen science participation: a motivational model, In Proc. of ICWSM
27. Open Data Toolkit, http://opendatakit.org
28. Pachube, http://pachube.com
29. Pascoe, J., N. Ryan, D. Morse, (2000). Using while moving: HCI issues in fieldwork environments. Transactions on Computer-Human Interaction, 417-437
30. Project Noah, http://www.projectnoah.org/
31. Raddick, M. et al. (2009). Galaxy Zoo: Exploring the Motivations of Citizen Science Volunteers, Arxiv preprint arXiv:0909.2925
32. Rotman, D., Preece, J., Hammock, J., Procita, K., Hansen, D., Parr, C., Jacobs, D. (2012). Dynamic changes in motivation in collaborative citizen-science projects. In Proc. of CSCW 2012
33. Sheppard, S.A. and Terveen, L. (2011). Quality is a verb: the operationalization of data quality in a citizen science community, In Proc. of the 7th International Symposium on Wikis and Open Collaboration, pp.29-38
34. Shilton, K., Burke, J., Estrin, D., Hansen, M., & Srivastava, M. B. (2008). Participatory Privacy in Urban Sensing. *Science*, *1596*, 1–7.
35. Shirk JL, Ballard HL, Wilderman CC, et al. (2012). Public participation in scientific research: a framework for deliberate design.Ecol Soc 17: 29
36. Smith, A. (2011). Smartphone Adoption and Usage, July, 2011. http://pewinternet.org/Reports/2011/Smartphones.aspx
37. Sullivan B.L., Wood, C.L., Iliff, M.I., Bonney, R.E., Fink, D., Kelling, S. (2009). eBird: A citizen-based bird observation network in the biological sciences. Biological Conservation.
38. Wiggins, A. and Crowston, K. (2011). From conservation to crowdsourcing: A typology of citizen science, In Proc. of Hawai'I International Conference on System Science
39. Willett, W., et al. (2010). Common Sense Community: Scaffolding Mobile Sensing and Analysis for Novice Users, In Proc. of Pervasive Computing
40. Williams, J. (2010). Help Find Genghis Khan's Tomb From the Comfort of Your Home,http://www.wired.com/geekdad/2010/07/mongolia-valley-of-the-khans/
41. Zerbe, F. and C. Wilderman. (2010). Monitoring IMPACTS of new gas-drilling technologies. Pages 1–4 in E. Ely, editor. The volunteer monitor. US Environmental Protection Agency Office of Water, Washington, D.C., USA

Comparing the Use of Social Networking and Traditional Media Channels for Promoting Citizen Science

Christine Robson[1,2,3]
crobson@cs.berkeley.edu

Marti A. Hearst[1]
hearst@ischool.berkeley.edu

Chris Kau[3]
ckau@us.ibm.com

Jeff Pierce[3,4]
j.pierce@sisa.samsung.com

[1]University of California, Berkeley
Berkeley, CA 94720 USA

[2]Google Research
1600 Amphitheater Pkwy
Mountain View, CA 94043

[3]IBM Research - Almaden
650 Harry Road,
San Jose, CA 95124 USA

[4]Samsung UX Innovations
3000 Orchard Parkway,
San Jose, CA 95134 USA

ABSTRACT
This paper examines how social networks can be used to recruit and promote a crowdsourced citizen science project and compares this recruiting method to the use of traditional media channels including press releases, news stories, and participation campaigns. The target studied is Creek Watch, a citizen science project that allows anyone with an iPhone to submit photos and observations of their local waterways to authorities who use the data for water management, environmental programs, and cleanup events. The results compare promotional campaigns using a traditional press release with news pickups, a participation campaign through local organizations, and a social networking campaign through Facebook and Twitter. Results also include the trial of a feature that allows users to post automatically to Facebook or Twitter. Social networking is found to be a worthwhile avenue for increasing awareness of the project, increasing the conversion rate from browsers to participants, but that targeting existing communities with a participation campaign was a more successful means for increasing the amount of data collected by volunteers.

Author Keywords
Citizen Science, Crowdsourcing, Social Networking

ACM Classification Keywords
H.5.3

General Terms
Human Factors; Design; Measurement

INTRODUCTION
Social networking presents opportunities for collaborative responses to community concerns. Advertisers exploit the networking power of Facebook to raise awareness about products, issues, and opportunities. Facebook Pages[1] are an increasingly popular way to voice support for issues or problems of concern. In parallel with the growth of social networking opportunities, a new data collection movement has emerged. Participatory sensing is used by activists to support data collection where participants use mobile devices and web services to collect actionable data on problems of concern to their communities (e.g. air pollution and trash data) [13]. The growth of mobile data collection is partly due to the increasing instrumentation of mobile phones, providing the means to easily collect data, and the opportunity to integrate data collection into daily activities.

With such a multitude of technologies to empower users, project managers are often ill equipped to choose the best technology or deployment plan. This is particularly the case for citizen science projects, in which volunteers collaborate to collect data or perform analysis on a project with scientific goals. Examples of citizen science range from volunteers in the field recording observations about wildlife and the environment, to those who donate their time or computing cycles for protein folding algorithms or processing signals from space. Citizen science projects typically operate on limited resources with a small budget and time constrained staff members frequently doubling as both administrators and as scientists who conduct experiment design and data analysis. Often, a decision to try a new method of recruiting or educating users comes at the expense of time to analyze data or take action on findings. Knowing what avenues to invest time and effort on are critical for the success of a project [3].

Recently, there has been a trend in citizen science projects towards the use of social networking tools to promote projects and encourage community, but it is unclear how successful such tools are for citizen science projects. While several prominent projects have established presences on Facebook and Twitter (e.g., Cornell's eBird[2], and Berkeley's SETI@Home[3]), the success of social networking as a means for raising project awareness, recruiting participants, and encouraging participation has not been well-explored [3].

In this paper, we report our experiences using social networking tools to promote and recruit users for a citizen science project, Creek Watch. Creek Watch was developed in

[2]http://www.ebird.org
[3]http://setiathome.berkeley.edu

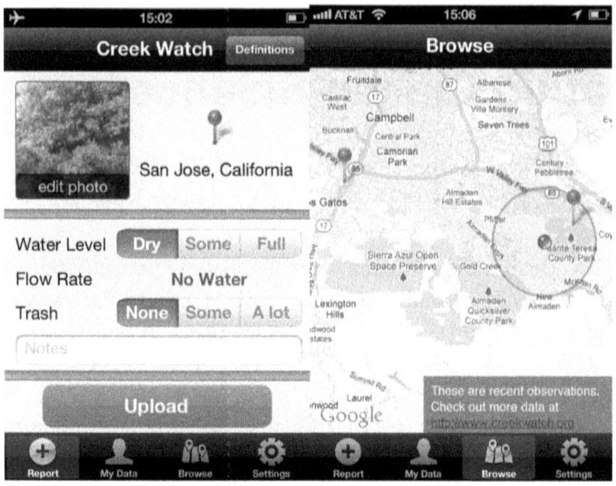

Figure 1: Creek Watch iPhone App.

collaboration between an HCI (human-computer interaction) research group and a government agency, as a means to encourage anyone with a smart phone help authorities manage freshwater resources. By employing user-centered iterative design in collaboration with scientists who need the data, Creek Watch was built to collect data that is useful to scientists and water authorities, while still being usable by untrained novices [8]. Users of Creek Watch submit a photo of their local creek, stream, or other water body along with simple observations about water level, water flow rate, and trash (see Figure 1). Observations are automatically time stamped and GPS tagged. Reports are submitted to a database at creekwatch.org, where scientists and members of the public alike can view reports and download data.

After the initial launch of the project in October 2010, we conducted three separate campaigns several months apart to recruit volunteers: (1) a press release with international web news coverage, (2) a participation campaign with targeted groups in two cities, and (3) a social networking campaign, promoting a new version of the app on Facebook and Twitter. The results of these campaigns on website visitors, iPhone App downloads, and report submissions are described in "Methods of Recruitment".

A second avenue for using social networking with Creek Watch is also described. In "Social Network Integration" we present the results of a new feature that enables users to notify their friends and followers automatically when they participate, and a user survey about this feature. The effect on participation of the Twitter and Facebook postings is described, with a discussion of why the difference in usage and communities might reflect the differences in participation from Twitter and Facebook followers.

BACKGROUND

Citizen science is a collaborative process of data collection, curation, and analysis, in which a network of individuals contribute towards a scientific project. While citizen science has a long history, most projects are now Internet based or facilitated [19]. Perhaps the most important recent development in citizen science is the shift towards open participation in every stage of the project. Early projects were usually organized with a central scientific authority gathering and analyzing data from distributed volunteers who only ever saw a fraction of the data, and were later able to read a final report [19]. For example, the Christmas Bird Count, the oldest citizen science project in North America that for over 100 years has collected annual data from bird watchers, was organized this way [17]. Many of today's projects are designed, implemented, and analyzed by the citizen scientists themselves. For instance, ReClam The Bay[4], a monitoring and shellfish restoration project in Barnegat Bay, New Jersey, is entirely operated by concerned community members, who collect data on shellfish rearing from their restoration initiatives, and then recruit scientists to help them analyze and understand the data [2].

Computers have created a new niche for citizen scientists who prefer to help with a minimum of effort. Volunteer computing platforms enable participants to use idle time on their computers, for instance in SETI@home[2] to search for signals in space, or Folding@home[5] to solve biochemistry problems. Participants in these projects have been shown to be motivated by knowing that their work contributes to a worthy goal, suggesting that they have overlapping motivations with citizen scientists who do field work [11].

Nov et. al have termed these new internet based citizen science projects "SciSourcing." In their work they have uncovered different motives for participants in SciSourcing, as compared to participants in crowdsourcing for non-scientific purposes. Specifically, SciSourcing participants were motivated foremost by the opportunity to learn, and not at all by reputation and identification [12].

The proliferation of mobile phones has also opened up a new era of citizen science. Most of today's phones carry a suite of sensors including GPS and cameras, with new models experimenting with additional sensors such as temperature and pollen & particulate count [13]. This is transforming the phone into a generic platform for gathering data about the environment, both actively and passively. Paulos et al have observed this phenomenon of mobile phones as data collection devices and termed it "participatory urbanism" or "participatory sensing" [13].

Field science is experiencing a push towards novel data collection techniques that employ volunteers and encourage the kinds of observations that can be recorded by participatory sensing approaches. The work of Kuzentsov et al. in situ with scientific field data collectors suggests a need for increasing data collection through non-digital sensors and enriched observation [9].

While these methods for data collection are new, and to some extent unstudied, study of the motivations for volunteers to collect such data and participate in projects has a

[4] http://www.reclamthebay.org
[5] http://folding.stanford.edu

long history. Community building is a key motivator for participation in citizen science [15], as contrasted with other volunteer activities for which acknowledgement and rewards are more common motivators (e.g. open source software development [5]). Indeed, the clearest difference between the motives of citizen scientists and those of professional scientists is just this: citizen scientists are much more motivated by collectivism [15]. This is consistent with established patterns of volunteerism. In Wilson and Musick's work on understanding volunteering, which involved a comprehensive survey of 3,617 individuals, they found that people are more likely to volunteer if they are more social (i.e., report more frequent conversations and meetings in their daily lives) [20]. Younger volunteers are also significantly more likely than older volunteers to be motivated by social or collaborative activities, such as meetings or other opportunities to interact with others [16]. These findings suggest that targeting younger, more social individuals may increase participation in citizen science projects. One of the best places to reach younger, more social individuals is on social networking sites such as Facebook [4].

METHODS OF RECRUITMENT

The question of how to best to recruit users to a citizen science project remains open. In an NSF sponsored workshop bringing together citizen science practitioners and Computer Science researchers [3], we explored several recruitment strategies used by practitioners. It became clear that there was no consensus or understanding of which recruitment methods work best, nor how to evaluate such methods. For some projects, data collection is the priority, and all efforts are focused on increasing the number of data reports so that more data is available for scientific research (e.g. eBird [18]). Other projects are more focused on awareness and education, focusing on engaging a large number of people about an issue (e.g. the World Water Monitoring Challenge[6]) [3].

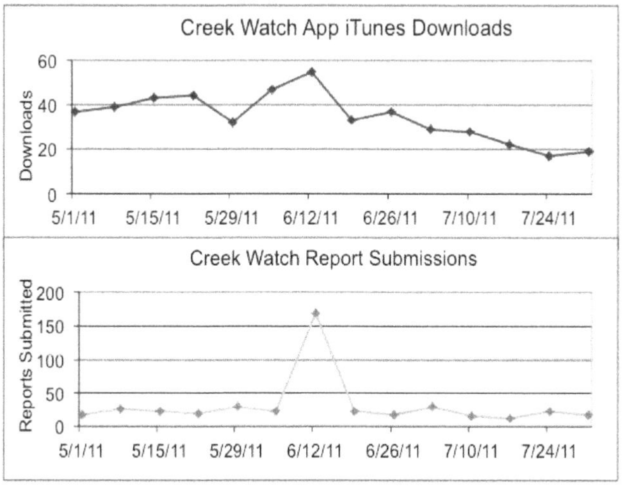

Figure 2: App Downloads and Report Submissions during Creek Watch Snapshot Day on June 16, 2011.

[6] http://www.wwmd.org

In the course of the Creek Watch project, we explored the effects of three different methods of recruitment: (1) a press release with international web news coverage, (2) a participation campaign with targeted groups in two cities, and (3) a social networking campaign, promoting a new version of the app on Facebook and Twitter. This paper describes the outcome of these three different methods.

Recruiting via Press Release and News Coverage

In Jan 2011, three months after the launch of Creek Watch, an international press release highlighted the project. The announcement was included in 23 web news articles and resulted in a spike in downloads of the Creek Watch App, as well as a spike in the number of report submissions (See Figures 3 and 4).

Participation Day

In June 2011, in collaboration with two city water boards, we launched a participation campaign dubbed "Creek Watch snapshot day." Participants were recruited through a community service outreach program to make coordinated observations of the waterways of greatest concern in their local areas. Over 100 people signed up to participate. This campaign, and the resulting press, resulted in an increase in downloads and report submissions, as seen in Figure 2.

Social Networking Campaign

In March 2012, we launched a new version of Creek Watch with social networking features. Instead of putting out press releases, we announced this feature through a social networking campaign, including a six-hour Q&A with 512,496 Facebook and Twitter followers. The Q&A resulted in 1,511 people "talking about this," (i.e., the number of people who interacted directly with the campaign by posting questions or re-posting/tweeting content) and a "viral reach" of 26,973 people (i.e., of the people "talking about this," the "viral reach" is the total number of their friends and followers who saw their activity). A YouTube video embedded in the Facebook conversation received 920 views.

Results

Comparing these three methods of recruitment, we can see that the international press release and the social networking campaign resulted in similarly sized download spikes

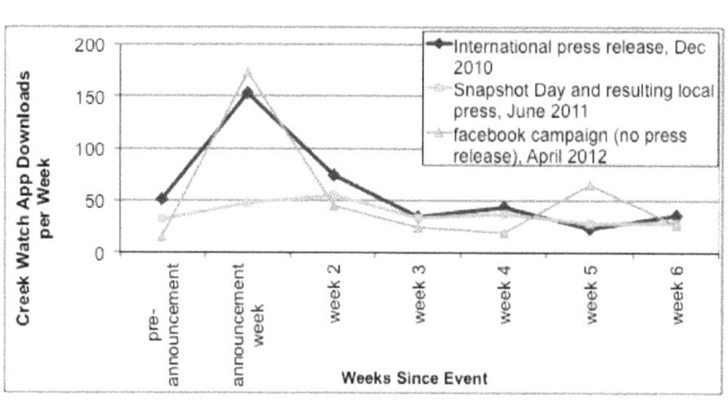

Figure 3: iTunes app downloads of Creek Watch during three different campaigns, spaced by more then a year apart, but overlaid based on start date to show relative effects.

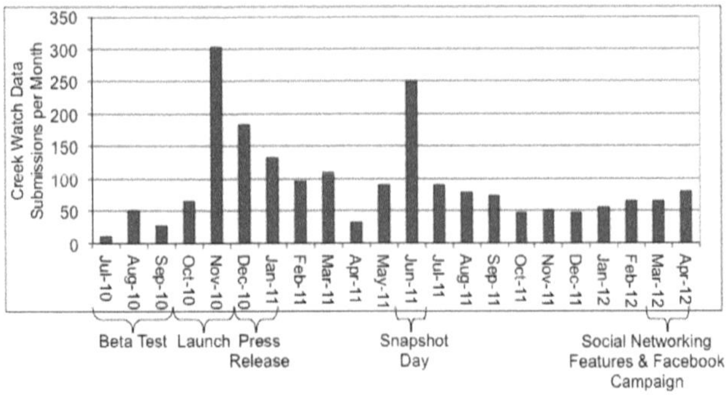

Figure 4: Creek Watch report submissions over all time.

(see Figure 3). This suggests that the Facebook campaign was just as effective at recruiting new users as a traditional press campaign.

The participation day, which was aimed primarily at encouraging data collection, not new user recruitment, did not result in a download spike. However, as can be seen in Figure 4, the participation day was very successful in increasing report submissions from users. By comparison, the social networking campaign resulted in very little increase in report submissions. This result is consistent with expectations from patterns of volunteer involvement, as established by Wilson and Musick [20]. Focusing on existing users who have an established interest in the project resulted in more work for the project being completed (i.e. more data collected), whereas recruiting new users had less immediate impact on data collection.

Comparison to Major News Coverage

The above three campaigns are in many ways comparable because they each took place after Creek Watch had launched, and at a time when we were exploring new ways to recruit participants but had not taken any action to promote the project in months. However, the effects of these campaigns are dwarfed by comparison to the Creek Watch launch. The project was launched in October 2010 with a combination of press releases, Facebook announcements, and targeted emails to mailing lists of potentially interested parties. Two weeks later, a spotlight on the evening TV news prompted a minor media frenzy. Creek Watch was featured in two television broadcasts, two radio broadcasts, and over 400 news articles including the front page of the *San Jose Mercury News*. The resulting spike in downloads, shown in Figure 5, was over four times the size of any subsequent campaign.

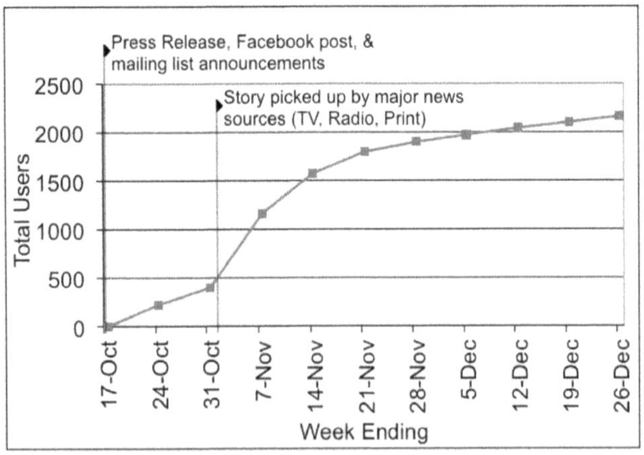

Figure 5: iTunes app downloads of Creek Watch after launch in Oct 2010.

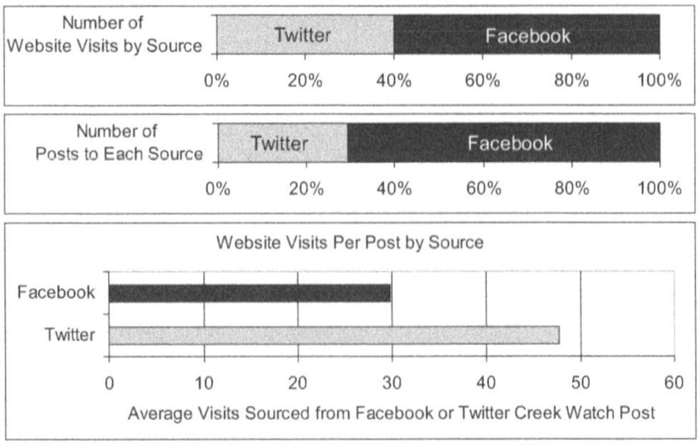

Figure 6: Visitors to creekwatch.org who clicked on a Creek Watch observation posted to Facebook or Twitter.

SOCIAL NETWORK INTEGRATION

As a second experiment with social networking, the new version of Creek Watch released in March 2012 includes integration with Facebook and Twitter. Users who submit reports have the option of automatically posting their observations to their Facebook Wall or Twitter Stream. Visitors to the Creek Watch website who have clicked on a link from one of these Facebook or Twitter posts are tracked anonymously to measure the effectiveness of this feature at recruiting new users and increasing web traffic. This feature is consistent with the observed uses of microblogging tools such as Twitter and Facebook, since microblogging is commonly used to announce casual or daily activities [6]. As can be seen in Figure 6, Creek Watch users more commonly (60%) post observations to Facebook than to Twitter, however Twitter posts generate more visits. This is consistent with observations of Lampe & Roth on use of Facebook and Twitter in the public sector [10], and with general use of Facebook [7]. While more people click on individual Twitter than Facebook posts, the audiences

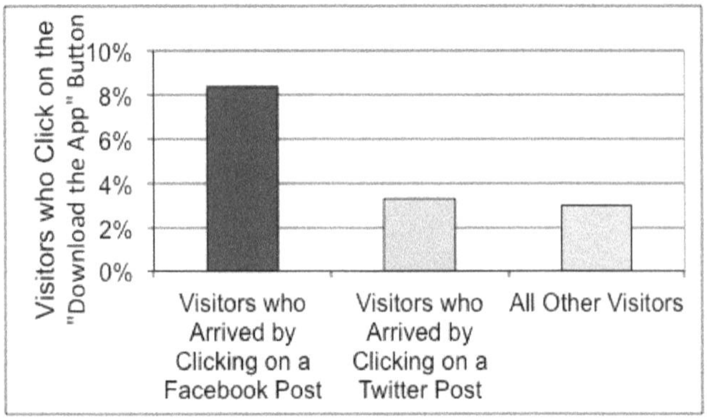

Figure 7: Percent of users who click on the download button on creekwatch.org, by referring website.

appear different. Click throughs from Facebook posts are 2.5 times more likely to result in a download of the iPhone app then click throughs from Twitter posts (see Figure 7). Indeed, visitors who clicked on a Twitter post are no more likely to download the app then any other web visitor, with a "conversion rate" of about 3%. The Twitter results are unsurprising when considering the work of Bansky et al.'s influence and diffusion of tweets, which suggests that it is difficult to predict what content will generate re-tweeting or which users will be the largest influencers, indicating that Twitter may not be a reliable means for promotion [1].

The effect of a Facebook or Twitter post is relatively local and highly transient. Each post generates between 0 and 152 website hits per Facebook/Twitter post, with an average of 29.52 hits per post (median 21). As shown in figure 9, the increase in web traffic resulting from the post is concentrated in the first 2-5 hours, with small peaks centered about 9 hours and 21 hours after posts. These peaks coincide with the evening of the day the post is made, and the morning of the following day, as most Creek Watch reports are made between 8am-1pm.

These results illustrate that integration with Facebook and Twitter resulted in an increase in web traffic (project awareness), but that only integration with Facebook resulted in an increase in downloads (recruitment).

Impressions of Facebook & Twitter Integration

While the social networking feature shows promise, we noticed that not many of our users are making use of it. In the first 8 weeks of use, only 21% of reports submitted to Creek Watch were also posted to Facebook or Twitter. To try to understand the reasons behind the low adoption rate of this feature and to investigate Creek Watch use patterns in general, we conducted a survey (N=139). Due to the anonymous nature of Creek Watch and of iTunes App downloads, we could not target Creek Watch users directly. Instead we sent the survey through three channels: (1) posting on the Creek Watch Facebook page and the pages of Creek Watch's sponsors (28 respondents), (2) a government mailing list for people who are interested in water conservation (97 respondents), and (3) a list of 121 people who had contacted the Creek Watch team directly at some point (14 respondents). There were 139 total survey respondents with

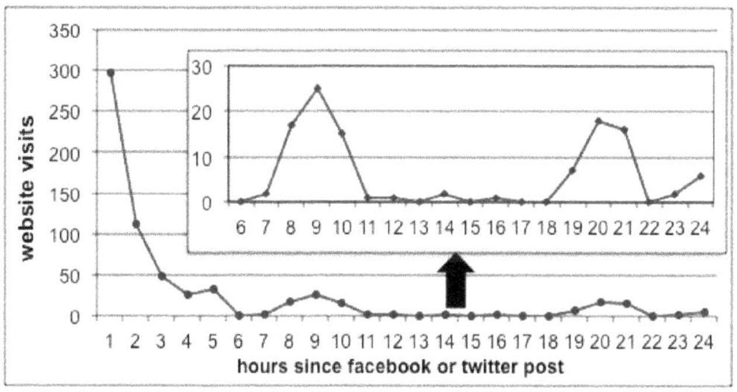

Figure 8: Visits to creekwatch.org from clicks on a Facebook or Twitter post, by time since post.

Age	under 25	25-35	35-45	45-55	55+
respondents	3	32	28	32	41

Table 1: Age breakdown of survey respondents.

a 47%-53% female-male breakdown. 94% of respondents have a college degree, of whom 52% also have a graduate level degree. A breakdown of the ages of respondents can be seen in Table 1; the average age is 47 (std. deviation 14).

About two-thirds (65%) of respondents had heard of Creek Watch, of whom 22% have downloaded the Creek Watch app. 55% of respondents who have downloaded the app indicated they have used it to submit at least one report, with only 15% indicating they submit frequent, regular reports. Interestingly, none of the survey respondents use the Facebook & Twitter feature. 41% of users were unaware of the feature, and 9% do not have a Facebook or Twitter account. 51% of users were aware of the feature but chose not to use it. Of those who chose not to use it, 46% indicated the reason as "I'm not interested in [this feature]", 46% indicated "I don't want to clutter my Facebook page or Twitter stream," and 8% cited privacy concerns. There were no write-ins.

We also asked survey respondents if they had "liked" Creek Watch on Facebook, or planned to. Of respondents with a Facebook account, only 10% had already done so, with a further 45% indicating they planned to do so, and 45% stating they did not plan to "like" Creek Watch. Of the subset of users who were aware of the Twitter & Facebook posting feature but chose not to use it, 53% indicated that they have "liked" Creek Watch on Facebook or plan to.

Respondents indicated they had heard of Creek Watch through several channels. 12% indicated they had heard of it through a social network, 15% from a news article, 21% through word of mouth, and 44% from a group or mailing list. As Creek Watch's launch was advertised on the same mailing list from which 70% of our respondents came, there is unavoidable bias in these numbers.

This survey is limited by several sources of bias including the demographics of the respondents, an unusually high percentage of whom have a college degree (94%). While 54% of respondents are over the age of 45, most Creek Watch users (84%) are under the age of 45. While 32% of users over the age of 45 do not have a Facebook account, those that do are no more or less likely than users under the age of 45 to "like" Creek Watch on Facebook. Another source of bias is the method of recruiting respondents. While only 30% of respondents were reached through Facebook or the targeted mailing list, 55% of Creek Watch users came from these sources.

CONCLUSION

Our experiences with promoting Creek Watch and with social network integration indicate that these were successful ways to get the word out about our project, and show potential for increasing the number of participants.

Our results are limited in several ways. In particular, our work applies to only one crowdsourced citizen science project. While the data from our campaigns, improvements, and surveys seems compelling, the possibility remains that the results are due to other factors, many of which were beyond our control. Other factors that certainly influenced the success of these campaigns included our own familiarity and experience with social media such as Facebook and Twitter, access to the press team for a large multi-national corporation, and the notoriety of the groups we partnered with. While we hope that this work provides some insight and guidance to other citizen science projects, we cannot presume that what worked for us will work for others.

That said, we are able to conclude that, in the case of Creek Watch, a social networking campaign was just as successful at recruiting participants as an international press release, and more successful then a participation campaign through existing communities. However, the participation campaign resulted in more data being collected (presumably by existing users) then either other campaign. We furthermore conclude that integrating Facebook and Twitter into our app was a worthwhile means for getting the word out about the project, but that only Facebook posts (and not Twitter posts) lead to more people signing up for Creek Watch. However, the low adoption rate of this feature combined with the fact that many users stated their unwillingness to use this feature but were willing to "like" Creek Watch on Facebook, suggests that developing a Facebook community may be more useful then adding a feature to post to Facebook & Twitter automatically.

As a result of this work, we plan to focus our efforts at recruitment on social networking platforms, but to focus our efforts for data collection on existing communities through local channels.

REFERENCES

[1] Eytan Bakshy, Jake M. Hofman, Winter A. Mason, and Duncan J. Watts. Everyone's an influencer: quantifying influence on Twitter. In WSDM '11, pages 65-74, ACM, 2011.

[2] Rick Bonney, et al. Public participation in scientific research: Defining the field and assessing its potential for informal science education. CAISE inquiry group report, Washington, DC, Tech. Report, 2009.

[3] Kevin Crowston and Andrea Wiggins. Design for citizen science. Final Workshop Report, NSF Grants 09-43049 & 11-11107, 2011.

[4] Nicole B. Ellison, Charles Steinfeld, and Cliff Lampe. The benefits of Facebook ''Friends:'' Social capital and college students' use of online social network sites. In Journal of Computer-Mediated Communication, volume 12(4), article 1, 2007.

[5] Alexander Hars and Shaosong Ou. Working for Free? - Motivations of Participating in Open Source Projects. In HICSS '01, volume 7, page 7014, IEEE, 2001.

[6] Akshay Java, Xiaodan Song, Tim Finin, and Belle Tseng. Why we Twitter: understanding microblogging usage and communities. In Proceedings of the 9th WebKDD, 56-65, ACM, 2007.

[7] Adam N. Joinson. Looking at, looking up or keeping up with people?: motives and use of Facebook. In CHI '08, pages 1027-1036, ACM, 2008.

[8] Sunyoung Kim, Christine Robson, Thomas Zimmerman, Jeffrey Pierce, and Eben M. Haber. Creek watch: pairing usefulness and usability for successful citizen science. In CHI'11. ACM, 2011

[9] Stacey Kuznetsov, William Odom, James Pierce, and Eric Paulos. Nurturing natural sensors. In UbiComp '11, ACM, 2011.

[10] Cliff Lampe and Rebecca Roth. Implementing social media in public sector organizations. In iConference '12, pages 191-198, ACM, 2012.

[11] Oded Nov, David Anderson, and Ofer Arazy. Volunteer computing: a model of the factors determining contribution to community-based scientific research. In WWW '10. ACM, 2010.

[12] Oded Nov, Ofer Arazy, and David Anderson. Crowdsourcing for science: understanding and enhancing SciSourcing contribution. Workshop on the Changing Dynamics of Scientific Collaborations, at CSCW'10. ACM, 2010.

[13] Eric Paulos, R.J. Honicky, and Ben Hooker. Citizen Science: Enabling Participatory Urbanism. In *Handbook of Research on Urban Informatics: The Practice and Promise of the Real-Time City*. IGI Global, 2008.

[14] Christine Robson, Sean Kandel, Jeffrey Heer, and Jeffrey S. Pierce. Data collection by the people, for the people. In CHI'11 Extended Abstracts, ACM 2012.

[15] Dana Rotman, et al. Dynamic changes in motivation in collaborative citizen science projects. In CSCW '12, pages 217-226, ACM, 2012.

[16] Shirley B. Rouse and Barbara Clawson. Motives and incentives of older adult volunteers. In Journal of Extension, Vol 30, pages 9-12, 1992.

[17] Paul A. Stewart. The Value of the Christmas Bird Counts. The Wilson Bulletin, volume 66 (3), pages 184-195, 1954.

[18] Chris Wood, Brian Sullivan, Marshall Iliff, Daniel Fink, and Steve Kelling. eBird: Engaging Birders in Science and Conservation. In PLoS Biol volume 9(12): document number e1001220, 2011.

[19] Andrea Wiggins and Kevin Crowston. From conservation to crowdsourcing: A typology of citizen science. In HICSS '11, 1- 10, Jan 2011.

[20] John Wilson and Marc Musick. Who cares? Toward an integrated theory of volunteer work. In American Sociological Review, Vol 62(5), pages 694-713, 1997.

Free As In Puppies: Compensating for ICT Constraints in Citizen Science

Andrea Wiggins
University of New Mexico & Cornell University
159 Sapsucker Woods Rd.
Ithaca, NY 14850 USA
andrea.wiggins@cornell.edu

ABSTRACT
Citizen science is a form of collaborative research engaging the public with professional scientists. Information and communication technologies (ICT) are a leading factor in the recent spread of this phenomenon. A common assumption is that money and ICT are the ideal solutions to issues of data quality and participant engagement. The reality is instead that resource limitations often require adopting suboptimal ICT, including tools that are "free as in puppies" with hidden costs from poor usability and lack of appropriate functionality.

A comparative case study of three citizen science projects, eBird, The Great Sunflower Project, and Mountain Watch, found that projects with few ICT resources employed a broader range of strategies to address these issues than expected. The most practical and effective strategies integrated available ICT with other resources to open up new solutions and options for supporting citizen science outcomes in spite of resource limitations.

Author Keywords
Citizen science; scientific collaboration; distributed work; case study; technology-mediated participation; data quality

ACM Classification Keywords
H.5.3 Information Interfaces and Presentation (e.g. HCI): Group and Organization Interfaces

INTRODUCTION
Citizen science involves the public with scientists in collaborative research [4]. Citizen science projects "hold out the possibility of scaling up the processes of scientific research so that they are truly global in scale and scope" [2, p. 125]. Many such projects rely upon geographically dispersed resources and contributors who work toward common goals via information and communication technologies (ICT). The dominant form of citizen science projects, found in the environmental sciences, focuses on monitoring ecosystems and wildlife populations; volunteers form a human sensor network for distributed data collection [3]. By contrast, in entirely online projects, volunteers provide data transcription and analysis services, applying basic human perception to computationally difficult image recognition tasks. The focus for this study was the more common observation-based projects traditionally called *volunteer monitoring*.

The term volunteer monitoring is now synonymous with citizen science, but is historically best known in the applied domain of natural resource management, where it has been practiced in North America for over a century [6]. Among other long-term citizen science projects, the Audubon Christmas Bird Count has been in continuous operation since 1901, with data quality and quantity reaching levels suitable for scientific research and policy decision support in the 1960's. In these projects, lay persons are trained to make scientific observations for long-term monitoring, offering new opportunities for large scale distributed scientific research.

While citizen science cannot replace conventional science, it is already acting as a complement to professional scientific research in fields like conservation biology [4]. Citizen science projects increasingly place more emphasis on scientifically sound practices and measurable goals for public education than similar historical efforts [1]. Ample evidence has shown that under the right circumstances, citizen science can work on a massive scale and is capable of producing high quality data as well as unexpected insights and innovations [19].

Citizen science represents massive scale collaboration in science as seen nowhere else, providing an opportunity for understanding aspects of other massively distributed collaborations. In addition, many online communities and distributed collaborations face similar issues of participation and product quality, particularly in peer production settings, a common focus of research in computer-supported cooperative work research (CSCW). Prior CSCW research specific to citizen science is scant, and relatively little work focuses on the critical issues of participant recruitment, retention, and data quality, which are the focus of this study.

The remainder of this paper discusses the motivation, related work, case selection, and methodology for this study. Descriptions of the cases are followed by discussion of the use of

ICT to support participation and data quality in observation-based citizen science projects and implications for practice. The conclusion identifies future directions for research related to technology-enabled citizen science.

MOTIVATION AND RELATED WORK

Despite the increasing popularity of citizen science, there are few guides to project design and implementation issues, such as selecting technologies and designing participation tasks to ensure the best possible outcomes for both the research and the participants. With the recent rise of technology-enabled citizen science, traditional citizen sciences practices are rapidly changing. In this context, successful scientific outcomes are dependent on participant recruitment, retention, and data quality, key issues facing citizen science project organizers.

Project organizers need effective mechanisms to support participant recruitment and retention, spurring research on participant motivations [15, 13]. Because the primary justification for a citizen science approach is a matter of fundamental feasibility (i.e., the research cannot be conducted in any other way, due to reliance on human cognitive competencies and/or observation over large geospatial and temporal scales), attracting large numbers of contributions from as many individuals as possible is a central goal for most project organizers.

In large-scale citizen science, the need to produce sound scientific results further conflicts with the usual conditions associated with crowdsourcing, namely that contributors are all but anonymous and their skills and knowledge base are largely unknown [8]. These challenges are compounded by the voluntary, uncompensated nature of participation: if the technologies, tasks, and goals are unappealing to would-be contributors, they simply choose not to participate. Project organizers' efforts to address these conditions are continually stymied by resource shortages endemic to volunteer work.

Participant characteristics and participation directly impact data quality. Scientists are consistently and rightfully concerned about ensuring the quality of research outputs, and public contributions come with no guarantees of expertise. Critical examination makes it apparent that the fundamental differentiating characteristic between conventional science and citizen science is the sheer number of non-professional volunteers contributing data, which has cascading effects on the research. In localized projects, typified by water quality monitoring, participation procedures may closely mimic professional protocols, with data quality addressed through extensive volunteer training and QA/QC processes [16]. For projects with a limited number of strongly motivated contributors, training volunteers in complex scientific processes can be both practical and highly successful, but this approach does not scale.

Large-scale citizen science can become truly massive: over a quarter million people have contributed classifications of images to Galaxy Zoo and related Zooniverse projects, making the contributor base orders of magnitude larger than the biggest professional scientific collaboration. In such technology-enabled projects, different approaches to participant engagement and data quality are needed. For example, using a very simple participation protocol can still yield useful data [10].

However, such simplicity is often inadequate for answering scientific research questions that demand a citizen science approach. Combined with the lack of direct oversight in distributed settings, scientists' unfamiliarity with this type of research collaboration fosters mistrust of project products despite the fact that most projects implement several strategies to ensure that the data are suitable for their intended purposes [24]. Concerns over contribution quality are the primary objections raised by critics [14], but are only a symptom of the underlying problem: researchers have yet to establish how to consistently select effective tools and mechanisms for contribution and coordination to achieve the desired scientific outcomes.

A common assumption is that money and ICT are the solution to issues of data quality and participant engagement: with more funding, superior and cheaper digital tools will yield more participation and better data quality, leading to improved scientific outcomes. The eBird project, which collects data on bird abundance and distribution, is a classic example of the basis for these assumptions. If all projects could follow suit, there would be little reason to doubt the value of citizen science.

Through comparison to Mountain Watch, a project monitoring alpine plant life cycles, and The Great Sunflower Project, which solicits observations of bees visiting sunflowers, this study revealed a different reality. Most citizen science project organizers are not well positioned to acquire adequate funding to build new ICT or improve existing tools, as their resources are consumed by project management and working to meet scientific research goals. Instead, they rely on less ideally suited technologies which may be "free as in beer" meaning that they are available at no charge [11], but are also "free as in puppies" with unexpected hidden costs of ownership. The situation faced by these projects is far more pervasive than the idealized conditions that high profile projects like eBird and Galaxy Zoo have enjoyed.

This set of assumptions and conflicting realities led to the research question for this work: *How do citizen science project organizers address key issues related to participation and data quality when resource constraints limit their ICT options?* The goal of this focus was to identify factors influencing the design and operation of citizen science projects with the greatest potential to improve project outcomes.

As the analysis presented here will show, these projects instead employed a broader range of technologies and strategies to increase participation and improve data quality than is typically assumed. Integrating this wider selection of tools and techniques with available ICT opens up new solutions and options for creating sociotechnical systems that optimize the value of citizen science for both participants and scientists in spite of resource limitations.

CASE SELECTION

A comparative case study, with theoretical sampling of three cases for in-depth study, was selected to enable a deeply contextualized understanding of the relationships between project organizers' decisions related to ICT, participation, and data quality, and their subsequent impacts. The focus of the research was on the organizers of citizen science projects rather than participants, as most prior research on citizen science focuses on participant motivations and experiences. This study therefore complements prior work and provides a foundation for integrating individual-level and group-level research for a more holistic understanding of the phenomenon.

Theoretical Sampling Criteria

Case selection included projects that are organized around primarily scientific goals and involve participants in collecting observational data about the natural world. Theoretical sampling criteria were selected from the set of project inputs identified in a conceptual framework based on literature review and prior work in small groups research [22]. The concepts of purpose, community, environment, and technologies were chosen as most likely to influence project organizers' decisions related to ICT, participation, and data quality. The application of these criteria to the selected cases are shown in Table 1.

Purpose

Two primary dimensions of purpose were considered for sampling: 1) scientific interests and goals, and 2) the mission of the project with respect to broader goals. In organizational and institutional contexts, "mission" is congruent with the guiding principles of the organization, institution, or project. Mission as used here represents explicit organizational mission or goals expressed as project mission. The missions of most observation-based citizen science projects frequently fall within the same subset of broader goals, so this dimension of the concept of purpose supports comparison. Instead, variation along the dimension of scientific interests was expected to be more important: the selected cases operate in different scientific domains, with different research goals.

Community

In citizen science, participant community is typically congruent with scientific domain variability; community as used here refers to communities of practice [20]. The intuitive expectation is that people who self-select for participation in citizen science projects focusing on birds come from a community of birders, and those who help with trailside invasive species monitoring are typically members of a hiking community.

Environment

Environment refers to organizational contexts and the broader organizational field in which a project is situated. Organizational and institutional support and constraints affect project resources and purpose. Citizen science projects are most frequently operated by academic researchers and public-sector groups, namely nonprofits and governmental agencies, so the selected cases vary across sectors. An additional related point of comparison is the resources that can be brought to the project. These include staffing and fiscal resources, summarized in full-time employee equivalents (FTEs) and approximate annual operating budget for the project.

Technologies

The technologies used for making, managing, and reporting field observations—common core tasks across the target population of citizen science projects—were one point of contrast. For example, paper-based record making in the field is very common in observational citizen science. The nature of these uses of paper, however, can differ substantially, from a protocol-based data sheet, to species lists that follow established community conventions, to free-form notes specific to individuals' field observation habits.

Two specific qualities of ICT were used in sampling, technology sophistication and data access for participants. The overall degree of technology sophistication was evaluated according to the type of web-based technologies (e.g., devoted purpose-built platforms, content management systems alone, or standard websites with data submission forms). The availability and breadth of means for data access by participants was categorized according to the extent to which contributors can interact with data. For example, very limited data access might include only a summary list of one's own observations and a static map of aggregated observation sites. Extensive data access for participants means multiple mechanisms for data access, such as: faceted data querying tools; APIs; animated and interactive maps, charts, and graphs; general audience publications; custom report generation; and/or open access to the entire data set.

Cases

The cases selected for this study are briefly introduced here; key characteristics will be discussed in more detail later.

eBird

eBird is a popular citizen science project developed by the Cornell Lab of Ornithology [18], a leading organization in the development of citizen science practice, in partnership with the National Audubon Society. Launched in 2002, eBird allows birders to report and manage birding observation records online and offers access to the full data set through a wide range of reports and data visualizations, as well as professionally curated research data products. By enticing birders to submit data through birder-centric features, eBird's data set has grown exponentially since 2005 to reach a landmark 100 million observations in August 2012, and by the start of 2013 was receiving approximately four to five million observations monthly.

eBird has generated the world's largest biodiversity data set, used not only by hobbyists and researchers, but also by land managers, policy makers, and many others. Due to its robust data validation system and enthusiastic adoption, eBird provides rich data on bird abundance and distribution at a variety of spatial and temporal scales. eBird represents a mature, well supported, and technologically sophisticated project that engages volunteers internationally on a massive scale.

Criterion		Mountain Watch	Great Sunflower	eBird
Purpose	Mission	Conservation, education, recreation	Research, education	Research, education, conservation
	Scientific Interests	Climate change effects on alpine habitats	Plant-bee relationships	Bird abundance & distribution
Intended Community		Hikers	Gardeners	Birders
Environment	Institutions	Single nonprofit	Academic	Nonprofit partnership
	Resources	1.5 FTEs, $15K	0.5 FTE, $13K	4.5 FTEs, $300K
Technologies	Paper	Structured data sheet	Structured data sheet	Variable, optional
	Digital	Organization website section	Open source CMS	Purpose-built software system
	Data access	Limited	Very limited	Extensive

Table 1. Theoretical sampling criteria in the selected cases.

The Great Sunflower Project

The Great Sunflower Project (GSP) focuses on pollinator service, that is, bee pollination activity. The project was founded in 2008 by a biology professor at San Francisco State University to collect data for her research on pollinator service, an important indicator of local ecological health. Participants grow sunflowers at homes across North America and report bee activity data online, enabling comparison of pollinator service across habitats, previously impossible at a continental scale.

While the project has been very successful in attracting volunteer interest, project leaders have struggled to turn interest into participation while also addressing pressing project sustainability concerns. The Great Sunflower Project represents a young, underfunded, and technologically disadvantaged citizen science project that has shown remarkable resilience despite substantial challenges.

Mountain Watch

Mountain Watch is a citizen science project designed and operated by the Research and Education departments of the Appalachian Mountain Club (AMC), a membership-based trail club whose mission is to support conservation, education, and recreation in the northeastern mountain ranges of the Appalachian ridge. Since 2004, Mountain Watch has enlisted hikers in evaluating air quality through visibility measurement and in collecting observations of flowering plants for climate change research. For all practical purposes, the project is geospatially constrained, collecting data primarily in the White Mountains of New Hampshire. The Whites feature the largest alpine region in the northeast U.S. with eight square miles of land above treeline, and are home to AMC's two primary visitor centers, administrative offices, and eight backcountry facilities ("High Huts").

Alpine plant monitoring, the primary focus of the project, gathers long-term data to monitor the effects of climate change on fragile alpine ecosystems by examining the timing of plant life cycle stages (phenology), such as flowering and fruiting (phenophases). Although hikers can report data online for any location in the northeastern U.S. where the target plants are found, the primary participants are hut guests. To date, hikers' data contributions show that climate change is having a stronger effect on forest plants at low elevations than high elevation alpine plants. Mountain Watch represents a mature project that has methodically fine-tuned its participation protocol over a period of several years to produce increasingly scientifically useful data.

METHODS

Field research methods were used to collect several types of data, including interviews, documents, and participant observation. As data were collected, analysis began with interview transcript coding and description of each case. Comparisons were drawn throughout the data collection and analysis process. The iterative and concurrent data collection and analysis strategy employed both inductive and deductive approaches. The remainder of this section discusses the data collection and analysis methods for this study, as well as strategies for ensuring research quality.

Data Collection

The overall case study data collection approach shared many of the characteristics of traditional ethnography, including negotiation of access, long-term participation and observation, longitudinal interviews, and field notes [17, 5]. Analytic procedures included ongoing memoing, coding, and description.

Interviews with project organizers comprised the primary data source. Interviewee selection included all project leaders and staff for each case (notably two of the projects have very limited staffing) plus representatives of diverse partner organizations both in the U.S. and internationally. Interviews also included several longitudinal interviews over a period of two to three years. In addition, hundreds of documents were used to provide background and context for the case studies, as well as to triangulate claims made in interviews.

Over 500 hours of participant observation spanning three years complemented interviews. Participant observation involved the researcher acting both as a participant contributing data for each project, and as a colleague attending citizen science organizer meetings and related events. Participating as a contributor to these citizen science projects involved hiking in the White Mountains of New Hampshire to observe alpine plants; growing sunflowers and counting bees; and learning to identify nearly 350 species of birds to report data at over 160 locations. Participation also included reading and posting to email listservs and online forums from the standpoint of a non-researcher [7].

Data Analysis

Data analysis consisted of iterative qualitative analysis guided by an existing theoretical framework [22]. The original framework was based in literature review and small groups theory, as previously mentioned, and follows an inputs-moderators-outputs-inputs structure [9], reflecting the feedback of project outputs into ongoing operation.

Throughout the course of analysis, the framework and associated schema evolved based on empirical evidence. For example, the original framework included individual processes of joining and contributing, and organizational processes of scientific research, volunteer management, and data management. The final framework included processes of science, design, organizing, and participation. These four categories encompassed prior concepts while also including other relevant subprocesses and omitting overly specific processes (e.g., joining and contributing, both part of participation) for which there was little support in the data due to the research focus on organizers.

The processes provided links between project inputs and outputs. For this analysis, the impacts on organizing and participation processes from resource constraints were evident in project-level inputs such as community, resources, institutions, and technologies. In turn, these concepts shed light on the influence of project characteristics and processes on outcomes, which included contributions, scientific knowledge, and broader impacts beyond data sets and academic publications.

The findings and interpretation were subject to review by the participants at two stages. Interview transcripts were sent to each participant for examination and verification. Key informants from each case site reviewed the case descriptions to verify factual accuracy as well as interpretation.

CASE STUDIES

The resources available in each of the cases described here varied substantially, as did their uses of ICT. This section provides background for comparison of the compensatory strategies applied when resource constraints do not permit ideal ICT-based solutions. The data contribution tasks, resources, and ICT in these projects are described below.

Data Contribution Tasks

Each of the cases collects similar data—observations about species in the natural world—but takes a different approach to participation protocols. These variations are based primarily on the expected participant base and the intended scientific applications of the data.

eBird

The basic process for contributing data to eBird is fairly simple. A birder goes birding, and makes a list of the birds observed, following one of several protocols (incidental, stationary, traveling, or area.) Along with the information about species encountered, details about the participation effort for the chosen protocol are also recorded: date, starting time, elapsed time, and number of observers, with some protocols requiring additional details about distance traveled or area surveyed. This process is only slightly more involved than traditional birding community practices, as most birders are not in the habit of collecting the effort information needed for data aggregation, nor counts of birds, records of all species seen or heard, or separate checklists for different locations. Without these details, the observations are less useful to all interested parties, including hobbyists, so eBirders often change their birding habits over time to generate more scientifically valuable data [21].

In most cases, the eBirder later enters the data through the eBird web interface or uploads data using specially-formatted email messages or Excel spreadsheets. As soon as the checklist is submitted, the birder's personal lists are automatically updated with new totals. Within 24 hours, the new observations are available through the eBird API, combined into range maps and other publicly available reports, and leaderboard rankings are updated. More recently, a third party has developed the BirdLog mobile app for data entry and submission in the field.

The Great Sunflower Project

The GSP bills its participation procedure as a four-step process, accurately describing the simplicity of the protocol. Volunteers plant Lemon Queen sunflowers (or other flowering plants added through project expansion) and can optionally report on the plant's development while they wait for their sunflowers to grow. Once the sunflowers bloom, participants choose a flower that is in the appropriate stage of development to attract bees (showing pollen) and describe the observation conditions. Next, they observe the selected bloom for fifteen minutes, recording the times at which bees visit, and optionally attempt to identify the bees. The majority of data are then entered by the volunteers into an online database, although some participants submit paper observation forms by postal mail.

Mountain Watch

Participation in Mountain Watch is largely constrained to the White Mountains. Starting at an AMC facility, hikers pick up a packet with a detailed instruction and identification guide, data sheet customized to location, and pencil in a plastic zip bag. Data sheets and reference information are also available on the Mountain Watch webpages.

Hikers locate monitoring plots using provided maps and text descriptions, and indicate which species are present and whether they are in any of the indicated phenophases (e.g., before flowering, flowering, after flowering.) The completed data sheets are then dropped off in collection boxes at any of the eight huts or the visitor centers. Observations can also be submitted online, giving contributors access to their own data, which is not currently possible for participants who submit their data on paper. While straightforward to describe, this participation protocol is quite difficult for most participants, as they are not familiar with the plant species or their phenophases.

Resources

The organizational settings were a primary factor in determining the fiscal, infrastructural, and human resources for each project. The Cornell Lab of Ornithology and Appalachian Mountain Club each had substantial but very different organizational assets that project leaders could access. For The GSP, however, institutional support was very limited; the project was just one of many faculty initiatives across a large university.

eBird

eBird's success has yielded substantial funding to support the project, with over $7 million in grant funding since the project's inception. Although this is a large figure, the grant awards were received and expended over a period of ten years, and expectations are high for a well funded project. Initially, the Lab of Ornithology provided internal venture capital funding to support project development, a particularly valuable benefit of starting the project in this unique institutional environment.

Since repaying the internal debt with grant funding from the U.S. National Science Foundation (NSF), the eBird team developed a project sustainability plan which has been recognized for its excellence as a model for sustaining digital resources [12]. The general approach is summarized very simply: "We use NSF money for innovation, and use other resources for sustainability" (Dendroica[1]). eBird's revenue sources included sponsorships, portal software licensing, endowment payouts, donations from Lab membership, and fees for location-based eBird TrailTracker kiosks at nature centers and wildlife refuges. Assuring project sustainability convinces top-level contributors and data consumers to rely on eBird as an authoritative data source and data management tool, and even more so as an increasingly longitudinal data set develops.

These income streams covered the costs of 4.25 full-time employee equivalents, including the project leaders, a web developer, department administrators, and a database administrator (all partial time with the exception of the web developer.) This represents more devoted staff time than the average citizen science project, and notably greater technical expertise. A broad skill and knowledge base was developed with lower direct investment, partly because most staff are assigned to the project part-time and partly through interorganizational partnerships. eBird is therefore able to draw upon the expertise of biologists, statisticians, computer scientists, social scientists, and complementary domain knowledge,.

The Great Sunflower Project

With less than 20 hours per week of staff time available, The GSP's most substantial ongoing challenge was the need for funding to support staffing for project coordination and communication. Early proposals for grant funding were consistently rejected due to recessionary economic conditions, so the project organizers had to explore other avenues for generating funding. Like eBird, the resultant diversification of project revenue sources is more sustainable. The GSP's new revenue streams took an entrepreneurial bent, in addition to solicitation of donations from participants.

From 2009–2011, the organizers worked with volunteers to create visually appealing calendars featuring professional quality beauty shots of bees, enhanced with additional details about each bee species and its pollination habits, emphasizing the connection between habitat conservation and food production. When calendar sales flagged, a second product was added in 2011: note cards featuring whimsical, biologically accurate illustrations of bees that further reinforce the link between bees and food.

Another strategy to bolster project sustainability was referral sales of sunflower seeds, which created an additional a revenue stream. As new revenue sources began to provide adequate funding to meet immediate operating costs, over time the organizers expressed increasing confidence in the year-to-year sustainability of the project, although the long-term outlook remained uncertain.

Mountain Watch

AMC's institutional structure and organizational resources, particularly the backcountry facilities with their constant flow of summer visitors, are a substantial asset for Mountain Watch. The eight High Huts are approximately six to eight miles apart along a 42-mile section of the 2,200-mile Appalachian Trail, operated by special permit from the U.S. Forest Service (USFS). Hut lodging capacities range from 36–90 people in bunkrooms; for a reasonable fee, guests enjoy spectacular views and hearty multi-course family-style meals.

During the summer, the huts are operated by a "hut croo"[2] of five to nine caretakers who provide hospitality, day-to-day maintenance, and emergency rescue; they are typically college students or recent graduates. The croos also include a resident naturalist with expertise or training in natural history, who makes daily educational presentations for guests on topics ranging from how Mt. Washington makes it own weather to Mountain Watch monitoring.

The internal partnership between the Research and Education departments also increased project resources, resulting in carefully designed materials for participants and Mountain Watch training for all hut croo members. The hut naturalists, who received additional training, served a special role by making regular observations at permanent plots near the huts and incorporating Mountain Watch into their presentations to hut guests. A research assistant noted, "When naturalists were giving a program about the alpine flowers, they tended to get more observations from that hut" (Clintonia).

In addition, Mountain Watch marketing materials are prominently displayed throughout the AMC facilities, with large posters in the huts and visitor centers, flyers posted on the insides of toilet stall doors, and participation materials in prominent locations. Hut croos encouraged participation in Mountain Watch at every evening presentation during dinner, at every hut, as a standard part of the croo's daily duties. Incorporating Mountain Watch into hut croo training supported ongoing participant recruitment from a constantly changing audience, as well as data validation through hut naturalists' data collection duties. Although it took considerable time to achieve, the pervasive messaging at AMC facilities demonstrated exceptional integration into the organizational culture.

[1]Latin names for species are used as pseudonyms.

[2]The term "croo" is the traditional name for these teams.

Information & Communication Technologies

As noted in the case sampling methods, the sophistication of the ICT implemented to support these projects varied substantially. The fiscal, human, and organizational resources available to each of these projects had a major impact on ICT use. While eBird had the resources to develop ICT infrastructure ideally suited to project audiences and goals, The GSP and Mountain Watch were not so fortunate.

eBird

eBird was the first citizen science project collecting data through the Internet at large scale, and online data submission is the only avenue to participation. The primary technology supporting eBird is custom online data submission and management software, developed in-house and wrapped in an open source content management system for essential communication functions, with a presentation layer for user interfaces. The unique core features include lists, alerts, and a wide variety of data reports, both personalized and general.

eBird's unique and extensive functionality is considered highly innovative by members of the birding community. During interviews, eBird was frequently identified by organizers of many other citizen science projects as having developed the most sophisticated citizen science ICT support they had encountered. The system evolved in this direction due to a consistent priority on developing functionality not available elsewhere. As an example, visualizations—particularly graphs and maps—are among these essential features because, as one organizer explained: "People like maps, and they've always liked maps, and if you can animate the maps they even like them more" (Dendroica).

The Great Sunflower Project

The Great Sunflower Project relies on the open source Drupal content management system (CMS) to support participation, although contributions are also accepted on paper data sheets. The modular system allowed organizers to pick and choose functionality to support participation, relying primarily on core features in the Drupal environment. A programmer was hired to ensure proper database management, form checking for data submissions, and usable table structures for research data retrieval. The rest of the technology development and administration is handled entirely by the project organizers. Drupal is a complex technology to learn and manage, but neither of the project's two organizers has any background in web development, a common situation in citizen science.

As the project founder quipped, open source software is "free as in puppies" for non-technologist end users, meaning that the associated costs are high when the necessary skills are not readily available. The choice to adopt an open source system kept operational costs low enough to fit a shoestring budget and permitted ongoing system upkeep without incurring substantial additional expense. The drawback, however, is that CMS like Drupal require skilled customization to function effectively for scientific data collection and need substantial work to improve usability. Many domain researchers must contract out such work because the necessary technology skills are not part of their repertoires. This challenge was exacerbated by the flat refusal of funders to provide any resources for the ICT infrastructure necessary to operate the project.

Mountain Watch

Mountain Watch contrasts sharply with the other cases in the degree to which it relies upon paper data sheets, an important non-digital technology for many field-based monitoring projects. Due to resource constraints, characteristics of the physical locations, and the natural flow of observation processes, paper remains the only practical approach for data collection at this time. For most Mountain Watch contributors participation involves *only* paper data sheets.

Online data entry and interactive map displays are a relatively new feature of the Mountain Watch webpages, which are integrated into the larger AMC website. Developed to enable participation in other northeastern forest regions and mountain ranges (e.g., the Catskill, Adirondack, and Green Mountains), this non-essential ICT provides capacity to substantially increase the scale of participation. With the exception of limited contributions from other mountain clubs (e.g., the Adirondack Mountain Club) online data entry has yet to deliver on this promise due to lack of human resources needed for outreach to promote participation outside of the Whites.

In 2009, AMC researchers also deployed plantcams, digital cameras for ongoing monitoring in outdoors environments. Most plantcams were located in established monitoring sites, so an additional benefit was that volunteers could use them to locate monitoring plots on public lands that cannot otherwise be marked due to U.S. Forest Service regulations. This technology investment was spurred by several factors: available grant funding; decreasing costs and wide availability of remote camera technologies; potential for verification of participant data; and the ability to do off-season monitoring. Some phenological events occur in late spring, when weather conditions are so severe that no one will venture out to make observations.

DISCUSSION

Differences in project resources profoundly impacted the use of ICT to support participant recruitment, retention, and data quality in each of these cases. As was expected, monetary and human resources had the most direct influences on project design and outcomes, but resources unique to organizational context were also a substantial and often overlooked factor. In the discussion of participant recruitment, retention, and data quality that follows, eBird provides an example of the expected uses of ICT tailored to the project, while The GSP and Mountain Watch demonstrate strategies that compensated for ICT limitations.

Recruiting Participants

Recruitment and retention of participants is a common concern for citizen science projects that need to accumulate a large data set. In many respects, all three projects used the same tried-and-true volunteer recruitment strategies employed in many other settings. Across the cases, ICT was not the most effective tool for recruitment. In theory, being open to web-based contributions would make project participation more visible to a broader audience and ease recruitment efforts. This was only partially true; contributors were recruited most effectively through direct in-person contact.

The three eBird project leaders estimated that they each spent approximately 100 days per year traveling to make presentations as keynote speakers at bird festivals and reach out to local groups such as bird clubs and Audubon chapters. Outside of the U.S., these efforts are extended by staff of partner organizations, such as Bird Studies Canada, who engage in similar outreach in their own communities. By contrast, The GSP had great success in initial recruitment by requesting only a few individuals email information about the project to their social networks. The level of follow-through from these initial recruits, however, was very low. Partnering with similarly focused organizations and hiring an Outreach Director to promote local participation generated better recruitment results, as did newspaper and magazine articles featuring The GSP. Mountain Watch organizers were able to employ a different strategy altogether, exploiting location-based organizational resources for ongoing recruitment of a high turnover volunteer base. ICT for online data submission, however, had yet to pay off in increased recruitment and participation.

Unlike the other two projects, eBird was able to create ICT-based features that further improved participant recruitment by leveraging existing birder community practices. eBird organizers did not attempt to displace the well established birding listservs through which individuals share sightings with their local communities. Instead, they created features to work with the existing community infrastructure: eBirders can have nicely formatted checklists emailed to them to forward to friends and local listservs. These messages are more easily produced, readable, and useful than the average trip report and include footer text that reads, "This report was generated automatically by eBird v3," a subtle form of social recommendation. Interviewees reported that in some areas the majority of messages on the email lists are forwarded eBird reports. The well established social structure of birding communities made emailed checklists an effective way to take advantage of participants' social networks to effortlessly extend recruitment.

Due to differences in community structures and the lack of ICT tools to accomplish similar ends, however, neither of the other two projects were able to mimic eBird's strategy. Instead, both The GSP and Mountain Watch used paper-based data submission as a means of expanding the contributor base and increasing data submissions. For Mountain Watch, this was a matter of practicality on several levels. Collecting paper data sheets at the AMC facilities yielded a higher return rate because participants did not have to go out of their way to submit data. Expecting hikers to enter this data online after returning home from an exhausting vacation in the Whites would be unrealistic: the records become lost, mangled, or forgotten, among other reasons for neglecting to submit data.

The GSP, on the other hand, emphasizes online data entry but accepts paper data sheets by postal mail. In addition to the practical considerations of outdoors data collection, paper data sheets are one way that The GSP organizers try to be inclusive of "die hard retirees that want to participate, that want to feel part of the project, but yet are really still very uncomfortable with online entry, who get confused by websites" (Bombus). The level of difficulty that older adult participants encountered with online data submission was a substantial barrier for some individuals, due in no small part to the lack of resources to devote to improving the usability of the Drupal site. The use of paper data sheets helped make up for the organizers' inability to make the ICT more accessible by expanding the means of participation.

While all three projects used many similar recruitment techniques from established volunteer management practices, each found that in-person recruitment was most effective. For eBird, ICT-based marketing was effective when spread by participants through their local social networks via emailed and shared checklists that dovetail with existing community practices, benefit participants, and advertise eBird functionality. For The GSP and Mountain Watch, however, developing such features was out of the question. Paper data sheets—a more accessible technology for some participants—and refinements to the participation protocols both helped compensate for this limitation in The GSP, and in Mountain Watch, saturation marketing throughout physical facilities and daily presentations to hut guests were highly effective.

Participant Retention

In most cases, retaining participants is nearly as high priority as recruiting them because ongoing participation is expected to yield more and better data submissions. Unfortunately, the ICT features that clearly supported retention for eBird were among the most expensive to develop, making them unrealistic options for The GSP and Mountain Watch.

eBird developers spent years developing rapid feedback in the form of birder-centric reports and visualizations that reward contributors for submitting data by providing access to information they want. These included leaderboards that built on long-standing traditions of friendly competition in the birding community, subtly incorporating social rewards based on community norms. Participants find the data displays very satisfying for their personal interests in bird data and for elevating their social standing in the birding community through visibility of their contributions.

While eBird's simple bar charts and ranked reports may seem an easy solution, they required extensive development time, and project staff remarked upon the continual difficulty of integrating custom software with the CMS and presentation layers that comprise the full system. The latest and greatest of these visualizations, animated migration maps, required millions of data points, invention of new spatiotemporal statistical modeling techniques, and high performance grid computing to generate. In short, the innovative and popular data visualizations cost a lot of money.

Interviewees connected these high quality visualizations with several benefits to participants that can also support retention. According to a project organizer, "the fact is that to see the dynamics, spatially and temporally, of how these things change, and to do it at such a broad scale as we can do it, is transformative in the way people think about biodiversity and natural history" (Dendroica). For many participants, the data visualizations may be just another way to find the information they desire, but for others, seeing the aggregated data in a different way can stimulate a change in the way they understand relationships between biodiversity and habitat preservation, reinforcing the value of participation.

These ICT-supported offerings, while in many ways ideal for a distributed contributor base, are practically impossible to implement for small underfunded citizen science projects. The Mountain Watch website now includes an interactive map of phenology observations, although the relatively low emphasis on ICT use for the primary contributor base makes the utility of this visualization for contributor retention questionable, and it may instead be more valuable for recruitment. In addition, most Mountain Watch participants are one-time contributors on a brief vacation in the mountains, and are therefore less invested in submitting more data or making use of data visualization tools. Instead of focusing on retention, the organizers therefore prioritized recruitment.

The GSP provided a static map on the project website showing locations of bee sightings, which took three years to produce. The alternate solutions the project organizers implemented to improve retention included modifying the observation protocol to make sampling times shorter (from 30 to 15 minutes) and accepting data for a wider variety of common garden flowers beyond sunflowers, in response to popular demand. These changes better supported participation by families with small children and those whose sunflowers fail, which reduced participation in the first few years due to bad seeds and unfavorable weather conditions.

Adding more monitoring species also encouraged additional contributions by volunteers whose gardens already contained multiple target species. Further, it will eventually enable new research by accumulating comparative data of bee visitation rates across plant species, which was not an initial goal but will make an additional novel and valuable scientific contribution. The GSP organizers also experimented with other strategies to support retention, including different modes of communication with participants and explicit rewards, such as sending sunflower seeds to participants who have submitted multiple data points for several years to encourage them to continue.

While project organizers often expressed yearning to provide reports and visualizations similar to those eBird features, The GSP and Mountain Watch organizers all felt that this was a pipe dream. The cost of ICT tailored to support specific project needs and goals was simply too high for their limited resources. Instead, they found other ways to support retention by expanding options available to participants, trying new communication strategies, or simply focusing instead on recruitment.

Maximizing Data Quality

Contribution quality is a high priority in the context of scientific research. Carefully structured participation tasks are a very important facet of quality assurance. Data verification is also needed, however, and ICT are among the few truly scalable solutions. Tools for expert data review, a favored strategy, usually require custom development that substantially increases the cost of scalable quality control.

Not surprisingly, the data quality strategies in these cases were differentiated primarily based on use of human resources versus reliance on ICT. eBird was again an exemplar, with several features of participation protocols to improve incoming data supported by rigorous, scalable data verification. This process employs both customized ICT and expert birders to generate scientifically reliable data. Notably, eBird was uniquely able to implement a set of observation protocol that mirrored existing birding practices and therefore have required no changes over time [22]. eBird's other data quality mechanisms are largely based on customized ICT.

First, the eBird data entry interfaces present predictive checklists that reinforce careful species identification by displaying only the most likely species for the specific place and time of year, based on both expert input and existing data. Second, eBird uses a custom taxonomy with less specific taxonomic categories for birds that are difficult to identify in the field. A project leader described the importance of the specialized taxonomy to data quality: "We are not going to do any great science with [those data], but we are going to keep someone from just pigeonholing a bird because they think that's what it is but they're not really sure" (Stercorarius). This is a valuable strategy, given the uncertainties of field observation and variability in observer skill, but required substantial effort to create.

Finally, data review by experts plays a crucial role in quality control. eBird's reviewer network includes approximately 500 hand-selected individuals in North America, plus a few international reviewers. Volunteers performing this role often consult historic records for the location, ply personal local knowledge, and engage data contributors in email exchanges. After reviewing algorithmically flagged records, the reviewers render a judgment of whether the sighting is valid or not, which is then added to the record; observations that are considered invalid still appear in the user's life list but are not added to the research data set.

Needless to say, the specialized review tools and network of experts that made eBird's system scalable and highly reliable are also out of reach for projects with less funding for ICT and personnel. However, as contribution rates continued to increase sharply, the stress on the reviewer system had started to limit project capacity, leading to development of increasingly sophisticated ICT functionality [23]. Instead, The GSP organizers spent two years ironing out the participation protocol, during which time most data could not be salvaged, and then integrated authoritative data sets (housing density data) upon discovering that participants' characterizations of their garden locations were too subjective to be reliable.

The GSP also invested limited funds in database design, according to the project founder: "When I spent money [on ICT], it's really been to manage the forms where data gets entered, because I want to make sure that there's no way I can screw it up" (Apis). As with other projects using online data submission forms, implementing these measures improved data quality at an additional but modest expense that was substantially outweighed by the benefit.

Mountain Watch responded to similar participation process issues with an in-depth study of factors affecting data quality, and used multiple sources of complementary data. The organizers based protocol modification on rigorous scientific research, complete with statistical analyses that conclusively identified problems related to task complexity.

Evaluation of the original protocol highlighted participants' difficulties with location description and identification tasks. These insights led organizers to shift from open-ended locations to specific monitoring plots on a map, with detailed descriptions for reference. They also added lists of the known monitoring species occurring at each of the plots, reducing uncertainty in species identification, and tested the new data sheet the following year to verify improved data quality.

> People hiking from Mizpah [Spring Hut] to Lakes [of the Clouds Hut] were providing better data than the people hiking from Lakes to Mizpah because [they] had the new data sheet and were going to specific places. People hiking from the other direction but on the same trail, they just didn't have the focus, and their data was kind of all over the place. (Clintonia)

Developing a viable protocol was a substantial human resource investment for Mountain Watch, but the experimental design for evaluation of data quality paid off with certainty of the benefits of making further changes. The statistical analyses that capitalized on the scientists' research skills were a more rigorous approach to appraisal of the data collection instrument than is typically seen in citizen science projects.

Another strategy to ensure scientific data quality was integration with conventional scientific research and use of complementary technologies. Mountain Watch organizers implemented three different methods to capture data about phenophases: citizen science volunteers, trained hut naturalists, and automated data collection using plantcams. These data sources also complemented ongoing data collection by scientists, as some of the observation sites were at existing research plots.

As previously mentioned, the installation of plantcams served multiple purposes, including potential application to verifying volunteers' data. Actually comparing plantcam data to hikers' observations, however, is a more complex undertaking than it might initially appear. Processing image data from plantcams for this type of phenology monitoring requires human effort. This is a common focus for analysis-oriented citizen science projects like Galaxy Zoo, but requires customized technological infrastructure that is not readily available to most citizen science projects and too costly to customize to their purposes.

While eBird used ICT to develop a scalable, reliable approach to data verification, such purpose-built technologies are not available for most citizen science projects. The GSP instead invested time in protocol development and data integration and spent some limited funds on database design. Mountain Watch, on the other hand, was able to take advantage of internal research skills and low-cost labor for a rigorous multi-season study that honed not only the participation protocol, but also the data collection instrument. Using multi-layered data collection to supplement volunteers' data with complementary data from scientists, trained naturalists, and plantcam images was another promising strategy for ensuring data quality.

Implications

Returning to the concepts from the theoretical framework, these cases verified the expected links between project inputs and outputs through processes of design, organizing, contribution, and science. The cases also demonstrated that these factors and processes are strongly intertwined: there is no single input that guarantees data quality, nor can any one process effectively support participant recruitment and retention. As a complex sociotechnical phenomenon, developing ICT for technology-supported citizen science requires a holistic understanding of project goals, practices, and resources.

These findings challenge the notion that better ICT is the best solution to participant recruitment, retention, and data quality in citizen science. The reality is instead that many projects' resource limitations require adopting suboptimal ICT, including tools that are "free as in puppies" with hidden costs in the form of poor usability and lack of appropriate functionality. The primary insight that emerged was a broader view of potential solutions beyond ICT, demonstrating that the most practical and effective strategies under these constraints involved combining ICT with other resources, particularly human expertise.

The implications of these findings suggest that ICT selection and development should focus primarily on project goals, known characteristics of the participant audience that influence recruitment and retention, and data quality requirements for scientific outcomes. Tempering the instinct to rely primarily on ICT to address these concerns, it is likewise important to identify ICT-related constraints and work to find compensatory strategies based on other available resources, which are sometimes taken for granted by organizers and overlooked by technologists.

CONCLUSION

For citizen science projects with few resources, managing ICT can be burdensome due to low levels of technology expertise among project organizers. In most cases, technologies with the least complexity and lowest cost are the only sustainable choices despite the fact that nearly all organizers are aware that far better results could be obtained with more sophisticated systems. The affordability of tailoring ICT to project needs and audiences, however, remains a constant limitation.

As the case studies showed, however, alternate strategies that rely less on ICT and instead leverage other types of resources can provide effective ways of compensating for less than ideal ICT support. Direct contact with potential participants was the most successful recruitment strategy, and although it can be bolstered with ICT functionality, this turned out to be a relatively low priority for ICT use. Participant retention was more challenging when organizers were unable to provide engaging data displays, but modifications to participation activities and communication strategies were useful techniques for improving retention. Those citizen science projects with adequate resources have successfully formulated robust, scalable systems to support the scientific rigor of the research [25], and while these tools are currently out of reach for most smaller projects, turning to other resources can achieve similar data quality for a wide range of citizen science projects.

Similarities between citizen science and online communities, distributed scientific collaboration, and peer production suggest opportunities for future work examining how findings from CSCW studies of massively distributed collaborations may generalize across contexts. Identifying means of improving engagement and product quality that do not rely solely on ICT provides a reminder for CSCW researchers that technologies are not a solution in and of themselves. Ideal technologies are not always available to practitioners, particularly in resource-constrained contexts, and remaining open to complementary strategies to support distributed collaboration can provide viable solutions. Case studies such as those presented here can also provide a frame of reference to both practitioners and researchers exploring alternate approaches for improving upon large-scale open collaboration.

As ICT supporting citizen science continues to evolve, the emergence of cyberinfrastructures and platforms to support projects faced with resource limitations will likely begin to address these issues more comprehensively. In the meantime, attention to the context of practical constraints surrounding ICT use, incorporating creative strategies that do not rely entirely on ICT, and leveraging small investments in ICT for maximum benefit are viable approaches to improving citizen science project outcomes.

ACKNOWLEDGMENTS

This research was supported in part by NSF Grants VOSS-0943049, SOCS-0968470, and OCI-0830944. I am deeply grateful to the organizers of eBird, The Great Sunflower Project, Mountain Watch, and their colleagues and partners who shared their time and experiences for this study. Finally, I thank the AC and anonymous reviewers, whose feedback substantially improved the work.

REFERENCES

1. Bonney, R., Cooper, C., Dickinson, J., Kelling, S., Phillips, T., Rosenberg, K., and Shirk, J. Citizen science: A developing tool for expanding science knowledge and scientific literacy. *BioScience 59*, 11 (2009), 977–984.
2. Bowker, G. *Memory Practices in the Sciences*. MIT Press, Cambridge, MA, 2005.
3. Cohn, J. Citizen science: Can volunteers do real research? *BioScience 58*, 3 (March 2008), 192–107.
4. Cooper, C., Dickinson, J., Phillips, T., and Bonney, R. Citizen science as a tool for conservation in residential ecosystems. *Ecology and Society 12*, 2 (2007).
5. Emerson, R., Fretz, R., and Shaw, L. *Writing Ethnographic Fieldnotes*. University of Chicago Press, Chicago, IL, 1995.
6. Firehock, K., and West, J. A brief history of volunteer biological water monitoring using macroinvertebrates. *Journal of the North American Benthological Society 14*, 1 (1995), 197–202.
7. Hine, C. *Virtual Ethnography*. Sage Publications Ltd, Thousand Oaks, CA, 2000.
8. Howe, J. The Rise of Crowdsourcing. *Wired Magazine 14*, 6 (2006), 1–4.
9. Ilgen, D., Hollenbeck, J., Johnson, M., and Jundt, D. Teams in organizations: From Input-Process-Output Models to IMOI Models. *Annual Review of Psychology 56* (2005), 517–543.
10. Kim, S., Robson, C., Zimmerman, T., Pierce, J., and Haber, E. Creek watch: Pairing usefulness and usability for successful citizen science. In *Proceedings of the 2011 International Conference on Human Factors in Computing Systems*, ACM (New York, NY, 2011), 2125–2134.
11. Klang, M. Free software and open source: The freedom debate and its consequences. *First Monday 10*, 3-7 (2005).
12. Maron, N., Smith, K., and Loy, M. Sustaining Digital Resources: An On-the-Ground View of Projects Today. Tech. rep., Ithaka S+R, New York, NY, 2009.
13. Nov, O., Arazy, O., and Anderson, D. Dusting for science: Motivation and participation of digital citizen science volunteers. In *Proceedings of iConference 2011*, ACM (New York, NY, 2011).
14. Roman, D. Crowdsourcing and the question of expertise. *Communications of the ACM 52*, 12 (2009), 12.
15. Rotman, D., Preece, J., Hammock, J., Procita, K., Hansen, D., Parr, C., Lewis, D., and Jacobs, D. Dynamic changes in motivation in collaborative ecological citizen science projects. In *Proceedings of the ACM 2012 conference on Computer supported cooperative work*, ACM (New York, NY, 2012).
16. Sheppard, S., and Terveen, L. Quality is a verb: The operationalization of data quality in a citizen science community. In *Proceedings of the Seventh International Symposium on Wikis and Open Collaboration*, ACM (2011), 29–38.
17. Spradley, J. *The Ethnographic Interview*. Wadsworth Publishing Company, 1979.
18. Sullivan, B., Wood, C., Iliff, M., Bonney, R., Fink, D., and Kelling, S. eBird: A citizen-based bird observation network in the biological sciences. *Biological Conservation 142*, 10 (2009), 2282–2292.

19. Trumbull, D., Bonney, R., Bascom, D., and Cabral, A. Thinking scientifically during participation in a citizen-science project. *Science Education 84*, 2 (2000), 265–275.
20. Wenger, E. *Communities of Practice: Learning, Meaning, and Identity*. Cambridge University Press, 1999.
21. Wiggins, A. eBirding: Technology adoption and the transformation of leisure into science. In *Proceedings of iConference 2011* (Seattle, WA, 2011).
22. Wiggins, A., and Crowston, K. Developing a conceptual model of virtual organisations for citizen science. *International Journal of Organisational Design and Engineering 1* (2010), 148–162.
23. Wiggins, A., Gerbracht, J., Lagoze, C., Yu, J., Wong, W., and Kelling, S. Crowdsourcing citizen science data quality with a human-computer learning network. In *Proceedings of the Workshop on Human Computation for Science and Computational Sustainability*, Neural Information Processing Systems Foundation (Lake Tahoe, NV, 2012).
24. Wiggins, A., Newman, G., Stevenson, R., and Crowston, K. Mechanisms for data quality and validation in citizen science. In *Proceedings of Workshops at the Seventh International Conference on eScience*, IEEE (2011).
25. Wood, C., Sullivan, B., Iliff, M., Fink, D., and Kelling, S. eBird: Engaging birders in science and conservation. *PLoS Biology 9*, 12 (12 2011).

Form Factor Matters

Joon-Suk Lee **Deborah Tatar**
Dept. of Computer Science, MC 0106
Virginia Tech
2202 Kraft Dr., Blacksburg, VA 24060
{joonlee, tatar}@vt.edu

ABSTRACT
Previous research reports a number of different variables that affect group processes. We examine situations in "triple space," in which people must manage (1) complex problem-solving tasks, (2) social interaction, and (3) the meaning making process of the changing representation created by others on shared mediums. In this case, the complex problem-solving task is solving a shared Sudoku puzzle. Two findings follow from the current study. People in both the laptop and tablet conditions talked less than people in the paper-control condition, but only people in the laptop condition experienced a significant decrease in positive emotion.

Author Keywords
Micro-coordination; Coordination; Form Factor

ACM Classification Keywords
H.5.m. Information interfaces and presentation (e.g., HCI): Miscellaneous.

INTRODUCTION
Questions such as "would you feel more positive if you played a crossword puzzle with your friends on an iPAD as compared to playing the same game as printed in a newspaper or with a laptop?" or "would you talk more if you played *Settlers of Catan* on a laptop rather than playing it on a tablet?" might sound absurd or obvious to some people. They might ask "why would people feel or act any differently by engaging in the same kind of activities using different forms of technologies?" or they might say "I know how to use technology, so it's all the same to me." Indeed, the person who expresses doubt might, in today's culture, feel a need to apologize or qualify him- or herself as "not a technical person."

Previous research, however, has shown differences in interactive technologies can affect and change users' behaviors and their feelings toward the artifacts. For instance, people prefer a computer that flatters or diagnoses them as happy regardless of the correctness of the assessment [13]. People act politely towards computers in general [14], but not towards small computers [6].

CSCW '13, February 23–27, 2013, San Antonio, Texas, USA.

In our study, unlike previous studies that looked at how people react to different interactive technologies, we investigate how mediating technologies affect people in group settings. In this case, we examine the role technological mediums play in influencing behaviors and emotional states in a "triple space" situation. Participants play a collaborative Sudoku game while in the same physical location. Baron [1] describes students solving a problem together as jointly inhabiting a "dual space" involving the management of both cognitive and social functions. Lee, Tatar and Harrison [10] have previously described the increasingly common situation shown in Figure 1 as representing a "triple space," in which participants are managing not only the cognitive and social functions described by Barron, but also the challenge of making sense of the changes to the shared medium caused by the other players.

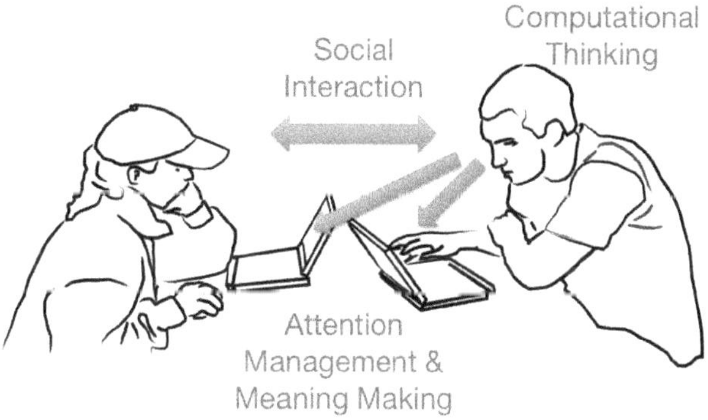

Figure 1. Interactions in Triple Space

Jean Twenge documents a rise in anxiety and depression among young adults, and argues that today's children see themselves as solitary actors, untied to others in *Generation Me* [16]. Sherry Turkle also portrayed people in our current society as becoming more and more detached from face-to-face interactions and increasingly attached to machinery in *Alone Together* [15].

While a recent Pew Internet Personal Networks and Community survey reports that the extent of social isolation has not changed since 1985 [7], Klinenberg reports that more than 50% of American adults today are single and one out of every seven adults lives alone [9]. Klinenberg assesses this change positively, claiming that the rise in rates of living alone is a transformative social experience that requires us to make changes in how we view ourselves and our intimate relationships. He claims living alone does not make people any lonelier, and goes on to explain how solitude can be beneficial in reviving personal energy in a hyper-networked, always-connected culture [9]. Klinenberg does not provide evidence about unhappiness (more generally than loneliness).

While the evidence for whether Americans are becoming evermore isolated is still mixed and controversial, and the interpretation for whether the use of social media is supplementing or replacing traditional interpersonal connections is debatable, it is an undeniable fact that we are living in the era of information technology, and that we do not necessarily understand all the ways that information technology affects us. For example, loneliness and unhappiness are closely related concepts but they are not identical, and questions about both may vary according to precise details in the framework in which the questions or assessments are made. We need to understand more and our understanding needs to come from many perspectives and levels of analysis. Tablets and smartphones are rapidly taking the place of desktops and laptops. However, we do not yet know what it means to use tablets and smartphones in the place of desktops and laptops.

Lee, Tatar and Harrison's investigation [10] suggested a more complex interaction between technology design and user experience than had emerged clearly in prior works. In particular, they found that proxies such as "amount of talk" or even "kinds of talk" proved poor indicators of the satisfactory nature of the system.

The current study explores the relation between talk, difference in the mediating technology and user's emotional state. It asks "How does the mediating artifact affect people's coordinative behaviors and possibly the way that people feel as they engage in joint activities?" It uses the same highly demanding Collaborative Sudoku task as in [10], but contrasts a Paper, a Tablet and a Laptop condition. It investigates whether and how the kinds and the form factors of mediating technology affect users' behaviors and their emotional state.

THE STUDY

To explore the possibilities of the differences in mediating technology having impacts on people's emotional states and behaviors, we asked groups of people to play Sudoku collectively on a 25 x 30.5 inch sheet (base-line, Paper Condition) and on two different form-configurations (Tablet Condition and Laptop Condition) of tablet PCs. In the paper condition (PC), researchers prepared the Sudoku game board manually on 25 x 30.5 inch sheets prior to the study and asked participants to solve the puzzles on that. In both computer conditions, groups were asked to collaboratively solve puzzles on specially designed multiplayer Sudoku software, Team Sudoku.

We made an explicit decision to use a type of computer that has a twist-and-swivel display so that we could configure the same computer both as a laptop and as a tablet. For the laptop condition (LC), mice were connected to the systems as the primary input devices, while for the tablet condition (TC), stylus pens were provided as the primary input devices. Keyboard input mechanisms were disabled in the systems to maintain compatibility between the laptop condition and the tablet condition in which keyboards are hidden under the laid-down screens, inaccessible to the users.

Clearly, there are many differences between the paper and the computer conditions that are consequences of the types of sharing that they enable. However, the differences between the LC and the TC include only the configuration and the input device.

Team Sudoku

Team Sudoku is a multi-user, parallel-distributed form of the Sudoku game. Sudoku presents the player with a 9x9 board with digits between 1 and 9 in some cells. The goal of Sudoku is to fill the board so that each of the nine columns, nine rows and nine distinct 3x3 blocks contain exactly one instance of each digit from 1 to 9. Games are differentiated from one another by the number and location of starting digits. In the computerized form, each distinct game initially contains digits that cannot be written over or changed except by starting a new game, and that are a different color (black) from those that are in play (green).

Team Sudoku provides users three distinct features for manipulating the board. A pen tool enables users to insert entries on the board, and a pencil tool allows users to tentatively mark possibilities (note-entries). Users can delete any entries on the game board with an eraser tool. Team Sudoku is a multi-user collaborative variation of Sudoku in which players have their own computers with their own copies of the shared game board. When one player fills in a number, erases a number, or uses an indicating tool, the results are promptly shared on all players' screens.

Procedures

Players were recruited from the Psychology Participant pool at our university, and received extra credit for participation. The advertisement for participation had two components: that the study was about a collaborative game, and that participants needed to have played Sudoku before. Players played in groups of two or three.

The study was designed as a two-phased, between-subject experiment. In phase 1, participants were asked to fill out online questionnaires about demographics, prior experiences with Sudoku as well as five personality self-report inventories (Big Five [8], Circumplex Scales of Interpersonal Values [11], Circumplex Scales of Interpersonal Efficacy [12], Beck Anxiety Inventory [2] and Beck Depression Inventory [3]). When participants reported that they did not have prior Sudoku experience, they were directed to a web site that had both descriptions of the Sudoku rules and sample Sudoku games.

Figure 2. Set-up for three Team Sudoku Players (Laptop Condition shown).

In phase 2, participants were brought into a small room and seated in close proximity to one another (Figure. 2). They were introduced to one another when they came into the room. After the informed consent process, participants were asked to fill out a pre-game questionnaire (Q1) including questions about their experiences with the game and with the other players, and also the 20-item *Positive and Negative Affect Schedule (PANAS)* [17] that measures how people are feeling in the moment. The groups were asked to work together on two Sudoku puzzles, in an order counter-balanced across groups. The groups were given 20 minutes to work on each game. After each game, participants filled out post-game questionnaires (Q2 and Q3), including retaking the PANAS. In Q3, we also asked them to rate how much they were satisfied with the group and the way it worked together on a scale of 1 (not at all) to 7 (very much). There was also a short discussion at the end of the study. Video and audio recordings of all the game sessions were collected as well as computer logs and screen shot movies of the games. Transcripts of the talk were made using a method modified from Chafe [4].

Participants

A total of 138 (75 female, 63 male) college students enrolled in the study, in 24 groups of two and 30 groups of three. Participants' age ranged from 18 to 41 ($M = 19$ $SD = 2.28$). 10 of 138 reported that their first language was not English, but none appeared to have difficulty because of this. Almost all the participants had prior experience with Sudoku. 15 reported initially that they did not know the Sudoku rules. But researchers confirmed that these 15 people were at least fully familiar with the Sudoku rules when they came in for the on-site experiment. Overall, participants reported playing Sudoku quite often ($M = 5.35$, $SD = 1.51$) on a scale of 1 (rarely) to 7 (several times a day).

If only two participants appeared at the agreed time, the game was run with them, resulting in 24 groups of two. In this paper, we address only the 30 three-person groups.

In this note, we focus on the data on mood change from the PANAS questionnaires and how many times individuals took turns in group conversation.

FINDINGS

How the form factor of a technological medium influences participants' emotions

The first mood state (PANAS) questionnaire was given before the first puzzle (P1), the second between the first and the second puzzle (P2), the third after the second puzzle (P3). As usual, the sum of scores for the Positive Affect (PA) items and the sum of scores for the Negative Affect (NA) items were calculated for each PANAS test. Difference scores were calculated to monitor the mood changes after playing the first game (P1-to-P2), and from the beginning to the end of the experience (P1-to-P3). P2-to-P3 differences are not reported, but continue the same trends.

No differences were found in across the study in NA. However, as shown in Tables 1 and 2, there were significant differences in the mean changes in PA by technological condition (from P1-to-P2, $F(2, 87) = 5.05$, $p < .01$) in which PA scores showed a gain of the most positive affect in the PC, a gain of only a bit in the TC, and a loss in the LC. These changes became more differentiated from one another after the second game ($F(2, 87) = 7.68$, $p = .001$). Despite reaching statistical significance P1-to-P2, the test of homogeneity of variances showed unequal variances among the three conditions. However, the Welch's adjusted F ratio confirmed and even strengthened the previous finding, ($F(2, 55.32) = 5.46$, $p = .007$). The effect size for P1-to-P2, calculated using eta-squared, was 0.10 and for P1-to-P3, was 0.15. In Cohen's terms, these effects fall between medium and large. (p.284-287, [5]).

Drilling down, post-hoc comparisons using the LSD test indicated that participants in PC had a significantly higher rise in PA scores than participants in the LC (P1-to-P2, Mean Dif. = 4.97; $p < 0.01$; P1-to-P3, Mean Dif. = 7.53; $p < 0.01$). They were quite a bit more happy with paper than on the laptop. This is, perhaps, not very surprising. More surprising were the differences between the TC and the LC. While these were only marginally different from P1-to-P2 (Mean Dif. = 2.83; $p = 0.07$), they were significantly different from P1-to-P3 (Mean Dif. = 4.43; $p < 0.03$). Instead of, for example, Laptop and Tablet resembling one another, Paper and Tablet were more aligned on this outcome measure, although the difference neared significance if examined from P1-to-P3 (P1-to-P2, Mean Dif. = 2.13, $p = 0.18$; P1-to-P3, Mean Dif. = 3.10, $p = 0.11$). Furthermore, the mean value for the LC ($M = -1.23$) decreased after the first game, while the mean value for the TC ($M=1.60$) and the PC increased ($M = 3.73$).

In other words, differences in people's positive emotional states are associated with the properties of the medium, and these differences are associated not only with the large and obvious differences between the PC and the computer conditions, but also with the more subtle differences between the LC and the TC. The difference between the LC and the TC shows that not only the differences in mediating technology, but also the differences in form factor, affect people's emotional states differently.

Condition	N	Mean	Std. Err
Paper	30	3.73	1.43
Tablet	30	1.60	0.99
Laptop	30	-1.23	0.79

Table 1: Positive Affect Changes Before to After First Game

Condition	N	Mean	Std. Err
Paper	30	3.07	1.69
Tablet	30	-0.03	1.28
Laptop	30	-4.47	1.06

Table 2: Positive Affect Changes from Before First Game to After Second Game

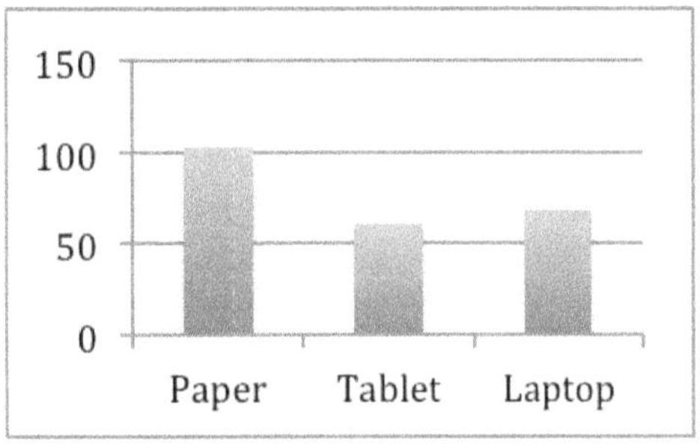

Figure 3: Mean number of conversational turns by individuals by technological condition

How technological medium influences participants' contributions to group discourse

As shown in Figure 3, the number of conversational turns individuals took differed from one technological condition to another (P1-to-P2, $F(2,87) = 5.86$, $p < .004$). People in the paper condition took significantly more conversational turns than individuals in either the LC (Mean Dif. = 33.73; $p = 0.01$) or the TC (Mean Dif. = 41.47; $p < 0.01$).

A related previous study [10] showed a statistically significant positive correlation between the amount of talk and participants' self-reported satisfaction. We were able to partially replicate that result in this study in that, overall, $r=0.28$ ($p < 0.01$). However, the current study did not have enough participants in the LC condition to adequately test the relationship reported in [10] (p. 1140) that $r = 0.26$ ($p < .006$, $N = 168$). Our LC had only 30 participants, and produced a correlation of $r = 0.31$, but a marginally significant p-value (0.10). However, the current findings suggest that the relationship between the amount of talk and participant satisfaction is more pronounced when they are working together on paper than when they are working together on separate laptops.

We also found a statistically significant positive correlation between the amount of talk and changes in individual's positive emotion ($r=0.24$; $p=0.02$). As with reported satisfaction with the group, this overall condition was driven primarily by the paper condition ($r=0.45$; $p=0.01$), with weaker contributions from the other two (TC, $r=0.27$, $p=0.15$; LC, $r=0.25$, $p=0.18$).

DISCUSSION & CONCLUSION

Our results show statistically significant differences in the amount of talk among the conditions. People talked more when they shared a big piece of paper to collectively work on a Sudoku puzzle. They talked significantly less when they were using computers. Our data also show that people's positive feelings rose more when they talked more. And from those two findings, we might conjecture that the evermore prevalent use of technologies in current society might be holding people back from engaging in face-to-face conversations, which in turn might cause a rise in anxiety and depression among the young adults as documented by Twenge [16].

On the other hand, we also found that people who used tablets were less susceptible to the changes in positive emotions. When participants used laptops, they talked significantly less and had a considerable decrease in their positive feelings than people who used paper. But when participants used tablets, the changes in their positive feelings weren't statistically different from the people in the paper condition, even though there were clear differences in the amount of talk between the two groups. We still do not decisively know why people using tablets had higher positive emotions than people using the laptop. However, the fact that these two groups of people used exactly the same computers, but in different form configurations hints to us that the form factor of technological medium might affect changes in people's emotional states differently.

Among the noticeable behavioral differences between TC and LC was that some participants in TC tried to glance over other players' screens during the sessions while none in LC exhibited such behavior. Even though, players shared the exact same information on their own screens, participants might have felt more connected by having a chance to physically share what is considered their private resource. This conjecture might also help in explaining the highest mean numbers in positive affect changes in PC, in which participants had a large shared resource. In LC, upright-positioned screens might have acted as physical barriers between players, whereas in TC, laid-down screens could have helped people to feel enhanced social presence by providing increased immediacy for social interactions [18].

Our findings are promising in the sense that the increasing use of tablets might alleviate the increasing rise in depression among young adults (if such a trend exists). They also suggest the importance of investigating the relationship between tablets and similar-yet-different form factors such as tabletops and smart phones. Indeed, we believe that comparing technologies with different screen sizes (tabletops, desktops, laptops, tablets in different sizes and mobile phones) will help us further test our hypothesis of having physically less obtrusive technologies increasing in positive emotional states. In this short paper, we have not advanced a theory of the relationship between these findings, but we point out that there may be important effects in an increasingly present situation. Form factor just might matter.

ACKNOWLEDGMENTS

This work was supported by NSF Grant. IIS-1018607 HCC-Small.

REFERENCES

1. Barron, B. (2003) When smart groups fail, *The Journal of the Learning Sciences*.
2. Beck, A. and Steer, R. (1993) Beck Anxiety Inventory. The Psychological Corporation.
3. Beck, A., Ward, C., Mendelson, M., Mock, J., and Erbaugh, J. (1961) An inventory for measuring depression. Archives of General Psychiatry.
4. Chafe,W.L. (1993) Prosodic and Functional Units of Language. In J. Edwards & M. Lampert (Eds) *Talking Data*, pp. 33-44, Lawrence Erlbaum Associates
5. Cohen, J. (1988) Statistical power analysis for the behavioral sciences. Lawrence Erlbaum.
6. Goldstein, M., Alsiö, G., and Werdenhoff, J. The media equation does not always apply: People are not polite towards small computers. Personal and ubiquitous computing 6, 2 (2002), 87–96.
7. Hampton, K.N., Sessions, L.F., Her, E.J., and Rainie, L., Social Isolation and New Technology. Pew Internet & American Life Project (2009) Available from: http://www.pewinternet.org/Reports/2009/18--Social-Isolation-and-New-Technology.aspx.
8. John, O. P. (1990). The "Big Five" factor taxonomy: Dimensions of personality in the natural language and in questionnaires. In L. Pervin (Ed.), Handbook of personality: Theory and research (pp. 66-100). Guilford Press.
9. Klinenberg, E. Going Solo: The Extraordinary Rise and Surprising Appeal of Living Alone. 2012.
10. Lee, J.S., Tatar, D., and Harrison, S. (2012) Micro-coordination: Because We did not Already Learn Everything We Need to Know about Working with Others in Kindergarten, In Proc. of CSCW.
11. Locke, K.D. (2000). Circumplex scales of interpersonal values: Reliability, validity, and applicability to interpersonal problems and personality disorders. Journal of Personality Assessment, 75, 249-267.
12. Locke, K.D. and Sadler, P. (2007). Self-efficacy, values, and complementarity in dyadic interactions: Integrating interpersonal and social-cognitive theory. Personality and Social Psychology Bulletin, 33, 94-109.
13. Nass, C.I. and Yen, C. The man who lied to his laptop: what machines teach us about human relationships. 2010.
14. Reeves, B. and Nass, C. The Media Equation: How People Treat Computers, Television, and New Media Like Real People and Places (Center for the Study of Language and In-formation - Lecture Notes). Center for the Study of Language and Inf, 2003.
15. Turkle, S. (2011) Alone Together: Why We Expect More from Technology and Less from Each Other. Basic Books.
16. Twenge, J.M. (2006) Generation Me: Why Today's Young Americans Are More Confident, Assertive, Entitled--and More Miserable Than Ever Before. Free Press.
17. Watson, D., Clark, L.A., Tellegen, A.(1988) Development and validation of brief measures of positive and negative affect: The PANAS scales. Journal of Personality and Social Psychology, 54(6), 1063-1070.
18. Weinel, M., Bannert, M., Zumbach, J., Hoppe, H.U., and Malzahn, N. A closer look on social presence as a causing factor in computer-mediated collaboration. Computers in Human Behavior 27, 1 (2011), 513–521.

Managing Mobile Multitasking: The Culture of iPhones on Stanford Campus

Morgan G. Ames
Department of Communication
Stanford University
morganya@stanford.edu

ABSTRACT
This paper discusses three concepts that govern technosocial practices among university students with iPhones. First is the social expectation of *constant connection* that requires multitasking to achieve. Second is the resulting *technosocial pecking order* of who gets interrupted or ignored for whom. Third is the way that many students push back against these demands with *techno-resistance*, deliberately curtailing constant connection to reduce the negative effects of multitasking, in spite of the risk of social censure. These concepts are developed from interviews with 57 students, 30 hours of field observations, and a survey of 177 students on Stanford campus, which in particular explored iPhone use. This research concludes that so-called "digital natives" must still navigate familiar social dynamics and personal desires, both online and off. Providing a detailed description of how students from across campus make sense of iPhones in their everyday technosocial assemblages, this research suggests opportunities for more socially and cognitively sensitive design of smartphone features.

Author Keywords
iPhones; mobile phones; smartphones; multitasking; ethnography; digital native; ANT; SCOT; technofeminism.

ACM Classification Keywords
H.5.m. Information interfaces and presentation (e.g., HCI): Miscellaneous.

INTRODUCTION
Mobile phones, and increasingly smartphones, are a ubiquitous part of student life on many college campuses in the United States and around the world. In spring 2009, when data collection for this research took place, an estimated one quarter of students on Stanford campus, the site of this study, owned an Apple iPhone. At the end of 2011, 43% of mobile phone users in the United States had smartphones, most of them either iPhones or Android devices [20]. However, there is still little scholarship that examines smartphone use specifically. This paper explores the rules, etiquette, and practices that governed the use of iPhones on campus, which tended to balance two competing desires. On one hand, students reported social expectations of *constant connection*, which often led to heavy multitasking, emphasized by iPhones but also enabled by other mobile phones, laptops, and other devices. On the other hand, two-thirds of students practiced *techno-resistance*, actively setting boundaries or disconnecting from their iPhones and other devices. This let them minimize the negative cognitive effects of multitasking and reinforce personal identities and values opposing constant connection. This latter finding in particular presents a contrasting perspective to the often celebratory tone of other research on mobile phone culture in discussing the constant connection mobile phones enable.

This tension underscores broader issues concerning the social effects of mediated communication, multitasking, and constant technology access, especially through smartphones. In particular, the prevalence of techno-resistance complicates the unilinear S-curve technology adoption model [26] as well as the monolithic category of "digital native," the generation who grew up with the Internet and mobile phones and, according to some, embrace these technologies and the multitasking they require in a fundamentally different way than older generations [24,32]. The digital natives in this study did have to negotiate the social expectations enabled by these new technologies, but almost none embraced them wholeheartedly, and those who did found that embracing them, like rejecting them, carried social consequences.

Life on Stanford campus—a wealthy, elite, and technological university—is almost certainly not typical. However, I posit that living so close to California's Silicon Valley, where new technologies are often quickly adopted and actively discussed, can act as a focusing lens for emergent practices involving new technologies, making people cognizant of issues that may otherwise lie dormant in more lightweight usage scenarios. In short, Stanford presents a self-conscious, if privileged, snapshot into how students make sense of smartphones and other technologies in their everyday lives. The emergent tensions may be accentuated by this environment, but as some of the findings presented here echo or amplify previous analyses of mobile culture or multitasking, they are likely not unique to it.

RESEARCH ON MOBILE PHONES AND MULTITASKING

University campuses are not the only places that have developed cultural practices around mobile phones or struggled to balance constant connection and techno-resistance. The human-computer interaction and the social studies of science communities both have rich ecologies of research on the social life of the mobile phone. Though lacking space for an exhaustive survey, I will highlight several that have particularly informed this research.

Katz and Aakhus's edited volume, published in 2002, provides one of the earliest comprehensive social analyses of mobile phone culture around the world, especially as it relates to "private talk" and "public performance" [15]. A common theme throughout the volume is the "perpetual contact" that mobile phones enable, as this paper's section on *constant connection* echoes. The next year, Katz edited another volume further exploring the development of mobile phone culture as distinct from landline telephone culture, particularly in negotiating technosocial control [16]. However, foreshadowing this project's finding of *techno-resistance*, Nafus and Tracey describe how mobile consumption was at times implicated in oppositional identities even when mobile phones were still relatively new [15:13]. This paper provides an updated and differently-articulated account of this identity-work in a world where mobile phones are ubiquitous and smartphones common.

More recently, Rich Ling has explored the ways in which mobile phones have affected social cohesion, borrowing from Durkheim's and Goffman's theories of ritual in social interactions to examine the ways that mobile phones have become part of ritual communication [18]. His findings that mobile phones strengthen close ties, though sometimes at the expense of copresent acquaintances (also discussed in [15:14]), are echoed in the discussion below of the technosocial pecking order of college students with iPhones.

Ito *et al.* have examined mobile phone use among Japanese teenagers, describing the many ways in which these *keitai* are negotiated in their everyday social worlds [13,14]. The authors also discuss the popularity of mobile email (defined broadly as any mobile textual communication) as a lightweight method of maintaining *ambient virtual copresence* [13:13], buttressing this research's finding that email (defined more narrowly) was the most popular mode of contact among the US college students in this study.

There are fewer studies of the social ecology of *smartphones* specifically, though the topic is still one of interest to the CSCW community as smartphones continue to grow in popularity. Here, a 'smartphone' is a portable computing device with a high-resolution screen (usually a touchscreen), Internet connectivity, a number of multimedia features, and an "app store" for fetching content and applications for the phone, in addition to standard mobile phone features of calling, SMS, and voicemail. This particular set of features was first established by the iPhone in 2007 and has since appeared on smartphones from various manufacturers.

Sherry Turkle implicates smartphones in her explorations of the brave new social worlds enabled by our many always-connected devices in *Alone Together*. She found that many of her participants—and, increasingly, she as well—were constantly tethered to a liminal space between the physical and virtual, not fully present to either but comforted (if coldly) by the simulation of personal connection in both [33:8]. Several of the themes explored in *Alone Together* are echoed in the following pages, particularly the cognitive and social consequences of constant connection and the multitasking it entails. Turkle does also touch on techno-resistance, but mostly in describing her own ambivalence toward her smartphone; this study suggests that her desire to disconnect from the virtual world in order to better connect to the physical is an increasingly prevalent aspect of many people's technosocial negotiations.

There have been a few other explorations of smartphone use in HCI literature as well. Studying early smartphones, Swallow, Blythe, and Wright describe the ways they became implicated in issues of identity, sociability, security, and organization among their participants [31], and Ames *et al.* explore photographic practices on early Nokia smartphones [1]. Focusing on the iPhone, Blythe and Cairns discuss the ways YouTube videos shaped perceptions of the iPhone 3G prior to its release [5], and Oren *et al.* provide user-tested guidelines for internationalizing the iPhone [22].

This paper adds to this literature a systematic exploration of iPhones (and, by extension, smartphones in general) in daily life. We will see that while iPhones did not differ from other mobile phones as social actors in some ways, there were instances where their smartphone capabilities did set them apart; in particular, the constant connection they enabled forced their users to be more deliberate in setting boundaries.

The social demands and cognitive costs of the multitasking that iPhones and other devices 'demanded' emerged as central concerns among the participants in this study. The implications of multitasking, interruptions, and fragmented work—especially in the workplace, but also in the classroom [10] and elsewhere—is a topic with extensive scholarship in CSCW, as well as the broader HCI community (e.g. see [4,6,11,19,30]). While research on multitasking in the workplace and classroom often focuses on productivity or learning outcomes rather than the broader social implications explored here, some have examined multitasking and interruptions beyond the workplace as well. Baron explores multitasking and discourse control, similar to and described in the "technosocial pecking order" section below [2]. Salvucci *et al.* propose a *multitasking continuum* defined by the rapidity of task-switching, from seconds (*e.g.* talking and driving) to hours (*e.g.* reading and cooking), and also theorize the elements of multitasking [28].

On a cognitive level, Ophir *et al.* show that chronic multitaskers are actually *less* able to keep track of multiple inputs than those who avoid multitasking in psychological testing [21]. Oulasvirta *et al.* measure the cognitive load of fragmented attention on mobile phones in particular, noting decreased reaction times and eventual interaction breakdowns [23]. To these studies, this account adds a qualitative, *in situ* perspective on the social expectations of mobile multitasking and how students resisted them.

This analysis utilizes two theoretical frameworks for understanding technology and social life. In discussing the social practices that have developed around iPhones and other technologies, it highlights how the iPhone both acts like and is treated as another *social actor*, much like humans and other machines in the influence it can have, in the way that Bruno Latour has described in Actor-Network Theory [17]. This research additionally discusses how iPhones became part of *networks* of friends and family, both local and extended. The use of 'networks' here also hails from actor-network theory, where both humans and non-humans (like iPhones) are actor-nodes constantly co-articulating both their identities and their connections.

This research also acknowledges a degree of *interpretive flexibility* in how the iPhone is understood (which was by no means stable) and also of distinct *relevant social groups* in its adoption (which can be summarized as a continuum between embracers and resisters, as well as the have-nots), in keeping with The Social Construction of Technology, or SCOT [25]. It also notes the how and why participants resisted the dominant meanings associated with iPhone use through *techno-resistance*, borrowing from technofeminism's critiques of SCOT to provide an oppositional perspective on SCOT's generally technology-positive adoption model [34]. It furthermore complicates the classic innovation-adoption model in which only 'laggards' (itself a socially loaded term) do not adopt technology, mainly because of low social standing or lack of knowledge [26]. In this study, even 'early adopters' cultivated habits of techno-resistance, indicating that technological adoption of iPhones was not a unilinear process of ever-increasing acceptance.

However, this research does not directly address the power differences between those who have iPhones and those who do not. While several interviewees mentioned elitism and iPhones, they felt that that was more of a concern between the campus and elsewhere than within the campus community. As this research is an analysis of practices on campus, addressing this concern is beyond the scope of this work.

RESEARCH METHODS

The field observations, interviews and survey data presented in this paper were collected by nine doctoral students over ten weeks in spring quarter 2009 as part of an anthropology class, in which we explored iPhone culture on campus. The bulk of the results presented here are drawn from open-ended interviews with 57 students, of which 45 owned iPhones, seven owned iPod Touch devices but no iPhone, and five owned neither. Of those who did not have an iPhone, four owned Android smartphones and the rest owned non-smartphone mobile phones. The twelve students without iPhones helped us contextualize our findings in the broader campus community.

We recruited students from many departments all across campus, including the humanities, engineering, social sciences, natural sciences, and various professional schools. We used a variety of recruitment techniques: some students were spotted with iPhones during field observations around campus and asked to participate, some were recruited through student dorms (which house 96% of undergraduates and 56% of graduate students, and are assigned by lottery[1]), and some through snowball sampling, using the initial participants and contacts of the researchers as seeds.

We developed and used an interview protocol to ensure that all interviewers covered the same topics, but kept the interviews open-ended and conversational to allow for the discovery of unexpected themes. These topics were formulated broadly and included questions about recent usage patterns, types of use (phone, text, email, apps, music, video, etc.), rules for use, thoughts on others' use, changing perceptions of space or time, privacy, cost, elitism/politics, friendships, family, romance, disconnection/breakage, and the proposed iStanford plan. We encouraged participants to corroborate what they were telling us by showing us examples on their phones during the interview. Finally, to understand how mobile phone use fit into students' broader sociotechnical ensembles, we asked similar questions about their use of laptops, iPods, other mobile phones, and other technologies in their day-to-day life.

The interviews were each one to two hours long. They included 46 individual interviews and three focus groups with two to four participants each; we used the same interview protocol for both types of interviews. We organized the three focus groups to explore whether the group setting might enable or inhibit certain kinds of discussions, but found that the results did not differ from those of individual interviews. Each researcher watched at least one interview conducted by another researcher to verify that our interview techniques were consistent. We offered tokens of appreciation to interview participants, either a free meal or a $5 gift card to a campus eatery. VerbalInk (http://verbalink.com), a professional transcription service, transcribed the interviews.

Along with these interviews, we collectively carried out 30 hours of field observations (about 3 hours per researcher) in various campus settings: the campus library, the student union lounge, the campus bookstore café, an outdoor campus café, two other cafés just off campus that are popular with students, a busy pedestrian intersection in the center of campus, two campus bus stops, a jogging track on the west end of campus, and a local pub popular with students. We discussed these locations ahead of time and also developed a guide to help us determine what to record, focusing on noting the context and content of mobile phone use, actions preceding and following mobile phone use, and instances of the passive presence of mobile phones not in use (*e.g.* on the table, attached to headphones, etc.). These observations

[1] http://facts.stanford.edu/campuslife.html

allowed us to triangulate the self-reported behavior collected in interviews.

We pooled the interview transcripts and fieldnotes generated by each of the researchers and distributed them for individual analysis. For this paper, the author analyzed the interviews and field observations using Atlas.TI software, iteratively coding to identify emergent themes based on the perspectives of the participants themselves, as described in [29].

To test whether the themes we had observed were shared by a larger proportion of the student population, we used the themes that we each uncovered in our individual analyses to develop a survey, which we distributed to 177 students who owned iPhones. We each generated several questions for the survey, which were then collated, organized, and edited for coherence. We recruited the 177 survey-takers from classes, dorms, and public locations (such as eateries and walkways) throughout campus; these settings were chosen collectively to create, in aggregate, a representative sample. This included 131 undergraduates, or approximately 8% of the estimated iPhone-owning undergraduate student population, and 44 graduate students, or approximately 2.5% of the estimated iPhone-owning graduate student population, as extrapolated from Stanford's 2008-2009 enrollment numbers. As before, we pooled the responses each researcher had collected and then distributed them for individual analysis; the author of this paper analyzed the survey results using SPSS.

Why focus on iPhones? After all, students used not just iPhones but a suite of technologies, and the majority of students did not own iPhones at all. We chose to focus data collection around iPhones for two reasons. The first was to limit our study to a reasonable scope by choosing one particular technology that has a relatively uniform set of features and a strong presence on campus. The iPhone fit this description. We estimated that in spring 2009, fully one quarter of students used iPhones, based on our systematic counts of iPhone ownership in freshman dorms and (non-engineering) undergraduate classes; this proportion has almost certainly risen since. Over half of our interviewees and survey respondents received their iPhones in the last 3-12 months, many as a gift for Christmas and some as hand-me-downs from family members upgrading to the iPhone 3G. Though ownership was not universal, the iPhone was still prominent in student interactions and often discussed on campus.

Second, the experimental iStanford program, led by the university registrar, proposed to replace student ID cards and dorm keys with iPhones and to develop a suite of iPhone-specific tools for students. Though the ID card part of the proposal was shelved shortly after our data collection concluded, iPhones were given to a group of residential computing consultants for the 2008-2009 school year as part of a pilot program, and Stanford's computer science department offered iPhone development classes. Because of this, we were interested in learning about iPhone culture to inform this initiative or similar initiatives elsewhere, should they ever come to pass.

IPHONE USE ON CAMPUS

This analysis will start with an illustration of the ubiquity of mobile phones and other technologies in general and iPhones in particular, which were present in sites of transit, quiet areas, and social areas all across campus. It will then turn to the dimensions of *constant connection*, discussing preferred methods of connection as well as strategies and reasons for social censure. The double-standard that constant connection created—of being present in one's immediate surroundings and over the network simultaneously—led to a *technosocial pecking order*, where students privileged some people and devices over others, though this often produced feelings of guilt and the stress of multitasking. This research will conclude with a discussion of the implications of some students' personal desires for *techno-resistance*.

Sunny with a Chance of 3G: a Snapshot of Campus Technology Use

Stanford University lies just west of the affluent town of Palo Alto and just north of Silicon Valley. Visitors typically arrive at the university via Palm Drive, a striking mile-long road lined with trees separating the pastoral campus from the city around it with a stretch of native forest. At the end of Palm Drive is grassy Palm Oval park surrounded by parking, and beyond that the arches and low-slung buildings of the main quad, built with Stanford's characteristic tan sandstone and brick red roof tiles. Both the park and the main quad bustle with students on a busy day between classes.

I will begin this technological snapshot of Stanford campus, based on our collective field observations, here. It is between classes on a sunny spring afternoon, and students whiz down Serra Mall on bicycles and longboards. Over half sport white earbud headphones leading to a pocket, backpack, or purse, suggestive of an iPhone or iPod. Approximately one in thirty hold a phone with one hand, using the other hand or sometimes balance alone to navigate the crowds. Even more pedestrians—one in ten—hold a phone to their ear or in their field of view, looking up occasionally to avoid obstacles but otherwise allowing bicyclists and others to swerve around them. Some walk bikes while they peck at their phones. Undergraduates in witty T-shirts and business school students in blazers crowd the bus stop on the left side of Palm Oval; some have phones out, though most of these are watching or listening, not talking. A couple resting on the grass in the park take pictures of one another and then peer together at the screen of an iPhone with a Stanford-branded cover.

One of the buildings bordering the main quad to the left is Green library, facing the quad with grand columns and arches and flanked by a hodgepodge of wings. The study desks and broad tables inside are half-full of students on this sunny spring day. Some have laptops and some have books in front of them, and many have mobile phones laying beside their study materials, at which they glance periodically. About half have earbuds and are listening to music off of their phones or laptops. Occasionally a student jumps up and hurries out of a study hall to the lobby, phone in hand, to take an incoming call, leaving books and laptop behind. "I'm in the library." "Oh, *now* you call." Some students stand at the public computers across from the lobby browsing the library website or Facebook, each with a mobile phone laid out beside the keyboard.

Outside of the lobby, on the other side of the library from the main quad, is a popular outdoor café, and another grassy area by a fountain. Here, we again find phones on tables or in hands while students study or chat. Students occasionally glance at their phones during their studies and conversations. One student has two phones out on the table, a clamshell and an iPhone. Another peers at her friend's iPhone, exclaiming, "Text him! Text him right now. Or send him a picture. He'll check it on his Blackberry." Occasionally a student pauses on the steps by the red hoop fountain, suggestive of a giant power button, across from the cafe to take out her phone and send a text before hurrying on her way to class or a meeting.

Other sites of campus—the clock tower, the bookstore café, Old Union lounge—are like one of the three described: sites of transit, where phones may be out or in pockets; quiet areas, with phones as electronic companions; and social places, where phones may be implicated in exchanges or themselves become a social actor. They all share the characteristic of extensive mobile phone use. Even in classrooms, some students keep phones beside their computers or (if laptops are banned, which has become increasingly common in lecture halls [10]) paper notebooks, or furtively between their knees, where they check their email, visit Facebook, play games, or surf the web during class.

Of the students surveyed, fully three-quarters of the respondents said they fell asleep with their iPhones in bed with them, and just as many checked their iPhones before getting out of bed in the morning. A few interviewees said that their sweeties joked about being "iPhone widows," left behind for this new, alluring social actor. One graduate student said her husband often said that he was "married to my wife and her iPhone," acknowledging the role the device had in their relationship. In short, the devices were a constant companion and often played an active role for many students throughout their daily activities: studying, eating, socializing, attending class, even sleeping.

We at first found the diversity of technology practices among students to be overwhelming. Analysis showed, however, that these practices tended to follow a coherent pattern primarily balancing two competing desires: to be available and responsive to one's extended network of friends and family via email, text, and voice on one hand, and to be present and focused on one's immediate surroundings on the other. As we will see in the following sections, both desires fulfilled various social obligations to friends, peers, and authority figures. I will first discuss the social expectations for constant connection, and how they are balanced with social expectations for being present with friends. The second desire—to be focused on one's immediate surroundings—allowed students to minimize the drawbacks to multitasking they have noticed in their own lives and to mitigate the perceived demands and stress of always-on technology.

Constant Connection: Demands of Extended Networks

All 57 interview subjects talked, sometimes at length, about the social expectation of constant connection: the demands others placed on them to be electronically available and the similar demands they placed on others. While students did alter the mode of communication they used—email, SMS, and voice—to fit their own circumstances and the expected circumstances of the remote party, they generally assumed that *some* mode should get through.

This section contributes an updated description of the social practices and expectations associated with each of these modes, including how the iPhone in particular shaped its use. It will then discuss the ways they are collectively enrolled to establish social expectations of connectedness, expectations that were heightened by the multi-featuredness and uniformity of iPhones.

Email: The Mode of Choice

Though email is often discussed in human-computer interaction literature as a method of asynchronous communication, where the recipient is expected to attend just a few times a day (or less) to a number of messages at once, the students we talked to said that those with iPhones, smartphones, and other always-present devices were expected to receive email as it arrived and in turn expected the same of others. One participant explained that because his phone buzzed when email arrived, he could check it anytime, in effect delegating the constant polling to his iPhone. Another said that if she didn't check email constantly, she'd have over fifty to deal with every evening, which was just too overwhelming. A third described email as by far the most-used feature on his iPhone, and actually encouraged multitasking *less* than a computer:

> *I probably check my mail thirty to fifty times a day [on my iPhone]. It used to be, I'd sit and check my email [at my computer], and then open Facebook and browse the web, but now I can check in about thirty seconds which makes my day way more productive.*

Moreover, email was the contact method of choice for many iPhone users because they found voice calls inconvenient and they did not want to risk incurring extra charges for text messages amongst their receivers. Thus, though some report that SMS has replaced email for the "digital generation" [24], these findings indicate otherwise.

Despite email's popularity on campus, many did not respond to email from their iPhones, or they responded tersely, because of the difficulty typing on the iPhone's small on-screen keyboard. One participant explained,

> *I keep pushing the physical button that would kick me out of the program, not the buttons on the screen [of his iPod Touch]. I am more of a tactile person.*

Another said,

> *I have big hands and thumbs, and you have to go [push keys] straight on. ... The learning curve is high.*

This echoes the findings of Haywood and Boguslawski that the iPhone's touchscreen interface presents a number of challenges for users that non-touchscreen mobile phones do not [9]. In most cases, iPhones provided a convenient, portable method of checking messages, but the device was largely read-only. Some students said they liked the "sent from my iPhone" addition because it excused terseness, and a few had customized this (e.g. adding "please excuse any typos") to make short replies more socially acceptable.

Many students reported having their laptops on hand around campus anyway, and would prefer to take those out to compose longer replies. (In fact, one longtime student pointed out that due to the ubiquity of laptops, constant connection through email had been a social expectation on campus—though to a somewhat lesser degree—before iPhones. According to her, iPhones simply heightened a social norm that was already present.) A few others carried iPhones instead of laptops through the day or to their homes, leaving laptops in offices, confident they were still reachable via email but wanting to loosen the electronic leash their advisors and peers had on them.

Text Messaging: The SMS Black Hole

While texting has been reported elsewhere as the mainstay of youth communication [3,13,18], Stanford students—iPhone users and not—said they tended not to use it much because it was less reliable, and often no more convenient, than email. Nearly one third of our iPhone-using interviewees said they refused to pay the surcharge of $20/month or $0.10/message that AT&T levied on text messages, choosing to disable messaging instead. Others reported disliking the silent failure that happened when they sent messages to friends who had disabled messaging, unbeknownst to them. In either case, students said that the fact that text messages that never reached their destinations were not reported to the sender led the sender to think that the recipient was ignoring or shunning them—a social faux pas committed by the mobile phone system itself, but with blame passed on to the intended recipient. One student explained the consequences of this:

> *They are ripping people off [so I opted out of getting texts]. ... Right now I'm using email to text, but people send me these texts that I don't get. My friend was mad at me not getting texts.*

SMS had thus failed to become a common mode of interaction among Stanford students largely for economic and technical reasons, especially the absence of enough users for beneficial network effects and the lack of feedback on failure.

The sites where texting did regularly occur were between close friends or sweethearts who had established one another's texting capabilities or were even on shared "family" plans. All interviewees agreed that texting was one of the most "casual" forms of contact, and that they would never text someone above them in the social hierarchy, such as a professor (echoing [27]). However, few students texted those closest to them throughout the day simply to maintain a sense of virtual copresence, contrasting what has been reported in research on other populations [13,15,18]. This may be due to frequent in-person contact on the relatively small campus. Several said they liked to be able to text when they did not want an "actual conversation"—when all they had to do was coordinate with someone or communicate one piece of information, without all the social niceties that went with calling someone.

Texting (along with email) was also particularly popular at the start of relationships, when new sweethearts could send "casual" (though of course very carefully-crafted) flirtatious messages, realizing a potential discussed in [31]. This interaction, many students felt, was less pressure than voice or even email because it seemed more transitory: texts were generally read once and then disappeared from view unless they were sought out, rather than lingering in an inbox, demanding a reply. However, a few interviewees specifically disliked the practice of flirtatious texting: as one student put it, a potential partner should "have the balls to call" rather than hiding behind texting.

Voice: Intimate but Bothersome

Students' thoughts on voice calls were mixed. Most interviewees said they used their iPhones for checking typed messages, surfing the web, or listening to music much more often than making voice calls, and our observations recorded many times more instances of students peering silently at their phones than talking on them. Some said voice calls were particularly annoying because of all of the required social niceties—"Hello, how are you" and "Thank you, I'll see you soon, goodbye"—even though Ling found that such rituals were the very fabric of social cohesion [18]. However, some preferred a 20-second phone conversation over multiple emails or texts when trying to reach consensus.

Overall, most agreed that it was more momentous to make a voice call than to send an email or text message. Phone conversations were naturally more intimate, students explained, and they demanded certain conditions on both ends: students had to be in a relatively quiet place, but able to talk (not in a classroom or library, for instance, and able to disengage from others); they had to be able to hold the phone to an ear or engage a hands-free device (more difficult when in transit); they had to be available right then; and most importantly, they had to be able to devote a fair amount of their attention to the conversation—they could not multitask in the same way they could with email or texting. One student explained,

> *It's kind of a big deal to make a phone call. You hear their voice. I don't keep up with 'phone people' very well because it's intimidating and you have to dedicate an hour to them.*

Thus, voice calls were reserved for—and signaled the need for—particularly urgent, formal, or intimate communication.

One may argue that one does *not* actually have to be immediately available to receive a voice call: this is what voicemail is for, of course. However, students largely disliked voicemail, even with the iPhone's flexible playback options. Like voice calls, voicemail demanded a quiet environment and a fair amount of attention. Moreover, many messages did not actually contain much content beyond the signal a missed call left already (namely, "call me back"), making the benefit to listening to many messages negligible. In fact, unless they were expecting the caller to add more information, some students we interviewed said they would often just contact the caller without even listening to the message they left. Around one dozen interviewees complained that "others" (though only one admitted to personally doing this) would go weeks without checking their voicemail.

Constant Connection and Social Censure

These sundry modes for contact all fed the expectation that others should be always available. The prevalence of iPhones in particular raised the bar on expectations of constant connection. However, we will see that students are *not* always available, sometimes by circumstance and sometimes by design. In interviews, students talked about no longer being able to use the excuses of not having their laptop with them or of being out of mobile range. Because the whole campus had wireless Internet access, iPhone owners had no infrastructural excuse for not responding to emails, and using behavioral excuses for these *butler lies* [8]—"I was in class," "I was sleeping," "I was biking," "I was studying"—were sometimes taken as mere pretexts for neglect by more demanding friends. Thus, some felt pressured to monitor their iPhones during times they would otherwise put them away.

Students reported that over time, they developed general expectations for their friends' degree of connectivity, a combination of the behaviors and the affordances of the device they owned. They learned that this friend always responded to email within an hour, and that friend *never* returned phone calls. Some students also talked about keeping track of which friends were not AT&T subscribers, which at the time was the only provider for iPhones as well as the only provider with decent reception on campus.

These expectations were not value-neutral. Students, especially the most heavily-connected ones, often judged their friends based on how responsive they were, and applied social pressure to make them more reachable, from teasing to anger to gradual shunning and estrangement. Corroborating our interviews, we also observed some instances of social censure in our field observations. We overheard one woman say to a friend, "Hey, I guess you don't reply to email anymore. You're not as fast as you used to be." Another teased into her handset, "Oh, *now* you call. I have nothing to say. I wanted to get a froyo [frozen yogurt] but I can't now." In interviews, two graduate students reported annoyance with others on their project who did not respond quickly, one because he did not own a mobile phone and the other because he did not respond to work-related email on weekends. Some students also described the experience of being on the receiving end of this social censure when they were not as connected as their friends expected. One student was cut out of an important decision with a rude email stating that "she did not have a say in this anymore" when she did not respond for twelve hours one weekend because she was visiting her parents. Another described how keeping track of who answered calls became part of the official policy for Resident Computing Consultants in the dorms:

> *In my staff meetings we would call late people, but they had two marks on them if they were late* and *didn't answer their phone.*

These judgments did not just result in social pressure. At times, they weakened the friendships between those who were heavily connected and those who were less so. "You can tell who's a real friend after a while," said one student. Another similarly stated,

> *There are some people that you say 'oh, don't even bother calling that person.' That in itself says something about a person. It defines true friends.*

A third explained,

> *People who don't answer their phone but call you when they need [you]—I ignore them. I always try to catch up with people before I ask them for something.*

While this may say as much about the friendship as the technology, we will see below that technology may play a larger role than is initially apparent.

Students reported additional problems when the expectations their friends had developed for them about their *usual* connectivity did not match their *current* connectivity. The student above who was cut out of an important decision after not being reachable via email for twelve hours one weekend is one example of the consequences of unexpected changes in connectivity—and she reported feeling a lot of anxiety about the lack of mobile signal and data connectivity at her parents' place, knowing that such a thing might happen. Another student whose parents live in a canyon in Los Angeles without mobile signal drove to the bottom of the canyon at least once a day when visiting in order to check his messages and to "stay in the loop" for both social and academic coordination. Other students took vacations where they did not have cell coverage and often expressed how strange and difficult it was to not be available to others. In fact, one student who went on a spring break cruise with friends carried his phone with him as a comfort even though it could not connect at sea, much to his companions' amusement. In our survey, about one-third of students said that if their iPhones broke, they would treat it as an emergency and skip class to get it fixed, which echoed a few stories from interviews of students doing just that.

Technosocial Pecking Orders: Balancing Extended Networks and Immediate Surroundings

While students often expected *others* to be constantly

connected, they were not always available themselves. This section explores how students balanced the social demands of extended networks with those of their immediate surroundings. It describes of a spectrum of behavior that on one side equally privileges the copresent and distant (as also discussed elsewhere), and on the other shuts out the distant in favor of the copresent. I describe this spectrum as a "technosocial pecking order" that stretches across both extended and copresent social obligations. This section then describes the consequences of the awkward double-standard in availability that many students described: they were expected to be "fully" available and attentive to *both* their immediate surroundings and their extended networks, leading to pressure to multitask. It concludes with a discussion of how iPhones affect being in "the moment."

On one side of the spectrum, some students applied the same rules to networked interruptions as they did to face-to-face interruptions, which were tied to general social hierarchies and accountabilities. One graduate student explicitly spelled out her hierarchy to us: her academic advisor was at the top, followed by the students she helped advise, then her colleagues, then her boyfriend, then her friends and parents. This work-focused hierarchy contrasts with the more intimate ones, focused on family and loved ones, described by other researchers [2,13,15:14,18]. Another student explained that his hierarchy was situation-specific—if he was expecting communication from a particular person, he would privilege that, whether it was face-to-face or over the phone.

One consequence of this policy is that these students said that they did poll their email and texts to check for high-importance messages throughout the day, in many different settings. Most would refrain only if they were in an important social situation such as a one-on-one meeting or job interview where they were directly interacting with someone in a position of power over them. But when talking with friends or in group situations (even classrooms or group meetings—or, as we found, our interviews), they would often have their iPhone out as well, like an uninvited companion, and would glance at it from time to time. These students were fully aware that this policy bothered some of their peers, but like Ling's plumber [18] or Turkle's tethered teens [33:8], they felt that they also have obligations to their extended network and did not want to treat them like second-class citizens just because they were not copresent. One student responded to a peer who chastised him about the 'bad etiquette' of taking a call when with him, "It's also bad etiquette to always miss your calls." In his study of earlier mobile phone culture, Gergen observed similar tendencies toward privileging a select few contacts, noting that "rather than the leveling of significance in relationships, the cell phone lends itself to a retrenchment of verticality" [15:240].

On the other side of the spectrum—and less present in previous research on mobile phone cultures—a few students reported almost never answering their phone or checking messages when they were with others. For them, the pull of the extended network was significantly weaker than the influence of immediate surroundings. These students said that they would never interrupt a face-to-face interaction with a phone call, regardless of who it was from, and also avoided checking messages or even having their phone out when with other people. One reported making a show of turning his mobile phone off in "special social situations" such as dinner with friends or dates, which he said others often found flattering. Others just ignored the vibration of always-on but always-silenced phones. One avoided getting an iPhone in favor of an iPod Touch specifically because "it doesn't make me accessible. I hate being accessible—my family had to cajole me to even get an answering machine before I got a cell phone."

Why did these students privilege their immediate surroundings over their extended networks? Many expressed concerns about being tethered to "electronic leashes," able to be yanked at any time out of the present, which Turkle also discusses [33] and which we will see echoed again below in students' more personal reasons for turning off and tuning out the media in their lives. Others adopted the values of those around them: when their families or friends derided them for not being fully present or even just having their phone out, they chose to yield to this social pressure. However, most also felt increased anxiety about what their extended network thought about them as a result.

While a few students occupied each of these extremes, most negotiated practices somewhere in between, balancing various social obligations and making choices about when to check their phones on a case-by-case basis. These kinds of negotiations have also described by other researchers, particularly Naomi Baron, who used of a "volume control" metaphor to describe communicative multitasking [2], and Lee Humphreys, who describes the in-person negotiations that take place when a mobile phone call arrives [12]. Almost all students kept their phones on vibrate—usually noticeable by them but not disruptive to others—throughout the day. (Several women complained that because much of their clothing lacked pockets and it was difficult to feel the phone's vibration from a backpack or handbag, they had to either carry their phone or risk ignoring their extended networks. One man mentioned frustration from not always being able to reach his girlfriend because of this.) While voice calls were most intrusive and least likely to be answered, students often checked messages throughout the day: in class, with friends, while eating, while walking, while biking, and while driving, though the last two are illegal in California.

Double-standards, Guilt, and Multitasking

Overall, the double-standard that students should be fully available to *both* their local and extended networks led to feelings of anxiety and guilt in about one third of our interviewees as well as one third of those surveyed. When they could not answer their phones or return messages, they felt guilty about neglecting their extended networks. When they did, they felt guilty about ignoring their surroundings. The double-standard also compelled them to try to multitask more than they would otherwise like to, behavior that the iPhone's multi-functionality exacerbated.

One student we interviewed, Nate [note: all names are pseudonymous], exemplified this culture of constant connection and the juggling of various inputs that it necessitated. Nate checked email at stoplights and made calls while riding his bike to utilize what he called the "dead time" of transit. Like many students [10,33:8], he multitasked throughout the day in many different settings, visiting Facebook and browsing the Internet in class while "selectively" taking notes on his laptop, with his iPhone out for checking email as well. "I keep my phone between my legs," he explained, laughing. "Just check for students looking down." (Another student explained away her use of Facebook and iPhone applications thusly: "isn't it better to stay semi-engaged by playing games than to fall asleep?")

After getting his iPhone, Nate told us that he had gotten "a lot worse" about spending too much time on his mobile phone because it enabled so many different kinds of connections and "time-wasting": not only was he keeping up with friends, but he enjoyed playing multi-player iPhone games with them and could easily check on Facebook and other sites on the go, rather than having to take out his laptop to do so. He also attested to the constant connection of Stanford students by commenting on how fast things advertised on campus mailing lists are sold—often in seconds.

Nate had established rules for himself about using his phone when with others: it was "okay to read email at dinner with a group but not one other person." However, if he was not able or willing to check his phone in a particular situation, he reported feeling anxious until he found an excuse to do so, and guilty about missed messages; if he did check, he felt guilty about neglecting friends or classes. Though he allowed himself to be 'tethered' [33:8] and feared the social censure of disconnection, Nate also recognized its cognitive and emotional tolls.

iPhones and "The Moment"

These discussions about immediate surroundings versus extended networks prompted us to ask, do iPhones only take one out of the present, or can they contribute to it as well? We certainly saw and heard of many instances of iPhones taking people out of "the moment." For some students, an iPhone was not only a connection device, but a time-killer, especially with the availability of "addictive" games (which were already popular on campus in 2009, even before the advent of Zynga's bestsellers or Angry Birds). One student explained, "The iPhone interface invites distraction by displaying too many options … it was designed to be a toy." In our field observations, we witnessed students walking around campus using their mobile phones and oblivious to their surroundings: one student walked the long way around a roundabout against traffic while pecking at her iPhone's screen, some were unaware of how loudly they were talking on their phones or of the irritated looks they were receiving from others, and a few initially missed turns while using their phones in transit and had to come back around.

A few students said they liked that they could use the many apps on their iPhone as an excuse to not make eye contact while walking around campus, much like shy book-readers do, or to create the appearance of busyness [7] while waiting. While other students derided these practices as "shallow" or "rude," it served an important function of giving students a relatively acceptable way to withdraw from the always-on culture of campus life. This simultaneous inhabitation of physical and virtual spaces—in essence, creating private spaces within a larger public space—is described by Turkle as "tethering" [33:8] and is similar to the lightweight *nagara* ("while-doing-something-else") culture of Japanese teens discussed by Fujimoto [13:4].

However, iPhones did not always detract from immediate surroundings, as Ito and Okabe also noted among Japanese youth and mobile phones more generally [13]. Interviewees told us cases when iPhones enhanced face-to-face interactions, often in ways that highlighted features that were unique to smartphones. Almost all interviewees talked about using their iPhones to show off applications, play music or videos for friends, or look up information on the fly to contribute to a conversation, sometimes doing so collaboratively to include the other person in what would otherwise be an exclusionary interaction with just the phone. In the words of one participant, "These apps are a great conversation starter." A few discussed the "YouTube time" at parties, which generally happened fairly late at night when those still present wound down by showing each other funny videos on their iPhones or laptops. Some played social games with friends on their iPhones, either over the network (competitive word games were particularly popular) or in person (*e.g.* two-player Tap Tap Revenge, played on opposite ends of the same screen).

Still relatively new, iPhones also served as a status symbol for their owners: three-quarters of survey respondents said their iPhones made them feel "cool" (see [16:15] for more on mobile phones, status, and fashion), though the technology fetishism surrounding the iPhone was often an uncomfortable topic of discussion in interviews. In fact, one student said she was "ashamed" when her family gave her one because "only pretentious people had them. I didn't want people to see me with it." (However, she explained that the maps feature later won her over, as she saw herself as "direction-impaired.")

Some students also said that their iPhones made them more aware of their surroundings by allowing them to explore new areas and discover local restaurants using the maps feature—though others said that this reduced the serendipity of getting lost and wandering. Other students did not think the seat-of-the-pants planning typical of mobile phone culture (discussed at more length in [13]) changed their overall awareness of their surroundings at all. In short, the evidence on whether iPhones took students "out of the moment" is mixed and highly idiosyncratic.

Techno-resistance and Oppositional Identities

A few of our interviewees had never thought of limiting the reach of technology in their lives. Some graduate students in particular reported that the constant connection that their multi-featured iPhones enabled freed them from being tethered to their computers all day, allowing them to work outside their office or run errands, confident that they can be reached by their advisors, peers, or sweeties as needed. "It helps me structure my life to be more efficient," one asserted. Another darkly joked, "If I didn't have my iPhone for a month I'd end up on the roof with a rifle. It's my lifeline."

About two-thirds of the 57 students we interviewed, however, and about as many survey respondents talked about balancing the myriad social demands of constant connection, in person and over the network, with personal desires for control, concentration, and peace by sometimes turning iPhones and others technologies off. I describe this active push-back to the perceived overreach of iPhones and other technologies as ***techno-resistance,*** and note that among our participants, techno-resistance was often expressed as a part of their identity. The practice of techno-resistance, whether minor or all-encompassing, allowed students to use their self-imposed limits on interactions with technology to make a broader statement about their values, particularly when they were in contrast to the values they thought that those around them held. More importantly, it allowed them to stand by these values when others censured them for not being available, and it even enabled some to censure others for multitasking. By suggesting that their behaviors and values were part of their identity, students could make them appear more fundamental and unchangeable than mere choices.

Specifically, the belief that technologies and the multitasking they demanded were to blame for stress and scattered brains were often entwined with beliefs about what it means to be an "authentic" or "present" individual. Beatrice, an undergraduate who lived in a campus co-op and was interviewed in the campus community garden, exemplified the anxiety and need for discipline that these students felt regarding technology. She felt guilty that she sometimes used her iPhone to "fill time." She did not want to be absorbed in her phone like others, oblivious to the world around her—in her words, she wanted to be able to "notice what's around me, and the friend around the corner," rather than being "addicted" or even "creepy" like some people she knew with iPhones. Though she brought both her iPhone and her Mac to Stanford's community garden and checked both during the interview despite teasing, she said that she was thinking of getting rid of her iPhone because she did not like that she felt compelled to check email all the time, and she had to force herself not to. In fact, when we followed up with her a few weeks after the interview, she had gotten rid of it.

To students like Beatrice, the constant connection that iPhones entailed limited their freedom and independence, ultimately making them feel less whole, less adult, even less human. She and several other interviewees derided people who were always consulting their extended social networks for all of their decisions—another student described this as a technological "security blanket" from which these people should wean themselves. Beatrice was also concerned with privacy and was against texting in romance. The reasons for this stance that she gave were more about her past than about technology: she pushed back because she was "from a ranch" and was thus "more on the nature side" (and, by implication, against pervasive technology). One female undergraduate described how technology "alienated" people from nature and face-to-face interaction and exacerbated "bad mental habits." Another participant told us about how he deliberately disconnecting himself on occasion, explaining his preference in naturalistic terms and adding that he could quit anytime:

> *I like to be in touch with the environment and the space I find myself in—not just for safety reasons, but because I prefer the experience. ... I could leave it [the iPhone] behind quite happily.*

Another student, though he used his iPhone all the time, expressed similar sentiments:

> *I don't want to be texting all the time instead of enjoying nature and the people around me. People are going to stop seeing the beauty of the world because they're so wrapped up in their iPhones.*

In this way, technology use became implicated—often negatively—in some students' sense of authenticity, naturalness, and the ways they perceived "real" relationships and connections as superior to virtual ones. While these students did use iPhones and other technologies, sometimes extensively, they also expressed age-old concerns about whether the social expectations enabled by these technologies were really what they wanted.

Moreover, by publicly defining themselves as in opposition to constant connection, they were, in a way, ensuring that they did not succumb to it themselves. About one quarter of the students who talked about their desire for techno-resistance compared their actions to what they saw as the "typical" iPhone user, finishing stories about this kind of user with some variation of the statement "I'm not one of *those* people." This echoes Nafus and Tracey's finding that some participants similarly defined themselves in opposition to the "the kinds of people [they] *think* use mobiles," though some uses and social expectations have evolved since their study [15:208]. Typical iPhone users, the students in this study said, were always peering down at their screens, unaware of their surroundings and oblivious to the social gaffes they were making. Like Turkle's tethered selves [33:8], they were "alone together," never fully present either physically or virtually: they talked loudly on their phones in public places, they texted when with their friends, they checked Facebook during class. They were always consulting their extended network for where to go to dinner or what to do with an extra five minutes. In short, they were *addicted* to their iPhones, and their addiction stifled their initiative and creativity, did not let them enjoy the moment, and made them dependent on being constantly connected. Some of the strong language students used to describe these strawman users stemmed from students' frustration with others, but it was also due to the fear that they could easily be making the same mistakes. A few students, in fact, reported that they feared becoming like this, and a few others said they had been like this at one time before, like Beatrice, "seeing the light" and imposing limits on themselves.

Students had a variety of strategies for shutting out technology's distractions and achieving techno-resistance. Several commented that being able to control intrusions was particularly challenging because both work and distractions were present on the same devices (whether laptops or iPhones), and the barrier to switch from one to the other was extremely low, making multitasking a constant temptation/threat. One student raised this barrier somewhat by putting his devices into "airplane mode" when he wanted to focus on something else, and another physically unplugged her wireless router and gave it to a friend while she studied. Others would try to *mentally* regulate their behaviors, though often with more limited success, by setting time or work goals for themselves, after which they would have a reward of a few minutes of distractions. (Though there are software tools that enforce these kinds of limits, none of the students in this study had used them.)

In sum, we can see that this generation of so-called digital natives was hardly uniform in embracing digital technologies. Rather than deterministically creating new sociotechnical worlds, iPhones and other technologies were integrated into existing webs of social relations, and their influence, like that of any social actor, varied across individuals and situations. These technologies were part of the ongoing social negotiations that all students faced, and their responses to the pressures of constant connection were heterogeneous. The prevalence of *techno-resistance* in particular pushes back at monolithic definitions of "digital natives": even in such a technologically-savvy population as Stanford students, such definitions are too technologically determinist and do not match the complexities of reality.

Thoughts on the iStanford Plan

Toward the end of our interviews, we asked students about the plan to replace their ID cards and possibly dorm keys with iPhones. How would they feel about this, and how would it change campus life? Though most expressed concerns about what it would cost and how the university would pay for it (raise tuition?) and some expressed concerns about Apple/AT&T monopolies, their further thoughts about what effect it might have on campus often mirrored their thoughts about constant connection.

On one side, one student who sheepishly (though otherwise unapologetically) described herself as "addicted" to email said she would welcome such a plan because it would make other students "accountable" for communications from the university, teachers, and peers—in effect, institutionally *enforcing* constant connection. Students practicing techno-resistance also expected that this plan would enforce constant connection—and the thought appalled them. They already had trouble getting away from technology, they cried; why would the university want to make that even more difficult? In short, institutionalizing a technology like the iPhone may also institutionalize certain aspects of the social culture that has developed around it, and Stanford's culture of constant connection was one that not all students welcomed.

CONCLUSION

This paper provides a window onto the technosocial lives of college students, centered around the iPhone. Mobile phones, and iPhones in particular, were often treated like social actors, playing a role in students' daily lives and social interactions. However, we have also seen that iPhone use was by no means stable or uniform: students exhibited an array of behaviors and rules regarding their use, some even rejecting the connectivity that iPhones enabled.

Throughout this paper, I have emphasized findings unique to iPhones. It is worth noting, however, that in many cases smartphones did *not* introduce a radical break in mobile phone culture. The iPhone's multi-functionality and uniformity introduced some new practices, but it merely intensified others, such as the expectation of constant connection, that were already present. Students visited Facebook, played games, and looked up directions before the iPhone; the iPhone just made these more accessible. This in itself is an important finding: rather than creating from whole cloth an entirely new mobile phone culture, iPhones more often shifted the focus, and perhaps the valence, of the ongoing negotiations between mobile technologies and users.

In *Born Digital*, John Palfrey and Urs Gasser posit that the generation in college now is the first generation of "digital natives" who interact with, understand, and incorporate technology into their everyday lives in a fundamentally different way than older generations [24]. These students grew up multitasking between their surroundings and their extended networks and, as Don Tapscott further describes in *Growing Up Digital*, have adapted to it [32]. Arguably, Stanford students, having generally grown up with easy access to mobile phones and the Internet and surrounded by a casual ubiquity of cutting-edge technology on campus, should be some of those most deeply engaged in these brave new digital worlds. They should be the 'innovators' and 'early adopters' of new technologies, not the 'laggards' [26].

However, these students were negotiating their iPhones, social lives, productivity, and more in ways that were multivalent and, moreover, remarkable for their ordinariness. Their concerns about maintaining relationships, being productive, and staying true to themselves would be familiar to both sides of the "digital native" divide. While these students do live in a world where their peers, and even their professors and parents, expect them to be constantly connected, there are still recognizable social rules and personal preferences governing behavior, both online and off. Students must also deal with the same concerns about the cognitive and social perils of multitasking. As a result, surprisingly large numbers of students pushed back against the stress and cognitive load of constant connection and the multitasking it entailed by actively *dis*connecting, invoking tropes of wholeness and authenticity to justify their actions. In short, even the most savvy and privileged "digital natives" make sense of their iPhones in the same ways as any of us.

ACKNOWLEDGEMENTS

I am indebted to Professor Tanya Luhrmann for teaching the class in which this data was collected. This would also have been impossible without the work and insights of fellow classmates in Anthropology 306: Hilary Chart, Damien Droney, Alejandro Feged, Patrick Gallagher, Mark Gardiner, Nicky Ramos-Beban, Sara Rutherford, and Anna West. Finally, thank you to the students who took time out of their perpetually busy schedules to patiently answer our questions.

REFERENCES

1. Ames, M., Eckles, D., Naaman, M., Spasojevic, M., & Van House, N. Requirements for Mobile Photoware. *Personal & Ubiquitous Computing 14*, 2 (2009), 95-109.
2. Baron, N. Adjusting the Volume: Technology and Multitasking in Discourse Control. In J. Katz, ed., *Mobile Communication and Social Change in a Global Context*. MIT Press, 2007, 177-194.
3. Battestini, A., Setlur, V., Sohn, T., & Road, P.M. A Large Scale Study of Text Messaging Use. *Proc. Mobile HCI 2010,* ACM Press, 229-238.
4. Bell, C., Compeau, D., & Olivera, F. Understanding the Social Implications of Technological Multitasking: A Conceptual Model. *Proc. CHI 2005,* ACM Press, 80-84.
5. Blythe, M., & Cairns, P. Critical Methods and User-Generated Content: the iPhone on YouTube. *Proc. CHI 2009,* ACM Press, 1467-1476.
6. Czerwinski, M., Horvitz, E., & Wilhite, S. A diary study of task switching and interruptions. *Proc. CHI 2004,* ACM Press, 175-182.
7. Gershuny, J. Busyness as the Badge of Honor for the New Superordinate Working Class. *Social Research 72*, 2 (2005), 287-315.
8. Hancock, J., Birnholtz, J., Bazarova, N., Guillory, J., Perlin, J., & Amos, B. Butler Lies: Awareness, Deception, and Design. *Proc. CHI 2004,* ACM Press, 129-134.
9. Haywood, A. & Boguslawski, G. I Love My iPhone But There Are Certain Things that 'Niggle' Me. In J.A. Jacko, ed., *Human-Computer Interaction, Part I*. Springer-Verlag Berlin Heildelberg, 2009, 421-430.
10. Hembrooke, H. & Gay, G. The Laptop and the Lecture: The effects of multitasking in learning environments. *Journal of Computing in Higher Education 15*, 1 (2003), 46-64.
11. Hudson, J.M., Christensen, J., Kellogg, W., & Erickson, T. "I'd Be Overwhelmed, But It's Just One More Thing to Do": Availability and Interruption in Research Management. *Proc. CHI 2002,* ACM Press, 97-104.
12. Humphreys, L. Cellphones in Public: Social Interactions in a Wireless Era. *New Media & Society 7*, 6 (2005), 810-833.
13. Ito, M., Okabe, D., & Matsuda, M. *Personal, Portable, Pedestrian: Mobile Phones in Japanese Life*. MIT Press, 2005.
14. Ito, M. & Okabe, D. Mobile Phones, Japanese Youth, and the Re-Placement of Social Contact. *Mobile Communications 31*, (2005), 131-148.
15. Katz, J. & Aakhus, M. *Perpetual Contact: Mobile Communication, Private Talk, Public Performance*. Cambridge University Press, 2002.
16. Katz, J. *Machines that Become Us: The Social Context of Communication Technology*. Transaction Pub., 2003.
17. Latour, B. *Reassembling the Social: An introduction to actor-network theory*. Oxford University Press, 2005.
18. Ling, R. *New Tech, New Ties: How Mobile Communication is Reshaping Social Cohesion*. MIT Press, 2008.
19. Mark, G., Gonzalez, V.M., & Harris, J. No Task Left Behind? Examining the Nature of Fragmented Work. *Proc. CHI 2005,* ACM Press, 321-330.
20. NielsenWire staff. Generation App: 62% of Mobile Users 25-34 own Smartphones. *NielsenWire*, 2011. http://blog.nielsen.com/nielsenwire/?p=29786.
21. Ophir, E., Nass, C., & Wagner, A.D. Cognitive Control in Media Multitaskers. *Proc. NAS 106*, 33 (2009).
22. Oren, M., Seth, U., Huang, F., & Kang, S. Cross-Cultural Design and Evaluation of the Apple iPhone. *Proc. IDGD 2009,* ACM Press, 79-88.
23. Oulasvirta, A., Tamminen, S., Roto, V., & Kuorelahti, J. Interaction in 4-second Bursts: The Fragmented Nature of Attentional Resources in Mobile HCI. *Proc. CHI 2005,* ACM Press, 919-928.
24. Palfrey, J. & Gasser, U. *Born Digital: Understanding the First Generation of Digital Natives*. Basic Books, 2008.
25. Pinch, T.J. & Bijker, W.E. The Social Construction of Facts and Artefacts: or How the Sociology of Science and the Sociology of Technology might Benefit Each Other. *Social Studies of Science 14*, 3 (1984), 399-441.
26. Rogers, E. *Diffusion of Innovations*. Free Press, 2003.
27. Rotman, D. Constant Connectivity, Selective Participation: Mobile-Social Interaction of Students and Faculty. *Ext. Abstrs. CHI 2010,* ACM Press, 4333-4338.
28. Salvucci, D.D. & Taatgen, N.A. Toward a Unified Theory of the Multitasking Continuum: From Concurrent Performance to Task Switching, Interruption, and Resumption. *Proc. CHI 2009,* ACM Press, 1819-1828.
29. Strauss, A. & Corbin, J. *Basics of Qualitative Research: Grounded Theory Procedures and Techniques*. Sage Publications, 1992.
30. Su, N.M. & Mark, G. Communication Chains and Multitasking. *Proc. CHI 2008,* ACM Press, 83-92.
31. Swallow, D., Blythe, M., & Wright, P. Grounding Experience: Relating Theory and Method to Evaluate the User Experience of Smartphones. *Proc. EACE 2005,* ACM Press, 91-98.
32. Tapscott, D. *Grown Up Digital: How the Net Generation in Changing Your World*. McGraw-Hill, 2009.
33. Turkle, S. *Alone Together: Why we expect more from technology and less from each other*. Basic Books, 2011.
34. Wajcman, J. *Technofeminism*. Polity, 2004.

Designing an Effective Vibration-Based Notification Interface for Mobile Phones

Bahador Saket, Chrisnawan Prasojo, Yongfeng Huang, Shengdong Zhao
NUS-HCI Lab, School of Computing, National University of Singapore
117418, Singapore
{bahador.saket, xgjonathan}@gmail.com, chris@prasojo.com, zhaosd@comp.nus.edu.sg

ABSTRACT
We conducted an experiment to understand how mobile phone users perceive the urgency of ten simple vibration alerts that were created from four basic signals: short on, short off, long on, and long off. The short and long signals correspond to 200 ms and 600 ms, respectively. To convey the level of urgency of notifications and help users prioritize them, the design of mobile phone vibration alerts should consider that the gap length preceding or succeeding a signal, the number of gaps in the vibration pattern, and the vibration's duration affect an alert's perceived level of urgency. Our study specifically shows that shorter gap lengths between vibrations (200 ms vs. 600 ms), a vibration pattern with one gap instead of two, and shorter vibration all contribute to making the user perceive the alert as more urgent.

Author Keywords
Vibration patterns; mobile phone; perceived urgency; notifications; alerts.

ACM Classification Keywords
H.5.3 [Information Interfaces and Presentation]: Group and Organization Interfaces – Computer-supported cooperative work, Synchronous interaction, Collaborative computing.

INTRODUCTION
Notification interfaces that inform users about the status and activities of others without overwhelming or distracting them are a key concern in computer-supported cooperative work (CSCW). This is reflected in dozens of studies on awareness and notification that were presented at the CSCW conference [2]. Among the different types of notification interface, the ones that use vibration are particularly important.

Vibration is an essential component of the mobile phone notification system today. It is useful especially when the user's auditory and visual modalities are occupied or limited due to social and environmental factors. While the vibration alert was typically used for signalling incoming calls and text messages in feature phones, in today's smartphone, it can represent a wide array of notifications from numerous sources, ranging from games, location-based services, and communication-related applications. However, the same general vibration alert is used for all notifications, which could otherwise have sounded differently if the smartphone were not in silent mode.

CSCW '13, February 23–27, 2013, San Antonio, Texas, USA.

In many previous projects, vibrotactile urgency perception was enhanced by increasing the range of tactile modality at the fingertips. These involved employing a range of amplitude [13], frequency [7, 13, 15], vibration direction [7], gap length, intensity [14], as well as multiple actuators [5]; or trying to perceive salient tactile cues by attaching the device to seated participants' waists [12].

Although many of these innovative solutions were successful, they were tested on delicate tactioception nerves in the fingertips and areas of the hand where idle mobile phones are less likely to be located [5, 7, 13, 15], or used extra vibrators [5, 14] or modified mobile phones [7, 13, 15]. These make the studies impractical and less realistic for mobile phones and smartphones that were manufactured in the past few years.

As such, users are still unable to distinguish the priority of incoming messages from the vibration alert generated by unmodified mobile phones (i.e., phones without any custom hardware modification). We designed a practical vibration notification interface for an unmodified mobile phone by:

a) Eliminating all features that are not currently supported by today's mobile phone, including frequency, amplitude, and intensity. This also excludes custom-made vibrators as they require hardware modifications.

b) Testing the phone in the trouser pocket of a user's pants instead of in other locations because this is where mobile phones are more commonly carried [8].

Three controllable factors affect the perceived urgency of basic vibration alerts in these types of phone: gap length, number of gaps, and vibration length.

A previous study by White [14] considered gap length a factor. This study used only a single gap length (with gap length vs. without) and was conducted using a customized adjustable tactile belt display system that is no longer available in current mobile phones. Thus, the results are not as relevant to today's mobile phone users. Our study uses short and long gap lengths.

One plausible way to alleviate tactile modality crowding is by assigning a level of urgency for the incoming alert through the vibration signal itself. Vibration alerts can be interpreted and associated with different objects and concepts [9], as well as encoded with three urgency levels according to the designer's preferences [4]. Users have to undergo an active learning process to interpret their meaning. Little is known on how mobile phone users naturally interpret a vibration alert's sense of urgency. Therefore, we aim to understand the perceived urgency of these vibration alerts through an empirical study on basic vibration patterns, and to answer the following questions:

1. How many levels of urgency can users reliably associate with simple vibration patterns?
2. What are the underlying factors that make users perceive certain vibration patterns as more urgent than others?
3. How does the combination of these factors amplify or diminish the degree of perceived urgency?

Future design of mobile phones vibration alerts can leverage our findings to convey its degree of urgency and help its users to understand and prioritise the incoming alerts.

Note that the study of Qian et al. [12] also uses the length of the vibration signal and the length of the gaps as parameters for vibration pattern design, but with a different focus. Their study tries to understand the differences between two types of vibration pattern design (static vs. dynamic) and which combination pair can yield the most distinguishing effect while our focus is to not only understand the differences, but also to construct an ordered list of distinguishable patterns and understand what is the limit in terms of number of patterns human can reliably distinguish.

Pilot Study

In a real world scenario, environmental noise is a constant distraction. It can easily interfere with sounds that accompany a vibration alert, making it difficult to determine their effect on the user's perception. To avoid such complications, we eliminated the potential influence of audio by providing an audio mask.

We carried out a pilot study on six participants with ages ranging from 21 to 25 years to determine the type of audible mask that should be used and to find out the appropriate lengths for short and long signals. We found that pink noise is more effective in masking audible cues than Brownian noise [3]. And, as determined in previous research [10], we confirmed that the appropriate lengths for short and long signals are 200 ms and 600 ms, respectively.

Pattern Design

A vibration pattern is defined as an arrangement of the simplest repeatable alternating sequence of an actuator's on and off state, with specific lengths (short and long) assigned to each state. We limited the variable of short to 200 ms and long to 600 ms, without any median values due to its susceptibility to detection errors. As shown in a previous vibrotactile study [3], participants could differentiate vibrotactile signals with extreme values well but were less able to do so with median values. We used four basic types of signal to form distinguishable vibration patterns: short on, short off, long on, and long off.

In order to produce unique repeatable sequences, an equal number of on and off signals must be alternated in arrangements that do not replicate any other sequence. A pair of short and long on-off signals forms four unique patterns, labelled 1 to 4 in Figure 1. Two pairs of such signals form additional 16 patterns, of which only six are unique. These unique patterns are labelled 5 to 10. An initial test on four undergraduate students confirmed that the ten patterns were distinguishable while those that were comprised of three pairs of on-off signals were hard to distinguish. Thus, we did not consider patterns consisting of three or more pairs of on-off signals in the study.

EXPERIMENT 1

The purpose of the first experiment is to determine how many levels of urgency users can distinguish and how the urgency of each of the ten vibration patterns is ranked.

White [14] simply presented all the vibration patterns sequentially, then asked users to rank them. However, this approach is infeasible due to the limitation of human short-term memory: remembering and comparing more than two patterns presented in sequential order is difficult. Therefore, we adopted pairwise comparison, in which users are only required to compare two patterns at a time. The ranking of all ten patterns was then derived from the aggregated comparison results of the individual pairs.

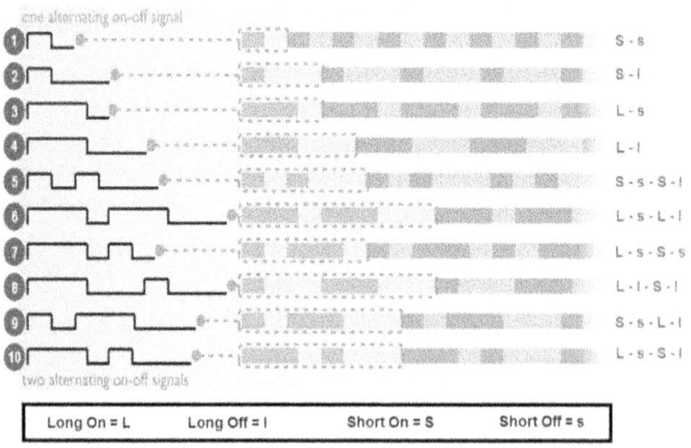

Figure 1. All possible distinguishable permutations of the four basic types of signal and the vibration patterns they produce, based on one and two pairs of 200 ms (short) or 600 ms (long) on-off signals. Each pattern is repeated (played) for a total duration of 4,500 ms.

Apparatus

We programmed an Android application to present the 45 comparisons in five rounds and installed it on a NexusOne smartphone running Android 2.1. The smartphone weighs 130 g and measures 119 x 59.8 x 11.5 mm. It contains one vibrating micro-motor that operates on 1–2 VDC with a weight of .05 oz, a dimension of .5 in long, and a diameter of .188 in [6].

Participants
Sixteen participants (10 male and 6 female) with ages ranging from 19 to 25 years from four different nationalities (mean: 23, SD: 1.83) took part in this experiment.

Procedure
At the beginning of the experiment, participants were briefed and asked to try the ten vibration patterns while adjusting the volume of the audible mask. We then placed the smartphone inside their right pants pocket, allowing the phone to rest naturally on the thigh.

During the experiment, the 45 pairs of vibration patterns were presented in a reduced Latin square to counterbalance learning and order effects. This prevents participants from extrapolating new judgments from previous ones. Each pairwise comparison was presented to the participants by playing the first pattern for 4.5 seconds, following it with a 1.5-second gap, and playing the second pattern for 4.5 seconds. The participants were then asked to compare the perceived urgency of the two patterns by selecting the most appropriate answer out of the following:

1: the first pattern is more urgent,
2: the second pattern is more urgent,
1≅ 2: the first and second patterns are comparable, and
Repeat: perform the comparison again.

The first three are equivalent to the options in a 3-point Likert scale. We choose the simpler 3-point scale because previous research [1] showed that having more options to select from may confuse participants. A post-experiment questionnaire asked the participants to describe the characteristics of the vibration patterns.

Results of Experiment 1
We analyzed the pairwise comparisons of the 45 comparison results we collected from each participant, and from that data ranked the ten vibration patterns in ten levels of urgency (Fig. 2). For instance, if Patterns 1, 2, and 3 show that:

- Pattern 1 is more urgent than Pattern 2,
- The urgency levels of Patterns 1 and 3 are comparable,
- Pattern 3 is more urgent than Pattern 2,

Patterns 1 and 3 are ranked Level 1 and Pattern 2 ranked Level 2.

Not all results were consistent. For instance, a participant judged the urgency levels of pattern pair 4-7 to be comparable and pattern pair 7-9 to be comparable. Logically, the urgency level of Patterns 4 and 9 should be comparable but the participant perceived their urgency levels to be different from each other. However, this inconsistency was observed only two times during the entire experiment and the participants were not made aware of it. We corrected it by simply repeating the comparisons for the pattern pairs in question until the results were consistent.

Figure 2 summarizes each participant's ranking of the ten vibration patterns. While there are individual differences, a number of common trends can also be observed. It was obvious which patterns occupied the extreme ends of the spectrum: all participants ranked Pattern 2 as the least urgent while almost all of them (14 out of 16) ranked Pattern 1 as the most urgent. The ranking of patterns in the middle range is less consistent.

DISCUSSION
The ranking of these patterns gives us a basis for discussing the reasons behind the differences in perceived urgency and the factors that contributed to these differences.

Descriptions of Individual Signals
We asked participants to describe the characteristics of the vibration patterns, then classified similar comments and adjectives into four groups: short on, long on, short off, and long off. Short on is often described as a firm and sharp vibration while long on is described as steady. Short off gives some participants the feeling of being hurried while the feeling long off imparts is slow and relaxed. These qualities describe each of the four basic signals that we used for creating the vibration patterns in this study.

On-Off Signal Pairs
We classified the results into two groups based on the number of consecutive on-off signals in each pattern's basic design.

	P1	P2	P3	P4	P5	P6	P7	P8
L1	6,3	1	1	1	1	1	1	1
L2	4	3, 6	3, 6	3, 6	6, 3, 9	3, 6	3,6, 9	3, 6
L3	1	9	9	7, 9	4, 7	9	4, 7	7, 9
L4	7	4	7	4	5	7	5	4
L5	9	7	4	5	8, 10	4	8, 10	5
L6	5	5	10	8, 10	2	8	2	8, 10
L7	8,10	8, 10	5, 8	2		5, 10		2
L8	2	2	2			2		
L9								
L10								

	P9	P10	P11	P12	P13	P14	P15	P16
L1	1	1	1	1	1	3,6,9	1	1
L2	3	3, 6	3,6,7,9	3, 6	3,4,6,7,9	1	3,6, 9	3
L3	6	9	4	4,7, 9	5	4	4, 7	6
L4	9	7	5	5, 8, 10	10	7	5,8, 10	9
L5	7	4	8,10	2	8	5,8, 10	2	4
L6	4	5	2		2	2		7
L7	5	8, 10						5
L8	10	2						8
L9	8							10
L10	2							2

Figure 2. Ranking results for the 16 participants. P1-P16 represents the participant IDs. The level of urgency is listed in descending order with Level 1 (L1) being the most urgent and Level 10 (L10) being the least urgent.

After ranking the ten vibration patterns, we computed the dissimilarity matrix by squared Euclidean distance. To derive an aggregated ranking from all the participants' ordinal data, we applied a hierarchical clustering algorithm based on the dissimilarity matrix calculation, as this method is recommended for clustering ordinal data [18]. Figure 3 shows the various clustering results and their ranking.

3 Clusters	4 Clusters	5 Clusters
L 1: Pattern 1	L 1: Pattern 1	L 1: Pattern 1
L 2: Patterns 3,4,5,6,7,8,9,10	L 2: Patterns 3,4,6,7,9	L 2: Patterns 3,6
L 3: Pattern 2	L 3: Patterns 5,8,10	L 3: Patterns 4,7,9
	L 4: Pattern 2	L 4: Patterns 5,8,10
		L 5: Pattern 2

6 Clusters	7 Clusters	8 Clusters
L 1: Pattern 1	L 1: Pattern 1	L 1: Pattern 1
L 2: Patterns 3,6	L 2: Patterns 3,6	L 2: Patterns 3, 6
L 3: Patterns 4,7,9	L 3: Patterns 7,9	L 3: Pattern 9
L 4: Pattern 5	L 4: Pattern 4	L 4: Pattern 7
L 5: Patterns 8,10	L 5: Pattern 5	L 5: Pattern 4
L 6: Pattern 2	L 6: Patterns 8, 10	L 6: Pattern 5
	L 7: Pattern 2	L 7: Patterns 8, 10
		L 8: Pattern 2

Figure 3. Classifying the 10 vibration patterns into various clusters based on dissimilarity matrix calculation. (L stands for level of urgency)

Patterns 1 through 4 are in the one on-off signal pair group. Patterns 5 through 10 are in the two on-off signal pair group. These groups shall be referred to as "one on-off" and "two on-off" respectively.

There was an extreme variation in results in the one on-off group because Patterns 1 and 2 were distinguishable in all the different clusters. A more direct cause-effect relationship was observed in this group because the single on and off signal limits attenuating effects on multivariate signal length.

On the other hand, variation in results in the two on-off group was milder. This could be due to the presence of two on-off signals, which attenuate the effects of each on or off signal. In addition, combinations of two on signals and two off signals increased the pattern's complexity and further moved its perceived urgency towards a neutral point. As a result, about half of the participants were undecided when asked to compare two patterns from the two on-off group. The majority of participants wanted the interviewer to play the pattern pair again.

It is worth noting that—as seen in the results of the post-experiment questionnaire—most of the participants were able to describe, through comparisons of the patterns within the one on-off group, the signal characteristics of the patterns in that group. They were also able to associate simpler patterns, i.e., those belonging to the one on-off group, with the appropriate level of urgency.

Characteristics of Vibration Patterns' Signals

Similarities among some of the ten vibration patterns were grouped based on their level of urgency and the characteristics of their signals (Fig. 4). These were marked accordingly for further analysis. In comparing each pattern's signal characteristics, we found similarities that potentially contributed to some patterns being perceived as more urgent than others. This can be observed particularly among the patterns in the one on-off group.

	Vibration Patterns									
	1	***3***	***6***	***9***	***7***	***4***	***5***	***8***	***10***	***2***
One Short Off	X	X								
One Long Off						X				X
Two Short Off					X					
Two Long Off								X		
Two Mixed Off			X	X			X		X	
One Short On	X									X
One Long On		X				X				
Two Short On							X			
Two Long On			X							
Two Mixed On				X	X			X	X	

Figure 4. A table of signal characteristics of vibration Patterns 1 to 10.

• Given the same gap length between vibrations, a pattern that contains short gap(s) was perceived to be more urgent than those with longer gap(s).

• Given the same number of gaps, a pattern with one gap was perceived to be more urgent than those with two gaps.

• Given the same length of vibration, a pattern with shorter vibration was perceived to be more urgent than those with longer vibration.

Factors that Influence the Perceived Level of Urgency

Three underlying factors contribute to users' perceived urgency of vibration alerts: gap length is the strongest factor, followed by number of gaps, and finally vibration length.

Experiment results and qualitative analysis reveal that the short on signal is highly susceptible to varying perceptions of its level of urgency, depending on the length of the gaps that precede and succeed it. A gap length of 200 ms between short on signals heighten perceived urgency because the short and sharp pulse is delivered in a stronger manner. On the other hand, a 600 ms gap length preceding or succeeding a short on signal diminishes its strength, making the pulse feel weaker.

White [14] showed that pulses with different intensities that have no gaps between them were perceived as more urgent than those with long gaps. This is reflected in the results of Patterns 1 and 2, which ranked as most urgent and least urgent, respectively. In comparison, the long on signal has a steady attribute that makes it less susceptible to fluctuations caused by gaps surrounding it. Therefore, the discrepancy between Patterns 3 and 4 is minimal.

EXPERIMENT 2

In Experiment 1, simple vibration patterns were clustered and ranked according to their perceived urgency, and factors that contributed to differences in perceived urgency were identified. Figure 3 shows how the 10 patterns can be grouped into different clusters (from three clusters to eight). However, how many different levels of urgency can a user reliably distinguish when receiving random, isolated vibration notification? If a smartphone uses N, which represents the number of clusters, how large can N be before a user can no longer reliably indentify each vibration pattern's corresponding urgency level?

In Experiment 2, we asked participants to identify the urgency level of individual vibration notifications. From Experiment 1, we know that the range for N is somewhere between 3 and 10. The initial candidates of our investigation were N=4 clusters, N=5 clusters, and N=6 clusters. The patterns from each N were selected from their corresponding levels of urgency: Patterns 1, 2, 10, and 6 were selected for N=4 clusters; Patterns 1, 2, 4, 10, and 6 were selected for N=5 clusters; and patterns 1, 2, 4, 10, 6 and 5 were selected for N=6 clusters.

Participants

Twelve new participants (six male and six female) with ages ranging from 19 to 25 years took part in this experiment.

Procedure

The participants were briefed and were asked to try each vibration pattern while adjusting the volume of the audible mask. The experiment was divided into three parts: in the first part, the participants were asked to rank four vibration patterns. In the second part, they were asked to rank five, and in the third part they were asked to rank six. The order of presentation was counterbalanced using a Latin Square.

For each part, the participants were given the total number of urgency levels that they will use for ranking, as well as the number of times the patterns will be played in random order. In the first part, for instance, the participants went through four trials to rank four patterns according to four levels of urgency. For each trial, the participant was asked to indicate the level by holding up a small placard with the appropriate sign. The interviewer recorded the response before playing the next set of patterns. The three parts of the experiment were separated by two-minute breaks.

Results of Experiment 2

We performed a one-way repeated measure ANOVA for the single factor, number of urgency levels on the dependent measure, accuracy of recognition. Accuracy of recognition was calculated using the number of correct recognition trials divided by the total number of trials, the value is shown as a percentage

The result showed that there is a significant main effect on the number of urgency levels for recognition accuracy ($F_{2, 22} = 26.78$, $p < .01$). Pairwise t-tests with a Bonferroni correction showed that the recognition accuracy of four urgency levels (95.8%) is not significantly different from the recognition accuracy of five urgency levels (81.7%, $p = .082$), but both of them are significantly higher than the recognition accuracy of six urgency levels (57%, $p < .01$). We found that 11 out of the 12 participants could clearly distinguish and rank all four vibration patterns into four levels correctly. Seven out of 12 participants could clearly distinguish and rank all five vibration patterns into five levels correctly. However, none of them could rank six vibration patterns into six levels correctly.

In all three parts of the experiment, all the participants were able to correctly identify and rank Pattern 1 as the most urgent pattern and Pattern 2 as the least urgent. This shows that the number of vibration patterns and levels of urgency that participants can distinguish is between four and five.

Based on the findings, we developed an Android application that can assign different levels of urgency to different contacts' incoming calls or messages. As demonstrated in the accompanying video, participants can distinguish the level of urgency of an incoming call or message even without an audio alert.

CONCLUSION

The perceived urgency of simple vibration alerts is affected by three primary factors. The basic signals that were used to create the ten vibration patterns had characteristics—short on, short off, long on, and long off—the combination of which had attenuating effects particularly in more complex patterns of two or more on-off signal pairs. Thus, to effectively impart the level of urgency, the vibration pattern design should be at its simplest form with the least number of on-off signal pairs.

The study investigated vibration patterns made of one and two on-off signal pairs with two distinct lengths. We found that users can reliably distinguish at least four levels of urgency based on the simple design of our vibration alerts. We implemented a system-level application so that notifications are more personalized, for instance by tailoring vibration alerts of incoming calls based on the user's communication history as well as application usage trends. More complex patterns can be explored in future studies to discover possible associations with more complex concepts.

A better understanding of perceived urgency associated with vibration patterns can help future designers create notification interfaces that effectively convey a vibration alert's level of urgency, help users understand and prioritize incoming alerts, and alleviate information overload. It is our hope that our findings contribute to more effective computer-supported cooperative work on awareness and notification.

Finally, such understanding can also contribute to the research of eyes-free interaction, as the vibration signals can complement existing eyes-free interaction techniques primarily based on auditory feedback (e.g., earPod [17]) to come up with more effective multi-modal interfaces. The resulting interfaces will have more expressive power to serve the variety of needs behind eyes-free interactions [16].

ACKNOWLEDGEMENTS

We thank anonymous reviewers for their constructive comments and feedback. We also thank Toni-Jan Keith Monserrat, Tai-Wei Kan, and other members of the NUS-HCI lab for their generous help throughout the project. This research is supported by National University of Singapore Academic Research Fund WBS R-252-000-414-101.

REFERENCES

1. Crawford, G., Williams, C. The Analysis of Subjective Judgment Matrices, Rand Corporation (1985)
2. Cadiz, JJ., Venolia, G.D., Jancke, G., Gupta, A. Designing and deploying an information awareness interface. In *Proc. CSCW 2002*, ACM (2002), 314-323
3. Enriquez, M., MacLean, K., Chita, C. Haptic phonemes: basic building blocks of haptic communication. In *Proc. Multimodal Interfaces 2006*, ACM (2006), 302-309.
4. Hoggan E., Brewster S. New parameters for tacton design. In *Proc. CHI 2007 extended abstracts*, ACM (2007), 2417-2422
5. Hoggan, E, Anwar, S., Brewster, S. Mobile multi-actuator tactile displays. *Haptic and Audio Interaction Design* (2007), 22–33.
6. OEM Google Nexus One Vibrating Motor, http://www.globaldirectparts.com/OEM-Google- Nexus-One-Vibrating-Motor-p/htc736660.htm
7. Hwang, J., Hwang, W. Vibration perception and excitatory direction for haptic devices. *Journal of Intelligent Manufacturing* (2010), 1-11
8. Ichikawa, F., Chipchase, J., Grignani, R. Where's the Phone? A Study of Mobile Phone Location in Public Spaces. In *Proc. IEEE Mobility Conference* (2005), 797 - 804.
9. Kaaresoja, T. Mobile phone using tactile icons. *US Patent App 20,020/177* (2002)*,471*
10. Kaaresoja, T., Linjama, J. Perception of Short Tactile Pulses Generated by a Vibration Motor in a Mobile Phone. In *Proc. World Haptics (2005),* 471–472
11. Miranda, E. Improving subjective estimates using paired comparisons. *IEEE Software* 18,1 (2001), 87 - 91
12. Qian, H., Kuber, R., Sears, A. Towards Identifying Distinguishable Tactons for Use with Mobile Devices. In *Proc. ASSETS (2009)*, 257-258
13. Ryu J., Jung J., Choi S. Perceived magnitudes of vibrations transmitted through mobile device. In *Proc. HAPTICS 2008*, IEEE (2008), 139-140.
14. White, T. The Perceived Urgency of Tactile Patterns. Human Research and Engineering Directorate, Army Research Laboratory. ARL-TR-5557 (2011)
15. Yao H. Y., Grant D., and Cruz-Hernandez J. M. Perceived vibration strength in mobile devices: The effect of weight and frequency. In *Proc. IEEE transactions on haptics 2009*, IEEE (2009), 56-62
16. Yi, B., Cao, X., Fjeld, M. Zhao, S. Exploring User Motivations for Eyes-free Interaction on Mobile Devices. In *Proc. CHI 2012*, ACM (2012), 2789–2792
17. Zhao S., Dragicevic, P., Chignell, M.H., Balakrishnan, R., Baudisch, P. earPod: Eyes-free Menu Selection with Touch Input and Reactive Audio Feedback. In *Proc CHI 2007*, ACM (2007), 1395-1404
18. Žiberna, A., Kejžar, N.,Golob, P. A comparison of different approaches to hierarchical clustering of ordinal data, Metodološki zvezki, Vol 1,1 (2004), 57-73

Emergent Roles in Decision-Making Tasks using Group Chat

Jordan B. Barlow
Indiana University
1309 East Tenth Street, BU 670
Bloomington, IN 47405
jbbarlow@indiana.edu

ABSTRACT
Individuals assume roles in all aspects of life, including in computer-supported collaborative settings. The concept of roles is particularly interesting in settings where no formal roles are defined, as in self-managing virtual teams. In these settings, roles often emerge not only as a result of individual characteristics, but also as participants interact with each other and develop norms of behavior. Using role theory and speech act theory, this study explores the emergence of roles in computer-mediated decision-making groups, using chat transcripts from a lab experiment. Results indicate that four distinct roles emerge as individuals come together in decision-making groups using synchronous computer-mediated communication. These emerging roles have implications for virtual teams in research and practice.

Author Keywords
Computer-mediated communication; virtual teams; decision-making; roles; role theory; speech acts; speech act theory; computer-mediated discourse analysis; group outcomes; cluster analysis.

ACM Classification Keywords
K.4.3 [Organizational Impacts]: Computer-supported collaborative work

INTRODUCTION
People assume roles in all aspects of life. Roles can be formal (e.g., manager) or informal (e.g., discussion leader); they can form naturally (e.g., father) or by appointment (e.g., professor). Roles are created or emerge in every situation where humans interact with each other [9, 19]. The concept of role emergence is particularly interesting in settings where no formal roles are defined. In such situations, people can fill roles without formal recognition or even recognizing the roles themselves [19].

One such setting is group decision-making tasks. Roles often emerge as participants interact with each other and develop norms of behavior [42]. These roles emerge not only as a result of differing individual characteristics [e.g., 51], but also as a result of social interaction within the group in an effort to facilitate positive outcomes [42].

While past research on emerging roles in face-to-face decision groups gives some insight into the issue of roles in decision teams [e.g., 9], research on computer-mediated teams indicates that members of such teams behave in different ways than those participating in traditional group processes [28, 39]. In addition to communication differences, prior research shows that group tasks requiring convergence are less likely to be successful virtually than face-to-face [31].

One way to enrich theoretical and practical understanding regarding virtual teams is to examine the roles that develop among such teams. These roles could play an important part in the behavior and outcomes of such groups [42]. Prior research on virtual teams shows that the configuration of individuals in a group influences team outcomes [40]. This research has shown that the geographic, cultural, and structural makeup of a team affects group outcomes including communication effectiveness, coordination, and performance [27, 28, 40, 51]. Together, this research indicates that the composition of the team will affect how the team communicates and performs.

In addition to individual factors (e.g., culture, location, gender, personality), the makeup of a group in terms of behavioral roles might affect group outcomes. Group members have a need for role definition, particularly in virtual teams where roles tend to be even more ambiguous [15]. Such role clarity leads to improved team identity [15] and could also lead to other improved team outcomes. For example, recent research shows that the emergence of certain roles in online study groups can ultimately affect the grades of the group members [11]. Given that roles drive outcomes in study groups, emerging roles in virtual decision-making teams could similarly affect group decisions and other behavioral outcomes such as team performance, influence, satisfaction, or trust.

Typically, roles are defined as norms or patterns of behavior [9]. In many computer-mediated environments, behavior takes place through written language [23, 29]. In other words, roles in these settings are based on communication patterns, such as types of speech acts used, level of participation in group communication, and who among participants communicates with others. Such communication patterns differ depending on situational variables such as the topic and purpose of the communication [24]. Thus, while some previous research has examined role emergence in CMC [3, 16, 20, 35, 44], none of this research, to my knowledge, has focused on synchronous online communication nor on virtual teams working together toward a consensus decision. For example, many of these studies focus on roles that emerge in Usenet or Wikipedia. However, individuals communicating on Usenet or Wikipedia often have disparate or unfocused goals. The purpose of online communication in these settings is not necessarily to reach a consensus on one specific topic. These studies do not examine nor interpret the roles that emerge as individuals come together in a common task-focused interaction.

The current study, grounded in role theory and speech act theory, uses computer-mediated discourse analysis (CMDA) tools to address the following research question:

> *What roles, as defined by unique patterns of speech acts and participation in group communication, emerge in synchronous computer-mediated decision-making tasks?*

The answer to this research question should inform research on virtual group interventions and outcomes as researchers and practitioners seek ways to improve decision-making tasks among computer-mediated teams.

THEORETICAL BACKGROUND

Role Theory

To pursue my research question, I use two complementary theoretical perspectives. First, I draw from role theory [9]. Role theory defines roles simply as characteristic behavior patterns [9]. Role theory assumes that people hold social positions while interacting, and that they hold expectations for their own and others' behavior [9]. Further, the concept of roles provides a means for explaining the relationship between individuals and social structures by explaining how social structures are built upon individual roles, or individual patterns of action [10]. While previous research on virtual teams has explored the effects of individual characteristics on team outcomes [e.g., 27, 39, 51], these studies do not consider the concept of behavioral roles that emerge during group communication.

Much traditional research on roles focuses exclusively on leadership roles. The emergence of leadership roles has been studied in offline groups for decades. Studies by Bales during the 1950's examined the types of leaders that emerge in face-to-face decision-making groups [5]. Bales concluded that, often, two complementary leaders emerge—one task leader and one social leader. While the emergence of a strong leader or pair of leaders is documented in many team settings [e.g., 38, 43, 47, 49], the present study seeks to explore a variety of roles from a more general, exploratory perspective—including, but not limited to, leadership roles.

Several researchers have examined the roles that people assume as they communicate through computer networks [3, 16, 20, 35, 44, 45]. These works have identified and analyzed different types of roles that emerge in asynchronous communication, including Usenet [20, 44] and Wikipedia [3, 19, 35]. For example, a myriad of roles emerge in asynchronous collaborative learning environments, such as 'encourager,' 'dominator,' and 'fellow-traveler' [11]. Researchers have used social network analysis [16] and visualization methods [44] to understand emerging social roles in Usenet groups such as 'discussion people' and 'answer people.' Other roles in Usenet include 'newbie,' 'celebrity,' 'elder,' 'lurker,' 'flamer,' 'troll,' and 'ranter' [20]. Roles that have emerged from research on Wikipedia [19, 35, 45] include 'substantive experts,' 'vandal fighters,' 'social networkers,' 'watchdogs,' 'starters,' 'content justifiers,' 'copy editors,' and 'cleaners.'

These roles are specific to asynchronous communication and do not fit well for synchronous decision tasks. For example, roles such as 'newbie' and 'elder' refer to people who are new or well established in the conversation. However, in synchronous decision tasks, individuals generally (though not always) start and end the conversation together. Other roles such as 'copy editors' and 'cleaners' refer to those who edit the communication of others, which generally does not occur in synchronous chat. These examples show that different types of communication and different types of tasks have different roles, and the CMC roles that have been defined thus far likely are not the best fit for synchronous CMC tasks such as decision-making.

Speech Act Theory

In addition to the role theory perspective as used by these researchers, I draw from an additional theory base, particularly suited to synchronous communication, to explore emerging roles in decision tasks—speech act theory. Speech act theory [4] posits that speech uttered in a particular way constitutes an act [29, 41]. Speech acts do not simply describe the world—they "bring about change to the world" [2: p. 252]. Speech act theory is particularly suited to virtual communication because in many computer-mediated environments, behavior is performed primarily (and sometimes only) through verbal language [23, 29]. In other words, to understand the behavior of individuals in mediated teams, one must understand their speech acts.

Surprisingly, no prior studies on role emergence in CMC [e.g., 3, 16, 20, 35, 44], to my knowledge, are grounded in speech act theory. Hence, they do not focus heavily on message content to understand roles, but rather focus on how much and with whom individuals communicate. However, according to speech act theory, behavior can only be truly understood by understanding the meaning of communicative acts. Further, these studies tend to focus more on social roles than task roles [16] by focusing solely on participation and interaction patterns rather than meaning of the messages. In order to understand task-based roles, such as those that should emerge in decision-making tasks in CMC, one must understand the speech acts performed by communicating individuals.

Using these perspectives from role theory and speech act theory, I propose that roles in virtual group decision-making tasks can be detected by studying the speech acts of individuals participating in the task.

METHODOLOGY

To explore emerging roles in synchronous decision tasks, I used CMDA methods to analyze 26 online group chat transcripts taken from a lab experiment. The experiment was originally conducted by the author and other colleagues to investigate the effects of priming on group decision-making tasks [7]; analysis of the participants' communication was not done for that study.

Participants

The participants in the lab experiment were 130 undergraduate business students (80 male, 49 female, one undisclosed gender) working in 26 groups of five. All students received extra credit for participating in the study.

Task

Participants were instructed to make university admissions decisions regarding a set of five possible candidates. To encourage discussion among team members, participants were not allowed to admit more than three of the five candidates. This task has been used in previous research on decision-making in virtual teams [22].

The admissions task is a hidden profile task, meaning the information given to each individual consists of both common information, known to all participants, and unique information, known to only one participant on each team. As a result, hidden profile tasks encourage team discussion. Hidden profile tasks are similar to the tasks real groups face; in real groups, not all participants have complete information to make the best decision individually.

Experiment Procedures

The experiment began with participants playing a priming game [13] for eight minutes. In one condition, participants were primed with achievement and attention words. The remaining participants were given neutral words. For more discussion on priming in virtual settings, the reader is referred to [13]. The priming did not have an effect on group decision quality.

Participants were then provided four minutes to read the candidate information and make an individual admissions decision. Next, participants worked together as a team for 15 minutes using Gmail Chat to arrive at a team decision. Pseudonyms were used in Gmail Chat so that participants did not know the identity of their team members or which people in the room were part of their group. The participants sat in separate cubicles in front of individual personal computers during the study so no audible communication occurred. Finally, participants were asked to fill out a survey indicating their team's decision and individual demographic information.

CMDA Procedures

At the end of the experiment, I downloaded the transcripts of each session from the Gmail accounts that were created for the experiment. The 26 transcripts contained 2996 messages, with an average of 115.23 messages per transcript.

CMDA methods were used to code and analyze the data. CMDA is a collection of discourse analysis methods tailored specifically for computer-mediated communication [23]. CMDA methods are particularly suited to my research question because roles reflect patterns of behavior, and behavior in virtual teams is reflected entirely by the way group members communicate [23]. Text analysis methods and other methods based on speech act theory are increasingly used by information systems researchers in a variety of contexts [1, 2, 29]. Abbasi and Chen [1] note that "CMC text analysis is important for evaluating the effectiveness and efficiency of electronic communication in various organizational settings, including virtual teams and group support systems" (p. 812). To explore the emerging roles of the participants of the lab experiment, I used two CMDA methods—participation analysis and speech act analysis—to measure how much and in what ways participants communicated.

Participation analysis is a common CMDA method used to detect roles in asynchronous CMC [e.g., 16, 44]. For example, work exploring collaboration in Wikipedia largely defines the roles 'zealot' and 'good Samaritan' based on the amount of participation in editing Wikipedia articles [3]. Participation analysis has also been used in studies of emergent leadership in virtual teams [43, 47, 49]. In this research, I analyze the number of messages by participant, the percentage of the team's messages by each participant, and the length (in words) of each message.

Previous research on roles in CMC generally combines participation analysis with another type of analysis—typically social network analysis because of the asynchronous nature of the studies [e.g., 19]. I chose to use speech act analysis, a better fit with the theoretical reasoning and methodological design of my research.

Speech act analysis has been used extensively in linguistics to analyze the meaning of utterances in speech and writing

[18, 37]. In speech act analysis, a technique based on speech act theory [4, 41], researchers read every utterance in a communication transcript and assign it to a speech act category describing the behavior portrayed by the utterance (e.g., "claim", "question", "reaction"). To apply speech act analysis, several taxonomies have been created by linguists [e.g., 17]. These taxonomies have been used to examine computer-mediated communication as well; for example, researchers have applied the Francis and Hunston [17] taxonomy to understand the seriousness of Internet Relay Chat [26].

However, due to challenges of previous speech act taxonomies, such as difficulty in distinguishing between closely related codes, missing codes, overlapping codes, and codes specific to certain types of datasets [c.f. 29], Herring et al. [25] developed a consolidated and simplified taxonomy specifically for the analysis of CMC. This CMC act taxonomy, which consists of 16 types of speech acts, was tested by Herring and her colleagues on blog posts, threaded bulletin boards, and synchronous chat. They found it to be easily applied and interpreted. The CMC act taxonomy has been used in previous research on computer-mediated communication [30].

I classified each of the 2996 messages of the sample according to its relevant speech act type using the CMC act taxonomy. Some messages contained multiple speech acts; these were divided and coded as separate messages, resulting in a classification of 3055 total speech acts. Because speech act analysis can be subjective, a second coder participated in the analysis to establish inter-rater reliability. The second coder and I jointly coded one transcript of 170 speech acts to ensure mutual understanding of the classification scheme. Next, we independently coded four more transcripts (458 speech acts, about 15 percent of the total sample), and obtained a Cohen's kappa reliability score of 0.708, indicating substantial agreement between raters [33]. The rest of the messages were then coded solely by the author.

ANALYSIS AND RESULTS

Participation and Speech Act Analyses

Summary statistics for the participation analysis (shown in Table 1) show that the messages in this type of conversation are typically short, with one-third of messages being only one or two words in length.

Average message length in words	5.60
Average number of messages per participant	23.05
1-word messages as % of total messages	24.4%
1- or 2-word messages of % of total messages	33.1%

Table 1. Participation summary statistics.

Speech Act Category	% of Total
INFORM	22.78%
CLAIM	19.87%
ACCEPT	16.24%
INQUIRE	9.92%
REACT	7.73%
INVITE	7.00%
MANAGE	4.22%
REQUEST	3.37%
REPAIR	2.62%
ELABORATE	2.52%
GREET	1.67%
Others (< 1%)	2.06%

Table 2. Speech act summary statistics

In addition to these overall summary statistics, participation statistics were calculated for each participant of the experiment in order to compare amounts of participation as an indicator of behavioral patterns.

The overall results from the speech act analysis (shown in Table 2) indicate that most of the acts performed by participants through their communication were sharing information, making claims about information, agreeing with others, and asking questions. These speech acts are consistent with the type of task completed by the group—a decision-making task. While this research focuses on such decision-making groups, research on different types of group tasks (e.g., brainstorming, planning) would likely result in differences in the types of speech acts used and length of messaged communicated by participants [24].

Cluster Analysis

Based on the summary results of the participation and speech act analyses and a qualitative analysis of the text, I determined a set of six relevant factors of role behavior to be used in a cluster analysis to explore roles: two participation factors and four speech act factors.

Though I collected three participation analysis metrics, I chose to use just two as factors in the cluster analysis: percentage of team messages contributed by an individual, and average message length. I chose not to use number of individual messages because this metric is redundant with percentage of team messages, which also accounts for between-group differences in the number of messages typed.

The four speech act factors used were the following: information shared (percentage of an individual's speech acts classified as 'inform' speech acts), opinions shared (percentage of speech acts classified as 'claim' speech acts), agreement with others (percentage of speech acts classified as 'accept' speech acts), and amount of discussion guiding (percentage of speech acts classified as 'inquire,' 'manage, 'request,' or 'direct' speech acts). I combined the 'inquire,' 'manage,' 'request,' and 'direct' speech acts because these were strikingly similar upon reviewing them in the transcripts. Each of these four factors accounted for over 10 percent of the overall number of speech acts, respectively.

I then performed a cluster analysis based on the six factors, as done in previous CMC role research [35] and virtual team leadership research [43]. For example, Liu and Ram [35] used cluster analysis to define roles in Wikipedia collaboration; the factors for the cluster analysis were behaviors exhibited by the Wikipedia users (e.g., sentence insertions, link modifications, etc.). In contrast, my cluster analysis used factors based on levels of participation and types of speech acts, as these are the most relevant indicators of behavior in synchronous virtual communication.

I first used Ward's method of hierarchical clustering to identify the proper number of clusters. The results suggested four distinct groups of participants in the sample based on the six factors. I then used non-hierarchical (k-means) clustering to refine the original clusters. No cluster contained all five members of any group, indicating that the clusters do not reflect characteristics of teams, but rather individuals. The means of each of the six factors for each of the four clusters are shown in Table 3. Distinguishing values for each cluster are highlighted in light grey (low values) and dark grey (high values).

Results

Table 4 provides a summary description of the four clusters. A qualitative reading of the transcripts confirms the emergence of these four roles as group members interacted with each other. Again, these roles are specific to a decision-making task.

The largest cluster was the cluster of organizers, those who directed the conversation of the group by asking questions and requesting information. The organizers tended to have more than the average number of messages, with moderate amounts of sharing, claiming, and agreeing. Often, teams had more than one organizer as individuals worked together to move the discussion forward in a limited period. In fact, it was not uncommon for groups to have 3-4 organizers.

The next largest group is the listeners, those who participated less in discussion and primarily agreed with others. While the listeners tended to share some information and make claims when they did speak, these individuals did not guide the discussion.

Cluster	% of team messages contributed	Average message length	% of acts classified as 'inform'	% of acts classified as 'claim'	% of acts classified as 'accept'	% of acts classified as discussion guiding
1	15.37%	5.12	45.76%	9.62%	20.11%	9.36%
2	16.90%	6.45	24.49%	18.02%	29.81%	10.84%
3	22.41%	5.57	20.59%	15.87%	14.65%	26.47%
4	24.79%	6.11	13.92%	32.95%	8.73%	14.94%

Table 3. Cluster analysis results. Distinctly high values in dark gray; distinctly low value in light gray.

Cluster	Distinguishing characteristics	Role name	# individuals
1	Mostly share information and agree with others; little guiding of discussion; few, short messages and few claims about information.	*Sharers*	24 (18.5%)
2	Few messages, mostly agreeing with others; little guiding of discussion; average amounts of sharing and interpreting information.	*Listeners*	37 (28.5%)
3	Mostly guide the discussion by managing or asking questions; above average amounts of sharing information, making claims, and agreeing with others.	*Organizers*	44 (33.8%)
4	Mostly make claims, but do not share many facts; little agreement with others; many messages, often long, but only moderate discussion guiding.	*Opinion-aters*	25 (19.2%)

Table 4. Interpretation of clusters / roles.

Fewer individuals filled the role of *sharers*, those who mostly shared facts about the candidates but did not interject many strong opinions. These individuals answered questions and shared what they knew so that the team would have enough information to make a good decision. However, they had fewer, shorter messages and usually did not propose solutions.

The last emerging role was that of *opinionaters*, those who primarily tried to convince others of their own opinions. Most of the individuals in this role shared a variety of opinions, but were slow to accept the opinions of others, some even showing high tendencies toward stubbornness in the transcripts. These individuals used many messages, often long messages, to try to persuade their teammates of their opinions.

The roles detected through this cluster analysis reflect the roles that emerge in a decision-making task by groups communicating through chat software. Different roles would likely emerge in situations where a different type of task or technology was used.

DISCUSSION

The results show that distinct roles emerge in synchronous CMC, likely as a result of individual characteristics, social interaction, and group needs [42]. These roles emerged in text-based communication; similar roles may emerge in other types of CMC, though the results cannot be perfectly generalized from this study. However, the techniques proposed by my research to detect roles could be used in future studies examining role emergence in other computer-mediated groups using a different technology or performing a different type of task.

Limitations

The results of this research should be considered in light of some limitations. First, the transcripts for this study were taken from a lab experiment using student participants. While the results are useful for a variety of settings, including student groups, careful consideration should be used in applying the results to other contexts where individuals have different characteristics than students. Because roles and behavior are dependent on a multitude of factors, including gender, education, and culture [27], roles may differ in other contexts outside of student groups. However, because the results demonstrate general human behavior, similar results could potentially hold in other groups.

Care should also be taken in generalizing the results to other types of CMC or other types of group tasks—this study only examined text-based chat for decision-making groups. Other types of communication technologies that more closely resemble face-to-face communication may have different results, especially for different types of tasks. However, a main contribution of this research is a demonstration of an appropriate technique for detecting roles in CMC. This technique can be applied to CMC in other contexts in future research.

Another limitation of the study is the small sample size. Because the data for the research were taken from a previous study, more data could not be collected. Using a larger sample, more research should further examine and verify the roles in synchronous CMC and then investigate how these roles truly affect group outcomes and interventions. Notwithstanding, this study is an important contribution in that role emergence was shown, and a pattern of investigating roles in synchronous CMC was set forth.

Finally, this study only examines roles in groups of individuals who are interacting for the first time and have no anticipation of interacting together in the future. However, research shows that both individuals and groups adapt to computer-mediated communication over time and shift behaviors to meet the unique demands of CMC [36, 48]. Future research should examine whether and how roles in synchronous decision tasks persist or change as groups adapt over time.

Interpretation of Findings

Interpretation of Individual Roles

Each of the roles detected in this study reflects distinct patterns of behavior exhibited by participants during a decision-making process in a text-based communication environment.

The most common role in the groups was the organizer. The organizers in a group were those who showed leadership behaviors as they directed the discussion, asked questions, and structured the communication. Often, teams would have more than one organizer as individuals worked together to move the discussion forward in a limited period of time. Some groups even had three or four organizers. This complex pattern of leading the discussion and communication is consistent with prior CMC research suggesting that a simple pattern of single or complementary leadership does not always hold in online contexts [e.g., 11, 19, 50] and emergent leadership patterns are different in virtual teams than in face-to-face teams [38]. Further research supports the notion that influence and leadership behaviors are displayed by individuals of all social positions [50]. In online contexts, even when task-related, the simple emergence of one or even two distinct leaders is not a given [38]; rather, individuals participating in CMC show more complex patterns of leading and following by assuming different types of roles.

Synchronous online decision-making groups also tend to have many listeners, those who were mostly passive and agreeing with others. This finding is consistent with research showing that social loafing tends to emerge in groups larger than two to three individuals [12]. These listeners were generally doing more than just lurking; when asked for information or an opinion they would share it, often elaborating—listeners tend to share longer messages than others. However, the amount of participation of these individuals, along with the high amount of agreement, showed a mostly passive role. Possible reasons that an individual would assume a listener role include a quiet personality, or an interest in the discussion while others dominate as organizers or opinionaters. In other words, for some listeners, it may be the case that they shared more messages at the beginning, but the percentage of team messages typed decreased as others in the group dominated and the listeners resorted to mostly agreement statements. Further, it may be that listeners type longer messages than others in an effort to share more information and opinions at one time to compensate for a lack of consistent active speaking during the discussion.

Fewer individuals assumed the role of sharers, those who simply shared facts but did not attempt to widely influence the discussion. Like listeners, sharers fell into a largely passive role. Sharers typed sparse, short messages, often in response to a question put forth by an organizer. Sharers avoid giving their opinions and only respond when needed. While all roles are affected by individual characteristics, possible reasons that people assume a sharer role during the task could be lack of care about the task, or too many other people in the group dominating the discussion.

Opinionaters were those whose primary goal was to convince others of their own opinions. Most of the individuals in this role shared a variety of opinions, but were slow to accept the opinions of others, some even showing high tendencies toward stubbornness in the transcripts. While the number of speech acts categorized as 'reject' was low in the overall sample, speech acts connoting a rejection of others' ideas was highest in this cluster. Further, opinionaters shared relatively low amounts of factual information with the team, relying on opinion more than evidence to argue a case.

Interpretation of Role Structure

A variety of all four roles emerged in groups at all levels of decision quality; that is, teams who performed better on the task did not have a unique role structure. The emergence of roles is affected by individual characteristics, but the transcripts indicated that in some cases, people assumed roles as a result of the group interaction. For example, if a group happened to have many organizers or opinionaters dominating the discussion, others who may have assumed these roles became more passive and assumed a listener or sharer role instead.

The roles are also dependent on the task that was used. For example, if the task had been more emotional than university admissions, there may have been more opinionaters. If the task had focused more on encouraging participations, there might have been fewer listeners. Different types of tasks such as brainstorming or planning, rather than decision-making, could result in different types of roles altogether. The interpretation of these roles is based on the decision-making task. However, the methods used to understand the roles can be applied to a wide variety of tasks.

Contributions

Practical Implications

The results of this study have implications for both research and practice. Awareness of the unique task-based roles that emerge during decision-making tasks using synchronous text-based CMC is important for groups that commonly use technology for such tasks. Understanding the types of behaviors that emerge in these settings is useful to better structure and facilitate communication among individuals. While determining exactly which roles are present in a given group is currently a manually intensive process that occurs after the fact, groups can be informed that, generally speaking, the four roles presented here are common in decision-making groups.

Research on Role Outcomes

This research also has implications for research on the relationship of roles to group outcomes. Previous research indicates that inclusion or exclusion of certain types of individuals can affect team processes and outcomes [21]. However, until recently, little research was done in exploring relationships between roles and team-level outcomes [42], and scholars have called for more research examining how the presence or absence of roles affects group outcomes such as productivity and longevity [19]. For example, the presence of certain roles in collaborative learning environments affects group project grades [11]; the quality of a Wikipedia article depends on the roles of the contributors and how they collaborate with each other [35]. Such relationships between roles and group outcomes should be further examined for virtual teams in decision-making tasks. Having clarity of roles in virtual teams will lead to improved team identity [15] and other group outcomes.

Several virtual group decision-making outcomes could be affected by the emergence of roles. For example, roles may affect the extent to which individuals change their decisions to conform to the group. Because individuals in different roles communicate (i.e., behave) differently, the behavior of some individuals may be more influential than the behavior of others. In this case, the sharers and listeners of the groups tend to be more passive than other roles. Because individuals in these roles largely agree with others without interjecting strong opinions, they could be more likely to change their original decisions to match the opinions of others in the group as they give up their own opinions to agree with the statements of others. Future research should more thoroughly examine what types of group outcomes are most influenced by these roles. Further, if roles affect group outcomes, and group performance is correlated with individual characteristics such as gender, educational background, and culture [e.g., 27, 46, 51], behavioral roles may act as a mediator between individual characteristics and group outcomes. Future research should further explore this relationship.

Research on Factors Influencing Role Formation

Next, if roles affect group outcomes, it may be important to shape role formation in group to achieve better outcomes of group decision-making. Traditional role research has viewed roles as somewhat static within individuals. For example, researchers argue that every user in online Q&A services behaves consistently and uses patterns of communication regardless of circumstances [6]. Indeed, roles are known to be influenced by individual characteristics [42]. However, research also shows that individual roles are adapted in real-time depending on the context and situational demands [42]. This opens up the possibility that individuals and organizations can use interventions to change the emerging roles in group contexts. In the context of synchronous CMC decision-making tasks, some interventions, whether intentional or resulting from context, could change the way that groups interact together and adapt their individual roles.

Researchers in the computer-supported collaboration and human-computer interaction fields have developed technological interventions to improve group collaboration [e.g., 8, 14, 32, 34], and more research is needed to understand how such interventions could affect role emergence in groups. For example, collaboration researchers developed a system that allows group members to give anonymous feedback in a backchannel in addition to the regular communication of the group [8]. This backchannel communication allows for more contributions from participants who may otherwise participate less. A group using such a system may have fewer people assuming a 'listener' role. Other researchers have proposed real-time systems that summarize individual participation to the group by highlighting the number of comments by individuals or summarizing contributions with keywords [14, 32]. These systems give feedback while groups are communicating, and have been shown to change group communication styles and facilitate cooperation among group members [32]. Technological interventions have also been designed to give real-time feedback to group members about the type of language they use during group discussion [34]. These intervention systems have the power to affect the roles that emerge during computer-mediated decision tasks. Future research should connect these two streams of research—while work on group intervention systems shows improvements in group processes, more research is needed to better understand exactly how such interventions affect the roles of individuals in the group.

In addition to technological interventions, other factors, such as unrelated interactions with other people before the meeting, could subconsciously encourage team members to listen and agree rather than interject and actively participate. For example, in the lab experiment from which transcripts were used for this study [7], individuals were primed with attention and achievement words in an effort to change the behavior of individuals to pay more attention to other group members. Unfortunately, the sample size of the data is too small to test whether the priming effect changed which roles emerged in the teams (e.g., whether the priming caused more listeners to emerge). Future studies should examine direct and indirect effects (such as priming) on role emergence.

Research Methods for Detecting Roles

Finally, this study has implications for the methods in carrying out further research on roles in virtual settings. This research successfully used speech act analysis, a form of CMDA, to detect and interpret roles in synchronous computer-mediated communication. Further research should build on this work by continuing to use speech act analysis and other CMDA methods that are theoretically related to the research question regarding roles in online communication. A study of speech acts directly reflects participant behavior in computer-mediated settings, and such techniques should be applied in studies of online behavior. While the current study examines roles for decision-making tasks, the procedures used can be applied to a variety of CMC settings.

ACKNOWLEDGMENTS

The author sincerely thanks Alan Dennis and Valerie Bartelt, who designed the lab experiment; Lingyao Yuan and Rosh Dhanawade, who helped in proctoring the experiment; Kayleen Barlow, the second coder of the speech act analysis; and Susan Herring and David Wilson, who provided helpful feedback on previous versions of this paper.

REFERENCES

1. Abbasi, A. and Chen, H. CyberGate: A design framework and system for text analysis of computer-mediated communication. *MIS Quarterly 32*, 4 (2008), 811-837.
2. Ågerfalk, P.J. Getting pragmatic. *European Journal of Information Systems 19*, 3 (2010), 251-256.
3. Anthony, D., Smith, S.W., and Williamson, T. Reputation and reliability in collective goods: The case of the online encyclopedia Wikipedia. *Rationality and Society 21*, 3 (2009), 283-306.
4. Austin, J.L. *How to Do Things with Words*. Harvard University Press (1962), Cambridge, MA, USA.
5. Bales, R.F. Task roles and social roles in problem-solving groups. In *Role Theory: Concepts and Research*,

B.J. Biddle and E.J. Thomas Eds. John Wiley & Sons, Inc. (1966), New York City, NY, USA, 254-263.

6. Barash, V., Smith, M.A., Getoor, L., and Welser, H.T. Distinguishing knowledge vs social capital in social media with roles and context. In *Proc. ICWSM 2009*, AAAI Press (2009), 1-4.
7. Bartelt, V., Dennis, A.R., Yuan, L.I., and Barlow, J.B. Individual priming in virtual team decision-making. *Group Decision and Negotiation* (accepted pending minor revisions).
8. Bergstrom, T. and Karahalios, K. Vote and be heard: Adding back-channel signals to social mirrors. In *INTERACT 2009*, International Federation for Information Processing (2009), 546-559.
9. Biddle, B.J. Recent developments in role theory. *Annual Review of Sociology 12* (1986), 67-92.
10. Callero, P.L. From role-playing to role-using: Understanding role as resource. *Social Psychology Quarterly 57*, 3 (1994), 228-243.
11. Chang, C.-K., Chen, G.-D., and Wang, C.-Y. Statistical model for predicting roles and effects in learning community. *Behaviour & Information Technology 30*, 1 (2011), 101-111.
12. Chidambaram, L. and Tung, L.L. Is out of sight, out of mind? An empirical study of social loafing in technology-supported groups. *Information Systems Research 16*, 2 (2005), 149-168.
13. Dennis, A.R., Minas, R.K., and Bhagwatwar, A. Sparking creativity: Improving electronic brainstorming with individual cognitive priming. In *Proc. 45th HICSS*, Computer Society Press (2012), 139-148.
14. Dimicco, J.M. and Bender, W. Second messenger: Increasing the visibility of minority viewpoints with a face-to-face collaboration tool. In *Proc. 9th Conf. IUI*, (2004), 232-234.
15. Fiol, C.M. and O'connor, E.J. Identification in face-to-face, hybrid, and pure virtual teams: Untangling the contradictions. *Organization Science 16*, 1 (2005), 19-32.
16. Fisher, D., Smith, M.A., and Welser, H.T. You are who you talk to: Detecting roles in Usenet newsgroups. In *Proc. 39th HICSS*, Computer Society Press (2006), 1-10.
17. Francis, G. and Hunston, S. Analysing everyday conversation. In *Advances in Spoken Discourse Analysis*, M. Coulthard Ed. Routledge (1992), London, UK, 1-34.
18. Fraser, B. Hedged performatives. In *Speech Acts: Syntax and Semantics*, P. Cole and J.L. Morgan Eds. Academic Press (1975), New York, NY, USA, 187-210.
19. Gleave, E., Welser, H.T., Lento, T.M., and Smith, M.A. A conceptual and operational definition of 'social role' in online community. In *Proc. 43rd HICSS*, Computer Society Press (2009), 1-11.
20. Golder, S.A. and Donath, J. Social roles in electronic communities. In *AoIR Conf. Internet Research 5.0*, (2004), 1-25.
21. Guzzo, R.A. and Dickson, M.W. Teams in organizations: Recent research on performance and effectiveness. *Annual Review of Psychology 47* (1996), 307-338.
22. Heninger, W.G., Dennis, A.R., and Hilmer, K.M. Individual cognition and dual-task interference in group support systems. *Information Systems Research 17*, 4 (2006), 415-424.
23. Herring, S.C. Computer-mediated discourse analysis: An approach to researching online behavior. In *Designing for virtual communities in the service of learning*, S.A. Barab, R. Kling, and J.H. Gray Eds. Cambridge University Press (2004), New York, NY, USA, 338-376.
24. Herring, S.C. A faceted classification scheme for computer-mediated discourse. *Language@Internet 4*, 1 (2007), 1-19.
25. Herring, S.C., Das, A., and Penumarthy, S., 2005. CMC act taxonomy. http://www.slis.indiana.edu/faculty/herring/cmc.acts.html.
26. Herring, S.C. and Nix, C.G. Is "serious chat" an oxymoron? Pedagogical vs. social uses of Internet Relay Chat. In *AAAL Conf.*, (1997), 1-19.
27. Hinds, P., Liu, L., and Lyon, J. Putting the global in global work: An intercultural lens on the practice of cross-national collaboration. *The Academy of Management Annals 5*, 1 (2011), 135-188.
28. Hinds, P.J. and Bailey, D.E. Out of sight, out of sync: Understanding conflict in distributed teams. *Organization Science 14*, 6 (2003), 615-632.
29. Janson, M.A. and Woo, C.C. A speech act lexicon: An alternative use of speech act theory in information systems. *Information Systems Journal 6*, 4 (1996), 301-329.
30. Kapidzic, S. and Herring, S.C. Gender, communication, and self-presentation in teen chatrooms revisited: Have patterns changed? *Journal of Computer-Mediated Communication 17*, 1 (2011), 39-59.
31. Kerr, D.S. and Murthy, U.S. Divergent and convergent idea generation in teams: A comparison of computer-mediated and face-to-face communication. *Group Decision and Negotiation 13*, 4 (2004), 381-399.
32. Kim, T., Hinds, P., and Pentland, A. Awareness as an antidote to distance: Making distributed groups cooperative and consistent. In *15th ACM Conf. CSCW*, ACM (2012), 1237-1246.

33. Landis, J.R. and Koch, G.G. The measurement of observer agreement for categorical data. *Biometrics 33*, 1 (1977), 159-174.

34. Leshed, G., Perez, D., Hancock, J.T., Cosley, D., Birnholtz, J., Lee, S., Mcleod, P.L., and Gay, G. Visualizing real-time language-based feedback on teamwork behavior in computer-mediated groups. In *CHI 2009*, ACM (2009), 537-546.

35. Liu, J. and Ram, S. Who does what: Collaboration patterns in the Wikipedia and their impact on article quality. *ACM Transactions on Management Information Systems 2*, 2 (2011), article 11.

36. Majchrzak, A., Rice, R., Malhotra, A., King, N., and Ba, S. Technology adaptation: The case of a computer-supported inter-organizational virtual team. *MIS Quarterly 24*, 4 (2000), 569-600.

37. Mclaughlin, M. Chapter 4: Acts. In *Conversation: How Talk is Organized* Sage (1984), Thousand Oaks, CA, USA, 133-168.

38. Misiolek, N.I. and Heckman, R. Patterns of emergent leadership in virtual teams. In *Proc. 38th HICSS*, IEEE Press (2005), 1-10.

39. Mortensen, M. and Hinds, P.J. Conflict and shared identity in geographically distributed teams. *International Journal of Conflict Management 12*, 3 (2001), 212-238.

40. O'Leary, M.B. and Mortensen, M. Go (con)figure: Subgroups, imbalance, and isolates in geographically dispersed teams. *Organization Science 21*, 1 (2010), 115-131.

41. Searle, J.R. A taxonomy of illocutionary acts. In *Expression and Meaning: Studies in the Theory of Speech Acts*, J.R. Searle Ed. Cambridge University Press (1979), Cambridge, UK, 1-29.

42. Stewart, G.L., Fulmer, I.S., and Barrick, M.R. An exploration of member roles as a multilevel linking mechanism for individual traits and team outcomes. *Personnel Psychology 58*, 2 (2005), 343-365.

43. Sudweeks, F. and Simoff, S. Leading conversations: Communication behaviours of emergent leaders in virtual teams. In *Proc. 38th HICSS*, IEEE Press (2005), 1-10.

44. Welser, H.T., Gleave, E., Fisher, D., and Smith, M.A. Visualizing the signatures of social roles in online discussion groups. *Journal of Social Structure 8*, 2 (2007), 1-32.

45. Welser, H.T., Kossinets, G., Smith, M.A., and Cosley, D. Finding social roles in Wikipedia. In *Annual Meeting of the ASA*, AllAcademic (2008), 1-8.

46. Woolley, A.W., Chabris, C.F., Pentland, A., Hashmi, N., and Malone, T.W. Evidence for a collective intelligence factor in the performance of human groups. *Science 330*, 29 Oct 2010 (2010), 686-688.

47. Yoo, Y. and Alavi, M. Emergent leadership in virtual teams: What do emergent leaders do? *Information and Organization 14*, 1 (2004), 27-58.

48. Zhang, P. and Sun, H. The complexity of different types of attitudes in initial and continued ICT use. *Journal of the American Society for Information Science and Technology 60*, 10 (2009), 2048-2063.

49. Zhang, S. and Fjermestad, J. Bridging the gap between traditional leadership theories and virtual team leadership. *International Journal of Technology, Policy and Management 6*, 3 (2006), 274-291.

50. Zhu, H., Kraut, R., and Kittur, A. Effectiveness of shared leadership in online communities. In *15th ACM Conf. CSCW*, (2012), 1-10.

51. Zolin, R., Hinds, P., Fruchter, R., and Levitt, R.E. Interpersonal trust in cross-functional, geographically distributed work: A longitudinal study. *Information and Organization 14*, 1 (2004), 1-2.

Appropriation by Unanticipated Users: Looking Beyond Design Intent and Expected Use

Pablo-Alejandro Quinones, Stephanie D. Teasley, & Steven Lonn
School of Information, University of Michigan–Ann Arbor
105 S. State St., Ann Arbor, MI
pabloq, steasley, slonn@umich.edu

ABSTRACT
Research in CSCW has demonstrated that people use technology in inventive ways, yet little work investigates the adoption and adaptation of collaborative technologies by unanticipated users. In this paper, we present a study investigating an unanticipated user group's appropriation of a leaning management system, CTools. This group of users, staff at a large research university, has adapted the system, which was designed to support student-content-faculty interactions at the University of Michigan. We present the User/Use Technology Appropriation Matrix (UTAM) as a way to frame our understanding of users and their system use. Based on findings from system log data and surveys, we show that staff use the system similarly to students and faculty, though they value the tools and work affordances differently in their varied work contexts. We discuss these findings, how UTAM can be used to frame these findings, and suggestions for future research.

Author Keywords
Appropriation; practice; groupware; unanticipated users

ACM Classification Keywords
H.5.3 **[Group and Organization Interfaces]:** Computer-supported cooperative work; H.4.0 **[Information Systems Applications]:** General.

INTRODUCTION
Groupware has become a staple in today's work environments for helping people communicate, coordinate and collaborate. The tools available in groupware systems are used to support groups that vary along a number of dimensions, such as group size, task types, and physical distance between group members. These systems have been widely studied in various contexts by CHI and CSCW researchers. This paper starts with the observation that groupware, like many other information technologies (IT), may not be used as expected by system designers [20]. We build on this knowledge by suggesting that *collaborative technologies may be appropriated by groups of users who were never targeted or anticipated by the system designers—users who may or may not be using the technologies in the expected ways and could have real impact on practices surrounding the system in question.* There are a number of papers documenting how users adapt to IT and how IT use evolves over time as users adapt it to their own evolving contexts [1, 6, 9, 36], an act often referred to as appropriation. A number of papers show how groupware use is itself the subject of evolution [20-23, 27]. With so many ways that users and technology use evolve, a consistent set of key terms has emerged across a number of fields to address evolving and unexpected use of technology. For example, Leonardi and Barley's meta-review of two decade's worth of research on technology's impacts [11] describes a number of terms for adapted use of IT (*appropriation*) and user's system adaptation in terms of their practices (*enactment*) and structures (*alignment*).

There are only a few examples in the literature showing how appropriation by unanticipated users benefits subsequent system design [1, 10], but the research on appropriation is mostly focused on aspects of technology use in the context of anticipated users. This paper describes a largely unexplored type of use: appropriation by users who constitute an audience unanticipated by the system designers—that is to say, a user group that designers neither included nor excluded in their conceptualization of the target user. Specifically, the system under scrutiny here was designed mainly for students and faculty to support activities related to teaching and learning at institutions of higher learning—not designed to support traditional workplace practices nor the particular needs of university staff.

By studying unanticipated users in detail and comparing them to users from the target audience (anticipated users), we can come to understand the appropriation of the learning management system as a collaborative platform. Such comparisons may have strong implications for the iterative design process of information technology, groupware, and collaboration tools. In this paper we propose a matrix that distinguishes between users (anticipated and unanticipated) and use (expected and unexpected) in order to better understand the appropriation process of collaborative systems.

GROUPWARE & EVOLVING USES: AN OVERVIEW

Groupware supports collaboration by providing tools that help users communicate, coordinate, and manage group activity. Groupware has been studied extensively utilizing a paradigm that typically frames successful design in terms of the system's ability to improve performance along pre-defined criteria. Prior studies have provided rich demonstrations of ways in which outcomes vary between groups due to differences in how those groups use IT across contexts [12]. These different modes of use suggest that groups alter their technology use based on shifting contexts, thus use isn't static. The evolving ways in which IT is used are generally called *appropriations*. The topic of evolving use of groupware has been important enough to warrant a special issue of the *CSCW Journal* [see 3, 6, 9, 36].

Appropriation

According to Orlikowski [20], "When users choose to use a technology, they are also choosing how to interact with that technology. Thus, they may, deliberately or inadvertently, use it in ways not anticipated by the developers" (p. 408). In CSCW, early work suggested that users are unpredictable in the way they will use technology [31]. Orlikowski and other researchers [e.g., 1] have used the term *appropriation* to refer to the various unexpected and unintended ways a technology is used. Other terms for technological appropriation include *re-invention* [30, 32], *tailoring* [37], *adaptation* [11, 15], and *hacking* [33]. These approaches to technology appropriation have clearly demonstrated that technology is transmutable—it is not static in its uses or roles in organizational practice, as both IT and its users go through a process of mutual adaptation and co-evolution [12, 19].

Interpretive Flexibility

As a part of the design process, users are specified and their needs are identified. While designers and researchers may develop systems that provide interventions for workflow and communication issues, users generate a variety of their own interpretations about these systems. The narratives that end users create are neither inherently obvious nor fully understood in the design phase. IT has varying degrees of *interpretive flexibility* [26]—that is, flexibility in the way its meaning and purposes can be interpreted. This point is well documented in the CSCW, HCI, and organizational science literatures. Nardi & Miller [16,17] detail a case where the use of spreadsheets evolved to support collaborative work in a business setting. In particular, various members of this organization interpreted the use of spreadsheets differently, developing practices that extended beyond the affordances typically assumed to be inherent to spreadsheets. Similarly, Orlikowski [20] showed how users of Lotus Notes interpreted the purpose of the system in a number of different ways, where some people used the system 'incorrectly' as a personal information management system rather than as a collaborative tool. Robinson [31] described a number of studies that highlight modes of use that didn't match designer's visions either because users found other ways of using the systems or because they ignored many of the features that designers spent time to create. In extreme cases of appropriation, users reinterpret the artifact at hand by changing its structure and functionality, such as when people manipulate pieces of IKEA products to create new home items [33].

Appropriation's Impact on Design

To date, only a few researchers have proposed design requirements for computer support that are based on observations of unexpected use (e.g., Robinson [31] and Pekkola [25]). Robinson's work has suggested that in addition to added functionality, computer support systems should be predictable, provide peripheral awareness, support implicit communication, provide a platform or basis for discussion and negotiation (double-level language), and afford overview of the work process. Pekkola revisited these requirements and confirmed that these requirements do lead to applications that are better suited for unanticipated use.

Contribution to Literature

Studies like those referenced above implicitly focus on intended users. However, as a growing number of users engage in appropriation, tailoring, and hacking, it is becoming more likely that groupware—or any IT for that matter—can be used by an unanticipated audience in any number of ways. Thus, interpretive flexibility can be compounded by what we call *flexibility of audience*, the extent to which IT affords interpretation by multiple user groups—anticipated or unanticipated. By identifying unanticipated users and understanding the ways they interact with a technology we can reveal opportunities for adding functionality not conceived of in the initial design phase.

There are a few examples in the existing literature where unanticipated users' appropriation of technologies is discussed. The most well known is the case of Internet use as we know it today. Abbate [1] describes how the Internet evolved from a research-focused network between universities and government labs to include many kinds of activities by users who saw that it could fulfill needs unrelated to research. The broad scale adoption of email is an obvious example of how Internet-based communication has extended beyond the originally targeted users. Ito [10] describes how mobile phones evolved from a tool supporting businessmen's needs to a personal device for everyday use, driven primarily by teen adopters. Ultimately, teen users, *unintended users*, drove the evolution of mobile phone design and infrastructure to include such features as SMS. These examples demonstrate that users who were never targeted by designers were able to interpret these technologies in ways that allowed them to appropriate them *because the system itself afforded both interpretive flexibility and flexibility of audience.* The examples also show that designers and implementers can benefit from considering both varied uses of groupware and users who fall outside of the primary design intent.

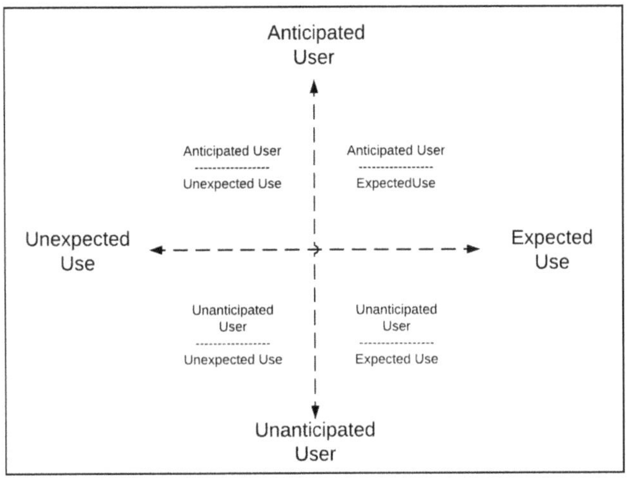

Figure 1. User/Use Technology Appropriation Matrix

Despite the benefits of considering possible unanticipated users, the current best practices of Participatory Design, User-Centered Design, etc., while able to capture use in the wild by continuously studying users, make few or no recommendations for designing for unanticipated users. The research literature, while thorough in its treatment and understanding of collaborative work and collaborative technologies, has treated appropriation as a matter of technology use in groups of interest—groups that are almost always the intended user group. Unanticipated users are rarely, if ever, studied for reasons of practicality, perceived value, etc. In many ways, unanticipated users may be 'designed out' of research studies, whether purposefully or unwittingly.

We argue that the two dimensions along which we can study end use and appropriation (users and their utilization of collaboration technologies) can be combined into a framework that we call the User/Use Technology Appropriation Matrix (UTAM). UTAM (see Figure 1) shows that when studying users and their use of a technology, we can characterize them as being on a continuum in terms of both their actual use versus the expected use of the system and the extent to which they are anticipated members of the target audience as envisioned by researchers, system designers, and implementers. While the use of a matrix renders these dimensions as dichotomies, we stress that they are each a spectrum, thus the matrix as we depict it emphasizes the extremes in the users and types of use under investigation. In our case, the anticipated user groups are university students, faculty, and researchers, which are positioned firmly at the top quadrants of the matrix. Meanwhile, the university staff users are unanticipated (lower left and right quadrants) and our analysis addresses whether the way they use the system is close to expected use (lower left vs. right quadrants).

Understanding system use by unanticipated users requires a new lens like the one we proposed—one that is sensitive to how these users differ from those the designer expected. This is true especially when we study collaborative systems; unanticipated users' ways of using collaborative technologies can lead to evolving practices that can further diffuse throughout their group and even beyond their immediate network of colleagues. Therefore *not* learning how these users employ technologies can have negative consequences for understanding overall use down the road.

Since iterative and participatory design techniques do not typically propose how to investigate unanticipated users, we see this work as a crucial first step towards addressing these gaps. Specifically, we detail a case where a group of users has adopted a system and adapted it to their work environments despite the fact that it was not designed with their needs in mind.

Understanding system use by unanticipated users requires a new lens like the one we have proposed—one that is sensitive to how these users differ from those the designer expected. This is true especially when we study collaborative systems; unanticipated users' ways of using collaborative technologies can lead to evolving practices that can further diffuse throughout their group and even beyond their immediate network of colleagues. Therefore *not* learning how these users employ technologies can have negative consequences for understanding overall use down the road.

Since iterative and participatory design techniques do not typically propose how to investigate unanticipated users, we see this work as a crucial first step towards addressing these gaps in the literature. Specifically, we detail a case where a group of users has adopted a system and adapted it to their work environments despite the fact that it was not designed with their needs in mind.

PROJECT SITES: USING A COURSEWARE SYSTEM AS GROUPWARE

This study of unanticipated users arose in the context of the University of Michigan, a large university setting, where staff members were found to be using a learning management system (LMS) in non-learning contexts. Learning management systems are an instance of courseware. Courseware systems are designed for use in educational settings to support learning activities where students and faculty interact with each other and with content. Courseware use is ubiquitous in higher education in the United States [34].

LMSs serve as a content management system and, especially in recent years, also function as communication systems. LMSs serve as a classroom-specific type of groupware employed for both online and "blended learning" [7]. Research in CSCW's sister field, CSCL (learning), has examined the use of LMSs to understand the kind of learning that occurs primarily in the context of higher education. Previous work has shown that students and faculty use these systems predominately as a repository for information and, to a lesser degree, to support learner-instructor and learner-learner interactions [14].

The LMS we examine here, CTools, is based on the Sakai architecture and is similar to other courseware systems, such as Blackboard, Moodle, and ANGEL. At the University of Michigan, an overwhelming majority of the anticipated audience uses this system: 91% of faculty and 99% of students. The primary use of the system is for "Course Sites", the de facto site type for classroom learning activities that can only be created by faculty for courses listed by the Registrar's office. The second type of site, a "Project Site" is growing rapidly in use; these sites can be created for any purpose by anyone on the campus.

Course Sites and Project Sites offer the same toolkit, including tools for one-way communication, interactive communication, content management, assessment, and coordination. Despite the different kinds of sites, the tools' labels are the same. For example, the tool for setting up a task is called "Assignments" on both types of sites even though this functionality is equally important in both contexts; the tool label does not reflect its possible uses outside of the classroom setting. This reflects the fact that Project Sites were designed to serve as a support for learning activities, primarily for a user in the instructor role to assign tasks to users in the learning role. The carbon-copy nature of Project Sites reflects the fact that they were designed to serve as a support for learning activities. By keeping the names for all tools the same across contexts, designers may have ensured that site types and tools are interpreted similarly.

The design for the architecture for Project Sites features and use of labels can be attributed to its predecessors. The availability of Project Sites in the CTools system is linked historically to a previous version of the LMS that was designed to support faculty research and teaching. In the conversion from the two pre-existing systems, Course Tools and Work Tools, Work Tools was incorporated into CTools and made available to the wider university audience under the name "Project Sites." Despite Project Sites' strong focus on teaching/learning and research, log data on site creation has shown that a rapidly increasing number of university staff members are creating Project Sites. While students create the majority of Project Sites, staff members actually create a higher number of these sites than faculty. Data from the site set-up tool suggests that staff members are not creating sites for faculty/student use (as would be the case for a staff member assigned to setting up sites on the behalf of faculty members or student group).

Table 1 shows that staff, students and faculty are creating sites for very different purposes. Two-thirds of all student-created Project Sites are primarily for group work, typically related to course assignments. Faculty members appear to create Project Sites for multiple reasons, including research, group projects and some administrative work. By contrast, just over half of all staff-created Project Sites are set up for administrative work. While these data are not necessarily surprising when we think of the typical type of work engaged in by each user group, it is important to emphasize

	Staff	Student	Faculty
Administrative	52.8	1.5	19.8
Club/ Organization	1.4	7.8	1.4
Group Project	15.1	69.0	27.7
Research	2.0	7.9	30.0
Study Group	14.3	7.3	5.5
Personal	3.2	4.2	5.0
Other	11.2	2.3	10.6

Table 1. Percentage of Project Sites created by each group for each purpose (Grey = Primary use)

that that staff were not expected to use this system beyond occasional participation in faculty sites. Functionality for supporting administrative tasks was not an intended type of use and therefore is not obviously supported by the LMS toolset. As mentioned previously, many tools are labeled with course-related terms, such as Syllabus, Gradebook, and Test Center. Other tools, such as Resources, Discussion, and Announcements, are more general and perhaps lend themselves to more interpretive flexibility—a point we will consider in the analyses that follow.

Because the staff users studied here are quite variable in terms of their work and IT needs, this research will have implications for the development of other groupware systems where a single interface and toolkit serves a large and diverse population, especially under the assumption that only a highly flexible system will support many such users with variable activities.

RESEARCH QUESTIONS

We believe that the ways in which staff perceive and value the system informs the ways in which they use the system. Specifically, these are our research questions:

- How do university staff use Project Sites?
    - How does staff use compare with how faculty and students use the LMS?
- How do university staff users of Project Sites value the system and its tools?
    - Do these values reflect the ways staff use the LMS?
    - Are these values different from how faculty and students value the LMS?

METHODS

The research agenda, as a whole, addresses ways of investigating these staff users and developing design recommendations for the system as a whole. To do this we have designed a number of studies, two of which we present in this paper. We obtained system log data from CTools to document how staff are using Project Sites and to compare their use with the two anticipated user populations – faculty and students. We also administered a survey that asked staff about their IT use in general and the system in particular. A number of questions probed users' perceptions of the overall value of this system and which specific tools were most valuable to them.

System Log Data

Our sample of 2,976 staff-created Project Sites came from staff that identified themselves as a Project Sites user on a survey about general technology use in the workplace (described below). We collected system data from January 1, 2010 through December 31, 2010. In cases where multiple staff respondents belonged to the same site, we used only one instance of log data from that site.

For comparison, we used log data from 1,621 randomly selected student-created Project Sites and 1,594 randomly selected faculty-created Project Sites, collecting this data during the same period as the log data from the staff sites.

Survey Overview

To assess how staff valued the system, we asked staff members at the University to participate in an online general technology use survey over a three-week period during October of 2010. We collected data about use of the LMS as part of a general technology use survey, using a branched design where respondents self-identified their current Project Site use. All self-identified users (any level of use) were asked to respond to questions about their use and experience. For the purposes of this paper, we focus our analysis only on responses from those users who self-identified as 'current users'.

We compared data from the staff survey to findings from a similar instrument used in a student/faculty survey administered in April - May 2010.

Survey Participants

We sampled all full time staff members at the university who had regular appointments at the time of the survey (i.e., not temporary staff). We excluded some staff members in job roles where previous surveys showed little to no technology use (such as athletics), as well as those who hold dual appointments as both faculty and staff. Out of the 27,477 staff invited to participate in the study, we received 6,590 responses, resulting in a 24% overall response rate. Out of these respondents, 990 self-identified as 'current users' of Project Sites. To ensure that the Project Site users were representative of the overall body of staff, we compared the job categories, departments, and overall computer expertise of Project Site users with all other participants and by the categories created by the branched design. We found no significant differences along these dimensions, suggesting that we were not collecting data from a biased group of staff (insofar as the above demographic variables were concerned).

All instructional faculty and a random sample of 25% of students (stratified by school/college) were invited via email to participate in a related survey. We received 1,017 faculty responses (13% response rate) and 1,415 student responses (16% response rate). Student users differ from staff in two ways: students are much younger and their use of the LMS is mandatory for almost all classes on this campus. Like students, faculty are also frequent users of the LMS because of their reliance on Course Sites, but they are more like staff in that Project Sites serve different needs than those of students. Faculty are also generally closer in age to staff members, which may have implications technology use and overall attitudes. To examine the differences between the anticipated and unanticipated users in this study, we make student/staff/ and faculty/staff comparisons. Our data and analyses take into consideration the student/faculty comparisons for purposes of determining statistical significance, but differences between the two intended user groups are not the focus of this paper.

Survey Method

All of our staff participants were recruited by an email inviting them to detail their attitudes towards IT and their use of information technology in their jobs. As an incentive, we offered gift certificates ($50 USD) to two randomly selected participants.

For staff, the first part of the survey consisted of questions concerning demographics and general information about job-related use of information technology (IT). At the end of this sections, staff were ask to self-report their Project Site use (no use, once, few times, past user, seasonal/current user). Staff members who identified themselves as seasonal/current Project Site users were next asked to respond to a series of questions concerning this use, including: rating the value of specific tools, rating the value of Project Sites for general tasks, and rating the value Project Sites for general and specific activities. Respondents provided ratings on a 5-point Likert scale (1 = Strongly Disagree to 5 = Strongly Agree, and 0=Have Not Used). The questions about tools, tasks, and activities were nearly identical to questions on the faculty and student survey (e.g., changing "your teaching" and "your coursework" to "your work"). We make note, in the results, of the few cases where items were different.

Log Data Collection

CTools creates "event" logs that capture when a user takes a particular action with a specific tool, such as downloading a document or posting an announcement. We aggregated the logged events for each tool (after removing extraneous site-level events) by Project Site in order to create a picture of system use that represents the activity on a site-by-site basis.

Procedure

The system log data captured a site's ID (system-generated) and name (user-generated), the number of users on the site, how many times the site had been logged into, and the number of times each tool had been used, which allowed us to calculate a number of other variables. We set the minimum threshold for what constitutes as 'tool use' at one event. This allows us not to overestimate the use of tools that were selected to be on the site but never used. Using the above criteria, we detected 2.28 million events from 2,976 staff sites. For comparison, we looked at 529,995 events from 1,594 faculty sites and 502,765 events from 1,621 student sites.

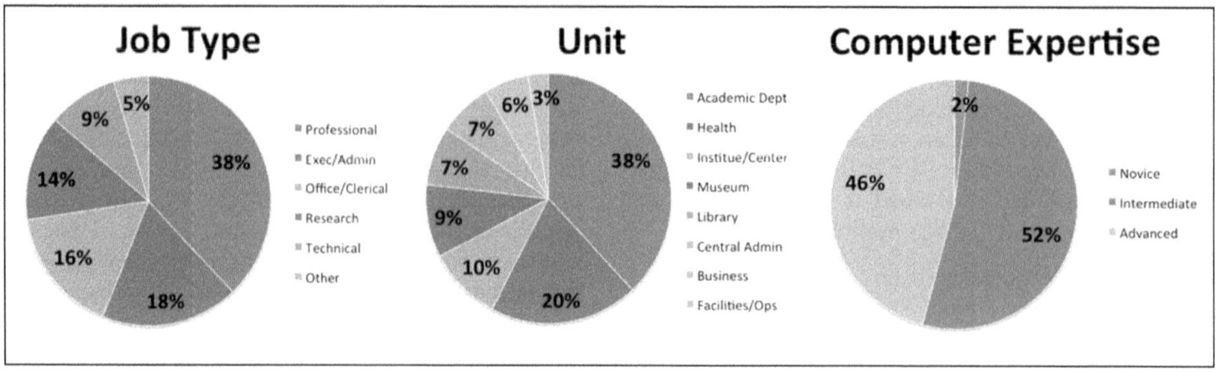

Figure 2. Staff Project Site users by job type (left), departmental unit (middle) and computer expertise (right)

RESULTS

Staff Demographics

Of our 6,590 staff member survey respondents, 990 (15%) reported being current users of Project Sites. We asked staff respondents to report their job categories, the unit they belong to within the larger organization, and their self-perceived level of computer expertise. Their responses are shown in Figure 2 (next page).

We asked staff Project Site users how many sites they belonged to and how often they visited their sites. Approximately 32.5% of users (N=354) belonged to 1-2 sites, 37.9% (N=413) belonged to 3-6 sites, 15.5% (N=169) belonged to 7-10 sites, and 14.1% (N=153) belonged to more than ten sites. The frequency of site visits varied greatly; 23.3% (N=251) visited their sites a few times per semester, 29.4% (N=317) visited their sites a few times a month, 13.5% (N=146) visited their sites once a week, 22.2% (N=240) visited their sites a few times a week, and 11.6 % (N=125) reported visiting their sites daily (at least once per day).

System Log Data

We analyzed the distribution of system log events across Project Sites using a top-level tool categorization scheme (communication, content, and management tools) and by a sub- categorization for communication tools (interaction and broadcast tools) and management tools (tracking and coordination tools). This descriptive analysis shows which categories and sub-categories of activity are predominant, as well as which tools get the most use within their categories and can be seen along with significant differences between user groups in Table 2 (next page).

Analysis of the tool categories (Table 2) revealed that the majority of events were related to the management of content (e.g., uploading, downloading). For individual tools, the results showed that the Resources tool alone accounted for the largest percentage of overall tool use across all sample populations.

The use of each tool follows a power law distribution where overall tool use is heavily concentrated in the relatively low to medium use range with a long tail [2] as use increases. For our analysis, rather than using counts, we used the percentage of overall use that is attributed to each tool category, sub-category and specific tool. By using this method of percentage scores, we avoid comparing large sites to smaller ones (e.g., all sites where half of all activity is due to the Resources tool are equal regardless of whether there are 500 events or 50 events).

Because of the non-normative distributions of the data, we conducted the non-parametric Kruskal-Wallis ANOVA (Table 2, center column). The ANOVA results show statistically significant differences between groups for the categories, the sub-categories, and at the individual tool level. There were statistically significant differences in mean rank scores between the comparison groups except for in the Coordination sub-category (marginally significant at p=.06) and the iTunesU (marginally significant at p=.076) and Podcast (not significant) tools.

To investigate pairwise differences between staff and the comparison groups, we used the Mann-Whitney U-test with a Holm's Sequential Bonferroni adjustment for post hoc analyses. Although all three pair-wise comparisons were tested, the two tests of particular interest to this paper are staff vs. faculty and staff vs. students. Rather than presenting the medians and mean ranks, we present the effect sizes to reduce the likelihood that large sample sizes make small differences between groups seem significant[1].

According to the post hoc test results, staff members were significantly different from faculty in all categories and significantly different from students in communication and content categories, but not the management category. The post hoc tests suggest that although all groups use Project Sites extensively for uploading and accessing content, staff members do so more than faculty and students. Staff use is focused more on management than communication, whereas the reverse is true for faculty and students. Though the results indicated that there were significant differences,

[1] Effect size is calculated in post hoc test (where df =1). Effect size $r = \frac{z}{\sqrt{N}}$, .1 (small), .3 (medium), .5 (large)

	Staff	Faculty	Student	K-W ANOVA			Post-Hoc Comparisons Staff/Students			Staff/Faculty		
	(N=2976)	(N=1621)	(N=1594)	*H*	*df*	*p*	|*Z*|	*p*	*r*	|*Z*|	*p*	*r*
Content Tools	**93.3%**	**92.9%**	**90.3%**	**388.2**	**2**	**≤ .001**	**14.87**	**≤ .001**	**> .1**	**5.55**	**≤ .001**	
- Resources	91.7%	91.0%	89.7%	167.6	2	≤ .001	13.04	≤ .001	> .1	6.51	≤ .001	> .1
- iTunes U	.3%	.4%	.0%	5.1	2	NS	.92	NS		1.60	NS	
- Podcast	.7%	.3%	.3%	0.4	2	NS	.05	NS		.59	NS	
- Wiki	.6%	1.2%	.3%	215.4	2	≤.001	.69	NS		4.46	≤ .001	
Communication Tools	**3.6%**	**5.4%**	**8.7%**	**364.6**	**2**	**≤.001**	**17.75**	**≤ .001**	**> .1**	**8.50**	**≤ .001**	**> .1**
Broadcast Tools	.5%	.8%	1.8%	465.1	2	≤ .001	19.26	≤ .001	> .3	7.40	≤ .001	> .1
- Announcements	.4%	.7%	1.7%	13.5	2	≤ .001	21.58	≤ .001	> .3	8.68	≤ .001	
- News	.1%	.1%	.1%	251.3	2	≤ .001	3.34	≤ .001		2.36	≤ .05	
Interaction Tools	3.1%	4.6%	6.9%	20.5	2	≤ .001	16.01	≤ .001	> .3	6.33	≤ .001	
- Forum/Discussion	1.5%	.5%	.4%	46.6	2	≤ .001	3.22	= .001		4.28	≤ .001	
- Messages	1.3%	2.8%	2.1%	27.2	2	≤ .001	6.68	≤ .001		4.15	≤ .001	
- Chat	.3%	1.3%	4.4%	742.5	2	≤ .001	24.82	≤ .001	> .3	3.86	≤ .001	
Management	**3.1%**	**1.9%**	**.9%**	**19.8**	**2**	**≤ .001**	**4.28**	**NS**		**.32**	**NS**	
Tracking Tools	2.1%	1.3%	.5%	49.8	2	≤ .001	5.18	≤.001		2.96	≤ .005	
- Test Center	1.4%	.2%	.1%	30.8	2	≤ .001	5.53	<.001		.21	NS	
- Assignments	.5%	.7%	.2%	26.2	2	≤ .001	2.01	≤ .05		3.60	≤ .001	
- Modules	.2%	.3%	.2%	8.8	2	≤ .001	2.23	≤ .05		1.22	NS	
- Gradebook	.0%	.1%	.0%	7.4	2	≤ .001	.86	NS		2.04	NS	
Coordination Tools	1.0%	.6%	.4%	5.4	2	NS	1.95	= .05		1.85	NS	
- Schedule	1.0%	.5%	.3%	22.3	2	≤ .001	3.71	≤ .001		3.86	≤ .001	
- Poll	.0%	.1%	.1%	22.8	2	≤ .001	4.61	≤ .001		1.07	NS	
- Syllabus	.0%	.0%	.0%	17.5	2	≤ .001	.38	NS		3.90	≤ .001	

Table 2. Percentage of use attributed to each tool (left) and Kruskal-Wallis ANOVA results of differences in tool use between sites created by each user type (middle), and post hoc significance and effect sizes (right).

	K-W ANOVA			Staff (N=2976)	Students (N=1621)	Faculty (N=1594)	Post Hoc Comparisons Staff/Faculty			Staff/Students		
	χ^2	*df*	*p*	Median	Median	Median	|Z|	*p*	*r*	|Z|	*p*	*r*
# Users	1245.7	2	≤ .001	13	5	4	24.10	< .001	> .3	32.9	< .001	> .5
# Total Site Events	50.80	2	≤ .001	97	88	153	1.14	NS		5.62	< .001	
Number of Logins	230.72	2	≤ .001	48	36	95	5.37	< .001		11.19	< .001	> .3

Table 3. K-W ANOVA results for differences between site types and number users, total number of events per site, and number of log-ins

the effect sizes were small and many were below the threshold to qualify as a small effect (See Table 2).

Staff users' mean rank scores were significantly different from faculty scores in all sub-categories and different from students in all sub-categories except Coordination, which was marginally significant. Further investigation shows that faculty and students consistently use both broadcast and interaction tools more frequently than staff. Faculty and students use Project Site tools for assessment more than staff, but the use of management tools (overall) remains higher among the staff. Differences between groups of users for the use of Project Sites for general management activities approached significance (p= .06). The effect sizes at the sub-category level were either small or none.

We explored pairwise comparisons at the tool level as well. While there were a surprising number of significant differences between staff/students and staff/faculty, most of those differences did not result in large effect sizes (see Table 2). The only medium effect sizes we found were between staff and student mean rank scores for the Announcements tool and the Chat tool.

We also collected some general usage statistics from Project Sites to explore whether there were differences between the comparison groups for the number of users on a site, the number of events on a site, and the number of times a site is visited. The ANOVA shows significant differences in the number of site visits between user groups, as well as differences in the number of users on a site and the total number of events on a given site (see left side of Table 3).

Post hoc tests indicate that staff typically have fewer users on their sites than do either students or faculty. Effect sizes corroborate these findings, showing a large effect size between staff/students and a moderate effect between

Staff Tool Value Ratings		ANOVA					Value Ratings & Post Hoc Comparisons			
							Faculty/Staff		Students/Staff	
TOOL	Mean (*SD*)	*df*	N	F	*p*	η^2	Mean (*SD*)	*p*	Mean (*SD*)	*p*
Resources	4.25 (0.78)	2	2585	54.30	≤ .001	.040	4.05 (1.70)	≤ .001	3.84 (1.65)	≤ .001
Announcements	3.77 (0.95)	2	2744	366.98	≤ .001	.211	4.46 (1.11)	≤ .001	4.57 (0.74)	≤ .001
Syllabus	3.67 (1.02)	2	2397	187.30	≤ .001	.135	3.98 (1.53)	≤ .001	4.31 (1.06)	≤ .001
Schedule	3.63 (1.02)	2	2010	16.03	≤ .001	.016	2.35 (2.09)	≤ .001	2.84 (1.94)	≤ .001
Assignments	3.57 (1.03)	2	2462	298.92	≤ .001	.195	3.70 (1.82)	≤ .001	4.45 (0.89)	≤ .001
Messages	3.57 (0.95)	2	2034	49.63	≤ .001	.047	2.34 (1.56)	≤ .001	3.01 (1.90)	≤ .001
Wiki	3.30 (0.94)	2	1399	1.65	NS	----	1.11 (1.70)	NS	1.64 (1.86)	NS
Forum	3.20 (0.97)	2	1488	0.86	NS	----	1.10 (1.68)	NS	1.82 (1.85)	NS
Discussion	3.20 (0.93)	2	1999	12.01	≤ .001	.012	1.85 (1.91)	NS	2.86 (1.71)	≤ .001
Polls	3.18 (0.87)	2	1367	5.20	≤ .01	≤.01	1.16 (1.72)	≤ .01	1.81 (1.83)	NS
Podcast	3.12 (0.92)	--	----	----	----	----	----	----	----	----
News	3.01 (0.89)	2	1291	8.05	≤ .001	.012	1.14 (1.67)	≤ .05	1.58 (1.77)	≤ .001
Chat	2.90 (0.97)	2	1864	30.89	≤ .001	.032	1.68 (1.83)	≤ .001	2.66 (1.71)	≤ .001

Table 4. Post hoc analyses of system value ratings for supporting general purposes and specific activities

Staff Value Ratings		ANOVA					Value Ratings & Post Hoc Comparisons			
							Faculty/Staff		Student/Staff	
General Purpose	**Mean (*SD*)**	*df*	*N*	*F*	*p*	η^2	**Mean (*SD*)**	*p*	**Mean (*SD*)**	*p*
Administration	3.85 (0.86)	2	2131	47.50	<.001	.042	4.00 (1.00)	< .001	3.43 (1.09)	< .05
Training	3.60 (0.91)	2	1634	11.13	<.001	.013	3.53 (1.14)	N.S.	3.32 (1.07)	< .001
Faculty-led research	3.53 (0.88)	2	1710	9.12	<.001	.010	3.55 (1.13)	N.S.	3.30 (1.09)	< .001
Managing events	3.50 (0.91)	2	1709	7.60	<.001	.008	3.59 (1.08)	N.S.	3.32 (1.07)	< .005
Non-academic use	3.48 (0.83)	2	1725	3.11	<.050	<.01	3.39 (1.11)	N.S.	3.57 (1.09)	N.S.
Personal use	3.19 (0.98)	2	1764	22.26	<.001	.027	3.54 (1.20)	< .001	3.52 (1.09)	< .001
Non-credit learning*	2.37 (1.80)	----	----	----	----	----	----	----	----	----
Specific Activity	**Mean (*SD*)**	*df*	*N*	*F*	*p*	η^2	**Mean (*SD*)**	*p*	**Mean (*SD*)**	*p*
Single Access Point	4.30 (0.69)	2	2791	18.55	<.001	.013	4.51 (0.78)	< .001	4.31 (0.87)	N.S.
Distance Work	3.93 (0.82)	2	1880	33.80	<.001	.035	3.53 (1.20)	< .001	3.55 (1.09)	< .001
Creating Groups*	3.90 (0.81)	----	----	----	----	----	----	----	----	----
Communication	3.84 (0.96)	2	2839	193.21	<.001	.120	4.57 (0.77)	< .001	4.42 (0.74)	< .001
Post Audio/Video	3.78 (0.90)	2	1983	8.71	<.001	<.01	3.69 (1.19)	N.S.	3.93 (1.01)	< .01
Edit Group Materials	3.67 (0.98)	----	----	----	----	----	----	----	----	----
Tracking Progress	3.53 (0.94)	2	1831	7.70	<.001	<.01	3.41 (1.17)	N.S.	3.31 (1.12)	< .001
Scheduling	3.21 (1.09)	2	2136	36.98	<.001	.033	3.60 (1.14)	< .001	3.66 (1.12)	< .001

Table 5. ANOVA and post hoc analyses for value ratings for supporting general purposes and specific activities

staff/faculty. Controlling for the number of site participants, students have more events on their sites and visit their sites more frequently than staff. There was a moderate effect for being a student on the number of visits, whereas the number of events was near the criteria for a weak effect. Staff have more events on their sites and visit their sites more frequently than faculty, but the effect sizes are small for both variables.

Survey Results

We analyzed the survey data collected from staff members to understand what they believe is valuable about the system, as well as the value of Project Sites for different general and specific purposes. Staff respondents rated the value of 14 of 17 tools in the toolkit (3 tools, Gradebook, Modules, and iTunesU, were excluded because previous surveys had established that there were very low-use tools and thus value ratings were not informative). Faculty and students did not rate one of the tools, Podcast, for which we present only the staff scores.

Tool ratings (shown in Table 4) indicate that staff gave the highest value ratings to Resources, whereas both faculty and students rated the Syllabus tool highest. Although neither faculty nor students rated Resources as the most valuable tool, it was the second most valuable tool for faculty and the fourth most valuable tool for students. Staff rated the Announcements tool and Syllabus tool as the top three most valuable tools. Similarly, faculty's three highest ratings were for the same tools, though in different ordering. Students, on the other hand, rated Announcements highest, followed by Syllabus and Assignments (course-related tools), respectively. There were statistically significant differences between staff and the other two user groups in value ratings for all tools except for the Wiki and Forum tools. Except for Polls, the effect sizes were small or higher.[2]

[2] **η^2 =.01 (small), .059 (medium), .138 (large)**

We asked our survey respondents to rate the value of Project Sites for accomplishing a number of purposes for computer support for collaboration and activities that most staff perform (see Table 5). We omit ANOVA results where staff responded to a prompt that did not appear on the faculty or student instrument. Staff rated the system most valuable for administrative purposes, similar to faculty. Students, on the other hand, valued the system more for non-academic activities. Staff rated the system more valuable for supporting central access to materials (sharing and retrieval), whereas faculty and students rated this use second most valuable, instead valuing the system more for communication activities. Value ratings were statistically significant for all comparisons between user groups for systems ability to support the listed general purposes and the activities. All of the effect sizes were above small except for in three instances.

DISCUSSION

Our first research question addressed how a group of unintended users—university staff—use Project Sites, and how their use compared to that of two intended user groups—faculty and students. The log data points to a number of differences. It was evident that most of the system activity for all groups could be attributed to the tools for access and management of content. This is not surprising for faculty and students given prior work that has also shown predominant use of LMSs for content management [14]. That staff also value this functionality suggests that university staff discovered the system's capacity to support centrally located information/content creation and management, a need that they share with their counterparts albeit in a different context of use.

We expected staff to use the communication tools as often, if not more, than faculty and students since communication is a central issue for group work. However, this was not the case. In comparison to the other two user groups, staff use of communication tools was lower. Staff members' higher use of the system for management-related activities reflects the kinds of work and practices these users engage in on a daily basis.

Overall, these results suggest that most of the activity on Project Sites, regardless of user type, is for document/information storage and retrieval. While we can not say with certainty this type of use is expected or unexpected (according to our UTAM matrix), we at least have evidence that users of all types look similar enough in terms of their overall usage that there is a good chance that their use aligns with the primary 'expected' use. Where the anticipated and unanticipated groups differ is in the way that staff differ from other users of the system. Staff use the system more for management tasks than for communication, whereas the reverse is true for faculty and students.

One limitation of this log analysis is the discrepancy between the high number of significant results and the relatively small effect sizes, likely a result of our large sample size. However, the findings do help point to ways in which the needs of the unanticipated users might differ from those of the anticipated users. Discovering these differences can lead to design recommendations for future system releases. For example, these findings suggest that further study of staff users would be useful, particularly looking at their use of content management/production tools. These tools are perhaps not as valuable from a student perspective, but may be of high value if staff needs are going to be considered in subsequent design decisions. Exploring how the system does and doesn't support management tasks performed by university staff can also lead to future design changes that may benefit all system users.

Beyond actual differences in use, the analyses of value ratings suggest that there are indeed some fundamental differences between the ways that the comparison groups value different aspects of the system. These differences make sense when one considers the different kinds of work that staff, faculty, and students are engaged in. The survey data supported the log data's depiction of the importance of content tools for all users, with relatively high ratings across the board for accessing materials, and high ratings for the Resources tool. Staff and faculty valued the system's applicability to administrative purposes, whereas students valued it more for non-academic purposes, with the latter having given administrative purposes the third highest ratings.

Staff valued the system's ability to support the activities related to the centralized storage and retrieval of documents, both being integral parts of administrative work. Faculty and students both gave the highest value ratings to communication activities. The importance of communication tools for faculty and students is mirrored by high use of Announcements, Chat, and Messages tools (compared to staff in the log analysis), the first being rated highly and the latter two being rated much lower. Whereas effect sizes for the log data were often small to none, the effect sizes for the survey were much stronger, with many medium or strong effect sizes regardless of whether we were looking at the value of tools or the value of the system for a certain purpose or its ability to support a certain activity.

One interesting observation from the survey data is that staff members generally rated the system tools more favorably than faculty and students, as exemplified by the range of mean value ratings and by the lowest given ratings for each group. Yet, value ratings had similar ranges when rating the value for purpose and types activities the system supports. A lingering question is whether staff would be more critical of Project Site's tools if they were designed for their use and/or if Project Sites were as central to their work as it is in the coursework environment.

Though we did not have specific hypotheses concerning expectations that minimally used tools would be unpopular, we found the extent to which infrequently used tools (e.g. Schedule, Announcements, and Assignments) were rated highly by staff to be interesting. This may be because some tools are very useful, but leave only small traces. For example, sending an announcement to all members of a site is a convenient feature that creates only one event (a mass e-mail)—even if 20 site members read it and discuss it offline. Other tools, like the Syllabus tool, are used only once by each site owner and users may create only one action to view and copy the contents even when the information is referenced multiple times.

In general, the survey findings suggest that staff are engaging in many of the same activities as students and faculty although their value ratings might suggest different intentions in visiting the toolkit, which has important design implications. Specifically, we suggest that these differences suggest ways that the system might be improved, showing where designers and implementers might employ task analysis, needs assessments, iterative design, and other design methods that get to the core of what staff users are actually doing, thereby being better able to refine collaborative systems. Also, because these particular research questions were motivated by differences between staff and faculty/students, this analysis did not look at differences within the staff community. Analyses that look at differences between staff show that there are even differences between the way staff value the system based on their job types and their home departmental units.

The finding that many staff users came from academic departments was not surprising, since we could expect that these staff would have access to faculty and students who might expose them to Project Sites. However, we did not expect to see avid Project Site users among the staff working in the university health system because these staff members are fairly removed (organizationally and geographically) from classroom teaching and learning. These users, although numerous relative to the overall staff users of Project Sites, actually only comprise a small percentage of total health services staff. Their use of the system poses further questions both in terms of how they interpret the system's use, their needs, and how future redesign might address health workers and administrators.

Referring back to our larger research question and the matrix (UTAM), it is evident that more work is needed in order to move ahead in placing staff users within the matrix. While the current studies can expose value judgments and look at comparative use in a very general sense, it doesn't allow us to truly understand fine-grain differences between staff and the comparison groups. For example, the current studies do not account for the types of content or analysis of communication exchanges. A more detailed analysis of site names and content might begin to unravel the ways in which groups' sites might differ. There are also general questions that the analyses we present here do not address such as motivations, causes, and sociological context surrounding use. Survey items that we don't discuss in this paper address some of this, but qualitative work is ultimately needed to better understand these contributing factors to unintended use.

We are currently conducting a large-scale interview study with staff members to better understand their roles within the university and to explore how they describe their use of Project Sites and the role they play within their greater information ecology [18] of colleagues, activities, and work tools. Early results have mirrored the finding that content tools are important as a central location for most work for a number of rich tasks that include forming committees. These early results also indicate that other Project Site tools, such as chat and announcements, are redundant with those that appear in other workplace collaboration systems in use (and often in more central and/or usable forms). Lastly, there is evidence building that points to a number of key people and groups that play a large role in the way Project Sites are used. One example of this is a push by the university IT office to migrate email to Google email services, which has already begun to affect the ways that users will choose to use or not use communication features in Project Sites.

CONCLUSION

In this paper we highlighted a gap in the CSCW work addressing the concept of appropriation of collaborative technologies. While the field has been investigating the evolution of technology in use, it has done so consistently with users who are in the anticipated (target) user group. Instead we propose that the concept of interpretive flexibility is as valuable for designing for unanticipated users *and* unexpected uses. The matrix we provide here highlights that interpretive flexibility is not just about how the system is interpreted, but also about who is doing the interpretation. By using these characterizations of users and use, we can better understand cases of technology appropriation and help the design process such that is sensitive to the kinds of uses and users that may adopt these systems.

It was clear that we had unanticipated users for the LMS, but lack knowledge of how their use compared to the expected user groups and if they were using it in unexpected ways. We created UTAM to frame our research questions for this research agenda concerning unanticipated users. The work presented here only presents part of the work that has been completed and it suggests that, on the surface, staff activity on the system looks like expected activities for students and faculty, though a look into their values suggests different foundational values. Even in light of superficially similar usage, the UTAM framework allows us to address how to study users through a different lens and design collaboration systems to better support users.

While considering Robinson's design requirements [31] and their application to our current study, it seemed clear that even though Robinson admitted that "specific actors are not determinable" (p. 190), this indeterminacy did not result in recommendations that could be applied to unanticipated users. In addition to the requirements of predictability, peripheral awareness, implicit communication, double-level language, and overview, we add that flexibility of use should be a requirement when for designing for appropriation (see also Dix [5]) and that flexibility of audience should be added as a requirement that would provide unanticipated users with access to tools that they may be able to appropriate.

Though it is quite easy for implementation teams to provide access to similar Project Site set-up tools to students and staff at their respective universities, few of them leverage the open-source Sakai-based LMSs like CTools to provide this added functionality. Instead, implementers tend to allow only faculty and their assistants to set up shared worksites specifically for teaching and learning [13]. In this case study, because the unanticipated users, staff at the University of Michigan, had to access the Project Sites toolkit, achieving 'flexibility of audience' was merely accidental. However, designers and implementers of collaborative systems may intentionally create this kind of flexibility. For example, flexibility of audience could have been achieved in this context if the designers had asked themselves who else is part of a campus community and made a conscious effort to not only leave the opportunity open for appropriation, but to create such an opportunity to make the detection of unanticipated users and their ways of using the technology easier. Though we focus on an academic setting, our recommendations generalize to commercial and industry settings. For example, it might be the case that a groupware system is targeted to management and administration, but gets appropriated by finance groups.

We have argued that studying unanticipated users is important because they may lead designers and implementers to explore opportunities that may be missed based on their conceptions of who the users are and what are the appropriate use of the system. While we may not always be able to identify these kinds of users a priori, knowing how to involve them in the iterative design process is crucial. These unanticipated user populations also cause designers to rethink and expand their notions of who the users are, what the original design is and how it can grow and evolve throughout its lifespan.

ACKNOWLEDGEMENTS
We would like to thank Steve Lonn and the USE Lab at the University of Michigan.

REFERENCES
1. Abbate, J. (1999). *Inventing the Internet.* MIT Press; Cambridge.
2. Anderson, C. (2004) "The Long Tail." *Wired*, October 2004.
3. Andriessen, J.H.E., Hettinga, M., & Wulf, V. (2003). Introduction to Special Issue on evolving use of groupware. *Computer Supported Cooperative Work*, 12, 367-380.
4. DeSanctis, G. & Poole, M.S. (1994). Capturing the Complexity in advanced technology use: Adaptive structuration theory. *Organization Science*, 5(2), 121-147.
5. Dix, A. (2007). Designing for appropriation. *Proceeding of the British HCI Group Annual Conference on People and Computers*, 2, 27-30.
6. Dourish, P. (2003). The Appropriation of Interactive Technologies. Computer Supported Cooperative Work, 12 (4), 465-490.
7. Garrison, D. R. & Kanuka, H. (2004). "Blended learning: Uncovering its transformative potential in higher education". *The Internet and Higher Education, 7* (2), 95–105.
8. Holm, S. (1979). A simple sequential rejective multiple test procedure. *Scandinavian Journal of Statistics* 6, 65-70.
9. Huysman, M., Steinfield, C., Jang, C., David, C., Huis in 't Veld, M., Poot, J., &Mulder, I. (2003). Virtual Teams and the Appropriation of Communication Technology: Exploring the Concept of Media Stickiness. *Computer Supported Cooperative Work*, 12 (4), 411-436.
10. Ito, M. (2005). Mobile Phones, Japanese Youth, and the Re-Placement of Social Contact, in R. Ling and P. Pederson, (eds.) *Mobile Communications: Re-Negotiation of the Social Sphere*, Springer-Verlag: London, 131-148.
11. Leonard-Barton, D. (1988). Implementation as mutual adaptation of technology and organization. Res. Policy 17(5) 251–267.
12. Leonardi, P.M. & Barley, S.R. (2010). What's Under Construction Here? Social Action, Materiality, and Power in Constructivist Studies of Technology and Organizing. *The Academy of Management Annals*, 4(1), 1-51.
13. Lonn, S. & Teasley, S. D., Conley, S., Leveque, J., Pavolka, R. (2010, June). *Quoth the User: The Multi-Institutional Survey Initiative.* Panel presentation at the Annual Sakai Conference, Denver, CO.
14. Lonn, S & Teasley, S.D. (2009). Saving time or innovating practice: Investigating perceptions and uses of Learning Management Systems. *Computers and Education*, 53, 686-694.
15. Majchrzak, A., Rice, R.E., Malhotra, A., & King, N. (2000). Technology Adaptation: The Case of a Computer-Supported Inter-Organizational Virtual Team. *MIS Quarterly*, 24 (4), 569-600.
16. Nardi, B. & Miller, J. (1990). An Ethnographic Study of Distributed Problem Solving in Spreadsheet Development. *CSCW Proceedings 90*, 197-208.

17. Nardi, B.A. & Miller, J.R. (1991). Twinkling lights and nested loops: distributed problem solving and spreadsheet development. *International Journal of Man-Machine Studies*, 34, 161-184.

18. Nardi, B. & O'Day, V. (1999). Information Ecology: Using Technology with Heart. Cambridge: MIT Press.

19. O'Day, V.L. Information Ecologies (2000). *The Serials Librarian*, 38(1/2), 31-40.

20. Orlikowski, W.J. (1992a). Learning from Notes: Organizational issues in groupware implementation. *CSCW Proceedings*.

21. Orlikowski, W.J. (1993). CASE Tools as organizational change: Investigating incremental and radical changes in systems development. *MIS Quarterly*, 309-340.

22. Orlikowski, W.J. (1996a). Evolving with Notes: Organizational change around groupwaretechnology. In C. Ciborra (ed.) *Groupware & Teamwor*. Chichester: Wiley, 23-60.

23. Orlikowski, W.J. (1996b). Improvising organizational transformation over time: A situated change perspective. *Information Systems Research*, 7, 63-92.

24. Orlikowski, W.J. (2000). Using Technology and constituting structures: A practice lens for studying technology in organizations. *Organization Science*, 11(4), 404-428.

25. Pekkola, S. (2003). Designed for unanticipated use: Common artefacts as design principle for CSCW Applications. *GROUP 2003 Proceedings*, 359-368.

26. Pinch, T.J. & Bijker, W.E. (1984). The Social Construction of Facts and Artefacts: or how the sociology of science and the sociology of technology might benefit each other. *Social Studies of Science*, 14, 399-441.

27. Pipek, V. & Wulf, V. (1999). A Groupware's Life. *ECSCW Proceedings*, 199-219.

28. Poole, M.S. & DeSanctis, G. (1990). Understanding the use of group decision support systems: The theory of adaptive structuration. In Fulk, J. & Steinfeld, C. (eds), *Organizations and communication technology*, 173-193, Newbury Park, CA: Sage.

29. Poole, M.S. & DeSanctis, G. (1992). Microlevel Structuration in computer-supported group decision making. *Human Communication Research*, 19(1), 5-49.

30. Rice, R.E. & Rogers, E.M. (1980). Reinvention in the innovation Process. *Science Communication*, 1 (4), 499-514.

31. Robinson, M (1993). Design for unanticipated use….. *Proceedings of ECSCW 1993, 187-202.*

32. Rogers, E.M. (2003). Diffusion of Innovations (5 ed). New York: Free Press.

33. Rosner, D & Bean, J (2009). Learning from IKEA Hacking: "I'm not One to Decoupage a Tabletop and Call it a Day". CHI Proceedings 2009, 419-422.

34. Smith, S. & Caruso, J.B. (2010). The ECAR Study of undergraduate students and information technology. Boulder: EDUCAUSE Center for Applied Research.

35. Star SL & Griesemer JR (1989). "Institutional Ecology, 'Translations' and Boundary Objects: Amateurs and Professionals in Berkeley's Museum of Vertebrate Zoology, 1907-39". *Social Studies of Science*, 19(4), 387–420.

36. Torpel, B., Pipek, V., & Rittenbruch, M. (2003). Creating Hetergeneity – Evolving use of groupware in a network of freelancers. *Computer Supported Cooperative Work*, 12, 381-409.

37. Trigg, R.H. and Bodker, S. (1994). From implementation to design: tailoring and the emergence of systematization in CSCW. Proceedings of CSCW 94, 45-54.

38. Wenger, Etienne (1998). Communities of Practice: Learning, Meaning, and Identity. Cambridge: Cambridge University Press.

The Work of Developing Cyberinfrastructure Middleware Projects

Matthew J. Bietz
University of California, Irvine
Department of Informatics
Irvine, CA 92697-3440
mbietz@uci.edu

Drew Paine
University of Washington
Department of Human Centered Design & Engineering
Seattle, WA 98195
pained@uw.edu

Charlotte P. Lee
University of Washington
Department of Human Centered Design & Engineering
Seattle, WA 98195
cplee@uw.edu

ABSTRACT

Middleware software, which provides an abstraction layer between low-level computational services and domain-specific applications, is a key component of cyberinfrastructure. This paper presents a qualitative study of how cyberinfrastructure middleware development is accomplished in two supercomputing centers. Our investigation highlights key development phases in the lives of middleware projects. Middleware development is typically undertaken as part of collaborations between technologists and domain scientists, and middleware developers must balance the pressure to meet specific scientific needs and the desire to explore their own R&D agendas. We explore how developers work to sustain an ongoing development trajectory by aligning their own work with particular domain science projects and funding streams. However, we find that the key transition from being a component in a domain-specific project to a stand-alone system that is useful across domains is particularly challenging for middleware development. We provide organizational and national policy implications for how to better support this transition.

Author Keywords

Cyberinfrastructure; middleware; sustaining development; qualitative methods.

ACM Classification Keywords

H.5.3 [Information Interfaces and Presentation]: Group and Organization Interfaces - Computer-supported cooperative work.

INTRODUCTION

The large-scale, advanced computational infrastructures known by terms such as collaboratories, cyberinfrastructures (CI), or e-Science, have been sites of study for CSCW for well over a decade [7,11,20]. In this paper we explore the development of a key element of cyberinfrastructure that has remained understudied: middleware. Middleware are software systems that act as an abstraction layer between low-level computational services and domain-specific applications. Understanding how to support the development of CI requires also understanding how middleware development is sustained over time.

Cyberinfrastructures are created to support collaboration in science and other academic disciplines. However the creation of cyberinfrastructure is also a collaborative enterprise, bringing together researchers in various academic domains with computer scientists and professional development teams. Cyberinfrastructures can be seen as large-scale, collaborative enterprises distributed over space and time, in other words, virtual organizations [8]. In this paper we examine the strategies developers undertake in order to enact collaborative cyberinfrastructures. Understanding the processes that shape the development of large-scale information infrastructures continues to be an important concern for CSCW [15].

Creating sustainable CI remains an important challenge [19]. Given the significant investment required to build cyberinfrastructures, they are expected to operate over decade-long (if not longer) time scales. Additionally, there are concerns about long-term preservation of the scientific record [12]. Here, however, we draw on an understanding of sustainability as "how to maintain the persistent human and technological arrangements that comprise cyberinfrastructure" [3]. We are primarily concerned with the ongoing work of sustainability; that is, the ways in which developers sustain (or sometimes don't) a development trajectory through significant social and technical disruptions and breakdowns. In this qualitative, interview-based study of software engineers at two supercomputing centers we ask: *how do developers sustain middleware projects in the context of cyberinfrastructure development?*

The sites for this study are two supercomputing centers in the United States. Formed in the mid-1980s to provide high-performance computing services to the nation's scientists, these organizations are central players in the development of cyberinfrastructure. Located at large research universities, these organizations bring together a wide range of domain stakeholders and systems developers to produce CI projects ranging from domain-specific science gateways & workflow systems down to the large-scale computing systems upon which computational scientific research relies.

The remainder of this paper is structured as follows: to position our work we first introduce cyberinfrastructure development, including previous work in CSCW, along with studies of the development of middleware. We then describe our research sites and methods before presenting our findings through a narrative that tells the story of the development of one successful middleware, along with analysis, commentary, and other examples from our data. We discuss three key aspects of CI middleware development and the work that supports this process. Finally, we reflect on the challenges of sustaining the development of CI middleware.

LITERATURE REVIEW

In our literature review we provide an introduction to the concept of cyberinfrastructure, define middleware and its role in cyberinfrastructure, and discuss the theoretical lens we use to examine our data on cyberinfrastructure middleware development.

Cyberinfrastructure Development

Cyberinfrastructure refers to a class of information and computation infrastructures in support of scientific and knowledge work. The term cyberinfrastructure was coined by a 2003 NSF Blue-Ribbon panel that examined the future of scientific computing [2]. Concepts like cyberinfrastructure, e-Science, and collaboratories are fundamentally concerned with distributed collaborative science which grows out of a trend in scientific research toward larger, collaborative projects studying large-scale phenomena through shared data sets [1,9]. Cyberinfrastructure refers to the infrastructural facilities needed to support this kind of science, and is based on information technology resources including high-performance computing and high-speed networking. Cyberinfrastructure relies not only on advanced technologies, but also on "human infrastructure," the rich and extensive arrangements of people, organizations, and communities that support the CI [14].

The cyberinfrastructure paradigm makes explicit comparisons between these new information infrastructures and traditional infrastructures such as roads and electricity distribution systems. This way of thinking focuses on the interconnectedness of the information systems more than on the individual software projects of which they are partially composed. Star & Ruhleder [24] emphasize that infrastructures are characterized by the relationships among the infrastructural components, they are embedded inside of other systems and infrastructures, and they are learned as part of membership in a community. Infrastructures form when separate components are consolidated into linked "networks" or "webs" of systems [6]. Infrastructure works because it structures the relationships among various entities in specific ways. Therefore to understand the development of cyberinfrastructures it is important to study the relationships between the various stakeholders of CI projects.

Lee et al. [14] posit the notion of the "human infrastructure" of cyberinfrastructure as a way to understand the myriad relationships that affect the work of building CI. Human infrastructure is the collaborative partnerships of researchers, software developers, managers, and other stakeholders who develop and maintain cyberinfrastructure. The notion of human infrastructure takes a perspective beyond that of teams to include organizational structures and personal networks as well. Using the notion of human infrastructure, the fluctuations in the relationships which support cyberinfrastructure development may be made visible and recognizable as multimorphous and constantly changing.

In the same vein, Bietz et. al [4] define the concept of synergizing to highlight the work of creating infrastructural relationships among individuals, technologies, and institutions. In this context, synergizing is the work necessary to enact productive infrastructural relationships. Synergy refers to the bringing together of two or more already existing entities to produce an effect greater than any of the single entities could produce alone. The overall lens of synergizing reveals that a major part of the work of developing cyberinfrastructure is concerned with building and managing the connections among people, technologies, and organizations. In other words, cyberinfrastructure development is inherently collaborative work. It is a sociotechnical process that relies upon the changing, multi-faceted relationships of software developers, domain-scientists, funding bodies, and institutions. Studying middleware development reveals the processes by which human infrastructure enables and supports cyberinfrastructure.

Middleware

Given this relational view of infrastructure, middleware provides a rich site for understanding cyberinfrastructure development. Middleware systems are a type of software that support distributed information systems. Middleware systems provide a common platform upon which domain-specific applications may be built. Fundamentally, middleware enables communication between disparate systems. Middleware, sometimes referred to as "glue software," are systems that "mediate communication and interaction between heterogeneous networked technologies" and provide "a kind of lingua franca that enables inscriptionally diverse systems to interact" [18]. In CI, middleware systems sit between lower-level systems like databases or authorization services and the applications designed for domain-specific user groups.

The term middleware dates to the original 1968 NATO conference report defining Software Engineering as a field [17]. Here d'Agapeyeff presented an inverted pyramid structure of software systems, with middleware placed between application programs and service routines. d'Agapeyeff stated that middleware is necessary because "no matter how good the manufacturer's software for items like file handling it is just not suitable; it's either inefficient or inappropriate" [17] (p.14). As software systems have grown in scale and complexity, middleware have maintained their role as an integral part of many systems that support a multitude of hardware platforms at low-level and domain-specific applications at the high-level.

Newman [18], in a study of corporate software development, finds that middleware development is subject to a number of organizational and business complexities. The development that we study takes place in an academic space where many of the organizational constraints differ, but many of Newman's insights apply. In particular, Newman finds that middleware development is particularly important because it "involves choices about standardization of new and important parts of the technical infrastructure that links parts of highly distributed enterprises together." Middleware not only allows technologies to interact; it also synergistically links people and organizations within collaborative enterprises.

Academic software development, at least in the contexts we studied, has key differences to corporate development. For example, Newman discusses how developers operate within a relatively hierarchical arrangement, where projects are subject to the whims of high-level managers and concerns of profitability and efficiency. In contrast, the middleware project teams we observed were relatively small and autonomous. Rather than being told what to work on, they depended on making successful proposals to grant agencies or other sources of funding, and metrics of success had more to do with providing novel solutions (or enabling transformative science) than profit. Given the importance of cyberinfrastructure in many areas of science, and the key role of middleware in enabling that cyberinfrastructure, understanding how development proceeds in this area will have important implications for scientific policy makers, developers, and other stakeholders.

We next introduce the research sites and methods of our study before presenting our findings on the middleware development process.

RESEARCH SITES & METHODS

Research that studies cyberinfrastructure development typically does so by studying particular domain-specific research and development projects. Our study is distinct from these approaches as we focus on how cyberinfrastructure middleware development crosses and transcends cyberinfrastructure domain project collaborations. We investigated projects and the groups developing them at two of the United States' most established supercomputing organizations, the National Center for Supercomputing Applications (NCSA) at the University of Illinois Urbana-Champaign and the San Diego Supercomputer Center (SDSC) at the University of California, San Diego.

Each center was founded in the mid-1980s when the US National Science Foundation established five national supercomputing centers to provide the nation's scientists with access to high-performance computing resources [5]. While originally funded through large facilities grants, today most development and research activities at these two centers are funded through project-level competitive grants. With their focus on scientific computing, the centers have been vital hubs for the development of cyberinfrastructure. Studying the middleware development activities at these centers affords the opportunity to discover commonalities between the two institutions that may be common to computing organizations throughout the United States, and around the world. Additionally the knowledge gained from studying the work to build these middleware projects may be transferable to researchers developing systems at smaller scales and in different research contexts so as to enhance and support their development activities.

Both SDSC and NCSA work with multiple scientific communities coming from various academic disciplines. Cyberinfrastructure developers at NCSA and SDSC are more often than not involved with more than one project at a given point in time. These projects range in size from one or two people up to the hundreds of people who are involved in projects like TeraGrid (www.teragrid.org) and its successor XSEDE (www.xsede.org). In addition to varying in size, projects also vary in the distribution of members, from entirely localized at a single center to those with members distributed around the United States and elsewhere in the world.

We conducted a qualitative, interview-based study with two rounds of semi-structured interviews. The first round of interviews was designed to elicit an understanding of the roles of each interviewee along with the projects that they work on and how CI development takes place in the organization that they work in. The second round was designed to provide depth to our understanding of the design and development practices of an individual's CI projects. The first round of interviews took place in the Spring and Summer of 2009 and the second in the Summer of 2011 after multiple rounds of data analysis were completed. We interviewed 20 participants at NCSA and 12 participants at SDSC during the first round of data collection, for a total of 32 participants. The second round of interviews included 8 participants at NCSA alone based upon access to our research sites. Of the 20 participants in the first round at NCSA and the 8 in the second round, three were interviewed both times providing elaboration and triangulation of our initial interviews.

The 37 individual participants in this study included upper-level management and directors (10 participants), software engineers and project developers (15 participants), and domain scientists and humanities scholars (12 participants) who work with NCSA or SDSC on cyberinfrastructure development. The participants in our study work on software rather than hardware development. We attempted to obtain a breadth of roles in the cyberinfrastructure development process who could convey perspectives from different positions in the organization. While our sampling focused on interviewing a breadth of the organization the interviews themselves resulted in discussion of several common projects. This provides us with multiple perspectives on projects that cut across the individuals involved in the development process. Many of the participants in our study act as principal investigators on funded projects enabling us to obtain data regarding this important aspect of project work. The first round of interviews were semi-structured, typically scheduled for an hour, and lasted between 15 and 86 minutes depending on participant availability and how the discussion developed (median: 56 min). Those conducted in the second round were again semi-structured and scheduled for an hour and lasted between 20 and 95 minutes (median: 53 min). Participants and projects have been assigned pseudonyms to ensure privacy.

The interviews were semi-structured to ensure consistency across interviews and also to allow for deeper questioning to draw out new insights regarding the projects each participant works on. All interviews were recorded and professionally transcribed for analysis. The second round of interviews was designed to elicit further depth as to the processes and strategies participants use when designing cyberinfrastructure systems. Data were analyzed using a grounded-theory approach. We began with closed coding of the initial interviews based on the semi-structured protocol, whereupon a codebook was iteratively developed and refined based on discussions within the research team. A series of memos were generated to express the thematic relationships the team found and to support further open coding of the data. This analysis process saw the emergence of themes surrounding the building of middleware systems which informed our semi-structured protocol for the second round of interviews.

FINDINGS: MIDDLEWARE Z AND OTHER MIDDLEWARE PROJECTS

In this section, we detail the development of a particular system, Middleware Z (a pseudonym) and other middleware projects, in order to illustrate the work of attempting to sustainably develop middleware for cyberinfrastructure. Based on our analysis of multiple middleware projects at both supercomputing centers, we believe Middleware Z followed a typical development trajectory. We heard about Middleware Z from several different interview participants, allowing us to construct a narrative about this project that covers its entire lifetime. The stages of development that we highlight create a common trajectory across the projects we studied. Of course, not every detail is shared by every project, and the stages and transitions may occur along different time scales. But combining the story of Middleware Z with details from other projects at NCSA and SDSC provides a rich set of examples that both gives a sense of the lifecycle of a middleware project and illuminates our analysis of cross-cutting themes. This narrative illustrates the complexities and challenges inherent in sustaining a middleware development project, one of the key activities participants in our study undertake.

Middleware Z is designed to provide seamless access to multiple database platforms for domain specific applications. Scientists often need to access multiple databases which each might have their own query language and constructs. Middleware Z provides an abstraction layer between the application and the databases that makes it easier to search across multiple databases and aggregate the results. Middleware Z has been developed over approximately the last decade, starting from the initial system conception to the second full version that is in use as part of multiple projects today. The developers of Middleware Z are part of a group that eventually became known as the Cyberinfrastructure Middleware and Applications (CIMA, a pseudonym) group. The software engineers and project managers in CIMA develop tools that integrate distributed computing resources and data sources for scientific purposes in various domains. The CIMA group, like the other groups at the centers in our study, must work with stakeholders in multiple scientific domains to write grants and obtain funding to develop systems. Beyond developing applications for domain projects the CIMA group works to develop middleware that they can use as a common base for any specific domain application they may end up developing. This middleware supports the group's domain applications by providing uniform access to various computational, data storage, and user management services, or by acting as a common platform for end-user portals. The CIMA group builds collaborations with stakeholders in each domain to obtain funding that is tied to that specific domain's research needs. This funding model typically only supports middleware development to the extent that it serves a particular domain application.

The narrative we construct below detailing the development of Middleware Z over time is compiled from our interviews with several participants, including the lead developer (John) and other members of his group. We use the narrative as a way to illuminate particular features of the story that are representative of middleware development in CI centers. In telling the story, **we use typographic distinctions, telling the Middleware Z story in italics and providing analysis, commentary, and other examples from our data in plain text.**

In the next sections we present key moments in the middleware development process that illustrate the overarching trajectory of the work being conducted throughout a project's lifecycle. Specifically, we discuss:

- Conceiving of a Problem and Solution: The Seeds of a Project Idea
- Pursuing Development through Domain Science Collaborations
- Developing a Standalone Project
- Managing Breakdown and Change

These four sections highlight salient phases and transitions that comprise the work of cyberinfrastructure middleware development.

Conceiving of a Problem and Solution: The Seeds of a Project Idea

Like infrastructures themselves, middleware as concepts and functioning systems tend to emerge gradually. They do not appear as fully-formed or obvious solutions to an immediate problem. Instead, a project's birth can often be traced to the emergent awareness of an unmet need or problem and a rough idea for a potential solution. Developers conceive of project ideas when stakeholders in a CI project are not in agreement about either the need or the solution or both. Before the formal naming and development of Middleware Z, a developer identified a problem and unsuccessfully proposed forming a group to solve it.

In the late 1990s, John, a developer and project lead, was working on an information management system and was frustrated by that project's inability to easily handle multiple different types of data. John states that the client for this project wanted to "merge two extremely different kinds of information." At the time, tools to handle such data queries were not readily available. John was part of a group tasked to "buil[d] a whole set of tools for performing distributed searches, so that when you issued a search, it would fan the search out to a bunch of different sub-searches, and then the sub-searches could translate the query into what was necessary to pull it from the different sources and then present a unified view." But John believed that the group was "doing it [the development] wrong." He proposed to the client that the group be funded to develop a new version that would be more capable and stable in the long-term. At this stage however John only had an initial concept for this new type of system, and importantly, nothing was yet implemented. The client felt the "technology [wasn't] really ready to go" and the utility of such a system was not apparent. This led John to "shelve" the idea for the time being.

John's project idea, for what later becomes Middleware Z, grows out of a recognition of a particular, perhaps better, way of meeting an information management need that could be applied to the existing application. We heard similar stories at SDSC. For example, one participant told us about the genesis of a middleware project: "This is something that we started a while ago because we realized that what we were doing for our research group—in dealing with how to move data and how to get it in one spot for people to analyze it…—these things are all coupled in it" (Roland, domain scientist). The technologists working with Roland realized, as John did, that there was a better way to deal with their data problems, and began building a middleware system to link their various archives and tools.

The middleware Roland described could be developed within an already-funded project, but when John went to the client to fund his new concept, he was unable to convince the client of both the viability and the utility of the project. This simple, seemingly mundane example, of an unmet need and modest failed proposal, indicates a fairly common scenario in which the ideas for new projects are conceived. Developers may decide not to pursue the realization of the idea, but they may also decide to find ways to continue pursuing development.

Pursuing Development through Domain Science Collaborations

Cyberinfrastructure developers and researchers alike bemoan that projects tend to be funded on relatively short time scales (from one to five years). The pressure to consistently come up with attractive, fundable projects results in a climate where developers are required to work on multiple projects simultaneously or start new ones. This offers both challenges and opportunities.

New projects can open up opportunities for developers to pursue their own interests in a new context. The middleware developers in our study are able to pursue their development activities in the context of domain-specific projects as a strategy to support their development work. Pursuing development within the context of domain science projects enables relationships to be formed that may be synergistically relied upon to support the transition from a concept into a functioning system.

As the initial information management system project ended, John began working on a different cyberinfrastructure development project in civil engineering. Importantly he was placed in the role of data architect for the entire project. John states that many of the other project members were not as "data-oriented" as himself, and thus from his perspective did not fully grasp the complexity of the data handling task at hand. From his point of view the larger group did not understand the need to standardize data handling which is why the project "wasn't really getting very far." As development work progressed, both CIMA and the domain science stakeholders began to realize that the data issues were in fact more difficult than originally thought. Given this opening, John was able to push to pursue his idea within the context of this project. The larger project team became convinced that the data storage portion of the software system was one of the more difficult problems and needed more resources, and John was able to take his idea off the shelf and pursue it within the mandate of this new project.

In the case of Middleware Z, John was able to find a way to pursue his idea within an existing cyberinfrastructure project. More often, senior developers within the centers must actively search for collaborations with domain scientists that can support their work. In order to pursue their own R&D agendas, the computer scientists in the supercomputing centers typically must find domain-specific application development projects with which to collaborate. Developers must both align with the current to near-future needs of the funding source and ensure that they can continue their own middleware development activities. In order to identify potential collaborators, the developers worked to maintain an awareness of domain science activities both inside and outside their host universities. They would attend seminars and conferences, follow trends in various domains, and watch the funding calls from various agencies for potential opportunities. Sometimes finding a collaborator seems serendipitous, as in the case of Middleware Z. However, a developer on another middleware project described actively seeking opportunities for collaboration:

"The other thing that I do is I go out and I look for new opportunities to fund applications that can drive our development.... To make [Middleware Q] viable and exciting to researchers in the application domains, I have collaborations with computer science departments, graduate schools, the library information sciences, bioinformatics groups that are developing new data management analysis and visualization techniques that we feed into this development environment.... So I'm looking for applications that can help fund this development and some of this research." (Mick, project lead, NCSA)

These supercomputing centers can also be seen as centers of expertise for e-science projects, and the depth of that expertise also attracts collaborators.

"A lot of e-science projects have a community portal and data management infrastructure, data analysis infrastructure, visualization, whatever is needed. These are the ingredients to build it up. We have the expertise here for all these different pieces…. We have a lot of PIs here who could work with domain scientists…. We're also [providing] the middleware infrastructure with our research groups to put this together" (Irene, project lead, SDSC).

For Irene, collaborating with domain scientists is a crucial driver in her work: "On a given day we have to have the computer science researcher that you're thinking how you can make this better, but it's also thinking about working with scientists, understanding what they want, and then turning them into requirements for what they're doing." Maintaining the right pool of expertise to serve the scientists' requirements helps to build those necessary collaborations.

Despite the opportunities, the strategy of pursuing a longer-term research and development agenda within the context of multiple domain science projects also presents significant challenges. Regardless of the length of a project that is scoped out as part of a collaboration, middleware developers must grapple with a tension between building systems that can be used across multiple projects (the middleware goal) while also ensuring that their software meets the specific requirements of a particular funded project. As we saw, John had recognized that his idea could be adapted to solve some of the data problems for the civil engineers, and that their project could provide a venue for his middleware development agenda. However, aligning the agenda to the specific domain project was difficult, as John explained when discussing an early version of Middleware Z.

Development work proceeded on the first version of what would become Middleware Z. But responding to the needs of the domain scientists resulted in software that "had an absurd amount of complexity for what it did because I had all these requirements that were being dumped on me." Development took place in the context of a domain-specific CI project with requirements drawn from a large and diverse scientific community. While there may have been scientific reasons for the requirements, for John's technological interests, they were "completely arbitrary." Collaborating with scientists was a mixed blessing: while it provided funding and a context to test the ideas, supporting functionality that was very domain specific led to complexity in the design and less focus on pushing the development of transformative technologies. And even though the middleware approach was showing promise, the domain project's funding was time limited and it came to an end.

The scientific needs of the stakeholders in a domain science project can place many changing and varied demands upon the developers building middleware. However, in order to maintain their collaborations, software developers must be proactive about aligning the existing and potential functionality of their middleware with scientific requirements. Ronnie, a project lead working with an astronomy community, described how his group ensured that their development would satisfy the domain scientists: "so, first of all, we set up some science priorities and we do that every year and things that we're going to deliver to the user." However, prioritizing scientific agendas over development agendas can make it difficult to create broadly applicable middleware.

The short-term nature of project funding is also a continual challenge for middleware developers. Rex, a senior research programmer in the CIMA group, explained that for one of the main projects that he works on they are funded on a yearly basis with no guarantee that they will receive continued funding the next year. To keep the money flowing, they work hard to keep the funder happy and deliver systems as close to what was promised in the grant proposal. By building a reputation as a group that delivers what they promise, they increase their opportunities for future projects.

With development activities typically arranged around a specific, short-term application context it can be difficult to enlist the resources for a long-term middleware vision. As was the case with Middleware Z, having to emphasize the needs of the immediate domain project may not leave room in the near term to focus on the middleware development. On the other hand, it does support working towards tangible artifacts that may be leveraged in future projects to obtain support for the work. For John, the opportunity to work on his own research agenda inside of the civil engineering project set up the possibility of future funding. Even though the concept became overly complex and did not play out as he envisioned in this project, the incomplete version 1 of Middleware Z offered a functioning example of the concept that he could carry forward into the next project. This use in a deployed system allowed John to illustrate the utility of the concept behind this data middleware and to argue that he was well-prepared for the next project.

Developing a Standalone Project

Once a middleware has been developed within the context of a domain science project, and if it shows promise as a system applicable to multiple projects such that enough collaborators, colleagues, and funders can be convinced, then a middleware may be able to become a standalone project. Middleware Z until this point had only existed as a piece of other cyberinfrastructure projects for specific domain uses. Based on the work that occurred in the context of a civil engineering CI, Middleware Z's next developmental point was to become its own project. This transition enabled Middleware Z to obtain an identity that is recognizable as a singular system outside of the context of any one domain-specific project.

John wanted to continue development of Middleware Z, but new funding sources would be required. John told us, "The result of that whole [civil engineering] process was kind of a half-baked version of [Middleware Z]. I sustained the funding for it. I called it [Middleware Z] after I left - after the [civil engineering] project ended.... It was just the data component of [the civil engineering project], and that provided the entire funding for the development of that first rev.... Then, after the [civil engineering] project ended, I had some support through [a grid computing] project.... I put [Middleware Z] in there as a data management component, but it was really dis-integrated from the rest of the package. It was a strange relationship, where I just sort of hung around with them, and helped them make sure my stuff would install correctly... but it provided bridge funding."

An important shift in middleware development occurs when the middleware develops its own identity. In our investigations, the seed idea for middleware typically was born from an attempt to solve a problem in a particular cyberinfrastructure project. Then, in part because developers, either individually or as a group, are always involved with multiple different domains, there is an emerging realization that the same approach could be useful across a range of domain contexts.

At SDSC, Irene told us about a middleware project that gained shape when several projects realized they were dealing with the same issue: "[The projects] were basically trying to do a similar thing.... We sort of put the streams together so we could learn from each other." At first, they began developing Middleware W as an informal package of shared software that was shared across several domain projects, but there was a need to create a more sustainable solution.

"MWC (Middleware W Central) is a specific project we put together... to lead Middleware W into something more shareable, more robust. Until MWC, Middleware W didn't have that driving force. Projects were taking a lot of the – [ProjectX] mainly was a big, big driving core for Middleware W until the end of the project. Projects end, and Middleware W didn't have this community self-sustainable structure. MWC is the project to bring it in and provide an infrastructure for Middleware W."

It was time for the next step, to move development out of the context of specific applications and into its own project. We saw this same progression—from a domain-specific solution to a stand-alone cross-domain middleware—in projects that ranged across data processing workflows, image processing, pattern analysis, and portal systems. Returning to Middleware Z, when our story began, there was no middleware. Instead, what became Middleware Z began as a simple idea for how to solve a particular problem of merging data - an idea that was not compelling enough to pursue. During development for the civil engineering project, it was just the "data component." Now, Middleware Z has a name (or, in our story, a pseudonym). Now it is possible for Middleware Z to be "dis-integrated" from the domain projects that fund it. While usefulness in particular contexts will remain a criteria for continued funding, developing this stand-alone identity makes it possible to consider Middleware Z as a project in itself.

As the grid project funding ended the CIMA group obtained a technology research "umbrella" grant. Timothy, the project manager of CIMA, told us that this umbrella grant funded John's group to "actually design and develop new capabilities" for Middleware Z so that it could be used by projects being built for multiple communities. John was now able to lead a small team focused just on developing Middleware Z. The umbrella grant also removed the constraints placed on the software by the original civil engineering project and the grid project. John states that Middleware Z "didn't need 50% of the features that [version 1]" had. The Middleware Z team could "really push it to the point of maturity to where it became useful."

John said, "I can't quite remember the chronology, but at some point, I decided to completely rewrite Middleware Z from the ground up." Over the next two to three years, Middleware Z became an important item in CIMA's cyberinfrastructure toolbox. Middleware Z was incorporated into several projects in multiple domains including education, environmental research, and the humanities.

Middleware Z found funding as a standalone project through an umbrella grant, but other middleware projects were able to make this transition using other models. For example, one workflow middleware project fostered an active open-source community to support the development, while another project spun off their middleware and founded a commercial start-up to take over the project. Regardless of the model, however, this progression from local problem solution to widely applicable middleware was a key transition in all of the projects.

Managing Breakdown and Change

Middleware development does not follow a purely linear trajectory, however, and any infrastructural middleware will be faced with moments of change and breakdown. Middleware Z became a popular tool inside the center where it was developed. It had been incorporated into a number of other systems developed by the CIMA group. However, Middleware Z had not gained traction in a wider community and there were changes on the horizon which led to support for further development to wane. This final point in the middleware development process in our data highlights the relational nature of CI and the constant synergistic activities that the developers behind a system must undertake throughout the development of a cyberinfrastructure middleware system.

When the umbrella grant funding ended Middleware Z had been through its second major re-write and was at a stable development point. John decided to leave the center for a position at another research institution. Before he left, the team conducted a code review with him ensuring that they had an overall grasp of the middleware system's design and implementation. The group also performed an internal analysis that revealed that CIMA's projects would soon run up against Middleware Z's "performance wall" with larger data sets. Due to this performance wall the group sought an "exit strategy" that would allow them to support existing projects while finding a solution for larger datasets. Timothy, the CIMA group manager now responsible for Middleware Z, explained that the CIMA group as a whole could maintain Middleware Z since they "have got enough experience on the team [with Middleware Z] that if [they] have to debug something, [they] will debug it." Timothy, Jerry, and the developers in the group decided to lock down a subset of Middleware Z's features as "Middleware Z Light." The Light version would strip out all but the essential and stable functions, since "when we were creating this, we were experimenting with all these different back ends to see which ones would behave best, you know, give us different characteristics and such" (Timothy). Any experimenting would cease, and Middleware Z would not be further developed. Instead of continuing development, the CIMA group began to evaluate open source middleware projects that could perform similar functions. "The reality is, [Middleware A] and [Middleware B] have become de facto middleware data store environments" (Timothy), and they decided to adopt one of those platforms rather than continue Middleware Z development.

Middleware Z had reached a turning point: would it become infrastructure or not? Infrastructure is a relational concept [24]. Inside this center, Middleware Z had become infrastructural. Many of their domain-specific projects were using Middleware Z as an underlying, black-boxed technology. But faced with two forms of impending infrastructural breakdown—John leaving the center and the performance limits of the software—the CIMA group was forced to reconsider the role that Middleware Z played in their activities. Change is not uncommon in these middleware projects; people come and go, funding streams end, organizations are restructured. Sometimes, as in the case of Middleware Z, these changes may lead to the end of the project. For other projects, this provides a chance to restructure the project or go in a new direction (as they did earlier in the Middleware Z project when the developers were able to do a complete rewrite of the software). These moments provide new opportunities for heedful synergizing by creating new infrastructural alignments or reinforcing those that are already in place.

The synergizing lens frames the work of infrastructure as a process of developing and managing infrastructural relationships among people, technologies, and institutions, and is useful for understanding how infrastructures deal with and manage change. [3] finds that "A change in one component of the infrastructure cannot be understood without understanding the way that the component is connected to others." In this case, Middleware Z has infrastructural relationships with a number of other middleware projects and domain-specific applications. In order to sustain the larger infrastructure that has been built up at NCSA, it would be necessary to either fix the breakdowns (for example, by assigning a new development lead and re-architecting Middleware Z to avoid its performance limitations), or find another way to provide the required functionality. In the end, the decision was made to turn to external middleware efforts to meet the same infrastructural needs. However, in order to manage the pace of that change and smooth the transition, the group decided to maintain the "light" version of Middleware Z until the replacement components were ready.

Overall the moments of articulation work that groups at NCSA and SDSC enact enable them to sustain work on many projects for specific domains while working to produce middleware that can be applied in many situations.

We find that middleware development typically begins in response to an emergent need within a domain science project. As developers work with different scientist collaborators, if they face similar needs in multiple contexts they tend to reuse and expand on what they have already developed and the middleware takes shape and grows. Eventually, if the need is broad enough, the middleware can become a project in itself and begin to stand alone from the particular contexts from which it emerged. Throughout the life of these projects, developers work collaboratively and must continually align their own interests with domain science needs. The growth of Middleware Z and the other examples provided here—from initial ideas to a functioning middleware leveraged as a key components of multiple domain science projects—demonstrates the work cyberinfrastructure developers must undertake to accomplish infrastructure.

DISCUSSION

Based on the findings presented we now discuss three key themes that emphasize the synergizing work necessary to support cyberinfrastructure middleware development in the supercomputing centers in our study. The first is that of the importance of research & development agendas to the work of building these systems. The second theme is the relationship among the multiple projects that provide the context for development over time. Finally, the third theme is that of recognizing that sustaining middleware development requires the marshaling of multiple stakeholders' interests.

R&D Agendas in Cyberinfrastructure Development

In all of the middleware projects in our study, it was clear that there was an individual project leader who played a key role in sustaining the middleware development. John is a dominant figure in the story of Middleware Z because John and his research interests were such an important part of its trajectory. Of course, John was working with other people in the various scientific projects, and then led a small team when the middleware was funded as a standalone project. What we see as important, however, is the role of people like John in sustaining the middleware across the gaps and transitions between funded projects.

Others have pointed out the importance of good leadership in cyberinfrastructure projects [23], but we believe there are structural properties to middleware development that go beyond having a strong or charismatic leader. In particular, what is important is that the developer has his or her own research and development agenda. This agenda is not, at least initially, tied to a particular system or approach. Instead, the agenda revolves around solving a particular class of problems, as in the case of Middleware Z, where John was interested in the challenges of data management when working with large and heterogeneous datasets. Prior research argues that cyberinfrastructure developers, like the domain scientists with whom they collaborate, have their own research agendas and face many of the same challenges related to pursuing a research agenda in the face of short-term grant-funded projects [13].

Our point here is similar but slightly different. In the stories we heard from our participants, a developer (or development group) with an agenda was *necessary* to shepherd the concept and prototypes through the multiple phases and moments of alignment necessary to realize a functioning middleware. With each of the middleware projects we encountered, there was an individual or small group of individuals who, at least in the early phases of the project, served as champions for the systems. These centers are working on cutting edge technologies, and most (although not all) of the people we spoke to leading development projects considered themselves technology researchers as much as software developers, and they modeled their groups on academic research laboratories. These individuals take responsibility for the necessary synergizing work to enable sustainable software. They identify the concepts in their current project that could have broader applicability. They advocate for their vision, and they gather the necessary resources and foster collaborations to develop prototypes. As the middleware matures, they work with other projects to convince them to use the middleware and help them incorporate it into their systems, all the while continuing development work to support additional use cases or make the middleware more stable. They monitor the system, anticipating breakdowns and repairing them when they occur. Without an interested party to carry the concept through prototypes and into a working system, middleware would not happen.

The Relationships Among Projects

The work of middleware infrastructure development cannot be understood without looking at the multiple and complex relationships among projects. Middleware is thought of as a technological component that sits in the 'middle' of and links other components together. If we take a sociotechnical approach, we see that it is not just a matter of interoperable software, but that there is a meshing of work practices that must also occur simultaneously. This work requires collaboration among developers, and between developers and domain scientists. Schmidt and Simone [22] point out that collaboration takes place within a "common field of work." The common field of work is the set of things that the cooperating individuals are working on, in other words, "the collective of things upon which an ensemble is enacting state changes" [4]. However, our data suggests that middleware development occurs in a complex, multiple, and sometimes ill-defined project space.

Consider the story of Middleware Z. It started out as an idea in an information management project, but did not become a prototype until it was picked up in a second (civil engineering) project. Then it had a "strange relationship" with the grid computing project before getting funding from the umbrella grant. As Middleware Z matured, it was adopted by many other projects within the CIMA group, requiring significant internal collaboration among the projects. The diversity of collaborations was a factor in all of the middleware projects, and all of the developers in our study were involved in developing components of multiple different domain projects at any one time. Rather than having a single common field of work, middleware developers are always participating simultaneously in multiple overlapping fields of work. That developers are working in multiple fields of work at once is not particularly new or remarkable in itself. What is important, however, is how the fields of work shift and blend over time.

Within a common field of work, cooperation requires that workers "articulate (divide, allocate coordinate, schedule, mesh, interrelate, etc.) their distributed individual activities" [21]. However, much of the work of middleware development goes beyond this sense of articulation work to involve defining the fields of work themselves and managing the relationships among fields of work. Building and managing these links across projects and infrastructural components draws more on the processes that Bietz, Lee and Baumer have called "synergizing" [4].

The point at which a middleware goes from existing only within other fields of work to being able to define its own field of work is a key transition. For example, in the case of Middleware Z, it was not until after John consolidated his work on the concept and named it "Middleware Z" that others viewed it as a specific project and area of focus. When middleware is defined as a project in itself, it becomes a target of a significant amount of synergizing work. The middleware is now a distinct entity, leverageable by other projects since it is a visible, known system. The alignment work which takes place to integrate middleware into other projects further strengthens its position in the larger infrastructure as other projects come to rely on its services.

The Sustainability of Infrastructure

Sustaining infrastructure requires an understanding of the organizational, individual, and technological aspects together. Middleware development occurs within cyberinfrastructure, domain science, and organizational contexts that shape long-term development trajectories. In the Middleware Z story, and all of the stories we heard, middleware development relies on successful marshaling of R&D agendas, domain science needs, and institutional interests.

Once a system has reached a point such that it is embedded in multiple projects it reaches a point that it is viewed as infrastructural middleware, at least from the perspective of the group relying upon it in multiple projects. The individual developers and the organizational group that they are a part of are able to make the case that supporting the continued development of the middleware is crucial to the needs of the many domain projects that it has been embedded within. Moments that may have major impacts on the sustainability of a middleware project include when the intellectual owner leaves for a new position and does not take the system with them or when it is determined that a performance wall has been reached. It is at points like these in a project's development that the opportunity to pull back and examine opportunities for alignment with other outside development projects arise. It may be the case that continuing to develop the internally developed middleware may no longer be the most sensible approach.

IMPLICATIONS

Cyberinfrastructures are complex sociotechnical collaborative systems that are comprised of and embedded in other systems. As the corpus of CSCW research in the area of cyberinfrastructure continues to grow in breadth and depth, CSCW researchers, without losing a necessary view of larger systems, are able to focus on key elements of cyberinfrastructure development such as the particular relationship and interaction between middleware developers, middleware, and larger organizations such as funded projects and supercomputing centers.

Implications for Middleware Development Organizations

Our data suggest that the ideas that eventually grew into fully fledged middleware systems all began as solutions to specific challenges that arose directly out of the scientific needs. However, we saw that the crucial transition from a system-specific component into a fully capable middleware was poorly supported. There is a need to envision new sustainability models that allow for earlier identification of candidate middleware systems and ease the transition from research prototype to sustainable system. Organizations can create procedures that help developers to detect when similar needs arise in multiple domains. For example, periodic cross-project reviews of development work and new technologies would allow for awareness of emergent trends. Also, while we recognize the constraints of current academic funding models, finding ways to give middleware developers the time and flexibility to pursue their own R&D interests would be productive. One developer we interviewed stated that she felt that she had to account for every working hour to the projects that funded her. However, allowing for some individually-directed work time (perhaps similar to Google's "twenty-percent time" [10]) could create space for innovation and encourage developers to take a seed concept from a domain-specific project and begin to develop it into its own distinct middleware system at an earlier stage in its lifecycle.

Implications for National Funding Policy

Our findings also suggest that there are important policy concerns around providing better support for the R&D agendas and careers of the individuals who lead cyberinfrastructure development efforts. Middleware is clearly an essential component of cyberinfrastructure. To achieve the stated goal of developing systems and infrastructures that can provide a broad array of services to scientists in multiple domains [2], it may be necessary to implement funding structures that can directly fund middleware development and provide greater stability and support for the long-term R&D agendas of middleware developers. The US National Science Foundation's (NSF) *Software Infrastructure for Sustained Innovation (SI^2)* program is a new program with the goal of transforming innovations in research and education into sustained software resources that are an integral part of the cyberinfrastructure [16]. This program is a good first step, but the program is currently limited to chemical science collaborations bridging the US and UK. A broader program is needed.

Implications for CSCW

Our research finds that the developers of middleware do not stand outside of infrastructure, but are integrally embedded in it, which is key to sustaining these projects. Lee et al. [14] refers to this as the "human infrastructure of cyberinfrastructure." We find that individual technology researchers pursuing their own career-level R&D agendas provide important continuity of expertise as well as a driving force that helps make the transition from domain-specific solutions to generalizable middleware systems. Thinking about enabling individual careers and building stable organizations must be as much of the discussion as creating a flexible and long lasting technological artifact.

Understanding how elements in the technical and human infrastructure interact over time is a step towards creating an increasingly sophisticated conceptual model that provides insight into two layers of sociotechnical design: *supporting collaborative development* of cyberinfrastructures and *developing cyberinfrastructure systems themselves* that support collaboration. Future work will further explore and qualitatively model how these layers interact and co-evolve and how cyberinfrastructures are created and maintained by multiple sociotechnical elements that are by turns stable and dynamic.

CONCLUSION

This paper is part of a growing corpus of work that is taking seriously the notion that cyberinfrastructures are relational, sociotechnical systems that are comprised of and embedded in other systems. The development of cyberinfrastructures not only necessarily spans geographic space, but also communities that have differing priorities and ways of working, and—importantly—time. Designing something as complex as a collaborative cyberinfrastructure is itself a complex collaborative activity that resembles a program that is more akin to a public works development project with a myriad of stakeholders and a changing political-economic environment.

This paper also highlights the importance of the everyday, seemingly mundane work, of middleware developers to cultivate and maintain infrastructural relationships over time. We addressed the question of "how do developers sustain middleware projects in the context of cyberinfrastructure development?" Building on the data from a qualitative study of middleware development at two supercomputing centers, we tell the story of the development of a representative project, Middleware Z, enriched with examples from other projects. Focusing on key transitions—from an early concept to a functional prototype to working infrastructure to managing breakdown and change—reveals the work required to nurture and sustain a middleware project through its different stages of development. Infrastructural middleware development requires not just understanding how to build sustainable technologies, but also how to build sustainable human and technological assemblages.

ACKNOWLEDGMENTS

We wish to thank the participants in this research for their time and insights, and the anonymous reviewers for their feedback. This work was supported by National Science Foundation Awards IIS-0712994, IIS-0954088 and OCI-0838601.

REFERENCES

1. Aronova, E., Baker, K. S., & Oreskes, N. Big science and big data in biology: From the International Geophysical Year through the International Biological Program to the Long Term Ecological Research (LTER) Network, 1957-present. *Historical Studies in the Natural Sciences, 40*, 2 (2010), 183-224.
2. Atkins, D. E., Droegemeier, K. K., Feldman, S. I., Garcia-Molina, H., Klein, M. L., et al. *Revolutionizing science and engineering through cyberinfrastructure: Report of the National Science Foundation blue-ribbon advisory panel on cyberinfrastructure*. National Science Foundation, Washington, D.C. (2003).
3. Bietz, M. J., Ferro, T., & Lee, C. P. Sustaining the development of cyberinfrastructure: An organization adapting to change. In Proc. *CSCW 2012*, ACM Press (2012), 901-910.
4. Bietz, M. J., Lee, C. P., & Baumer, E. P. S. Synergizing in cyberinfrastructure development. *Computer Supported Cooperative Work, 19*, 3-4 (2010), 245-281.
5. Branscomb, L., Belytschko, T., Bridenbaugh, P., Chay, T., Dozier, J., et al. *From Desktop To Teraflop: Exploiting the U.S. Lead in High Performance Computing*. National Science Foundation, Washington, D.C. (1993).
6. Edwards, P. N., Jackson, S. J., Bowker, G. C., & Knobel, C. P. *Understanding infrastructure: Dynamics, tensions, and design.* http://hdl.handle.net/2027.42/49353
7. Finholt, T. A. Collaboratories. In *Annual Review of Information Science and Technology*. B. Cronin, Ed., (Vol. 36). Information Today Publishers, Medford, NJ (2002), 73-107.
8. Foster, I., & Kesselman, C. *The Grid: Blueprint for a New Computing Infrastructure* (second ed.). Morgan Kaufmann, Boston (2004).

9. Galison, P. *Big Science: The Growth of Large-Scale Research*. Stanford University Press, Stanford, CA (1992).
10. Iyer, B., & Davenport, T. H. Reverse engineering Google's innovation machine. *Harvard Business Review, 86*, 4 (2008), 58-68.
11. Jirotka, M., Proctor, R., Rodden, T., & Bowker, G. C. Special Issue: Collaboration in e-Research. *Computer Supported Cooperative Work, 15*, 4 (2006), 251-255.
12. Karasti, H., & Baker, K. S. Infrastructuring for the long-term: Ecological information management. In *Proc. HICSS 2004*, IEEE Computer Society (2004), 10020c.
13. Lee, C. P., Bietz, M. J., Derthick, K., & Paine, D. A sociotechnical exploration of infrastructural middleware development. In Proc. *CSCW 2012,* ACM Press (2012), 1347-1350.
14. Lee, C. P., Dourish, P., & Mark, G. The human infrastructure of cyberinfrastructure. In *Proc. CSCW 2006*. ACM Press (2006), 483-492.
15. Monteiro, E., Pollock, N., Hanseth, O., & Williams, R. From artefacts to infrastructures. *Computer Supported Cooperative Work (CSCW)* (2012), 1-33. DOI=10.1007/s10606-012-9167-1.
16. National Science Foundation. (2012). *Software infrastructure for sustained innovation (SI2)*. http://www.nsf.gov/pubs/2012/nsf12576/nsf12576.htm.
17. Naur, P., & Randell, B. Software Engineering Report of a conference sponsored by the NATO Science Committee Garmisch Germany 7th-11th October 1968: Scientific Affairs Division, NATO (1969).
18. Newman, S. E. Here, there, and nowhere at all: Distribution, negotiation, and virtuality in postmodern ethnography and engineering. *Knowledge and Society, 11* (1998), 235-267.
19. Ribes, D., & Finholt, T. A. The long now of technology infrastructure: Articulating tensions in development. *Journal of the Association for Information Systems, 10* (2009), 375-398.
20. Ribes, D., & Lee, C. Sociotechnical studies of cyberinfrastructure and e-research: Current themes and future trajectories. *Computer Supported Cooperative Work (CSCW), 19*, 3 (2010), 231-244.
21. Schmidt, K., & Bannon, L. Taking CSCW seriously: Supporting articulation work. *Computer Supported Cooperative Work, 1*, 1 (1992), 7-40.
22. Schmidt, K., & Simone, C. Coordination mechanisms: Towards a conceptual foundation of CSCW systems design. *Computer Supported Cooperative Work (CSCW), 5*, 2 (1996), 155-200.
23. Spencer, B. F., Jr., Butler, R., Ricker, K., Marcusiu, D., Finholt, T. A., et al. NEESgrid: Lessions learned for future cyberinfrastructure development. In *Scientific Collaboration on the Internet*. G. M. Olson & A. Zimmerman & N. Bos, Eds. MIT Press, Cambridge, MA (2008), 331-347.
24. Star, S. L., & Ruhleder, K. Steps toward an ecology of infrastructure: Design and access for large information spaces. *Information Systems Research, 7*, 1 (1996), 111-134.

Come Drive with Me: An Ethnographic Study of Driver-Passenger Pairs to Inform Future In-Car Assistance

Nicole Perterer, Petra Sundström, Alexander Meschtscherjakov, David Wilfinger and Manfred Tscheligi
University of Salzburg
{nicole.perterer, petra.sundstroem, alexander.meschtscherjakov, david.wilfinger, manfred.tscheligi|}@sbg.ac.at

ABSTRACT

There is today a large number of ADAS used while driving. These systems are mainly technology driven and most often fail to make use of the social nature and the collaborative mechanisms between driver-passenger pairs. To inform the development of future automotive user interface designs we need to develop a deeper understanding of collaboration in general. In addition, we need to develop an understanding of how, and in what way, other platforms (e.g., the mobile phones) are and will be used in combination with these systems while driving. This paper presents the results of a participative ethnographic study with nine driver-passenger pairs recruited from two online car-sharing portals. Results are categorized in three areas: *common ground as a base for successful in-car communication, types and strategies of front-seat passenger assistance,* and lastly *the impact of technology on collaboration.*

Author Keywords

Driver assistance; in-car technology; ethnographic study; collaboration.

ACM Classification Keywords

H.5.m **[Information interfaces and presentation (e.g., HCI)]**: Miscellaneous.

General Terms

Design and Human Factors

INTRODUCTION

Most modern cars are equipped with various Advanced Driver Assistance Systems (ADAS), sometimes referred to as in-vehicle information systems. Mostly discussed in HCI and CSCW is GPS, but there are also cruise control systems, lane detection systems, break assistance systems, and belt pre-tensioners, just to mention a few. The main goal of all ADAS, as the name suggests, is to support the driver with the primary task of driving the car. There are many benefits to ADAS. As 37% of all US traffic accidents are associated with inadequate attention due to drivers' engagement in tertiary tasks (such as mobile phone conversations) [9], it is not difficult to understand how all these additional systems in the car also add potential risks. High complexity and demanding functionality add to the distraction of the driver. Therefore, the design and development of future ADAS is of great importance in the field of HCI.

Additionally, drivers are not often alone in the car. Especially, longer trips and unfamiliar routes make more use of supportive systems such as GPS [10]. In these situations, it is not uncommon that front-seat passengers help with activities such as reading and handling these assistance systems. Most ADAS are, however, neither designed for this kind of collaborative usage, nor for being used by front-seat passengers alone. Current ADAS consistently fail to make use of the collaborative aspects of driving.

Automation in the form of ADAS is an opportunity, but as we know, drivers are remarkably good at ignoring automated safety warning alerts, or suggestions made by friends, partners, or other passengers. Also, misunderstandings between drivers and passengers are not uncommon. For successful communication and collaboration, there needs to be a shared understanding of some of the basic principles of what characterizes the situation [5, 6]. This is something a more cooperative, future ADAS could potentially support. But to understand how and what kind of information, we need to develop a deeper understanding of how collaboration and communication already take place in the car while driving with one or more passengers.

There is an important, yet small number of works that exists on the topic of ethnographic studies in the car [e.g., 2]. Our focus, however, is on driver-passenger interaction in general, and the role that ADAS and additional equipment play. The focus of previous studies [e.g., 10] has been almost exclusively on GPS usage so far. Our work departs from related previous work, in that our focus is on *lived contextual experiences* really covering the essence of the various aspects in and around a car. In this paper, we present the results of a two-month ethnographically informed empirical case study of nine driver-passenger pairs recruited through two online car-sharing communities. Because we focused on lived experiences, it was decided not to use any additional technical equipment (e.g., video cameras) as that would take us time to set up, and/or have too much of an effect on the experience that evolved together with the driver and the other passengers. Instead, it was decided to rely on the careful notes we could take on these drives as back-seat passenger.

In the results section of this paper, we draw attention to some of the mechanisms of driver-passenger collaboration we find important for the development of future, more collaboratively used ADAS, and thereby important to the CSCW community. The results are presented in three categories: *common ground as a base for successful in-car communication*, *types and strategies of front-seat passenger assistance*, and last *impact of technology on collaboration.*

BACKGROUND AND RELATED WORK

Before the presentation of the set up and the results of this study, we first discuss current types of ADAS in some more detail. Further we describe the role of the social car and lastly, we discuss how the theory of *common ground* [5,6], could be take as base for understanding in how these collaboration takes place in the automotive domain.

Current Advanced Driver Assistance Systems

Advanced Driver Assistance Systems (ADAS) are in-vehicle systems that use environment sensors (e.g., radar, laser, and/or vision). The main goal of such technology is to improve driving comfort and traffic safety by assisting the driver in recognizing and reacting to potentially dangerous traffic situations. In modern cars, there are several such systems. GPS is perhaps the widely known of device in HCI related fields, but there are many such devices, e.g., break assistance or belt pre-tensioners.

To provide some guidance in this highly technical field, Gietelink and colleagues [12] classify ADAS into:

- *Driver Information Systems* – systems that increase the driver's situational awareness (e.g., GPS).
- *Driver Warning Systems* – systems that actively warn the driver of a potential danger (e.g., a lane departure warning system).
- *Intervening Systems* – systems that provide active support to the driver (e.g., an adaptive cruise control).
- *Integrated Passive and Active Safety Systems* – systems that act to keep the driver and passengers safe and react when triggered (e.g., break assistance or seat belt pre-tensioners).
- *Fully Automated Systems* –systems that are beyond state of the art and operate without a human driver in the control loop (i.e., cars that drive without a driver).

Within the automotive domain, the popularity of ADAS has prompted specific attention to the design of these systems. Such (semi-) autonomous systems have the potential to assist with the task of driving; however, there are problems to be expected from the usage of these systems. For instance, Hipp and colleagues [16] have found how commercial GPS units frequently fail to provide directions that correspond with drivers' intentions. Kun and colleagues [22] have pointed out that navigation systems may even distract drivers and lead to additional driving errors. A few studies [e.g., 7] have also found signs of complacency (i.e., unjustified over-reliance on ADAS). These forms of behavioral adaptations or compensations should be taken into account when designing and developing future ADAS. Another issue is the time it takes to interact with these systems. (Semi-) autonomous systems may help drivers react faster to a specific event, but several studies [e.g., 25] have shown that humans are poor *process monitors* and how enforced vigilance in the operational environment is stressful [13].

This is why we, and others [e.g., 2, 10, 23], point to how these systems do not necessarily need to be used by drivers alone. According to, Forlizzi [10], a move from an individually-focused design paradigm to one based upon collaborative human interaction holds a great deal of potential in improving mediated human-human interaction during secondary or tertiary driving tasks of both drivers and front-seat passengers (e.g., operating with the navigation device). The development of collaborative workspaces in the car is of high relevance to the CSCW and HCI community, where one solution is to make ADAS more sensitive to social and collaborative aspects of driving together as driver-passenger pairs.

The Social Car

Driving a car in traffic is fundamentally a collaborative and social activity. Collaboration is essential when two drivers meet on the same part of the road at the same time [7]. This not only includes sharing the road with other vehicles, but also with cyclists and pedestrians. In addition, the car itself is a place where encounters with other people occur. Most of us travel from time to time with family and friends for social or convenient reasons. It might also be that individuals share their commutes to save money or for environment reasons. Many professionals additionally have colleagues drive together as a pair or work force. These reasons are examples as why carpooling has gained more importance in the last decades. Many platforms are available for people to get in contact with other individuals who share the same destinations.

From a social standpoint, the relationship between driver-passenger pairs can take many forms. One notable dimension of these relationships relates to whether or not the passenger pays for the ride. Based on a study of Inbar and Tractinsky [18], non-paying passengers (e.g., family members or friends) who have a personal relationship with the driver are far more likely to take on the role of co-driver (e.g., answering a phone call or setting a destination on the navigation system). Passengers receiving a service are unlikely to actively operate in-car systems and may even hesitate to ask the driver for travel information, fearing it may be impolite to ask. Their study indicates how passengers in a carpool or car-sharing situation usually fall into one of these two categories.

It is clear that the car has become a ubiquitous social object, where different forms of driver-passenger pairs interact with each other in various ways and for various reasons. This is why a deeper understanding of social and collaborative in-car activities is important.

Collaboration

What we propose in this paper is not just assistance, but more of a collaborative usage of ADAS. As we have seen in previous research and also in our data, collaborative activities are triggered by *situational cues* [11]. These cues signal to a person that an action or event may occur or that a person needs to respond in a particular way. For the collaboration between a driver and a passenger, we define a trigger a cue that causes the assistance of a front-seat passenger. An example would be when the driver asks for help with the navigation device in a stressful traffic situation. In such situations, the trigger is the specific request of the driver. The driver-passenger pair is then collaborating with the main goal of increasing traffic safety. In such situations, it might be that the front-seat passenger is the one handling the navigation device while the driver attends to the traffic situation at hand. Here, Forlizzi and colleagues [10] point to how important it is that ADAS displays information in a way that is also accessible for the front-seat passenger, supporting this collaborative usage.

There can also be implicit triggers, such as how it might start to rain and the front-seat passenger feels the need to assist the driver. Another example is when the front-seat passenger interprets a traffic situation as dangerous and assumes the driver is not able to maneuver the situation without assistance. In such situations, the passenger may misinterpret the situation and exacerbates the problem or induces an even more dangerous situation. This takes us to the issue of how successful communication and collaboration is based upon a shared understanding of the situation at hand, often referred to as a common ground, which is mutual knowledge, beliefs, and assumptions [5, 6]. Clark and Marshall state how common ground is the joint action that emerges when speakers and listeners perform their individual actions in coordination as an ensemble. In any conversation, participants are continuously and dynamically assessing what the other parties know; this knowledge is used to form subsequent utterances. Clark and Brennan`s theory [5] describes that communicating parties have to coordinate both the *content* and the *process* of what they are doing. They explain how the content is what the parties want to accomplish together, *such as playing a song on the piano together* [5, p.1] or as in our case, let the driver drive the car safely from A to B. Of course, the situation is slightly different here as it is the driver that drives and the passenger can only assist, but the goal, i.e. the content (as Clark and Brennan refer to it), is the same for both. The means, though, are different (i.e., driving and assisting). A driver-passenger pair also must synchronize their entrances and exits, and coordinate how loud to speak under different driving situations, as well as adjust to each other's resources and tempo. This is the coordination of the process. In this coordination, the driver and passenger do not explicitly state what sets their individual knowledge, beliefs, and assumptions about the situation. Here it is more of an implicit understanding, which is something future ADAS potentially could help with making decisive factors more explicit.

To do this, we need to build up deeper knowledge in how these collaborations specifically take place in the automotive domain. This task has already been initiated by a few researchers [e.g., 23]. Our intention is to add to this small body of research by going back to the essence of collaboration as it happens and takes place already with current ADAS in cars of today. We are also interested in what additional tools that may be used in combination with ADAS (e.g., drivers and passengers' personal mobile phones).

METHOD AND SETTING

Ethnographic research methods have become important in the field of HCI and CSCW. This qualitative approaches has gained growing awareness as a technique for investigating how individuals work in groups or teams and how they can be supported by information communication technology. Before continuing to the procedure and results of our study, we first want to outline some related ethnographic fieldwork in the car domain which also has acted as an inspiration for our ethnographic study, thereafter presented.

Ethnographic Approaches in the Automotive Domain

Indeed, there is a growing body of ethnographic studies in the automotive domain. There are, for example, studies investigating how the car reconfigures urban life [e.g., 28] and studies investigating the pleasures of various in-car activities, such as the activity of listening to music while driving [e.g., 4]. We want to especially mention the research group directed by Oskar Juhlin [e.g., 20]. Based on various ethnographic studies [e.g., 7] they have designed a range of systems related to the social dimensions of driving, such as the SoundPryer system [26]. Their fieldwork underlines the ways in which driving is a social process whereby road users *solve coordination problems with other road users and try to influence each other* [20, p. 49].

In relation to our work more specifically, Leshed and colleagues [24] present an ethnographically informed study with GPS users, showing evidence for practices of disengagement as well as new opportunities for engagement. The use of GPS was also discussed in Brown and Laurier's recent ethnographic paper aiming to understand the navigation practices employed by drivers and passengers while driving [2]. While Brown and Laurier used an interactional analysis approach of video data collected without their presence in the car, we were interested in understanding collaborative mechanisms between driver-passengers pairs. Based on the goal to capture *contextually lived experiences,* we decided to go for a more participatory ethnographic approach. This is inspired by Bubb [3], who emphasizes the *lived experience* of ethnographic approaches and how it should also be practiced in the domain of automotive research, although the car is small and very much a private space for many people. We argue that the rich experiences between driver-passenger pairs can only be collected by being present in the car. This allows the researcher to experience the situation as it takes place in all its multiplicity.

Based on our contextually lived, note-recorded experiences, we were able to focus on natural social interaction elements well-known in CSCW. We drew on interactional analysis [14], describing how front-seat passengers assist drivers and which collaborative activities took place between driver-passenger pairs. Our data was interpreted by specific episodes. This solution is seen as providing different kinds of aspects of driver-passenger cooperation than those given by video-recorded approaches [2, 7, 23].

A main advantage of our study was that we could observe real-interactions without artifacts caused by technical devices. The importance of that goal was confirmed when we recruited participants. Many of the participants asked us skeptically if we would record them. As soon as we told them that we were only joining them as a "normal" passenger sitting in the back seat and taking some notes, they immediately gave their informed consent. Our experiences also showed that with our study set up, we did not cause any delays on departure due to installing any equipment. That fact was important for our setup, where we joined driver-passenger pairs in their natural behavior, which also includes them being in a hurry to get somewhere. Installing equipment would have caused delays and potential frustration with participants. With our study set we could observe real interactions by using the two car-sharing platforms in an unobtrusive manner.

Our Study

Our study took place in wintertime from January to March 2011. For this study were the online car-sharing communities from which we recruited our participants were significant. A car-sharing community is most often a group of people who, for various reasons, have decided not to own a car for themselves, but instead share a collection of cars with a group of people. Most often they live in the same neighborhood, such as a person who picks up his/her work colleagues with his/her car in the morning. In our case though, the situation was slightly different. The car-sharing communities we joined were two online platforms where car owners register to bring people with them as passengers in their car and non-car owners register to take a ride with someone going in the same direction. We chose to join the Compano (www. campano.at) and the Mitfahrgelegenheit (www.mitfahrgelegenheit.at) communities. These two platforms are active in Europe.

In our case, we were not only looking not just for someone driving from A to B, but for a ride that already had a front-seat passenger registered for the drive. Based on this information, we then called the driver to ask if he or she would allow us (as researchers) to sign up for a particular ride. As previously mentioned, it was a significant aim of ours to live the experience of these shared rides as much as possible, so we decided not to use video or audio recording tools but instead to take part in the rides in the same way as other travelers do. In order to record our experiences, we relied on the notes we were able to take during the drives. Although we acknowledge the advantages of technical support for the purpose of replicating certain situations, we wanted to avoid the effect that the installation of permanent recording devices would have on the naturalness of the situation. Of course, we presented ourselves as researchers and asked for permission to take notes. On one hand, our aim was to intervene as a researcher and, on the other hand, to minimize the social distance from the participants.

Nine driver-passenger pairs were recruited, aged between 20 and 32 years (27.9 on average), seven male and two female drivers. A driver-passenger pair consisted of two persons, a driver and a front-seat passenger. On two of the trips there was also another back-seat passenger (in addition to one of us). One of the drivers tested the car-sharing platform for the first time; the others were regular members. All rated themselves as good to excellent drivers and were familiar with taking other people in their car. Three of the nine driver-passenger pairs were partners. Two of them were either friends or work colleagues. The rest of them (four) met each other through the community. Both drivers and passengers had driving licenses; two of them additionally had the permission to drive a truck. The cars were all different, e.g., Audi A3, BMW 1er, Peugeot 207, Volkswagen Polo, or Mercedes Vito. Four out of nine drivers used a mobile navigation device, but additionally switched on the radio to hear either music or traffic news. In one specific case, a driver had a laptop mounted on the center stack with Google Earth running.

ANALYSIS

The observed episodes collected in this study were analyzed using an interaction analysis approach [14]. The detailed stories are direct observations of what we could hear and see while observing the driver-passenger pairs. In total we collected data from 9 journeys, lasting over 21hr 30min in total. Journey times ranged from 1hr 30min to 3hr 30min; the average trip duration took 2hr 23min. In this chapter, we will focus on observational data, along with fragments from informal interviews and discussions we had with the drivers and passengers while driving together.

The data will be presented in the form of short stories, which we believe come closest to describing the richness of human assistance and collaboration that we observed. The first recalled episode describes how different kinds of communication affect participants' mutual knowledge and, thereby, how it influences collaboration. With episode II and III, we want to indicate different forms of assistance (e.g., implicit assistance by telling the stories of some self-experienced accidents). The reason why those particular episodes are chosen is that they highlight the multiplicity of types and strategies in front-seat passenger assistance. Finally, two stories IV and V show common activities and how the devices in use support the shared goal of drivers and passengers.

Common Ground as a Base for successful In-Car Communication

Our first observed episode involves Mr. Draco, the driver, and his front-seat passenger, Mr. Frederick (both fictional names[1]). They met through the car-sharing community and are now friends. Mr. Draco has been registered on the website since 2010. He drives home every Friday evening, and Mr. Frederick joins him. Mr. Fredrick is also a member of the online-platform. They have an agreement that every Friday at 6 p.m. Mr. Draco is waiting for Mr. Frederick on a taxi stand at the railway station.

Episode I: Mr. Draco is driving on the two-lane highway, chatting with Mr. Frederick. At the moment, Mr. Draco is driving on the right lane. In front of him are some cars and a truck which are driving a little bit slower. As soon as the gap to the car in front of him is getting smaller, Mr. Frederick is answering the questions of Mr. Draco with a little bit of a delay. Mr. Frederick is observing the lane, and turning to Mr. Draco alternately. The position of his head is lowered toward the street and is sloped to the face of Mr. Draco. In the meantime, Mr. Draco looks at the left-side mirror to ensure that he can make a lane change. Once Frederick realizes Draco will overtake the car in front, he stops the conversation. Simultaneously, Mr. Frederick is observing Mr. Draco carefully. During the whole overtaking maneuver Mr. Frederick and Mr. Draco are quiet. They resume their conversation as soon as Mr. Draco aligns on the right lane again.

In this episode Mr. Frederick (the front-seat passenger) stopped the conversation and monitored Mr. Draco (the driver) carefully during the overtake maneuvers. The silence between the two lasted from the first lane change until the maneuver was completed. Our data from this specific trip indicate an example of *no communication* between driver-passenger pairs. This form of communication also happened when the Mr. Draco overtook any larger-sized vehicle, such as a semi-truck. Mr. Fredrick then took a short break from speaking, looked out the right side window, and did not remove his eyes from that side of the car until Mr. Draco, the driver had sufficient distance to change back to the right lane.

A *delay in communication* (no immediate reply to a question from the driver) between Mr. Frederick and Mr. Draco could be identified when there was a truck and other road users in front of, or behind the car. This identified communication behavior seemed to be dependent on the distance from the moving larger-sized vehicle: the closer the car came to the vehicle, the more delayed and shorter the answers from the front-seat passenger were. Mr. Frederick seemed to recognize that some situations needed more concentration from Mr. Draco (i.e., overtaking a truck) and did then not reply immediately to his question.

Frequent and spry communication between the driver and front-seat passenger was observed, though not supported by Episode I but later described in Episode IV. This type of communication was mainly shown when there were specific circumstances, such as the danger of black ice or snow-covered roads. Thereby, the front-seat passenger (later called Mr. Freeman in Episode IV) spoke to the driver about his current state, "*Is everything okay?*" or "*You seemed to be worn out by the heavy driving conditions", or "If you like, we could swap position?*". Under these conditions, the front-seat passenger was talking continuously with the driver to enquire about the other's well-being.

In summation, successful communication acts as a base for successful collaboration and it relies on common ground. In other words, mutual knowledge, mutual beliefs, and mutual assumptions are essential for successful *in-car communication* – indeed for all collective actions [5,6]. This means, once we have formulated a message, we must do more than just send it off. We need to assure ourselves that it will be understood by the other person (i.e., the driver) as well as adapt our communication behavior in the specific context or situation (i.e., taking a break from speaking when needed). Otherwise, we have little assurance that the discourse we are taking part in will proceed in an orderly manner [5]. The different communication strategies, such as *no*, *delayed,* and *frequent and spry communication* allow Mr. Frederick to support the driver, but require a common ground of the context and coordinated actions (i.e., stopping the discussion triggered by a contextual cue). Thereby, the front-seat passenger signals to the driver that he is aware of the current situation (e.g., workload caused by overtaking a truck) by adapting his communication strategies, something that introduces a common ground and further achieves a joint activity.

Types and Strategies of Front-seat passenger Assistance

In second observed episode, Mr. Drew (the driver) and a work colleague, Mr. Franklin (the front-seat passenger), are the protagonists. Mr. Franklin uses the car-sharing opportunity for the first time, whereas Mr. Drew uses it regularly. The recalled episode starts when Mr. Franklin is

[1] In the following fictional driver names begin with "Dr" and front-seat passenger names with "Fr".

in a phone conversation with his wife and Mr. Drew enters the highway as it begins to snow. Mr. Drew then turns the music down, winds down the side window, and switches on the car heater because the windshield is fogging up.

Episode II: Mr. Drew answers and complains about how he has a hard time seeing anything. Mr. Franklin takes a peek at the driver while is speaking to his wife on the telephone. He does not stop the conversation. At the same time, Mr. Franklin tells his wife how lovely it is; the landscape looks so beautiful. Intermittently, Mr. Franklin changes his posture, moves his seat forward, and looks up at Mr. Drew, yet says nothing to him. After a while, the driving conditions get worse and the windshield fogs up again. From that moment on, Mr. Franklin makes some longer breaks between words to his wife and turns on the car heater; the situation does not change. Mr. Franklin ends his conversation with this wife and takes out a package of tissues from the shelf on the center stack. Without the request of Mr. Drew, Mr. Franklin wipes off the windshield, first on the driver's side and then his own side. In the meantime Mr. Drew concentrates on the task of driving. After that, Mr. Franklin bends his upper body closer to Mr. Drew. After that, Mr. Franklin opens the side window. Unfortunately, the windshield fogs again but this time only on the driver's side. Mr. Franklin notices and mentions, "It is really surprising! Your side is always getting fogged up. Why is that?" Mr. Drew answers that he does not know why. Mr. Franklin replies and emphasizes that the current situation is really unusual. Mr. Franklin quips, "Look out of the upper half of the window – and I will look out the bottom of the window on my side". Mr. Drew sighs with relief and laughs. Then he adds that this could be an exciting trip.

The second recalled episode underpins the difference between *non-verbal* and *verbal actions* that depends on the context. Contrary to non-verbal forms of assistance, *verbal actions* are an active form of communication. In the beginning, Mr. Franklin used nonverbal actions by changing his posture and moving his seat forward, showing his attention to the situation. He paid closer attention to the reactions of Mr. Drew and stood by to help if necessary. In this situation, he kept an eye on Mr. Drew but did not stop the telephone call. As soon as the problem (i.e., fogged up windows) could not be solved by Mr. Drew alone, he stopped the phone conversation. Mr. Franklin then opened the window without the request of Mr. Drew. According to [15], *non-verbal* actions include (shown in this recalled episode) orientations towards each other, changing posture, and other aspects of language (e.g., breaks between words or sentences). It is also noteworthy that not only common active interventions such as suggestions or complaints (e.g., "*Pay attention, the traffic light is red!*) were used to support the driver. Jokes were also used to ease the situation and to reduce driver's workload (i.e., caused by a fogged-up windshield, illustrated in Episode II).

In the following episode, Ms. Dream (the driver) and Mr. Fruggle (the front-seat passenger) are on a highway. During the last half year, Mr. Fruggle joins Ms. Dream every Sunday and Thursday. They met through an online-platform.

Episode III: Today, the weather is really bad, but typical for the time of year. It is snowing slightly all the time. Mr. Fruggle explains to us (the driver and the researcher) that he is a good skier, but he does not like having snow on the road. After a while Mr. Fruggle further comments: "In my opinion the majority of the road users are driving too fast under these circumstances, aren't they?" After saying that, Mr. Fruggle looks towards Ms. Dream, then to her dashboard, then to Ms. Dream again. Ms. Dream notices, but does not immediately answer Mr. Fruggle. After about ten seconds (only a estimation of the researcher), she agrees with her car passenger but is mainly concentrating on the road: "Yes, you are [...]". Mr. Fruggle repeats his statement from before and mentions that almost everybody is driving too fast. Mr. Fruggle looks at Ms. Dream's dashboard again. After that Mr. Fruggle begins to narrate about his own-experienced accident to us. Mr. Fruggle tells us that especially ambulance drivers sometimes drive too fast. He recalled a story where an emergency vehicle skidded off the road during a call.

Within this episode, we want to explain how two different types of verbal strategies could be observed: the *explicit* and *implicit* form. Implicit assistance can be described as indirect instructions from the driver, whereas explicit assistance is a strong demand for action. The explicit form was shown as the front-seat passenger's appealed to the driver to slow down (see Episode V). This type of human assistance is characterized as: assignments, requests, warnings, complaints, suggestions, explanations, or considerations. In reference to implicit assistance, Mr. Fruggle (the front-seat passenger) focused Ms. Dream's (the driver) attention indirectly by using two different implicit strategies: (1) generating compliance [i.e., "*The majority of the road users are driving too fast under these circumstances, aren`t they*?", *"Yes, you are ... ."*] and (2) explaining self-experienced accidents, as happened in Episode III.

Impact of Technology on Collaboration

In the fourth episode, we describe Mr. Dragon (the driver), who has switched on the radio to hear the traffic news: "Today, *there are heavy snowfalls in the South of Bavaria, which have caused some traffic jams. Many motor trucks are getting stuck in the snow*." After hearing that news Mr. Dragon decides to take another route because he is afraid of getting stuck in traffic jam that evening. At that, Mr. Dragon leaves the highway. Two other passengers are sitting in the car, one of them is Mr. Freeman (the front-seat passenger), and the other one is Mr. Barnes (the back-seat passenger). Mr. Barnes, a friend of Mr. Dragon, has already fallen asleep on the backseat.

Episode IV: Mr. Dragon explains to Mr. Freeman that the best way for reaching their destination is to drive on rural roads. That is the reason why Mr. Dragon enters an alternative route using a navigation system, which he then follows. At increasingly short intervals, Mr. Dragon observes the screen in order to estimate the arrival time. He seems to be anxious about the weather conditions. Mr. Freeman notices his behavior and asks him, "What a trip, driving is really hard today, particularly at night. Is everything ok?" Mr. Dragon answers that it is okay for him. Mister Freeman asks again, "If you like, we could swap positions?". About fifteen minutes later, Mr. Dragon is unsure where he is and how far away they are from the main route. From that moment on, Mr. Freeman turns restless and looks with more attention outside the window. After a while, Mr. Freeman remembers that he has a navigation app on his smartphone. He starts his application and looks on the map to clarify their position. While states, "Look, we are here". Mr. Freeman lifts his smartphone to Mister Dragon`s navigation device.

[It looks a little bit like a two-distributed display, which consists of screen of an iPhone and a screen of a mobile device]. In the meantime, Mr. Barnes (the passenger on the backseat) wakes up. Mr. Barnes notices that they are not on the highway anymore and asks if he could help. Mr. Dragon gives thanks to Mr. Barnes`s aid After that, Mr. Dragon continues the conversation with Mr. Freeman and says, " Would you be so nice to look at [...]. Mr. Freeman requests Mr. Dragon to take care of the turn-by-turn instructions provided by his navigation. Mr. Freeman suggests Mr. Dragon that he would keep his eyes on both screens. If Mr. Freeman notices that the information of the mobile navigation device is not sufficient, he immediately staffs off his iPhone closer to Mr. Dragon`s device.

In particular, at night Mr. Freeman (the front-seat passenger) did not sleep, he was alert, and assisted Mr. Dragon (the driver) by asking him, *"What a trip, driving is really hard today, particularly at night. Is everything ok? [...]"* Also the intensity and frequency of human assistance and collaborative activity depended on the driver`s mental state. (i.e., to be anxious). Repeatedly, Mr. Freeman looked at Mr. Dragon and monitored his state. Mr. Dragon literally told Mr. Freeman that he was overstrained with the specific situation and needed help from him, because Mr. Dragon had already been anxious about finding the right way in the unfamiliar area under those bad weather conditions. At the beginning of the trip, the sun was shining, and Mr. Freeman was more relaxed; he was playing a game on his notebook.

In Episode IV, it is apparent that current ADAS are not always sufficient for turn-by-turn navigation under such circumstances. Mr. Dragon (the driver) and Mr. Freeman (the front-seat passenger) interacted with two navigation systems simultaneously to interpret and resume routing. Mr. Dragon used the portable unit (mounted on the center stack) for detailed information, whereas Mr. Freeman simultaneously assisted him using his smartphone that then provided them with an overview picture. In terms of satellite-based GPS systems Brown and Laurier [2] have already mentioned that the situated instructions are not "simply" instructions but are puzzle pieces that must be assembled by the driver or someone helping him. During night trips through unfamiliar areas drivers seemed overloaded with the information presented on the display and needed more help from the front-seat passenger. In our findings, we could also see how driver-passenger pairs made use of additional equipment. They found their own way to achieve the common goal, which was not supported by the customized navigation system. Within our study, we found that the collaborative activity between the driver-passenger pairs varied among different situations and was highly dependent on context factors, such as the mental state of the driver, weather, and light conditions. For instance, the view of the driver in Episode II was limited by heavy snowfall. This required more concentration on the road from both the front-seat passenger and the driver; they shared the view out of the front windshield. The front-seat passenger (i.e., Mr. Franklin (the front-seat passenger) suggested to Mr. Drew (the driver) to look through the upper half of the window. He would then focus his attention on the lower part of the window.

In the last brief recalled episode, we describe Ms. Dry (the driver) and Mr. Frog (the front-seat passenger) who are students and regularly drive between European cities. Now, however, they are in urban traffic that is mostly regulated between 40 and 50 kilometers per hour. They are driving through a part of the city which is fitted with integrated speed controls at traffic lights.

Episode V: Ms. Dry drives faster than allowed. She exceeds the speed limit by more than ten percent. At first, Mr. Frog does not intervene at all; Mr. Frog says nothing. But this does not stop him from looking at the speedometer. Mr. Frog bends his head for a moment to the driver`s side to see the current speed. After that, Mr. Frog reminds Ms. Dry not to forget to look at the speedometer and says, "We should not risk getting a ticket." Later, the driver-passenger pair approaches an intersection with many cars. At the moment the traffic light turns red; Mr. Frog suddenly stops watching the current YouTube clip on his mobile phone and tells Ms. Dry a second time to slow down. According to him, there may be traffic lights, which have integrated speed controls.

Mr. Frog (the front-seat passenger) paid attention on the driving speed of Ms. Dry (the driver) saying, *"Don't forget to look at the speedometer [...]"*. Furthermore, special attention was given to specific traffic situations (i.e., approaching traffic lights with integrated speed controls). If there were many vehicles waiting at a red traffic light, Mr. Frog stopped his tasks. This episode showed that the front-seat passengers also took care of the speed controls. They alerted drivers not to drive too fast. The current speed, which is presented on the dashboard, specifically led to more collaboration and human assistance.

DISCUSSION

Current research focuses mainly on drivers and, therefore, has lead to a lack of knowledge on how passengers assist and collaborate with drivers. This paper shows how passengers perceive what is happening on the road and tailors their interactions with drivers accordingly (a finding refines the simple mode of passengers being a distraction from the driving task, see e.g., [27]). Further, this paper describes how passengers can assist drivers (e.g., wiping clean a steamed-up window). In addition to seeing front-seat passenger as just an aid, the paper describes how they could be more involved in the driving task itself (see e.g., monitoring the speed of the car or assisting with the navigation device). Our study not only shows what some driver-passenger pairs do together, but it also presents how they make their devices fit to achieve a common goal.

Derived from our findings, we can make suggestions concerning the design of future ADAS that support a more cooperative use. We pay special attention to three topics that can enrich social and collaborative in-car activities. First, we argue for a broader conception of shared activities between driver-passenger pairs and discuss how a shared tool can help to achieve their common goals. Second, we discuss "common ground as a base for successful in-car communication" and how it relates to design. Finally, we explain how the implicit form of human assistance influences new designs for politeness.

Control vs. Sharing

We admit that ADAS in some cases have advantages over human assistance in preventing accidents (e.g., active brake assistant to reduce the risk of a collision) or in maneuvering (e.g., keeping a safe distance to vehicles in front). But human assistance can sometimes be superior to these technical assistance systems, as humans are more flexible and capable of adapting to a range of different conditions. Humans can react to contextual changes during a journey in more subtle ways and adapt their assistance accordingly. Based on our data, we see that one mobile navigation device, which was mounted on the windshield, was not sufficient for the specific navigation task. Instead, the specific driver-passenger pair used two systems simultaneously and shared information. This helped them to understand their environment in more detail and simultaneously reduced the driver's uncertainty.

A customized navigation system could serve as a good example for bridging the gap between keeping the driver in control while sharing tasks and duties with the front-seat passenger. A joint activity could be providing information about the navigation task (i.e., turn right in 500 meters) to the driver and also to the front-seat passenger. As stated above, front-seat passengers often keep track of more detailed information (e.g., points of interest) especially in unfamiliar areas, while the driver focus more on the primary task of driving. The findings from our study to raise awareness and an enhanced feeling of control indicate that front-seat passengers also like to share basic information about the car (e.g., speed) in terms of displays in the dashboard. This means that front-seat passengers want be informed about the current speed of the car (see Episode V), preferably on their own screen. ADAS could, therefore, be oriented towards front-seat passengers.

We argue not to provide only basic information about the car to the front-seat passenger but also specific situation based information. This gives the driver the opportunity to use the front-seat passenger as a reminder. That is the reason why we envisage a collaborative system which keeps the front-seat passenger and the driver updated on the current driving situation through personalized information (a concept is illustrated in Figure 1). It consists of two movable displays, which provide different contents. Figure 1a shows the basic configuration, where only one display is visible to the driver. This display can be used similar to conventional in-car dashboard navigation devices. If the driver needs additional information in special situations (e.g., in a traffic jam) the visible area of the navigation unit is enlarged with a second display, which can be seen in Figure 1b. To this point, the navigation unit only supports the driver.

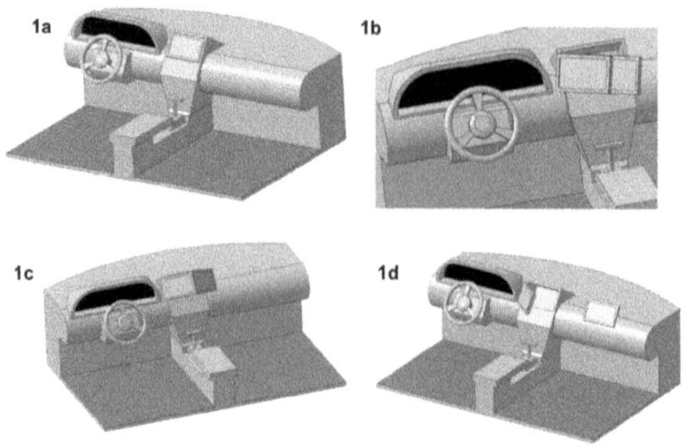

Figure 1: Idea of an Information-Sharing Prototype

By splitting the two displays and turning the second display towards the front-seat passenger, the driver and front-seat passenger get information using the two displays in the center stack (see Figure 1). This arrangement is especially useful in situations where a high amount of interaction is needed between the driver-passenger pair. The interaction is conducted on the center stack and they are facing each other allowing a social collaboration. In situations, where the interaction is reduced, a setup shown in Figure 1d could be useful. A display is then set up in front of the front-seat passenger who can gather information easily without turning towards the driver and also with his/her hand. This setup is useful, for example, during long trips where the front-seat passenger can monitor, e.g., the speed or the route and give the driver appropriate help and act as a reminder in critical situations. However, our aim here is not to provide specific designs but more to guide and to provide inspiration for designers. With the idea of an initial sketch, we want to explain how a shared tool potentially can support the collaborative activities between driver-passenger pairs.

Establishing a Common Ground Space

Having the right sensitivity in interpreting drivers' reactions and desires is sometimes difficult for many front-seat passengers. Misunderstandings between driver-passenger pairs can arise quickly. While people who are friends or in a relationship might be able to interpret the other's intentions, this is not always the case for all driver-passenger pairs. As in social interaction in general [20], front-seat passengers have to interpret the driver's intentions by being aware of what is happing and adapt their assistance to the specific situation. To succeed with coordinated actions and to achieve common ground [5,6], front-seat passengers in our data used various communication strategies such as *no, delayed, and frequent and spry* forms of communication. In our study, the front-seat passengers adapted their communication style for example, by making short speech breaks in their conversation. Another front-seat passenger, for instance, started to talk continuously with the driver to enquire about his well-being. He recognized that the situation needed more assistance from him and, therefore, required knowledge on the driver's state to communicate effectively. From a human-human mediated design perspective we see two fundamental questions which have to be taken into account. The first question addresses the issue of how can we achieve a common ground between driver-passenger pairs; the second focuses on how can we design and evaluate assistance systems to address this need.

Looking at evidence from our data, some drivers did not ask the front-seat passengers directly for help. Instead, they often had "hidden intentions", something that led to misunderstandings or wrong assistance in some cases by the front-seat passenger. We believe that future ADAS can be designed to display some of the context-related information contributing to mutual knowledge, believes, and assumptions. By being displayed, this kind of information might help driver-passenger pairs to understand the other`s intention. Based on Clark and Marshall`s theory [6], we state, that it is a good solution to make the implicit mechanism of common grounding more visible for the front-seat passenger. By presenting the driver`s mental state on a front-seat passenger display, we argue that a front-seat passenger can take care of the driver`s feelings and implicit needs. The obtained data, for example, measured by physiological equipment on the steering wheel could describe the driver`s mental state. The knowledge of the driver`s state (i.e., workload caused by heavy snowfalls) allows the front-seat passenger to support the driver earlier. The front-seat passenger could then be in a better position to assist the driver adequately and adapt his communication styles based on the current situation in order to avoid misunderstanding. Additionally, the interpretation of the data could be supported by the system (e.g., level of risk could be analyzed and visualized). We suggest to empower users, (e.g., the front-seat passenger like [17]), with more explicit contextual information in order to foster mutual knowledge about contextual factors. Also, by supplying this kind of information to front-seat passengers, we want to put focus on how any passenger in the car has control of their life in addition to the driver. Without taking away any responsibility of the driver, we believe we can increase the comfort of front-seat passengers by supplying them with more information on what is the current status of the car and the traffic situation (e.g., the outside temperature and the status of the road). This way, we do not see front-seat passengers as the person in charge of the primary task of driving, but as an important resource to assist the driver and as a person that deserves to feel more in control of what is currently happening.

Design for Politeness

In carpools, registered drivers offer rides for passengers. In doing that they become responsible for the welfare and comfort of his/her guest. Passengers have the responsibility to show gratitude. Often passengers feel the need to be polite and to not criticize the driving (i.e., that they are driving too fast in snowy weather conditions) of the person offering their driving service. Therefore, providing assistance to the driver is to be done in a careful manner. In our data we can see how front-seat passengers used two implicit strategies of human assistance (i.e., generating compliance to the majority of driver is too fast and explaining self-experienced stories). With this data, we can also confirm the results of Jonsson and colleagues [19] in identifying the importance of word usage in driver assistance systems. The front-seat passengers in our study were highly aware of the effects of their words and used them very consciously. This also can be seen as an essential factor in politeness. For instance, jokes were used to ease the situation and indicate how front-seat passengers attempted to reduce the driver`s workload politely. We argue that this form of interaction is a considerable issue and absolutely key to successful passenger-driver interactions. Yet this topic is almost completely unaddressed. We believe that future in-car assistive systems should employ the same implicit usage of polite vocabulary, showing that the system is not blaming the drivers for mistakes, but making them aware of potential effects of their behavior.

CONCLUSION

Today a huge number of ADAS systems are available on the market. In addition to these technology passengers often support the driver with supplemental information or with emotional assistance. Often though, these systems fail to make use of the social nature and collaborative mechanisms of driving where in the car there sometimes is also a skilled front-seat passenger. How and under what contextual conditions a front-seat passenger assists the driver is a relevant concern for design-oriented areas such as CSCW. The common understanding of collaboration and assistance that happens in the car between the driver and the front-seat passenger will contribute and inform the development of future automotive user interface designs; Driving has, for too long, been researched and designed for passenger-blind. In this paper, we have argued for a way forward based on ethno-methodological approaches in particular work. We used the ethnographic technique by travelling in the car. This is different from other studies conducted in similar settings, where video recordings would be captured without the presence of a researcher and later analyzed. By presenting material from our ethnographic contextually lived experiences of how and under what contextual influences front-seat passengers assist and collaborate with drivers, we point out a few potential ways in which future ADAS better can support collaboration between driver-passenger pairs. A shared understanding of the current situation can lead to better communication and collaboration between drivers and front-seat passengers. We highlight how the simple step of sharing or making contextual information visible for the front-seat passenger can have a large effect on the collaborative dimensions of driving. By presenting this data we hope we have succeeded in providing a foundation for reconsidering human-system interaction in the car and allow for more collaboration while driving also on the level of assisting technology.

ACKNOWLEDGEMENT

The financial support by the Federal Ministry of Economy, Family and Youth and the National Foundation for Research, Technology and Development is gratefully acknowledged (Christian Doppler Laboratory for "Contextual Interfaces"). Our thanks to ACM SIGCHI for allowing us to modify templates they had developed.

REFERENCES

1. Boyle, E.A., Anderson, A.H., and Newlands, A. The effects of visibility on dialogue and performance in a cooperative problem-solving task. *Language and Speech 37*, 1 (1994), 1-20.
2. Brown, B. and Laurier, E. The normal natural troubles of driving with GPS. In *Proc. CHI 2012*, ACM Press (2012), 1621-1630.
3. Bubb, H. Fahrerassistenz-Primär ein Beitrag zum Komfort oder für die Sicherheit. VDI-Berichte 1768 VDI-Verlag (2003), 25-44.
4. Bull, M. Automobility and the power of sound. *Theory, Culture & Society*, 21(2005), 243-260.
5. Clark, H.H., and Brennan, E. Grounding in communication. In L.B. Resnick, R.M. Levine, and S.D. Tesley (Eds.): Perspectives on Socially Shared Cognition, APA Press (1991), 127-149.
6. Clark, H.H., and Marshall, C.R. Definite reference and mutual knowledge. In B.L. Webber, A.K. Joshi, and I.A. Sag (Eds.): Elements of discourse understanding. Cambridge, Univ. Press (1981), 1-63.
7. De Waard, D., et al. Driver behavior in an emergency situation in the Automated Highway System. *Transportation Human Factors*, 1 (1999), 67-82.
8. Esbjörnsson, M., Juhlin, O. and Weilenmann, A. Drivers using mobile phones in traffic: An ethnographic study of interactional adaptation. *INT. J. HUM-COMPUT INT 22*, 1 (2007), 37-58.
9. Federal Motor Carrier Saftey Administration. The 100-Car Naturalistic Driving study. Report FMCSA-RRR-06-004. Virginia (2006). U.S. Department of Transportation.
10. Forlizzi J., Barley. W.C., and Seder T. Where should I turn: moving from individual to collaborative navigation strategies to inform the interaction design of future navigation systems. In *Proc. CHI 2010*, ACM Press (2010), 1261-1270.
11. Friija, N. Facial expressions and situational cues. *Abnormal and Social Psychology*, 54, 2(1958), 149-154.
12. Gietelink, O., et al. Development of Advanced Driver Assistance Systems with vehicle hardware-in-the-loop simulations. *Vehicle System Dynamics* 44, 7 (2006), 569-590.
13. Hancock, P.A. and Parasuraman, R. Human Factors and safety in the design of Intelligent Vehicle-Highway Systems. *J. SAF. RES*, 23 (1992), 181-198.
14. Heath, C. and Luff, P. *Technology in Action*. Cambridge, Univ. Press, (2000).
15. Hinde, R. A. *Non-verbal communication*. Cambridge, Cambridge, Univ. Press, (1975).
16. Hipp, M., Schaub, F. et al. Interaction weaknesses of personal navigation devices. In *Proc. AutomotiveUI 2010*, ACM Press (2010), 129-136.
17. Höök, K., Stahl, A. et al. Interactional Empowerment. In *Proc. CHI 2008*, ACM Press (2008), 647-656.
18. Inbar, O. and Tractinsky, N. Make a trip an experience: sharing in-car information with passengers. In *Proc. CHI 2011*, ACM Press (2011), 1243-1248.
19. Jonsson, I., Nass, C. et al. Don't blame me I am only the driver: impact of blame attribution on attitudes and attention to driving task. *Ext. Abstracts CHI 2004*, ACM Press (2004), 1219–1222.
20. Juhlin, O. *Social Media on the Road* -The future of car based computing, Monography. Springer Verlag, London, (2010).
21. Juhlin, O. Traffic Behavior as social interaction – Implications for the design of the artificial driver. In *Proc. ITS 1999*, Transport Research Laboratory (1999).
22. Kun, A. L., Paek, T. et al. (2009). Glancing at personal navigation devices can affect driving: experimental results and design implications. In *Proc. AutomotiveUI 2009*, ACM Press (2009), 129- 136.
23. Laurier, B., Lorimer, H. et al. A. Driving and 'Passengering': Notes on the Ordinary Organization of Car Travel. *Mobilities 3*, 1 (2008), 1-23.
24. Leshed, G., Velden, T. et al. In-car GPS navigation: engagement with and disengagement from the environment. In *Proc. CHI 2008*, ACM Press (2008), 1675-1684.
25. Molloy, R. and Parasuraman, R. Monitoring an automated system for single failure: vigilance and task complexity effects. *Human Factors*, 38 (1996), 311-322.
26. Östergren, M. and Juhlin, O. Sound Pryer: truly mobile joint music listening. Int. workshop on mobile music technology, (2004).
27. Regan, M., and Mitsopoulos, E. Understanding passenger influences on driver behavior: Implications for road safety and recommendations for countermeasure development. Tech. rep., (2001).
28. Sheller, M. and Urry, J. The city and the car. *IJUR 24*, 4 (2000), 737-757.

Exploring Pet Video Chat: The Remote Awareness and Interaction Needs of Families with Dogs and Cats

Carman Neustaedter
School of Interactive Arts & Technology
Simon Fraser University
Surrey, BC, Canada
carman_neustaedter@sfu.ca

Jennifer Golbeck
Human-Computer Interaction Lab
University of Maryland
College Park, MD, USA
golbeck@cs.umd.edu

ABSTRACT
Many people have pets such as dogs and cats that they would consider to be family. Along with this comes a need to stay aware of one's pet and, possibly, interact with it when away from home. There has even been a recent push by companies to create video-mediated communication (VMC) systems to connect pet owners and pets over distance. Yet the problem is that we do not know how such systems should be designed to meet the real needs of pet owners. To investigate this, we conducted a survey with dog and cat owners that explores their needs for remotely monitoring and interacting with their pets. Our results show that many family members would value being able to maintain an awareness of their pets and interact with them over distance using VMC systems. Such systems would be particularly valuable when pet owners are away from home for extended time periods. However, VMC systems for pets must be designed cautiously to avoid issues of owner disembodiment and other ethical challenges.

Author Keywords
Awareness; interaction; pets; dogs; cats; video-mediated communication

ACM Classification Keywords
H5.3. Information interfaces and presentation: Group and Organization Interfaces – *Computer-supported cooperative work;*

INTRODUCTION
Family members naturally want to stay aware of one another when they are separated by distance [17]. For example, couples wish to stay connected when they travel and parents desire to know the whereabouts of their children throughout the day [17]. For many people, the idea of 'family' extends beyond just people to include pets. In fact, over 63% of households in the United States have pets [2] where 98% of pet owners consider their pets to be family or close friends [7]. The most commonly owned pets in the United States are dogs followed by cats [12].

Given the above need, researchers and companies have started to design systems that allow pet owners to monitor or interact with their pets over distance when they are not at home (e.g., [15,26]). For example, there now exists a plethora of commercial remote monitoring systems for pets such as dogs (e.g., Panasonic's Pet Cam). Such 'doggie cams' are focused at supporting remote awareness for family members who might be away from their home (and dog) for periods of time during the day [8], dog kennels where people leave their pets while traveling (e.g., [9,21]), and even dog groomers or spas [21]. Despite these initial attempts at creating useful technologies for pet owners and companies, it is not clear if they map to families' real needs for remotely monitoring and interacting with their pets.

Our paper addresses this by exploring the potential for family members to monitor and interact with their dogs and cats over distance through video-mediated communication (VMC) systems. By VMC systems, we refer to Skype-like 'video chat' systems that can provide two-way audio and video connections between locations [13,14]. This goes somewhat beyond the capabilities of existing pet cams to explore additional opportunities for remote interaction in addition to just awareness.

We conducted a survey with 86 family members who owned dogs and/or cats. Our results show that most pet owners like to know the same awareness information about their pets as they do about their family members: activities, location, and well-being. We also found that pet owners would value awareness and interaction features that could be incorporated within a VMC system, but that there is some concern with owner disembodiment as perceived by the pet. Thus, such video-based systems must be designed cautiously in order to avoid stress on the pet.

RELATED WORK
Recently, a number of studies have explored the use of VMC systems by families. Results showed that families appreciate the additional feelings of connectedness they received from being able to actually see their remote family members [1,13,14]. Yet VMC systems were found to be challenging to use with bootstrapping and connectivity issues [1,13,14]. Studies of children using VMC showed that parents must do a lot of "scaffold" work to keep children engaged in conversation [1] as children can easily lose interest in the remote people [25]. We expect that such

issues may extend to instances where VMC is used to monitor or interact with pets over distance. Researchers have also found that families with small children find benefit in leaving a video connection going for an extended period of time to show remote family members the children's activities [13]. Given the feelings many family members have for their pets, some of this knowledge is likely to extend to and apply in the context of connecting family members with their pets.

Turning to technologies for pets, we see a recent increase in the design of systems to support human-pet interaction. These include a game-like training environment for dogs called CAT (Canine Amusement and Training) [24]; Cat Cat Revolution (CCR) [18] which shows a moving mouse on an iPad that cats can follow; a dog-owner interaction system with sounds and a remote tennis-ball throwing device [15]; and a remotely monitored and controlled 'cat condo' with play activities [26].

There also exists a body of research that provides initial investigations into pet awareness. Studies of online social networking sites aimed at pets (e.g., Dogster) showed that pet owners use such sites to share pictures and information about their pets, view profiles of other pets, and receive advice [10]. Studies with hunters and typical pet owners showed that hunters desire location tracking of their pets, while everyday pet owners desire to know about their pets' well being while they were away from home and want ways to comfort them remotely [20]. Weilenmann and Juhlin describe a GPS dog tracking-device that allows hunters to track their dog's locations outdoors [24]. Paasovaara et al. explored dog monitoring via an enhanced collar containing indoor and outdoor location tracking and audio sensing [19]. They found that people valued the idea of monitoring their dog's activities and location (inside/outside the home) in real time. Participants also felt there was value in being able to see video recordings of their dogs.

Our research builds on the related work by exploring the situations when family members would value remote interaction systems and the needs they would have for these systems. We focus on pet awareness and interaction, as well as, video-based systems. We also extend the literature by exploring the needs for *both* dog and cat owners.

ONLINE SURVEY METHODOLOGY

We chose to use a survey for our study because we wanted to get an understanding from people who owned a variety of types of dogs and cats. We wanted to see if this would influence their thoughts on the topic (yet we actually found a large degree of similarities). We also value the depth of knowledge gained from interviews and, as such, structured our survey to be open-ended where we asked for stories of pet interactions and expected use (if any) of VMC systems.

Survey Questions and Topics

We asked for background information about the respondents and their pets, what their remote monitoring needs were when not at home with their pets, and how they would want to see or interact with their pets over distance (if at all). Examples of specific questions include: 'What would you like to know about your pet(s) when you are not with them?' and 'If you could interact with your pet(s) over the Internet when you are not at home, what would you like to be able to do with them?' As a cautionary note, our questions asked pet owners for their *opinions* on what technologies they felt would benefit their pets and themselves; thus, they used their own knowledge as a pet owner to comment on our survey as opposed to knowledge that might come from a trained expert on pets.

Respondents

We advertised our survey via snowball sampling where we emailed links to it to friends/family who then forwarded it on to others they knew. We also posted links to the survey on Twitter, Facebook, and online forums devoted to pet owners. We received completed surveys from 86 people (26 male, 59 female, 1 not said). Respondents varied from 19 to 65+ years; however, about half of our respondents were in their late 20s to mid 30s. Respondents' occupations varied heavily and only one had professional experience with animals (a veterinarian). All resided in the United States or Canada. Six people lived alone, and the rest lived with at least one other person. Nearly half of the respondents (42 of 86) had children where their ages and numbers varied. Respondents also had various numbers and types of dogs and cats: 25 had just cats, 37 had just dogs, and 24 had at least one of both. At the extreme, and likely outliers, one had 4 dogs, and another had 16 cats.

Analysis

We inductively analyzed our interviews using open, axial, and selective coding [22] to draw out the important themes from our data. Quotes have been carefully selected to present examples from our survey responses. Next to each quote is the gender and age range of the respondent and type and number of animals owned.

BEING AWAY FROM HOME

We first wanted to understand at what times it might be valuable for pet owners to maintain remote awareness of their pets or potentially interact with them.

Short Time Durations

Nearly all dog owners did not have issues being away from their pet for *short durations* of time, e.g., going to work, shopping, or visiting a friend. In fact, they were generally okay with being gone the length of a typical workday (e.g., 6-10 hours). This was the point at which most people felt that the dogs would be 'fine' physically. For example, they would not need to use the bathroom in this time period if they were trained to go outside. Beyond this time frame, there was a sense of guilt that they should be with their dogs for a portion of the day and return home.

"if we've been at work and a friend asks us to do something that will have us away the entire evening and we won't have

time to walk the dog, we'll usually say no." – F, 19-25, Basset Hound

In cases where pets had health issues or other concerns such as social anxiety, dog owners would ensure they came home more often, e.g., every 2 to 4 hours.

In the case of cats, all but one pet owner did not have concerns about being away from home for short durations of time. This is expected as most cats are trained to use a litter box indoors. Interestingly, compared to dog owners, cat owners did not report feelings of guilt associated with not being at home. For the one cat owner who did have concerns, it was because the cat had health issues. This is certainly an outlier yet still important, as it would likely generalize to all situations where a pet has health issues.

Long Time Durations

Most respondents (66 of 86) left home for vacations or trips several times a year where the trips spanned several days to a week or two. Sixteen people did not leave their home for more than a day and only four people had more extreme situations and would be gone from home repeatedly throughout the year for weeks or months at a time.

Knowledge of Pet Activities. Most people (50 of 86) said they didn't know what their pets did when they were gone for long durations of time and the pets were either at home (being fed by a friend or neighbor), at a kennel, or at another person's house. Yet the remaining 36 respondents had technology-based routines to stay aware of their pets while away. In these cases, people said that the person watching the pet would send updates while they were gone or the owner would contact them to get information. This might be over the phone, email, or Facebook, and sometimes even included the sharing of pictures.

"Yes. I ask the operator of the kennel about what the dog's schedule is to be. I also call the kennel frequently while I'm away." – F, 37-50, Yellow Labrador

"We sometimes email catsitter; he always leaves detailed report on time spent, what he did, what cats did." – M, 51-65, 3 Cats

Two people even talked about using Skype to connect with their dogs over VMC while away. For example:

"At the dog boarding facility we do not know what she's doing, but the facility provides a "schedule" of what the dogs do (i.e. go to the play area at 10am-noon, etc etc.). When the dog is staying with family, we sometimes video skype, or our family members will send pictures via phone, email, or Facebook." – M, 26-36, English Bulldog

One respondent described a situation where their dog kennel had previously provided an online webcam system for pet owners but had to discontinue it because it did not always capture what pet owners wanted to see:

"They use to have a webcam but stopped it as people would constantly call them and disrupt their routine to make petty requests like they can't see the dogs water bowl on the webcam , to call back and say that wasnt their dogs blanket. It got too much so they had to discontinue it." – F, 37-50, Great Pyrenees and Black Labrador

REMOTE AWARENESS AND INTERACTION

Next we looked specifically at what information pet owners wanted to know about their pets when away and how they wanted to interact with their pets remotely, if at all. We asked general questions about remote awareness and interaction followed by questions asking if/how they might use a VMC system with a pet.

Awareness of Pets

A small number of people (5 dog owners, 2 dog/cat owners) were completely fine knowing nothing about their pets while away from home. On the other hand, the large majority of people (79 of 86) wanted details about their pets when they were not at home with them. This included knowledge of the pets' activities (35 people), temperament or mood (23 people), safety or health (17 people), and location (5 people) where each was desired by both cat and dog owners. Most respondents wanted to know this information simply out of concern for their pets' well being.

"what they are doing (especially my dog) and whether they miss us/have seperation anxiety" – F, 19-25, Pitbull and 2 Cats

"What they are doing, like how much they move around the house and where. It would be good to have a sense of how much exercise they get ... It would be nice to know that especially for the cat, since if she spends all her alone time cowering in a tiny hot corner of the attic... – F, 26-36, Pound Puppy and Cat

Some people wanted to be able discipline their pets based on this knowledge or ensure they were not misbehaving.

"I want to make sure she doesn't bark all day, want to know if she just sleeps, want to make sure she isn't trying to get into the frig or garbage." – F, 37-50, Retriever and Cat

"Does my Shiba Inu even hesitate before he chews on something that he knows he's not supposed to when we're not around? lol" – F, 26-36, Shiba Inu & 3 Cats

Remote Interaction and Viewing

Over half of respondents, 65 of 86 people, (28 dog owners, 18 cat owners, 19 dog/cat owners) thought that some form of remote interaction with their pets would be valuable.

Talking with Pets. About a third of our respondents (28 people) wanted to be able to talk with their pets while away from home using some type of VMC system. These respondents felt that by being able to talk to their pets they might be able to calm them, if needed, or provide comfort and companionship through their voice when they weren't able to physically be there. Some people even wanted to be able to tell their dog specific things related to obedience or discipline through an audio connection.

"Let them hear my voice and the inflection they hear daily when i converse with them ... I know when using FaceTime with the iPhone they respond VERY positively to sound alone." – M, 26-36, Shepherd, Dalmation, and Corgi Mix

"We have a webcam and it's frustrating to watch her chew on the couch or generally get into things without being able to do anything about. Maybe if we had a way to talk to her or let her see our image, we could stop her behavior remotely." – F, 37-50, Husky Mix

Watching Pets. Another one-third of our respondents (27 people) wanted to be able to watch or see their pets and saw benefit in this. Here VMC was seen as a means to know what activities their pets were doing to ensure they were not getting into trouble or to check to make sure they were safe. Thus, people saw a VMC system as a way to ensure peace-of-mind when away from home.

"We've actually used Skype before to keep an eye on the animals for fun. We just setup an open laptop with a restricted skype account that would accept any call from a specific account. It was kind of fun, but mostly my dog just sleeps. We just used it to see what she was up to at random times of the day and to see if she ever barked at people outside, etc." – F, 19-25, Bassett Hound and Cat

Providing Play or Exercise. A small number of people (9 of 86) said they would like to be able to play with their pets over distance through some form of physical interaction; this was without prompting and we note that some may simply have not realized it was possible to do this. Respondents felt that these interactions would allow them to engage with their pets while remote so that the pets would not feel lonely. They also saw this as a means to provide needed exercise or mental stimulation. Here the focus was mostly on remotely controlled toys.

Additional Activities. We also had four people say they would like some mechanism that would allow them to touch or pet their animal, though these could be considered outliers. Additionally, two people wanted to open and shut doors to let pets inside and outside.

No Need or Desire for Remote Interaction

On the other hand, 21 people (10 dog owners, 6 cat owners, 5 dog/cat owners) said they would not use remote interaction technologies with their pets. Respondents were either uninterested, did not think they would have enough time, or, in some cases, they saw issues with such technologies that would complicate their usage.

In the case of VMC systems, some respondents did not think their pet would stay near a computer display with a VMC system long enough for it to be useful. Others were concerned about their own disembodiment, as perceived by the pets. That is, if pets heard their owner talking through a VMC system, they might not understand where the voice was coming from, or why they did not actually see the physical presence of their owner. Thus, respondents felt pets may be confused and receive no benefit from the system and, even worse, it may cause increased loneliness or anxiety. Respondents also felt that seeing a live video stream of their owner may additionally confuse pets. For some pet owners who had tried existing VMC systems with their pets, this was indeed the case:

"we tried talking to the dogs when we had the laptop set up, but they found that confusing, so we just observed" – F, 37-50, Mutt

"I would like to see them but I don't think interaction is fair because they don't understand and if they hear my voice they would be confused as to why I'm not there with them. THey want me to touch them and play with them and I can't do that over the internet." – F, 26-36, Entlebucher

A few dog owners even expressed strong opposition to remote interaction because of this. For example:

"I dont want to interact with them over the Internet and I strongly feel that this is a mistake. Their communication with me is extremely strong and at a level totally inappropriate for remote or disembodied contact. Disembodied contact would in fact DAMAGE my relationship and effect the girls adversely ... It would be far far better to be able to manage water, food, shelter, toys than dogs." – M, 51-65, 2 German Shepherds

In the case of remotely controlled toys, some pet owners felt that their pets might be afraid of them or could easily damage them (e.g., energetic or large animals).

DISCUSSION

Compared to the existing research on family communication [17], we see that pet owners largely want to be able to know the same types of information about their pets as they would their family members or close friends (e.g., activities, location, and well being). These findings are similar to past studies [19,20]. Reactions varied but there was generally positive responses for viewing and interacting with pets. Long trips are when people feel especially detached from their pets; this suggests value for VMC systems in these times.

Yet the more one attempts to incorporate interaction into a VMC system for pets, the more problematic the topic becomes. For example, showing a video feed of an owner may cause confusion for the pet (if the video is presented in a pet-viewable way). Similarly, pets may not understand where a voice is coming from if it is sent over an audio link. Thus, if owners want to truly interact with their pet by talking to it, akin to how they might in person, disembodied voices could be problematic. This suggests that VMC systems for pets be designed and used cautiously. For example, one should carefully consider whether audio links are critical to a VMC design, if interaction is desired. Similarly, owners should be careful to monitor and understand their own behavior over such systems to ensure that it is not causing distress to their pets. The 'safest' designs, in terms of not causing distress to the pet, may simply be those that allow pet owners to monitor their pet from afar using a video link, where the owner sees the pet, but not vice-versa, and the interaction is limited.

Reflecting on the CSCW literature, we can see that the challenge with disembodiment is certainly not new. Research on the design of VMC systems for human-human communication has shown that the disembodiment of people can also be problematic [4]; however, in the human-human case, it is because people may not know who is able to see or hear them over a video link (e.g., someone standing outside of the camera's view). It is also clear that another challenge with designing VMC systems for pets is that pets have few ways to actually control how they participate in a system. In human-human communications, people are able to regulate their autonomy and choose how and when they participate in a VMC system [4,6]. For example, they can start and stop the video call at the push of a button. This type of interaction is so pivotal that it has garnered decades of CSCW literature exploring it and the privacy implications (e.g., [4,5,6,11]).

Yet pets are not people. With pets, this control is lost and it is left in the hands of the pet's owner. For example, if a pet becomes confused or anxious because of a VMC system, the pet cannot turn it off to alleviate the feelings. One might imagine being able to design system features that *could* allow a pet to turn a VMC system on and off; however, it is unlikely that most dogs or cats could be trained to perform such an action (while understanding it). Like children using VMC systems [1], pets will require some type of 'scaffolding' by others to interact and work the system. Yet in VMC systems for pets, the scaffolding will need to occur at the remote location by the pet owner (for children, this occurs in a collocated fashion by parents [1]). This might involve the remote pet owner monitoring the pet to observe anxiety levels or trying to 'coax' them to come in front of a system. It would likely also include mechanisms for the pet owner to easily close a video connection if distress is detected, or selectively stopping the features that might be causing the distress.

Because of challenges like these, ethical issues certainly arise for the design and use of VMC systems for pets. Ethical review boards have strict rules governing the study of animals [16] and the Special Interest Group on Animal-Computer Interaction provides similar guidelines [3]. These include (in the least) not causing unnecessary distress or pain and stopping procedures if this occurs. The challenge, however, is that detecting mental confusion or anxiety in pets could be very difficult, especially for technology researchers. For example, in the case of designing a VMC system for pets, it would be difficult to know just how much distress seeing or hearing a remote owner would cause. One could also imagine issues with systems that support interaction through physical devices (e.g., a remotely controlled ball thrower). For example, a pet could easily be injured by such a system if it did not fully understand how the system worked and an owner was not present to monitor it. Issues such as these and more should be carefully thought about by researchers exploring designs for remote pet awareness and interaction.

CONCLUSION

Our paper has reported on the awareness and interaction needs of families with dogs and cats through an online survey. We have specifically focused on understanding when and how families might value a video chat system designed for them to monitor and interact with their pets. Our findings show potential benefits for such systems, yet there are also challenges that must be overcome such as owner disembodiment and ethical concerns. We hope that our work provides designers and practitioners with a new understanding for designing solutions that mitigate these concerns while still providing owners with the benefits that such systems may offer. We also recognize that there are many other types of pets beyond dogs and cats and hope that other researchers will continue this area of exploration to understand how systems may be designed to best meet the needs of these pet owners.

ACKNOWLEDGEMENTS

We thank the Natural Sciences and Engineering Research Council of Canada for funding this research. We also thank Kirstin Neustaedter for her help recruiting participants.

REFERENCES

1. Ames, M., Go, J., Kaye, J., Spasojevic, M., Making Love in the Network Closet: The Benefits and Work of Family Videochat, *Proc. CSCW,* ACM Press (2010).
2. AAPMA National Pet Owners Survey, American Pet Products Manufacturers Association (2008).
3. Animal-Computer Interaction, http://www.open.ac.uk/blogs/ACI
4. Bellotti, V. Design for Privacy in Multimedia Computing and Communications Environments, in *Technology and Privacy: The New Landscape*, MIT Press (1998) 63-98.
5. Bellotti, V., and Sellen, A. Design for Privacy in Ubiquitous Computing Environments, *Proc. ECSCW*, Kluwer Academic Publishers (1993), 77-92.
6. Boyle, M., Neustaedter, C., and Greenberg, S. Privacy Factors in Video-based Media Spaces, *in Media Spaces: 20+ Years of Mediated Life,* Springer (2009).
7. Cain, A. Pets as Family Members, *Pets and Family,* Hawthorn Press (1985), 5-10.
8. Dogs in Canada, Furveillance, http://dogsincanada.com/furveillance-the-latest-on-pet-cams
9. Downtown Dog Lounge, downtowndoglounge.com
10. Golbeck, J. The more people I meet, the more I like my dog: A study of pet-oriented social networks on the web. *First Monday*. 16(2), February 7, 2011.
11. Harrison, S., *Media Spaces: 20+ Years of Mediated Life,* Springer (2009).
12. Household Pet Ownership: 2001, *US Census Bureau.*

13. Judge, T.K. and Neustaedter, C., Sharing Conversation and Sharing Life: Video Conferencing in the Home. *Proc. CHI*, ACM Press (2010), 655-658.

14. Kirk, D., Sellen, A., and Cao, X., Home Video Communication, *Proc. CSCW,* ACM Press (2010).

15. Mankoff, D., Dey, A., Mankoff, J., Mankoff, K. Supporting interspecies social awareness: using peripheral displays for distributed pack awareness, *Proc. UIST,* ACM Press (2005).

16. National Research Council, Guide for the Care and Use of Laboratory Animals: Eighth Edition, The National Academies Press (2011).

17. Neustaedter, C., Elliot, K. and Greenberg, S., Interpersonal awareness in the domestic realm. *Proc. OzCHI*, ACM Press (2006), 15-22

18. Noz, F. and An, J. Cat cat revolution: an interspecies gaming experience. *Proc. CHI*, ACM Press (2011).

19. Paasovaara, S., Paldanius, M., Saarinen, P., Hakkila, J., and Vaananen-Vainio-Mattila, K. The Secret Life of My Dog – Design and Evaluation of Paw Tracker Concept, *Proc. MobileHCI,* ACM Press (2011).

20. Paldanius, M., Tuula Kärkkäinen, Väänänen-Vainio-Mattila, K., Juhlin, O. and Häkkilä, J. Communication technology for human-dog interaction, *Proc. CHI*, ACM Press (2011), 2641-2650.

21. Playful Paws, www.playfulpawskennel.ca/

22. Strauss, A. and Corbin, J. Basics of Qualitative Research, 2nd Edition, Sage Publications (1998).

23. Weilenmann, A., and Juhlin, O. Understanding People and Animals: The Use of a Positioning System in Ordinary Human-Canine Interaction, *Proc. CHI,* ACM Press (2011).

24. Wingrave, C.A., Rose, J. Langston, T. and LaViola, J.J. Early explorations of CAT: canine amusement and training. *Proc. CHI EA.* (2010), 2661-2670.

25. Yarosh, S., Inkpen, K.M., and Brush, A.J. Video Playdate: Toward Free Play across Distance. Proc. CHI, ACM Press (2010), 1251-1260.

26. Young, J., Young, N., Greenberg, S. and Sharlin, E. Feline Fun Park: A Distributed Interface for Pets and Owners, *Video Proc. Pervasive Computing,* (2007).

Engaging Robots: Easing Complex Human-Robot Teamwork using Backchanneling

Malte F. Jung[1], Jin Joo Lee[2], Nick DePalma[2], Sigurdur O. Adalgeirsson[2], Pamela J. Hinds[1], Cynthia Breazeal[2]

[1]Stanford University
Stanford, CA 94305 USA
{mjung, phinds}@stanford.edu

[2]Massachusetts Institute of Technology
Cambridge, MA 02139 USA
{jinjoo, ndepalma}@mit.edu, {siggi, cynthiab}@media.mit.edu

ABSTRACT
People are increasingly working with robots in teams and recent research has focused on how human-robot teams function, but little attention has yet been paid to the role of social signaling behavior in human-robot teams. In a controlled experiment, we examined the role of backchanneling and task complexity on team functioning and perceptions of the robots' engagement and competence. Based on results from 73 participants interacting with autonomous humanoid robots as part of a human-robot team (one participant, one confederate, and three robots), we found that when robots used backchanneling team functioning improved and the robots were seen as more engaged. Ironically, the robots using backchanneling were perceived as less competent than those that did not. Our results suggest that backchanneling plays an important role in human-robot teams and that the design and implementation of robots for human-robot teams may be more effective if backchanneling capability is provided.

Author Keywords
Affect; human-robot interaction; human-robot teams; team performance; urban search and rescue.

ACM Classification Keywords
I.2.9; K.4.3.

INTRODUCTION
Robots are part of high-stakes search and rescue operations [36], high-risk surgeries [25], and exploration missions. With ever-increasing capabilities, autonomous robots are becoming an integral part of professional and operational teams as people try to extend human capabilities. A burgeoning human-robot interaction research agenda is exploring the dynamics of human-robot teams with the goal of understanding more about how to enable coordination between people and robots [15, 44]. To date, this research has primarily focused on cognitive aspects of team functioning such as the development of situational awareness [37], common ground [48], task coordination [27, 44], and decision making.

CSCW '13, February 23–27, 2013, San Antonio, Texas, USA.

The role of subtle social signaling behavior in facilitating human robot teamwork, however, remains underexplored despite encouraging initial research highlighting the need for robots to be more adept at social interaction. By social signaling behaviors we mean behaviors that do not have their primary role in communicating content but rather in coordinating (e.g. when is it appropriate to speak?) and orienting (e.g. status and affect) participants of an interaction. By studying robot supported rescue teams in the field, the need for robots to have social interaction capabilities became evident when Fincannon et. al., [22] observed that rescue specialists engaged in social interactions with the robots even though the robots were not designed with social signaling capabilities. Bethel and colleagues [5, 6] proceeded to explore how robots without human-like social interfaces could exhibit socio-emotional behavior. Additional studies have demonstrated the powerful effects that simple social signaling behaviors can have in human-robot interaction. Only slight orientation towards a person, for example, can indicate attentiveness and caring [7, 11, 23]. The human-robot interaction community has so far primarily focused on how this signaling makes people think and feel *about the robot* itself [6], often with the goal of improving communication between the person and the robot. The primary goal of this research has been to make robots more understandable, intuitive, and predictable (or "believable") by using patterns that allow people to apply mental models and heuristics from interactions with people to infer a robot's internal states and intentions [9, 10, 24, 38, 42].

With the exception of two studies, the role of social signaling in improving *task-related outcomes* in human-machine interaction settings has been overlooked. In an experimental study, Breazeal and colleagues [8], for example, show that nonverbal social behaviors such as gaze, shifts in posture or orientation serve not only a cosmetic but also a pragmatic role in improving team functioning. Parasuraman and Miller [40] also demonstrate that adhering to social etiquette rules such as when and how to interrupt in an automated system can drastically improve overall human-machine system reliability.

The possibility that subtle, and seemingly task-unrelated, social signaling can have important implications for the performance of human robot teamwork is intriguing, and past research leaves two important questions unanswered.

First, it is not clear how these social signaling behaviors affect task outcomes that go beyond the interaction itself. For example do these behaviors have direct task-related benefits rather than only benefits in improving perceptions such as liking or naturalness? Second, it is not clear from past research whether the effects of social signaling behaviors extend beyond the simple dyadic human-robot scenarios to more complex human-robot team configurations.

A specific social signaling behavior that has been examined in the context of dyadic human robot interactions but not in complex human-robot teamwork settings is backchanneling [34, 46, 56]. Even though backchanneling is reported to have powerful effects in human-robot interaction, it is unclear whether those effects exist in complex scenarios in which the task, rather than the robot is the focus of attention. In the study presented here, we show that backchanneling is a subtle nonverbal social behavior that can have substantial effects on team functioning and perceptions of engagement in a complex teamwork scenario.

Backchanneling in Interactions

Backchanneling refers to a set of mostly nonverbal behaviors by a listener in a conversation, which signals to the speaker that the listener is actively engaged in the interaction. It includes behaviors such as "mm-hmm" vocalizations, slight nodding, eye contact, and orientation towards the speaker.

Within the CSCW community, backchanneling has largely been treated as form of concurrent feedback. Dennis and Kinney [19], for example, describe that backchanneling serves four cognitive functions including indicating understanding, indicating lack of understanding, repair or clarification of the message, and sentence completion. From this perspective backchanneling's main function is in establishing common ground by signaling that the receiver has understood the message [17]. Backchanneling, however, not only has a coordination function but also has a positive "gestalt emotional tone" [41]. It signals emotional attunement towards the speaker as an indication of emotionally positive validation, interest, and care about the partner's opinions [18].

Backchanneling In Human-Robot Teamwork

Given these broad cognitive and affective functions, backchanneling is a particularly promising behavior in the context of human robot interaction. First, it can be enacted nonverbally, which is important, as it can be manipulated without affecting the robot's verbal content. Second, it can be implemented mechanically and computationally less expensive by using simple head movements and reactive timings based on speaker cues. Third, its effectiveness in conveying responsiveness and smoothing coordination has been demonstrated in the context of human-robot interactions. Yamasaki et. al. [56], for example, showed that robot backchanneling in the form of simple turns towards the speaker was consistently reciprocated by human participants when being guided by a robot in a museum. Backchanneling, even when it is only embodied through head movement indicates engagement [45] and when expressed by an artificial agent over longer periods of time has been shown to communicate caring [7]. Despite previous research, however, the role of backchanneling in complex human-robot teamwork is, as of yet, underexplored.

Study Overview

To explore the implications of backchanneling for the functioning of teams, we designed a 2 (backchanneling present: yes vs. no) by 2 (complexity: low vs. high) experiment.

HYPOTHESES

Theories about human-human interaction have been shown to be transferrable not only to human-computer interactions [39] but also to human-robot interactions [49] and human-robot teams [48]. We therefore expect that the cognitive and emotional effects associated with backchanneling such as establishing common ground and signaling engagement can be leveraged to understand how people will behave in human-robot teams.

Backchanneling improves team functioning

We specifically anticipate that the benefits of backchanneling will aid team functioning in human-robot teams. Although subtle, the presence or absence of backchanneling indicated through nods, gaze, and "mhm" vocalizations has been shown to be a key factor in distinguishing high performance from low performance work teams [28]. Backchanneling has also shown to matter when people are interacting with robots. Bickmore and Picard [7], for example, showed that nonverbal behaviors such as head nodding when expressed by a computer agent strongly affected participants' willingness to work with the computer agent in a future task. Further, Wang and colleagues [52] found that a robot tracking and following a person's face increased enjoyment over a condition in which the robot remained still. In human-robot teams, we therefore predict that when robots use backchanneling, it will enhance team functioning. We further argue that this effect will be strongest when the task is complex. Complex tasks create more demand on team members, require more coordination as a result of greater uncertainty, and can generate more tension among team members than simple tasks [13]. We expect backchanneling through its cognitive role in establishing common ground and through its affective role in signaling positive attunement to alleviate the negative impact of increased complexity on a team.

H1: The presence of backchanneling by robots will improve team functioning (by decreasing stress and cognitive load and by increasing team coordination and performance) in human-robot teams, especially when the task is complex.

Backchanneling increases perceived engagement

Backchanneling can convey engagement in a task, suggesting that a team member is emotionally engaged and fully present [29]. This is true for robots as well. Sidner et al. [45], for example, showed that a robot capable of backchanneling behavior was perceived as more engaging to participants who were asked to jointly give a demo with a robot. We anticipate that this effect in human-robot interaction will transfer to human-robot team interaction. That is, we expect that when robots use backchanneling in a collaborative task, they will be seen as more engaged in the task.

We also argue that this effect will increase when the task is complex. A relationship between complexity and engagement was suggested by Carl Weick in his study of an airplane crew failure that led to a deadly collision [55]. He proposed that task complexity decreases as group engagement improves. That is, when people are fully engaged in a team task, they are better able to manage the complexity. We therefore anticipate that backchanneling will particularly help in complex tasks in which participants are trying to manage multiple activities and may need more overt signals from team members to help them cope with the complexity. In less complex tasks, however, backchanneling may be seen as less useful and therefore not an indicator of engagement.

H2: Backchanneling by robots will be seen as positively related to robots' engagement in the task when the task is complex, but less so when the task is not complex.

Backchanneling decreases perceived competence
Simple backchanneling used by robots might also have negative consequences. Human-like backchanneling behaviors can increase expectations team members have about the capabilities of a robot. Hinds, Roberts, and Jones [32], for example, showed that the more human-like a robot the more task responsibility people defer to it. If then expectations of the robot are not met, it might lead to disappointment and lowered perceptions of a robot's competence. Backchanneling can also directly indicate a lack of competence. Johnson [26], for example, conducted an experimental study and found that in a dyadic work interaction low authority employees, responsible only for mundane tasks, exhibited more backchanneling such as "mmm-hmm" vocalizations than their high authority counterparts who were responsible for complex decision making . That is, backchanneling was associated with lower status. This is in line with findings that associate backchanneling with decreased perceptions of reliability in robots [45]. Taken together, this research suggests that backchanneling can signal that the actor is lower status and less competent. We therefore anticipate that while a backchanneling robot may ease team functioning and be perceived as more engaged, it may also be seen as less competent and intelligent than a robot that does not exhibit any backchanneling behavior.

H3: Backchanneling by robots will decrease perceived competence and intelligence of the robot in human-robot teams, especially when the task is complex.

TASK DESIGN
To investigate our research questions, we required a task that utilized a human-robot team in which the people and robots were interdependent, required a high level of coordination and clear performance criteria, enabled us to vary task complexity, and created a sense of urgency for participants, thus fully engaging them in the task. Consistent with these requirements, we designed an urban search and retrieval (USAR) game in which human-robot teams worked together collaboratively to retrieve as many items as possible following a building collapse.

Urban Search and Retrieval Scenario
Based on available Urban Search and Rescue (USAR) scenario descriptions [36], we abstracted a USAR game described to participants as taking place in a large building that has recently collapsed, and in which the human-robot team needs to search and retrieve as many items as possible in 10 minutes. The USAR team consisted of the participant, two ground robots, and an aerial robot. The ground robots were mobile, upper-torso humanoid robots named Nexi and Maddox, and the aerial robot (UAV) was remotely controlled by a human operator (confederate) who was also described as a member of the team.

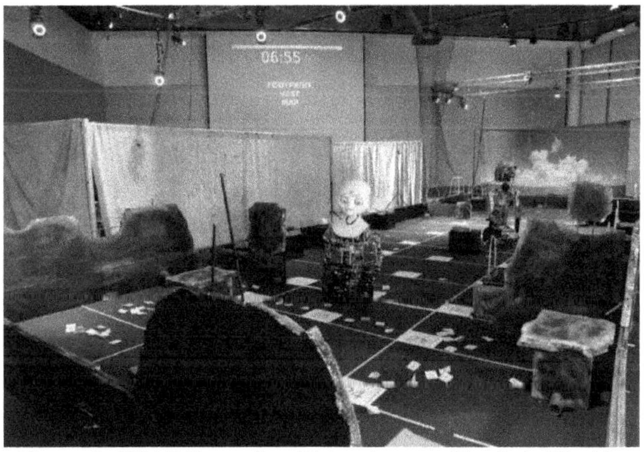

Figure 1. USAR Sencario with two humanoid robots (Nexi in front and Maddox in back)

Items (e.g. a briefcase, necklace, flashlight) were drawn onto small cards that were then covered by a post-it. Items could be found everywhere in the arena (see Figure 1) on the floor and also in baskets. Players needed to flip open the post-it to see what item was hidden underneath (see Figure 2). The goal of the game was to collect as many items as possible in 10 minutes. The team needed to coordinate together as each member has his/her own unique capabilities and skills in searching and retrieving the items that if utilized strategically could lead to better success.

The arena was split into three *danger zones* (low, medium, and high), mimicking the varying levels of safety and searchable access in USAR situations. A player could safely search in the low danger zone, but was not allowed in the high danger zone. To enter the medium danger zone, the player needed to check with the ground robots to see if access was safe. The ground robots were capable of searching in all danger zones, and if an item was in an area too dangerous for humans, the robot could retrieve that item for the player, when instructed to do so. The ground robots were also described as having a "special scanner" that allowed them to quick-scan a square (that it was currently in) to reveal all the items in that square. Acting as the "eyes in the sky" and flying in the high danger zone, the UAV+O (unmanned aerial vehicle and the operator) had better global situational awareness of where items were hidden and could give information about the specific location of an item to the participant. The confederate, acting as the UAV operator, responded with information from a script and had preplanned actions in controlling the flying robot.

A projector at the back of the arena displayed a set of three items to find for the current round and also a countdown clock indicating how much time remained. For example, Figure 2 displays a time of 3 minutes 18 seconds remaining and for the current round the player needs to find the items: footprint, vest, and map.

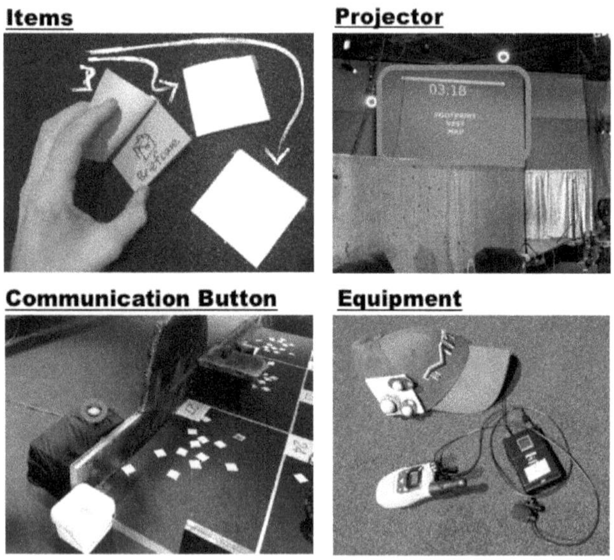

Figure 2. Photos of elements of the USAR game.

Game Play

The following narrative illustrates a typical game play from a player's point of view:

The game starts with a loud buzzer ringing in the arena, and I look up at the projector and see that time is counting down! Okay! We need to find the footprint, vest, and map for the first round. I get down on the floor and start looking in square 27 in the low danger zone. I frantically flip the post-its one by one to see what item is hidden underneath. I then remember that the ground robots have a special scanner and ask Nexi, "Can you scan square 25?" Nexi replies, "Okay I will go to square 25." Nexi and I both search in the low danger zone as Maddox goes off and searches around in the medium danger zone. I flip open a post-it and found the vest inside! I exclaim, "I have found the vest" into the mic so the robots can stop looking for that particular item. Nexi finally arrives in square 25 and after scanning the square says "I've found the footprint in square 25." I scramble over and start flipping and indeed found the footprint! Great, okay, just need to find the map to finish this round. I ask Maddox, "Have you found anything?" And he replies, "No, I have not found anything in particular yet." I grab my walkie-talkie and say, "Aerial operator, can you tell me where the map is?" He replies, "Okay, I'm on it!" I then see the UAV fly up into the air in the high danger zone as it surveys the entire scene. I continue looking around in the low danger zone, and I look over to see that both Nexi and Maddox are searching in the medium danger zone. The aerial operator finally reports back through the walkie-talkie, "The map is in the medium danger zone in square 8." I ask Maddox, "Is square 8 safe?" and he replies "No, it is not safe." I then ask Maddox to go into square 8 and once he arrives he says, "I have found the map in square 8, would you like for me to bring it to you?" I reply "Yes!" and moments later Maddox brings me a basket with the map inside of it and now its time for round 2!

TECHNOLOGY IMPLEMENTATION

Robot Platforms

The ground robots (Maddox and Nexi) are mobile, upper torso humanoid robots that are a part of the MDS (Mobile-Dexterous-Social) robot line as seen in Figure 1. The MDS robots are 4 to 5-feet tall with a hokuyo sensor mounted near the base of the robot and a kinect sensor mounted near the torso. They have 15 facial degrees of freedom (DoFs), 4 neck DoFs, a pair of 3 DoF shoulders, a pair of 5 DoF lower arms and hands, DoFs, a mobile wheel base with 2 DoFs, and a torso DoF. The neck and head mechanisms have 4 DoFs to support a lower bending at the base of the neck as well as pan-tilt-yaw of the head. The head can move at human-like speeds to support human head gestures such as nodding, shaking, and orienting.

The ground robots are fully autonomous agents (see below for system details), and the AR.Drone, a commercially available aerial robot, was teleoperated by a remote operator using its tablet interface.

System Overview

Autonomous Humanoid Robots

The role of the ground robots is to collaborate with the co-located human participant to successfully complete the USAR task. As such, these robots were capable of listening and recognizing human requests, verbally and nonverbally responding to humans, searching and navigating the arena, being aware of the task and environment states, and picking up baskets with items. To ensure consistent behavior of the robots, we developed fully autonomous robotic agents rather than utilizing a Wizard of Oz approach.

System Modules

By combining commercially available software solutions, open-source software packages, and custom in-house code, we created the following necessary technical modules relevant to the experiment:

Navigation: Laser range values from the hokuyo are used to estimate the robot's current position and orientation in a pre-made map of the arena through the Carnegie Mellon Robot Navigation Toolkit (CARMEN)[14]. We then used A* to path-plan to target destinations while avoiding static and moving obstacles. We included dynamic re-planning A* when an obstacle is hit.

Manipulation: The RGB image from the kinect was sent to ARToolKit [1], a software library that tracks special markers in physical space, to locate baskets in the 2D image. Unfortunately, since the robot's grasping range is outside the min range of the kinect's depth sensor, we estimated the 3D location of the basket in real coordinates using the z-depth value provided by the hokuyo, which can sense at a shorter minimum distance. We then used CCD (Cyclic Coordinate Descent [53]), an inverse kinematics method, to hook onto the basket's handle.

Speech: To understand the human utterances, we used the CMU Sphinx [47], an open source toolkit for speech recognition along with a human monitoring the speech input and either filtering or correcting misinterpreted speech. The robots spoke using synthesized voice through Cereproc [16], a real-time text-to-speech commercial technology, while also generating corresponding readable mouth positions with its articulated jaw. Nexi, the smaller robot, was given a female voice, and Maddox a male voice to make them easily distinguishable.

Human Localization: We used the Vicon [51] motion capture system to track a specially marked hat worn by the participant (see figure 2) and localize the human's position in the low danger zone. And by fusing the Vicon and CARMEN virtual spaces, the robots could also localize the human's relative position in the entire arena even when they were outside the vicon space.

Backchanneling: Backchanneling was provided through articulation of the head, eyes and upper torso. The feedback module was implemented by processing speech volume of the participant and then triggering the backchanneling response whenever the speech volume increased beyond a certain threshold. (For more detail, please consult the Experimental Manipulations section.)

System Behavior

The robot's primary behavior system was structured within a finite state machine that drove the main interaction, dialogue, and the random coverage search of the arena. A pilot study was performed early in the study design stage to determine the phrases most likely uttered in the task scenario, which served as event triggers for many states. The behavior system was a mixed initiative design in which an action queue could be self-populated and also managed by the interaction state machine. When a question or request was made to the robot, the robot responded by looking into its own memory or by addressing the command by prioritizing it in the action queue. In general, a separate action queue was maintained for managing the dialogue.

Task Management

The robot's task system was based on a common interaction policy between groups that was determined during the pilot study. A number of subsystems interacted by queuing and prioritizing social actions such as speech and gesture. The task model works closely with the dialogue in that the human can explicitly queue certain action policies such as searching for specific objects or visiting certain regions for exploration. Constraints were hard coded into the system to limit the potential actions. For instance, the robot could not go searching for an item once it had been asked to retrieve an object and the object was in its hand.

METHOD

To test our hypotheses, we conducted a 2 (presence of backchanneling: no vs. yes) x 2 (task complexity: low vs. high) between-subject experiment (N = 73).

Participants

We recruited ninety-six participants from a university community who were randomly assigned to one of the four conditions. Of the ninety-six participants seventy-three completed the study successfully and were included in the analysis – the others were dropped due to various malfunctions of the robots. Participants ranged in age from 18 to 40 ($M = 25.0$, SD = 6.1).

Experimental Manipulations

We manipulated backchanneling by adding or omitting nonverbal look-at and nodding behavior. In the backchanneling condition the robots oriented their body and turned their heads and eyes towards the participant, which composed of the "look-at" behavior, and nodded slightly whenever the participant made an utterance. We involved the entire "body" of the robots in the enactment of this behavior as the social perception of physical behavior is dependent on the entire body, rather than just the face [2]. We carefully timed the behavior so that it occurred in parallel with the utterances of a speaker and we chose a subtle, quick nod that was designed by a professional animator. The timing was to ensure that the looking-at and nodding would indicate concurrent backchanneling and listening feedback rather than an explicit "yes" response by the robot to something said by the participant. In the no backchanneling conditions, the robots did not exhibit any look-at or nodding behavior. As shown in Figure 3 below, requests by the human were always acknowledged verbally across conditions. Backchanneling was only manipulated through the presence and absence of nonverbal behavior.

We manipulated task complexity by altering two characteristics previously identified as fundamental task complexity characteristics [13], including multiple paths to a desired end state and conflicting interdependence. The presence of these characteristics alone or in combination distinguishes non-complex from complex tasks [13]. In the low complexity condition, we told participants that they would get one point for each item found. In the high-complexity condition we told participants that they would get one point for each item found, however, if they found all three items of one set in the color blue their points would double, if they found all in green their points would triple, and if they found all in red their points would quadruple. Each item was available in all three colors across conditions. Operationally the only change between low and high complexity was whether the task description gave the color added significance. This change in the task description opened up "multiple pathways to the desired end-state." Participants could vary their strategy to balance speed and the value of the combination of items. Participants also had to make tradeoffs as to whether they wanted to find more items within the time available or find the matching colors, which satisfied the "presence of conflicting inter-dependence" condition for task complexity. The order and composition of item sets were identical across conditions.

Materials and Measures

We used a range of subjective and objective measures that were administered during and after the task to test our hypotheses. Our dependent measures include four items for team functioning, two for robot engagement, and two for perceptions of the robots' competence.

Manipulation Checks

As a manipulation check of the robots' backchanneling, we asked participants to rate the extent to which they thought the ground robots were looking at them on a seven-point Likert type scale between "strongly disagree" and "strongly agree."

Our second manipulation, task complexity, was measured using a two-item scale (α = .70) comprised of items taken from [20] "I found this to be a complex task" and [35] "The task required me to coordinate many different things at the same time". Participants rated the items on a seven point scale from "totally disagree" to "totally agree."

Team Functioning

To address the first hypothesis, we measured stress, cognitive load, team coordination, and team performance. We measured participants' level of stress with a three-item sub-scale (α = .72) of the Positive and Negative Affect Schedule (PANAS) [54] administered as part of the post-task survey. Participants were asked to report on a five-point scale ranging from "very slightly or not at all" to "extremely" with regard to how much they were distressed, upset, and irritable during the task.

To measure cognitive load, we took a direct, objective measure using a dual task paradigm [12, 50]. Participants were instructed to monitor and press a big red "communication button" as soon as possible when it started to blink (see figure 2). The blinking button, they were told, meant that other responders were trying to verify that they were okay and pushing the button would signal that the team was safe. The button blinked three times at 3, 5, and 9 minutes into the task, and we measured the reaction times

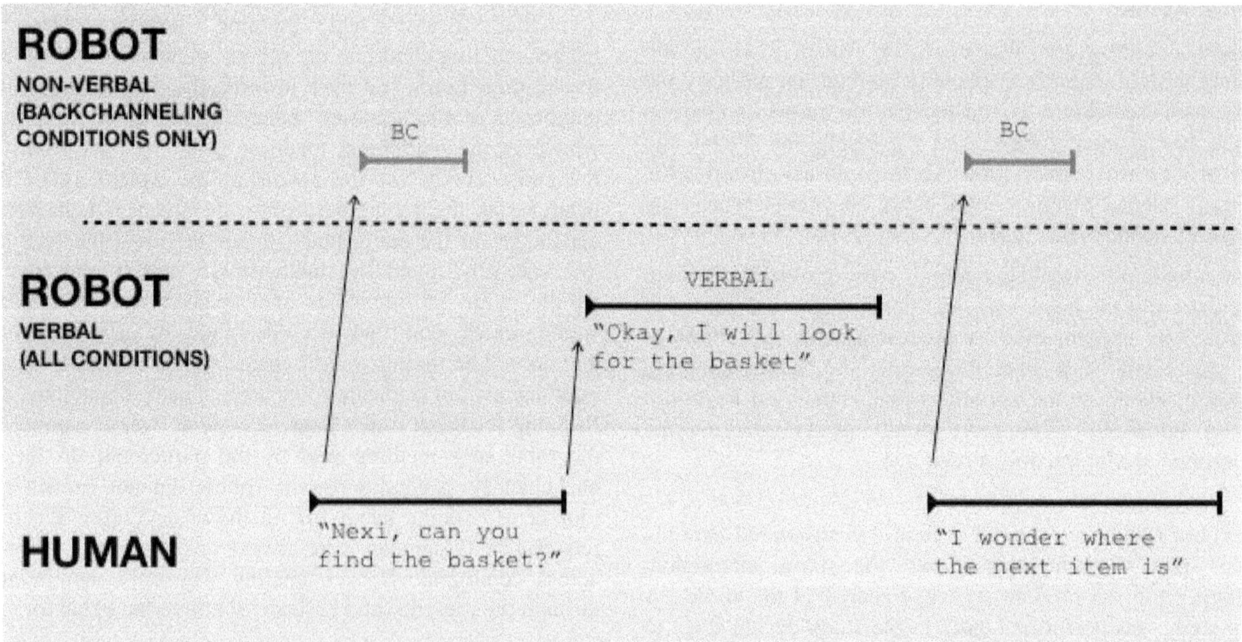

Figure 3. Temporal visualization of backchanneling manipulation. The robots respond verbally to requests across conditions, however the nonverbal backchanneling is only triggered in the backchanneling condition.

between the time the button started to blink and the moment the participant hit the button. We averaged across three measurements to account for the possibly varying travel distances by the participants. Our objective cognitive load measure was computed by taking the sum of all three reaction times and dividing the sum by the number of button presses that were made before the timeout. Several participants forgot about the button entirely and therefore reaction time was only used as a measure if the button was pressed at least once during the task (N = 55). We also used a self-report measure of cognitive load in which, as part of the post-task survey, we asked participants the extent to which "the task was mentally demanding" on a 7-point scale ranging from "totally disagree" to "totally agree."

We measured perceived team coordination with the five-item coordination subscale ($\alpha = .83$) from the Transactive Memory System (TMS) scale by Lewis and colleagues [33]. Participants rated items such as "Our team worked together in a well-coordinated fashion" on a 5-point Likert type scale ranging between "strongly disagree", and "strongly agree."

Finally, we measured team performance by recording the number of items found by each team. We counted how many correct items participants placed in the container within the allotted ten minutes of the task.

Perception of Robots' Engagement
To address our second hypothesis focusing on how backchanneling from the robots and task complexity would affect perceptions of the robots' engagement, we measured perceived distraction and responsiveness by using 7-point scale items ranging from "totally disagree" to "totally agree". Perceived distractedness used a 2-item measure including questions about the extent to which the ground robots seemed distracted and unfocused ($\alpha = .70$). We measured responsiveness by asking respondents about the extent to which they "felt that the ground robots were responsive."

Perception of Robots' Competence
To address our third hypothesis focusing on how robot backchanneling and task complexity would affect perceptions of the robots' competence, we employed two measures of robot perception in our post-task survey. First we measured perceived intelligence with a 5-point scale by asking "How much did you feel as if you were accompanied by intelligent beings?" borrowed from [32]. Second, we measured perceived competence by asking participants to rate the extent to which they "felt that the ground robots are very competent." on a 7-point scale.

Procedure
Upon arrival in the lab participants were asked to sit at a table separated from the task arena by a curtain and were asked for their informed consent to participate in our study. First, each participant filled out the pre-task section of our online survey, which asked about their demographic background, knowledge and experience of robots, and prior knowledge of the MDS robot platform that we used in our study.

Next, participants were introduced to the task through an instructional slide presentation – either the "low complexity" or "high complexity" version, depending on the condition to which they were assigned. Each participant was then asked to enter the task arena and was introduced to the physical setup of the space. An experimenter re-iterated the main points of the task and participants were given the opportunity to ask further clarification questions about the task. Before starting the main task, participants performed a trial search and retrieval task by finding and retrieving a specific item without the help of the robot. Participants were informed that the best performing team would win an additional $200. This task introduction and training procedure took approximately 15 minutes.

For the main task, participants conducted the ten-minute search and retrieval task as outlined in the previous section. Participants were asked to find and retrieve as many items as possible. After reaching the ten-minute time limit, we congratulated participants for their performance and asked them to return to the table behind the curtain to complete the post-task survey. Participants were then thanked and paid.

Data Analysis
We used a two-way analysis of variance (ANOVA) to investigate whether robot backchanneling and task complexity influenced team functioning and participants' perceptions of the robot. In each ANOVA we used robot backchanneling (no vs. yes) and task complexity (low vs. high) as independent variables. We also included participant gender, age, and prior knowledge about robots as covariates, but none of them had any significant influence on our dependent measures. We therefore omitted the covariates from further discussion.

RESULTS

Manipulation Checks
Participants in the backchanneling condition felt more strongly that the ground robots were looking at them ($M = 4.78$, $SE = 0.21$) as compared with those in the no-backchanneling condition ($M = 4.03$, $SE = 0.23$), $F(1, 65) = 5.93$, $p < .05$, providing evidence that our backchanneling manipulation was effective.

Interestingly, the main effect for perceived task complexity was not significant because the backchanneling manipulation interacted with perceived task complexity. We found a main effect for robot backchanneling on task complexity ($F(1, 69) = 4.78$, $p < .05$), as participants perceived the task as significantly less complex in the backchanneling condition ($M = 5.16$, $SD = 1.16$) than in the no-backchanneling condition ($M = 5.76$, $SD = 1.16$).

Team Functioning

In our first hypothesis, we argued that backchanneling by a robot would improve team functioning, especially when the task is complex. To test this, we examined participants' self-reported stress during the task, cognitive load as measured by reaction time, self-reported team coordination, and performance measured by number of items found in the task. H1 was partially supported.

Stress

As expected, we found a significant interaction between backchanneling and complexity of the task when predicting the amount of stress perceived by the participant $F(1,69) = 7.63$, $p < .01$. This indicates that when task complexity was low, the perceived stress of participants was similar in the no-backchanneling ($M = 1.72$, $SD = 0.70$) and backchanneling condition ($M = 1.87$, $SD = 0.50$). However, when task complexity was high, the perceived stress of participants was significantly higher in the no-backchanneling condition ($M = 2.55$, $SD = 0.86$) than in the backchanneling condition ($M = 1.78$, $SD = 0.73$). Additionally, there was a significant (positive) main effect of task complexity on perceived stress, $F(1, 69) = 5.00$, $p < .05$ (see left graph in Figure 4).

Cognitive Load

Consistent with hypothesis 1, we also found a significant main effect of robot backchanneling when predicting our behavioral measure of cognitive load $F(1, 51) = 6.70$, $p < .05$. The presence of backchanneling reduced the reaction time on the parallel task of pressing the button by an average 46% between the backchanneling condition ($M = 101.28$ sec, $SD = 62.40$) and the no-backchanneling condition ($M = 184.87$ sec, $SD = 157.21$), suggesting that people experienced significantly less cognitive load when the robot used backchanneling. Our self-report measure of cognitive load confirmed that the task was perceived as less mentally demanding when the robot used backchanneling, $F(1,69) = 4.91$, $p < .05$. There was, however, no interaction between backchanneling and task complexity, so hypothesis 1 was only partially supported (see right graph in Figure 4).

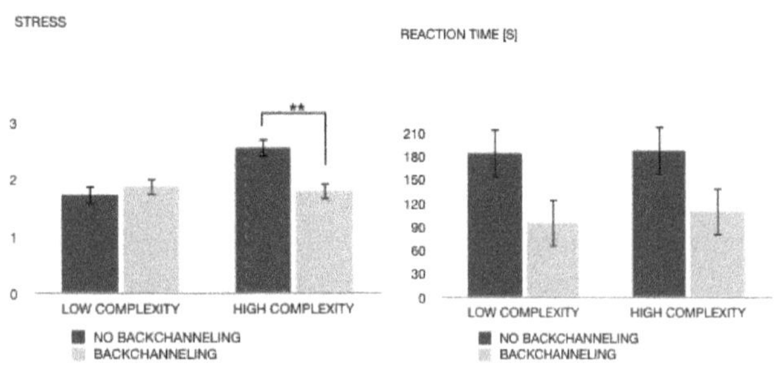

Figure 4. Left Graph: Effect of robots' backchanneling and task complexity on stress. Right graph: Effect of robots' backchanneling and task complexity on cognitive load (measured as response time in seconds). Error bars = ±1SE

Team Coordination

We found a significant main effect of task complexity on participants' sense of overall team coordination $F(1, 70) = 5.45$, $p < .05$. Participants found their teams to be more coordinated when task complexity was low ($M = 3.44$, $SD = 0.75$) in comparison to when task complexity was high ($M = 3.03$, $SD = 0.80$). There was not, however, any main effect of robots' backchanneling, nor an interaction effect between backchanneling and complexity, as predicted in hypothesis 1 (see left graph in Figure 5).

Team Performance

Our last indicator of team functioning was team performance measured by the number of items found during the task. Although the main effect of backchanneling on the number of items found was not significant, $F(1, 69) = 2.31$, $p = .13$, the direction was as predicted. That is, participants performed better, albeit not significantly, when the robot used backchanneling (see right graph in Figure 5).

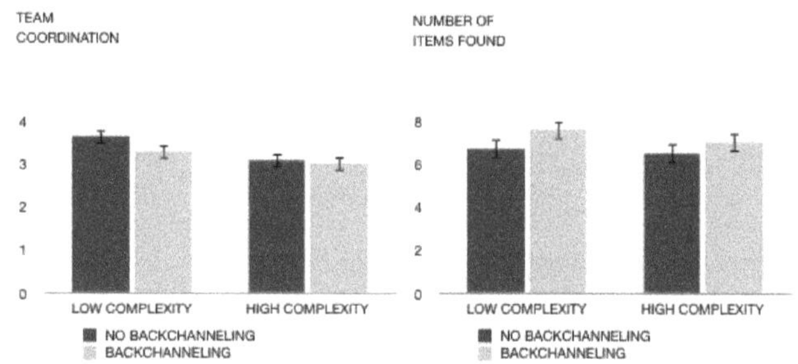

Figure 5. Left graph: Effect of robots' backchanneling and task complexity on perceived team coordination. Right graph: Effect of robots' backchanneling and task complexity on team performance (number of items found). Error bars = ±1S

Perceptions of the Robots' Engagement

We argued in hypothesis 2 that participants would perceive robots that used backchanneling to be more engaged and that this would be strongest in the high task complexity conditions.

Perceived responsiveness

Our analysis predicting perceived responsiveness supports hypothesis 2. The interaction between robots' backchanneling and task complexity was significant, $F(1,69) = 6.17$, $p < .05$, indicating that when the task was complex, the robots that gave feedback were seen as more responsive whereas in the less complex task, the robots that gave no backchanneling were seen as more responsive. There were no main effects (see left graph in Figure 6).

Perceived distractedness

Our analysis predicting distraction yielded a similar result. That is, when the task was complex, robots that used backchanneling were seen as less distracted whereas, in the low task complexity conditions, the robots that provided feedback were seen as more distracted, $F(1, 69) = 4.50$, $p < .05$. Thus H2 was partially supported (see right graph in Figure 6).

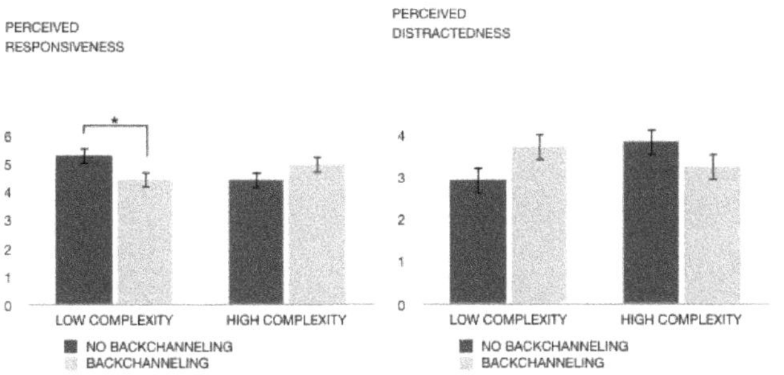

Figure 6 Left graph: Effect of robots' backchanneling and task complexity on perceived responsiveness of robots. Right graph: Effect of robots' backchanneling and task complexity on perceived distraction of robots. Error bars = ± 1 SE

Perceptions of the Robots' Competence

In hypothesis 3, we argued that participants, despite the positive effects of robots that use backchanneling, would perceive affective robots more negatively.

Perceived Intelligence

As expected, we found a significant main effect of robot backchanneling on perceived intelligence of the robots $F(1, 69) = 4.53$, $p < .05$. Participants found the robots that used backchanneling ($M = 2.68$, $SD = 1.02$) to be on average 16% less intelligent than the robots that did not use backchanneling ($M = 3.20$, $SD = 1.02$). We did not, however, find an interaction effect, as hypothesized (see left graph in Figure 7).

Perceived Competence

As with perceived intelligence, our analysis of perceived competence of the robot showed that robots that used backchanneling were perceived as less competent than robots that did not, $F(1,69) = 4.65$, $p < .04$. Again, there was no interaction effect, so hypothesis 3 was only partially supported (see right graph in Figure 7).

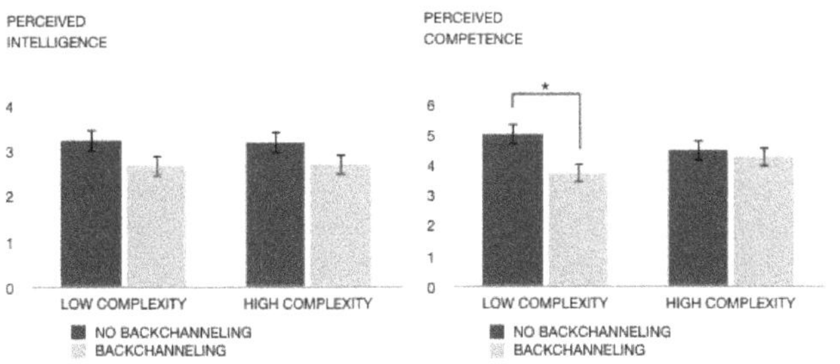

Figure 7 Left graph: Effect of robots' backchanneling and task complexity on perceived intelligence of robots. Right graph: Effect of robots' backchanneling and task complexity on perceived competence of robots.

DISCUSSION

We argued and found that subtle backchanneling by robots in human-robot teams helped team functioning (lower stress, lower cognitive load) and perceived engagement of the robots, especially when the task was complex, but at the same time lead to robots being seen as less competent. We also found that task complexity had a significant effect on peoples' responses to the robots' backchanneling. In general, we saw a pattern in which more benefits (less stress, less cognitive load, more perceived engagement) were found from backchanneling in high complexity conditions over low complexity conditions. Complexity, however, did not interact significantly with perceptions of robots' competence. These results suggest that the biggest benefits from backchanneling in human-robot teams may be seen when tasks are demanding and complex.

Although the trend was in the right direction, we were not able to demonstrate a significant effect of backchanneling on the number of items found. We attribute this to a ceiling effect. One of the items in the fourth round of the USAR game could only be picked up by a robot as the item was in the high danger zone at the far end of the arena. Retrieving this item took the robots an especially long time due to travel time. Even if all other items in that set had already been found, the participants waited for the robot to retrieve the item in the danger zone. All participants ran out of time before the robot retrieved that item and therefore no participant advanced from round 4. It would be useful if future research included more sensitive measures of performance to better detect the effects of backchanneling on performance.

Previous research has highlighted both a cognitive and an affective role of backchanneling in interactions. Cognitively, backchanneling is a key factor in establishing common ground [17] and affectively backchanneling indicates emotionally positive engagement and listening [18]. Contrary to our expectations, backchanneling did not have any effects on participants' perceptions of team coordination. This suggests that our particular way of embodying backchanneling was not successful in tapping into the cognitive benefits of backchanneling to build common ground. If our manipulation had worked primarily at a cognitive level, we would have expected the robots to be seen as more competent and intelligence, especially in high complexity conditions, because they would have been seen as instrumental in establishing common ground. We found, however, that backchanneling reduced perceptions of competence and intelligence independent of task complexity. Backchanneling might also have raised participants' expectations about the robots' cognitive capabilities. When these cognitive expectations were not met, people thought of the robots as less competent collaborators.

The results we obtained are more consistent with theories of backchanneling as an affective phenomenon. To understand backchanneling as affective, we take what Keltner and Haidt [30] called a social-functional perspective on affect. This perspective emphasizes the interpersonal functions of emotion and the notion that the emotional meaning of behavior is not inherent in behavior itself. Rather than assuming a one-to-one coherence between a specific behavior and its emotional meaning (such as a smile for happiness, or an eye-roll for contempt) it is assumed first, that the affective meaning of behavior is constructed in the context of the interaction itself, and second, that there are an infinite number of ways to express a certain affective quality in an interaction. A smile, for example, can be condescending, and an eye-roll can be seen as empathetic if a team member complains about a vendor and his colleague rolls his eyes in agreement. The condescending comment and the eye-roll form what Schegloff [43] called an adjacency pair as the interpretation of the colleague's eye-roll is directly contingent upon the teammate's complaint. In the same way, the emotional interpretation of backchanneling behavior is contingent upon its placement within the interaction. The slight nodding and looking by the listener when placed concurrently with the speaker as implemented in our study can transform backchanneling to convey positive listening and engagement.

Backchanneling from a social-functional perspective can be seen as an interactive device for regulating emotions in teams. Emotions are contagious. They easily spread within a team and it only takes one person's negative emotions to spoil an entire team [3, 21]. Since emotions are crucial determinants of team performance [4], this opens up the possibility that robots, through their backchanneling behavior, can help to regulate the emotions of a team and through that ultimately affect the team's performance. Understanding when and what robot affective displays are contagious will be important in designing more effective robot team members. At the extreme, robots' backchanneling and displays could be used to intentionally regulate the emotions of work teams, for example, diffusing stressful situations when the work is demanding and dangerous.

More broadly, it becomes important to consider the affective meanings and effects of the interactive capabilities currently being developed in the field of robotics (nodding, speech modulation, gaze, body orientation, etc). A social-functional perspective applied to these behaviors might reveal affective implications for behaviors that have been thought of as purely cognitive. For example, simple pointing gestures can have important positive functions in directing attention but they can also be interpreted as a domineering or even condescending gesture. Focusing on these social interpretations of behavior is particularly important since brief exposure to a nonverbal expression is enough for people to infer a complex image of a person's (and perhaps a robot's) personality [31] and capabilities.

In sum, our results confirm that subtle forms of backchanneling by robots may ease team functioning and improve perceptions of robots' engagement in complex tasks, but at the same time create more negative impressions of the robots' competence. These results suggest that more attention is needed to subtle affective cues and their role in human-robot teams.

ACKNOWLEDGMENTS

We thank our anonymous reviewers for their helpful comments on previous versions of this document. The authors gratefully acknowledge two grants by the Office of Naval Research that supported the work presented here (#N000140710749, #N000140910112).

REFERENCES

1. ARToolKit. *[Software]*. Available from: http://www.hitl.washington.edu/artoolkit/.
2. Aviezer, H., et al., *Angry, Disgusted, or Afraid?* Psychological Science, 2008. 19(7): p. 724-732.
3. Barsade, S.G., *The Ripple Effect: Emotional Contagion and its Influence on Group Behavior.* Administrative Science Quarterly, 2002. 47(4): p. 644-675.
4. Barsade, S.G. and D.E. Gibson, *Why does affect matter in organizations?* The Academy of Management Perspectives, 2007. 21(1): p. 36-59.
5. Bethel, C.L. and R.R. Murphy, *Affective expression in appearance constrained robots*, in *Proceedings of the 1st ACM SIGCHI/SIGART conference on Human-robot interaction*. 2006, ACM: Salt Lake City, Utah, USA. p. 327-328.
6. Bethel, C.L. and R.R. Murphy, *Non-facial/non-verbal methods of affective expression as applied to robot-assisted victim assessment*, in *Proceedings of the ACM/IEEE international conference on Human-robot interaction*. 2007, ACM: Arlington, Virginia, USA. p. 287-294.
7. Bickmore, T.W. and R.W. Picard, *Towards caring machines*, in *CHI '04 extended abstracts on Human factors in computing systems*. 2004, ACM: Vienna, Austria. p. 1489-1492.
8. Breazeal, C., et al. *Effects of nonverbal communication on efficiency and robustness in human-robot teamwork*. in *Intelligent Robots and Systems, 2005. (IROS 2005). 2005 IEEE/RSJ International Conference on*. 2005.
9. Breazeal, C. and B. Scassellati. *How to build robots that make friends and influence people*. in *Intelligent Robots and Systems, 1999. IROS '99. Proceedings. 1999 IEEE/RSJ International Conference on*. 1999.
10. Breazeal, C.L., *Designing sociable robots*. 2004: The MIT Press.
11. Bruce, A., I. Nourbakhsh, and R. Simmons. *The role of expressiveness and attention in human-robot interaction*. in *Robotics and Automation, 2002. Proceedings. ICRA '02. IEEE International Conference on*. 2002.
12. Brunken, R., J.L. Plass, and D. Leutner, *Direct Measurement of Cognitive Load in Multimedia Learning*. Educational Psychologist, 2003. 38(1): p. 53-61.
13. Campbell, D.J., *Task complexity: A review and analysis*. The Academy of Management Review, 1988. 13(1): p. 40-52.

14. CARMEN. *Robot Navigation Toolkit*. Available from: http://carmen.sourceforge.net/.

15. Casper, J. and R.R. Murphy, *Human-robot interactions during the robot-assisted urban search and rescue response at the World Trade Center.* Systems, Man, and Cybernetics, Part B: Cybernetics, IEEE Transactions on, 2003. 33(3): p. 367-385.

16. Cereproc. *[Software]*. Available from: http://www.cereproc.com/.

17. Clark, H.H. and S.A. Brennan, *Grounding in Communication*, in *Perspectives on socially shared cognition*, L.B. Resnick, J.M. Levine, and S.D. Teasley, Editors. 1991, APA Book.: Washington.

18. Coan, J.A. and J.M. Gottman, *The Specific Affect Coding System (SPAFF)*, in *Handbook of emotion elicitation and assessment.*, J.A. Coan and J.J.B. Allen, Editors. 2007, New York, NY, US: Oxford University Press. p. 267-285.

19. Dennis, A.R. and S.T. Kinney, *Testing Media Richness Theory in the New Media: The Effects of Cues, Feedback, and Task Equivocality.* Information Systems Research, 1998. 9(3): p. 256-274.

20. Earley, P.C., *Influence of information, choice and task complexity upon goal acceptance, performance, and personal goals.* Journal of Applied Psychology, 1985. 70(3): p. 481-491.

21. Felps, W., T.R. Mitchell, and E. Byington, *How, when, and why bad apples spoil the barrel: Negative group members and dysfunctional groups.* Research in organizational behavior, 2006. 27: p. 175-222.

22. Fincannon, T., et al. *Evidence of the need for social intelligence in rescue robots*. in *2004 IEEE/RSJ International Conference on Intelligent Robots and Systems*. 2004. Sendai, Japan: IEEE.

23. Fong, T., I. Nourbakhsh, and K. Dautenhahn, *A survey of socially interactive robots.* Robotics and Autonomous Systems, 2003. 42(3): p. 143-166.

24. Gockley, R., R. Simmons, and J. Forlizzi. *Modeling Affect in Socially Interactive Robots*. in *Robot and Human Interactive Communication, 2006. ROMAN 2006. The 15th IEEE International Symposium on*. 2006.

25. Jacob, M., et al., *Gestonurse: a robotic surgical nurse for handling surgical instruments in the operating room.* Journal of Robotic Surgery, 2012. 6(1): p. 53-63.

26. Johnson, C., *Gender, Legitimate Authority, and Leader-Subordinate Conversations.* American Sociological Review, 1994. 59(1): p. 122-135.

27. Jones, H. and P. Hinds. *Extreme work teams: using swat teams as a model for coordinating distributed robots*. in *ACM conference on Computer supported cooperative work, CSCW'02*. 2002. New Orleans, Louisiana, USA.: ACM.

28. Jung, M.F., J. Chong, and L.J. Leifer. *Group Hedonic Balance and Pair Programming Performance: Affective Interaction Dynamics as indicators of Performance*. in *ACM SIGCHI Conference on Human Factors in Computing Systems (CHI'12)*. 2012. Austin, Texas, USA.

29. Kahn, W.A., *Psychological Conditions of Personal Engagement and Disengagement at Work.* Academy of Management Journal, 1990. 33(4): p. 692-724.

30. Keltner, D. and J. Haidt, *Social functions of emotions*, in *Emotions: Currrent issues and future directions*, T.J.M.G.A. Bonanno, Editor. 2001, Guilford Press: New York, NY, US. p. 192-213.

31. Knutson, B., *Facial expressions of emotion influence interpersonal trait inferences.* Journal of Nonverbal Behavior, 1996. 20(3): p. 165-182.

32. Lee, K.M., et al., *Can Robots Manifest Personality?: An Empirical Test of Personality Recognition, Social Responses, and Social Presence in Human–Robot Interaction.* Journal of Communication, 2006. 56(4): p. 754-772.

33. Lewis, K., *Measuring transactive memory systems in the field: Scale development and validation.* Journal of Applied Psychology, 2003. 88(4): p. 587-604.

34. Liu, C., et al. *Generation of nodding, head tilting and eye gazing for human-robot dialogue interaction*. in *7th ACM/IEEE International Conference on Human-Robot Interaction (HRI)*. 2012. Kyoto, Japan: IEEE.

35. Maynard, D.C. and M.D. Hakel, *Effects of objective and subjective task complexity on performance.* Human Performance;Human Performance, 1997. 10(4): p. 303-330.

36. Murphy, R.R., *Human-robot interaction in rescue robotics.* Systems, Man, and Cybernetics, Part C: Applications and Reviews, IEEE Transactions on, 2004. 34(2): p. 138-153.

37. Murphy, R.R. and J.L. Burke, *Up from the Rubble: Lessons Learned about HRI from Search and Rescue.* Proceedings of the Human Factors and Ergonomics Society Annual Meeting, 2005. 49(3): p. 437-441.

38. Murphy, R.R., et al., *Emotion-based control of cooperating heterogeneous mobile robots.* Robotics and Automation, IEEE Transactions on, 2002. 18(5): p. 744-757.

39. Nass, C. and B. Reeves, *The media equation: How people treat computers, televisions, and new media as real people and places*. 1996, Cambridge University Press.

40. Parasuraman, R. and C.A. Miller, *Trust and etiquette in high-criticality automated systems.* Commun. ACM, 2004. 47(4): p. 51-55.

41. Pasupathi, M., et al., *Responsive Listening in Long-Married Couples: A Psycholinguistic Perspective.* Journal of Nonverbal Behavior, 1999. 23(2): p. 173-193.

42. Rose, R., M. Scheutz, and P. Schermerhorn. *Empirical investigations into the believability of robot affect.* in *Proceedings of the AAAI Spring Symposium.* 2008.

43. Schegloff, E.A., *Sequence organization in interaction: A primer in conversation analysis I.* Vol. 1. 2007: Cambridge Univ Pr.

44. Shah, J., et al., *Improved human-robot team performance using chaski, a human-inspired plan execution system*, in *Proceedings of the 6th international conference on Human-robot interaction.* 2011, ACM: Lausanne, Switzerland. p. 29-36.

45. Sidner, C.L., et al., *Explorations in engagement for humans and robots.* Artificial Intelligence, 2005. 166(1): p. 140-164.

46. Sidner, C.L., et al., *The effect of head-nod recognition in human-robot conversation*, in *Proceedings of the 1st ACM SIGCHI/SIGART conference on Human-robot interaction.* 2006, ACM: Salt Lake City, Utah, USA. p. 290-296.

47. Sphinx, C. *[Software].* Available from: http://cmusphinx.sourceforge.net/.

48. Stubbs, K., P.J. Hinds, and D. Wettergreen, *Autonomy and Common Ground in Human-Robot Interaction: A Field Study.* Intelligent Systems, IEEE, 2007. 22(2): p. 42-50.

49. Takayama, L., V. Groom, and C. Nass, *I'm sorry, Dave: i'm afraid i won't do that: social aspects of human-agent conflict*, in *Proceedings of the 27th international conference on Human factors in computing systems.* 2009, ACM: Boston, MA, USA. p. 2099-2108.

50. van Gerven, P.W.M., et al., *Modality and variability as factors in training the elderly.* Applied Cognitive Psychology, 2006. 20(3): p. 311-320.

51. Vicon. *[Software].* Available from: http://www.vicon.com/.

52. Wang, E., et al., *Effects of head movement on perceptions of humanoid robot behavior*, in *Proceedings of the 1st ACM SIGCHI/SIGART conference on Human-robot interaction.* 2006, ACM: Salt Lake City, Utah, USA. p. 180-185.

53. Wang, L. and C. Chen, *A Combined Optimization Method for Solving the Inverse Kinematics Problem of Mechanical Manipulators, .* IEEE Trans. On Robotics and Applications, 1991. 7(4): p. 489-499.

54. Watson, D., L.A. Clark, and A. Tellegen, *Development and validation of brief measures of positive and negative affect: The PANAS scales.* Journal of Personality and Social Psychology, 1988. 54(6): p. 1063-1070.

55. Weick, K.E., *The Vulnerable System: An Analysis of the Tenerife Air Disaster.* Journal of Management, 1990. 16(3): p. 571-593.

56. Yamazaki, A., et al., *Precision timing in human-robot interaction: coordination of head movement and utterance*, in *Proceedings of the twenty-sixth annual SIGCHI conference on Human factors in computing systems CHI'08.* 2008, ACM: Florence, Italy. p. 131-140.

APPENDIX: SURVEY ITEMS

Manipulation Checks

Back-channeling:
"I felt that the ground robots were looking at me" (7pt, "strongly disagree" – "strongly agree")

Task Complexity:
"I found this to be a complex task"
"The task required me to coordinate many different things at the same time". (7pt, "totally disagree" – "totally agree")

Team Functioning

Stress:
"Indicate to what extent you have felt distressed during the interaction task"
"Indicate to what extent you have felt upset during the interaction task"
"Indicate to what extent you have felt irritable during the interaction task" (5pt, "very slightly or not at all" – "extremely")

Cognitive Load:
"The task was mentally demanding" (7pt, "totally disagree" – "totally agree")

Perceived Team Coordination:
"Our team worked together in a well-coordinated fashion."
"Our team had very few misunderstandings about what to do."
"Our team needed to backtrack and start over a lot." (reverse scored)
"We accomplished the task smoothly and efficiently."
"There was much confusion about how we would accomplish the task." (reverse scored) (5pt, "strongly disagree" – "strongly agree")

Perceptions of robots' engagement

Perceived Distractedness
"I felt that the ground robots were distracted"
"I felt that the ground robots were unfocused" (7pt, "strongly disagree" – "strongly agree")

Perceived Responsiveness
"I felt that the ground robots were responsive" (7pt, "strongly disagree" – "strongly agree")

Perceptions of robots' competence

Perceived Intelligence
"How much did you feel as if you were accompanied by intelligent beings?" (5pt, "not at all" – "absolutely")

Perceived Competence
"The ground robots are very competent" (7pt, "strongly disagree" – "strongly agree")

Author Index

www.ingramcontent.com/pod-product-compliance
Ingram Content Group UK Ltd.
Pitfield, Milton Keynes, MK11 3LW, UK
UKHW051420290926
15471UKWH00009B/1708

9 781450 320993